DATA
COMMUNICATIONS
AND
NETWORKING

McGraw-Hill Forouzan Networking Series

Titles by Behrouz A. Forouzan:

Data Communications and Networking
TCP/IP Protocol Suite
Local Area Networks
Business Data Communications

DATA COMMUNICATIONS AND NETWORKING

Third Edition

Behrouz A. Forouzan

DeAnza College

with

Sophia Chung Fegan

Boston   Burr Ridge, IL   Dubuque, IA   Madison, WI   New York   San Francisco   St. Louis
Bangkok   Bogotá   Caracas   Kuala Lumpur   Lisbon   London   Madrid   Mexico City
Milan   Montreal   New Delhi   Santiago   Seoul   Singapore   Sydney   Taipei   Toronto

The **McGraw·Hill** Companies

DATA COMMUNICATIONS AND NETWORKING, THIRD EDITION
International Edition 2003

Exclusive rights by McGraw-Hill Education (Asia), for manufacture and export. This book cannot
be re-exported from the country to which it is sold by McGraw-Hill. The International Edition is
not available in North America.

10 09 08 07 06 05
20 09 08 07 06 05 04
CTF   SLP

Cover image: © *Stone 996673-005 (RM), Skydivers in free fall formation, low angle view, KenFisher*

Library of Congress Cataloging-in-Publication Data
Forouzan, Behrouz A.
    Data communications and networking / Behrouz A. Forouzan.— 3rd ed.
        p. cm.
    Includes index.
    ISBN 007-251584-8
    1.   Data transmission systems. 2. Computer networks. I. Title.
    TK5105.F6617   2004
    004.6—dc21   2003011267
                                                                 CIP

When ordering this title, use ISBN 007-123241-9

Printed in Singapore

www.mhhe.com

To Faezeh with love.

Table of Contents

Preface to the Third Edition   xxix

Part 1   **Overview of Data Communications and Networking   1**

Chapter 1   *Introduction   3*

1.1   DATA COMMUNICATIONS   3
      Components   4
      Data Representation   5
      Direction of Data Flow   6
1.2   NETWORKS   8
      Distributed Processing   8
      Network Criteria   8
      Physical Structures   8
      Categories of Networks   13
1.3   THE INTERNET   15
      A Brief History   15
      The Internet Today   16
1.4   PROTOCOLS AND STANDARDS   18
      Protocols   18
      Standards   18
      Standards Organizations   19
      Internet Standards   20
1.5   KEY TERMS   20
1.6   SUMMARY   21
1.7   PRACTICE SET   22
      Review Questions   22
      Multiple-Choice Questions   23
      Exercises   25

Chapter 2   *Network Models   27*

2.1   LAYERED TASKS   27
      Sender, Receiver, and Carrier   27

Hierarchy   28
Services   29
2.2   INTERNET MODEL   29
Peer-to-Peer Processes   30
Functions of Layers   31
Summary of Layers   39
2.3   OSI MODEL   40
2.4   KEY TERMS   41
2.5   SUMMARY   41
2.6   PRACTICE SET   42
Review Questions   42
Multiple-Choice Questions   42
Exercises   44

Part 2   **Physical Layer**   **45**

Chapter 3   *Signals*   *49*

3.1   ANALOG AND DIGITAL   49
Analog and Digital Data   49
Analog and Digital Signals   49
Periodic and Aperiodic Signals   50
3.2   ANALOG SIGNALS   50
Sine Wave   51
Phase   54
Examples of Sine Waves   54
Time and Frequency Domains   54
Composite Signals   56
Bandwidth   59
3.3   DIGITAL SIGNALS   62
Bit Interval and Bit Rate   62
Digital Signal as a Composite Analog Signal   63
Digital Signal Through a Wide-Bandwidth Medium   63
Digital Signal Through a Band-Limited Medium   63
Digital versus Analog Bandwidth   65
Higher Bit Rate   66
3.4   ANALOG VERSUS DIGITAL   66
Low-pass versus Band-pass   66
Digital Transmission   66
Analog Transmission   67
3.5   DATA RATE LIMITS   67
Noiseless Channel: Nyquist Bit Rate   67
Noisy Channel: Shannon Capacity   68
Using Both Limits   69
3.6   TRANSMISSION IMPAIRMENT   69
Attenuation   69
Distortion   71
Noise   71

3.7   MORE ABOUT SIGNALS   72
           Throughput   72
           Propagation Speed   72
           Propagation Time   73
           Wavelength   73
3.8   KEY TERMS   74
3.9   SUMMARY   75
3.10   PRACTICE SET   75
           Review Questions   75
           Multiple-Choice Questions   76
           Exercises   80

Chapter 4 *Digital Transmission* 85

4.1   LINE CODING   85
           Some Characteristics of Line Coding   85
           Line Coding Schemes   88
           Some Other Schemes   94
4.2   BLOCK CODING   95
           Steps in Transformation   96
           Some Common Block Codes   97
4.3   SAMPLING   98
           Pulse Amplitude Modulation (PAM)   99
           Pulse Code Modulation   99
           Sampling Rate: Nyquist Theorem   101
           How Many Bits per Sample?   102
           Bit Rate   103
4.4   TRANSMISSION MODE   103
           Parallel Transmission   104
           Serial Transmission   104
4.5   KEY TERMS   107
4.6   SUMMARY   108
4.7   PRACTICE SET   108
           Review Questions   108
           Multiple-Choice Questions   109
           Exercises   112

Chapter 5 *Analog Transmission* 115

5.1   MODULATION OF DIGITAL DATA   115
           Aspects of Digital-to-Analog Conversion   116
           Amplitude Shift Keying (ASK)   117
           Frequency Shift Keying (FSK)   120
           Phase Shift Keying (PSK)   122
           Quadrature Amplitude Modulation (QAM)   125
           Bit/Baud Comparison   127
5.2   TELEPHONE MODEMS   128
           Modem Standards   130
5.3   MODULATION OF ANALOG SIGNALS   133
           Amplitude Modulation (AM)   134

Frequency Modulation (FM)   136
Phase Modulation (PM)   138

5.4   KEY TERMS   138
5.5   SUMMARY   139
5.6   PRACTICE SET   140
Review Questions   140
Multiple-Choice Questions   141
Exercises   145

Chapter 6   *Multiplexing*   *149*

6.1   FDM   150
Multiplexing Process   151
Demultiplexing Process   151
The Analog Hierarchy   153
Other Applications of FDM   155
Implementation   155
6.2   WDM   155
6.3   TDM   157
Time Slots and Frames   157
Interleaving   158
Synchronizing   160
Bit Padding   161
Digital Signal (DS) Service   162
T Lines   163
Inverse TDM   165
More TDM Applications   165
6.4   KEY TERMS   166
6.5   SUMMARY   166
6.6   PRACTICE SET   167
Review Questions   167
Multiple-Choice Questions   167
Exercises   169

Chapter 7   *Transmission Media*   *173*

7.1   GUIDED MEDIA   174
Twisted-Pair Cable   174
Coaxial Cable   177
Fiber-Optic Cable   179
7.2   UNGUIDED MEDIA: WIRELESS   184
Radio Waves   186
Microwaves   188
Infrared   189
7.3   KEY TERMS   190
7.4   SUMMARY   190
7.5   PRACTICE SET   191
Review Questions   191

     Multiple-Choice Questions 192
     Exercises 195

Chapter 8 *Circuit Switching and Telephone Network 197*

8.1 CIRCUIT SWITCHING 197
     Space-Division Switch 199
     Time-Division Switch 201
     TDM Bus 203
     Space- and Time-Division Switch Combinations 203
8.2 TELEPHONE NETWORK 204
     Major Components 204
     LATAs 205
     Making a Connection 207
     Analog Services 208
     Digital Services 209
     A Brief History 210
8.3 KEY TERMS 211
8.4 SUMMARY 211
8.5 PRACTICE SET 212
     Review Questions 212
     Multiple-Choice Questions 213
     Exercises 215

Chapter 9 *High-Speed Digital Access: DSL, Cable Modems,*
       and SONET 219

9.1 DSL TECHNOLOGY 219
     ADSL 219
     Other DSL Technologies 222
9.2 CABLE MODEM 223
     Traditional Cable Networks 223
     HFC Network 224
     Sharing 226
     CM and CMTS 226
     Data Transmission Schemes: DOCSIS 227
9.3 SONET 228
     SONET Devices 229
     SONET Frame 229
     Frame Transmission 230
     Synchronous Transport Signals 230
     STS-1 230
     Virtual Tributaries 231
     Higher-Rate Services 232
9.4 KEY TERMS 232
9.5 SUMMARY 233
9.6 PRACTICE SET 234
     Review Questions 234
     Multiple-Choice Questions 234
     Exercises 237

Part 3 Data Link Layer **239**

Chapter 10 *Error Detection and Correction* *243*

10.1 TYPES OF ERRORS 243
  Single-Bit Error 243
  Burst Error 244
10.2 DETECTION 245
  Redundancy 245
  Parity Check 246
  Cyclic Redundancy Check (CRC) 249
  Checksum 253
10.3 ERROR CORRECTION 256
  Error Correction by Retransmission 256
  Forward Error Correction 256
  Burst Error Correction 260
10.4 KEY TERMS 260
10.5 SUMMARY 261
10.6 PRACTICE SET 261
  Review Questions 261
  Multiple-Choice Questions 262
  Exercises 265

Chapter 11 *Data Link Control and Protocols* *267*

11.1 FLOW AND ERROR CONTROL 267
  Flow Control 267
  Error Control 268
  Flow and Error Control Mechanisms 268
11.2 STOP-AND-WAIT ARQ 268
  Operation 269
  Bidirectional Transmission 272
11.3 GO-BACK-*N* ARQ 272
  Sequence Numbers 273
  Sender Sliding Window 273
  Receiver Sliding Window 274
  Control Variables 274
  Timers 274
  Acknowledgment 275
  Resending Frame 275
  Operation 275
  Sender Window Size 277
  Bidirectional Transmission and Piggybacking 277
11.4 SELECTIVE REPEAT ARQ 278
  Sender and Receiver Windows 278
  Operation 278
  Sender Window Size 279
  Bidirectional Transmission and Piggybacking 280

Bandwidth-Delay Product   280
Pipelining   281
11.5   HDLC   281
Configurations and Transfer Modes   281
Frames   282
Frame Format   282
Frame Type   283
Examples   287
Data Transparency   288
11.6   KEY TERMS   290
11.7   SUMMARY   290
11.8   PRACTICE SET   291
Review Questions   291
Multiple-Choice Questions   291
Exercises   293

Chapter 12   *Point-to-Point Access: PPP*   *295*

12.1   POINT-TO-POINT PROTOCOL   295
Frame Format   295
Transition States   296
12.2   PPP STACK   297
Link Control Protocol (LCP)   297
Authentication Protocols   300
Network Control Protocol (NCP)   302
An Example   304
12.3   KEY TERMS   305
12.4   SUMMARY   305
12.5   PRACTICE SET   305
Review Questions   305
Multiple-Choice Questions   306
Exercises   308

Chapter 13   *Multiple Access*   *311*

13.1   RANDOM ACCESS   311
Multiple Access (MA)   312
Carrier Sense Multiple Access (CSMA)   314
CSMA/CD   315
CSMA/CA   316
13.2   CONTROLLED ACCESS   317
Reservation   318
Polling   318
Token Passing   319
13.3   CHANNELIZATION   320
FDMA   321
TDMA   321
CDMA   321
13.4   KEY TERMS   326

13.5   SUMMARY   326
13.6   PRACTICE SET   327
            Review Questions   327
            Multiple-Choice Questions   327
            Exercises   330

Chapter 14   *Local Area Networks: Ethernet*   *333*

14.1   TRADITIONAL ETHERNET   334
            MAC Sublayer   334
            Physical Layer   337
            Physical Layer Implementation   339
            Bridged Ethernet   341
            Switched Ethernet   342
            Full-Duplex Ethernet   343
14.2   FAST ETHERNET   344
            Mac Sublayer   344
            Physical Layer   345
            Physical Layer Implementation   346
14.3   GIGABIT ETHERNET   350
            MAC Sublayer   350
            Physical Layer   350
            Physical Layer Implementation   351
14.4   KEY TERMS   354
14.5   SUMMARY   355
14.6   PRACTICE SET   356
            Review Questions   356
            Multiple-Choice Questions   356
            Exercises   358

Chapter 15   *Wireless LANs*   *361*

15.1   IEEE 802.11   361
            Architecture   361
            Physical Layer   363
            MAC Layer   365
            Addressing Mechanism   370
15.2   BLUETOOTH   372
            Architecture   373
            Bluetooth Layers   374
            Radio Layer   375
            Baseband Layer   375
            L2CAP   378
            Other Upper Layers   379
15.3   KEY TERMS   380
15.4   SUMMARY   380
15.5   PRACTICE SET   381
            Review Questions   381
            Multiple-Choice Questions   381
            Exercises   385

Chapter 16   *Connecting LANs, Backbone Networks,
and Virtual LANs*   387

16.1   CONNECTING DEVICES   387
Repeaters   387
Hubs   389
Bridges   390
Two-Layer Switch   396
Router and Three-Layer Switches   396
16.2   BACKBONE NETWORKS   396
Bus Backbone   397
Star Backbone   398
Connecting Remote LANs   398
16.3   VIRTUAL LANS   399
Membership   401
Configuration   402
Communication Between Switches   403
IEEE Standard   403
Advantages   403
16.4   KEY TERMS   404
16.5   SUMMARY   404
16.6   PRACTICE SET   405
Review Questions   405
Multiple-Choice Questions   405
Exercises   407

Chapter 17   *Cellular Telephone and Satellite Networks*   409

17.1   CELLULAR TELEPHONY   409
Frequency-Reuse Principle   409
Transmitting   410
Receiving   411
Handoff   411
Roaming   411
First Generation   411
Second Generation   412
Third Generation   419
17.2   SATELLITE NETWORKS   420
Orbits   420
Footprint   421
Three Categories of Satellites   422
GEO Satellites   423
MEO Satellites   424
LEO Satellites   425
17.3   KEY TERMS   428
17.4   SUMMARY   428
17.5   PRACTICE SET   429
Review Questions   429
Multiple-Choice Questions   429
Exercises   433

Chapter 18   *Virtual Circuit Switching: Frame Relay and ATM   435*

18.1   VIRTUAL CIRCUIT SWITCHING   435
      Global Addressing   436
      Virtual Circuit Identifier   436
      Three Phases   436
      Data Transfer Phase   437
      Setup Phase   437
      Teardown Phase   440

18.2   FRAME RELAY   441
      Architecture   442
      Frame Relay Layers   443
      FRADs   444
      VOFR   445
      LMI   445
      Congestion Control and Quality of Service   446

18.3   ATM   446
      Design Goals   446
      Problems   446
      Architecture   449
      Switching   452
      ATM Layers   453
      Congestion Control and Quality of Service   459
      ATM LANs   459

18.4   KEY TERMS   460
18.5   SUMMARY   460
18.6   PRACTICE SET   461
      Review Questions   461
      Multiple-Choice Questions   462
      Exercises   464

Part 4   Network Layer   467

Chapter 19   *Host-to-Host Delivery: Internetworking, Addressing, and Routing   471*

19.1   INTERNETWORKS   471
      Need for Network Layer   472
      Internet as a Packet-Switched Network   474
      Internet as a Connectionless Network   476

19.2   ADDRESSING   477
      Internet Address   477
      Classful Addressing   479
      Subnetting   486
      Supernetting   490
      Classless Addressing   491
      Dynamic Address Configuration   492

    Network Address Translation (NAT) 494

19.3 ROUTING 497
    Routing Techniques 497
    Static versus Dynamic Routing 499
    Routing Table for Classful Addressing 500
    Routing Table for Classless Addressing: CIDR 501
19.4 KEY TERMS 503
19.5 SUMMARY 503
19.6 PRACTICE SET 504
    Review Questions 504
    Multiple-Choice Questions 505
    Exercises 508

Chapter 20 *Network Layer Protocols: ARP, IPv4, ICMP, IPv6,*
      and ICMPv6 513

20.1 ARP 514
    Mapping 514
    Packet Format 516
    Encapsulation 517
    Operation 517
20.2 IP 519
    Datagram 520
    Fragmentation 523
20.3 ICMP 525
    Types of Messages 526
20.4 IPV6 528
    IPv6 Addresses 529
    Categories of Addresses 530
    IPv6 Packet Format 531
    Fragmentation 532
    ICMPv6 532
    Transition from IPv4 to IPv6 533
20.5 KEY TERMS 535
20.6 SUMMARY 535
20.7 PRACTICE SET 536
    Review Questions 536
    Multiple-Choice Questions 537
    Exercises 540

Chapter 21 *Unicast and Multicast Routing: Routing*
      Protocols 543

21.1 UNICAST ROUTING 543
    Metric 544
    Interior and Exterior Routing 544
21.2 UNICAST ROUTING PROTOCOLS 545
    RIP 546
    OSPF 548

BGP   557
21.3   MULTICAST ROUTING   560
    IGMP   561
    Multicast Trees   567
    MBONE   568
21.4   MULTICAST ROUTING PROTOCOLS   569
    DVMRP   570
    MOSPF   572
    CBT   574
    PIM   576
    Applications   576
21.5   KEY TERMS   577
21.6   SUMMARY   577
21.7   PRACTICE SET   579
    Review Questions   579
    Multiple-Choice Questions   579
    Exercises   586

Part 5   **Transport Layer**   **589**

Chapter 22   *Process-to-Process Delivery: UDP and TCP*   *593*

22.1   PROCESS-TO-PROCESS DELIVERY   593
    Client-Server Paradigm   594
    Addressing   594
    Multiplexing and Demultiplexing   597
    Connectionless versus Connection-Oriented Service   597
    Reliable versus Unreliable   600
22.2   USER DATAGRAM PROTOCOL (UDP)   601
    Port Numbers   601
    User Datagram   601
    Applications   602
22.3   TRANSMISSION CONTROL PROTOCOL (TCP)   603
    Port Numbers   603
    TCP Services   603
    Numbering Bytes   606
    Sequence Number   607
    Segment   608
    Connection   609
    State Transition Diagram   612
    Flow Control   614
    Silly Window Syndrome   618
    Error Control   619
    TCP Timers   621
    Congestion Control   624
    Other Features   624
22.4   KEY TERMS   625
22.5   SUMMARY   626
22.6   PRACTICE SET   626

Review Questions   626
Multiple-Choice Questions   627
Exercises   631

Chapter 23   *Congestion Control and Quality of Service*   633

23.1   DATA TRAFFIC   633
          Traffic Descriptor   633
          Traffic Profiles   634
23.2   CONGESTION   636
          Network Performance   636
23.3   CONGESTION CONTROL   638
          Open-Loop Congestion Control   638
          Closed-Loop Congestion Control   639
23.4   TWO EXAMPLES   639
          Congestion Control in TCP   639
          Congestion Control in Frame Relay   641
23.5   QUALITY OF SERVICE   643
          Flow Characteristics   643
          Flow Classes   644
23.6   TECHNIQUES TO IMPROVE QOS   644
          Scheduling   644
          Traffic Shaping   646
          Resource Reservation   649
          Admission Control   649
23.7   INTEGRATED SERVICES   649
          Signaling   649
          Flow Specification   649
          Admission   650
          Service Classes   650
          RSVP   650
          Problems with Integrated Services   653
23.8   DIFFERENTIATED SERVICES   653
23.9   QOS IN SWITCHED NETWORKS   655
          QoS in Frame Relay   655
          QoS in ATM   657
23.10   KEY TERMS   659
23.11   SUMMARY   660
23.12   PRACTICE SET   660
          Review Questions   660
          Multiple-Choice Questions   661
          Exercises   665

Part 6   **Application Layer**   667

Chapter 24   *Client-Server Model: Socket Interface*   671

24.1   CLIENT-SERVER MODEL   671

Relationship   671
Concurrency   673
Processes   674

24.2   SOCKET INTERFACE   675
Sockets   675
Connectionless Iterative Server   677
Connection-Oriented Concurrent Server   678
Client and Server Programs   680

24.3   KEY TERMS   680
24.4   SUMMARY   680
24.5   PRACTICE SET   681
Review Questions   681
Multiple-Choice Questions   681
Exercises   684

Chapter 25   *Domain Name System (DNS)   685*

25.1   NAME SPACE   685
Flat Name Space   685
Hierarchical Name Space   686

25.2   DOMAIN NAME SPACE   686
Label   686
Domain Name   687
Domain   688

25.3   DISTRIBUTION OF NAME SPACE   689
Hierarchy of Name Servers   689
Zone   689
Root Server   690
Primary and Secondary Servers   690

25.4   DNS IN THE INTERNET   691
Generic Domains   691
Country Domains   693
Inverse Domain   693

25.5   RESOLUTION   694
Resolver   694
Mapping Names to Addresses   695
Mapping Addresses to Names   695
Recursive Resolution   695
Iterative Resolution   696
Caching   696

25.6   DNS MESSAGES   697
Header   697
Question Section   698
Answer Section   698
Authoritative Section   698
Additional Information Section   698

25.7   DDNS   698
25.8   ENCAPSULATION   699
25.9   KEY TERMS   699

25.10 SUMMARY   699
25.11 PRACTICE SET   700
    Review Questions   700
    Multiple-Choice Questions   701
    Exercises   703

Chapter 26   *Electronic Mail (SMTP) and File Transfer (FTP)*   *705*

26.1 ELECTRONIC MAIL   705
    Sending Mail   705
    Receiving Mail   706
    Addresses   706
    User Agent (UA)   707
    Multipurpose Internet Mail Extensions (MIME)   708
    Mail Transfer Agent (MTA)   714
    Mail Delivery   715
    Mail Access Protocols   717
    Web-Based Mail   718
26.2 FILE TRANSFER   718
    Connections   720
    Communication   720
    File Transfer   722
    User Interface   723
    Anonymous FTP   724
26.3 KEY TERMS   725
26.4 SUMMARY   725
26.5 PRACTICE SET   726
    Review Questions   726
    Multiple-Choice Questions   726
    Exercises   729

Chapter 27   *HTTP and WWW*   *731*

27.1 HTTP   731
    Transaction   732
    Request Messages   732
    Response Message   734
    Headers   735
    Some Examples   736
    Some Other Features   738
27.2 WORLD WIDE WEB   738
    Hypertext and Hypermedia   739
    Browser Architecture   740
    Static Documents   740
    HTML   741
    Examples   743
    Dynamic Documents   745
    Common Gateway Interface (CGI)   746
    Examples   746

Active Documents   747
Java   748
Examples   751

27.3   KEY TERMS   752
27.4   SUMMARY   752
27.5   PRACTICE SET   753
Review Questions   753
Multiple-Choice Questions   753
Exercises   758

Chapter 28   *Multimedia   761*

28.1   DIGITIZING AUDIO AND VIDEO   762
Digitizing Audio   762
Digitizing Video   762
28.2   AUDIO AND VIDEO COMPRESSION   763
Audio Compression   763
Video Compression   764
28.3   STREAMING STORED AUDIO/VIDEO   769
First Approach: Using a Web Server   769
Second Approach: Using a Web Server with Metafile   770
Third Approach: Using a Media Server   770
Fourth Approach: Using a Media Server and RTSP   771
28.4   STREAMING LIVE AUDIO/VIDEO   772
28.5   REAL-TIME INTERACTIVE AUDIO/VIDEO   772
Characteristics   773
Real-Time Transport Protocol   777
Real-Time Transport Control Protocol (RTCP)   778
28.6   VOICE OVER IP   779
SIP   779
H.323   781
28.7   KEY TERMS   784
28.8   SUMMARY   784
28.9   PRACTICE SET   785
Review Questions   785
Multiple-Choice Questions   786
Exercises   789

Part 7   Security   **791**

Chapter 29   *Cryptography   795*

29.1   INTRODUCTION   795
29.2   SYMMETRIC-KEY CRYPTOGRAPHY   796
Traditional Ciphers   797
Block Cipher   801
Operation Modes   805
29.3   PUBLIC-KEY CRYPTOGRAPHY   808
RSA   809

Choosing Public and Private Keys   810
29.4   KEY TERMS   810
29.5   SUMMARY   810
29.6   PRACTICE SET   811
Review Questions   811
Multiple-Choice Questions   811
Exercises   813

Chapter 30   *Message Security, User Authentication, and Key Management   815*

30.1   MESSAGE SECURITY   815
Privacy   816
Message Authentication   817
Integrity   817
Nonrepudiation   817
30.2   DIGITAL SIGNATURE   817
Signing the Whole Document   817
Signing the Digest   818
30.3   USER AUTHENTICATION   820
User Authentication with Symmetric-Key Cryptography   820
User Authentication with Public-Key Cryptography   822
30.4   KEY MANAGEMENT   823
Symmetric Key Distribution   823
Public-Key Certification   829
30.5   KERBEROS   831
Servers   831
Operation   832
Using Different Servers   834
Kerberos Version 5   834
Realms   834
30.6   KEY TERMS   835
30.7   SUMMARY   835
30.8   PRACTICE SET   836
Review Questions   836
Multiple-Choice Questions   836
Exercises   839

Chapter 31   *Security Protocols in the Internet   841*

31.1   IP LEVEL SECURITY: IPSEC   841
Security Association   842
Two Modes   842
Two Security Protocols   842
Encapsulating Security Payload   844
31.2   TRANSPORT LAYER SECURITY   846
Position of TLS   846
Two Protocols   846

31.3 APPLICATION LAYER SECURITY: PGP 848
31.4 FIREWALLS 849
        Packet-Filter Firewall 849
        Proxy Firewall 850
31.5 VIRTUAL PRIVATE NETWORK 851
        Private Networks 851
        Achieving Privacy 852
        VPN Technology 854
31.6 KEY TERMS 855
31.7 SUMMARY 855
31.8 PRACTICE SET 856
        Review Questions 856
        Multiple-Choice Questions 856
        Exercises 859

Appendix A *ASCII Code* *861*

Appendix B *Numbering Systems and Transformation* *865*

B.1 NUMBERING SYSTEMS 865
        Decimal Numbers 865
        Binary Numbers 866
        Octal Numbers 867
        Hexadecimal Numbers 868
B.2 TRANSFORMATION 869
        From Other Systems to Decimal 870
        From Decimal to Other Systems 870
        From Binary to Octal or Hexadecimal 871
        From Octal or Hexadecimal to Binary 872

Appendix C *The OSI Model* *873*

C.1 THE MODEL 873
C.2 LAYERS IN THE OSI MODEL 873
        First Four Layers 873
        Session Layer 874
        Presentation Layer 874
        Application Layer 876
C.3 COMPARISON 877

Appendix D *8B/6T Code* *878*

Appendix E *Checksum Calculation* *881*

E.1 BINARY NOTATION 881
        Partial Sum 881
        Sum 881
        Checksum 881
E.2 HEXADECIMAL NOTATION 882

Partial Sum   882
Sum   883
Checksum   884

Appendix F   *Structure of a Router*   885

F.1   COMPONENTS   885
Input Ports   885
Output Ports   886
Routing Processor   886
Switching Fabrics   886

Appendix G   *ATM LANs*   889

G.1   ATM LAN ARCHITECTURE   889
Pure ATM Architecture   890
Legacy LAN Architecture   890
Mixed Architecture   891
G.2   LAN EMULATION (LANE)   891
G.3   CLIENT-SERVER MODEL   892
LAN Emulation Client (LEC)   892
LAN Emulation Configuration Server (LECS)   893
LAN Emulation Server (LES)   893
Broadcast/Unknown Server (BUS)   893

Appendix H   *Client-Server Programs*   895

H.1   UDP CLIENT-SERVER PROGRAMS   895
Server Program   895
Client Program   896
H.2   TCP CLIENT-SERVER PROGRAMS   897
Server Program   898
Client Program   899

Appendix I   *RFCs*   901

Appendix J   *UDP and TCP Ports*   903

Appendix K   *Contact Addresses*   905

Acronyms   *907*

Glossary   *911*

Index   *949*

Website and Online Learning Center for Data Communications and Networking, Third Edition

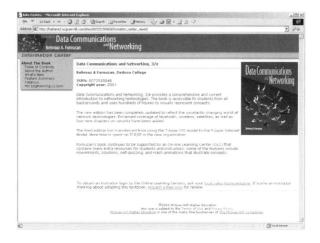

Online Learning Center at www.mhhe.com/forouzan

The online learning center provides additional resources for both instructor and student.

For the instructor:

PowerPoint Slides. A full set of color PowerPoints for every chapter provides excellent supplemental lecture materials.

Solutions are available (password-protected).

PageOut. This McGraw-Hill product offers instant course website development. An interactive course syllabus allows you to post content to coincide with your lectures. When students visit your PageOut website, your syllabus will direct them to components of Forouzan's Online Learning Center, or specific material of your own.

For the student:

Approximately 80 automated quiz questions per chapter. This resource allows you to test your knowledge of concepts online. An immediate response will let you know how you are doing.

Animated figures from the book. Flash animations of selected figures from the book help networking concepts come to life. You can watch as the diagrams actively demonstrate their concepts.

Preface to the Third Edition

Data communications and networking may be the fastest growing technologies in our culture today. One of the ramifications of that growth is a dramatic increase in the number of professions where an understanding of these technologies is essential for success—and a proportionate increase in the number and types of students taking courses to learn about them.

Features of the Book

Several features of this text are designed to make it particularly easy for students to understand data communications and networking.

Structure

We have used the five-layer Internet model as the framework for the text not only because a thorough understanding of the model is essential to understanding most current networking theory but also because it is based on a structure of interdependencies: Each layer builds upon the layer beneath it and supports the layer above it. In the same way, each concept introduced in our text builds upon the concepts examined in the previous sections. The Internet model was chosen because it is a protocol that is fully implemented.

This text is designed for students with little or no background in telecommunications or data communications. For this reason, we use a bottom-up approach. In this approach, students can learn first about data communications (lower layers) before learning about networking (upper layers). For example, students can learn about signaling, encoding, modulation, and error detection before learning about data transfer across the Internet. This eliminates the need for two courses: one for data communications and one for networking concepts.

Visual Approach

The book presents highly technical subject matter without complex formulas by using a balance of text and figures. More than 700 figures accompanying the text provide a visual and intuitive opportunity for understanding the material. Figures are particularly important in explaining networking concepts, which are based on connections and transmission. Both of these are easy to grasp visually.

Highlighted Points

We have repeated important concepts in boxes for quick reference and immediate attention.

Examples and Applications

Whenever appropriate, we have included examples that illustrate the concepts introduced in the text. They also help students do the exercises at the end of each chapter. Also, we have added real-life applications throughout each chapter.

Key Terms

Each chapter includes a list of key terms for the student.

Summary

Each chapter ends with a summary of the material covered in that chapter. The summary is a brief overview of all the important points in the chapter.

Practice Set

Each chapter includes a practice set designed to reinforce and apply salient concepts. It consists of three parts: review questions, multiple-choice questions, and exercises. Review questions are intended to test the student's first-level understanding of the material presented in the chapter. Multiple-choice questions test the student's grasp of basic concepts and terminology. Exercises require deeper understanding of the material.

Appendixes

The appendixes are intended to provide quick reference material or a review of materials needed to understand the concepts discussed in the book.

Glossary and Acronyms

The book contains an extensive glossary and a list of acronyms.

Contents

The book is divided into seven parts. The first part is an overview; the last part concerns network security. The middle five parts are designed to represent the five layers of the Internet model. The following summarizes the contents of each part.

Part One: Overview of Data Communications and Networking

The first part gives a general overview of data communications and networking. It contains two chapters. Chapter 1 covers introductory concepts needed for the rest of the book. Chapter 2 introduces the Internet model.

Part Two: Physical Layer

The second part is a discussion of the physical layer of the Internet model. This part includes Chapters 3 to 9. Chapters 3 to 6 discusses telecommunication aspects of the physical layer. Chapter 7 introduces the transmission media, which, although not part of the physical layer, is controlled by it. Chapters 8 and 9 introduce several protocols related mainly to the physical layer.

Part Three: Data Link Layer

The third part is devoted to the discussion of the data link layer of the Internet model. This part includes Chapters 10 to 18. Chapter 10 is devoted to error detection. Chapters 11, 12, and 13 discuss issues related to data link control. Some common data link protocols are also introduced in these three chapters. Chapters 14 through 16 are about LANs. LANs operate in the physical and data link layers. Chapter 14 is about the dominant wired LAN called Ethernet. Chapter 15 is about wireless LANs. Chapter 16 shows how to connect LANs to create backbone networks. Chapters 17 and 18 are about WANs, another technology that uses the physical and data link layers. Chapter 17 discusses mobile telephone systems and satellite systems. Chapter 18 explains switched WANs such as Frame Relay and ATM.

Part Four: Network Layer

The fourth part is devoted to the discussion of the network layer of the Internet model. This part includes Chapters 19 to 21. Chapter 19 is devoted to the concept and services of the network layer. This chapter also discusses routing and internetworking in the Internet. Chapter 20 covers the internetworking protocols in the Internet. The main internetworking protocol, IP, is discussed in some depth. Other protocols such as ARP, ICMP, and IGMP are discussed briefly to show how they support the operation of the IP protocol. Chapter 21 opens the discussion about routing protocols, both unicast and multicast. In unicast routing, the emphasis is mostly on concepts such as *distance vector routing, link state routing,* and *path vector routing.* However, RIP, OSPF, and BGP are also discussed in some depth as examples of unicast routing protocols. In multicast routing, the emphasis is on spanning tree methods. In addition, protocols such as DVMRP, MOSPF, CBT, PIM-DM, and PIM-SM are discussed to show real life applications. IGMP is introduce in this chapter to provide the necessary vehicle for multicast routing. At the end of the chapter, we introduce MBONE as a temporary multicast method.

Part Five: Transport Layer

The fifth part is devoted to the discussion of the transport layer of the Internet model. This part includes Chapters 22 and 23. Chapter 22 is an overview of the transport layer and discusses the services and duties of this layer. It also introduces the two transport layer protocols of the Internet, UDP and TCP. Chapter 23, although included in this part, discusses congestion control and quality of service, two issues related to the transport layer and the previous two layers. These topics are becoming increasingly important with the booming popularity of multimedia applications on the Internet.

Part Six: Application Layer

The sixth part is devoted to the discussion of the application layer of the Internet model. This part includes Chapters 24 and 28. Services in the application layer are the objective of the model. All the other layers exist so that users can access applications in this layer. We can not cover all applications in an introductory book like this; we have chosen some examples to show the concept. Chapter 24 defines the general idea, the client-server paradigm. We also briefly introduce the socket interface in this chapter as the prelude to client-server programming. Chapter 25 is about DNS, the application program that is used by other application programs to map application layer addresses to network layer addresses. Chapter 26 is about two popular applications, email and file transfer. We introduce the World Wide Web and the protocol that accesses it, HTTP, in Chapter 27. Chapter 28 is about multimedia. We introduce multimedia applications and the problems and issues involved. We also discuss some protocols that are used to provide Internet telephony, Internet teleconferencing, and audio/video streaming.

Part Seven: Network Security

The seventh part is devoted to a discussion of network security. Security today does not belong to just one specific layer; it is a concern of all layers. This part is a very brief discussion of the main ideas affecting security. Three chapters are included in this part. Chapter 29 discusses the general idea of cryptography. Symmetric (secret key) and asymmetric (public-key) cryptography are described without involving number theory. Chapter 30 introduces security services (message confidentiality, message authentication, message integrity, and message non-repudiation). It also shows some methods to authenticate users' access to the system. Finally there is a discussion on key management in both types of cryptography. Chapter 31 focuses on Internet security. It explores protocols used in the network, transport, and application layers. It also discusses firewalls and private virtual networks.

Online Supplementary Material at www.mhhe.com/forouzan

Online Learning Center

The McGraw-Hill Online Learning Center is a "digital cartridge" that contains the book's pedagogy and supplements. As students read through *Data Communications and Networking,* they can go online to take self-grading quizzes. They also get appropriate access to lecture materials such as PowerPoint slides and animated figures from the book. Solutions are also available over the Web. The solutions to odd-numbered problems are provided to students, and instructors can use a password to access the complete set of solutions.

Additionally, McGraw-Hill makes it easy to create a website for your networking course with an exclusive McGraw-Hill product called PageOut. It requires no prior knowledge of HTML, no long hours, and no design skills on your part. Instead, PageOut offers a series of templates. Simply fill them with your course information and click on one of 16 designs. The process takes under an hour and leaves you with a professionally designed website.

Although PageOut offers "instant" development, the finished website offers powerful features. An interactive course syllabus allows you to post content to coincide with your lectures, so when students visit your PageOut website, your syllabus will direct them to components of Forouzan's Online Learning Center, or specific material of your own.

How to Use the Book

This book is written for both an academic and a professional audience. The book can be used as a self-study guide for interested professionals. As a textbook, it can be used for a one-semester or one-quarter course. The following are some guidelines.

- Parts one to three are strongly recommended.
- Parts four to six can be covered if there is no following course in TCP/IP protocol.
- Part seven is recommended if there is no following course in network security.

Acknowledgments

It is obvious that the development of a book of this scope needs the support of many people. We especially thank Ying-Ping Sarah Liu and Gregory Yee for their tremendous assistance in reading the manuscript and checking the solutions to the end materials.

The most important contribution to the development of a book such as this comes from peer reviews. We cannot express our gratitude in words to the many reviewers who spent numerous hours reading the manuscript and providing us with helpful comments and ideas. We would especially like to acknowledge the contributions of the following reviewers for the third edition of this book.

Anthony Barnard, *University of Alabama, Birmingham*
Rayman Meservy, *Brigham Young University*
Arnold Patton, *Bradley University*
Scott Campbell, *Miami University*
Arnold C. Meltzer, *George Washington University*
Christophe Veltsos, *Minnesota State University, Mankato*
Wenhang Liu, *California State University, Los Angeles*
Sandeep Gupta, *Arizona State University*
Alvin Sek See Lim, *Auburn University*
Sherali Zeadally, *Wayne State University*
Tom Hilton, *Utah State University*
Ten-Hwang Lai, *Ohio State University*
Hung Z Ngo, *SUNY, Buffalo*
A. T. Burrell, *Oklahoma State University*
Hans-Peter Dommel, *Santa Clara University*
Louis Marseille, *Harford Community College*

Special thanks go to the staff of McGraw-Hill. Betsy Jones, our publisher, proved how a proficient publisher can make the impossible possible. Emily Lupash, the developmental editor, gave us help whenever we needed it. Sheila Frank, our project manager, guided us through the production process with enormous enthusiasm. We also thank Kara Kudronowicz in production, Rick Noel in design, and Patti Scott, the copy editor.

Trademark Notices

Throughout the text we have used several trademarks. Rather than insert a trademark symbol with each mention of the trademarked name, we acknowledge the trademarks here and state that they are used with no intention of infringing upon them. Other product names, trademarks, and registered trademarks are the property of their respective owners.

- Apple, AppleTalk, EtherTalk, LocalTalk, TokenTalk, and Macintosh are registered trademarks of Apple Computer, Inc.
- Bell and StarLan are registered trademarks of AT&T.
- DEC, DECnet, VAX, and DNA are trademarks of Digital Equipment Corp.
- IBM, SDLC, SNA, and IBM PC are registered trademarks of International Business Machines Corp.
- Novell, Netware, IPX, and SPX are registered trademarks of Novell, Inc.
- Network File System and NFS are registered trademarks of Sun Micro-systems, Inc.
- PostScript is a registered trademark of Adobe Systems, Inc.
- UNIX is a registered trademark of UNIX System Laboratories, Inc., a wholly owned subsidiary of Novell, Inc.
- Xerox is a trademark and Ethernet is a registered trademark of Xerox Corp.

PART 1

Overview of Data Communications and Networking

Data communications and networking are topics that have moved from the technical world to the public realm. Products such as MP3 players and cellular phones are no longer the manifestations of high tech wizardry, but are gadgets toted by everyone from preteens to grandparents. Progress in data communications and networking technologies is proceeding at a rapid rate. Bunny-ear antennas on televisions have gone the way of the dinosaurs, phased out by digital cable and satellite dishes. The home office is moving toward wireless connections as well. The end user of such technologies is only required to know how to use the systems. A student in this field, however, must be familiar with the issues and concepts shown in Figure 1.

Figure 1   *Overview of data communications and networking*

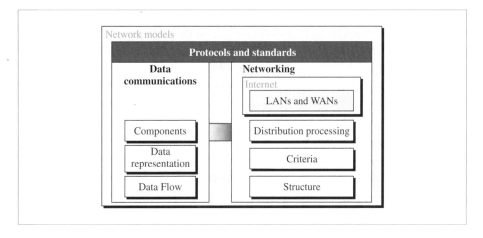

Data Communications

Networks exist so that data may be sent from one place to another—the basic concept of data communications. To fully grasp this subject, we must understand the physical network components, how different types of data can be represented, and how to create a data flow.

Networking

Data communications between remote parties can be achieved through a process called networking, involving the connection of computers, media, and networking devices. When we talk about networks, we need to keep in mind three concepts: distributed processing, network criteria, and network structure.

Local and Wide Area Networks

Networks are divided into two main categories: local area networks (LANs) and wide area networks (WANs). These two types of networks have different characteristics and different functionalities. In general, a LAN is a collection of computers and peripheral devices in a limited area such as a building or campus. A LAN is usually under the domain of a single organization such as a company or department. A WAN, however, is a collection of LANs and spans a large geographical distance.

Internet

The Internet, the main of focus of the book, is a collection of LANs and WANs held together by internetworking devices. In the figure, we demonstrate this relationship by having the box entitled *Internet* enclose LANs and WANs. The Internet is, however, more than just a physical connection of LANs and WANs; internetworking protocols and standards are also needed.

Protocols and Standards

Protocols and standards are vital to the implementation of data communication and networking. Protocols refer to the rules; a standard is a protocol that has been adopted by vendors and manufacturers. In the diagram, the *Protocols and Standards* box spans both data communications and networking to emphasize that each area falls under its jurisdiction.

Network Models

Network models serve to organize, unify, and control the hardware and software components of data communication and networking. Although the term "network model" suggests a relationship to networking, the model also encompasses data communications.

Chapters

In Chapter 1 we briefly discuss the first three topics—data communications, networking, and protocols and standards. Network models, the cornerstones for the rest of the book, are described in Chapter 2.

CHAPTER 1

Introduction

Data communications and networking are changing the way we do business and the way we live. Business decisions have to be made ever more quickly, and the decision makers require immediate access to accurate information. Why wait a week for that report from Germany to arrive by mail when it could appear almost instantaneously through computer networks? Businesses today rely on computer networks and internetworks. But before we ask how quickly we can get hooked up, we need to know how networks operate, what types of technologies are available, and which design best fills which set of needs.

The development of the personal computer brought about tremendous changes for business, industry, science, and education. A similar revolution is occurring in data communications and networking. Technological advances are making it possible for communications links to carry more and faster signals. As a result, services are evolving to allow use of the expanded capacity, including the extension to established telephone services such as conference calling, call waiting, voice mail, and caller ID.

Data communications and networking are in their infancy. The goal is to be able to exchange data such as text, audio, and video from any point in the world. We want to access the Internet to download and upload information quickly and accurately and at any time.

This chapter addresses four issues: data communications, networks, the Internet, and protocols and standards. First we give a broad definition of data communications. Then we define networks as a highway on which data can travel. The Internet is discussed as a good example of an internetwork (i.e., a network of networks). Finally, we discuss different types of protocols, the difference between protocols and standards, and the organizations that set those standards.

1.1   DATA COMMUNICATIONS

When we communicate, we are sharing information. This sharing can be local or remote. Between individuals, local communication usually occurs face to face, while remote communication takes place over distance. The term **telecommunication,** which includes telephony, telegraphy, and television, means communication at a distance (*tele* is Greek for "far").

The word **data** refers to information presented in whatever form is agreed upon by the parties creating and using the data.

Data communications is the exchange of data between two devices via some form of transmission medium such as a wire cable. For data communications to occur, the communicating devices must be part of a communication system made up of a combination of hardware (physical equipment) and software (programs). The effectiveness of a data communications system depends on three fundamental characteristics: delivery, accuracy, and timeliness.

1. **Delivery.** The system must deliver data to the correct destination. Data must be received by the intended device or user and only by that device or user.

2. **Accuracy.** The system must deliver the data accurately. Data that have been altered in transmission and left uncorrected are unusable.

3. **Timeliness.** The system must deliver data in a timely manner. Data delivered late are useless. In the case of video and audio, timely delivery means delivering data as they are produced, in the same order that they are produced, and without significant delay. This kind of delivery is called *real-time* transmission.

Components

A data communications system has five components (see Fig. 1.1).

Figure 1.1   *Five components of data communication*

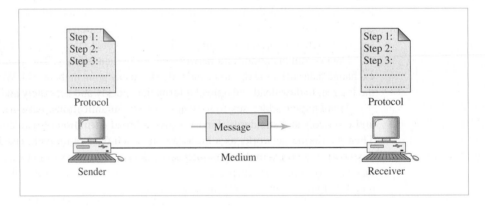

1. **Message.** The **message** is the information (data) to be communicated. It can consist of text, numbers, pictures, sound, or video—or any combination of these.

2. **Sender.** The **sender** is the device that sends the data message. It can be a computer, workstation, telephone handset, video camera, and so on.

3. **Receiver.** The **receiver** is the device that receives the message. It can be a computer, workstation, telephone handset, television, and so on.

4. **Medium.** The **transmission medium** is the physical path by which a message travels from sender to receiver. It could be a twisted-pair wire, coaxial cable, fiber-optic cable, or radio waves (terrestrial or satellite microwave).

5. **Protocol.** A **protocol** is a set of rules that governs data communications. It represents an agreement between the communicating devices. Without a protocol, two devices may be connected but not communicating, just as a person speaking French cannot be understood by a person who speaks only Japanese.

Data Representation

Information today comes in different forms such as text, numbers, images, audio, and video.

Text

In data communications, text is represented as a bit pattern, a sequence of bits (0s or 1s). The number of bits in a pattern depends on the number of symbols in the language. For example, the English language uses 26 symbols (A, B, C, . . . , Z) to represent uppercase letters, 26 symbols (a, b, c, . . . , z) to represent lowercase letters, 10 symbols (0, 1, 2, . . . , 9) to represent numeric characters, and symbols (., ?, :, ; . . . , !) to represent punctuation. Other symbols such as the blank, the newline, and the tab are used for text alignment and readability.

Different sets of bit patterns have been designed to represent text symbols. Each set is called a **code,** and the process of representing symbols is called coding.

ASCII The American National Standards Institute (ANSI) developed a code called the American Standard Code for Information Interchange (ASCII). This code uses 7 bits for each symbol. This means 128 (2^7) different symbols can be defined by this code. The full bit patterns for ASCII code are found in Appendix A.

Extended ASCII To make the size of each pattern 1 byte (8 bits), the ASCII bit patterns are augmented with an extra 0 at the left. Now each pattern is exactly 1 byte of memory. In other words, in extended ASCII, the first pattern is 00000000 and the last one is 01111111.

Unicode Neither of the foregoing codes represents symbols belonging to languages other than English. For that, a code with much greater capacity is needed. A coalition of hardware and software manufacturers have designed a code called Unicode that uses 16 bits and can represent up to 65,536 (2^{16}) symbols. Different sections of the code are allocated to symbols from different languages in the world. Some parts of the code are used for graphical and special symbols.

ISO The International Organization for Standardization, known as ISO, has designed a code using a 32-bit pattern. This code can represent up to 4,294,967,296 (2^{32}) symbols, which is definitely enough to represent any symbol in the world today.

Numbers

Numbers are also represented by using bit patterns. However, a code such as ASCII is not used to represent numbers; the number is directly converted to a binary number. The reason is to simplify mathematical operations on numbers. Appendix B lists the binary numbers and their equivalents.

Images

Images today are also represented by bit patterns. However, the mechanism is different. In its simpler form, an image is divided into a matrix of pixels (picture elements), where each pixel is a small dot. The size of the pixel depends on what is called the *resolution.* For example, an image can be divided into 1000 pixels or 10,000 pixels. In the second case, there is a better representation of the image (better resolution), but more memory is needed to store the image.

After an image is divided into pixels, each pixel is assigned a bit pattern. The size and the value of the pattern depend on the image. For an image made of only black-and-white dots (e.g., a chessboard), a 1-bit pattern is enough to represent a pixel.

If an image is not made of pure white and pure black pixels, you can increase the size of the bit pattern to include gray scale. For example, to show four levels of gray scale, you can use 2-bit patterns. A black pixel can be represented by 00, a dark gray pixel by 01, a light gray pixel by 10, and a white pixel by 11.

To represent color images, each colored pixel is decomposed into three primary colors: red, green, and blue (RGB). Then the intensity of each color is measured, and a bit pattern (usually 8 bits) is assigned to it. In other words, each pixel has three bit patterns: one to represent the intensity of the red color, one to represent the intensity of the green color, and one to represent the intensity of the blue color.

Audio

Audio is a representation of sound. Audio is by nature different from text, numbers, or images. It is continuous, not discrete. Even when we use a microphone to change voice or music to an electric signal, we create a continuous signal. In Chapters 4 and 5, we learn how to change audio to a digital or an analog signal.

Video

Video can be produced either as a continuous entity (e.g., by a TV camera), or it can be a combination of images, each a discrete entity, arranged to convey the idea of motion. Again we can change video to a digital or an analog signal, as we will see in Chapters 4 and 5.

Direction of Data Flow

Communication between two devices can be simplex, half-duplex, or full-duplex.

Simplex

In **simplex mode,** the communication is unidirectional, as on a one-way street. Only one of the two devices on a link can transmit; the other can only receive (see Fig. 1.2).

Figure 1.2 *Simplex*

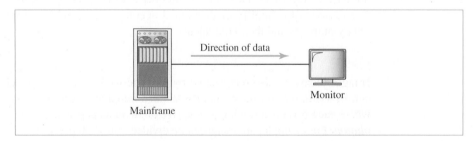

Keyboards and traditional monitors are both examples of simplex devices. The keyboard can only introduce input; the monitor can only accept output.

Half-Duplex

In **half-duplex mode,** each station can both transmit and receive, but not at the same time. When one device is sending, the other can only receive, and vice versa (see Fig. 1.3).

Figure 1.3   *Half-duplex*

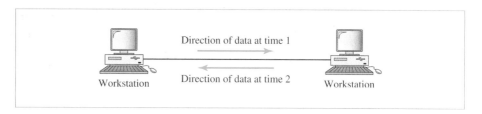

The half-duplex mode is like a one-lane road with two-directional traffic. While cars are traveling one direction, cars going the other way must wait. In a half-duplex transmission, the entire capacity of a channel is taken over by whichever of the two devices is transmitting at the time. Walkie-talkies and CB (citizens band) radios are both half-duplex systems.

Full-Duplex

In **full-duplex mode** (also called **duplex**), both stations can transmit and receive simultaneously (see Fig. 1.4).

Figure 1.4   *Full-duplex*

The full-duplex mode is like a two-way street with traffic flowing in both directions at the same time. In full-duplex mode, signals going in either direction share the capacity of the link. This sharing can occur in two ways: Either the link must contain two physically separate transmission paths, one for sending and the other for receiving; or the capacity of the channel is divided between signals traveling in both directions.

One common example of full-duplex communication is the telephone network. When two people are communicating by a telephone line, both can talk and listen at the same time.

1.2   NETWORKS

A **network** is a set of devices (often referred to as *nodes*) connected by communication links. A node can be a computer, printer, or any other device capable of sending and/or receiving data generated by other nodes on the network.

Distributed Processing

Most networks use **distributed processing,** in which a task is divided among multiple computers. Instead of a single large machine being responsible for all aspects of a process, separate computers (usually a personal computer or workstation) handle a subset.

Network Criteria

A network must be able to meet a certain number of criteria. The most important of these are performance, reliability, and security.

Performance

Performance can be measured in many ways, including transit time and response time. Transit time is the amount of time required for a message to travel from one device to another. Response time is the elapsed time between an inquiry and a response. The performance of a network depends on a number of factors, including the number of users, the type of transmission medium, the capabilities of the connected hardware, and the efficiency of the software.

Reliability

In addition to accuracy of delivery, network **reliability** is measured by the frequency of failure, the time it takes a link to recover from a failure, and the network's robustness in a catastrophe.

Security

Network **security** issues include protecting data from unauthorized access.

Physical Structures

Before discussing networks, we need to define some network attributes.

Type of Connection

A network is two or more devices connected together through links. A link is a communications pathway that transfers data from one device to another. For visualization purposes, it is simplest to imagine any link as a line drawn between two points. For communication to occur, two devices must be connected in some way to the same link at the same time. There are two possible type of connections: point-to-point and multipoint.

Point-to-Point A **point-to-point** connection provides a dedicated link between two devices. The entire capacity of the link is reserved for transmission between those two devices. Most point-to-point connections use an actual length of wire or cable to connect the two ends, but other options, such as microwave or satellite links, are also possible (see Fig. 1.5). When you change television channels by infrared remote control, you are establishing a point-to-point connection between the remote control and the television's control system.

Figure 1.5 *Point-to-point connection*

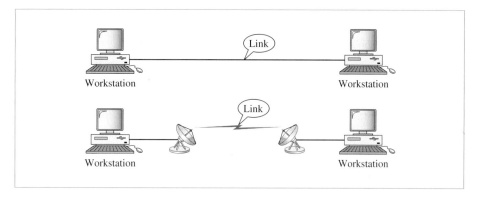

Multipoint A **multipoint** (also called **multidrop**) connection is one in which more than two specific devices share a single link (see Fig. 1.6).

In a multipoint environment, the capacity of the channel is shared, either spatially or temporally. If several devices can use the link simultaneously, it is a *spatially shared* connection. If users must take turns, it is a *timeshare* connection.

Figure 1.6 *Multipoint connection*

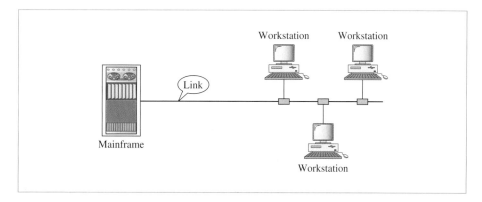

Physical Topology

The term **physical topology** refers to the way in which a network is laid out physically. Two or more devices connect to a link; two or more links form a topology. The topology of a network is the geometric representation of the relationship of all the links and

Figure 1.7   *Categories of topology*

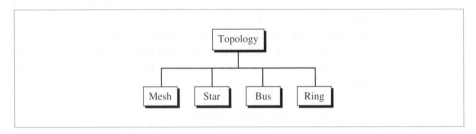

linking devices (usually called **nodes**) to one another. There are four basic topologies possible: mesh, star, bus, and ring (see Fig. 1.7).

Mesh   In a **mesh topology,** every device has a dedicated point-to-point link to every other device. The term *dedicated* means that the link carries traffic only between the two devices it connects. A fully connected mesh network therefore has $n(n-1)/2$ physical channels to link n devices. To accommodate that many links, every device on the network must have $n-1$ input/output (I/O) ports (see Fig. 1.8).

Figure 1.8   *Fully connected mesh topology (for five devices)*

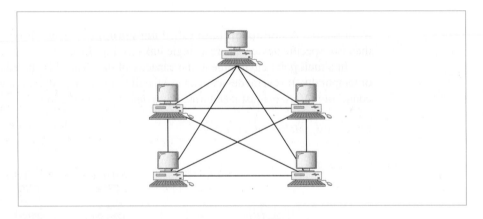

A mesh offers several advantages over other network topologies. First, the use of dedicated links guarantees that each connection can carry its own data load, thus eliminating the traffic problems that can occur when links must be shared by multiple devices. Second, a mesh topology is robust. If one link becomes unusable, it does not incapacitate the entire system. Another advantage is privacy or security. When every message travels along a dedicated line, only the intended recipient sees it. Physical boundaries prevent other users from gaining access to messages. Finally, point-to-point links make fault identification and fault isolation easy. Traffic can be routed to avoid links with suspected problems. This facility enables the network manager to discover the precise location of the fault and aids in finding its cause and solution.

The main disadvantages of a mesh are related to the amount of cabling and the number of I/O ports required. First, because every device must be connected to every other device, installation and reconnection are difficult. Second, the sheer bulk of the wiring can be greater than the available space (in walls, ceilings, or floors) can accommodate. Finally, the hardware required to connect each link (I/O ports and cable) can be prohibitively expensive. For these reasons a mesh topology is usually implemented in a limited fashion—for example, as a backbone connecting the main computers of a hybrid network that can include several other topologies.

Star   In a **star topology,** each device has a dedicated point-to-point link only to a central controller, usually called a **hub.** The devices are not directly linked to one another. Unlike a mesh topology, a star topology does not allow direct traffic between devices. The controller acts as an exchange: If one device wants to send data to another, it sends the data to the controller, which then relays the data to the other connected device (see Fig. 1.9).

Figure 1.9   *Star topology*

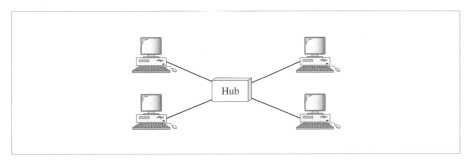

A star topology is less expensive than a mesh topology. In a star, each device needs only one link and one I/O port to connect it to any number of others. This factor also makes it easy to install and reconfigure. Far less cabling needs to be housed, and additions, moves, and deletions involve only one connection: between that device and the hub.

Other advantages include robustness. If one link fails, only that link is affected. All other links remain active. This factor also lends itself to easy fault identification and fault isolation. As long as the hub is working, it can be used to monitor link problems and bypass defective links.

However, although a star requires far less cable than a mesh, each node must be linked to a central hub. For this reason, often more cabling is required in a star than in some other topologies (such as ring or bus).

Bus   The preceding examples all describe point-to-point connections. A **bus topology,** on the other hand, is multipoint. One long cable acts as a **backbone** to link all the devices in a network (see Fig. 1.10).

Nodes are connected to the bus cable by drop lines and taps. A drop line is a connection running between the device and the main cable. A tap is a connector that either splices into the main cable or punctures the sheathing of a cable to create a contact with the metallic core. As a signal travels along the backbone, some of its energy is transformed into heat. Therefore, it becomes weaker and weaker as it has to travel farther

Figure 1.10   *Bus topology*

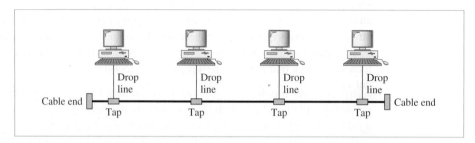

and farther. For this reason there is a limit on the number of taps a bus can support and on the distance between those taps.

Advantages of a bus topology include ease of installation. Backbone cable can be laid along the most efficient path, then connected to the nodes by drop lines of various lengths. In this way, a bus uses less cabling than mesh or star topologies. In a star, for example, four network devices in the same room require four lengths of cable reaching all the way to the hub. In a bus, this redundancy is eliminated. Only the backbone cable stretches through the entire facility. Each drop line has to reach only as far as the nearest point on the backbone.

Disadvantages include difficult reconnection and fault isolation. A bus is usually designed to be optimally efficient at installation. It can therefore be difficult to add new devices. Signal reflection at the taps can cause degradation in quality. This degradation can be controlled by limiting the number and spacing of devices connected to a given length of cable. Adding new devices may therefore require modification or replacement of the backbone.

In addition, a fault or break in the bus cable stops all transmission, even between devices on the same side of the problem. The damaged area reflects signals back in the direction of origin, creating noise in both directions.

Ring   In a **ring topology,** each device has a dedicated point-to-point connection only with the two devices on either side of it. A signal is passed along the ring in one direction, from device to device, until it reaches its destination. Each device in the ring incorporates a repeater. When a device receives a signal intended for another device, its repeater regenerates the bits and passes them along (see Fig. 1.11).

Figure 1.11   *Ring topology*

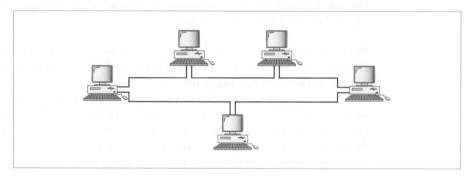

A ring is relatively easy to install and reconfigure. Each device is linked only to its immediate neighbors (either physically or logically). To add or delete a device requires changing only two connections. The only constraints are media and traffic considerations (maximum ring length and number of devices). In addition, fault isolation is simplified. Generally in a ring, a signal is circulating at all times. If one device does not receive a signal within a specified period, it can issue an alarm. The alarm alerts the network operator to the problem and its location.

However, unidirectional traffic can be a disadvantage. In a simple ring, a break in the ring (such as a disabled station) can disable the entire network. This weakness can be solved by using a dual ring or a switch capable of closing off the break.

Categories of Networks

Today when we speak of networks, we are generally referring to three primary categories: local area networks, metropolitan area networks, and wide area networks. Into which category a network falls is determined by its size, its ownership, the distance it covers, and its physical architecture (see Fig. 1.12).

Figure 1.12 *Categories of networks*

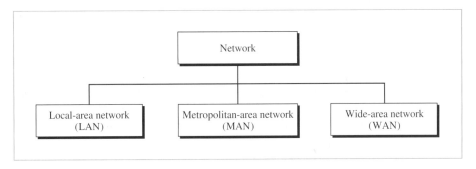

Local Area Network (LAN) A **local area network (LAN)** is usually privately owned and links the devices in a single office, building, or campus (see Fig. 1.13). Depending on the needs of an organization and the type of technology used, a LAN can be as simple as two PCs and a printer in someone's home office; or it can extend throughout a company and include audio and video peripherals. Currently, LAN size is limited to a few kilometers.

LANs are designed to allow resources to be shared between personal computers or workstations. The resources to be shared can include hardware (e.g., a printer), software (e.g., an application program), or data. A common example of a LAN, found in many business environments, links a workgroup of task-related computers, for example, engineering workstations or accounting PCs. One of the computers may be given a large-capacity disk drive and may become a server to the other clients. Software can be stored on this central server and used as needed by the whole group. In this example, the size of the LAN may be determined by licensing restrictions on the number of users per copy of software, or by restrictions on the number of users licensed to access the operating system.

Figure 1.13   *LAN*

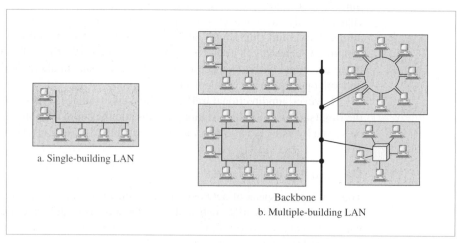

a. Single-building LAN

Backbone

b. Multiple-building LAN

In addition to size, LANs are distinguished from other types of networks by their transmission media and topology. In general, a given LAN will use only one type of transmission medium. The most common LAN topologies are bus, ring, and star.

Traditionally, LANs have data rates in the 4 to 16 megabits per second (Mbps) range. Today, however, speeds are increasing and can reach 100 Mbps with gigabit systems in development. LANs are discussed at length in Chapters 14, 15, and 16.

Metropolitan-Area Network (MAN)   A **metropolitan-area network (MAN)** is designed to extend over an entire city. It may be a single network such as a cable television network, or it may be a means of connecting a number of LANs into a larger network so that resources may be shared LAN-to-LAN as well as device-to-device. For example, a company can use a MAN to connect the LANs in all its offices throughout a city (see Fig. 1.14).

A MAN may be wholly owned and operated by a private company, or it may be a service provided by a public company, such as a local telephone company. Many

Figure 1.14   *MAN*

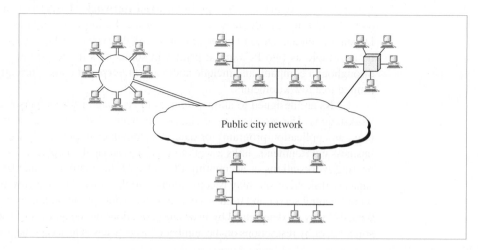

Public city network

telephone companies provide a popular MAN service called Switched Multi-megabit Data Services (SMDS).

Wide Area Network (WAN) A **wide area network (WAN)** provides long-distance transmission of data, voice, image, and video information over large geographic areas that may comprise a country, a continent, or even the whole world (see Fig. 1.15).

Figure 1.15 *WAN*

In contrast to LANs (which depend on their own hardware for transmission), WANs may utilize public, leased, or private communication equipment, usually in combinations, and can therefore span an unlimited number of miles.

A WAN that is wholly owned and used by a single company is often referred to as an *enterprise network*. WANs are discussed in Chapters 17 and 18.

Internetworks When two or more networks are connected, they become an **internetwork,** or **internet.**

1.3   THE INTERNET

The Internet has revolutionized many aspects of our daily lives. It has affected the way we do business as well as the way we spend our leisure time. Count the ways you've used the Internet recently. Perhaps you've sent electronic mail (email) to a business associate, paid a utility bill, read a newspaper from a distant city, or looked up a local movie schedule—all by using the Internet. Or maybe you researched a medical topic, booked a hotel reservation, chatted with a fellow Trekker, or comparison-shopped for a car. The Internet is a communication system that has brought a wealth of information to our fingertips and organized it for our use.

The Internet is a structured, organized system. We begin with a brief history of the Internet. We follow with a description of the Internet today.

A Brief History

A **network** is a group of connected communicating devices such as computers and printers. An internet (note the lowercase letter i) is two or more networks that can communicate with each other. The most notable internet is called the **Internet** (upper-case letter I), a collaboration of more than hundreds of thousands interconnected networks. Private individuals as well as various organizations such as government agencies, schools, research facilities, corporations, and libraries in more than 100 countries use the Internet. Millions of people are users. Yet this extraordinary communication system only came into being in 1969.

In the mid-1960s, mainframe computers in research organizations were stand-alone devices. Computers from different manufacturers were unable to communicate with one another. The **Advanced Research Projects Agency (ARPA)** in the Department of Defense (DOD) was interested in finding a way to connect computers so that the researchers they funded could share their findings, thereby reducing costs and eliminating duplication of effort.

In 1967, at an Association for Computing Machinery (ACM) meeting, ARPA presented its ideas for **ARPANET,** a small network of connected computers. The idea was that each host computer (not necessarily from the same manufacturer) would be attached to a specialized computer, called an *interface message processor* (IMP). The IMPs, in turn, would be connected to one another. Each IMP had to be able to communicate with other IMPs as well as with its own attached host.

By 1969, ARPANET was a reality. Four nodes, at the University of California at Los Angeles (UCLA), the University of California at Santa Barbara (UCSB), Stanford Research Institute (SRI), and the University of Utah, were connected via the IMPs to form a network. Software called the *Network Control Protocol* (NCP) provided communication between the hosts.

In 1972, Vint Cerf and Bob Kahn, both of whom were part of the core ARPANET group, collaborated on what they called the *Internetting Project*. Cerf and Kahn's landmark 1973 paper outlined the protocols to achieve end-to-end delivery of packets. This paper on Transmission Control Protocol (TCP) included concepts such as encapsulation, the datagram, and the functions of a gateway.

Shortly thereafter, authorities made a decision to split TCP into two protocols: **Transmission Control Protocol (TCP)** and **Internetworking Protocol (IP).** IP would handle datagram routing while TCP would be responsible for higher-level functions such as segmentation, reassembly, and error detection. The internetworking protocol became known as TCP/IP.

The Internet Today

The Internet has come a long way since the 1960s. The Internet today is not a simple hierarchical structure. It is made up of many wide- and local area networks joined by connecting devices and switching stations. It is difficult to give an accurate representation of the Internet because it is continuously changing—new networks are being added, existing networks are adding addresses, and networks of defunct companies are being removed. Today most end users who want Internet connection use the services of Internet service providers (ISPs). There are international service providers, national service providers, regional service providers, and local service providers. The Internet today is run by private companies, not the government. Figure 1.16 shows a conceptual (not geographic) view of the Internet.

Figure 1.16   *Internet today*

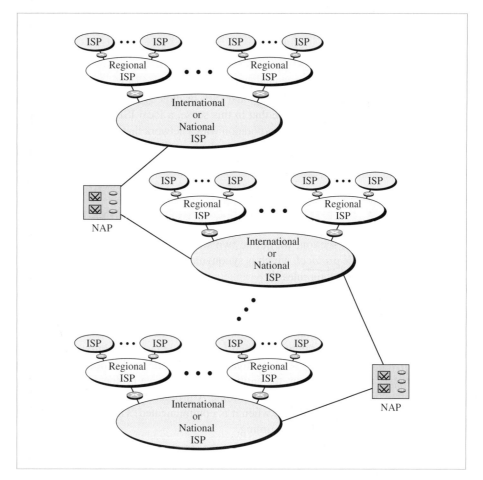

International Service Providers

At the top of the hierarchy are the international service providers that connect nations together.

National Service Providers (NSPs)

National service providers (NSPs) are backbone networks created and maintained by specialized companies. There are many NSPs operating in North America; some of the most well known are SprintLink, PSINet, UUNet Technology, AGIS, and internet MCI. To provide connectivity between the end users, these backbone networks are connected by complex switching stations (normally run by a third party), called **network access points (NAPs).** Some NSP networks are also connected to one another by private switching stations called *peering points*. NSPs normally operate at a high data rate (up to 600 Mbps).

Regional Internet Service Providers

Regional internet service providers or **regional ISPs** are smaller ISPs that are connected to one or more NSPs. They are at the third level of hierarchy with a lesser data rate.

Local Internet Service Providers

Local Internet service providers provide direct service to the end users. The local ISPs can be connected to regional ISPs or directly to NSPs. Most end users are connected to the local ISPs. Note that in this sense, a local ISP can be a company that just provides Internet services, a corporation with a network that supplies services to its own employees, or a nonprofit organization, such as a college or a university, that runs its own network. Each of these local ISPs can be connected to a regional or national service provider.

1.4   PROTOCOLS AND STANDARDS

In this section, we define two widely used terms: protocols and standards. First, we define *protocol,* which is synonymous with *rule*. Then we discuss *standards,* which are agreed-upon rules.

Protocols

In computer networks, communication occurs between entities in different systems. An **entity** is anything capable of sending or receiving information. However, two entities cannot simply send bit streams to each other and expect to be understood. For communication to occur, the entities must agree on a protocol. A **protocol** is a set of rules that governs data communications. A protocol defines what is communicated, how it is communicated, and when it is communicated. The key elements of a protocol are syntax, semantics, and timing.

- **Syntax.** Syntax refers to the structure or format of the data, meaning the order in which they are presented. For example, a simple protocol might expect the first 8 bits of data to be the address of the sender, the second 8 bits to be the address of the receiver, and the rest of the stream to be the message itself.

- **Semantics.** Semantics refers to the meaning of each section of bits. How is a particular pattern to be interpreted, and what action is to be taken based on that interpretation? For example, does an address identify the route to be taken or the final destination of the message?

- **Timing.** Timing refers to two characteristics: when data should be sent and how fast they can be sent. For example, if a sender produces data at 100 Mbps but the receiver can process data at only 1 Mbps, the transmission will overload the receiver and data will be largely lost.

Standards

Standards are essential in creating and maintaining an open and competitive market for equipment manufacturers and in guaranteeing national and international interoperability of data and telecommunications technology and processes. They provide guidelines to manufacturers, vendors, government agencies, and other service providers to ensure the kind of interconnectivity necessary in today's marketplace and in international communications. Data communication standards fall into two categories: *de facto* (meaning "by fact" or "by convention") and *de jure* (meaning "by law" or "by regulation").

■ **De facto.** Standards that have not been approved by an organized body but have been adopted as standards through widespread use are **de facto standards.** De facto standards are often established originally by manufacturers that seek to define the functionality of a new product or technology.

■ **De jure.** Those that have been legislated by an officially recognized body are **de jure standards.**

Standards Organizations

Standards are developed through the cooperation of standards creation committees, forums, and government regulatory agencies.

Standards Creation Committees

While many organizations are dedicated to the establishment of standards, data telecommunications in North America rely primarily on those published by the following:

■ **International Organization for Standardization (ISO).** The ISO is a multinational body whose membership is drawn mainly from the standards creation committees of various governments throughout the world. The ISO is active in developing cooperation in the realms of scientific, technological, and economic activity.

■ **International Telecommunication Union—Telecommunication Standards Sector (ITU-T).** By the early 1970s, a number of countries were defining national standards for telecommunications, but there was still little international compatibility. The United Nations responded by forming, as part of its International Telecommunication Union (ITU), a committee, the **Consultative Committee for International Telegraphy and Telephony (CCITT).** This committee was devoted to the research and establishment of standards for telecommunications in general and for phone and data systems in particular. On March 1, 1993, the name of this committee was changed to the International Telecommunication Union— Telecommunication Standards Sector (ITU-T).

■ **American National Standards Institute (ANSI).** Despite its name, the American National Standards Institute is a completely private, nonprofit corporation not affiliated with the U.S. federal government. However, all ANSI activities are undertaken with the welfare of the United States and its citizens occupying primary importance.

■ **Institute of Electrical and Electronics Engineers (IEEE).** The Institute of Electrical and Electronics Engineers is the largest professional engineering society in the world. International in scope, it aims to advance theory, creativity, and product quality in the fields of electrical engineering, electronics, and radio as well as in all related branches of engineering. As one of its goals, the IEEE oversees the development and adoption of international standards for computing and communications.

■ **Electronic Industries Association (EIA).** Aligned with ANSI, the Electronic Industries Association is a nonprofit organization devoted to the promotion of electronics manufacturing concerns. Its activities include public awareness education and lobbying efforts in addition to standards development. In the field of information technology, the EIA has made significant contributions by defining physical connection interfaces and electronic signaling specifications for data communication.

Forums

Telecommunications technology development is moving faster than the ability of standards committees to ratify standards. Standards committees are procedural bodies and by nature slow-moving. To accommodate the need for working models and agreements and to facilitate the standardization process, many special-interest groups have developed *forums* made up of representatives from interested corporations. The forums work with universities and users to test, evaluate, and standardize new technologies. By concentrating their efforts on a particular technology, the forums are able to speed acceptance and use of those technologies in the telecommunications community. The forums present their conclusions to the standards bodies.

Regulatory Agencies

All communications technology is subject to regulation by government agencies such as the **Federal Communications Commission (FCC)** in the United States. The purpose of these agencies is to protect the public interest by regulating radio, television, and wire/cable communications. The FCC has authority over interstate and international commerce as it relates to communications.

Internet Standards

An **Internet standard** is a thoroughly tested specification that is useful to and adhered to by those who work with the Internet. It is a formalized regulation that must be followed. There is a strict procedure by which a specification attains Internet standard status. A specification begins as an Internet draft. An **Internet draft** is a working document (a work in progress) with no official status and a 6-month lifetime. Upon recommendation from the Internet authorities, a draft may be published as a **Request for Comment (RFC).** Each RFC is edited, assigned a number, and made available to all interested parties. RFCs go through maturity levels and are categorized according to their requirement level.

1.5   KEY TERMS

Advanced Research Projects Agency
   (ARPA)
American National Standards Institute
   (ANSI)
ARPANET
audio
backbone
bus topology

code
Consultative Committee for International Telegraphy and Telephony
   (CCITT)
CSNET
data
data communications
de facto standards

de jure standards
distributed processing
Electronic Industries Association (EIA)
entity
Federal Communications Commission
  (FCC)
forum
full-duplex mode
half-duplex mode
hub
image
Institute of Electrical and Electronics
  Engineers (IEEE)
International Organization for
  Standardization (ISO)
International Telecommunication
  Union–Telecommunication
  Standards Sector (ITU-T)
Internet
Internet draft
Internet service provider (ISP)
Internet standard
internetwork (internet)
local area network (LAN)
local Internet service providers
maturity levels
mesh topology
message

metropolitan area network (MAN)
multipoint connection
national service provider (NSP)
network
node
performance
physical topology
point-to-point connection
protocol
receiver
regional ISPs
reliability
Request for Comment (RFC)
ring topology
security
semantics
sender
simplex mode
star topology
syntax
telecommunications
timing
Transmission Control Protocol/
  Internetworking Protocol (TCP/IP)
transmission medium
video
wide area network (WAN)

1.6   SUMMARY

❏ Data communication is the transfer of data from one device to another via some
   form of transmission medium.

❏ A data communications system must transmit data to the correct destination in an
   accurate and timely manner.

❏ The five components that make up a data communications system are the message,
   sender, receiver, medium, and protocol.

❏ Text, numbers, images, audio, and video are different forms of information.

❏ Data flow between two devices can occur in one of three ways: simplex, half-
   duplex, or full-duplex.

❏ A network is a set of communication devices connected by media links.

❏ In a point-to-point connection, two and only two devices are connected by a
   dedicated link. In a multipoint connection, three or more devices share a link.

❏ Topology refers to the physical or logical arrangement of a network. Devices may be arranged in a mesh, star, bus, or ring topology.

❏ A network can be categorized as a local area network (LAN), a metropolitan-area network (MAN), or a wide area network (WAN).

❏ A LAN is a data communication system within a building, plant, or campus, or between nearby buildings.

❏ A MAN is a data communication system covering an area the size of a town or city.

❏ A WAN is a data communication system spanning states, countries, or the whole world.

❏ An internet is a network of networks.

❏ The Internet is a collection of many separate networks.

❏ TCP/IP is the protocol suite for the Internet.

❏ There are local, regional, national, and international Internet service providers (ISPs).

❏ A protocol is a set of rules that governs data communication; the key elements of a protocol are syntax, semantics, and timing.

❏ Standards are necessary to ensure that products from different manufacturers can work together as expected.

❏ The ISO, ITU-T, ANSI, IEEE, and EIA are some of the organizations involved in standards creation.

❏ Forums are special-interest groups that quickly evaluate and standardize new technologies.

❏ A Request for Comment (RFC) is an idea or concept that is a precursor to an Internet standard.

1.7   PRACTICE SET

Review Questions

1. Identify the five components of a data communications system.
2. What are the advantages of distributed processing?
3. What are the three criteria necessary for an effective and efficient network?
4. What are the advantages of a multipoint connection over a point-to-point connection?
5. What are the two types of line configuration?
6. Categorize the four basic topologies in terms of line configuration.
7. What is the difference between half-duplex and full-duplex transmission modes?
8. Name the four basic network topologies, and give an advantage for each type.
9. For *n* devices in a network, what is the number of cable links required for a mesh, ring, bus, and star topology?
10. What are some of the factors that determine whether a communication system is a LAN, MAN, or WAN?
11. What is an internet? What is the Internet?

12. Why are protocols needed?
13. Why are standards needed?

Multiple-Choice Questions

14. The _____ is the physical path over which a message travels.
    a. Protocol
    b. Medium
    c. Signal
    d. All the above
15. The information to be communicated in a data communications system is the _____.
    a. Medium
    b. Protocol
    c. Message
    d. Transmission
16. Frequency of failure and network recovery time after a failure are measures of the _____ of a network.
    a. Performance
    b. Reliability
    c. Security
    d. Feasibility
17. An unauthorized user is a network _____ issue.
    a. Performance
    b. Reliability
    c. Security
    d. All the above
18. Which topology requires a central controller or hub?
    a. Mesh
    b. Star
    c. Bus
    d. Ring
19. Which topology requires a multipoint connection?
    a. Mesh
    b. Star
    c. Bus
    d. Ring
20. Communication between a computer and a keyboard involves _____ transmission.
    a. Simplex
    b. Half-duplex
    c. Full-duplex
    d. Automatic

21. In a network with 25 computers, which topology would require the most extensive cabling?

    a. Mesh

    b. Star

    c. Bus

    d. Ring

22. A television broadcast is an example of _____ transmission.

    a. Simplex

    b. Half-duplex

    c. Full-duplex

    d. Automatic

23. A _____ connection provides a dedicated link between two devices.

    a. Point-to-point

    b. Multipoint

    c. Primary

    d. Secondary

24. In a _____ connection, more than two devices can share a single link.

    a. Point-to-point

    b. Multipoint

    c. Primary

    d. Secondary

25. In _____ transmission, the channel capacity is shared by both communicating devices at all times.

    a. Simplex

    b. Half-duplex

    c. Full-duplex

    d. Half-simplex

26. A cable break in a _____ topology stops all transmission.

    a. Mesh

    b. Bus

    c. Star

    d. Primary

27. Which organization has authority over interstate and international commerce in the communications field?

    a. ITU-T

    b. IEEE

    c. FCC

    d. ISO

Exercises

28. Assume six devices are arranged in a mesh topology. How many cables are needed? How many ports are needed for each device?

29. For each of the following four networks, discuss the consequences if a connection fails.
    a. Five devices arranged in a mesh topology
    b. Five devices arranged in a star topology (not counting the hub)
    c. Five devices arranged in a bus topology
    d. Five devices arranged in a ring topology

30. Draw a hybrid topology with a star backbone and three ring networks.

31. Draw a hybrid topology with a ring backbone and two bus networks.

32. Draw a hybrid topology with a bus backbone connecting two ring backbones. Each ring backbone connects three star networks.

33. Draw a hybrid topology with a star backbone connecting two bus backbones. Each bus backbone connects three ring networks.

34. Find three standards defined by ISO.

35. Find three standards defined by ITU-T.

36. Find three standards defined by ANSI.

37. Find three standards defined by IEEE.

38. Find three standards defined by EIA.

39. Give two instances of how networks are a part of your life today.

40. When a party makes a local telephone call to another party, is this a point-to-point or multipoint connection? Explain your answer.

CHAPTER 2

Network Models

A network uses a combination of hardware and software to send data from one location to another. The hardware consists of the physical equipment that carries signals from one point of the network to another. However, the services that we expect from a network are more complex than just sending a signal from a source computer to a destination computer. In addition to hardware, we need software.

We can compare the task of networking to the task of solving a mathematics problem with a computer. The fundamental job of solving the problem in a computer is done by computer hardware. However, this is a very tedious task if only hardware is used. We would need switches for every memory location to store and manipulate data. The task is much easier if software is in the picture. At the highest level, a program can direct the problem-solving process; the details of how this is done by the actual hardware can be left to the layers of software that are called by higher levels.

There is a comparable situation with the computer network. The task of sending an email from one point in the world to another can be broken into several tasks, each performed by a separate software package. Each piece of software uses the services of another software package to do its job. At the lowest layer, a signal, or a set of signals, is sent from the source computer to the destination computer.

In this chapter, we give a general idea of the layers of a network and discuss the functions of each. Detailed descriptions of these layers follow in later chapters.

2.1 LAYERED TASKS

We use the concept of layers in our daily life. As an example, let us consider two friends who communicate through postal mail. The process of sending a letter to a friend would be complex if there were not services available from the post office. Figure 2.1 shows how this task is done.

Sender, Receiver, and Carrier

It is obvious that we have a sender, a receiver, and a carrier that transports the letter. There is a hierarchy of tasks.

Figure 2.1   *Sending a letter*

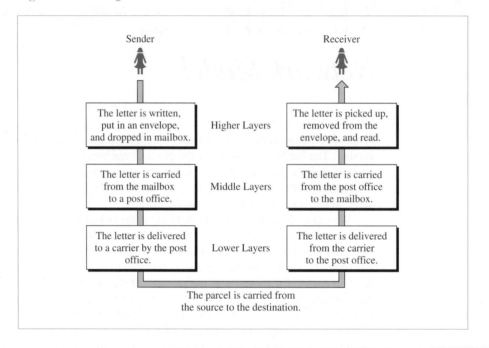

At the Sender Site

Let us first describe, in order, the activities that take place at the sender site.

- **Higher layer.** The sender writes the letter, inserts the letter in an envelope, writes the sender and receiver addresses, and drops the letter in a mailbox.
- **Middle layer.** The letter is picked up by a letter carrier and delivered to the post office.
- **Lower layer.** The letter is sorted at the post office; a carrier transports the letter.

On the Way

The letter is then on its way to the recipient. On the way to the recipient's local post office, it may actually go through a central office. In addition, the letter may be transported by truck, train, airplane, boat, or a combination.

At the Receiver Site

- **Lower layer.** The carrier transports the letter to the post office.
- **Middle layer.** The letter is sorted and delivered to the recipient's mailbox.
- **Higher layer.** The receiver picks up the letter, opens the envelope, and reads it.

Hierarchy

According to our analysis, there are three different activities at the sender site and another three activities at the receiver site. The task of transporting the letter between the sender and the receiver is done by the carrier. Something which is not obvious immediately is that the tasks must be done in the order given in the hierarchy. At the sender site, the letter must be written and dropped in the mailbox before being picked up by the letter carrier and delivered to the post office. At the receiver site, the letter must be dropped in the recipient mailbox before being picked up and read by the recipient.

Services

Each layer at the sending site uses the services of the layer immediately below it. The sender at the higher layer uses the services of the middle layer. The middle layer uses the services of the lower layer. The lower layer uses the services of the carrier.

2.2   INTERNET MODEL

The layered protocol stack that dominates data communications and networking today is the five-layer **Internet model,** sometimes called the **TCP/IP protocol suite** (see Fig. 2.2). The model is composed of five ordered layers: physical (layer 1), data link (layer 2), network (layer 3), transport (layer 4), and application (layer 5). Figure 2.3 shows the layers involved when a message is sent from device A to device B. As the message travels from A to B, it may pass through many intermediate nodes. These intermediate nodes usually involve only the first three layers of the model.

Figure 2.2   *Internet layers*

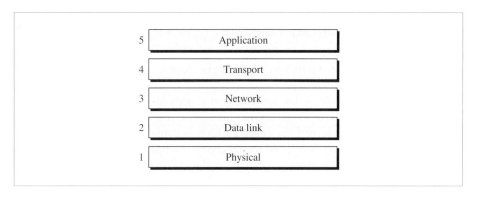

In developing the model, the designers distilled the process of transmitting data to its most fundamental elements. They identified which networking functions had related uses and collected those functions into discrete groups that became the layers. Each layer defines a family of functions distinct from those of the other layers. By defining and localizing functionality in this fashion, the designers created an architecture that is both comprehensive and flexible.

Within a single machine, each layer calls upon the services of the layer just below it. Layer 3, for example, uses the services provided by layer 2 and provides services for layer 4. Between machines, layer x on one machine communicates with layer x on another machine. This communication is governed by an agreed-upon series of rules

Figure 2.3 *Peer-to-peer processes*

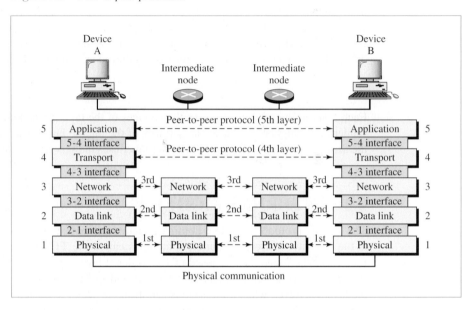

and conventions called protocols. The processes on each machine that communicate at a given layer are called **peer-to-peer processes.** Communication between machines is therefore a peer-to-peer process using the protocols appropriate to a given layer.

Peer-to-Peer Processes

At the physical layer, communication is direct: In Figure 2.3, device A sends a stream of bits to device B. At the higher layers, however, communication must move down through the layers on device A, over to device B, and then back up through the layers. Each layer in the sending device adds its own information to the message it receives from the layer just above it and passes the whole package to the layer just below it.

At layer 1 the entire package is converted to a form that can be transferred to the receiving device. At the receiving machine, the message is unwrapped layer by layer, with each process receiving and removing the data meant for it. For example, layer 2 removes the data meant for it, then passes the rest to layer 3. Layer 3 then removes the data meant for it and passes the rest to layer 4, and so on.

Interfaces Between Layers

The passing of the data and network information down through the layers of the sending device and back up through the layers of the receiving device is made possible by an **interface** between each pair of adjacent layers. Each interface defines what information and services a layer must provide for the layer above it. Well-defined interfaces and layer functions provide modularity to a network. As long as a layer provides the expected services to the layer above it, the specific implementation of its functions can be modified or replaced without requiring changes to the surrounding layers.

Organization of the Layers

The five layers can be thought of as belonging to three subgroups. Layers 1, 2, and 3—physical, data link, and network—are the network support layers; they deal with the physical aspects of moving data from one device to another (such as electrical specifications, physical connections, physical addressing, and transport timing and reliability). Layer 5—application—can be thought of as the user support layer; it allows interoperability among unrelated software systems. Layer 4, the transport layer, links the two subgroups and ensures that what the lower layers have transmitted is in a form that the upper layers can use.

In Figure 2.4, which gives an overall view of the layers, L5 data means the data unit at layer 5, L4 data means the data unit at layer 4, and so on. The process starts at layer 5 (the application layer), then moves from layer to layer in descending, sequential order. At each layer, a **header** can be added to the data unit. At layer 2, a **trailer** is added as well. When the formatted data unit passes through the physical layer (layer 1), it is changed into an electromagnetic signal and transported along a physical link.

Figure 2.4   *An exchange using the Internet model*

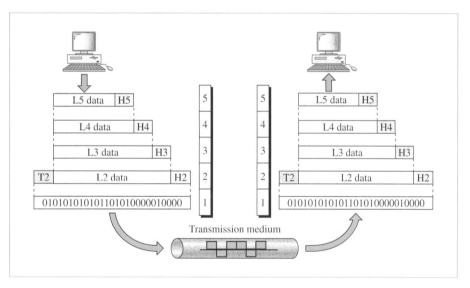

Upon reaching its destination, the signal passes into layer 1 and is transformed back into digital form. The data units then move back up through the layers. As each block of data reaches the next-higher layer, the headers and trailers attached to it at the corresponding sending layer are removed, and actions appropriate to that layer are taken. By the time it reaches layer 5, the message is again in a form appropriate to the application and is made available to the recipient.

Functions of Layers

In this section we briefly describe the functions of each layer.

Physical Layer

The **physical layer** coordinates the functions required to transmit a bit stream over a physical medium. It deals with the mechanical and electrical specifications of the interface and transmission media. It also defines the procedures and functions that physical devices and interfaces have to perform for transmission to occur. Figure 2.5 shows the position of the physical layer with respect to the transmission media and the data link layer.

Figure 2.5   *Physical layer*

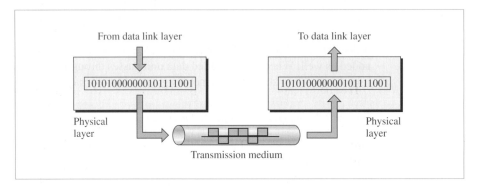

The physical layer is responsible for transmitting individual bits from one node to the next.

We discuss the physical layer in Part II of this book and include the dominant protocols designed for this layer. The major duties of the physical layer are as follows:

- **Physical characteristics of interfaces and media.** The physical layer defines the characteristics of the interface between the devices and the transmission media. It also defines the type of transmission medium (see Chapter 7).

- **Representation of bits.** The physical layer data consists of a stream of **bits** (sequence of 0s or 1s) without any interpretation. To be transmitted, bits must be encoded into signals—electrical or optical. The physical layer defines the type of representation (how 0s and 1s are changed to signals).

- **Data rate.** The **transmission rate**—the number of bits sent each second—is also defined by the physical layer. In other words, the physical layer defines the duration of a bit, which is how long it lasts.

- **Synchronization of bits.** The sender and receiver not only must use the same bit rate but also must be synchronized at the bit level. In other words, the sender and the receiver clocks must be synchronized.

Data Link Layer

The **data link layer** transforms the physical layer, a raw transmission facility, to a reliable link. It makes the physical layer appear error-free to the upper layer (network layer). Figure 2.6 shows the relationship of the data link layer to the network and physical layers.

Figure 2.6 *Data link layer*

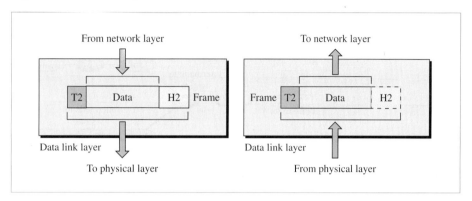

The data link layer is responsible for transmitting frames from one node to the next.

We discuss the data link layer in Part III of this book and include the dominant protocols designed for this layer. The major duties of the data link layer are as follows:

- **Framing.** The data link layer divides the stream of bits received from the network layer into manageable data units called **frames.**

- **Physical addressing.** If frames are to be distributed to different systems on the network, the data link layer adds a header to the frame to define the sender and/or receiver of the frame. If the frame is intended for a system outside the sender's network, the receiver address is the address of the connecting device that connects the network to the next one.

- **Flow control.** If the rate at which the data are absorbed by the receiver is less than the rate produced in the sender, the data link layer imposes a flow control mechanism to prevent overwhelming the receiver.

- **Error control.** The data link layer adds reliability to the physical layer by adding mechanisms to detect and retransmit damaged or lost frames. It also uses a mechanism to prevent duplication of frames. Error control is normally achieved through a trailer added to the end of the frame.

- **Access control.** When two or more devices are connected to the same link, data link layer protocols are necessary to determine which device has control over the link at any given time.

Figure 2.7 illustrates **hop-to-hop (node-to-node) delivery** by the data link layer.

Example 1

In Figure 2.8 a node with physical address 10 sends a frame to a node with physical address 87. The two nodes are connected by a link. At the data link level this frame contains physical addresses in the header. These are the only addresses needed. The rest of the header contains other information needed at this level. The trailer usually contains extra bits needed for error detection.

Figure 2.7   *Node-to-node delivery*

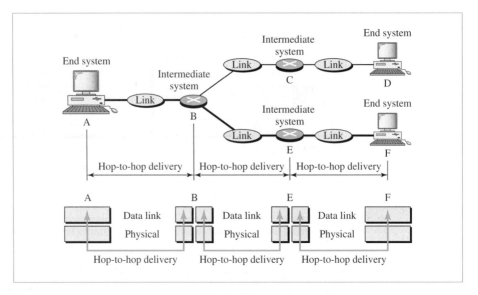

Figure 2.8   *Example 1*

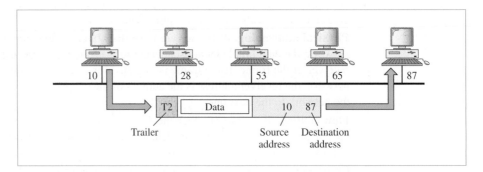

Network Layer

The **network layer** is responsible for the **source-to-destination delivery** of a packet possibly across multiple networks. Whereas the data link layer oversees the delivery of the packet between two systems on the same network, the network layer ensures that each packet gets from its point of origin to its final destination.

■   If two systems are connected to the same link, there is usually no need for a network layer. However, if the two systems are attached to different networks with connecting devices between the networks, there is often a need for the network layer to accomplish source-to-destination delivery. Figure 2.9 shows the relationship of the network layer to the data link and transport layers.

We discuss the network layer in Part IV of this book and include the dominant protocols designed for this layer. The major duties of the network layer are as follows:

■   **Logical addressing.** The physical addressing implemented by the data link layer handles the addressing problem locally. If a packet passes the network boundary,

Figure 2.9   *Network layer*

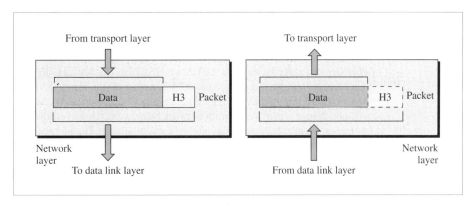

The network layer is responsible for the delivery of packets from the original source to the final destination.

we need another addressing system to help distinguish the source and destination systems. The network layer adds a header to the packet coming from the upper layer that, among other things, includes the logical addresses of the sender and receiver.

■ **Routing.** When independent networks or links are connected to create an **internetwork** (network of networks) or a large network, the connecting devices (called *routers* or *switches*) route or switch the packets to their final destination. One of the functions of the network layer is to provide this mechanism.

Figure 2.10 illustrates source-to-destination delivery by the network layer.

Figure 2.10   *Source-to-destination delivery*

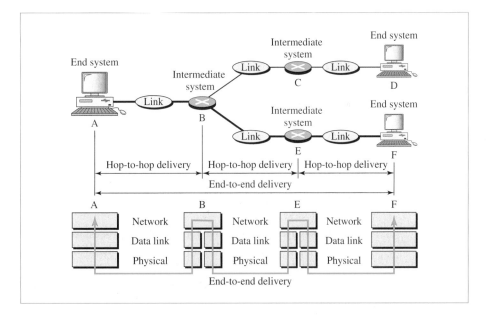

Example 2

In Figure 2.11 we want to send data from a node with network address A and physical address 10, located on one LAN, to a node with a network address P and physical address 95, located on another LAN. Because the two devices are located on different networks, we cannot use physical addresses only; the physical addresses only have local jurisdiction. What we need here are universal addresses that can pass through the LAN boundaries. The network (logical) addresses have this characteristic. The packet at the network layer contains the logical addresses, which remain the same from the original source to the final destination (A and P, respectively, in the figure). They will not change when we go from network to network. However, the physical addresses will change as the packet moves from one network to another. The box with the R is a router (inter-network device), which we will discuss in Chapter 16.

Figure 2.11   *Example 2*

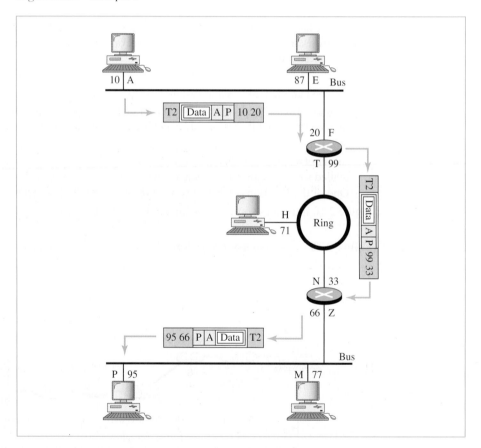

Transport Layer

The **transport layer** is responsible for **process-to-process delivery** of the entire message. Whereas the network layer oversees host-to-destination delivery of individual packets, it does not recognize any relationship between those packets. It treats each one independently, as though each piece belonged to a separate message, whether or not it does. The transport layer, on the other hand, ensures that the whole message arrives intact and in order, overseeing both error control and flow control at the process-to-process level. Figure 2.12 shows the relationship of the transport layer to the network and session layers.

Figure 2.12 *Transport layer*

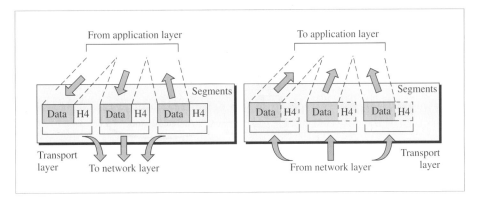

The transport layer is responsible for delivery of a message from one process to another.

We discuss the transport layer in Part V of this book and include the dominant protocols designed for this layer. The major duties of the transport layer are as follows:

- **Port addressing.** Computers often run several processes (running programs) at the same time. For this reason, process-to-process delivery means delivery not only from one computer to the next but also from a specific process on one computer to a specific process on the other. The transport layer header must therefore include a type of address called a **port address.** The network layer gets each packet to the correct computer; the transport layer gets the entire message to the correct process on that computer.

- **Segmentation and reassembly.** A message is divided into transmittable segments, each segment containing a sequence number. These numbers enable the transport layer to reassemble the message correctly upon arrival at the destination and to identify and replace packets that were lost in the transmission.

- **Connection control.** The transport layer can be either connectionless or connection-oriented. A connectionless transport layer treats each segment as an independent packet and delivers it to the transport layer at the destination machine. A connection-oriented transport layer makes a connection with the transport layer at the destination machine first before delivering the packets. After all the data are transferred, the connection is terminated.

- **Flow control.** Like the data link layer, the transport layer is responsible for flow control. However, flow control at this layer is performed end to end rather than across a single link.

- **Error control.** Like the data link layer, the transport layer is responsible for error control. However, error control at this layer is performed end to end rather than across a single link. The sending transport layer makes sure that the entire message arrives at the receiving transport layer without **error** (damage, loss, or duplication). Error correction is usually achieved through retransmission.

Figure 2.13 illustrates a process-to-process delivery by the transport layer.

Figure 2.13 *Reliable process-to-process delivery of a message*

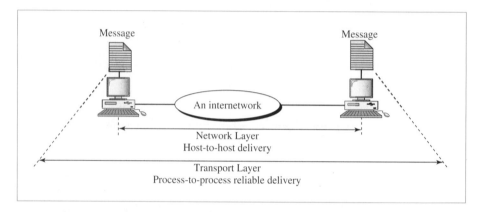

Example 3

Figure 2.14 shows an example of transport layer communication. Data coming from the upper layers have port addresses j and k (j is the address of the sending process, and k is the address of the receiving process). Since the data size is larger than the network layer can handle, the data are split into two packets, each packet retaining the port addresses (j and k). Then in the network layer, network addresses (A and P) are added to each packet. The packets can travel on different

Figure 2.14 *Example 3*

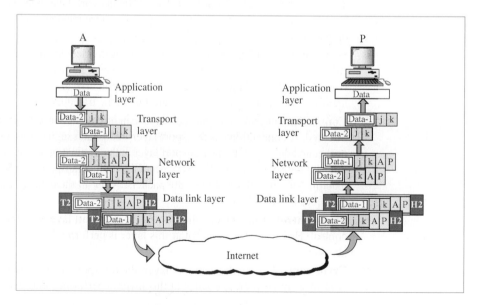

paths and arrive at the destination either in order or out of order. The two packets are delivered to the destination transport layer, which is responsible for removing the transport layer headers and combining the two pieces of data for delivery to the application layer.

Application Layer

The **application layer** enables the user, whether human or software, to access the network. It provides user interfaces and support for services such as electronic mail, remote file access and transfer, access to the World Wide Web, and so on.

Figure 2.15 shows the relationship of the application layer to the user and the transport layer.

Figure 2.15   *Application layer*

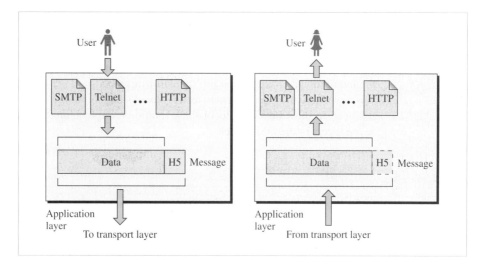

The application layer is responsible for providing services to the user.

We discuss the application layer in Part VI of this book and include the dominant protocols designed for this layer. The major duties of the application layer are as follows:

- **Mail services.** This application is the basis for email forwarding and storage.
- **File transfer and access.** This application allows a user to access files in a remote host (to make changes or read data), to retrieve files from a remote computer for use in the local computer, and to manage or control files in a remote computer locally.
- **Remote log-in.** A user can log into a remote computer and access the resources of that computer.
- **Accessing the World Wide Web.** The most common application today is the access of the World Wide Web (WWW).

Summary of Layers

Figure 2.16 summarizes the duties of each layer.

Figure 2.16   *Summary of duties*

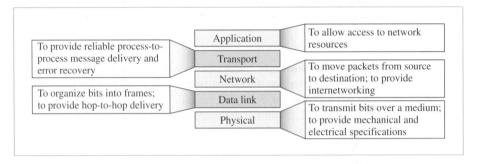

2.3   OSI MODEL

Another model, the **Open Systems Interconnection,** or **OSI,** model, was designed by the International Organization for Standardization (ISO). It is a seven-layer model. OSI was never seriously implemented as a protocol stack, however; it is a theoretical model designed to show how a protocol stack should be implemented. Figure 2.17 shows the seven layers in the OSI model.

Figure 2.17   *OSI model*

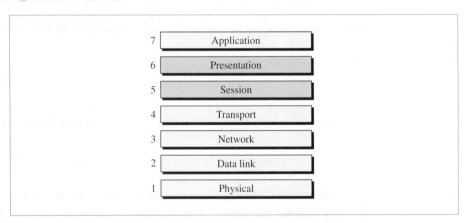

As Figure 2.17 shows, OSI defines two extra layers: the session and presentation layers. The **session layer** is the network *dialog controller*. It was designed to establish, maintain, and synchronize the interaction between communicating systems.

The **presentation layer** was designed to handle the syntax and semantics of the information exchanged between the two systems. It was designed for data translation, encryption, decryption, and compression.

The OSI model is briefly discussed in Appendix C.

Today, however, the duties of these two layers are handled by other layers; for example, encryption and decryption occur at several layers. Data are compressed at the application layer by the protocols at that level. For these reasons, we concentrate on the five-layer Internet model.

2.4 KEY TERMS

access control	node-to-node delivery
application layer	Open Systems Interconnection (OSI)
connection control	model
data link layer	peer-to-peer process
error	physical addressing
error control	physical layer
flow control	port address
frame	presentation layer
header	process-to-process delivery
hop-to-hop delivery	routing
interface	segmentation
Internet model	session layer
internetwork	source-to-destination delivery
logical addressing	TCP/IP protocol suite
mail service	trailer
network layer	transport layer

2.5 SUMMARY

❏ The five-layer model provides guidelines for the development of universally compatible networking protocols.

❏ The physical, data link, and network layers are the network support layers.

❏ The application layer is the user support layer.

❏ The transport layer links the network support layers and the user support layer.

❏ The physical layer coordinates the functions required to transmit a bit stream over a physical medium.

❏ The data link layer is responsible for delivering data units from one station to the next without errors.

❏ The network layer is responsible for the source-to-destination delivery of a packet across multiple network links.

❏ The transport layer is responsible for the process-to-process delivery of the entire message.

❏ The application layer enables the users to access the network.

2.6   PRACTICE SET

Review Questions

1. List the layers of the Internet model.
2. Which layers in the Internet model are the network support layers?
3. Which layer in the Internet model is the user support layer?
4. What is the difference between network layer delivery and transport layer delivery?
5. What is a peer-to-peer process?
6. How does information get passed from one layer to the next in the Internet model?
7. What are headers and trailers, and how do they get added and removed?
8. What are the concerns of the physical layer in the Internet model?
9. What are the responsibilities of the data link layer in the Internet model?
10. What are the responsibilities of the network layer in the Internet model?
11. What are the responsibilities of the transport layer in the Internet model?
12. What is the difference between a port address, a logical address, and a physical address?
13. Name some services provided by the application layer in the Internet model.
14. How do the layers of the Internet model correlate to the layers of the OSI model?

Multiple-Choice Questions

15. The Internet model consists of _____ layers.
    a. Three
    b. Five
    c. Seven
    d. Eight
16. The process-to-process delivery of the entire message is the responsibility of the _____ layer.
    a. Network
    b. Transport
    c. Application
    d. Physical
17. The _____ layer is the layer closest to the transmission medium.
    a. Physical
    b. Data link
    c. Network
    d. Transport
18. Mail services are available to network users through the _____ layer.
    a. Data link
    b. Physical

    c. Transport

    d. Application

19. As the data packet moves from the lower to the upper layers, headers are _____.

    a. Added

    b. Subtracted

    c. Rearranged

    d. Modified

20. As the data packet moves from the upper to the lower layers, headers are _____.

    a. Added

    b. Removed

    c. Rearranged

    d. Modified

21. The _____ layer lies between the network layer and the application layer.

    a. Physical

    b. Data link

    c. Transport

    d. None of the above

22. Layer 2 lies between the physical layer and the _____ layer.

    a. Network

    b. Data link

    c. Transport

    d. None of the above

23. When data are transmitted from device A to device B, the header from A's layer 4 is read by B's _____ layer.

    a. Physical

    b. Transport

    c. Application

    d. None of the above

24. The _____ layer changes bits into electromagnetic signals.

    a. Physical

    b. Data link

    c. Transport

    d. None of the above

25. The physical layer is concerned with the transmission of _____ over the physical medium.

    a. Programs

    b. Dialogs

    c. Protocols

    d. Bits

26. Which layer functions as a liaison between user support layers and network support layers?
    a. Network layer
    b. Physical layer
    c. Transport layer
    d. Application layer
27. What is the main function of the transport layer?
    a. Node-to-node delivery
    b. Process-to-process delivery
    c. Synchronization
    d. Updating and maintenance of routing tables
28. Which of the following is an application layer service?
    a. Remote log-in
    b. File transfer and access
    c. Mail service
    d. All the above

Exercises

29. Match the following to one of the five Internet layers.
    a. Route determination
    b. Flow control
    c. Interface to physical world
    d. Provides access to the network for the end user
    e. Packet switching
30. Match the following to one of the five Internet layers.
    a. Reliable process-to-process data transportation
    b. Network selection
    c. Routing
    d. Provides user services such as email and file transfer
    e. Transmission of bit stream across physical medium
31. Match the following to one of the five Internet layers.
    a. Communicates directly with user's application program
    b. Error correction and retransmission
    c. Mechanical, electrical, and functional interface
    d. Responsibility for delivery between adjacent nodes
    e. Reassembly of data packets

PART 2

Physical Layer

We start the discussion of the Internet model with the bottom-most layer, the physical layer. It is the layer that actually interacts with the transmission media, the physical part of the network that connects network components together. This layer is involved in physically carrying information from one node in the network to the next. Figure 1 shows the position of the physical layer in the 5-layer Internet model.

Figure 1 *Position of the physical layer*

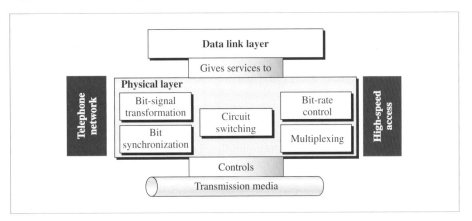

The physical layer has complex tasks to perform. One major task is to provide services for the data link layer. The data in the data link layer consists of 0s and 1s organized into frames that are ready to be sent across the transmission medium. This stream of 0s and 1s must first be converted into another entity: signals. One of the services provided by the physical layer is to create a signal that represents this stream of bits.

The physical layer must also take care of the physical network, the transmission medium. The transmission medium is a passive entity; it has no internal program or logic for control like other layers. The transmission medium must be controlled by the physical layer. The physical layer decides on the directions of data flow. The physical layer decides on the number of logical channels for transporting data coming from different sources.

Services

The physical layer transfers a stream of bits (in the form of a signal) from the sender to the receiver. The transfer is node-to-node, from one node to the next. The physical layers of the two adjacent nodes provide a logical pipe through which the bits can travel. Figure 2 shows the general services offered by the physical layer.

Figure 2   *Physical layer services*

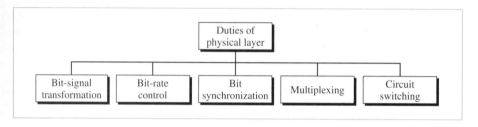

Bit-to-Signal Transformation

The logical pipe under the physical layer is the transmission media (cable or air). Since a transmission medium cannot carry bits, we need to represent the bits by a signal, electromagnetic energy that can propagate through a medium.

Bit-Rate Control

Although the transmission medium determines the upper limit of the data rate, the physical layer is the controller. The design of the physical-layer hardware and software determine the data rate.

Bit-Synchronization

The timing of the bit transfer is crucial in data communications. The physical layer governs the synchronization of the bits by providing clocking mechanisms that control both the sender and the receiver.

Multiplexing

Multiplexing is the process of dividing a link, the physical medium, into logical channels for better efficiency. The physical layer, using different techniques, can do this. Although the medium itself is not actually changed, the result is several channels instead of one. Multiplexing defined in this section of the text is needed to understand access methods in later chapters.

Switching

Switching in data communications can be done in several layers. We have circuit-switching, packet-switching, and message switching. Circuit switching, a method that allows two nodes to have a dedicated link, is mostly a function of the physical layer.

Packet switching is discussed in Chapter 18 as a data-link-layer issue and in Chapter 19 as a network-layer issue.

Transmission Media

The physical layer is dependent on the transmission media to carry its bits (in signal form). Although the transmission media are not actually a part of the physical layer, the media are controlled by this layer. Media can be guided and unguided. Twisted-pair cable, coaxial cable, and fiber-optic cables are discussed in the guided media section. Radio and microwave communication are included in the unguided section.

Networks and Technologies

To connect the issues discussed in Chapters 3 to 7, we have included several examples of networks and technologies which provide services at the physical layer.

Telephone Network

Most of the networks today have their beginnings in the telephone network. Telephone networks have been around for some time and provide voice communication around the world. When the need for data communication started, the telephone network was the foundation. Data were transformed into analog signals and sent over the same networks that sent voice. We discuss the telephone network as a prelude to other specific data networks and also as a good example of a network with the physical layer issues covered in this part of the book. We also give a brief historical background of the telephone network to understand the reasons for some recent developments such as LATAs.

High Speed Access

Accessing the Internet requires a physical connection between the user and a company known as the Internet service provider. We introduce modems, an Internet access method that many users find too slow. We present two alternative technologies. DSL technology provides a faster physical connection, again using the existing telephone line. The cable TV network allows the use of some channels previously assigned for video broadcasting for data transfer to and from the Internet.

Chapters

Part two of the book covers seven chapters. Chapters 3 introduces the concepts and characteristics of signals as the vehicle for carrying data. Chapters 4 and 5 show how we can change bits into digital or analog signals. Chapter 6 is about multiplexing, an important issue due to the improvements in transmission media bandwidth. Although transmission media are located below the physical layer, it is controlled by the physical layer. We have included the discussion of media in Chapter 7. Chapter 8 discusses switching, a topic that can be related to several layers. We have, however, discussed only circuit switching, which is mostly a physical-layer issue. To show an application of circuit switching, we have introduced the telephone network and several topics related to this network. The main purpose of most networks today is to access the Internet. Chapter 9 introduces several technologies that allow the user to access the Internet.

CHAPTER 3

Signals

One of the major concerns of the physical layer lies in moving data in the form of electromagnetic signals across a transmission medium. Whether you are collecting numerical statistics from another computer, sending animated pictures from a design workstation, or causing a bell to ring at a distant control center, you are working with the transmission of *data* across network connections.

Generally, the data usable to a person or application are not in a form that can be transmitted over a network. For example, you cannot roll up a photograph, insert it into a wire, and transmit it across town. You can, however, transmit an encoded description of the photograph. Instead of sending the actual photograph, you can use an encoder to create a stream of 1s and 0s that tells the receiving device how to reconstruct the image of the photograph.

But even 1s and 0s cannot be sent as such across network links. They must be further converted to a form that transmission media can accept. Transmission media work by conducting energy along a physical path. So a data stream of 1s and 0s must be turned into energy in the form of electromagnetic signals.

To be transmitted, data must be transformed to electromagnetic signals.

3.1 ANALOG AND DIGITAL

Both data and the signals that represent them can take either *analog* or *digital* form.

Analog and Digital Data

Data can be analog or digital. An example of **analog data** is the human voice. When someone speaks, an analog wave is created in the air. This can be captured by a microphone and converted to an analog signal or sampled later and converted to a digital signal.

An example of **digital data** is data stored in the memory of a computer in the form of 0s and 1s. It can be converted to a digital signal when it is transferred from one position to another inside or outside the computer or modulated into an analog signal and then sent through a transmission medium to another computer.

Analog and Digital Signals

Like the data they represent, **signals** can be either analog or digital. An **analog signal** has infinitely many levels of intensity over a period of time. As the wave moves from value A to value B, it passes through and includes an infinite number of values along its path. A **digital signal,** on the other hand, can have only a limited number of defined values, often as simple as 1 and 0.

The simplest way to show signals is by plotting them on a pair of perpendicular axes. The vertical axis represents the value or strength of a signal. The horizontal axis represents the passage of time. Figure 3.1 illustrates an analog and a digital signal. The curve representing the analog signal is passing through an infinite number of points. The vertical lines of the digital signal, however, demonstrate the sudden jump the signal makes from value to value.

> **Signals can be analog or digital. Analog signals can have an infinite number of values in a range; digital signals can have only a limited number of values.**

Figure 3.1   *Comparison of analog and digital signals*

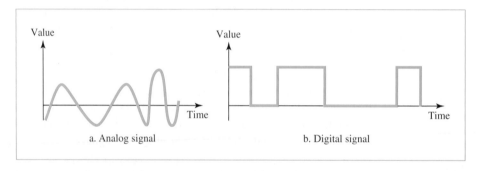

Periodic and Aperiodic Signals

Both analog and digital signals can take one of two forms: *periodic* and *aperiodic* (nonperiodic).

A **periodic signal** completes a pattern within a measurable time frame, called a **period,** and repeats that pattern over subsequent identical periods. The completion of one full pattern is called a **cycle.** An **aperiodic signal** changes without exhibiting a pattern or cycle that repeats over time.

Both analog and digital signals can be periodic or aperiodic. In data communication, however, we commonly use periodic analog signals and aperiodic digital signals to send data from one point to another.

> **In data communication, we commonly use periodic analog signals and aperiodic digital signals.**

3.2   ANALOG SIGNALS

Analog signals can be classified as simple or composite. A simple analog signal, a **sine wave,** cannot be decomposed into simpler signals. A composite analog signal is composed of multiple sine waves.

Sine Wave

The sine wave is the most fundamental form of a periodic analog signal. Visualized as a simple oscillating curve, its change over the course of a cycle is smooth and consistent, a continuous, rolling flow. Figure 3.2 shows a sine wave. Each cycle consists of a single arc above the time axis followed by a single arc below it.

Figure 3.2   *A sine wave*

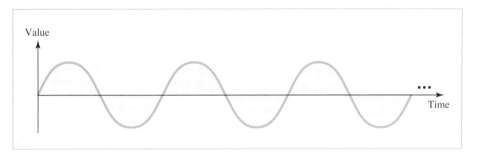

We can mathematically describe a sine wave as

$$s(t) = A\sin(2\pi ft + \phi)$$

where *s* is the *instantaneous amplitude, A* the *peak amplitude, f* the *frequency,* and ϕ the *phase*. These three characteristics fully describe a sine wave.

Peak Amplitude

The **peak amplitude** of a signal represents the absolute value of its highest intensity, proportional to the energy it carries. For electric signals, peak amplitude is normally measured in *volts* (see Fig. 3.3).

Figure 3.3   *Amplitude*

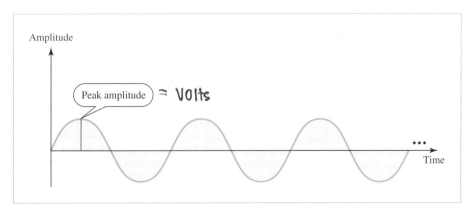

Period and Frequency

Period refers to the amount of time, in seconds, a signal needs to complete one cycle. **Frequency** refers to the number of periods in one second. Note that period and frequency are just one characteristic defined in two ways. Period is the inverse of frequency, and frequency is the inverse of period, as shown in the following formulas.

$$f = \frac{1}{T} \quad \text{and} \quad T = \frac{1}{f}$$

Frequency and period are inverses of each other.

Figure 3.4 shows the concept of period and frequency.

Figure 3.4   *Period and frequency*

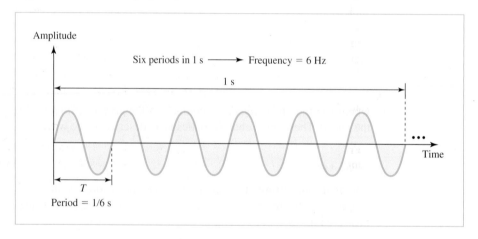

Period is formally expressed in seconds. Frequency is formally expressed in **hertz (Hz),** as shown in Table 3.1.

Table 3.1   *Units of period and frequency*

Unit	Equivalent	Unit	Equivalent
Seconds (s)	1 s	hertz (Hz)	1 Hz
Milliseconds (ms)	10^{-3} s	kilohertz (KHz)	10^{3} Hz
Microseconds (µs)	10^{-6} s	megahertz (MHz)	10^{6} Hz
Nanoseconds (ns)	10^{-9} s	gigahertz (GHz)	10^{9} Hz
Picoseconds (ps)	10^{-12} s	terahertz (THz)	10^{12} Hz

Example 1

Express a period of 100 ms in microseconds, and express the corresponding frequency in kilohertz.

Solution

Let us first express 100 ms in microseconds. From Table 3.1 we find the equivalent of 1 ms (1 ms is 10^{-3} s) and 1 s (1 s is 10^6 μs). We make the following substitutions:

$$100 \text{ ms} = 100 \times 10^{-3} \text{ s} = 100 \times 10^{-3} \times 10^6 \text{ μs} = 10^5 \text{ μs}$$

Now we use the inverse relationship to find the frequency, changing hertz to kilohertz (1 Hz is 10^{-3} KHz).

$$100 \text{ ms} = 100 \times 10^{-3} \text{ s} = 10^{-1} \text{ s} \longrightarrow f = \frac{1}{10^{-1}} \text{ Hz} = 10 \times 10^{-3} \text{ KHz} = 10^{-2} \text{ KHz}$$

More About Frequency

We know already that frequency is the relationship of a signal to time and that the frequency of a wave is the number of cycles it completes per second. But another way to look at frequency is as a measurement of the rate of change. Electromagnetic signals are oscillating waveforms; that is, they fluctuate continuously and predictably above and below a mean energy level. A 40-Hz signal has one-half the frequency of an 80-Hz signal; it completes one cycle in twice the time of the 80-Hz signal, so each cycle also takes twice as long to change from its lowest to its highest voltage levels. Frequency, therefore, though described in cycles per second (hertz), is a general measurement of the rate of change of a signal with respect to time.

Frequency is the rate of change with respect to time. Change in a short span of time means high frequency. Change over a long span of time means low frequency.

If the value of a signal changes over a very short span of time, its frequency is high. If it changes over a long span of time, its frequency is low.

Two Extremes

What if a signal does not change at all? What if it maintains a constant voltage level for the entire time it is active? In such a case, its frequency is zero. Conceptually, this idea is a simple one. If a signal does not change at all, it never completes a cycle, so its frequency is 0 Hz.

But what if a signal changes instantaneously? What if it jumps from one level to another in no time? Then its frequency is infinite. In other words, when a signal changes instantaneously, its period is zero; since frequency is the inverse of period, in this case, the frequency is 1/0, or infinite (unbounded).

If a signal does not change at all, its frequency is zero. If a signal changes instantaneously, its frequency is infinite.

Phase

The term **phase** describes the position of the waveform relative to time zero. If we think of the wave as something that can be shifted backward or forward along the time axis, phase describes the amount of that shift. It indicates the status of the first cycle.

Phase describes the position of the waveform relative to time zero.

Phase is measured in degrees or radians [360° is 2π rad; 1° is $2\pi/360$ rad, and 1 rad is $360/(2\pi)$]. A phase shift of 360° corresponds to a shift of a complete period; a phase shift of 180° corresponds to a shift of one-half of a period; and a phase shift of 90° corresponds to a shift of one-quarter of a period (see Fig. 3.5).

Figure 3.5   *Relationships between different phases*

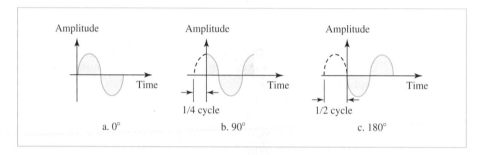

Example 2

A sine wave is offset one-sixth of a cycle with respect to time zero. What is its phase in degrees and radians?

Solution

We know that one complete cycle is 360°. Therefore, 1/6 cycle is

$$\frac{1}{6} \times 360 = 60° = 60 \times \frac{2\pi}{360} \text{ rad} = \frac{\pi}{3} \text{ rad} = 1.046 \text{ rad}$$

Examples of Sine Waves

A visual comparison of signals with different characteristics can give a better understanding of these characteristics. Figure 3.6 shows three sine waves with different peak amplitudes, frequencies, and phases.

Time and Frequency Domains

A sine wave is comprehensively defined by its amplitude, frequency, and phase. We have been showing a sine wave by using what is called a **time-domain plot.** The time-domain plot shows changes in signal amplitude with respect to time (it is an amplitude versus time plot). Phase and frequency are not explicitly measured on a time-domain plot.

Figure 3.6   *Sine wave examples*

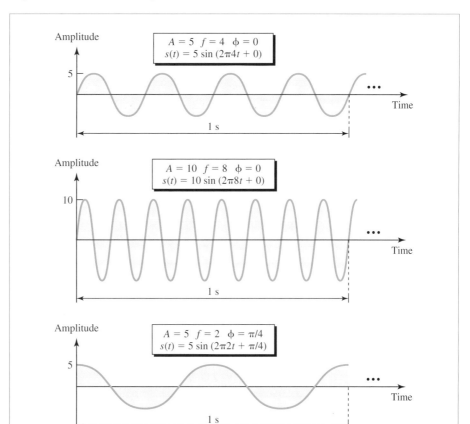

To show the relationship between amplitude and frequency, we can use what is called a **frequency-domain plot.** Figure 3.7 compares the time domain (instantaneous amplitude with respect to time) and the frequency domain (peak amplitude with respect to frequency).

The figure shows three signals with varying frequencies. Compare the models within each pair to see which sort of data each is best suited to convey. All three signals have a peak amplitude of 5 volts (V). The frequency of the first signal is 0; we show it in the frequency domain with a spike at frequency 0 and a height of 5 (its amplitude). The second signal has a frequency of 8, so we show it in the frequency domain with a spike of height 5 and a frequency of 8. Finally, the third is shown with a frequency of 16 at the same height. Note that in the frequency domain we can show two characteristics of a signal with only one spike; the position is the frequency, and the height is the peak amplitude. The phase of a signal cannot be shown in the frequency domain; we need another domain that we won't discuss in this book.

An analog signal is best represented in the frequency domain.

Figure 3.7   *Time and frequency domains*

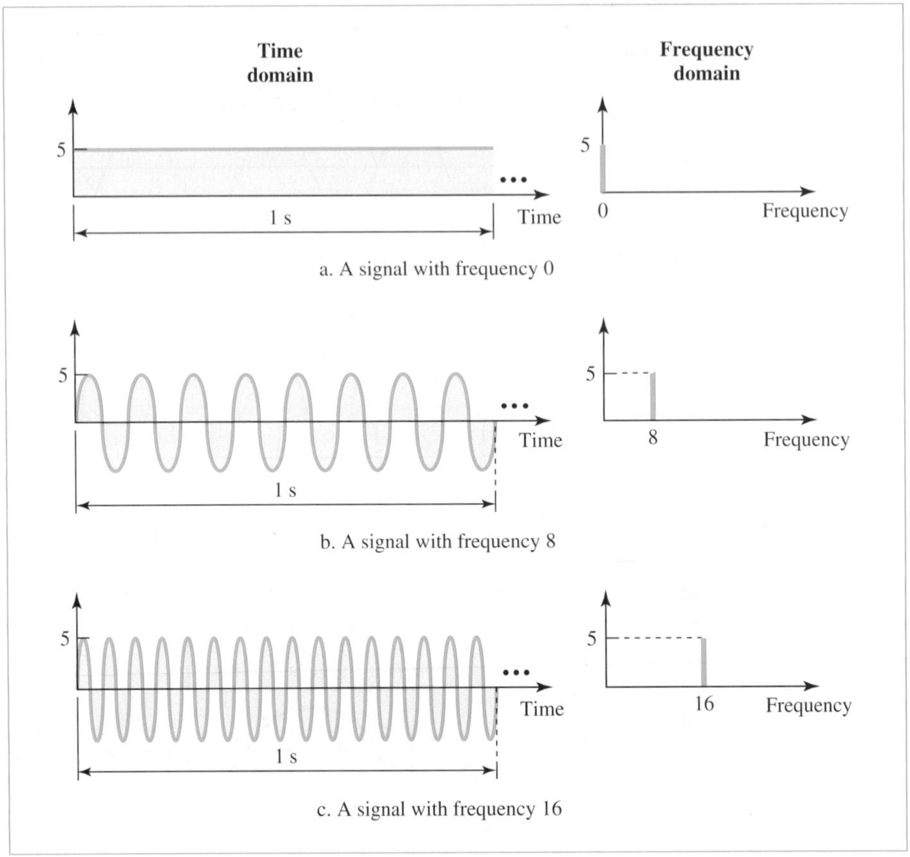

a. A signal with frequency 0

b. A signal with frequency 8

c. A signal with frequency 16

Composite Signals

So far, we have focused attention on simple signals (sine waves). Although a simple sine wave signal is very useful for some purposes, it is useless for data communications. We can send a single sine wave to carry electric energy from one place to another. For example, the power company sends a single sine wave with a frequency of 60 Hz to distribute electric energy to our houses and businesses. We can use a single sine wave to send an alarm to a security center when a burglar opens a door or a window in our house. In the first case, the sine wave is carrying energy; in the second, the presence of the signal infers danger.

If we used one single sine wave to convey a conversation over the phone, we would always hear a buzz; it would make no sense and carry no information. If we sent one single sine wave to convey data, we would always be sending alternating 1s and 0s, which does not have any communication value.

A single-frequency sine wave is not useful in data communications; we need to change one or more of its characteristics to make it useful.

If we want to use a sine wave for communication, we need to change one or more of its characteristics. For example, when the data to be sent are a 1 bit, we can send a maximum amplitude; when it is a 0 bit, we can send a minimum amplitude. However, we need to keep in mind that when we change one or more characteristics of a sine wave, it is no longer a simple sine wave. Instead, it is a **composite signal** made of many simple sine waves. A mere change in the amplitude, frequency, or phase creates a new set of frequencies. Intuively, change is related to frequency; more change means creating more new frequencies.

When we change one or more characteristics of a single-frequency signal, it becomes a composite signal made of many frequencies.

Fourier Analysis

In the early 1900s, the French mathematician Jean-Baptiste Fourier showed that any composite signal is a sum of a set of sine waves of different frequencies, phases, and amplitudes. In other words, we can write a composite signal as

$$s(t) = A_1 \sin (2\pi f_1 t + \phi_1) + A_2 \sin (2\pi f_2 t + \phi_2) + A_3 \sin (2\pi f_3 t + \phi_3) + \cdots$$

According to Fourier analysis, any composite signal can be represented as a combination of simple sine waves with different frequencies, phases, and amplitudes.

For example, let us consider the square wave of Figure 3.8 with a peak amplitude of A and a frequency of f (period T). According to **Fourier analysis,** we can prove that this signal can be decomposed into a series of sine waves as shown below.

Figure 3.8 *Square wave*

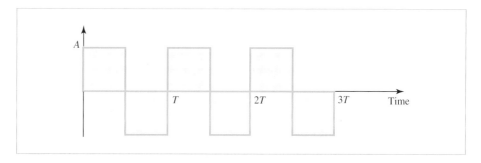

$$s(t) = \frac{4A}{\pi} \sin 2\pi ft + \frac{4A}{3\pi} \sin [2\pi(3f)t] + \frac{4A}{5\pi} \sin [2\pi(5f)t] + \cdots$$

In other words, we have a series of sine waves with frequencies f, $3f$, $5f$, $7f$, ... and amplitudes $4A/\pi$, $4A/3\pi$, $4A/5\pi$, $4A/7\pi$, and so on. The term with frequency f is dominant and is called the **fundamental frequency.** The term with frequency $3f$ is called the third harmonic, the term with frequency $5f$ is the fifth harmonic, and so on. To recreate the complete square wave signal requires all the odd harmonics up to infinity. For example, if the square wave has a frequency of 5000, the components have frequencies 5000, 15,000, 25,000, and so on. Figure 3.9 shows three of the harmonics.

Figure 3.9   *Three harmonics*

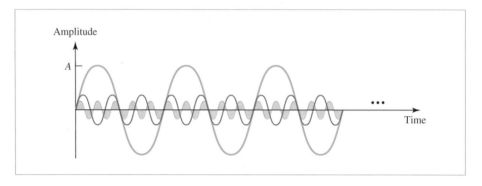

Of course, if we add these three harmonics, we do not get a square wave—we get something which is close, but not exact, as shown in Figure 3.10. If we need something closer to a square wave, we need to add more harmonics.

Figure 3.10   *Adding first three harmonics*

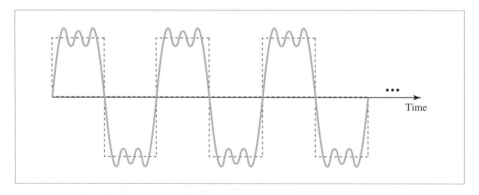

Frequency Spectrum

The description of a signal using the frequency domain and containing all its components is called the **frequency spectrum** of that signal. For example, Figure 3.11 shows the frequency spectrum of a square wave and the frequency spectrum of a signal which is very close to a square wave (only three harmonics).

Composite Signal and Transmission Medium

A signal needs to pass through a transmission medium (cable or air). However, each medium has its own characteristics. One of the characteristics of a medium is related to

Figure 3.11 *Frequency spectrum comparison*

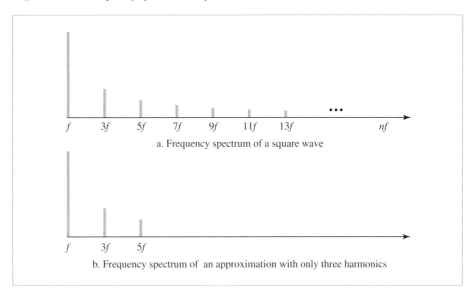

a. Frequency spectrum of a square wave

b. Frequency spectrum of an approximation with only three harmonics

frequency. A medium may pass some frequencies and may block or weaken others. This means that when we send a composite signal, containing many frequencies, at one end of a transmission medium, we may not receive the same signal at the other end. To maintain the integrity of the signal, the medium needs to pass every frequency (and also preserve the amplitude and phase, as we shall see later).

What we must realize is that no transmission medium is perfect. Each medium passes some frequencies, weakens others, and blocks still others. This means that when we send our square wave signal through a medium, we get something at the other end which is not a square wave at all. Figure 3.12 shows the concept.

Figure 3.12 *Signal corruption*

frequency. Input signal   Transmission medium   Output signal

Bandwidth

The range of frequencies that a medium can pass is called its **bandwidth.** Because no medium can pass or block all frequencies, the bandwidth normally refers to the range of frequencies that a medium can pass without losing one-half of the power contained in that signal. The bandwidth is a range and is normally referred to as the difference between two numbers. For example, if a medium can pass frequencies between 1000 and 5000 without losing most of the power contained in this range, its bandwidth is 5000 – 1000, or 4000.

> **The bandwidth is a property of a medium: It is the difference between the highest and the lowest frequencies that the medium can satisfactorily pass.**

If the bandwidth of a medium does not match the spectrum of a signal, some of the frequencies are lost. For example, the square wave signal in Figure 3.8 has a spectrum that expands to infinity. No transmission medium has such a bandwidth. This means that passing a square wave through any medium will always deform the signal. As another example, voice normally has a spectrum of 300 to 3300 Hz (a bandwidth of 3000 Hz). If we use a transmission line with a bandwidth of 1000 (between 1500 and 2500 Hz), we lose some frequencies in our voice; it may not even be recognizable.

Sometimes people use the term *bandwidth* with regard to a signal. For example, they say, "This signal has a bandwidth of 1000 Hz." In this case, what they mean is that the signal has a spectrum with significant frequencies that span 1000 Hz. In other words, they mean, "We need a medium with a bandwidth of 1000 Hz if we want to send this signal without losing a significant part of it." We can say that today, people use the term *bandwidth* for media and signals interchangeably, but it was not always so.

> **In this book, we use the term *bandwidth* to refer to the property of a medium or the width of a single spectrum.**

Figure 3.13 shows the concept of bandwidth. The figure depicts the range of frequencies a medium can pass and the relative amplitude of the frequencies passed. Note that the media may pass some frequencies above the 5000 and below 1000, but according to the criteria we mentioned before, the amplitudes of those frequencies are less than those in the middle.

Figure 3.13 *Bandwidth*

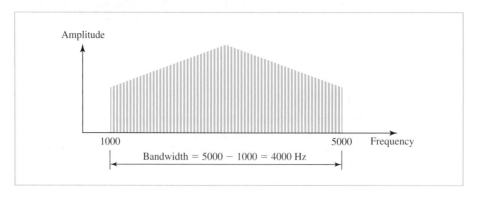

Example 3

If a periodic signal is decomposed into five sine waves with frequencies of 100, 300, 500, 700, and 900 Hz, what is the bandwidth? Draw the spectrum, assuming all components have a maximum amplitude of 10 V.

Solution

Let f_h be the highest frequency, f_l the lowest frequency, and B the bandwidth. Then

$$B = f_h - f_l = 900 - 100 = 800 \text{ Hz}$$

The spectrum has only five spikes, at 100, 300, 500, 700, and 900 (see Fig. 3.14).

Figure 3.14   *Example 3*

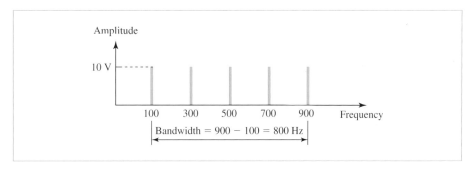

Example 4

A signal has a bandwidth of 20 Hz. The highest frequency is 60 Hz. What is the lowest frequency? Draw the spectrum if the signal contains all integral frequencies of the same amplitude.

Solution

Let f_h be the highest frequency, f_l the lowest frequency, and B the bandwidth. Then

$$B = f_h - f_l$$
$$20 = 60 - f_l$$
$$f_l = 60 - 20 = 40 \text{ Hz}$$

The spectrum contains all integral frequencies. We show this by a series of spikes (see Fig. 3.15).

Figure 3.15   *Example 4*

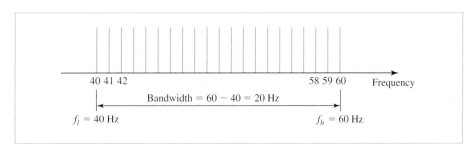

Example 5

A signal has a spectrum with frequencies between 1000 and 2000 Hz (bandwidth of 1000 Hz). A medium can pass frequencies from 3000 to 4000 Hz (a bandwidth of 1000 Hz). Can this signal faithfully pass through this medium?

Solution

The answer is definitely no. Although the signal can have the same bandwidth (1000 Hz), the range does not overlap. The medium can only pass the frequencies between 3000 and 4000 Hz; the signal is totally lost.

3.3 DIGITAL SIGNALS

In addition to being represented by an analog signal, data can be represented by a digital signal. For example, a 1 can be encoded as a positive voltage and a 0 as zero voltage (see Fig. 3.16).

Figure 3.16 *A digital signal*

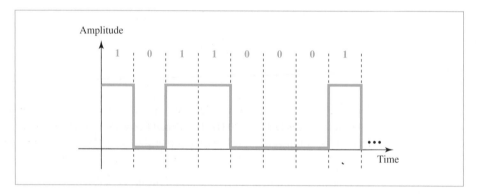

Bit Interval and Bit Rate

Most digital signals are aperiodic, and thus period or frequency is not appropriate. Two new terms—*bit interval* (instead of *period*) and *bit rate* (instead of *frequency*)— are used to describe digital signals. The **bit interval** is the time required to send one single bit. The **bit rate** is the number of bit intervals per second. This means that the bit rate is the number of bits sent in 1 s, usually expressed in **bits per second (bps).** See Figure 3.17.

Example 6

A digital signal has a bit rate of 2000 bps. What is the duration of each bit (bit interval)?

Solution

The bit interval is the inverse of the bit rate.

$$\text{Bit interval} = \frac{1}{\text{bit rate}} = \frac{1}{2000} = 0.000500 \text{ s} = 0.000500 \times 10^6 \text{ μs} = 500 \text{ μs}$$

Figure 3.17 *Bit rate and bit interval*

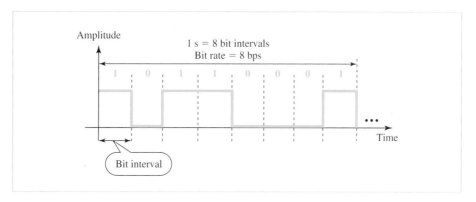

Digital Signal as a Composite Analog Signal

It should be clear so far that a digital signal, with all its sudden changes, is actually a composite signal having an infinite number of frequencies. In other words, the bandwidth of a digital signal is infinite.

A digital signal is a composite signal with an infinite bandwidth.

Digital Signal Through a Wide-Bandwidth Medium

If a medium has a wide bandwidth, we can send a digital signal through it. Of course, some of the frequencies are blocked by the medium, but still enough frequencies are passed to preserve a decent signal shape. We will see that we can use a dedicated medium such as a coaxial cable to send a digital signal through a local area network.

Digital Signal Through a Band-Limited Medium

Can we send digital data through a band-limited medium? The answer to this question is definitely yes. We send data by using band-limited telephone lines to the Internet every day. But what is the minimum required bandwidth B in hertz if we want to send n bps? In other words, what is the relationship between the number of bits per second and the required bandwidth? We will formally answer this question when we discuss the Nyquist theorem and the Shannon capacity. In this section, we take an intuitive approach to understand the foundation of data transmission.

Using Only One Harmonic

To simplify the discussion, imagine that our computer creates just 6 bps. We make this unrealistic assumption just to be able to show things graphically. Every second, 6 bits are produced by the computer. One second, we may have 111111, another second 001010, another second 101010, and so on. We use an encoding method that uses a positive value to represent 1 and a negative value to represent 0. Figure 3.18 shows two signals.

Figure 3.18 *Digital versus analog*

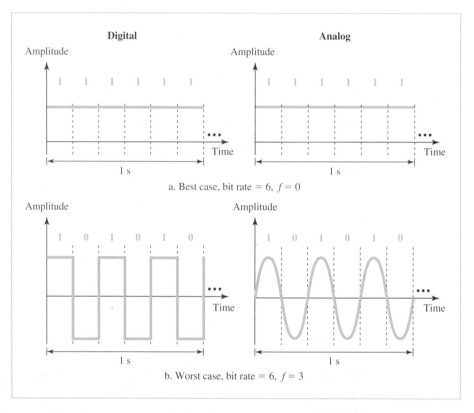

a. Best case, bit rate = 6, $f = 0$

b. Worst case, bit rate = 6, $f = 3$

Let us see if we can simulate any of these patterns by using a single-frequency signal. The best case is 111111 or 000000. We can simulate this case by sending a signal of frequency zero. The worst case is definitely 101010 or 010101. These are the worst cases, because there are more changes in this pattern than in any other pattern; with each succeeding bit there is a change. More change means higher frequency. However, we can simulate this digital signal by using a single-frequency analog signal with a frequency of 3 Hz, one-half of the bit rate. So we have

Best case:	bit rate = 6	frequency = 0
Worst case:	bit rate = 6	frequency = 3

We can say that all other cases are between the best and the worst cases. We can simulate other cases with a single frequency of 1 or 2 Hz (using the appropriate phase).

In other words, if we need to simulate this digital signal of data rate 6 bps, sometimes we need to send a signal of frequency 0, sometimes 1, sometimes 2, and sometimes 3 Hz. We need our medium to be able to pass frequencies of 0 to 3 Hz. Our medium needs to have a bandwidth of 3 Hz (3 − 0).

If we generalize this simple example, we come to a very simple relationship between the bit rate and bandwidth. To send *n* bps through an analog channel using the above approximation, we need a bandwidth B such that

$$B = \frac{n}{2}$$

Using More Harmonics

The above discussion was based on one harmonic. For each pattern we send a single-frequency signal using a frequency of 0 to 3 Hz. However, in many situations, a one-frequency signal is not very appropriate; the analog signal may look very different from the digital signal. The receiver may not recognize the signal correctly.

To improve the shape of the signal for better communication, particularly for high data rates, we need to add some harmonics. It is clear from our previous discussions that we need to add some odd harmonics. If we add the third harmonic to each case, we need $B = n/2 + 3n/2 = 4n/2$ Hz; if we add third and fifth harmonics, we need $B = n/2 + 3n/2 + 5n/2 = 9n/2$ Hz; and so on. In other words, we have

$$B >= \frac{n}{2} \quad \text{or} \quad n <= 2B$$

Table 3.2 shows how much bandwidth we need to send 1000 bps using this method.

Table 3.2   *Bandwidth requirements*

Bit Rate	Harmonic 1	Harmonics 1, 3	Harmonics 1, 3, 5	Harmonics 1, 3, 5, 7
$n = 1$ Kbps	$B = 500$ Hz	$B = 2$ KHz	$B = 4.5$ KHz	$B = 8$ KHz
$n = 10$ Kbps	$B = 5$ KHz	$B = 20$ KHz	$B = 45$ KHz	$B = 80$ KHz
$n = 100$ Kbps	$B = 50$ KHz	$B = 200$ KHz	$B = 450$ KHz	$B = 800$ KHz

We want to emphasize the following: In this method as well as others, the required bandwidth is proportional to the bit rate. If we double the bit rate, we need to double the bandwidth.

The bit rate and the bandwidth are proportional to each other.

Digital versus Analog Bandwidth

The above discussion on the proportionality of bandwidth and bit rate leads to the idea of digital bandwidth. If we are sending analog data through a medium, we are concerned with analog bandwidth (expressed in hertz); if we are sending digital data through a medium, we are concerned with digital bandwidth (in bits per second). Analog bandwidth is the range of frequencies that a medium can pass. Digital bandwidth is the maximum bit rate that a medium can pass. They represent the same property of a medium, but in different scales and units.

The analog bandwidth of a medium is expressed in hertz; the digital bandwidth, in bits per second.

Higher Bit Rate

Some readers may be puzzled by the above discussion, especially if they consider data transmission over telephone lines. Telephone lines have a bandwidth of 3 to 4 KHz for the regular user; we know that sometimes we send more than 30,000 bps using a traditional modem. According to the above discussion, we should not be able to send more than 8000 bps. How can this be reconciled? It's so because we are using a modem with modulation techniques that allow the representation of multiple bits in one single period of an analog signal. We discuss these techniques in Chapter 5.

3.4 ANALOG VERSUS DIGITAL

Finally we come to this question: Should we use analog or digital signals? It really depends on the situation and on the available bandwidth.

Low-pass versus Band-pass

A channel or a link is either low-pass or band-pass. A **low-pass channel** has a bandwidth with frequencies between 0 and *f*. The lower limit is 0, the upper limit can be any frequency (including infinity). On the other hand, a **band-pass channel** has a bandwidth with frequencies between f_1 and f_2. Figure 3.19 shows the bandwidth of a low-pass channel and a band-pass channel.

Figure 3.19 *Low-pass and band-pass*

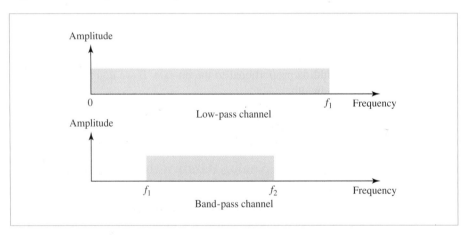

Digital Transmission

A digital signal theoretically needs a bandwidth between 0 and infinity. The lower limit (0) is fixed; the upper limit (infinity) can be relaxed if we lower our standards by accepting a limited number of harmonics. This means a bandwidth between 0 and *f* for a low-pass signal.

We have a low-pass channel only if the medium is dedicated to two devices (point-to-point) or shared between several devices in time (not in frequency). For example, in a wired local area network, a cable can be shared between stations. We can transmit data digitally in this system.

Digital transmission needs a low-pass channel.

Analog Transmission

An analog signal normally has a narrower bandwidth than a digital signal with frequencies between f_1 and f_2. In other words, an analog signal requires a band-pass channel. In addition, the bandwidth of an analog signal can always be shifted. For example, we can always shift a signal with a bandwidth from f_1 to f_2 to a signal with a bandwidth from f_3 to f_4 as long as the width of the bandwidth remains the same.

A band-pass channel is more available than a low-pass channel. The bandwidth of a medium can be divided into several band-pass channels to carry several analog transmissions. For example, in analog cellular telephony, a limited bandwidth is divided between many telephone users. Each user has a bandwidth between 0 to 30 KHz, with each signal shifted appropriately.

Analog transmission can use a band-pass channel.

This is not to say that an analog transmission cannot use a low-pass channel; it just means that it can use the more available band-pass channel. A low-pass channel is a special case of a band-pass channel with $f_1 = 0$.

3.5   DATA RATE LIMITS

A very important question is how fast we can send data, in bits per second, over a channel. Data rate depends on three factors:

1. The bandwidth available
2. The levels of signals we can use
3. The quality of the channel (the level of the noise).

Two theoretical formulas were developed to calculate the data rate: one by Nyquist for a noiseless channel, another by Shannon for a noisy channel.

Noiseless Channel: Nyquist Bit Rate

For a noiseless channel, the **Nyquist bit rate** formula defines the theoretical maximum bit rate

$$\text{BitRate} = 2 \times \text{Bandwidth} \times \log_2 L$$

In this formula, Bandwidth is the bandwidth of the channel, L is the number of signal levels used to represent data, and BitRate is the bit rate in bits per second.

Example 7

Consider a noiseless channel with a bandwidth of 3000 Hz transmitting a signal with two signal levels. The maximum bit rate can be calculated as:

$$\text{BitRate} = 2 \times 3000 \times \log_2 2 = 6000 \text{ bps}$$

Example 8

Consider the same noiseless channel, transmitting a signal with four signal levels (for each level, we send two bits). The maximum bit rate can be calculated as:

$$\text{BitRate} = 2 \times 3000 \times \log_2 4 = 12{,}000 \text{ bps}$$

Noisy Channel: Shannon Capacity

In reality, we cannot have a noiseless channel; the channel is always noisy. In 1944, Claude Shannon introduced a formula, called the **Shannon capacity,** to determine the theoretical highest data rate for a noisy channel:

$$\text{Capacity} = \text{Bandwidth} \times \log_2 (1 + \text{SNR})$$

In this formula, Bandwidth is the bandwidth of the channel, SNR is the **signal-to-noise ratio,** and Capacity is the capacity of the channel in bits per second. The signal-to-noise ratio is the statistical ratio of the power of the signal to the power of the noise. Note that in the Shannon formula there is no indication of the signal level, which means that no matter how many levels we use, we cannot achieve a data rate higher than the capacity of the channel. In other words, the formula defines a characteristic of the channel, not the method of transmission.

Example 9

Consider an extremely noisy channel in which the value of the signal-to-noise ratio is almost zero. In other words, the noise is so strong that the signal is faint. For this channel the capacity is calculated as

$$C = B \log_2 (1 + \text{SNR}) = B \log_2 (1 + 0) = B \log_2 (1) = B \times 0 = 0$$

This means that the capacity of this channel is zero regardless of the bandwidth. In other words, we cannot receive any data through this channel.

Example 10

We can calculate the theoretical highest bit rate of a regular telephone line. A telephone line normally has a bandwidth of 3000 Hz (300 Hz to 3300 Hz). The signal-to-noise ratio is usually 3162. For this channel the capacity is calculated as

$$C = B \log_2 (1 + \text{SNR}) = 3000 \log_2 (1 + 3162) = 3000 \log_2 (3163)$$
$$C = 3000 \times 11.62 = 34{,}860 \text{ bps}$$

This means that the highest bit rate for a telephone line is 34,860 Kbps. If we want to send data faster than this, we can either increase the bandwidth of the line or improve the signal-to-noise ratio.

Using Both Limits

In practice, we need to use both methods to find what bandwidth of what signal level we need. Let us show this by an example.

Example 11

We have a channel with a 1 MHz bandwidth. The SNR for this channel is 63; what is the appropriate bit rate and signal level?

Solution

First, we use the Shannon formula to find our upper limit.

$$C = B \log_2 (1 + SNR) = 10^6 \log_2 (1 + 63) = 10^6 \log_2 (64) = 6 \text{ Mbps}$$

Although the Shannon formula gives us 6 Mbps, this is the upper limit. For better performance we choose something lower, for example 4 Mbps. Then we use the Nyquist formula to find the number of signal levels.

$$4 \text{ Mbps} = 2 \times 1 \text{ MHz} \times \log_2 L \longrightarrow L = 4$$

3.6 TRANSMISSION IMPAIRMENT

Signals travel through transmission media, which are not perfect. The imperfections cause impairment in the signal. This means that the signal at the beginning and end of the medium are not the same. What is sent is not what is received. Three types of impairment usually occur: attenuation, distortion, and noise (see Fig. 3.20).

Figure 3.20   *Impairment types*

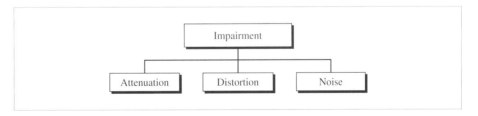

Attenuation

Attenuation means loss of energy. When a signal, simple or composite, travels through a medium, it loses some of its energy so that it can overcome the resistance of the medium. That is why a wire carrying electrical signals gets warm, if not hot, after a while. Some of the electrical energy in the signal is converted to heat. To compensate for this loss, amplifiers are used to amplify the signal. Figure 3.21 shows the effect of attenuation and amplification.

Figure 3.21   *Attenuation*

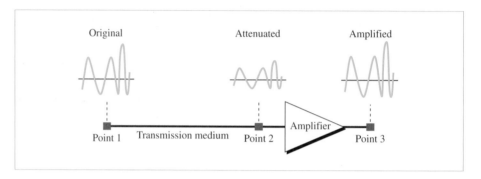

Decibel

To show that a signal has lost or gained strength, engineers use the concept of the decibel. The **decibel (dB)** measures the relative strengths of two signals or a signal at two different points. Note that the decibel is negative if a signal is attenuated and positive if a signal is amplified.

$$dB = 10 \log_{10} (P_2 / P_1)$$

where P_1 and P_2 are the powers of a signal at points 1 and 2, respectively.

Example 12

Imagine a signal travels through a transmission medium and its power is reduced to half. This means that $P_2 = 1/2\ P_1$. In this case, the attenuation (loss of power) can be calculated as

$$10 \log_{10} (P_2/P_1) = 10 \log_{10} (0.5P_1/P_1) = 10 \log_{10} (0.5) = 10(-0.3) = -3\ dB$$

Engineers know that −3 dB or a loss of 3 dB is equivalent to losing half the power.

Example 13

Imagine a signal travels through an amplifier and its power is increased ten times. This means that $P_2 = 10 \times P_1$. In this case, the amplification (gain of power) can be calculated as

$$10 \log_{10} (P_2/P_1) = 10 \log_{10} (10P_1/P_1) = 10 \log_{10} (10) = 10 (1) = 10\ dB$$

Example 14

One reason that engineers use the decibel to measure the changes in the strength of a signal is that decibel numbers can be added (or subtracted) when we are talking about several points instead of just two (cascading). In Figure 3.22 a signal travels a long distance from point 1 to point 4. The signal is attenuated by the time it reaches point 2. Between points 2 and 3, the signal is amplified.

Again, between points 3 and 4, the signal is attenuated. We can find the resultant decibel for the signal just by adding the decibel measurements between each set of points.

Figure 3.22 *Example 14*

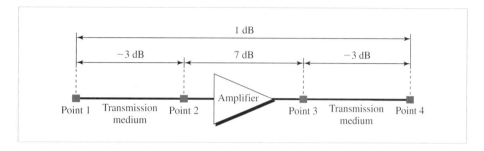

In this case, the decibel can be calculated as

$$dB = -3 + 7 - 3 = +1$$

which means that the signal has gained power.

Distortion

Distortion means that the signal changes its form or shape. Distortion occurs in a composite signal, made of different frequencies. Each signal component has its own propagation speed (see the next section) through a medium and, therefore, its own delay in arriving at the final destination. Figure 3.23 shows the effect of distortion on a composite signal.

Figure 3.23 *Distortion*

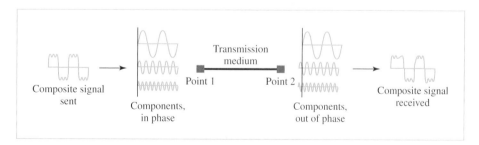

Noise

Noise is another problem. Several types of noise such as thermal noise, induced noise, crosstalk, and impulse noise may corrupt the signal. Thermal noise is the random motion of electrons in a wire which creates an extra signal not originally sent by the transmitter. Induced noise comes from sources such as motors and appliances. These devices act as a sending antenna and the transmission medium acts as the receiving antenna. Crosstalk is the effect of one wire on the other. One wire acts as a sending antenna and the other as the receiving antenna. Impulse noise is a spike (a signal with high energy in a very short period of time) that comes from power lines, lightning, and so on. Figure 3.24 shows the effect of noise on a signal.

Figure 3.24   *Noise*

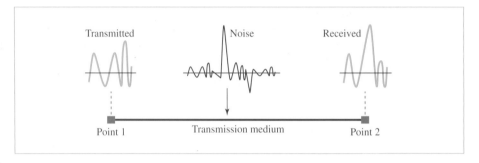

3.7   MORE ABOUT SIGNALS

Four other measurements used in data communications are throughput, propagation speed, propagation time, and wavelength. We discuss these in this section before closing the chapter.

Throughput

The **throughput** is the measurement of how fast data can pass through an entity (such as a point or a network). In other words, if we consider this entity as a wall through which bits pass, throughput is the number of bits that can pass this wall in one second. Figure 3.25 shows the concept.

Figure 3.25   *Throughput*

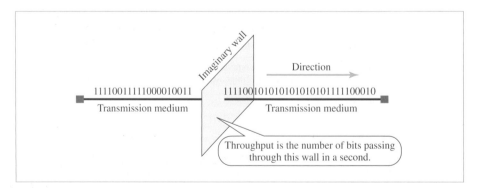

Propagation Speed

Propagation speed measures the distance a signal or a bit can travel through a medium in one second. The propagation speed of electromagnetic signals depends on the medium and on the frequency of the signal. For example, in a vacuum, light is propagated with a speed of 3×10^8 m/s. It is lower in air. It is much lower in a cable.

Propagation Time

Propagation time measures the time required for a signal (or a bit) to travel from one point of the transmission medium to another. The propagation time is calculated by dividing the distance by the propagation speed. Figure 3.26 shows the concept.

$$\text{Propagation time} = \text{Distance/Propagation speed}$$

Figure 3.26 *Propagation time*

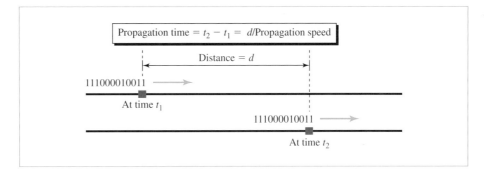

Wavelength

Wavelength is another characteristic of a signal traveling through a transmission medium. Wavelength binds the period or the frequency of a simple sine wave to the propagation speed of the medium. In other words, while the frequency of a signal is independent of the medium, the wavelength depends on both the frequency and the medium. Although wavelength can be associated with electrical signals, it is customary to use wavelengths when talking about the transmission of light in an optical fiber. The wavelength is the distance a simple signal can travel in one period (see Fig. 3.27).

Figure 3.27 *Wavelength*

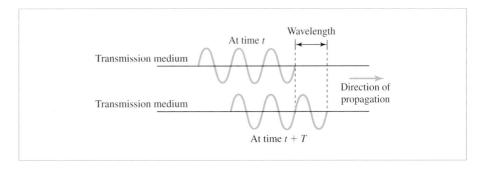

Wavelength can be calculated given the propagation speed and the period of the signal

$$\text{Wavelength} = \text{Propagation speed} \times \text{Period}$$

However, since period and frequency are related to each other, we can also say

$$\text{Wavelength} = \text{Propagation speed} \times (1/\text{Frequency}) = \text{Propagation speed}/\text{Frequency}$$

If we represent wavelength by λ, propagation speed by c (speed of light), and frequency by f, we get

$$\lambda = c/f$$

The wavelength is normally measured in micrometers (microns) instead of meters. For example, the wavelength of red light (frequency $= 4 \times 10^{14}$) in air is

$$\lambda = c/f = (3 \times 10^8)/(4 \times 10^{14}) = 0.75 \times 10^{-6} \text{ m} = 0.75 \text{ μm}$$

In a coaxial or fiber-optic cable, however, the wavelength is lower (0.5 μm) because the propagation speed in the cable is less than in the air.

3.8   KEY TERMS

analog data	fundamental frequency
analog signal	harmonics
aperiodic signal	hertz (Hz)
attenuation	low-pass channel
band-pass channel	noise
bandwidth	Nyquist bit rate
bit interval	peak amplitude
bit rate	period
bits per second (bps)	periodic signal
composite signal	phase
cycle	propagation speed
decibel (dB)	propagation time
digital	Shannon capacity
digital data	signal
digital signal	signal-to-noise ratio (SNR)
distortion	sine wave
Fourier analysis	throughput
frequency	time-domain plot
frequency-domain plot	wavelength
frequency spectrum	

3.9 SUMMARY

❑ Data must be transformed into electromagnetic signals prior to transmission across a network.

❑ Data and signals can be either analog or digital.

❑ A signal is periodic if it consists of a continuously repeating pattern.

❑ Each sine wave can be characterized by its amplitude, frequency, and phase.

❑ Frequency and period are inverses of each other.

❑ A time-domain graph plots amplitude as a function of time.

❑ A frequency-domain graph plots each sine wave's peak amplitude against its frequency.

❑ By using Fourier analysis, any composite signal can be represented as a combination of simple sine waves.

❑ The spectrum of a signal consists of the sine waves that make up the signal.

❑ The bandwidth of a signal is the range of frequencies the signal occupies. Bandwidth is determined by finding the difference between the highest and lowest frequency components.

❑ Bit rate (number of bits per second) and bit interval (duration of 1 bit) are terms used to describe digital signals.

❑ A digital signal is a composite signal with an infinite bandwidth.

❑ Bit rate and bandwidth are proportional to each other.

❑ The Nyquist formula determines the theoretical data rate for a noiseless channel.

❑ The Shannon capacity determines the theoretical maximum data rate for a noisy channel.

❑ Attenuation, distortion, and noise can impair a signal.

❑ Attenuation is the loss of a signal's energy due to the resistance of the medium.

❑ The decibel measures the relative strength of two signals or a signal at two different points.

❑ Distortion is the alteration of a signal due to the differing propagation speeds of each of the frequencies that make up a signal.

❑ Noise is the external energy that corrupts a signal.

❑ We can evaluate transmission media by throughput, propagation speed, and propagation time.

❑ The wavelength of a frequency is defined as the propagation speed divided by the frequency.

3.10 PRACTICE SET

Review Questions

1. Describe the three characteristics of a sine wave.
2. What is the spectrum of a signal?
3. Contrast an analog signal with a digital signal.

4. A signal has been received that only has values of −1, 0, and 1. Is this an analog or a digital signal?

5. What is the relationship between period and frequency?

6. What are the units of period and frequency?

7. What does the amplitude of a signal measure?

8. What does the frequency of a signal measure?

9. What does the phase of a signal measure?

10. Which type of plot shows the amplitude of a signal at a given time?

11. How can a composite signal be decomposed into its individual frequencies?

12. What is a bit interval, and what is its counterpart in an analog signal?

13. What is bit rate, and what is its counterpart in an analog signal?

14. Name three types of transmission impairment.

15. What does a decibel measure?

16. What is the relationship between propagation speed and propagation time?

17. What is the wavelength of a signal and how is it calculated?

18. What does the Shannon capacity have to do with communications?

Multiple-Choice Questions

19. Before data can be transmitted, they must be transformed to _____.
    a. Periodic signals
    b. Electromagnetic signals
    c. Aperiodic signals
    d. Low-frequency sine waves

20. A periodic signal completes one cycle in 0.001 s. What is the frequency?
    a. 1 Hz
    b. 100 Hz
    c. 1 KHz
    d. 1 MHz

21. Which of the following can be determined from a frequency-domain graph of a signal?
    a. Frequency
    b. Phase
    c. Power
    d. All the above

22. Which of the following can be determined from a frequency-domain graph of a signal?
    a. Bandwidth
    b. Phase
    c. Power
    d. All the above

23. In a frequency-domain plot, the vertical axis measures the _____.
    a. Peak amplitude
    b. Frequency
    c. Phase
    d. Slope
24. In a frequency-domain plot, the horizontal axis measures the _____.
    a. Peak amplitude
    b. Frequency
    c. Phase
    d. Slope
25. In a time-domain plot, the vertical axis is a measure of _____.
    a. Amplitude
    b. Frequency
    c. Phase
    d. Time
26. In a time-domain plot, the horizontal axis is a measure of _____.
    a. Signal amplitude
    b. Frequency
    c. Phase
    d. Time
27. If the bandwidth of a signal is 5 KHz and the lowest frequency is 52 KHz, what is the highest frequency?
    a. 5 KHz
    b. 10 KHz
    c. 47 KHz
    d. 57 KHz
28. What is the bandwidth of a signal that ranges from 40 KHz to 4 MHz?
    a. 36 MHz
    b. 360 KHz
    c. 3.96 MHz
    d. 396 KHz
29. When one of the components of a signal has a frequency of zero, the average amplitude of the signal _____.
    a. Is greater than zero
    b. Is less than zero
    c. Is zero
    d. (a) or (b)
30. A periodic signal can always be decomposed into _____.
    a. Exactly an odd number of sine waves
    b. A set of sine waves

c. A set of sine waves, one of which must have a phase of 0°

d. None of the above

31. As frequency increases, the period _____.

   a. Decreases

   b. Increases

   c. Remains the same

   d. Doubles

32. Given two sine waves A and B, if the frequency of A is twice that of B, then the period of B is _____ that of A.

   a. One-half

   b. Twice

   c. The same as

   d. Indeterminate from

33. A sine wave is _____.

   a. Periodic and continuous

   b. Aperiodic and continuous

   c. Periodic and discrete

   d. Aperiodic and discrete

34. If the maximum amplitude of a sine wave is 2 V, the minimum amplitude is _____ V.

   a. 2

   b. 1

   c. –2

   d. Between –2 and 2

35. A signal is measured at two different points. The power is P_1 at the first point and P_2 at the second point. The dB is 0. This means _____.

   a. P_2 is zero

   b. P_2 equals P_1

   c. P_2 is much larger than P_1

   d. P_2 is much smaller than P_1

36. _____ is a type of transmission impairment in which the signal loses strength due to the resistance of the transmission medium.

   a. Attenuation

   b. Distortion

   c. Noise

   d. Decibel

37. _____ is a type of transmission impairment in which the signal loses strength due to the different propagation speeds of each frequency that makes up the signal.

   a. Attenuation

   b. Distortion

     c. Noise

     d. Decibel

38. _____ is a type of transmission impairment in which an outside source such as crosstalk corrupts a signal.

     a. Attenuation

     b. Distortion

     c. Noise

     d. Decibel

39. The _____ has units of meters/second or kilometers/second.

     a. Throughput

     b. Propagation speed

     c. Propagation time

     d. (b) or (c)

40. _____ has units of bits/second.

     a. Throughput

     b. Propagation speed

     c. Propagation time

     d. (b) or (c)

41. The _____ has units of seconds.

     a. Throughput

     b. Propagation speed

     c. Propagation time

     d. (b) or (c)

42. When propagation speed is multiplied by propagation time, we get the _____.

     a. Throughput

     b. Wavelength of the signal

     c. Distortion factor

     d. Distance a signal or bit has traveled

43. Propagation time is _____ proportional to distance and _____ proportional to propagation speed.

     a. Inversely; directly

     b. Directly; inversely

     c. Inversely; inversely

     d. Directly; directly

44. Wavelength is _____ proportional to propagation speed and _____ proportional to period.

     a. Inversely; directly

     b. Directly; inversely

     c. Inversely; inversely

     d. Directly; directly

45. The wavelength of a signal depends on the _____.
    a. Frequencies of the signal
    b. Medium
    c. Phase of the signal
    d. (a) and (b)
46. The wavelength of green light in air is _____ the wavelength of green light in fiber-optic cable.
    a. Less than
    b. Greater than
    c. Equal to
    d. None of the above
47. Using the Shannon formula to calculate the data rate for a given channel, if $C = B$, then _____.
    a. The signal is less than the noise
    b. The signal is greater than the noise
    c. The signal is equal to the noise
    d. Not enough information is given to answer the question

Exercises

48. Given the frequencies listed below, calculate the corresponding periods. Express the result in seconds, milliseconds, microseconds, nanoseconds, and picoseconds.
    a. 24 Hz
    b. 8 MHz
    c. 140 KHz
    d. 12 THz
49. Given the following periods, calculate the corresponding frequencies. Express the frequencies in hertz, kilohertz, megahertz, gigahertz, and terahertz.
    a. 5 s
    b. 12 μs
    c. 220 ns
    d. 81 ps
50. What is the phase shift for the following?
    a. A sine wave with the maximum amplitude at time zero
    b. A sine wave with maximum amplitude after 1/4 cycle
    c. A sine wave with zero amplitude after 3/4 cycle and increasing
    d. A sine wave with minimum amplitude after 1/4 cycle
51. Show the phase shift in degrees corresponding to each of the following delays in cycles.
    a. 1 cycle
    b. 1/2 cycle

c. 3/4 cycle

d. 1/3 cycle

52. Show the delay in cycles corresponding to each of the following.

a. 45°

b. 90°

c. 60°

d. 360°

53. Draw the time-domain plot of a sine wave (for only 1 s) with a maximum amplitude of 15 V, a frequency of 5, and a phase of 270°.

54. Draw two sine waves on the same time-domain plot. The characteristics of each signal are as follows:

signal *A*: amplitude 40, frequency 9, phase 0;

signal *B*: amplitude 10, frequency 9, phase 90.

55. Draw two periods of a sine wave with a phase shift of 90°. On the same diagram, draw a sine wave with the same amplitude and frequency but with a 90° phase shift from the first.

56. What is the bandwidth of a signal that can be decomposed into four sine waves with frequencies at 0, 20, 50, and 200 Hz? All maximum amplitudes are the same. Draw the frequency spectrum.

57. A periodic composite signal with a bandwidth of 2000 Hz is composed of two sine waves. The first one has a frequency of 100 Hz with a maximum amplitude of 20 V; the second one has a maximum amplitude of 5 V. Draw the frequency spectrum.

58. Show how a sine wave can change its phase by drawing two periods of an arbitrary sine wave with phase shift of 0° followed by the two periods of the *same signal* with a phase shift of 90°.

59. Imagine we have a sine wave called *A*. Show the negative of *A*. In other words, show the signal −*A*. Can we relate the negation of a signal to the phase shift? How many degrees?

60. Which signal has a higher bandwidth, a signal that changes 100 times per second or a signal that changes 200 times per second?

61. What is the bit rate for each of the following signals?

a. A signal in which 1 bit lasts 0.001 s

b. A signal in which 1 bit lasts 2 ms

c. A signal in which 10 bits last 20 μs

d. A signal in which 1000 bits last 250 ps

62. What is the duration of 1 bit for each of the following signals?

a. A signal with a bit rate of 100 bps

b. A signal with a bit rate of 200 Kbps

c. A signal with a bit rate of 5 Mbps

d. A signal with a bit rate of 1 Gbps

63. A device is sending out data at the rate of 1000 bps.
   a. How long does it take to send out 10 bits?
   b. How long does it take to send out a single character (8 bits)?
   c. How long does it take to send a file of 100,000 characters?
64. What is the bit rate for the signal in Figure 3.28?

Figure 3.28 Exercise 64

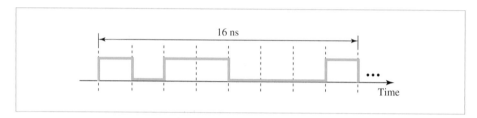

65. What is the frequency of the signal in Figure 3.29?

Figure 3.29 Exercise 65

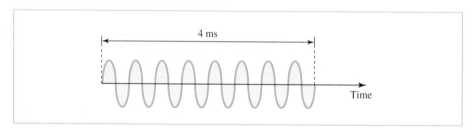

66. Draw the time-domain representation (for the first 1/100 s) of the signal shown in Figure 3.30.

Figure 3.30 Exercise 66

67. Draw the frequency-domain representation of the signal shown in Figure 3.31.
68. What is the bandwidth of the composite signal shown in Figure 3.32?
69. What is the bandwidth of the signal shown in Figure 3.33?
70. A composite signal contains frequencies from 10 to 30 KHz, each with an amplitude of 10 V. Draw the frequency spectrum.
71. A composite signal contains frequencies from 10 to 30 KHz. The amplitude is zero for the lowest and the highest signals and is 30 V for the 20-KHz signal. Assuming

Figure 3.31 *Exercise 67*

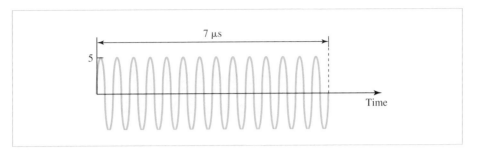

Figure 3.32 *Exercise 68*

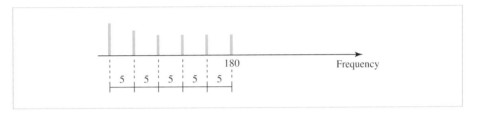

Figure 3.33 *Exercise 69*

that the amplitudes change gradually from the minimum to the maximum, draw the frequency spectrum.

72. Two signals have the same frequencies. However, whenever the first signal is at its maximum amplitude, the second signal has an amplitude of zero. What is the phase shift between the two signals?

73. What is the mathematical representation of a signal with an amplitude of 10 V, a frequency of 2500 Hz, a phase of 30°?

74. Show the frequency domain of the following signal:

$$s(t) = 8 + 3 \sin 100\pi t + 5 \sin 200\pi t$$

75. What is the period of the following signal?

$$s(t) = 4 \sin 628t$$

76. A cosine wave is a sine wave with a 90° phase shift. Show the equivalent of the following signal in sine format.

$$s(t) = \cos (2\pi ft + \pi)$$

77. A TV channel has a bandwidth of 6 MHz. If we send a digital signal using one channel, what are the data rates if we use one harmonic, three harmonics, and five harmonics?

78. A signal travels from point A to point B. At point A, the signal power is 100 W. At point B, the power is 90 W. What is the attenuation in decibel?

79. The attenuation of a signal is −10 dB. What is the final signal power if it was originally 5 W?

80. A signal has passed through three cascaded amplifiers, each with a 4 dB gain. What is the total gain? How much is the signal amplified?

81. If the throughput at the connection between a device and the transmission medium is 5 Kbps, how long does it take to send 100,000 bits out of this device?

82. The light of the sun takes approximately eight minutes to reach the earth. What is the distance between the sun and the earth?

83. A signal has a wavelength of 1 μm in air. How far can the front of the wave travel during five periods?

84. A line has a signal-to-noise ratio of 1000 and a bandwidth of 4000 KHz. What is the maximum data rate supported by this line?

85. We measure the performance of a telephone line (4 KHz of bandwidth). When the signal is 10 V, the noise is 5 mV. What is the maximum data rate supported by this telephone line?

CHAPTER 4

Digital Transmission

A computer network is designed to send information from one point in the network to another. In designing a network, we have two choices: convert information to either a digital signal or an analog signal. In this chapter, we discuss the first choice, using digital signals; in Chapter 5, we discuss the second choice, using analog signals.

We discussed the advantages and disadvantages of digital transmission over analog transmission in Chapter 3. In this chapter, we show the schemes and techniques that we can use to transmit data digitally. First, we discuss line coding, which is a technique to convert binary data to digital signals. Second, we show how to improve the efficiency of line coding. Third, we discuss sampling, a technique for changing analog data to binary data. After data are in binary form, we can then use line coding or a combination of block coding and line coding to change them to a digital signal. Finally, we discuss the parallel and serial transmission of digital signals.

4.1 LINE CODING

Line coding is the process of converting binary data, a sequence of bits, to a digital signal. For example, data, text, numbers, graphical images, audio, and video that are stored in computer memory are all sequences of bits (see Chapter 1). Line coding converts a sequence of bits to a digital signal. Figure 4.1 shows the concept of line coding.

Figure 4.1 *Line coding*

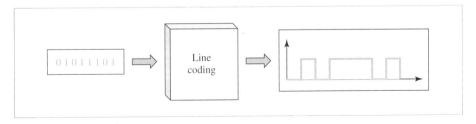

Some Characteristics of Line Coding

Before we discuss the different types of line coding, we need to understand some characteristics of line coding: signal level versus data level, pulse rate versus bit rate, dc components, and self-synchronization.

Signal Level versus Data Level

As discussed previously, a digital signal can have a limited number of values. However, only some of these values can be used to represent data; the rest are used for other purposes, as we will see shortly. We refer to the number of values allowed in a particular signal as the number of **signal levels;** we refer to the number of values used to represent data as the number of **data levels.** Figure 4.2 shows two examples of digital signals. The first signal has two signal levels and two data levels. The second signal has three signal levels and two data levels.

Figure 4.2   *Signal level versus data level*

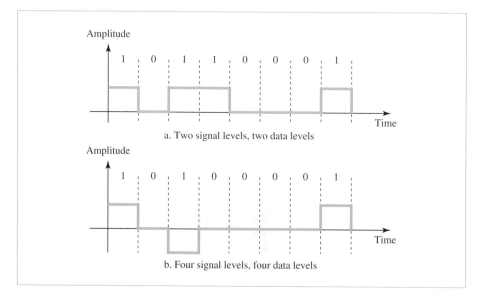

a. Two signal levels, two data levels

b. Four signal levels, four data levels

Pulse Rate versus Bit Rate

The **pulse rate** defines the number of pulses per second. A pulse is the minimum amount of time required to transmit a symbol. The **bit rate** defines the number of bits per second. If a pulse carries only 1 bit, the pulse rate and the bit rate are the same. If the pulse carries more than 1 bit, then the bit rate is greater than the pulse rate. In general, we have the following formula, in which L is the number of data levels of the signal:

$$\text{BitRate} = \text{PulseRate} \times \log_2 L$$

Example 1

A signal has two data levels with a pulse duration of 1 ms. We calculate the pulse rate and bit rate as follows:

$$\text{PulseRate} = \frac{1}{1 \times 10^{-3}} = 1000 \text{ pulses/s}$$

$$\text{BitRate} = \text{PulseRate} \times \log_2 L = 1000 \times \log_2 2 = 1000 \text{ bps}$$

Example 2

A signal has four data levels with a pulse duration of 1 ms. We calculate the pulse rate and bit rate as follows:

$$\text{PulseRate} = \frac{1}{1 \times 10^{-3}} = 1000 \text{ pulses/s}$$

$$\text{BitRate} = \text{PulseRate} \times \log_2 L = 1000 \times \log_2 4 = 2000 \text{ bps}$$

DC Components

Some line coding schemes leave a residual direct-current (dc) component (zero-frequency). This component is undesirable for two reasons. First, if the signal is to pass through a system (such as a transformer) that does not allow the passage of a **dc component,** the signal is distorted and may create errors in the output. Second, this component is extra energy residing on the line and is useless. Figure 4.3 shows two line coding schemes. The first has a dc component; the positive voltages are not canceled by the negative voltages. The second has no dc component; the positive voltages are canceled by any negative voltages. The first does not pass through a transformer properly; the second does.

Figure 4.3 *DC component*

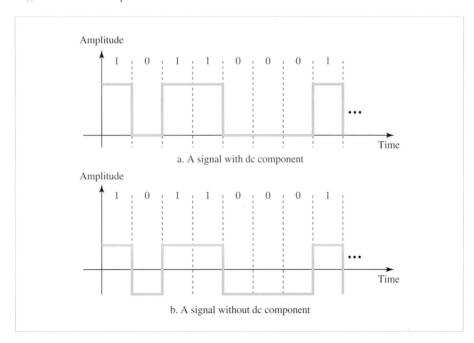

a. A signal with dc component

b. A signal without dc component

Self-Synchronization

To correctly interpret the signals received from the sender, the receiver's bit intervals must correspond exactly to the sender's bit intervals. If the receiver clock is faster or slower, the bit intervals are not matched and the receiver might interpret the signals differently than the sender intended. Figure 4.4 shows a situation in which the receiver has a shorter bit duration. The sender sends 10110001, while the receiver receives 110111000011 (exaggerated situation).

Figure 4.4   *Lack of synchronization*

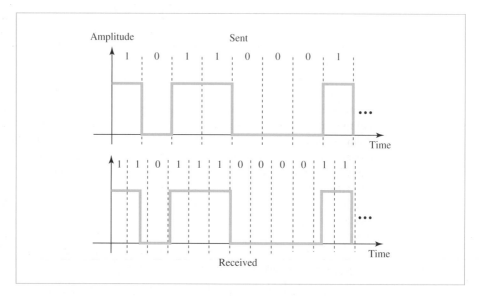

A **self-synchronizing** digital signal includes timing information in the data being transmitted. This can be achieved if there are transitions in the signal that alert the receiver to the beginning, middle, or end of the pulse. If the receiver's clock is out of synchronization, these alerting points can reset the clock.

Example 3

In a digital transmission, the receiver clock is 0.1 percent faster than the sender clock. How many extra bits per second does the receiver receive if the data rate is 1 Kbps? How many if the data rate is 1 Mbps?

Solution

At 1 Kbps, the receiver receives 1001 bps instead of 1000 bps.

$$1000 \text{ bits sent} \longrightarrow 1001 \text{ bits received} \longrightarrow 1 \text{ extra bps}$$

At 1 Mbps, the receiver receives 1,001,000 bps instead of 1,000,000 bps.

$$1{,}000{,}000 \text{ bits sent} \longrightarrow 1{,}001{,}000 \text{ bits received} \longrightarrow 1000 \text{ extra bps}$$

Line Coding Schemes

We can divide line coding schemes into three broad categories—*unipolar, polar,* and *bipolar*—as shown in Figure 4.5.

Figure 4.5   *Line coding schemes*

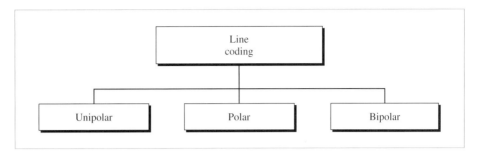

Unipolar

Unipolar encoding is very simple and very primitive. Although it is almost obsolete today, its simplicity provides an easy introduction to the concepts developed with the more complex encoding systems and allows us to examine the kinds of problems that any digital transmission system must overcome.

Digital transmission systems work by sending voltage pulses along a medium link, usually a wire or cable. In many types of encoding, one voltage level stands for binary 0, and another level stands for binary 1. The polarity of a pulse refers to whether it is positive or negative. Unipolar encoding is so named because it uses only one polarity. This polarity is assigned to one of the two binary states, usually the 1. The other state, usually the 0, is represented by zero voltage.

Unipolar encoding uses only one voltage level.

Figure 4.6 shows the idea of unipolar encoding. In this example, the 1s are encoded as a positive value, and the 0s are encoded as a zero value. In addition to being straightforward, unipolar encoding is inexpensive to implement.

However, unipolar encoding has at least two problems that make it undesirable: a dc component and a lack of synchronization. The average amplitude of a unipolar

Figure 4.6   *Unipolar encoding*

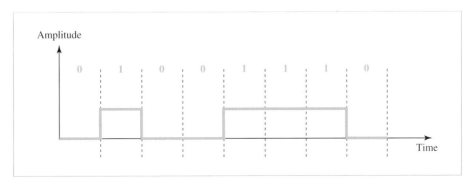

encoded signal is nonzero. This creates a dc component. Lack of synchronization is also an issue in unipolar encoding. If the data contain a long sequence of 0s or 1s, there is no change in the signal during this duration that can alert the receiver to potential synchronization problems.

Polar

Polar encoding uses two voltage levels, one positive and one negative. By using two levels, in most polar encoding methods the average voltage level on the line is reduced and the dc component problem seen in unipolar encoding is alleviated.

Polar encoding uses two voltage levels (positive and negative).

Of the many existing variations of polar encoding, we examine four of the most popular: **nonreturn to zero (NRZ), return to zero (RZ), Manchester,** and **differential Manchester** (see Fig. 4.7).

Figure 4.7   *Types of polar encoding*

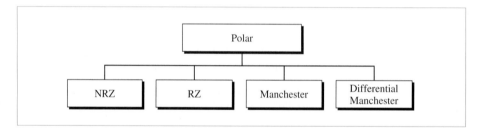

Nonreturn to Zero (NRZ)   In NRZ encoding, the value of the signal is always either positive or negative. There are two popular forms of NRZ.

In **NRZ-L** (NRZ-level) encoding, the level of the signal depends on the type of bit that it represents. A positive voltage usually means the bit is a 0, while a negative voltage means the bit is a 1; thus, the level of the signal is dependent upon the state of the bit. A problem can arise when the data contain a long stream of 0s or 1s. The receiver receives a continuous voltage and determines how many bits are sent by relying on its clock, which may or may not be synchronized with the sender clock.

In NRZ-L the level of the signal is dependent upon the state of the bit.

In **NRZ-I** (NRZ-invert), an inversion of the voltage level represents a 1 bit. It is the transition between a positive and a negative voltage, not the voltage itself, that represents a 1 bit. A 0 bit is represented by no change. NRZ-I is superior to NRZ-L due to the synchronization provided by the signal change each time a 1 bit is encountered. The existence of 1s in the data stream allows the receiver to synchronize its timer to the actual arrival of the transmission. A string of 0s can still cause problems, but because 0s are not as likely, they are less of a problem.

In NRZ-I the signal is inverted if a 1 is encountered.

Figure 4.8 shows the NRZ-L and NRZ-I representations of the same series of bits. In the NRZ-L sequence, positive and negative voltages have specific meanings: positive for 0 and negative for 1. In the NRZ-I sequence, the voltages per se are meaningless. Instead, the receiver looks for changes from one level to another as its basis for recognition of 1s.

Figure 4.8 *NRZ-L and NRZ-I encoding*

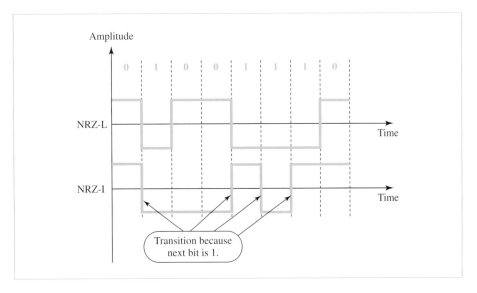

Return to Zero (RZ) As you can see, anytime the original data contain strings of consecutive 1s or 0s, the receiver can lose its place. A solution is to somehow include synchronization in the encoded signal, something like the solution provided by NRZ-I, but one capable of handling strings of 0s as well as 1s.

To ensure synchronization, there must be a signal change for each bit. The receiver can use these changes to build up, update, and synchronize its clock. As we saw above, NRZ-I accomplishes this for sequences of 1s. But to change with every bit, we need more than just two values. One solution is return to zero (RZ) encoding, which uses three values: positive, negative, and zero. In RZ, the signal changes not between bits but during each bit. Like NRZ-L, a positive voltage means 1 and a negative voltage means 0. But, unlike NRZ-L, halfway through each bit interval, the signal returns to zero. A 1 bit is actually represented by positive-to-zero and a 0 bit by negative-to-zero, rather than by positive and negative alone. Figure 4.9 illustrates the concept.

Figure 4.9 *RZ encoding*

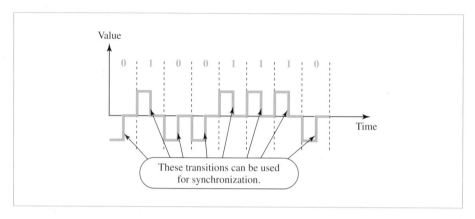

The main disadvantage of RZ encoding is that it requires two signal changes to encode 1 bit and therefore occupies more bandwidth. But of the three alternatives we have examined so far, it is the most effective.

A good encoded digital signal must contain a provision for synchronization.

Manchester Manchester encoding uses an inversion at the middle of each bit interval for both synchronization and bit representation. A negative-to-positive transition represents binary 1, and a positive-to-negative transition represents binary 0. By using a single transition for a dual purpose, Manchester encoding achieves the same level of synchronization as RZ but with only two levels of amplitude. Figure 4.10 shows Manchester encoding.

Figure 4.10 *Manchester encoding*

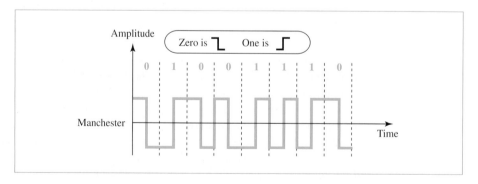

In Manchester encoding, the transition at the middle of the bit is used for both synchronization and bit representation.

Differential Manchester   In differential Manchester encoding, the inversion at the middle of the bit interval is used for synchronization, but the presence or absence of an additional transition at the beginning of the interval is used to identify the bit. A transition means binary 0, and no transition means binary 1. Differential Manchester encoding requires two signal changes to represent binary 0 but only one to represent binary 1. Figure 4.11 shows differential Manchester encoding.

Figure 4.11   *Differential Manchester encoding*

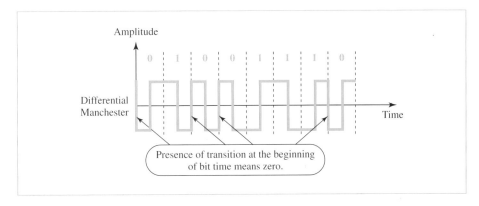

In differential Manchester encoding, the transition at the middle of the bit is used only for synchronization. The bit representation is defined by the inversion or noninversion at the beginning of the bit.

Bipolar

Bipolar encoding, like RZ, uses three voltage levels: positive, negative, and zero. Unlike RZ, however, the zero level in bipolar encoding is used to represent binary 0. The 1s are represented by alternating positive and negative voltages. If the first 1 bit is represented by the positive amplitude, the second will be represented by the negative amplitude, the third by the positive amplitude, and so on. This alternation occurs even when the 1 bits are not consecutive.

In bipolar encoding, we use three levels: positive, zero, and negative.

A common bipolar encoding scheme is called bipolar **alternate mark inversion (AMI).** In the term *alternate mark inversion,* the word *mark* comes from telegraphy and means 1. So AMI means alternate 1 inversion. A neutral, zero voltage represents binary 0. Binary 1s are represented by alternating positive and negative voltages. Figure 4.12 gives an example.

A modification of bipolar AMI has been developed to solve the problem of synchronizing sequential 0s, especially for long-distance transmission. It is called **B*n*ZS (bipolar *n*-zero substitution).** In this scheme, wherever *n* consecutive zeros occur in the sequence, some of the bits in these *n* bits become positive or negative which

Figure 4.12   *Bipolar AMI encoding*

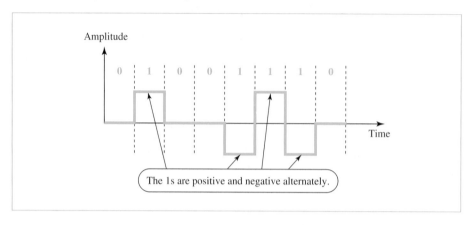

helps synchronization. This substitution violates the rules of AMI in a specified manner such that the receiver knows that these bits are actually 0s and not 1s.

Some Other Schemes

There are some other line coding schemes created for special purposes in data communications. We discuss two interesting ones here: 2B1Q and MLT-3.

2B1Q

The 2B1Q (two binary, one quaternary) uses four voltage levels. Each pulse can then represent 2 bits, making each pulse more efficient. Figure 4.13 shows an example of a 2B1Q signal.

Figure 4.13   *2B1Q*

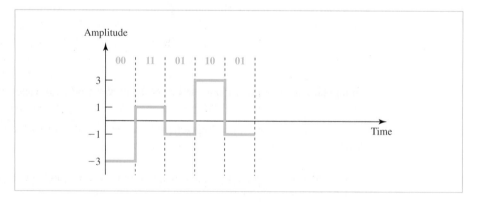

MLT-3

Multiline transmission, three level (MLT-3) is very similar to NRZ-I (nonreturn to zero, invert), but it uses three levels of signals (+1, 0, and −1). The signal transitions from one level to the next at the beginning of a 1 bit; there is no transition at the beginning of a 0 bit. Figure 4.14 shows a sample MLT-3 signal.

Figure 4.14 *MLT-3 signal*

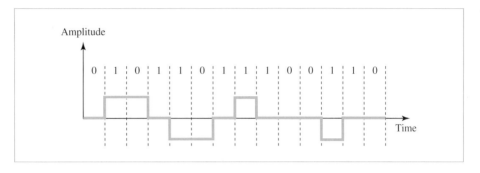

4.2 BLOCK CODING

To improve the performance of line coding, **block coding** was introduced. We need some kind of redundancy to ensure synchronization. In addition, we need to include other redundant bits (as we will see in Chapter 10) to detect errors. Block coding can achieve, to some extent, these two goals. Figure 4.15 shows the procedure.

Figure 4.15 *Block coding*

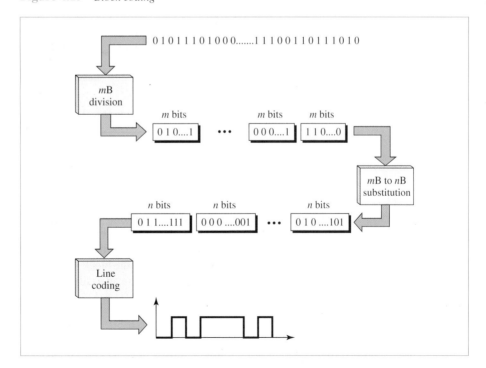

Steps in Transformation

In this method, there are three steps: division, substitution, and line coding.

Step 1: Division

In this step, the sequence of bits is divided into groups of *m* bits. For example, in 4B/5B encoding, the original bit sequence is divided into 4-bit groups.

Step 2: Substitution

The heart of block coding is the substitution step. In this step, we substitute an *m*-bit code for an *n*-bit group. For example, in 4B/5B encoding we substitute a 5-bit code for a 4-bit group. With a 4-bit block, we can have 16 (2^4) different groups. With a 5-bit code, we can have 32 (2^5) possible codes. This means that we can map some of the 5-bit groups to the 4-bit groups. Some of the 5-bit codes are not used. We can apply a strategy or a policy to choose only the 5-bit codes that help us in synchronization and error detection. Figure 4.16 shows how we can use just one-half of the 5-bit codes.

Figure 4.16   *Substitution in block coding*

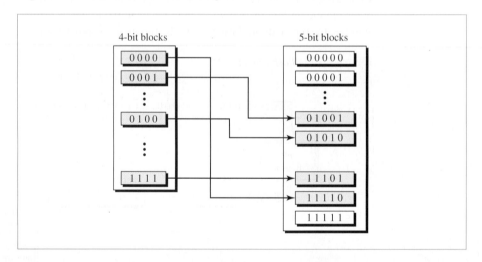

To achieve synchronization, we can use the 5-bit codes in such a way that, for example, we do not have more than three consecutive 0s or 1s.

Block coding can definitely help in error detection. Because only a subset of the 5-bit codes is used, if one or more of the bits in the block is changed in such a way that one of the unused codes is received, the receiver can easily detect the error.

Step 3: Line Coding

After the substitution, we can use one of the line coding schemes to create a signal. Normally a very simple line coding scheme is chosen because the block coding procedure provides two desirable features of complex line coding schemes. Sometimes, as we will see, the second step (substitution) and the third step (line coding) are combined.

Some Common Block Codes

In this section, we discuss some common block codes.

4B/5B

As described above, in 4B/5B, every 4 bits of data is encoded into a 5-bit code. The selection of the 5-bit code is such that each code contains no more than one leading 0 and no more than two trailing 0s. Therefore, when these 5-bit codes are sent in sequence, no more than three consecutive 0s are encountered. The 5-bit codes are normally line coded using NRZ-I. Table 4.1 shows the 4B/5B encoding. The encoded sequences for control characters (column 3) do not follow the 4B/5B rules of coding.

Table 4.1   *4B/5B encoding*

Data Sequence	Encoded Sequence	Data Sequence	Encoded Sequence
0000	11110	Q (Quiet)	00000
0001	01001	I (Idle)	11111
0010	10100	H (Halt)	00100
0011	10101	J (start delimiter)	11000
0100	01010	K (start delimiter)	10001
0101	01011	T (end delimiter)	01101
0110	01110	S (Set)	11001
0111	01111	R (Reset)	00111
1000	10010		
1001	10011		
1010	10110		
1011	10111		
1100	11010		
1101	11011		
1110	11100		
1111	11101		

8B/10B

This is similar to 4B/5B encoding except that a group of 8 bits of data is now substituted by a 10-bit code. It provides more error detection capability than 4B/5B. The **8B/10B encoding** table is very long and is not shown here.

8B/6T

We saw that 4B/5B encoding and 8B/10B encoding provide good synchronization and error detection capabilities, but they come with a price; the required bandwidth is increased. Sometimes, we cannot afford this extra bandwidth. **8B/6T encoding** is designed to substitute an 8-bit group with a six-symbol code. However, each symbol is ternary, having one of three signal levels. This means that each block of 8-bit data is encoded as units of ternary signals (three levels, +1, 0, and −1 V). An 8-bit code can represent one of 256 possibilities (2^8); a six-symbol ternary signal can represent one of 729 possibilities (3^6). This means that some of the codes are not used. Encoding can be designed to maintain synchronization and error-checking capability. Appendix D shows the full table of 8B/6T encoded values. Figure 4.17 shows an example of 8B/6T encoding.

Figure 4.17   *Example of 8B/6T encoding*

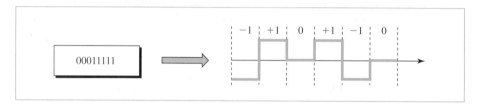

4.3   SAMPLING

Line coding and block coding can be used to convert binary data to a digital signal. Sometimes, however, our data are analog, such as audio. Voice and music, for example, are by nature analog, so when we record voice or video, we have created an analog electric signal. If we want to store the recording in the computer or send it digitally, we need to change it through a process called **sampling.** After the analog signal is sampled, we can store the binary data in the computer or use line coding (or a combination of block coding and line coding) to further change the signal to a digital one so it can be transmitted digitally.

The idea of digitizing analog signals started with telephone companies. To provide long-distance services, they have to carry analog signals, produced from voice channels, over long metallic media (cables). Electric signals lose their strength over metallic wire, which means amplifiers are needed to amplify signals. However, the amplifiers create distortion in the signal due to frequency spectrum and phase changes and also add some noise. The received signal is not the exact replica of the original signal. If you used the telephone system for long-distance communication some decades ago, you have noticed this phenomenon.

The solution found by the telephone companies was to digitize the analog signal at the sender. The signal is transmitted as a digital signal and converted back to an analog signal at the receiver.

As discussed in Chapter 3, digital signals are less prone to noise and distortion. A small change in an analog signal can change the received voice substantially, but it takes a considerable change to convert a 0 to 1 or a 1 to 0.

Pulse Amplitude Modulation (PAM)

One analog-to-digital conversion method is called **pulse amplitude modulation (PAM).** This technique takes an analog signal, samples it, and generates a series of pulses based on the results of the sampling. The term **sampling** means measuring the amplitude of the signal at equal intervals.

The method of sampling used in PAM is more useful to other areas of engineering than it is to data communication. However, PAM is the foundation of an important analog-to-digital conversion method called **pulse code modulation (PCM).**

In PAM, the original signal is sampled at equal intervals, as shown in Figure 4.18. PAM uses a technique called *sample and hold*. At a given moment, the signal level is read, then held briefly. The sampled value occurs only instantaneously in the actual waveform, but is generalized over a still short but measurable period in the PAM result.

Figure 4.18 *PAM*

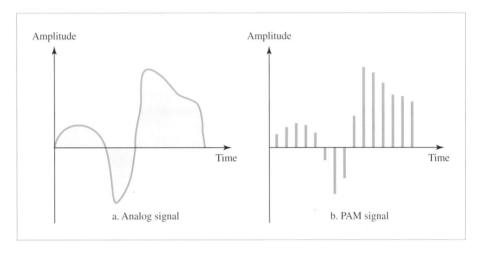

a. Analog signal

b. PAM signal

PAM is not useful to data communications because even though it translates the original waveform to a series of pulses, these pulses are still of any amplitude (still an analog signal, not digital). To make them digital, we must modify them by using pulse code modulation.

> **Pulse amplitude modulation has some applications, but it is not used by itself in data communication. However, it is the first step in another very popular conversion method called pulse code modulation.**

Pulse Code Modulation

PCM modifies the pulses created by PAM to create a completely digital signal. To do so, PCM first quantizes the PAM pulses. **Quantization** is a method of assigning integral values in a specific range to sampled instances. The result of quantization is presented in Figure 4.19.

Figure 4.19   *Quantized PAM signal*

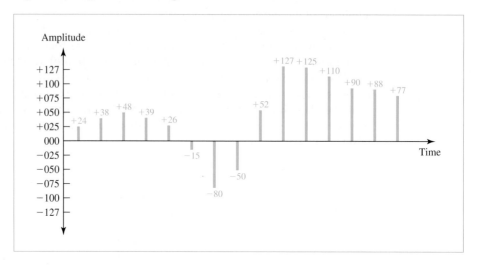

Figure 4.20 shows a simple method of assigning sign and magnitude to quantized samples. Each value is translated into its 7-bit binary equivalent. The eighth bit indicates the sign.

Figure 4.20   *Quantizing by using sign and magnitude*

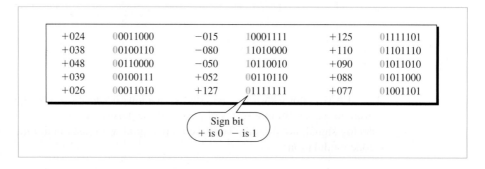

The binary digits are then transformed to a digital signal by using one of the line coding techniques. Figure 4.21 shows the result of the pulse code modulation of the original signal encoded finally into a unipolar signal. Only the first three sampled values are shown.

PCM is actually made up of four separate processes: PAM, quantization, binary encoding, and line coding. Figure 4.22 shows the entire process in graphical form. PCM is the sampling method used to digitize voice in T-line transmission in the North American telecommunication system (see Chapter 6).

Figure 4.21 *PCM*

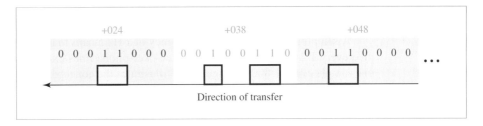

Figure 4.22 *From analog signal to PCM digital code*

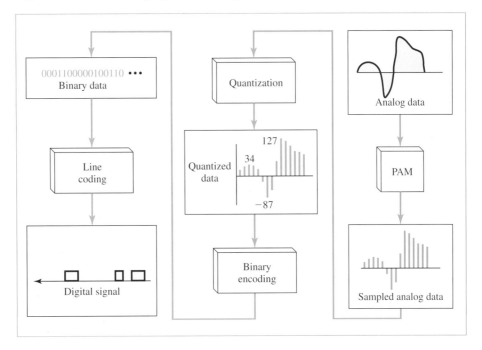

Sampling Rate: Nyquist Theorem

The accuracy of any digital reproduction of an analog signal depends on the number of samples taken. Using PAM and PCM, we can reproduce the waveform exactly by taking infinite samples, or we can reproduce the barest generalization of its direction of change by taking three samples. Obviously, we prefer to find a number somewhere between these two extremes. So the question is, How many samples are sufficient?

Actually, it requires remarkably little information for the receiving device to reconstruct an analog signal. According to the **Nyquist theorem,** to ensure the accurate reproduction of an original analog signal using PAM, the **sampling rate** must be at least twice the highest frequency of the original signal. So if we want to sample telephone voice with a maximum frequency 4000 Hz, we need a sampling rate of 8000 samples per second.

> **According to the Nyquist theorem, the sampling rate must be at least 2 times the highest frequency.**

A sampling rate of twice the frequency of x Hz means that the signal must be sampled every $1/2x$ seconds. Using the voice-over-phone-lines example above, that means one sample every $1/8000$ s. Figure 4.23 illustrates the concept.

Figure 4.23 *Nyquist theorem*

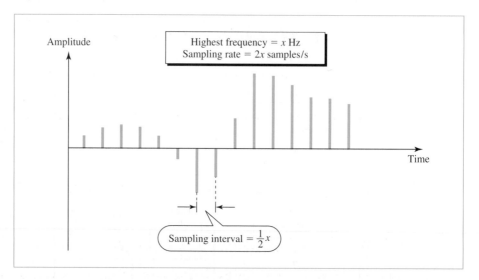

> **Note that we can always change a band-pass signal to a low-pass signal before sampling. In this case, the sampling rate is twice the bandwidth.**

Example 4

What sampling rate is needed for a signal with a bandwidth of 10,000 Hz (1000 to 11,000 Hz)?

Solution

The sampling rate must be twice the highest frequency in the signal:

$$\text{Sampling rate} = 2 \times (11{,}000) = 22{,}000 \text{ samples/s}$$

How Many Bits per Sample?

After we have found the sampling rate, we need to determine the number of bits to be transmitted for each sample. This depends on the level of precision needed. The number of bits is chosen such that the original signal can be reproduced with the desired precision in amplitude.

Example 5

A signal is sampled. Each sample requires at least 12 levels of precision (+0 to +5 and −0 to −5). How many bits should be sent for each sample?

Solution

We need 4 bits; 1 bit for the sign and 3 bits for the value. A 3-bit value can represent $2^3 = 8$ levels (000 to 111), which is more than what we need. A 2-bit value is not enough since $2^2 = 4$. A 4-bit value is too much because $2^4 = 16$.

Bit Rate

After finding the number of bits per sample, we can calculate the bit rate by using the following formula:

$$\text{Bit rate} = \text{sampling rate} \times \text{number of bits per sample}$$

Example 6

We want to digitize the human voice. What is the bit rate, assuming 8 bits per sample?

Solution

The human voice normally contains frequencies from 0 to 4000 Hz. So the sampling rate is

$$\text{Sampling rate} = 4000 \times 2 = 8000 \text{ samples/s}$$

The bit rate can be calculated as

$$\text{Bit rate} = \text{sampling rate} \times \text{number of bits per sample} = 8000 \times 8 = 64{,}000 \text{ bps} = 64 \text{ Kbps}$$

4.4 TRANSMISSION MODE

Of primary concern when we are considering the transmission of data from one device to another is the wiring, and of primary concern when we are considering the wiring is the data stream. Do we send 1 bit at a time; or do we group bits into larger groups and, if so, how? The transmission of binary data across a link can be accomplished in either parallel or serial mode. In parallel mode, multiple bits are sent with each clock tick. In serial mode, 1 bit is sent with each clock tick. While there is only one way to send parallel data, there are two subclasses of serial transmission: synchronous and asynchronous (see Fig. 4.24).

Figure 4.24   *Data transmission*

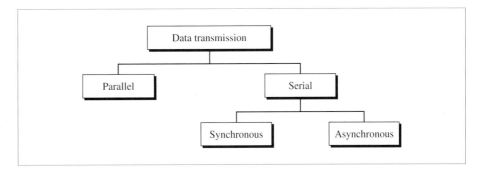

Parallel Transmission

Binary data, consisting of 1s and 0s, may be organized into groups of n bits each. Computers produce and consume data in groups of bits much as we conceive of and use spoken language in the form of words rather than letters. By grouping, we can send data n bits at a time instead of 1. This is called **parallel transmission.**

The mechanism for parallel transmission is a conceptually simple one: Use n wires to send n bits at one time. That way each bit has its own wire, and all n bits of one group can be transmitted with each clock tick from one device to another. Figure 4.25 shows how parallel transmission works for $n = 8$. Typically, the eight wires are bundled in a cable with a connector at each end.

Figure 4.25   *Parallel transmission*

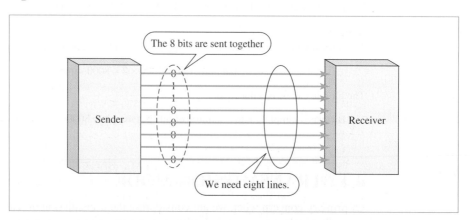

The advantage of parallel transmission is speed. All else being equal, parallel transmission can increase the transfer speed by a factor of n over serial transmission. But there is a significant disadvantage: cost. Parallel transmission requires n communication lines (wires in the example) just to transmit the data stream. Because this is expensive, parallel transmission is usually limited to short distances.

Serial Transmission

In **serial transmission** one bit follows another, so we need only one communication channel rather than n to transmit data between two communicating devices (see Fig. 4.26).

The advantage of serial over parallel transmission is that with only one communication channel, serial transmission reduces the cost of transmission over parallel by roughly a factor of n.

Since communication within devices is parallel, conversion devices are required at the interface between the sender and the line (parallel-to-serial) and between the line and the receiver (serial-to-parallel).

Serial transmission occurs in one of two ways: asynchronous or synchronous.

Figure 4.26 *Serial transmission*

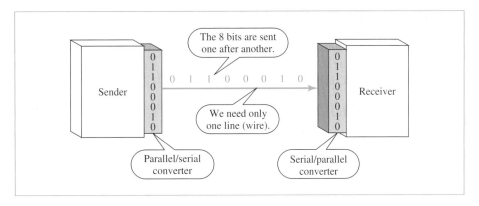

Asynchronous Transmission

Asynchronous transmission is so named because the timing of a signal is unimportant. Instead, information is received and translated by agreed-upon patterns. As long as those patterns are followed, the receiving device can retrieve the information without regard to the rhythm in which it is sent. Patterns are based on grouping the bit stream into bytes. Each group, usually 8 bits, is sent along the link as a unit. The sending system handles each group independently, relaying it to the link whenever ready, without regard to a timer.

Without synchronization, the receiver cannot use timing to predict when the next group will arrive. To alert the receiver to the arrival of a new group, therefore, an extra bit is added to the beginning of each byte. This bit, usually a 0, is called the **start bit.** To let the receiver know that the byte is finished, 1 or more additional bits are appended to the end of the byte. These bits, usually 1s, are called **stop bits.** By this method, each byte is increased in size to at least 10 bits, of which 8 are information and 2 or more are signals to the receiver. In addition, the transmission of each byte may then be followed by a gap of varying duration. This gap can be represented either by an idle channel or by a stream of additional stop bits.

In asynchronous transmission, we send 1 start bit (0) at the beginning and 1 or more stop bits (1s) at the end of each byte. There may be a gap between each byte.

The start and stop bits and the gap alert the receiver to the beginning and end of each byte and allow it to synchronize with the data stream. This mechanism is called asynchronous because, at the byte level, sender and receiver do not have to be synchronized. But within each byte, the receiver must still be synchronized with the incoming bit stream. That is, some synchronization is required, but only for the duration of a single byte. The receiving device resynchronizes at the onset of each new byte. When the receiver detects a start bit, it sets a timer and begins counting bits as they come in. After *n* bits, the receiver looks for a stop bit. As soon as it detects the stop bit, it waits until it detects the next start bit.

> **Asynchronous here means "asynchronous at the byte level," but the bits are still synchronized; their durations are the same.**

Figure 4.27 is a schematic illustration of asynchronous transmission. In this example, the start bits are 0s, the stop bits are 1s, and the gap is represented by an idle line rather than by additional stop bits.

Figure 4.27   *Asynchronous transmission*

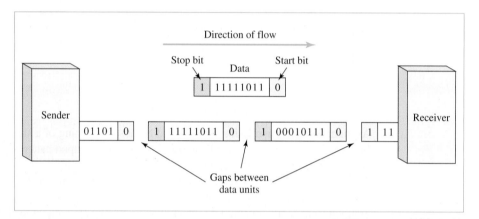

The addition of stop and start bits and the insertion of gaps into the bit stream make asynchronous transmission slower than forms of transmission that can operate without the addition of control information. But it is cheap and effective, two advantages that make it an attractive choice for situations such as low-speed communication. For example, the connection of a keyboard to a computer is a natural application for asynchronous transmission. A user types only one character at a time, types extremely slowly in data processing terms, and leaves unpredictable gaps of time between each character.

Synchronous Transmission

In **synchronous transmission,** the bit stream is combined into longer "frames," which may contain multiple bytes. Each byte, however, is introduced onto the transmission link without a gap between it and the next one. It is left to the receiver to separate the bit stream into bytes for decoding purposes. In other words, data are transmitted as an unbroken string of 1s and 0s, and the receiver separates that string into the bytes, or characters, it needs to reconstruct the information.

> **In synchronous transmission, we send bits one after another without start/stop bits or gaps. It is the responsibility of the receiver to group the bits.**

Figure 4.28 gives a schematic illustration of synchronous transmission. We have drawn in the divisions between bytes. In reality, those divisions do not exist; the sender puts its data onto the line as one long string. If the sender wishes to send data in separate bursts, the gaps between bursts must be filled with a special sequence of 0s and 1s that means *idle*. The receiver counts the bits as they arrive and groups them in 8-bit units.

Figure 4.28 *Synchronous transmission*

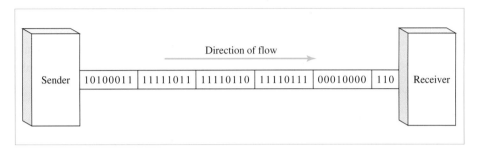

Without gaps and start/stop bits, there is no built-in mechanism to help the receiving device adjust its bit synchronization midstream. Timing becomes very important, therefore, because the accuracy of the received information is completely dependent on the ability of the receiving device to keep an accurate count of the bits as they come in.

The advantage of synchronous transmission is speed. With no extra bits or gaps to introduce at the sending end and remove at the receiving end and, by extension, with fewer bits to move across the link, synchronous transmission is faster than asynchronous transmission. For this reason, it is more useful for high-speed applications such as the transmission of data from one computer to another. Byte synchronization is accomplished in the data link layer.

4.5   KEY TERMS

2B1Q encoding
4B/5B encoding
8B/6T encoding
8B/10B encoding
alternate mark inversion (AMI)
asynchronous transmission
bipolar encoding
bipolar *n*-zero substitution (B*n*ZS)
bit rate
block coding
data level
dc component
differential Manchester encoding
line coding
Manchester encoding

multiline transmission, 3 level (MLT-3)
  encoding
nonreturn to zero (NRZ)
nonreturn to zero, invert (NRZ-I)
nonreturn to zero, level (NRZ-L)
Nyquist theorem
parallel transmission
polar encoding
pulse amplitude modulation (PAM)
pulse code modulation (PCM)
pulse rate
quantization
return to zero (RZ)
sampling
sampling rate

self-synchronization   stop bit
serial transmission   synchronous transmission
signal level   unipolar encoding
start bit

4.6   SUMMARY

❏   Line coding is the process of converting binary data to a digital signal.

❏   The number of different values allowed in a signal is the signal level. The number of symbols that represent data is the data level.

❏   Bit rate is a function of the pulse rate and data level.

❏   Line coding methods must eliminate the dc component and provide a means of synchronization between the sender and the receiver.

❏   Line coding methods can be classified as unipolar, polar, or bipolar.

❏   NRZ, RZ, Manchester, and differential Manchester encoding are the most popular polar encoding methods.

❏   AMI is a popular bipolar encoding method.

❏   Block coding can improve the performance of line coding through redundancy and error correction.

❏   Block coding involves grouping the bits, substitution, and line coding.

❏   4B/5B, 8B/10B, and 8B/6T are common block coding methods.

❏   Analog-to-digital conversion relies on PCM (pulse code modulation).

❏   PCM involves sampling, quantizing, and line coding.

❏   The Nyquist theorem says that the sampling rate must be at least twice the highest-frequency component in the original signal.

❏   Digital transmission can be either parallel or serial in mode.

❏   In parallel transmission, a group of bits is sent simultaneously, with each bit on a separate line.

❏   In serial transmission, there is only one line and the bits are sent sequentially.

❏   Serial transmission can be either synchronous or asynchronous.

❏   In asynchronous serial transmission, each byte (group of 8 bits) is framed with a start bit and a stop bit. There may be a variable-length gap between each byte.

❏   In synchronous serial transmission, bits are sent in a continuous stream without start and stop bits and without gaps between bytes. Regrouping the bits into meaningful bytes is the responsibility of the receiver.

4.7   PRACTICE SET

Review Questions

1. Give the signal level for each line coding method discussed (NRZ, RZ, etc.).

2. What is the dc component?

3. Can the bit rate be less than the pulse rate? Why or why not?
4. Why is synchronization a problem in data communications?
5. How does NRZ-L differ from NRZ-I?
6. What is the major disadvantage in using NRZ encoding? How does RZ encoding attempt to solve the problem?
7. Compare and contrast RZ and bipolar AMI.
8. What are the three major steps in block coding?
9. How can block coding aid in synchronization?
10. How can block coding aid in error detection?
11. Discuss the relationship between the sampling rate and the received signal.
12. Discuss the relationship between the number of bits allotted for each sample and the received signal.
13. What is the Nyquist theorem?
14. Explain the two modes for transmitting binary data across a link.
15. What are the advantages and disadvantages of parallel transmission?
16. Compare the two methods of serial transmission. Discuss the advantages and disadvantages of each.

Multiple-Choice Questions

17. Unipolar, bipolar, and polar encoding are types of _____ encoding.
    a. Line
    b. Block
    c. NRZ
    d. Manchester
18. If a symbol is composed of 3 bits, there are _____ data levels.
    a. 2
    b. 4
    c. 8
    d. 16
19. Pulse rate is always _____ the bit rate.
    a. Greater than
    b. Less than
    c. Greater than or equal to
    d. Less than or equal to
20. _____ encoding has a transition at the middle of each bit.
    a. RZ
    b. Manchester
    c. Differential Manchester
    d. All the above

21. _____ encoding has a transition at the beginning of each 0 bit.
    a. RZ
    b. Manchester
    c. Differential Manchester
    d. All the above

22. PCM is an example of _____ conversion.
    a. Digital-to-digital
    b. Digital-to-analog
    c. Analog-to-analog
    d. Analog-to-digital

23. If the frequency spectrum of a signal has a bandwidth of 500 Hz with the highest frequency at 600 Hz, what should be the sampling rate, according to the Nyquist theorem?
    a. 200 samples/s
    b. 500 samples/s
    c. 1000 samples/s
    d. 1200 samples/s

24. The Nyquist theorem specifies the minimum sampling rate to be_____.
    a. Equal to the lowest frequency of a signal
    b. Equal to the highest frequency of a signal
    c. Twice the bandwidth of a signal
    d. Twice the highest frequency of a signal

25. One factor in the accuracy of a reconstructed PCM signal is the _____.
    a. Signal bandwidth
    b. Carrier frequency
    c. Number of bits used for quantization
    d. Baud rate

26. Which encoding type always has a nonzero average amplitude?
    a. Unipolar
    b. Polar
    c. Bipolar
    d. All the above

27. Which of the following encoding methods does not provide for synchronization?
    a. NRZ-L
    b. RZ
    c. NRZ-I
    d. Manchester

28. Which encoding method uses alternating positive and negative values for 1s?
    a. NRZ-I
    b. RZ

c. Manchester

d. AMI

29. In PCM, an analog-to- _____ conversion occurs.

a. Analog

b. Digital

c. QAM

d. Differential

30. If the maximum value of a PCM signal is 31 and the minimum value is −31, how many bits were used for coding?

a. 4

b. 5

c. 6

d. 7

31. RZ encoding involves _____ signal levels.

a. Two

b. Three

c. Four

d. Five

32. Which quantization level results in a more faithful reproduction of the signal?

a. 2

b. 8

c. 16

d. 32

33. Which encoding technique attempts to solve the loss of synchronization due to long strings of 0s?

a. BnZS

b. NRZ

c. AMI

d. (a) and (b)

34. Block coding can help in _____ at the receiver.

a. Synchronization

b. Error detection

c. Attenuation

d. (a) and (b)

35. In _____ transmission, bits are transmitted simultaneously, each across its own wire.

a. Asynchronous serial

b. Synchronous serial

c. Parallel

d. (a) and (b)

36. In _____ transmission, bits are transmitted over a single wire, one at a time.
    a. Asynchronous serial
    b. Synchronous serial
    c. Parallel
    d. (a) and (b)

37. In _____ transmission, a start bit and a stop bit frame a character byte.
    a. Asynchronous serial
    b. Synchronous serial
    c. Parallel
    d. (a) and (b)

38. In asynchronous transmission, the gap time between bytes is _____.
    a. Fixed
    b. Variable
    c. A function of the data rate
    d. Zero

39. Synchronous transmission does not have _____.
    a. A start bit
    b. A stop bit
    c. Gaps between bytes
    d. All the above

Exercises

40. If the bit rate of a signal is 1000 bps, how many bits can be sent in 5 s? How many bits in 1/5 s? How many bits in 100 ms?

41. Assume a data stream is made of ten 0s. Encode this stream, using the following encoding schemes. How many changes (vertical line) can you find for each scheme?
    a. Unipolar
    b. NRZ-L
    c. NRZ-I
    d. RZ
    e. Manchester
    f. Differential Manchester
    g. AMI

42. Repeat Exercise 41 for a data stream of ten 1s.

43. Repeat Exercise 41 for a data stream of 10 alternating 0s and 1s.

44. Repeat Exercise 41 for a data stream of three 0s followed by two 1s followed by two 0s and another three 1s.

45. Figure 4.29 is the unipolar encoding of a data stream. What is the data stream?

46. Figure 4.30 is the NRZ-L encoding of a data stream. What is the data stream?

Figure 4.29   *Exercise 45*

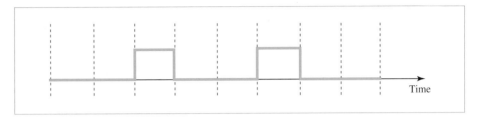

Figure 4.30   *Exercises 46 and 47*

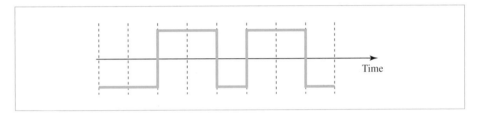

47. Repeat Exercise 46 if the figure is the NRZ-I encoding of a data stream.

48. Figure 4.31 is the RZ encoding of a data stream. What is the data stream?

Figure 4.31   *Exercise 48*

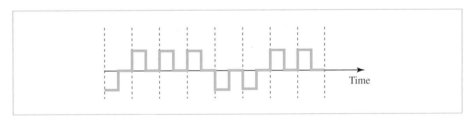

49. Figure 4.32 is the Manchester encoding of a data stream. What is the data stream?

Figure 4.32   *Exercises 49 and 50*

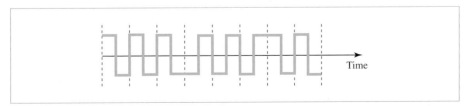

50. Repeat Exercise 49 if the figure is the differential Manchester encoding of a data stream.

51. Figure 4.33 is the AMI encoding of a data stream. What is the data stream?

Figure 4.33 *Exercises 51 and 52*

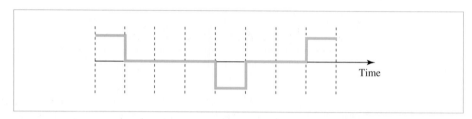

52. How many amplitude levels are there for each of the following methods?
    a. Unipolar
    b. NRZ-L
    c. NRZ-I
    d. RZ
    e. Manchester
    f. Differential Manchester
53. What is the sampling rate for PCM if the frequency ranges from 1000 to 4000 Hz?
54. Using the Nyquist theorem, calculate the sampling rate for the following analog signals.
    a. An analog signal with bandwidth of 2000 Hz
    b. An analog signal with frequencies from 2000 to 6000 Hz
    c. A signal with a horizontal line in the time-domain representation
    d. A signal with a vertical line in the time-domain representation
55. If a signal is sampled 8000 times per second, what is the interval between each sample?
56. If the interval between two samples in a digitized signal is 125 μs, what is the sampling rate?
57. A signal is sampled. Each sample represents one of four levels. How many bits are needed to represent each sample? If the sampling rate is 8000 samples per second, what is the bit rate?
58. If we want to transmit 1000 ASCII (see Appendix A) characters asynchronously, what is the minimum number of extra bits needed? What is the efficiency in percentage?

CHAPTER 5

Analog Transmission

In Chapter 3, we discussed the advantages and disadvantages of digital transmission and analog transmission. We mentioned that digital transmission is very desirable, but a low-pass channel with a very large bandwidth is needed. We also mentioned that analog transmission is the only choice if we have a channel which is band-pass in nature. Digital transmission was discussed in Chapter 4; we discuss analog transmission in this chapter.

Converting binary data or a low-pass analog signal to a band-pass analog signal is traditionally called *modulation*. In this chapter, we first discuss modulation of binary data. We then discuss modems, devices that actually do the modulation; we finally discuss modulation of low-pass analog signals.

5.1   MODULATION OF DIGITAL DATA

Modulation of binary data or **digital-to-analog modulation** is the process of changing one of the characteristics of an analog signal based on the information in a digital signal (0s and 1s). When you transmit data from one computer to another across a public access phone line, for example, the original data are digital, but because telephone wires carry analog signals, the data must be converted. The digital data must be modulated on an analog signal that has been manipulated to look like two distinct values corresponding to binary 1 and binary 0. Figure 5.1 shows the relationship between the digital information, the digital-to-analog modulating hardware, and the resultant analog signal.

Of the many mechanisms for digital-to-analog modulation, we will discuss only those most useful for data communications.

As discussed in Chapter 3, a sine wave is defined by three characteristics: amplitude, frequency, and phase. When we vary any one of these characteristics, we create a different version of that wave. If we then say that the original wave represents binary 1, the variation can represent binary 0, or vice versa. So, by changing one aspect of a simple electric signal back and forth, we can use it to represent digital data. Any of the three characteristics listed above can be altered in this way, giving us at least three mechanisms for modulating digital data into an analog signal: *amplitude shift keying (ASK), frequency shift keying (FSK),* and *phase shift keying (PSK)*. In addition, there is a fourth (and better) mechanism that combines changes in both

Figure 5.1   *Digital-to-analog modulation*

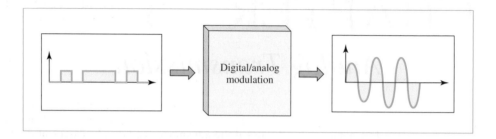

Figure 5.2   *Types of digital-to-analog modulation*

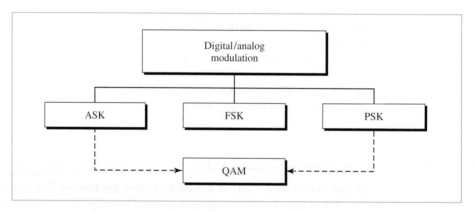

amplitude and phase called *quadrature amplitude modulation (QAM)*. QAM is the most efficient of these options and is the mechanism used in all modern modems (see Fig. 5.2).

Aspects of Digital-to-Analog Conversion

Before we discuss specific methods of digital-to-analog modulation, two basic issues must be defined: bit and baud rates and carrier signal.

Bit Rate and Baud Rate

Two terms used frequently in data communication are *bit rate* and *baud rate*. **Bit rate** is the number of bits transmitted during 1 s. **Baud rate** refers to the number of signal units per second that are required to represent those bits. A signal unit is composed of 1 or more bits. In discussions of computer efficiency, the bit rate is the more important—we want to know how long it takes to process each piece of information. In data transmission, however, we are more concerned with how efficiently we can move those data from place to place, whether in pieces or blocks. The fewer signal units required, the more efficient the system and the less bandwidth required to transmit more bits; so we are more concerned with the baud rate. The baud rate determines the bandwidth required to send the signal.

Bit rate equals the baud rate times the number of bits represented by each signal unit. The baud rate equals the bit rate divided by the number of bits represented by each signal unit. Bit rate is always greater than or equal to the baud rate.

> **Bit rate is the number of bits per second. Baud rate is the number of signal units per second. Baud rate is less than or equal to the bit rate.**

An analogy can clarify the concept of bauds and bits. In transportation, a baud is analogous to a car, and a bit is analogous to a passenger. A car can carry one or more passengers. If 1000 cars go from one point to another, carrying only one passenger (the driver), then 1000 passengers are transported. However, if each car carries four passengers (carpooling), then 4000 passengers are transported. Note that the number of cars, not the number of passengers, determines the traffic and, therefore, the need for wider highways. Similarly, the number of bauds determines the required bandwidth, not the number of bits.

Example 1

An analog signal carries 4 bits in each signal unit. If 1000 signal units are sent per second, find the baud rate and the bit rate.

Solution

$$\text{Baud rate} = \text{number of signal units per second} = 1000 \text{ bauds per second (baud/s)}$$
$$\text{Bit rate} = \text{baud rate} \times \text{number of bits per signal unit} = 1000 \times 4 = 4000 \text{ bps}$$

Example 2

The bit rate of a signal is 3000. If each signal unit carries 6 bits, what is the baud rate?

Solution

$$\text{Baud rate} = \frac{\text{bit rate}}{\text{number of bits per signal unit}} = \frac{3000}{6} = 500 \text{ baud/s}$$

Carrier Signal

In analog transmission, the sending device produces a high-frequency signal that acts as a basis for the information signal. This base signal is called the **carrier signal** or carrier frequency. The receiving device is tuned to the frequency of the carrier signal that it expects from the sender. Digital information then modulates the carrier signal by modifying one or more of its characteristics (amplitude, frequency, or phase). This kind of modification is called **modulation** (or shift keying), and the information signal is called the *modulating signal.*

Amplitude Shift Keying (ASK)

In **amplitude shift keying,** the strength of the carrier signal is varied to represent binary 1 or 0. Both frequency and phase remain constant while the amplitude changes. Which voltage represents 1 and which represents 0 are left to the system designers. A bit duration is the period of time that defines 1 bit. The peak amplitude of the signal during each bit duration is constant, and its value depends on the bit (0 or 1). Figure 5.3 gives a conceptual view of ASK.

Figure 5.3   *ASK*

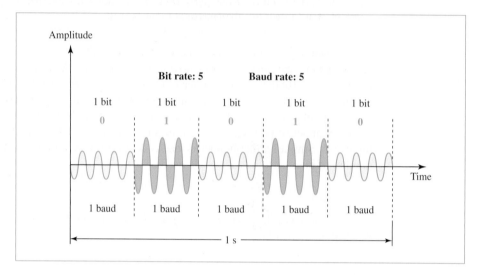

Unfortunately, ASK transmission is highly susceptible to noise interference. The term *noise* refers to unintentional voltages introduced onto a line by various phenomena such as heat or electromagnetic induction created by other sources. These unintentional voltages combine with the signal to change the amplitude. A 0 can be changed to 1, and a 1 to 0. You can see how noise would be especially problematic for ASK, which relies solely on amplitude for recognition. Noise usually affects the amplitude; therefore, ASK is the modulation method most affected by noise.

A popular ASK technique is called on/off keying (OOK). In OOK one of the bit values is represented by no voltage. The advantage is a reduction in the amount of energy required to transmit information.

Bandwidth for ASK

As you will recall from Chapter 3, the bandwidth of a signal is the total range of frequencies occupied by that signal. When we decompose an ASK-modulated signal, we get a spectrum of many simple frequencies. However, the most significant ones are those between $f_c - N_{baud}/2$ and $f_c + N_{baud}/2$ with the carrier frequency f_c at the middle (see Fig. 5.4).

Bandwidth requirements for ASK are calculated using the formula

$$BW = (1 + d) \times N_{baud}$$

where BW is the bandwidth, N_{baud} is the baud rate, and d is a factor related to the modulation process (with a minimum value of 0).

As you can see, the minimum bandwidth required for transmission is equal to the baud rate.

Figure 5.4 *Relationship between baud rate and bandwidth in ASK*

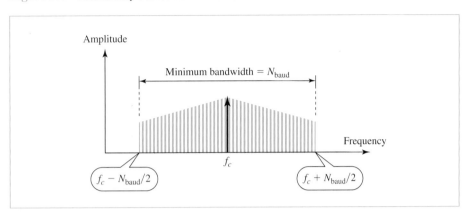

Although there is only one carrier frequency, the process of modulation produces a complex signal that is a combination of many simple signals, each with a different frequency.

Example 3

Find the minimum bandwidth for an ASK signal transmitting at 2000 bps. The transmission mode is half-duplex.

Solution

In ASK the baud rate and bit rate are the same. The baud rate is therefore 2000. An ASK signal requires a minimum bandwidth equal to its baud rate. Therefore, the minimum bandwidth is 2000 Hz.

Example 4

Given a bandwidth of 5000 Hz for an ASK signal, what are the baud rate and bit rate?

Solution

In ASK the baud rate is the same as the bandwidth, which means the baud rate is 5000. But because the baud rate and the bit rate are also the same for ASK, the bit rate is 5000 bps.

Example 5

Given a bandwidth of 10,000 Hz (1000 to 11,000 Hz), draw the full-duplex ASK diagram of the system. Find the carriers and the bandwidths in each direction. Assume there is no gap between the bands in the two directions.

Solution

For full-duplex ASK, the bandwidth for each direction is

$$\text{BW} = \frac{10{,}000}{2} = 5000 \text{ Hz}$$

The carrier frequencies can be chosen at the middle of each band (see Fig. 5.5).

$$f_{c\,(\text{forward})} = 1000 + \frac{5000}{2} = 3500 \text{ Hz}$$

$$f_{c\,(\text{backward})} = 11{,}000 - \frac{5000}{2} = 8500 \text{ Hz}$$

Figure 5.5 *Solution to Example 5*

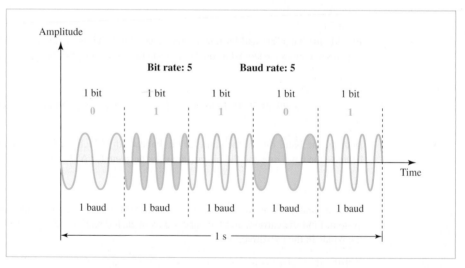

Frequency Shift Keying (FSK)

In **frequency shift keying,** the frequency of the carrier signal is varied to represent binary 1 or 0. The frequency of the signal during each bit duration is constant, and its value depends on the bit (0 or 1): Both peak amplitude and phase remain constant. Figure 5.6 gives a conceptual view of FSK.

Figure 5.6 *FSK*

FSK avoids most of the problems from noise. Because the receiving device is looking for specific frequency changes over a given number of periods, it can ignore voltage spikes. The limiting factors of FSK are the physical capabilities of the carrier.

Bandwidth for FSK

Although FSK shifts between two carrier frequencies, it is easier to analyze as two coexisting frequencies. We can say that the FSK spectrum is a combination of two

ASK spectra centered on f_{c0} and f_{c1}. The bandwidth required for FSK transmission is equal to the baud rate of the signal plus the frequency shift (difference between the two carrier frequencies): BW = $f_{c1} - f_{c0} + N_{baud}$. See Figure 5.7.

Figure 5.7 *Relationship between baud rate and bandwidth in FSK*

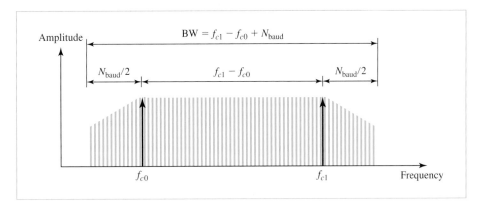

Although there are only two carrier frequencies, the process of modulation produces a composite signal that is a combination of many simple signals, each with a different frequency.

Example 6

Find the minimum bandwidth for an FSK signal transmitting at 2000 bps. Transmission is in half-duplex mode, and the carriers are separated by 3000 Hz.

Solution

For FSK, if f_{c1} and f_{c0} are the carrier frequencies, then

$$BW = \text{baud rate} + f_{c1} - f_{c0}$$

However, the baud rate here is the same as the bit rate. Therefore,

$$BW = \text{bit rate} + f_{c1} - f_{c0} = 2000 + 3000 = 5000 \text{ Hz}$$

Example 7

Find the maximum bit rates for an FSK signal if the bandwidth of the medium is 12,000 Hz and the difference between the two carriers is 2000 Hz. Transmission is in full-duplex mode.

Solution

Because the transmission is full duplex, only 6000 Hz is allocated for each direction. For FSK, if f_{c1} and f_{c0} are the carrier frequencies,

$$BW = \text{baud rate} + f_{c1} - f_{c0}$$

$$\text{Baud rate} = BW - (f_{c1} - f_{c0}) = 6000 - 2000 = 4000$$

But because the baud rate is the same as the bit rate, the bit rate is 4000 bps.

Phase Shift Keying (PSK)

In **phase shift keying,** the phase of the carrier is varied to represent binary 1 or 0. Both peak amplitude and frequency remain constant as the phase changes. For example, if we start with a phase of 0° to represent binary 0, then we can change the phase to 180° to send binary 1. The phase of the signal during each bit duration is constant, and its value depends on the bit (0 or 1). Figure 5.8 gives a conceptual view of PSK.

Figure 5.8   *PSK*

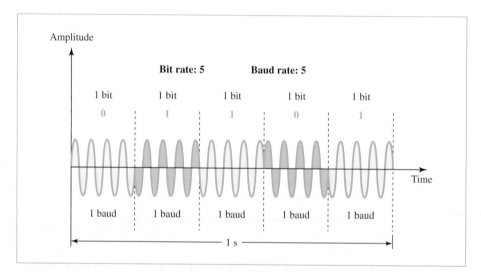

The above method is often called 2-PSK, or binary PSK, because two different phases (0° and 180°) are used. Figure 5.9 makes this point clearer by showing the relationship of phase to bit value. A second diagram, called a **constellation** or phase-state diagram, shows the same relationship by illustrating only the phases.

Figure 5.9   *PSK constellation*

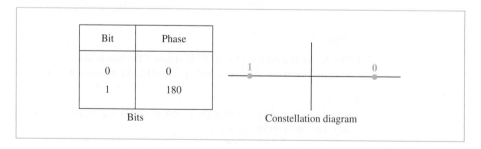

PSK is not susceptible to the noise degradation that affects ASK or to the bandwidth limitations of FSK. This means that smaller variations in the signal can be detected reliably by the receiver. Therefore, instead of utilizing only two variations of a signal, each representing 1 bit, we can use four variations and let each phase shift represent 2 bits (see Fig. 5.10).

Figure 5.10   *The 4-PSK method*

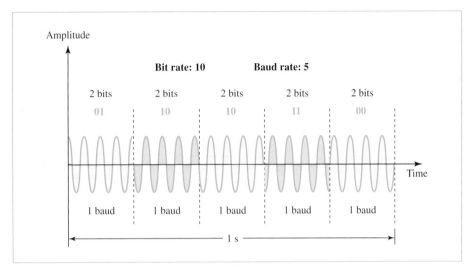

The constellation diagram for the signal in Figure 5.10 is given in Figure 5.11. A phase of 0° now represents 00; 90° represents 01; 180° represents 10; and 270° represents 11. This technique is called 4-PSK or Q-PSK. The pair of bits represented by each phase is called a **dibit.** We can transmit data twice as efficiently using 4-PSK as we can using 2-PSK.

Figure 5.11   *The 4-PSK characteristics*

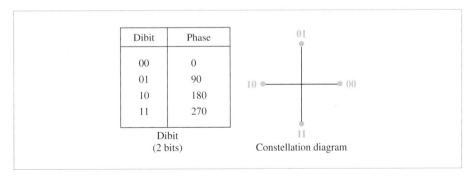

We can extend this idea to 8-PSK. Instead of 90°, we now vary the signal by shifts of 45°. With eight different phases, each shift can represent 3 bits (1 **tribit**) at a time. (As you can see, the relationship of number of bits per shift to number of phases is a power of 2. When we have four possible phases, we can send 2 bits at a time—2^2 equals 4. When we have eight possible phases, we can send 3 bits at a time—2^3 equals 8).

Figure 5.12 shows the relationships between the phase shifts and the tribits each one represents: 8-PSK is 3 times as efficient as 2-PSK.

Figure 5.12   *The 8-PSK characteristics*

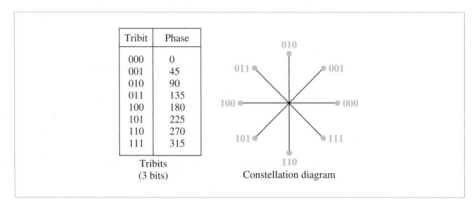

Tribit	Phase
000	0
001	45
010	90
011	135
100	180
101	225
110	270
111	315

Tribits
(3 bits)

Constellation diagram

Bandwidth for PSK

The minimum bandwidth required for PSK transmission is the same as that required for ASK transmission—and for the same reasons (see Fig. 5.13). As we have seen, the maximum bit rate in PSK transmission, however, is potentially much greater than that of ASK. So while the maximum baud rates of ASK and PSK are the same for a given bandwidth, PSK bit rates using the same bandwidth can be 2 or more times greater.

Figure 5.13   *Relationship between baud rate and bandwidth in PSK*

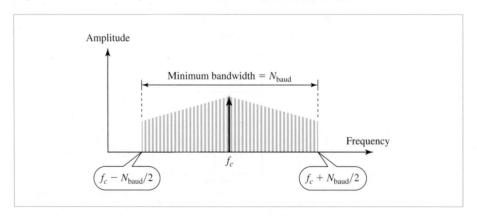

Amplitude

Minimum bandwidth = N_{baud}

Frequency

f_c

$f_c - N_{baud}/2$

$f_c + N_{baud}/2$

Example 8

Find the bandwidth for a 4-PSK signal transmitting at 2000 bps. Transmission is in half-duplex mode.

Solution

For 4-PSK the baud rate is one-half of the bit rate. The baud rate is therefore 1000. A PSK signal requires a bandwidth equal to its baud rate. Therefore, the bandwidth is 1000 Hz.

Example 9

Given a bandwidth of 5000 Hz for an 8-PSK signal, what are the baud rate and bit rate?

Solution

For PSK the baud rate is the same as the bandwidth, which means the baud rate is 5000. But in 8-PSK the bit rate is 3 times the baud rate, so the bit rate is 15,000 bps.

Quadrature Amplitude Modulation (QAM)

PSK is limited by the ability of the equipment to distinguish small differences in phase. This factor limits its potential bit rate.

So far, we have been altering only one of the three characteristics of a sine wave at a time, but what if we alter two? Bandwidth limitations make combinations of FSK with other changes practically useless. But why not combine ASK and PSK? Then we could have *x* variations in phase and *y* variations in amplitude, giving us *x* times *y* possible variations and the corresponding number of bits per variation. **Quadrature amplitude modulation (QAM)** does just that.

Quadrature amplitude modulation is a combination of ASK and PSK so that a maximum contrast between each signal unit (bit, dibit, tribit, and so on) is achieved.

Possible variations of QAM are numerous. Theoretically, any measurable number of changes in amplitude can be combined with any measurable number of changes in phase. Figure 5.14 shows two possible configurations, 4-QAM and 8-QAM. In both cases, the number of amplitude shifts is fewer than the number of phase shifts. Because amplitude changes are susceptible to noise and require greater shift differences than do phase changes, the number of phase shifts used by a QAM system is always larger than the number of amplitude shifts. The time-domain plot corresponding to the 8-QAM signal in Figure 5.14 is shown in Figure 5.15.

Figure 5.14   *The 4-QAM and 8-QAM constellations*

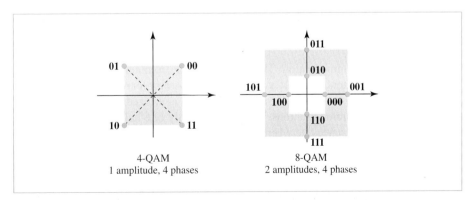

Other geometric relationships are also possible. Three popular 16-QAM configurations are shown in Figure 5.16. The first example, 3 amplitudes and 12 phases, handles noise best because of a greater ratio of phase shift to amplitude. It is the ITU-T

Figure 5.15 *Time domain for an 8-QAM signal*

Amplitude

Bit rate: 24   **Baud rate: 8**

3 bits	3 bits	3 bits	3 bits	3 bits	3 bits	3 bits	3 bits
101	100	001	000	010	011	110	111

Time

| 1 baud | 1 baud | 1 baud | 1 baud | 1 baud | 1 baud | 1 baud | 1 baud |

|←——————————————— 1 s ———————————————→|

Figure 5.16 *16-QAM constellations*

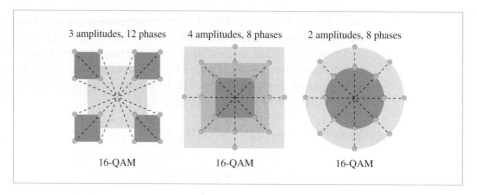

3 amplitudes, 12 phases   4 amplitudes, 8 phases   2 amplitudes, 8 phases

16-QAM   16-QAM   16-QAM

recommendation. The second example, four amplitudes and eight phases, is the OSI recommendation. If you examine the graph carefully, you will notice that not every intersection of phase and amplitude is utilized. In fact, 4 times 8 should allow for 32 possible variations. But by using only one-half of those possibilities, the measurable differences between shifts are increased and greater signal readability is ensured. In addition, several QAM designs link specific amplitudes with specific phases. This means that even with the noise problems associated with amplitude shifting, the meaning of a shift can be recovered from phase information. In general, therefore, a second advantage of QAM over ASK is its lower susceptibility to noise.

Bandwidth for QAM

The minimum bandwidth required for QAM transmission is the same as that required for ASK and PSK transmission. QAM has the same advantages as PSK over ASK.

Bit/Baud Comparison

Assuming that an FSK signal over voice-grade phone lines can send 1200 bps, the bit rate is 1200 bps. Each frequency shift represents a single bit; so it requires 1200 signal units to send 1200 bits. Its baud rate, therefore, is also 1200 bps. Each signal variation in an 8-QAM system, however, represents 3 bits. So a bit rate of 1200 bps, using 8-QAM, has a baud rate of only 400. As Figure 5.17 shows, a dibit system has a baud rate of one-half the bit rate, a tribit system has a baud rate of one-third the bit rate, and a **quadbit** system has a baud rate of one-fourth the bit rate.

Figure 5.17 *Bit and baud*

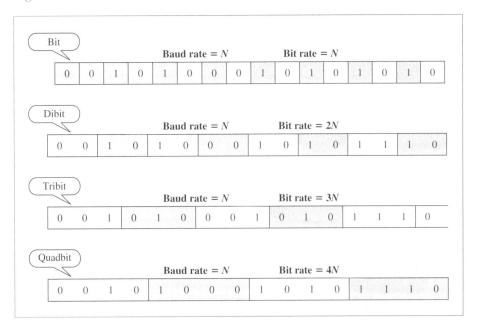

Table 5.1 shows the comparative bit and baud rates for the various methods of digital-to-analog modulation.

Table 5.1 *Bit and baud rate comparison*

Modulation	Units	Bits/Baud	Baud Rate	Bit Rate
ASK, FSK, 2-PSK	Bit	1	N	N
4-PSK, 4-QAM	Dibit	2	N	$2N$
8-PSK, 8-QAM	Tribit	3	N	$3N$
16-QAM	Quadbit	4	N	$4N$
32-QAM	Pentabit	5	N	$5N$
64-QAM	Hexabit	6	N	$6N$
128-QAM	Septabit	7	N	$7N$
256-QAM	Octabit	8	N	$8N$

Example 10

A constellation diagram consists of eight equally spaced points on a circle. If the bit rate is 4800 bps, what is the baud rate?

Solution

The constellation indicates 8-PSK with the points 45° apart. Since $2^3 = 8$, 3 bits are transmitted with each signal unit. Therefore, the baud rate is

$$\frac{4800}{3} = 1600 \text{ baud}$$

Example 11

Compute the bit rate for a 1000-baud 16-QAM signal.

Solution

A 16-QAM signal has 4 bits per signal unit since $\log_2 16 = 4$. Thus,

$$(1000)(4) = 4000 \text{ bps}$$

Example 12

Compute the baud rate for a 72,000-bps 64-QAM signal.

Solution

A 64-QAM signal has 6 bits per signal unit since $\log_2 64 = 6$. Thus,

$$\frac{72,000}{6} = 12,000 \text{ baud}$$

5.2   TELEPHONE MODEMS

Traditional telephone lines can carry frequencies between 300 and 3300 Hz, giving them a bandwidth of 3000 Hz. All this range is used for transmitting voice, where a great deal of interference and distortion can be accepted without loss of intelligibility. As we have seen, however, data signals require a higher degree of accuracy to ensure integrity. For safety's sake, therefore, the edges of this range are not used for data communications. In general, we can say that the signal bandwidth must be smaller than the cable bandwidth. The effective bandwidth of a telephone line being used for data transmission is 2400 Hz, covering the range from 600 to 3000 Hz. Note that today some telephone lines are capable of handling more bandwidth than traditional lines. However, modem design is still based on traditional capability (see Fig. 5.18).

> A telephone line has a bandwidth of almost 2400 Hz for data transmission.

This bandwidth defines a baseband nature, which means we need to modulate if we want to use this bandwidth for data transmission. Devices that were traditionally used to do so are called modems.

The term **modem** is a composite word that refers to the two functional entities that make up the device: a signal *mo*dulator and a signal *dem*odulator. A **modulator**

Figure 5.18   *Telephone line bandwidth*

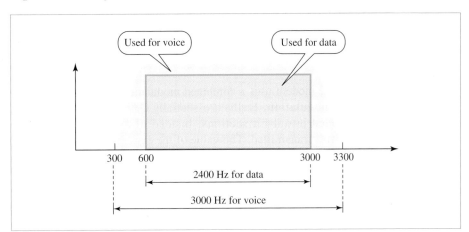

creates a band-pass analog signal from binary data. A **demodulator** recovers the binary data from the modulated signal.

Modem **stands for modulator/demodulator.**

Figure 5.19 shows the relationship of modems to a communications link. The computer on the left sends binary data to the modulator portion of the modem; the data is sent as an analog signal on the telephone lines. The modem on the right receives the analog signal, demodulates it through its demodulator, and delivers data to the computer on the right. The communication can be bidirectional, which means the computer on the right can also send data to the computer on the left using the same modulation/ demodulation processes.

Figure 5.19   *Modulation/demodulation*

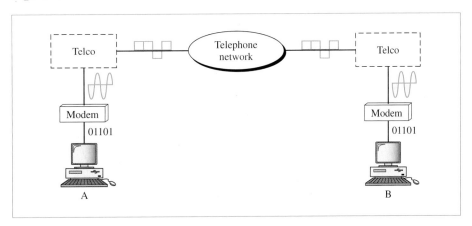

Modem Standards

Today, many of the most popular modems available are based on the **V-series** standards published by the ITU-T. We discuss just the most recent series.

V.32

The **V.32** modem uses a combined modulation and encoding technique called **trellis-coded modulation.** Trellis is essentially QAM plus a redundant bit. The data stream is divided into 4-bit sections. Instead of a quadbit, however, a pentabit (5-bit pattern) is transmitted. The value of the extra bit is calculated from the values of the data bits.

In any QAM system, the receiver compares each received signal point to all valid points in the constellation and selects the closest point as the intended value. A signal distorted by transmission noise can arrive closer in value to an adjacent point than to the intended point, resulting in a misidentification of the point and an error in the received data. The closer the points are in the constellation, the more likely it is that transmission noise can result in a signal's being misidentified. By adding a redundant bit to each quadbit, trellis-coded modulation increases the amount of information used to identify each bit pattern and thereby reduces the number of possible matches. For this reason, a trellis-encoded signal is much less likely than a plain QAM signal to be misread when distorted by noise.

The V.32 calls for 32-QAM with a baud rate of 2400. Because only 4 bits of each pentabit represents data, the resulting speed is $4 \times 2400 = 9600$ bps. The constellation diagram and bandwidth are shown in Figure 5.20.

Figure 5.20   *The V.32 constellation and bandwidth*

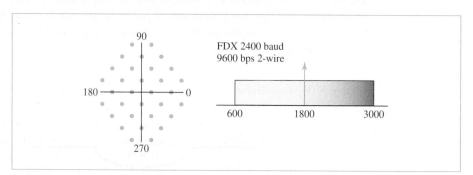

V.32bis

The **V.32bis** modem was the first of the ITU-T standards to support 14,400-bps transmission. The V.32bis uses 128-QAM transmission (7 bits/baud with 1 bit for error control) at a rate of 2400 baud ($2400 \times 6 = 14{,}400$ bps).

An additional enhancement provided by V.32bis is the inclusion of an automatic fall-back and fall-forward feature that enables the modem to adjust its speed upward or downward depending on the quality of the line or signal. The constellation diagram and bandwidth are shown in Figure 5.21.

Figure 5.21 *The V.32bis constellation and bandwidth*

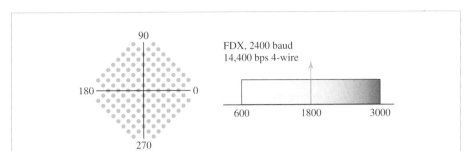

V.34bis

The **V.34bis** modem provides a bit rate of 28,800 with a 960-point constellation to a bit rate of 33,600 with a 1664-point constellation.

V.90

Traditional modems have a limitation on the data rate (maximum of 33.6 Kbps), as determined by the Shannon formula (see Chapter 3). However, **V.90** modems with a bit rate of 56,000 bps, called **56K modems,** are available. These modems may be used only if one party is using digital signaling (such as through an Internet provider). They are asymmetric in that the downloading rate (flow of data from the Internet provider to the PC) is a maximum of 56 Kbps, while the uploading rate (flow of data from the PC to the Internet provider) can be a maximum of 33.6 Kbps. Do these modems violate the Shannon capacity principle? No, the approach is different. Let us compare the two approaches.

Traditional Modems   In traditional modems data exchange is between two computers, A and B, through the digital telephone network, as shown in Figure 5.22.

After modulation by the modem, an analog signal reaches the telephone company switching station, where it is sampled and digitized to be passed through the digital network. The quantization noise introduced into the signal at the sampling point limits the data rate according to the Shannon capacity. This limit is 33.6 Kbps.

Because the sampling point exists in both directions, the maximum data rate is 33.6 Kbps.

56K Modems   Communication today is via the Internet. We still use modems to upload data to the Internet and download data from the Internet, as shown in Figure 5.23.

In **uploading,** the analog signal must still be sampled at the switching station, which means the data rate in uploading is limited to 33.6 Kbps. However, there is

Figure 5.22   *Traditional modems*

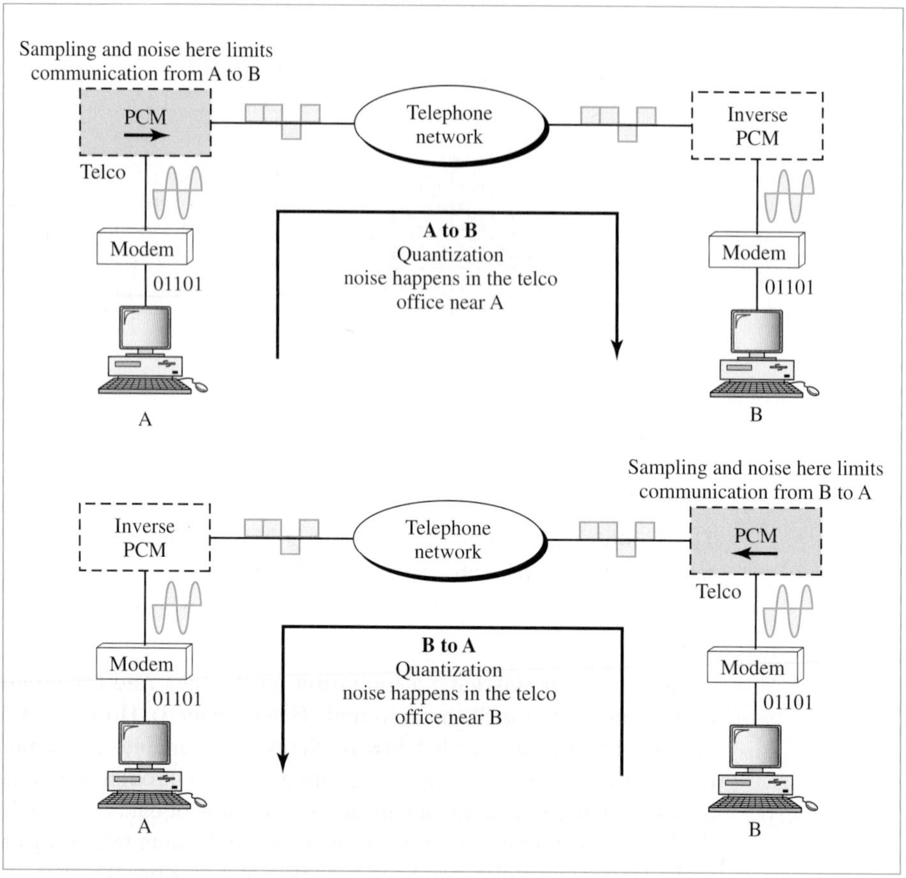

no sampling in the **downloading.** The signal is not affected by quantization noise and not subject to the Shannon capacity limitation. The maximum data rate in the uploading direction is still 33.6 Kbps, but the data rate in the downloading direction is now 56 Kbps.

One may wonder why 56 Kbps. The telephone companies sample 8000 times per second with 8 bits per sample. One of the bits in each sample is used for control purposes, which means each sample is 7 bits. The rate is therefore 8000×7, or 56,000, bps or 56 Kbps.

V.92

The standard above V.90 is called **V.92.** These modems can adjust their speed, and if the noise allows, they can upload data at the rate of 48 Kbps. The downloading rate is still 56 Kbps. The modem has additional features. For example, the modem can interrupt the Internet connection when there is an incoming call if the line has call-waiting service.

Figure 5.23   *56K modems*

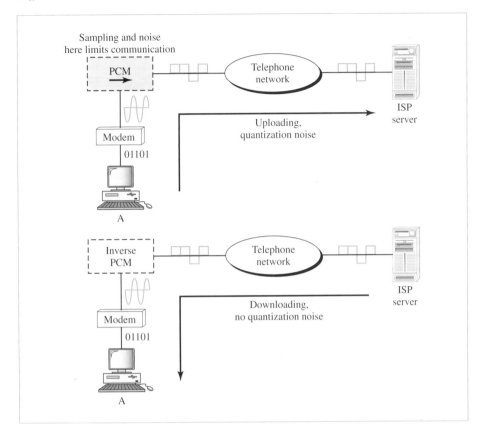

5.3   MODULATION OF ANALOG SIGNALS

Modulation of an analog signal or analog-to-analog conversion is the representation of analog information by an analog signal. One may ask why we need to modulate an analog signal; it is already analog. Modulation is needed if the medium has a band-pass nature or if only band-pass bandwidth is available to us. An example is radio. The government assigns a baseband bandwidth to each radio station. The analog signal produced by each station is a low-pass signal, all in the same range. To be able to listen to different stations, the low-pass signals need to be shifted, each to a different range.

Figure 5.24 shows the relationship between the analog information, the analog-to-analog conversion hardware, and the resultant analog signal.

Analog-to-analog modulation can be accomplished in three ways: **amplitude modulation (AM), frequency modulation (FM),** and **phase modulation (PM).** See Figure 5.25.

Figure 5.24   *Analog-to-analog modulation*

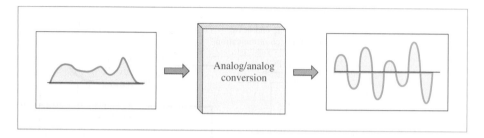

Figure 5.25   *Types of analog-to-analog modulation*

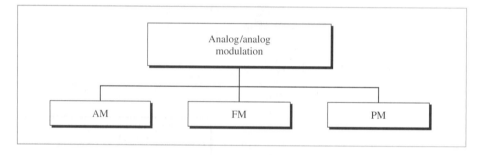

Amplitude Modulation (AM)

In AM transmission, the carrier signal is modulated so that its amplitude varies with the changing amplitudes of the modulating signal. The frequency and phase of the carrier remain the same; only the amplitude changes to follow variations in the information. Figure 5.26 shows how this concept works. The modulating signal becomes an envelope to the carrier.

AM Bandwidth

The bandwidth of an AM signal is equal to twice the bandwidth of the modulating signal and covers a range centered on the carrier frequency (see Fig. 5.27). The shaded portion of the graph is the frequency spectrum of the signal.

The bandwidth of an audio signal (speech and music) is usually 5 KHz. Therefore, an AM radio station needs a minimum bandwidth of 10 KHz. In fact, the Federal Communications Commission (FCC) allows 10 KHz for each AM station.

AM stations are allowed carrier frequencies anywhere between 530 and 1700 KHz (1.7 MHz). However, each station's carrier frequency must be separated from those on either side of it by at least 10 KHz (one AM bandwidth) to avoid interference. If one station uses a carrier frequency of 1100 KHz, the next station's carrier frequency cannot be lower than 1110 KHz (see Fig. 5.28).

The total bandwidth required for AM can be determined from the bandwidth of the audio signal: $BW_t = 2 \times BW_m$.

Figure 5.26 *Amplitude modulation*

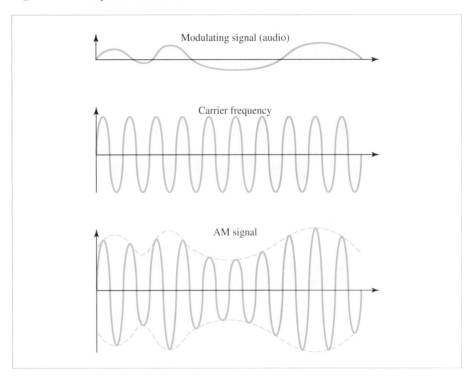

Figure 5.27 *AM bandwidth*

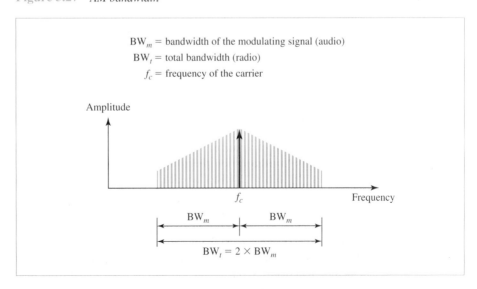

Figure 5.28   *AM band allocation*

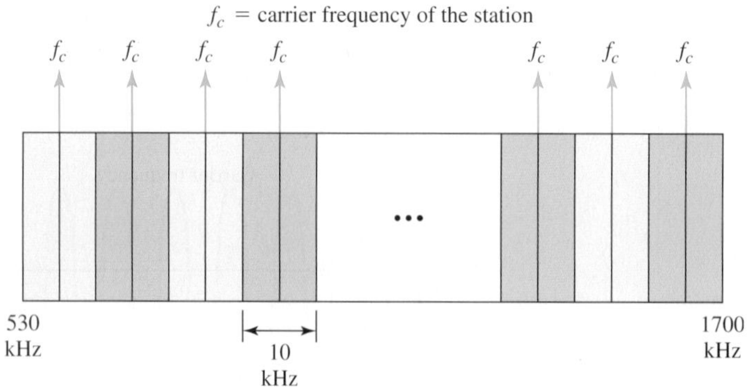

Example 13

We have an audio signal with a bandwidth of 4 KHz. What is the bandwidth needed if we modulate the signal using AM? Ignore FCC regulations.

Solution

An AM signal requires twice the bandwidth of the original signal:

$$BW = 2 \times 4 \text{ KHz} = 8 \text{ KHz}$$

Frequency Modulation (FM)

In FM transmission, the frequency of the carrier signal is modulated to follow the changing voltage level (amplitude) of the modulating signal. The peak amplitude and phase of the carrier signal remain constant, but as the amplitude of the information signal changes, the frequency of the carrier changes correspondingly. Figure 5.29 shows the relationships of the modulating signal, the carrier signal, and the resultant FM signal.

FM Bandwidth

The bandwidth of an FM signal is equal to 10 times the bandwidth of the modulating signal and, like AM bandwidths, covers a range centered on the carrier frequency. Figure 5.30 shows both the bandwidth and, in the shaded portion, the frequency spectrum of an FM signal.

   The bandwidth of an audio signal (speech and music) broadcast in stereo is almost 15 KHz. Each FM radio station, therefore, needs a minimum bandwidth of 150 KHz. The FCC allows 200 KHz (0.2 MHz) for each station to provide some room for guard bands.

   FM stations are allowed carrier frequencies anywhere between 88 and 108 MHz. Stations must be separated by at least 200 KHz to keep their bandwidths from overlapping. To create even more privacy, the FCC requires that in a given area, only alternate bandwidth allocations may be used. The others remain unused to prevent any possibility

---

The total bandwidth required for FM can be determined from the bandwidth of the audio signal: $BW_t = 10 \times BW_m$.

Figure 5.29   *Frequency modulation*

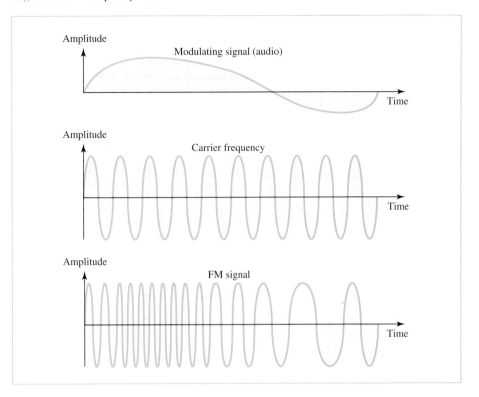

Figure 5.30   *FM bandwidth*

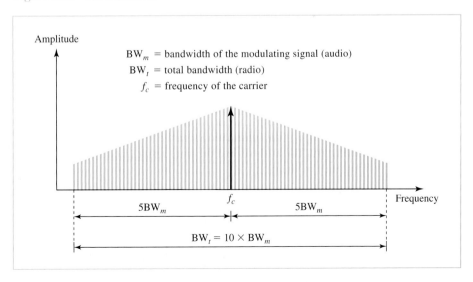

> The bandwidth of a stereo audio signal is usually 15 KHz. Therefore, an FM station needs at least a bandwidth of 150 KHz. The FCC requires the minimum bandwidth to be at least 200 KHz (0.2 MHz).

of two stations interfering with each other. Given 88 to 108 MHz as a range, there are 100 potential FM bandwidths in an area, of which 50 can operate at any one time. Figure 5.31 illustrates this concept.

Figure 5.31   *FM band allocation*

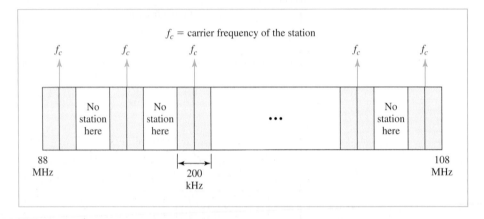

Example 14

We have an audio signal with a bandwidth of 4 MHz. What is the bandwidth needed if we modulate the signal using FM? Ignore FCC regulations.

Solution

An FM signal requires 10 times the bandwidth of the original signal:

$$BW = 10 \times 4 \text{ MHz} = 40 \text{ MHz}$$

Phase Modulation (PM)

Due to simpler hardware requirements, phase modulation (PM) is used in some systems as an alternative to frequency modulation. In PM transmission, the phase of the carrier signal is modulated to follow the changing voltage level (amplitude) of the modulating signal. The peak amplitude and frequency of the carrier signal remain constant, but as the amplitude of the information signal changes, the phase of the carrier changes correspondingly. The analysis and the final result (modulated signal) are similar to those of frequency modulation.

5.4   KEY TERMS

56K modem
amplitude modulation (AM)
amplitude shift keying (ASK)

analog-to-analog modulation
bit rate
baud rate

carrier signal
constellation
demodulation
demodulator
dibit
digital-to-analog modulation
downloading
frequency modulation (FM)
frequency shift keying (FSK)
modem
modulation
modulator
phase modulation (PM)

phase shift keying (PSK)
quadbit
quadrature amplitude modulation (QAM)
trellis-coded modulation
tribit
uploading
V series
V.32
V.32bis
V.34bis
V.90
V.92

5.5 SUMMARY

❏ Digital-to-analog modulation can be accomplished using the following:
   Amplitude shift keying (ASK)—the amplitude of the carrier signal varies.
   Frequency shift keying (FSK)—the frequency of the carrier signal varies.
   Phase shift keying (PSK)—the phase of the carrier signal varies.
   Quadrature amplitude modulation (QAM)—both the phase and amplitude of the carrier signal vary.

❏ QAM enables a higher data transmission rate than other digital-to-analog methods.

❏ Baud rate and bit rate are not synonymous. Bit rate is the number of bits transmitted per second. Baud rate is the number of signal units transmitted per second. One signal unit can represent one or more bits.

❏ The minimum required bandwidth for ASK and PSK is the baud rate. ·

❏ The minimum required bandwidth (BW) for FSK modulation is $BW = f_{c1} - f_{c0} + N_{baud}$, where f_{c1} is the frequency representing a 1 bit, f_{c0} is the frequency representing a 0 bit, and N_{baud} is the baud rate.

❏ A regular telephone line uses frequencies between 600 and 3000 Hz for data communication.

❏ ASK modulation is especially susceptible to noise.

❏ Because it uses two carrier frequencies, FSK modulation requires more bandwidth than ASK and PSK.

❏ PSK and QAM modulation have two advantages over ASK:
   They are not as susceptible to noise.
   Each signal change can represent more than one bit.

❏ Trellis coding is a technique that uses redundancy to provide a lower error rate.

❏ The 56K modems are asymmetric; they download at a rate of 56 Kbps and upload at 33.6 Kbps.

❑ Analog-to-analog modulation can be implemented by using the following:
Amplitude modulation (AM)
Frequency modulation (FM)
Phase modulation (PM)

❑ In AM radio, the bandwidth of the modulated signal must be twice the bandwidth of the modulating signal.

❑ In FM radio, the bandwidth of the modulated signal must be 10 times the bandwidth of the modulating signal.

5.6   PRACTICE SET

Review Questions

1. What is digital-to-analog modulation?
2. What is analog-to-analog modulation?
3. Why is frequency modulation superior to amplitude modulation?
4. What is the advantage of QAM over ASK or PSK?
5. What are the methods that convert a digital signal to an analog signal?
6. What is the difference between bit rate and baud rate? Give an example where both are the same. Give an example where they are different.
7. What is modulation?
8. What is the purpose of a carrier signal in modulation?
9. How is baud rate related to transmission bandwidth in ASK?
10. How is baud rate related to transmission bandwidth in FSK?
11. How is baud rate related to transmission bandwidth in PSK?
12. What kind of information can be obtained from a constellation diagram?
13. How is baud rate related to transmission bandwidth in QAM?
14. How is QAM related to ASK and PSK?
15. What is the major factor that makes PSK superior to ASK?
16. What does the term *modem* stand for?
17. What is the function of a modulator? What is the function of a demodulator?
18. Explain the asymmetry of 56K modems.
19. Why are modems needed for telephone communications?
20. The minimum bandwidth of an ASK signal could be equal to the bit rate. Explain why this is impossible for FSK.
21. How does AM differ from ASK?
22. How does FM differ from FSK?
23. Compare the FM bandwidth with the AM bandwidth in terms of the modulating signal.

Multiple-Choice Questions

24. ASK, PSK, FSK, and QAM are examples of _____ modulation.
    a. Digital-to-digital
    b. Digital-to-analog
    c. Analog-to-analog
    d. Analog-to-digital

25. AM and FM are examples of _____ modulation.
    a. Digital-to-digital
    b. Digital-to-analog
    c. Analog-to-analog
    d. Analog-to-digital

26. In QAM, both phase and _____ of a carrier frequency are varied.
    a. Amplitude
    b. Frequency
    c. Bit rate
    d. Baud rate

27. Which of the following is most affected by noise?
    a. PSK
    b. ASK
    c. FSK
    d. QAM

28. If the baud rate is 400 for a 4-PSK signal, the bit rate is _____ bps.
    a. 100
    b. 400
    c. 800
    d. 1600

29. If the bit rate for an ASK signal is 1200 bps, the baud rate is _____.
    a. 300
    b. 400
    c. 600
    d. 1200

30. If the bit rate for an FSK signal is 1200 bps, the baud rate is _____.
    a. 300
    b. 400
    c. 600
    d. 1200

31. If the bit rate for a QAM signal is 3000 bps and a signal unit is represented by a tribit, what is the baud rate?
    a. 300
    b. 400

c. 1000

d. 1200

32. If the baud rate for a QAM signal is 3000 and a signal unit is represented by a tribit, what is the bit rate?

a. 300

b. 400

c. 1000

d. 9000

33. If the baud rate for a QAM signal is 1800 and the bit rate is 9000, how many bits are there per signal unit?

a. 3

b. 4

c. 5

d. 6

34. In 16-QAM, there are 16 _____.

a. Combinations of phase and amplitude

b. Amplitudes

c. Phases

d. bps

35. Which modulation technique involves tribits, eight different phase shifts, and one amplitude?

a. FSK

b. 8-PSK

c. ASK

d. 4-PSK

36. Given an AM radio signal with a bandwidth of 10 KHz and the highest-frequency component at 705 KHz, what is the frequency of the carrier signal?

a. 700 KHz

b. 705 KHz

c. 710 KHz

d. Cannot be determined from given information

37. A modulated signal is formed by _____.

a. Changing the modulating signal by the carrier wave

b. Changing the carrier wave by the modulating signal

c. Quantization of the source data

d. Sampling at the Nyquist frequency

38. If FCC regulations are followed, the carrier frequencies of adjacent AM radio stations are _____ apart.

a. 5 KHz

b. 10 KHz

c. 200 KHz

d. 530 KHz

39. If FCC regulations are followed, _____ potential FM stations are theoretically possible in a given area.

    a. 50

    b. 100

    c. 133

    d. 150

40. When an ASK signal is decomposed, the result is _____.

    a. Always one sine wave

    b. Always two sine waves

    c. An infinite number of sine waves

    d. None of the above

41. The bandwidth of an FM signal requires 10 times the bandwidth of the _____ signal.

    a. Carrier

    b. Modulating

    c. Bipolar

    d. Sampling

42. Modulation of an analog signal can be accomplished through changing the _____ of the carrier signal.

    a. Amplitude

    b. Frequency

    c. Phase

    d. Any of the above

43. For a telephone line, the bandwidth for voice is usually _____ the bandwidth for data.

    a. Equivalent to

    b. Less than

    c. Greater than

    d. Twice

44. For a given bit rate, the minimum bandwidth for ASK is _____ the minimum bandwidth for FSK.

    a. Equivalent to

    b. Less than

    c. Greater than

    d. Twice

45. As the bit rate of an FSK signal increases, the bandwidth _____.

    a. Decreases

    b. Increases

    c. Remains the same

    d. Doubles

46. For FSK, as the difference between the two carrier frequencies increases, the bandwidth _____.

    a. Decreases

    b. Increases

    c. Remains the same

    d. Halves

47. Which ITU-T modem standard uses trellis coding?

    a. V.32

    b. V.33

    c. V.34

    d. (a) and (b)

48. In trellis coding the number of data bits is _____ the number of transmitted bits.

    a. Equal to

    b. Less than

    c. More than

    d. Double that of

49. What is the object of trellis coding?

    a. To narrow the bandwidth

    b. To simplify modulation

    c. To increase the data rate

    d. To reduce the error rate

50. The bit rate always equals the baud rate in which type of signal?

    a. FSK

    b. QAM

    c. 4-PSK

    d. All the above

51. A modulator converts a(n)_____ signal to a(n) _____ signal.

    a. Digital; analog

    b. Analog; digital

    c. PSK; FSK

    d. FSK; PSK

52. A 56K modem can download at a rate of _____ Kbps and upload at a rate of _____ Kbps.

    a. 33.6; 33.6

    b. 33.6; 56.6

    c. 56.6; 33.6

    d. 56.6; 56.6

Exercises

53. Calculate the baud rate for the given bit rate and type of modulation:
    a. 2000 bps, FSK
    b. 4000 bps, ASK
    c. 6000 bps, 2-PSK
    d. 6000 bps, 4-PSK
    e. 6000 bps, 8-PSK
    f. 4000 bps, 4-QAM
    g. 6000 bps, 16-QAM
    h. 36,000 bps, 64-QAM

54. Calculate the baud rate for the given bit rate and bit combination:
    a. 2000 bps, dibit
    b. 6000 bps, tribit
    c. 6000 bps, quadbit
    d. 6000 bps, bit

55. Calculate the bit rate for the given baud rate and type of modulation.
    a. 1000 baud, FSK
    b. 1000 baud, ASK
    c. 1000 baud, 8-PSK
    d. 1000 baud, 16-QAM

56. Draw the constellation diagram for the following:
    a. ASK, amplitudes of 1 and 3
    b. 2-PSK, amplitude of 1 at 0° and 180°

57. Data from a source ranges in value between −1.0 and 1.0. To what do the data points 0.91, −0.25, 0.56, and 0.71 transform if 8-bit quantization is used?

58. The data points of a constellation are at (4, 0) and (6, 0). Draw the constellation. Show the amplitude and phase for each point. Is the modulation ASK, PSK, or QAM? How many bits per baud can one send with this constellation?

59. Repeat Exercise 58 if the data points are at (4, 5) and (8, 10).

60. Repeat Exercise 58 if the data points are at (4, 0) and (−4, 0).

61. Repeat Exercise 58 if the data points are at (4, 4) and (−4, 4).

62. Repeat Exercise 58 if the data points are at (4, 0), (4, 4), (−4, 0), and (−4, −4).

63. Does the constellation in Figure 5.32 represent ASK, FSK, PSK, or QAM?

Figure 5.32 *Exercise 63*

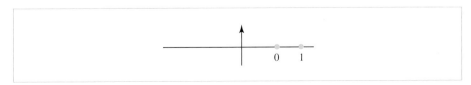

64. Does the constellation in Figure 5.33 represent ASK, FSK, PSK, or QAM?

Figure 5.33 *Exercise 64*

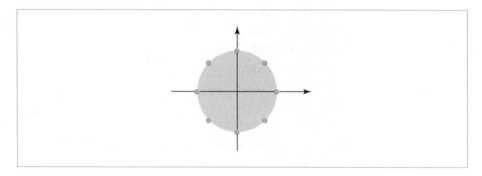

65. Does the constellation in Figure 5.34 represent ASK, FSK, PSK, or QAM?

Figure 5.34 *Exercise 65*

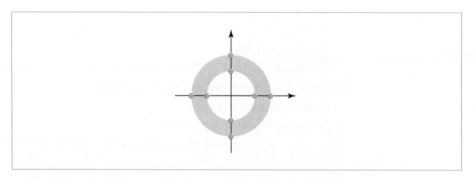

66. Does the constellation in Figure 5.35 represent ASK, FSK, PSK, or QAM?

Figure 5.35 *Exercise 66*

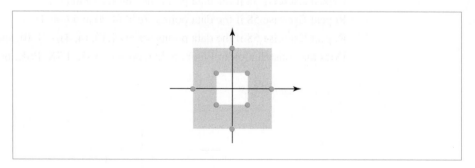

67. Can a constellation have 12 points? Why or why not?

68. Can a constellation have 18 points? Why or why not?

69. Can you define a general rule for the number of points in a constellation?

70. If the number of points in a constellation is 8, how many bits can we send per baud?

71. Calculate the bandwidth required for each of the following AM stations. Disregard FCC rules.

    a. Modulating signal with a bandwidth of 4 KHz

    b. Modulating signal with a bandwidth of 8 KHz

    c. Modulating signal with frequencies of 2000 to 3000 Hz

72. Calculate the bandwidth required for each of the following FM stations. Disregard FCC rules.

    a. Modulating signal with a bandwidth of 12 KHz

    b. Modulating signal with a bandwidth of 8 KHz

    c. Modulating signal with frequencies of 2000 to 3000 Hz

CHAPTER 6

Multiplexing

Whenever the bandwidth of a medium linking two devices is greater than the bandwidth needs of the devices, the link can be shared. **Multiplexing** is the set of techniques that allows the simultaneous transmission of multiple signals across a single data link.

As data and telecommunications usage increases, so does traffic. We can accommodate this increase by continuing to add individual lines each time a new channel is needed, or we can install higher-bandwidth links and use each to carry multiple signals. As described in Chapter 7, today's technology includes high-bandwidth media such as optical fiber and terrestrial and satellite microwaves. Each of these has a bandwidth far in excess of that needed for the average transmission signal. If the bandwidth of a link is greater than the bandwidth needs of the devices connected to it, the bandwidth is wasted. An efficient system maximizes the utilization of all resources; bandwidth is one of the most precious resources we have in data communications.

In a multiplexed system, *n* lines share the bandwidth of one **link.** Figure 6.1 shows the basic format of a multiplexed system.

Figure 6.1   *Dividing a link into channels*

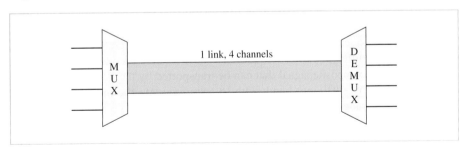

The four lines on the left direct their transmission streams to a **multiplexer (MUX),** which combines them into a single stream (many to one). At the receiving end, that stream is fed into a **demultiplexer (DEMUX),** which separates the stream back into its component transmissions (one to many) and directs them to their corresponding lines.

In Figure 6.1 the word **link** refers to the physical path. The word **channel** refers to the portion of a link that carries a transmission between a given pair of lines. One link can have many (*n*) channels.

Signals are multiplexed by one of three basic techniques: frequency-division multiplexing (FDM), wave-division multiplexing (WDM), and time-division multiplexing (TDM). The first two are techniques used for analog signals; the third for digital signals (see Figure 6.2).

Figure 6.2   *Categories of multiplexing*

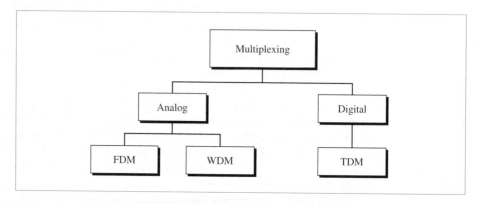

6.1   FDM

Frequency-division multiplexing (FDM) is an analog technique that can be applied when the **bandwidth** of a link (in hertz) is greater than the combined bandwidths of the signals to be transmitted. In FDM, signals generated by each sending device modulate different carrier frequencies. These modulated signals are then combined into a single composite signal that can be transported by the link. Carrier frequencies are separated by sufficient bandwidth to accommodate the modulated signal. These bandwidth ranges are the channels through which the various signals travel. Channels must be separated by strips of unused bandwidth (**guard bands**) to prevent signals from overlapping. In addition, carrier frequencies must not interfere with the original data frequencies. Failure to adhere to either condition can result in the unsuccessful recovery of the original signals.

Figure 6.3 gives a conceptual view of FDM. In this illustration, the transmission path is divided into three parts, each representing a channel to carry one transmission. As an analogy, imagine a point where three narrow streets merge to form a three-lane highway. Each of the three streets corresponds to a lane of the highway. Each car merging onto the highway from one of the streets still has its own lane and can travel without interfering with cars in other lanes.

Figure 6.3 *FDM*

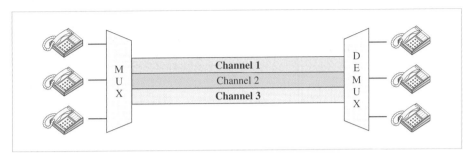

FDM is an analog multiplexing technique that combines signals.

Multiplexing Process

Figure 6.4 is a conceptual illustration of the multiplexing process. FDM is an analog process, and we show it here using telephones as the input devices. Each telephone generates a signal of a similar frequency range. Inside the multiplexer, these similar signals are modulated onto different carrier frequencies (f_1, f_2, and f_3). The resulting modulated signals are then combined into a single composite signal that is sent out over a media link that has enough bandwidth to accommodate it.

Figure 6.4 *FDM process*

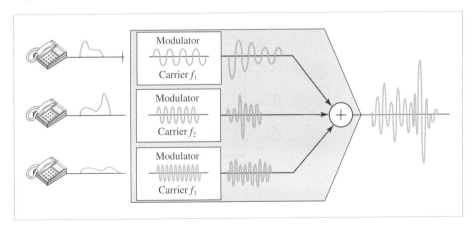

Demultiplexing Process

The demultiplexer uses a series of filters to decompose the multiplexed signal into its constituent component signals. The individual signals are then passed to a demodulator that separates them from their carriers and passes them to the waiting receivers. Figure 6.5 is a conceptual illustration of FDM, again using three telephones as the communication devices.

Figure 6.5   *FDM demultiplexing example*

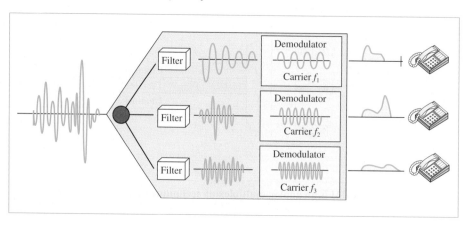

Example 1

Assume that a voice channel occupies a bandwidth of 4 KHz. We need to combine three voice channels into a link with a bandwidth of 12 KHz, from 20 to 32 KHz. Show the configuration using the frequency domain without the use of guard bands.

Solution

Shift (modulate) each of the three voice channels to a different bandwidth, as shown in Figure 6.6.

Figure 6.6   *Example 1*

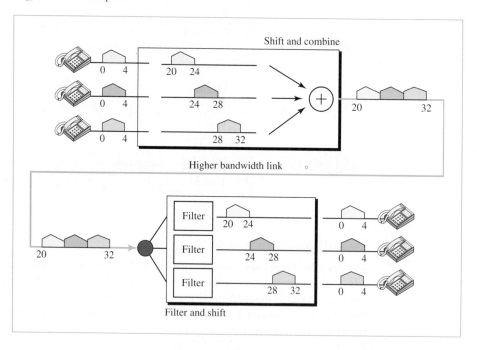

We use the 20- to 24-KHz bandwidth for the first channel, the 24- to 28-KHz bandwidth for the second channel, and the 28- to 32-KHz bandwidth for the third one. Then we combine them as shown in Figure 6.6. At the receiver, each channel receives the entire signal, using a filter to separate out its own signal. The first channel uses a filter that passes frequencies between 20 and 24 KHz and filters out (discards) any other frequencies. The second channel uses a filter that passes frequencies between 24 and 28 KHz, and the third channel uses a filter that passes frequencies between 28 and 32 KHz. Each channel then shifts the frequency to start from zero.

Example 2

Five channels, each with a 100-KHz bandwidth, are to be multiplexed together. What is the minimum bandwidth of the link if there is a need for a guard band of 10 KHz between the channels to prevent interference?

Solution

For five channels, we need at least four guard bands. This means that the required bandwidth is at least $5 \times 100 + 4 \times 10 = 540$ KHz, as shown in Figure 6.7.

Figure 6.7　*Example 2*

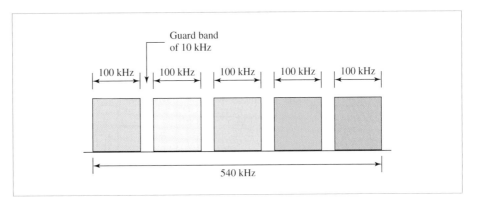

Example 3

Four data channels (digital), each transmitting at 1 Mbps, use a satellite channel of 1 MHz. Design an appropriate configuration using FDM.

Solution

The satellite channel is analog. We divide it into four channels, each channel having a 250-KHz bandwidth. Each digital channel of 1 Mbps is modulated such that each 4 bits are modulated to 1 Hz. One solution is 16-QAM modulation. Figure 6.8 shows one possible configuration.

The Analog Hierarchy

To maximize the efficiency of their infrastructure, telephone companies have traditionally multiplexed signals from lower-bandwidth lines onto higher-bandwidth lines. In this way, many switched or leased lines can be combined into fewer but bigger channels. For analog lines, FDM is used.

One of these hierarchical systems used by AT&T is made up of groups, supergroups, master groups, and jumbo groups (see Figure 6.9).

Figure 6.8   *Example 3*

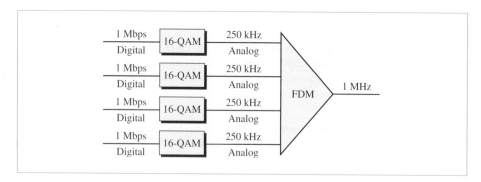

Figure 6.9   *Analog hierarchy*

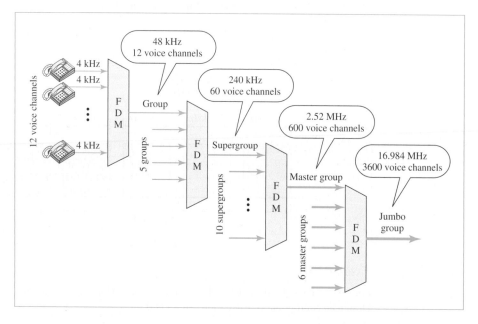

In this **analog hierarchy,** 12 voice channels are multiplexed onto a higher-bandwidth line to create a **group.** A group has 48 KHz of bandwidth and supports 12 voice channels.

At the next level, up to five groups can be multiplexed to create a composite signal called a **supergroup.** A supergroup has a bandwidth of 240 KHz and supports up to 60 voice channels. Supergroups can be made up of either five groups or 60 independent voice channels.

At the next level, 10 supergroups are multiplexed to create a **master group.** A master group must have 2.40 MHz of bandwidth, but the need for guard bands between the supergroups increases the necessary bandwidth to 2.52 MHz. Master groups support up to 600 voice channels.

Finally, six master groups can be combined into a **jumbo group.** A jumbo group must have 15.12 MHz (6 × 2.52 MHz) but is augmented to 16.984 MHz to allow for guard bands between the master groups.

Other Applications of FDM

A very common application of FDM is AM and FM radio broadcasting. Radio uses the air as the transmission medium. A special band, from 530 to 1700 KHz, is assigned to AM radio. All radio stations need to share this band. As discussed in Chapter 5, each AM station needs 10 KHz of bandwidth. Each station uses a different carrier frequency, which means it is shifting its signal and multiplexing. The signal which goes to the air is a combination of all signals. A receiver receives all these signals, but filters (by tuning) only the one which is desired. Without multiplexing only one AM station could broadcast to the common link, the air.

The situation is similar with FM broadcasting. However, FM uses a wider band, 88 to 108 MHz, because each station needs more bandwidth, 200 KHz.

Another common use of FDM is in television broadcasting. Each TV channel has its own bandwidth of 6 MHz.

The first generation of cellular telephones (still in operation) also uses FDM. Each user is assigned two 30-KHz channels, one for sending voice and one for receiving. The voice signal, which has a bandwidth of 3 KHz (from 300 to 3300 Hz), is modulated using FM. Remember that an FM signal has a bandwidth 10 times that of the modulating signal, which means each channel has 30 KHz (10×3) of bandwidth. Therefore, each user is given, by the base station, a 60-KHz bandwidth in a range available at the time of the call.

Example 4

The Advanced Mobile Phone System (AMPS) uses two bands. The first band, 824 to 849 MHz, is used for sending; and 869 to 894 MHz is used for receiving. Each user has a bandwidth of 30 KHz in each direction. The 3-KHz voice is modulated using FM, creating 30 KHz of modulated signal. How many people can use their cellular phones simultaneously?

Solution

Each band is 25 MHz. If we divide 25 MHz into 30 KHz, we get 833.33. In reality, the band is divided into 832 channels. Of these, 42 channels are used for control, which means only 790 channels are available for cellular phone users. We discuss AMPS in greater detail in Chapter 17.

Implementation

FDM can be implemented very easily. In many cases, such as radio and television broadcasting, there is no need for a physical multiplexer or demultiplexer. As long as the stations agree to send their broadcasts to the air using different carrier frequencies, multiplexing is achieved. In other cases, such as the cellular telephone system, a base station needs to assign a carrier frequency to the telephone user. There is not enough bandwidth available, in a cell, to be assigned permanently to every telephone user. When a user hangs up, the bandwidth is assigned to another caller.

6.2 WDM

Wave-division multiplexing (WDM) is designed to use the high data rate capability of fiber-optic cable. The optical fiber data rate is higher than the data rate of metallic transmission cable. Using a fiber-optic cable for one single line wastes the available bandwidth. Multiplexing allows us to connect several lines into one.

WDM is conceptually the same as FDM, except that the multiplexing and demultiplexing involve optical signals transmitted through fiber-optic channels. The idea is the same: We are combining different signals of different frequencies. However, the difference is that the frequencies are very high.

Figure 6.10 gives a conceptual view of a WDM multiplexer and demultiplexer. Very narrow bands of light from different sources are combined to make a wider band of light. At the receiver, the signals are separated by the demultiplexer.

Figure 6.10   *WDM*

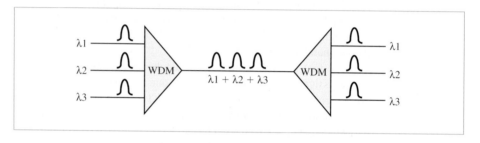

WDM is an analog multiplexing technique to combine optical signals.

One may wonder about the mechanism of WDM. Although the technology is very complex, the idea is very simple. We want to combine multiple light sources into one single light at the multiplexer and do the reverse at the demultiplexer. Combining and splitting of light sources are easily handled by a prism. Recall from basic physics that a prism bends a beam of light based on the angle of incidence and the frequency. Using this technique, a multiplexer can be made to combine several input beams of light, each containing a narrow band of frequencies, into one output beam of a wider band of frequencies. A demultiplexer can also be made to reverse the process. Figure 6.11 shows the concept.

Figure 6.11   *Prisms in WDM multiplexing and demultiplexing*

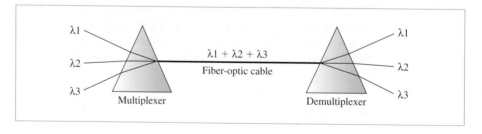

One application of WDM is the SONET network in which multiple optical fiber lines are multiplexed and demultiplexed. We discuss SONET in Chapter 9.

A new method, called **DWDM (dense WDM),** can multiplex a very large number of channels by spacing channels closer to one another. It achieves even greater efficiency.

6.3 TDM

Time-division multiplexing (TDM) is a digital process that allows several connections to share the high bandwidth of a link. Instead of sharing a portion of the bandwidth as in FDM, time is shared. Each connection occupies a portion of time in the link. Figure 6.12 gives a conceptual view of TDM. Note that the same link is used as in FDM; here, however, the link is shown sectioned by time rather than by frequency. In the figure, portions of signals 1, 2, 3, and 4 occupy the link sequentially.

Figure 6.12 *TDM*

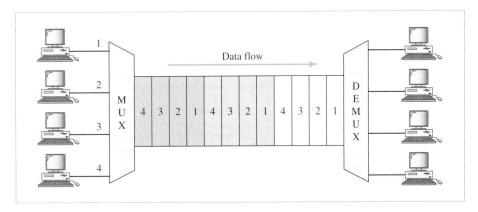

TDM is a digital multiplexing technique to combine data.

Time Slots and Frames

The data flow of each connection is divided into units, and the link combines one unit of each connection to make a frame. The size of the unit can be 1 bit or several bits. For *n* input connections, a frame is organized into a minimum of *n* time slots, each slot carrying one unit from each connection. Figure 6.13 shows an example where *n* is 3.

In TDM, the data rate of the link that carries data from *n* connections must be *n* times the data rate of a connection to guarantee the flow of data. Therefore, the duration of a unit in a connection is *n* times the duration of a time slot in a frame. If we consider that the bit duration and bit rate are the inverse of each other, the above requirement makes sense. In Figure 6.13, the data rate of the link is 3 times the data rate of a connection; likewise, the duration of a unit on a connection is 3 times that of the time slot (duration of a unit on the link). In the figure we represent the data prior to multiplexing as 3 times the size of the data after multiplexing. This is just to convey the idea that each unit is 3 times longer in duration before multiplexing than after.

Figure 6.13   *TDM*

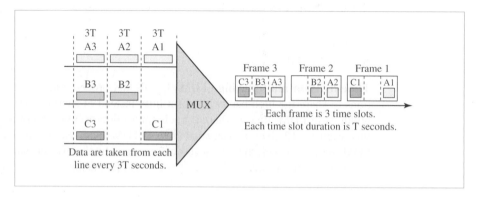

In a TDM, the data rate of the link is *n* times faster, and the unit duration is *n* times shorter.

Time slots are grouped into frames. A frame consists of one complete cycle of time slots, with one slot dedicated to each sending device. In a system with *n* input lines, each frame has *n* slots, with each slot allocated to carrying data from a specific input line.

Example 5

Four 1-Kbps connections are multiplexed together. A unit is 1 bit. Find (1) the duration of 1 bit before multiplexing, (2) the transmission rate of the link, (3) the duration of a time slot, and (4) the duration of a frame?

Solution

We can answer the questions as follows:

1. The duration of 1 bit before multiplexing is 1/1 Kbps, or 0.001 s (1 ms).
2. The rate of the link is 4 times the rate of a connection, or 4 Kbps.
3. The duration of each time slot is one-fourth of the duration of each bit before multiplexing, or 1/4 ms or 250 µs. Note that we can also calculate this from the data rate of the link, 4 Kbps. The bit duration is the inverse of the data rate, or 1/4 Kbps or 250 µs.
4. The duration of a frame is always the same as the duration of each unit before multiplexing, or 1 ms. We can also calculate this in another way. Each frame in this case includes four time slots. So the duration of a frame is 4 times of 250 µs, or 1 ms.

Interleaving

TDM can be visualized as two fast rotating switches, one on the multiplexing side and the other on the demultiplexing side. The switches are synchronized and rotate at the same speed, but in opposite directions. On the multiplexing side, as the switch opens in front of a connection, that connection has the opportunity to send a unit onto the path. This process is called **interleaving.** On the demultiplexing side, as the switch opens in front of a connection, that connection has the opportunity to receive a unit from the path.

Figure 6.14 shows the interleaving process for the connection shown in Figure 6.13. In this figure, we assume that no switching is involved and that the data from the first connection at the multiplexer site go to the first connection at the demultiplexer. We discuss switching in Chapter 8.

Figure 6.14 *Interleaving*

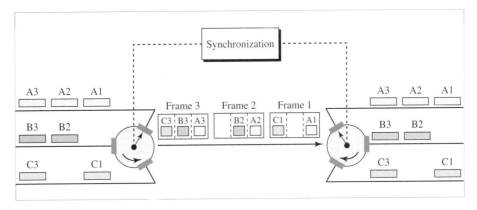

Example 6

Four channels are multiplexed using TDM. If each channel sends 100 bytes/s and we multiplex 1 byte per channel, show the frame traveling on the link, the size of the frame, the duration of a frame, the frame rate, and the bit rate for the link.

Solution

The multiplexer is shown in Figure 6.15. Each frame carries 1 byte from each channel. So the size of each frame is 4 bytes or 32 bits. Because each channel is sending 100 bytes per second and a frame carries 1 byte from each channel, the frame rate must be 100 frames per second. The duration of a frame is therefore 1/100 s. The link is carrying 100 frames per second, and each frame contains 32 bits, so the bit rate is 100×32 or 3200 bps. This is actually 4 times the bit rate for each channel, which is $100 \times 8 = 800$ bps.

Figure 6.15 *Example 6*

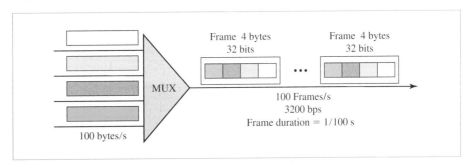

Example 7

A multiplexer combines four 100-Kbps channels using a time slot of 2 bits. Show the output with four arbitrary inputs. What is the frame rate? What is the frame duration? What is the bit rate? What is the bit duration?

Solution

Figure 6.16 shows the output for four arbitrary inputs. The link carries 50,000 frames per second since each frame contains 2 bits per channel. The frame duration is therefore 1/50,000 s or 20 μs. The frame rate is 50,000 frames per second, and each frame carries 8 bits; the bit rate is 50,000 × 8 = 400,000 bits or 400 Kbps. The bit duration is 1/400,000 s, or 2.5 μs. Note that the frame duration is 8 times the bit duration because each frame is carrying 8 bits.

Figure 6.16   *Example 7*

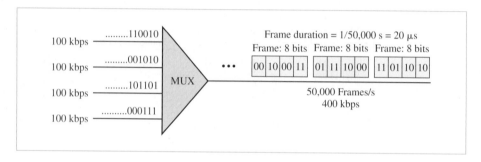

Synchronizing

You may have noticed that the implementation of TDM is not as easy as that of FDM. Synchronization between the multiplexer and demultiplexer is a major issue. If the multiplexer and the demultiplexer are out of synchronization, a bit belonging to one channel may be received by the wrong channel. For this reason, one or more synchronization bits are usually added to the beginning of each frame. These bits, called **framing bits,** follow a pattern, frame to frame, that allows the demultiplexer to synchronize with the incoming stream so that it can separate the time slots accurately. In most cases, this synchronization information consists of 1 bit per frame, alternating between 0 and 1, as shown in Figure 6.17.

Figure 6.17   *Framing bits*

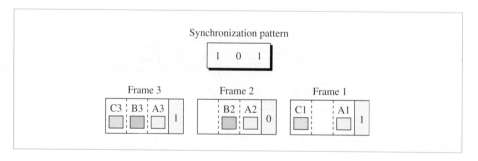

Example 8

We have four sources, each creating 250 characters per second. If the interleaved unit is a character and 1 synchronizing bit is added to each frame, find (1) the data rate of each source, (2) the duration of each character in each source, (3) the frame rate, (4) the duration of each frame, (5) the number of bits in each frame, and (6) the data rate of the link.

Solution

We can answer the questions as follows:

1. The data rate of each source is $250 \times 8 = 2000$ bps = 2 Kbps.
2. Each source sends 250 characters per second; therefore, the duration of a character is 1/250 s, or 4 ms.
3. Each frame has one character from each source, which means the link needs to send 250 frames per second to keep the transmission rate of each source.
4. The duration of each frame is 1/250 s, or 4 ms. Note that the duration of each frame is the same as the duration of each character coming from each source.
5. Each frame carries 4 characters and 1 extra synchronizing bit. This means that each frame is $4 \times 8 + 1 = 33$ bits.
6. The link sends 250 frames per second, and each frame contains 33 bits. This means that the data rate of the link is 250×33, or 8250 bps. Note that the bit rate of the link is more than the combined bit rates of the four channels. If we add the bit rates of four channels, we get 8000 bps. Because 250 frames are traveling per second and each contains 1 extra bit for synchronizing, we need to add 250 to the sum to get 8250 bps.

Bit Padding

It is possible to multiplex data from devices of different data rates. For example, device A could use one time slot, while the faster device B could use two. The number of slots in a frame and the input lines to which they are assigned remain fixed throughout a given system, but devices of different data rates may control different numbers of those slots. *Remember,* the time slot length is fixed. For this technique to work, therefore, the different data rates must be integer multiples of each other. For example, we can accommodate a device that is 5 times faster than the other devices by giving it five slots to one for each of the other devices. We, however, cannot accommodate a device that is 5.5 times faster by this method, because we cannot introduce one-half of a time slot into a frame.

When the speeds are not integer multiples of each other, they can be made to behave as if they were, by a technique called **bit padding.** In bit padding, the multiplexer adds extra bits to a device's source stream to force the speed relationships among the various devices into integer multiples of each other. For example, if we have one device with a bit rate of 2.75 times that of the other devices, we can add enough bits to raise the rate to 3 times that of the others. The extra bits are then discarded by the demultiplexer.

Example 9

Two channels, one with a bit rate of 100 Kbps and another with a bit rate of 200 Kbps, are to be multiplexed. How this can be achieved? What is the frame rate? What is the frame duration? What is the bit rate of the link?

Solution

We can allocate one slot to the first channel and two slots to the second channel. Each frame carries 3 bits. The frame rate is 100,000 frames per second because it carries 1 bit from the first channel. The frame duration is 1/100,000 s, or 10 ms. The bit rate is 100,000 frames/s × 3 bits/frame, or 300 Kbps. Note that because each frame carries 1 bit from the first channel, the bit rate for the first channel is preserved. The bit rate for the second channel is also preserved because each frame carries 2 bits from the second channel.

Digital Signal (DS) Service

Telephone companies implement TDM through a hierarchy of digital signals, called **digital signal (DS) service.** Figure 6.18 shows the data rates supported by each level.

Figure 6.18 *DS hierarchy*

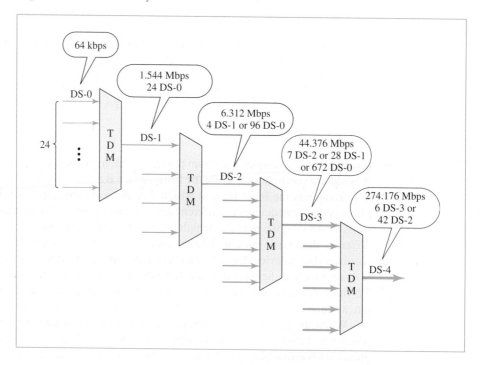

- A DS-0 service is a single digital channel of 64 Kbps.
- DS-1 is a 1.544-Mbps service; 1.544 Mbps is 24 times 64 Kbps plus 8 Kbps of overhead. It can be used as a single service for 1.544-Mbps transmissions, or it can be used to multiplex 24 DS-0 channels or to carry any other combination desired by the user that can fit within its 1.544-Mbps capacity.
- DS-2 is a 6.312-Mbps service; 6.312 Mbps is 96 times 64 Kbps plus 168 Kbps of overhead. It can be used as a single service for 6.312-Mbps transmissions, or it can be used to multiplex 4 DS-1 channels, 96 DS-0 channels, or a combination of these service types.
- DS-3 is a 44.376-Mbps service; 44.376 Mbps is 672 times 64 Kbps plus 1.368 Mbps of overhead. It can be used as a single service for 44.376-Mbps

transmissions, or it can be used to multiplex 7 DS-2 channels, 28 DS-1 channels, 672 DS-0 channels, or a combination of these service types.

- DS-4 is a 274.176-Mbps service; 274.176 is 4032 times 64 Kbps plus 16.128 Mbps of overhead. It can be used to multiplex 6 DS-3 channels, 42 DS-2 channels, 168 DS-1 channels, 4032 DS-0 channels, or a combination of these service types.

T Lines

DS-0, DS-1, and so on are the names of services. To implement those services, the telephone companies use **T lines** (T-1 to T-4). These are lines with capacities precisely matched to the data rates of the DS-1 to DS-4 services (see Table 6.1).

Table 6.1   *DS and T line rates*

Service	Line	Rate (Mbps)	Voice Channels
DS-1	**T-1**	1.544	24
DS-2	**T-2**	6.312	96
DS-3	**T-3**	44.736	672
DS-4	**T-4**	274.176	4032

The T-1 line is used to implement DS-1, T-2 is used to implement DS-2, and so on. As you can see from Table 6.1, DS-0 is not actually offered as a service, but it has been defined as a basis for reference purposes.

T Lines for Analog Transmission

T lines are digital lines designed for the transmission of digital data, audio, or video. However, they also can be used for analog transmission (regular telephone connections), provided the analog signals are sampled first, then time-division multiplexed.

The possibility of using T lines as analog carriers opened up a new generation of services for the telephone companies. Earlier, when an organization wanted 24 separate telephone lines, it needed to run 24 twisted-pair cables from the company to the central exchange. (Remember those old movies showing a busy executive with 10 telephones lined up on his desk? Or the old office telephones with a big fat cable running from them? Those cables contained a bundle of separate lines.) Today, that same organization can combine the 24 lines into one T-1 line and run only the T-1 line to the exchange. Figure 6.19 shows how 24 voice channels can be multiplexed onto one T-1 line. (Refer to Chapter 5 for PCM encoding.)

The T-1 Frame

As noted above, DS-1 requires 8 Kbps of overhead. To understand how this overhead is calculated, we must examine the format of a 24-voice-channel frame.

The frame used on a T-1 line is usually 193 bits divided into 24 slots of 8 bits each plus 1 extra bit for synchronization ($24 \times 8 + 1 = 193$); see Figure 6.20. In other words, each slot contains one signal segment from each channel; 24 segments are interleaved

Figure 6.19 *T-1 line for multiplexing telephone lines*

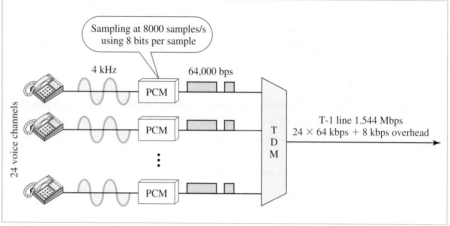

in one frame. If a T-1 line carries 8000 frames, the data rate is 1.544 Mbps ($193 \times 8000 = 1.544$ Mbps)—the capacity of the line.

Figure 6.20 *T-1 frame structure*

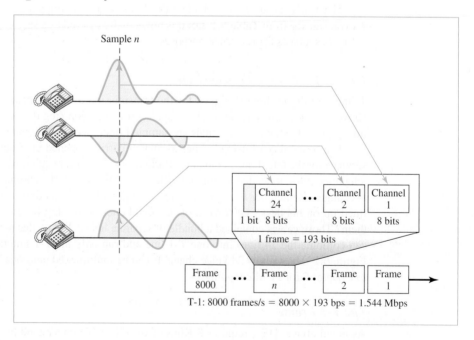

E Lines

Europeans use a version of T lines called **E lines.** The two systems are conceptually identical, but their capacities differ. Table 6.2 shows the E lines and their capacities.

Table 6.2   *E line rates*

Line	Rate (Mbps)	Voice Channels
E-1	2.048	30
E-2	8.448	120
E-3	34.368	480
E-4	139.264	1920

Inverse TDM

As its name implies, **inverse multiplexing** is the opposite of multiplexing. Inverse multiplexing takes the data stream from one high-speed line and breaks it into portions that can be sent across several lower-speed lines simultaneously, with no loss in the collective data rate (see Figure 6.21).

Figure 6.21   *Multiplexing and inverse multiplexing*

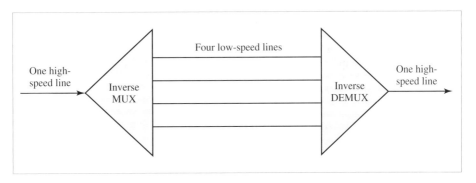

Why do we need inverse multiplexing? Think of an organization that wants to send data, audio, and video, each of which requires a different data rate. To send audio, it may need a 64-Kbps link. To send data, it may need a 128-Kbps link. And to send video, it may need a 1.544-Mbps link. To accommodate all these needs, the organization has two options. It can lease a 1.544-Mbps channel from a common carrier (the telephone company) and use the full capacity only sometimes, which is not an efficient use of the facility. Or it can lease several separate channels of lower data rates. Using an agreement called **bandwidth on demand,** the organization can use any of these channels whenever and however it needs them. Voice transmissions can be sent intact over any of the channels. Data or video signals can be broken up and sent over two or more lines. In other words, the data and video signals can be inversely multiplexed over multiple lines.

More TDM Applications

Some second-generation cellular telephone companies use TDM. For example, the digital version of the cellular telephony we discussed before still divides the available bandwidth into 30-KHz bands and uses FDM to combine these bands. For each band, it applies TDM so that six users share the band. This means that each 30-KHz band is now made of six time slots, and the digitized voice signals of the users are inserted in the slots. Using TDM, the number of telephone users in each area is now six times greater. We discuss second-generation cellular telephony in Chapter 17.

6.4   KEY TERMS

analog hierarchy	guard band
bandwidth on demand	interleaving
bit padding	inverse multiplexing
channel	jumbo group
demultiplexer (DEMUX)	link
dense wave-division multiplexing (DWDM)	master group
	multiplexer (MUX)
digital signal (DS) service	multiplexing
E lines	supergroup
framing bit	T lines
frequency-division multiplexing (FDM)	time-division multiplexing (TDM)
group	wave-division multiplexing (WDM)

6.5   SUMMARY

- ❏ Multiplexing is the simultaneous transmission of multiple signals across a single data link.
- ❏ Frequency-division multiplexing (FDM) and wave-division multiplexing (WDM) are techniques for analog signals, while time-division multiplexing (TDM) is for digital signals.
- ❏ In FDM, each signal modulates a different carrier frequency. The modulated carriers are combined to form a new signal that is then sent across the link.
- ❏ In FDM, multiplexers modulate and combine signals while demultiplexers decompose and demodulate.
- ❏ In FDM, guard bands keep the modulated signals from overlapping and interfering with one another.
- ❏ Telephone companies use FDM to combine voice channels into successively larger groups for more efficient transmission.
- ❏ Wave-division multiplexing is similar in concept to FDM. The signals being multiplexed, however, are light waves.
- ❏ In TDM, digital signals from *n* devices are interleaved with one another, forming a frame of data (bits, bytes, or any other data unit).
- ❏ Framing bits allow the TDM multiplexer to synchronize properly.
- ❏ Digital signal (DS) is a hierarchy of TDM signals.

❑ T lines (T-1 to T-4) are the implementation of DS services. A T-1 line consists of 24 voice channels.

❑ T lines are used in North America. The European standard defines a variation called E lines.

❑ Inverse multiplexing splits a data stream from one high-speed line onto multiple lower-speed lines.

6.6 PRACTICE SET

Review Questions

1. What are the three major multiplexing techniques?
2. How does FDM combine multiple signals into one?
3. What is the purpose of a guard band?
4. How is one FDM signal separated into its original components?
5. Describe the analog hierarchy in which groups of signals are successively multiplexed onto higher-bandwidth lines.
6. How is WDM similar to FDM? How are they different?
7. How does TDM combine multiple signals into one?
8. How is one TDM signal separated into its original components?
9. Discuss the duration of a data unit before and after the TDM process.
10. Describe the DS hierarchy.
11. How are T lines related to DS service?
12. How can T lines be used for analog transmission?
13. What is the relationship between the number of slots in a frame and the number of input lines for TDM?
14. Is bit padding a technique for FDM or TDM? Is the framing bit used in FDM or TDM?
15. What is inverse multiplexing?

Multiple-Choice Questions

16. The sharing of a medium and its link by two or more devices is called _____.
    a. Modulation
    b. Encoding
    c. Line discipline
    d. Multiplexing
17. Which multiplexing technique transmits analog signals?
    a. FDM
    b. TDM
    c. WDM
    d. (a) and (c)

18. Which multiplexing technique transmits digital signals?
    a. FDM
    b. TDM
    c. WDM
    d. None of the above

19. Which multiplexing technique shifts each signal to a different carrier frequency?
    a. FDM
    b. TDM
    c. Both (a) and (b)
    d. None of the above

20. In TDM, for *n* signal sources of the same data rate, each frame contains _____ slots.
    a. *n*
    b. *n* + 1
    c. *n* − 1
    d. 0 to *n*

21. In TDM, the transmission rate of the multiplexed path is usually _____ the sum of the transmission rates of the signal sources.
    a. Greater than
    b. Less than
    c. Equal to
    d. 1 less than

22. In AT&T's FDM hierarchy, the bandwidth of each group type can be found by multiplying _____ and adding extra bandwidth for guard bands.
    a. The number of voice channels by 4000 Hz
    b. The sampling rate by 4000 Hz
    c. The number of voice channels by 8 bits/sample
    d. The sampling rate by 8 bits/sample

23. DS-1 through DS-4 are _____ while T-1 through T-4 are _____.
    a. Services; multiplexers
    b. Services; signals
    c. Services; lines
    d. Multiplexers; signals

24. In a T-1 line, _____ interleaving occurs.
    a. Bit
    b. Byte
    c. DS-0
    d. Switch

25. Guard bands increase the bandwidth for _____.
    a. FDM
    b. TDM

c. Both (a) and (b)

d. None of the above

26. Which multiplexing technique involves signals composed of light beams?

a. FDM

b. TDM

c. WDM

d. None of the above

Exercises

27. Given the following information, find the minimum bandwidth for the path.

a. FDM multiplexing

b. Five lines, each requiring 4000 Hz

c. 200-Hz guard separating each band

28. Given the following information, find the maximum bandwidth for each signal source.

a. FDM multiplexing

b. Total available bandwidth = 7900 Hz

c. Three signal sources

d. A 200-Hz guard band between each signal source

29. Five signal sources are multiplexed using TDM. Each source produces 100 characters per second. Assume that there is byte interleaving and that each frame requires 1 bit for synchronization. What is the frame rate? What is the bit rate on the path?

30. Draw the TDM frames showing the character data, given the following information:

a. Four signal sources

b. Source 1 message: T E G

c. Source 2 message: A

d. Source 3 message:

e. Source 4 message: E F I L

31. What is the time duration for a T-1 frame?

32. The T-2 line offers a 6.312-Mbps service. Why is this number not 4×1.544 Mbps?

33. In Figure 6.19 the sampling rate is 8000 samples/s. Why?

34. If a single-mode optical fiber can transmit at 2 Gbps, how many telephone channels can one cable carry?

35. Calculate the overhead (in bits) per voice channel for each T line. What is the percentage of overhead per voice channel?

36. Three voice-grade lines, each using 4 KHz, are frequency multiplexed together by using AM and canceling the lower modulated band. Draw the frequency-domain representation of the resulting signal if the carrier frequencies are at 4, 10, and 16 KHz, respectively. What is the bandwidth of the resulting signal?

37. Show the frequency-domain representation of the resulting signals in each stage in Figure 6.22. Assume no guard band. Choose appropriate carrier frequencies.

Figure 6.22   *Exercise 37*

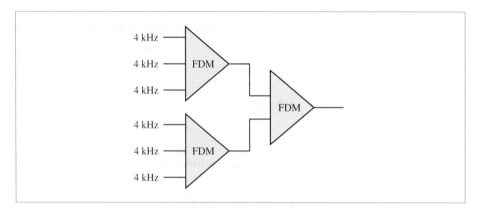

38. We have multiplexed 100 computers using synchronous TDM. If each computer sends data at the rate of 14.4 Kbps, what is the minimum bit rate of the line? Can a T-1 line handle this situation?

39. What is the minimum bit rate of each line in Figure 6.23 if we are using synchronous TDM? Ignore framing (synchronization) bits.

Figure 6.23   *Exercise 39*

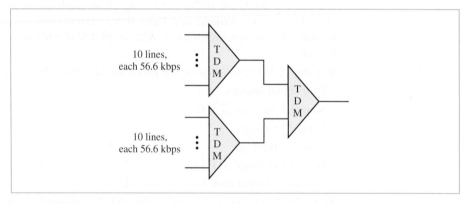

40. Figure 6.24 shows a multiplexer. If the slot is only 10 bits long (3 bits taken from each input plus 1 framing bit), what is the output bit stream? What is the output bit

Figure 6.24   *Exercise 40*

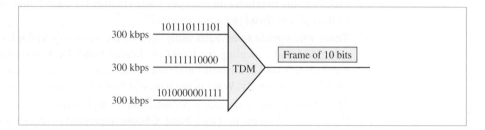

rate? What is the duration of each bit in the output line? How many slots are sent per second? What is the duration of each slot?

41. Figure 6.25 shows a demultiplexer. If the input slot is 12 bits long (ignore framing bits), what is the bit stream in each output? What is the bit rate for each output line?

Figure 6.25   *Exercise 41*

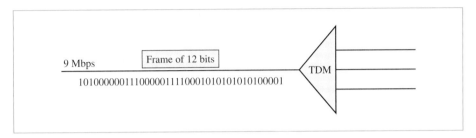

42. Figure 6.26 shows an inverse multiplexer. If the input data rate is 15 Mbps, what is the rate for each line? Can we use the service of T-1 lines for this purpose? Ignore the framing bits.

Figure 6.26   *Exercise 42*

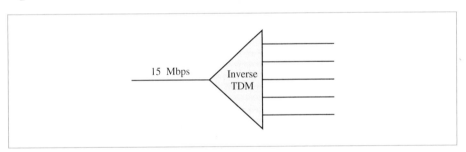

43. What is the overhead (number of extra bits per second) in a T-1 line?

44. If we want to connect two Ethernet LANs with 10-Mbps data rates, how many T-1 lines do we need? Do we need multiplexers or inverse multiplexers? Show the configuration.

CHAPTER 7

Transmission Media

We discussed many issues related to the physical layer in Chapters 3 through 6. In this chapter, we discuss transmission media. Transmission media are actually located below the physical layer and directly controlled by the physical layer. We can say that transmission media belong to layer zero. Figure 7.1 shows the position of transmission media in relation to the physical layer.

Figure 7.1   *Transmission medium and physical layer*

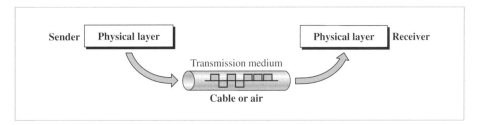

As discussed in Chapter 3, computers and other telecommunication devices use signals to represent data. These signals are transmitted from one device to another in the form of electromagnetic energy, which is propagated through transmission media.

Electromagnetic energy, a combination of electric and magnetic fields vibrating in relation to each other, includes power, radio waves, infrared light, visible light, ultraviolet light, and X, gamma, and cosmic rays. Each of these constitutes a portion of the **electromagnetic spectrum.** Not all portions of the spectrum are currently usable for telecommunications, however. The media to harness those that are usable are also limited to a few types.

For the purpose of telecommunications, transmission media can be divided into two broad categories: guided and unguided. Guided media include twisted-pair cable, coaxial cable, and fiber-optic cable. Unguided medium is usually air. Figure 7.2 shows this taxonomy.

Figure 7.2   *Classes of transmission media*

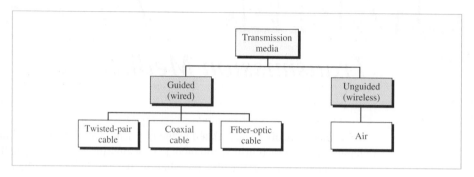

7.1   GUIDED MEDIA

Guided media, which are those that provide a conduit from one device to another, include **twisted-pair cable, coaxial cable,** and **fiber-optic cable.** A signal traveling along any of these media is directed and contained by the physical limits of the medium. Twisted-pair and coaxial cable use metallic (copper) conductors that accept and transport signals in the form of electric current. **Optical fiber** is a glass cable that accepts and transports signals in the form of light.

Twisted-Pair Cable

A twisted pair consists of two conductors (normally copper), each with its own plastic insulation, twisted together, as shown in Figure 7.3.

Figure 7.3   *Twisted-pair cable*

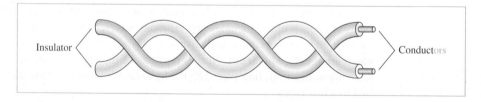

One of the wires is used to carry signals to the receiver, and the other is used only as a ground reference. The receiver uses the difference between the two levels.

In addition to the signal sent by the sender on one of the wires, interference (noise) and crosstalk may affect both wires and create unwanted signals. The receiver at the end, however, operates only on the difference between these unwanted signals. This means that if the two wires are affected by noise or crosstalk equally, the receiver is immune (the difference is zero).

If the two wires are parallel, the effect of these unwanted signals is not the same in both wires because they are at different locations relative to the noise or crosstalk sources (e.g., one closer and one farther). This results in a difference at the receiver. By twisting the pairs, a balance is maintained. For example, suppose in one twist, one wire is closer to the noise source and the other farther; in the next twist, the reverse is true. Twisting makes it probable that both wires are equally affected by external influences (noise or crosstalk). This means that the receiver, which calculates the difference between the two, receives no unwanted signals. From the above discussion, it is clear that the number of twists per unit of length (e.g., inch) determines the quality of the cable; more twists mean better quality.

Unshielded versus Shielded Twisted-Pair Cable

The most common twisted-pair cable used in communications is referred to as **unshielded twisted-pair (UTP).** IBM has also produced a version of twisted-pair cable for its use called **shielded twisted-pair (STP).** STP cable has a metal foil or braided-mesh covering that encases each pair of insulated conductors. Although metal casing improves the quality of cable by preventing the penetration of noise or crosstalk, it is bulkier and more expensive. Figure 7.4 shows the difference between UTP and STP. Our discussion focuses primarily on UTP because STP is seldom used outside of IBM.

Figure 7.4 *UTP and STP*

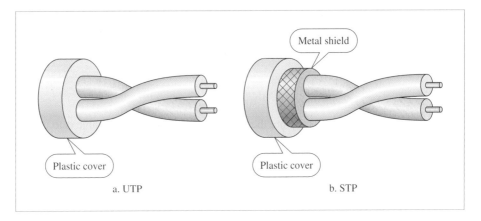

a. UTP   b. STP

Categories

The Electronic Industries Association (EIA) has developed standards to classify unshielded twisted-pair cable into seven categories (categories 6 and 7 are still in the draft stage). Categories are determined by cable quality, with 1 as the lowest and 7 as the highest. Each EIA category is suitable for specific uses. Table 7.1 shows these categories.

Table 7.1   *Categories of unshielded twisted-pair cables*

Category	Bandwidth	Data Rate	Digital/Analog	Use
1	Very low	<100 Kbps	Analog	Telephone
2	<2 MHz	2 Mbps	Analog/digital	T-1 lines
3	16 MHz	10 Mbps	Digital	LANs
4	20 MHz	20 Mbps	Digital	LANs
5	100 MHz	100 Mbps	Digital	LANs
6 (draft)	200 MHz	200 Mbps	Digital	LANs
7 (draft)	600 MHz	600 Mbps	Digital	LANs

Connectors

The most common UTP connector is **RJ45** (RJ stands for Registered Jack), as shown in Figure 7.5. The RJ45 is a keyed connector, meaning the connector can be inserted in only one way.

Figure 7.5   *UTP connector*

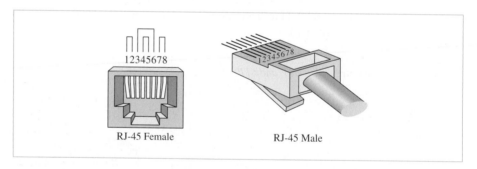

RJ-45 Female   RJ-45 Male

Performance

One way to measure the performance of twisted-pair cable is to compare attenuation versus frequency and distance. A twisted-pair cable can pass a wide range of frequencies. However, Figure 7.6 shows that with increasing frequency, the attenuation, measured in decibels per mile (dB/mi), sharply increases with frequencies above 100 KHz. Note that *gauge* is the measure of the thickness of the wire.

Applications

Twisted-pair cables are used in telephone lines to provide voice and data channels. The local loop—the line that connects subscribers to the central telephone office—is most commonly unshielded twisted-pair cables. We discuss telephone networks in Chapter 8.

The DSL lines that are used by the telephone companies to provide high data rate connections also use the high-bandwidth capability of unshielded twisted-pair cables. We discuss DSL technology in Chapter 9.

Local area networks, such as 10Base-T and 100Base-T, also use twisted-pair cables. We discuss these networks in Chapter 14.

Figure 7.6 *UTP performance*

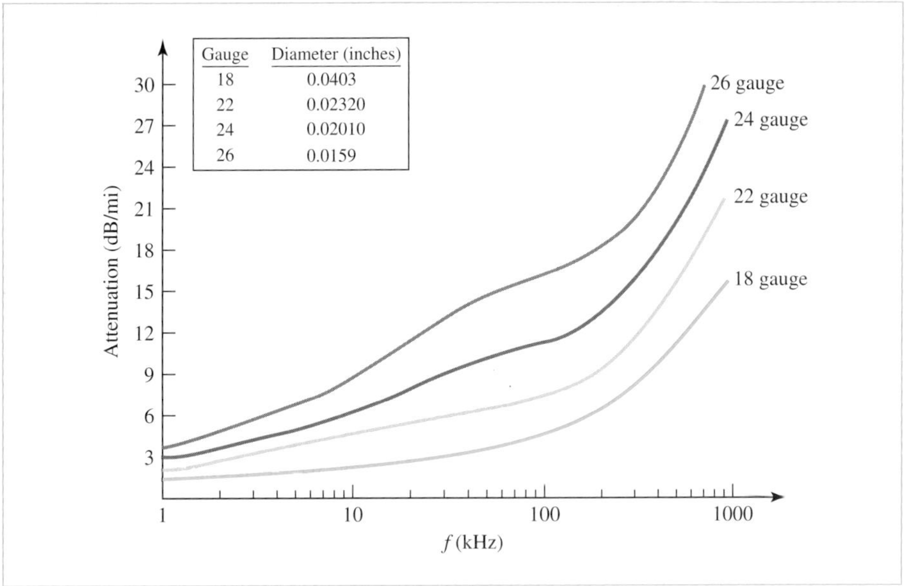

Gauge	Diameter (inches)
18	0.0403
22	0.02320
24	0.02010
26	0.0159

(graph: Attenuation (dB/mi) vs. f (kHz), showing curves labeled 26 gauge, 24 gauge, 22 gauge, and 18 gauge)

Coaxial Cable

Coaxial cable (or *coax*) carries signals of higher frequency ranges than twisted-pair cable, in part because the two media are constructed quite differently. Instead of having two wires, coax has a central core conductor of solid or stranded wire (usually copper) enclosed in an insulating sheath, which is, in turn, encased in an outer conductor of metal foil, braid, or a combination of the two. The outer metallic wrapping serves both as a shield against noise and as the second conductor, which completes the circuit. This outer conductor is also enclosed in an insulating sheath, and the whole cable is protected by a plastic cover (see Fig. 7.7).

Figure 7.7 *Coaxial cable*

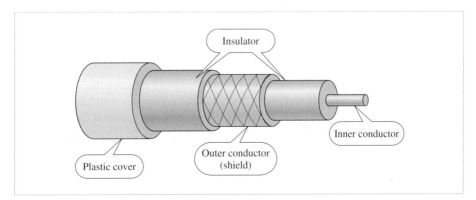

Coaxial Cable Standards

Coaxial cables are categorized by their radio government (RG) ratings. Each RG number denotes a unique set of physical specifications, including the wire gauge of the inner conductor, the thickness and type of the inner insulator, the construction of the shield, and the size and type of the outer casing. Each cable defined by RG ratings is adapted for a specialized function, as shown in Table 7.2.

Table 7.2   *Categories of coaxial cables*

Category	Impedance	Use
RG-59	75 Ω	Cable TV
RG-58	50 Ω	Thin Ethernet
RG-11	50 Ω	Thick Ethernet

Coaxial Cable Connectors

To connect coaxial cable to devices, we need coaxial connectors. The most common type of connector used today is the Bayone-Neill-Concelman, or BNC, connectors. Figure 7.8 shows three popular types of these connectors: the BNC connector, the BNC T connector, and the BNC terminator.

Figure 7.8   *BNC connectors*

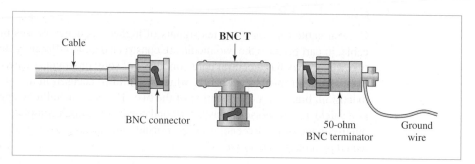

The **BNC connector** is used to connect the end of the cable to a device, such as a TV set. The BNC T connector is used in Ethernet networks (see Chapter 14) to branch out a cable for connection to a computer or other devices. The BNC terminator is used at the end of the cable to prevent the reflection of the signal.

Performance

As we did with twisted-pair cables, we can measure the performance of a coaxial cable. We notice from Figure 7.9 that the attenuation is much higher in coaxial cables than in twisted-pair cable. In other words, although coaxial cable has a much higher bandwidth, the signal weakens rapidly and needs the frequent use of repeaters.

Applications

The use of coaxial cable started in analog telephone networks where a single coaxial network could carry 10,000 voice signals. Later it was used in digital telephone networks

Figure 7.9 *Coaxial cable performance*

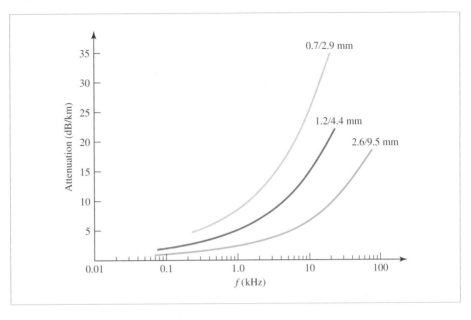

where a single coaxial cable could carry digital data up to 600 Mbps. However, coaxial cable in telephone networks has largely been replaced today with fiber-optic cable.

Cable TV networks (see Chapter 9) also used coaxial cables. In the traditional cable TV network, the entire network used coaxial cable. Later, however, cable TV providers replaced most of the network with fiber-optic cable; hybrid networks use coaxial cable only at the network boundaries, near the consumer premises. Cable TV uses RG-59 coaxial cable.

Another common application of coaxial cable is in traditional Ethernet LANs (see Chapter 14). Because of its high bandwidth, and consequently high data rate, coaxial cable was chosen for digital transmission in early Ethernet LANs. 10Base-2, or Thin Ethernet, uses RG-58 coaxial cable with BNC connectors to transmit data at 10 Mbps with a range of 185 m. 10Base5, or Thick Ethernet, uses RG-11 (thick coaxial cable) to transmit 10 Mbps with a range of 5000 m. Thick Ethernet has specialized connectors.

Fiber-Optic Cable

A fiber-optic cable is made of glass or plastic and transmits signals in the form of light. To understand optical fiber, we first need to explore several aspects of the nature of light.

Light travels in a straight line as long as it is moving through a single uniform substance. If a ray of light traveling through one substance suddenly enters another (more or less dense), the ray changes direction. Figure 7.10 shows how a ray of light changes direction when going from a more dense to a less dense substance.

As the figure shows, if the **angle of incidence** (the angle the ray makes with the line perpendicular to the interface between the two substances) is less than the **critical angle,** the ray **refracts** and moves closer to the surface. If the angle of incidence is equal to the critical angle, the light bends along the interface. If the angle is greater than

Figure 7.10   Bending of light ray

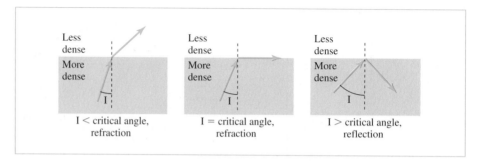

the critical angle, the ray **reflects** (makes a turn) and travels again in the denser substance. Note that the critical angle is a property of the substance, and its value is different from one substance to another.

Optical fibers use reflection to guide light through a channel. A glass or plastic **core** is surrounded by a **cladding** of less dense glass or plastic. The difference in density of the two materials must be such that a beam of light moving through the core is reflected off the cladding instead of being refracted into it. See Figure 7.11.

Figure 7.11   Optical fiber

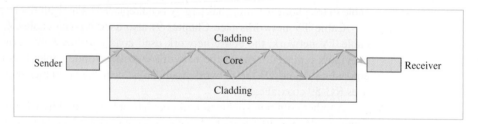

Propagation Modes

Current technology supports two modes (multimode and single mode) for propagating light along optical channels, each requiring fiber with different physical characteristics. Multimode can be implemented in two forms: step-index or graded-index (see Fig. 7.12).

Multimode   Multimode is so named because multiple beams from a light source move through the core in different paths. How these beams move within the cable depends on the structure of the core, as shown in Figure 7.13.

In **multimode step-index fiber,** the density of the core remains constant from the center to the edges. A beam of light moves through this constant density in a straight line until it reaches the interface of the core and the cladding. At the interface, there is an abrupt change to a lower density that alters the angle of the beam's motion. The term *step index* refers to the suddenness of this change.

A second type of fiber, called **multimode graded-index fiber,** decreases this distortion of the signal through the cable. The word *index* here refers to the index of refraction.

Figure 7.12   *Propagation modes*

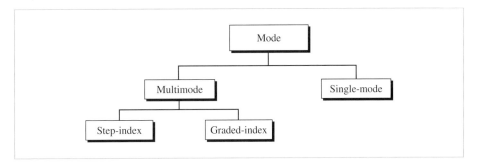

Figure 7.13   *Modes*

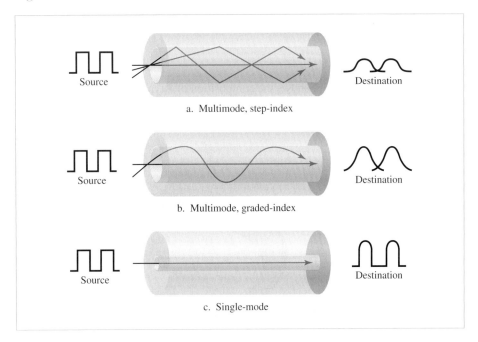

a. Multimode, step-index

b. Multimode, graded-index

c. Single-mode

As we saw above, the index of refraction is related to density. A graded-index fiber, therefore, is one with varying densities. Density is highest at the center of the core and decreases gradually to its lowest at the edge. Figure 7.13 shows the impact of this variable density on the propagation of light beams.

Single-Mode   Single-mode uses step-index fiber and a highly focused source of light that limits beams to a small range of angles, all close to the horizontal. The **single-mode fiber** itself is manufactured with a much smaller diameter than that of multimode fiber, and with substantially lower density (index of refraction). The decrease in density results in a critical angle that is close enough to 90° to make the propagation of beams almost horizontal. In this case, propagation of different beams is almost identical, and delays are negligible. All the beams arrive at the destination "together" and can be recombined with little distortion to the signal (see Fig. 7.13).

Fiber Sizes

Optical fibers are defined by the ratio of the diameter of their core to the diameter of their cladding, both expressed in micrometers. The common sizes are shown in Table 7.3. The last size listed is only for single-mode.

Table 7.3　*Fiber types*

Type	Core (μm)	Cladding (μm)	Mode
50/125	50	125	Multimode, graded-index
62.5/125	62.5	125	Multimode, graded-index
100/125	100	125	Multimode, graded-index
7/125	7	125	Single-mode

Cable Composition

Figure 7.14 shows the composition of a typical fiber-optic cable.

Figure 7.14　*Fiber construction*

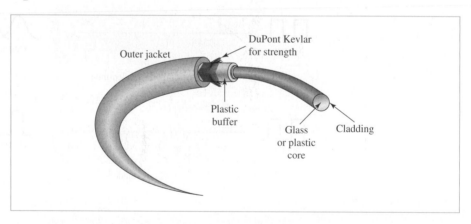

The outer jacket is made of either PVC or Teflon. Inside the jacket are Kevlar strands to strengthen the cable. Kevlar is a strong material used in the fabrication of bulletproof vests. Below the Kevlar is another plastic coating to cushion the fiber. The fiber is at the center of the cable, and it consists of cladding and core.

Fiber-Optic Cable Connectors

Fiber-optic cables use three different types of connectors, as shown in Figure 7.15.

The **subscriber channel (SC) connector** is used in cable TV. It uses a push/pull locking system. The **straight-tip (ST) connector** is used for connecting cable to

Figure 7.15 *Fiber-optic cable connectors*

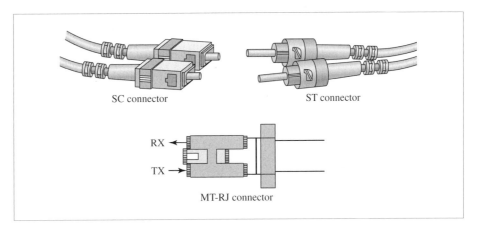

networking devices. It uses a bayonet locking system and is more reliable than SC. **MT-RJ** is a new connector with the same size as RJ45.

Performance

The measurement of attenuation versus wavelength shows a very interesting phenomenon in fiber-optic cable. Attenuation is flatter than in the case of twisted-pair cable and coaxial cable. The performance is such that we need fewer (actually 10 times less) repeaters when we use fiber-optic cable.

Figure 7.16 *Optical fiber performance*

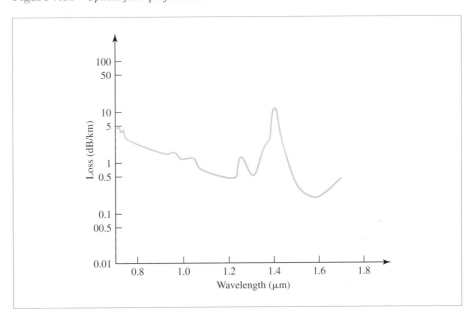

Applications

Fiber-optic cable is often found in backbone networks because its wide bandwidth is cost-effective. Today, with WDM, we can transfer data at a rate of 1600 Gbps. The SONET network that we discuss in Chapter 9 provides such a backbone.

Some cable TV companies use a combination of optical fiber and coaxial cable, thus creating a hybrid network. Optical fiber provides the backbone structure while coaxial cable provides the connection to the user premises. This is a cost-effective configuration since the narrow bandwidth requirement at the user end does not justify the use of optical fiber.

Local area networks such as 100Base-FX network (Fast Ethernet) and 1000Base-X also use fiber-optic cable.

Advantages and Disadvantages of Optical Fiber

Advantages   Fiber-optic cable has several advantages over metallic cable (twisted-pair or coaxial).

- **Higher bandwidth.** Fiber-optic cable can support dramatically higher bandwidths (and hence data rates) than either twisted-pair or coaxial cable. Currently, data rates and bandwidth utilization over fiber-optic cable are limited not by the medium but by the signal generation and reception technology available.

- **Less signal attenuation.** Fiber-optic transmission distance is significantly greater than that of other guided media. A signal can run for 50 km without requiring regeneration. We need repeaters every 5 km for coaxial or twisted-pair cable.

- **Immunity to electromagnetic interference.** Electromagnetic noise cannot affect fiber-optic cables.

- **Resistance to corrosive materials.** Glass is more resistant to corrosive materials than copper.

- **Light weight.** Fiber-optic cables are much lighter than copper cables.

- **More immune to tapping.** Fiber-optic cables are definitely more immune to tapping than copper cables. Copper cables create antennas that can easily be tapped.

Disadvantages   There are some disadvantages in the use of optical fiber.

- **Installation/maintenance.** Fiber-optic cable is a relatively new technology. Installation and maintenance need expertise that is not yet available everywhere.

- **Unidirectional.** Propagation of light is unidirectional. If we need bidirectional communication, two fibers are needed.

- **Cost.** The cable and the interfaces are relatively more expensive than those of other guided media. If the demand for bandwidth is not high, often the use of optical fiber cannot be justified.

7.2   UNGUIDED MEDIA: WIRELESS

Unguided media transport electromagnetic waves without using a physical conductor. This type of communication is often referred to as **wireless communication.** Signals are normally broadcast through air and thus are available to anyone who has a device capable of receiving them.

Figure 7.17 shows part of the electromagnetic spectrum, ranging from 3 KHz to 900 THz, used for wireless communication.

Figure 7.17 *Electromagnetic spectrum for wireless communication*

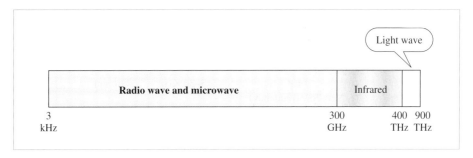

Unguided signals can travel from the source to destination in several ways. There is ground propagation, sky propagation, and line-of-sight propagation, as shown in Figure 7.18.

Figure 7.18 *Propagation methods*

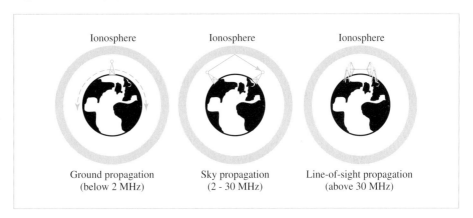

In **ground propagation,** radio waves travel through the lowest portion of the atmosphere, hugging the earth. These low-frequency signals emanate in all directions from the transmitting antenna and follow the curvature of the planet. Distance depends on the amount of power in the signal: The greater the power, the greater the distance. In **sky propagation,** higher-frequency radio waves radiate upward into the ionosphere (the layer of atmosphere where particles exist as ions) where they are reflected back to earth. This type of transmission allows for greater distances with lower power output. In **line-of-sight propagation,** very high-frequency signals are transmitted in straight lines directly from antenna to antenna. Antennas must be directional, facing each other, and either tall enough or close enough together not to be affected by the curvature of the earth. Line-of-sight propagation is tricky because radio transmissions cannot be completely focused.

The section of the electromagnetic spectrum defined as radio waves and microwaves is divided into eight ranges, called *bands,* each regulated by government authorities. These bands are rated from very low frequency (VLF) to extremely high frequency (EHF). Table 7.4 lists these bands, their ranges, propagation methods, and some applications.

Table 7.4   *Bands*

Band	Range	Propagation	Application
VLF (Very low frequency)	3–30 KHz	Ground	Long-range radio navigation
LF (Low frequency)	30–300 KHz	Ground	Radio beacons and navigational locators
MF (Middle frequency)	300 KHz–3 MHz	Sky	AM radio
HF (High frequency)	3–30 MHz	Sky	Citizens band (CB), ship/aircraft communication
VHF (Very high frequency)	30–300 MHz	Sky and line-of-sight	VHF TV, FM radio
UHF (Ultra high frequency)	300 MHz–3 GHz	Line-of-sight	UHF TV, cellular phones, paging, satellite
SHF (Super high frequency)	3–30 GHz	Line-of-sight	Satellite communication
EHF (Extremely high frequency)	30–300 GHz	Line-of-sight	Radar, satellite

We can divide wireless transmission into three broad groups: radio waves, microwaves, and infrared waves. See Figure 7.19.

Figure 7.19   *Wireless transmission waves*

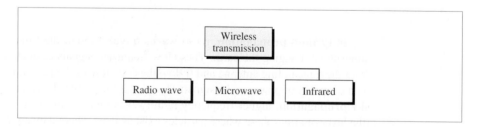

Radio Waves

Although there is no clear-cut demarcation between radio waves and microwaves, electromagnetic waves ranging in frequencies between 3 KHz and 1 GHz are normally called **radio waves;** waves ranging in frequencies between 1 and 300 GHz are called

microwaves. However, the behavior of the waves, rather than the frequencies, is a better criterion for classification.

Radio waves, for the most part, are omnidirectional. When an antenna transmits radio waves, they are propagated in all directions. This means that the sending and receiving antennas do not have to be aligned. A sending antenna can send waves that can be received by any receiving antenna. The omnidirectional property has a disadvantage, too. The radio waves transmitted by one antenna are susceptible to interference by another antenna that may send signals using the same frequency or band.

Radio waves, particularly those waves that propagate in the sky mode, can travel long distances. This makes radio waves a good candidate for long-distance broadcasting such as AM radio.

Radio waves, particularly those of low and medium frequencies, can penetrate walls. This characteristic can be both an advantage and a disadvantage. It is an advantage because, for example, an AM radio can receive signals inside a building. It is a disadvantage because we cannot isolate a communication to just inside or outside a building. The radio wave band is relatively narrow, just under 1 GHz, compared to the microwave band. When this band is divided into subbands, the sidebands are also narrow, leading to a low data rate for digital communications.

Almost the entire band is regulated by authorities (e.g., the FCC in the United States). Using any part of the band requires permission from the authorities.

Omnidirectional Antenna

Radio waves use **omnidirectional antennas** that send out signals in other directions. Based on the wavelength, strength, and the purpose of transmission, we can have several types of antennas. Figure 7.20 shows an omnidirectional antenna.

Figure 7.20 *Omnidirectional antennas*

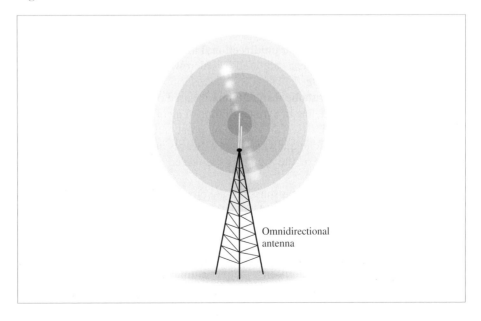

Omnidirectional antenna

Applications

The omnidirectional characteristics of radio waves make them useful for multicasting, in which there is one sender but many receivers. AM and FM radio, television, maritime radio, cordless phones, and paging are examples of multicasting.

> **Radio waves are used for multicast communications, such as radio and television, and paging systems.**

Microwaves

Electromagnetic waves having frequencies between 1 and 300 GHz are called microwaves.

Microwaves are unidirectional. When an antenna transmits microwave waves, they can be narrowly focused. This means that the sending and receiving antennas need to be aligned. The unidirectional property has an obvious advantage. A pair of antennas can be aligned without interfering with another pair of aligned antennas.

Microwave propagation is line-of-sight. Since the towers with the mounted antennas need to be in direct sight of each other, towers that are far apart need to be very tall. The curvature of the earth as well as other blocking obstacles do not allow two short towers to communicate using microwaves. Repeaters are often needed for long-distance communication.

Very high-frequency microwaves cannot penetrate walls. This characteristic can be a disadvantage if receivers are inside buildings.

The microwave band is relatively wide, almost 299 GHz. Therefore wider subbands can be assigned, and a high data rate is possible

Use of certain portions of the band requires permission from authorities.

Unidirectional Antenna

Microwaves need **unidirectional antennas** that send out signals in one direction. Two types of antennas are used for microwave communications: the parabolic dish and the horn (see Fig. 7.21).

A **parabolic dish antenna** is based on the geometry of a parabola: Every line parallel to the line of symmetry (line of sight) reflects off the curve at angles such that all the lines intersect in a common point called the focus. The parabolic dish works as a funnel, catching a wide range of waves and directing them to a common point. In this way, more of the signal is recovered than would be possible with a single-point receiver.

Outgoing transmissions are broadcast through a horn aimed at the dish. The microwaves hit the dish and are deflected outward in a reversal of the receipt path.

A **horn antenna** looks like a gigantic scoop. Outgoing transmissions are broadcast up a stem (resembling a handle) and deflected outward in a series of narrow parallel beams by the curved head. Received transmissions are collected by the scooped shape of the horn, in a manner similar to the parabolic dish, and are deflected down into the stem.

Figure 7.21 *Unidirectional antennas*

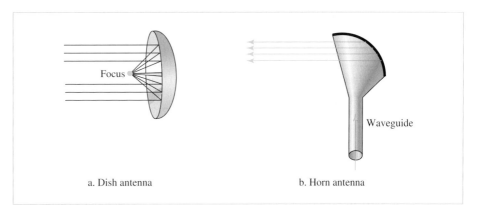

a. Dish antenna   b. Horn antenna

Applications

Microwaves, due to their unidirectional properties, are very useful when unicasting (one-to-one) communication is needed between the sender and the receiver. They are used in cellular phones (Chapter 17), satellite networks (Chapter 17), and wireless LANs (Chapter 15).

> **Microwaves are used for unicast communication such as cellular telephones, satellite networks, and wireless LANs.**

Infrared

Infrared signals, with frequencies from 300 GHz to 400 THz (wavelengths from 1 mm to 770 nm), can be used for short-range communication. Infrared signals, having high frequencies, cannot penetrate walls. This advantageous characteristic prevents interference between one system and another; a short-range communication system in one room cannot be affected by another system in the next room. When we use our infrared remote control, we do not interfere with the use of the remote by our neighbors. However, this same characteristic makes infrared signals useless for long-range communication. In addition, we cannot use infrared waves outside a building because the sun's rays contain infrared waves that can interfere with the communication.

Applications

The infrared band, almost 400 THz, has an excellent potential for data transmission. Such a wide bandwidth can be used to transmit digital data with a very high data rate. The Infrared Data Association (IrDA), an association for sponsoring the use of infrared waves, has established standards for using these signals for communication between devices such as keyboards, mice, PCs, and printers. For example, some manufacturers provide a special port called the **IrDA** port that allows a wireless keyboard to communicate with a PC. The standard originally defined a data rate of 75 Kbps for a distance up to 8 m. The recent standard defines a data rate of 4 Mbps.

Infrared signals defined by IrDA transmit through line of sight; the IrDA port on the keyboard needs to point to the PC for transmission to occur.

> **Infrared signals can be used for short-range communication in a closed area using line-of-sight propagation.**

7.3 KEY TERMS

angle of incidence	optical fiber
BNC connector	parabolic dish antenna
cladding	radio wave
coaxial cable	reflection
core	refraction
critical angle	RG number
electromagnetic spectrum	RJ45
fiber-optic cable	shielded twisted-pair (STP)
ground propagation	single-mode fiber
guided media	sky propagation
horn antenna	straight-tip (ST) connector
infrared wave	subscriber channel (SC) connector
IrDA port	transmission media
line-of-sight propagation	twisted-pair cable
microwave	unguided medium
MT-RJ	unidirectional antenna
multimode graded-index fiber	unshielded twisted-pair (UTP)
multimode step-index fiber	wireless communication
omnidirectional antenna	

7.4 SUMMARY

❑ Transmission media lie below the physical layer.

❑ A guided medium provides a physical conduit from one device to another.

❑ Twisted-pair cable, coaxial cable, and optical fiber are the most popular types of guided media.

❑ Twisted-pair cable consists of two insulated copper wires twisted together. Twisting allows each wire to have approximately the same noise environment.

❑ Twisted-pair cable is used in telephone lines for voice and data communications.

❑ Coaxial cable has the following layers (starting from the center): a metallic rod-shaped inner conductor, an insulator covering the rod, a metallic outer conductor (shield), an insulator covering the shield, and a plastic cover.

❏ Coaxial cable can carry signals of higher frequency ranges than twisted-pair cable.

❏ Coaxial cable is used in cable TV networks and traditional Ethernet LANs.

❏ Fiber-optic cables are composed of a glass or plastic inner core surrounded by cladding, all encased in an outside jacket.

❏ Fiber-optic cables carry data signals in the form of light. The signal is propagated along the inner core by reflection.

❏ Fiber-optic transmission is becoming increasingly popular due to its noise resistance, low attenuation, and high-bandwidth capabilities.

❏ Signal propagation in optical fibers can be multimode (multiple beams from a light source) or single-mode (essentially one beam from a light source).

❏ In multimode step-index propagation, the core density is constant and the light beam changes direction suddenly at the interface between the core and the cladding.

❏ In multimode graded-index propagation, the core density decreases with distance from the center. This causes a curving of the light beams.

❏ Fiber-optic cable is used in backbone networks, cable TV networks, and Fast Ethernet networks.

❏ Unguided media (usually air) transport electromagnetic waves without the use of a physical conductor.

❏ Wireless data are transmitted through ground propagation, sky propagation, and line-of-sight propagation.

❏ Wireless data can be classified as radio waves, microwaves, or infrared waves.

❏ Radio waves are omnidirectional. The radio wave band is under government regulation.

❏ Microwaves are unidirectional; propagation is line of sight. Microwaves are used for cellular phone, satellite, and wireless LAN communications.

❏ The parabolic dish antenna and the horn antenna are used for transmission and reception of microwaves.

❏ Infrared waves are used for short-range communications such as those between a PC and a peripheral device.

7.5   PRACTICE SET

Review Questions

1. Is the transmission medium a part of the physical layer? Why or why not?
2. Name the two major categories of transmission media.
3. How do guided media differ from unguided media?
4. What are the three major classes of guided media?
5. What is the form of the signal in twisted-pair cable and coaxial cable? How does this differ from the signal in fiber-optic cable?
6. Give a use for each class of guided media.

7. What is the major advantage of shielded twisted-pair over unshielded twisted-pair cable?

8. What is the significance of the twisting in twisted-pair cable?

9. Why is coaxial cable superior to twisted-pair cable?

10. What is reflection?

11. Discuss the modes for propagating light along optical channels.

12. What is the purpose of cladding in an optical fiber? Discuss its density relative to the core.

13. Name the advantages of optical fiber over twisted-pair and coaxial cable.

14. What are the disadvantages of optical fiber as a transmission medium?

15. Name the three ways for wireless data to be propagated.

16. Give a use for each class of unguided media.

17. How does sky propagation differ from line-of-sight propagation?

18. What is the difference between omnidirectional waves and unidirectional waves?

19. What is an IrDA port?

Multiple-Choice Questions

20. Transmission media are usually categorized as _____.
    a. Fixed or unfixed
    b. Guided or unguided
    c. Determinate or indeterminate
    d. Metallic or nonmetallic

21. Transmission media are closest to the _____ layer.
    a. Physical
    b. Network
    c. Transport
    d. Application

22. Category 1 UTP cable is most often used in _____ networks.
    a. Fast Ethernet
    b. Traditional Ethernet
    c. Infrared
    d. Telephone

23. BNC connectors are used by _____ cables.
    a. UTP
    b. STP
    c. Coaxial
    d. Fiber-optic

24. _____ cable consists of an inner copper core and a second conducting outer sheath.
    a. Twisted-pair
    b. Coaxial

    c. Fiber-optic

    d. Shielded twisted-pair

25. In fiber optics, the signal source is _____ waves.

    a. Light

    b. Radio

    c. Infrared

    d. Very low-frequency

26. Smoke signals are an example of communication through _____.

    a. A guided medium

    b. An unguided medium

    c. A refractive medium

    d. A small or large medium

27. Which of the following primarily uses guided media?

    a. Cellular telephone system

    b. Local telephone system

    c. Satellite communications

    d. Radio broadcasting

28. Which of the following is not a guided medium?

    a. Twisted-pair cable

    b. Coaxial cable

    c. Fiber-optic cable

    d. Atmosphere

29. In an environment with many high-voltage devices, the best transmission medium would be _____.

    a. Twisted-pair cable

    b. Coaxial cable

    c. Optical fiber

    d. The atmosphere

30. What is the major factor that makes coaxial cable less susceptible to noise than twisted-pair cable?

    a. Inner conductor

    b. Diameter of cable

    c. Outer conductor

    d. Insulating material

31. The RG number gives us information about _____.

    a. Twisted pairs

    b. Coaxial cables

    c. Optical fibers

    d. All the above

32. In an optical fiber, the inner core is _____ the cladding.
    a. Denser than
    b. Less dense than
    c. The same density as
    d. Another name for

33. The inner core of an optical fiber is _____ in composition.
    a. Glass or plastic
    b. Copper
    c. Bimetallic
    d. Liquid

34. Optical fibers, unlike wire media, are highly resistant to _____.
    a. High-frequency transmission
    b. Low-frequency transmission
    c. Electromagnetic interference
    d. Refraction

35. When a beam of light travels through media of two different densities, if the angle of incidence is greater than the critical angle, _____ occurs.
    a. Reflection
    b. Refraction
    c. Incidence
    d. Criticism

36. When the angle of incidence is _____ the critical angle, the light beam bends along the interface.
    a. More than
    b. Less than
    c. Equal to
    d. None of the above

37. In _____ propagation, the beam of propagated light is almost horizontal, and the low-density core has a small diameter compared to the cores of the other propagation modes.
    a. Multimode step-index
    b. Multimode graded-index
    c. Multimode single-index
    d. Single-mode

38. _____ is the propagation method subject to the greatest distortion.
    a. Multimode step-index
    b. Multimode graded-index
    c. Multimode single-index
    d. Single-mode

39. In _____ propagation, the core is of varying densities.
    a. Multimode step-index
    b. Multimode graded-index
    c. Multimode single-index
    d. Single-mode
40. When we talk about unguided media, usually we are referring to _____.
    a. Metallic wires
    b. Nonmetallic wires
    c. The air
    d. None of the above
41. Radio wave and microwave frequencies range from _____.
    a. 3 to 300 KHz
    b. 300 KHz to 3 GHz
    c. 3 KHz to 300 GHz
    d. 3 KHz to 3000 GHz
42. In _____ propagation, low-frequency radio waves hug the earth.
    a. Ground
    b. Sky
    c. Line of sight
    d. Space
43. The VLF and LF bands use _____ propagation for communications.
    a. Ground
    b. Sky
    c. Line of sight
    d. Space
44. A parabolic dish antenna is a(n) _____ antenna.
    a. Omnidirectional
    b. Bidirectional
    c. Unidirectional
    d. Horn
45. The _____ is an association that sponsors the use of infrared waves.
    a. IrDA
    b. EIA
    c. FCC
    d. PUD

Exercises

46. A beam of light moves from one medium to another, less dense medium. The critical angle is 60°. Draw the path of the light through both media when the

angle of incidence is

a. 40°

b. 50°

c. 60°

d. 70°

e. 80°

47. A twisted-pair cable has an attenuation of 2 dB/km at 1 KHz. What is the attenuation for 20 km?

48. How can we infer from Figure 7.6 that the bandwidth of a twisted-pair cable is related to distance?

49. How can we infer from Figure 7.9 that the bandwidth of a coaxial cable is related to distance?

50. Can we infer from Figure 7.16 that the bandwidth of a fiber is related to distance?

51. If the speed of light in fiber is 2×10^8 m/sec, what is the bandwidth of a fiber that passes light from 1000 nm to 1500 nm without significant loss in magnitude?

CHAPTER 8

Circuit Switching and Telephone Network

Whenever we have multiple devices, we have the problem of how to connect them to make one-to-one communication possible. One solution is to install a **point-to-point connection** between each pair of devices (a mesh topology) or between a central device and every other device (a star topology). These methods, however, are impractical and wasteful when applied to very large networks. The number and length of the links require too much infrastructure to be cost-efficient, and the majority of those links would be idle most of the time. Imagine a network of six devices: A, B, C, D, E, and F. If device A has point-to-point links to devices B, C, D, E, and F, then when only A and B are connected, the links connecting A to each of the other devices are idle and wasted.

Other topologies employing multipoint connections, such as a bus, are ruled out because the distances between devices and the total number of devices increase beyond the capacities of the media and equipment.

A better solution is switching. A switched network consists of a series of inter-linked nodes, called **switches.** Switches are hardware and/or software devices capable of creating temporary connections between two or more devices linked to the switch but not to each other. In a switched network, some of these nodes are connected to the communicating devices. Others are used only for routing.

Traditionally, three methods of switching have been important: circuit switching, packet switching, and message switching.

In this chapter, we discuss circuit switching, which normally takes place in the physical layer. We then discuss an application of circuit switching, the telephone network.

8.1   CIRCUIT SWITCHING

Circuit switching creates a direct physical connection between two devices such as phones or computers. For example, in Figure 8.1, instead of point-to-point connections between the three telephones on the left (A, B, and C) to the four telephones on the right (D, E, F, and G), requiring 12 links, we can use four switches to reduce the number and the total length of the links. In Figure 8.1, telephone A is connected through switches I,

II, and III to telephone D. By moving the levers of the switches, any telephone on the left can be connected to any telephone on the right.

Figure 8.1 *Circuit-switched network*

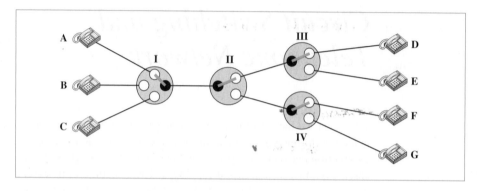

A circuit switch is a device with n inputs and m outputs that creates a temporary connection between an input link and an output link (see Fig. 8.2). The number of inputs does not have to match the number of outputs.

Figure 8.2 *A circuit switch*

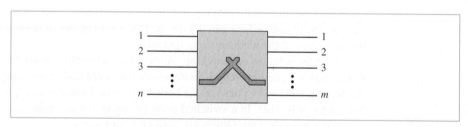

An n-by-n folded switch can connect n lines in full-duplex mode. For example, it can connect n telephones in such a way that each phone can be connected to every other phone (see Fig. 8.3).

Figure 8.3 *A folded switch*

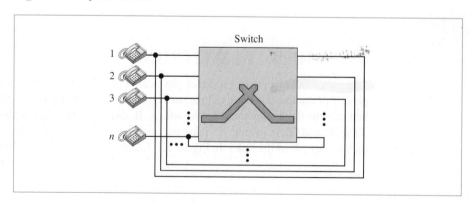

Circuit switching today can use either of two technologies: the space-division switch or the time-division switch.

Space-Division Switch

In **space-division switching,** the paths in the circuit are separated from each other spatially. This technology was originally designed for use in analog networks but is used currently in both analog and digital networks. It has evolved through a long history of many designs.

Crossbar Switch

A **crossbar switch** connects n inputs to m outputs in a grid, using electronic micro-switches (transistors) at each **crosspoint** (see Fig. 8.4). The major limitation of this design is the number of crosspoints required. Connecting n inputs to m outputs using a crossbar switch requires $n \times m$ crosspoints. For example, to connect 1000 inputs to 1000 outputs requires a crossbar with 1,000,000 crosspoints. A crossbar with this number of crosspoints is impractical. Such a switch is also inefficient because statistics show that, in practice, fewer than 25 percent of the crosspoints are in use at any given time. The rest are idle.

Figure 8.4   *Crossbar switch*

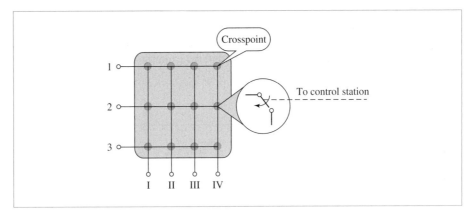

Multistage Switch

The solution to the limitations of the crossbar switch is the **multistage switch,** which combines crossbar switches in several stages. In multistage switching, devices are linked to switches that, in turn, are linked to other switches (see Fig. 8.5).

The design of a multistage switch depends on the number of stages and the number of switches required (or desired) in each stage. Normally, the middle stages have fewer switches than do the first and last stages. For example, imagine that we want a multi-stage switch as in Figure 8.5 to do the job of a single 15-by-15 crossbar switch. Assume that we have decided on a three-stage design that uses three switches in the first and final

Figure 8.5 *Multistage switch*

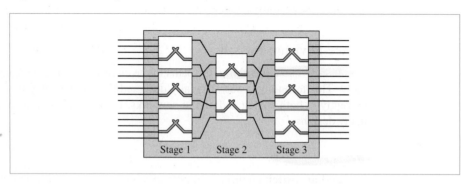

stages and two switches in the middle stage. Because there are three of them, each of the first-stage switches has inputs from one-third of the input devices, giving them five inputs each ($5 \times 3 = 15$).

Next, each of the first-stage switches must have an output to each of the intermediate switches. There are two intermediate switches; therefore, each first-stage switch has two outputs. Each third-stage switch must have inputs from each of the intermediate switches; two intermediate switches means two inputs. The intermediate switches must connect to all three first-stage switches and all three last-stage switches, and so must have three inputs and three outputs each.

Multiple Paths Multistage switches provide several options for connecting each pair of linked devices. Figure 8.6 shows two ways traffic can move from an input to an output using the switch designed in the example above.

Figure 8.6 *Switching path*

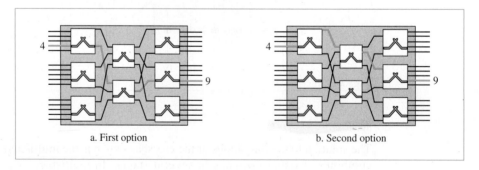

In Figure 8.6*a*, a pathway is established between input line 4 and output line 9. In this instance, the path uses the lower intermediate switch and that switch's center output line to reach the last-stage switch connected to line 9. Figure 8.6*b* shows a pathway between the same input line 4 and the same output line 9 using the upper intermediate switch.

Let us compare the number of crosspoints in a 15-by-15 single-stage crossbar switch with the 15-by-15 multistage switch that we described above. In the single-stage switch, we need 225 crosspoints (15 × 15). In the multistage switch, we need

■ Three first-stage switches, each with 10 crosspoints (5 × 2), for a total of 30 crosspoints at the first stage.

■ Two second-stage switches, each with 9 crosspoints (3 × 3), for a total of 18 crosspoints at the second stage.

■ Three third-stage switches, each with 10 crosspoints (5 × 2), for a total of 30 crosspoints at the last stage.   *30 → 18 → 30*

The total number of crosspoints required by our multistage switch is 78. In this example, the multistage switch requires only 35 percent as many crosspoints as the single-stage switch.

Blocking   This savings comes at a cost, however. The reduction in the number of crosspoints results in a phenomenon called **blocking** during periods of heavy traffic. Blocking refers to times when one input cannot be connected to an output because there is no path available between them—all the possible intermediate switches are occupied.

In a single-stage switch, blocking does not occur. Because every combination of input and output has its own crosspoint, there is always a path. (Cases where two inputs are trying to contact the same output don't count. That path is not blocked; the output is merely busy.) In the multistage switch described in the example above, however, only two of the first five inputs can use the switch at a time, only two of the second five inputs can use the switch at a time, and so on. The small number of outputs at the middle stage further increases the restriction on the number of available links.

In large systems, such as those having 10,000 inputs and outputs, the number of stages can be increased to cut down the number of crosspoints required. As the number of stages increases, however, possible blocking increases as well. Many people have experienced blocking on public telephone systems in the wake of a natural disaster when calls being made to check on or reassure relatives far outnumber the regular load of the system. In those cases, it is often impossible to get a connection. Under normal circumstances, however, blocking is not usually a problem. In countries that can afford it, the number of switches between lines is calculated to make blocking unlikely. The formula for finding this number is based on statistical analysis, which is beyond the scope of this book.

Time-Division Switch

Time-division switching uses time-division multiplexing to achieve switching. There are two popular methods used in time-division multiplexing: the time-slot interchange and the TDM bus.

Time-Slot Interchange (TSI)

Figure 8.7 shows a system connecting four input lines to four output lines. Imagine that each input line wants to send data to an output line according to the following pattern:

1 ⟶ 3   2 ⟶ 4   3 ⟶ 1   4 ⟶ 2

Figure 8.7   *Time-division multiplexing, without and with a time-slot interchange*

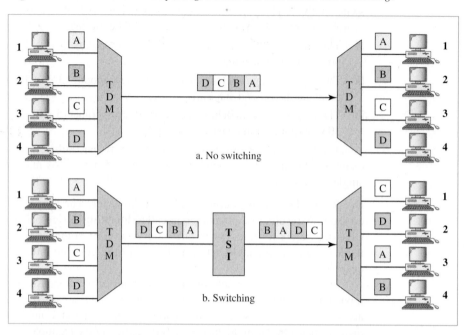

Figure 8.7a shows the results of ordinary time-division multiplexing. As you can see, the desired task is not accomplished. Data are output in the same order as they are input. Data from 1 go to 1, from 2 go to 2, from 3 go to 3, and from 4 go to 4.

In Figure 8.7b, however, we insert a device called a **time-slot interchange (TSI)** into the link. A TSI changes the ordering of the slots based on the desired connections. In this case, it changes the order of data from A, B, C, D to C, D, A, B. Now, when the demultiplexer separates the slots, it passes them to the proper outputs.

How a TSI works is shown in Figure 8.8. A TSI consists of random access memory (RAM) with several memory locations. The size of each location is the same as the

Figure 8.8   *Time-slot interchange*

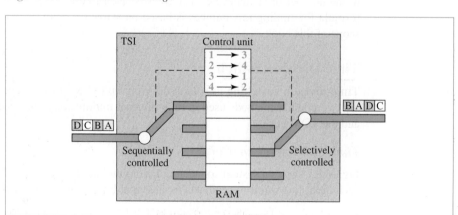

size of a single time slot. The number of locations is the same as the number of inputs (in most cases, the numbers of inputs and outputs are equal). The RAM fills up with incoming data from time slots in the order received. Slots are then sent out in an order based on the decisions of a control unit.

TDM Bus

Figure 8.9 shows a very simplified version of a **TDM bus.** The input and output lines are connected to a high-speed bus through input and output gates (microswitches). Each input gate is closed during one of the four time slots. During the same time slot, only one output gate is also closed. This pair of gates allows a burst of data to be transferred from one specific input line to one specific output line using the bus. The control unit opens and closes the gates according to switching need. For example, in the figure, at the first time slot, input gate 1 and output gate 3 will be closed; during the second time slot, input gate 2 and output gate 4 will be closed; and so on.

A folded TDM bus can be made with duplex lines (input and output) and dual gates.

Figure 8.9 *TDM bus*

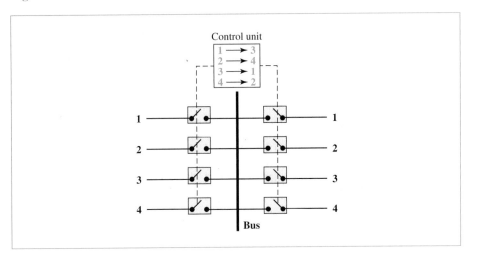

Space- and Time-Division Switch Combinations

When we compare space-division and time-division switching, some interesting facts emerge. The advantage of space-division switching is that it is instantaneous. Its disadvantage is the number of crosspoints required to make space-division switching acceptable in terms of blocking.

The advantage of time-division switching is that it needs no crosspoints. Its disadvantage, in the case of TSI, is that processing each connection creates delays. Each time slot must be stored by the RAM, then retrieved and passed on.

In a third option, we combine space-division and time-division technology to take advantage of the best of both. Combining the two results in switches that are optimized both physically (the number of crosspoints) and temporally (the amount of delay). Multi-stage switches of this sort can be designed as time-space-time (TST), time-space-space-time (TSST), space-time-time-space (STTS), or other possible combinations.

Figure 8.10 shows a simple TST switch that consists of two time stages and one space stage and has 12 inputs and 12 outputs. Instead of one time-division switch, it divides the inputs into three groups (of four inputs each) and directs them to three time-slot interchanges. The result in this case is that the average delay is one-third of that which would result from using one time-slot interchange to handle all 12 inputs.

Figure 8.10   *TST switch*

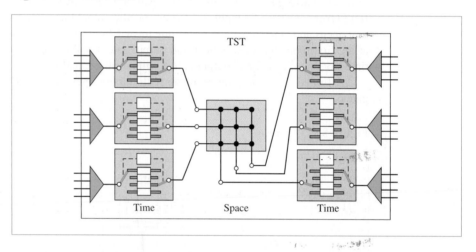

The last stage is a mirror image of the first stage. The middle stage is a space-division switch (crossbar) that connects the TSI groups to allow connectivity between all possible input and output pairs (e.g., to connect input 3 of the first group to output 7 of the second group).

8.2   TELEPHONE NETWORK

Telephone networks use circuit switching. The telephone network had its beginnings in the late 1800s. The entire network, which is referred to as the plain old telephone system (POTS), was originally an analog system using analog signals to transmit voice. With the advent of the computer era, the network, in the 1980s, began to carry data in addition to voice. During the last decade, the telephone network has undergone many technical changes. The network is now digital as well as analog.

Major Components

The telephone network, as shown in Figure 8.11, is made of three major components: local loops, trunks, and switching offices. The telephone network has several levels of switching offices such as end offices, tandem offices, and regional offices.

Figure 8.11   *A telephone system*

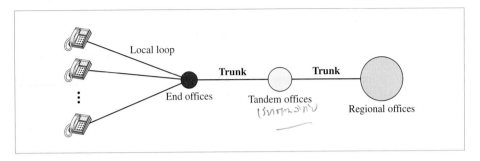

Local Loops

One component of the telephone network is the **local loop,** a twisted-pair cable that connects the subscriber telephone to the nearest **end office** or local central office. The local loop, when used for voice, has a bandwidth of 4000 Hz (4 KHz). It is interesting to examine the telephone number associated with each local loop. The first three digits of a local telephone number define the office, and the next four digits define the local loop number.

Trunks

Trunks are transmission media that handle the communication between offices. A trunk normally handles hundreds or thousands of connections through multiplexing. Transmission is usually through optical fibers or satellite links.

Switching Offices

To avoid having a permanent physical link between any two subscribers, the telephone company has switches located in a **switching office.** A switch connects several local loops or trunks and allows a connection between different subscribers.

LATAs

After the divestiture of 1984 (see *A Brief History* section), the United States of America was divided into more than 200 **local access transport areas (LATAs).** The number of LATAs has increased since then. A LATA can be a small or large metropolitan area. A small state may have one single LATA; a large state may have several LATAs. A LATA boundary may overlap the boundary of a state; part of a LATA can be in one state, part in another state.

Intra-LATA Services

The services offered by the **common carriers** (telephone companies) inside a LATA are called intra-LATA services. The carrier that handles these services is called a **local exchange carrier (LEC).** Before the Telecommunications Act of 1996, intra-LATA services were granted to one single carrier. This was a monopoly. After 1996, more than one carrier could provide services inside a LATA. The carrier that provided services before 1996 owns the cabling system (local loops) and is called the **incumbent** local exchange carrier (ILEC). The new carriers that can provide services are called competitive local exchange carriers (CLECs). To avoid the costs of new cabling, it was agreed that the ILECs would continue to provide the main services, and the CLECs would provide other services such as mobile telephone service, toll calls inside a LATA, and so on. Figure 8.12 shows a LATA and switching offices.

> Intra-LATA services are provided by local exchange carriers. Since 1996, there are two types of LECs: incumbent local exchange carriers and competitive local exchange carriers.

Figure 8.12   *Switching offices in a LATA*

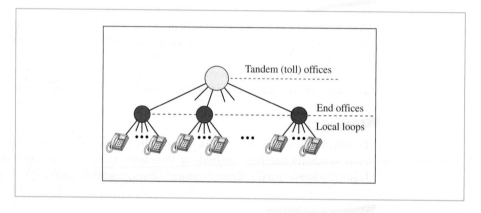

Communication inside a LATA is handled by end switches and tandem switches. A call that can be completed by using only end offices is considered toll-free. A call that has to go through a tandem office (intra-LATA toll office) is charged.

Inter-LATA Services

The services between LATAs are handled by **interexchange carriers (IXCs).** These carriers, sometimes called **long-distance companies,** provide communication services between two customers in different LATAs. After the act of 1996, these services can be provided by any carrier, including those involved in intra-LATA services. The field is wide open. Carriers providing inter-LATA services include AT&T, MCI, WorldCom, Sprint, and Verizon.

The IXCs are long-distance carriers that provide general data communications services including telephone service. A telephone call going through an IXC is normally digitized, with the carriers using several types of networks to provide service.

Points of Presence (POPs)

As we discussed, intra-LATA services can be provided by several LECs (one ILEC and possibly more than one CLEC). We also said that inter-LATA services can be provided by several IXCs. How do these carriers interact with one another? The answer is a switching office called a **point of presence (POP).** Each IXC that wants to provide inter-LATA services in a LATA must have a POP in that LATA. The LECs that provide services inside the LATA must provide connections so that every subscriber can have access to all POPs. Figure 8.13 illustrates the concept.

Figure 8.13 *POPs*

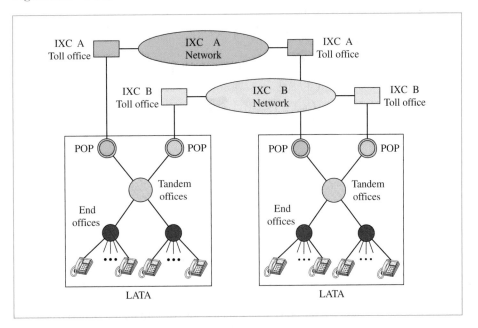

A subscriber who needs to make a connection with another subscriber is connected first to an end switch and then, either directly or through a tandem switch, to a POP. The call now goes from the POP of an IXC (the one the subscriber has chosen) in the source LATA to the POP of the same IXC in the destination LATA. The call will be passed through the toll office of the IXC and is carried through the network provided by the IXC.

Making a Connection

Subscriber telephones are connected, through local loops, to end offices (or central offices).

Accessing the switching station at the end offices is accomplished through dialing. In the past, telephones featured rotary or pulse dialing, in which a digital signal was sent to the end office for each number dialed. This type of dialing was prone to errors due to the inconsistency of humans during the dialing process.

Today, dialing is accomplished through the touch-tone technique. In this method, instead of sending a digital signal, the user sends two small bursts of analog signals, called *dual tone*. The frequency of the signals sent depends on the row and column of the pressed pad.

Figure 8.14 *Rotary and touch-tone dialing*

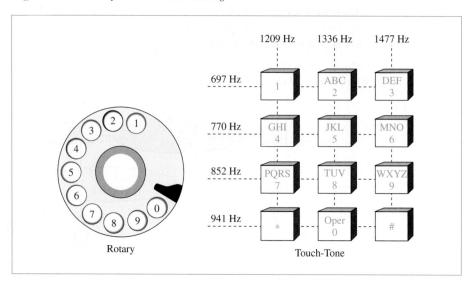

Rotary

Touch-Tone

Figure 8.14 shows a **rotary** and a **touch-tone dialing** system. In Figure 8.14, if a user has a rotary telephone, the number 8 is represented by a digital signal. On the other hand, if a user has a touch-tone telephone, two bursts of analog signals with frequencies 852 and 1336 Hz are sent to the end office.

> **Voice communication used analog signals in the past, but is now moving to digital signals. On the other hand, dialing started with digital signals (rotary) and is now moving to analog signals (touch-tone).**

Analog Services

Early on, telephone companies provided their subscribers with analog services. These services still continue today. We can categorize these services as either analog switched services or analog leased services.

Analog Switched Service

Analog switched service is the familiar dial-up service most often encountered when a home telephone is used. The signal on a local loop is analog, and the bandwidth is usually between 0 and 4000 Hz. With switched lines, when the caller dials a number, the call is conveyed to a switch, or series of switches, at the exchange. The appropriate switches are then activated to link the caller's line to that of the person being called. The switch connects the two lines for the duration of the call.

The LECs and IXCs provide optional services for their residential and business customers. We discuss the most common.

Local Call Services A **local call service** is normally provided for a flat monthly rate, although in some LATAs, the carrier charges for each call or a set of calls. The rationale for a non-flat-rate charge is to provide cheaper service for those customers who do not make many calls.

Toll Call Services A **toll call** can be intra-LATA or inter-LATA. If the LATA is geographically large, a call may go through a tandem office (toll office) and the subscriber will pay a fee for the call. The inter-LATA calls are long-distance calls and are charged as such.

800 Services If a subscriber (normally an organization) needs to provide free connections for other subscribers (normally customers), it can request an **800 service** (also 888, 877, 866 because 800 numbers are already exhausted). In this case, the call is free for the caller, but it is paid by the callee. An organization uses this service to encourage customers to call. The rate is less expensive than a normal long-distance call.

WATS The **wide-area telephone service (WATS)** is the opposite of 800/888 service. The latter are inbound calls paid by the organization; the former are outbound calls paid by the organization. This service is a less expensive alternative to regular toll calls; charges are based on the number of calls. The service can be specified as outbound calls to the same state, to several states, or to the whole country, with rates charged accordingly.

900 Services The **900 services** are like 800/888 services, in that they are inbound calls to a subscriber. However, unlike 800/888 services, the call is paid by the caller and is normally much more expensive than a normal long-distance call. The reason is that the carrier charges two fees; the first is the long-distance toll, and the second is the fee paid to the callee for each call. This service is used by an organization that needs to charge customers for its services. For example, a software company may need to charge a customer for technical support.

Analog Leased Service

An **analog leased service** offers customers the opportunity to lease a line, sometimes called a dedicated line, that is permanently connected to another customer. Although the connection still passes through the switches in the telephone network, subscribers experience it as a single line because the switch is always closed; no dialing is needed.

Digital Services

Recently telephone companies began offering **digital services** to their subscribers. Digital services are less sensitive than analog services to noise and other forms of interference. The two most common digital services are switched/56 and digital data service (DDS). We have already discussed high-speed digital services, the T lines, in Chapter 6. We discuss residential high-speed access in Chapter 9.

Switched/56 Service

Switched/56 service is the digital version of an analog switched line. It is a switched digital service that allows data rates of up to 56 Kbps. To communicate through this service, both parties must subscribe. A caller with normal telephone service cannot connect to a telephone or computer with switched/56 even if using a modem. On the whole, digital and analog services represent two completely different domains for the telephone companies.

Because the line in a switched/56 service is already digital, subscribers do not need modems to transmit digital data. However, they do need another device called a **digital service unit (DSU).** This device changes the rate of the digital data created by the subscriber's device to 56 Kbps and encodes them in the format used by the service provider. Switched/56 supports bandwidth on demand, allowing subscribers to obtain higher speeds by using more than one line (see the section on inverse multiplexing in Chapter 6). This option allows switched/56 to support video conferencing, fast facsimile, multimedia, and fast data transfer, among other services.

Digital Data Service (DDS)

Digital data service (DDS) is the digital version of an analog leased line; it is a digital leased line with a maximum data rate of 64 Kbps.

A Brief History

Before we leave this topic, let us review the history of telephone companies. The history of common carriers in the United States can be divided into three eras: prior to 1984, between 1984 and 1996, and after 1996.

Before 1984

Before 1984, almost all local and long-distance services were provided by the AT&T Bell System. In 1970, the U.S. government, believing that the Bell System was monopolizing the telephone service industry, sued the company. The verdict was in the favor of the government, and based on a document called the Modified Final Judgment (MFJ), beginning on January 1, 1984, AT&T was broken into AT&T Long Lines, 23 Bell Operating Companies (BOCs), and others. The 23 BOCs were grouped together to make several Regional Bell Operating Systems (RBOCs). This landmark event, the AT&T divestiture of 1984, was beneficial to customers of telephone services. Telephone rates were lower.

Between 1984 and 1996

The divestiture divided the country into more than 200 LATAs; some companies were allowed to provide services inside a LATA (LECs) and others were allowed to provide services between LATAs (IXCs). Competition, particularly between long-distance carriers, increased as new companies were formed. However, no LEC could provide long-distance services, and no IXCs could provide local services.

After 1996

Another major change in telecommunications occurred in 1996. The Telecommunications Act of 1996 combined the different services provided by different companies under the umbrella of telecommunication services; this included local services, long-distance voice and data services, video services, and so on. In addition, the act allowed any company to provide any of these services at the local and long-distance levels. In other words, a common carrier company provides services both inside the LATA and between the LATAs. However, to prevent the recabling of residents, the carrier that was given intra-LATA services (ILEC) continues to provide the main services; the new competitors (CLECs) provide other services.

8.3 KEY TERMS

800 service	local exchange carrier (LEC)
900 service	local loop
analog leased service	long-distance company
analog switched service	multistage switch
blocking	point-to-point connection
circuit switching	point of presence (POP)
common carrier	rotary dialing
competitive local exchange carrier (CLEC)	space-division switching
crossbar switch	switch
crosspoint	switched/56 service
digital data service (DDS)	switching office
digital service	TDM bus
digital service unit (DSU)	time-division switching
end office	time-slot interchange (TSI)
incumbent local exchange carrier (ILEC)	toll call service
interexchange carrier (IXC)	touch-tone dialing
local access and transport area (LATA)	trunk
local call service	wide-area telephone service (WATS)

8.4 SUMMARY

❏ Switching is a method in which communication devices are connected to one another efficiently.

❏ A switch is intermediary hardware or software that links devices together temporarily.

❏ There are three fundamental switching methods: circuit switching, packet switching, and message switching.

❏ In circuit switching, a direct physical connection between two devices is created by space-division switches, time-division switches, or both.

❏ In a space-division switch, the path from one device to another is spatially separate from other paths.

❏ A crossbar is the most common space-division switch. It connects n inputs to m outputs via $n \times m$ crosspoints.

❏ Multistage switches can reduce the number of crosspoints needed, but blocking may result.

❏ Blocking occurs when not every input has its own unique path to every output.

❏ In a time-division switch, the inputs are divided in time, using TDM. A control unit sends the input to the correct output device.

❏ The time-slot interchange and the TDM bus are two types of time-division switches.

❏ Space- and time-division switches may be combined.

❏ A telephone network is an example of a circuit-switched network.

❏ A telephone system has three major components: local loops, trunks, and switching offices.

❏ The United States is divided into more than 200 local access and transport areas (LATAs).

❏ Intra-LATA services are provided by incumbent local exchange carriers (ILECs) and competitive local exchange carriers (CLECs). Inter-LATA services are handled by interexchange carriers (IXCs).

❏ Telephone companies provide analog switched services such as local calls, toll calls, 800/888 services, WATS, and 900 services.

❏ Telephone companies provide digital services such as switched/56 services and digital data services.

❏ The AT&T monopoly was broken in 1984 through a government suit.

8.5 PRACTICE SET

Review Questions

1. What are the three major switching methods?
2. What are two types of switches used in circuit switching?
3. What is a crosspoint in a crossbar switch?
4. What is the limiting factor in a crossbar switch? How does a multistage switch alleviate the problem?
5. How is blocking related to a crossbar switch?
6. How is blocking related to a multistage switch?
7. Compare the mechanism of a space-division switch to the mechanism of a time-division switch.
8. Name the two technologies used in a time-division switch.
9. Compare a TSI to a TDM bus.
10. What is the function of the control unit in a TSI and a TDM bus?
11. How is space-division switching superior to time-division switching?
12. How is time-division switching superior to space-division switching?
13. What are the three main components of a telephone system?
14. What is the local loop?
15. What is the bandwidth of a traditional telephone line?
16. What is the function of a trunk?

17. How is an ILEC different from a CLEC?
18. What is the function of a POP?
19. How are telephone services between LATAs handled?
20. Compare the signals used in rotary dialing with the signals used in touch-tone dialing.
21. How does 800 service differ from 900 service?
22. What is the difference between an analog switched service and an analog leased service?
23. What is the function of a DSU?

Multiple-Choice Questions

24. The _____ is a device that connects *n* inputs to *m* outputs.
    a. Crosspoint
    b. Crossbar
    c. Modem
    d. RAM

25. How many crosspoints are needed in a single-stage switch with 40 inputs and 50 outputs?
    a. 40
    b. 50
    c. 90
    d. 2000

26. In a crossbar with 1000 crosspoints, approximately how many are in use at any time?
    a. 100
    b. 250
    c. 500
    d. 1000

27. The _____ of a TSI controls the order of delivery of slot values that are stored in RAM.
    a. Crossbar
    b. Crosspoint
    c. Control unit
    d. Transceiver

28. In _____ circuit switching, delivery of data is delayed because data must be stored and retrieved from RAM.
    a. Space-division
    b. Time-division
    c. Virtual
    d. Packet

29. To create a _____, combine crossbar switches in stages.
    a. Multistage switch
    b. Crosspoint
    c. Packet switch
    d. TSI

30. Which of the following is a time-division switch?
    a. TSI
    b. TDM bus
    c. Crosspoint
    d. (a) and (b)

31. In a time-division switch, a _____ governs the destination of a packet stored in RAM.
    a. TDM bus
    b. Crosspoint
    c. Crossbar
    d. Control unit

32. A telephone network is an example of a _____ network.
    a. Packet-switched
    b. Circuit-switched
    c. Message-switched
    d. None of the above

33. The local loop has _____ cable that connects the subscriber telephone to the nearest end office.
    a. Twisted-pair
    b. Coaxial
    c. Fiber-optic
    d. (b) and (c)

34. Trunks are transmission media such as _____ that handle the telephone communication between offices.
    a. Twisted-pair cable
    b. Fiber-optic cable
    c. Satellite links
    d. (b) and (c)

35. The established telephone company that provided services in a LATA before 1966 and owns the cabling system is called _____.
    a. An ILEC
    b. A CLEC
    c. An IXC
    d. A POP

36. A new telephone company that provides services in a LATA after 1966 is called
    _____.
    a. An ILEC
    b. A CLEC
    c. An IXC
    d. A POP

37. The telephone service handled between two LATAs is called _____.
    a. An ILEC
    b. A CLEC
    c. An IXC
    d. A POP

38. If the end office receives two bursts of analog signals with frequencies of 697 and
    1477 Hz, then the number _____ has been punched.
    a. 1
    b. 2
    c. 3
    d. 4

39. Data from a computer are _____; the local loop handles _____ signals.
    a. Analog; analog
    b. Analog; digital
    c. Digital; digital
    d. Digital; analog

40. A traditional telephone line has a bandwidth of _____.
    a. 2000 Hz
    b. 4000 Hz
    c. 2000 MHz
    d. 4000 MHz

Exercises

41. How many crosspoints are needed if we use a crossbar switch to connect 1000 tele-
    phones in a small town?

42. In Figure 8.15, find the number of crosspoints needed.

43. How many crosspoints are needed if we use only one crossbar switch in Fig-
    ure 8.15?

44. Using Exercises 42 and 43, how much is the efficiency improved if we use three
    stages instead of one?

45. In Figure 8.15, how many users connected to each first-stage switch can access the
    system at the same time? How many total users can access the whole system? Is

Figure 8.15 *Exercises 42, 43, 45, and 46*

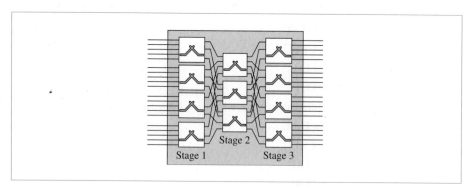

there any relationship between the first and the second answers? Can you say that the second answer can be obtained from the first answer?

46. In Figure 8.15, can we alleviate the blocking problem by adding more second-stage switches?

47. Which of the three-stage switches in Figure 8.16 has a better performance in terms of blocking? Justify your answer. Find the number of input/output connections for the middle switches.

Figure 8.16 *Exercise 47*

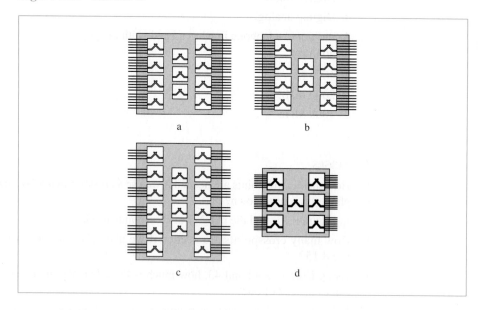

48. What is the formula to find, in a three-stage crossbar switch, the number of cross-points n in terms of the number of input/output lines N, the number of first- and third-stage switches K, and the number of second-stage switches L?

49. In Figure 8.9, what goes to the output lines if the input lines receive A, B, C, and D?

50. Design a folded TDM bus with four lines.

51. Design a TSSST switch with 48 inputs and 48 outputs. The input multiplexers should be 4×1; the output multiplexers should be 1×4.

52. Design an STS switch with 10 inputs and 10 outputs. The first-stage switches should be 5×2, and the last-stage switches should be 2×5.

CHAPTER 9

High-Speed Digital Access: DSL, Cable Modems, and SONET

We discussed in Chapter 5 how modems create a digital signal so that subscribers can access the Internet through their telephones. Traditional modems impose an upper limit on the data rate available for this type of access. In this chapter, we discuss three dominant technologies that surpass the limit of traditional modems: the DSL technology, cable modem, and SONET.

9.1 DSL TECHNOLOGY

After traditional modems reached their peak data rate, telephone companies developed another technology, DSL, to provide higher-speed access to the Internet. **Digital subscriber line (DSL)** technology is one of the most promising for supporting high-speed digital communication over the existing local loops. DSL technology is a set of technologies, each differing in the first letter (ADSL, VDSL, HDSL, and SDSL). The set is often referred to as *x*DSL, where *x* can be replaced by A, V, H, or S.

ADSL

The first technology in the set is **asymmetrical DSL (ADSL).** ADSL, like a 56K modem, provides higher speed (bit rate) in the downstream direction (from the Internet to the resident) than in the upstream direction (from the resident to the Internet). That is the reason it is called asymmetric. Unlike the asymmetry in 56K modems, the designers of ADSL specifically divided the available bandwidth of the local loop unevenly for the residential customer. The service is not suitable for business customers who need a large bandwidth in both directions.

> **ADSL is an asymmetric communication technology designed for residential users; it is not suitable for businesses.**

Using Existing Local Loops

One interesting point is that ADSL uses the existing local loop. But how does ADSL reach a data rate that was never achieved with traditional modems? The answer is that

219

the twisted-pair local loop is actually capable of handling bandwidths up to 1.1 MHz, but the filter installed at the end of the line by the telephone company limits the bandwidth to 4 KHz (sufficient for voice communication). This was done to allow the multiplexing of a large number of voice channels. If the filter is removed, however, the entire 1.1 MHz is available for data and voice communications.

> **The existing local loops can handle bandwidths up to 1.1 MHz.**

Adaptive Technology

Unfortunately, 1.1 MHz is just the theoretical bandwidth of the local loop. Factors such as the distance between the residence and the switching office, the size of the cable, the signaling used, and so on affect the bandwidth. The designers of ADSL technology were aware of this problem and used an adaptive technology that tests the condition and bandwidth availability of the line before settling on a data rate. The data rate of ADSL is not fixed; it changes based on the condition and type of the local loop cable.

> **ADSL is an adaptive technology. The system uses a data rate based on the condition of the local loop line.**

DMT

The modulation technique that has become standard for ADSL is called the **discrete multitone technique (DMT)** which combines QAM and FDM. There is no set way that the bandwidth of a system is divided. Each system can decide on its bandwidth division. Typically, an available bandwidth of 1.104 MHz is divided into 256 channels. Each channel uses a bandwidth of 4.312 KHz, as shown in Figure 9.1.

Figure 9.1   *DMT*

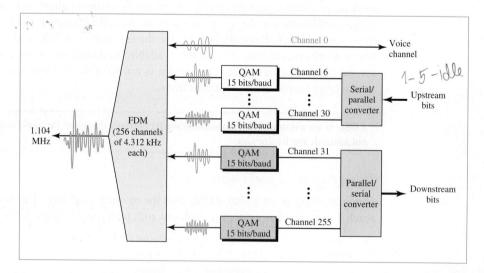

Figure 9.2 shows how the bandwidth can be divided into the following:

- **Voice.** Channel 0 is reserved for voice communication.
- **Idle.** Channels 1 to 5 are not used, to allow a gap between voice and data communication.
- **Upstream data and control.** Channels 6 to 30 (25 channels) are used for upstream data transfer and control. One channel is for control, and 24 channels are for data transfer. If there are 24 channels, each using 4 KHz (out of 4.312 KHz available) with QAM modulation, we have $24 \times 4000 \times 15$, or a 1.44-Mbps bandwidth, in the upstream direction.
- **Downstream data and control.** Channels 31 to 255 (225 channels) are used for downstream data transfer and control. One channel is for control, and 224 channels are for data. If there are 224 channels, we can achieve up to $224 \times 4000 \times 15$, or 13.4 Mbps.

Figure 9.2 *Bandwidth division*

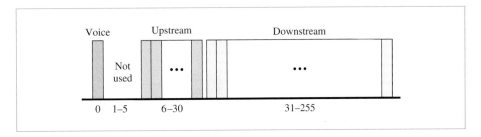

Actual Bit Rate

Because of the high signal/noise ratio, the actual bit rate is much lower than the above-mentioned rate. The bit rates are normally as follows:

Upstream: 64 Kbps to 1 Mbps
Downstream: 500 Kbps to 8 Mbps

downstream > upstream

Customer Site: ADSL modem

Figure 9.3 shows an ADSL modem installed at a customer's site. The local loop connects to the filter which separates voice and data communication. The ADSL modem modulates the data, using DMT, and creates downstream and upstream channels.

Telephone Company Site: DSLAM

At the telephone company site, the situation is different. Instead of an ADSL modem, a device called a **digital subscriber line access multiplexer (DSLAM)** is installed that functions similarly to ADSL. In addition, it packetizes the data to be sent to the Internet (ISP server). Figure 9.4 shows the configuration.

Figure 9.3   *ADSL modem*

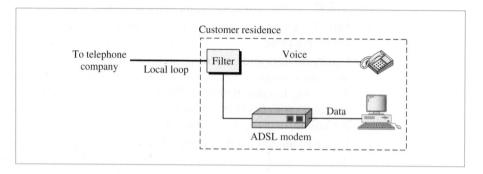

Figure 9.4   *DSLAM*

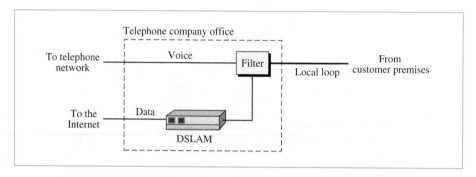

Other DSL Technologies

SDSL

ADSL provides asymmetric communication. The downstream bit rate is much higher than the upstream bit rate. Although this feature meets the needs of most residential subscribers, it is not suitable for businesses that send and receive data in large volumes in both directions. The **symmetric digital subscriber line (SDSL)** is designed for these types of businesses. It divides the available bandwidth equally between the downstream and upstream directions.

HDSL

The **high-bit-rate digital subscriber line (HDSL)** was designed as an alternative to the T-1 line (1.544 Mbps). The T-1 line uses alternate mark inversion (AMI) encoding, which is very susceptible to attenuation at high frequencies. This limits the length of a T-1 line to 1 km. For longer distances, a repeater is necessary, which means increased costs.

HDSL uses 2B1Q encoding (see Chapter 4), which is less susceptible to attenuation. A data rate of almost 2 Mbps can be achieved without repeaters up to a distance of 3.6 km. HDSL uses two twisted-pair wires to achieve full-duplex transmission.

VDSL

The **very-high-bit-rate digital subscriber line (VDSL),** an alternative approach that is similar to ADSL, uses coaxial, fiber-optic, or twisted-pair cable for short distances (300 to 1800 m). The modulating technique is DMT with a bit rate of 50 to 55 Mbps downstream and 1.5 to 2.5 Mbps upstream.

9.2   CABLE MODEM

Cable companies are now competing with telephone companies for the residential customer who wants high-speed access to the Internet. DSL technology provides high-data-rate connections for residential subscribers over the local loop. However, DSL uses the existing unshielded twisted-pair cable, which is very susceptible to interference. This imposes an upper limit on the data rate. Another solution is the use of the cable TV network. In this section, we briefly discuss this technology.

Traditional Cable Networks

Cable TV started to distribute broadcast video signals to locations with poor or no reception in the late 1940s. It was called **community antenna TV (CATV)** because an antenna at the top of a tall hill or building received the signals from the TV stations and distributed them, via coaxial cables, to the community. Figure 9.5 shows a schematic diagram of a traditional cable TV network.

Figure 9.5   *Traditional cable TV network*

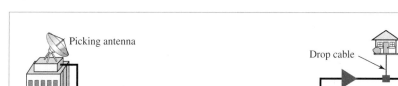

The cable TV office, called the **head end,** receives video signals from broadcasting stations and feeds the signals into coaxial cables. The signals became weaker and weaker, so amplifiers were installed through the network to amplify the signals. There could be up to 35 amplifiers between the head end and the subscriber premises. At the other end, splitters split the cable, and taps and drop cables make the connections to the subscriber premises.

The traditional cable TV system used coaxial cable end to end. Due to attenuation of the signals and the use of a large number of amplifiers, communication in the traditional network was unidirectional (one-way). Video signals were transmitted downstream, from the head end to the subscriber premises.

Communication in the traditional cable TV network is unidirectional.

HFC Network

The second generation of cable networks is called a **hybrid fiber-coaxial (HFC) network.** The network uses a combination of fiber-optic and coaxial cable. The transmission medium from the cable TV office to a box, called the **fiber node,** is optical fiber; from the fiber node through the neighborhood and into the house is still coaxial cable. Figure 9.6 shows a schematic diagram of an HFC network.

Figure 9.6   *HFC network*

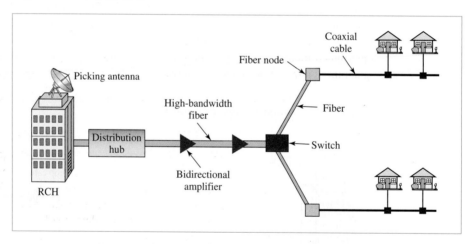

The **regional cable head (RCH)** normally serves up to 400,000 subscribers. The RCHs feed the **distribution hubs,** each of which serves up to 40,000 subscribers. The distribution hub plays an important role in the new infrastructure. Modulation and distribution of signals are done here; the signals are then fed to the fiber nodes through fiber-optic cables. The fiber node splits the analog signals so that the same signal is sent to each coaxial cable. Each coaxial cable serves up to 1000 subscribers. The use of fiber-optic cable reduces the need for amplifiers down to eight or less.

One reason for moving from traditional to hybrid infrastructure is to make the cable network bidirectional (two-way).

Communication in an HFC cable TV network can be bidirectional.

Bandwidth

Even in an HFC system, the last part of the network, from the fiber node to the sub-scriber premises, is still a coaxial cable. This coaxial cable has a bandwidth that ranges from 5 to 750 MHz (approximately). The cable company has divided this bandwidth into three bands: video, downstream data, and upstream data, as shown in Figure 9.7.

Figure 9.7   *Coaxial cable bands*

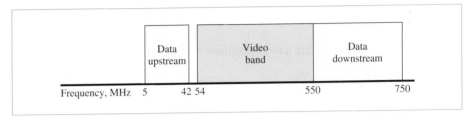

Video Band

The downstream-only **video band** occupies frequencies from 54 to 550 MHz. Since each TV channel occupies 6 MHz, this can accommodate more than 80 channels.

Downstream Data Band

The downstream data (from the Internet to the subscriber premises) occupies the upper band, from 550 to 750 MHz. This band is also divided into 6-MHz channels.

Modulation   Downstream data are modulated using the 64-QAM (or possibly 256-QAM) modulation technique.

Downstream data are modulated using the 64-QAM modulation technique.

Data Rate   There are 6 bits for each baud in 64-QAM. One bit is used for forward error correction; this leaves 5 bits of data per baud. The standard specifies 1 Hz for each baud; this means that, theoretically, downstream data can be received at 30 Mbps (5 bits/Hz × 6 MHz). The standard specifies only 27 Mbps. However, since the cable modem is connected to the computer through a 10base-T cable (see Chapter 14), this limits the data rate to 10 Mbps.

The theoretical downstream data rate is 30 Mbps.

Upstream Data Band

The upstream data (from the subscriber premises to the Internet) occupies the lower band, from 5 to 42 MHz. This band is also divided into 6-MHz channels.

Modulation   The **upstream data band** uses lower frequencies that are more suscepti-ble to noise and interference. For this reason, the QAM technique is not suitable for this band. A better solution is QPSK.

Upstream data are modulated using the QPSK modulation technique.

Data Rate   There are 2 bits for each baud in QPSK. The standard specifies 1 Hz for each baud; this means that, theoretically, downstream data can be sent at 12 Mbps (2 bits/Hz × 6 MHz). However, the data rate is usually less than 12 Mbps.

The theoretical upstream data rate is 12 Mbps.

Sharing

Both upstream and downstream bands are shared by the subscribers.

Upstream Sharing

The upstream data bandwidth is only 37 MHz. This means that there are only six 6-MHz channels available in the upstream direction. A subscriber needs to use one channel to send data in the upstream direction. The question is, How can six channels be shared in an area with 1000, 2000, or even 100,000 subscribers? The solution is timesharing. The band is divided into channels using FDM; these channels must be shared between subscribers in the same neighborhood. The cable provider allocates one channel, statically or dynamically, for a group of subscribers. If one subscriber wants to send data, she or he contends for the channel with others who want access; the subscriber must wait until the channel is available.

Downstream Sharing

We have a similar situation in the downstream direction. The downstream band has 33 channels of 6 MHz. A cable provider probably has more than 33 subscribers; therefore, each channel must be shared between a group of subscribers. However, the situation is different for the downstream direction; here we have a multicasting situation. If there are data for any of the subscribers in the group, the data are sent to that channel. Each subscriber is sent the data. But since each subscriber also has an address registered with the provider, the cable modem for the group matches the address carried with the data to the address assigned by the provider. If the address matches, the data are kept; otherwise, they are discarded.

CM and CMTS

To use a cable network for data transmission, we need two key devices: a CM and a CMTS.

CM

The **cable modem (CM)** is installed on the subscriber premises. It is similar to an ADSL modem. Figure 9.8 shows its location.

CMTS

The **cable modem transmission system (CMTS)** is installed inside the distribution hub by the cable company. It receives data from the Internet and passes them to the

Figure 9.8   *Cable modem*

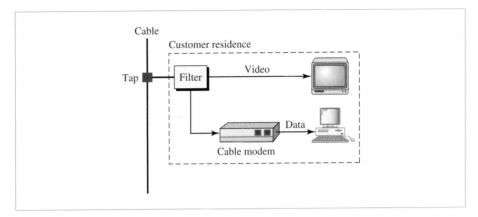

combiner, which sends them to the subscriber. The CMTS also receives data from the subscriber and passes them to the Internet. Figure 9.9 shows the location of the CMTS.

Figure 9.9   *CMTS*

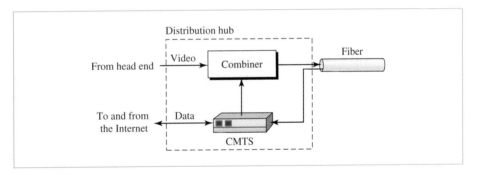

Data Transmission Schemes: DOCSIS

During the last few decades, several schemes have been designed to create a standard for data transmission over an HFC network. Prevalent is the one devised by Multimedia Cable Network Systems (MCNS), called **Data over Cable System Interface Specification (DOCSIS).** DOCSIS defines all the protocols necessary to transport data from a CMTS to a CM.

Upstream Communication

The following is a very simplified version of the protocol defined by DOCSIS for upstream communication. It describes the steps that must be followed by a CM:

1. The CM checks the downstream channels for a specific packet periodically sent by the CMTS. The packet asks any new CM to announce itself on a specific upstream channel.
2. The CMTS sends a packet to the CM, defining its allocated downstream and upstream channels.

3. The CM then starts a process, called **ranging,** which determines the distance between the CM and CMTS. This process is required for synchronization between all CMs and CMTSs for the **minislots** used for timesharing of the upstream channels. We will learn about this timesharing when we discuss contention protocols in Chapter 13.

4. The CM sends a packet to the ISP, asking for the Internet address.

5. The CM and CMTS then exchange some packets to establish security parameters, which are needed for a public network such as cable TV.

6. The CM sends its unique identifier to the CMTS.

7. Upstream communication can start in the allocated upstream channel; the CM can contend for the minislots to send data.

Downstream Communication

In the downstream direction, the communication is much simpler. There is no contention because there is only one sender. The CMTS sends the packet with the address of the receiving CM, using the allocated downstream channel.

9.3   SONET

The high bandwidths of fiber-optic cable are suitable for today's highest data rate technologies (such as video conferencing) and for carrying large numbers of lower-rate technologies at the same time. For this reason, the importance of optical fibers grows in conjunction with the development of technologies requiring high data rates or wide bandwidths for transmission. With their prominence came a need for standardization. The ANSI standard is called the **Synchronous Optical Network (SONET).** The ITU-T standard is called the **Synchronous Digital Hierarchy (SDH).** These two standards are nearly identical.

Among the concerns addressed by the designers of SONET and SDH, three are of particular interest to us. First, SONET is a synchronous network. A single clock is used to handle the timing of transmissions and equipment across the entire network. Network-wide synchronization adds a level of predictability to the system. This predictability, coupled with a powerful frame design, enables individual channels to be multiplexed, thereby improving speed and reducing cost.

Second, SONET contains recommendations for the standardization of fiber-optic transmission system (FOTS) equipment sold by different manufacturers. Third, the SONET physical specifications and frame design include mechanisms that allow it to carry signals from incompatible tributary systems (such as DS-0 and DS-1). It is this flexibility that gives SONET a reputation for universal connectivity.

SONET is a good example of a time-division multiplexing (TDM) system. The bandwidth of the fiber is considered as one channel divided into time slots to define subchannels. SONET, as a TDM network, is a synchronous system controlled by a master clock with a very high level of accuracy. The transmission of bits is controlled by the master clock.

SONET is a synchronous TDM system controlled by a master clock.

SONET Devices

SONET transmission relies on three basic devices: **synchronous transport signal (STS)** multiplexers, regenerators, and add/drop multiplexers. Figure 9.10 shows an example of a SONET.

Figure 9.10 *A SONET*

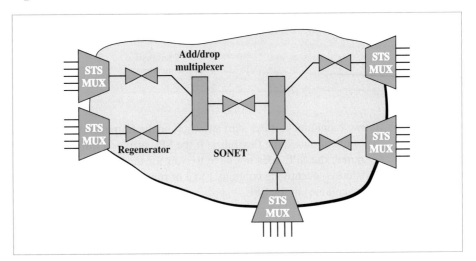

- **STS multiplexer/demultiplexer.** An STS multiplexer/demultiplexer either multiplexes signals from multiple sources into an STS or demultiplexes an STS into different destination signals.
- **Regenerator.** An STS **regenerator** is a repeater (see Chapter 16) that takes a received optical signal and regenerates it. Regenerators in this system, however, add a function to those of physical layer repeaters. A SONET regenerator replaces some of the existing overhead information (header information) with new information. These devices function at the data link layer.
- **Add/drop multiplexer.** An **add/drop multiplexer** can add signals coming from different sources into a given path or remove a desired signal from a path and redirect it without demultiplexing the entire signal.

SONET Frame

A SONET frame can be viewed as a matrix of nine rows of 90 octets each, for a total of 810 octets (see Fig. 9.11). Some of the octets are used for control; they are not positioned at the beginning or end of the frame (like a header or trailer).

The first three columns of the frame are used for administration overhead. The rest of the frame is called the **synchronous payload envelope (SPE)**. The SPE contains transmission overhead and user data. The payload, however, does not have to start at

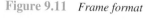

Figure 9.11   *Frame format*

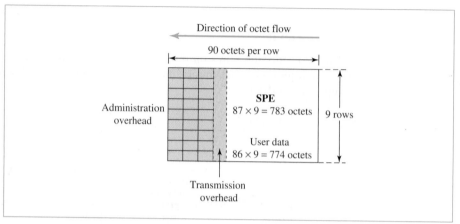

row 1, column 4; it can start anywhere in the frame and can even span two frames. This feature allows some flexibility; if the SPE arrives a little late, after a frame has already started, the SPE does not have to wait for the beginning of the next frame. A pointer (address) occupying columns 1 to 3 of row 4 can determine the beginning address (row and column) of the SPE.

Frame Transmission

SONET frames are transmitted one after another without any gap in between, even if there are no real data. Empty frames carry dummy data. In other words, a sequence of frames looks like a sequence of bits. However, the first 2 bytes of each frame, called alignment bytes, F628 in hexadecimal, define the beginning of each frame. The third byte is the frame identification.

Synchronous Transport Signals

SONET defines a hierarchy of signaling levels called synchronous transport signals (STSs). Each STS level (STS-1 to STS-192) supports a certain data rate, specified in megabits per second (see Table 9.1). The physical links defined to carry each level of STS are called **optical carriers (OCs).** OC levels describe the conceptual and physical specifications of the links required to support each level of signaling. Actual implementation of those specifications is left up to the manufacturers. Currently, the most popular implementations are OC-1, OC-3, OC-12, and OC-48.

STS-1

STS-1 or OC-1 is the lowest-rate service provided by SONET. STS-1 transmits 8000 frames per second. Figure 9.12 compares the raw, SPE, and user bit rates. The rates reflect the number of columns available. For example, the SPE bit rate is less than the raw bit rate due to the three columns for management.

Table 9.1   *SONET rates*

STS	OC	Raw (Mbps)	SPE (Mbps)	User (Mbps)
STS-1	OC-1	51.84	50.12	49.536
STS-3	OC-3	155.52	150.336	148.608
STS-9	OC-9	466.56	451.008	445.824
STS-12	OC-12	622.08	601.344	594.432
STS-18	OC-18	933.12	902.016	891.648
STS-24	OC-24	1244.16	1202.688	1188.864
STS-36	OC-36	1866.23	1804.032	1783.296
STS-48	OC-48	2488.32	2405.376	2377.728
STS-192	OC-192	9953.28	9621.604	9510.912

Figure 9.12

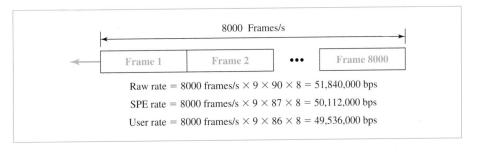

Virtual Tributaries

SONET is designed to carry broadband payloads. Current digital hierarchy data rates (DS-1 to DS-3), however, are lower than STS-1. To make SONET backward-compatible with the current hierarchy, its frame design includes a system of **virtual tributaries (VTs).** A virtual tributary is a partial payload that can be inserted into a frame and combined with other partial payloads to fill out the frame. Instead of using all 87 payload columns of an SPE frame for data from one source, we can subdivide the SPE and call each component a VT.

Four types of VTs have been defined to accommodate existing digital hierarchies (see Fig. 9.13). Notice that the number of columns allowed for each type of VT can be determined by doubling the type identification number (VT1.5 gets three columns, VT2 gets four columns, etc.).

- **VT1.5.** The VT1.5 accommodates the U.S. DS-1 service (1.544 Mbps).
- **VT2.** The VT2 accommodates the European CEPT-1 service (2.048 Mbps).
- **VT3.** The VT3 accommodates the DS-1C service (fractional DS-1, 3.152 Mbps).
- **VT6.** The VT6 accommodates the DS-2 service (6.312 Mbps).

When two or more tributaries are inserted into a single STS-1 frame, they are interleaved column by column. SONET provides mechanisms for identifying each VT and

Figure 9.13   *VT types*

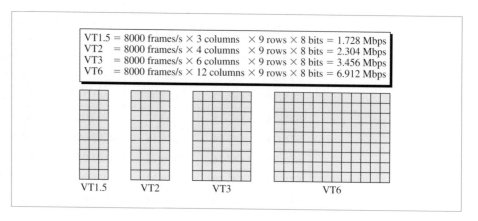

VT1.5 = 8000 frames/s × 3 columns × 9 rows × 8 bits = 1.728 Mbps
VT2 = 8000 frames/s × 4 columns × 9 rows × 8 bits = 2.304 Mbps
VT3 = 8000 frames/s × 6 columns × 9 rows × 8 bits = 3.456 Mbps
VT6 = 8000 frames/s × 12 columns × 9 rows × 8 bits = 6.912 Mbps

VT1.5   VT2   VT3   VT6

separating them without demultiplexing the entire stream. Discussion of these mechanisms and the control issues behind them is beyond the scope of this book.

Higher-Rate Services

Lower-rate STSs can be multiplexed to make them compatible with higher-rate systems. For example, three STS-1's can be combined into one STS-3, four STS-3's can
be multiplexed into one STS-12, and so on. Figure 9.14 shows how three STS-1's are
multiplexed into a single STS-3. To create an STS-12 out of lower-rate services, we
could multiplex either 12 STS-1's or 4 STS-3's.

Figure 9.14   *STS multiplexing*

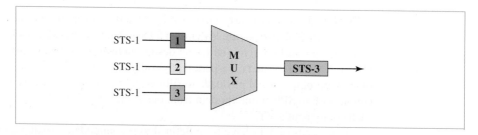

9.4   KEY TERMS

add/drop multiplexer
asymmetric DSL (ADSL)
cable modem (CM)
cable modem transmission system
   (CMTS)
cable TV

community antenna TV (CATV)
Data Over Cable System Interface
   Specification (DOCSIS)
digital subscriber line (DSL)
digital subscriber line access
   multiplexer (DSLAM)

discrete multitone technique (DMT)
distribution hub
downstream data band
fiber node
head end
high-bit-rate DSL (HDSL)
hybrid fiber-coaxial (HFC) network
minislot
optical carrier (OC)
ranging
regenerator

regional cable head (RCH)
STS multiplexer/demultiplexer
symmetric DSL (SDSL)
Synchronous Digital Hierarchy (SDH)
Synchronous Optical Network (SONET)
synchronous payload envelope (SPE)
synchronous transport signal (STS)
upstream data band
very-high-bit-rate DSL (VDSL)
video band
virtual tributary (VT)

9.5   SUMMARY

☐ A home computer can access the Internet through the existing telephone system or through a cable TV system.

☐ DSL supports high-speed digital communications over the existing telephone local loops.

☐ ADSL technology allows customers a bit rate of up to 1 Mbps in the upstream direction and up to 8 Mbps in the downstream direction.

☐ ADSL uses a modulation technique called DMT which combines QAM and FDM.

☐ SDSL, HDSL, and VDSL are other DSL technologies.

☐ Theoretically, the coaxial cable used for cable TV allows Internet access with a bit rate of up to 12 Mbps in the upstream direction and up to 30 Mbps in the downstream direction.

☐ An HFC network allows Internet access through a combination of fiber-optic and coaxial cables.

☐ The coaxial cable bandwidth is divided into a video band, a downstream data band, and an upstream data band. Both upstream and downstream bands are shared among subscribers.

☐ DOCSIS defines all protocols needed for data transmission on an HFC network.

☐ Synchronous Optical Network (SONET) is a synchronous high-data-rate TDM network for fiber-optic networks.

☐ SONET has defined a hierarchy of signals (similar to the DS hierarchy) called synchronous transport signals (STSs).

☐ Optical carrier (OC) levels are the implementation of STSs.

☐ A SONET frame can be viewed as a matrix of nine rows of 90 octets each.

☐ A SONET system can use the following equipment:

   a. STS multiplexer—combines several optical signals to make an STS signal.

   b. Regenerator—removes noise from an optical signal.

   c. Add/drop multiplexer—adds STSs from different paths and removes STSs from a path.

❏ SONET is backward compatible with the current DS hierarchy through the virtual tributary (VT) concept. VTs are a partial payload consisting of an *m*-by-*n* block of octets. An STS payload can be a combination of several VTs.

❏ STSs can be multiplexed to get a new STS with a higher data rate.

9.6 PRACTICE SET

Review Questions

1. Name two technologies that have a higher data rate than traditional modems.
2. Why is ADSL unsuitable for businesses? Which DSL technology is best suited for businesses?
3. Who are the main users of ADSL technology?
4. How do filters limit the bandwidth size of the local loop?
5. What is the modulation technique used by ADSL technology?
6. What kinds of devices at the customer premises are needed by an ADSL subscriber?
7. What is the purpose of a DSLAM?
8. How is HDSL superior to a T-1 line?
9. What is the function of the head end in a traditional cable TV network?
10. Discuss the transmission media in an HFC network.
11. Why is QAM not used in the modulation of upstream data in an HFC network?
12. How is a CM different from a CMTS?
13. What is the purpose of DOCSIS?
14. How is an STS multiplexer different from an add/drop multiplexer, since both can add signals?
15. What is the relationship between STS levels and OC levels?
16. What is the relationship between SONET and Synchronous Digital Hierarchy (SDH)?
17. Why is SONET called a synchronous network?
18. What is the function of a SONET regenerator?
19. How is an STS-1 frame organized?
20. What is a virtual tributary?
21. How can lower-data-rate STSs be made compatible with higher-data-rate STSs?

Multiple-Choice Questions

22. _____ has a higher transmission rate in the downstream direction than in the upstream direction.
    a. VDSL
    b. ADSL
    c. SDSL
    d. (a) and (b)

23. _____ is suitable for businesses that require comparable upstream and down-
    stream data rates.
    a. VDSL
    b. ADSL
    c. SDSL
    d. (a) and (b)

24. _____ limit the bandwidth of the local loop to 4 KHz.
    a. Fiber nodes
    b. Filters
    c. Repeaters
    d. Hubs

25. DMT is a modulation technique that combines elements of _____ and _____.
    a. FDM; TDM
    b. QDM; QAM
    c. FDM; QAM
    d. PSK; FSK

26. The largest portion of the bandwidth for ADSL carries _____.
    a. Voice communication
    b. Upstream data
    c. Downstream data
    d. Control data

27. The actual bit rate of ADSL downstream data is _____.
    a. 64 Kbps to 1 Mbps
    b. 6 to 30 Kbps
    c. 31 Kbps to 255 Mbps
    d. 500 Kbps to 8 Mbps

28. _____ is a device at the telephone company site that can packetize data to be
    sent to the ISP server.
    a. A DSLAM
    b. An ADSL modem
    c. A filter
    d. A splitter

29. _____ was designed as an alternative to the T-1 line.
    a. VDSL
    b. ADSL
    c. SDSL
    d. HDSL

30. HDSL encodes data using _____.
    a. 4B/5B
    b. 2B1Q

    c. 1B2Q

    d. 6B/8T

31. _____ encoded signal is more susceptible to attenuation than _____ encoded signal.

    a. An AMI; a 2B2Q

    b. A 2B1Q; an AMI

    c. An AMI; a 2B1Q

    d. None of the above

32. Another name for the cable TV office is the _____.

    a. Splitter

    b. Fiber node

    c. Combiner

    d. Head end

33. A traditional cable TV network transmits signals _____.

    a. Upstream

    b. Downstream

    c. Upstream and downstream

    d. None of the above

34. An HFC network uses _____ as the medium from the switch to the fiber node.

    a. Optical fiber

    b. Coaxial cable

    c. UTP

    d. STP

35. In an HFC network, the distribution hub handles the _____ of signals.

    a. Modulation

    b. Distribution

    c. Splitting

    d. (a) and (b)

36. A TV channel in an HFC network needs a _____-MHz bandwidth.

    a. 6

    b. 100

    c. 250

    d. 369

37. _____ data go from the subscriber to the Internet.

    a. Upstream

    b. Downstream

    c. Midstream

    d. None of the above

38. In an HFC network, the upstream data are modulated using the _____ modulation technique.

    a. QAM

    b. QPSK

    c. PCM

    d. ASK

39. The standard for data transmission over an HFC network is called _____.

    a. MCNS

    b. DOCSIS

    c. CMTS

    d. ADSL

40. The _____ is an HFC network device installed inside the distribution hub that receives data from the Internet and passes them to the combiner.

    a. CM

    b. CMTS

    c. DOCSIS

    d. MCNS

41. SONET is a standard for _____ networks.

    a. Twisted-pair cable

    b. Coaxial cable

    c. Ethernet

    d. Fiber-optic cable

42. SONET is an acronym for _____ Network.

    a. Synchronous Optical

    b. Standard Optical

    c. Symmetric Open

    d. Standard Open

43. In a SONET system, _____ can remove signals from a path.

    a. An STS multiplier

    b. A regenerator

    c. An add/drop multiplexer

    d. A repeater

44. The synchronous payload envelope of an STS-1 frame contains _____.

    a. Pointers

    b. User data

    c. Overhead

    d. (b) and (c)

Exercises

45. Show how STS-9's can be multiplexed to create an STS-36. Is there any extra overhead involved in this type of multiplexing? Why or why not?

46. What is the duration of a frame in STS-1?

47. What is the duration of a frame in STS-3, STS-9, ..., STS-192?

48. How many VT1.5's can be carried in an STS-1 frame?

49. How many VT2's can be carried in an STS-1 frame?

50. How many VT3's can be carried in an STS-1 frame?

51. How many VT6's can be carried in an STS-1 frame?

52. A user needs to send data at 3 Mbps. Which VT (or combination of VTs) can be used?

53. A user needs to send data at 7 Mbps. Which VT (or combination of VTs) can be used?

54. A user needs to send data at 12 Mbps. Which VT (or combination of VTs) can be used?

55. Which VT transmits at almost the same data rate as a T-1 line?

56. Which VT or STS transmits at almost the same data rate as a T-3 line?

57. A company wants to use SONET to multiplex up to 100 digitized voices. Which VT (or combination of VTs) is suitable for this company?

58. Draw a SONET using all the following devices. Label all lines, sections, and paths.

    a. Three STS multiplexers (two as input and one as output)

    b. Four add/drop multiplexers

    c. Five regenerators

PART 3

Data Link Layer

The data link layer lies between the network layer and the physical layer in the Internet model. It receives services from the physical layer and provides services to the network layer. Figure 1 shows the position of the data link layer in the Internet model.

Figure 1 *Position of data link layer*

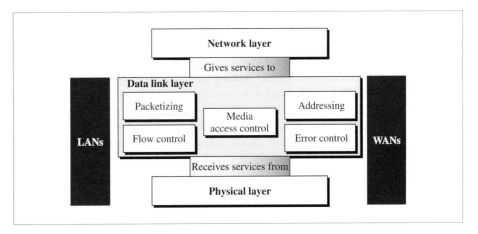

The **data link layer** is responsible for carrying a packet from one hop (computer or router) to the next hop. Unlike the network layer which has a global responsibility, the data link layer has a local responsibility. Its responsibility lies between two hops. In other words, because LANs and WANs in the Internet are delimited by hops, we can say that the responsibility of the data link layer is to carry a packet through a LAN or WAN.

The journey through a LAN or a WAN (between two hops) must preserve the integrity of the packet; the data link layer must make sure that the packet arrives safe and sound. If the packet is corrupted during the transmission, it must either be corrected or retransmitted. The data link layer must also make sure that the next hop is not overwhelmed with data by the previous hop; the flow of data must be controlled.

Access to a LAN or a WAN for the sending of data is also an issue. If several computers or routers are connected to a common medium (link), and more than one want to send data at the same time, which has the right to send? What is the access method?

Duties

The duties of the data link layer include packetizing, addressing, error control, flow control, and medium access control as shown in Figure 2.

Figure 2   *Data link layer duties*

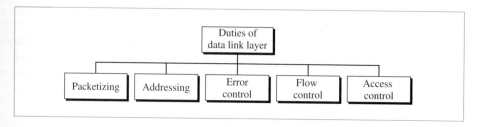

Packetizing

The data link layer is responsible for moving data from one hop to the next. To get to the next hop, the data must pass through a LAN or a WAN, each of which has its own protocols. The packet coming from the upper layer must therefore be encapsulated in the appropriate packet defined by the data link layer of the underlying LAN or WAN. Different protocols have different names for the packet at the data link layer. However, most LANs refer to the packet as a frame. The ATM WAN refers to a packet as a cell. We see examples of packetizing in Chapters 12–18.

Addressing

We need one addressing mechanism at the data link layer. The data link layer addresses are called physical addresses (or MAC addresses) and are used to find the address of the next hop in hop-to-hop delivery. The physical address used by a LAN is totally different from that used by a WAN. A LAN uses a next-hop address to carry a frame across the LAN; a WAN normally uses a virtual circuit address. We discuss addressing mechanisms in Chapters 14 to 18.

Error Control

In data communications, errors are inevitable. Using better equipment and more reliable transmission media may reduce the severity or the frequency of occurrence, but it can never eliminate errors. Networks must be able to transfer data from one device to another with complete accuracy. As a prelude to error control, we discuss error detection in Chapter 10. We then discuss error control in Chapter 11 as part of data link control.

Flow Control

Another responsibility of the data link layer is flow control. In most protocols, flow control is a set of procedures that tells the sender how much data it can transmit before it must wait for an acknowledgment from the receiver. The flow of data must not be allowed to overwhelm the receiver. The receiving device must be able to inform the sending device before some limit is reached and request that the transmitting device send fewer frames or stop temporarily. We discuss flow control as part of data link control in Chapter 11.

Medium Access Control

When computers use a shared medium (cable or air), there must be a method to control access to the medium at any moment. To prevent this conflict or collision on a network, there is a need for a medium access control (MAC) method. This method defines the procedure a computer follows when it needs to send a frame or frames. We devote two chapters to this issue, Chapter 12 and Chapter 13.

Local Area Networks

Local Area Networks (LANs) operate at the physical and data link layer. The obvious place to discuss local area networks is after these layers have been discussed. We have devoted Chapter 14 to Ethernet, the most common LAN today and Chapter 15 to wireless LANs, the most promising LAN today. After discussing these two subjects, we show how to connect LANs in Chapter 16.

IEEE Standards

The Internet does not spell out specifications for LANs or WANs. The Internet accepts any LAN as a communications pathway for transferring its network layer packet. There must other protocols to handle LANs. In 1985, the Computer Society of the IEEE started a project, called Project 802, to set standards to enable intercommunication between equipment from a variety of manufacturers. The IEEE has subdivided the data link layer into two sublayers: logical link control (LLC) and media access control (MAC) as shown in Figure 3. The LLC is nonarchitecture specific; that is, it is the same for all IEEE-defined LANs. It is not widely used today. The MAC sublayer, on the other hand, contains a number of distinct modules; each carries proprietary information specific to the LAN product being used. Figure 4 shows some IEEE 802 standards defined for specific LANs.

Figure 3 *LLC and MAC sublayers*

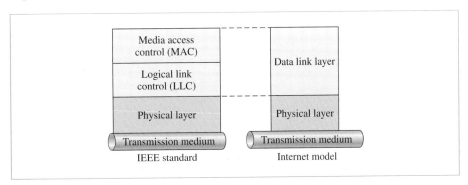

Figure 4   *IEEE standards for LANs*

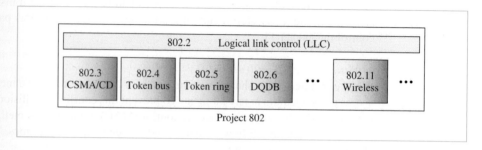

Wide Area Networks

Wide Area Networks (WANs) also operate in the physical and data link layer and are discussed in this part of the text. We discuss the mobile telephone systems and satellites, as wireless WANs, in Chapter 17. We discuss Frame Relay and ATM as switched WANs in Chapter 18.

Chapters

Part III of the book covers nine chapters 10–18. Chapters 10–13 discuss general services provided by the data link layer: error control, flow control, and media access. Chapter 10 is about error detection, a prelude to error control. Chapter 11 is about flow and error control. Chapter 12 explains media access control for point-to-point connections. Chapter 13 does the same for multiple access connections.

Chapters 14 to 16 are devoted to LANs. Chapter 14 discuss the most common LAN, Ethernet. Chapter 15 discusses wireless LANs. Chapter 16 discusses the connection of LANs.

Chapters 17 and 18 are devoted to WANs. Chapter 17 is about wireless WANs, mobile telephone networks and satellite networks. Chapter 18 is about switched WANs, Frame Relay, and ATM.

CHAPTER 10

Error Detection and Correction

Networks must be able to transfer data from one device to another with complete accuracy. A system that cannot guarantee that the data received by one device are identical to the data transmitted by another device is essentially useless. Yet anytime data are transmitted from one node to the next, they can become corrupted in passage. Many factors can alter or wipe out one or more bits of a given data unit. Reliable systems must have a mechanism for detecting and correcting such **errors.**

> **Data can be corrupted during transmission. For reliable communication, errors must be detected and corrected.**

10.1 TYPES OF ERRORS

Whenever bits flow from one point to another, they are subject to unpredictable changes because of interference. This interference can change the shape of the signal. In a single-bit error, a 0 is changed to a 1 or a 1 to a 0. In a burst error, multiple bits are changed. For example, a 0.01-s burst of impulse noise on a transmission with a data rate of 1200 bps might change all or some of 12 bits of information.

Single-Bit Error

The term **single-bit error** means that only one bit of a given data unit (such as a byte, character, data unit, or packet) is changed from 1 to 0 or from 0 to 1.

> **In a single-bit error, only one bit in the data unit has changed.**

Figure 10.1 shows the effect of a single-bit error on a data unit. To understand the impact of the change, imagine that each group of 8 bits is an ASCII character with a 0 bit added to the left. In the figure, 00000010 (ASCII *STX*) was sent, meaning *start of text*, but 00001010 (ASCII *LF*) was received, meaning *line feed*. (For more information about ASCII code, see Appendix A.)

Figure 10.1 *Single-bit error*

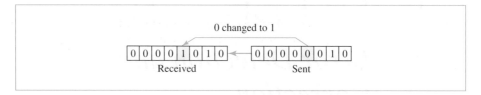

Single-bit errors are the least likely type of error in serial data transmission. To understand why, imagine a sender sends data at 1 Mbps. This means that each bit lasts only 1/1,000,000 s, or 1 μs. For a single-bit error to occur, the noise must have a duration of only 1 μs, which is very rare; noise normally lasts much longer than this.

However, a single-bit error can happen if we are sending data using parallel transmission. For example, if eight wires are used to send all 8 bits of 1 byte at the same time and one of the wires is noisy, one bit can be corrupted in each byte. Think of parallel transmission inside a computer, between CPU and memory, for example.

Burst Error

The term **burst error** means that 2 or more bits in the data unit have changed from 1 to 0 or from 0 to 1.

> **A burst error means that 2 or more bits in the data unit have changed.**

Figure 10.2 shows the effect of a burst error on a data unit. In this case, 0100010001000011 was sent, but 0101110101000011 was received. Note that a burst error does not necessarily mean that the errors occur in consecutive bits. The length of the burst is measured from the first corrupted bit to the last corrupted bit. Some bits in between may not have been corrupted.

Figure 10.2 *Burst error of length 5*

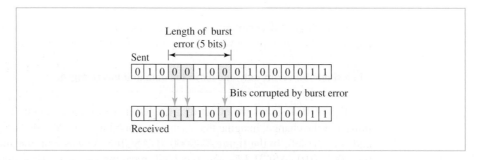

Burst error is most likely to occur in a serial transmission. The duration of noise is normally longer than the duration of one bit, which means that when noise affects data, it affects a set of bits. The number of bits affected depends on the data rate and duration of noise. For example, if we are sending data at 1 Kbps, a noise of 1/100 s can affect 10 bits; if we are sending data at 1 Mbps, the same noise can affect 10,000 bits.

10.2 DETECTION

Although the goal of error checking is to correct errors, most of the time, we first need to detect errors. Error detection is simpler than error correction and is the first step in the error correction process.

Redundancy

One **error detection** mechanism would be to send every data unit twice. The receiving device would then be able to do a bit-for-bit comparison between the two versions of the data. Any discrepancy would indicate an error, and an appropriate correction mechanism could be set in place. This system would be completely accurate (the odds of errors being introduced onto exactly the same bits in both sets of data are infinitesimally small), but it would also be insupportably slow. Not only would the transmission time double, but also the time it takes to compare every unit bit by bit must be added.

The concept of including extra information in the transmission for error detection is a good one. But instead of repeating the entire data stream, a shorter group of bits may be appended to the end of each unit. This technique is called **redundancy** because the extra bits are redundant to the information; they are discarded as soon as the accuracy of the transmission has been determined.

> **Error detection uses the concept of redundancy, which means adding extra bits for detecting errors at the destination.**

Figure 10.3 shows the process of using redundant bits to check the accuracy of a data unit. Once the data stream has been generated, it passes through a device that analyzes it and adds on an appropriately coded redundancy check. The data unit, now enlarged by several bits, travels over the link to the receiver. The receiver puts

Figure 10.3 *Redundancy*

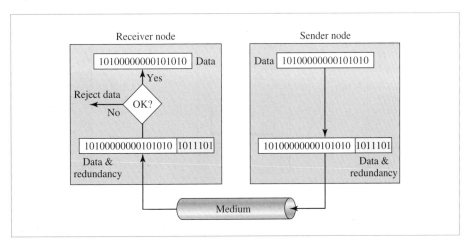

the entire stream through a checking function. If the received bit stream passes the checking criteria, the data portion of the data unit is accepted and the redundant bits are discarded.

Three types of redundancy checks are common in data communications: parity check, cyclic redundancy check (CRC), and checksum (see Fig. 10.4).

Figure 10.4 *Detection methods*

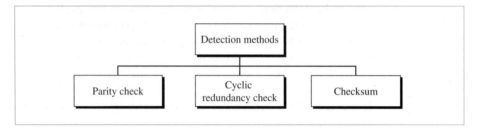

Parity Check

The most common and least expensive mechanism for error detection is the **parity check.** Parity checking can be simple or two-dimensional.

Simple Parity Check

In this technique, a redundant bit, called a **parity bit,** is added to every data unit so that the total number of 1s in the unit (including the parity bit) becomes even (or odd). Suppose we want to transmit the binary data unit 1100001 [ASCII *a* (97)]; see Figure 10.5.

Figure 10.5 *Even-parity concept*

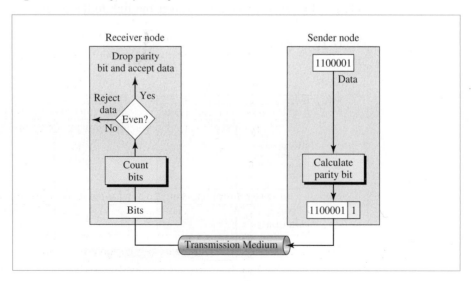

Adding the number of 1s gives us 3, an odd number. Before transmitting, we pass the data unit through a parity generator. The parity generator counts the 1s and appends the parity bit (a 1 in this case) to the end. The total number of 1s is now 4, an even number. The system now transmits the entire expanded unit across the network link. When it reaches its destination, the receiver puts all 8 bits through an **even-parity** checking function. If the receiver sees 11000011, it counts four 1s, an even number, and the data unit passes. But what if the data unit has been damaged in transit? What if, instead of 11000011, the receiver sees 11001011? Then when the parity checker counts the 1s, it gets 5, an odd number. The receiver knows that an error has been introduced into the data somewhere and therefore rejects the whole unit. Note that for the sake of simplicity, we are discussing here even-parity checking, where the number of 1s should be an even number. Some systems may use **odd-parity** checking, where the number of 1s should be odd. The principle is the same.

In parity check, a parity bit is added to every data unit so that the total number of 1s is even (or odd for odd-parity).

Example 1

Suppose the sender wants to send the word *world*. In ASCII (see Appendix A), the five characters are coded as

$$\longleftarrow \quad 1110111 \quad 1101111 \quad 1110010 \quad 1101100 \quad 1100100$$
$$\quad\quad\quad w \quad\quad\quad o \quad\quad\quad r \quad\quad\quad l \quad\quad\quad d$$

Each of the first four characters has an even number of 1s, so the parity bit is a 0. The last character (d), however, has three 1s (an odd number), so the parity bit is a 1 to make the total number of 1s even. The following shows the actual bits sent (the parity bits are underlined).

$$\longleftarrow \quad 1110111\underline{0} \quad 1101111\underline{0} \quad 1110010\underline{0} \quad 1101100\underline{0} \quad 1100100\underline{1}$$

Example 2

Now suppose the word *world* in Example 1 is received by the receiver without being corrupted in transmission.

$$\longleftarrow \quad 1110111\underline{0} \quad 1101111\underline{0} \quad 1110010\underline{0} \quad 1101100\underline{0} \quad 1100100\underline{1}$$

The receiver counts the 1s in each character and comes up with even numbers (6, 6, 4, 4, 4). The data are accepted.

Example 3

Now suppose the word *world* in Example 1 is corrupted during transmission.

$$\longleftarrow \quad 1111111\underline{0} \quad 1101111\underline{0} \quad 1110110\underline{0} \quad 1101100\underline{0} \quad 1100100\underline{1}$$

The receiver counts the 1s in each character and comes up with even and odd numbers (7, 6, 5, 4, 4). The receiver knows that the data are corrupted, discards them, and asks for retransmission.

Performance

Simple parity check can detect all single-bit errors. It can also detect burst errors as long as the total number of bits changed is odd (1, 3, 5, etc.). Let's say we have an even-parity data unit where the total number of 1s, including the parity bit, is 6: 1000111011. If any 3 bits change value, the resulting parity will be odd and the error will be detected: 1*111*111011:9, *01*10111011:7, 1*1000*10011:5—all odd. The checker would return a result of 1, and the data unit would be rejected. The same holds true for any odd number of errors.

Suppose, however, that 2 bits of the data unit are changed: 1*11*0111011:8, 1*100*011011:6, 1000011010:4. In each case the number of 1s in the data unit is still even. The parity checker will add them and return an even number although the data unit contains two errors. This method cannot detect errors where the total number of bits changed is even. If any two bits change in transmission, the changes cancel each other and the data unit will pass a parity check even though the data unit is damaged. The same holds true for any even number of errors.

> **Simple parity check can detect all single-bit errors. It can detect burst errors only if the total number of errors in each data unit is odd.**

Two-Dimensional Parity Check

A better approach is the **two-dimensional parity check.** In this method, a block of bits is organized in a table (rows and columns). First we calculate the parity bit for each data unit. Then we organize them into a table. For example, as shown in Figure 10.6, we have four data units shown in four rows and eight columns. We then calculate the parity bit for each column and create a new row of 8 bits; they are the parity bits for the whole block. Note that the first parity bit in the fifth row is calculated based on all first

Figure 10.6 *Two-dimensional parity*

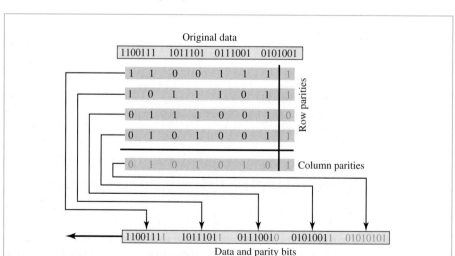

bits; the second parity bit is calculated based on all second bits; and so on. We then attach the 8 parity bits to the original data and send them to the receiver.

Example 4

Suppose the following block is sent:

⟵ 10101001 00111001 11011101 11100111 10101010

However, it is hit by a burst noise of length 8, and some bits are corrupted.

⟵ 1010*0011* *1000*1001 11011101 11100111 10101010

When the receiver checks the parity bits, some of the bits do not follow the even-parity rule and the whole block is discarded (the nonmatching bits are shown in bold).

⟵ 1010*0011* *1000*1001   11011101   11100111   **1010101 0**

(parity bits)

> **In two-dimensional parity check, a block of bits is divided into rows and a redundant row of bits is added to the whole block.**

Performance

Two-dimensional parity check increases the likelihood of detecting burst errors. As we showed in Example 4, a redundancy of n bits can easily detect a burst error of n bits. A burst error of more than n bits is also detected by this method with a very high probability. There is, however, one pattern of errors that remains elusive. If 2 bits in one data unit are damaged and two bits *in exactly the same positions* in another data unit are also damaged, the checker will not detect an error. Consider, for example, two data units: 11110000 and 11000011. If the first and last bits in each of them are changed, making the data units read *0*111000*1* and *0*100001*0*, the errors cannot be detected by this method.

Cyclic Redundancy Check (CRC)

The third and most powerful of the redundancy checking techniques is the **cyclic redundancy check (CRC).** Unlike the parity check which is based on addition, CRC is based on binary division. In CRC, instead of adding bits to achieve a desired parity, a sequence of redundant bits, called the CRC or the CRC remainder, is appended to the end of a data unit so that the resulting data unit becomes exactly divisible by a second, predetermined binary number. At its destination, the incoming data unit is divided by the same number. If at this step there is no remainder, the data unit is assumed to be intact and is therefore accepted. A remainder indicates that the data unit has been damaged in transit and therefore must be rejected.

The redundancy bits used by CRC are derived by dividing the data unit by a predetermined divisor; the remainder is the CRC. To be valid, a CRC must have two qualities: It must have exactly one less bit than the divisor, and appending it to the end of the data string must make the resulting bit sequence exactly divisible by the divisor.

Both the theory and the application of CRC error detection are straightforward. The only complexity is in deriving the CRC. To clarify this process, we will start with an overview and add complexity as we go. Figure 10.7 provides an outline of the three basic steps.

Figure 10.7   *CRC generator and checker*

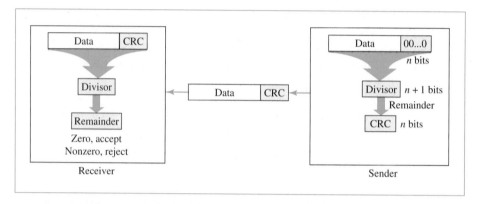

First, a string of n 0s is appended to the data unit. The number n is 1 less than the number of bits in the predetermined divisor, which is $n + 1$ bits.

Second, the newly elongated data unit is divided by the divisor, using a process called binary division. The remainder resulting from this division is the CRC.

Third, the CRC of n bits derived in step 2 replaces the appended 0s at the end of the data unit. Note that the CRC may consist of all 0s.

The data unit arrives at the receiver data first, followed by the CRC. The receiver treats the whole string as a unit and divides it by the same divisor that was used to find the CRC remainder.

If the string arrives without error, the CRC checker yields a remainder of zero and the data unit passes. If the string has been changed in transit, the division yields a non-zero remainder and the data unit does not pass.

The CRC Generator

A **CRC generator** uses modulo-2 division. Figure 10.8 shows this process. In the first step, the 4-bit divisor is subtracted from the first 4 bits of the dividend. Each bit of the divisor is subtracted from the corresponding bit of the dividend without disturbing the next-higher bit. In our example, the divisor, 1101, is subtracted from the first 4 bits of the dividend, 1001, yielding 100 (the leading 0 of the remainder is dropped). The next unused bit from the dividend is then pulled down to make the number of bits in the remainder equal to the number of bits in the divisor. The next step, therefore, is 1000 − 1101, which yields 101, and so on.

In this process, the divisor always begins with a 1; the divisor is subtracted from a portion of the previous dividend/remainder that is equal to it in length; the divisor can only be subtracted from a dividend/remainder whose leftmost bit is 1. Anytime the left-most bit of the dividend/remainder is 0, a string of 0s, of the same length as the divisor, replaces the divisor in that step of the process. For example, if the divisor is 4 bits long, it is replaced by four 0s. (Remember, we are dealing with bit patterns, not with quantitative values; 0000 is not the same as 0.) This restriction means that, at any step, the leftmost

Figure 10.8   *Binary division in a CRC generator*

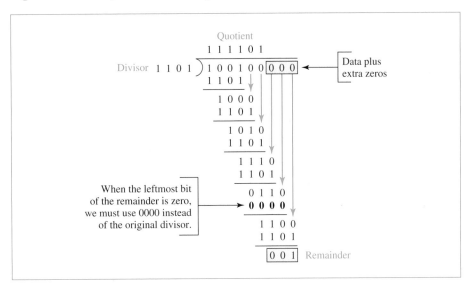

subtraction will be either $0 - 0$ or $1 - 1$, both of which equal 0. So, after subtraction, the leftmost bit of the remainder will always be a leading zero, which is dropped, and the next unused bit of the dividend is pulled down to fill out the remainder. Note that only the first bit of the remainder is dropped—if the second bit is also 0, it is retained, and the dividend/remainder for the next step will begin with 0. This process repeats until the entire dividend has been used.

The CRC Checker

A **CRC checker** functions exactly as the generator does. After receiving the data appended with the CRC, it does the same modulo-2 division. If the remainder is all 0s, the CRC is dropped and the data are accepted; otherwise, the received stream of bits is discarded and data are resent. Figure 10.9 shows the same process of division in the receiver. We assume that there is no error. The remainder is therefore all 0s, and the data are accepted.

Polynomials

The divisor in the CRC generator is most often represented not as a string of 1s and 0s, but as an algebraic **polynomial** (see Fig. 10.10). The polynomial format is useful for two reasons: It is short, and it can be used to prove the concept mathematically (which is beyond the scope of this book).

The relationship of a polynomial to its corresponding binary representation is shown in Figure 10.11.

A polynomial should be selected to have at least the following properties:

■ It should not be divisible by x.

■ It should be divisible by $x + 1$.

Figure 10.9   *Binary division in CRC checker*

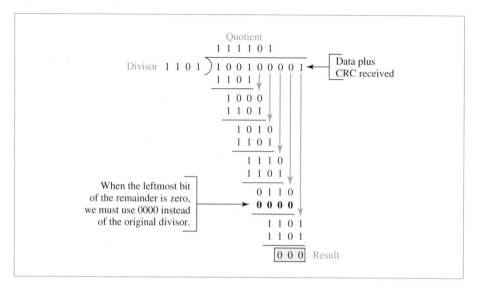

Figure 10.10   *A polynomial*

$$x^7 + x^5 + x^2 + x + 1$$

Figure 10.11   *A polynomial representing a divisor*

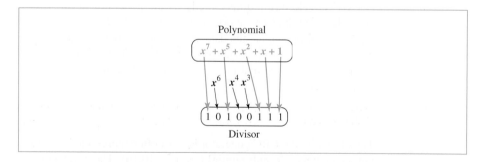

The first condition guarantees that all burst errors of a length equal to the degree of the polynomial are detected. The second condition guarantees that all burst errors affecting an odd number of bits are detected (the proof is beyond the scope of this book).

Example 5

It is obvious that we cannot choose x (binary 10) or $x^2 + x$ (binary 110) as the polynomial because both are divisible by x. However, we can choose $x + 1$ (binary 11) because it is not divisible by x, but is divisible by $x + 1$. We can also choose $x^2 + 1$ (binary 101) because it is divisible by $x + 1$ (binary division).

Standard Polynomials

Some standard polynomials used by popular protocols for CRC generation are shown in Table 10.1.

Table 10.1   *Standard polynomials*

Name	Polynomial	Application
CRC-8	$x^8 + x^2 + x + 1$	ATM header
CRC-10	$x^{10} + x^9 + x^5 + x^4 + x^2 + 1$	ATM AAL
ITU-16	$x^{16} + x^{12} + x^5 + 1$	HDLC
ITU-32	$x^{32} + x^{26} + x^{23} + x^{22} + x^{16} + x^{12} + x^{11} + x^{10} +$ $x^8 + x^7 + x^5 + x^4 + x^2 + x + 1$	LANs

Performance

CRC is a very effective error detection method. If the divisor is chosen according to the previously mentioned rules,

1. CRC can detect all burst errors that affect an odd number of bits.
2. CRC can detect all burst errors of length less than or equal to the degree of the polynomial.
3. CRC can detect, with a very high probability, burst errors of length greater than the degree of the polynomial.

Example 6

The CRC-12 ($x^{12} + x^{11} + x^3 + x + 1$), which has a degree of 12, will detect all burst errors affecting an odd number of bits, will detect all burst errors with a length less than or equal to 12, and will detect, 99.97 percent of the time, burst errors with a length of 12 or more.

Checksum

The third error detection method we discuss here is called the **checksum.** Like the parity checks and CRC, the checksum is based on the concept of redundancy.

Checksum Generator

In the sender, the checksum generator subdivides the data unit into equal segments of n bits (usually 16). These segments are added using **ones complement** arithmetic (see Appendices B and E) in such a way that the total is also n bits long. That total (sum) is then complemented and appended to the end of the original data unit as redundancy bits, called the checksum field. The extended data unit is transmitted across the network. So if the sum of the data segment is T, the checksum will be $-T$ (see Figs. 10.12 and 10.13).

Figure 10.12 *Checksum*

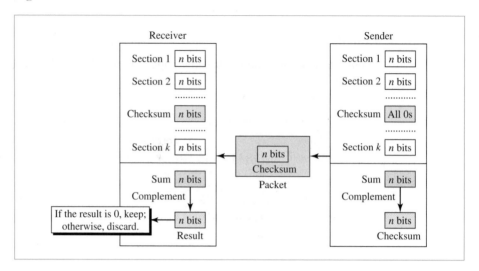

Figure 10.13 *Data unit and checksum*

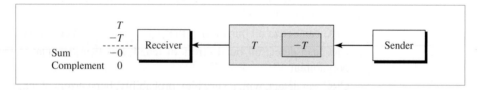

The sender follows these steps:

- The unit is divided into k sections, each of n bits.
- All sections are added using ones complement to get the sum.
- The sum is complemented and becomes the checksum.
- The checksum is sent with the data.

Checksum Checker

The receiver subdivides the data unit as above and adds all segments and complements the result. If the extended data unit is intact, the total value found by adding the data

The receiver follows these steps:

- The unit is divided into k sections, each of n bits.
- All sections are added using ones complement to get the sum.
- The sum is complemented.
- If the result is zero, the data are accepted; otherwise, they are rejected.

segments and the checksum field should be zero. If the result is not zero, the packet contains an error and the receiver rejects it (see Appendix E).

Example 7

Suppose the following block of 16 bits is to be sent using a checksum of 8 bits.

10101001   00111001

The numbers are added using ones complement arithmetic (see Appendix E).

	10101001
	00111001
Sum	11100010
Checksum	00011101

The pattern sent is

10101001   00111001   00011101
                      Checksum

Example 8

Now suppose the receiver receives the pattern sent in Example 7 and there is no error.

10101001   00111001   00011101

When the receiver adds the three sections, it will get all 1s, which, after complementing, is all 0s and shows that there is no error.

	10101001	
	00111001	
	00011101	
Sum	11111111	
Complement	00000000	means that the pattern is OK.

Example 9

Now suppose there is a burst error of length 5 that affects 4 bits.

10101*111*   *11*111001   00011101

When the receiver adds the three sections, it gets

		10101111	
		11111001	
		00011101	
Result	1	11000101	
Carry		1	
Sum		11000110	
Complement		00111001	means that the pattern is corrupted.

Performance

The checksum detects all errors involving an odd number of bits as well as most errors involving an even number of bits. However, if one or more bits of a segment are damaged and the corresponding bit or bits of opposite value in a second segment are also damaged, the sums of those columns will not change and the receiver will not detect a problem. If the last digit of one segment is a 0 and it gets changed to a 1 in transit, then the last 1 in another segment must be changed to a 0 if the error is to go undetected. In two-dimensional parity check, two 0s could both change to 1s without altering the parity because carries were discarded. Checksum retains all carries; so although two 0s becoming 1s would not alter the value of their own column, it would change the value of the next-higher column. But anytime a bit inversion is balanced by an opposite bit inversion in the corresponding digit of another data segment, the error is invisible.

10.3   ERROR CORRECTION

The mechanisms that we have discussed up to this point detect errors but do not correct them. **Error correction** can be handled in several ways. The two most common are error correction by retransmission and forward error correction.

Error Correction by Retransmission

In **error correction by retransmission,** when an error is discovered, the receiver can have the sender retransmit the entire data unit. This type of error correction is discussed along with flow and error control protocols in Chapter 11.

Forward Error Correction

In **forward error correction (FEC),** a receiver can use an error-correcting code, which automatically corrects certain errors. In theory, it is possible to correct any errors automatically. Error-correcting codes, however, are more sophisticated than error detection codes and require more redundancy bits.

The concept underlying error correction can be most easily understood by examining the simplest case: single-bit errors. As we saw earlier, single-bit errors can be detected by the addition of a redundant (parity) bit. A single additional bit can detect single-bit errors in any sequence of bits because it must distinguish between only two conditions: error or no error. A bit has two states (0 and 1). These two states are sufficient for this level of detection.

But what if we want to correct as well as detect single-bit errors? Two states are enough to detect an error but not to correct it. An error occurs when the receiver reads a 1 bit as a 0 or a 0 bit as a 1. To correct the error, the receiver simply reverses the value of the altered bit. To do so, however, it must know which bit is in error. The secret of error correction, therefore, is to locate the invalid bit or bits.

For example, to correct a single-bit error in an ASCII character, the error correction code must determine which of the 7 bits has changed. In this case, we have to distinguish between eight different states: no error, error in position 1, error in position 2, and so on, up to error in position 7. To do so requires enough redundancy bits to show all eight states.

At first glance, it seems that a 3-bit redundancy code should be adequate because 3 bits can show eight different states (000 to 111) and can therefore indicate the locations of eight different possibilities. But what if an error occurs in the redundancy bits themselves? Seven bits of data (the ASCII character) plus 3 bits of redundancy equals 10 bits. Three bits, however, can identify only eight possibilities. Additional bits are necessary to cover all possible error locations.

To calculate the number of redundancy bits r required to correct a given number of data bits m, we must find a relationship between m and r. With m bits of data and r bits of redundancy added to them, the length of the resulting code is $m + r$.

If the total number of bits in a transmittable unit is $m + r$, then r must be able to indicate at least $m + r + 1$ different states. Of these, one state means no error, and $m + r$ states indicate the location of an error in each of the $m + r$ positions.

So $m + r + 1$ states must be discoverable by r bits; and r bits can indicate 2^r different states. Therefore, 2^r must be equal to or greater than $m + r + 1$:

$$2^r >= m + r + 1$$

The value of r can be determined by plugging in the value of m (the original length of the data unit to be transmitted). For example, if the value of m is 7 (as in a 7-bit ASCII code), the smallest r value that can satisfy this equation is 4:

$$2^4 >= 7 + 4 + 1$$

Table 10.2 shows some possible m values and the corresponding r values.

Table 10.2   *Relationship between data and redundancy bits*

Number of Data Bits m	Number of Redundancy Bits r	Total Bits $m + r$
1	2	3
2	3	5
3	3	6
4	3	7
5	4	9
6	4	10
7	4	11

Hamming Code

Hamming provides a practical solution. The **Hamming code** can be applied to data units of any length and uses the relationship between data and redundancy bits discussed above. For example, a 7-bit ASCII code requires 4 redundancy bits that can be added to the end of the data unit or interspersed with the original data bits. In Figure 10.14, these bits are placed in positions 1, 2, 4, and 8 (the positions in an 11-bit sequence that are powers of 2). For clarity in the examples below, we refer to these bits as r_1, r_2, r_4, and r_8.

Figure 10.14   *Positions of redundancy bits in Hamming code*

11	10	9	8	7	6	5	4	3	2	1
d	d	d	r_8	d	d	d	r_4	d	r_2	r_1

In the Hamming code, each *r* bit is the parity bit for one combination of data bits, as shown below:

r_1:   bits 1, 3, 5, 7, 9, 11

r_2:   bits 2, 3, 6, 7, 10, 11

r_4:   bits 4, 5, 6, 7

r_8:   bits 8, 9, 10, 11

Each data bit may be included in more than one calculation. In the sequences above, for example, each of the original data bits is included in at least two sets, while the *r* bits are included in only one (see Fig. 10.15).

Figure 10.15   *Redundancy bits calculation*

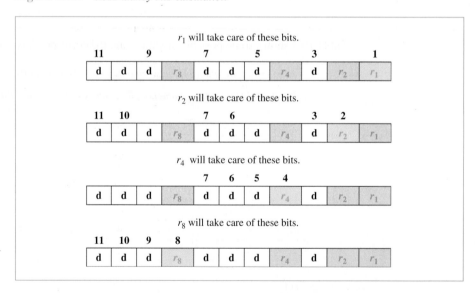

Calculating the *r* Values   Figure 10.16 shows a Hamming code implementation for an ASCII character. In the first step, we place each bit of the original character in its appropriate position in the 11-bit unit. In the subsequent steps, we calculate the even parities for the various bit combinations. The parity value for each combination is the value of the corresponding *r* bit.

Error Detection and Correction   Now imagine that by the time the above transmission is received, the number 7 bit has been changed from 1 to 0. The receiver takes the

Figure 10.16 *Example of redundancy bit calculation*

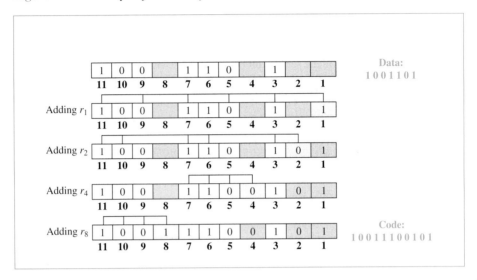

transmission and recalculates 4 new parity bits, using the same sets of bits used by the sender plus the relevant parity r bit for each set (see Fig. 10.17). Then it assembles the new parity values into a binary number in order of r position (r_8, r_4, r_2, r_1). In our example, this step gives us the binary number 0111 (7 in decimal), which is the precise location of the bit in error.

Figure 10.17 *Error detection using Hamming code*

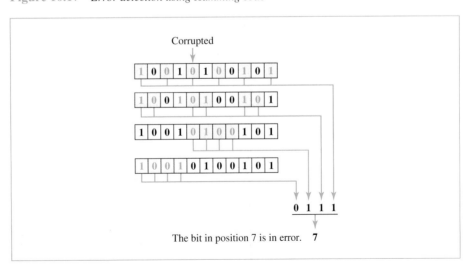

Once the bit is identified, the receiver can reverse its value and correct the error. The beauty of the technique is that it can easily be implemented in hardware and the code is corrected before the receiver knows about it.

Burst Error Correction

Although the Hamming code cannot correct a burst error directly, it is possible to rearrange the data and then apply the code. Instead of sending all the bits in a data unit together, we can organize N units in a column and then send the first bit of each, followed by the second bit of each, and so on. In this way, if a burst error of M bits occurs ($M < N$), then the error does not corrupt M bits of one single unit; it corrupts only 1 bit of a unit. With the Hamming scheme, we can then correct the corrupted bit in each unit. Figure 10.18 shows an example.

Figure 10.18 *Burst error correction example*

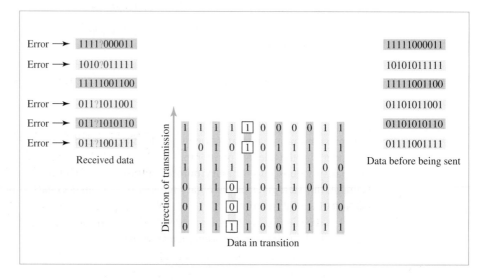

In Figure 10.18 we need to send six data units where each unit is a character with Hamming redundant bits. We organize the bits in columns and rows. We send the first column, then the second column, and so on. The bits that are corrupted by a burst error are shown in squares. Five consecutive bits are corrupted during the actual transmission. However, when these bits arrive at the destination and are reorganized into data units, each corrupted bit belongs to one unit and is automatically corrected. The trick here is to let the burst error corrupt only 1 bit of each unit.

10.4   KEY TERMS

burst error	error correction
checksum	error correction by retransmission
CRC checker	error detection
CRC generator	even parity
cyclic redundancy check (CRC)	forward error correction
error	Hamming code

odd parity
one's complement
parity bit
parity check

polynomial
redundancy
single-bit error
two-dimensional parity check

10.5 SUMMARY

❏ Errors can be categorized as a single-bit error or a burst error. A single-bit error has one bit error per data unit. A burst error has two or more bit errors per data unit.

❏ Redundancy is the concept of sending extra bits for use in error detection.

❏ Three common redundancy methods are parity check, cyclic redundancy check (CRC), and checksum.

❏ An extra bit (parity bit) is added to the data unit in the parity check.

❏ The parity check can detect only an odd number of errors; it cannot detect an even number of errors.

❏ In the two-dimensional parity check, a redundant data unit follows *n* data units.

❏ CRC, a powerful redundancy checking technique, appends a sequence of redundant bits derived from binary division to the data unit.

❏ The divisor in the CRC generator is often represented as an algebraic polynomial.

❏ Errors are corrected through retransmission and by forward error correction.

❏ The Hamming code is an error correction method using redundant bits. The number of bits is a function of the length of the data bits.

❏ In the Hamming code, for a data unit of *m* bits, use the formula $2^r >= m + r + 1$ to determine r, the number of redundant bits needed.

❏ By rearranging the order of bit transmission of the data units, the Hamming code can correct burst errors.

10.6 PRACTICE SET

Review Questions

1. How does a single-bit error differ from a burst error?
2. Discuss the concept of redundancy in error detection.
3. What are three types of redundancy checks used in data communications?
4. How can the parity bit detect a damaged data unit?
5. What is the difference between even parity and odd parity?
6. Discuss the parity check and the types of errors it can and cannot detect.
7. How is the simple parity check related to the two-dimensional parity check?
8. Discuss the two-dimensional parity check and the types of errors it can and cannot detect.

9. What does the CRC generator append to the data unit?

10. What is the relationship between the size of the CRC remainder and the divisor?

11. How does the CRC checker know that the received data unit is undamaged?

12. What are the conditions for the polynomial used by the CRC generator?

13. How is CRC superior to the two-dimensional parity check?

14. What is the error detection method used by upper-layer protocols?

15. What kind of arithmetic is used to add segments in the checksum generator and checksum checker?

16. List the steps involved in creating a checksum.

17. How does the checksum checker know that the received data unit is undamaged?

18. What kind of error is undetectable by the checksum?

19. What is the formula to calculate the number of redundancy bits required to correct a bit error in a given number of data bits?

20. What is the purpose of the Hamming code?

21. How can we use the Hamming code to correct a burst error?

Multiple-Choice Questions

22. Which error detection method consists of a parity bit for each data unit as well as an entire data unit of parity bits?
    a. Simple parity check
    b. Two-dimensional parity check
    c. CRC
    d. Checksum

23. Which error detection method uses ones complement arithmetic?
    a. Simple parity check
    b. Two-dimensional parity check
    c. CRC
    d. Checksum

24. Which error detection method consists of just one redundant bit per data unit?
    a. Simple parity check
    b. Two-dimensional parity check
    c. CRC
    d. Checksum

25. Which error detection method involves polynomials?
    a. Simple parity check
    b. Two-dimensional parity check
    c. CRC
    d. Checksum

26. Which of the following best describes a single-bit error?
    a. A single bit is inverted.
    b. A single bit is inverted per data unit.

c. A single bit is inverted per transmission.

d. Any of the above

27. If the ASCII character G is sent and the character D is received, what type of error is this?

a. Single-bit

b. Multiple-bit

c. Burst

d. Recoverable

28. If the ASCII character H is sent and the character I is received, what type of error is this?

a. Single-bit

b. Multiple-bit

c. Burst

d. Recoverable

29. In cyclic redundancy checking, what is the CRC?

a. The divisor

b. The quotient

c. The dividend

d. The remainder

30. In cyclic redundancy checking, the divisor is _____ the CRC.

a. The same size as

b. 1 bit less than

c. 1 bit more than

d. 2 bits more than

31. If the data unit is 111111, the divisor 1010, and the remainder 110, what is the dividend at the receiver?

a. 111111011

b. 111111110

c. 1010110

d. 110111111

32. If the data unit is 111111 and the divisor 1010, what is the dividend at the transmitter?

a. 111111000

b. 1111110000

c. 111111

d. 1111111010

33. If odd parity is used for ASCII error detection, the number of 0s per 8-bit symbol is _____.

a. Even

b. Odd

c. Indeterminate

d. 42

34. The sum of the checksum and data at the receiver is _____ if there are no errors.
    a. −0
    b. +0
    c. The complement of the checksum
    d. The complement of the data

35. The Hamming code is a method of _____.
    a. Error detection
    b. Error correction
    c. Error encapsulation
    d. (a) and (b)

36. In CRC there is no error if the remainder at the receiver is _____.
    a. Equal to the remainder at the sender
    b. Zero
    c. Nonzero
    d. The quotient at the sender

37. In CRC the quotient at the sender _____.
    a. Becomes the dividend at the receiver
    b. Becomes the divisor at the receiver
    c. Is discarded
    d. Is the remainder

38. Which error detection method involves the use of parity bits?
    a. Simple parity check
    b. Two-dimensional parity check
    c. CRC
    d. (a) and (b)

39. Which error detection method can detect a single-bit error?
    a. Simple parity check
    b. Two-dimensional parity check
    c. CRC
    d. All the above

40. Which error detection method can detect a burst error?
    a. The parity check
    b. Two-dimensional parity check
    c. CRC
    d. (b) and (c)

41. At the CRC generator, _____ added to the data unit before the division process.
    a. 0s are
    b. 1s are
    c. A polynomial is
    d. A CRC remainder is

42. At the CRC generator, _____ added to the data unit after the division process.
    a. 0s are
    b. 1s are
    c. The polynomial is
    d. The CRC remainder is

43. At the CRC checker, _____ means that the data unit is damaged.
    a. A string of 0s
    b. A string of 1s
    c. A string of alternating 1s and 0s
    d. A nonzero remainder

Exercises

44. What is the maximum effect of a 2-ms burst of noise on data transmitted at
    a. 1500 bps?
    b. 12,000 bps?
    c. 96,000 bps?

45. Assuming even parity, find the parity bit for each of the following data units.
    a. 1001011
    b. 0001100
    c. 1000000
    d. 1110111

46. A receiver receives the bit pattern 01101011. If the system is using even parity, is the pattern in error?

47. A system uses two-dimensional parity. Find the parity unit for the following two data units. Assume even parity.
    10011001 01101111

48. Given a 10-bit sequence 1010011110 and a divisor of 1011, find the CRC. Check your answer.

49. Given a remainder of 111, a data unit of 10110011, and a divisor of 1001, is there an error in the data unit?

50. Find the checksum for the following bit sequence. Assume a 16-bit segment size.
    1001001110010011
    1001100001001101

51. Find the complement of 1110010001110011.

52. Add 11100011 and 00011100 in ones complement. Interpret the result.

53. For each data unit of the following sizes, find the minimum number of redundancy bits needed to correct one single-bit error.
    a. 12
    b. 16
    c. 24
    d. 64

54. Construct the Hamming code for the bit sequence 10011101.

55. Find the parity bits for the following bit pattern, using simple parity. Do the same for two-dimensional parity. Assume even parity.

    ← 0011101 1100111 1111111 0000000

56. A sender sends 01110001; the receiver receives 01000001. If simple parity is used, can the receiver detect the error?

57. The following block is received by a system using two-dimensional even parity. Which bits are in error?

    ← 10010101 01001111 11010000 11011011

58. A system using two-dimensional even parity sends a block of 8 bytes. How many redundant bits are sent per block? What is the ratio of useful bits to total bits?

59. If a divisor is 101101, how many bits long is the CRC?

60. Find the binary equivalent of $x^8 + x^3 + x + 1$.

61. Find the polynomial equivalent of 100001110001.

62. A receiver receives the code 11001100111. When it uses the Hamming encoding algorithm, the result is 0101. Which bit is in error? What is the correct code?

63. In single-bit error correction, a code of 3 bits can be in one of four states: no error, first bit in error, second bit in error, and third bit in error. How many of these 3 bits should be redundant to correct this code? How many bits can be the actual data?

64. Using the logic in Exercise 63, find out how many redundant bits should be in a 10-bit code to detect an error.

65. The code 11110101101 was received. Using the Hamming encoding algorithm, what is the original code sent?

CHAPTER 11

Data Link Control and Protocols

Data communication requires at least two devices working together, one to send and one to receive. Even such a basic arrangement requires a great deal of coordination for an intelligible exchange to occur. The most important responsibilities of the data link layer are **flow control** and **error control.** Collectively, these functions are known as **data link control.**

In this chapter, we first informally define flow and error control. We then introduce three mechanisms that handle flow and error control. We finally discuss a popular data link protocol, HDLC.

11.1 FLOW AND ERROR CONTROL

Flow and error control are the main functions of the data link layer. Let us informally define each.

Flow Control

Flow control coordinates the amount of data that can be sent before receiving acknowledgment and is one of the most important duties of the data link layer. In most protocols, flow control is a set of procedures that tells the sender how much data it can transmit before it must wait for an acknowledgment from the receiver. The flow of data must not be allowed to overwhelm the receiver. Any receiving device has a limited speed at which it can process incoming data and a limited amount of memory in which to store incoming data. The receiving device must be able to inform the sending device before those limits are reached and to request that the transmitting device send fewer frames or stop temporarily. Incoming data must be checked and processed before they can be used. The rate of such processing is often slower than the rate of transmission. For this reason, each receiving device has a block of memory, called a *buffer*, reserved for storing incoming data until they are processed. If the buffer begins to fill up, the receiver must be able to tell the sender to halt transmission until it is once again able to receive.

> **Flow control refers to a set of procedures used to restrict the amount of data that the sender can send before waiting for acknowledgment.**

Error Control

Error control is both error detection and error correction. It allows the receiver to inform the sender of any frames lost or damaged in transmission and coordinates the retransmission of those frames by the sender. In the data link layer, the term *error control* refers primarily to methods of error detection and retransmission. Error control in the data link layer is often implemented simply: Anytime an error is detected in an exchange, specified frames are retransmitted. This process is called **automatic repeat request (ARQ)**.

> **Error control in the data link layer is based on automatic repeat request, which is the retransmission of data.**

Flow and Error Control Mechanisms

In this section we introduce three common flow and error control mechanisms: Stop-and-Wait ARQ, Go-Back-*N* ARQ, and Selective-Repeat ARQ. Although these are sometimes referred to as protocols, we prefer the term *mechanisms*.

11.2 STOP-AND-WAIT ARQ

Stop-and-Wait ARQ is the simplest flow and error control mechanism. It has the following features:

- The sending device keeps a copy of the last frame transmitted until it receives an acknowledgment for that frame. Keeping a copy allows the sender to retransmit lost or damaged frames until they are received correctly.

- For identification purposes, both data frames and **acknowledgment (ACK)** frames are numbered alternately 0 and 1. A data 0 frame is acknowledged by an ACK 1 frame, indicating that the receiver has received data frame 0 and is now expecting data frame 1. This numbering allows for identification of data frames in case of duplicate transmission (important in the case of lost acknowledgment or delayed acknowledgment, as we will see shortly).

- A damaged or lost frame is treated in the same manner by the receiver. If the receiver detects an error in the received frame, it simply discards the frame and sends no acknowledgment. If the receiver receives a frame that is out of order (0 instead of 1 or 1 instead of 0), it knows that a frame is lost. It discards the out-of-order received frame.

- The sender has a control variable, which we call S, that holds the number of the recently sent frame (0 or 1). The receiver has a control variable, which we call R, that holds the number of the next frame expected (0 or 1).

■ The sender starts a timer when it sends a frame. If an acknowledgment is not received within an allotted time period, the sender assumes that the frame was lost or damaged and resends it.

■ The receiver sends only positive acknowledgment for frames received safe and sound; it is silent about the frames damaged or lost. The acknowledgment number always defines the number of the next expected frame. If frame 0 is received, ACK 1 is sent; if frame 1 is received, ACK 0 is sent.

Operation

In the transmission of a frame, we can have four situations: normal operation, the frame is lost, the acknowledgment is lost, or the acknowledgment is delayed.

Normal Operation

In a normal transmission, the sender sends frame 0 and waits to receive ACK 1. When ACK 1 is received, it sends frame 1 and then waits to receive ACK 0, and so on. The ACK must be received before the timer set for each frame expires. Figure 11.1 shows successful frame transmissions.

Figure 11.1 *Normal operation*

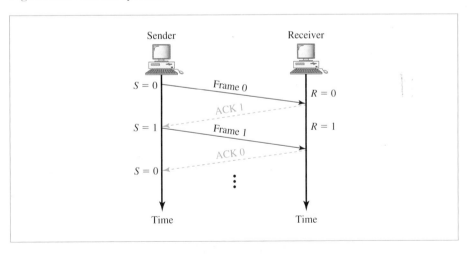

Lost or Damaged Frame

A lost or damaged frame is handled in the same way by the receiver; when the receiver receives a damaged frame, it discards it, which essentially means the frame is lost. The receiver remains silent about a lost frame and keeps its value of R. For example, in Figure 11.2, the sender transmits frame 1, but it is lost. The receiver does nothing, retaining the value of R (1). After the timer at the sender site expires, another copy of frame 1 is sent.

Figure 11.2 *Stop-and-Wait ARQ, lost frame*

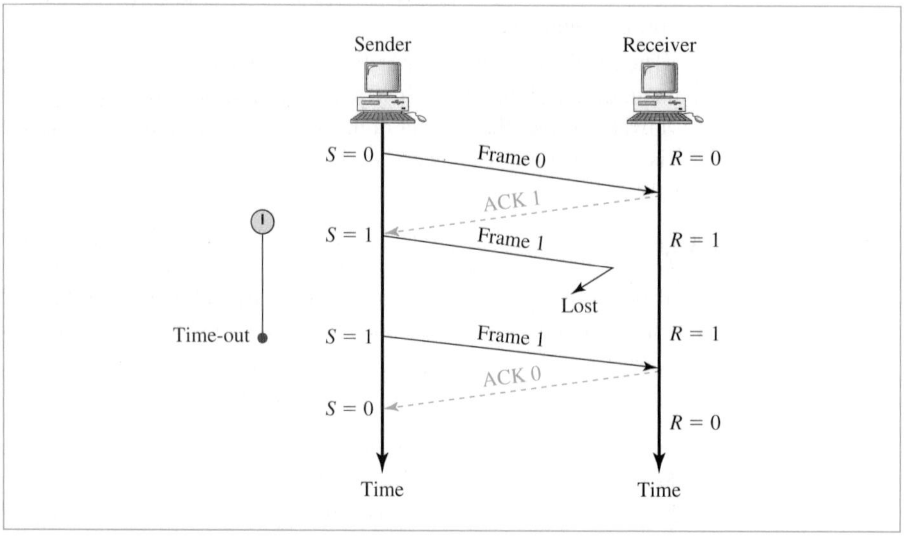

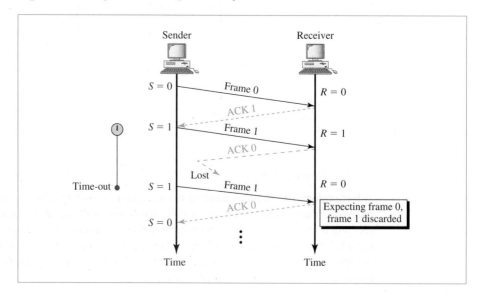

Lost Acknowledgment

A lost or damaged acknowledgment is handled in the same way by the sender; if the sender receives a damaged acknowledgment, it discards it. Figure 11.3 shows a lost ACK 0. The waiting sender does not know if frame 1 has been received. When the timer for frame 1 expires, the sender retransmits frame 1. Note that the receiver has already received frame 1 and is expecting to receive frame 0 ($R = 0$). Therefore, it silently discards the second copy of frame 1.

Figure 11.3 *Stop-and-Wait ARQ, lost ACK frame*

The reader may have discovered through this example the need to number frames. If the frames were not numbered, the receiver, thinking that frame 1 is a new frame (not a duplicate), keeps it.

In Stop-and-Wait ARQ, numbering frames prevents the retaining of duplicate frames.

Delayed Acknowledgment

Another problem that may occur is delayed acknowledgment. An acknowledgment can be delayed at the receiver or by some problem with the link. Figure 11.4 shows the delay of ACK 1; it is received after the timer for frame 0 has already expired. The sender has already retransmitted a copy of frame 0. However, the value of R at the receiver site is still 1, which means that the receiver expects to see frame 1. The receiver, therefore, discards the duplicate frame 0.

Figure 11.4 *Stop-and-Wait ARQ, delayed ACK*

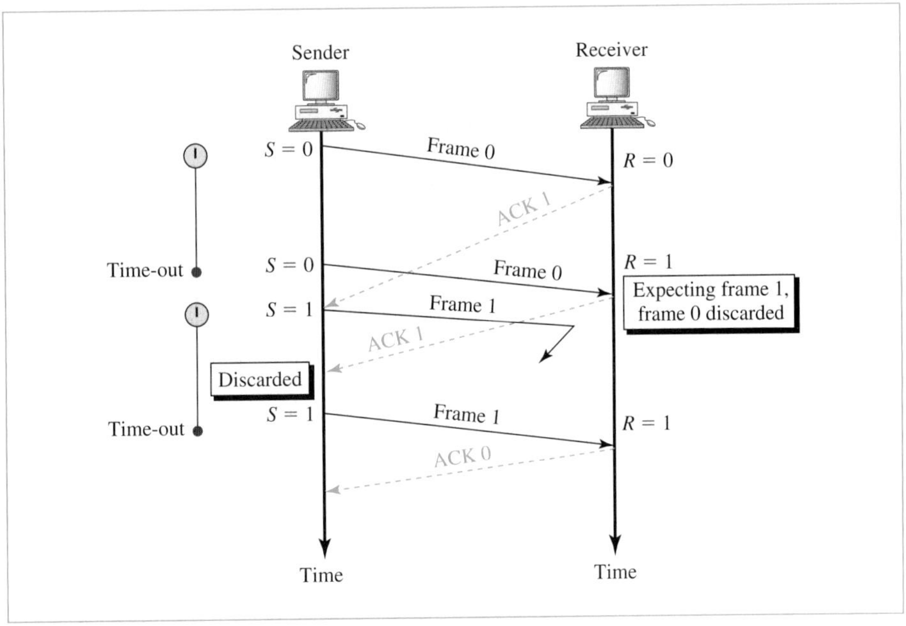

The sender has now received two ACKs, one that was delayed and one that was sent after the duplicate frame 0 arrived. The second ACK 1 is discarded.

To understand why we need to number the acknowledgments, let us examine Figure 11.4 again. After the delayed ACK 1 reaches the sender, frame 1 is sent. However, frame 1 is lost and never reaches the receiver. The sender then receives an ACK 1 for the duplicate frame sent. If the ACKs were not numbered, the sender would interpret the second ACK as the acknowledgment for frame 1. Numbering the ACKs provides a method to keep track of the received data frames.

> **Numbered acknowledgments are needed if an acknowledgment is delayed and the next frame is lost.**

Bidirectional Transmission

The stop-and-wait mechanism we have discussed is unidirectional. However, we can have bidirectional transmission if the two parties have two separate channels for full-duplex transmission or share the same channel for half-duplex transmission. In this case, each party needs both S and R variables to track frames sent and expected.

Piggybacking

Piggybacking is a method to combine a data frame with an acknowledgment. For example, in Figure 11.5, Stations A and B both have data to send. Instead of sending separate data and ACK frames, station A sends a data frame that includes an ACK. Station B behaves in a similar manner.

Figure 11.5   *Piggybacking*

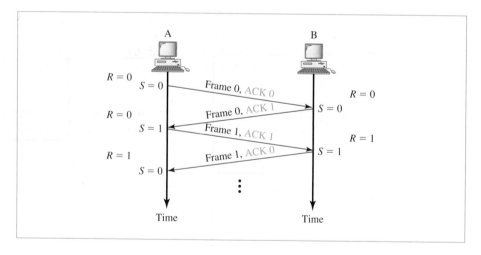

Piggybacking can save bandwidth because the overhead from a data frame and an ACK frame (addressees, CRC, etc.,) can be combined into just one frame.

11.3   GO-BACK-*N* ARQ

In Stop-and-Wait ARQ, at any point in time for a sender, there is only one frame, the outstanding frame, that is sent and waiting to be acknowledged. This is not a good use of the transmission medium. To improve the efficiency, multiple frames should be in transition while waiting for acknowledgment. In other words, we need to let more than one frame be outstanding. Two protocols use this concept: **Go-Back-*N* ARQ** and **Selective Repeat ARQ.** We discuss the first in this section and the second in Section 11.4.

In Go-Back-*N* ARQ, we can send up to *W* frames before worrying about acknowledgments; we keep a copy of these frames until the acknowledgments arrive. This procedure requires additional features to be added to Stop-and-Wait ARQ.

Sequence Numbers

Frames from a sending station are numbered sequentially. However, because we need to include the sequence number of each frame in the header, we need to set a limit. If the header of the frame allows *m* bits for the sequence number, the sequence numbers range from 0 to $2^m - 1$. For example, if *m* is 3, the only sequence numbers are 0 through 7 inclusive. However, we can repeat the sequence. So the sequence numbers are

$$0, 1, 2, 3, 4, 5, 6, 7, 0, 1, 2, 3, 4, 5, 6, 7, 0, 1, \ldots$$

Sender Sliding Window

At the sender site, to hold the outstanding frames until they are acknowledged, we use the concept of a window. We imagine that all frames are stored in a buffer. The outstanding frames are enclosed in a window. The frames to the left of the window are those that have already been acknowledged and can be purged; those to the right of the window cannot be sent until the window slides over them. The size of the window is at most $2^m - 1$ for reasons that we discuss later.

The size of the window in this protocol is fixed, although we can have a variable-size window in other protocols such as TCP (see Chapter 22). The window slides to include new unsent frames when the correct acknowledgments are received. The window is a **sliding window.** For example, in Figure 11.6*a*, frames 0 through 6 have been sent. In part *b*, the window slides two frames over because an acknowledgment was received for frames 0 and 1.

Figure 11.6 *Sender sliding window*

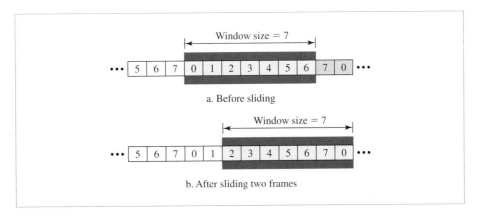

a. Before sliding

b. After sliding two frames

Receiver Sliding Window

The size of the window at the receiver site in this protocol is always 1. The receiver is always looking for a specific frame to arrive in a specific order. Any frame arriving out of order is discarded and needs to be resent. The receiver window also slides as shown in Figure 11.7. In part *a* the receiver is waiting for frame 0. When that arrives, the window slides over.

Figure 11.7   *Receiver sliding window*

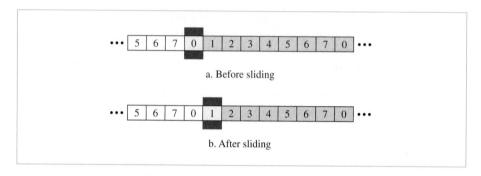

a. Before sliding

b. After sliding

Control Variables

The sender has three variables, S, S_F, and S_L. The S variable holds the sequence number of the recently sent frame; S_F holds the sequence number of the first frame in the window; and S_L holds the sequence number of the last frame in the window. The size of the window is W, where $W = S_L - S_F + 1$.

The receiver only has one variable, R, that holds the sequence number of the frame it expects to receive. If the sequence number of the received frame is the same as the value of R, the frame is accepted; if not, it is rejected. Figure 11.8 shows the sender and receiver window with their control variables.

Figure 11.8   *Control variables*

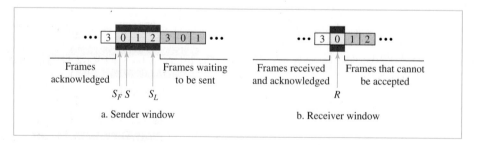

a. Sender window

b. Receiver window

Timers

The sender sets a timer for each frame sent. The receiver has no timers.

Acknowledgment

The receiver sends positive acknowledgments if a frame has arrived safe and sound and in order. If a frame is damaged or is received out of order, the receiver is silent and will discard all subsequent frames until it receives the one it is expecting. The silence of the receiver causes the timer of the unacknowledged frame to expire. This, in turn, causes the sender to go back and resend all frames, beginning with the one with the expired timer. The receiver does not have to acknowledge each frame received. It can send one cumulative acknowledgment for several frames.

Resending Frame

When a frame is damaged, the sender goes back and sends a set of frames starting from the damaged one up to the last one sent. For example, suppose the sender has already sent frame 6, but the timer for frame 3 expires. This means that frame 3 has not been acknowledged, so the sender goes back and sends frames 3, 4, 5, 6 again. That is why the protocol is called Go-Back-*N* ARQ.

Operation

Let us see what happens in various situations.

Normal Operation

Figure 11.9 shows a normal operation of this mechanism. The sender keeps track of the outstanding frames and updates the variables and windows as the acknowledgments arrive.

Figure 11.9   *Go-Back-N ARQ, normal operation*

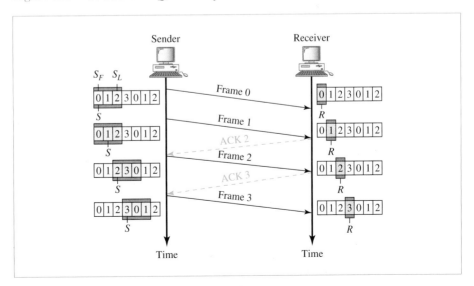

Damaged or Lost Frame

Now let us see what happens if a frame is lost. Figure 11.10 shows that frame 2 is lost. Note that when the receiver receives frame 3, it is discarded because the receiver is expecting frame 2, not frame 3 (according to its window). After the timer for frame 2 expires at the sender site, the sender sends frames 2 and 3 (it goes back to 2).

Figure 11.10 *Go-Back-N ARQ, lost frame*

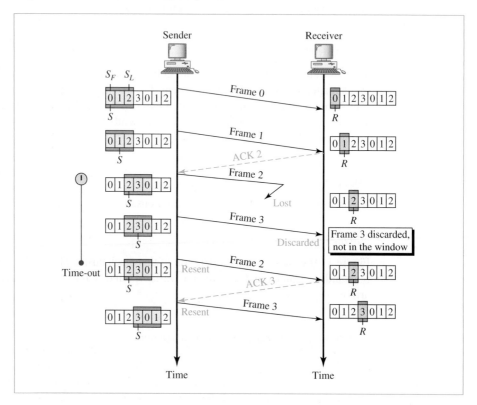

Damaged or Lost Acknowledgment

If an acknowledgment is damaged or lost, we can have two situations. If the next acknowledgment arrives before the expiration of any timer, there is no need for retransmission of frames because acknowledgments are cumulative in this protocol. ACK 4 means ACK 1 to ACK 4. So if ACK 1, ACK 2, and ACK 3 are lost, ACK 4 covers them. However, if the next ACK arrives after the time-out, the frame and all the frames after that are resent. Note that the receiver never resends an ACK. We leave the figure and details as an exercise.

Delayed Acknowledgment

A delayed acknowledgment also triggers the resending of frames. Again, we leave the figure and details as an exercise.

Sender Window Size

We can now show why the size of the sender window must be less than 2^m. As an example, we choose $m = 2$, which means the size of the window can be $2^m - 1$, or 3. Figure 11.11 compares a window size of 3 and 4.

Figure 11.11 *Go-Back-N ARQ: sender window size*

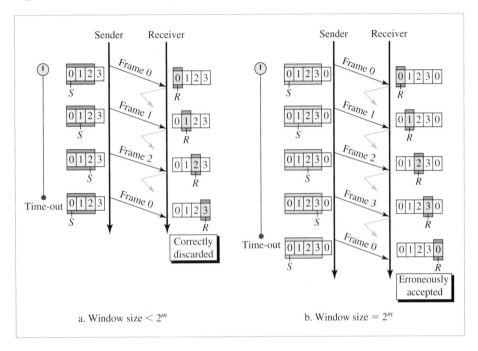

a. Window size $< 2^m$

b. Window size $= 2^m$

If the size of the window is 3 (less than 2^2) and all three acknowledgments are lost, the frame 0 timer expires and all three frames are resent. However, the window of the receiver is now expecting frame 3, not frame 0, so the duplicate frame is correctly discarded. On the other hand, if the size of the window is 4 (equal to 2^2) and all acknowledgments are lost, the sender will send the duplicate of frame 0. However, this time the window of the receiver expects to receive frame 0, so it accepts frame 0, not as a duplicate, but as the first frame in the next cycle. This is an error.

In Go-Back-*N* ARQ, the size of the sender window must be less than 2^m; the size of the receiver window is always 1.

Bidirectional Transmission and Piggybacking

As in the case of Stop-and-Wait ARQ, Go-Back-*N* ARQ can also be bidirectional. We can also use piggybacking to improve the efficiency of the transmission. However, note that each direction needs both a sender window and a receiver window. We leave the configuration of the windows as an exercise.

11.4   SELECTIVE REPEAT ARQ

Go-Back-*N* ARQ simplifies the process at the receiver site. The receiver keeps track of only one variable, and there is no need to buffer out-of-order frames; they are simply discarded. However, this protocol is very inefficient for a noisy link. In a noisy link a frame has a higher probability of damage, which means the resending of multiple frames. This resending uses up the bandwidth and slows down the transmission. For noisy links, there is another mechanism that does not resend *N* frames when just one frame is damaged; only the damaged frame is resent. This mechanism is called Selective Repeat ARQ. It is more efficient for noisy links, but the processing at the receiver is more complex.

Sender and Receiver Windows

The configuration of the sender and its control variables for Selective Repeat ARQ are the same as those for Go-Back-*N* ARQ. However, for reasons to be discussed later, the size of the window should be at most one-half of the value 2^m. The receiver window size must also be this size. This window, however, specifies the range of the accepted received frame. In other words, in Go-Back-*N*, the receiver is looking for one specific sequence number; in Selective Repeat, the receiver is looking for a range of sequence numbers. The receiver has two control variables R_F and R_L to define the boundaries of the window. Figure 11.12 shows the sender and receiver windows.

Figure 11.12   *Selective Repeat ARQ, sender and receiver windows*

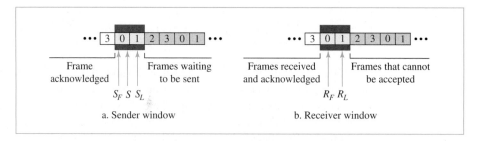

Selective Repeat ARQ also defines a **negative acknowledgment (NAK)** that reports the sequence number of a damaged frame before the timer expires.

Operation

Let us show the operation of the mechanism with an example of a lost frame, as shown in Figure 11.13.

Frames 0 and 1 are accepted when received because they are in the range specified by the receiver window. When frame 3 is received, it is also accepted for the same reason. However, the receiver sends a NAK 2 to show that frame 2 has not been received. When the sender receives the NAK 2, it resends only frame 2, which is then accepted because it is in the range of the window.

Figure 11.13   *Selective Repeat ARQ, lost frame*

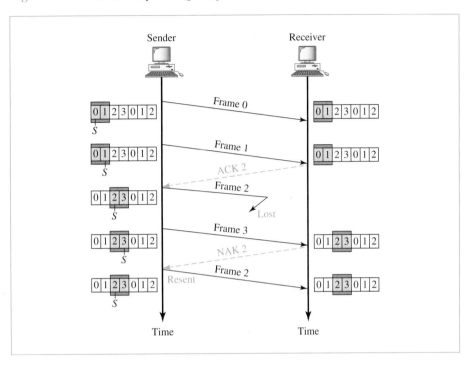

Lost and Delayed ACKs and NAKs

We leave lost and delayed ACKs and NAKs as exercises. Note that the sender also sets a timer for each frame sent.

Sender Window Size

We can now show why the size of the sender and receiver windows must be at most one-half of 2^m. For an example, we choose $m = 2$, which means the size of the window should be $2^m/2$, or 2. Figure 11.14 compares a window size of 2 with a window size of 3.

If the size of the window is 2 and all acknowledgments are lost, the timer for frame 0 expires and frame 0 is resent. However, the window of the receiver is now expecting frame 2, not frame 0, so this duplicate frame is correctly discarded. When the size of the window is 3 and all acknowledgments are lost, the sender sends a duplicate of frame 0. However, this time, the window of the receiver expects to receive frame 0 (0 is part of the window), so it accepts frame 0, not as a duplicate, but as the first frame in the next cycle. This is clearly an error.

> **In Selective Repeat ARQ, the size of the sender and receiver window must be at most one-half of 2^m.**

Figure 11.14   *Selective Repeat ARQ, sender window size*

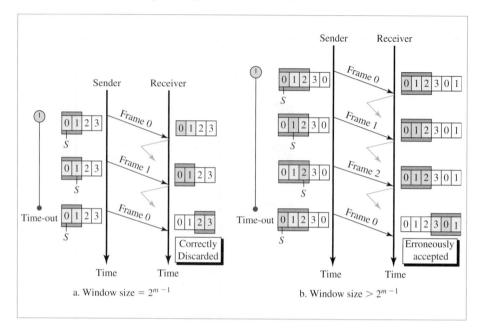

Bidirectional Transmission and Piggybacking

As in the case of Stop-and-Wait ARQ and the Go-Back-*N* ARQ, Selective Repeat ARQ can also be bidirectional. We can use piggybacking to improve the efficiency of the transmission. However, note that each direction needs both a sender window and a receiver window. We leave the configuration of the windows as an exercise.

Bandwidth-Delay Product

A measure of the efficiency of an ARQ system is the product of the bandwidth (in bits per second) and the round-trip delay (in seconds). If the link has an adequate bandwidth, the sender will exhaust its window quickly and will wait for the acknowledgments to come. If the delay is long, the sender can also exhaust its window while waiting. So the product of these two factors can be used to define the efficiency of an ARQ system. The **bandwidth-delay product** is a measure of the number of bits we can send out of our system while waiting for news from the receiver.

Example 1

In a Stop-and-Wait ARQ system, the bandwidth of the line is 1 Mbps, and 1 bit takes 20 ms to make a round trip. What is the bandwidth-delay product? If the system data frames are 1000 bits in length, what is the utilization percentage of the link?

Solution
The bandwidth-delay product is

$$1 \times 10^6 \times 20 \times 10^{-3} = 20{,}000 \text{ bits}$$

The system can send 20,000 bits during the time it takes for the data to go from the sender to the receiver and then back again. However, the system sends only 1000 bits. We can say that the link utilization is only 1000/20,000, or 5%. For this reason, for a link with high bandwidth or long delay, use of Stop-and-Wait ARQ wastes the capacity of the link.

Example 2

What is the utilization percentage of the link in Example 1 if the link uses Go-Back-*N* ARQ with a 15-frame sequence?

Solution

The bandwidth-delay product is still 20,000. The system can send up to 15 frames or 15,000 bits during a round trip. This means the utilization is 15,000/20,000, or 75 percent. Of course, if there are damaged frames, the utilization percentage is much less because frames have to be resent.

Pipelining

In networking and in other areas, a task is often begun before the previous task has ended. This is known as **pipelining.** There is no pipelining in Stop-and-Wait ARQ because we need to wait for a frame to reach the destination and be acknowledged before the next frame can be sent. However, pipelining does apply to Go-Back-*N* ARQ and Selective Repeat ARQ because several frames can be sent before we receive news about the previous frames.

Pipelining improves the efficiency of the transmission if the number of bits in transition is large with respect to the bandwidth-delay product.

11.5 HDLC

High-level Data Link Control (HDLC) is an actual protocol designed to support both half-duplex and full-duplex communication over point-to-point and multipoint links. It implements the ARQ mechanisms we discussed in this chapter.

Configurations and Transfer Modes

HDLC provides two common modes of transmission: NRM and ABM.

NRM

In **normal response mode (NRM),** the station configuration is unbalanced. We have one primary station and multiple secondary stations. A **primary station** can send commands; a **secondary station** can only respond. The NRM is used for both point-to-point and multiple-point links. See Figure 11.15.

ABM

In **asynchronous balanced mode (ABM),** the configuration is balanced. The link is point-to-point, and each station can function as a primary and a secondary, as shown in Figure 11.16.

Figure 11.15   *NRM*

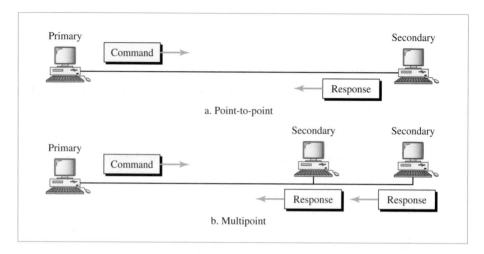

a. Point-to-point

b. Multipoint

Figure 11.16   *ABM*

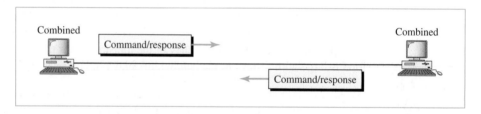

Frames

To provide the flexibility necessary to support all the options possible in the modes and configurations described above, HDLC defines three types of frames: **information frames (I-frames), supervisory frames (S-frames),** and **unnumbered frames (U-frames).** Each type of frame works as an envelope for the transmission of a different type of message. I-frames are used to transport user data and control information relating to user data (piggybacking). S-frames are used only to transport control information. U-frames are reserved for system management. Information carried by U-frames is intended for managing the link itself.

Frame Format

Each frame in HDLC may contain up to six fields, as shown in Figure 11.17: a beginning flag field, an address field, a control field, an information field, a frame check sequence (FCS) field, and an ending flag field. In multiple-frame transmissions, the ending flag of one frame can serve as the beginning flag of the next frame.

Flag Field

The **flag field** of an HDLC frame is an 8-bit sequence with a bit pattern 01111110 that identifies both the beginning and end of a frame and serves as a synchronization

Figure 11.17 *HDLC frame*

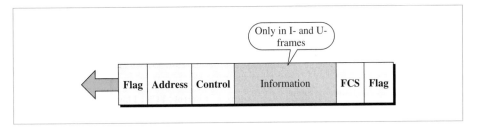

pattern for the receiver. The flag field is discussed further in the section on data transparency.

Address Field

The second field of an HDLC frame contains the address of the secondary station that is either the originator or the destination of the frame (or the station acting as secondary in the case of combined stations). If a primary station creates a frame, it contains a *to* address. If a secondary creates the frame, it contains a *from* address. An **address field** can be 1 byte or several bytes long, depending on the needs of the network. One byte can identify up to 128 stations (because 1 bit is used for another purpose). Larger networks require multiple-byte address fields.

If the address field is only 1 byte, the last bit is always a 1. If the address is more than 1 byte, all bytes but the last one will end with 0; only the last will end with 1. Ending each intermediate byte with 0 indicates to the receiver that there are more address bytes to come. The networks that do not use primary/secondary configuration, such as Ethernet (see Chapter 14), use two address fields: the sender address and the receiver address.

Control Field

The **control field** is a 1- or 2-byte segment of the frame used for flow and error control. The interpretation of bits in this field is different for different frame types. We discuss this field when we discuss the frame types.

Information Field

The **information field** contains the user's data from the network layer or network management information. Its length can vary from one network to another but is always fixed within each network.

FCS Field

The **frame check sequence (FCS)** is HDLC's error detection field. It can contain either a 2- or 4-byte ITU-T CRC.

Frame Type

HDLC defines three types of frames: the I-frame, S-frame, and U-frame, as shown in Figure 11.18.

Figure 11.18   *HDLC frame types*

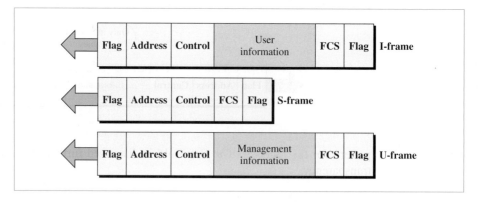

I-Frame

I-frames are designed to carry user data from the network layer. In addition, they can include flow and error control information (piggybacking). Figure 11.19 shows the format of the control field for an I-frame.

Figure 11.19   *I-frame*

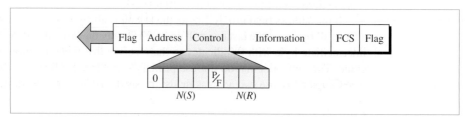

The bits in the control field of the I-frame are interpreted as follows:

- If the first bit of the control field is 0, this means the frame is an I-frame.
- The next 3 bits, called $N(S)$, define the sequence number of the frame in travel. Note that with 3 bits, we can only define a sequence number between 0 and 7. The value of this field corresponds to the value of control variable S, as discussed for the three ARQ mechanisms.
- The next bit is called the P/F bit. The P/F field is a single bit with a dual purpose. It has meaning only when it is set (bit = 1) and can mean poll or final. It means *poll* when the frame is sent by a primary station to a secondary (when the address field contains the address of the receiver). It means *final* when the frame is sent by a secondary to a primary (when the address field contains the address of the sender).
- The next 3 bits, called $N(R)$, correspond to the value of the ACK when piggybacking is used.

S-Frames

Supervisory frames are used for flow and error control whenever piggybacking is either impossible or inappropriate (when the station either has no data of its own to send or needs to send a command or response other than an acknowledgment). S-frames do not have information fields. Figure 11.20 shows the format of the control field for an S-frame.

Figure 11.20   S-frame control field in HDLC

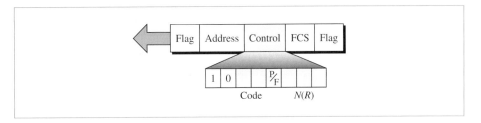

The bits in the control field are interpreted as follows:

■ If the first 2 bits of the control field are 10, this means the frame is an S-frame.

■ The second 2 bits of the control field of an S-frame is a code that defines the four types of S-frames: receive ready (RR), receive not ready (RNR), reject (REJ), and selective reject (SREJ).

a. **Receive ready (RR).** If the value of the code subfield is 00, it is an RR S-frame. This kind of frame acknowledges a safe and sound frame or group of frames.

b. **Receive not ready (RNR).** If the value of the code subfield is 10, it is an RNR S-frame. This kind of frame is the RR frame with additional duties. It acknowledges the receipt of a frame or group of frames, and it announces that the receiver is busy and cannot receive more frames. It acts as a kind of congestion control mechanism by asking the sender to slow down.

c. **Reject (REJ).** If the value of the code subfield is 01, it is a REJ S-frame. This is a NAK frame, but not like the one used for Selective Repeat ARQ. It is a NAK that can be used in Go-Back-N ARQ to improve the efficiency of the process by informing the sender, before the sender time expires, that the last frame is lost or damaged.

d. **Selective reject (SREJ).** If the value of the code subfield is 11, it is an SREJ S-frame. This is a NAK frame used in Selective Repeat ARQ. Note that the HDLC protocol uses the term *selective reject* instead of *selective repeat*.

■ The fifth bit in the control field is the P/F bit, as discussed before.

■ The next 3 bits, called $N(R)$, correspond to the ACK or NAK value.

U-Frames

Unnumbered frames are used to exchange session management and control information between connected devices. Unlike S-frames, U-frames contain an information field, but one used for system management information, not user data. As with S-frames, however, much of the information carried by U-frames is contained in codes included in the control field. U-frame codes are divided into two sections: a 2-bit prefix before the P/F bit and a 3-bit suffix after the P/F bit. Together, these two segments (5 bits) can be used to create up to 32 different types of U-frames. Some of the more common combinations are shown in Figure 11.21.

Figure 11.21 *U-frame control field in HDLC*

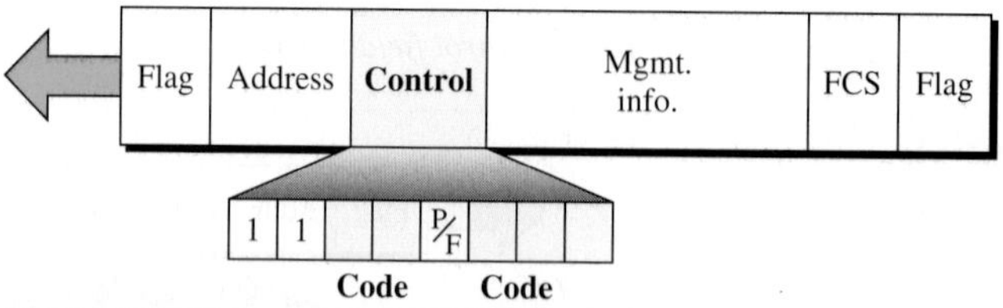

Code		Command	Response
00	001	SNRM	
11	011	SNRME	
11	100	SABM	DM
11	110	SABME	
00	000	UI	UI
00	110		UA
00	010	DISC	RD
10	000	SIM	RIM
00	100	UP	
11	001	RSET	
11	101	XID	XID
10	001		FRMR

The U-frame commands and responses listed in Table 11.1 can be used for different purposes such as mode setting, exchanging unnumbered frames, and connection and disconnection of the link.

Table 11.1 *U-frame control command and response*

Command/Response	*Meaning*
SNRM	Set normal response mode
SNRME	Set normal response mode (extended)
SABM	Set asynchronous balanced mode
SABME	Set asynchronous balanced mode (extended)
UP	Unnumbered poll
UI	Unnumbered information
UA	Unnumbered acknowledgment
RD	Request disconnect
DISC	Disconnect
DM	Disconnect mode
RIM	Request information mode
SIM	Set initialization mode
RSET	Reset
XID	Exchange ID
FRMR	Frame reject

Examples

We give examples of communication using HDLC in this section.

Example 3: Piggybacking without Error

Figure 11.22 shows an exchange.

Figure 11.22   *Example 3*

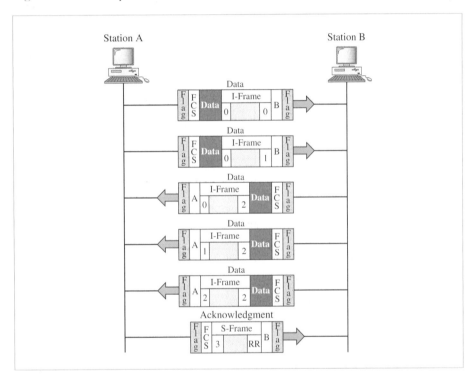

Station A begins the exchange of information with an I-frame numbered 0 followed by another I-frame numbered 1. Station B piggybacks its acknowledgment of both frames onto an I-frame of its own. Station B's first I-frame is also numbered 0 [$N(S)$ field] and contains a 2 in its $N(R)$ field, acknowledging the receipt of A's frames 1 and 0 and indicating that it expects frame 2 to arrive next. Station B transmits its second and third I-frames (numbered 1 and 2) before accepting further frames from station A. Its $N(R)$ information, therefore, has not changed: B frames 1 and 2 indicate that station B is still expecting A frame 2 to arrive next.

Station A has sent all its data. Therefore, it cannot piggyback an acknowledgment onto an I-frame and sends an S-frame instead. The RR code indicates that A is still ready to receive. The number 3 in the $N(R)$ field tells B that frames 0, 1, and 2 have all been accepted and that A is now expecting frame number 3.

Example 4: Piggybacking with Error

In Example 3, suppose frame 1 sent from station B to station A has an error. Station A informs station B to resend frames 1 and 2 (the system is using the Go-Back-N mechanism). Station A sends a reject supervisory frame to announce the error in frame 1. Figure 11.23 shows the exchange.

Figure 11.23   *Example 4*

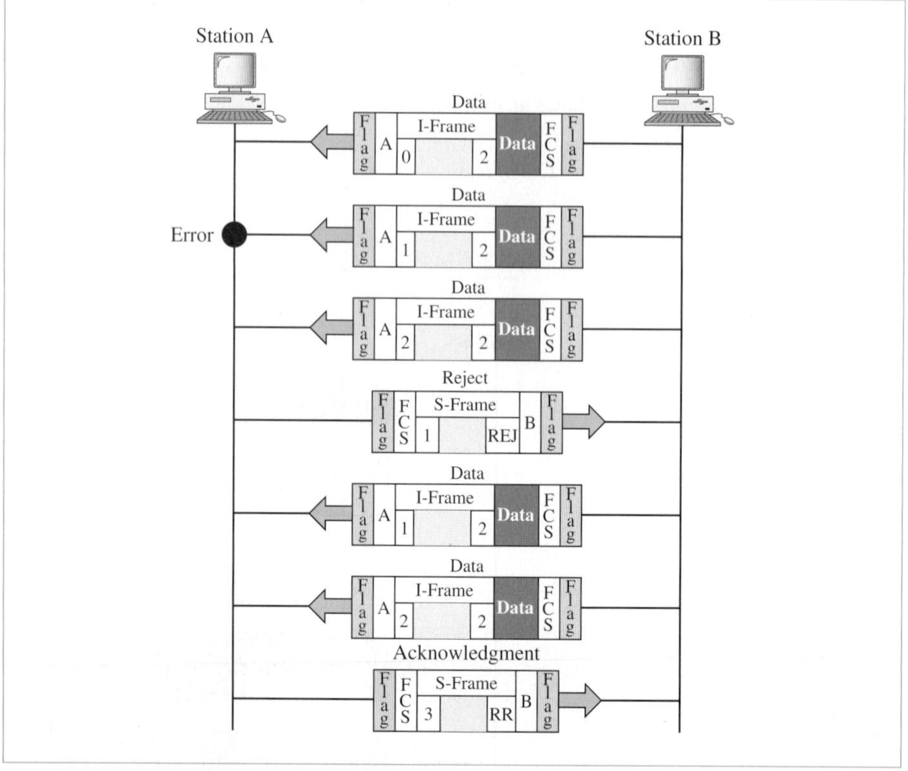

Data Transparency

The data field of the HDLC frame can carry text as well as nontextual information such as graphics, audio, video, or other bit sequences. Unfortunately, some message types can create problems during transmission. For example, if the data field of an HDLC frame contains a pattern that is the same as the sequence reserved for the flag field 01111110, the receiver interprets that sequence as the ending flag. The rest of the bits are assumed to belong to the next frame. This phenomenon is called a lack of **data transparency.** When data are transparent, all data are recognized as data and all control information is recognized as control information. There is no ambiguity as to which is which.

Bit Stuffing

To guarantee that the flag field sequence does not appear inadvertently anywhere else in the frame, HDLC uses a process called **bit stuffing.** Every time a sender wants to transmit a bit sequence having more than five consecutive 1s, it inserts (stuffs) one redundant 0 after the fifth 1. For example, the sequence 011111111000 becomes 0111110111000. This extra 0 is inserted regardless of whether the sixth bit is another 1. Its presence tells the receiver that the current sequence is not a flag. Once the receiver has seen the stuffed 0, the 0 is dropped from the data and the original bit stream is restored.

Bit stuffing is the process of adding one extra 0 whenever there are five consecutive 1s in the data so that the receiver does not mistake the data for a flag.

Figure 11.24 shows bit stuffing at the sender and bit removal at the receiver. Note that even if we have a 0 after five 1s, we still stuff a 0. The 0 will be removed by the receiver.

Figure 11.24 *Bit stuffing and removal*

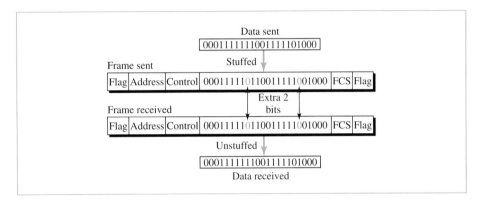

With three exceptions, bit stuffing is required whenever five 1s occur consecutively. The exceptions are when the bit sequence really is a flag, when the transmission is being aborted, and when the channel is idle. The flowchart in Figure 11.25 shows the

Figure 11.25 *Bit stuffing in HDLC*

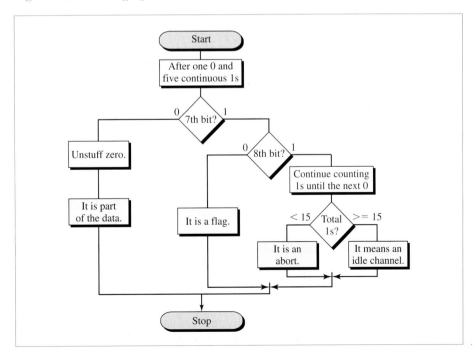

process the receiver follows to identify and discard a stuffed bit. As the receiver reads the incoming bits, it counts 1s. When it finds five consecutive 1s after a 0, it checks the next (seventh) bit. If the seventh bit is a 0, the receiver recognizes it as a stuffed bit, discards it, and resets its counter. If the seventh bit is a 1, the receiver checks the eighth bit. If the eighth bit is a 0, the sequence is recognized as a flag and treated accordingly. If the eighth bit is another 1, the receiver continues counting. A total of 7 to 14 consecutive 1s indicates an abort. A total of 15 or more 1s indicates an idle channel.

11.6   KEY TERMS

acknowledgment (ACK)	information field
address field	information frame (I-frame)
asynchronous balanced mode (ABM)	negative acknowledgment (NAK)
automatic repeat request (ARQ)	normal response mode (NRM)
bandwidth-delay product	piggybacking
bit stuffing	pipelining
data link control	primary station
data transparency	secondary station
error control	Selective Repeat ARQ
flag field	sliding window
flow control	Stop-and-Wait ARQ
frame check sequence (FCS)	supervisory frame (S-frame)
Go-Back-*N* ARQ	unnumbered frame (U-frame)
High-level Data Link Control (HDLC)	

11.7   SUMMARY

❑ Flow control is the regulation of the sender's data rate so that the receiver buffer does not become overwhelmed.

❑ Error control is both error detection and error correction.

❑ In Stop-and-Wait ARQ, the sender sends a frame and waits for an acknowledgment from the receiver before sending the next frame.

❑ In Go-Back-*N* ARQ, multiple frames can be in transit at the same time. If there is an error, retransmission begins with the last unacknowledged frame even if subsequent frames have arrived correctly. Duplicate frames are discarded.

❑ In Selective Repeat ARQ, multiple frames can be in transit at the same time. If there is an error, only the unacknowledged frame is retransmitted.

❑ Flow control mechanisms with sliding windows have control variables at both sender and receiver sites.

❑ Piggybacking couples an acknowledgment with a data frame.

❑ The bandwidth-delay product is a measure of the number of bits a system can have in transit.

❑ HDLC is a protocol that implements ARQ mechanisms. It supports communication over point-to-point or multipoint links.

❑ HDLC stations communicate in normal response mode (NRM) or asynchronous balanced mode (ABM).

❑ HDLC protocol defines three types of frames: the information frame (I-frame), the supervisory frame (S-frame), and the unnumbered frame (U-frame).

❑ HDLC handles data transparency by adding a 0 whenever there are five consecutive 1s following a 0. This is called bit stuffing.

11.8   PRACTICE SET

Review Questions

1. Why is flow control needed?
2. What are three popular ARQ mechanisms?
3. How does ARQ correct an error?
4. Stop-and-Wait ARQ has two control variables S and R. What are their functions?
5. How does Go-Back-N ARQ differ from Selective Repeat ARQ?
6. What is the purpose of the timer at the sender site in systems using ARQ?
7. Discuss the size of the Go-Back-N ARQ sliding window at both the sender site and the receiver site.
8. How are a lost acknowledgment and a lost frame handled at the sender site?
9. Discuss the size of the Selective Repeat ARQ sliding window at both the sender site and the receiver site.
10. Which ARQ mechanisms utilize pipelining?
11. How is the bandwidth-delay product related to the system efficiency?
12. In HDLC, what is bit stuffing and why is it needed?
13. Name the types of HDLC frames, and give a brief description of each.
14. Name and discuss briefly the bits in the HDLC control field.
15. What is piggybacking?
16. Name the four types of S-frames.

Multiple-Choice Questions

17. In a Go-Back-N ARQ, if the window size is 63, what is the range of sequence numbers?
    a. 0 to 63
    b. 0 to 64
    c. 1 to 63
    d. 1 to 64
18. Flow control is needed to prevent _____.
    a. Bit errors
    b. Overflow of the sender buffer
    c. Overflow of the receiver buffer
    d. Collision between sender and receiver

19. In Go-Back-N ARQ, if frames 4, 5, and 6 are received successfully, the receiver may send an ACK _____ to the sender.

    a. 5

    b. 6

    c. 7

    d. Any of the above

20. For a sliding window of size $n - 1$ (n sequence numbers), there can be a maximum of _____ frames sent but unacknowledged.

    a. 0

    b. $n - 1$

    c. n

    d. $n + 1$

21. In _____ ARQ, if a NAK is received, only the specific damaged or lost frame is retransmitted.

    a. Stop-and-Wait

    b. Go-Back-N

    c. Selective Repeat

    d. (a) and (b)

22. ARQ stands for _____.

    a. Automatic repeat quantization

    b. Automatic repeat request

    c. Automatic retransmission request

    d. Acknowledge repeat request

23. A timer is set when _____ is (are) sent out.

    a. A data frame

    b. An ACK

    c. A NAK

    d. All the above

24. For Stop-and-Wait ARQ, for n data packets sent, _____ acknowledgments are needed.

    a. n

    b. $2n$

    c. $n - 1$

    d. $n + 1$

25. HDLC is an acronym for _____.

    a. High-duplex line communication

    b. High-level data link control

    c. Half-duplex digital link combination

    d. Host double-level circuit

26. The address field of a frame in HDLC protocol contains the address of the _____ station.
    a. Primary
    b. Secondary
    c. Tertiary
    d. (a) or (b)

27. The HDLC _____ field defines the beginning and end of a frame.
    a. Flag
    b. Address
    c. Control
    d. FCS

28. What is present in all HDLC control fields?
    a. P/F bit
    b. $N(R)$
    c. $N(S)$
    d. Code bits

29. The shortest frame in HDLC protocol is usually the _____ frame.
    a. Information
    b. Supervisory
    c. Management
    d. None of the above

30. When data and acknowledgment are sent on the same frame, this is called _____.
    a. Piggybacking
    b. Backpacking
    c. Piggypacking
    d. A good idea

Exercises

31. Draw the sender and receiver windows for a system using Go-Back-N ARQ, given the following:
    a. Frame 0 is sent; frame 0 is acknowledged.
    b. Frames 1 and 2 are sent; frames 1 and 2 are acknowledged.
    c. Frames 3, 4, and 5 are sent; frame 4 is acknowledged; timer for frame 5 expires.
    d. Frames 5, 6, and 7 are sent; frames 4 through 7 are acknowledged.

32. Repeat Exercise 31, using Selective Repeat ARQ.

33. What does the number on a NAK frame mean for Selective Repeat ARQ?

34. What does the number on an ACK frame mean for Selective Repeat ARQ?

35. ACK 7 has been received by the sender in a Go-Back-*N* sliding window system. Now frames 7, 0, 1, 2, and 3 are sent. For each of the following separate scenarios, discuss the significance of the receiving of

    a. An ACK 1

    b. An ACK 4

    c. An ACK 3

36. A Go-Back-*N* ARQ uses a window of size 15. How many bits are needed to define the sequence number?

37. A Selective Repeat ARQ is using 7 bits to represent the sequence numbers. What is the size of the window?

38. A computer is using a sliding window of size 7. Complete the following sequence numbers for 20 packets:

$$0, 1, 2, 3, 4, 5, 6, \ldots$$

39. A computer is using the following sequence numbers. What is the size of the window?

$$0, 1, 2, 3, 4, 5, 6, 7, 8, 9, 10, 11, 12, 13, 14, 15, 0, 1, \ldots$$

40. Computer A uses Stop-and-Wait ARQ protocol to send packets to computer B. If the distance between A and B is 4000 km, how long does it take computer A to receive acknowledgment for a packet? Use the speed of light for propagation speed, and assume the time between receiving and sending the acknowledgment is zero.

41. In Exercise 40, how long does it take for computer A to send out a packet of size 1000 bytes if the throughput is 100,000 Kbps?

42. Using the results of Exercises 40 and 41, for how much time is computer A idle?

43. Repeat Exercise 42 for a system that uses a sliding window ARQ with a window size of 255.

44. Bit-stuff the following data:

    00011111101111100111100111111001

45. Bit-stuff the following data:

    00011111111111111111111111111111110011111001

CHAPTER 12

Point-to-Point Access: PPP

In a network, two devices can be connected by a dedicated link or a shared link. In the first case, the link can be used by the two devices at any time. We refer to this type of access as **point-to-point access.** In the second case, the link is shared between pairs of devices that need to use the link. We refer to this type of access as multiple access.

Multiple access can involve point-to-point access. When two devices in a multiple-access situation get access to the link or a channel in the link, they may need to use a point-to-point access protocol to exchange data. We discuss point-to-point access in this chapter; we defer the discussion of multiple access to Chapter 13.

12.1 POINT-TO-POINT PROTOCOL

One of the most common protocols for point-to-point access is the **Point-to-Point Protocol (PPP).** Today, millions of Internet users who need to connect their home computers to the server of an Internet service provider use PPP. The majority of these users have a traditional modem, a DSL modem, or a cable modem. They are connected to the Internet through either a telephone line or a TV cable connection. The telephone line or the cable TV connection provides a physical link, but to control and manage the transfer of data, there is a need for a point-to-point protocol; PPP is by far the most common.

PPP provides several services that we discuss here:

1. It defines the format of the frame to be exchanged between devices.
2. It defines how two devices can negotiate the establishment of the link and the exchange of data.
3. It defines how network layer data are encapsulated in the data link frame.
4. It defines how two devices can authenticate each other.

Frame Format

PPP employs a version of HDLC. Figure 12.1 shows the format of a PPP frame. The description of each field follows:

■ **Flag field.** The flag fields, like the one in HDLC, identify the boundaries of a PPP frame. Its value is 01111110.

Figure 12.1   *PPP frame*

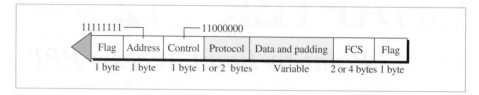

- **Address field.** Because PPP is used for a point-to-point connection, it uses the broadcast address of HDLC, 11111111, to avoid a data link address in the protocol.
- **Control field.** The control field uses the format of the U-frame in HDLC. The value is 11000000 to show that the frame does not contain any sequence numbers and that there is no flow or error control.
- **Protocol field.** The protocol field defines what is being carried in the data field: user data or other information. We discuss this field in detail shortly.
- **Data field.** This field carries either the user data or other information that we will discuss shortly.
- **Frame check sequence (FCS) field.** The FCS, as in HDLC, is simply a 2-byte or 4-byte CRC.

Transition States

A PPP connection goes through different phases which can be shown in a **transition state** diagram (see Fig. 12.2).

Figure 12.2   *Transition states*

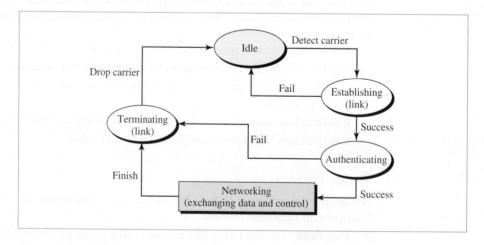

- **Idle state.** The **idle state** means that the link is not being used. There is no active carrier, and the line is quiet.
- **Establishing state.** When one of the endpoints starts the communication, the connection goes into the **establishing state.** In this state, options are negotiated

between the two parties. If the negotiation is successful, the system goes to the authenticating state (if authentication is required) or directly to the networking state. The link control protocol packets, discussed shortly, are used for this purpose. Several packets may be exchanged during this state.

■ **Authenticating state.** The **authenticating state** is optional; the two endpoints may decide, during the establishing state, not to go through this state. However, if they decide to proceed with authentication, they send several authentication packets, discussed in a later section. If the result is successful, the connection goes to the networking state; otherwise, it goes to the terminating state.

■ **Networking state.** The **networking state** is the heart of the transition states. When a connection reaches this state, the exchange of user control and data packets can be started. The connection remains in this state until one of the endpoints wants to terminate the connection.

■ **Terminating state.** When the connection is in the **terminating state,** several packets are exchanged between the two ends for house cleaning and closing the link.

12.2 PPP STACK

Although PPP is a data-link layer protocol, PPP uses a stack of other protocols to establish the link, to authenticate the parties involved, and to carry the network layer data. Three sets of protocols are defined to make PPP a powerful protocol: Link Control Protocol, authentication protocols, and Network Control Protocol. At any moment, a PPP packet can carry packets related to one of these protocols in its data field, as shown in Figure 12.3.

Figure 12.3 *Protocol stack*

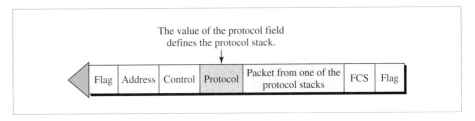

Link Control Protocol (LCP)

One of the protocols in the protocol stack is the **Link Control Protocol (LCP).** It is responsible for establishing, maintaining, configuring, and terminating links. It also provides negotiation mechanisms to set options between the two endpoints. Both endpoints of the link must reach an agreement about the options before the link can be established.

Note that when PPP is carrying an LCP packet, it is either in the establishing state or in the terminating state. No user data are carried during these states.

All LCP packets are carried in the data field of the PPP frame. What defines the frame as one carrying an LCP packet is the value of the protocol field, which is set to $C021_{16}$. Figure 12.4 shows the format of the LCP packet.

Figure 12.4   *LCP packet encapsulated in a frame*

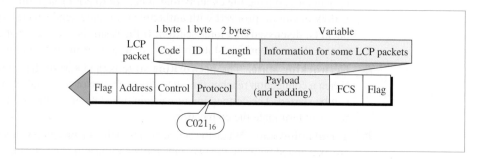

The descriptions of the fields are as follows:

■ **Code.** This field defines the type of LCP packet. We will discuss these packets and their purpose in the next section.

■ **ID.** This field holds a value used to match a request with the reply. One endpoint inserts a value in this field, which will be copied in the reply packet.

■ **Length.** This field defines the length of the entire LCP packet.

■ **Information.** This field contains extra information needed for some LCP packets.

LCP Packets

Table 12.1 lists some LCP packets.

Table 12.1   *LCP packets and their codes*

Code	Packet Type	Description
01_{16}	Configure-request	Contains the list of proposed options and their values
02_{16}	Configure-ack	Accepts all options proposed
03_{16}	Configure-nak	Announces that some options are not acceptable
04_{16}	Configure-reject	Announces that some options are not recognized
05_{16}	Terminate-request	Requests to shut down the line
06_{16}	Terminate-ack	Accepts the shut down request
07_{16}	Code-reject	Announces an unknown code
08_{16}	Protocol-reject	Announces an unknown protocol
09_{16}	Echo-request	A type of hello message to check if the other end is alive
$0A_{16}$	Echo-reply	The response to the echo-request message
$0B_{16}$	Discard-request	A request to discard the packet

Configuration Packets   Configuration packets are used to negotiate the options between two ends. Four different packets are used for this purpose: configure-request, configure-ack, configure-nak, and configure-reject.

- **Configure-request.** The endpoint that wishes to start a connection sends a configure-request message with a list of zero or more options to the other endpoint. Note that all the options are negotiated in one packet.

- **Configure-ack.** If all the options listed in the configure-request packet are accepted by the receiving end, it sends a configure-ack packet, which repeats all the options requested.

- **Configure-nak.** If the receiver of the configure-request packet recognizes all the options but finds that some need to be omitted or revised (the values must be changed), it sends a configure-nak packet to the sender. The sender then omits or revises the options and sends a totally new configure-request packet.

- **Configure-reject.** If some of the options are not recognized by the receiving party, it responds with a configure-reject packet, marking those options that are not recognized. The sender of the request must revise the configure-request message and send a totally new one.

Link Termination Packets   The link termination packets are used to disconnect the link between two endpoints.

- **Terminate-request.** Either party can terminate the link by sending a terminate-request packet.

- **Terminate-ack.** The party that receives the terminate-request packet must answer with a terminate-ack packet.

Link Monitoring and Debugging Packets   These packets are used for monitoring and debugging the link.

- **Code-reject.** If the endpoint receives a packet with an unrecognized code in the packet, it sends a code-reject packet.

- **Protocol-reject.** If the endpoint receives a packet with an unrecognized protocol in the frame, it sends a protocol-reject packet.

- **Echo-request.** This packet is sent to monitor the link. Its purpose is to see if the link is functioning. The sender expects to receive an echo-reply packet from the other side as proof.

- **Echo-reply.** This packet is sent in response to an echo-request. The information field in the echo-request packet is exactly duplicated and sent back to the sender of the echo-request packet.

- **Discard-request.** This is a kind of loopback test packet. It is used by the sender to check its internal condition. The receiver of the packet just discards it.

Options

There are many options that can be negotiated between the two endpoints. Options are inserted in the information field of the configuration packets. We list some of the most common options in Table 12.2.

Table 12.2 *Common options*

Option	Default
Maximum receive unit	1500
Authentication protocol	None
Protocol field compression	Off
Address and control field compression	Off

Authentication Protocols

Authentication plays a very important role in PPP because PPP is designed for use over dial-up links where verification of user identity is necessary. **Authentication** means validating the identity of a user who needs to access a set of resources. PPP has created two protocols for authentication: Password Authentication Protocol (PAP) and Challenge Handshake Authentication Protocol (CHAP). Note that these protocols are used during the authentication state. During this state, no user data are exchanged, only the corresponding packets to authenticate the user.

PAP

The **Password Authentication Protocol (PAP)** is a simple authentication procedure with a two-step process:

1. The user who wants to access a system sends an authentication identification (usually the user name) and a password.
2. The system checks the validity of the identification and password and either accepts or denies connection.

For those systems that require greater security, PAP is not enough; a third party with access to the link can easily pick up the password and access the system resources. Figure 12.5 shows the PAP concept.

Figure 12.5 *PAP*

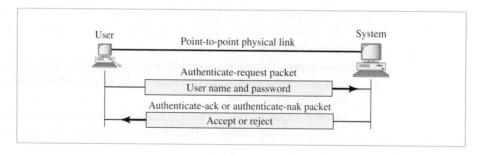

PAP Packets   PAP packets are encapsulated in a PPP frame. What distinguishes a PAP packet from other packets is the value of the protocol field, $C023_{16}$. There are three PAP packets: authenticate-request, authenticate-ack, and authenticate-nak. The first packet is used by the user to send the user name and password. The second is used by the system to allow access. The third is used by the system to deny access. Figure 12.6 shows the format of the three packets.

Figure 12.6 *PAP packets*

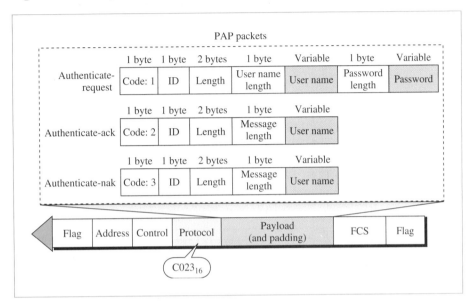

CHAP

The **Challenge Handshake Authentication Protocol (CHAP)** is a three-way hand-shaking authentication protocol that provides greater security than PAP. In this method, the password is kept secret; it is never sent on-line.

- The system sends to the user a challenge packet containing a challenge value, usually a few bytes.
- The user applies a predefined function that takes the challenge value and the user's own password and creates a result. The user sends the result in the response packet to the system.
- The system does the same. It applies the same function to the password of the user (known to the system) and the challenge value to create a result. If the result created is the same as the result sent in the response packet, access is granted; otherwise, it is denied.

CHAP is more secure than PAP, especially if the system continuously changes the challenge value. Even if the intruder learns the challenge value and the result, the password is still secret. Figure 12.7 shows the concept.

CHAP Packets

CHAP packets are encapsulated in the PPP frame. What distinguishes a CHAP packet from other packets is the value of the protocol field, $C223_{16}$. There are four CHAP packets: challenge, response, success, and failure. The first packet is used by the system to

Figure 12.7   *CHAP*

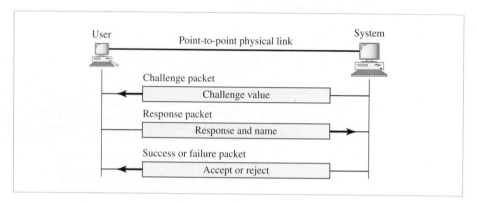

Figure 12.8   *CHAP packets*

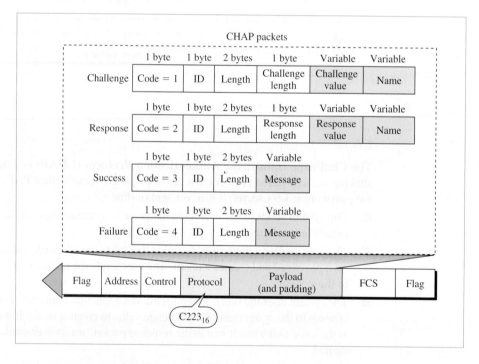

send the challenge value. The second is used by the user to return the result of the calculation. The third is used by the system to allow access to the system. The fourth is used by the system to deny access to the system. Figure 12.8 shows the format of the four packets.

Network Control Protocol (NCP)

After the link is established and authentication (if any) is successful, the connection goes to the networking state. In this state, PPP uses another protocol called **Network**

Control Protocol (NCP). NCP is a set of control protocols to allow the encapsulation of data coming from network layer protocols into the PPP frame.

IPCP

PPP requires two parties to negotiate not only at the data link layer, but also at the network layer. Before user data can be sent, a connection must be established at this level. The set of packets that establish and terminate a network layer connection for IP packets (see Chapter 19) is called **Internetwork Protocol Control Protocol (IPCP).** The format of an IPCP packet is shown in Figure 12.9. Note that the value of the protocol field, 8021_{16}, defines the packet encapsulated in the protocol as an IPCP packet.

Figure 12.9   *IPCP packet encapsulated in PPP frame*

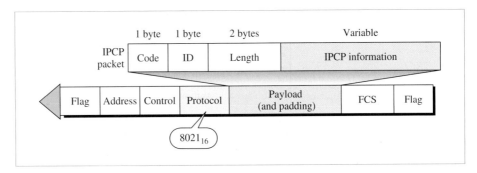

Seven packets are defined for the IPCP, distinguished by their code values, as shown in Table 12.3.

Table 12.3   *Code value for IPCP packets*

Code	IPCP Packet
01	Configure-request
02	Configure-ack
03	Configure-nak
04	Configure-reject
05	Terminate-request
06	Terminate-ack
07	Code-reject

A party uses the configure-request packet to negotiate options with the other party, to set the IP addresses, and so on.

After configuration, the link is ready to carry IP data in the payload field of a PPP frame. This time, the value of the protocol field is 0021_{16}, to show that an IP data packet, not the IPCP packet, is being carried across the link.

After IP has sent all its packets, the IPCP can take control and use the terminate-request and terminate-ack packets to end the network connection.

Other Protocols

Although our discussion here is limited to the use of Internet packets, PPP can carry different packets belonging to other protocols.

An Example

Let us go through the states when network layer packets are transmitted through a PPP connection. Figure 12.10 shows the steps:

Figure 12.10   *An example*

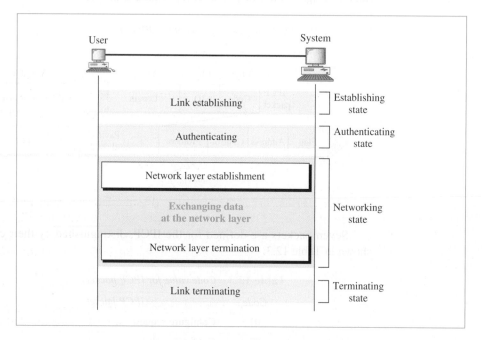

- ■ **Establishing.** The user sends a configure-request packet to negotiate the options for establishing the link. The user requests PAP authentication. After the user receives a configure-ack packet, link establishment is over.
- ■ **Authenticating.** The user sends an authenticate-request packet which includes the user name and password. After it receives the configure-ack packet, the authentication phase is over.
- ■ **Networking.** Now the user sends an configure-request packet to negotiate the options for the network layer activity. After it receives a configure-ack packet, the user can send the network layer data, which may take multiple frames. After all data are sent, the user sends the terminate-request packet to terminate the network layer activity. When the terminate-ack packet is received, the networking phase is complete. The connection goes to the terminating state.
- ■ **Terminating.** The user sends the terminate-request packet to terminate the link. With the receipt of the terminate-ack packet, the link is terminated.

12.3   KEY TERMS

authenticating state

authentication

Challenge Handshake Authentication
  Protocol (CHAP)

establishing state

idle state

Internetwork Protocol Control Protocol
  (IPCP)

Link Control Protocol (LCP)

Network Control Protocol (NCP)

networking state

Password Authentication Protocol (PAP)

point-to-point access

Point-to-Point Protocol (PPP)

terminating state

transition state diagram

12.4   SUMMARY

❑   The Point-to-Point Protocol (PPP) was designed to provide a dedicated line for
    users who need Internet access via a telephone line or a cable TV connection.

❑   A PPP connection goes through these phases: idle, establishing, authenticating
    (optional), networking, and terminating.

❑   At the data link layer, PPP employs a version of HDLC.

❑   The Link Control Protocol (LCP) is responsible for establishing, maintaining,
    configuring, and terminating links.

❑   Password Authentication Protocol (PAP) and Challenge Handshake Authentication
    Protocol (CHAP) are two protocols used for authentication in PPP.

❑   PAP is a two-step process. The user sends authentication identification and a
    password. The system determines the validity of the information sent.

❑   CHAP is a three-step process. The system sends a value to the user. The user
    manipulates the value and sends its result. The system verifies the result.

❑   Network Control Protocol (NCP) is a set of protocols to allow the encapsulation of
    data coming from network layer protocols; each set is specific for a network layer
    protocol that requires the services of PPP.

❑   Internetwork Protocol Control Protocol (IPCP), an NCP protocol, establishes and
    terminates a network layer connection for IP packets.

12.5   PRACTICE SET

Review Questions

1. Which type of user needs PPP?
2. Describe each of the states of a PPP connection.
3. Name three protocols that make up the PPP stack.
4. What is the purpose of the protocol field in the PPP frame?
5. Discuss the control field of the PPP frame.
6. What is the purpose of the LCP?

7. Discuss the relationship between the LCP packet and the PPP frame.

8. What are the categories of LCP packets? What is the function of each category?

9. What two protocols are used for authentication in PPP?

10. How does PAP work? What is its primary deficiency?

11. How does CHAP work? Why is it superior to PAP?

12. How does the PPP frame carry authentication packets from PAP and CHAP?

13. What is the purpose of NCP?

14. What is the relationship between IPCP and NCP?

Multiple-Choice Questions

15. According to the PPP transition state diagram, exchange of user control and data packets occurs in the _____ state.
    a. Establishing
    b. Authenticating
    c. Networking
    d. Terminating

16. According to the PPP transition state diagram, options are negotiated in the _____ state.
    a. Establishing
    b. Authenticating
    c. Networking
    d. Terminating

17. According to the PPP transition state diagram, verification of user identification occurs in the _____ state.
    a. Establishing
    b. Authenticating
    c. Networking
    d. Terminating

18. According to the PPP transition state diagram, the link is disconnected in the _____ state.
    a. Establishing
    b. Authenticating
    c. Networking
    d. Terminating

19. In the PPP frame, the _____ field defines the contents of the data field.
    a. Flag
    b. Control
    c. Protocol
    d. FCS

20. In the PPP frame, the _____ field is similar to that of the U-frame in HDLC.

a. Flag

b. Control

c. Protocol

d. FCS

21. In the PPP frame, the _____ field has a value of 11111111 to indicate the broadcast address of HDLC.

a. Address

b. Control

c. Protocol

d. FCS

22. In the PPP frame, the _____ field is for error control.

a. Flag

b. Control

c. Protocol

d. FCS

23. What is the purpose of LCP packets?

a. Configuration

b. Termination

c. Option negotiation

d. All the above

24. _____ is a three-way handshake for user verification.

a. PPP

b. CHAP

c. PAP

d. (b) and (c)

25. A PAP packet and a CHAP packet can be distinguished by the value of the _____ field of the PPP frame.

a. Address

b. Control

c. Protocol

d. FCS

26. PAP requires _____ and _____ from the user.

a. A password; a calculated value

b. Authentication identification; a password

c. A challenge value; a password

d. Authentication identification; a calculated value

27. For CHAP authentication, the user takes the system's _____ and its own _____ to create a result that is then sent to the system.

a. Authentication identification; password

b. Password; challenge value

c. Password; authentication identification

d. Challenge value; password

28. _____, an (a)_____ protocol, establishes and terminates a network layer connection for IP packets.

a. NCP; IPCP

b. CHAP; NCP

c. IPCP; NCP

d. SLIP; PPP

Exercises

29. What are the values of the flag, address, and control fields in hexadecimal?

30. Make a table to compare the PPP frame with the U-frame of HDLC. Which fields are the same? Which fields are different?

31. The value of the first few bytes of a frame is $7EFFC0C02105_{16}$. What is the protocol of the encapsulated payload? What is the type of packet?

32. The value of the first few bytes of a frame is $7EFFC0C02109110014_{16}$. What is the protocol of the encapsulated payload? What type of packet is being carried? How many bytes of information are in the packet?

33. Show the contents of a configure-nak packet in the LCP. Encapsulate the packet in a PPP frame.

34. Show the contents of a configure-nak packet in the NCP. Encapsulate the packet in a PPP frame.

35. Compare the results of Exercises 33 and 34. What differences do you see?

36. Show the contents of an echo-request packet with the message "Hello." Write the whole packet in hexadecimal. Encapsulate the packet in a PPP frame, and show the contents in hexadecimal.

37. Show the contents of an echo-reply in response to the packet in Exercise 36. Write the whole packet in hexadecimal. Encapsulate the packet in a PPP frame, and show the contents in hexadecimal.

38. Show the contents of an authenticate-request packet using "Forouzan" as the user name and "797979" as the password. Encapsulate the packet in a PPP frame.

39. Show the contents of the authenticate-ack that is received in response to the packet in Exercise 38.

40. Show the contents of a challenge packet (CHAP) using $A4253616_{16}$ as the challenge value. Encapsulate the packet in a PPP frame.

41. Show the contents of a response packet (CHAP) using $6163524A_{16}$ as the response value. Encapsulate the packet in a PPP frame.

42. A system sends the challenge value $2A2B1425_{16}$. The password of the user is 22112211_{16}. The function to be used by the user adds the challenge value to the password; the result should be split into two and swapped to get the response. Show the response of the user.

43. If a user sends an LCP packet with code 02_{16}, what is the state of the connection after this event?

44. A connection is in the establishing state. If the user receives an LCP configure-nak packet, what is the new state?

45. A connection is in the networking state. If the user receives an NCP configure-nak packet, what is the new state?

46. Show the contents of all frames in Figure 12.10. What protocol (LCP, NCP, authentication, and so on) is involved in each transmission?

CHAPTER 13

Multiple Access

When nodes or stations are connected to or use a common link, called a multipoint or broadcast link, we need a multiple-access protocol to coordinate access to the link. The problem of controlling the access to the medium is similar to the rules of speaking in an assembly. Different procedures guarantee that the right to speak is upheld and ensure that two people do not speak at the same time, do not interrupt each other, do not monopolize the discussion, and so on.

The situation is the same with multipoint networks. Many formal protocols have been devised to handle access to the shared link. We categorize them into three groups. Protocols belonging to each group are shown in Figure 13.1.

Figure 13.1 *Multiple-access protocols*

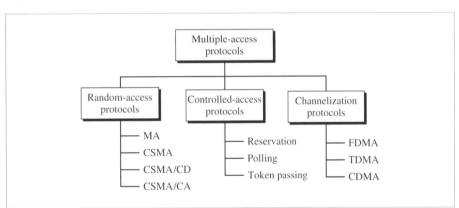

13.1 RANDOM ACCESS

In a random access method, each station has the right to the medium without being controlled by any other station. However, if more than one station tries to send, there is an access conflict (**collision**) and the frames will be either destroyed or modified. To avoid access conflict or to resolve it when it happens, we need a procedure that answers the following questions:

- When can the station access the medium?
- What can the station do if the medium is busy?
- How can the station determine the success or failure of the transmission?
- What can the station do if there is an access conflict?

The random-access methods we study in this chapter have evolved as shown in Figure 13.2.

Figure 13.2   *Evolution of random-access methods*

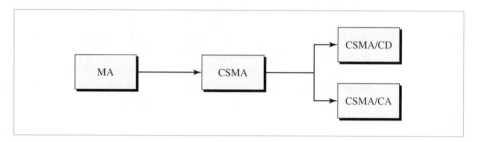

The first method, known as ALOHA, used a very simple procedure called **multiple access (MA).** The method was improved with the addition of a procedure that forced the station to sense the medium before transmitting. This was called carrier sense multiple access (CSMA). This method later evolved into two parallel methods: CSMA/CD and CSMA/CA. CSMA/CD (CSMA with collision detection) defines procedures to be followed if a collision is detected while CSMA/CA (CSMA with collision avoidance) defines procedures to avoid the collision.

Multiple Access (MA)

ALOHA, the earliest random-access method, was developed at the University of Hawaii in the early 1970s. It was designed to be used on a radio (wireless) local area network (LAN) with a data rate of 9600 bps.

Figure 13.3 shows the basic idea behind an ALOHA network. A base station is the central controller. Every station that needs to send a frame to another station first sends it to the base station. The base station receives the frame and relays it to the intended destination. In other words, the base station acts as a hop. The uploading transmission (from a station to the base station) uses modulation with a carrier frequency of 407 MHz. The downloading transmission (from the base station to any station) uses a carrier frequency of 413 MHz.

It is obvious that there are potential collisions in this arrangement. The medium (air) is shared between the stations. When a station sends data at frequency 407 MHz to the base station, another station may attempt to do so at the same time. The data from the two stations collide and become garbled. The ALOHA protocol is very simple. It is

Figure 13.3 *ALOHA network*

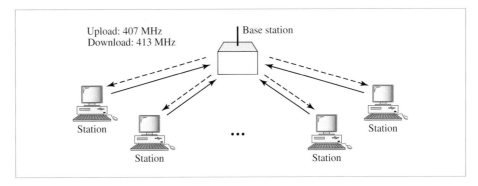

based on the following rules:

- **Multiple access.** Any station sends a frame when it has a frame to send.
- **Acknowledgment.** After sending the frame, the station waits for an acknowledgment (explicit or implicit). If it does not receive an acknowledgment during the allotted time, which is 2 times the maximum propagation delay (the time it takes for the first bit of the frame to reach every station), it assumes that the frame is lost; it tries sending again after a random amount of time.

The protocol flowchart is shown in Figure 13.4. A station that has a frame to send sends it. It then waits for a period of time, which is 2 times the maximum propagation delay. If it receives an acknowledgment, the transmission is successful. If there is no acknowledgment during this period, the station uses a backoff strategy (explained later) and sends the packet again. After several tries, if there is no acknowledgment, the station gives up.

Figure 13.4 *Procedure for ALOHA protocol*

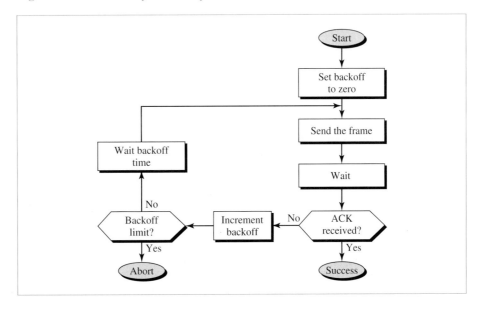

Carrier Sense Multiple Access (CSMA)

To minimize the chance of collision and, therefore, increase the performance, the CSMA method was developed. The chance of collision can be reduced if a station senses the medium before trying to use it. **Carrier sense multiple access (CSMA)** requires that each station first listen to the medium (or check the state of the medium) before sending. In other words, the CSMA is based on the principle "sense before transmit" or "listen before talk."

CSMA can reduce the possibility of collision, but it cannot eliminate it. One might ask why there may be a collision if each station listens to the medium before transmitting a frame. The possibility of collision still exists because of the propagation delay; when a station sends a frame, it takes a while (although very short) for the first bit to reach every station and for every station to sense it. In other words, a station may sense the medium and find it idle, only because propagation by another station has not yet reached this station. Figure 13.5 shows how a collision may happen.

Figure 13.5 *Collision in CSMA*

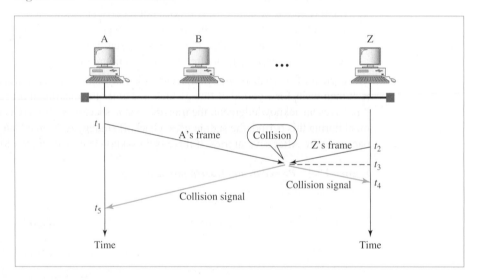

At time t_1, station A at the left end of the medium senses the medium. The medium is idle, so it sends a frame. At time t_2 ($t_2 > t_1$), station Z at the right end of the medium senses the medium and finds it idle because, at this time, propagation from station A has not reached station Z. Station Z also sends a frame. The two signals collide at time t_3 ($t_3 > t_2 > t_1$). Note that the result of the collision, which is a garbled signal, will also propagate now in both directions. It reaches station Z at time t_4 ($t_4 > t_3 > t_2 > t_1$) and station A at time t_5 ($t_5 > t_4 > t_3 > t_2 > t_1$).

Persistence Strategy

The **persistence strategy** defines the procedures for a station that senses a busy medium. Two substrategies have been devised: nonpersistent and persistent. (see Fig. 13.6).

Figure 13.6 *Persistence strategies*

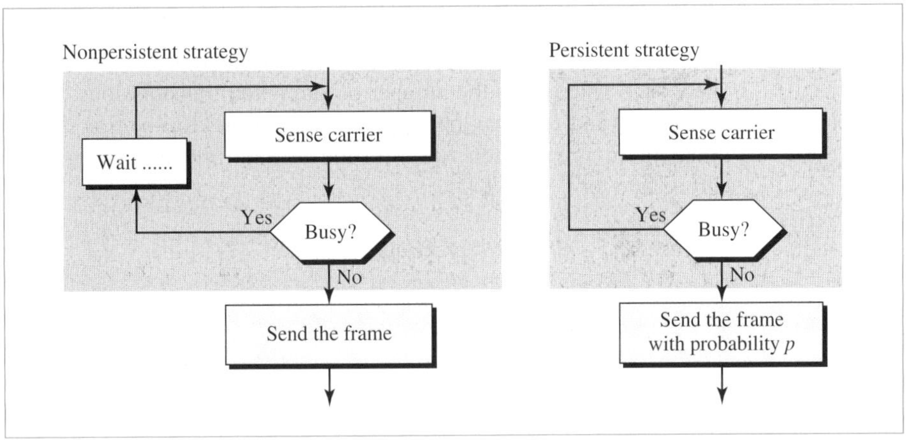

Nonpersistent strategy

Persistent strategy

Sense carrier

Wait ......

Yes

Busy?

No

Send the frame

Sense carrier

Yes

Busy?

No

Send the frame
with probability *p*

Nonpersistent   In a **nonpersistent strategy,** a station that has a frame to send senses the line. If the line is idle, the station sends immediately. If the line is not idle, the station waits a random period of time and then senses the line again. The nonpersistent approach reduces the chance of collision because it is unlikely that two or more stations wait the same amount of time and retry again simultaneously. However, this method reduces the efficiency of the network if the medium is idle when there are stations that have frames to send.

Persistent   In a **persistent strategy,** a station senses the line. If the line is idle, the station sends a frame. This method has two variations: **1-persistent** and **p-persistent.**

In the 1-persistent method, if the station finds the line idle, the station sends its frame immediately (with a probability of 1). This method increases the chance of collision because two or more stations may send their frames after finding the line idle.

In the *p*-persistent method, if the station finds the line idle, the station may or may not send. It sends with probability *p* and refrains from sending with probability $1 - p$. For example, if *p* is 0.2, it means that each station, after sensing an idle line, sends with a probability of 0.2 (20 percent of the time) and refrains from sending with a probability of 0.8 (80 percent of the time). The station generates a random number between 1 and 100. If the random number is less than 20, the station will send; otherwise the station refrains from sending. The *p*-persistent strategy combines the advantages of the other two strategies. It reduces the chance of collision and improves the efficiency.

CSMA/CD

The CSMA method does not define the procedure for a collision. That is the reason CSMA was never implemented. **Carrier sense multiple access with collision detection (CSMA/CD)** adds a procedure to handle a collision.

In this method, any station can send a frame. The station then monitors the medium to see if transmission was successful. If so, the station is finished. If, however, there was a collision, the frame needs to be sent again. To reduce the probability of collision the second time, the station waits—it needs to **back off.** The question is,

How much? It is reasonable that the station waits a little the first time, more if a collision occurs again, much more if it happens a third time, and so on.

In the exponential backoff method, the station waits an amount of time between 0 and $2^N \times$ maximum_propagation_time (the time needed for a bit to reach the end of the network), where N is the number of attempted transmissions. In other words, it waits between 0 and $2 \times$ (maximum_propagation_time) for the first time, between 0 and $2^2 \times$ (maximum_propagation_time) for the second time, and so on. Figure 13.7 shows the procedure for CSMA/CD.

Figure 13.7   *CSMA/CD procedure*

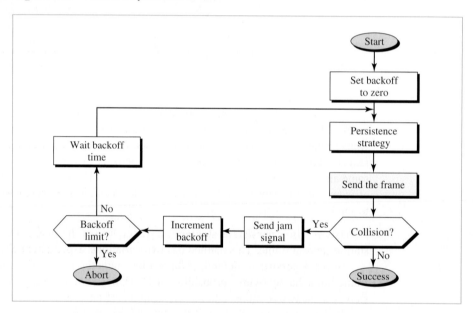

The station that has a frame to send sets the backoff parameter N to zero. It then senses the line using one of the persistence strategies. After sending the frame, if it does not hear a collision until the whole frame has been sent, the transmission is successful. However, if the station hears a collision, it sends a jam signal to the line to inform other stations of the situation and to alert them that a collision has occurred; all stations discard the part of the frame received. The station then increments the value of the backoff parameter by 1. It checks to see if the value of the backoff parameter exceeds the limit (usually 15). If this value exceeds the limit, it means that the station has tried enough and should give up the attempt; the station should abort the procedure. If the value has not exceeded the limit, the station waits a random backoff time based on the current value of the backoff parameter and senses the line again. CSMA/CD is used in traditional Ethernet (discussed in Chapter 14).

CSMA/CA

The CSMA/CA procedure differs from the previous procedures in that there is no collision. The procedure avoids collision (see Fig. 13.8). The station uses one of the

Figure 13.8   *CSMA/CA procedure*

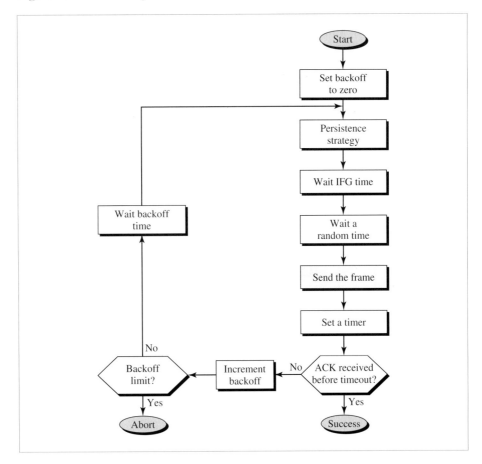

persistence strategies. After it finds the line idle, the station waits an IFG (interframe gap) amount of time. It then waits another random amount of time. After that, it sends the frame and sets a timer. The station waits for an acknowledgment from the receiver. If it receives the acknowledgment before the timer expires, the transmission is successful. If the station does not receive an acknowledgment, it knows that something is wrong (the frame is lost or the acknowledgment is lost). The station increments the value of the backoff parameter, waits for a backoff amount of time, and resenses the line. CSMA/CA is used in wireless LANs (see Chapter 15).

13.2   CONTROLLED ACCESS

In **controlled access,** the stations consult one another to find which station has the right to send. A station cannot send unless it has been authorized by other stations. We discuss three popular controlled-access methods.

Reservation

In the reservation access method, a station needs to make a reservation before sending data. Time is divided into intervals. In each interval, a reservation frame precedes the data frames sent in that interval.

If there are N stations in the system, there are exactly N reservation minislots in the reservation frame. Each minislot belongs to a station. When a station needs to send a data frame, it makes a reservation in its own minislot. The stations that have made reservations can send their data frames after the reservation frame.

Figure 13.9 shows a situation with five stations and a five-minislot reservation frame. In the first interval, only stations 1, 3, and 4 have made reservations. In the second interval, only station 1 has made a reservation.

Figure 13.9   *Reservation access method*

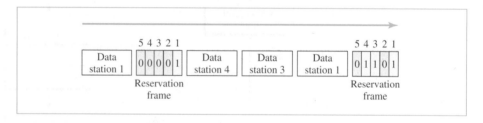

Polling

Polling works with topologies in which one device is designated as a **primary station** and the other devices are **secondary stations.** All data exchanges must be made through the primary device even when the ultimate destination is a secondary device. The primary device controls the link; the secondary devices follow its instructions. It is up to the primary device to determine which device is allowed to use the channel at a given time. The primary device, therefore, is always the initiator of a session. If the primary wants to receive data, it asks the secondaries if they have anything to send; this function is called **polling.** If the primary device wants to send data, it tells the secondary target to get ready to receive; this function is called selecting.

Select

The **select mode** is used whenever the primary device has something to send. Remember that the primary controls the link. If the primary is neither sending nor receiving data, it knows the link is available. If it has something to send, the primary device sends it. What it does not know, however, is whether the target device is prepared to receive. So the primary must alert the secondary to the upcoming transmission and wait for an acknowledgment of the secondary's ready status. Before sending data, the primary creates and transmits a select (SEL) frame, one field of which includes the address of the intended secondary. See Figure 13.10.

Poll

The polling function is used by the primary device to solicit transmissions from the secondary devices. Figure 13.11 shows the situation.

Figure 13.10   *Select*

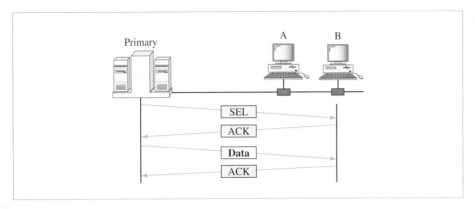

Figure 13.11   *Poll*

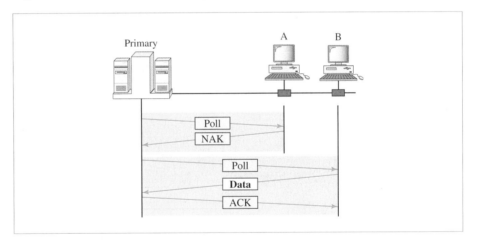

When the primary is ready to receive data, it must ask (poll) each device in turn if it has anything to send. When the first secondary is approached, it responds either with a NAK frame if it has nothing to send or with data (in the form of a data frame) if it does. If the response is negative (a NAK frame), the primary then polls the next secondary in the same manner until it finds one with data to send. When the response is positive (a data frame), the primary reads the frame and returns an acknowledgment (ACK frame), verifying its receipt.

Token Passing

In the **token-passing** method, a station is authorized to send data when it receives a special frame called a token. In this method, stations are arranged around a ring. Each station has a predecessor and a successor. Frames are coming from the predecessor and going to the successor. Figure 13.12 shows the idea.

Figure 13.12   *Token-passing network*

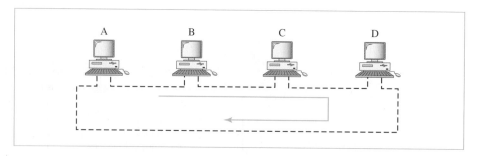

When no data are being sent, a token circulates around the ring. If a station needs to send data, it waits for the token. The station captures the token and sends one or more frames (as long as it has frames to send or the allocated time has not expired), and finally it releases the token to be used by the successor station (the next station on the physical or logical ring). Figure 13.13 shows a very simplified procedure for token passing. In reality, other features (such as priority and reservation) are added to the process.

Figure 13.13   *Token-passing procedure*

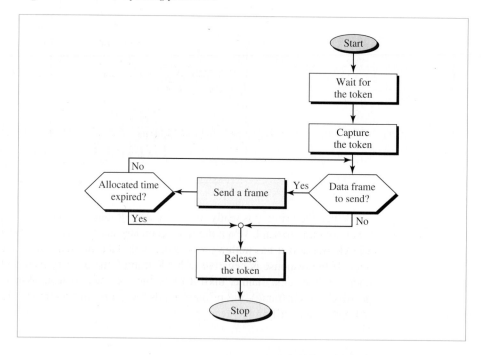

13.3   CHANNELIZATION

Channelization is a multiple-access method in which the available bandwidth of a link is shared in time, frequency, or through code, between different stations. In this section, we discuss three channelization protocols: FDMA, TDMA, and CDMA. The first two are related to procedures previously discussed in the physical layer. CDMA is a data link multiple-access protocol.

FDMA

In **frequency-division multiple access (FDMA),** the available bandwidth is shared by all stations. Each station uses its allocated band to send its data. Each band is reserved for a specific station. The band belongs to the station all the time. FDMA is a data link layer protocol that uses FDM at the physical layer (see Chapter 6). We will see how FDMA is used in cellular telephone and satellite networks in Chapter 17.

In FDMA, the bandwidth is divided into channels.

TDMA

In **time-division multiple access (TDMA),** the entire bandwidth is just one channel. The stations share the capacity of the channel in time. Each station is allocated a time slot during which it can send data. TDMA is a data link layer protocol that uses TDM at the physical layer (see Chapter 6). We will see how TDMA is used in the cellular telephone network in Chapter 17.

In TDMA, the bandwidth is just one channel that is timeshared.

CDMA

Code-division multiple access (CDMA) was conceived several decades ago. Recent advances in electronic technology have finally made its implementation possible. CDMA differs from FDMA because only one channel occupies the entire bandwidth of the link. It differs from TDMA because all stations can send data simultaneously; there is no timesharing.

In CDMA, one channel carries all transmissions simultaneously.

CDMA is based on coding theory. Each station is assigned a code, which is a sequence of numbers called **chips.** Suppose we have four stations; each has a sequence of chips which we designate as A, B, C, and D (see Fig. 13.14). Later in this chapter we show how we chose these sequences.

Figure 13.14 *Chip sequences*

$+1, +1, +1, +1$	$+1, -1, +1, -1$	$+1, +1, -1, -1$	$+1, -1, -1, +1$
A	B	C	D

We follow these rules for encoding: If a station needs to send a 0 bit, it sends a −1; if it needs to send a 1 bit, it sends a +1. When a station is idle, it sends no signal, which is represented by a 0. These are shown in Figure 13.15.

Figure 13.15   *Encoding rules*

Data bit 0 ⟶ −1   Data bit 1 ⟶ +1   Silence ⟶ 0

As a simple example, we show how four stations share the link during 1-bit interval. The procedure can easily be repeated for additional intervals. We assume that stations 1 and 2 are sending a 0 bit and channel 4 is sending a 1 bit. Station 3 is silent.

Multiplexer

Figure 13.16 shows the situation at the multiplexer. The steps are as follows:

Figure 13.16   *CDMA multiplexer*

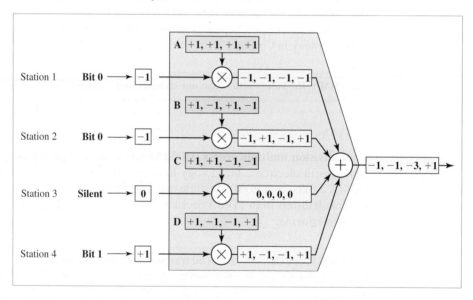

1. The multiplexer receives one encoded number from each station (−1, −1, 0, and +1).
2. The encoded number sent by station 1 is multiplied by each chip in sequence A. A new sequence is the result (−1, −1, −1, −1). Likewise, the encoded number sent by station 2 is multiplied by each chip in sequence B. The same is true for the remaining two encoded numbers. The result is four new sequences.
3. All first chips are added, as are all second, third, and fourth chips. The result is one new sequence.
4. The sequence is transmitted through the link.

Demultiplexer

Figure 13.17 shows the situation at the demultiplexer. The steps are as follows:

Figure 13.17 *CDMA demultiplexer*

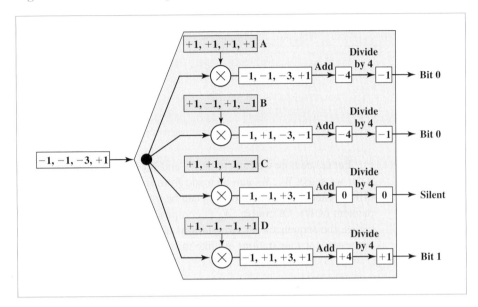

1. The demultiplexer receives the sequence sent across the link.
2. It multiplies the sequence by the code for each receiver. The multiplication is done chip by chip.
3. The chips in each sequence are added. The result is always +4, −4, or 0.
4. The result of step 3 is divided by 4 to get −1, +1, or 0.
5. The number in step 4 is decoded to 0, 1, or silence by the receiver.

Observation

We see that each station receives what is sent by the sender. Note that the third receiver does not receive data because the sender was idle. There is only one sequence flowing through the channel, the sum of the sequences. However, each receiver detects its own data from the sum.

Orthogonal Sequences   Let us return to the chip sequences. We did not choose the sequences randomly; they were carefully selected. The sequences in our example are called **orthogonal sequences.** We show how to generate orthogonal sequences, and then we discuss their properties.

Sequence Generation   To generate sequences, we use a **Walsh table,** a two-dimensional table with an equal number of rows and columns. Each row is a sequence of chips. The Walsh table W_1 for a one-chip sequence has one row and one column. We can choose −1 or +1 for the chip for this trivial table (we chose +1). According to Walsh, if we know the table for N sequences W_N, we can create the table for $2N$ sequences W_{2N}, as shown in Figure 13.18. The W_N with the overhead bar stands for the complement of W_N, where each +1 is changed to −1 and vice versa.

Figure 13.18   *W_1 and W_{2N}*

$$W_1 = \begin{bmatrix} +1 \end{bmatrix} \qquad W_{2N} = \begin{bmatrix} W_N & W_N \\ W_N & \overline{W_N} \end{bmatrix}$$

Let us see how we can create W_2 and W_4 from W_1. Figure 13.19 shows the process. After we select W_1, W_2 can be made from four W_1's, with the last one the complement of W_1. After W_2 is generated, W_4 can be made of four W_2's, with the last one the complement of W_2. Of course, W_8 is composed of four W_4's, and so on. According to the tables, the sequences for two stations accessing one link are +1, +1 and +1, −1. The sequences for four stations are like those used in our example (see Fig. 13.16).

Figure 13.19   *Sequence generation*

$$W_1 = \begin{bmatrix} +1 \end{bmatrix}$$

$$W_2 = \begin{bmatrix} +1 & +1 \\ +1 & -1 \end{bmatrix} \qquad W_4 = \begin{bmatrix} +1 & +1 & +1 & +1 \\ +1 & -1 & +1 & -1 \\ +1 & +1 & -1 & -1 \\ +1 & -1 & -1 & +1 \end{bmatrix}$$

Properties of Orthogonal Sequences   Orthogonal sequences have properties that are suitable for CDMA. They are as follows:

1. If we multiply a sequence by −1, every element in the sequence is complemented (+1 becomes −1 and −1 becomes +1). We can see that when a station is sending −1 (bit 0), it is sending its complement.

2. If we multiply two sequences, element by element, and add the results, we get a number called the **inner product.** If the two sequences are the same, we get N, where N is the number of sequences; if they are different, we get 0. The inner product uses a dot as the operator. So $A \cdot A$ is N, but $A \cdot B$ is 0.

3. The inner product of a sequence by its complement is $-N$. So $A \cdot (-A)$ is $-N$.

Example 1

Check to see if the second property about orthogonal codes holds for our CDMA example.

Solution

The inner product of each code by itself is N. This is shown for code C; you can prove for yourself that it holds true for the other codes.

$$C \cdot C = [+1, +1, -1, -1] \cdot [+1, +1, -1, -1] = 1 + 1 + 1 + 1 = 4$$

If two sequences are different, the inner product is 0.

$$B \cdot C = [+1, -1, +1, -1] \cdot [+1, +1, -1, -1] = 1 - 1 - 1 + 1 = 0$$

Example 2

Check to see if the third property about orthogonal codes holds for our CDMA example.

Solution

The inner product of each code by its complement is $-N$. This is shown for code C; you can prove for yourself that it holds true for the other codes.

$$C \cdot (-C) = [+1, \ +1, -1, -1] \cdot [-1, -1, +1, +1] = -1 - 1 - 1 - 1 = -4$$

The inner product of a code with the complement of another code is 0.

$$B \cdot (-C) = [+1, \ -1, +1, -1] \cdot [-1, -1, +1, +1] = -1 + 1 + 1 - 1 = 0$$

Orthogonal Codes in CDMA

Now we can understand why our trivial example of CDMA works.

In the Multiplexer   In the multiplexer, each station is sending the appropriate sequence:

- Station 1 is sending $-A$ (-1 was multiplied by A), station 2 is sending $-B$, station 3 is sending an empty sequence (all zeros), and station 4 is sending D.
- The sequence that comes out of the multiplexer is the sum of all sequences.

$$S = -A - B + D$$

In the Demultiplexer   In the demultiplexer, all stations receive S:

- Station 1 finds the inner product of S and A.

$$S \cdot A = (-A - B + D) \cdot A \ = -A \cdot A - B \cdot A + D \cdot A = -4 + 0 + 0 = -4$$

The result is then divided by 4, which is -1. This is interpreted as a 0 bit.
- Station 2 finds the inner product of S and B.

$$S \cdot B \ = (-A - B + D) \cdot B \ = -A \cdot B - B \cdot B + D \cdot B = 0 - 4 + 0 = -4$$

The result is then divided by 4, which is -1. This is interpreted as a 0 bit.
- Station 3 finds the inner product of S and C.

$$S \cdot C \ = (-A - B + D) \cdot C \ = -A \cdot C - B \cdot C + D \cdot C = 0 + 0 + 0 = 0$$

This is interpreted as a silent station.
- Station 4 finds the inner product of S and D.

$$S \cdot D \ = (-A - B + D) \cdot D \ = -A \cdot D - B \cdot D + D \cdot D = 0 + 0 + 4 = 4$$

The result is then divided by 4, which is $+1$. This is interpreted as a 1 bit.

13.4 KEY TERMS

1-persistent strategy

ALOHA

back off

carrier sense multiple access (CSMA)

carrier sense multiple access/collision avoidance (CSMA/CA)

carrier sense multiple access/collision detection (CSMA/CD)

channelization

chip

code-division multiple access (CDMA)

collision

controlled access

frequency-division multiple access (FDMA)

inner product

multiple access (MA)

nonpersistent strategy

orthogonal sequence

persistence strategy

poll mode

polling

p-persistent strategy

primary station

random access

reservation

secondary station

select mode

time-division multiple access (TDMA)

token passing

Walsh table

13.5 SUMMARY

❏ Medium access methods can be categorized as random, controlled, or channelized.

❏ In the carrier sense multiple-access (CSMA) method, a station must listen to the medium prior to sending data onto the line.

❏ A persistence strategy defines the procedure to follow when a station senses an occupied medium.

❏ Carrier sense multiple access with collision detection (CSMA/CD) is CSMA with a postcollision procedure.

❏ Carrier sense multiple access with collision avoidance (CSMA/CA) is CSMA with procedures that avoid a collision.

❏ Reservation, polling, and token passing are controlled-access methods.

❏ In the reservation access method, a station reserves a slot for data by setting its flag in a reservation frame.

❏ In the polling access method, a primary station controls transmissions to and from secondary stations.

❏ In the token-passing access method, a station that has control of a frame called a token can send data.

❏ Channelization is a multiple-access method in which the available bandwidth of a link is shared in time, frequency, or through code, between stations on a network.

❏ FDMA, TDMA, and CDMA are channelization methods.

❏ In FDMA, the bandwidth is divided into bands; each band is reserved for the use of a specific station.

❏ In TDMA, the bandwidth is not divided into bands; instead the bandwidth is timeshared.

❏ In CDMA, the bandwidth is not divided into bands, yet data from all inputs are transmitted simultaneously.

❏ CDMA is based on coding theory and uses sequences of numbers called chips. The sequences are generated using Walsh tables.

13.6 PRACTICE SET

Review Questions

1. What is the advantage of controlled access over random access?
2. List in order the protocols that evolved from MA.
3. When do we increment the backoff in a network that uses ALOHA?
4. How do the two persistent strategies differ?
5. What is the purpose of the jam signal in CSMA/CD?
6. How does CSMA/CD differ from CSMA/CA?
7. Name three popular controlled-access methods.
8. Is the reservation access method suitable for a very large network in which many stations are idle? Why or why not?
9. Discuss the difference between polling and selecting.
10. Why is token passing a controlled-access procedure?
11. Name three channelization protocols.
12. Discuss the number of bands per medium bandwidth for FDMA, TDMA, and CDMA.
13. How is CDMA superior to FDMA? How is CDMA superior to TDMA?
14. What is a collision?
15. What is an inner product?

Multiple-Choice Questions

16. The most primitive random access method is _____.
    a. ALOHA
    b. CSMA
    c. Channelization
    d. Token passing
17. In the _____ random-access method there is no collision.
    a. ALOHA
    b. CSMA/CD
    c. CSMA/CA
    d. Token-passing

18. In the _____ random-access method, stations do not sense the medium.
    a. ALOHA
    b. CSMA/CD
    c. CSMA/CA
    d. Ethernet

19. In the 1-persistent approach, when a station finds an idle line, it _____.
    a. Waits 0.1 s before sending
    b. Waits 1 s before sending
    c. Waits a time equal to $1 - p$ before sending
    d. Sends immediately

20. In the p-persistent approach, when a station finds an idle line, it _____.
    a. Waits 1 s before sending
    b. Sends with probability $1 - p$
    c. Sends with probability p
    d. Sends immediately

21. A network using the CSMA random-access method with p equal to 0.25 will send _____ percent of the time after accessing an idle line.
    a. 25
    b. 50
    c. 75
    d. 100

22. The 1-persistent approach can be considered a special case of the p-persistent approach with p equal to _____.
    a. 0.1
    b. 0.5
    c. 1.0
    d. 2.0

23. _____ is a random-access protocol.
    a. MA
    b. Polling
    c. FDMA
    d. CDMA

24. _____ is a controlled-access protocol.
    a. Reservation
    b. FDMA
    c. TDMA
    d. CSMA

25. _____ is (are) a channelization protocol.
    a. FDMA
    b. TDMA

c. CDMA

d. All the above

26. _____ is the access protocol used by traditional Ethernet.

a. CSMA

b. CSMA/CD

c. CSMA/CA

d. Token ring

27. When a collision is detected in a network using CSMA/CD, _____.

a. The frame is immediately resent

b. A jam signal is sent by the station

c. The backoff value is set to 0

d. The backoff value is decremented by 1

28. In the reservation access method, if there are 10 stations on a network, then there are _____ reservation minislots in the reservation frame.

a. 5

b. 9

c. 10

d. 11

29. _____ requires one primary station and one or more secondary stations.

a. Reservation

b. Polling

c. Token ring

d. CSMA

30. When a primary device asks a secondary device if it has data to send, this is called _____.

a. Polling

b. Selecting

c. Reserving

d. Backing off

31. If an FDMA network has eight stations, the medium bandwidth has _____ bands.

a. 1

b. 2

c. 8

d. 16

32. If a TDMA network has eight stations, the medium bandwidth has _____ bands.

a. 1

b. 2

c. 8

d. 16

33. If a CDMA network has eight stations, the medium bandwidth has _____ bands.
    a. 1
    b. 2
    c. 8
    d. 16

34. A Walsh table for 16 stations has a chip sequence of _____ chips.
    a. 4
    b. 8
    c. 16
    d. 32

Exercises

35. Explain how the ALOHA protocol answers this question: When should the station access the medium?

36. Explain how the ALOHA protocol answers this question: What should be done if the medium is busy?

37. Explain how the ALOHA protocol answers this question: How should the station determine the success or failure of the transmission?

38. Explain how the ALOHA protocol answers this question: What should the station do if there is an access conflict?

39. Explain how the CSMA/CD protocol answers this question: When should the station access the medium?

40. Explain how the CSMA/CD protocol answers this question: What should be done if the medium is busy?

41. Explain how the CSMA/CD protocol answers this question: How should the station determine the success or failure of the transmission?

42. Explain how the CSMA/CD protocol answers this question: What should the station do if there is an access conflict?

43. Explain how the CSMA/CA protocol answers this question: When should the station access the medium?

44. Explain how the CSMA/CA protocol answers this question: What should be done if the medium is busy?

45. Explain how the CSMA/CA protocol answers this question: How should the station determine the success or failure of the transmission?

46. Explain how the CSMA/CA protocol answers this question: What should the station do if there is an access conflict?

47. Explain how the token-passing protocol answers this question: When should the station access the medium?

48. Explain how the token-passing protocol answers this question: What should be done if the medium is busy?

49. Explain how the token-passing protocol answers this question: How should the station determine the success or failure of the transmission?

50. Explain how the token-passing protocol answers this question: What should the station do if there is an access conflict?

51. Complete Table 13.1 for the different protocols discussed in this chapter. Answer yes or no.

Table 13.1 *Exercise 51*

Characteristic	ALOHA	CSMA/CD	CSMA/CA	Token Passing	Channel-ization
Multiple access					
Carrier sense					
Collision checking					
Acknowledgment					

52. Show the Walsh table for W_{16}.

53. Prove the second property of orthogonal sequences for any two entries of your choice in W_{16}.

54. Prove the third property of orthogonal sequences for any two entries of your choice in W_{16}.

55. Show the output of multiplexer in Figure 13.16 if station 1 is silent and every other station is sending a 1 bit.

56. Redraw Figure 13.17 for Problem 55.

CHAPTER 14

Local Area Networks: Ethernet

In Chapter 1, we learned that a local area network (LAN) is a computer network that is designed for a limited geographic area such as a building or a campus. Although a LAN can be used as an isolated network to connect computers in an organization for the sole purpose of sharing resources, most LANs today are also links in a wide area network (WAN) or the Internet.

The LAN market has seen several technologies, but the most dominant today is **Ethernet.** In this chapter, we concentrate on Ethernet; in Chapter 15 we discuss wireless LANs.

Figure 14.1 compares three generations of Ethernet.

Figure 14.1 *Three generations of Ethernet*

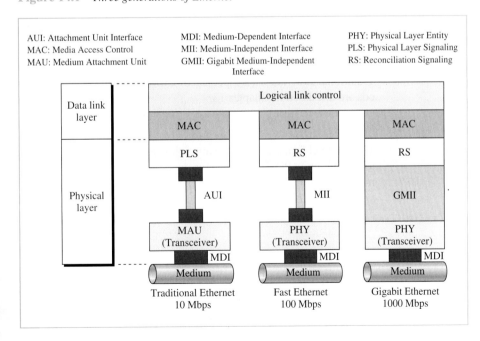

AUI: Attachment Unit Interface
MAC: Media Access Control
MAU: Medium Attachment Unit

MDI: Medium-Dependent Interface
MII: Medium-Independent Interface
GMII: Gigabit Medium-Independent Interface

PHY: Physical Layer Entity
PLS: Physical Layer Signaling
RS: Reconciliation Signaling

The original Ethernet was created in 1976 at Xerox's Palo Alto Research Center (PARC). Since then, it has evolved. We designate the original, with a data rate of 10 Mbps, as traditional Ethernet. Fast Ethernet operates at 100 Mbps; Gigabit Ethernet at 1 Gbps.

A computer connected via a LAN to the Internet needs all five layers of the Internet model. The three upper layers (network, transport, and application) are common to all LANs. The data link layer is divided into the logical link control (LLC) sublayer and the medium access control (MAC) sublayer. The LLC sublayer was originally designed to be the same for all LANs for interoperability, but it is not used often today. Instead, the interoperability is provided by a common network layer protocol, as we will see in a future chapter. This means that local area networks differ only in their MAC sublayers and in their physical layers. While the MAC sublayer is slightly different for each Ethernet version, the physical layer is quite different.

14.1   TRADITIONAL ETHERNET

Traditional Ethernet was designed to operate at 10 Mbps. Access to the network by a device is through a contention method (CSMA/CD). The media are shared between all stations.

MAC Sublayer

The **MAC sublayer** governs the operation of the access method. It also frames data received from the upper layer and passes them to the PLS sublayer for encoding.

Access Method: CSMA/CD

Traditional Ethernet uses 1-persistent CSMA/CD as the access method. Access methods are discussed in Chapter 13.

Frame

The Ethernet frame contains seven fields: preamble, SFD, DA, SA, length/type of protocol data unit (PDU), upper layer data, and the CRC. Ethernet does not provide any mechanism for acknowledging received frames, making it what is known as an unreliable medium. Acknowledgments must be implemented at the higher layers. The format of the MAC frame is shown in Figure 14.2.

Figure 14.2   *802.3 MAC frame*

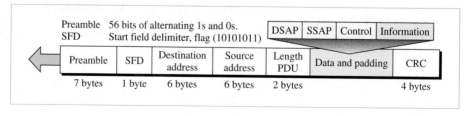

- **Preamble.** The first field of the 802.3 frame contains 7 bytes (56 bits) of alternating 0s and 1s that alert the receiving system to the coming frame and enable it to synchronize its input timing. The pattern provides only an alert and a timing pulse. The 56-bit pattern allows the stations to miss some bits at the beginning of the frame. The **preamble** is actually added at the physical layer and is not (formally) part of the frame.

- **Start frame delimiter (SFD).** The second field (1 byte: 10101011) signals the beginning of the frame. The SFD tells the stations that they have a last chance for synchronization. The last 2 bits are 11 and alert the receiver that the next field is the destination address.

- **Destination address (DA).** The DA field is 6 bytes and contains the physical address of the destination station or stations to receive the packet. We will discuss the destination address in greater detail later.

- **Source address (SA).** The SA field is also 6 bytes and contains the physical address of the sender of the packet. We will discuss the source address in greater detail later.

- **Length/type.** This field is defined as a length or type field. If the value of the field is less than 1518, it is a length field and defines the length of the data field that follows. On the other hand, if the value of this field is greater than 1536, it defines the type of the PDU packet that is encapsulated in the frame.

- **Data.** This field carries data encapsulated from the upper-layer protocols. It is a minimum of 46 and a maximum of 1500 bytes, as we will see later.

- **CRC.** The last field contains the error detection information, in this case a CRC-32.

Frame Length   Ethernet has imposed restrictions on both the minimum and maximum length of a frame, as shown in Figure 14.3.

Figure 14.3   *Minimum and maximum length*

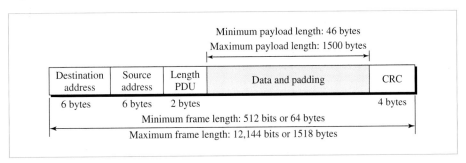

The minimum length restriction is required for the correct operation of CSMA/CD. If there is a collision before the physical layer sends a frame out of a station, it must be heard by all stations. If the entire frame is sent out before a collision is detected, it is too late. The MAC layer has already discarded the frame, thinking that the frame has reached the destination. This situation is aggravated as the frame length diminishes in size since smaller frames are sent out faster. The standard has therefore defined the smallest frame length for every 10-Mbps Ethernet LAN as 512 bits or 64 bytes (without the preamble or SFD field).

An Ethernet frame must therefore have a minimum length of 512 bits or 64 bytes. Part of this length is the header and the trailer. If we count 18 bytes of header and trailer (6 bytes source address, 6 bytes destination address, 2 bytes length/type, and 4 bytes CRC), then the minimum length of data from the upper layer is 64 − 18 = 46 bytes. If the upper-layer packet is less than 46 bytes, padding is added to make up the difference. The standard defines the maximum length of a frame (without preamble and SFD field) as 1518 bytes. If we subtract the 18 bytes of header and trailer, the maximum length of the payload is 1500 bytes. The maximum length restriction is only historical.

Addressing

Each station on an Ethernet network (such as a PC, workstation, or printer) has its own **network interface card (NIC).** The NIC fits inside the station and provides the station with a 6-byte physical address. The Ethernet address is 6 bytes (48 bits) that is normally written in **hexadecimal notation** using a hyphen to separate bytes from each other, as shown in Figure 14.4.

Figure 14.4   *Ethernet addresses in hexadecimal notation*

06-01-02-01-2C-4B

Unicast, Multicast, and Broadcast Addresses   A source address is always a **unicast address**—the frame comes from only one station. The destination address, however, can be unicast, **multicast,** or **broadcast.** Figure 14.5 shows how to distinguish a unicast address from a multicast address.

Figure 14.5   *Unicast and multicast addresses*

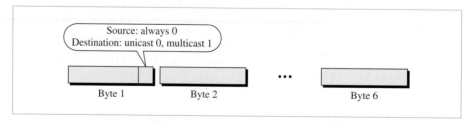

A unicast destination address defines only one recipient; the relationship between the sender and the receiver is one-to-one. A multicast destination address defines a group of addresses; the relationship between the sender and the receiver is one-to-many.

The broadcast address is a special case of the multicast address; the recipients are all the stations on the network. A destination broadcast address is forty-eight 1s.

Physical Layer

Figure 14.6 shows the physical layer for 10-Mbps Ethernet.

Figure 14.6 *Physical layer*

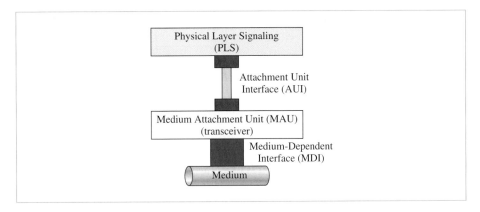

PLS

The **PLS sublayer** encodes and decodes data. Traditional Ethernet uses Manchester encoding (see Chapter 4) with a data rate of 10 Mbps. Note that for this data rate a bandwidth of 20 Mbaud is needed. Figure 14.7 shows the functions of the PLS sublayer.

Figure 14.7 *PLS*

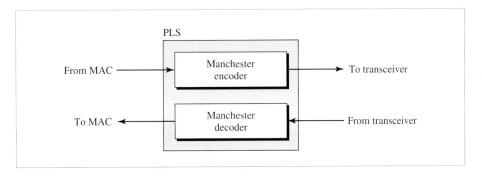

AUI

The **attachment unit interface (AUI)** is a specification that defines the interface between the PLS and MAU. The AUI was developed to create a kind of *medium-independent interface* between the PLS and the MAU. The interface was designed for the first implementation of Ethernet, which used thick coaxial cable. The whole idea was that if in the future we want to connect the PLS sublayer to a different MAU (using a different medium), we do not have to change the PLS. Figure 14.8 shows the AUI, AUI cable, and connector.

Figure 14.8   *AUI*

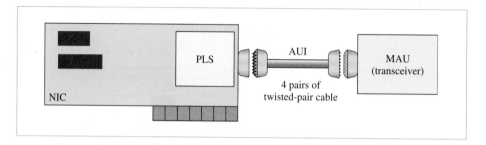

MAU (Transceiver)

The **medium attachment unit (MAU),** or transceiver, is medium-dependent. It creates the appropriate signal for each particular medium. There is a MAU for each type of medium used in 10-Mbps Ethernet. The coaxial cable needs its own type of MAU, the twisted-pair medium needs a twisted-pair MAU, and fiber-optic cable needs a fiber-optic MAU.

The **transceiver** is a transmitter and a receiver. It transmits signals over the medium; it receives signals over the medium; it also detects collisions. Figure 14.9 shows the position and functions of a transceiver.

Figure 14.9   *MAU (transceiver)*

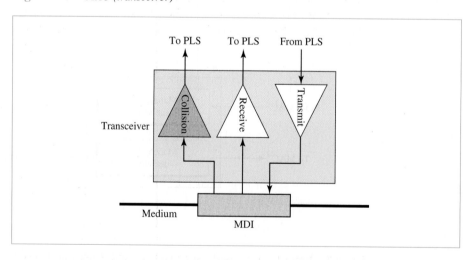

A transceiver can be external or internal. An external transceiver is installed close to the media and is connected via an AUI to the station. An internal transceiver is installed inside the station (on the interface card) and does not need an AUI cable.

MDI

To connect the transceiver (internal or external) to the medium, we need a **medium-dependent interface (MDI).** The MDI is just a piece of hardware for connecting a transceiver to the medium. For an external transceiver, it can be a tap or a tee connector. For an internal transceiver, it can be a jack.

Physical Layer Implementation

The standard defines four different implementations for baseband (digital), 10-Mbps Ethernet, as shown in Figure 14.10. We discuss each implementation separately.

Figure 14.10 *Categories of traditional Ethernet*

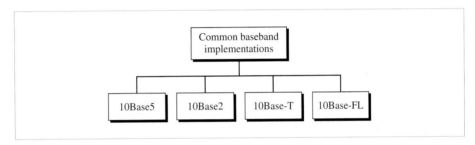

10Base5: Thick Ethernet

The first implementation is called **10Base5, thick Ethernet,** or Thicknet. The nickname derives from the size of the cable, which is roughly the size of a garden hose and too stiff to bend with your hands. 10Base5 was the first Ethernet specification.

10Base5 uses a bus topology with an external transceiver connected via a tap to a thick coaxial cable. Figure 14.11 shows how a station can be connected to the medium.

Figure 14.11 *Connection of a station to the medium using 10Base5*

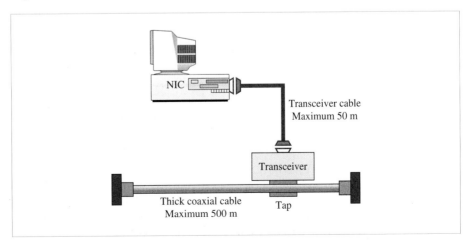

10Base2: Thin Ethernet

The second implementation is called **10Base2, thin Ethernet,** or Cheapernet. 10Base2 uses a bus topology with an internal transceiver or a point-to-point connection via an external transceiver. Figure 14.12 shows the connection of two stations to the medium. Note that if the station uses an internal transceiver, there is no need for an AUI cable. If the station lacks a transceiver, then an external transceiver can be used in conjunction with the AUI.

Figure 14.12   *Connection of stations to the medium using 10Base2*

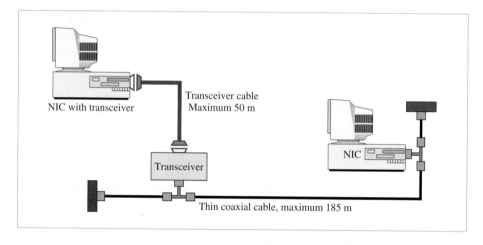

10Base-T: Twisted-Pair Ethernet

The third implementation is called **10Base-T** or **twisted-pair Ethernet.** 10Base-T uses a physical star topology. The stations are connected to a hub with an internal transceiver or an external transceiver. When the internal transceiver is used, there is no need for an AUI cable; the interface card is directly connected to the medium connector. When an external transceiver is used, the transceiver is connected through an AUI cable to the interface. The transceiver is connected then to the hub, as shown in Figure 14.13.

Figure 14.13   *Connection of stations to the medium using 10Base-T*

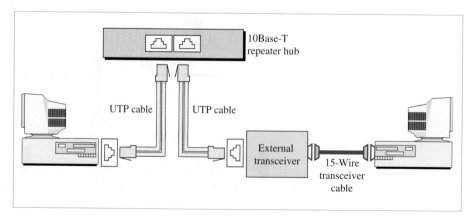

10Base-FL: Fiber Link Ethernet

Although several types of fiber-optic 10-Mbps Ethernet are defined, the one implemented by vendors is called **10Base-FL** or **fiber link Ethernet.** 10Base-FL uses a star topology to connect stations to a hub. The standard is normally implemented using an external transceiver called fiber-optic MAU. The station is connected to the external transceiver by an AUI cable. The transceiver is connected to the hub by using two pairs of fiber-optic cables, as shown in Figure 14.14.

Figure 14.14   *Connection of stations to the medium using 10Base-FL*

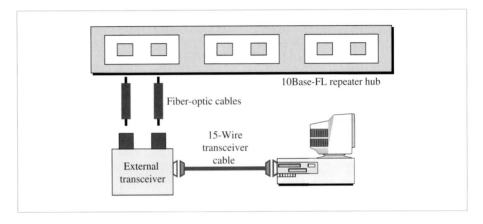

Bridged Ethernet

The first step in the Ethernet evolution was the division of a LAN by **bridges.** Bridges have two effects on an Ethernet LAN: They raise the bandwidth and separate collision domains. We discuss bridges in Chapter 16.

Raising the Bandwidth

In an unbridged Ethernet network, the total capacity (10 Mbps) is shared between all stations with a frame to send; the stations share the bandwidth of the network. If only one station has frames to send, it benefits from the total capacity (10 Mbps). But if more than one station needs to use the network, the capacity is shared. For example, if two stations have a lot of frames to send, they probably alternate in usage. When one station is sending, the other one refrains from sending. We can say that, on average, each station sends at the rate of 5 Mbps. Figure 14.15 shows the situation.

The bridge, as we will learn in Chapter 16, can help here. A bridge divides the network into two or more networks. Bandwidthwise, each network is independent. For example, in Figure 14.16, a network with 12 stations is divided into two networks, each with 6 stations. Now each network has a capacity of 10 Mbps. The 10-Mbps capacity in each segment is now shared between 6 stations (actually 7 because the bridge acts as a station in each segment), not 12 stations. In a network with a heavy load, each station

Figure 14.15   *Sharing bandwidth*

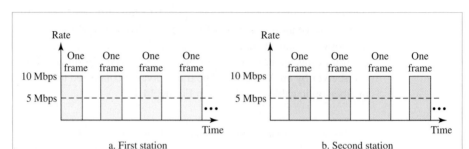

a. First station

b. Second station

Figure 14.16   *A network with and without a bridge*

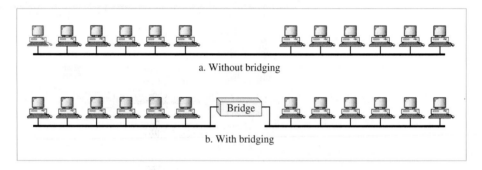

a. Without bridging

b. With bridging

theoretically is offered 10/6 Mbps instead of 10/12 Mbps, assuming that the traffic is not going through the bridge.

It is obvious that if we further divide the network, we can gain more bandwidth for each segment. For example, if we use a four-port bridge, each station is now offered 10/3 Mbps, which is 4 times more than a nonbridged network.

Separating Collision Domains

Another advantage of a bridge is the separation of the **collision domain.** Figure 14.17 shows the collision domains for an unbridged and a bridged network. You can see that the collision domain becomes much smaller and the probability of collision is reduced tremendously. Without bridging, 12 stations contend for access to the medium; with bridging only 3 stations contend for access to the medium.

Switched Ethernet

The idea of a bridged LAN can be extended to a switched LAN. Instead of having two to four networks, why not have N networks, where N is the number of stations on the LAN? In other words, if we can have a multiple-port bridge, why not have an N-port switch? In this way, the bandwidth is shared only between the station and the switch (5 Mbps each). In addition, the collision domain is divided into N domains.

Figure 14.17 *Collision domains in a nonbridged and bridged network*

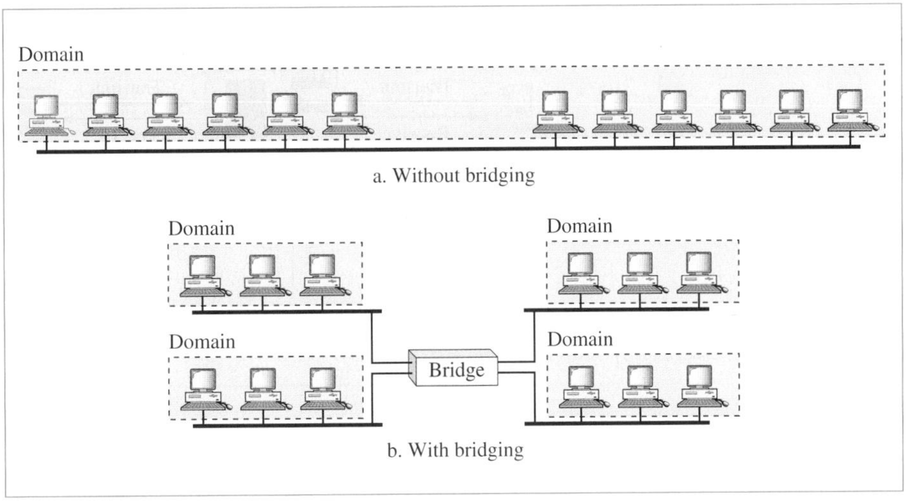

Domain

a. Without bridging

Domain

Domain

Domain

Bridge

Domain

b. With bridging

A layer 2 **switch** is an *N*-port bridge with additional sophistication that allows faster handling of the packets. Evolution from a bridged Ethernet to a **switched Ethernet** was a big step that opened the way to an even faster Ethernet, as we will see. Figure 14.18 shows a switched LAN.

Figure 14.18 *Switched Ethernet*

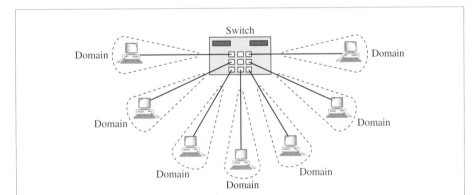

Switch

Domain

Domain

Domain

Domain

Domain

Domain

Domain

Full-Duplex Ethernet

One of the limitations of 10Base5 and 10Base2 is that communication is half-duplex (10Base-T is always full-duplex); a station can either send or receive, but not at the same time. The next step in the evolution was to move from switched Ethernet to **full-duplex switched Ethernet.** The full-duplex mode increases the capacity of each domain

Figure 14.19 *Full-duplex switched Ethernet*

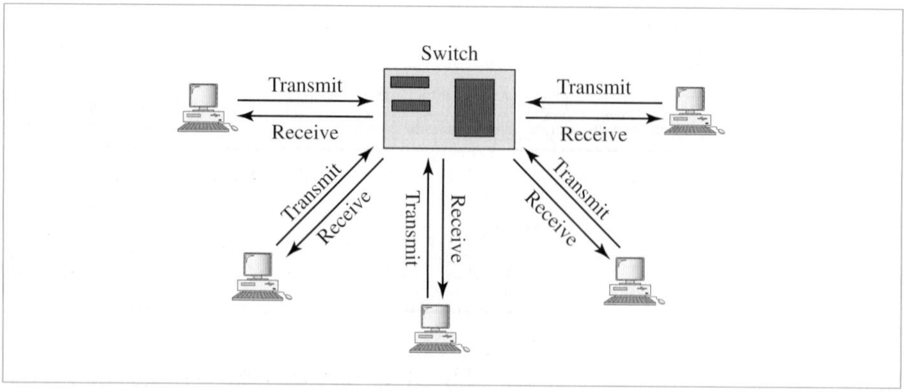

from 10 to 20 Mbps. Figure 14.19 shows a switched Ethernet in full-duplex mode. Note that, instead of using one link between the station and the switch, the configuration uses two links: one to transmit and one to receive.

No Need for CSMA/CD

In full-duplex switched Ethernet, there is no need for the CSMA/CD method. In a switched full-duplex Ethernet, each station is connected to the switch via two separate links. Each station or switch can send and receive independently without worrying about collision. Each link is a point-to-point dedicated path between the station and the switch. There is no more need for carrier sensing; there is no more need for collision detection. The job of the MAC layer becomes much easier. The carrier sense and collision detection functionality of the MAC sublayer can be turned off.

MAC

Traditional Ethernet was designed as a connectionless protocol at the MAC sublayer. There is no explicit flow control or error control to inform the sender that the frame has arrived at the destination without error. When the receiver receives the frame it does not send any positive or negative acknowledgment.

To provide for flow and error control in full-duplex switched Ethernet, a new sublayer, called the MAC control, is added between the LLC sublayer and the MAC sublayer.

14.2 FAST ETHERNET

The need for a higher data rate resulted in the design of the **Fast Ethernet** protocol (100 Mbps).

Mac Sublayer

The whole idea in the evolution of Ethernet from 10 to 100 Mbps is to keep the MAC sublayer untouched. The access method is the same (CSMA/CD). Of course, for full-duplex

Fast Ethernet, there is no need for CSMA/CD. However, the implementations keep CSMA/CD for backward compatibility with traditional Ethernet. Frame format, minimum and maximum frame lengths, and addressing are the same for 10- and 100-Mbps Ethernet.

Autonegotiation

A new feature added to Fast Ethernet is called **autonegotiation.** It allows a station or a hub a range of capabilities. Auto negotiation allows two devices to negotiate the mode or data rate of operation. It was particularly designed for the following purposes:

- To allow incompatible devices to connect to one another. For example, a device with a maximum capacity of 10 Mbps can communicate with a device that is designed for 100 Mbps (but can work at a lower rate).
- To allow one device to have multiple capabilities.
- To allow a station to check a hub's capabilities.

Physical Layer

Figure 14.20 shows the physical layer for 100-Mbps Ethernet.

Figure 14.20   *Fast Ethernet physical layer*

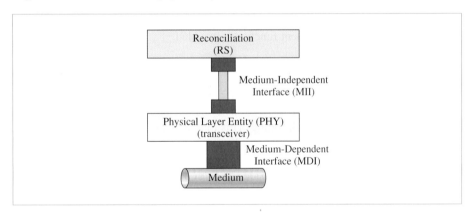

The physical layer is made up of four sublayers: RS, MII, PHY, and MDI. The reconciliation sublayer is common to all implementations. The PHY and MDI are medium-dependent.

RS

The **reconciliation sublayer** in Fast Ethernet replaces the PLS sublayer in 10-Mbps Ethernet. Encoding and decoding, which were performed by the PLS, are moved to the PHY sublayer (transceiver) because encoding in Fast Ethernet is medium-dependent. The reconciliation sublayer is responsible for whatever is left over, specifically, the passing of data in 4-bit format (nibble) to the MII, as we will see shortly.

MII

In the design of Fast Ethernet, the AUI was replaced with the **medium-independent interface (MII).** The MII is an improved interface that can be used with both a 10- and 100-Mbps data rate. Figure 14.21 shows the MII.

Figure 14.21   *MII*

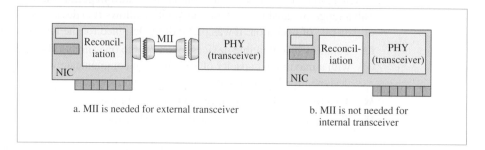

a. MII is needed for external transceiver

b. MII is not needed for internal transceiver

We summarize the features of MII as follows:

- It operates at both 10 and 100 Mbps. In other words, it is backward-compatible with the AUI.
- It features a parallel data path (4 bits at a time) between the PHY sublayer and the reconciliation sublayer.
- Management functions are added.

PHY (Transceiver)

The transceiver in Fast Ethernet is called the **PHY sublayer.** Besides the regular functions mentioned in 10-Mbps Ethernet, the transceiver in Fast Ethernet is responsible for encoding and decoding. This function was moved from the PLS layer to the PHY sublayer. A transceiver can be external or internal. An external transceiver is installed close to the medium and is connected via an MII cable to the station. An internal transceiver is installed inside the station (on the interface card) and does not need an MII cable. Because a transceiver is medium-dependent, we will discuss the transceiver designed for each implementation in the implementation section.

MDI

To connect the transceiver (internal or external) to the medium, we need a medium-dependent interface (MDI). The MDI is just a piece of hardware that is implementation-specific.

Physical Layer Implementation

Fast Ethernet can be categorized as either a two-wire or a four-wire implementation. The two-wire implementation is called 100Base-X, which can be either twisted-pair

Figure 14.22 *Fast Ethernet implementations*

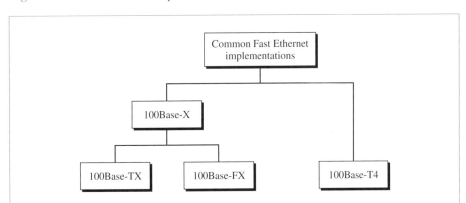

cable (100Base-TX) or fiber-optic cable (100Base-FX). The four-wire implementation is designed only for twisted-pair cable (100Base-T4). In other words, we have three implementations: 100Base-TX, 100Base-FX, and 100Base-T4, as shown in Figure 14.22.

100Base-TX

100Base-TX uses two pairs of twisted-pair cable (either category 5 UTP or STP) in a physical star topology. The implementation allows either an external transceiver (with an MII cable) or an internal transceiver. Figure 14.23 shows both types of connections.

Figure 14.23 *100Base-TX implementation*

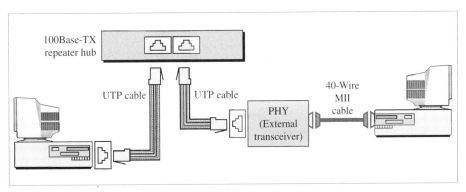

Transceiver In Fast Ethernet, the transceiver is responsible for transmitting, receiving, detecting collisions, and encoding/decoding of data.

Encoding and Decoding   To achieve a 100-Mbps data rate, encoding (and decoding) is implemented in two steps, as shown in Figure 14.24.

Figure 14.24   *Encoding and decoding in 100Base-TX*

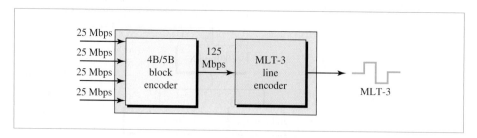

To maintain synchronization, the encoder first performs block encoding. The 4 parallel bits received from the NIC are encoded into 5 serial bits using 4B/5B, discussed in Chapter 4. This requires a bandwidth of 125 MHz (125 Mbps).

The data at the 125-Mbps rate are then encoded into a signal using MLT-3 (see Chapter 4).

100Base-FX

100Base-FX uses two pairs of fiber-optic cables in a physical star topology. The implementation allows either an external transceiver (with an MII cable) or an internal transceiver. Figure 14.25 shows both types of connections.

Figure 14.25   *100Base-FX implementation*

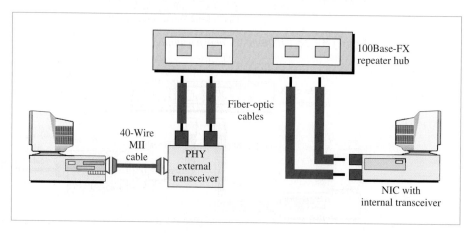

Transceiver   The transceiver is responsible for transmitting, sending, detecting the collision, and encoding/decoding.

Encoding and Decoding   100Base-FX uses two levels of encoding, as shown in Figure 14.26.

Figure 14.26 *Encoding and decoding in 100Base-FX*

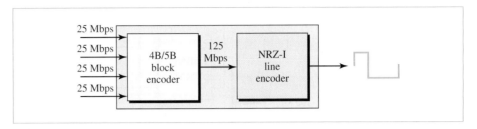

To maintain synchronization, the encoder first performs block encoding. The 4 parallel bits received from the NIC is encoded into 5 serial bits using 4B/5B. This requires a bandwidth of 125 MHz (125 Mbps).

The data at the 125-Mbps rate are then encoded into a signal using NRZ-I (see Chapter 4).

100Base-T4

A 100Base-TX network can provide a data rate of 100 Mbps, but it requires the use of category 5 UTP or STP cable. This is not cost-efficient for buildings that already have been wired for voice-grade twisted-pair (category 3). A new standard, called **100Base-T4,** was designed to use category 3 or higher UTP. The implementation uses four pairs of UTP for transmitting 100 Mbps. Figure 14.27 shows the connection of a station in a 100Base-T4 network.

Figure 14.27 *100Base-T4 implementation*

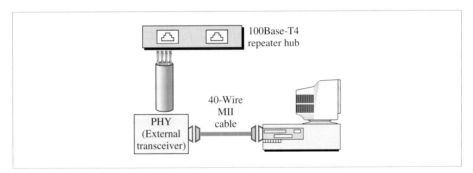

Transceiver

While the transceiver function in 100Base-T4 is similar to the other implementations, encoding and decoding are more complex.

Encoding and Decoding   To maintain synchronization and at the same time reduce the bandwidth, 8B/6T (see Chapter 4) is used.

Transmission Using Four Wires   The 8B/6T encoding reduces the bandwidth from 100 to 75 Mbaud (ratio of 8/6). However, a voice-grade UTP is not capable of handling even this bandwidth. 100Base-T4 is designed to operate on 25-Mbaud bandwidths. For unidirectional transmission, this would require six cable pairs (three pairs in each direction).

Figure 14.28   *Using four wires in 100Base-T4*

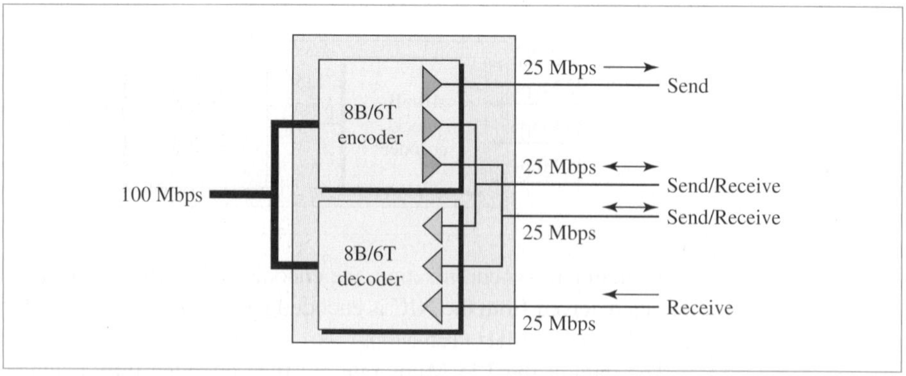

To cut down the number of pairs to four, two pairs are designed for unidirectional transmission and the other two for bidirectional transmission. The two unidirectional pairs are
always free in one direction to carry collision signals. Figure 14.28 shows the wiring.

14.3   GIGABIT ETHERNET

Recent need for an even higher data rate resulted in the design of the **Gigabit Ethernet**
protocol (1000 Mbps).

MAC Sublayer

The whole idea in the evolution of Ethernet was to keep the MAC sublayer untouched.
However, when it came to sending at a 1-Gbps rate, this was no longer possible.

Access Method

Gigabit Ethernet has two distinctive approaches for medium access: half-duplex using
CSMA/CD or full-duplex with no need for CSMA/CD. Although the half-duplex
approach is very interesting, it is complicated and not in use today. In the full-duplex
approach, there is no need for CSMA/CD. Almost all implementations of Gigabit
Ethernet follow the full-duplex approach.

Physical Layer

Figure 14.29 shows the physical layer of Gigabit Ethernet. The physical layer is made
up of four sublayers: reconciliation, GMII, PHY, and MDI. The reconciliation sublayer
is common to all implementations. The PHY and MDI are medium-dependent. In this
section, we discuss these sublayers briefly. In the next section, we define GMII, PHY,
and MDI for each particular implementation.

RS

The reconciliation sublayer sends 8-bit parallel data to the PHY sublayer via a GMII
interface.

Figure 14.29 *Physical layer in Gigabit Ethernet*

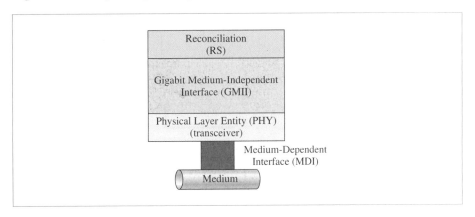

GMII

GMII (gigabit medium-independent interface) is a specification that defines how the reconciliation sublayer is to be connected to the PHY sublayer (transceiver). It is the counterpart of MII in Fast Ethernet. However, GMII is not an external physical component. It does not exist outside the NIC. In other words, it is primarily a logical, rather than a physical, interface. It is a specification for integrated circuits or circuit boards for the Gigabit Ethernet NIC. Some features of GMII are as follows:

- It operates only at 1000 Mbps. However, there are chips that support both MII and GMII. This means a station can operate at 10, 100, and 1000 Mbps while using such a chip.
- GMII specifies a parallel data path (8 bits at a time) between the RS sublayer and the transceiver.
- Management functions are included.
- There is no GMII cable.
- There is no GMII connector.

PHY (Transceiver)

Just as in Fast Ethernet, the transceiver is medium-dependent and also encodes and decodes. However, in Gigabit Ethernet, the transceiver can only be internal because there is no external GMII to provide the connection. We discuss the transceivers for each implementation in the implementation section.

MDI

Just as in Fast Ethernet, the MDI connects the transceiver to the medium. For Gigabit Ethernet, only the RJ-45 and fiber-optic connectors are defined.

Physical Layer Implementation

Gigabit Ethernet can be categorized as either a two-wire or a four-wire implementation. The two-wire implementation is called **1000Base-X,** which can use shortwave optical

Figure 14.30   *Gigabit Ethernet implementations*

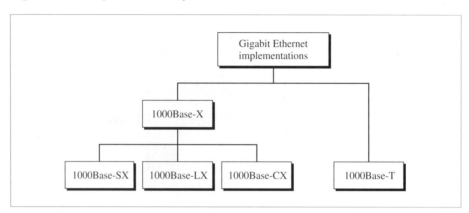

fiber **(1000Base-SX),** long-wave optical fiber **(1000Base-LX),** or short copper jumpers **(1000Base-CX).** The four-wire version uses twisted-pair cable **(1000Base-T).** In other words, we have four implementations, as shown in Figure 14.30.

1000Base-X

Both 1000Base-SX and 1000Base-LX use two fiber-optic cables. The only difference between them is that the former uses shortwave laser and the latter uses long-wave laser. As we said before, all implementations are designed with an internal transceiver, so there is no external GMII cable or connector. Figure 14.31 shows the connection of a station to the hub.

Figure 14.31   *1000Base-X implementation*

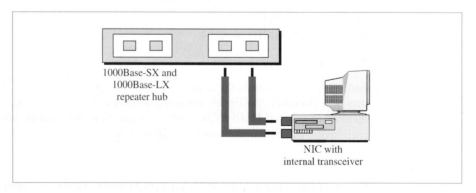

The 1000Base-CX implementation was designed to use STP cable, but it has never been implemented.

Transceiver   The transceiver in Gigabit Ethernet is internal. Its functions are encoding and decoding, transmitting, receiving, and collision detection (if appropriate).

Figure 14.32 *Encoding in 1000Base-X*

Figure 14.32 *Encoding in 1000Base-X*

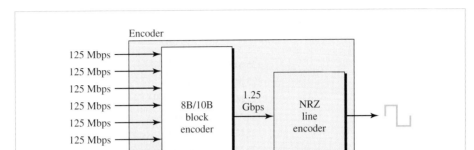

Encoding To achieve a 1000-Mbps data rate, encoding (and decoding) occurs in two steps, as shown in Figure 14.32.

To maintain synchronization, the encoder first performs block encoding. The 8 parallel bits received from the NIC is encoded into 10 serial bits using 8B/10B. This requires a bandwidth of 1.25 GHz (1.25 Gbps).

The data at the 1.25-Gbps rate are then encoded into a signal using NRZ encoding, as discussed in Chapter 4.

1000Base-T

1000Base-T was designed to use category 5 UTP. Four twisted pairs achieve a transmission rate of 1 Gbps. Figure 14.33 shows the connection of a station to the medium in this implementation.

Figure 14.33 *1000Base-T implementation*

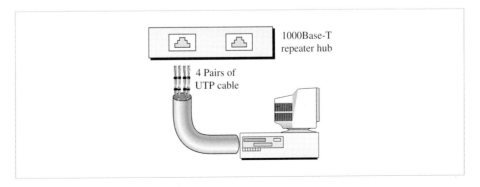

Transceiver To send 1.25 Gbps over four pairs of UTP, 1000Base-T uses an encoding scheme called **4D-PAM5 (4-dimensional, 5-level pulse amplitude modulation).**

Figure 14.34   *Encoding in 1000Base-T*

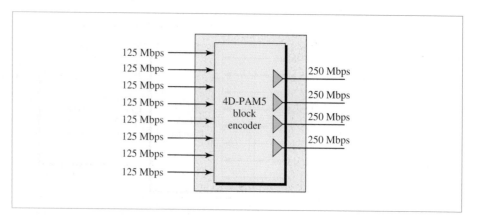

Five levels of pulse amplitude modulation are used. The technique is very complicated and beyond the scope of this book. Figure 14.34 shows the overall concept.

14.4   KEY TERMS

1000Base-CX
1000Base-LX
1000Base-SX
1000Base-T
1000Base-X
100Base-FX
100Base-T4
100Base-TX
100Base-X
10Base2
10Base5
10Base-FL
10Base-T
4-dimensional, 5-level pulse amplitude
   modulation (4D-PAM5)
attachment unit interface (AUI)
autonegotiation
bridge
broadcast address
collision domain
destination address (DA)
Ethernet
Fast Ethernet
fiber link Ethernet

full-duplex switched Ethernet
Gigabit Ethernet
gigabit medium-independent interface
   (GMII)
hexadecimal notation
medium access control (MAC)
   sublayer
medium attachment unit (MAU)
medium-dependent interface (MDI)
medium-independent interface (MII)
multicast address
network interface card (NIC)
PHY sublayer
physical layer signaling (PLS) sublayer
preamble
reconciliation sublayer
source address (SA)
start frame delimiter (SFD)
switched Ethernet
thick Ethernet
thin Ethernet
transceiver
twisted-pair Ethernet
unicast address

14.5 SUMMARY

❏ Ethernet is the most widely used local area network protocol.

❏ The IEEE 802.3 standard defines 1-persistent CSMA/CD as the access method for first-generation 10-Mbps Ethernet.

❏ The data link layer of Ethernet consists of the LLC sublayer and the MAC sublayer.

❏ The MAC sublayer is responsible for the operation of the CSMA/CD access method.

❏ Each station on an Ethernet network has a unique 48-bit address imprinted on its network interface card (NIC).

❏ The minimum frame length for 10-Mbps Ethernet is 64 bytes; the maximum is 1518 bytes.

❏ The physical layer of 10-Mbps Ethernet can be composed of four sublayers: the physical layer signaling (PLS) sublayer, the attachment unit interface (AUI) sublayer, the medium attachment unit (MAU) sublayer, and the medium-dependent interface (MDI) sublayer.

❏ The common baseband implementations of 10-Mbps Ethernet are 10Base5 (thick Ethernet), 10Base2 (thin Ethernet), 10Base-T (twisted-pair Ethernet), and 10Base-FL (fiber link Ethernet).

❏ The 10Base5 implementation of Ethernet uses thick coaxial cable. The 10Base2 implementation of Ethernet uses thin coaxial cable. The 10Base-T implementation of Ethernet uses twisted-pair cable that connects each station to a port in a hub. The 10Base-FL implementation of Ethernet uses fiber-optic cable.

❏ A bridge can raise the bandwidth and separate the collision domains on an Ethernet LAN.

❏ A switch allows each station on an Ethernet LAN to have the entire capacity of the network to itself.

❏ Full-duplex mode doubles the capacity of each domain and deletes the need for the CSMA/CD method.

❏ Fast Ethernet has a data rate of 100 Mbps.

❏ In Fast Ethernet, autonegotiation allows two devices to negotiate the mode or data rate of operation.

❏ The Fast Ethernet reconciliation sublayer is responsible for the passing of data in 4-bit format to the MII.

❏ The Fast Ethernet MII is an interface that can be used with both a 10- and a 100-Mbps interface.

❏ The Fast Ethernet PHY sublayer is responsible for encoding and decoding.

❏ The common Fast Ethernet implementations are 100Base-TX (two pairs of twisted-pair cable), 100Base-FX (two fiber-optic cables), and 100Base-T4 (four pairs of voice-grade, or higher, twisted-pair cable).

❏ Gigabit Ethernet has a data rate of 1000 Mbps.

❏ Gigabit Ethernet access methods include half-duplex using traditional CSMA/CD (not common) and full-duplex (most popular method).

❏   The Gigabit Ethernet reconciliation sublayer is responsible for sending 8-bit parallel data to the PHY sublayer via a GMII interface.

❏   The Gigabit Ethernet GMII defines how the reconciliation sublayer is to be connected to the PHY sublayer.

❏   The Gigabit Ethernet PHY sublayer is responsible for encoding and decoding.

❏   The common Gigabit Ethernet implementations are 1000Base-SX (two optical fibers and a shortwave laser source), 100Base-LX (two optical fibers and a long-wave laser source), and 100Base-T (four twisted pairs).

14.6   PRACTICE SET

Review Questions

1. How is the preamble field different from the SFD field?
2. What is the purpose of an NIC?
3. What is the purpose of a transceiver?
4. What is the difference between a multicast address and a broadcast address?
5. What are the advantages of dividing an Ethernet LAN with a bridge?
6. What is the relationship between a switch and a bridge?
7. Why is there no need for CSMA/CD on a full-duplex Ethernet LAN?
8. Compare the data rates for traditional Ethernet, Fast Ethernet, and Gigabit Ethernet.
9. What are the common traditional Ethernet implementations?
10. What are the common Fast Ethernet implementations?
11. What are the common Gigabit Ethernet implementations?
12. What is the purpose of autonegotiation?
13. Compare the reconciliation sublayer in Fast Ethernet with the PLS sublayer in traditional Ethernet.
14. What is the GMII in Gigabit Ethernet?
15. What Internet model layers are of concern to LANs?

Multiple-Choice Questions

16. What is the hexadecimal equivalent of the Ethernet address 01011010 00010001 01010101 00011000 10101010 00001111?
    a. 5A-88-AA-18-55-F0
    b. 5A-81-BA-81-AA-0F
    c. 5A-18-5A-18-55-0F
    d. 5A-11-55-18-AA-0F
17. If an Ethernet destination address is 07-01-02-03-04-05, then this is a _____ address.
    a. Unicast
    b. Multicast

c. Broadcast

d. Any of the above

18. If an Ethernet destination address is 08-07-06-05-44-33, then this is a _____ address.

a. Unicast

b. Multicast

c. Broadcast

d. Any of the above

19. Which of the following could not be an Ethernet source address?

a. 8A-7B-6C-DE-10-00

b. EE-AA-C1-23-45-32

c. 46-56-21-1A-DE-F4

d. 8B-32-21-21-4D-34

20. Which of the following could not be an Ethernet unicast destination?

a. 43-7B-6C-DE-10-00

b. 44-AA-C1-23-45-32

c. 46-56-21-1A-DE-F4

d. 48-32-21-21-4D-34

21. Which of the following could not be an Ethernet multicast destination?

a. B7-7B-6C-DE-10-00

b. 7B-AA-C1-23-45-32

c. 7C-56-21-1A-DE-F4

d. 83-32-21-21-4D-34

22. A 10-station Ethernet LAN uses a _____-port bridge if the effective average data rate for each station is 2 Mbps.

a. 1

b. 2

c. 5

d. 10

23. A _____-station Ethernet LAN uses a four-port bridge. Each station has an effective average data rate of 1.25 Mbps.

a. 32

b. 40

c. 80

d. 160

24. Forty stations are on an Ethernet LAN. A 10-port bridge segments the LAN. What is the effective average data rate of each station?

a. 1.0 Mbps

b. 2.0 Mbps

c. 2.5 Mbps

d. 5.0 Mbps

25. An 80-station traditional Ethernet is divided into four collision domains. This means that a maximum of _____ stations contend for medium access at any one time.
    a. 320
    b. 80
    c. 76
    d. 20

26. What is the efficiency of 4B/5B block encoding?
    a. 20 percent
    b. 40 percent
    c. 60 percent
    d. 80 percent

27. What is the efficiency of a frame in half-duplex Gigabit Ethernet carrying 46 bytes of data?
    a. 97 percent
    b. 70 percent
    c. 56 percent
    d. 12 percent

28. Which of the following is a four-wire Gigabit Ethernet implementation?
    a. 1000Base-SX
    b. 1000Base-LX
    c. 1000Base-CX
    d. 1000Base-T

29. What is the efficiency of 8B/10B encoding?
    a. 20 percent
    b. 40 percent
    c. 60 percent
    d. 80 percent

Exercises

30. What is the average size of an Ethernet frame?

31. What is the ratio of useful data to the entire packet for the smallest Ethernet frame? What is the ratio for the largest frame? What is the average ratio?

32. Why do you think that an Ethernet frame should have a minimum data size?

33. Imagine the length of a 10Base5 cable is 2500 m. If the speed of propagation in a thick coaxial cable is 200,000,000 m/s, how long does it take for a bit to travel from the beginning to the end of the network? Ignore any propagation delay in the equipment.

34. The data rate of 10Base5 is 10 Mbps. How long does it take to create the smallest frame? Show your calculation.

35. An Ethernet MAC sublayer receives 42 bytes of data from the LLC sublayer. How many bytes of padding must be added to the data?

36. An Ethernet MAC sublayer receives 1510 bytes of data from the LLC layer. Can the data be encapsulated in one frame? If not, how many frames need to be sent? What is the size of the data in each frame?

37. Complete Table 14.1.

Table 14.1 *Exercise 37*

Characteristics	10Base5	10Base2	10Base-T	10Base-FL
Type of cable				
Type of transceiver				
Need for cable end				

38. Compare the physical sublayers of Fast and Gigabit Ethernet, using Table 14.2.

Table 14.2 *Exercise 38*

Sublayers	Fast Ethernet	Gigabit Ethernet
Reconciliation		
MII		
GII		
PHY		
MDI		

39. Compare the different Fast Ethernet implementations using Table 14.3.

Table 14.3 *Exercise 39*

Implementation	Media	Encoding Methods
100Base-TX		
100Base-FX		
100Base-T4		

40. Compare the different Gigabit Ethernet implementations using Table 14.4.

Table 14.4 *Exercise 40*

Implementation	Media	Encoding Methods
1000Base-SX		
1000Base-LX		
1000Base-CX		
1000Base-T		

CHAPTER 15

Wireless LANs

Wireless communication is one of the fastest growing technologies. The demand for connecting devices without cable is increasing everywhere. Wireless LANs are found on college campuses, office buildings, and public areas. At home, a **wireless LAN** can connect roaming devices to the Internet.

In this chapter, we concentrate on two promising wireless technologies for LANs: IEEE 802.11 wireless LANs, sometimes called wireless Ethernet, and Bluetooth, a complex technology for small wireless LANs.

Although both protocols need several layers to operate, we mostly concentrate on the physical and data link layer in this part of the book. In this chapter, we study these technologies as wireless links, links that can connect us to the Internet. How the connection is made and how end-to-end communication is accomplished are the subjects of future chapters.

15.1 IEEE 802.11

IEEE has defined the specification for a wireless LAN, called **IEEE 802.11,** which covers the physical and data link layers. But before discussing these layers, we describe the architecture of the protocol in general.

Architecture

The standard defines two kinds of services: the basic service set (BSS) and the extended service set (ESS).

Basic Service Set

IEEE 802.11 defines the **basic service set (BSS)** as the building block of a wireless LAN. A basic service set is made of stationary or mobile wireless stations and a possible central base station, known as the **access point (AP).** Figure 15.1 shows two sets in this standard.

The BSS without an AP is a stand-alone network and cannot send data to other BSSs. It is what is called an *ad hoc architecture*. In this architecture, stations can

Figure 15.1   *BSSs*

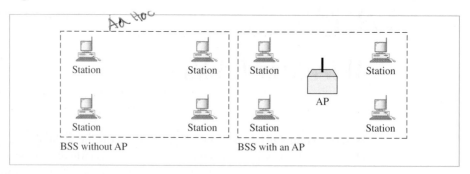

form a network without the need of an AP; they can locate each other and agree to be part of a BSS.

Extended Service Set

An **extended service set (ESS)** is made up of two or more BSSs with APs. In this case, the BSSs are connected through a *distribution system,* which is usually a wired LAN. The distribution system connects the APs in the BSSs. IEEE 802.11 does not restrict the distribution system; it can be any IEEE LAN such as an Ethernet. Note that the extended service set uses two types of stations: mobile and stationary. The mobile stations are normal stations inside a BSS. The stationary stations are AP stations that are part of a wired LAN. Figure 15.2 shows an ESS.

Figure 15.2   *ESS*

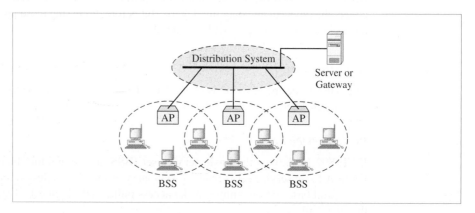

When BSSs are connected, we have what is called an *infrastructure network*. In this network, the stations within reach of one another can communicate without the use of an AP. However, communication between two stations in two different BSSs usually occurs via two APs. The idea is similar to communication in a cellular network if we consider each BSS to be a cell and each AP to be a base station. Note that a mobile station can belong to more than one BSS at the same time.

Station Types

IEEE 802.11 defines three types of stations based on their mobility in a wireless LAN: **no-transition, BSS-transition,** and **ESS-transition.**

No-Transition Mobility   A station with no-transition mobility is either stationary (not moving) or moving only inside a BSS.

BSS-Transition Mobility   A station with BSS-transition mobility can move from one BSS to another, but the movement is confined inside one ESS.

ESS-Transition Mobility   A station with ESS-transition mobility can move from one ESS to another. However, IEEE 802.11 does not guarantee that communication is continuous during the move.

Physical Layer

IEEE 802.11 defines specifications for the conversion of bits to a signal in the physical layer; one specification is in the infrared frequencies and is not discussed here. The other five specifications are in the radio frequency range as shown in Figure 15.3.

Figure 15.3   *Physical layer specifications*

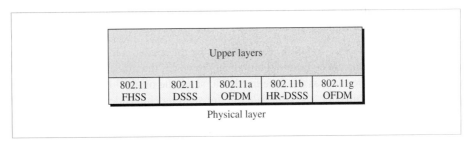

IEEE 802.11 FHSS

IEEE 802.11 FHSS describes the **frequency-hopping spread spectrum (FHSS)** method for signal generation in a 2.4-GHz ISM band.

FHSS   FHSS is a method in which the sender sends on one carrier frequency for a short amount of time, then hops to another carrier frequency for the same amount of time, hops again to still another for the same amount of time, and so on. After N hoppings, the cycle is repeated (see Fig. 15.4). If the bandwidth of the original signal is B, the allocated spread spectrum bandwidth is $N \times B$.

Spreading makes it difficult for unauthorized persons to make sense of transmitted data. In FHSS the sender and receiver agree on the sequence of the allocated bands. In the figure, the first bit (or group of bits) is sent in subband 1, the second bit (or group of bits) is sent in subband 2, and so on. An intruder who tunes his or her receiver to frequencies for one subband may receive the first group of bits, but receives nothing in this subband during the second interval. The amount of time spent at each subband, called the dwell time, is 400 ms or more. Note that this is not a case of multiple access; all stations contend to use the same subbands to send their data. Contention is a function of the MAC sublayer, as we will see shortly.

Figure 15.4   *FHSS*

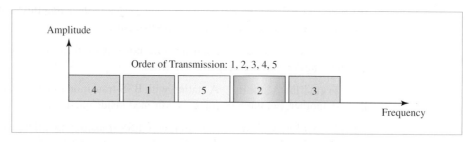

Band   FHSS uses a 2.4-GHz industrial, scientific, and medical (ISM) band. The band in North America is from 2.4 GHz to 2.48 GHz. The band is divided into 79 subbands of 1 MHz. A pseudorandom number generator selects the hopping sequence.

Modulation and Data Rate   The modulation technique in this specification is FSK at 1 Mbaud/s. The system allows 1 or 2 bits/baud (two-level FSK or four-level FSK), which results in a data rate of 1 or 2 Mbps.

IEEE 802.11 DSSS

IEEE 802.11 DSSS describes the **direct sequence spread spectrum (DSSS)** method for signal generation in a 2.4-GHz ISM band.

DSSS   In DSSS, each bit sent by the sender is replaced by a sequence of bits called a chip code. To avoid buffering, however, the time needed to send one chip code must be the same as the time needed to send one original bit. If N is the number of bits in each chip code, then the data rate for sending chip codes is N times the data rate of the original bit stream. Figure 15.5 shows an example of DSSS.

Figure 15.5   *DSSS*

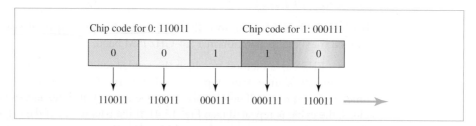

Although this scheme looks similar to CDMA (see Chapter 13), there is a major difference. DSSS is implemented at the physical layer. It is not a multiple-access method for the data link layer. We need a contention method at the data link layer, and that will be discussed shortly.

Band   DSSS uses a 2.4-GHz ISM band. The bit sequence uses the entire band.

Modulation and Data Rate   The modulation technique in this specification is PSK at 1 Mbaud/s. The system allows 1 or 2 bits/baud (BPSK or QPSK), which results in a data rate of 1 or 2 Mbps.

IEEE 802.11a OFDM

IEEE 802.11a OFDM describes the **orthogonal frequency-division multiplexing (OFDM)** method for signal generation in a 5-GHz ISM band.

OFDM   OFDM is the same as FDM, with one major difference: All the subbands are used by one source at a given time. Sources contend with one another at the data link layer for access.

Band   The specification uses a 5-GHz ISM band. The band is divided into 52 subbands, with 48 subbands for sending 48 groups of bits at a time and 4 subbands for control information. The scheme is similar to ADSL, as discussed in Chapter 9. Dividing the band into subbands diminishes the effects of interference. If the subbands are used randomly, security can also be increased.

Modulation and Data Rate   OFDM uses PSK and QAM for modulation. The common data rates are 18 Mbps (PSK) and 54 Mbps (QAM).

IEEE 802.11b HR-DSSS

IEEE 802.11b HR-DSSS describes the **high-rate DSSS (HR-DSSS)** method for signal generation in a 2.4-GHz ISM band.

HR-DSSS   HR-DSSS is similar to DSSS except for the encoding method, which is called **complementary code keying (CCK).** CCK encodes 4 or 8 bits to one CCK symbol.

Band   The specification uses a 2.4-GHz ISM band.

Modulation and Data Rate   To be backward-compatible with DSSS, HR-DSSS defines four data rates: 1, 2, 5.5, and 11 Mbps. The first two use the same modulation techniques as DSSS. The 5.5-Mbps version uses BPSK and transmits at 1.375 Mbaud/s with 4-bit CCK encoding. The 11-Mbps version uses QPSK and transmits at 1.375 Mbps with 8-bit CCK encoding. Note that the 11-Mbps version has a data rate close to 10-Mbps Ethernet.

IEEE 802.11g OFDM

This relatively new specification uses OFDM with a 2.4-GHz ISM band. The complex modulation technique achieves a 54-Mbps data rate.

MAC Layer

IEEE 802.11 defines two MAC sublayers: the **distributed coordination function (DCF)** and **point coordination function (PCF)** as shown in Figure 15.6.

PCF is an optional and complex access method that can be implemented in an infrastructure network (not in an ad hoc network). We do not discuss this here; for more information refer to Forouzan, *Local Area Networks,* McGraw-Hill. DCF is similar to CSMA/CA, as discussed in Chapter 13, with some additional control features. We discuss only the access method.

Figure 15.6   *MAC layers in IEEE 802.11 standard*

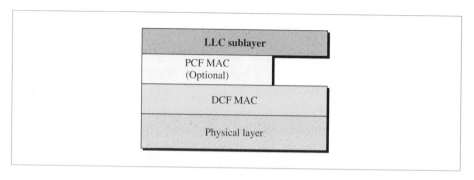

CSMA/CA

Wireless LANs cannot implement CSMA/CD for three reasons:

1. Collision detection implies that the station must be able to send data and receive collision signals at the same time. This implies costly stations and increased bandwidth requirements.

2. Collision may not be detected because of the hidden terminal problem. A terminal may be hidden from another in a wireless environment (due to natural obstacles such as mountains or artificial obstacles such as buildings). Suppose stations A and B both have data to send to station C. Station B is hidden from A, so if there is a collision near B, A will not hear. This does not happen in wired LANs because all stations are connected by wire and any collision is heard by all stations.

3. The distance between stations in wireless LANs can be great. Signal fading could prevent a station at one end from hearing a collision at the other end.

Process Flowchart   Figure 15.7 shows a flowchart similar to one in Chapter 13. This one has modifications that we will explain shortly.

Frame Exchange Time Line   Figure 15.8 shows the exchange of data and control frames in time.

1. Before sending a frame, the source station senses the medium by checking the energy level at the carrier frequency.

   a. The channel uses a persistence strategy with backoff until the channel is idle.

   b. After the station is found idle, the station waits for a period of time, called the **distributed interframe space (DIFS);** then the station sends a control frame called the request to send (RTS).

2. After receiving the RTS and waiting a short period of time, called the **short interframe space (SIFS),** the destination station sends a control frame, called the clear to send (CTS), to the source station. This control frame indicates that the destination station is ready to receive data.

3. The source station sends data after waiting an amount of time equal to SIFS.

4. The destination station, after waiting for an amount of time equal to SIFS, sends an acknowledgment to show that the frame has been received. Acknowledgment

Figure 15.7   *CSMA/CA flowchart*

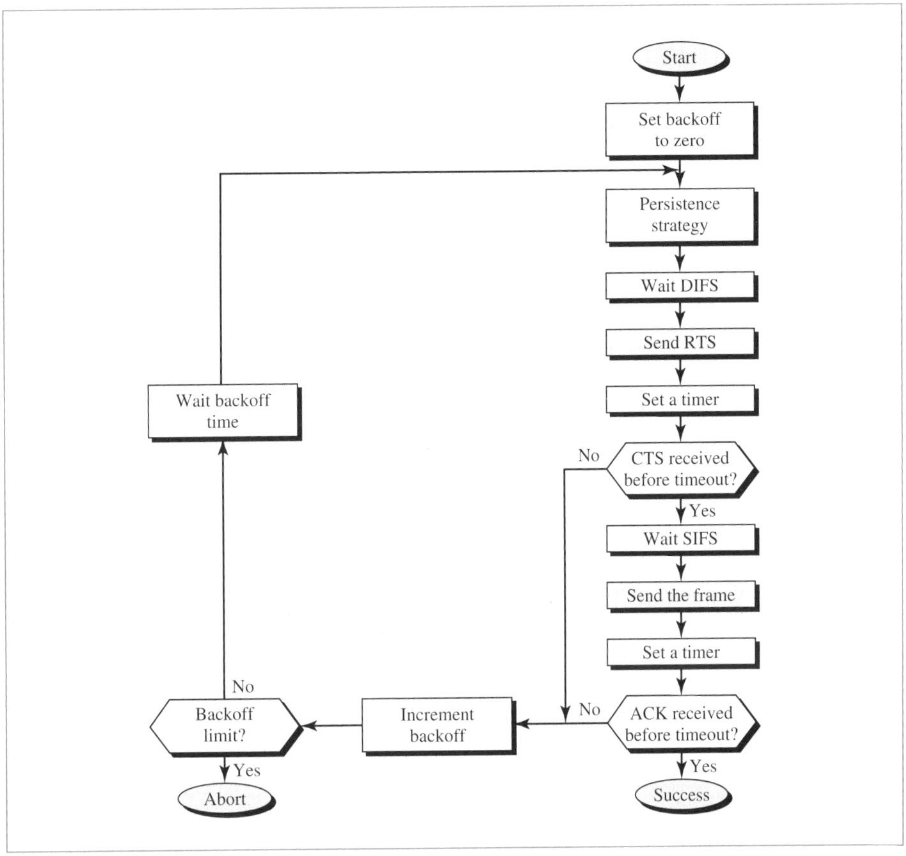

is needed in this protocol because the station does not have any means to check for the successful arrival of its data at the destination. On the other hand, the lack of collision in CSMA/CD is a kind of indication to the source that data have arrived.

Network Allocation Vector   How do other stations defer sending their data if one station acquires access? In other words, how is the *collision avoidance* aspect of this protocol accomplished? The key is a feature called NAV.

When a station sends an RTS frame, it includes the duration of the time that it needs to occupy the channel. The stations that are affected by this transmission create a timer called a **network allocation vector (NAV)** that shows how much time must pass before these stations are allowed to check the channel for idleness. Each time a station accesses the system and sends an RTS frame, other stations start their NAV. In other words, each station, before sensing the physical medium to see if it is idle, first checks its NAV to see if it has expired. Figure 15.8 shows the idea of NAV.

Figure 15.8 *CSMA/CA and NAV*

Source
Destination
All other stations
DIFS
RTS
SIFS
CTS
SIFS
Data
SIFS
ACK
NAV
(No carrier sensing)
Time
Time
Time
Time

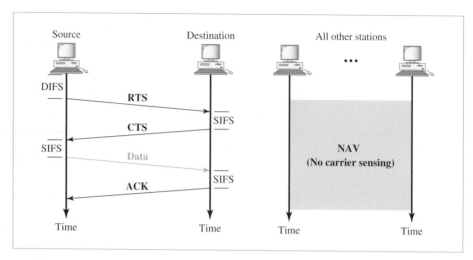

Collision During Handshaking What happens if there is collision during the time when RTS or CTS control frames are in transition, often called the **handshaking period?** Two or more stations may try to send RTS frames at the same time. These control frames may collide. However, because there is no mechanism for collision detection, the sender assumes there has been a collision if it has not received a CTS frame from the receiver. The backoff strategy is employed, and the sender tries again.

Fragmentation

The wireless environment is very noisy; a corrupt frame has to be retransmitted. The protocol, therefore, recommends fragmentation—the division of a large frame into smaller ones. It is more efficient to replace a small frame than a large one.

Frame Format

The MAC layer frame consists of nine fields, as shown in Figure 15.9.

Figure 15.9 *Frame format*

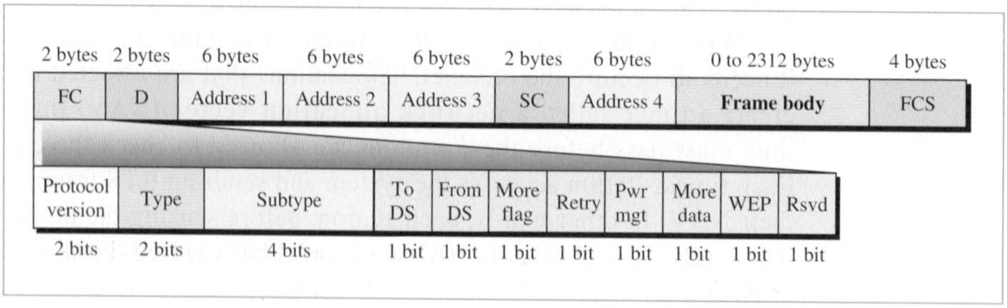

2 bytes
2 bytes
6 bytes
6 bytes
6 bytes
2 bytes
6 bytes
0 to 2312 bytes
4 bytes
FC
D
Address 1
Address 2
Address 3
SC
Address 4
Frame body
FCS
Protocol version
Type
Subtype
To DS
From DS
More flag
Retry
Pwr mgt
More data
WEP
Rsvd
2 bits
2 bits
4 bits
1 bit
1 bit
1 bit
1 bit
1 bit
1 bit
1 bit
1 bit

■ **Frame control (FC).** The FC field is 2 bytes long and defines the type of the frame and some control information. Table 15.1 describes the subfields. We will discuss each frame type later in this chapter.

Table 15.1 *Subfields in FC field*

Field	Explanation
Protocol version	The current version is 0.
Type	Defines type of information carried in the frame body: management (00), control (01), or data (10).
Subtype	Defines the subtype of each type (see Table 15.2).
To DS	Defined later.
From DS	Defined later.
More flag	When set to 1, means more fragments.
Retry	When set to 1, means retransmitted frame.
Pwr mgt	When set to 1, means station is in power management mode.
More data	When set to 1, means station has more data to send.
WEP	Wired equivalent privacy. When set to 1, means encryption implemented.
Rsvd	Reserved.

■ **D.** In all frame types except one, this field defines the duration of the transmission that is used to set the value of NAV. In one control frame, this field defines the ID of the frame.

■ **Addresses.** There are four address fields, each 6 bytes long. The meaning of each address field depends on the value of the *To DS* and the *From DS* subfields and will be discussed later.

■ **Sequence control.** This field defines the sequence number of the frame to be used in flow control.

■ **Frame body.** This field, which can be between 0 and 2312 bytes, contains information based on the type and the subtype defined in the FC field.

■ **FCS.** The FCS field is 4 bytes long and contains a CRC-32 error detection sequence.

Frame Types

A wireless LAN defined by IEEE 802.11 has three categories of frames: management frames, control frames, and data frames.

Management Frames Management frames are used for the initial communication between stations and access points.

Control Frames Control frames are used for accessing the channel and acknowledging frames. Figure 15.10 shows the format.

Figure 15.10   *Control frames*

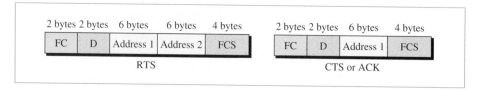

For control frames the value of the type field is 01; the values of the subtype fields for frames we have discussed are shown in Table 15.2.

Table 15.2   *Values of subfields in control frames*

Subtype	Meaning
1011	Request to send (RTS)
1100	Clear to send (CTS)
1101	Acknowledgment (ACK)

Data Frames   Data frames are used for carrying data and control information.

Addressing Mechanism

The IEEE 802.11 addressing mechanism is complicated. The complexity stems from the fact that there may be intermediate stations (APs). There are four cases, defined by the value of the two flags in the FC field, *To DS* and *From DS*. Each flag can be either 0 or 1, thus defining four different situations. The interpretation of the four addresses (address 1 to address 4) in the MAC frame depends on the value of these flags, as shown in Table 15.3.

Table 15.3   *Addresses*

To DS	From DS	Address 1	Address 2	Address 3	Address 4
0	0	Destination station	Source station	BSS ID	N/A
0	1	Destination station	Sending AP	Source station	N/A
1	0	Receiving AP	Source station	Destination station	N/A
1	1	Receiving AP	Sending AP	Destination station	Source station

Note that address 1 is always the address of the next device. Address 2 is always the address of the previous device. Address 3 is the address of the final destination station if it is not defined by address 1. Address 4 is the address of the original source station if it is not the same as address 2.

Case 1

In this case, *To DS* = 0 and *From DS* = 0. This means that the frame is not going to a distribution system (*To DS* = 0) and is not coming from a distribution system (*From DS* = 0). The frame is going from one station in a BSS to another without passing through the distribution system. The ACK frame should be sent to the original sender. The addresses are as shown in Figure 15.11.

Figure 15.11 *Addressing mechanism: case 1*

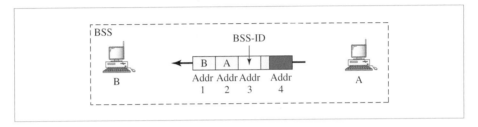

Case 2

In this case, *To DS* = 0 and *From DS* = 1. This means that the frame is coming from a distribution system (*From DS* = 1). The frame is coming from an AP and going to a station. The ACK should be sent to the AP. The addresses are as shown in Figure 15.12. Note that address 3 contains the original sender of the frame (in another BSS).

Figure 15.12 *Addressing mechanism: case 2*

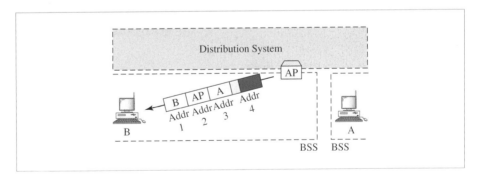

Case 3

In this case, *To DS* = 1 and *From DS* = 0. This means that the frame is going to a distribution system (*To DS* = 1). The frame is going from a station to an AP. The ACK is sent to the original station. The addresses are as shown in Figure 15.13. Note that address 3 contains the final destination of the frame (in another BSS).

Case 4

In this case, *To DS* = 1 and *From DS* = 1. This is the case in which the distribution system is also wireless. The frame is going from one AP to another AP in a wireless

Figure 15.13 *Addressing mechanism: case 3*

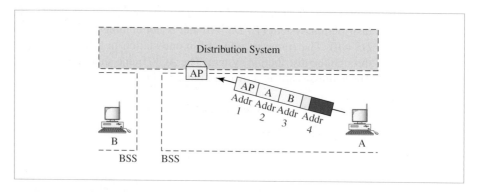

distribution system. We do not need to define addresses if the distribution system is a wired LAN because the frame in these cases has the format of a wired LAN frame (Ethernet, for example). Here, we need four addresses to define the original sender, the final destination, and two intermediate APs. Figure 15.14 shows the situation.

Figure 15.14 *Addressing mechanism: case 4*

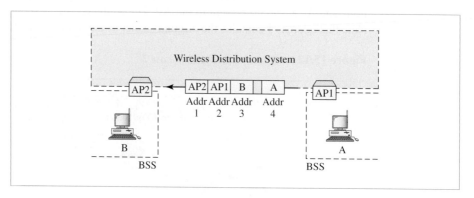

15.2 BLUETOOTH

Bluetooth is a wireless LAN technology designed to connect devices of different functions such as telephones, notebooks, computers (desktop and laptop), cameras, printers, coffee makers, and so on. A Bluetooth LAN is an ad hoc network, which means that the network is formed spontaneously; the devices, sometimes called gadgets, find each other and make a network called piconet. A Bluetooth LAN can even be connected to the Internet if one of the gadgets has this capability. A Bluetooth LAN, by nature, cannot be large. If there are many gadgets that try to connect, there is chaos.

Bluetooth technology has several applications. Peripheral devices of a computer can communicate with the computer through this technology (wireless mouse or keyboard).

Monitoring devices can communicate with sensor devices in a small health care center. Home security devices can use this technology to connect different sensors to the main security controller. Conference attendees can synchronize their palmtop computers at a conference.

Bluetooth was originally started as a project by the Ericsson Company. It is named for Harald Blaatand, the king of Denmark (940-981) who united Denmark and Norway. *Blaatand* translates to *Bluetooth* in English.

Today, Bluetooth technology is the implementation of a protocol defined by the IEEE 802.15 standard. The standard defines a wireless personal-area network (PAN) operable in an area the size of a room or a hall.

Architecture

Bluetooth defines two types of networks: piconets and scatternet.

Piconets

A Bluetooth network is called a **piconet,** or a small net. A piconet can have up to eight stations, one of which is called the **master;** the rest are called **slaves.** All the slave stations synchronize their clocks and hopping sequence with the master slave. Note that a piconet can have only one master station. The communication between the master and the slaves can be one-to-one or one-to-many. Figure 15.15 shows a piconet.

Figure 15.15 *Piconet*

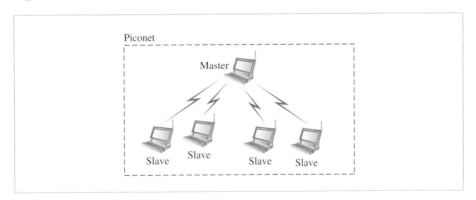

Although a piconet can have a maximum of seven slaves, an additional eight slaves can be in the *parked state*. A slave in a parked state is synchronized with the master, but cannot take part in communication until it is moved from the parked state. Because only eight stations can be active in a piconet, activating a station from the parked state means that an active station must go to the parked state.

Scatternet

Piconets can be combined to form what is called a **scatternet.** A slave station in one piconet can become the master in another piconet. This station can receive messages from the master in the first piconet (as a slave) and, acting as a master, deliver it to slaves in the second piconet. A station can be a member of two piconets. Figure 15.16 illustrates a scatternet.

Figure 15.16   *Scatternet*

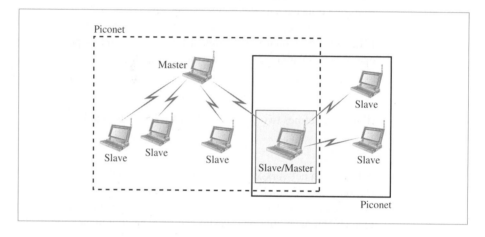

Bluetooth Devices

A Bluetooth device has a built-in short-range radio transmitter. The current data rate is 1 Mbps with a 2.4-GHz bandwidth. This means that there is a possibility of interference between the IEEE 802.11b wireless LANs and Bluetooth LANs.

Bluetooth Layers

Bluetooth uses several layers that do not exactly match those of the Internet model we have defined in this book. Figure 15.17 shows these layers.

Figure 15.17   *Bluetooth layers*

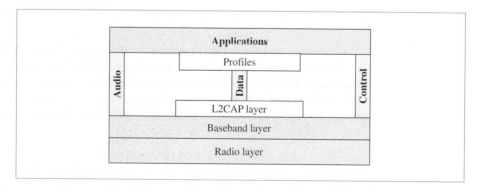

Radio Layer

The radio layer is roughly equivalent to the physical layer of the Internet model. Bluetooth devices are low-power and have a range of 10 m.

Band

Bluetooth uses a 2.4-GHz ISM band divided into 79 channels of 1 MHz each.

FHSS

Bluetooth uses the frequency-hopping spread spectrum method in the physical layer to avoid interference from other devices or other networks. Bluetooth hops 1600 times per second, which means that each device changes its modulation frequency 1600 times per second. A device uses a frequency for only 625 μs (1/1600 s) before it hops to another frequency; the dwell time is 625 μs.

Modulation

To transform bits to a signal, Bluetooth uses a sophisticated version of FSK, called GFSK (FSK with Gaussian bandwidth filtering; a discussion of this topic is beyond the scope of this book). FSK has a carrier frequency. Bit 1 is represented by a frequency deviation above the carrier; bit 0 is represented by a frequency deviation below the carrier. The carrier frequencies, in megahertz, are defined according to the following formula for each channel:

$$f_c = 2402 + n \qquad n = 0, 1, 2, 3, \ldots, 78$$

For example, the first channel uses carrier frequency 2402 MHz (2.402 GHz), and the second channel uses carrier frequency 2403 MHz (2.403 GHz).

Baseband Layer

The baseband layer is roughly equivalent to the MAC sublayer in LANs. The access method is TDMA (see Chapter 13). The master and slave communicate with each other using time slots. The length of a time slot is exactly the same as the dwell time, 625 μs. This means that during the time that one frequency is used, a sender sends a frame to a slave, or a slave sends a frame to the master. Note that the communication is only between the master and a slave; slaves cannot communicate directly with one another.

TDMA

Bluetooth uses a form of TDMA (see Chapter 13) that is called **TDD-TDMA (time-division duplexing TDMA).** TDD is a kind of half-duplex communication in which the slave and receiver send and receive data, but not at the same time (half-duplex); however, the communication for each direction uses different hops. This is similar to walkie-talkies using different carrier frequencies.

Single-Slave Communication   If the piconet has only one slave, the TDMA operation is very simple. The time is divided into slots of 625 μs. The master uses even-numbered slots (0, 2, 4, . . .); the slave uses odd-numbered slots (1, 3, 5, . . .). TDD-TDMA allows the master and the slave to communicate in half-duplex mode. In slot 0, the master sends, and the slave receives; in slot 1, the slave sends, and the master receives. The cycle is repeated. Figure 15.18 shows the concept.

Figure 15.18   *Single-slave communication*

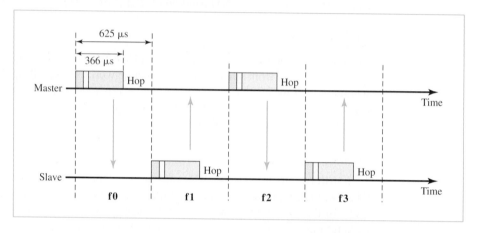

Multiple-Slave Communication   The process is a little more complex if there is more than one slave in the piconet. Again, the master uses the even-numbered slots, but a slave sends in the next odd-numbered slot if the packet in the previous slot was addressed to it. All slaves listen on even-numbered slots, but only one slave sends in any odd-numbered slot. Figure 15.19 shows a scenario.

Figure 15.19   *Multiple-slave communication*

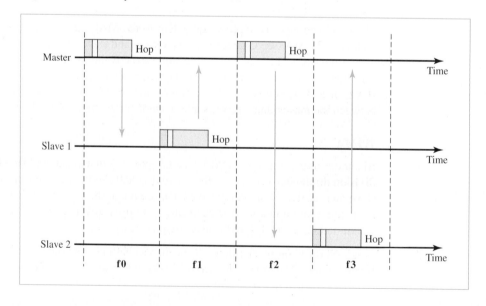

Let us elaborate on the figure.

1. In slot 0, the master sends a frame for slave 1.
2. In slot 1, only slave 1 sends a frame to the master because the previous frame was addressed to slave 1; other slaves are silent.
3. In slot 2, the master sends a frame for slave 2.
4. In slot 3, only slave 2 sends a frame to the master because the previous frame was addressed to slave 2; other slaves are silent.
5. The cycle continues.

We can say that this access method is similar to a poll/select operation with reservations. When the master selects a slave, it also polls it. The next time slot is reserved for the polled station to send its frame. If the polled slave has no frame to send, the channel is silent.

Physical Links

Two types of links can be created between a master and a slave: SCO links and ACL links.

SCO A **synchronous connection-oriented (SCO) link** is used when avoiding latency (delay in data delivery) is more important than integrity (error-free delivery). In SCO, a physical link is created between a master and a slave by reserving specific slots at regular intervals. The basic unit of connection is two slots, one for each direction. In SCO, if a packet is damaged, it is never retransmitted. SCO is used for real-time audio where avoiding delay is all-important. A slave can create up to three SCO links with the master, sending 64 Kbps digitized audio (PCM) in each link.

ACL An **asynchronous connectionless link (ACL)** is used when data integrity is more important than avoiding latency. In this type of link, if a payload encapsulated in the frame is corrupted, it is retransmitted. A slave returns an ACL frame in the available odd-numbered slot if and only if the previous slot has been addressed to it. ACL can use one, three, or more slots and can achieve a data rate up to 721 KbpsKbps.

Frame Format

A frame in the baseband layer can be one of three types: one-slot, three-slot, or five-slot. A slot, as we said before, is 625 μs. However, in a one-slot frame exchange, 259 μs is needed for hopping and control mechanisms. This means that a one-slot frame can last only 625 − 259, or 366 μs. With a 1-MHz bandwidth and 1 bit/Hz, the size of a one-slot frame is 366 bits.

A three-slot frame occupies three slots. However, since 259 μs is used for hopping, the length of the frame is $3 \times 625 - 259$ or 1616 μs or 1616 bits. A device that uses a three-slot frame remains at the same hop (at the same carrier frequency) for three slots. Even though only one hop number is used, three hop numbers are consumed. That means the hop number for each frame is equal to the first slot of the frame.

A five-slot frame also uses 259 bits for hopping, which means that the length of the frame is $5 \times 625 - 259$, or 2866, bits.

Figure 15.20 shows the format of the three frame types.

Figure 15.20   *Frame format types*

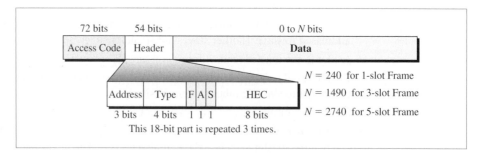

The following describes each field:

- **Access code.** This 72-bit field normally contains synchronization bits and the identifier of the master to distinguish the frame of one piconet from another.

- **Header.** This 54-bit field is a repeated 18-bit pattern. Each pattern has the following subfields:

  - **Address.** The 3-bit address subfield can define up to seven slaves (1 to 7). If the address is zero, it is used for broadcast communication from the master to all slaves.

  - **Type.** The 4-bit type subfield defines the type of data coming from the upper layers. We discuss these types later.

  - **F.** This 1-bit subfield is for flow control. When set (1), it indicates that the device is unable to receive more frames (buffer is full).

  - **A.** This 1-bit subfield is for acknowledgment. Bluetooth uses Stop-and-Wait ARQ; 1 bit is enough for acknowledgment.

  - **S.** This 1-bit subfield holds a sequence number. Bluetooth uses Stop-and-Wait ARQ; 1 bit is enough for sequence numbering.

  - **HEC.** The 8-bit header error correction subfield is a checksum to detect errors in each 18-bit header section.

  The header has three 18-bit sections, which the sender creates exactly the same. The receiver compares these three sections, bit by bit. If each of the three corresponding bits is the same, the bit is accepted; if not, the majority opinion wins. This is a form of forward error correction (for the header only). This double error control is needed because the nature of the communication, via air, is very noisy. Note that there is no retransmission in this sublayer.

- **Payload.** This subfield can be 0 to 2740 bits long. It contains data or control coming from the upper layers.

L2CAP

The **Logical Link Control and Adaptation Protocol,** or **L2CAP** (L2 here means LL) is roughly equivalent to the LLC sublayer in LANs. It is used for data exchange on an ACL link; SCO channels do not use L2CAP. Figure 15.21 shows the format of the data packet in this level.

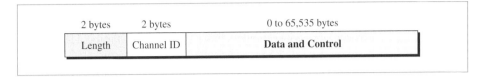

Figure 15.21 *L2CAP data packet format*

The 16-bit length field defines the size of the data, in bytes, coming from the upper layers. Data can be up to 65,535 bytes. The channel ID (CID) defines a unique identifier for the virtual channel created at this level (see below).

The L2CAP has several specific duties: multiplexing, segmentation and reassembly, quality of service, and group management.

Multiplexing

The L2CAP can do multiplexing. At the sender site, it accepts data from one of the upper-layer protocols, frames them, and delivers them to the baseband layer for delivery. At the receiver site, it accepts a frame from the baseband layer, extracts the data, and delivers them to the appropriate protocol layer. It creates a kind of virtual channel that we will discuss in future chapters on higher-level protocols.

Segmentation and Reassembly

The maximum size of the payload field in the baseband layer is 2774 bits, or 343 bytes. This includes 4 bytes to define the packet and packet length. Therefore, the size of the packet that can arrive from an upper layer can only be 339 bytes. However, application layers sometimes need to send a data packet that can be up to 65,535 bytes (an Internet packet, for example). The L2CAP divides these large packets into segments and adds extra information to define the location of the segments in the original packet. The L2CAP segments the packet at the source and reassembles them at the destination.

QoS

Bluetooth allows the stations to define a quality of service level. We discuss quality of service in Chapter 23. For the moment, it is enough to know that if no quality of service level is defined, Bluetooth defaults to what is called *best-effort* service; it will do its best under the circumstances.

Group Management

Another functionality of L2CAP is to allow devices to create a type of logical addressing between them. This is similar to multicasting. For example, two or three slave devices can be part of a multicast group to receive data from the master.

Other Upper Layers

Bluetooth defines several protocols for the upper layers that use the services of L2CAP; these protocols are specific for different purposes. They are very complex and involved and will not be discussed here.

15.3　KEY TERMS

access point (AP)

asynchronous connectionless link (ACL)

basic service set (BSS)

Bluetooth

BSS-transition mobility

complementary code keying (CCK)

direct sequence spread spectrum (DSSS)

distributed coordination function (DCF)

distributed interframe space (DIFS)

ESS-transition mobility

extended service set (ESS)

frequency-hopping spread spectrum (FHSS)

handshaking period

high-rate direct sequence spread spectrum (HR-DSSS)

IEEE 802.11

Logical Link Control and Adaptation Protocol (L2CAP)

master

network allocation vector (NAV)

no-transition mobility

orthogonal frequency-division multiplexing (OFDM)

piconet

point coordination function (PCF)

scatternet

short interframe space (SIFS)

slave

synchronous connection-oriented (SCO) link

time-division duplexing TDMA (TDD-TDMA)

wireless LAN

15.4　SUMMARY

❑ The IEEE 802.11 standard for wireless LANs defines two services: basic service set (BSS) and extended service set (ESS). An ESS consists of two or more BSSs; each BSS must have an access point (AP).

❑ The physical layer methods used by wireless LANs include frequency-hopping spread spectrum (FHSS), direct sequence spread spectrum (DSSS), orthogonal frequency-division multiplexing (OFDM), and high-rate direct sequence spread spectrum (HR-DSSS).

❑ FHSS is a signal generation method in which repeated sequences of carrier frequencies are used for protection against hackers.

❑ One bit is replaced by a chip code in DSSS.

❑ OFDM specifies that one source must use all the channels of the bandwidth.

❑ HR-DSSS is DSSS with an encoding method called complementary code keying (CCK).

❑ The wireless LAN access method is CSMA/CA.

❑ The network allocation vector (NAV) is a timer for collision avoidance.

❑ The MAC layer frame has nine fields. The addressing mechanism can include up to four addresses.

❑ Wireless LANs use management frames, control frames, and data frames.

❑ Bluetooth is a wireless LAN technology that connects devices (called gadgets) in a small area.

❑ A Bluetooth network is called a piconet. Multiple piconets form a network called a scatternet.

❏ The Bluetooth radio layer performs functions similar to those in the Internet model's physical layer.

❏ The Bluetooth baseband layer performs functions similar to those in the Internet model's MAC sublayer.

❏ A Bluetooth network consists of one master device and up to seven slave devices.

❏ A Bluetooth frame consists of data as well as hopping and control mechanisms. A frame is one, three, or five slots in length with each slot equal to 625 μs.

15.5 PRACTICE SET

Review Questions

1. What is the difference between a BSS and an ESS?
2. Discuss the three types of mobility in a wireless LAN.
3. What is FHSS?
4. What is DSSS?
5. How is OFDM different from FDM?
6. What is the access method used by wireless LANs?
7. What is the purpose of the NAV?
8. What are the three types of frames used by wireless LANs?
9. How does a control frame differ from a management frame?
10. Name two applications for a Bluetooth network.
11. Compare a piconet and a scatternet.
12. Match the layers in Bluetooth and the Internet model.
13. What are the two types of links between a Bluetooth master and a Bluetooth slave?
14. In multiple-slave communication, who uses the even-numbered slots and who uses the odd-numbered slots?
15. How much time in a Bluetooth one-slot frame is used for the hopping mechanism? What about a three slot frame and a five slot frame?
16. What is the purpose of L2CAP?

Multiple-Choice Questions

17. A wireless LAN using FHSS hops 10 times per cycle. If the bandwidth of the original signal is 10 MHz, the spread spectrum is _____ MHz.
    a. 10
    b. 100
    c. 1000
    d. 10,000

18. A wireless LAN using FHSS hops 10 times per cycle. If the bandwidth of the original signal is 10 MHz and 2 GHz is the lowest frequency, the highest frequency of the system is _____ GHz.

    a. 1.0

    b. 2.0

    c. 2.1

    d. 3.0

19. An FHSS wireless LAN has a spread spectrum of 1 GHz. The bandwidth of the original signal is 250 MHz, and there are _____ hops per cycle.

    a. 1

    b. 2

    c. 3

    d. 4

20. A wireless LAN using DSSS with an 8-bit chip code needs _____ MHz for sending data that originally required a 10-MHz bandwidth.

    a. 2

    b. 8

    c. 20

    d. 80

21. A wireless LAN using DSSS with _____-bit chip code needs 320 MHz for sending data that originally required a 20-MHz bandwidth.

    a. A 2

    b. An 8

    c. A 16

    d. A 32

22. A wireless LAN using DSSS with a 4-bit chip code needs 10 MHz for sending data that originally required a _____-MHz bandwidth.

    a. 2.5

    b. 20

    c. 25

    d. 40

23. In an ESS the _____ station is not mobile.

    a. AP

    b. Server

    c. BSS

    d. None of the above

24. In an ESS the _____ stations are part of a wired LAN.

    a. AP

    b. Server

    c. BSS

    d. All the above

25. A station with _____ mobility can move from one BSS to another.
    a. No-transition
    b. BSS-transition
    c. ESS-transition
    d. (b) and (c)

26. A station with _____ mobility can move from one ESS to another.
    a. No-transition
    b. BSS-transition
    c. ESS-transition
    d. (b) and (c)

27. A station with _____ mobility is either stationary or moving only inside a BSS.
    a. No-transition
    b. BSS
    c. ESS
    d. (a) and (b)

28. A _____ frame usually precedes a CTS frame.
    a. DIFS
    b. SIFS
    c. RTS
    d. Any of the above

29. A _____ frame usually precedes an RTS frame.
    a. DIFS
    b. CIFS
    c. CTS
    d. None of the above

30. Stations do not sense the medium during _____ time.
    a. RTS
    b. CTS
    c. SIFS
    d. NAV

31. Wireless transmission is _____ prone to error than/as wired transmission.
    a. More
    b. Less
    c. Half as
    d. None of the above

32. Which MAC sublayer does IEEE 802.11 define?
    a. LLC
    b. PCF
    c. DCF
    d. (b) and (c)

33. What is the basic access method for wireless LANs as defined by IEEE 802.11?
    a. LLC
    b. DCF
    c. PCF
    d. BFD

34. The access method for wireless LANs as defined by IEEE 802.11 is based on _____.
    a. CSMA
    b. CSMA/CD
    c. CSMA/CA
    d. Token passing

35. FHSS, DSSS, and OFDM are _____ layer specifications.
    a. Physical
    b. Data link
    c. Network
    d. Transport

36. In the _____ method, the sender hops from frequency to frequency in a specific order.
    a. FHSS
    b. DSSS
    c. OFDM
    d. HR-DSSS

37. A wireless LAN uses _____ frames for acknowledgment.
    a. Management
    b. Control
    c. Data
    d. None of the above

38. A wireless LAN uses _____ frames for the initial communication between stations and the access points.
    a. Management
    b. Control
    c. Data
    d. None of the above

39. A Bluetooth network can have _____ master(s).
    a. One
    b. Two
    c. Three
    d. Eight

40. _____ combine to form a scatternet.
    a. BSSs
    b. ESSs
    c. APs
    d. Piconets

41. Bluetooth uses _____ in the physical layer.
    a. FHSS
    b. DSSS
    c. DHSS
    d. OFDM

42. A Bluetooth frame needs _____ μs for hopping and control mechanisms.
    a. 625
    b. 259
    c. 3
    d. A multiple of 259

Exercises

43. Use Table 15.4 to compare and contrast the three types of mobility for a station defined in IEEE 802.11.

Table 15.4   Exercise 43

Types of Mobility	Movement Inside BSS	Movement Between BSSs	Movement Between ESSs
No transition			
BSS transition			
ESS transition			

44. Compare and contrast CSMA/CD with CSMA/CA.

45. Use Table 15.5 to compare and contrast the fields in IEEE 802.3 and 802.11.

Table 15.5   Exercise 45

Fields	IEEE 802.3 Field Size	IEEE 802.11 Field Size
Destination address		
Source address		
Address 1		
Address 2		
Address 3		
Address 4		
FC		
D/ID		
SC		
PDU length		
Data and padding		
Frame body		
FCS (CRC)		

CHAPTER 16

Connecting LANs, Backbone Networks, and Virtual LANs

LANs do not normally operate in isolation. They are connected to one another or to the Internet. To connect LANs, or segments of LANs, we use connecting devices. Connecting devices can operate in different layers of the Internet model. In this chapter, we discuss only those that operate in the physical and data link layer; we discuss those that operate in the first three layers in Chapter 19.

After discussing some connecting devices, we show how they are used to create backbone networks. Finally, we discuss virtual local area networks (VLANs).

16.1   CONNECTING DEVICES

There are five kinds of **connecting devices:** repeaters, hubs, bridges, and two- and three-layer switches. Repeaters and hubs operate in the first layer of the Internet model. Bridges and two-layer switches operate in the first two layers. Routers and three-layer switches operate in the first three layers. Figure 16.1 shows the layers in which each device operates.

Figure 16.1   *Connecting devices*

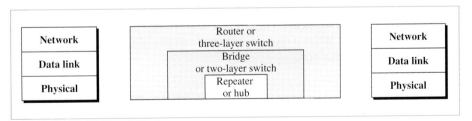

Repeaters

A **repeater** is a device that operates only in the physical layer. Signals that carry information within a network can travel a fixed distance before attenuation endangers the integrity of the data. A repeater receives a signal and, before it becomes too weak or corrupted, regenerates the original bit pattern. The repeater then sends the refreshed signal. A repeater can extend the physical length of a LAN, as shown in Figure 16.2.

Figure 16.2 *Repeater*

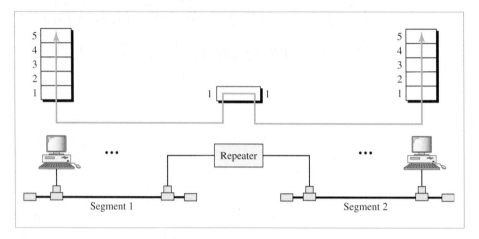

Segment 1   Repeater   Segment 2

A repeater does not actually connect two LANs; it connects two segments of the same LAN. The segments connected are still part of one single LAN. A repeater is not a device that can connect two LANs of different protocols.

A repeater connects segments of a LAN.

A repeater can overcome the 10Base5 Ethernet length restriction. In this standard, the length of the cable is limited to 500 m. To extend this length, we divide the cable into segments and install repeaters between segments. Note that the whole network is still considered one LAN, but the portions of the network separated by repeaters are called **segments.** The repeater acts as a two-port node, but operates only in the physical layer. When it receives a frame from any of the ports, it regenerates and forwards it to the other port.

A repeater forwards every frame; it has no filtering capability.

It is tempting to compare a repeater to an amplifier, but the comparison is inaccurate. An **amplifier** cannot discriminate between the intended signal and noise; it amplifies equally everything fed into it. A repeater does not amplify the signal; it regenerates the signal. When it receives a weakened or corrupted signal, it creates a copy, bit for bit, at the original strength.

A repeater is a regenerator, not an amplifier.

The location of a repeater on a link is vital. A repeater must be placed so that a signal reaches it before any noise changes the meaning of any of its bits. A little noise can alter the precision of a bit's voltage without destroying its identity (see Fig. 16.3). If the corrupted bit travels much farther, however, accumulated noise can change its meaning completely. At that point, the original voltage is not recoverable, and the error needs to be corrected. A repeater placed on the line before the legibility of the signal becomes lost can still read the signal well enough to determine the intended voltages and replicate them in their original form.

Figure 16.3 *Function of a repeater*

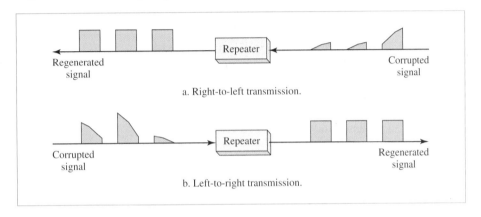

a. Right-to-left transmission.

b. Left-to-right transmission.

Hubs

Although, in a general sense, the word *hub* can refer to any connecting device, it does have a specific meaning. A **hub** is actually a multiport repeater. It is normally used to create connections between stations in a physical star topology. We have seen examples of hubs in some Ethernet implementations (10Base-T, for example). However, hubs can also be used to create multiple levels of hierarchy, as shown in Figure 16.4.

The hierarchical use of hubs removes the length limitation of 10Base-T (100 m).

Figure 16.4 *Hubs*

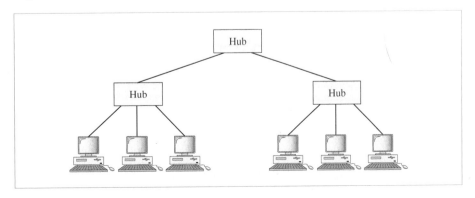

Bridges

A **bridge** operates in both the physical and the data link layers. As a physical-layer device, it regenerates the signal it receives. As a data link layer device, the bridge can check the physical (MAC) addresses (source and destination) contained in the frame.

Filtering

One may ask, What is the difference in functionality between a bridge and a repeater? A bridge has **filtering** capability. It can check the destination address of a frame and decide if the frame should be forwarded or dropped. If the frame is to be forwarded, the decision must specify the port. A bridge has a table that maps addresses to ports.

A bridge has a table used in filtering decisions.

Let us give an example. In Figure 16.5, two LANs are connected by a bridge.

Figure 16.5   *Bridge*

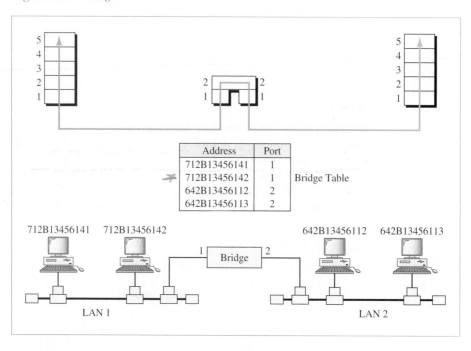

If a frame destined for station 712B1345642 arrives at port 1, the bridge consults its table to find the departing port. According to its table, frames for 712B1345642 leave through port 1; therefore, there is no need for forwarding; the frame is dropped. On the other hand, if a frame for 712B1345641 arrives at port 2, the departing port is port 1 and the frame is forwarded. In the first case, LAN 2 remains free of traffic; in the second case, both LANs have traffic. In our example, we show a two-port bridge; in reality a bridge usually has more ports.

Note also that a bridge does not change the physical addresses contained in the frame.

> **A bridge does not change the physical (MAC) addresses in a frame.**

Transparent Bridges

A **transparent bridge** is a bridge in which the stations are completely unaware of the bridge's existence. If a bridge is added or deleted from the system, reconfiguration of the stations is unnecessary. According to the IEEE 802.1d specification, a system equipped with transparent bridges must meet three criteria:

1. Frames must be forwarded from one station to another.
2. The forwarding table is automatically made by learning frame movements in the network.
3. Loops in the system must be prevented.

Forwarding   A transparent bridge must correctly forward the frames, as discussed in the previous section.

Learning   The earliest bridges had forwarding tables that were static. The systems administrator would manually enter each table entry during bridge setup. Although the process was simple, it was not practical. If a station was added or deleted, the table had to be modified manually. The same was true if a station's MAC address changed, which is not a rare event. For example, putting in a new network card means a new MAC address.

A better solution to the static table is a dynamic table that maps addresses to ports automatically. To make a table dynamic, we need a bridge that gradually learns from the frame movements. To do this, the bridge inspects both the destination and the source addresses. The destination address is used for the forwarding decision (table lookup); the source address is used for adding entries to the table and for updating purposes. Let us elaborate on this process using Figure 16.6.

1. When station A sends a frame to station D, the bridge does not have an entry for either D or A. The frame goes out from all three ports; the frame floods the network. However, by looking at the source address, the bridge learns that station A must be located on the LAN connected to port 1. This means that frames destined for A, in the future, must be sent out through port 1. The bridge adds this entry to its table. The table has its first entry now.
2. When station E sends a frame to station A, the bridge has an entry for A, so it forwards the frame only to port 1. There is no flooding. In addition, it uses the source address of the frame, E, to add a second entry to the table.
3. When station B sends a frame to C, the bridge has no entry for C, so once again it floods the network and adds one more entry to the table.
4. The process of learning continues as the bridge forwards frames.

Figure 16.6   *Learning bridge*

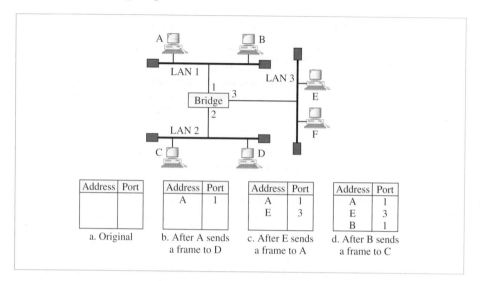

Loop Problem   Transparent bridges work fine as long as there are no redundant bridges in the system. Systems administrators, however, like to have redundant bridges (more than one bridge between a pair of LANs) to make the system more reliable. If a bridge fails, another bridge takes over until the failed one is repaired or replaced. Redundancy can create loops in the system, which is very undesirable. Figure 16.7 shows a very simple example of a loop created in a system with two LANs connected by two bridges.

1. Station A sends a frame to station D. The tables of both bridges are empty. Both forward the frame and update their tables based on the source address A.

2. Now there are two copies of the frame on LAN 2. The copy sent out by bridge 1 is received by bridge 2, which does not have any information about the destination address D; it floods the bridge. The copy sent out by bridge 2 is received by bridge 1 and is sent out for lack of information about D. Note that each frame is handled separately because bridges, as two nodes on a network sharing the medium, use an access method such as CSMA/CD. The tables of both bridges are updated, but still there is no information for destination D.

3. Now there are two copies of the frame on LAN 1. Step 2 is repeated, and both copies flood the network.

4. The process continues on and on. Note that bridges are also repeaters and regenerate frames. So in each iteration, there are newly generated fresh copies of the frames.

To solve the looping problem, the IEEE specification requires that bridges use the spanning tree algorithm to create a loopless topology.

Spanning Tree

In graph theory, a **spanning tree** is a graph in which there is no loop. In a bridged LAN, this means creating a topology in which each LAN can be reached from any other LAN

Figure 16.7 *Loop problem*

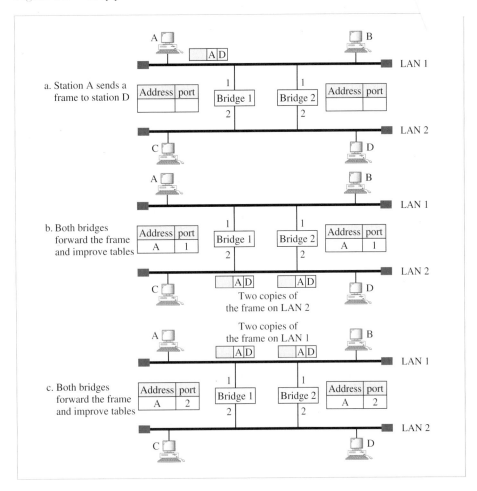

through one path only (no loop). We cannot change the physical topology of the system because of physical connections between cables and bridges, but we can create a logical topology that overlays the physical one. The process involves three steps:

1. Every bridge has a built-in ID. The one with the smallest ID is selected as the *root* bridge (as the root of the tree).

2. Mark one port of each bridge (except for the root bridge) as the *root* port. A root port is the port with the least-cost path from the bridge to the root bridge. The interpretation of the least-cost path is left up to the systems administrator. It may be the minimum number of hops (going from a bridge to a LAN); it may be the path with minimum delay or the path with maximum bandwidth. If two ports have the same least-cost value, the systems administrator just chooses one.

3. Choose a *designated* bridge for each LAN. A designated bridge has the least-cost path between the LAN and the root bridge. Make the corresponding port (the port

that connects the LAN to its designated bridge) the *designated* port. If two bridges have the same least-cost value, choose the one with the smaller ID.

4. Mark the root port and designated port as *forwarding* ports, the others as *blocking* ports. A **forwarding port** forwards a frame that it receives; a **blocking port** does not.

Let us give an example. The algorithm written in the C language can be found in Gilberg and Forouzan, *Data Structures: With Pseudocode Using C,* Thomson Learning. In Figure 16.8 we have four LANs and five bridges.

Figure 16.8 *Prior to spanning tree application*

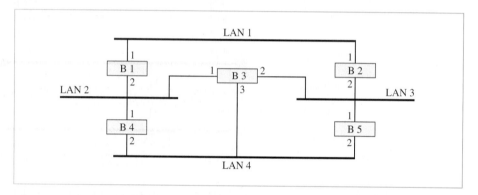

Figure 16.9 shows the first three steps. Assuming it has the least ID, we have chosen B1 as the root bridge. The root ports are marked with one star. The designated bridges have an arrow pointing to them from the corresponding LAN. Finally, designated ports are marked by two stars.

Figure 16.9 *Applying spanning tree*

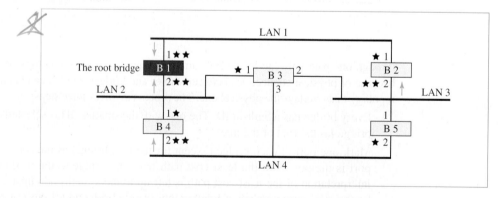

Now we can mark the root ports and the designated ports as forwarding ports; the others are blocking ports. In Figure 16.10 we show a blocking port with a broken line. The physical connection is there, but the bridge never forwards any frame from these ports.

Figure 16.10   *Forwarding ports and blocking ports*

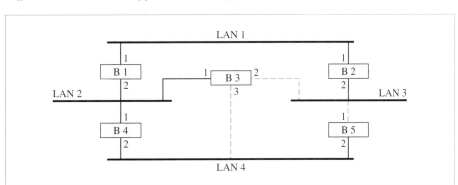

Note that there is only one single path from any LAN to any other LAN in the spanning tree system. This means there is only one single path from one LAN to any other LAN. No loops are created. You can prove to yourself that there is only one path from LAN 1 to LAN 2, LAN 3, or LAN 4. Similarly, there is only one path from LAN 2 to LAN 1, LAN 3, and LAN 4. The same is true for LAN 3 and LAN 4.

Dynamic Algorithm   We have described the spanning tree algorithm as though it requires manual entries. This is not true. Each bridge is equipped with a software package that does this process dynamically. The bridges send special messages to each other, called bridge protocol data units (BPDUs), to update the spanning tree. The spanning tree is updated when there is a change in the system such as a failure of a bridge or an addition or deletion of bridges.

Source Routing Bridges

Another way to prevent loops in a system with redundant bridges is to use **source routing bridges.** A transparent bridge's duties includes filtering frames, forwarding, and blocking. In a system that has source routing bridges, these duties are performed by the source station and, to some extent, the destination station.

In source routing, a sending station defines the bridges that the frame must visit. The addresses of these bridges are included in the frame. In other words, the frame contains not only the source and destination addresses, but also the addresses of all bridges to be visited.

The source gets these bridge addresses through the exchange of special frames with the destination prior to sending the data frame.

Source routing bridges were designed by IEEE to be used with Token Ring LANs. These LANs are not very common today.

Bridges Connecting Different LANs

Theoretically a bridge should be able to connect LANs using different protocols at the data link layer, such as an Ethernet LAN to a wireless LAN. However, there are many issues to be considered:

■   **Frame format.** Each LAN type has its own frame format (compare an Ethernet frame with a wireless LAN frame).

■ **Maximum data size.** If an incoming frame's size is too large for the destination LAN, the data must be fragmented into several frames. The data then need to be reassembled at the destination. However, no protocol at the data link layer allows the fragmentation and reassembly of frames. We will see in Chapter 19 that this is allowed in the network layer. The bridge must therefore discard any frames too large for its system.

■ **Data rate.** Each LAN type has its own data rate. (Compare the 10-Mbps data rate of an Ethernet with the 1-Mbps data rate of a wireless LAN.) The bridge must buffer the frame to compensate for this difference.

■ **Bit order.** Each LAN type has its own strategy in the sending of bits. Some send the most significant bit in a byte first; others send the least significant bit first.

■ **Security.** Some LANs, such as wireless LANs, implement security measures in the data link layer. Other LANs, such as Ethernet, do not. Security often involves encryption (see Chapter 29). When a bridge receives a frame from a wireless LAN, it needs to decrypt the message before forwarding it to an Ethernet LAN.

■ **Multimedia support.** Some LANs support multimedia and the quality of services needed for this type of communication; others do not.

Two-Layer Switch

When we use the term *switch,* we must be careful because a switch can mean two different things. We must clarify the term by adding the level at which the device operates. We can have a two-layer switch or a three-layer switch. A **three-layer switch** is used at the network layer; it is a kind of router. The **two-layer switch** performs at the physical and data link layer.

A two-layer switch is a bridge, a bridge with many ports and a design that allows better (faster) performance. A bridge with a few ports can connect a few LANs together. A bridge with many ports may be able to allocate a unique port to each station, with each station on its own independent entity. This means no competing traffic (no collision as we saw in Ethernet). In this book, to avoid confusion, we use the term *bridge* for a two-layer switch.

More information about switches will be given in our discussion on routers in Chapter 19 and Appendix F.

Router and Three-Layer Switches

A discussion of **routers** and **three-layer switches** is postponed until we cover the network layer in Chapters 19, 21, and Appendix F.

16.2 BACKBONE NETWORKS

Some of the connecting devices discussed in this chapter can be used to connect LANs in a backbone network. A backbone network allows several LANs to be connected. In a backbone network, no station is directly connected to the backbone; the stations are part of a LAN, and the backbone connects the LANs. The backbone is itself a LAN that uses a LAN protocol such as Ethernet; each connection to the backbone is itself another LAN.

Although many different architectures can be used for a backbone, we discuss only the two most common: the bus and the star.

Bus Backbone

In a **bus backbone,** the topology of the backbone is a bus. The backbone itself can use one of the protocols that supports a bus topology such as 10Base5 or 10Base2.

In a bus backbone, the topology of the backbone is a bus.

Bus backbones are normally used as a distribution backbone to connect different buildings in an organization. Each building can comprise either a single LAN or another backbone (normally a star backbone). A good example of a bus backbone is one that connects single- or multiple-floor buildings on a campus. Each single-floor building usually has a single LAN. Each multiple-floor building has a backbone (usually a star) that connects each LAN on a floor. A bus backbone can interconnect these LANs and backbones. Figure 16.11 shows an example of a bridge-based backbone with four LANs.

Figure 16.11 *Bus backbone*

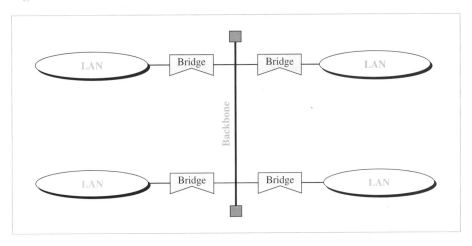

In the figure, if a station in a LAN needs to send a frame to another station in the same LAN, the corresponding bridge blocks the frame; the frame never reaches the backbone. However, if a station needs to send a frame to a station in another LAN, the bridge passes the frame to the backbone, which is received by the appropriate bridge and is delivered to the destination LAN. Each bridge connected to the backbone has a table that shows the stations on the LAN side of the bridge. The blocking or delivery of a frame is based on the contents of this table.

Star Backbone

In a **star backbone,** sometimes called a collapsed or switched backbone, the topology of the backbone is a star. In this configuration, the backbone is just one switch (that is why it is called, erroneously, a collapsed backbone) that connects the LANs.

> In a star backbone, the topology of the backbone is a star; the backbone is just one switch.

Figure 16.12 shows a star backbone. Note that, in this configuration, the switch does the job of the backbone and, at the same time connects the LANs.

Figure 16.12   *Star backbone*

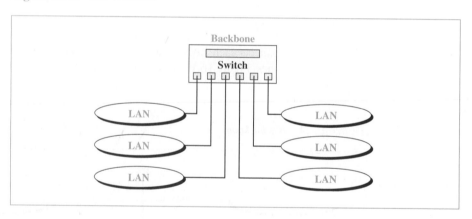

Star backbones are mostly used as a distribution backbone inside a building. In a multifloor building, we usually find one LAN that serves each particular floor. A star backbone connects these LANs. The backbone network, which is just a switch, can be installed in the basement or the first floor, and separate cables can run from the switch to each LAN. If the individual LANs have a physical star topology, either the hubs (or switches) can be installed in a closet on the corresponding floor, or all can be installed close to the switch. We often find a rack or chassis in the basement where the backbone switch and all hubs or switches are installed.

Connecting Remote LANs

Another common application for a backbone network is to connect remote LANs. This type of backbone network is useful when a company has several offices with LANs and needs to connect them. The connection can be done through bridges, sometimes called **remote bridges.** The bridges act as connecting devices connecting LANs and point-to-point networks, such as leased telephone lines or ADSL lines.

The point-to-point network in this case is considered a LAN without stations. The point-to-point link can use a protocol such as PPP. Figure 16.13 shows a backbone connecting remote LANs.

Figure 16.13   *Connecting remote LANs*

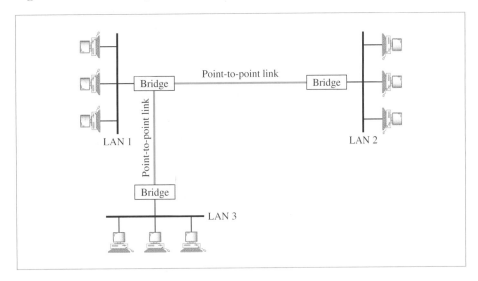

A point-to-point link acts as a LAN in a remote backbone connected by remote bridges.

16.3   VIRTUAL LANS

A station is considered part of a LAN if it physically belongs to that LAN. The criterion of membership is geographic. What happens if we need a virtual connection between two stations belonging to two different physical LANs? We can roughly define a **virtual local area network (VLAN)** as a local area network configured by software, not by physical wiring.

Let us use an example to elaborate on this definition. Figure 16.14 shows a switched LAN in an engineering firm in which 10 stations are grouped into three LANs that are connected by a switch. The first four engineers work together as the first group, the next three engineers work together as the second group, and the last three engineers work together as the third group. The LAN is configured to allow this arrangement.

But what would happen if the administrators needed to move two engineers from the first group to the third group to speed up the project being done by the third group? The LAN configuration would need to be changed. The network technician must rewire. The problem is repeated if in another week, the two engineers move back to their previous group. In a switched LAN, changes in the workgroup mean physical changes in the network configuration.

Figure 16.14   *A switch connecting three LANs*

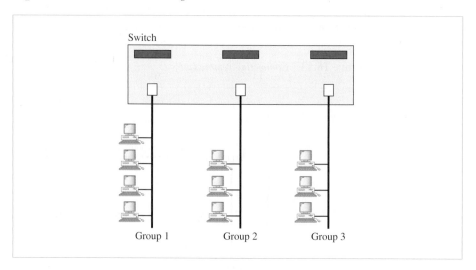

Figure 16.15   *A switch using VLAN software*

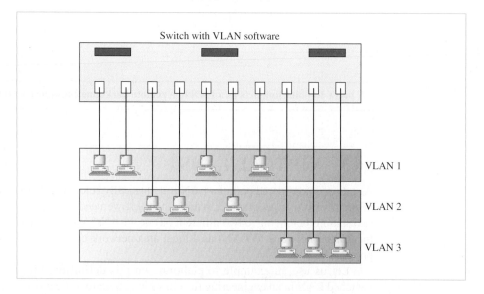

Figure 16.15 shows the same switched LAN divided into VLANs. The whole idea of VLAN technology is to divide a LAN into logical, instead of physical, segments. A LAN can be divided into several logical LANs called VLANs. Each VLAN is a work-group in the organization. If a person moves from one group to another, there is no need to change the physical configuration. The group membership in VLANs is defined by software, not hardware. Any station can be logically moved to another VLAN. All members belonging to a VLAN can receive broadcast messages sent to that particular VLAN. This means if a station moves from VLAN 1 to VLAN 2, it receives broadcast messages sent to VLAN 2, but no longer receives broadcast messages sent to VLAN 1.

It is obvious that the problem in our previous example can easily be solved by using VLANs. Moving engineers from one group to another through software is easier than changing the configuration of the physical network.

VLAN technology even allows the grouping of stations connected to different switches in a VLAN. Figure 16.16 shows a backbone local area network with two switches and three VLANs. Stations from switches A and B belong to each VLAN.

Figure 16.16   *Two switches in a backbone using VLAN software*

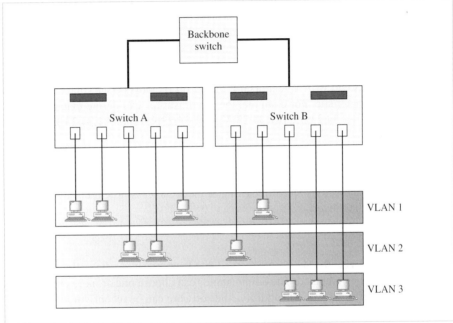

This is a good configuration for a company with two separate buildings. Each building can have its own switched LAN connected by a backbone. People in the first building and people in the second building can be in the same workgroup even though they are connected to different physical LANs.

From these three examples, we can define a VLAN characteristic:

VLANs create broadcast domains.

VLANs group stations belonging to one or more physical LANs into broadcast domains. The stations in a VLAN communicate with one another as though they belonged to a physical segment.

Membership

What characteristic can be used to group stations in a VLAN? Vendors use different characteristics such as port numbers, MAC addresses, IP addresses, IP multicast address, or a combination of two or more of the above.

Port Numbers

Some VLAN vendors use switch port numbers as a membership characteristic. For example, the administrator can define that stations connecting to ports 1, 2, 3, and 7 belong to VLAN 1; stations connecting to ports 4, 10, and 12 belong to VLAN 2; and so on.

MAC Addresses

Some VLAN vendors use the 48-bit MAC address as a membership characteristic. For example, the administrator can define that stations having MAC addresses E21342A12334 and F2A123BCD341 belong to VLAN 1.

IP Addresses

Some VLAN vendors use the 32-bit IP address (see Chapter 19) as a membership characteristic. For example, the administrator can define that stations having IP addresses 181.34.23.67, 181.34.23.72, 181.34.23.98, and 181.34.23.112 belong to VLAN 1.

Multicast IP Addresses

Some VLAN vendors use the multicast IP address (see Chapter 19) as a membership characteristic. Multicasting at the IP layer is now translated to multicasting at the data link layer.

Combination

Recently, the software available from some vendors allows all these characteristics to be combined. The administrator can choose one or more characteristics when installing the software. In addition, the software can be reconfigured to change the settings.

Configuration

How are the stations grouped into different VLANs? Stations are configured in one of three ways: manual, semiautomatic, and automatic.

Manual Configuration

In a manual configuration, the network administrator uses the VLAN software to manually assign the stations into different VLANs at setup. Later migration from one VLAN to another is also done manually. Note that this is not a physical configuration; it is a logical configuration. The term *manually* here means that the administrator types the port numbers, the IP addresses, or other characteristics using the VLAN software.

Automatic Configuration

In an automatic configuration, the stations are automatically connected or disconnected from a VLAN using criteria defined by the administrator. For example, the administrator can define the project number as the criterion for being a member of a group. When a user changes the project, he or she automatically migrates to a new VLAN.

Semiautomatic Configuration

A semiautomatic configuration is somewhere between a manual configuration and an automatic configuration. Usually, the initializing is done manually, with migrations done automatically.

Communication Between Switches

In a multiswitched backbone, each switch must know not only which station belongs to which VLAN, but also the membership of stations connected to other switches. For example, in Figure 16.16, switch A must know the membership status of stations connected to switch B, and switch B must know the same about switch A. Three methods have been devised for this purpose: table maintenance, frame tagging, and time-division multiplexing.

Table Maintenance

In this method, when a station sends a broadcast frame to its group members, the switch creates an entry in a table and records station membership. The switches send their tables to each other periodically for updating.

Frame Tagging

In this method, when a frame is traveling between switches, an extra header is added to the MAC frame to define the destination VLAN. The frame tag is used by the receiving switches to determine the VLANs to be receiving the broadcast message.

Time-Division Multiplexing (TDM)

In this method, the connection (trunk) between switches is divided into timeshared channels (see TDM in Chapter 6). For example, if the total number of VLANs in a backbone is five, each trunk is divided into five channels. The traffic destined for VLAN 1 travels in channel 1, the traffic destined for VLAN 2 travels in channel 2, and so on. The receiving switch determines the destination VLAN by checking the channel from which the frame arrived.

IEEE Standard

In 1996, the IEEE 802.1 subcommittee passed a standard called 802.1Q that defines the format for frame tagging. The standard also defines the format to be used in multiswitched backbones and enables the use of multivendor equipment in VLANs. IEEE 802.1Q has opened the way for further standardization in other issues related to VLANs. Most vendors have already accepted the standard.

Advantages

There are several advantages to using VLANs.

Cost and Time Reduction

VLANs can reduce the migration cost of stations going from one group to another. Physical reconfiguration takes time and is costly. Instead of physically moving one station to another segment or even to another switch, it is much easier and quicker to move it using software.

Creating Virtual Workgroups

VLANs can be used to create virtual workgroups. For example, in a campus environment, professors working on the same project can send broadcast messages to one another without the necessity of belonging to the same department. This can reduce traffic if the multicasting capability of IP was previously used.

Security

VLANs provide an extra measure of security. People belonging to the same group can send broadcast messages with the guaranteed assurance that users in other groups will not receive these messages.

16.4   KEY TERMS

amplifier
blocking port
bridge
bus backbone
connecting device
filtering
forwarding port
hub
remote bridge
repeater

router
segment
source routing bridge
spanning tree
star backbone
three-layer switch
transparent bridge
two-layer switch
virtual local area network (VLAN)

16.5   SUMMARY

- A repeater is a connecting device that operates in the physical layer of the Internet model. A repeater regenerates a signal, connects segments of a LAN, and has no filtering capability.
- A bridge is a connecting device that operates in the physical and data link layers of the Internet model.
- A transparent bridge can forward and filter frames and automatically build its forwarding table.
- A bridge can use the spanning tree algorithm to create a loopless topology.
- A backbone LAN allows several LANs to be connected.
- A backbone is usually a bus or a star.
- A virtual local area network (VLAN) is configured by software, not by physical wiring.
- Membership in a VLAN can be based on port numbers, MAC addresses, IP addresses, IP multicast addresses, or a combination of these features.

❏ VLANs are cost- and time-efficient, can reduce network traffic, and provide an extra measure of security.

16.6   PRACTICE SET

Review Questions

1. How is a repeater different from an amplifier?
2. What do we mean when we say that a bridge can filter traffic? Why is filtering important?
3. What is a transparent bridge?
4. How does a repeater extend the length of a LAN?
5. How is a hub related to a repeater?
6. What is the difference between a root bridge and a designated bridge?
7. What is the difference between a forwarding port and a blocking port?
8. What is the difference between a bus backbone and a star backbone?
9. How does a VLAN save a company time and money?
10. How does a VLAN provide extra security for a network?
11. How does a VLAN reduce network traffic?
12. What is the basis for membership in a VLAN?
13. How is TDM involved in VLAN communication?

Multiple-Choice Questions

14. Which of the following is a connecting device?
    a. Bridge
    b. Repeater
    c. Hub
    d. All the above
15. A bridge forwards or filters a frame by comparing the information in its address table to the frame's _____.
    a. Layer 2 source address
    b. Source node's physical address
    c. Layer 2 destination address
    d. Layer 3 destination address
16. A bridge can _____.
    a. Filter a frame
    b. Forward a frame
    c. Extend a LAN
    d. Do all the above

17. Repeaters function in the _____ layer(s).
    a. Physical (MAC)
    b. Data link
    c. Network
    d. (a) and (b)

18. A _____ is actually a multiport repeater.
    a. Bridge
    b. Router
    c. VLAN
    d. Hub

19. Bridges function in the _____ layer(s).
    a. Physical (MAC)
    b. Data link
    c. Network
    d. (a) and (b)

20. A repeater takes a weakened or corrupted signal and _____ it.
    a. Amplifies
    b. Regenerates
    c. Resamples
    d. Reroutes

21. A bridge has access to the _____ address of a station on the same network.
    a. Physical (MAC)
    b. Network
    c. Service access point
    d. All the above

22. A system with redundant bridges might have a problem with _____ in the system.
    a. Loops
    b. Filters
    c. Spanning trees
    d. All the above

23. A _____ bridge has the smallest ID.
    a. Root
    b. Designated
    c. Forwarding
    d. Blocking

24. The bridge with the least-cost path between the LAN and the root bridge is called the _____ bridge.
    a. Designated
    b. Forwarding
    c. Blocking
    d. (a) and (b)

25. A bridge never forwards frames out of the _____ port.
    a. Root
    b. Designated
    c. Forwarding
    d. Blocking

26. Which type of bridge builds and updates its tables from address information on frames?
    a. Simple
    b. Transparent
    c. (a) and (b)
    d. None of the above

27. VLAN technology divides a LAN into _____ groups.
    a. Physical
    b. Logical
    c. Multiplexed
    d. Framed

28. Which station characteristic can be used to group stations into a VLAN?
    a. Port numbers
    b. MAC addresses
    c. IP addresses
    d. All the above

29. In a VLAN, stations are separated into groups by _____.
    a. Physical methods
    b. Software methods
    c. Location
    d. Switches

Exercise

30. Complete the table in Figure 16.6 after each station has sent a packet to another station.

31. Create a system of 3 LANs with 4 bridges. The bridges (B1 to B4) connect the LANs as follows:
    a. B1 connects LAN 1 and LAN 2
    b. B1 connects LAN 1 and LAN 3
    c. B3 connects LAN 2 and LAN 3
    d. B4 connects LAN 1, LAN 2, and LAN 3
    Choose B1 as the root bridge. Show the forwarding and blocking ports after applying the spanning tree procedure.

CHAPTER 17

Cellular Telephone and Satellite Networks

We discussed wireless LANs in Chapter 15. Wireless technology is also used in cellular telephony and satellite networks. We discuss the former in this chapter as well as examples of channelization access methods (see Chapter 13). We also briefly discuss satellite networks, a technology that eventually will be linked to cellular telephony to access the Internet directly.

17.1 CELLULAR TELEPHONY

Cellular telephony is designed to provide communications between two moving units, called mobile stations (MSs), or between one mobile unit and one stationary unit, often called a land unit. A service provider must be able to locate and track a caller, assign a channel to the call, and transfer the channel from base station to base station as the caller moves out of range.

To make this tracking possible, each cellular service area is divided into small regions called cells. Each cell contains an antenna and is controlled by a small office, called the base station (BS). Each base station, in turn, is controlled by a switching office, called a **mobile switching center (MSC).** The MSC coordinates communication between all the base stations and the telephone central office. It is a computerized center that is responsible for connecting calls, recording call information, and billing (see Fig. 17.1).

Cell size is not fixed and can be increased or decreased depending on the population of the area. The typical radius of a cell is 1 to 12 miles. High-density areas require more geographically smaller cells to meet traffic demands than do lower-density areas. Once determined, cell size is optimized to prevent the interference of adjacent cell signals. The transmission power of each cell is kept low to prevent its signal from interfering with those of other cells.

Frequency-Reuse Principle

In general, neighboring cells cannot use the same set of frequencies for communication because it may create interference for the users located near the cell boundaries. However,

Figure 17.1 *Cellular system*

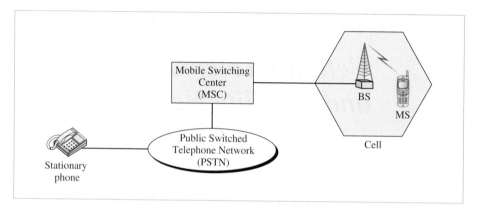

the set of frequencies available is limited, and frequencies need to be reused. A frequency reuse pattern is a configuration of N cells, N being the **reuse factor,** in which each cell uses a unique set of frequencies. When the pattern is repeated, the frequencies can be reused. There are several different patterns. Figure 17.2 shows two of them.

Figure 17.2 *Frequency reuse patterns*

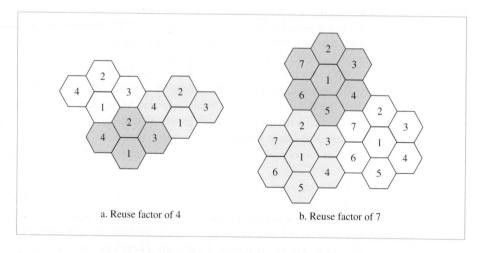

a. Reuse factor of 4   b. Reuse factor of 7

The cells with the same number in a pattern can use the same set of frequencies. We call these cells the *reusing cells.* As the figure shows, in a pattern with reuse factor 4, only one cell separates the cells using the same set of frequencies. In the pattern with reuse factor 7, two cells separate the reusing cells.

Transmitting

To place a call from a mobile station, the caller enters a code of 7 or 10 digits (a phone number) and presses the send button. The mobile station then scans the band, seeking a setup channel with a strong signal, and sends the data (phone number) to the closest base station using that channel. The base station relays the data to the MSC. The MSC sends the data on to the telephone central office. If the called party is available, a connection is made and the result is relayed back to the MSC. At this point, the MSC assigns an unused voice channel to the call, and a connection is established. The mobile station automatically adjusts its tuning to the new channel, and communication can begin.

Receiving

When a mobile phone is called, the telephone central office sends the number to the MSC. The MSC searches for the location of the mobile station by sending query signals to each cell in a process called *paging*. Once the mobile station is found, the MSC transmits a ringing signal and, when the mobile station answers, assigns a voice channel to the call, allowing voice communication to begin.

Handoff

It may happen that, during a conversation, the mobile station moves from one cell to another. When it does, the signal may become weak. To solve this problem, the MSC monitors the level of the signal every few seconds. If the strength of the signal diminishes, the MSC seeks a new cell that can better accommodate the communication. The MSC then changes the channel carrying the call (hands the signal off from the old channel to a new one).

Hard Handoff Early systems used a hard **handoff.** In a hard handoff, a mobile station only communicates with one base station. When the MS moves from one cell to another, communication must first be broken with the previous base station before communication can be established with the new one. This may create a rough transition.

Soft Handoff New systems use a soft handoff. In this case, a mobile station can communicate with two base stations at the same time. This means that, during handoff, a station may continue with the new base station before breaking from the old one.

Roaming

One feature of cellular telephony is called **roaming.** Roaming means, in principle, that a user can have access to communication or can be reached where there is coverage. A service provider usually has limited coverage. Neighboring service providers can provide extended coverage through a roaming contract. The situation is similar to snail mail between countries. The charge for delivery of a letter between two countries can be divided upon agreement by the two countries.

First Generation

Cellular telephony is now in its second generation with the third on the horizon. The first generation was designed for voice communication using analog signals. We discuss one first-generation mobile system used in North America, AMPS.

AMPS

Advanced Mobile Phone System (AMPS) is one of the leading analog cellular systems in North America. It uses FDMA to separate channels in a link.

> **AMPS is an analog cellular phone system using FDMA.**

Bands   AMPS operates in the ISM 800-MHz band. The system uses two separate analog channels for forward (base station to mobile station) and reverse (mobile station to base station) communication. The band between 824 and 849 MHz carries reverse communication; the band between 869 and 894 MHz carries forward communication. See Figure 17.3.

Figure 17.3   *Cellular bands for AMPS*

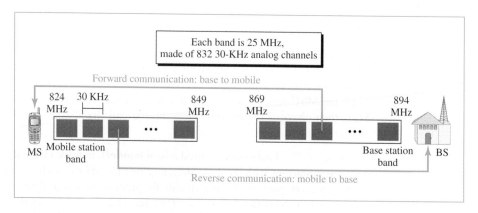

Each band is divided into 832 channels. However, two providers can share an area, which means 416 channels in each cell for each provider. Out of these 416, 21 channels are used for control, which leaves 395 channels. AMPS has a frequency reuse factor of 7; this means only one-seventh of these 395 traffic channels are actually available in a cell.

Transmission   AMPS uses FM and FSK for modulation. Figure 17.4 shows the transmission in the reverse direction. Voice channels are modulated using FM, and control channels use FSK to create 30-KHz analog signals. AMPS uses FDMA to divide each 25-MHz band into 30-KHz channels.

Second Generation

To provide higher-quality (less noise-prone) mobile voice communications, the second generation of the cellular phone network was developed. While the first generation was designed for analog voice communication, the second generation was mainly designed for digitized voice. Three major systems evolved in the second generation, as shown in Figure 17.5. We will discuss each system separately.

Figure 17.4 *AMPS reverse communication band*

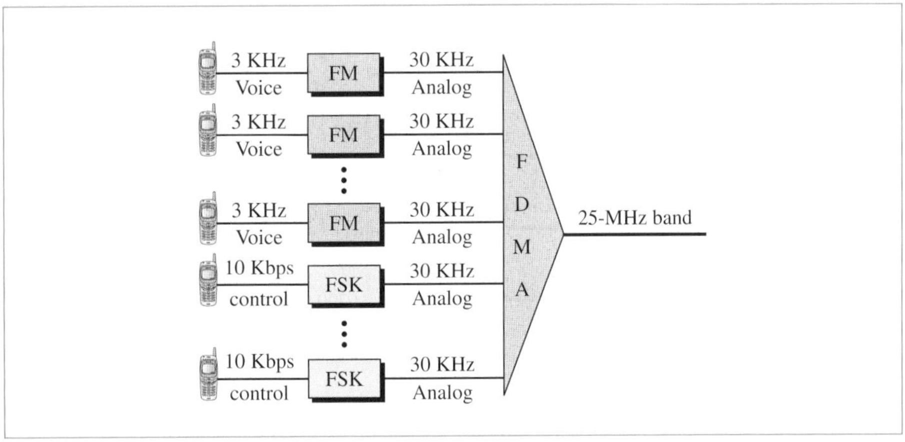

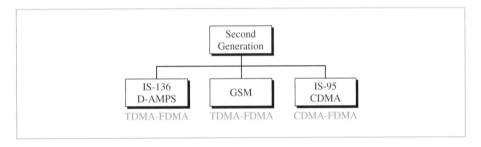

Figure 17.5 *Second-generation cellular phone systems*

D-AMPS

The product of the evolution of the analog AMPS into a digital system is **digital AMPS (D-AMPS).** D-AMPS was designed to be backward-compatible with AMPS. This means that in a cell, one telephone can use AMPS and another D-AMPS. D-AMPS was first defined by IS-54 (Interim Standard 54) and later revised by IS-136.

Band   D-AMPS uses the same bands and channels as AMPS.

Transmission   Each voice channel is digitized using a very complex PCM and compression technique. A voice channel is digitized to 7.95 Kbps. Three 7.95-Kbps digital voice channels are combined using TDMA. The result is 48.6 Kbps of digital data; much of this is overhead.

As Figure 17.6 shows, the system sends 25 frames per second, with 1944 bits per frame. Each frame lasts 40 ms (1/25) and is divided into six slots shared by three digital channels; each channel is allotted two slots.

Each slot holds 324 bits. However, only 159 bits comes from the digitized voice; 64 bits for control, and 101 bits for error correction. In other words, each channel drops 159 bits of data in each of the two channels assigned to it. The system adds 64 control bits and 101 error-correcting bits.

Figure 17.6   *D-AMPS*

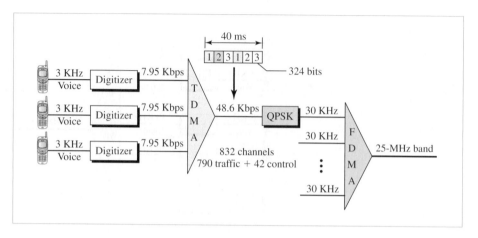

The resulting 48.6 Kbps of digital data modulates a carrier using QPSK; the result is a 30-KHz analog signal. Finally, the 30-KHz analog signals are frequency-multiplexed in the 25-MHz band. D-AMPS has a frequency reuse factor of 7.

> **D-AMPS, or IS-136, is a digital cellular phone system using TDMA and FDMA.**

GSM

The **Global System for Mobile Communication (GSM)** is a European standard that was developed to provide a common second-generation technology for all of Europe. The aim was to replace a number of incompatible first-generation technologies.

Bands   GSM uses two bands for duplex communication. Each band is 25 MHz in width, shifted toward 900 MHz, as shown in Figure 17.7. Each band is divided into 124 channels of 200 KHz separated by guard bands.

Transmission   Figure 17.8 shows a GSM system. Each voice channel is digitized and compressed to a 13-Kbps digital signal. Each slot carries 156.25 bits. Eight slots are

Figure 17.7   *GSM bands*

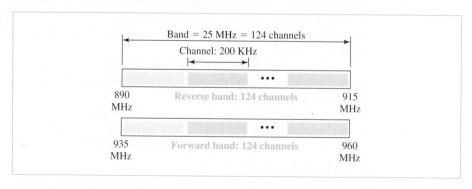

Figure 17.8   *GSM*

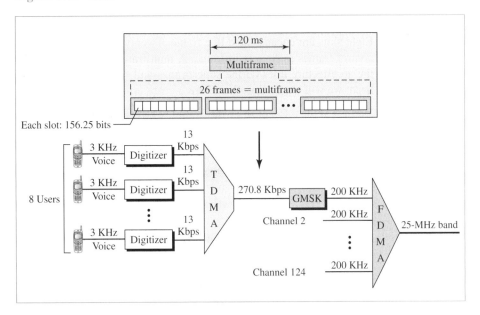

multiplexed together, creating a TDM frame. Twenty-six frames are combined to form a multiframe. We can calculate the bit rate of each channel as follows:

$$\text{Channel data rate} = (1/120 \text{ ms}) \times 26 \times 8 \times 156.25 = 270.8 \text{ Kbps}$$

Each 270.8-Kbps digital channel modulates a carrier using GMSK (a form of FSK used mainly in European systems); the result is a 200-KHz analog signal. Finally 124 analog channels of 200 KHz are multiplexed together using FDMA. The result is a 25-MHz band.

Figure 17.9 shows the user data and overhead in a multiframe.

Figure 17.9   *Multiframe components*

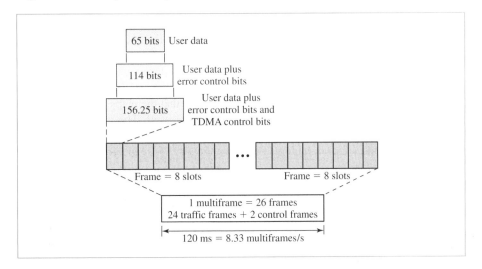

The reader may have noticed the large amount of overhead in TDMA. The user data is only 65 bits per slot. The system adds extra bits for error correction to make it 114 bits per slot. To this, control bits are added to bring it up to 156.25 bits per slot. Eight slots are encapsulated in a frame. Twenty-four traffic frames and two additional control frames make a multiframe. A multiframe has a duration of 120 ms. However, the architecture does define superframes and hyperframes that do not add any overhead; we will not discuss them here.

Reuse Factor   Because of the complex error correction mechanism, GSM allows a reuse factor as low as 3.

> **GSM is a digital cellular phone system using TDMA and FDMA.**

IS-95

One of the dominating second-generation standards in North America is **Interim Standard 95 (IS-95).** It is based on CDMA and DSSS.

Bands and Channels   IS-95 uses two bands for duplex communication. The bands can be the traditional ISM 800-MHz band or the ISM 1900-MHz band. Each band is divided into 20 channels of 1.228 MHz separated by guard bands. Each service provider is allotted 10 channels. IS-95 can be used in parallel with AMPS. Each IS-95 channel is equivalent to 41 AMPS channels (41×30 KHz = 1.23 MHz).

Synchronization   All base channels need to be synchronized to use CDMA. To provide synchronization, bases use the services of GPS (Global Positioning System), a satellite system that we discuss in the next section.

Forward Transmission   IS-95 has two different transmission techniques: one for use in the forward (base to mobile) direction and another for use in the reverse (mobile to base) direction. In the forward direction, communications between the base and all mobiles are synchronized; the base sends synchronized data to all mobiles. Figure 17.10 shows a simplified diagram for the forward direction.

Each voice channel is digitized, producing data at a basic rate of 9.6 Kbps. After adding error-correcting and repeating bits, and interleaving, the result is a signal of 19.2 ksps (kilosignals per seconds). This output is now scrambled using a 19.2-ksps signal. The scrambling signal is produced from a long code generator that uses the electronic serial number (ESN) of the mobile station and generates 2^{42} pseudorandom chips, each chip having 42 bits. Note that the chips are generated pseudorandomly, not randomly, because the pattern repeats itself. The output of the long code generator is fed to a decimator, which chooses 1 bit out of 64 bits. The output of the decimator is used for scrambling. The scrambling is used to create privacy; the ESN is unique for each station.

The result of the scrambler is fed to the CDMA multiplexer. For each traffic channel, one Walsh 64×64 row chip is selected. The result is a signal of 1.288 Mcps (megachips per second).

$$19.2 \text{ Ksps} \times 64 \text{ cps} = 1.288 \text{ Mcps}$$

Figure 17.10 *IS-95 forward transmission*

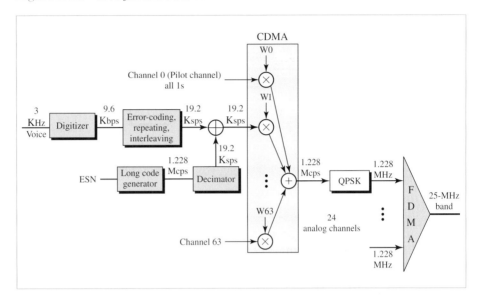

The CDMA-multiplexed signal is fed into a QPSK modulator to produce a signal of 1.288 MHz. The resulting bandwidth is shifted appropriately, using FDMA.

An analog channel creates 64 digital channels, of which 55 channels are traffic channels (carrying digitized voice). Nine channels are used for control and synchronization:

■ Channel 0 is a pilot channel. This channel sends a continuous stream of 1s to mobile stations. The stream provides bit synchronization, serves as a phase reference for demodulation, and allows the mobile station to compare the signal strength of neighboring bases for handoff decisions.

■ Channel 32 gives information about the system to the mobile station.

■ Channels 1 to 7 are used for paging, to send messages to one or more mobile stations.

■ Channels 8 to 31 and 33 to 63 are traffic channels carrying digitized voice from the base station to the corresponding mobile station.

Reverse Transmission The use of CDMA in the forward direction is possible because the pilot channel sends a continuous sequence of 1s to synchronize transmission. The synchronization is not used in the reverse direction because we need an entity to do that, which is not feasible. Instead of CDMA, the reverse channels use DSSS (direct sequence spread spectrum), which we discussed in Chapter 15. Figure 17.11 shows a simplified diagram for reverse transmission.

Each voice channel is digitized, producing data at a rate of 9.6 Kbps. However, after adding error-correcting and repeating bits, plus interleaving, the result is a signal of 28.8 Ksps. The output is now passed through a 6/64 symbol modulator. The symbols are divided into six-symbol chunks, and each chunk is interpreted as a binary number (from 0 to 63). The binary number is used as the index to a 64 × 64 Walsh matrix for

Figure 17.11   *IS-95 reverse transmission*

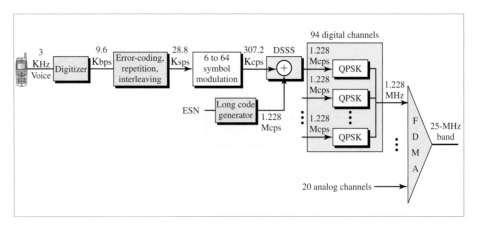

selection of a row of chips. Note that this procedure is not CDMA; each bit is not multiplied by the chips in a row. Each six-symbol chunk is replaced by a 64-chip code. This is done to provide a kind of orthogonality; it differentiates the streams of chips from the different mobile stations. The result creates a signal of 307.2 kcps or (28.8/6) × 64.

Spreading is the next step; each chip is spread into 4. Again the ESN of the mobile station creates a long code of 42 bits at a rate of 1.228 Mcps, which is 4 times 307.2. After spreading, each signal is modulated using QPSK, which is slightly different from the one used in the forward direction; we do not go into details here. Note that there is no multiple-access mechanism here; all reverse channels send their analog signal into the air, but the correct chips will be received by the base station due to spreading.

Although we can create $2^{42} - 1$ digital channels in the reverse direction (because of the long code generator), normally 94 channels are used; 62 are traffic channels, and 32 are channels used to gain access to the base station.

IS-95 is a digital cellular phone system using CDMA/DSSS and FDMA.

Two Data Rate Sets   IS-95 defines two data rate sets, with four different rates in each set. The first set defines 9600, 4800, 2400, and 1200 bps. If, for example, the selected rate is 1200 bps, each bit is repeated 8 times to provide a rate of 9600 bps. The second set defines 14,400, 7200, 3600, and 1800 bps. This is possible by reducing the number of bits used for error correction. The bit rates in a set are related to the activity of the channel. If the channel is silent, only 1200 bits can be transferred, which improves the spreading by repeating each bit 8 times.

Frequency Reuse Factor   In an IS-95 system, the frequency reuse factor is normally 1 because the interference from neighboring cells cannot affect CDMA or DSSS transmission.

Soft Handoff   Every base station continuously broadcasts signals using its pilot channel. This means a mobile station can detect the pilot signal from its cell and neighboring cells. This enables a mobile station to do a soft handoff in contrast to a hard handoff.

PCS

Before we leave the discussion on second-generation cellular telephones, let us explain a term generally heard in relation to this generation: PCS. **Personal Communications System (PCS)** does not refer to a single technology such as GSM, IS-136, or IS-95. It is a generic name for a commercial system that offers several kinds of communication services. Common features of these systems can be summarized:

1. They may use any second-generation technology (GSM, IS-136, or IS-95).
2. They use the 1900-MHz band, which means that a mobile station needs more power because higher frequencies have a shorter range than lower ones. However, since a station's power is limited by the FCC, the base station and the mobile station need to be close to each other (smaller cells).
3. They offer communication services such as short message service (SMS) and limited Internet access.

Third Generation

The third generation of cellular telephony refers to a combination of technologies that provide a variety of services. Ideally, when it matures, the third generation can provide both digital data and voice communication. Using a small portable device, a person should be able to talk to anyone else in the world with a voice quality similar to that of the existing fixed telephone network. A person can download and watch a movie, can download and listen to music, can surf the Internet or play games, can have a video conference, and can do much more. One of the interesting characteristics of a third-generation system is that the portable device is always connected; you do not need to dial a number to connect to the Internet.

The third-generation concept started in 1992, when ITU issued a blueprint called **Internet Mobile Communication for year 2000 (IMT-2000).** The blueprint defines some criteria for 3G technology as outlined below:

- Voice quality comparable to that of the existing public telephone network.
- Data rate of 144 Kbps for access in a moving vehicle (car), 384 Kbps for access as the user walks (pedestrians), and 2 Mbps for the stationary user (office or home).
- Support for packet-switched and circuit-switched data services.
- A band of 2 GHz.
- Bandwidths of 2 MHz.
- Interface to the Internet.

The main goal of third-generation cellular telephony is to provide universal personal communication.

IMT-2000 Radio Interface

Figure 17.12 shows the radio interfaces (wireless standards) adopted by IMT-2000. All five are developed from second-generation technologies. The first two evolve from CDMA technology. The third evolves from a combination of CDMA and TDMA. The fourth evolves from TDMA, and the last evolves from both FDMA and TDMA.

Figure 17.12   *IMT-2000 radio interfaces*

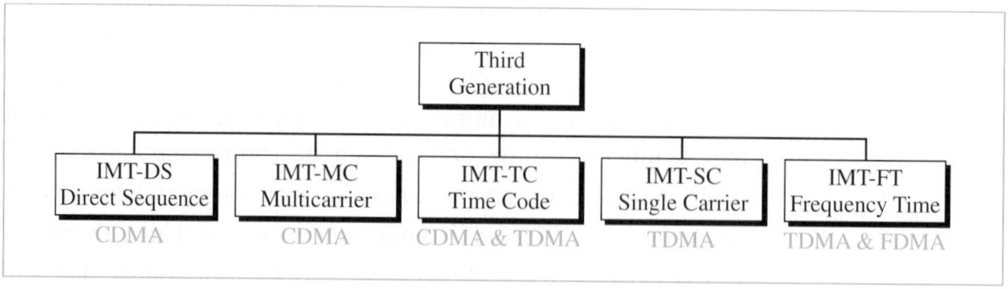

IMT-DS   This approach uses a version of CDMA called wideband CDMA or W-CDMA. W-CDMA uses a 5-MHz bandwidth. It was developed in Europe, and it is compatible with the CDMA used in IS-95.

IMT-MC   This approach was developed in North America and is known as CDMA 2000. It is an evolution of CDMA technology used in IS-95 channels. It combines the new wideband (15-MHz) spread spectrum with the narrowband (1.25-MHz) CDMA of IS-95. It is backward-compatible with IS-95. It allows communication on multiple 1.25-MHz channels (1, 3, 6, 9, 12 times), up to 15 MHz. The use of the wider channels allows it to reach the 2-Mbps data rate defined for the third generation.

IMT-TC   This standard uses a combination of W-CDMA and TDMA. The standard tries to reach the IMT-2000 goals by adding TDMA multiplexing to W-CDMA.

IMT-SC   This standard only uses TDMA.

IMT-FT   This standard uses a combination of FDMA and TDMA.

17.2   SATELLITE NETWORKS

A **satellite network** is a combination of nodes that provides communication from one point on the earth to another. A node in the network can be a satellite, an earth station, or an end-user terminal or telephone. Although a real satellite, such as the moon, can be used as a relaying node in the network, the use of artificial satellites is preferred because we can install electronic equipment on the satellite to regenerate the signal that has lost its energy during travel. Another restriction on using natural satellites is their distances from the earth, which create a long delay in communication.

Satellite networks are like cellular networks in that they divide the planet into large cells. Satellites can provide transmission capability to and from any location on earth, no matter how remote. This advantage makes high-quality communication available to undeveloped parts of the world without requiring a huge investment in ground-based infrastructure.

Orbits

An artificial satellite needs to have an **orbit,** the path in which it travels around the earth. The orbit can be equatorial, inclined, or polar, as shown in Figure 17.13.

Figure 17.13 *Satellite orbits*

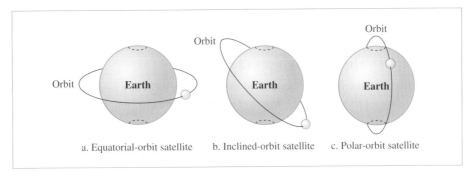

a. Equatorial-orbit satellite   b. Inclined-orbit satellite   c. Polar-orbit satellite

The period of a satellite, the time required for a satellite to make a complete trip around the earth, is determined by Kepler's law, which defines the period as a function of the distance of the satellite from the center of the earth.

$$\text{Period} = C \times \text{distance}^{1.5}$$

Here C is a constant approximately equal to 1/100. The period is in seconds and the distance in kilometers.

Example 1

What is the period of the moon according to Kepler's law?

Solution

The moon is located approximately 384,000 km above the earth. The radius of the earth is 6378 km. Applying the formula, we get

$$\text{Period} = (1/100) \, (384{,}000 + 6378)^{1.5} \longrightarrow 2{,}439{,}090 \text{ s} \longrightarrow 1 \text{ month}$$

Example 2

According to Kepler's law, what is the period of a satellite that is located at an orbit approximately 35,786 km above the earth?

Solution

Applying the formula, we get

$$\text{Period} = (1/100) \, (35{,}786 + 6378)^{1.5} \longrightarrow 86{,}579 \text{ s} \longrightarrow 24 \text{ h}$$

This means that a satellite located at 35,786 km has a period of 24 h, which is the same as the rotation period of the earth. A satellite like this is said to be *stationary* to the earth. The orbit, as we will see, is called a geosynchronous orbit.

Footprint

Satellites process microwaves with bidirectional antennas (line-of-sight). Therefore, the signal from a satellite is normally aimed at a specific area called the **footprint.** The signal power at the center of the footprint is maximum. The power decreases as we move from the footprint center. The boundary of the footprint is the location where the power reaches a predefined threshold.

Three Categories of Satellites

Based on the location of the orbit, satellites can be divided into three categories: GEO, LEO, and MEO. Figure 17.14 shows the taxonomy.

Figure 17.14   *Satellite categories*

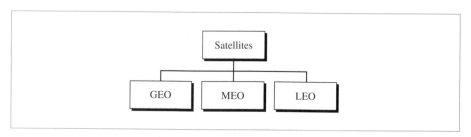

Figure 17.15 shows the satellite altitudes with respect to the surface of the earth. There is only one orbit, at an altitude of 35,786 km for the GEO satellite. MEO satellites are located at altitudes between 5000 and 15,000 km. LEO satellites are normally below an altitude of 2000 km.

Figure 17.15   *Satellite orbit altitudes*

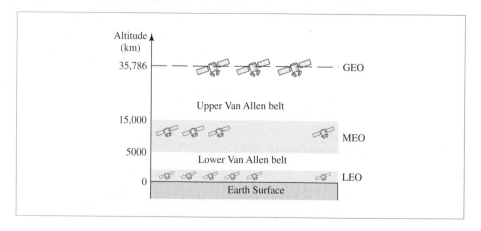

One reason for having different orbits is due to the existence of two Van Allen belts. A Van Allen belt is a layer that contains charged particles. A satellite orbiting in one of these two belts would be totally destroyed by the energetic charged particles. The MEO orbits are located between these two belts.

Frequency Bands for Satellite Communication

The frequencies reserved for satellite microwave communication are in the gigahertz (GHz) range. Each satellite sends and receives over two different bands. Transmission from the earth to the satellite is called **uplink.** Transmission from the satellite to the earth is called **downlink.** Table 17.1 gives the band names and frequencies for each range.

Table 17.1   *Satellite frequency bands*

Band	Downlink, GHz	Uplink, GHz	Bandwidth, MHz
L	1.5	1.6	15
S	1.9	2.2	70
C	4	6	500
Ku	11	14	500
Ka	20	30	3500

GEO Satellites

Line-of-sight propagation requires that the sending and receiving antennas be locked onto each other's location at all times (one antenna must have the other in sight). For this reason, a satellite that moves faster or slower than the earth's rotation is useful only for short periods of time. To ensure constant communication, the satellite must move at the same speed as the earth so that it seems to remain fixed above a certain spot. Such satellites are called *geosynchronous.*

Because orbital speed is based on distance from the planet, only one orbit can be geosynchronous. This orbit occurs at the equatorial plane and is approximately 22,000 miles from the surface of the earth.

But one geosynchronous satellite cannot cover the whole earth. One satellite in orbit has line-of-sight contact with a vast number of stations, but the curvature of the earth still keeps much of the planet out of sight. It takes a minimum of three satellites equidistant from each other in **geosynchronous Earth orbit (GEO)** to provide full global transmission. Figure 17.16 shows three satellites, each 120° from another in geosynchronous orbit around the equator. The view is from the North Pole.

Figure 17.16   *Satellites in geosynchronous orbit*

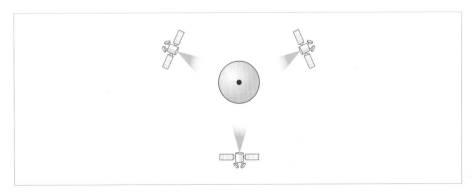

MEO Satellites

Medium-Earth orbit (MEO) satellites are positioned between the two Van Allen belts. A satellite at this orbit takes approximately 6 hours to circle the earth.

GPS

One example of a MEO satellite system is the **Global Positioning System (GPS)** orbiting at an altitude about 18,000 km (11,000 miles) above the Earth. Although GPS was put in place by the Department of Defense, it is now a public system. The system consists of 24 satellites and is used for land and sea navigation to provide time and locations for vehicles and ships. The GPS is not used for communications.

GPS is based on a principle called **triangulation.** On a plane, if we know our distance from three points, we know exactly where we are. Let us say that we are 10 miles away from point A, 12 miles away from point B, and 15 miles away from point C. If we draw three circles with the centers at A, B, and C, we must be somewhere on circle A, somewhere on circle B, and somewhere on circle C. These three circles meet at one single point (if our distances are correct), our position. Figure 17.17 shows the concept. In space, however, the situation is different. Three spheres meet in two points; we need four spheres. If we know our distance from four points, we can find out where we are.

Figure 17.17 *Triangulation*

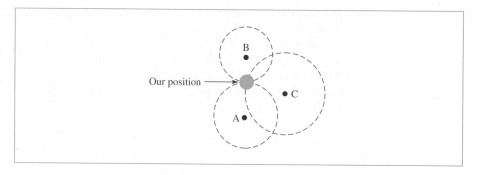

GPS uses 24 satellites in six orbits, as shown in Figure 17.18. The orbits and the locations of the satellites in each orbit are designed in such a way that, at any time, four satellites are visible from any point on Earth. A GPS receiver has an almanac that tells the current position of a satellite. It then sends a signal to four satellites and measures how long it takes for the signal to return. It calculates your position on the Earth. A GPS receiver can also show you where you are on a map.

GPS is used by military forces. For example, thousands of portable GPS receivers were used during the Persian Gulf war by foot soldiers, vehicles, and helicopters. Another use of GPS is in navigation. The driver of a car can find the location of the car. The driver can then consult a database in the memory of the automobile to be directed to the destination. In other words, GPS gives the location of the car, and the database uses this information to find a path to the destination. As we mentioned previously, the IS-95 cellular telephone system uses GPS to create synchronization between the base stations.

Figure 17.18 *GPS*

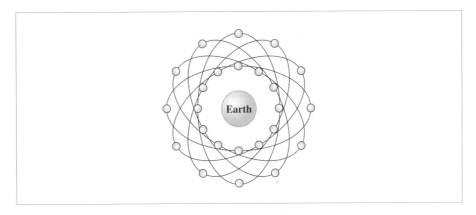

LEO Satellites

Low-Earth orbit (LEO) satellites have polar orbits. The altitude is between 500 to 2000 km, with a rotation period of 90 to 120 min. The satellite has a speed of 20,000 to 25,000 km/h. An LEO system usually has a cellular type of access, similar to the cellular telephone system. The footprint normally has a diameter of 8000 km. Because LEO satellites are close to the Earth, the round-trip time propagation delay is normally less than 20 ms, which is acceptable for audio communication.

A LEO system is made of a constellation of satellites that work together as a network; each satellite acts as a switch. Satellites that are close to each other are connected through intersatellite links (ISLs). A mobile system communicates with the satellite through a user mobile link (UML). A satellite can also communicate with an earth station (gateway) through a gateway link (GWL). Figure 17.19 shows a typical LEO satellite network.

LEO satellites can be divided into three categories: little LEOs, big LEOs, and broadband LEOs. The little LEOs operate under 1 GHz. They are mostly used for low-data-rate messaging. The big LEOs operate between 1 and 3 GHz. Globalstar and Iridium systems are examples of big LEOs. The broadband LEOs provide communication similar to fiber-optic networks. The first broadband LEO system was Teledesic.

Figure 17.19 *LEO satellite system*

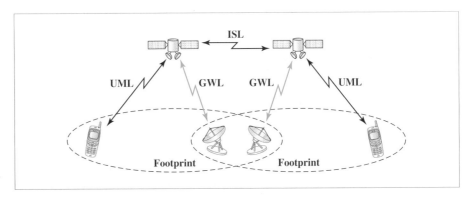

Iridium System

The concept of the **Iridium** system, a 77-satellite network, was started by Motorola in 1990. The project took 8 years to materialize. During this period, the number of satellites was reduced. Finally, in 1998, the service started with 66 satellites. The original name, Iridium, came from the name of the 77th chemical element; a more appropriate name is Dysprosium (the name of element 66).

Iridium has gone through rough times. The system was halted in 1999 due to financial problems; it was sold and restarted in 2001 under new ownership.

The system has 66 satellites divided into six orbits, with 11 satellites in each orbit. The orbits are at an altitude of 750 km. The satellites in each orbit are separated from one another by approximately 32° of latitude. Figure 17.20 shows a schematic diagram of the constellation.

Figure 17.20   *Iridium constellation*

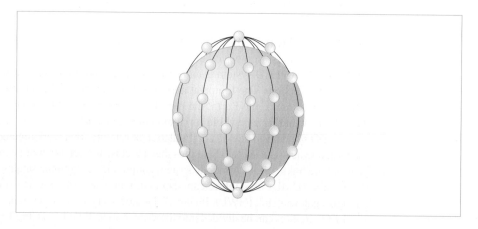

The Iridium system has 66 satellites in six LEO orbits, each at an altitude of 750 km.

Since each satellite has 48 spot beams, the system can have up to 3168 beams. However, some of the beams are turned off as the satellite approaches the pole. The number of active spot beams at any moment is approximately 2000. Each spot beam covers a cell on the earth, which means that the earth is divided into approximately 2000 (overlapping) cells.

In the Iridium system, communication between two users takes place through satellites. When a user calls another user, the call can go through several satellites before reaching the destination. This means that relaying is done in space and each satellite needs to be sophisticated enough to do relaying. This strategy eliminates the need for many terrestrial stations.

The whole purpose of Iridium is to provide direct worldwide communication using handheld terminals (same concept as cellular telephony). The system can be used for voice, data, paging, fax, and even navigation. The system can provide connectivity between users at locations where other types of communication are not possible. The system provides 2.4- to 4.8-Kbps voice and data transmission between portable telephones.

Transmission occurs in the 1.616- to 1.6126-GHz frequency band. Intersatellite communication occurs in the 23.18- to 23.38-GHz frequency band.

Iridium is designed to provide direct worldwide voice and data communication using handheld terminals, a service similar to cellular telephony but on a global scale.

Globalstar

Globalstar is another LEO satellite system. The system uses 48 satellites in six polar orbits with each orbit hosting eight satellites. The orbits are located at an altitude of almost 1400 km.

The Globalstar system is similar to the Iridium system; the main difference is the relaying mechanism. Communication between two distant users in the Iridium system requires relaying between several satellites; Globalstar communication requires both satellites and earth stations, which means that ground stations can create more powerful signals.

Teledesic

Teledesic is a system of satellites that provides fiber-optic-like (broadband channels, low error rate, and low delay) communication. Its main purpose is to provide broadband Internet access for users all over the world. It is sometimes called "Internet in the sky."

The project was started in 1990 by Craig McCaw and Bill Gates; later, other investors joined the consortium. The project is scheduled to be fully functional in 2005.

Constellation   Teledesic provides 288 satellites in 12 polar orbits with each orbit hosting 24 satellites. The orbits are at an altitude of 1350 km, as shown in Figure 17.21.

Figure 17.21   *Teledesic*

Teledesic has 288 satellites in 12 LEO orbits, each at an altitude of 1350 km.

Communication   The system provides three types of communication. Intersatellite communication allows eight neighboring satellites to communicate with one another. Communication is also possible between a satellite and an earth gateway station. Users can communicate directly with the network using terminals. The earth is divided into tens of thousands of cells. Each cell is assigned a time slot, and the satellite focuses its beam to the cell at the corresponding time slot. The terminal can send data during its time slot. A terminal receives all packets intended for the cell, but selects only those intended for its address.

Bands   Transmission occurs in the Ka bands.

Data Rate   The data rate is up to 155 Mbps for the uplink and up to 1.2 Gbps for the downlink.

17.3   KEY TERMS

Advanced Mobile Phone System (AMPS)	Iridium
cellular telephony	low-Earth orbit (LEO)
digital AMPS (D-AMPS)	medium-Earth orbit (MEO)
downlink	mobile switching center (MSC)
footprint	orbit
geosynchronous Earth orbit (GEO)	personal communications system
Global Positioning System (GPS)	(PCS)
Global System for Mobile Communica-	reuse factor
tion (GSM)	roaming
Globalstar	satellite network
handoff	Teledesic
Interim Standard 95 (IS-95)	triangulation
Internet Mobile Communication for	uplink
year 2000 (IMT-2000)	

17.4   SUMMARY

❏   Cellular telephony provides communication between two devices. One or both may be mobile.

❏   A cellular service area is divided into cells.

❏   Advanced Mobile Phone System (AMPS) is a first-generation cellular phone system.

❏   Digital AMPS (D-AMPS) is a second-generation cellular phone system that is a digital version of AMPS.

❏   Global System for Mobile Communication (GSM) is a second-generation cellular phone system used in Europe.

❏   Interim Standard 95 (IS-95) is a second-generation cellular phone system based on CDMA and DSSS.

❏ The third-generation cellular phone system will provide universal personal communication.

❏ A satellite network uses satellites to provide communication between any points on earth.

❏ A geosynchronous Earth orbit (GEO) is at the equatorial plane and revolves in phase with the earth.

❏ Global Positioning System (GPS) satellites are medium-Earth-orbit (MEO) satellites that provide time and location information for vehicles and ships.

❏ Iridium satellites are low-Earth-orbit (LEO) satellites that provide direct universal voice and data communications for handheld terminals.

❏ Teledesic satellites are low-Earth-orbit satellites that will provide universal broadband Internet access.

17.5   PRACTICE SET

Review Questions

1. What is the relationship between a base station and a mobile switching center?
2. What are the functions of a mobile switching center?
3. Which is better, a low reuse factor or a high reuse factor? Explain your answer.
4. What is the difference between a hard handoff and a soft handoff?
5. What is AMPS?
6. What is the relationship between D-AMPS and AMPS?
7. What is GSM?
8. What is the function of the CDMA multiplexer in IS-95?
9. What are the three types of orbits?
10. Which type of orbit does a GEO satellite have? Explain your answer.
11. What is a footprint?
12. What is the relationship between the Van Allen belts and satellites?
13. Compare an uplink with a downlink.
14. What is the purpose of GPS?
15. What is the main difference between Iridium and Globalstar?

Multiple-Choice Questions

16. A _____ is a computerized center that is responsible for connecting calls, recording call information, and billing.
    a. Base station
    b. Mobile switching center
    c. Cell
    d. Mobile station

17. In _____, a mobile station always communicates with just one base station.
   a. Roaming
   b. A hard handoff
   c. A soft handoff
   d. A roaming handoff

18. _____ is a first-generation cellular phone system.
   a. AMPS
   b. D-AMPS
   c. GSM
   d. IS-95

19. _____ is a second-generation cellular phone system.
   a. D-AMPS
   b. GSM
   c. IS-95
   d. All the above

20. AMPS uses _____ for modulation.
   a. FM
   b. FSK
   c. PM
   d. (a) and (b)

21. _____ separates the AMPS voice channels.
   a. CDMA
   b. TDMA
   c. FDMA
   d. (b) and (c)

22. _____ is a cellular telephone system popular in Europe.
   a. AMPS
   b. D-AMPS
   c. GSM
   d. IS-95

23. D-AMPS uses _____ for multiplexing.
   a. CDMA
   b. TDMA
   c. FDMA
   d. (b) and (c)

24. GSM uses _____ for multiplexing.
   a. CDMA
   b. TDMA
   c. FDMA
   d. (b) and (c)

25. DSSS is used by the _____ cellular phone system.
    a. AMPS
    b. D-AMPS
    c. GSM
    d. IS-95

26. _____ base stations use GPS for synchronization.
    a. AMPS
    b. D-AMPS
    c. GSM
    d. IS-95

27. IS-95 has a frequency reuse factor of _____.
    a. 1
    b. 5
    c. 7
    d. 95

28. The path that a satellite makes around the world is called _____.
    a. A period
    b. A footprint
    c. An orbit
    d. An uplink

29. A GEO satellite has _____ orbit.
    a. An equatorial
    b. A polar
    c. An inclined
    d. An equilateral

30. The signal from a satellite is aimed at a specific area called the _____.
    a. Period
    b. Footprint
    c. Orbit
    d. Uplink

31. Which orbit has the highest altitude?
    a. GEO
    b. MEO
    c. LEO
    d. HEO

32. MEO satellites orbit _____ Van Allen belts.
    a. In the
    b. Between the
    c. Above both
    d. Below both

33. Transmission from the Earth to the satellite is called the _____.
   a. Footlink
   b. Up print
   c. Downlink
   d. Uplink

34. The _____ is not used for voice communication.
   a. IS-95 system
   b. Globalstar system
   c. GPS
   d. Iridium system

35. _____ is often used for navigation purposes.
   a. AMPS
   b. IS-95
   c. Iridium
   d. GPS

36. An LEO satellite has _____ orbit.
   a. An equatorial
   b. An inclined
   c. A polar
   d. All the above

37. Teledesic is a _____ LEO satellite system.
   a. Little
   b. Big
   c. Passband
   d. Broadband

38. _____ has 66 satellites in six LEOs.
   a. Globalstar
   b. Iridium
   c. Teledesic
   d. GPS

39. _____ has 48 satellites in six polar orbits.
   a. Globalstar
   b. Iridium
   c. Teledesic
   d. GPS

40. _____ will have 288 satellites in 12 polar orbits.
   a. Globalstar
   b. Iridium
   c. Teledesic
   d. GPS

Exercises

41. Draw a cell pattern with a frequency reuse factor of 3.

42. What is the maximum number of callers in each cell in AMPS?

43. What is the maximum number of callers in each cell in an IS-136 (D-AMPS) system?

44. What is the maximum number of callers in each cell in a GSM?

45. What is the maximum number of callers in each cell in an IS-95 system?

46. What is the efficiency of AMPS in terms of callers per megahertz of bandwidth?

47. What is the efficiency of D-AMPS in terms of callers per megahertz of bandwidth?

48. What is the efficiency of GSM in terms of callers per megahertz of bandwidth?

49. What is the efficiency of IS-95 in terms of callers per megahertz of bandwidth?

50. Guess the relationship between a 3-KHz voice channel and a 30-KHz modulated channel in a stem using AMPS.

51. How many slots are sent in each second in a system using D-AMPS? How many slots are sent by each user in 1 s?

52. Can you find out why the basic user data rate is only 13 Kbps for GSM?

53. In IS-95, how many digital channels are available in each cell?

54. What happens if a satellite is placed above the GEO?

55. Use Kepler's formula to check the accuracy of a given period and altitude for a GPS satellite.

56. Use Kepler's formula to check the accuracy of a given period and altitude for an Iridium satellite.

57. Use Kepler's formula to check the accuracy of a given period and altitude for a Globalstar satellite.

CHAPTER 18

Virtual Circuit Switching: Frame Relay and ATM

This is our last chapter on the data link layer. Previously, we introduced flow and error control and data link layer protocols such as HDLC. We explained multiple-access mechanism in wired LANs and wireless LANs. We need to discuss one last issue: switching in WANs.

First we introduce the concept of **virtual circuit switching,** the technique used in a switched WAN. We show how it is different from circuit switching at the physical layer.

Two common WAN technologies use virtual circuit switching. Frame Relay is a relatively high-speed protocol that can provide some services not available in other WAN technologies such as DSL, cable TV, and T lines.

ATM, as a high-speed protocol, can be the superhighway of communication when it deploys physical layer carriers such as SONET.

18.1 VIRTUAL CIRCUIT SWITCHING

In Chapter 8, we discussed circuit switching. Circuit switching is mostly used at the physical layer to create *real* circuits, dedicated lines, between a source and destination. Real circuits were designed for real-time audio (telephony). For data communication, packet switching networks were designed; data are packetized and sent packet by packet. The main difference between a circuit-switched and a packet-switched network is that in the latter the links are shared, channelized between different communication paths. A link between switch 1 and 2 may carry several packets at the same time, each sent by a different source and going to different destinations.

Packet switching uses two different approaches: the datagram approach and the virtual circuit approach. The datagram approach is mostly used in the network layer; therefore, we postpone its discussion until later chapters. The virtual circuit approach is a data link layer technology; we discuss this approach in this chapter.

Figure 18.1 is an example of a virtual circuit wide area network. The network has switches that allow traffic from sources to destinations. A source or destination can be a computer, router, bridge, or any other device that connects other networks (LANs, for example) to the switched WAN.

Figure 18.1   *Virtual circuit wide area network*

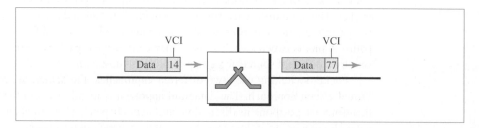

Global Addressing

A source or a destination needs to have a global address, an address that can be unique in the scope of the WAN or internationally if the WAN is used as part of an international network. However, we will see that global addressing in virtual circuit networks is used only to create a virtual circuit identifier, as discussed next.

Virtual Circuit Identifier

The identifier that is actually used for data transfer is called the **virtual circuit identifier (VCI).** A VCI, unlike a global address, is a small number that only has switch scope; it is used by a frame between two switches. When a frame arrives at a switch, it has one VCI; when it leaves, it has another. Figure 18.2 shows how the VCI in a data frame changes from one switch to another.

Figure 18.2   *VCI*

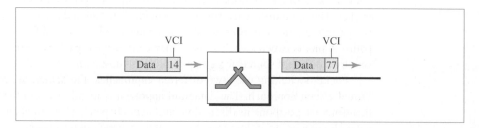

Note that a VCI does not need to be a large number since each switch can use its own unique set of VCIs.

Three Phases

To communicate, a source and destination need to go through three phases: **setup, data transfer,** and **teardown,** as shown in Figure 18.3.

Figure 18.3 *VCI phases*

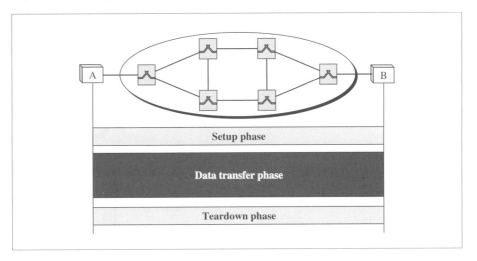

In the setup phase, the source and destination use their global addresses to help switches make table entries for the connection. In the teardown phase, the source and destination inform the switches to erase the corresponding entry. Data transfer occurs between these two phases. We first discuss the data transfer phase, which is more straightforward; we then talk about the setup and teardown phases.

Data Transfer Phase

To transfer a frame from a source to its destination, all switches need to have a table entry for this virtual circuit. The table, in its simplest form, has four columns. This means that the switch holds four pieces of information for each virtual circuit that is already set up. We show later how the switches make their table entries, but for the moment we assume that each switch has a table with entries for all active virtual circuits. Figure 18.4 shows such a switch and its corresponding table.

The figure shows a frame arriving at port 1 with a VCI of 14. When the frame arrives, the switch looks in its table to find port 1, and VCI 14. When it is found, the switch knows to change the VCI to 22 and send out the frame from port 3.

Figure 18.5 shows how a frame from source A reaches destination B and how its VCI changes during the trip. Each switch changes the VCI and routes the frame.

The data transfer phase is active until the source sends all its frames to the destination. The procedure at the switch is the same for each frame of a message. The process creates a virtual circuit, not a real circuit, between the source and destination.

Setup Phase

The setup phase is interesting. How does a switch create an entry for a virtual circuit? There are two approaches here: the **permanent virtual circuit (PVC)** approach and the **switched virtual circuit (SVC)** approach.

Figure 18.4   Switch and table

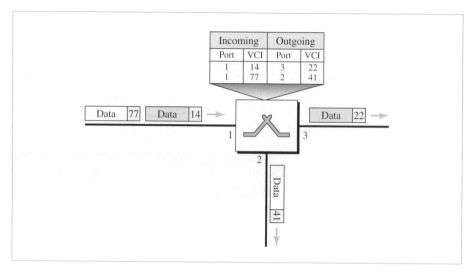

Figure 18.5   Source-to-destination data transfer

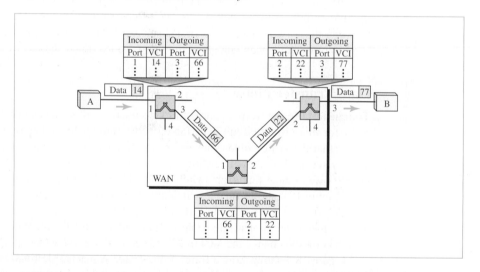

Permanent Virtual Circuit

A source and a destination may choose to have a permanent virtual circuit. In this case, the connection setup is simple. The corresponding table entry is recorded for all switches by the administrator (of course remotely and electronically). An outgoing VCI is given to the source, and an incoming VCI is given to the destination. The source always uses this VCI to send frames to that particular destination; the destination knows that the frame is coming from that particular source if the frame carries the corresponding incoming VCI. If there is a need for duplex communication, two virtual circuits are established. The PVC is like a leased telephone line. If there is a leased telephone line between party A and party B, A can pick up the receiver and talk with B without dialing.

Switched Virtual Circuit

PVC connections have two drawbacks. First, they are costly because two parties pay for the connection all the time even when it is not in use. Second, a connection is created from one source to one single destination. If a source needs connections with several destinations, it needs a PVC for each connection. An alternate approach is the SVC. The SVC creates a temporary, short connection that exists only when data are being transferred between source and destination. An SVC requires a connection phase.

Suppose source A needs to create a virtual circuit to B. Two steps are required, the setup request and the acknowledgment.

Setup Request A setup request frame is sent from the source to the destination. Figure 18.6 shows the process.

Figure 18.6 *SVC setup request*

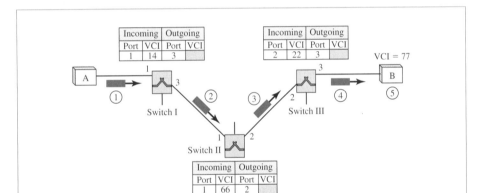

1. Source A sends a setup frame to switch I.
2. Switch I receives the setup request frame. It knows that a frame going from A to B goes out through port 3. How the switch has this information is a point covered in future chapters. The switch, in the setup phase, acts as a router; it has a routing table which is different from the switching table. For the moment, assume that it knows the output port. The switch creates an entry in its table for this virtual circuit, but it is only able to fill three of the four columns. The switch assigns the incoming port (1) and chooses an available incoming VCI (14) and the outgoing port (3). It does not yet know the outgoing VCI, which will be found during the acknowledgment step. The switch then forwards the frame through port 3 to switch II.
3. Switch II receives the setup request frame. The same events happen here as at switch I; three columns of the table are completed: in this case, incoming port (1), incoming VCI (66), and outgoing port (2).

4. Switch III receives the setup request frame. Again, three columns are completed: incoming port (2), incoming VCI (22), and outgoing port (3).

5. Destination B receives the setup frame, and if it is ready to receive frames from A, it assigns a VCI to the incoming frames that come from A, in this case 77. This VCI lets the destination know that the frames come from A, and not other sources.

Acknowledgment   A special frame, called the acknowledgment frame, can complete the entries in the switching tables. Figure 18.7 shows the process.

Figure 18.7   *SVC setup acknowledgment*

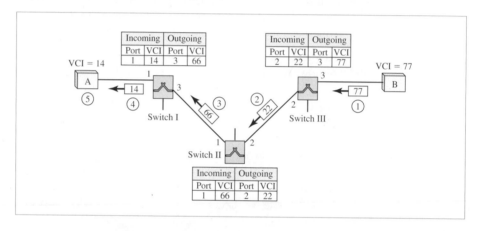

1. The destination sends an acknowledgment to switch III. The acknowledgment carries the global source and destination addresses so the switch knows which entry in the table is to be completed. The frame also carries VCI 77, chosen by the destination as the incoming VCI for frames from A. Switch III uses this VCI to complete the outgoing VCI column for this entry. Note that 77 is the incoming VCI for destination B, but outgoing VCI for switch III.

2. Switch III sends an acknowledgment to switch II that contains its incoming VCI in the table, chosen in the previous step. Switch II uses this as the outgoing VCI in the table.

3. Switch II sends an acknowledgment to switch I that contains its incoming VCI in the table, chosen in the previous step. Switch I uses this as the outgoing VCI in the table.

4. Finally switch I sends an acknowledgment to source A that contains its incoming VCI in the table, chosen in the previous step.

5. The source uses this as the outgoing VCI for the data frames to be sent to destination B.

Teardown Phase

In this phase, source A, after sending all frames to B, sends a special frame called a teardown request. Destination B responds with a teardown confirmation frame. All switches erase the corresponding entry from their tables.

18.2 FRAME RELAY

Frame Relay is a virtual circuit wide area network that was designed to respond to demands for a new type of WAN in the late 1980s and early 1990s.

1. Prior to Frame Relay, some organizations were using a virtual circuit switching network called **X.25** that performed switching at the network layer. For example, the Internet, which needs wide area networks to carry its packets from one place to another, used X.25. X.25 is still being used by the Internet, but it is being replaced by other WANs. However, X.25 has several drawbacks:

   a. X.25 has a low 64-Kbps data rate. By the 1990s, there was a need for higher-data-rate WANs.

   b. X.25 has extensive flow and error control at both the data link layer and the network layer. This was so because X.25 was designed in 1970s, when the available transmission media were more prone to errors. Flow and error control at both layers create a large overhead and slow down transmissions. X.25 requires acknowledgments for both data link layer frames and network layer packets that are sent between nodes and between source and destination.

   c. Originally X.25 was designed for private use, not for the Internet. X.25 has its own network layer. This means that the user's data are encapsulated in the network-layer packets of X.25. The Internet, however, has its own network layer, which means if the Internet wants to use X.25, the Internet must deliver its network-layer packet, called a datagram, to X.25 for encapsulation in the X.25 packet. This doubles the overhead.

2. Disappointed with X.25, some organizations started their own private WAN by leasing T-1 or T-3 lines from public service providers. This approach also has some drawbacks.

   a. If an organization has n branches spread over an area, it needs $n(n-1)/2$ T-1 or T-3 lines. The organization pays for all these lines although it may use the lines only 10 percent of the time. This can be very costly.

   b. The services provided by T-1 and T-3 lines assume that the user has fixed-rate data all the time. For example, a T-1 line is designed for a user who wants to use the line at a consistent 1.544 Mbps. This type of service is not suitable for the many users today that need to send **bursty data.** For example, a user may want to send data at 6 Mbps for 2 s, 0 Mbps (nothing) for 7 s, and 3.44 Mbps for 1 s for a total of 15.44 Mbits during a period of 10 s. Although the average data rate is still 1.544 Mbps, the T-1 line cannot accept this type of demand because it is designed for fixed-rate data, not bursty data. Bursty data requires what is called **bandwidth on demand.** The user needs different bandwidth allocations at different times.

In response to the above drawbacks, Frame Relay was designed. Frame Relay is a wide area network with the following features:

1. Frame Relay operates at a higher speed (1.544 Mbps and recently 44.376 Mbps). This means that it can easily be used instead of a mesh of T-1 or T-3 lines.

2. Frame Relay operates in just the physical and data link layers. This means it can easily be used as a backbone network to provide services to protocols that already have a network layer protocol, such as the Internet.

3. Frame Relay allows bursty data.

4. Frame Relay allows a frame size of 9000 bytes, which can accommodate all local area network frame sizes.

5. Frame Relay is less expensive than other traditional WANs.

6. Frame Relay has error detection at the data link layer only. There is no flow control or error control. There is not even a retransmission policy if a frame is damaged; it is silently dropped. Frame Relay was designed in this way to provide fast transmission capability for more reliable media and for those protocols that have flow and error control at the higher layers.

Architecture

Frame Relay provides permanent virtual circuits and switched virtual circuits. Figure 18.8 shows an example of a Frame Relay network connected to the Internet. The routers are used, as we will see in Chapter 19, to connect LANs and WANs in the Internet. In the figure, Frame Relay WAN is used as one link in the global Internet.

Figure 18.8   *Frame Relay network*

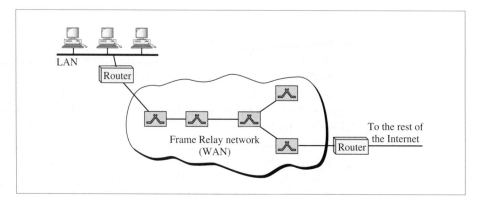

Virtual Circuits

Frame Relay is a virtual circuit network. A virtual circuit in Frame Relay is identified by a number called a **data link connection identifier (DLCI).** Frame Relay uses both PVCs and SVCs.

VCIs in Frame Relay are called DLCIs.

Switches

Each switch in a Frame Relay network has a table to route frames. The table matches an incoming port–DLCI combination with an outgoing port–DLCI combination as we described for general virtual circuit networks. The only difference is that VCIs are replaced by DLCIs.

Frame Relay Layers

Figure 18.9 shows the Frame Relay layers. Frame Relay has only physical and data link layers.

Figure 18.9 *Frame Relay layers*

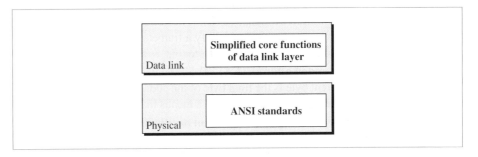

Frame Relay operates only at the physical and data link layers.

Physical Layer

No specific protocol is defined for the physical layer in Frame Relay. Instead, it is left to the implementer to use whatever is available. Frame Relay supports any of the protocols recognized by ANSI.

Data Link Layer

At the data link layer, Frame Relay employs a simplified version of HDLC. The simpler version is used because HDLC provides extensive error and flow control fields that are not needed in Frame Relay.

Figure 18.10 shows the format of a Frame Relay frame. The frame is similar to that of HDLC. In fact, the flag, FCS, and information fields are the same. However, the control field is missing because this field was needed for flow and error control which is not provided by Frame Relay. The address field defines the DLCI as well as some bits used to control congestion and traffic.

Figure 18.10 *Frame Relay frame*

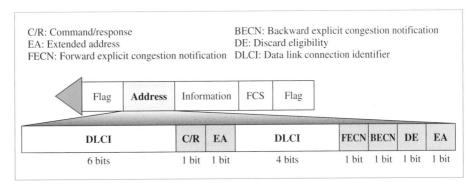

The descriptions of the fields are as follows:

- **Address (DLCI) field.** The first 6 bits of the first byte make up part 1 of the DLCI. The second part of the DLCI uses the first 4 bits of the second byte. These bits are part of the 10-bit data link connection identifier defined by the standard. The function of the DLCI was discussed previously. We will discuss extended addressing at the end of this section.

- **Command/response (C/R).** The command/response (C/R) bit is provided to allow upper layers to identify a frame as either a command or a response. It is not used by the Frame Relay protocol.

- **Extended address (EA).** The extended address (EA) bit indicates whether the current byte is the final byte of the address. An EA of 0 means that another address byte is to follow. An EA of 1 means that the current byte is the final one.

- **Forward explicit congestion notification (FECN).** The **forward explicit congestion notification (FECN)** bit can be set by any switch to indicate that traffic is congested in the direction in which the frame is traveling. This bit informs the destination that congestion has occurred. We will discuss the use of this bit when we discuss congestion control in Chapter 23.

- **Backward explicit congestion notification (BECN).** The **backward explicit congestion notification (BECN)** bit is set to indicate a congestion problem in the direction opposite to the one in which the frame is traveling. This bit informs the sender that congestion has occurred. We will discuss the use of this bit when we discuss congestion control in Chapter 23.

- **Discard eligibility (DE).** The **discard eligibility (DE)** bit indicates the priority level of the frame. In emergency situations, switches may have to discard frames to relieve bottlenecks and keep the network from collapsing due to overload. When set (DE 1), this bit tells the network to discard this frame if there is congestion. This bit can be set either by the sender of the frames (user) or by any switch in the network. We will discuss the use of this bit when we discuss congestion control in Chapter 23.

> **Frame Relay does not provide flow or error control; they must be provided by the upper-layer protocols.**

Extended Address

To increase the range of DLCIs, the Frame Relay address has been extended from the original 2-byte address to 3- or 4-byte addresses. Figure 18.11 shows the different addresses. Note that the EA field defines the number of bytes; it is 1 in the last byte of the address, and it is 0 in the other bytes. Note that in the 3- and 4-byte formats, the bit before the last bit is set to 0.

FRADs

To handle frames arriving from other protocols, Frame Relay uses a device called a **Frame Relay assembler/disassembler (FRAD).** A FRAD assembles and disassembles frames coming from other protocols to allow them to be carried by Frame Relay frames.

Figure 18.11   *Three address formats*

DLCI			C/R	EA=0
DLCI	FECN	BECN	DE	EA=1

a. Two-byte address (10-bit DLCI)

DLCI			C/R	EA=0
DLCI	FECN	BECN	DE	EA=0
DLCI			0	EA=1

b. Three-byte address (16-bit DLCI)

DLCI			C/R	EA=0
DLCI	FECN	BECN	DE	EA=0
DLCI				EA=0
DLCI			0	EA=1

c. Four-byte address (23-bit DLCI)

Figure 18.12   *FRAD*

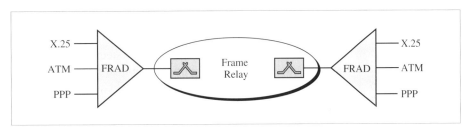

A FRAD can be implemented as a separate device or as part of a switch. Figure 18.12 shows two FRADs connected to a Frame Relay network.

VOFR

Frame Relay networks offer an option called **Voice Over Frame Relay (VOFR)** that sends voice through the network. Voice is digitized using PCM and then compressed. The result is sent as data frames over the network. This feature allows the inexpensive sending of voice over long distances. However, note that the quality of voice is not as good as voice over a circuit-switched network such as the telephone network. Also, the varying delay mentioned earlier sometimes corrupts real-time voice.

LMI

Frame Relay was originally designed to provide PVC connections. There was not, therefore, a provision for controlling or managing interfaces. **Local management information (LMI)** is a protocol added recently to the Frame Relay protocol to provide more management features. In particular, LMI can provide

- A keep-alive mechanism to check if data are flowing.
- A multicast mechanism to allow a local end system to send frames to more than one remote end system.
- A mechanism to allow an end system to check the status of a switch (e.g., to see if the switch is congested).

Congestion Control and Quality of Service

One of the nice features of Frame Relay is that it provides **congestion control** and **quality of service.** We have not discussed these features yet. In Chapter 23, we introduce these two important aspects of networking and discuss how they are implemented in Frame Relay and some other networks.

18.3   ATM

Asynchronous Transfer Mode (ATM) is the **cell relay** protocol designed by the ATM Forum and adopted by the ITU-T. The combination of ATM and SONET will allow high-speed interconnection of all the world's networks. In fact, ATM can be thought of as the "highway" of the information superhighway.

Design Goals

Among the challenges faced by the designers of ATM, six stand out.

1. Foremost is the need for a transmission system to optimize the use of high-data-rate transmission media, in particular optical fiber. In addition to offering large bandwidths, newer transmission media and equipment are dramatically less susceptible to noise degradation. A technology is needed to take advantage of both factors and thereby maximize data rates.

2. The system must interface with existing systems and provide wide area interconnectivity between them without lowering their effectiveness or requiring their replacement.

3. The design must be implemented inexpensively so that cost would not be a barrier to adoption. If ATM is to become the backbone of international communications, as intended, it must be available at low cost to every user who wants it.

4. The new system must be able to work with and support the existing telecommunications hierarchies (local loops, local providers, long-distance carriers, and so on).

5. The new system must be connection-oriented to ensure accurate and predictable delivery.

6. Last but not least, one objective is to move as many of the functions to hardware as possible (for speed) and eliminate as many software functions as possible (again for speed).

Problems

Before we discuss the solutions to these design requirements, it is useful to examine some of the problems associated with existing systems.

Frame Networks

Before ATM, data communications at the data link layer had been based on frame switching and frame networks. Different protocols use frames of varying size and intricacy. As networks become more complex, the information that must be carried in the header becomes more extensive. The result is larger and larger headers relative to the size of the data unit. In response, some protocols have enlarged the size of the data unit to make header use more efficient (sending more data with the same size header). Unfortunately, large data fields create waste. If there is not much information to transmit, much of the field goes unused. To improve utilization, some protocols provide variable frame sizes to users.

Mixed Network Traffic

As you can imagine, the variety of frame sizes makes traffic unpredictable. Switches, multiplexers, and routers must incorporate elaborate software systems to manage the various sizes of frames. A great deal of header information must be read, and each bit counted and evaluated to ensure the integrity of every frame. Internetworking among the different frame networks is slow and expensive at best, and impossible at worst.

Another problem is that of providing consistent data rate delivery when frame sizes are unpredictable and can vary so dramatically. To get the most out of broadband technology, traffic must be time-division-multiplexed onto shared paths. Imagine the results of multiplexing frames from two networks with different requirements (and frame designs) onto one link (see Fig. 18.13). What happens when line 1 uses large frames (usually data frames) while line 2 uses very small frames (the norm for audio and video information)?

Figure 18.13 *Multiplexing using different frame sizes*

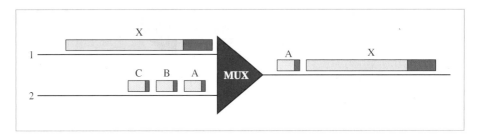

If line 1's gigantic frame X arrives at the multiplexer even a moment earlier than line 2's frames, the multiplexer puts frame X onto the new path first. After all, even if line 2's frames have priority, the multiplexer has no way of knowing to wait for them and processes the frame that has arrived. Frame A must therefore wait for the entire X bit stream to move into place before it can follow. The sheer size of X creates an unfair delay for frame A. The same imbalance can affect all the frames from line 2.

Because audio and video frames ordinarily are small, mixing them with conventional data traffic often creates unacceptable delays of this type and makes shared frame links unusable for audio and video information. Traffic must travel over different paths, in much the same way that automobile and train traffic does. But to fully utilize broad bandwidth links, we need to be able to send all kinds of traffic over the same links.

Cell Networks

Many of the problems associated with frame internetworking are solved by adopting a concept called cell networking. A cell is a small data unit of fixed size. In a **cell network,** which uses the **cell** as the basic unit of data exchange, all data are loaded into identical cells that can be transmitted with complete predictability and uniformity. As frames of different sizes and formats reach the cell network from a tributary network, they are split into multiple small data units of equal length and are loaded into cells. The cells are then multiplexed with other cells and routed through the cell network. Because each cell is the same size and all are small, the problems associated with multiplexing different-sized frames are avoided.

> A cell network uses the cell as the basic unit of data exchange. A cell is defined as a small, fixed-sized block of information.

Figure 18.14 shows the multiplexer from Figure 18.13 with the two lines sending cells instead of frames. Frame X has been segmented into three cells: X, Y, and Z. Only the first cell from line 1 gets put on the link before the first cell from line 2. The cells from the two lines are interleaved so that none suffers a long delay.

Figure 18.14   *Multiplexing using cells*

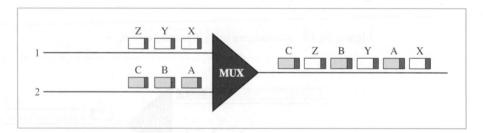

A second point in this same scenario is that the high speed of the links coupled with the small size of the cells means that, despite interleaving, cells from each line arrive at their respective destinations in an approximation of a continuous stream (much as a movie appears to your brain to be continuous action when in fact it is really a series of separate still photographs). In this way, a cell network can handle real-time transmissions, such as a phone call, without the parties being aware of the segmentation or multiplexing at all.

Asynchronous TDM

ATM uses asynchronous time-division multiplexing—that is why it is called Asynchronous Transfer Mode—to multiplex cells coming from different channels. It uses fixed-size slots (size of a cell). ATM multiplexers fill a slot with a cell from any input channel that has a cell; the slot is empty if none of the channels has a cell to send.

Figure 18.15 shows how cells from three inputs are multiplexed. At the first tick of the clock, channel 2 has no cell (empty input slot), so the multiplexer fills the slot with

Figure 18.15   *ATM multiplexing*

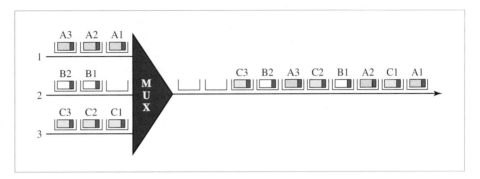

a cell from the third channel. When all the cells from all the channels are multiplexed, the output slots are empty.

Architecture

ATM is a cell-switched network. The user access devices, called the endpoints, are connected through a **user-to-network interface (UNI)** to the switches inside the network. The switches are connected through **network-to-network interfaces (NNIs).** Figure 18.16 shows an example of an ATM network.

Figure 18.16   *Architecture of an ATM network*

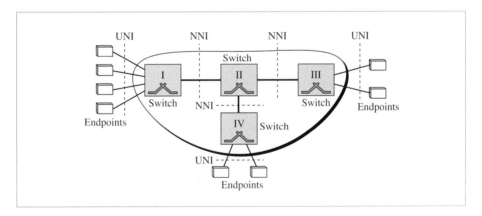

Virtual Connection

Connection between two endpoints is accomplished through transmission paths (TPs), virtual paths (VPs), and virtual circuits (VCs). A **transmission path (TP)** is the physical connection (wire, cable, satellite, and so on) between an endpoint and a switch or between two switches. Think of two switches as two cities. A transmission path is the set of all highways that directly connects the two cities.

A transmission path is divided into several virtual paths. A **virtual path (VP)** provides a connection or a set of connections between two switches. Think of a virtual path as a highway that connects two cities. Each highway is a virtual path; the set of all highways is the transmission path.

Cell networks are based on **virtual circuits (VCs).** All cells belonging to a single message follow the same virtual circuit and remain in their original order until they reach their destination. Think of a virtual circuit as the lanes of a highway (virtual path). Figure 18.17 shows the relationship between a transmission path (a physical connection), virtual paths (a combination of virtual circuits that are bundled together because parts of their paths are the same), and virtual circuits that logically connect two points.

Figure 18.17 *TP, VPs, and VCs*

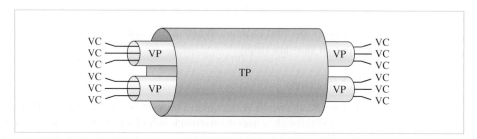

To better understand the concept of VPs and VCs, look at Figure 18.18. In this figure, eight endpoints are communicating using four VCs. However, the first two VCs seem to share the same virtual path from switch I to switch III, so it is reasonable to bundle these two VCs together to form one VP. On the other hand, it is clear that the other two VCs share the same path from switch I to switch IV, so it is also reasonable to combine them to form one VP.

Figure 18.18 *Example of VPs and VCs*

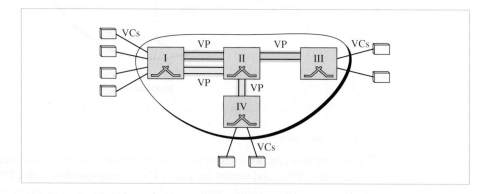

Identifiers

In a virtual circuit network, to route data from one endpoint to another, the virtual connections need to be identified. For this purpose, the designers of ATM created a hierarchical identifier with two levels: a **virtual path identifier (VPI)** and a **virtual circuit identifier (VCI).** The VPI defines the specific VP, and the VCI defines a particular VC inside the VP. The VPI is the same for all virtual connections that are bundled (logically) into one VP.

Note that a virtual connection is defined by a pair of numbers: the VPI and the VCI.

Figure 18.19 shows the VPIs and VCIs for a transmission path. The rationale for dividing an identifier into two parts will become clear when we discuss routing in an ATM network.

Figure 18.19   *Connection identifiers*

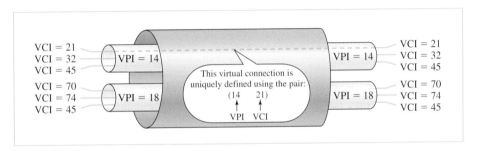

The lengths of the VPIs for UNIs and NNIs are different. In a UNI, the VPI is 8 bits, whereas in an NNI, the VPI is 12 bits. The length of the VCI is the same in both interfaces (16 bits). We therefore can say that a virtual connection is identified by 24 bits in a UNI and by 28 bits in an NNI (see Fig. 18.20).

The whole idea behind dividing a virtual connection identifier into two parts is to allow hierarchical routing. Most of the switches in a typical ATM network are routed using VPIs. The switches at the boundaries of the network, those that interact directly with the endpoint devices, use both VPIs and VCIs.

Figure 18.20   *Virtual connection identifiers in UNIs and NNIs*

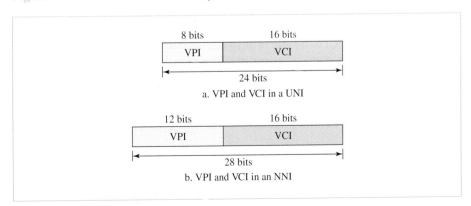

Cells

The basic data unit in an ATM network is called a cell. A cell is only 53 bytes long with 5 bytes allocated to header and 48 bytes carrying payload (user data may be less than 48 bytes). We will study in detail the fields of a cell, but for the moment it suffices to say that most of the header is occupied by the VPI and VCI that define the virtual connection through which a cell should travel from an endpoint to a switch or from a switch to another switch. Figure 18.21 shows the cell structure.

Figure 18.21   *An ATM cell*

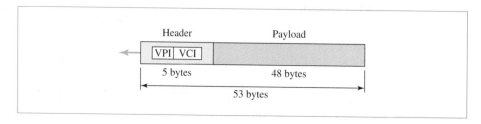

Connection Establishment and Release

Like Frame Relay, ATM uses two types of connections: PVC and SVC.

PVC   A permanent virtual circuit connection is established between two endpoints by the network provider. The VPIs and VCIs are defined for the permanent connections, and the values are entered for the tables of each switch.

SVC   In a switched virtual circuit connection, each time an endpoint wants to make a connection with another endpoint, a new virtual circuit must be established. ATM cannot do the job by itself, but needs network layer addresses and the services of another protocol (such as IP). The signaling mechanism of this other protocol makes a connection request using the network layer addresses of the two endpoints. The actual mechanism depends on the network layer protocol.

Switching

ATM uses switches to route the cell from a source endpoint to the destination endpoint. A switch routes the cell using both the VPIs and the VCIs. The routing requires the whole identifier. Figure 18.22 shows how a VPC switch routes the cell. A cell with a VPI of 153 and VCI of 67 arrives at switch interface (port) 1. The switch checks its switching table, which stores six pieces of information per row: arrival interface number, incoming VPI, incoming VCI, corresponding outgoing interface number, the new VPI, and the new VCI. The switch finds the entry with the interface 1, VPI 153, and VCI 67 and discovers that the combination corresponds to output interface 3, VPI 140, and VCI 92. It changes the VPI and VCI in the header to 140 and 92, respectively, and sends the cell out through interface 3.

Switching Fabric

The switching technology has created many interesting features to increase the speed of switches to handle data. Because switches are used in both data link layer and

Figure 18.22   *Routing with a switch*

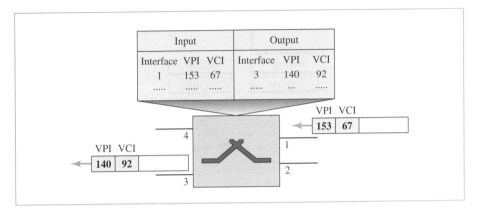

network layer, we do not discuss these variations here. For more information, see Appendix F.

ATM Layers

The ATM standard defines three layers. They are, from top to bottom, the application adaptation layer, the ATM layer, and the physical layer (see Fig. 18.23).

Figure 18.23   *ATM layers*

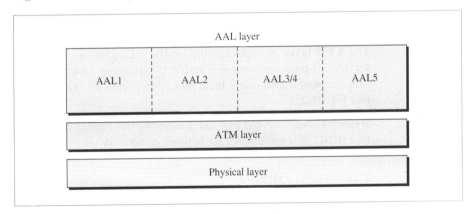

The endpoints use all three layers while the switches use only the two bottom layers (see Fig. 18.24).

Physical Layer

Like Ethernet and wireless LANs, ATM cells can be carried by any physical layer carrier.

SONET   The original design of ATM was based on **SONET** (see Chapter 9) as the physical layer carrier. SONET is preferred for two reasons. First, the high data rate

Figure 18.24   *ATM layers in endpoint devices and switches*

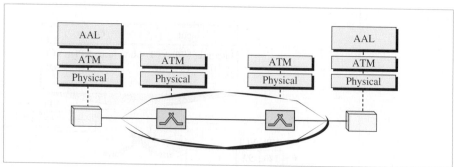

of SONET's carrier reflects the design and philosophy of ATM. Second, in using SONET, the boundaries of cells can be clearly defined. As we saw in Chapter 9, SONET specifies the use of a pointer to define the beginning of a payload. If the beginning of the first ATM cell is defined, the rest of the cells in the same payload can easily be identified because there are no gaps between cells. Just count 53 bytes ahead to find the next cell.

Other Physical Technologies   ATM does not limit the physical layer to SONET. Other technologies, even wireless, may be used. However, the problem of cell boundaries must be solved. One solution is for the receiver to guess the end of the cell and apply the CRC to the 5-byte header. If there is no error, the end of the cell is found, to a high probability, correctly. Count 52 bytes back to find the beginning of the cell.

ATM Layer

The **ATM layer** provides routing, traffic management, switching, and multiplexing services. It processes outgoing traffic by accepting 48-byte segments from the AAL sublayers and transforming them into 53-byte cells by the addition of a 5-byte header (see Fig. 18.25).

Header Format   ATM uses two formats for this header, one for user-to-network interface (UNI) cells and another for network-to-network interface (NNI) cells. Figure 18.26

Figure 18.25   *ATM layer*

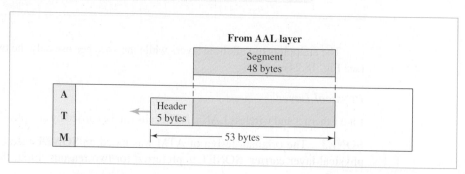

Figure 18.26   *ATM headers*

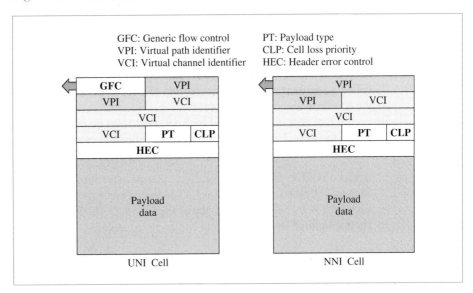

shows these headers in the byte-by-byte format preferred by the ITU-T (each row represents a byte).

- **Generic flow control (GFC).** The 4-bit GFC field provides flow control at the UNI level. The ITU-T has determined that this level of flow control is not necessary at the NNI level. In the NNI header, therefore, these bits are added to the VPI. The longer VPI allows more virtual paths to be defined at the NNI level. The format for this additional VPI has not yet been determined.

- **Virtual path identifier (VPI).** The VPI is an 8-bit field in a UNI cell and a 12-bit field in an NNI cell (see above).

- **Virtual channel identifier (VCI).** The VCI is a 16-bit field in both frames.

- **Payload type (PT).** In the three-bit PT field, the first bit defines the payload as user data or managerial information. The interpretation of the last 2 bits depends on the first bit.

- **Cell loss priority (CLP).** The 1-bit CLP field is provided for congestion control. A cell with its CLP bit set to 1 must be retained as long as there are cells with a CLP of 0. We discuss congestion control and quality of service in an ATM network in Chapter 23.

- **Header error correction (HEC).** The HEC is a code computed for the first 4 bytes of the header. It is a CRC with the divisor $x^8 + x^2 + x + 1$ that is used to correct single-bit errors and a large class of multiple-bit errors.

Application Adaptation Layer (AAL)

The **application adaptation layer (AAL)** was designed to enable two ATM concepts. First, ATM must accept any type of payload, both data frames and streams of bits. A data frame can come from an upper-layer protocol that creates a clearly defined frame to be sent to a carrier network such as ATM. A good example is the Internet. ATM must also carry multimedia payload. It can accept continuous bit streams and break them into chunks to be encapsulated into a cell at the ATM layer. AAL uses two sublayers to accomplish these tasks.

Whether the data are a data frame or a stream of bits, the payload must be segmented into 48-byte segments to be carried by a cell. At the destination, these segments need to be reassembled to recreate the original payload. The AAL defines a sublayer, called a **segmentation and reassembly (SAR)** sublayer, to do so. Segmentation is at the source; reassembly, at the destination.

Before data are segmented by SAR, they must be prepared to guarantee the integrity of the data. This is done by a sublayer called the **convergence sublayer (CS).**

ATM defines four versions of the AAL: **AAL1, AAL2, AAL3/4,** and **AAL5.**

AAL1   **AAL1** supports applications that transfer information at constant bit rates, such as video and voice. It allows ATM to connect existing digital telephone networks such as voice channels and T-lines. Figure 18.27 shows how a bit stream of data is chopped into 47-byte chunks and encapsulated in cells.

Figure 18.27   *AAL1*

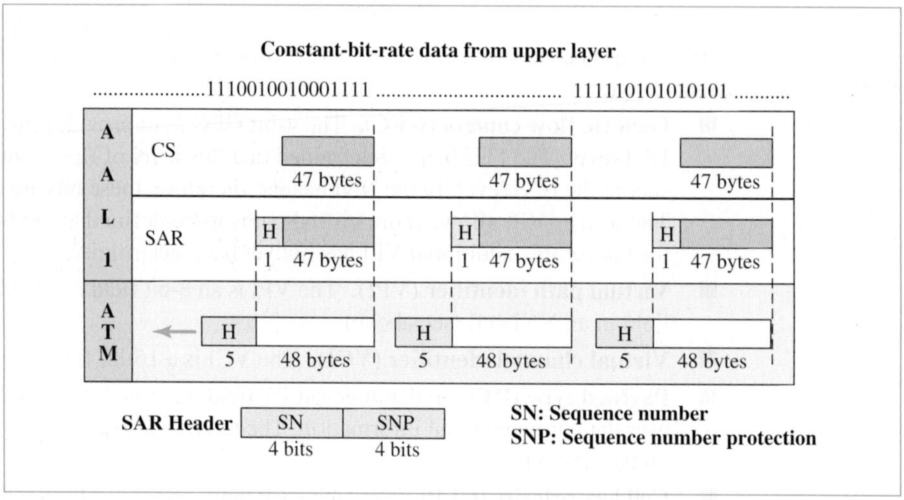

The CS sublayer divides the bit stream into 47-byte segments and passes them to the SAR sublayer below. Note that the CS sublayer does not add a header.

The SAR sublayer adds 1 byte of header and passes the 48-byte segment to the ATM layer. The header has two fields:

■ **Sequence number (SN).** This 4-bit field defines a sequence number to order the bits. The first bit is sometimes used for timing, which leaves 3 bits for sequencing (modulo 8).

■ **Sequence number protection (SNP).** The second 4-bit field protects the first field. The first 3 bits automatically correct the SN field. The last bit is a parity bit that detects error over all 8 bits.

■ **Length indicator (LI).** This field defines how much of the packet is data, not padding.

■ **CRC.** The last 10 bits of the trailer is a CRC for the entire data unit.

AAL5 AAL3/4 provides comprehensive sequencing and error control mechanisms that are not necessary for every application. For these applications, the designers of ATM have provided a fifth AAL sublayer, called the **simple and efficient adaptation layer (SEAL). AAL5** assumes that all cells belonging to a single message travel sequentially and that control functions are included in the upper layers of the sending application. Figure 18.30 shows the AAL5 sublayer.

Figure 18.30 *AAL5*

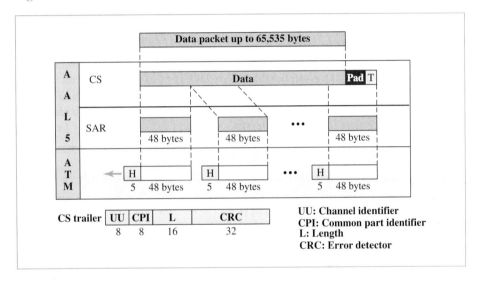

The four trailer fields in the CS layer are

■ **User-to-user (UU).** This field is used by end users, as described previously.

■ **Common part identifier (CPI).** This field is the same as defined previously.

■ **Length (L).** The 2-byte L field indicates the length of the original data.

■ **CRC.** The last 4 bytes are for error control on the entire data unit.

Congestion Control and Quality of Service

ATM has a very developed congestion control and quality of service that we discuss in Chapter 23.

ATM LANs

A lot of effort has been made to apply ATM technology to LANs. The result is the ATM LAN. We talk about ATM LANs in Appendix G.

18.4   KEY TERMS

AAL1

AAL2

AAL3/4

AAL5

application adaptation layer (AAL)

Asynchronous Transfer Mode (ATM)

ATM layer

bandwidth on demand

bursty data

cell

cell network

cell relay

congestion control

convergence sublayer (CS)

data link connection identifier (DLCI)

data transfer phase

Frame Relay

Frame Relay assembler/disassembler
   (FRAD)

Local Management Information (LMI)

network-to-network interface (NNI)

permanent virtual circuit (PVC)

quality of service (QoS)

segmentation and reassembly (SAR)

setup phase

Simple and Efficient Adaptation
   Layer (SEAL)

switched virtual circuit (SVC)

teardown phase

transmission path (TP)

user-to-network interface (UNI)

virtual circuit (VC)

virtual circuit identifier (VCI)

virtual circuit switching

virtual path (VP)

virtual path identifier (VPI)

Voice Over Frame Relay (VOFR)

X.25

18.5   SUMMARY

- ❏ Virtual circuit switching is a data link technology in which links are shared.
- ❏ A virtual circuit identifer (VCI) identifies a frame between two switches.
- ❏ The three phases in virtual circuit switching are setup, data transfer, and teardown.
- ❏ The setup phase can use the permanent virtual circuit (PVC) approach or the switched virtual circuit (SVC) approach.
- ❏ Frame Relay is a relatively high-speed, cost-effective technology that can handle bursty data.
- ❏ Both PVC and SVC connections are used in Frame Relay.
- ❏ The data link connection identifier (DLCI) identifies a virtual circuit in Frame Relay.
- ❏ Asynchronous Transfer Mode (ATM) is a cell relay protocol that, in combination with SONET, allows high-speed connections.
- ❏ A cell is a small, fixed-size block of information.
- ❏ The ATM data packet is a cell composed of 53 bytes (5 bytes of header and 48 bytes of payload).
- ❏ ATM eliminates the varying delay times associated with different-sized packets.
- ❏ ATM can handle real-time transmission.
- ❏ A user-to-network interface (UNI) is the interface between a user and an ATM switch.

❏ A network-to-network interface (NNI) is the interface between two ATM switches.

❏ In ATM, connection between two endpoints is accomplished through transmission paths (TPs), virtual paths (VPs), and virtual circuits (VCs).

❏ In ATM, a combination of a virtual path identifier (VPI) and a virtual circuit identifier identifies a virtual connection.

❏ The ATM standard defines three layers:

    a. Application adaptation layer (AAL) accepts transmissions from upper-layer services and maps them into ATM cells.

    b. ATM layer provides routing, traffic management, switching, and multiplexing services.

    c. Physical layer defines the transmission medium, bit transmission, encoding, and electrical-to-optical transformation.

❏ The AAL is divided into two sublayers: convergence sublayer (CS) and segmentation and reassembly (SAR).

❏ There are four different AALs, each for a specific data type:

    a. AAL1 for constant-bit-rate stream.

    b. AAL2 for short packets.

    c. AAL3/4 for conventional packet switching (virtual circuit approach or datagram approach).

    d. AAL5 for packets requiring no sequencing and no error control mechanism.

18.6 PRACTICE SET

Review Questions

1. Compare the format of an HDLC protocol frame with a Frame Relay protocol frame. Which fields are missing in the Frame Relay protocol frame? Which fields are added in the Frame Relay protocol frame?

2. Why is the control field from HDLC totally dropped from Frame Relay?

3. HDLC has three types of frames (I-frame, S-frame, and U-frame). Which one corresponds to the Frame Relay frame?

4. There are no sequence numbers in Frame Relay. Why?

5. Can two devices connected to the same Frame Relay network use the same DLCIs?

6. Why is Frame Relay a better solution for connecting LANs than T-1 lines?

7. Compare an SVC with a PVC.

8. Discuss the Frame Relay physical layer.

9. Why is multiplexing more efficient if all the data units are the same size?

10. How does an NNI differ from a UNI?

11. What is the relationship between TPs, VPs, and VCs?

12. How is an ATM virtual-connection identified?

13. Name the ATM layers and their functions.

Multiple-Choice Questions

14. Frame Relay operates in the _____.
    a. Physical layer
    b. Data link layer
    c. Physical and data link layers
    d. Physical, data link, and network layers

15. In the data link layer, Frame Relay uses _____.
    a. BSC protocol
    b. A simplified HDLC protocol
    c. LAPB
    d. Any ANSI standard protocol

16. Routing and switching in Frame Relay are performed by the _____ layer.
    a. Physical
    b. Data link
    c. Network
    d. (b) and (c)

17. Frame Relay is unsuitable for _____ due to possible delays in transmission resulting from variable frame sizes.
    a. Real-time video
    b. File transfers
    c. Fixed-rate data communication
    d. All the above

18. Frame Relay provides _____ connections.
    a. PVC
    b. SVC
    c. (a) and (b)
    d. None of the above

19. The Frame Relay address field is _____ in length.
    a. 4 bytes
    b. 2 bytes
    c. 3 bytes
    d. Any of the above

20. A device called a(n) _____ allows frames from an ATM network to be transmitted across a Frame Relay network.
    a. LMI
    b. VOFR
    c. FRAD
    d. DLCI

21. _____ is a protocol to control and manage interfaces in Frame Relay networks.

   a. LMI

   b. VOFR

   c. FRAD

   d. DLCI

22. _____ is a Frame Relay option that transmits voice through the network.

   a. LMI

   b. VOFR

   c. FRAD

   d. DLCI

23. In data communications, ATM is an acronym for _____.

   a. Automated Teller Machine

   b. Automatic Transmission Model

   c. Asynchronous Telecommunication Method

   d. Asynchronous Transfer Mode

24. Because ATM _____, which means that cells follow the same path, the cells do not usually arrive out of order.

   a. Is asynchronous

   b. Is multiplexed

   c. Is a network

   d. Uses virtual circuit routing

25. Which layer in ATM protocol reformats the data received from other networks?

   a. Physical

   b. ATM

   c. Application adaptation

   d. Data adaptation

26. Which layer in ATM protocol has a 53-byte cell as an end product?

   a. Physical

   b. ATM

   c. Application adaptation

   d. Cell transformation

27. Which AAL type is designed to support a data stream that has a constant bit rate?

   a. AAL1

   b. AAL2

   c. AAL3/4

   d. AAL5

28. Which AAL type is designed to support SEAL?

   a. AAL1

   b. AAL2

   c. AAL3/4

   d. AAL5

29. In an ATM network, all cells belonging to a single message follow the same _____ and remain in their original order until they reach their destination.
   a. Transmission path
   b. Virtual path
   c. Virtual circuit
   d. None of the above

30. A _____ provides a connection or a set of connections between switches.
   a. Transmission path
   b. Virtual path
   c. Virtual circuit
   d. None of the above

31. A _____ is the physical connection between an endpoint and a switch or between two switches.
   a. Transmission path
   b. Virtual path
   c. Virtual circuit
   d. None of the above

32. The VPI of a UNI is _____ bits in length.
   a. 8
   b. 12
   c. 16
   d. 24

33. The VPI of an NNI is _____ bits in length.
   a. 8
   b. 12
   c. 16
   d. 24

Exercises

34. The address field of a Frame Relay frame is 1011000100010110. What is the DLCI (in decimal)?
35. The address field of a Frame Relay frame is 101100000101001. Is this valid?
36. Find the DLCI value if the first 3 bytes received is 7C 74 E1 in hexadecimal.
37. Find the value of the 2-byte address field in hexadecimal if the DLCI is 178. Assume no congestion.
38. In Figure 18.31 a virtual connection is established between A and B. Show the DLCI for each link.
39. In Figure 18.32 a virtual connection is established between A and B. Show the corresponding entries in the tables of each switch.
40. An AAL1 layer receives data at 2 Mbps. How many cells are created per second by the ATM layer?

Figure 18.31   Exercise 38

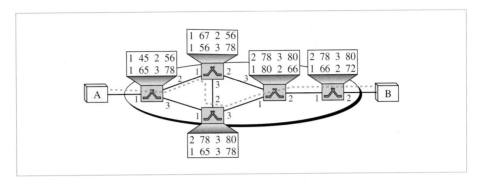

Figure 18.32   Exercise 39

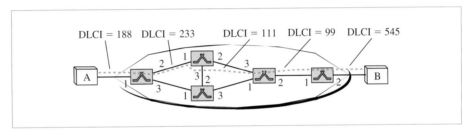

41. What is the total efficiency of ATM using AAL1 (the ratio of received bits to sent bits)?

42. If an application uses AAL3/4 and there are 47,787 bytes of data coming into the CS, how many padding bytes are necessary? How many data units get passed from the SAR to the ATM layer? How many cells are produced?

43. Does the efficiency of ATM using AAL3/4 depend on the size of the packet? Explain your answer.

44. What is the minimum number of cells resulting from an input packet in the AAL3/4 layer? What is the maximum number of cells resulting from an input packet?

45. What is the minimum number of cells resulting from an input packet in the AAL5 layer? What is the maximum number of cells resulting from an input packet?

46. Explain why padding is unnecessary in AAL1, but necessary in other AALs.

47. Using AAL3/4, show the situation where we need _____ of padding.

   a. 0 bytes (no padding)
   b. 40 bytes
   c. 43 bytes

48. Using AAL5, show the situation where we need _____ of padding.

   a. 0 bytes (no padding)
   b. 40 bytes
   c. 47 bytes

49. In a 53-byte cell, how many bytes belong to the user in the following (assume no padding)?

    a. AAL1

    b. AAL2

    c. AAL3/4 (not the first or last cell)

    d. AAL5 (not the first or last cell)

50. Complete Table 18.1 by entering the size of the data unit at the SAR sublayer for all AALs.

    Table 18.1   *Exercise 50*

Sublayer	AAL1	AAL2	AAL3/4	AAL5
SAR				

51. How many virtual connections can be defined in a UNI? How many virtual connections can be defined in an NNI?

PART 4

Network Layer

The network layer in the Internet model is responsible for carrying a packet from one computer to another; it is responsible for *host-to-host* delivery. In other words, when we send a packet from San Francisco to Miami, the two network-layer protocols in the two computers cooperate to supervise the delivery of a message.

Figure 1 shows the position of the network layer in the 5-layer Internet model. The network layer is the third layer in the model. It receives services from the data link layer and provides services to the transport layer. The main service it receives from the data link layer is the delivery of data, node-to-node. If there are N nodes between the source and destination hosts, there are N node-to-node deliveries to achieve a host-to-host delivery at the network layer.

Figure 1   *Position of network layer*

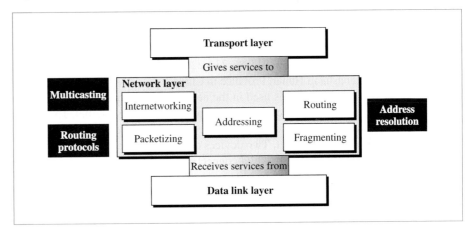

The two hosts are often separated by several physical networks. The data link layer is responsible for carrying data through a physical network; the network layer, or the internetwork layer, as it is sometimes called, is responsible for carrying the packets through the Internet, through several physical networks.

Duties

The network layer has a defined set of duties as shown in Figure 2.

Figure 2   *Network layer duties*

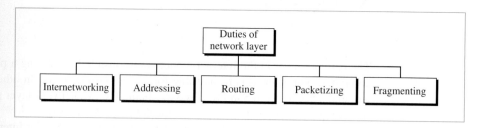

Internetworking

The main duty of the network layer is to provide internetworking, the logical gluing of heterogeneous physical networks together to look like a single network to the upper transport and application layers.

Addressing

At the network layer, we need to uniquely identify each device on the Internet to allow global communication between all devices. This is analogous to the telephone system, where each telephone subscriber has a unique telephone number (the country code and the area code as part of the identifying scheme must be considered). For example, the telephone number 011 86 731 220 8098 uniquely identifies a number in the city of Changsha in Hunan Province in China.

The addresses used in the network layer must *uniquely* and *universally* define the connection of a host (computer) or a router to the Internet. The addresses at the network layer must be unique in the sense that each address defines one, and only one, connection to the Internet. Two devices on the Internet can never have the same address. However, if a device has two connections to the Internet, it has two addresses. We devote most of Chapter 19 to addressing and all its issues.

Routing

Have you ever been faced with this dilemma? You want to reach a destination, but there are several routes from which you can choose. One route is shorter, but the road is in bad condition. Another route is longer, but safer. One route, which is normally congested during rush hour, connects you to the destination for a fee. Another route goes through a mountainous road that may be icy.

Whenever there are multiple routes to a destination, we must make a decision and choose one route. Our decision is usually based on some criteria that are important for us. If we have a car that is not so reliable, we might choose the longer road to avoid the danger associated with an icy road. If time is of the essence we might choose the shortest route. The Internet too is a combination of roads through which the IP packets travel to reach their destinations. Each IP packet can normally reach its destination via several routes. The difference is that the packet cannot choose the route; the routers connecting the LANs and WANs makes this decision. We discuss routing in Chapter 19.

Packetizing

The network layer encapsulates packets received from upper-layer protocols and makes new packets out of them. In the Internet model, packetizing is done by a network layer protocol called IP (Internetworking Protocol). We discuss this protocol along with other network-layer protocols in Chapter 20.

Fragmenting

A datagram can travel through different networks. Each router decapsulates the IP datagram from the received frame, processes it, and then encapsulates it in another frame. The format and size of the received frame depend on the protocol used by the physical network from which the frame has just arrived. The format and size of the departing frame depend on the protocol used by the physical network to which the frame is going. We discuss fragmentation in Chapter 20 when we introduce the IP protocol.

Other Issues

There are other Internet issues that are not directly related to the duties of the network, but need to be discussed in this part of the text.

Address Resolution

When a packet needs to be delivered from a host to destination, it needs to pass from one node to the next. The network layer provides only host-to-host addressing; the data link layer needs physical (MAC) addresses for node-to-node delivery. There must be a method to map these two addresses. A protocol, called the Address Resolution Protocol, ARP, can do this mapping. We discuss this issue in Chapter 20.

Multicasting

Another issue in the Internet today is multicasting, delivery of data from one host to many destinations. Multicasting is becoming a very important issue in the Internet because of multimedia. Multimedia, in the form of audio and video, need multicasting routes to reach many destinations, destinations that belong to a group. We discuss multicasting in Chapter 21.

Routing Protocols

Routing protocols have been created in response to the demand for dynamic routing tables. A routing protocol is a combination of rules and procedures that lets routers in an internet inform each other of changes. It allows routers to share whatever they know about the internet or their neighborhood. The sharing of information allows a router in San Francisco to know about the failure of a network in Texas. The routing protocols also include procedures for combining information received from other routers. We discuss routing protocols in Chapter 21.

Other Supporting Protocols

An internetworking protocol such as IP needs the support of another protocol to help it achieve host-to-host delivery. This protocol, called the Internet Control Message Protocol (ICMP) is discussed in Chapter 20.

Chapters

We have included three chapters in this part of the book. Chapter 19 discusses the general concept of a network layer; process-to-process communication and routing. Chapter 20 covers the internetworking protocols in the Internet: ARP, IP, ICMP, and IGMP. Chapter 21 is devoted to unicast and multicast routing protocols.

CHAPTER 19

Host-to-Host Delivery: Internetworking, Addressing, and Routing

In this chapter we discuss the primary issues related to the network layer. We first need to understand the concept of internetworking and the need for the network layer in an internetwork. We also need to understand the type of switching used in the Internet. We show that the Internet, at the network layer, is a packet-switched network that uses connectionless communication.

Any internetwork, and particularly the Internet, needs global addressing. We discuss the global addresses used in the Internet and the issues related to addressing.

No one can deny that routing is the most important and complex issue in the Internet. Routing is needed to guarantee that a packet from an obscure corner of the world reaches an office in California's Silicon Valley. We discuss routing in this chapter, but we postpone the discussion of routing protocols until Chapter 21.

19.1   INTERNETWORKS

The physical and data link layers of a network operate locally. These two layers are jointly responsible for data delivery on the network from one node to the next.

So, how can data be exchanged *between* networks? They need to be connected to make an internetwork. Figure 19.1 shows an example of an internetwork.

Figure 19.1   *Internetwork*

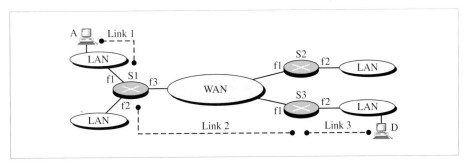

The internetwork is made of five networks: four LANs and one WAN. If host A needs to send a data packet to host D, the packet first needs to go from A to S1 (a switch or router), then from S1 to S3, and finally from S3 to host D. We say that the data packet passes through three links.

In each link, two physical and data link layers are involved, as shown in Figure 19.2.

Figure 19.2   *Links in an internetwork*

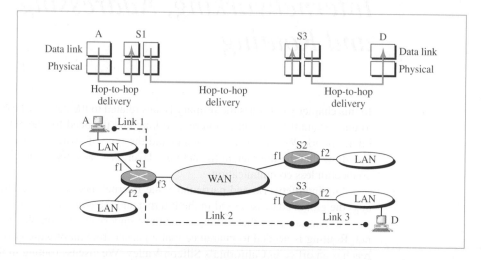

However, there is a big problem here. When data arrive at interface f1 of S1, how does S1 know that they should be sent out from interface f3? There is no provision in the data link (or physical) layer to help S1 make the right decision. The frame does not carry any routing information either. The frame contains the MAC address of A as the source and the MAC address of S1 as the destination. For a LAN or a WAN, delivery means carrying the frame through one link, not beyond.

Need for Network Layer

To solve the problem of delivery through several links, the network layer (or the inter-network layer, as it is sometimes called) was designed. The network layer is responsible for host-to-host delivery and for routing the packets through the routers or switches. Figure 19.3 shows the same internetwork with a network layer added.

Network Layer at Source

The network layer at the source is responsible for creating a packet that carries two universal addresses: a destination address and a source address. The source network layer receives data from the transport layer, adds the universal address of host A, adds the universal address of D, and makes sure the packet is the correct size for passage through the next link. If the packet is too large, the packet is fragmented (fragmentation is discussed in Chapter 20). The network layer at the source may also add fields for error control; these are mostly for error detection. See Figure 19.4.

Figure 19.3 *Network layer in an internetwork*

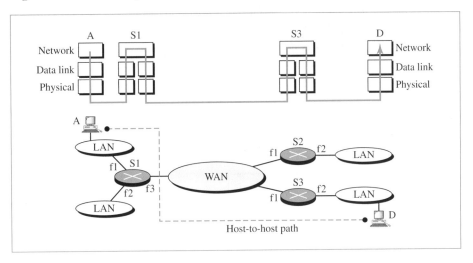

Figure 19.4 *Network layer at the source*

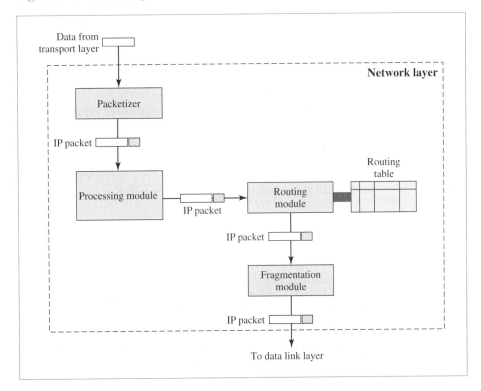

Network Layer at Router or Switch

The network layer at the switch or router is responsible for routing the packet. When a packet arrives, the router or switch finds the interface from which the packet must be sent. This is done by using a routing table. In addition, the packet may go through another fragmentation, if necessary. See Figure 19.5.

Figure 19.5   *Network layer at a router*

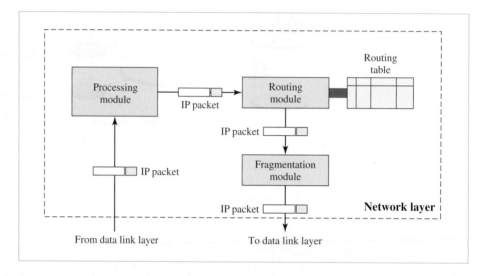

Network Layer at Destination

The network layer at the destination is responsible for address verification; it makes sure that the destination address on the packet is the same as the address of the host. It is also checks to see if the packet has been corrupted during transmission. If it has, the network layer discards the packet. If the packet is a fragment, the network layer waits until all fragments have arrived, and then it reassembles them and delivers the reassembled packet to the transport layer. See Figure 19.6.

Internet as a Packet-Switched Network

The Internet, at the network layer, is a packet-switched network. We discussed switching in Chapters 8 and 18. In general, switching can be divided into two broad categories: circuit switching and packet switching. Packet switching itself uses either the virtual circuit approach or the datagram approach. Figure 19.7 shows the taxonomy.

In circuit switching, a physical link is dedicated between a source and a destination. In this case, data can be sent as a stream of bits without the need for packetizing. In **packet switching,** on the other hand, data are transmitted in discrete units of potentially variable-length blocks called **packets.** The maximum length of the packet is established by the network. Longer transmissions are broken up into multiple packets. Each packet contains not only data but also a header with control information (such as priority codes and source and destination addresses). The packets are sent over the network, node to

Figure 19.6 *Network layer at the destination*

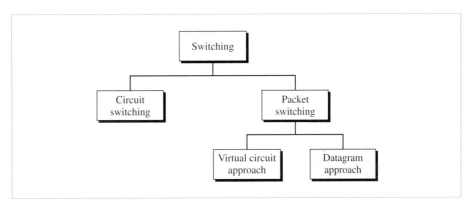

Figure 19.7 *Switching*

node. At each node, the packet is stored briefly before being routed according to the information in its header. There are two popular approaches to packet switching: the datagram approach and the virtual circuit approach.

Virtual Circuit Approach

In the **virtual circuit approach** to packet switching, the relationship between all packets belonging to a message or session is preserved. A single route is chosen between sender and receiver at the beginning of the session. When the data are sent, all packets of the transmission travel one after another along that route. Wide area networks use the virtual circuit approach to packet switching. As we discussed in Chapter 18, the virtual circuit approach needs a call setup to establish a virtual circuit between the source and destination. A call teardown deletes the virtual circuit. After the setup, routing takes place based on the virtual circuit identifier. This approach is used in WANs, Frame Relay, and ATM and is implemented at the data link layer.

Datagram Approach

In the **datagram approach** to packet switching, each packet is treated independently of all others. Even if one packet is just a piece of a multipacket transmission, the network treats it as though it existed alone. Packets in this approach are referred to as **datagrams.**

Figure 19.8 shows how the datagram approach can be used to deliver four packets from station A to station X. In this example, all four packets (or datagrams) belong to the same message but may go by different paths to reach their destination.

Figure 19.8   *Datagram approach*

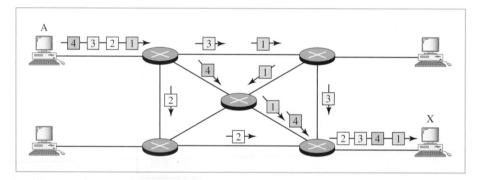

This approach can cause the datagrams of a transmission to arrive at their destination out of order. In most protocols, it is the responsibility of an upper layer to reorder the datagrams before passing them on to the destination port.

The datagram approach has some advantages, too. It does not need call setup and virtual circuit identifiers. The routing and delivery of the packet are based on the source and destination addresses included in the packet itself. The switches or routers each have a routing table that can decide on the route based on these two addresses.

The Internet has chosen the datagram approach to switching in the network layer. It uses the universal addresses defined in the network layer to route packets from the source to the destination.

> **Switching at the network layer in the Internet is done using the datagram approach to packet switching.**

Internet as a Connectionless Network

Delivery of a packet can be accomplished using either a connection-oriented or a connectionless network service. In a **connection-oriented service,** the source first makes a connection with the destination before sending a packet. When the connection is established, a sequence of packets from the same source to the same destination can be sent one after another. In this case, there is a relationship between packets. They are sent on the same path in sequential order. A packet is logically connected to the packet traveling before it and to the packet traveling after it. When all packets of a message have been delivered, the connection is terminated.

In a connection-oriented protocol, the decision about the route of a sequence of packets with the same source and destination addresses can be made only once, when the connection is established. Switches do not recalculate the route for each individual packet. This type of service is used in a virtual circuit approach to packet switching such as in Frame Relay and ATM.

In **connectionless service,** the network layer protocol treats each packet independently, with each packet having no relationship to any other packet. The packets in a message may or may not travel the same path to their destination. This type of service is used in the datagram approach to packet switching. The Internet has chosen this type of service at the network layer.

The reason for this decision is that the Internet is made of so many heterogeneous networks that it is almost impossible to create a connection from the source to the destination without knowing the nature of the networks in advance.

> **Communication at the network layer in the Internet is connectionless.**

19.2   ADDRESSING

From the discussion in Section 19.1, it is obvious that we need addresses and routing mechanisms for delivery at the network layer, from host to host. We discuss addressing in this section and routing in Section 19.3. At the network layer, we need to uniquely identify each device on the Internet to allow global communication between all devices. This is analogous to the telephone system, where each telephone subscriber has a unique telephone number, given that the country code and the area code are part of the identifying scheme.

Internet Address

The identifier used in the network layer of the Internet model to identify each device connected to the Internet is called the **Internet address** or **IP address.** An IP address, in the current version of the protocol, is a 32-bit binary address that *uniquely* and *universally* defines the connection of a host or a router to the Internet.

> **An IP address is a 32-bit address.**

IP addresses are unique. They are unique in the sense that each address defines one, and only one, connection to the Internet. Two devices on the Internet can never have the same address at the same time. However, if a device has two connections to the Internet, via two networks, it has two IP addresses.

The IP addresses are universal in the sense that the addressing system must be accepted by any host that wants to be connected to the Internet.

The IP addresses are unique and universal.

There are two common notations to show an IP address: binary notation and dotted-decimal notation.

Binary Notation

In **binary notation,** the IP address is displayed as 32 bits. To make the address more readable, one or more spaces is usually inserted between each octet (8 bits). Each octet is often referred to as a *byte*. So it is common to hear an IP address referred to as a 32-bit address, a 4-octet address, or a 4-byte address. The following is an example of an IP address in binary notation:

```
01110101   10010101   00011101   11101010
```

Dotted-Decimal Notation

To make the IP address more compact and easier to read, Internet addresses are usually written in decimal form with a decimal point (dot) separating the bytes. Figure 19.9 shows an IP address in **dotted-decimal notation.** Note that because each byte (octet) is only 8 bits, each number in the dotted-decimal notation is between 0 and 255.

Figure 19.9   *Dotted-decimal notation*

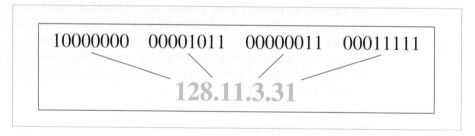

The binary, decimal, and hexadecimal number systems are reviewed in Appendix B.

Example 1

Change the following IP addresses from binary notation to dotted-decimal notation.
  a. 10000001 00001011 00001011 11101111
  b. 11111001 10011011 11111011 00001111

Solution

We replace each group of 8 bits with its equivalent decimal number (see Appendix B) and add dots for separation:
  a. 129.11.11.239
  b. 249.155.251.15

Example 2

Change the following IP addresses from dotted-decimal notation to binary notation.

    a. 111.56.45.78

    b. 75.45.34.78

Solution

We replace each decimal number with its binary equivalent (see Appendix B):

    a. 01101111 00111000 00101101 01001110

    b. 01001011 00101101 00100010 01001110

Classful Addressing

IP addresses, when started a few decades ago, used the concept of classes. This architecture is called **classful addressing.** In the mid-1990s, a new architecture, called **classless addressing,** was introduced which will eventually supersede the original architecture. However, most of the Internet is still using classful addressing, and the migration is slow. We first discuss classful addressing.

In classful addressing, the IP address space is divided into five classes: **classes A, B, C, D,** and **E.** Each class occupies some part of the whole **address space.**

In classful addressing, the address space is divided into five classes: A, B, C, D, and E.

We can find the class of an address when the address is given in binary notation or dotted-decimal notation.

Finding the Class in Binary Notation

If the address is given in binary notation, the first few bits can immediately tell us the class of the address, as shown in Figure 19.10.

Figure 19.10 *Finding the class in binary notation*

	First byte	Second byte	Third byte	Fourth byte
Class A	0			
Class B	10			
Class C	110			
Class D	1110			
Class E	1111			

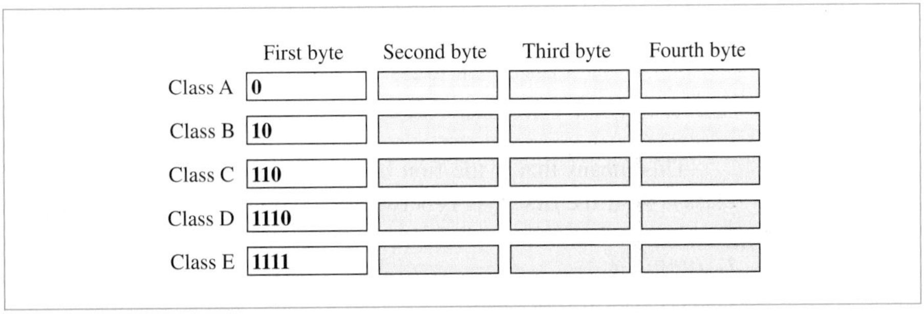

One can follow the procedure shown in Figure 19.11 to systematically check the bits and find the class.

Figure 19.11   *Finding the address class*

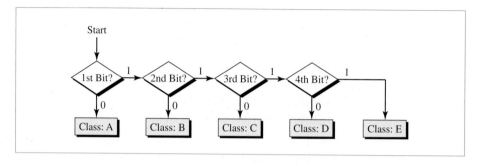

Example 3

Find the class of each address:

    a. **00000001** 00001011 00001011 11101111

    b. **1111**0011 10011011   11111011 00001111

Solution

See the procedure in Figure 19.11.

    a. The first bit is 0; this is a class A address.

    b. The first 4 bits are 1s; this is a class E address.

Finding the Class in Dotted-Decimal Notation   When the address is given in dotted-decimal notation, then we need to look only at the first byte (number) to determine the class of the address. Each class has a specific range of numbers. Figure 19.12 shows the idea.

Figure 19.12   *Finding the class in decimal notation*

	First byte	Second byte	Third byte	Fourth byte
Class A	**0 to 127**			
Class B	**128 to 191**			
Class C	**192 to 223**			
Class D	**224 to 239**			
Class E	**240 to 255**			

This means that if the first byte (in decimal) is between 0 and 127 inclusive, the class is A. If the first byte is between 128 and 191 inclusive, the class is B. And so on.

Example 4

Find the class of each address:

    a. **227**.12.14.87

    b. **252**.5.15.111

    c. **134**.11.78.56

Solution

    a. The first byte is 227 (between 224 and 239); the class is D.
    b. The first byte is 252 (between 240 and 255); the class is E.
    c. The first byte is 134 (between 128 and 191); the class is B.

Unicast, Multicast, and Reserved Addresses

Addresses in classes A, B, and C are for unicast communication, from one source to one destination. A host needs to have at least one **unicast address** to be able to send or receive packets.

    Addresses in class D are for multicast communication, from one source to a group of destinations. If a host belongs to a group or groups, it may have one or more multicast addresses. A **multicast address** can be used only as a destination address, but never as a source address.

    Addresses in class E are reserved. The original idea was to use them for special purposes. They have been used only in a few cases.

Netid and Hostid

In classful addressing, an IP address in classes A, B, and C is divided into **netid** and **hostid.** These parts are of varying lengths, depending on the class of the address. Figure 19.13 shows the netid and hostid bytes. Note that classes D and E are not divided into netid and hostid for reasons that we will discuss later.

Figure 19.13 *Netid and hostid*

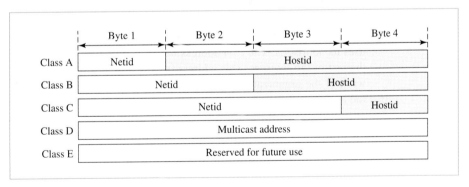

    In class A, one byte defines the netid and three bytes define the hostid. In class B, two bytes define the netid and two bytes define the hostid. In class C, three bytes define the netid and one byte defines the hostid.

Classes and Blocks

One problem with classful addressing is that each class is divided into a fixed number of blocks with each block having a fixed size. Let us look at each class.

Class A   Class A is divided into 128 blocks with each block having a different netid. The first block covers addresses from 0.0.0.0 to 0.255.255.255 (netid 0). The second block covers addresses from 1.0.0.0 to 1.255.255.255 (netid 1). The last block covers addresses from 127.0.0.0 to 127.255.255.255 (netid 127). Note that for each block of addresses the first byte (netid) is the same, but the other 3 bytes (hostid) can take any value in the given range. Figure 19.14 shows the blocks in class A.

Figure 19.14   *Blocks in class A*

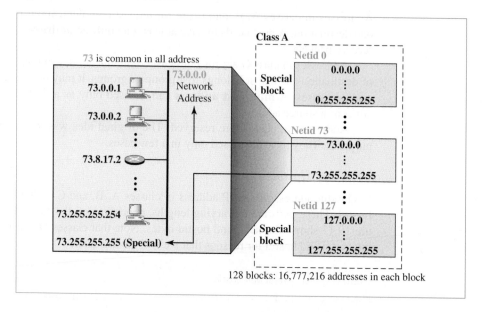

Figure 19.14 also shows how an organization that is granted a block with netid 73 uses its addresses. The first address in the block is used to identify the organization to the rest of the Internet. This address is called the **network address;** it defines the network of the organization, not individual hosts. The organization is not allowed to use the last address; it is reserved for a special purpose, as we will see shortly.

Class A addresses were designed for large organizations with a large number of hosts or routers attached to their network. However, the number of addresses in each block, 16,777,216, is probably larger than the needs of almost all organizations. Many addresses are wasted in this class.

Millions of class A addresses are wasted.

Class B   Class B is divided into 16,384 blocks with each block having a different netid. Sixteen blocks are reserved for private addresses, leaving 16,368 blocks for assignment to organizations. The first block covers addresses from 128.0.0.0 to 128.0.255.255 (netid 128.0). The last block covers addresses from 191.255.0.0 to 191.255.255.255 (netid 191.255). Note that for each block of addresses the first 2 bytes (netid) is the same, but the other 2 bytes (hostid) can take any value in the given range.

There are 16,368 blocks that can be assigned. This means that the total number of organizations that can have a class B address is 16,368. However, since each block in

Figure 19.15   *Blocks in class B*

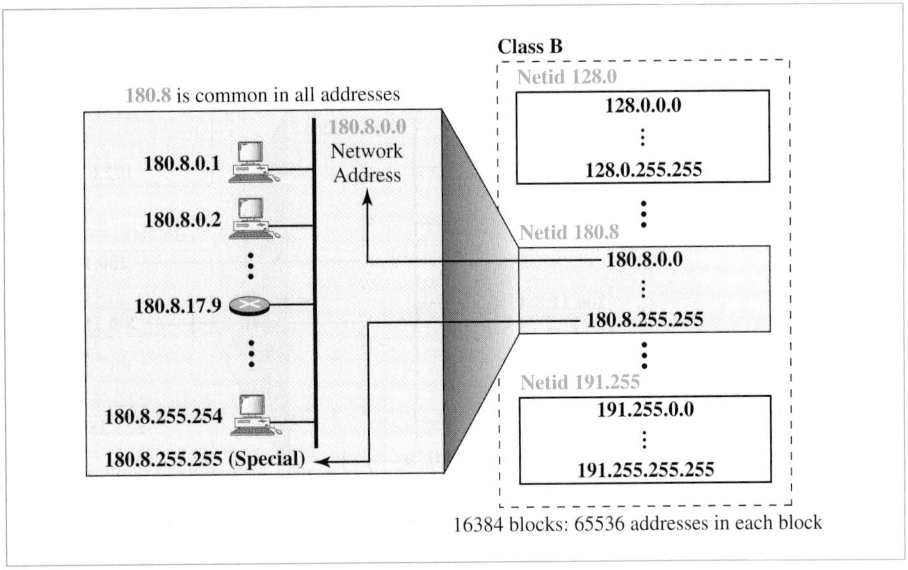

this class contains 65,536 addresses, the organization should be large enough to use all these addresses. Figure 19.15 shows the blocks in class B.

Class B addresses were designed for midsize organizations that may have tens of thousands of hosts or routers attached to their networks. However, the number of addresses in each block, 65,536, is larger than the needs of most midsize organizations. Many addresses are also wasted in this class.

Many class B addresses are wasted.

Class C   Class C is divided into 2,097,152 blocks with each block having a different netid. Two hundred fifty-six blocks are used for private addresses, leaving 2,096,896 blocks for assignment to organizations. The first block covers addresses from 192.0.0.0 to 192.0.0.255 (netid 192.0.0). The last block covers addresses from 223.255.255.0. to 223.255.255.255 (netid 223.255.255). Note that for each block of addresses the first 3 bytes (netid) are the same, but the remaining byte (hostid) can take any value in the given range.

There are 2,096,902 blocks that can be assigned. This means that the total number of organizations that can have a class C address is 2,096,902. However, each block in this class contains 256 addresses, which means the organization should be small enough to need less than 256 addresses. Figure 19.16 shows the blocks in class C.

Class C addresses were designed for small organizations with a small number of hosts or routers attached to their networks. The number of addresses in each block is so limited that most organizations do not want a block in this class.

The number of addresses in class C is smaller than the needs of most organizations.

Figure 19.16 *Blocks in class C*

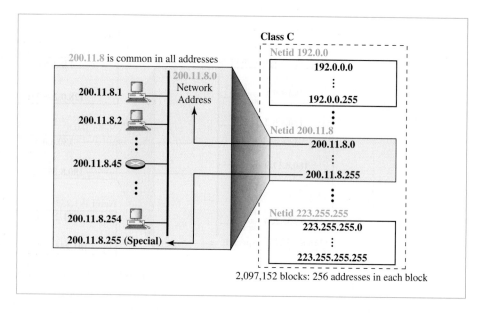

Class D   There is just one block of class D addresses. It is designed for multicasting.

Class E   There is just one block of class E addresses. It was designed for use as reserved addresses.

Network Address

The network address is an address that defines the network itself; it cannot be assigned to a host. Figure 19.17 shows three examples of network addresses, one for each class.

Figure 19.17 *Network address*

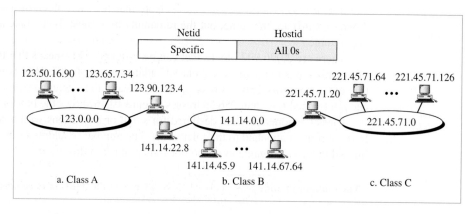

Network addresses play a very important role in classful addressing. A network address has several properties:

1. All hostid bytes are 0s.
2. The network address defines the network to the rest of the Internet. Later, we learn that routers can route a packet based on the network address.
3. The network address is the first address in the block.
4. Given the network address, we can find the class of the address.

In classful addressing, the network address is the one that is assigned to the organization.

Example 5

Given the address 23.56.7.91, find the network address.

Solution
The class is A. Only the first byte defines the netid. We can find the network address by replacing the hostid bytes (56.7.91) with 0s. Therefore, the network address is 23.0.0.0.

Example 6

Given the address 132.6.17.85, find the network address.

Solution
The class is B. The first 2 bytes defines the netid. We can find the network address by replacing the hostid bytes (17.85) with 0s. Therefore, the network address is 132.6.0.0.

Example 7

Given the network address 17.0.0.0, find the class.

Solution
The class is A because the netid is only 1 byte.

A network address is different from a netid. A network address has both netid and hostid, with 0s for the hostid.

A Sample Internet with Classful Addresses

Figure 19.18 shows a part of an internet with five networks.

1. A Token Ring LAN with network address 220.3.6.0 (class C).
2. An Ethernet LAN with network address 134.18.0.0 (class B).
3. An Ethernet LAN with network address 124.0.0.0 (class A).
4. A point-to-point WAN (broken line). This network (a T-1 line, for example) just connects two routers; there are no hosts. In this case, to save addresses, no network address is assigned to this type of WAN. A switched WAN (such as Frame Relay or ATM) can be connected to many routers. We have shown three. One router connects the WAN to the Token Ring network. One connects the WAN to one of the Ethernet networks, and one router connects the WAN to the rest of the Internet.

Figure 19.18   *Sample internet*

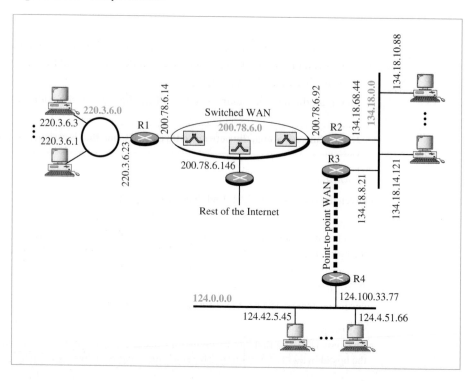

Subnetting

When an organization is given a block of class A, B, or C addresses, the first address in the block defines the network address. This address is used by routers outside the organization, as we see later, to route the packets destined for the network. The outside world, when it comes to routing, recognizes the network, not the individual hosts on the network.

A portion of a 32-bit address indicates the network (netid), and a portion indicates the host (hostid) on the network. This means that there is a sense of hierarchy in IP addressing. To reach a host on the Internet, we must first reach the network by using the first portion of the address (netid). Then we must reach the host itself by using the second portion (hostid). In other words, IP addresses are designed with two levels of hierarchy. Figure 19.19 shows the concept.

IP addresses are designed with two levels of hierarchy.

However, often an organization needs to assemble the hosts into groups; the network needs to be divided into several **subnetworks** (subnets). For example, a university may want to group its hosts according to department. In this case, the university has one network address, but needs several subnetwork addresses. The outside world knows the organization by its network address. Inside the organization each subnetwork is

Figure 19.19   *A network with two levels of hierarchy*

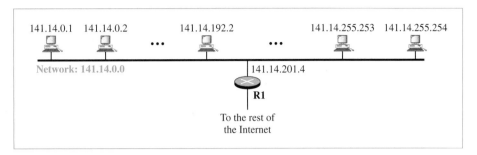

recognized by its subnetwork address. In **subnetting,** a network is divided into several smaller groups with each subnetwork (or subnet) having its own subnetwork address.

When we divide a network into several subnets, we have three levels of hierarchy (see Fig. 19.20). In this figure, the rest of the Internet is not aware that the network is divided into physical subnetworks: The subnetworks still appear as a single network to the rest of the Internet. A packet destined for host 141.14.192.2 still reaches router R1.

Figure 19.20   *A network with three levels of hierarchy (subnetted)*

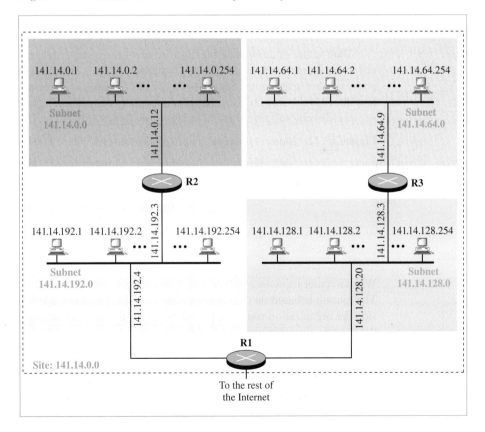

However, when the datagram arrives at router R1, the interpretation of the IP address changes. Router R1 knows that network 141.14 is physically divided into subnetworks. It knows that the packet must be delivered to subnetwork (subnet) 141.14.192.0.

Adding subnetworks creates an intermediate level of hierarchy in the IP addressing system. Now we have three levels: site, subnet, and host. The site is the first level. The second level is the **subnet.** The host is the third level; it defines the connection of the host to the subnetwork. See Figure 19.21.

Figure 19.21   *Addresses in a network with and without subnetting*

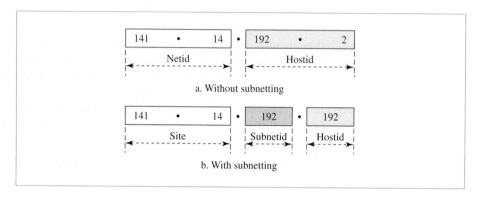

Figure 19.22   *Hierarchy concept in a telephone number*

The routing of an IP datagram now involves three steps: delivery to the site, delivery to the subnetwork, and delivery to the host. This is analogous to the 10-digit telephone number in the United States. As Figure 19.22 shows, a telephone number is divided into three levels: area code, exchange number, and connection number.

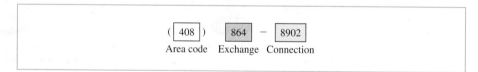

Mask

When a router receives a packet with a destination address, it needs to route the packet. The routing is based on the network address and subnetwork address. The routers outside the organization route the packet based on the network address; the router inside the organization routes the packet based on the subnetwork address. An analogy will help. When parcels reach a post office, they are routed according to Zip code. When they reach the post office serving that Zip code, the parcels are routed according to the street address.

The question is, How can a router find the network address or subnetwork address? A network administrator knows the network address and the subnetwork addresses, but a router does not. The router outside the organization has a routing table with one column based on the network addresses; the router inside the organization has a routing table based on the subnetwork addresses. A 32-bit number called the **mask** is the key. The routers outside the organization use a **default mask;** the routers inside the organization use a **subnet mask.**

Default Mask A default mask is a 32-bit binary number that gives the network address when ANDed with an address in the block. For our purpose, it is enough to know that the AND operation does the following:

1. If the bit in the mask is 1, the corresponding bit in the address is retained in the output (no change).
2. If the bit in the mask is 0, a 0 bit in the output is the result.

In other words, the bits in the address corresponding to the 1s in the mask are preserved (remain 0 or 1, as they were), and the bits corresponding to the 0s in the mask change to 0.

Table 19.1 shows the default mask for each class. For class A, the mask is eight 1s and twenty-four 0s. For class B, the mask is sixteen 1s and sixteen 0s. For class C, the mask is twenty-four 1s and eight 0s. The 1s preserve the netid; the 0s set the hostid to 0. Remember that the network address in any class is the netid with the hostid all 0s. An alternative mask notation is a slash followed by the number of 1s. This is called **slash notation.**

Table 19.1 *Default masks*

Class	In Binary	In Dotted-Decimal	Using Slash
A	11111111 00000000 00000000 00000000	255.0.0.0	/8
B	11111111 11111111 00000000 00000000	255.255.0.0	/16
C	11111111 11111111 11111111 00000000	255.255.255.0	/24

Note that the number of 1s in each class matches the number of bits in the netid, and the number of 0s matches the number of bits in the hostid. In other words, when a mask is ANDed with an address, the netid is retained and the hostid is set to 0s.

The network address can be found by applying the default mask to any address in the block (including itself). It retains the netid of the block and sets the hostid to 0s.

Example 8

A router outside the organization receives a packet with destination address 190.240.7.91. Show how it finds the network address to route the packet.

Solution

The router follows three steps:

a. The router looks at the first byte of the address to find the class. It is class B.
b. The default mask for class B is 255.255.0.0. The router ANDs this mask with the address to get 190.240.0.0.
c. The router looks in its routing table to find out how to route the packet to this destination. Later, we will see what happens if this destination does not exist.

Subnet Mask   The number of 1s in a subnet mask is more than the number of 1s in the corresponding default mask. In other words, in a subnet mask, we change some of the leftmost 0s in the default mask to make a subnet mask. Figure 19.23 shows the difference between a class B default mask and subnet mask for the same block.

Figure 19.23   *Subnet mask*

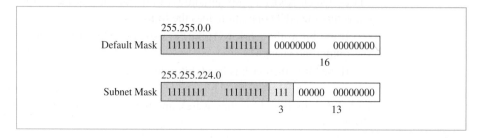

The number of subnets is determined by the number of extra 1s. If the number of extra 1s is n, the number of subnets is 2^n. If the number of subnets is N, the number of extra 1s is $\log_2 N$.

Example 9

A router inside the organization receives the same packet with destination address 190.240.33.91. Show how it finds the subnetwork address to route the packet.

Solution

The router follows three steps:

    a. The router must know the mask. We assume it is /19, as shown in Figure 19.23.

    b. The router applies the mask to the address, 190.240.33.91. The subnet address is 190.240.32.0.

    c. The router looks in its routing table to find how to route the packet to this destination. Later, we will see what happens if this destination does not exist.

Supernetting

Although class A and B addresses are almost depleted, class C addresses are still available. However, the size of a class C block with a maximum number of 256 addresses may not satisfy the needs of an organization. Even a midsize organization may need more addresses.

    One solution is **supernetting.** In supernetting, an organization can combine several class C blocks to create a larger range of addresses. In other words, several networks are combined to create a supernetwork. By doing this, an organization can apply for a set of class C blocks instead of just one. For example, an organization that needs 1000 addresses can be granted four class C blocks. The organization can then use these addresses in one supernetwork. There are so many issues involved in supernetting that it is beyond the scope of this book. For further information, see Forouzan's *TCP/IP Protocol Suite,* 2d ed., McGraw-Hill, 2002.

Classless Addressing

The idea of classful addressing has created many problems. Until the mid-1990s, a range of addresses meant a block of addresses in class A, B, or C. The minimum number of addresses granted to an organization was 256 (class C); the maximum was 16,777,216 (class A). In between these limits an organization could have a class B block or several class C blocks. However, the choices were limited. In addition, what about a small business that needed only 16 addresses? Or a household that needed only two addresses?

During the 1990s, Internet Service Providers (ISPs) came into prominence. An ISP is an organization that provides Internet access for individuals, small businesses, and mid-size organizations that do not want to create an Internet site and become involved in providing Internet services (such as email services) for their employees. An ISP can provide these services. An ISP can be granted several class B or class C blocks and then subdivide the range of addresses (in groups of 2, 4, 8, or 16 addresses), giving a range to a household or a small business. The customers are connected via a dial-up modem, DSL, or cable modem to the ISP. However, each customer still needs an IP address (we will discuss other solutions such as address translation later).

In 1996, the Internet authorities announced a new architecture called **classless addressing** that will eventually render classful addressing obsolete.

Variable-Length Blocks

The whole idea of classless addressing is to have variable-length blocks that belong to no class. We can have a block of 2 addresses, 4 addresses, 128 addresses, and so on. There are some restrictions that we will discuss shortly, but in general a block can range from very small to very large. In this architecture, the whole address space (2^{32} addresses) is divided into blocks of different sizes. An organization will be granted a block suitable for its purposes. There is only one condition on the number of addresses in a block; it must be a power of 2 (2, 4, 8, . . .). A household may be given a block of 2 addresses. A small business may be given 16 addresses. A large organization may be given 1024 addresses. The beginning address must be evenly divisible by the number of addresses. For example, if a block contains 4 addresses, the beginning address, as a 32-bit integer, must be divisible by 4.

Mask

If you remember, when an organization was given a block in classful addressing, the organization was given the beginning address of the block and a mask (default mask). In subnetting, when an organization was assigned a subblock, it was given the first address and the subnet mask. The same concept is carried over to classless addressing. When an organization is given a block, it is given the first address and the mask. These two pieces of information can define the whole block. The mask is normally given in slash notation, as we discussed before.

Finding the Network Address

Can we find the network address (the first address in the block) if one of the addresses is in the block and the mask is given? The answer is definitely yes. When we have the mask, we can AND the mask and the address to find the first address.

Subnetting

We can, of course, use subnetting with classless addressing. When an organization is granted a block of addresses, it can create subnets to meet its needs. The network administrator can design a subnet mask just as we discussed in classful addressing. The procedure is even simpler here. The number of 1s in the mask (n) increases to define the subnet mask. For example, if the mask is /17, the subnet mask can be /20 to create eight subnets ($2^3 = 8$).

CIDR

The idea behind classless addressing is **Classless InterDomain Routing (CIDR).** Although classless addressing alleviates the depletion of addresses, we now need classless routing or CIDR instead of classful routing. We discuss this issue in Section 19.3.

Dynamic Address Configuration

Each computer that is attached to the Internet must have the following information:

- Its IP address.
- Its subnet mask.
- The IP address of a router.
- The IP address of a name server.

This information is usually stored in a configuration file and accessed by the computer during the bootstrap (boot) process. But what about a diskless workstation or a computer with a disk that is booted for the first time, or a computer that has moved from one subnet to another? **Dynamic Host Configuration Protocol (DHCP)** is a protocol designed to provide the information dynamically (based on demand). DHCP is also used to assign addresses to a host dynamically. When a computer in an organization needs an address, it can use DHCP.

DHCP is a client-server program, which we will discuss in Chapter 24. Basically, DHCP server has two databases. The first database statically binds physical addresses to IP addresses. The second database makes DHCP dynamic. When a DHCP client requests a temporary IP address, the DHCP server goes to the pool of available (unused) IP addresses and assigns an IP address for a negotiable period of time.

When a DHCP client sends a request to a DHCP server, the server first checks its static database. If an entry with the requested physical address exists in the static database, the permanent IP address of the client is returned. On the other hand, if the entry does not exist in the static database, the server selects an IP address from the available pool, assigns the address to the client, and adds the entry to the dynamic database.

Leasing

The addresses assigned from the pool are temporary addresses. The DHCP server issues a lease for a specific period of time. When the lease expires, the client must either stop using the IP address or renew the lease. The server can choose to agree or disagree to the renewal. If the server disagrees, the client stops using the address.

Transition States

The DHCP client transitions from one state to another depending on the messages it receives or sends. See Figure 19.24.

Figure 19.24   *DHCP transition diagram*

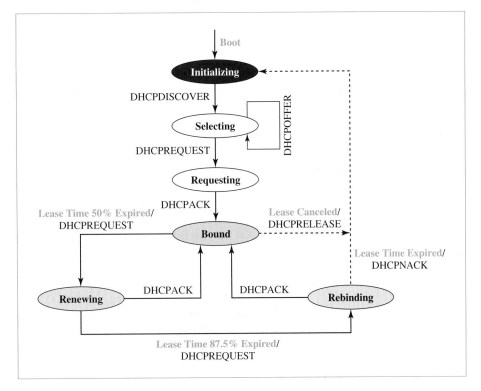

Initializing State   When the DHCP client first starts, it is in the initializing state. The client broadcasts a DHCPDISCOVER message.

Selecting State   After sending the DHCPDISCOVER message, the client goes to the selecting state. Those servers that can provide this type of service respond with a DHCPOFFER message. In these messages, the servers offer an IP address. They can also offer the lease duration. The default is 1 h. The server that sends a DHCPOFFER locks the offered IP address so that it is not available to any other clients. The client chooses one of the offers and sends a DHCPREQUEST message to the selected server. It then goes to the requesting state. If the client receives no DHCPOFFER message, it tries four more times, each with a span of 2 s. If there is no reply to any of these DHCPDISCOVERs, the client sleeps for 5 min before trying again.

Requesting State   The client remains in the requesting state until it receives a DHC-PACK message from the server which creates the binding between the client's physical address and its IP address.

Bound State In this state, the client can use the IP address until the lease expires. When 50 percent of the lease period is reached, the client sends another DHCPRE-QUEST to ask for renewal. It then goes to the renewing state. When in the bound state, the client can also cancel the lease and go to the initializing state.

Renewing State The client remains in the renewing state until one of the two events happens. It can receive a DHCPACK, which renews the lease agreement. In this case, the client resets its timer and goes back to the bound state. Or, if a DHCPACK is not received and 87.5 percent of the lease time expires, the client goes to the rebinding state.

Rebinding State The client remains in the rebinding state until one of the three events happens. If the client receives a DHCPNACK or the lease expires, the client goes back to the initializing state and tries to get another IP address. If the client receives a DHCPACK, it goes to the bound state and resets the timer.

Network Address Translation (NAT)

The number of home users and small businesses that want to use the Internet is ever increasing. In the beginning, these users were connected to the Internet with a dial-up line, which means that they were connected for a specific period of time. An ISP with a block of addresses could dynamically assign addresses to this user. An address was given to a user when it was needed. But the situation is different today. Home users and small business can be connected by an ADSL line or cable modem. In addition, many are not happy with one address; many have created small networks with several hosts and need an IP address for each host. With the shortage of addresses, this is a serious problem.

A quick solution to this problem is called **network address translation (NAT).** NAT enables a user to have a large set of addresses internally and one address, or a small set of addresses, externally. The traffic inside can use the large set; the traffic outside, the small set.

To separate the addresses used inside the home or business and the ones used in the Internet, the Internet authorities have reserved three sets of addresses as private addresses, shown in Table 19.2.

Table 19.2   *Addresses for private networks*

Range			Total
10.0.0.0	to	10.255.255.255	2^{24}
172.16.0.0	to	172.31.255.255	2^{20}
192.168.0.0	to	192.168.255.255	2^{16}

Any organization can use an address out of this set without permission from the Internet authorities. Everybody knows that these reserved addresses are for private networks. They are unique inside the organization, but they are not unique globally. No router will forward a packet that has one of these addresses as the destination address.

The site must have only one single connection to the global Internet through a router that runs the NAT software. Figure 19.25 shows a simple implementation of NAT.

Figure 19.25 *NAT*

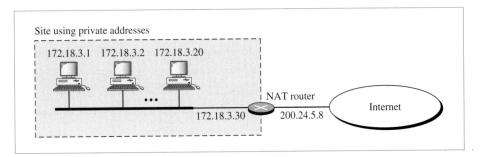

As the figure shows, the private network uses private addresses. The router that connects the network to the global address uses one private address and one global address. The private network is transparent to the rest of the Internet; the rest of the internet sees only the NAT router with the address 200.24.5.8.

Address Translation

All the outgoing packets go through the NAT router, which replaces the *source address* in the packet with the global NAT address. All incoming packets also pass through the NAT router, which replaces the *destination address* in the packet (the NAT router global address) with the appropriate private address. Figure 19.26 shows an example of address translation.

Figure 19.26 *Address translation*

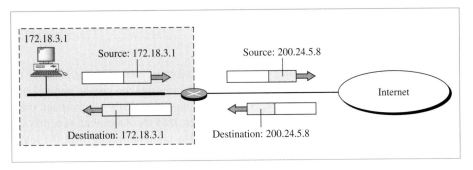

Translation Table

The reader may have noticed that translating the source addresses for an outgoing packets is straightforward. But how does the NAT router know the destination address for a packet coming from the Internet? There may be tens or hundreds of private IP addresses, each belonging to one specific host. The problem is solved if the NAT router has a translation table.

Using One IP Address In its simplest form, a translation table has only two columns: the private address and the external address (destination address of the packet).

When the router translates the source address of the outgoing packet, it also makes note of the destination address—where the packet is going. When the response comes back from the destination, the router uses the source address of the packet (as the external address) to find the private address of the packet. Figure 19.27 shows the idea. Note that the addresses that are changed (translated) are shown in color.

Figure 19.27   *Translation*

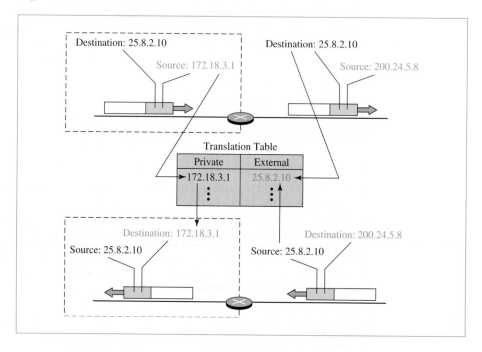

In this strategy, communication must always be initiated by the private network. The NAT mechanism described requires that the private network start the communication. As we will see, NAT is used mostly by ISPs which assign one single address to a customer. The customer, however, may be a member of a private network that has many private addresses. In this case, communication with the Internet is always initiated from the customer site, using a client program such as HTTP, TELNET, or FTP to access the corresponding server program. For example, when email that originates from a noncustomer site is received by the ISP email server, the email is stored in the mailbox of the customer until retrieved. A private network cannot run a server program for clients outside of its network if it is using NAT technology.

Using a Pool of IP Addresses   Since the NAT router has only one global address, only one private-network host can access the same external host. To remove this restriction, the NAT router uses a pool of global addresses. For example, instead of using only one global address (200.24.5.8), the NAT router can use four addresses (200.24.5.8, 200.24.5.9, 200.24.5.10, and 200.24.5.11). In this case, four private-network hosts can communicate with the same external host at the same time because each pair of addresses defines a connection. However, there are still some drawbacks. No more than four connections can be made to the same destination. No private-network host can access two external server programs (e.g., HTTP and FTP) at the same time.

Using Both IP Addresses and Port Numbers   To allow a many-to-many relationship between private-network hosts and external server programs, we need more information in the translation table. For example, suppose two hosts inside a private network with addresses 172.18.3.1 and 172.18.3.2 need to access the HTTP server on external host 25.8.3.2. If the translation table has five columns, instead of two, that include the source and destination port numbers of the transport layer protocol, the ambiguity is eliminated. We discuss port numbers in Chapter 22. Table 19.3 shows an example of such a table.

Table 19.3   *Five-column translation table*

Private Address	Private Port	External Address	External Port	Transport Protocol
172.18.3.1	1400	25.8.3.2	80	TCP
172.18.3.2	1401	25.8.3.2	80	TCP
...	...	...	...	...

Note that when the response from HTTP comes back, the combination of source address (25.8.3.2) and destination port number (1400) defines the private network host to which the response should be directed. Note also that for this translation to work, the temporary port numbers (1400 and 1401) must be unique.

19.3   ROUTING

As we discussed in Section 19.2, we need addresses and routing to handle delivery of packets. We discussed addressing; we now focus on routing.

Routing Techniques

Routing requires a host or a router to have a **routing table.** When a host has a packet to send or when a router has received a packet to be forwarded, it looks at this table to find the route to the final destination. However, this simple solution is impossible today in an internetwork such as the Internet because the number of entries in the routing table makes table lookups inefficient. Several techniques can make the size of the routing table manageable and handle issues such as security. We will discuss these methods here.

Next-Hop Routing

One technique to reduce the contents of a routing table is called **next-hop routing.** In this technique, the routing table holds only the information that leads to the next hop instead of holding information about the complete route. The entries of a routing table must be consistent with each other. Figure 19.28 shows how routing tables can be simplified by using this technique.

Figure 19.28 *Next-hop routing*

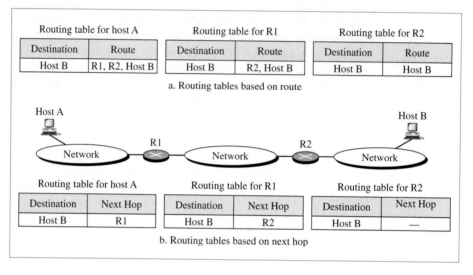

a. Routing tables based on route

b. Routing tables based on next hop

Network-Specific Routing

A second technique to reduce the routing table and simplify the searching process is called **network-specific routing.** Here, instead of having an entry for every host connected to the same physical network, we have only one entry to define the address of the network itself. In other words, we treat all hosts connected to the same network as one single entity. For example, if 1000 hosts are attached to the same network, only one entry exists in the routing table instead of 1000. Figure 19.29 shows the concept.

Figure 19.29 *Network-specific routing*

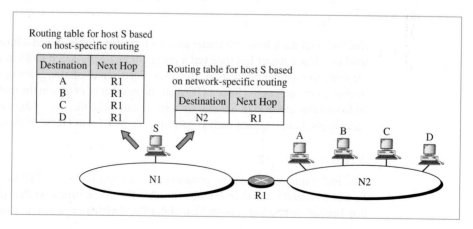

Host-Specific Routing

In **host-specific routing,** the destination host address is given in the routing table. The idea of host-specific routing is the inverse of network-specific routing. Here efficiency is sacrificed for other advantages: Although it is not efficient to put the host address in the routing table, there are occasions in which the administrator wants to have greater control over routing. For example, in Figure 19.30 if the administrator wants all packets destined for host B delivered via router R3 instead of R1, one single entry in the routing table of host A can explicitly define the route.

Host-specific routing is used for specific purposes such as checking the route or providing security measures.

Figure 19.30 *Host-specific routing*

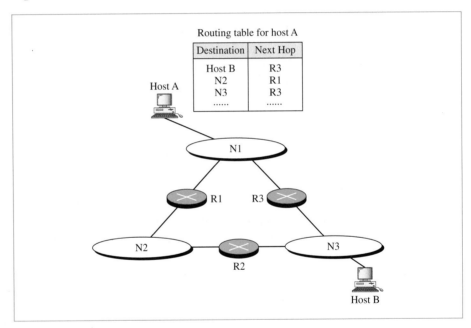

Default Routing

Another technique to simplify routing is **default routing.** In Figure 19.31 host A is connected to a network with two routers. Router R1 is used to route the packets to hosts connected to network N2. However, for the rest of the Internet, router R2 is used. So instead of listing all networks in the entire Internet, host A can just have one entry called the *default* (network address 0.0.0.0).

Static Versus Dynamic Routing

A host or a router keeps a routing table, with an entry for each destination, to route IP packets. The routing table can be either static or dynamic.

Figure 19.31   *Default routing*

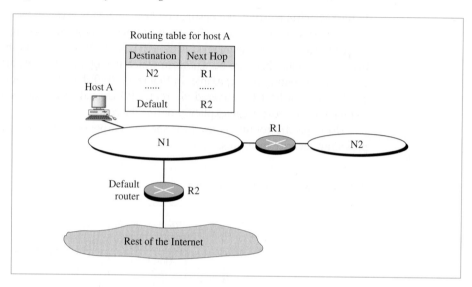

Static Routing Table

A **static routing table** contains information entered manually. The administrator enters the route for each destination into the table. When this type of table is created, it cannot update automatically when there is a change in the Internet. The table must be manually altered by the administrator.

A static routing table can be used in a small internet that does not change very often, or in an experimental internet for troubleshooting. It is not good strategy to use a static routing table in a big internet such as the Internet.

Dynamic Routing Table

A **dynamic routing table** is updated periodically using one of the dynamic routing protocols such as RIP, OSPF, or BGP (see Chapter 21). Whenever there is a change in the Internet, such as a shutdown of a router or breaking of a link, the dynamic routing protocols update all the tables in the routers (and eventually in the host).

The routers in a big internet such as the Internet need to be updated dynamically for efficient delivery of the IP packets. We will discuss in detail three dynamic routing protocols in Chapter 21.

Routing Table for Classful Addressing

In classful addressing, with or without subnetting, a routing table needs a minimum of four columns (it normally has more): mask, destination network address, next-hop address, and interface, as shown in Figure 19.32.

When a packet arrives, the router applies the mask to the **destination address** to find the corresponding destination network address. If found, the packet is sent out from the corresponding interface in the table. If the destination network address is not

Figure 19.32   *Classful addressing routing table*

	Mask	Destination address	Next-hop address	Interface
	/8	14.0.0.0	118.45.23.8	m1
Host-specific ───▶	/32	192.16.7.1	202.45.9.3	m0
	/24	193.14.5.0	84.78.4.12	m2
Default ───▶	/0	/0	145.11.10.6	m0

found, the packet is delivered to the default interface which carries the packet to the default router.

Example 10

Using the table in Figure 19.32, the router receives a packet for destination 192.16.7.1. For each row, the mask is applied to the destination address until a match with the destination address is found. In this example, the router sends the packet through interface m0 (host specific).

Example 11

Using the table in Figure 19.32, the router receives a packet for destination 193.14.5.22. For each row, the mask is applied to the destination address until a match with the next-hop address is found. In this example, the router sends the packet through interface m2 (network specific).

Example 12

Using the table in Figure 19.32, the router receives a packet for destination 200.34.12.34. For each row, the mask is applied to the destination address, but no match is found. In this example, the router sends the packet through the default interface m0.

Routing Table for Classless Addressing: CIDR

So far, the discussion on routing tables concentrated on classful addressing. Now we need to consider classless addressing and Classless InterDomain Routing (CIDR). The shift to classless addressing requires changes to the routing table organization and routing algorithms.

Routing Table Size

When we use classful addressing, there is only one entry in the routing table for each site outside the organization. The entry defines the site even if that site is subnetted. When a packet arrives at the router, the router checks the corresponding entry and forwards the packet accordingly.

When we use classless addressing, the number of entries in the router's table can either decrease or increase. It can decrease if the block of addresses assigned to an organization is larger than the block in classful addressing. For example, instead of having four entries for an organization that creates a supernet from four class C blocks, we can have one entry in classless routing.

It is more likely, however, that the number of routing table entries will increase. This is so because the intent of classless addressing is to divide up the blocks of class A and class B addresses. For example, instead of assigning over 16 million addresses to just one organization, the addresses can be portioned out to many organizations. The problem is that whereas there was just one routing table entry for a block in a class A address, now there are many entries in classless addressing. For example, if a class B block (over 64,000 addresses) is divided up between 60 organizations, there are now 60 routing table entries where before there was just one.

Hierarchical Routing

To solve the problem of gigantic routing tables, we create a sense of hierarchy in the Internet architecture and create **hierarchical routing** tables. In Chapter 1, we mentioned that the Internet today has a sense of hierarchy. We said that the Internet is divided into international and national ISPs. National ISPs are divided into regional ISPs, and regional ISPs are divided into local ISPs. If the routing table has a sense of hierarchy like the Internet architecture, the routing table can decrease in size.

Let us take the case of a local ISP. A local ISP can be assigned a single, but large block of addresses with a certain mask. The local ISP can divide this block into smaller blocks of different sizes and can assign these to individual users and organizations, both large and small. If the block assigned to the local ISP is A.B.C.D/n, the ISP can create blocks of E.F.G.H/m, where m may vary for each customer and is greater than n.

How does this reduce the size of the routing table? The rest of the Internet does not have to be aware of this division. All customers of the local ISP are defined as A.B.C.D/n to the rest of the Internet. Every packet destined for one of the addresses in this large block is routed to the local ISP. There is only one entry in every router in the world for all these customers. They all belong to the same group. Of course, inside the local ISP, the router must recognize the subblocks and route the packet to the destined customer. If one of the customers is a large organization, it also can create another level of hierarchy by subnetting and dividing its subblock into smaller subblocks (or sub-subblocks). In classless routing, the levels of hierarchy are unlimited as long as we follow the rules of classless addressing.

Geographic Routing

To decrease the size of the routing table even further, we need to extend hierarchical routing to include **geographic routing.** We must divide the entire address space into a few large blocks. We assign a block to North America, a block to Europe, a block to Asia, a block to Africa, and so on. The routers of ISPs outside of Europe will have only one entry for packets to Europe in their routing tables. The routers of ISPs outside of North America will have only one entry for packets to North America in their routing tables. And so on. Part of this idea has already been implemented for class C addressing. But, for real efficiency, all of classes A and B need to be recycled and reassigned.

Routing Table Search Algorithms

In classless addressing, searching is definitely more complex. We need to change the **search algorithms** to make the CIDR as efficient as possible. Many new algorithms have been proposed, but their discussions are beyond the scope of this book.

19.4 KEY TERMS

address space	Internet address
binary notation	IP address
class A address	mask
class B address	multicast address
class C address	netid
class D address	network address
class E address	network address translation (NAT)
classful addressing	network-specific routing
classless addressing	next-hop routing packet
Classless InterDomain Routing (CIDR)	packet-switched network
connectionless service	packet switching
connection-oriented service	routing table
datagram	search algorithm
datagram approach (to packet switching)	slash notation
default mask	static routing table
default routing	subnet
dotted-decimal notation	subnet mask
Dynamic Host Configuration Protocol (DHCP)	subnetting
	subnetwork
dynamic routing table	supernetting
geographic routing	unicast address
hierarchical routing	virtual-circuit approach (to packet switching)
hostid	
host-specific routing	

19.5 SUMMARY

❏ There are two popular approaches to packet switching: the datagram approach and the virtual circuit approach.

❏ In the datagram approach, each packet is treated independently of all other packets.

❏ At the network layer, a global addressing system that uniquely identifies every host and router is necessary for delivery of a packet from network to network.

❏ The Internet address (or IP address) is 32 bits (for IPv4) that uniquely and universally defines a host or router on the Internet.

❏ The portion of the IP address that identifies the network is called the netid.

❏ The portion of the IP address that identifies the host or router on the network is called the hostid.

❏ There are five classes of IP addresses. Classes A, B, and C differ in the number of hosts allowed per network. Class D is for multicasting, and class E is reserved.

❏ The class of a network is easily determined by examination of the first byte.

❏ Unicast communication is one source sending a packet to one destination.

❏ Multicast communication is one source sending a packet to multiple destinations.

❏ Subnetting divides one large network into several smaller ones.

❏ Subnetting adds an intermediate level of hierarchy in IP addressing.

❏ Default masking is a process that extracts the network address from an IP address.

❏ Subnet masking is a process that extracts the subnetwork address from an IP address.

❏ Supernetting combines several networks into one large one.

❏ In classless addressing, there are variable-length blocks that belong to no class. The entire address space is divided into blocks based on organization needs.

❏ The first address and the mask in classless addressing can define the whole block.

❏ A mask can be expressed in slash notation which is a slash followed by the number of 1s in the mask.

❏ Every computer attached to the Internet must know its IP address, the IP address of a router, the IP address of a name server, and its subnet mask (if it is part of a subnet).

❏ DHCP is a dynamic configuration protocol with two databases.

❏ The DHCP server issues a lease for an IP address to a client for a specific period of time.

❏ Network address translation (NAT) allows a private network to use a set of private addresses for internal communication and a set of global Internet addresses for external communication.

❏ NAT uses translation tables to route messages.

❏ The IP protocol is a connectionless protocol. Every packet is independent and has no relationship to any other packet.

❏ Every host or router has a routing table to route IP packets.

❏ In next-hop routing, instead of a complete list of the stops the packet must make, only the address of the next hop is listed in the routing table.

❏ In network-specific routing, all hosts on a network share one entry in the routing table.

❏ In host-specific routing, the full IP address of a host is given in the routing table.

❏ In default routing, a router is assigned to receive all packets with no match in the routing table.

❏ A static routing table's entries are updated manually by an administrator.

❏ Classless addressing requires hierarchical and geographic routing to prevent immense routing tables.

19.6 PRACTICE SET

Review Questions

1. What is the fundamental difference between circuit switching and packet switching?

2. What are the two popular approaches to packet switching?

3. A message is broken up into three pieces. Discuss the transmission of the packets using the datagram approach to packet switching.

4. Why does the Internet use a connectionless network service?

5. Why is the largest octet in an Internet address 255?

6. Name the five current IP address classes. Which are used for unicast communication?

7. Which class of IP addresses is used for multicast communication?

8. What is the network address?

9. What is the purpose of subnetting?

10. What is a default mask?

11. Give an example of supernetting.

12. How can classless addressing alleviate the problem of diminishing IP addresses?

13. What is the function of DHCP?

14. What is the purpose of NAT?

15. How does next-hop routing decrease the number of table entries in a router?

16. How does network-specific routing decrease the number of table entries in a router?

17. How does host-specific routing decrease the number of table entries in a router?

18. How does default routing decrease the number of table entries in a router?

19. What is geographic routing?

Multiple-Choice Questions

20. In which type of switching do all the packets of a message follow the same channels of a path?
    a. Datagram packet switching
    b. Virtual circuit packet switching
    c. Message switching
    d. None of the above

21. In _____, each packet of a message need not follow the same path from sender to receiver.
    a. Message switching
    b. The virtual approach to packet switching
    c. The datagram approach to packet switching
    d. None of the above

22. An IP address consists of _____ bits.
    a. 4
    b. 8
    c. 32
    d. Any of the above

23. Identify the class of IP address 4.5.6.7.
    a. Class A
    b. Class B
    c. Class C
    d. Class D

24. Identify the class of IP address 229.1.2.3.
    a. Class A
    b. Class B
    c. Class C
    d. Class D

25. Identify the class of IP address 191.1.2.3.
    a. Class A
    b. Class B
    c. Class C
    d. Class D

26. A subnet mask in class A can have _____ 1s with the remaining bits 0s.
    a. Nine
    b. Four
    c. Thirty-three
    d. Three

27. A subnet mask in class B can have _____ 1s with the remaining bits 0s.
    a. Nine
    b. Fourteen
    c. Seventeen
    d. Three

28. A subnet mask in class C can have _____ 1s with the remaining bits 0s.
    a. Ten
    b. Twenty-five
    c. Twelve
    d. Seven

29. A subnet mask in class A has fourteen 1s. How many subnets does it define?
    a. 32
    b. 8
    c. 64
    d. 128

30. A subnet mask in class B has nineteen 1s. How many subnets does it define?
    a. 8
    b. 32
    c. 64
    d. 128

31. A subnet mask in class C has twenty-five 1s. How many subnets does it define?
    a. 2
    b. 8
    c. 16
    d. 0

32. Given the IP address 201.14.78.65 and the subnet mask 255.255.255.224, what is the subnet address?

    a. 201.14.78.32

    b. 201.14.78.65

    c. 201.14.78.64

    d. 201.14.78.12

33. Given the IP address 180.25.21.172 and the subnet mask 255.255.192.0, what is the subnet address?

    a. 180.25.21.0

    b. 180.25.0.0

    c. 180.25.8.0

    d. 180.0.0.0

34. Given the IP address 18.250.31.14 and the subnet mask 255.240.0.0, what is the subnet address?

    a. 18.0.0.14

    b. 18.31.0.14

    c. 18.240.0.0

    d. 18.9.0.14

35. Class _____ has the greatest number of hosts per given network address.

    a. A

    b. B

    c. C

    d. D

36. _____ is a client-server program that provides an IP address, subnet mask, IP address of a router, and IP address of a name server to a computer.

    a. NAT

    b. CIDR

    c. ISP

    d. DHCP

37. On a network that uses NAT, the _____ has a translation table.

    a. Switch

    b. Router

    c. Server

    d. None of the above

38. On a network that uses NAT, _____ initiates the communication.

    a. An external host

    b. An internal host

    c. The router

    d. (a) or (b)

39. On a network that uses NAT, the router can use _____ global address(es).
    a. One
    b. Two
    c. A pool of
    d. None of the above

40. In _____ routing, the full IP address of a destination is given in the routing table.
    a. Next-hop
    b. Network-specific
    c. Host-specific
    d. Default

41. In _____ routing, the mask and destination addresses are both 0.0.0.0 in the routing table.
    a. Next-hop
    b. Network-specific
    c. Host-specific
    d. Default

42. In _____ routing, the destination address is a network address in the routing table.
    a. Next-hop
    b. Network-specific
    c. Host-specific
    d. Default

Exercises

43. Complete Table 19.4 to compare a circuit-switched network with a packet-switched network.

    Table 19.4   *Exercise 43*

Issue	Circuit-Switched	Packet-Switched
Dedicated path		
Store and forward		
Need for connection establishment		
Routing table		

44. Complete Table 19.5 to compare a datagram approach with a virtual circuit approach of a packet-switching network.

    Table 19.5   *Exercise 44*

Issue	Datagram	Virtual Circuit
All packets follow the same route		
Table lookup		
Connection establishment		
Packet may arrive out of order		

45. Change the following IP addresses from dotted-decimal notation to binary notation.
    a. 114.34.2.8
    b. 129.14.6.8
    c. 208.34.54.12
    d. 238.34.2.1
    e. 241.34.2.8
46. Change the following IP addresses from binary notation to dotted-decimal notation.
    a. 01111111 11110000 01100111 01111101
    b. 10101111 11000000 11111000 00011101
    c. 11011111 10110000 00011111 01011101
    d. 11101111 11110111 11000111 00011101
    e. 11110111 11110011 10000111 11011101
47. Find the class of the following IP addresses.
    a. 208.34.54.12
    b. 238.34.2.1
    c. 114.34.2.8
    d. 129.14.6.8
    e. 241.34.2.8
48. Find the class of the following IP addresses.
    a. 11110111 11110011 10000111 11011101
    b. 10101111 11000000 11110000 00011101
    c. 11011111 10110000 00011111 01011101
    d. 11101111 11110111 11000111 00011101
    e. 01111111 11110000 01100111 01111101
49. Find the netid and the hostid of the following IP addresses.
    a. 114.34.2.8
    b. 19.34.21.5
    c. 23.67.12.1
    d. 127.23.4.0
50. Find the netid and the hostid of the following IP addresses.
    a. 129.14.6.8
    b. 132.56.8.6
    c. 171.34.14.8
    d. 190.12.67.9
51. Find the netid and the hostid of the following IP addresses.
    a. 192.8.56.2
    b. 220.34.8.9
    c. 208.34.54.12
    d. 205.23.67.8

52. In a class A subnet, we know the IP address of one of the hosts and the mask as given below:

    IP address: 25.34.12.56
    Mask: 255.255.0.0

    What is the first address (network address)?

53. In a class B subnet, we know the IP address of one of the hosts and the mask as given below:

    IP address: 125.134.112.66
    Mask: 255.255.224.0

    What is the first address (network address)?

54. In a class C subnet, we know the IP address of one of the hosts and the mask as given below:

    IP address: 182.44.82.16
    Mask: 255.255.255.192

    What is the first address (network address)?

55. Find the masks that create the following number of subnets in class A.
    a. 2
    b. 6
    c. 30
    d. 62
    e. 122
    f. 250

56. Find the masks that create the following number of subnets in class B.
    a. 2
    b. 5
    c. 30
    d. 62
    e. 120
    f. 250

57. What is the maximum number of subnets in class A using the following masks?
    a. 255.255.192.0
    b. 255.192.0.0
    c. 255.255.224.0
    d. 255.255.255.0

58. What is the maximum number of subnets in class B using the following masks?
    a. 255.255.192.0
    b. 255.255.0.0
    c. 255.255.224.0
    d. 255.255.255.0

59. What is the maximum number of subnets in class C using the following masks?
    a. 255.255.255.192
    b. 255.255.255.224
    c. 255.255.255.240
    d. 255.255.255.0

60. For each of the following subnet masks used in class A, find the number of 1s that defines the subnet.
    a. 255.255.192.0
    b. 255.192.0.0
    c. 255.255.224.0
    d. 255.255.255.0

61. For each of the following subnet masks used in class B, find the number of 1s that defines the subnet.
    a. 255.255.192.0
    b. 255.255.0.0
    c. 255.255.224.0
    d. 255.255.255.0

62. For each of the following subnet masks used in class C, find the number of 1s that defines the subnet.
    a. 255.255.255.192
    b. 255.255.255.224
    c. 255.255.255.240
    d. 255.255.255.0

63. Write the following masks in the /n format.
    a. 255.255.255.0
    b. 255.0.0.0
    c. 255.255.224.0
    d. 255.255.240.0

64. Find the range of addresses in the following blocks.
    a. 123.56.77.32/29
    b. 200.17.21.128/27
    c. 17.34.16.0/23
    d. 180.34.64.64/30

CHAPTER 20

Network Layer Protocols: ARP, IPv4, ICMP, IPv6, and ICMPv6

In the Internet model, or the TCP/IP suite, there are five network layer protocols: ARP, RARP, IP, ICMP, and IGMP, as shown in Figure 20.1.

Figure 20.1 *Protocols at network layer*

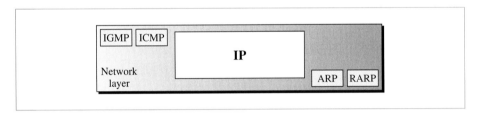

The main protocol in this layer is IP, which is responsible for host-to-host delivery of datagrams from a source to a destination. However, IP needs the services of other protocols.

IP needs a protocol called ARP to find the MAC (physical) address of the next hop. This address must be passed to the data link layer, with the IP datagram, to be inserted into the encapsulating frame.

During datagram delivery, IP needs the services of ICMP to handle unusual situations such as the occurrence of an error.

IP is designed for unicast delivery, one source to one destination. Multimedia and other new applications in the Internet need multicasting delivery, one source to many destinations. For multicasting, IP uses the services of another protocol called IGMP.

In this chapter, we discuss only ARP, IP, and ICMP. RARP is becoming obsolete. IGMP is discussed in Chapter 21 when we talk about multicasting.

The current version of IP is called IPv4. The new version, which may or may not become dominant, is IPv6. At the end of this chapter, we give a glance at this new protocol and the rationale for its existence.

20.1   ARP

The Internet is made of a combination of physical networks connected by devices such as routers. A packet starting from a source host may pass through several different physical networks before finally reaching the destination host.

The hosts and routers are recognized at the network level by their IP addresses. An **IP address** is an internetwork address. Its jurisdiction is universal. An IP address is universally unique. Every protocol that deals with interconnecting networks requires IP addresses.

However, packets pass through physical networks to reach these hosts and routers. At the physical network, the hosts and routers are recognized by their MAC addresses. A MAC address is a local address. Its jurisdiction is a local network. It should be unique locally, but not necessarily universally.

The MAC address and the IP address are two different identifiers. We need both of them because a physical network, such as Ethernet, can have two different protocols at the network layer, such as IP and IPX (Novell), at the same time. Likewise, a packet at a network layer such as IP may pass through different physical networks, such as Ethernet and Token Ring.

This means that delivery of a packet to a host or a router requires two levels of addressing: IP and MAC. We need to be able to map an IP address to its corresponding MAC address.

Mapping

We can have two types of address mapping: static and dynamic.

Static Mapping

Static mapping means creating a table that associates an IP address with a MAC address. This table is stored in each machine on the network. Each machine that knows, for example, the IP address of another machine but not its MAC address can look it up in the table. This has some limitations because MAC addresses may change in the following ways:

1. A machine could change its network card, resulting in a new MAC address.
2. In some LANs, such as LocalTalk (Apple), the MAC address changes every time the computer is turned on.
3. A mobile computer can move from one physical network to another, resulting in a change in its MAC address.

To implement these changes, a static mapping table must be updated periodically. This overhead could affect the network performance.

Dynamic Mapping

In **dynamic mapping** each time a machine knows one of the two addresses, it can use a protocol to find the other one.

Two protocols have been designed to perform dynamic mapping: **Address Resolution Protocol (ARP)** and **Reverse Address Resolution Protocol (RARP).** The first maps an IP address to a MAC address; the second maps a MAC address to an IP address. However, we discuss only ARP because RARP has been replaced by DHCP (see Chapter 19); it is becoming obsolete.

ARP associates an IP address with its MAC address. On a typical physical network, such as a LAN, each device on a link is identified by a physical or station address that is usually imprinted on the NIC (network interface card).

Anytime a host, or a router, needs to find the MAC address of another host or router on its network, it sends an ARP query packet. The packet includes the physical and IP addresses of the sender and the IP address of the receiver. Because the sender does not know the physical address of the receiver, the query is broadcast over the network (see Fig. 20.2).

Figure 20.2 *ARP operation*

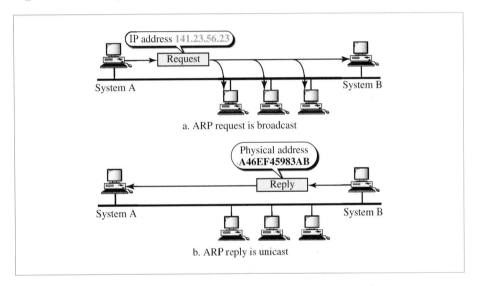

a. ARP request is broadcast

b. ARP reply is unicast

Every host or router on the network receives and processes the ARP query packet, but only the intended recipient recognizes its IP address and sends back an ARP response packet. The response packet contains the recipient's IP and physical addresses. The packet is unicast directly to the inquirer using the physical address received in the query packet.

In Figure 20.2a, the system on the left (A) has a packet that needs to be delivered to another system (B) with IP address 141.23.56.23. System A needs to pass the packet to its data link layer for the actual delivery, but it does not know the physical address of the recipient. It uses the services of ARP to send a broadcast request packet to ask for the physical address of a system with an IP address of 141.23.56.23.

This packet is received by every system on the physical network, but only system B will answer it, as shown in Figure 20.2b. System B sends an ARP reply packet that includes its physical address. Now system A can send all the packets it has for this destination, using the physical address it received.

Packet Format

Figure 20.3 shows the format of an ARP packet.

Figure 20.3   *ARP packet*

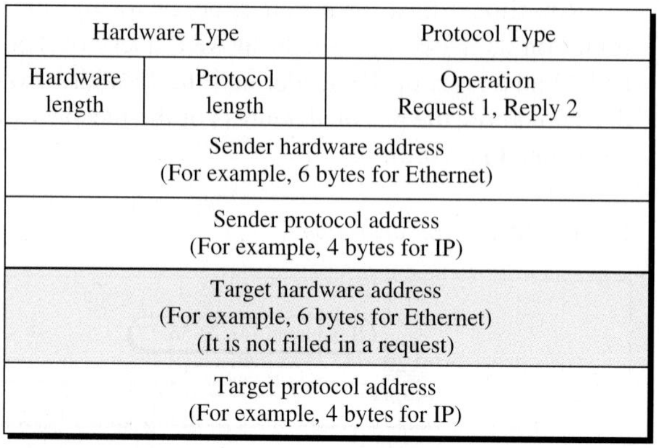

The fields are as follows:

■ **HTYPE (hardware type).** This is a 16-bit field defining the type of network on which ARP is running. Each LAN has been assigned an integer based on its type. For example, Ethernet is given type 1. ARP can be used on any physical network.

■ **PTYPE (protocol type).** This is a 16-bit field defining the protocol using ARP. For example, the value of this field for the IPv4 protocol is 0800_{16}. ARP can be used with any higher-level protocol.

■ **HLEN (hardware length).** This is an 8-bit field defining the length of the physical address in bytes. For example, for Ethernet the value is 6.

■ **PLEN (protocol length).** This is an 8-bit field defining the length of the IP address in bytes. For example, for the IPv4 protocol the value is 4.

■ **OPER (operation).** This is a 16-bit field defining the type of packet. Two packet types are defined: ARP request (1) and ARP reply (2).

■ **SHA (sender hardware address).** This is a variable-length field defining the physical address of the sender. For example, for Ethernet this field is 6 bytes long.

■ **SPA (sender protocol address).** This is a variable-length field defining the logical (for example, IP) address of the sender. For the IP protocol, this field is 4 bytes long.

■ **THA (target hardware address).** This is a variable-length field defining the physical address of the target. For example, for Ethernet this field is 6 bytes long. For an ARP request message, this field is all 0s because the sender does not know the physical address of the target.

■ **TPA (target protocol address).** This is a variable-length field defining the logical (for example, IP) address of the target. For the IPv4 protocol, this field is 4 bytes long.

Encapsulation

An ARP packet is **encapsulated** directly into a data link frame. For example, in Figure 20.4 an ARP packet is encapsulated in an Ethernet frame. Note that the type field indicates that the data carried by the frame are an ARP packet.

Figure 20.4 *Encapsulation of ARP packet*

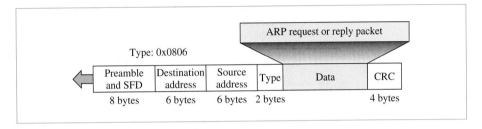

Operation

Let us see how ARP functions on the Internet. First we describe the steps involved. Then we discuss the four cases in which a host or router needs to use ARP.

Steps Involved

These are the steps involved in the delivery of the datagram:

1. The sender knows the IP address of the target. We will see how the sender obtains this shortly.
2. IP asks ARP to create an ARP request message, filling in the sender physical address, the sender IP address, and the target IP address. The target physical address field is filled with 0s.
3. The message is passed to the data link layer where it is encapsulated in a frame, using the physical address of the sender as the source address and the physical broadcast address as the destination address.
4. Every host or router receives the frame. Because the frame contains a broadcast destination address, all stations remove the message and pass it to ARP. All machines except the one targeted drop the packet. The target machine recognizes the IP address.
5. The target machine replies with an ARP reply message that contains its physical address. The message is unicast.
6. The sender receives the reply message. It now knows the physical address of the target machine.
7. The IP datagram, which carries data for the target machine, is now encapsulated in a frame and is unicast to the destination.

Four Different Cases

The following are four different cases in which the services of ARP can be used (see Fig. 20.5).

Figure 20.5   *Four cases using ARP*

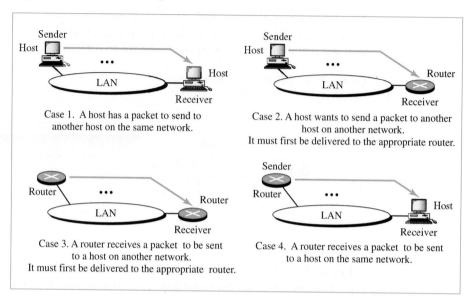

1. The sender is a host and wants to send a packet to another host on the same network. In this case, the IP address that must be mapped to a physical address is the destination IP address in the datagram header.

2. The sender is a host and wants to send a packet to another host on another network. In this case, the host looks at its routing table and finds the IP address of the next hop (router) for this destination. The IP address of the router becomes the IP address that must be mapped to a physical address.

3. The sender is a router that has received a datagram destined for a host on another network. It checks its routing table and finds the IP address of the next router. The IP address of the next router becomes the IP address that must be mapped to a physical address.

4. The sender is a router that has received a datagram destined for a host in the same network. The destination IP address of the datagram becomes the IP address that must be mapped to a physical address.

An ARP request is broadcast; an ARP reply is unicast.

Example 1

A host with IP address 130.23.3.20 and physical address B23455102210 has a packet to send to another host with IP address 130.23.43.25 and physical address A46EF45983AB. The two hosts are on the same Ethernet network. Show the ARP request and reply packets encapsulated in Ethernet frames.

Solution

Figure 20.6 shows the ARP request and reply packets. Note that the ARP data field in this case is 28 bytes, and that the individual addresses do not fit in the 4-byte boundary. That is why we do not show the regular 4-byte boundaries for these addresses. Note that we use hexadecimal for every field except the IP addresses.

Figure 20.6 *Example 1*

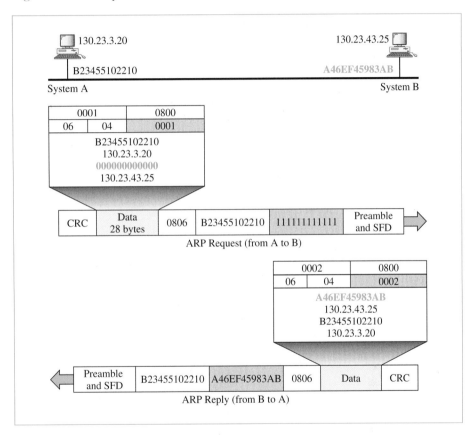

20.2 IP

The **Internet Protocol (IP)** is the host-to-host network layer delivery protocol for the Internet. IP is an unreliable and connectionless datagram protocol—a **best-effort delivery** service. The term *best-effort* means that IP provides no error control or flow control. IP uses only an error detection mechanism and discards the packet if it is corrupted. IP does its best to deliver a packet to its destination, but with no guarantees.

If reliability is important, IP must be paired with a reliable protocol such as TCP (at the transport layer). An example of a more commonly understood best-effort delivery service is the post office. The post office does its best to deliver the mail but might not always succeed. If an unregistered letter is lost, it is up to the sender or would-be recipient to discover the loss and rectify the problem. The post office itself does not keep track of every letter and cannot notify a sender of loss or damage.

IP is also a connectionless protocol for a packet-switching network which uses the datagram approach (see Chapter 19). This means that each datagram is handled independently, and each datagram can follow a different route to the destination. This implies that datagrams sent by the same source to the same destination could arrive out of order. Also, some could be lost or corrupted during transition. Again, IP relies on a higher-level protocol to take care of all these problems.

Datagram

Packets in the IP layer are called **datagrams.** Figure 20.7 shows the IP datagram format. A datagram is a variable-length packet consisting of two parts: header and data. The **header** is 20 to 60 bytes in length and contains information essential to routing and delivery. It is customary in the Internet to show the header in 4-byte sections. A brief description of each field is in order.

Figure 20.7   *IP datagram*

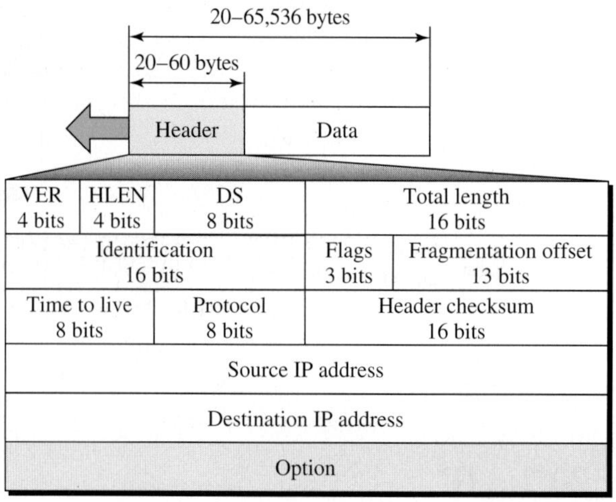

- **Version (VER).** This field defines the version of the IP. Currently the version is 4 (IPv4). However, version 6 (or IPv6) might totally replace version 4 in the near future.
- **Header length (HLEN).** Because of the option field, the length of the header is variable. This field defines the length of the datagram header in 4-byte words. Its value must be multiplied by 4 to give the length in bytes.

■ **Differentiated services.** This field defines the class of the datagram for quality-of-service purposes. We discuss quality of service in Chapter 23.

■ **Total length.** This field defines the total length (header plus data) of the IP datagram in bytes. To find the length of the data coming from the upper layer, subtract the header length from the total length. The header length can be found by multiplying the value in the HLEN field by 4.

$$\text{Length of data} = \text{total length} - \text{header length}$$

Since the field length is 16 bits, the total length of the IP datagram is limited to 65,535 ($2^{16} - 1$) bytes, of which 20 to 60 bytes are the header and the rest is data from the upper layer.

The total length field defines the total length of the datagram including the header.

Although a size of 65,535 bytes might seem large, the size of the IP datagram may increase in the near future as the underlying technologies allow even more throughput (using more bandwidth).

■ **Identification, flag, and offset.** We discuss these three fields when we discuss fragmentation in the next section.

■ **Time to live.** This field is used to control the maximum number of hops (routers) visited by the datagram. When a source host sends the datagram, it stores a number in this field. This value is approximately 2 times the maximum number of routes between any two hosts. Each router that processes the datagram decrements this number by 1. If this value, after being decremented, is zero, the router discards the datagram. The whole purpose is to prevent a datagram from becoming errant, going from one router to another.

■ **Protocol.** This field defines the higher-level protocol that uses the services of the IP layer. An IP datagram can encapsulate data from several higher-level protocols such as TCP, UDP, ICMP, and IGMP. This field specifies the final destination protocol to which the IP datagram should be delivered. In other words, since the IP multiplexes and demultiplexes data from different higher-level protocols, the value of this field helps in the demultiplexing process when the datagram arrives at its final destination (see Fig. 20.8).

The value of this field for different higher-level protocols is shown in Table 20.1.

Figure 20.8 *Multiplexing*

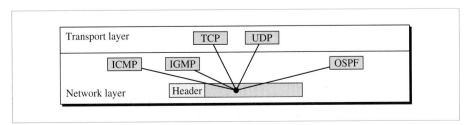

Table 20.1 *Protocols*

Value	Protocol
1	ICMP
2	IGMP
6	TCP
17	UDP
89	OSPF

■ **Checksum.** The checksum in the IP packet covers only the header, not the data. There are two good reasons for this. First, all higher-level protocols that encapsulate data in the IP datagram have a checksum field that covers the whole packet. Therefore, the checksum for the IP datagram does not have to check the encapsulated data. Second, the header of the IP packet changes with each visited router, but the data do not. So the checksum includes only the part that has changed. If the data are included, each router must recalculate the checksum for the whole packet, which means increased processing time for each router. Figure 20.9 shows an example of a checksum calculation for an IP header without options. The header is divided into 16-bit sections. The value of the checksum field is set to zero. All the sections are added and the sum is complemented. The result is inserted in the checksum field.

Figure 20.9   *Example of checksum calculation*

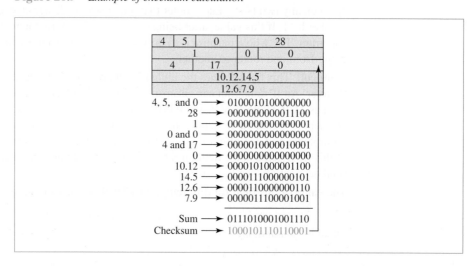

■ **Source address.** This field defines the IP address of the source. This field must remain unchanged during the time the IP datagram travels from the source host to the destination host.

■ **Destination address.** This field defines the IP address of the destination. This field must remain unchanged during the time the IP datagram travels from the source host to the destination host.

■ **Options.** Options, as the name implies, are not required for every datagram. They are used for network testing and debugging. Although options are not a required part of the IP header, option processing is required of the IP software. This means that all standards must be able to handle options if they are present in the header. There are several types of options, but we do not discuss them here. For more information see Forouzan, *TCP/IP Protocols Suite,* 2d ed., McGraw-Hill, 2002.

Fragmentation

A datagram can travel through different networks. Each router decapsulates the IP datagram from the frame it receives, processes it, and then encapsulates it in another frame. The format and size of the received frame depend on the protocol used by the physical network through which the frame has just traveled. The format and size of the sent frame depend on the protocol used by the physical network through which the frame is going to travel. For example, if a router connects an Ethernet network to an ATM network, it receives a frame in the Ethernet format and sends a frame in the ATM format.

Maximum Transfer Unit (MTU)

Each data link layer protocol has its own frame format. One of the fields defined in the format is the maximum size of the data field. In other words, when a datagram is encapsulated in a frame, the total size of the datagram must be less than this maximum size, which is defined by the restriction imposed by the hardware and software used in the network (see Fig. 20.10).

Figure 20.10 *MTU*

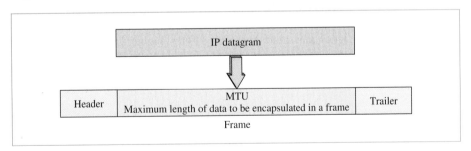

To make the IP independent of the physical network, the packagers decided to make the maximum length of the IP datagram equal to the largest **maximum transfer unit (MTU)** defined so far (65,535 bytes). This makes transmission more efficient if we use a protocol with an MTU of this size. However, for other physical networks, we must divide the datagram to make it possible to pass through these networks. This is called **fragmentation.**

When a datagram is fragmented, each fragment has its own header with most of the fields repeated, but some changed. A fragmented datagram may itself be fragmented if it encounters a network with an even smaller MTU. In other words, a datagram can be fragmented several times before it reaches the final destination.

A datagram can be fragmented by the source host or any router in the path. The reassembly of the datagram, however, is done only by the destination host because each fragment becomes an independent datagram. Whereas the fragmented datagram can travel through different routes, and we can never control or guarantee which route a fragmented datagram may take, all the fragments belonging to the same datagram should finally arrive at the destination host. So it is logical to do the reassembly at the final destination.

Fields Related to Fragmentation

The fields that are related to fragmentation and reassembly of an IP datagram are the identification, flags, and fragmentation offset fields.

- **Identification.** This field identifies a datagram originating from the source host. When a datagram is fragmented, the value in the identification field is copied into all fragments. In other words, all fragments have the same identification number, which is also the same as the original datagram. The identification number helps the destination in reassembling the datagram. It knows that all fragments having the same identification value should be assembled into one datagram.

- **Flags.** This is a 3-bit field. The first bit is reserved. The second bit is called the *do not fragment* bit. If its value is 1, the machine must not fragment the datagram. If it cannot pass the datagram through any available physical network, it discards the datagram and sends an ICMP error message to the source host (next section). If its value is 0, the datagram can be fragmented if necessary. The third bit is called the *more fragment* bit. If its value is 1, it means the datagram is not the last fragment; there are more fragments after this one. If its value is 0, it means this is the last or only fragment.

- **Fragmentation offset.** This 13-bit field shows the relative position of this fragment with respect to the whole datagram. It is the offset of the data in the original datagram measured in units of 8 bytes. Figure 20.11 shows a datagram with a data size of 4000 bytes fragmented into three parts. The bytes in the original datagram are numbered 0 to 3999. The first fragment carries bytes 0 to 1399. The offset for this

Figure 20.11   *Fragmentation example*

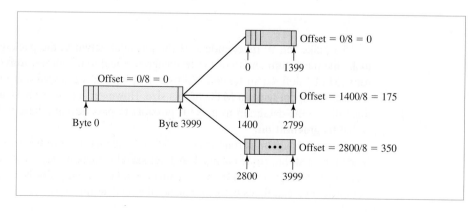

datagram is 0/8 = 0. The second fragment carries bytes 1400 to 2799; the offset value for this fragment is 1400/8 = 175. Finally, the third fragment carries bytes 2800 to 3999. The offset value for this fragment is 2800/8 = 350.

Remember that the value of the offset is measured in units of 8 bytes. This is done because the length of the offset field is only 13 bits long and cannot represent a sequence of bytes greater than 8191. This forces hosts or routers that fragment datagrams to choose the size of each fragment so that the first byte number is divisible by 8.

20.3 ICMP

As discussed in Section 20.2, the IP provides unreliable and connectionless datagram delivery. It was designed this way to make efficient use of network resources. IP is a best-effort delivery service that delivers a datagram from its original source to its final destination. However, it has two deficiencies: lack of error control and lack of assistance mechanisms.

IP has no error-reporting or error-correcting mechanism. What happens if something goes wrong? What happens if a router must discard a datagram because it cannot find a router to the final destination, or because the time-to-live field has a zero value? What happens if the final destination host must discard all fragments of a datagram because it has not received all fragments within a predetermined time limit? These are examples of situations where an error has occurred and IP has no built-in mechanism to notify the original host.

IP also lacks a mechanism for host and management queries. A host sometimes needs to determine if a router or another host is alive. And sometimes a network manager needs information from another host or router.

The **Internet Control Message Protocol (ICMP)** has been designed to compensate for the above two deficiencies. It is a companion to the IP.

ICMP itself is a network layer protocol. However, its messages are not passed directly to the data link layer as would be expected. Instead, the messages are first encapsulated inside IP datagrams before going to the lower layer (see Fig. 20.12).

The value of the protocol field in the IP datagram is 1 to indicate that the IP data are an ICMP message.

Figure 20.12 *ICMP encapsulation*

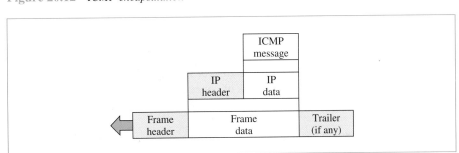

Types of Messages

ICMP messages are divided into two broad categories: error-reporting messages and query messages.

Error Reporting

One of the main responsibilities of ICMP is to report errors. Although technology has produced increasingly reliable transmission media, errors still exist and must be handled. IP is an unreliable protocol. This means that error checking and error control are not a concern of IP. ICMP was designed, in part, to compensate for this shortcoming. However, ICMP does not correct errors; it simply reports them. Error correction is left to the higher-level protocols. **Error-reporting messages** are always sent to the original source because the only information available in the datagram about the route is the source and destination IP addresses. ICMP uses the source IP address to send the error message to the source (originator) of the datagram.

ICMP always reports error messages to the original source.

Five types of errors are handled: destination unreachable, source quench, time exceeded, parameter problems, and redirection. See Figure 20.13.

Figure 20.13   *Error-reporting messages*

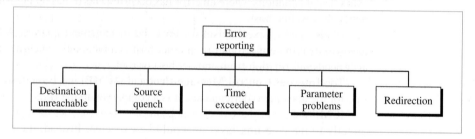

Destination Unreachable   When a router cannot route a datagram or a host cannot deliver a datagram, the datagram is discarded and the router or the host sends a **destination-unreachable message** back to the source host that initiated the datagram.

Source Quench   IP is a connectionless protocol. There is no communication between the source host, which produces the datagram; the routers, which forward it; and the destination host, which processes it. One of the ramifications of this absence of communication is the lack of *flow control* and *congestion control* (see Chapter 23). The lack of flow control can create a major problem in the operation of source-destination delivery. The source host never knows if the destination host has been overwhelmed with datagrams. The lack of congestion control can create a major problem in the routers that are supposed to forward the packets.

There is no flow control or congestion control mechanism in IP.

The **source-quench message** in ICMP has been designed to add a kind of flow control and congestion control to IP. When a router or host discards a datagram due to congestion, it sends a source-quench message to the sender of the datagram. This message has two purposes. First, it informs the source that the datagram has been discarded. Second, it warns the source that there is congestion somewhere in the path and that the source should slow down (quench) the sending process.

Time Exceeded   The **time-exceeded message** is generated in two cases. First, the router that receives a datagram with a value of 0 in the TTL field discards the datagram. However, when the datagram is discarded, a time-exceeded message must be sent by the router to the original source. Second, a time-exceeded message is also generated when all fragments that make up a message do not arrive at the destination host within a certain time limit.

Parameter Problem   Any ambiguity in the header part of a datagram can create serious problems as the datagram travels through the Internet. If a router or the destination host discovers an ambiguous or missing value in any field of the datagram, it discards the datagram and sends a **parameter-problem message** back to the source.

Redirection   When a router needs to send a packet destined for another network, it must know the IP address of the next appropriate router. The same is true if the sender is a host. Both routers and hosts, then, must have a routing table to find the address of the router or the next router. Routers take part in the routing update process, as we will see in Chapter 21, and are supposed to be updated constantly. Routing is dynamic.

However, for efficiency, hosts do not take part in the routing update process because there are many more hosts in an internet than routers. Updating the routing tables of hosts dynamically produces unacceptable traffic. The hosts usually use static routing. When a host comes up, its routing table has a limited number of entries. It usually knows only the IP address of one router, the default router. For this reason, the host may send a datagram, which is destined for another network, to the wrong router. In this case, the router that receives the datagram will forward the datagram to the correct router. However, to update the routing table of a host, it sends a **redirection message** back to this host.

Query

In addition to error reporting, ICMP can diagnose some network problems. This is accomplished through the **query messages,** a group of four different pairs of messages, as shown in Figure 20.14. In this type of ICMP message, a node sends a message that is answered in a specific format by the destination node.

Figure 20.14   *Query messages*

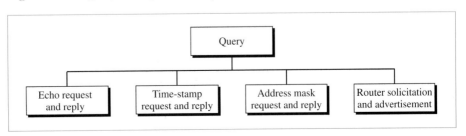

Echo Request and Reply   The **echo-request** and **echo-reply** messages are designed for diagnostic purposes. Network managers and users utilize this pair of messages to identify network problems. The combination of echo-request and echo-reply messages determines whether two systems (hosts or routers) can communicate with each other.

Time-stamp Request and Reply   Two machines (hosts or routers) can use the **time-stamp-request** and **time-stamp-reply messages** to determine the round-trip time needed for an IP datagram to travel between them. It can also be used to synchronize the clocks in two machines.

Address Mask Request and Reply   The IP address of a host contains a network address, subnet address, and host identifier. A host may know its full IP address, but it may not know which part of the address defines the network and subnetwork address and which part corresponds to the host identifier. In this case, the host can send an **address mask request message** to a router. The router then sends a mask in an **address mask reply message.**

Router Solicitation and Advertisement   As we discussed in the redirection-message section, a host that wants to send data to a host on another network needs to know the address of routers connected to its own network. Also, the host must know if the routers are alive and functioning. The **router-solicitation** and **router-advertisement** messages can help in this situation. A host can broadcast (or multicast) a router-solicitation message. The router or routers that receive the solicitation message broadcast their routing information using the router-advertisement message. A router can also periodically send router-advertisement messages even if no host has solicited. Note that when a router sends out an advertisement, it announces not only its own presence but also the presence of all routers on the network of which it is aware.

20.4   IPV6

The network layer protocol in the Internet is currently **IPv4**. IPv4 provides the host-to-host communication between systems in the Internet. Although IPv4 is well designed, data communication has evolved since the inception of IPv4 in the 1970s. IPv4 has some deficiencies that make it unsuitable for the fast-growing Internet, including the following:

- IPv4 has a two-level address structure (netid and hostid) categorized into five classes (A, B, C, D, and E). The use of address space is inefficient.
- The Internet must accommodate real-time audio and video transmission. This type of transmission requires minimum delay strategies and reservation of resources not provided in the IPv4 design.
- The Internet must accommodate encryption and authentication of data for some applications. Originally, no security mechanism was provided by IPv4.

To overcome these deficiencies, **Internet Protocol, version 6 (IPv6),** also known as **Internetworking Protocol, next generation (IPng),** was proposed and is now a standard. In IPv6, the Internet protocol was extensively modified to accommodate the unforeseen growth of the Internet. The format and the length of the IP addresses were changed along with the packet format.

The next-generation IP, or IPv6, has some advantages over IPv4 that can be summarized as follows:

- **Larger address space.** An IPv6 address is 128 bits long. Compared with the 32-bit address of IPv4, this is a huge (2^{96}) increase in the address space.
- **Better header format.** IPv6 uses a new header format in which options are separated from the base header and inserted, when needed, between the base header and the upper-layer data. This simplifies and speeds up the routing process because most of the options do not need to be checked by routers.
- **New options.** IPv6 has new options to allow for additional functionalities.
- **Allowance for extension.** IPv6 is designed to allow the extension of the protocol if required by new technologies or applications.
- **Support for resource allocation.** In IPv6, the type-of-service field has been removed, but a mechanism called **flow label** has been added to enable the source to request special handling of the packet. This mechanism can be used to support traffic such as real-time audio and video.
- **Support for more security.** The encryption and authentication options in IPv6 provide confidentiality and integrity of the packet.

IPv6 Addresses

An IPv6 address consists of 16 bytes (octets); it is 128 bits long (see Fig. 20.15).

Figure 20.15 *IPv6 address*

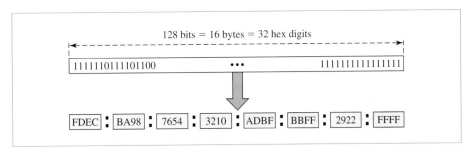

Hexadecimal Colon Notation

To make addresses more readable, IPv6 specifies **hexadecimal colon notation.** In this notation, 128 bits are divided into eight sections, each 2 bytes in length. Two bytes in hexadecimal notation requires four hexadecimal digits. Therefore, the address consists of 32 hexadecimal digits, with every 4 digits separated by a colon.

Abbreviation

Although the IP address, even in hexadecimal format, is very long, many of the digits are zeros. In this case, we can **abbreviate** the address. The leading zeros of a section (four digits between two colons) can be omitted. Only the leading zeros can be dropped, not the trailing zeros. For an example, see Figure 20.16.

Figure 20.16   *Abbreviated address*

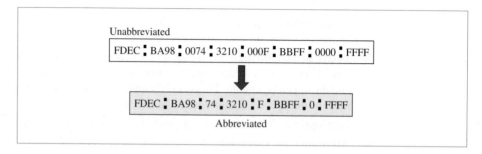

Using this form of abbreviation, 0074 can be written as 74, 000F as F, and 0000 as 0. Note that 3210 cannot be abbreviated. Further abbreviations are possible if there are consecutive sections consisting of zeros only. We can remove the zeros altogether and replace them with a double semicolon. Figure 20.17 shows the concept.

Figure 20.17   *Abbreviated address with consecutive zeros*

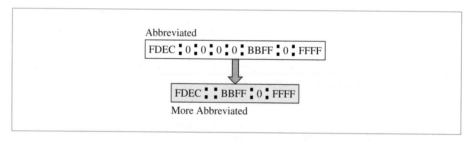

Note that this type of abbreviation is allowed only once per address. If there are two runs of zero sections, only one of them can be abbreviated. Reexpansion of the abbreviated address is very simple: Align the unabbreviated portions and insert zeros to get the original expanded address.

CIDR Notation

IPv6 allows classless addressing and CIDR notation. For example, Figure 20.18 shows how we can define a prefix of 60 bits using CIDR.

Figure 20.18   *CIDR address*

FDEC : 0 : 0 : 0 : 0 : BBFF : 0 : FFFF/60

Categories of Addresses

IPv6 defines three types of addresses: unicast, anycast, and multicast.

Unicast Addresses

A unicast address defines a single computer. The packet sent to a unicast address must be delivered to that specific computer.

Anycast Addresses

An **anycast address** defines a group of computers with addresses that have the same prefix. For example, all computers connected to the same physical network share the same prefix address. A packet sent to an anycast address must be delivered to exactly one of the members of the group—the closest or the most easily accessible.

Multicast Addresses

A multicast address defines a group of computers that may or may not share the same prefix and may or may not be connected to the same physical network. A packet sent to a multicast address must be delivered to each member of the set.

IPv6 Packet Format

The IPv6 packet is shown in Figure 20.19. Each packet is composed of a mandatory base header followed by the payload. The payload consists of two parts: optional extension headers and data from an upper layer. The base header occupies 40 bytes, whereas the extension headers and data from the upper layer contain up to 65,535 bytes of information.

Figure 20.19 *Format of an IPv6 datagram*

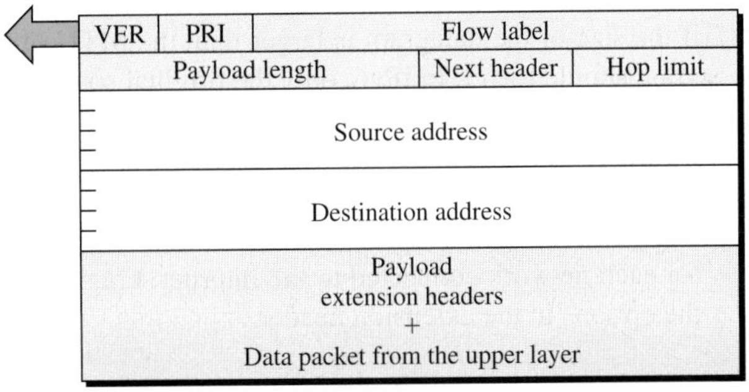

Base Header

Figure 20.19 shows the **base header** with its eight fields.
   These fields are as follows:

■   **Version.** This 4-bit field defines the version number of the IP. For IPv6, the value is 6.

- **Priority.** The 4-bit priority field defines the priority of the packet with respect to traffic congestion.
- **Flow label.** The flow label is a 3-byte (24-bit) field that is designed to provide special handling for a particular flow of data.
- **Payload length.** This 2-byte payload length field defines the total length of the IP datagram excluding the base header.
- **Next header.** The next header is an 8-bit field defining the header that follows the base header in the datagram. The next header is either one of the optional extension headers used by IP or the header for an upper-layer protocol such as UDP or TCP. Each extension header also contains this field.
- **Hop limit.** This 8-bit hop limit field serves the same purpose as the TTL (time to live) field in IPv4.
- **Source address.** The source address field is a 16-byte (128-bit) Internet address that identifies the original source of the datagram.
- **Destination address.** The destination address field is a 16-byte (128-bit) Internet address that usually identifies the final destination of the datagram. However, if source routing is used, this field contains the address of the next router.

Extension Headers

The length of the base header is fixed at 40 bytes. However, to give more functionality to the IP datagram, the base header can be followed by up to six **extension headers.** Many of these headers are options in IPv4. For more details see Forouzan, *TCP/IP Protocol Suite,* 2d ed., McGraw-Hill.

Fragmentation

The concept of fragmentation is the same as that in IPv4. However, the place where fragmentation takes place differs. In IPv4, the source or a router is required to fragment if the size of the datagram is larger than the MTU of the network over which the datagram should travel. In IPv6, only the original source can fragment. A source must use a path MTU discovery technique to find the smallest MTU supported by any network on the path. The source then fragments, using this knowledge.

If the source does not use the path MTU discovery technique, it must fragment the datagram to a size of 576 bytes or smaller. This is the minimum size of MTU required for each network connected to the Internet. Fragmentation in IPv6 is handled by one of the options in the extension header.

Authentication and Privacy

IPv6 provides authentication and privacy using options in the extension header. We will discuss network security in Chapter 31.

ICMPv6

Another protocol that has been modified in version 6 of the Internet is ICMP (**ICMPv6**). This new version follows the same strategy and purposes as version 4. ICMPv4 has been modified to make it more suitable for IPv6. In addition, some protocols that were independent in version 4 are now part of ICMPv6. Figure 20.20 compares the network layer of version 4 to that of version 6.

Figure 20.20 *Comparison of network layers in version 4 and version 6*

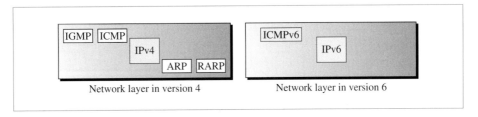

ARP and IGMP in version 4 are combined in ICMPv6. RARP is dropped from the suite because it is seldom used.

Transition from IPv4 to IPv6

Because of the huge number of systems on the Internet, the transition from IPv4 to IPv6 cannot happen suddenly. It takes a considerable amount of time before every system in the Internet can move from IPv4 to IPv6. The transition should be smooth to prevent any problems between IPv4 and IPv6 systems.

Three strategies have been devised by the IETF to make the transition period smoother (see Fig. 20.21).

Figure 20.21 *Three transition strategies*

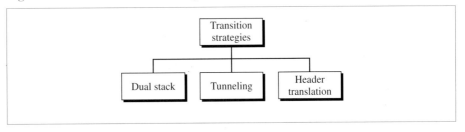

Dual Stack

It is recommended that all hosts, before migrating completely to version 6, have a **dual stack** of protocols. In other words, a station should run IPv4 and IPv6 simultaneously until all the Internet uses IPv6. See Figure 20.22 for the layout of dual-stack configuration.

To determine which version to use when sending a packet to a destination, the source host queries the DNS (see Chapter 25). If the DNS returns an IPv4 address, the source host sends an IPv4 packet. If the DNS returns an IPv6 address, the source host sends an IPv6 packet.

Tunneling

Tunneling is a strategy used when two computers using IPv6 want to communicate with each other when the packet must pass through a region that uses IPv4. To pass through

Figure 20.22   *Dual stack*

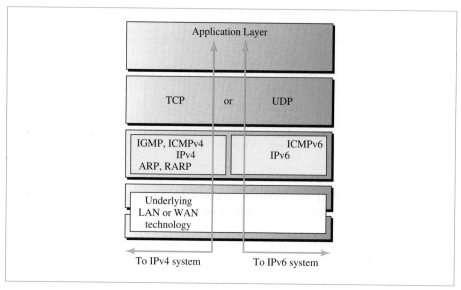

this region, the packet must have an IPv4 address. So the IPv6 packet is encapsulated in an IPv4 packet when it enters the region, and the IPv6 packet leaves its capsule when it exits the region. It seems as if the IPv6 packet enters a tunnel at one end and emerges at the other end. To make it clear that the IPv4 packet is carrying an IPv6 packet as data, the protocol value is set to 41. See Figure 20.23.

Figure 20.23   *Tunneling*

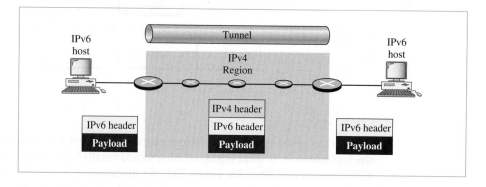

Header Translation

Header translation is necessary when the majority of the Internet has moved to IPv6 but some systems still use IPv4. The sender wants to use IPv6, but the receiver does not understand IPv6. Tunneling does not work in this situation because the packet must be in the IPv4 format to be understood by the receiver. In this case, the header format must be changed totally through header translation. The header of the IPv6 packet is converted to an IPv4 header (see Fig. 20.24).

Figure 20.24   *Header translation*

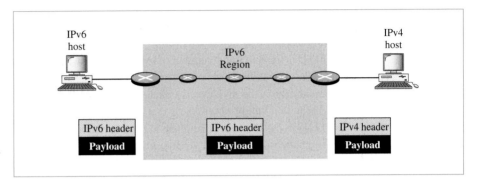

20.5   KEY TERMS

abbreviation
address mask request and reply
Address Resolution Protocol (ARP)
anycast address
base header
best-effort delivery
datagram
destination address
destination-unreachable message
dual stack
dynamic mapping
echo-request and -reply message
error-reporting message
extension header
flow label
fragmentation
fragmentation offset
header translation
hexadecimal colon notation
hop limit
Internet Control Message Protocol
   (ICMP)

Internet Protocol (IP)
Internetworking Control Message
   Protocol, version 6 (ICMPv6)
Internetworking Protocol, next generation
   (IPng)
Internetworking Protocol, version 4 (IPv4)
Internetworking Protocol, version 6 (IPv6)
maximum transfer unit (MTU)
next header
parameter-problem message
query message
redirection message
Reverse Address Resolution Protocol
   (RARP)
router-solicitation and -advertisement
   message
source-quench message
static mapping
time to live
time-exceeded message
time-stamp request and reply message
tunneling

20.6   SUMMARY

❑   The Address Resolution Protocol (ARP) is a dynamic mapping method that finds a
     physical address, given an IP address.
❑   An ARP request is broadcast to all devices on the network.
❑   An ARP reply is unicast to the host requesting the mapping.

❏ IP is an unreliable connectionless protocol responsible for source-to-destination delivery.

❏ Packets in the IP layer are called datagrams.

❏ A datagram consists of a header (20 to 60 bytes) and data.

❏ The MTU is the maximum number of bytes that a data link protocol can encapsulate. MTUs vary from protocol to protocol.

❏ Fragmentation is the division of a datagram into smaller units to accommodate the MTU of a data link protocol.

❏ The fields in the IP header that relate to fragmentation are the identification number, the fragmentation flags, and the fragmentation offset.

❏ The Internet Control Message Protocol (ICMP) sends five types of error-reporting messages and four pairs of query messages to support the unreliable and connectionless Internet Protocol (IP).

❏ ICMP messages are encapsulated in IP datagrams.

❏ The destination-unreachable error message is sent to the source host when a datagram is undeliverable.

❏ The source-quench error message is sent in an effort to alleviate congestion.

❏ The time-exceeded message notifies a source host that (1) the time-to-live field has reached zero or (2) fragments of a message have not arrived in a set amount of time.

❏ The parameter-problem message notifies a host that there is a problem in the header field of a datagram.

❏ The redirection message is sent to make the routing table of a host more efficient.

❏ The echo-request and echo-reply messages test the connectivity between two systems.

❏ The time-stamp-request and time-stamp-reply messages can determine the round-trip time between two systems or the difference in time between two systems.

❏ The address-mask request and address-mask reply messages are used to obtain the subnet mask.

❏ The router-solicitation and router-advertisement messages allow hosts to update their routing tables.

❏ IPv6, the latest version of the Internet Protocol, has a 128-bit address space, a revised header format, new options, an allowance for extension, support for resource allocation, and increased security measures.

❏ IPv6 uses hexadecimal colon notation with abbreviation methods available.

❏ Three strategies used to make the transition from version 4 to version 6 are dual stack, tunneling, and header translation.

20.7 PRACTICE SET

Review Questions

1. Name the five protocols in the network layer.
2. What is the purpose of ARP?
3. Why is an ARP request broadcast? Why is an ARP reply unicast?

4. What do we mean when we say IP is a best-effort delivery service?
5. What is the name of a packet in the IP layer?
6. What is purpose of the protocol field in the IP header?
7. Why does the IP checksum cover just the header?
8. What is the MTU and how is fragmentation related to it?
9. Which fields in the IP header remain the same as the packet travels from source host to destination host?
10. What is the function of ICMP?
11. What is the purpose of an ICMP redirection message?
12. How many bits is an IPv4 address? How many bits is an IPv6 address?
13. Name and describe the three types of IPv6 addresses.
14. Why are RARP and IGMP missing from IPv6?
15. What strategies have been devised for the transition of IPv4 to IPv6?

Multiple-Choice Questions

16. _____ is a dynamic mapping protocol in which a physical address is found for a given IP address.
   a. ARP
   b. RARP
   c. ICMP
   d. None of the above
17. A router reads the _____ address on a packet to determine the next hop.
   a. IP
   b. MAC
   c. Source
   d. ARP
18. The target hardware address on an Ethernet is _____ in an ARP request.
   a. 0x000000000000
   b. 0.0.0.0
   c. Variable
   d. Class-dependent
19. An ARP reply is _____ to _____.
   a. Broadcast; all hosts
   b. Multicast; one host
   c. Unicast; all hosts
   d. Unicast; one host
20. An ARP request is _____ to _____.
   a. Broadcast; all hosts
   b. Multicast; one host
   c. Unicast; all hosts
   d. Unicast; one host

21. What is the maximum size of the data portion of the IP datagram?
    a. 65,535 bytes
    b. 65,515 bytes
    c. 65,475 bytes
    d. 65,460 bytes

22. A best-effort delivery service such as IP does not include _____.
    a. Error checking
    b. Error correction
    c. Datagram acknowledgment
    d. All the above

23. An HLEN value of decimal 10 means _____.
    a. There is 10 bytes of options
    b. There is 40 bytes of options
    c. There is 10 bytes in the header
    d. There is 40 bytes in the header

24. In IPv4, what is the value of the total length field in bytes if the header is 28 bytes and the data field is 400 bytes?
    a. 428
    b. 407
    c. 107
    d. 427

25. In IPv4, what is the length of the data field given an HLEN value of 12 and total length value of 40,000?
    a. 39,988
    b. 40,012
    c. 40,048
    d. 39,952

26. A datagram is fragmented into three smaller datagrams. Which of the following is true?
    a. The *do not fragment* bit is set to 1 for all three datagrams.
    b. The *more fragment* bit is set to 0 for all three datagrams.
    c. The identification field is the same for all three datagrams.
    d. The offset field is the same for all three datagrams.

27. If the fragment offset has a value of 100, it means that _____.
    a. The datagram has not been fragmented
    b. The datagram is 100 bytes in size
    c. The first byte of the datagram is byte 100
    d. The first byte of the datagram is byte 800

28. What is needed to determine the number of the last byte of a fragment?
    a. Identification number
    b. Offset number

  c. Total length

  d. (b) and (c)

29. The IP header size _____.

  a. Is 20 to 60 bytes long

  b. Is 20 bytes long

  c. Is 60 bytes long

  d. Depends on the MTU

30. If a host needs to synchronize its clock with another host, it sends a _____ message.

  a. Time-stamp-request

  b. Source-quench

  c. Router-advertisement

  d. Time-exceeded

31. Which of the following types of ICMP messages needs to be encapsulated into an IP datagram?

  a. Time-exceeded

  b. Multicasting

  c. Echo reply

  d. All the above

32. The purpose of echo request and echo reply is to _____.

  a. Report errors

  b. Check node-to-node communication

  c. Check packet lifetime

  d. Find IP addresses

33. In error reporting the encapsulated ICMP packet goes to _____.

  a. The sender

  b. The receiver

  c. A router

  d. Any of the above

34. When the hop-count field reaches zero and the destination has not been reached, a _____ error message is sent.

  a. Destination-unreachable

  b. Time-exceeded

  c. Parameter-problem

  d. Redirection

35. When not all fragments of a message have been received within the designated amount of time, a _____ error message is sent.

  a. Source-quench

  b. Time-exceeded

  c. Parameter-problem

  d. Time-stamp-request

36. Errors in the header or option fields of an IP datagram require a _____ error message.
    a. Parameter-problem
    b. Source-quench
    c. Router-solicitation
    d. Redirection

37. A _____ can learn about network _____ by sending out a router-solicitation packet.
    a. Router; routers
    b. Router; hosts
    c. Host; hosts
    d. Host; routers

38. One method to alert a source host of congestion is the _____ message.
    a. Redirection
    b. Echo-request
    c. Source-quench
    d. Destination-unreachable

39. A time-exceeded message is generated if _____.
    a. The round-trip time between hosts is close to zero
    b. The time-to-live field has a zero value
    c. Fragments of a message do not arrive within a set time
    d. (b) and (c)

40. To determine whether a node is reachable, _____ message can be sent.
    a. An echo-reply
    b. An echo-request
    c. A redirection
    d. A source-quench

41. Which of the following is a necessary part of the IPv6 datagram?
    a. Base header
    b. Extension header
    c. Data packet from the upper layer
    d. (a) and (c)

42. In IPv6, the _____ field in the base header restricts the lifetime of a datagram.
    a. Version
    b. Priority
    c. Next-header
    d. Hop limit
    e. Neighbor-advertisement

Exercises

43. Is the size of the ARP packet fixed? Explain.

44. What is the size of an ARP packet when the protocol is IP and the hardware is Ethernet?

45. What is the size of an Ethernet frame carrying an ARP packet?

46. Which fields of the IP header change from router to router?

47. Calculate the HLEN value if the total length is 1200 bytes, 1176 of which is data from the upper layer.

48. Can the value of the header length in an IP packet be less than 5? When is it exactly 5?

49. The value of the total length field in an IP datagram is 36, and the value of the header length field is 5. How many bytes of data is the packet carrying?

50. A datagram is carrying 1024 bytes of data. If there is no option information, what is the value of the header length field? What is the value of the total-length field?

51. An IP datagram arrives whose fragmentation offset is 0 and whose M bit (more fragment bit) is 0. Is this a fragment?

52. An IP fragment has arrived whose offset value is 100. How many bytes of data were originally sent by the source before the data in this fragment?

53. What is the minimum size of an ICMP packet? What is the maximum size of an ICMP packet?

54. What is the minimum size of an IP packet that carries an ICMP packet? What is the maximum size?

55. What is the minimum size of an Ethernet frame that carries an IP packet which in turn carries an ICMP packet? What is the maximum size?

56. How can we determine if an IP packet is carrying an ICMP packet?

57. Show the shortest form of the following addresses.
    a. 2340:1ABC:119A:A000:0000:0000:0000:0000
    b. 0000:00AA:0000:0000:0000:0000:119A:A231
    c. 2340:0000:0000:0000:0000:119A:A001:0000
    d. 0000:0000:0000:2340:0000:0000:0000:0000

58. Show the original (unabbreviated) form of the following addresses.
    a. 0::0
    b. 0:AA::0
    c. 0:1234::3
    d. 123::1:2

59. How many more addresses are available with IPv6 than with IPv4?

CHAPTER 21

Unicast and Multicast Routing: Routing Protocols

An internet is a combination of networks connected by routers. When a packet goes from a source to a destination, it will probably pass through many routers until it reaches the router attached to the destination network. A router consults a routing table when a packet is ready to be forwarded. The routing table specifies the optimum path for the packet. However, the table can be either static or dynamic. A *static table* does not change frequently. A *dynamic table,* on the other hand, is updated automatically when there is a change somewhere in the internet. Today, an internet needs dynamic routing tables. The tables need to be updated as soon as there is a change in the internet. For instance, they need to be updated when a route is down, and they need to be updated whenever a better route has been created.

Routing protocols have been created in response to the demand for dynamic routing tables. A routing protocol is a combination of rules and procedures that lets routers in the internet inform one another of changes. It allows routers to share whatever they know about the internet or their neighborhood. The sharing of information allows a router in San Francisco to know about the failure of a network in Texas. The routing protocols also include procedures for combining information received from other routers.

In this chapter, we first discuss unicast routing, one source to one destination. We then define multicast routing, one source to a group of destinations.

21.1   UNICAST ROUTING

In unicast communication, there is one source and one destination. The relationship between the source and the destination is one-to-one. In this type of communication, both the source and the destination addresses, in the IP datagram, are the unicast addresses assigned to the host (or host port, to be more exact). In Figure 21.1, a unicast packet starts from source S1 and passes through routers to reach destination D1. We have shown the networks as a link between the routers to simplify the figure.

Note that in **unicast routing,** when a router receives a packet, it forwards the packet through only one of its ports (the one belonging to the optimum path) as defined

Figure 21.1 *Unicasting*

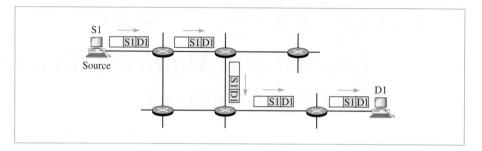

in the routing table. The router may discard the packet if it cannot find the destination address in its routing table.

> **In unicast routing, the router forwards the received packet through only one of its ports.**

Metric

A router receives a packet from a network and passes it to another network. A router is usually attached to several networks. When it receives a packet, to which network should it pass the packet? The decision is based on optimization: Which of the available pathways is the optimum pathway? A **metric** is a cost assigned for passing through a network. The total metric of a particular route is equal to the sum of the metrics of networks that comprise the route. A router chooses the route with the shortest (smallest) metric.

The metric assigned to each network depends on the type of protocol. Some simple protocols, such as the **Routing Information Protocol (RIP),** treat all networks as equals. The cost of passing through each network is the same; it is one hop count. So if a packet passes through 10 networks to reach the destination, the total cost is 10 hop counts.

Other protocols, such as **Open Shortest Path First (OSPF),** allow the administrator to assign a cost for passing through a network based on the type of service required. A route through a network can have different costs (metrics). For example, if maximum throughput is the desired type of service, a satellite link has a lower metric than a fiber-optic line. On the other hand, if minimum delay is the desired type of service, a fiber-optic line has a lower metric than a satellite line. OSPF allows each router to have several routing tables based on the required type of service.

Other protocols define the metric totally differently. In the **Border Gateway Protocol (BGP),** the criterion is the policy, which can be set by the administrator. The policy defines what paths should be chosen.

Interior and Exterior Routing

Today, an internet can be so large that one routing protocol cannot handle the task of updating the routing tables of all routers. For this reason, an internet is divided into autonomous systems. An **autonomous system (AS)** is a group of networks and routers under the authority of a single administration. Routing inside an autonomous system is referred to as **interior routing.** Routing between autonomous systems is referred to as **exterior routing.** Each autonomous system can choose an interior routing protocol to handle routing inside the autonomous system. However, only one exterior routing protocol is usually chosen to handle routing between autonomous systems.

21.2 UNICAST ROUTING PROTOCOLS

Several interior and exterior routing protocols are in use. In this section, we cover only the most popular ones. We discuss two interior routing protocols, RIP and OSPF, and one exterior routing protocol, BGP (see Fig. 21.2).

Figure 21.2 *Popular routing protocols*

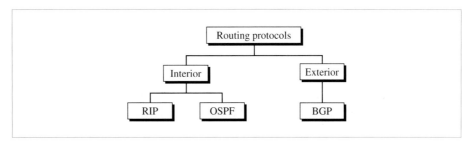

RIP and OSPF can be used to update routing tables inside an autonomous system. BGP can be used to update routing tables for routers that join the autonomous systems together.

In Figure 21.3, routers R1, R2, R3, and R4 use an interior and an exterior routing protocol. The other routers use only interior routing protocols. The solid lines show the

Figure 21.3 *Autonomous systems*

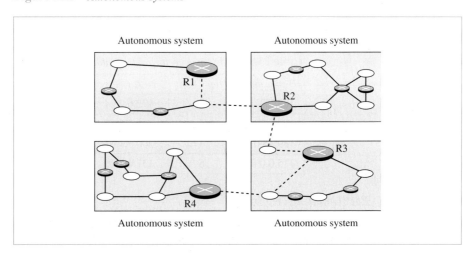

communication between routers that use interior routing protocols. The broken lines show the communication between the routers that use an exterior routing protocol.

RIP

The Routing Information Protocol (RIP) is an interior routing protocol used inside an autonomous system. It is a very simple protocol based on *distance vector routing,* which uses the Bellman-Ford algorithm for calculating the routing tables. In this section, we first study the principle of distance vector routing as it is applied to RIP, and we then discuss RIP itself.

Distance Vector Routing

In **distance vector routing,** each router periodically shares its knowledge about the entire internet with its neighbors. The three keys to understanding how this algorithm works are as follows:

1. **Sharing knowledge about the entire autonomous system.** Each router shares its knowledge about the entire autonomous system with its neighbors. At the outset, a router's knowledge may be sparse. How much it knows, however, is unimportant; it sends whatever it has.

2. **Sharing only with neighbors.** Each router sends its knowledge only to neighbors. It sends whatever knowledge it has through all its interfaces.

3. **Sharing at regular intervals.** Each router sends its knowledge to its neighbors at fixed intervals, for example, every 30 s.

Routing Table

Every router keeps a **routing table** that has one entry for each destination network of which the router is aware. The entry consists of the destination network address, the shortest distance to reach the destination in hop count, and the next router to which the packet should be delivered to reach its final destination. The hop count is the number of networks that a packet encounters to reach its final destination.

The table may contain other information such as the subnet mask or the time this entry was last updated. Table 21.1 shows an example of a routing table.

Table 21.1 *A distance vector routing table*

Destination	Hop Count	Next Router	Other Information
163.5.0.0	7	172.6.23.4	
197.5.13.0	5	176.3.6.17	
189.45.0.0	4	200.5.1.6	
115.0.0.0	6	131.4.7.19	

RIP Updating Algorithm

The routing table is updated upon receipt of a RIP response message. The following shows the updating algorithm used by RIP.

RIP Updating Algorithm
Receive: a response RIP message
1. Add one hop to the hop count for each advertised destination.
2. Repeat the following steps for each advertised destination:
1. If (destination not in the routing table)
1. Add the advertised information to the table.
2. Else
1. If (next-hop field is the same)
1. Replace entry in the table with the advertised one.
2. Else
1. If (advertised hop count smaller than one in the table)
1. Replace entry in the routing table.
3. Return.

In Figure 21.4 a router receives a RIP message from router C. The message lists destination networks and their corresponding hop counts. The first step according to the updating algorithm is to increase the hop count by 1. Next, this updated RIP packet and the old routing table are compared. The result is a routing table with an up-to-date hop count for each destination. For Net1 there is no new information, so the Net1 entry remains the same.

For Net2, information in the table and in the message identifies the same next hop (router C). Although the value of the hop count in the table (2) is less than the one in

Figure 21.4 *Example of updating a routing table*

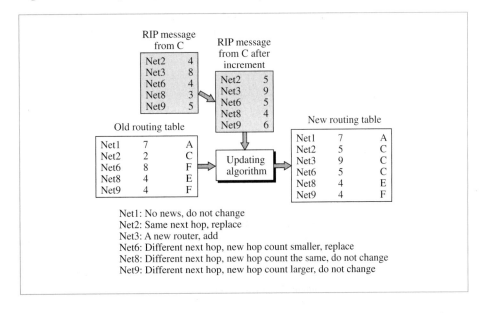

RIP message from C

Net2	4
Net3	8
Net6	4
Net8	3
Net9	5

RIP message from C after increment

Net2	5
Net3	9
Net6	5
Net8	4
Net9	6

Old routing table

Net1	7	A
Net2	2	C
Net6	8	F
Net8	4	E
Net9	4	F

Updating algorithm

New routing table

Net1	7	A
Net2	5	C
Net3	9	C
Net6	5	C
Net8	4	E
Net9	4	F

Net1: No news, do not change
Net2: Same next hop, replace
Net3: A new router, add
Net6: Different next hop, new hop count smaller, replace
Net8: Different next hop, new hop count the same, do not change
Net9: Different next hop, new hop count larger, do not change

the message (5), the algorithm selects the one received in the message because the original value came from router C. This value is now invalid because router C is advertising a new value.

Net3 is added as a new destination. For Net6, the RIP packet contains a lower hop count, and this shows up on the new routing table. Both Net8 and Net9 retain their original values since the corresponding hop counts in the message are not an improvement.

Initializing the Routing Table

When a router is added to a network, it initializes a routing table for itself, using its configuration file. The table contains only the directly attached networks and the hop counts, which are initialized to 1. The next-hop field, which identifies the next router, is empty. Figure 21.5 shows the initial routing tables in a small autonomous system.

Figure 21.5 *Initial routing tables in a small autonomous system*

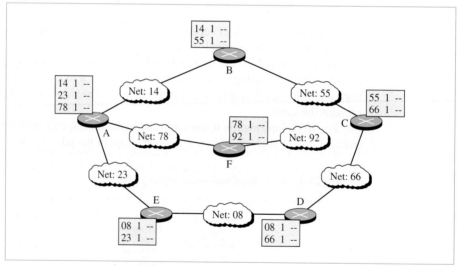

Updating the Routing Table

Each routing table is updated upon receipt of RIP messages using the RIP updating algorithm shown previously. Figure 21.6 shows our previous autonomous system with final routing tables.

OSPF

The **Open Shortest Path First (OSPF)** protocol is another interior routing protocol that is gaining in popularity. Its domain is also an autonomous system. Special routers called **autonomous system boundary routers** are responsible for dissipating information about other autonomous systems into the current system. To handle routing efficiently and in a timely manner, OSPF divides an autonomous system into areas.

Figure 21.6 *Final routing tables for Figure 21.5*

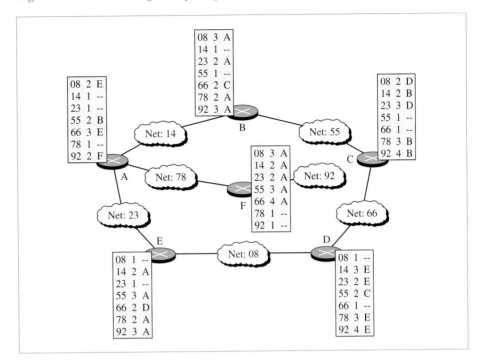

Areas

An **area** is a collection of networks, hosts, and routers all contained within an autonomous system. An autonomous system can also be divided into many different areas. All networks inside an area must be connected.

Routers inside an area flood the area with routing information. At the border of an area, special routers called **area border routers** summarize the information about the area and send it to other areas. Among the areas inside an autonomous system is a special area called the *backbone*; all the areas inside an autonomous system must be connected to the backbone. In other words, the backbone serves as a primary area, and the other areas serve as the secondary areas. However, this does not mean that the routers within areas cannot be connected with one another.

The routers inside the backbone are called the **backbone routers.** Note that a backbone router can also be an area border router.

If, due to some problem, the connectivity between a backbone and an area is broken, a **virtual link** between routers must be created by the administration to allow continuity of the functions of the backbone as the primary area.

Each area has an area identification. The area identification of the backbone is zero. Figure 21.7 shows an autonomous system and its areas.

Metric

The OSPF protocol allows the administrator to assign a cost, called the **metric,** to each route. The metric can be based on a type of service (minimum delay, maximum

Figure 21.7   *Areas in an autonomous system*

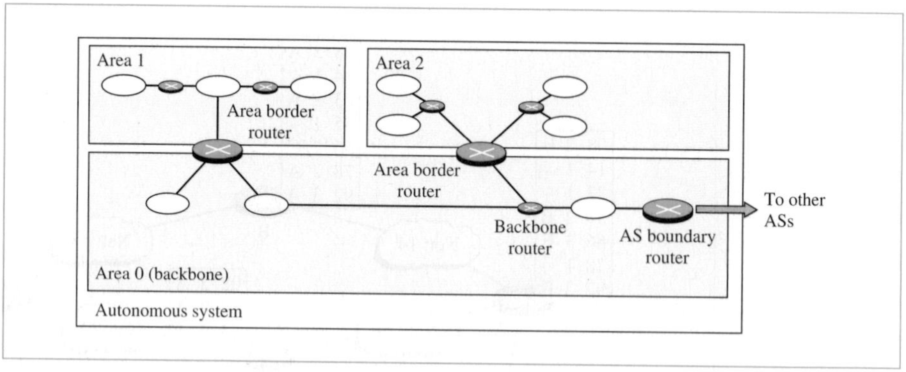

throughput, and so on). As a matter of fact, a router can have multiple routing tables, each based on a different type of service.

Link State Routing

OSPF uses **link state routing** to update the routing tables in an area. Before we discuss the details of the OSPF protocol, let us discuss link state routing, a process by which each router shares its knowledge about its neighborhood with every router in the area. The three keys to understanding how this method works are as follows:

1. **Sharing knowledge about the neighborhood.** Each router sends the *state of its neighborhood* to every other router in the area.

2. **Sharing with every other router.** Each router sends the state of its neighborhood to *every other router in the area*. It does so by **flooding,** a process whereby a router sends its information to all its neighbors (through all its output ports). Each neighbor sends the packet to all its neighbors, and so on. Every router that receives the packet sends copies to each of its neighbors. Eventually, every router (without exception) has received a copy of the same information.

3. **Sharing when there is a change.** Each router shares the state of its neighborhood only when there is a change. This rule contrasts with distance vector routing, where information is sent out at regular intervals regardless of change. This characteristic results in lower internet traffic than that required by distance vector routing.

The idea behind link state routing is that each router should have the exact topology of the internet at every moment. In other words, every router should have the whole "picture" of the internet. From this topology, a router can calculate the shortest path between itself and each network. The topology represented here means a graph consisting of nodes and edges. To represent an internet by a graph, however, we need more definitions.

Types of Links

In OSPF terminology, a connection is called a *link*. Four types of links have been defined: point-to-point, transient, stub, and virtual (see Fig. 21.8).

Figure 21.8 *Types of links*

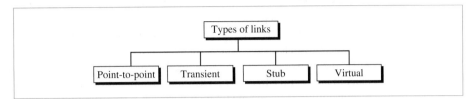

Point-to-Point Link   A **point-to-point link** connects two routers without any other host or router in between. In other words, the purpose of the link (network) is just to connect the two routers. An example of this type of link is two routers connected by a telephone line or a T-line. There is no need to assign a network address to this type of link. Graphically, the routers are represented by nodes, and the link is represented by a bidirectional edge connecting the nodes. The metrics, which are usually the same, are shown at the two ends, one for each direction. In other words, each router has only one neighbor at the other side of the link (see Fig. 21.9).

Figure 21.9 *Point-to-point link*

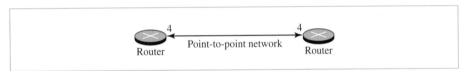

Transient Link   A **transient link** is a network with several routers attached to it. The data can enter through any of the routers and leave through any router. All LANs and some WANs with two or more routers are of this type. In this case, each router has many neighbors. For example, consider the Ethernet in Figure 21.10*a*. Router A has routers B, C, D, and E as neighbors. Router B has routers A, C, D, and E as neighbors. If we want to show the neighborhood relationship in this situation, we have the graph shown in Figure 21.10*b*.

Figure 21.10 *Transient link*

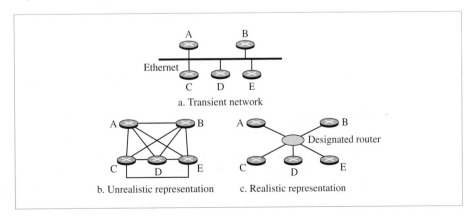

This is neither efficient nor realistic. It is not efficient because each router needs to advertise the neighborhood of four other routers, for a total of 20 advertisements. It is not realistic, because there is no single network (link) between each pair of routers; there is only one network that serves as a crossroad between all five routers.

To show that each router is connected to every other router through one single network, the network itself is represented by a node. However, because a network is not a machine, it cannot function as a router. One of the routers in the network takes this responsibility. It is assigned a dual purpose; it is a true router and a designated router. We can use the topology shown in Figure 21.10c to show the connections of a transient network.

Now each router has only one neighbor, the designated router (network). On the other hand, the designated router (the network) has five neighbors. We see that the number of neighbor announcements is reduced from 20 to 10. Still, the link is represented as a bidirectional edge between the nodes. However, while there is a metric from each node to the designated router, there is no metric from the designated router to any other node. The reason is that the designated router represents the network. We can only assign a cost to a packet that is passing through the network. We cannot charge for this twice. When a packet enters a network, we assign a cost; when a packet leaves the network to go to the router, there is no charge.

Stub Link A **stub link** is a network that is connected to only one router. The data packets enter the network through this single router and leave the network through this same router. This is a special case of the transient network. We can show this situation using the router as a node and using the designated router for the network. However, the link is only unidirectional, from the router to the network (see Fig. 21.11).

Figure 21.11 *Stub link*

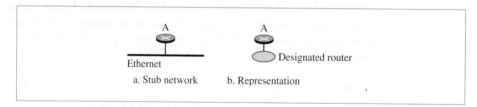

a. Stub network   b. Representation

Virtual Link When the link between two routers is broken, the administration may create a virtual link between them, using a longer path that probably goes through several routers.

Graphical Representation

Let us now examine a small internet using link state routing and see how we can represent it graphically. Figure 21.12 shows a small internet with seven networks and six routers. Two of the networks are point-to-point networks. We use symbols such as N1 and N2 for transient and stub networks. There is no need to assign a symbol to a point-to-point network.

Figure 21.12 *Example of an internet*

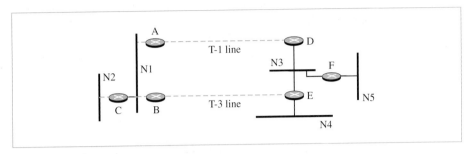

To show the above internet graphically, we use square nodes for the routers and ovals for the networks (represented by designated routers); see Figure 21.13. Note that we have three stub networks.

Figure 21.13 *Graphical representation of an internet*

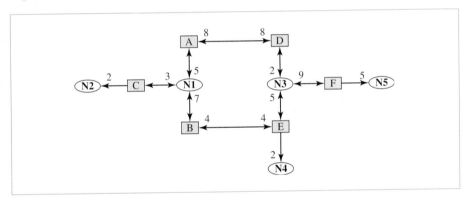

Link State Advertisements

To share information about their neighbors, each entity distributes **link state advertisements (LSAs).** An LSA announces the states of entity links. Depending on the type of entity, we can define five different LSAs (see Fig. 21.14).

Figure 21.14 *Types of LSAs*

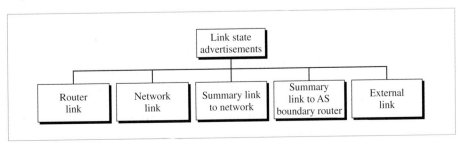

Router Link   A router link advertisement defines the links of a true router. A true router uses this advertisement to announce information about all its links and what is at the other side of the link (neighbors). See Figure 21.15 for a depiction of a router link.

Figure 21.15   *Router link*

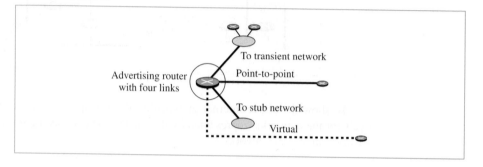

Network Link   A network link advertisement defines the links of a network. A designated router, on behalf of the transient network, distributes this type of LSA packet. The packet announces the existence of all the routers connected to the network (see Fig. 21.16).

Figure 21.16   *Network link*

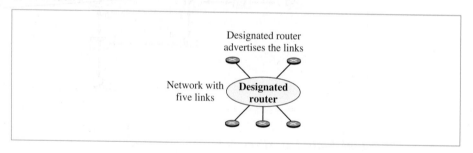

Summary Link to Network   Router link and network link advertisements flood the area with information about the router links and network links inside an area. But a router must also know about the networks outside its area, and the area border routers can provide this information. An area border router is active in more than one area. It receives router link and network link advertisements and creates a routing table for each area. For example, in Figure 21.17, router R1 is an area border router. It has two routing tables, one for area 1 and one for area 0. Router R1 floods area 1 with information about how to reach a network located in area 0. In the same way, router R2 floods area 2 with information about how to reach the same network in area 0.

Summary Link to AS Boundary Router   The previous advertisement lets every router know the cost to reach all the networks inside the autonomous system. But what about a network outside the autonomous system? If a router inside an area wants to send a packet outside the autonomous system, it should first know the route to an autonomous

Figure 21.17 *Summary link to network*

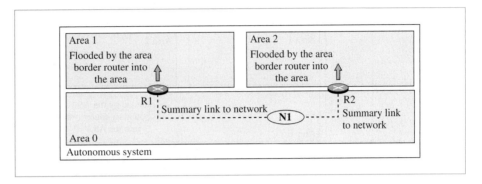

Figure 21.18 *Summary link to AS boundary router*

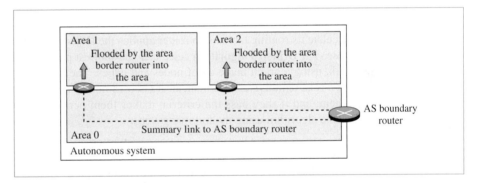

boundary router; the summary link to AS boundary router provides this information. The area border routers flood their areas with this information (see Fig. 21.18).

External Link   Although the previous advertisement lets each router know the route to an AS boundary router, this information is not enough. A router inside an autonomous system wants to know which networks are available outside the autonomous system; the external link advertisement provides this information. The AS boundary router floods the autonomous system with the cost of each network outside the autonomous system, using a routing table created by an exterior routing protocol. Each advertisement announces one single network. If there is more than one network, separate announcements are made. Figure 21.19 depicts an external link.

Link State Database

Every router in an area receives the router link and network link LSAs from every other router and forms a **link state database.** Note that every router in the same area has the same link state database.

A link state database is a tabular representation of the topology of the internet inside an area. It shows the relationship between each router and its neighbors including the metrics.

Figure 21.19   *External link*

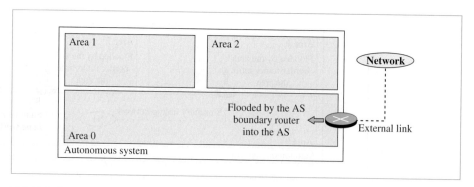

In OSPF, all routers have the same link state database.

Dijkstra Algorithm

To calculate its routing table, each router applies the Dijkstra algorithm to its link state database. The **Dijkstra algorithm** calculates the shortest path between two points on a network, using a graph made up of nodes and edges. The algorithm divides the nodes into two sets: tentative and permanent. It chooses nodes, makes them tentative, examines them, and if they pass the criteria, makes them permanent. We can informally define the algorithm using the following steps:

Dijkstra Algorithm
1. Start with the local node (router): the root of the tree.
2. Assign a cost of 0 to this node and make it the first permanent node.
3. Examine each neighbor node of the node that was the last permanent node.
4. Assign a cumulative cost to each node and make it tentative.
5. Among the list of tentative nodes
1. Find the node with the smallest cumulative cost and make it permanent.
2. If a node can be reached from more than one direction
1. Select the direction with the shortest cumulative cost.
6. Repeat steps 3 to 5 until every node becomes permanent.

Figure 21.20 shows some steps of the Dijkstra algorithm applied to node A of our sample internet in Figure 21.13. The number next to each node represents the cumulative cost from the root node. Note that if a network can be reached through two directions with two cumulative costs, the direction with the smaller cumulative cost is kept, and the other one is deleted.

Routing Table

Each router uses the shortest-path tree method to construct its routing table. The routing table shows the cost of reaching each network in the area. To find the cost of reaching

Figure 21.20 *Shortest-path calculation*

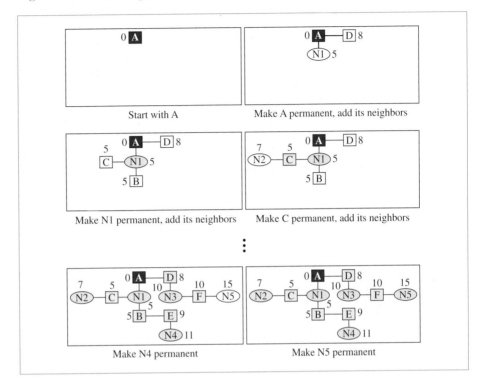

Table 21.2 *Link state routing table for router A*

Network	Cost	Next Router	Other Information
N1	5		
N2	7	C	
N3	10	D	
N4	11	B	
N5	15	D	

networks outside of the area, the routers use the summary link to network, the summary link to boundary router, and the external link advertisements. Table 21.2 shows the routing table for router A.

BGP

Border Gateway Protocol (BGP) is an **interautonomous system routing protocol.** It first appeared in 1989 and has gone through four versions. BGP is based on a routing method called **path vector routing.** However, before we describe the principle behind path vector routing, let us see why the two previously discussed methods—namely, distance vector routing and link state routing—are not good candidates for interautonomous system routing.

Distance vector is not a good candidate because there are occasions in which the route with the smallest hop count is not the preferred route. For example, we may not want a packet to pass through an autonomous system that is not secure, even though it is the shortest route. Also, distance vector routing is unstable due to the fact that the routers announce only the number of hop counts to the destination without actually defining the path that leads to that destination. A router that receives a distance vector advertisement packet may be fooled if the shortest path is actually calculated through the receiving router itself.

Link state routing is also not a good candidate for interautonomous system routing because an internet is usually too big for this routing method. To use link state routing for the whole internet would require each router to have a huge link state database. It would also take a long time for each router to calculate its routing table using the Dijkstra algorithm.

Path Vector Routing

Path vector routing is different from both distance vector routing and link state routing. Each entry in the routing table contains the destination network, the next router, and the path to reach the destination. The path is usually defined as an ordered list of autonomous systems that a packet should travel through to reach the destination. Table 21.3 shows an example of a path vector routing table.

Table 21.3   Path vector routing table

Network	Next Router	Path
N01	R01	AS14, AS23, AS67
N02	R05	AS22, AS67, AS05, AS89
N03	R06	AS67, AS89, AS09, AS34
N04	R12	AS62, AS02, AS09

Path Vector Messages

The autonomous boundary routers that participate in path vector routing advertise the reachability of the networks in their own autonomous systems to neighbor autonomous boundary routers. The concept of neighborhood here is the same as the one described in the RIP or OSPF protocol. Two autonomous boundary routers connected to the same network are neighbors.

We should mention here that an autonomous boundary router receives its information from an interior routing algorithm such as RIP or OSPF.

Each router that receives a path vector message verifies that the advertised path is in agreement with its policy (a set of rules imposed by the administrator controlling the routes). If it is, the router updates its routing table and modifies the message before sending it to the next neighbor. The modification consists of adding its AS number to the path and replacing the next router entry with its own identification.

For example, Figure 21.21 shows an internet with four autonomous systems. Router R1 sends a path vector message advertising the reachability of N1. Router R2 receives the message, updates its routing table, and after adding its autonomous system to the path and inserting itself as the next router, sends the message to router R3.

Figure 21.21   *Path vector messages*

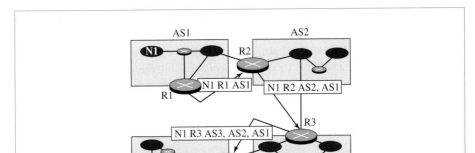

Router R3 receives the message, updates its routing table, and sends the message, after changes, to router R4.

Loop Prevention

The instability of distance vector routing and the creation of loops can be avoided in path vector routing. When a router receives a message, it checks to see if its autonomous system is in the path list to the destination. If it is, looping is involved and the message is ignored.

Policy Routing

Policy routing can be easily implemented through path vector routing. When a router receives a message, it can check the path. If one of the autonomous systems listed in the path is against its policy, the router can ignore that path and that destination. It does not update its routing table with this path, and it does not send this message to its neighbors. This means that the routing tables in path vector routing are not based on the smallest hop count or the minimum metric; they are based on the policy imposed on the router by the administrator.

Path Attributes

In our previous example, we discussed a path for a destination network. The path was presented as a list of autonomous systems, but is, in fact, a list of attributes. Each attribute gives some information about the path. The list of attributes helps the receiving router make a better decision when applying its policy.

Attributes are divided into two broad categories: well-known and optional. A *well-known attribute* is one that every BGP router should recognize. An **optional attribute** is one that need not be recognized by every router.

Well-known attributes are themselves divided into two categories: mandatory and discretionary. A **well-known mandatory attribute** is one that must appear in the description of a route. A **well-known discretionary attribute** is one that must be recognized by each router, but is not required to be included in every update message. One well-known mandatory attribute is ORIGIN. This defines the source of the routing information (RIP,

OSPF, and so on). Another well-known mandatory attribute is AS_PATH. This defines the list of autonomous systems through which the destination can be reached. Still another well-known mandatory attribute is NEXT_HOP, which defines the next router to which the data packet should be sent.

The optional attributes can also be subdivided into two categories: transitive and nontransitive. An *optional transitive attribute* is one that must be passed to the next router by the router that has not implemented this attribute. An *optional nontransitive attribute* is one that should be discarded if the receiving router has not implemented it.

Types of Packets

BGP uses four different types of messages: open, update, keep-alive, and notification (see Fig. 21.22).

Figure 21.22   *Types of BGP messages*

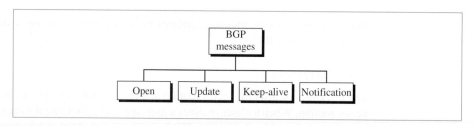

Open Message   To create a neighborhood relationship, a router running BGP opens a connection with a neighbor and sends an **open message.** If the neighbor accepts the neighborhood relationship, it responds with a *keep-alive* message, which means that a relationship has been established between the two routers.

Update Message   The **update message** is the heart of the BGP protocol. It is used by a router to withdraw destinations that have been advertised previously, announce a route to a new destination, or do both. Note that BGP can withdraw several destinations that were advertised before, but it can only advertise one new destination in a single update message.

Keep-Alive Message   The routers (called *peers* in BGP parlance) running the BGP protocols exchange **keep-alive messages** regularly (before their hold time expires) to tell each other that they are alive.

Notification Message   A **notification message** is sent by a router whenever an error condition is detected or a router wants to close the connection.

21.3   MULTICAST ROUTING

In **multicast routing,** there is one source and a group of destinations. The relationship is one-to-many. In this type of communication, the source address is a unicast address, but the destination address is a group address (class D). The group address defines the members of the group. Figure 21.23 shows the idea behind multicasting. A multicast packet starts from source S1 and goes to all destinations that belong to group G1.

In multicast routing, when a router receives a packet, it may forward it through several of its ports. The router may discard the packet if it is not in the multicast path.

Figure 21.23 *Multicasting*

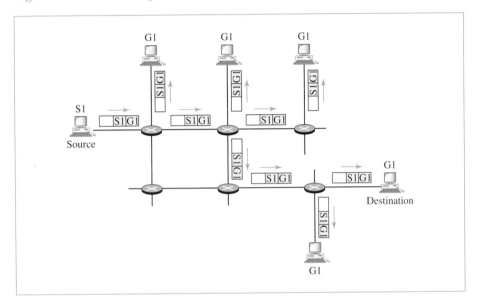

In multicast routing, the router may forward the received packet through several of its ports.

Broadcasting is a special case of multicasting in which the group contains all hosts. The Internet does not explicitly support broadcasting because of the huge amount of traffic it would create and because of the bandwidth it would need. Imagine the traffic generated in the Internet if 1000 people wanted to send a message to everyone else connected to the Internet. However, as we will see shortly, broadcasting is used implicitly as a prelude to multicasting.

Another term used in multicasting is **flooding.** Flooding is related to both multicasting and broadcasting. In flooding, a router forwards a packet out of all its ports except the one from which the packet came. Flooding provides broadcasting, but it also creates loops. A router will receive the same packet over and over from different ports. Several copies of the same packet are circulated, creating traffic jams.

In this section, we first discuss IGMP, a protocol at the network layer that is responsible for group membership management. We then define multicasting trees.

IGMP

The **Internet Group Management Protocol (IGMP)** is one of the necessary, but not sufficient (as we will see), protocols involved in multicasting.

Group Management

For multicasting in the Internet we need routers that are able to route multicast packets. The routing tables of these routers must be updated using one of the multicasting routing protocols that we will discuss later.

IGMP is not a multicasting routing protocol; it is a protocol that manages **group membership.** In any network, there are one or more **multicast routers** that distribute multicast packets to hosts or other routers. IGMP gives the multicast routers information about the membership status of hosts or routers connected to the network.

A multicast router may receive thousands of multicast packets every day for different groups. If a router has no knowledge about the membership status of the hosts, it must broadcast all these packets. This creates a lot of traffic and consumes bandwidth. A better solution is to keep a list of groups in the network for which there is at least one loyal member. IGMP helps the multicast router create and update this list.

> **IGMP is a group management protocol. It helps a multicast router create and update a list of loyal members related to each router interface.**

Messages

IGMP has gone through two versions. We discuss IGMPv2, the current version. IGMPv2 has three types of messages: the **query message,** the **membership report,** and the **leave report.** There are two types of query messages, general and special (see Fig. 21.24).

Figure 21.24   *IGMP message types*

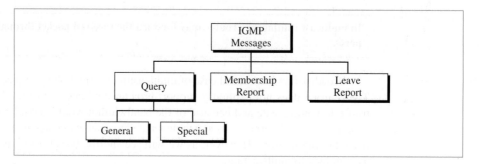

Message Format

Figure 21.25 shows the format of an IGMP (version 2) message.

Figure 21.25   *IGMP message format*

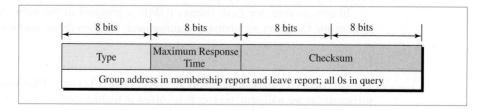

- **Type.** This 8-bit field defines the type of message, as shown in Table 21.4. The value of the type is shown in both hexadecimal and binary notation.

Table 21.4   *IGMP type field*

Type	Value
General or special query	0x11 or 00010001
Membership report	0x16 or 00010110
Leave report	0x17 or 00010111

- **Maximum response time.** This 8-bit field defines the amount of time in which a query must be answered. The value is in tenths of a second; for example, if the value is 100, it means 10 s. The value is nonzero in the query message; it is set to zero in the other two message types. We will see its use shortly.
- **Checksum.** This is a 16-bit field carrying the checksum. The checksum is calculated over the 8-byte message.
- **Group address.** The value of this field is 0 for a general query message. The value defines the groupid (multicast address of the group) in the special query, the membership report, and the leave report messages.

Operation

IGMP operates locally. A multicast router connected to a network has a list of multicast addresses of the groups for which the router distributes packets to groups with at least one loyal member in that network (see Fig. 21.26).

Figure 21.26   *IGMP operation*

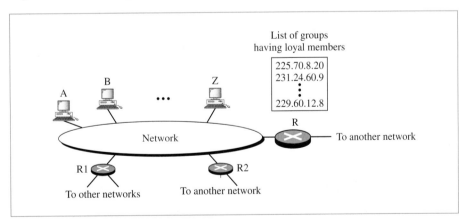

For each group, there is one router which has the duty of distributing the multicast packets destined for that group. This means that if there are three multicast routers connected to a network, their lists of groupids are mutually exclusive. For example, in the figure only router R distributes packets with the multicast address of 225.70.8.20.

A host or multicast router can have membership in a group. When a host has membership, it means that one of its processes (an application program) receives multicast packets from some group. When a router has membership, it means that a network connected to one of its other interfaces receives these multicast packets. We say that the host or the router has an *interest* in the group. In both cases, the host and the router keep a list of groupids and relay their interest to the distributing router.

For example, in Figure 21.26, router R is the distributing router. There are two other multicast routers (R1 and R2) which, depending on the group list maintained by router R, could be the recipients of router R in this network. Routers R1 and R2 may be distributors for some of these groups in other networks, but not on this network.

Joining a Group   A host or a router can join a group. A host maintains a list of processes that have membership in a group. When a process wants to join a new group, it sends its request to the host. The host adds the name of the process and the name of the requested group to its list. If this is the first entry for this particular group, the host sends a membership report message. If this is not the first entry, there is no need to send the membership report since the host is already a member of the group; it already receives multicast packets for this group.

A router also maintains a list of groupids that shows membership for the networks connected to each interface. When there is new interest in a group for any of these interfaces, the router sends out a membership report. In other words, a router here acts as a host, but its group list is much broader because it is the accumulation of all loyal members that are connected to its interfaces. Note that the membership report is sent out of all interfaces except the one from which the new interest comes. Figure 21.27 shows a membership report sent by a host or a router.

Figure 21.27   *Membership report*

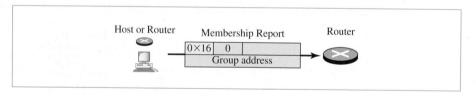

The protocol requires that the membership report be sent twice, one after the other within a few moments. In this way, if the first one is lost or damaged, the second one replaces it.

> **In IGMP, a membership report is sent twice, one after the other.**

Leaving a Group   When a host sees that no process is interested in a specific group, it sends a leave report. Similarly, when a router sees that none of the networks connected to its interfaces is interested in a specific group, it sends a leave report about that group.

However, when a multicast router receives a leave report, it cannot immediately purge that group from its list because the report comes from just one host or a router; there may be other hosts or routers that are still interested in that group. To make sure, the router sends a special query message and inserts the groupid (multicast address) related to the group. The router allows a specified response time for any host or router. If, during this time, no interest (membership report) is received, the router assumes that there are no loyal members in the network and it purges the group from its list. Figure 21.28 shows the mechanism for leaving a group.

Figure 21.28 *Leave report*

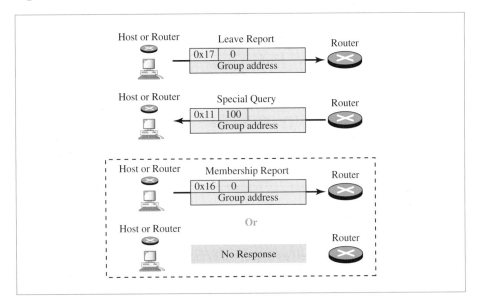

Monitoring Membership A host or router can join a group by sending a membership report message. They can leave a group by sending a leave report message. However, sending these two types of reports is not enough. Consider the situation in which there is only one host interested in a group, but the host is shut down or removed from the system. The multicast router will never receive a leave report. How is this handled? The multicast router is responsible for monitoring all the hosts or routers in a LAN to see if they want to continue their membership in a group.

The router periodically (by default, every 125 s) sends a **general query message.** In this message, the group address field is set to 0.0.0.0. This means the query for membership continuation is for all groups in which a host is involved, not just one.

The general query message does not define a particular group.

The router expects an answer for each group in its group list; even new groups may respond. The query message has a maximum response time of 10 s (the value of the field is actually 100, but this is in tenths of a second). When a host or router receives the general query message, it responds with a membership report if it is interested in a group. However, if there is a common interest (two hosts, for example, are interested in the same group), only one response is sent for that group to prevent unnecessary traffic. This is called a delayed response and is discussed next. Note that the query message must be sent by only one router (normally called the query router), also to prevent unnecessary traffic. We discuss this issue shortly. Figure 21.29 shows the query mechanism.

Figure 21.29   *General query message*

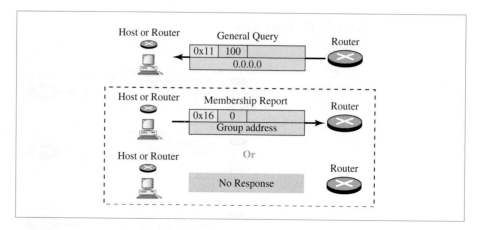

Delayed Response

To prevent unnecessary traffic, IGMP uses a **delayed-response strategy.** When a host or router receives a query message, it does not respond immediately; it delays the response. Each host or router uses a random number to create a timer, which expires between 1 and 10 s. The expiration time can be in steps of 1 s or less. A timer is set for each group in the list. For example, the timer for the first group may expire in 2 s, but the timer for the third group may expire in 5 s. Each host or router waits until its timer has expired before sending a membership report message. During this waiting time, if the timer of another host or router, for the same group, expires earlier, that host or router sends a membership report. Because, as we will see shortly, the report is broadcast, the waiting host or router receives the report and knows that there is no need to send a duplicate report for this group; thus, the waiting station cancels its corresponding timer.

Example 1

Imagine there are three hosts in a network, as shown in Figure 21.30. A query message was received at time 0; the random delay time (in tenths of seconds) for each group is shown next to the group address. Show the sequence of report messages.

Solution

The events occur in this sequence:

1. **Time 12.** The timer for 228.42.0.0 in host A expires and a membership report is sent, which is received by the router and every host including host B which cancels its timer for 228.42.0.0.

2. **Time 30.** The timer for 225.14.0.0 in host A expires and a membership report is sent, which is received by the router and every host including host C which cancels its timer for 225.14.0.0.

Figure 21.30   *Example 1*

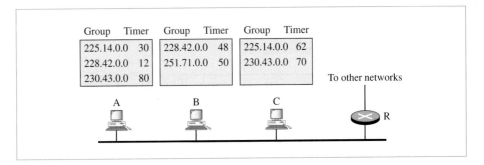

Group	Timer	Group	Timer	Group	Timer
225.14.0.0	30	228.42.0.0	48	225.14.0.0	62
228.42.0.0	12	251.71.0.0	50	230.43.0.0	70
230.43.0.0	80				

3. **Time 50.** The timer for 251.71.0.0 in host B expires and a membership report is sent, which is received by the router and every host.

4. **Time 70.** The timer for 230.43.0.0 in host C expires and a membership report is sent, which is received by the router and every host including host A which cancels its timer for 230.43.0.0.

Note that if each host had sent a report for every group in its list, there would have been seven reports; with this strategy only four reports are sent.

Query Router

Query messages may create a lot of responses. To prevent unnecessary traffic, IGMP designates one router as the **query router** for each network. Only this designated router sends the query message, and the other routers are passive (they receive responses and update their lists).

Multicast Trees

The objectives of multicasting are as follows:

■ Every member of the group should receive one, and only one, copy of the multicast packet. Receipt of multiple copies is not allowed.

■ Nonmembers must not receive a copy.

■ There must be no loops in routing; that is, a packet must not visit a router more than once.

■ The path traveled from the source to each destination must be optimal (the shortest path).

These objectives of multicasting can be achieved using a spanning tree, as discussed in Chapter 16. Two types of trees are used for multicasting: source-based trees and group-shared trees.

Source-Based Tree

In the **source-based tree** method, a single tree is made for each combination of source and group. In other words, the formation of the tree is based on both the source and the group. If there are N different groups and M different sources in the system, there can be a maximum of $N \times M$ different trees, one for each source–group combination. For example, if at this moment, a source needs to send a multicast packet to a group with a class D address of 228.9.28.40, a corresponding tree is made for this purpose. If 2 minutes later the same source wants to send a multicast packet to group 230.6.4.2 (a different group), the tree changes. In the source-based approach, the combination of source and group determines the tree.

> **In a source-based tree approach, the combination of source and group determines the tree.**

Two approaches have been used to create optimal source-based multicast trees. The first approach, used in DVMRP, is an extension of unicast distance vector routing (such as RIP). The second approach, used in MOSPF, is an extension of unicast link state routing (such as OSPF). Another protocol, PIM-DM, uses either RIP or OSPF, depending on need. All these approaches are discussed later.

Group-Shared Tree

In the **group-shared tree** method, each group in the system shares the same tree. If there are N groups in the whole system, there is a maximum of N trees, one for each group. For example, if at this moment, a source needs to send a multicast packet to a group with a class D address of 226.7.18.10, a corresponding tree is made for this purpose. If, a few seconds later, another source needs to send another packet to the same group, the corresponding tree is the same. But if the previous source, or any other source, needs to send a packet to group 229.5.80.10, a new tree is made. In other words, the tree changes when the group changes; the tree remains the same for the group regardless of the source. In the group-shared tree method, the group determines the tree, not the source.

> **In the group-shared tree approach, the group determines the tree.**

This method also has two approaches to find the multicast tree: the Steiner tree and **rendezvous-point tree.** We discuss only the rendezvous-point tree when we introduce CBT and PIM-SP protocols (discussed later). The Steiner tree is only theoretical and not implemented yet.

MBONE

Multimedia and real-time communication have increased the need for multicasting in the Internet. However, only a small fraction of Internet routers are multicast routers. In other words, a multicast router may not find another multicast router in the neighborhood to forward the multicast packet. Although this problem may be solved in the next few years by adding more and more multicast routers, there is another solution for this problem. The solution is **tunneling.** The multicast routers are seen as a group of routers on the top of unicast routers. The multicast routers may not be connected physically, but they are connected logically. Figure 21.31 shows the idea. In this figure, only the routers enclosed in the broken circles are capable of multicasting. Without tunneling, these routers are isolated islands. To enable multicasting, we

Figure 21.31 *Logical tunneling*

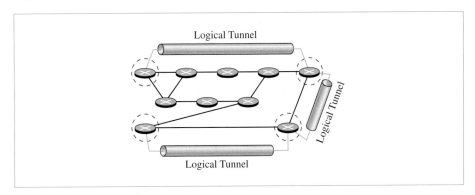

make a **multicast backbone (MBONE)** out of these isolated routers, using the concept of tunneling.

A **logical tunnel** is established by encapsulating the multicast packet inside a unicast packet. The multicast packet becomes the payload (data) of the unicast packet. The intermediate (nonmulticast) routers route the packet as unicast routers and deliver the packet from one island to another. It is as if the unicast routers do not exist and the two multicast routers are neighbors. So far the only protocol that supports MBONE and tunneling is DVMRP. Figure 21.32 shows the concept.

Figure 21.32 *MBONE*

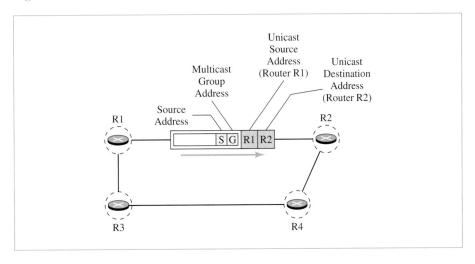

21.4 MULTICAST ROUTING PROTOCOLS

Now that we have discussed the management tool and general ideas in multicasting, let us introduce multicast routing protocols. DVMRP, MOSPF, CBT, PIM-DM, and

PIM-SM are multicast routing protocols that have been used or proposed for use in the Internet (see Fig. 21.33).

Figure 21.33 *Multicast routing protocols*

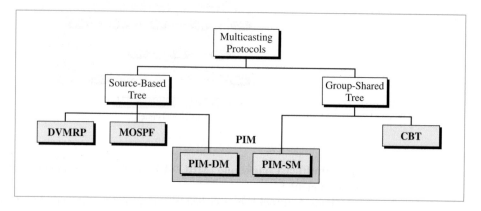

DVMRP

The **Distance Vector Multicast Routing Protocol (DVMRP),** a source-based routing protocol, is an extension of the distance vector routing used in unicast routing.

Formation of Shortest-Path Tree

DVMRP follows the same strategy followed by distance vector routing in which no router knows the complete route for a particular destination; there is no predefined route. Each router knows from which port to send out a unicast packet based *on the destination address*. The route is made gradually; each router contributes to the formation of the route when it receives the packet.

In DVMRP, the optimal tree is not predefined either. No router knows what should be the optimal tree. The tree is made gradually. When a router receives a packet, the router forwards the packet through some of the ports, *based on the source address,* and contributes to the formation of the tree; the rest of the tree is made by other downstream routers. This protocol must achieve the following:

1. It must prevent the formation of loops.
2. It must prevent duplications; no network receives more than one copy. In addition, the path traveled by a copy is the shortest path from the source to the destination.
3. It must provide for dynamic membership.

Reverse Path Forwarding (RPF)

The original idea in DVMRP was to use **reverse path forwarding (RPF).** In RPF, a router forwards the copy that has traveled the shortest path from the source to the router. To find if the packet has traveled the shortest path, RPF uses the unicast routing table of RIP. It pretends that it needs to send a packet to the source and finds if the port given by the routing table is the same from which the packet has arrived. Figure 21.34 shows the concept of RPF.

Figure 21.34 *Reverse path forwarding*

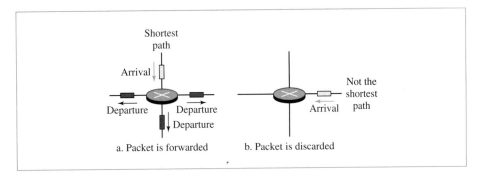

a. Packet is forwarded   b. Packet is discarded

> In reverse path forwarding, the router forwards only the packets that have traveled the shortest path from the source to the router; all other copies are discarded. RPF prevents the formation of loops.

Reverse Path Broadcasting (RPB)

RPF guarantees that each network receives a copy of the multicast packet without formation of loops. However, RPF does not guarantee that each network receives only one copy; a network may receive two or more copies. The reason is that forwarding is not based on the destination address (a group address); forwarding is based on the source address. To eliminate duplication, we must define only one parent router for each network. We must have this restriction: A network can receive a multicast packet from a particular source only through a *designated parent router.*

Now the policy is clear. For each source, the router sends the packet only out of those ports for which it is the designated parent. This policy is called **reverse path broadcasting (RPB)**. RPB guarantees that the packet reaches every network and that every network receives only one copy. Figure 21.35 shows the difference between RPF and RPB.

The reader may ask how the parent is determined. The designated parent router can be selected using one of several different strategies; the most common is to select the router with the shortest path to the source as the designated parent router.

Figure 21.35 *RPF versus RPB*

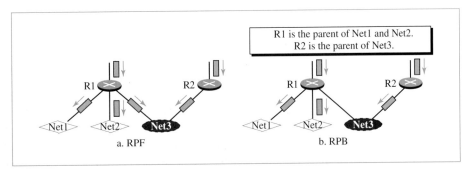

a. RPF   b. RPB

> **RPB creates a shortest-path broadcast tree from the source to each destination. It guarantees that each destination receives one and only one copy of the packet.**

Reverse Path Multicasting (RPM)

As you may have noticed, RPB does not multicast the packet, it broadcasts it. This is not efficient. To be more efficient, the multicast packet must reach only those networks that have active members for that particular group. However, the designers of DVMRP decided that the first packet is broadcast to every network. The decision regarding the remainder of the packets is the result of two procedures, *pruning* and *grafting*. This is sometimes called **reverse path multicasting (RPM).** Figure 21.36 shows the idea of pruning and grafting. Pruning is a procedure that stops the sending of messages from an interface. Grafting is a procedure that resumes the sending of multicast messages from an interface. Pruning and grafting are done by IGMP.

Figure 21.36   *RPF, RPB, and RPM*

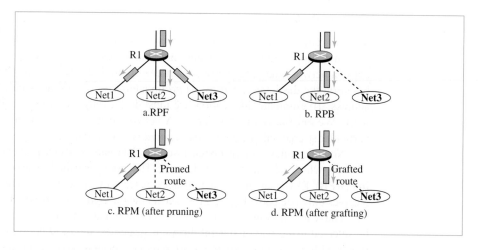

> **RPM adds pruning and grafting to RPB to create a multicast shortest-path tree that supports dynamic membership changes.**

MOSPF

The **Multicast Open Shortest Path First (MOSPF)** protocol is an extension of the OSPF protocol that uses multicast link state routing to create source-based trees. MOSPF uses an approach different from DVMRP. First, the tree is a **least-cost tree** (using a metric) instead of a shortest-path tree. Second, the tree is made all at once instead of gradually (the tree is said to be premade, prepruned, and ready to be used).

Least-Cost Trees

This approach uses the fact that in unicast link state routing there is a common link state database and, based on this database, each router knows the topology of the entire network. In addition, each router can use Dijkstra's algorithm to create a least-cost tree that has the router as the root and the rest of the routers as nodes of the tree. However, the least-cost trees generated by Dijkstra's algorithm in MOSPF are different for each router, unlike the database and the topology, which are the same for each router.

The tree we need in multicasting routing is slightly different from the one used in least-cost unicast routing. We need one tree for each source–group pair, and the root must be the source. The solution is not difficult, because the database is the same; we can ask each router to use Dijkstra's algorithm to create a tree with the source as the root. In this case, each router creates exactly the same tree, with the router itself as a node in the tree. Figure 21.37 shows the difference between trees.

Figure 21.37 *Unicast tree and multicast tree*

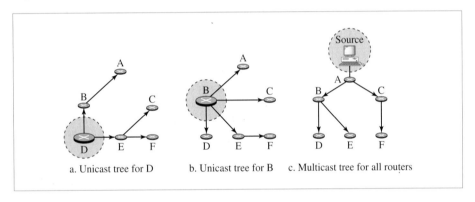

a. Unicast tree for D   b. Unicast tree for B   c. Multicast tree for all routers

Although a tree made this way looks like a perfect solution, there are still some problems.

1. The tree based on Dijkstra's algorithm uses unicast addresses (which are unique for each host); the tree we need requires group addresses, which are not unique (more than one host can belong to a group, and a host may belong to several groups).

2. The membership may change frequently. A host may belong to a group at one moment but not in the next, and vice versa.

3. Dijkstra's algorithm is very complex. Using the algorithm for each multicast packet is very expensive timewise.

To solve the first problem, we can add a new **link state update packet** to associate the unicast address of a host with the group address or addresses the host is sponsoring. It is called a *group membership LSA*. In this way, we can include in the tree only the hosts (using their unicast addresses) that belong to a particular group. In other words, we make a tree that contains all the hosts belonging to a group, but we use the unicast address of the host in the calculation.

The new link state packets can also solve the second problem if they are sent whenever there is a change in the membership.

To solve the third problem, we can make the router calculate the least-cost trees on demand (when it receives the first multicast packet). In addition, the tree can be saved in the cache memory for future use by the same source–group pair. MOSPF is a *data-driven* protocol; the first time a MOSPF router sees a datagram with a given source and group address, the router calculates the Dijkstra shortest-path tree calculation.

CBT

The **Core-Based Tree (CBT)** protocol is a group-shared protocol that uses a core as the root of the tree. The autonomous system is divided into regions, and a core (center router or rendezvous router) is chosen for each region. The procedure for selecting a rendezvous router is complex and beyond the scope of this book.

Formation of the Tree

After the rendezvous router is selected, every router is informed of the unicast address of the selected router. Each router then sends a unicast join message to show that it wants to join the group. This message passes through all routers that are located between the sender and the **rendezvous router.** Each intermediate router extracts the necessary information from the message, such as the unicast address of the sender and the port through which the packet has arrived, and forwards the message to the next router in the path. When the rendezvous router has received all join messages from every member of the group, the tree is formed. Now every router knows its upstream router and downstream router.

If a router wants to leave the group, it sends a leave message to its upstream router. The upstream router removes the link to that router from the tree and forwards the message to the upstream router, and so on. Figure 21.38 shows a shared-group tree with rendezvous router.

Figure 21.38   *Shared-group tree with rendezvous router*

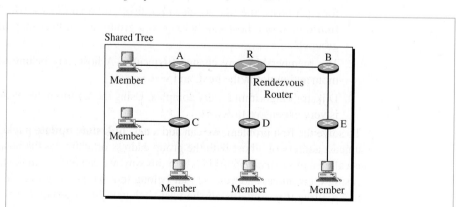

The reader may have noticed two differences between DVMRP and MOSPF, on one hand, and CBT, on the other. First, the tree for the first two is made from the root; the tree for CBT is formed from the leaves. Second, in DVMRP, the tree is first made (broadcasting) and then pruned; in CBT, there is no tree at the beginning; the joining (grafting) gradually makes the tree.

Sending Multicast Packets

After formation of the tree, any source (belonging to the group or not) can send a multicast packet to all members of the group. It simply sends the packet to the rendezvous router, using the unicast address of the rendezvous router; the rendezvous router distributes the packet to all members of the group. Figure 21.39 shows how a host can send a multicast packet to all members of the group. Note that the source host can be any of the hosts inside the shared tree or any host outside the shared tree. In the figure we show one located outside the shared tree.

Figure 21.39 *Sending a multicast packet to the rendezvous router*

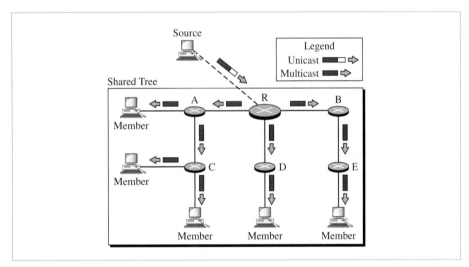

In summary, the Core-Based Tree (CBT) is a shared-group tree, center-based protocol using one tree per group. One of the routers in the tree is called the core. A packet is sent from the source to members of the group following this procedure:

1. The source, which may or may not be part of the tree, encapsulates the multicast packet inside a unicast packet with the unicast destination address of the core and sends it to the core. This part of delivery is done using a unicast address; the only recipient is the core router.

2. The core decapsulates the unicast packet and forwards it to all "interested" ports, which is part of the tree and is not pruned by IGMP.

3. Each router that receives the multicast packet, in turn, forwards it to all interested ports.

> **In CBT, the source sends the multicast packet to the core router. The core router decapsulates the packet and forwards it to all interested hosts.**

PIM

Protocol Independent Multicast (PIM) is the name given to two independent multicast routing protocols: **Protocol Independent Multicast, Dense Mode (PIM-DM)** and **Protocol Independent Multicast, Sparse Mode (PIM-SM).** Both protocols are unicast-protocol-dependent, but the similarity ends here. We discuss each separately.

PIM-DM

PIM-DM is used when there is a possibility that each router is involved in multicasting (dense mode). In this environment, the use of a protocol that broadcasts the packet is justified because almost all routers are involved in the process.

PIM-DM is a source-based routing protocol that uses RPF and pruning/grafting strategies for multicasting. Its operation is like DVMRP; however, unlike DVMRP, it does not depend on a specific unicasting protocol. It assumes that the autonomous system is using a unicast protocol and each router has a table that can find the outgoing port that has an optimal path to a destination. This unicast protocol can be a distance vector protocol (RIP) or link state protocol (OSPF).

> **PIM-DM uses RPF and pruning and grafting strategies to handle multicasting. However, it is independent of the underlying unicast protocol.**

PIM-SM

PIM-SM is used when there is slight possibility that each router is involved in multicasting (sparse mode). In this environment, the use of a protocol that broadcasts the packet is not justified, but a protocol such as CBT that uses a group-shared tree is more appropriate.

PIM-SM is a group-shared routing protocol that has a rendezvous point (RP) as the source of the tree. Its operation is like that of CBT; however, it is simpler because it does not require acknowledgment from a join message. In addition, it creates a backup set of RPs for each region to cover RP failures.

One of the characteristics of PIM-SM is that it can switch from a group-shared tree strategy to a source-based tree strategy when necessary. This can happen if there is a dense area of activity far from the RP. That area can be more efficiently handled with a source-based tree strategy instead of a group-shared tree strategy.

> **PIM-SM is similar to CBT but uses a simpler procedure.**

Applications

Multicasting has many applications today such as access to distributed databases, information dissemination, distance learning, and particularly multimedia communications.

21.5   KEY TERMS

area
area border router
area identification
autonomous system (AS)
autonomous system boundary router
backbone router
Border Gateway Protocol (BGP)
Core-Based Tree (CBT)
delayed-response strategy
Dijkstra algorithm
distance vector routing
Distance Vector Multicast Routing
   Protocol (DVMRP)
exterior routing
external link LSA
flooding
grafting
group membership
group-shared tree
hop count
interautonomous system routing protocol
interior routing
Internet Group Management Protocol
   (IGMP)
keep-alive message
least-cost tree
leave report
link state advertisement (LSA)
link state database
link state routing
link state update packet
logical tunnel
membership report
metric
multicast backbone (MBONE)
Multicast Open Shortest Path First
   (MOSPF)

multicast router
multicast routing
multicasting
network LSA
notification message
open message
Open Shortest Path First (OSPF)
optional attribute
path vector routing
point-to-point link
policy routing
Protocol Independent Multicast (PIM)
Protocol Independent Multicast, Dense
   Mode (PIM-DM)
Protocol Independent Multicast, Sparse
   Mode (PIM-SM)
pruning
query message
rendezvous-point tree
rendezvous router
reverse path broadcasting (RPB)
reverse path forwarding (RPF)
reverse path multicasting (RPM)
router link LSA
Routing Information Protocol (RIP)
routing table
source-based tree
stub link
summary link to AS boundary router LSA
summary link to network LSA
transient link
tunneling
unicast routing
update message
virtual link
well-known attribute

21.6   SUMMARY

❏   A metric is the cost assigned for passage of a packet through a network.

❏   A router consults its routing table to determine the best path for a packet.

❑ An autonomous system (AS) is a group of networks and routers under the authority of a single administration.

❑ RIP and OSPF are popular interior routing protocols used to update routing tables in an AS.

❑ RIP is based on distance vector routing, in which each router shares, at regular intervals, its knowledge about the entire AS with its neighbors.

❑ A RIP routing table entry consists of a destination network address, the hop count to that destination, and the IP address of the next router.

❑ OSPF divides an AS into areas, defined as collections of networks, hosts, and routers.

❑ OSPF is based on link state routing, in which each router sends the state of its neighborhood to every other router in the area. A packet is sent only if there is a change in the neighborhood.

❑ OSPF defines four types of links (networks): point-to-point, transient, stub, and virtual.

❑ Five types of link state advertisements (LSAs) disperse information in OSPF: router link, network link, summary link to network, summary link to AS boundary router, and external link.

❑ A router compiles all the information from the LSAs it receives into a link state database. This database is common to all routers in an area.

❑ An LSA is a multifield entry in a link state update packet.

❑ BGP is an interautonomous system routing protocol used to update routing tables.

❑ BGP is based on a routing method called path vector routing. In this method, the ASs through which a packet must pass are explicitly listed.

❑ There are four types of BGP messages: open, update, keep-alive, and notification.

❑ The Internet Group Management Protocol (IGMP) helps multicast routers create and update a list of loyal members related to a router interface.

❑ The three IGMP message types are the query message, the membership report, and the leave report.

❑ A host or router can have membership in a group.

❑ A host maintains a list of processes that have membership in a group.

❑ A router maintains a list of groupids that shows group membership for each interface.

❑ Multicasting applications include distributed databases, information dissemination, teleconferencing, and distance learning.

❑ For efficient multicasting we use a shortest-path spanning tree to represent the communication path.

❑ In a source-based tree approach to multicast routing, the source–group combination determines the tree.

❑ In a group-shared tree approach to multicast routing, the group determines the tree.

❑ DVRMP is a multicast routing protocol that uses the distance routing protocol to create a source-based tree.

❑ In reverse path forwarding (RPF), the router forwards only the packets that have traveled the shortest path from the source to the router.

❏ Reverse path broadcasting (RPB) creates a shortest-path broadcast tree from the source to each destination. It guarantees that each destination receives one and only one copy of the packet.

❏ Reverse path multicasting (RPM) adds pruning and grafting to RPB to create a multicast shortest-path tree that supports dynamic membership changes.

❏ MOSPF is a multicast protocol that uses multicast link state routing to create a source-based least-cost tree.

❏ The Core-Based Tree (CBT) protocol is a multicast routing protocol that uses a core as the root of the tree.

❏ PIM-DM is a source-based routing protocol that uses RPF and pruning and grafting strategies to handle multicasting.

❏ PIM-SM is a group-shared routing protocol that is similar to CBT and uses a rendezvous point as the source of the tree.

❏ For multicasting between two noncontiguous multicast routers, we make a multicast backbone (MBONE) to enable tunneling.

21.7 PRACTICE SET

Review Questions

1. What is the difference between unicast routing and multicast routing?
2. Why would an internet need an Autonomous System?
3. What is the difference between an interior routing protocol and an exterior routing protocol? Name an example of each.
4. What kind of information is in a routing table?
5. Name the four types of OSPF connections.
6. What is the difference between a transient link and a stub link?
7. What is the purpose of a Link State Advertisement?
8. What is path vector routing?
9. What is the role of the Dijkstra algorithm in unicast routing?
10. Name the three main categories of IGMP messages and briefly discuss their functions.
11. What is the difference between a source-based tree and a group-shared tree?
12. How does reverse path forwarding differ from reverse path broadcasting?
13. What is the purpose of a multicast backbone (MBONE)?

Multiple-Choice Questions

14. RIP is based on _____.
    a. Link state routing
    b. Distance vector routing
    c. Dijkstra's algorithm
    d. Path vector routing

15. In distance vector routing each router receives information directly from _____.

    a. Every router on the network

    b. Every router less than two units away

    c. A table stored by the network hosts

    d. Its neighbors only

16. In distance vector routing a router sends out information _____.

    a. At regularly scheduled intervals

    b. Only when there is a change in its table

    c. Only when a new host is added

    d. Only when a new network is added

17. A routing table contains _____.

    a. The destination network ID

    b. The hop count to reach the network

    c. The router ID of the next hop

    d. All the above

18. Router B receives an update from router A that indicates Net1 is two hops away. The next update from A says Net1 is five hops away. What value is entered in B's routing table for Net1? Assume the basic RIP is being used.

    a. 2

    b. 3

    c. 6

    d. 7

19. If the routing table contains four new entries, how many update messages must the router send to its one neighbor router?

    a. 1

    b. 2

    c. 3

    d. 4

20. The cost field of a router's first table from itself always has a value of _____.

    a. 0

    b. 1

    c. Infinity

    d. Some positive integer

21. Dijkstra's algorithm is used to _____.

    a. Create LSAs

    b. Flood an internet with information

    c. Calculate the routing tables

    d. Create a link state database

22. An area is _____.

    a. Part of an AS

    b. Composed of at least two ASs

   c. Another term for an internet

   d. A collection of stub areas

23. In an autonomous system with *n* areas, how many areas are connected to the backbone?

   a. 1

   b. *n* − 1

   c. *n*

   d. *n* + 1

24. An area border router can be connected to _____.

   a. Only another router

   b. Another router or another network

   c. Only another network

   d. Only another area border router

25. Which of the following usually has the least number of connections to other areas?

   a. An area

   b. An autonomous system

   c. A transient link

   d. A stub link

26. Which type of network using the OSPF protocol always consists of just two connected routers?

   a. Point-to-point

   b. Transient

   c. Stub

   d. Virtual

27. Which type of network using the OSPF protocol is the result of a break in a link between two routers?

   a. Point-to-point

   b. Transient

   c. Stub

   d. Virtual

28. Which type of network using the OSPF protocol can have five routers attached to it?

   a. Point-to-point

   b. Transient

   c. Stub

   d. All the above

29. A WAN using the OSPF protocol that connects two routers is an example of a _____ type of OSPF network.

   a. Point-to-point

   b. Transient

   c. Stub

   d. Virtual

30. An Ethernet LAN using the OSPF protocol with five attached routers can be called
    a _____ network.
    a. Point-to-point
    b. Transient
    c. Stub
    d. Virtual

31. Which layer produces the OSPF message?
    a. Data link
    b. Network
    c. Transport
    d. Application

32. Which of the following is an exterior routing protocol?
    a. RIP
    b. OSPF
    c. BGP
    d. (a) and (b)

33. Which of the following is an interior routing protocol?
    a. RIP
    b. OSPF
    c. BGP
    d. (a) and (b)

34. OSPF is based on _____.
    a. Distance vector routing
    b. Link state routing
    c. Path vector routing
    d. (a) and (b)

35. BGP is based on _____.
    a. Distance vector routing
    b. Link state routing
    c. Path vector routing
    d. (a) and (b)

36. Which type of BGP message creates a relationship between two routers?
    a. Open
    b. Update
    c. Keep-alive
    d. Notification

37. Which type of BGP message announces a route to a new destination?
    a. Open
    b. Update

    c. Keep-alive

    d. Notification

38. Which type of BGP message is sent by a system to notify another router of the sender's existence?

    a. Open

    b. Update

    c. Keep-alive

    d. Notification

39. Which type of BGP message is sent by a router to close a connection?

    a. Open

    b. Update

    c. Keep-alive

    d. Notification

40. The _____ is an IGMP message.

    a. Query message

    b. Membership report

    c. Leave report

    d. All the above

41. An IGMP query is sent from a _____ to a _____.

    a. Host; host

    b. Host; router

    c. Router; router

    d. Router; host or router

42. The _____ is used by a router in response to a received-leave report.

    a. General query message

    b. Special query message

    c. Membership report

    d. Leave report

43. The _____ field of the IGMP message is all zeros in a query message.

    a. Version

    b. Type

    c. Checksum

    d. Group address

44. The _____ field of the IGMP message is $0x11$ for a query message.

    a. Version

    b. Type

    c. Checksum

    d. (a) and (b)

45. If four hosts on a network belong to the same group, a total of _____ sent in response to a general query message.

    a. One membership report is

    b. Two membership reports are

    c. Three membership reports are

    d. Four membership reports are

46. A one-to-all communication between a source and all hosts on a network is classi-fied as a _____ communication.

    a. Unicast

    b. Multicast

    c. Broadcast

    d. (a) and (b)

47. A one-to-many communication between a source and a specific group of hosts is classified as a _____ communication.

    a. Unicast

    b. Multicast

    c. Broadcast

    d. (a) and (b)

48. A one-to-one communication between a source and one destination is classified as a _____ communication.

    a. Unicast

    b. Multicast

    c. Broadcast

    d. (a) and (b)

49. _____ is a multicasting application.

    a. Teleconferencing

    b. Distance learning

    c. Information dissemination

    d. All the above

50. A _____ is a data structure with nodes and edges and a hierarchical structure.

    a. Tree

    b. Graph

    c. Leaf

    d. Root

51. A system uses source-based trees for multicasting. If there are 100 sources and 5 groups, there is a maximum of _____ different trees.

    a. 5

    b. 20

    c. 100

    d. 500

52. In a _____ tree approach to multicasting, the combination of source and group determines the tree.

    a. Spanning-source

    b. Shortest-group

    c. Source-based

    d. Group-shared

53. In a _____ tree approach to multicasting, the group determines the tree.

    a. Spanning-source

    b. Shortest-group

    c. Source-based

    d. Group-shared

54. A system uses group-shared trees for multicasting. If there are 100 sources and 5 groups, there is a maximum of _____ different trees.

    a. 5

    b. 20

    c. 100

    d. 500

55. _____ is a multicast routing protocol using source-based trees.

    a. DVRMP

    b. MOSPF

    c. CBT

    d. (a) and (b)

56. _____ is a multicast routing protocol using group-shared trees.

    a. DVRMP

    b. MOSPF

    c. CBT

    d. (a) and (b)

57. In _____ a network can receive a multicast packet from a particular source only through a designated parent router.

    a. RPF

    b. RPB

    c. RPM

    d. All the above

58. Pruning and grafting are strategies used in _____.

    a. RPF

    b. RPB

    c. RPM

    d. All the above

59. A _____ message tells an upstream router to stop sending multicast messages for a specific group through a specific router.

    a. Weed

    b. Graft

    c. Prune

    d. Plum

60. A _____ message tells an upstream router to start sending multicast messages for a specific group through a specific router.

    a. Weed

    b. Graft

    c. Prune

    d. Plum

61. _____ uses multicast link state routing concepts to create source-based trees.

    a. DVMRP

    b. MOSPF

    c. CBT

    d. BVD

62. In the _____ protocol, a multicast packet is encapsulated inside a unicast packet with the core router as the destination.

    a. DVMRP

    b. MOSPF

    c. CBT

    d. BVD

63. _____ is used in a dense multicast environment while _____ is used in a sparse multicast environment.

    a. PIM-DM; PIM-SM

    b. PIM-SM; PIM-DM

    c. PIM; PIM-DM

    d. PIM; PIM-SM

64. When a multicast router is not directly connected to another multicast router, a _____ can be formed to connect the two.

    a. Physical tunnel

    b. Logical tunnel

    c. Logical core

    d. Spanning tree

Exercises

65. What is the basis of classification for the four types of links defined by OSPF?

66. Contrast and compare distance vector routing with link state routing.

67. Draw a flowchart of the steps involved when a router receives a distance vector message from a neighbor.

68. Why do OSPF messages propagate faster than RIP messages?

69. A router has the following RIP routing table:

Net1	4	B
Net2	2	C
Net3	1	F
Net4	5	G

What would be the contents of the table if the router receives the following RIP message from router C:

Net1	2
Net2	1
Net3	3
Net4	7

70. Show the autonomous system with the following specifications:

   a. There are eight networks (N1 to N8)
   b. There are eight routers (R1 to R8)
   c. N1, N2, N3, N4, and N5 are Ethernet networks
   d. N6 is a token ring
   e. N7 and N8 are point-to-point networks
   f. R1 connects N1 and N2
   g. R2 connects N1 and N7
   h. R3 connects N2 and N8
   i. R4 connects N7 and N6
   j. R5 connects N6 and N3
   k. R6 connects N6 and N4
   l. R7 connects N6 and N5
   m. R8 connects N8 and N5

71. Draw the graphical representation of the autonomous system of Exercise 70 as seen by OSPF.

72. Which of the networks in Exercise 70 is a transient network? Which is a stub network?

73. Why is there no need for the IGMP message to travel outside its own network?

74. A multicast router list contains four groups (W, X, Y, and Z). There are three hosts on the LAN. Host A has three loyal members belonging to group W and one loyal member belonging to group X. Host B has two loyal members belonging to group W and one loyal member belonging to group Y. Host C has no processes belonging to any group. Show the IGMP messages involved in monitoring.

75. If a router has 20 entries in its group table, should it send 20 different queries periodically or just 1?

76. If a host wants to continue the membership in five groups, should it send five different membership report messages or just one?

77. A router with IP address 202.45.33.21 and physical Ethernet address 234A4512ECD2 sends an IGMP general query message. Show all the entries in the message.

78. A host with IP address 124.15.13.1 and physical Ethernet address 4A224512E1E2 sends an IGMP membership report message about groupid 228.45.23.11. Show all the entries in the message.

79. A router on an Ethernet network has received a multicast IP packet with groupid 226.17.18.4. When the host checks its multicast group table, it finds this address. Show how the router sends this packet to the recipients by encapsulating the IP packet in an Ethernet frame. Show all the entries of the Ethernet frame. The outgoing IP address of the router is 185.23.5.6, and its outgoing physical address is 4A224512E1E2. Does the router need the services of ARP?

80. A host with IP address 114.45.7.9 receives an IGMP query. When it checks its group table, it finds no entries. What action should the host take? Should it send any messages? If so, show the packet fields.

81. A host with IP address 222.5.7.19 receives an IGMP query. When it checks its routing table, it finds two entries in its table: 227.4.3.7 and 229.45.6.23. What action should the host take? Should it send any messages? If so, what type and how many? Show the fields.

82. A host with IP address 186.4.77.9 receives a request from a process to join a group with groupid 230.44.101.34. When the host checks its group table, it does not find an entry for this groupid. What action should the host take? Should it send any messages? If so, show the packet field.

83. A router with IP address 184.4.7.9 receives a report from a host that wants to join a group with groupid 232.54.10.34. When the router checks its group table, it does not find an entry for this groupid. What action should the router take? Should it send any messages? If so, show the packet fields.

84. A router sends a query and receives only three reports about groupids 225.4.6.7, 225.32.56.8, and 226.34.12.9. When it checks its routing table, it finds five entries: 225.4.6.7, 225.11.6.8, 226.34.12.9, 226.23.22.67, and 229.12.4.89. What action should be taken?

85. A router using DVMRP receives a packet with source address 10.14.17.2 from port 2. If the router forwards the packet, what are the contents of the entry related to this address in the unicast routing table?

86. Router A sends a unicast RIP update packet to router B that says 134.23.0.0/16 is 7 hops away. Network B sends an update packet to router A that says 13.23.0.0/16 is 4 hops away. If these two routers are connected to the same network, which one is the designated parent router?

87. Does RPF actually create a spanning tree? Explain.

88. Does RPB actually create a spanning tree? Explain.

89. Does RPM actually create a spanning tree? Explain.

PART 5

Transport Layer

The transport layer is the core of the Internet model. Protocols at this layer oversee the delivery of data from a process, a running application program, on one computer to a process on another computer. More importantly, they act as a liaison between the application-layer protocols and the services provided by the lower layers (network, data link, and physical). The application layer programs interact with each other, using the services of the transport layer without even being aware of the existence of the lower layers. In other words, the application layer programs are oblivious to the intricacies of the physical network and are not dependent on the physical network type. Only one set of upper layer software needs to be developed. To the application layer program, the physical networks are simply a homogeneous cloud that somehow takes data and delivers it to its destination safe and sound.

Figure 1 shows the position of the transport layer in the 5-layer Internet model. The transport layer is the fourth layer in the model. Above it is the application layer and below it is the network layer. This means that transport layer receives services from the network layer and provides services to the application layer.

Figure 1   *Position of transport layer*

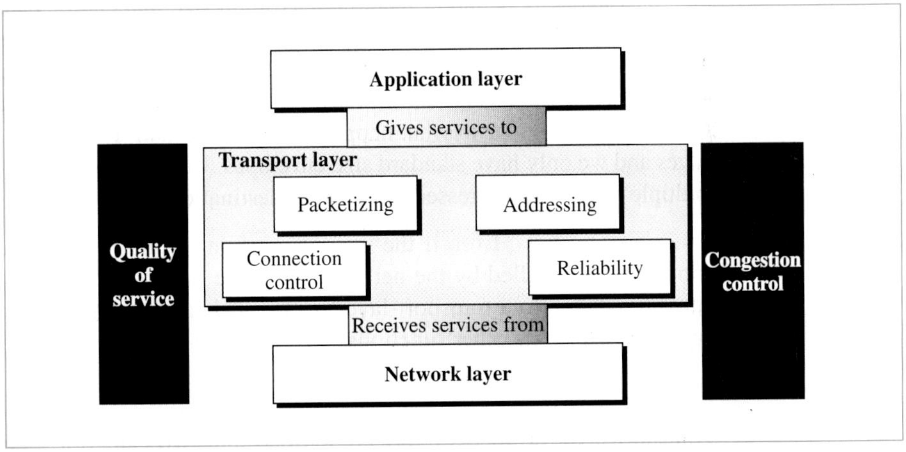

Duties

Process-to-process delivery is achieved through a set of functions performed by the transport layer. The most important are packetizing, connection control, addressing, and providing reliability as shown in Figure 2.

Figure 2   *Duties*

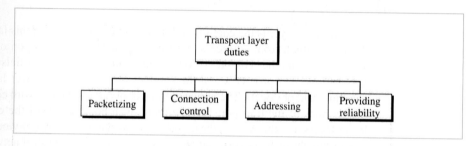

We discuss these duties in detail in Chapter 22; we give an overview below.

Packetizing

The transport layer creates packets out of the message received from the application layer. Packetizing divides a long message into smaller ones; these smaller units are encapsulated into the data field of the transport-layer packet and headers are added.

Dividing Large Messages   The message an application program sends can vary in length. For example, an SMTP client (email protocol) may send a short message (several lines) or a long message with several attachments and multimedia documents. A long message may be larger than the maximum size that can be handled by the lower-layer protocols. For example, some network layers can handle packets with only a few thousand characters or less. This means that long messages from the application layer must be divided into sections with each section inserted (encapsulated) into a separate packet. This is similar to what happens using snail mail. If we have a letter with many pages and we only have standard size envelopes, we need to separate the letter and send multiple envelopes addressed to the same destination.

Adding a Header   Even if the message arriving from the application layer is small enough to be handled by the network layer, the transport layer still inserts (encapsulates) the data into a transport-layer packet. A header is added to allow the transport layer to perform its other functions.

Connection Control

Transport-layer protocols today are divided into two categories: connection-oriented and connectionless.

Connection-Oriented Delivery   A connection-oriented transport layer protocol first establishes a connection (a virtual path) between the sender and receiver. The connection is virtual; that is, the application layer perceives that a single path has been created;

in reality, the packets may travel through different physical paths. We can say that a session exists between the sender and the receiver. The session remains intact until it is broken by one of the parties. In the meantime, the two parties can send multiple packets related to each other, traveling one after another through the virtual path. Of course, the packets may travel out of order, but the transport layer ensures that this is transparent to the application program. The packets are numbered consecutively and communication can take place in both directions.

Connectionless Delivery A connectionless transport protocol treats each packet independently without any connection between them.

Addressing

Imagine an HTTP client (a browser) on a local computer needs to send a request to an HTTP server on a remote computer. First, the client needs the address of the remote computer, which must be unique to distinguish it from all the computers in the world. This addressing is implemented in the network layer, which we discussed in Chapter 19. For the moment, let us assume that the client knows the address of this remote computer.

There is, however, another problem that must be solved. The remote computer may be running several server programs, such as HTTP, SMTP, and TELNET, at the same time. When the request arrives at the remote computer, the computer must deliver the request to the HTTP server program, not to any other server program. In other words, the packet carrying the request must specify to which server program the request must be delivered.

The request packet must also specify the client program that sent the packet. The server uses this when it responds to the request. The reason is that the local computer may also be running several clients. People normally open several client programs at the same time (using different windows, for example).

Providing Reliability

A transport layer can provide reliability for the application program that uses its services. Reliability, as we learned from the data link layer involves flow control and error control.

Flow Control Like the data link layer, the transport layer can provide flow control. However, flow control at this layer is performed end to end rather than across a single link.

Error Control Like the data link layer, the transport layer can provide error control. However, error control at this layer is performed end to end rather than across a single link. The sending transport layer makes sure that the entire message arrives at the receiving transport layer without error (damage, loss, or duplication). Error correction is usually achieved through retransmission.

Congestion Control and QoS

Although congestion in the network can happen in the data link, network, or transport layer, the effect of the congestion is normally seen in the transport layer because this is the layer that directly gives services to the application layer. We have not discussed congestion control as yet. We discuss it in this part of the text.

Quality of Service (QoS) is another issue that we have postponed. Although QoS can be implemented in other layers, its actual effect is also felt in the transport layer.

We discuss congestion control and quality of service in Chapter 23.

Chapters

We have included two chapters in this part of the book: Chapter 22 discusses the concepts and duties of the transport layer and explains the two transport-layer protocols used in the Internet: UDP and TCP. Chapter 23 discusses two issues, congestion control and quality of service, that can be applied to three layers: data link, network, and transport.

CHAPTER 22

Process-to-Process Delivery:
UDP and TCP

We begin the chapter by giving the rationale for the existence of the transport layer—the need for process-to-process delivery. We discuss the issues arising from this type of delivery, and we discuss methods to handle them.

The Internet model has two protocols at the transport layer, UDP and TCP. First we discuss UDP, which is the simpler of the two. We see how we can use this very simple transport-layer protocol that lacks some of the features of TCP.

We then discuss TCP, a complex transport-layer protocol. We see how our previously presented concepts are applied to TCP. We postpone the discussion of congestion control and quality of service in TCP until Chapter 23 because these two topics apply to the data link layer and network layer as well.

22.1   PROCESS-TO-PROCESS DELIVERY

The data link layer is responsible for delivery of frames between two neighboring nodes over a link. This is called *node-to-node delivery*. The network layer is responsible for delivery of datagrams between two hosts. This is called *host-to-host delivery*. Communication on the Internet is not defined as the exchange of data between two nodes or between two hosts. Real communication takes place between two processes (application programs). We need **process-to-process delivery.** However, at any moment, several processes may be running on the source host and several on the destination host. To complete the delivery, we need a mechanism to deliver data from one of these processes running on the source host to the corresponding process running on the destination host.

The transport layer is responsible for process-to-process delivery, the delivery of a packet, part of a message, from one process to another. Two processes communicate in a client-server relationship, as we will see later. Figure 22.1 shows these three types of deliveries and their domains.

The transport layer is responsible for process-to-process delivery.

Figure 22.1 *Types of data deliveries*

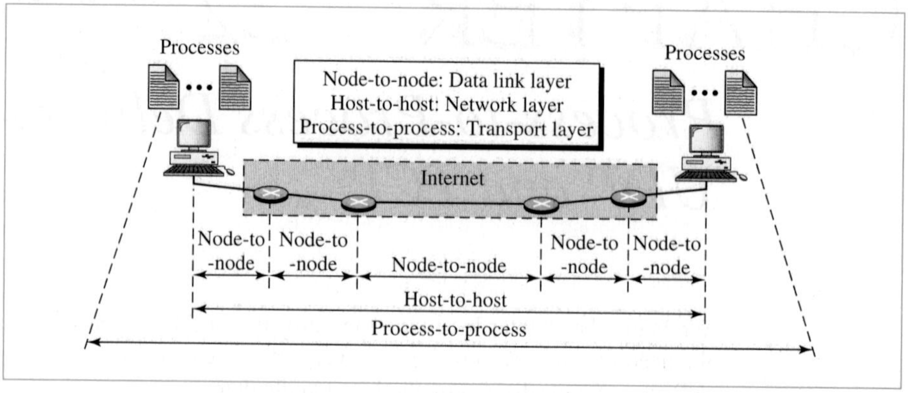

Client-Server Paradigm

Although there are several ways to achieve process-to-process communication, the most common one is through the **client-server paradigm.** A process on the local host, called a **client,** needs services from a process usually on the remote host, called a **server.**

Both processes (client and server) have the same name. For example, to get the day and time from a remote machine, we need a Daytime client process running on the local host and a Daytime server process running on a remote machine.

Operating systems today support both multiuser and multiprogramming environments. A remote computer can run several server programs at the same time, just as local computers can run one or more client programs at the same time. For communication, we must define the following:

1. Local host
2. Local process
3. Remote host
4. Remote process

Addressing

Whenever we need to deliver something to one specific destination among many, we need an address. At the data link layer, we need a MAC address to choose one node among several nodes if the connection is not point-to-point. A frame in the data link layer needs a destination MAC address for delivery and a source address for the next node's reply.

At the network layer, we need an IP address to choose one host among millions. A datagram in the network layer needs a destination IP address for delivery and a source IP address for the destination's reply.

At the transport layer, we need a transport-layer address, called a **port number,** to choose among multiple processes running on the destination host. The destination port number is needed for delivery; the source port number is needed for the reply.

In the Internet model, the port numbers are 16-bit integers between 0 and 65,535. The client program defines itself with a port number, chosen randomly by the transport-layer software running on the client host. This is the **ephemeral port number.**

The server process must also define itself with a port number. This port number, however, cannot be chosen randomly. If the computer at the server site runs a server process and assigns a random number as the port number, the process at the client site that wants to access that server and use its services will not know the port number. Of course, one solution would be to send a special packet and request the port number of a specific server, but this requires more overhead. The Internet has decided to use universal port numbers for servers; these are called **well-known port numbers.** There are some exceptions to this rule; for example, there are clients that are assigned well-known port numbers. Every client process knows the well-known port number of the corresponding server process. For example, while the Daytime client process, discussed above, can use an ephemeral (temporary) port number 52,000 to identify itself, the Daytime server process must use the well-known (permanent) port number 13. Figure 22.2 shows this concept.

Figure 22.2   *Port numbers*

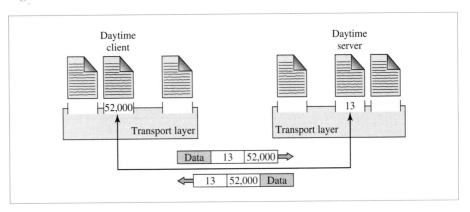

It should be clear by now that the IP addresses and port numbers play different roles in selecting the final destination of data. The destination IP address defines the host among the different hosts in the world. After the host has been selected, the port number defines one of the processes on this particular host (see Fig. 22.3).

IANA Ranges

The IANA (Internet Assigned Number Authority) has divided the port numbers into three ranges: well-known, registered, and dynamic (or private), as shown in Figure 22.4.

■ **Well-known ports.** The ports ranging from 0 to 1023 are assigned and controlled by IANA. These are the well-known ports.

■ **Registered ports.** The ports ranging from 1024 to 49,151 are not assigned or controlled by IANA. They can only be registered with IANA to prevent duplication.

■ **Dynamic ports.** The ports ranging from 49,152 to 65,535 are neither controlled nor registered. They can be used by any process. These are the ephemeral ports.

Figure 22.3   *IP addresses versus port numbers*

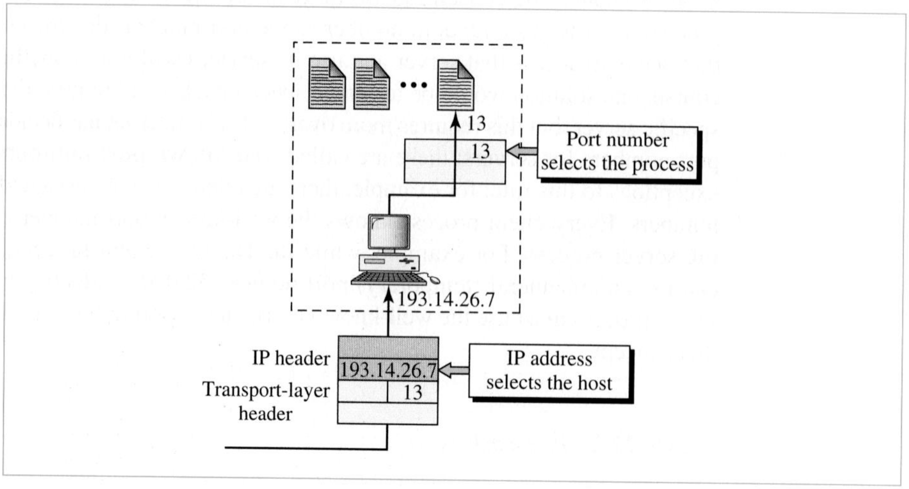

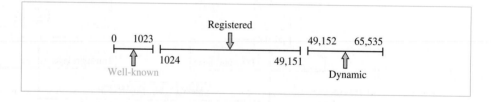

Figure 22.4   *IANA ranges*

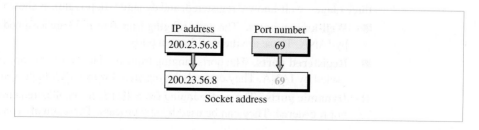

Socket Addresses

Process-to-process delivery needs two identifiers, IP address and the port number, at each end to make a connection. The combination of an IP address and a port number is called a **socket address.** The client socket address defines the client process uniquely just as the server socket address defines the server process uniquely (see Fig. 22.5).

A transport-layer protocol needs a pair of socket addresses: the client socket address and the server socket address. These four pieces of information are part of the IP header

Figure 22.5   *Socket address*

and the transport-layer protocol header. The IP header contains the IP addresses; the UDP or TCP header contains the port numbers.

Multiplexing and Demultiplexing

The addressing mechanism allows multiplexing and demultiplexing by the transport layer, as shown in Figure 22.6.

Figure 22.6 *Multiplexing and demultiplexing*

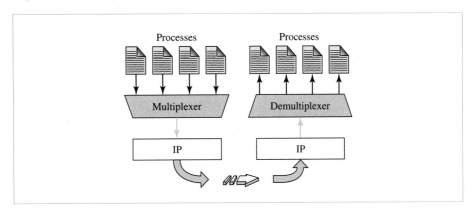

Multiplexing

At the sender site, there may be several processes that need to send packets. However, there is only one transport-layer protocol (UDP or TCP). This is a many-to-one relationship and requires multiplexing. The protocol accepts messages from different processes, differentiated by their assigned port numbers. After adding the header, the transport layer passes the packet to the network layer.

Demultiplexing

At the receiver site, the relationship is one-to-many and requires demultiplexing. The transport layer receives datagrams from the network layer. After error checking and dropping of the header, the transport layer delivers each message to the appropriate process based on the port number.

Connectionless versus Connection-Oriented Service

A transport-layer protocol can either be connectionless or connection-oriented.

Connectionless Service

In a **connectionless service,** the packets are sent from one party to another with no need for connection establishment or connection release. The packets are not numbered; they may be delayed, lost, or arrive out of sequence. There is no acknowledgment either. We will see shortly that one of the transport-layer protocols in the Internet model, UDP, is connectionless.

Connection-Oriented Service

In a **connection-oriented service,** a connection is first established between the sender and the receiver. Data are transferred. At the end, the connection is released. We will see shortly that TCP is a connection-oriented protocol.

Connection Establishment   Connection establishment involves the following:

1. Host A sends a packet to announce its wish for connection and includes its initialization information about traffic from A to B.
2. Host B sends a packet to acknowledge (confirm) the request of A.
3. Host B sends a packet that includes its initialization information about traffic from B to A.
4. Host A sends a packet to acknowledge (confirm) the request of B.

This connection establishment implies four steps. However, since steps 2 and 3 can occur at the same time, they can be combined into one step. That is, host B can confirm the request of host A and send its own request at the same time. Figure 22.7 shows the situation.

Figure 22.7   *Connection establishment*

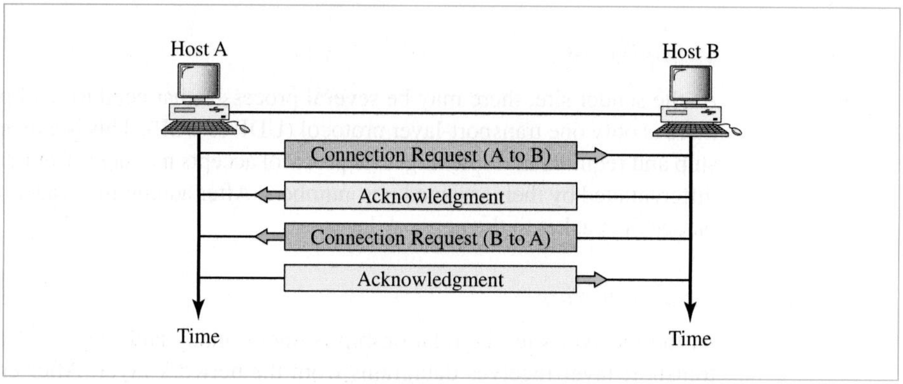

Although the above process seems very simple, we need to elaborate on it.

- Each connection request needs to have a sequence number to recover from the loss or duplication of the packet. Also each acknowledgment needs to have an acknowledgment number for the same reason.

- The first sequence number in each direction must be random for each connection established. In other words, a sender cannot create several connections that start with the same sequence number (for example, 1). The reason is to prevent a situation called **playback.** A classic example is a bank transaction. A bank customer makes a connection and requests a transfer of $1 million to a third party. If the network somehow duplicates the transaction after the first connection is closed, the bank may assume that this is a new connection and transfer another $1 million to the third party. This would probably not happen if the protocol required that the sender use a different sequence number each time it made a new connection. The bank would recognize a repeated sequence number and know that the request was a duplicate.

▪ Using a sequence number for each connection requires that the receiver keep a history of sequence numbers for each remote host for a specified time.

Connection Termination Any of the two parties involved in exchanging data can close the connection. When connection in one direction is terminated, the other party can continue sending data in the other direction. Therefore, four actions are needed to close the connections in both directions:

1. Host A sends a packet announcing its wish for connection termination.

2. Host B sends a segment acknowledging (confirming) the request of A. After this, the connection is closed in one direction, but not in the other. Host B can continue sending data to A.

3. When host B has finished sending its own data, it sends a segment to indicate that it wants to close the connection.

4. Host A acknowledges (confirms) the request of B.

The four-step connection termination cannot be reduced to three steps because the two parties may not wish to terminate at the same time. In other words, connection termination is asymmetric. Figure 22.8 shows the situation.

Figure 22.8 *Connection termination*

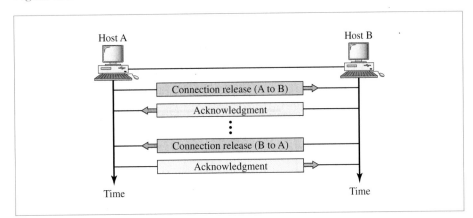

The question that often comes to the mind is, How can we make a connection-oriented transport-layer protocol over a connectionless network-layer protocol such as IP? The answer is that, according to the design goal of the Internet model, the two layers are totally independent. The transport layer only uses the services of network layer. Let us give an analogy. The post office service is connectionless. Each parcel delivered to the post office is independent from the next even if we deliver 100 parcels to the same destination. The post office cannot guarantee that the parcels arrive at the destination in order even if the parcels are numbered. But we can create a connection-oriented service on top of this service. We can have an agent at the destination city and send the numbered parcels to her. The agent can keep the parcels until all have arrived, put them in order, and deliver them to the destination. If a parcel is lost, the agent can ask for a duplicate. We can create a connection with our agent by telephone, for example, when the parcels are ready to be delivered to the post office and get her confirmation. After all parcels have been received, we can call again to announce the disconnection of service.

Reliable versus Unreliable

The transport-layer service can be reliable or unreliable. If the application-layer program needs reliability, we use a reliable transport-layer protocol by implementing flow and error control at the transport layer. This means a slower and more complex service. On the other hand, if the application program does not need reliability because it uses its own flow and error control mechanism or it needs fast service or the nature of the service does not demand flow and error control (real-time applications), then an unreliable protocol can be used.

In the Internet, there are two different transport-layer protocols, as we have already mentioned. UDP is connectionless and unreliable; TCP is connection-oriented and reliable. These two can respond to the demands of the application-layer programs.

One question often comes to the mind. If the data link layer is reliable and has flow and error control, do we need this at the transport layer, too? The answer is yes. Reliability at the data link layer is between two nodes; we need reliability between two ends. Because the network layer in the Internet is unreliable (best-effort delivery), we need to implement reliability at the transport layer. To understand that error control at the data link layer does not guarantee error control at the transport layer, let us look at Figure 22.9.

Figure 22.9 *Error control*

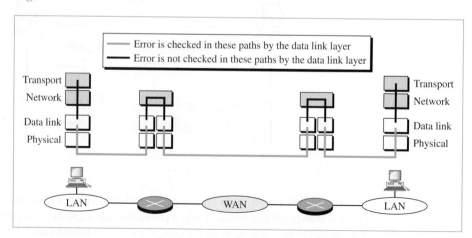

As we will see, flow and error control in TCP is implemented by the sliding window protocol, as discussed in Chapter 11. The window, however, is character-oriented, instead of frame oriented.

22.2 USER DATAGRAM PROTOCOL (UDP)

The simple unreliable transport-layer protocol in the Internet is called the **User Datagram Protocol (UDP).** UDP is a *connectionless, unreliable* transport protocol. It does not add anything to the services of IP except for providing process-to-process communication instead of host-to-host communication. Also, it performs very limited error checking. If UDP is so powerless, why would a process want to use it? With the disadvantages come some advantages. UDP is a very simple protocol with a minimum of overhead. If a process wants to send a small message and does not care much about reliability, it can use UDP. Sending a small message using UDP takes much less inter-action between the sender and receiver than using TCP. In addition, UDP is a convenient protocol for multimedia and multicasting applications.

> UDP is a connectionless, unreliable protocol that has no flow and error control. It uses port numbers to multiplex data from the application layer.

Port Numbers

UDP uses port numbers as the addressing mechanism in the transport layer. Table 22.1 shows some well-known port numbers used by UDP.

Table 22.1   *Well-known ports used by UDP*

Port	Protocol	Description
7	Echo	Echoes a received datagram back to the sender
9	Discard	Discards any datagram that is received
11	Users	Active users
13	Daytime	Returns the date and the time
17	Quote	Returns a quote of the day
19	Chargen	Returns a string of characters
53	Nameserver	Domain Name Service
67	Bootps	Server port to download bootstrap information
68	Bootpc	Client port to download bootstrap information
69	TFTP	Trivial File Transfer Protocol
111	RPC	Remote Procedure Call
123	NTP	Network Time Protocol
161	SNMP	Simple Network Management Protocol
162	SNMP	Simple Network Management Protocol (trap)

User Datagram

UDP packets, called **user datagrams,** have a fixed-size header of 8 bytes. Figure 22.10 shows the format of a user datagram.

Figure 22.10 *User datagram format*

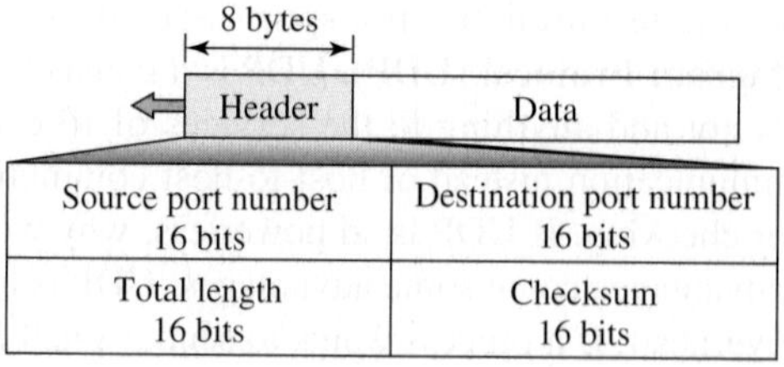

The fields are as follows:

■ **Source port number.** This is the port number used by the process running on the source host. It is 16 bits long, which means that the port number can range from 0 to 65,535.

■ **Destination port number.** This is the port number used by the process running on the destination host. It is also 16 bits long.

■ **Length.** This is a 16-bit field that defines the total length of the user datagram, header plus data. The 16 bits can define a total length of 0 to 65,535 bytes.

■ **Checksum.** This field is used to detect errors over the entire user datagram (header plus data). We have already talked about the concept of the checksum and the way it is calculated in Chapter 10. Although it seems that the UDP checksum should be based on the UDP header and payload (data coming from the application layer), the designers added a part of the IP header (only those fields not changed by routers) as part of the checksum calculation. This ensures that those fields have not been changed from the source to the destination. The calculation of the checksum and its inclusion in a user datagram are optional. If the checksum is not calculated, the field is filled with 0s.

> The calculation of checksum and its inclusion in the user datagram are optional.

Applications

The following are some uses of UDP:

■ UDP is suitable for a process that requires simple request-response communication with little concern for flow and error control. It is not usually used for a process that needs to send bulk data, such as FTP (see Chapter 26).

■ UDP is suitable for a process with internal flow and error control mechanisms. For example, the Trivial File Transfer Protocol (TFTP) includes flow and error control. It can easily use UDP.

■ UDP is a suitable transport protocol for multicasting. Multicasting capabilities are embedded in the UDP software but not in the TCP software.

■ UDP is used for some route updating protocols such as Routing Information Protocol (RIP) (see Chapter 21).

■ UDP is used in conjunction with the Real Time Transport Protocol (RTP) to provide a transport-layer mechanism for real-time data (see Chapter 28).

UDP is a convenient transport-layer protocol for applications that provide flow and error control. It is also used by multimedia applications.

22.3 TRANSMISSION CONTROL PROTOCOL (TCP)

The reliable, but complex transport-layer protocol in the Internet is called **Transmission Control Protocol (TCP).** TCP is called a *stream connection-oriented* and *reliable* transport protocol. It adds connection-oriented and reliability features to the services of IP.

Port Numbers

Like UDP, TCP uses port numbers as transport-layer addresses. Table 22.2 lists some well-known port numbers used by TCP. Note that if an application can use both UDP and TCP, the same port number is assigned to this application.

Table 22.2 *Well-known ports used by TCP*

Port	Protocol	Description
7	Echo	Echoes a received datagram back to the sender
9	Discard	Discards any datagram that is received
11	Users	Active users
13	Daytime	Returns the date and the time
17	Quote	Returns a quote of the day
19	Chargen	Returns a string of characters
20	FTP, Data	File Transfer Protocol (data connection)
21	FTP, Control	File Transfer Protocol (control connection)
23	TELNET	Terminal Network
25	SMTP	Simple Mail Transfer Protocol
53	DNS	Domain Name Server
67	BOOTP	Bootstrap Protocol
79	Finger	Finger
80	HTTP	Hypertext Transfer Protocol
111	RPC	Remote Procedure Call

TCP Services

Let us explain the services offered by TCP to the processes at the application layer.

Stream Delivery Service

TCP, unlike UDP, is a stream-oriented protocol. In UDP, a process (an application program) sends a chunk of bytes to UDP for delivery. UDP adds its own header to this chunk of data, which is now called a user datagram, and delivers it to IP for transmission. The process may deliver several chunks of data to the UDP, but UDP treats each chunk independently without seeing any connection between them.

TCP, on the other hand, allows the sending process to deliver data as a stream of bytes and the receiving process to obtain data as a stream of bytes. TCP creates an environment in which the two processes seem to be connected by an imaginary "tube" that carries their data across the Internet. This imaginary environment is depicted in Figure 22.11. The sending process produces the stream of bytes, and the receiving process consumes it.

Figure 22.11   *Stream delivery*

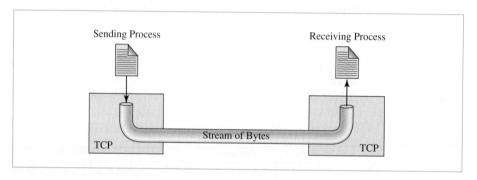

Sending and Receiving Buffers

Because the sending and the receiving processes may not produce and consume data at the same speed, TCP needs buffers for storage. There are two buffers, the sending buffer and the receiving buffer, for each direction. (We will see later that these buffers are also used in flow and error control mechanisms used by TCP.) One way to implement a buffer is to use a circular array of 1-byte locations, as shown in Figure 22.12.

Figure 22.12   *Sending and receiving buffers*

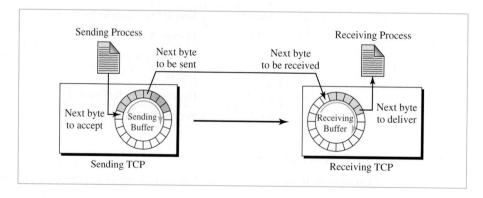

For simplicity, we have shown two buffers of 20 bytes each; normally the buffers are hundreds or thousands of bytes, depending on the implementation. We also show the buffers as the same size, which is not always the case.

The figure shows the movement of the data in one direction. At the sending site, the buffer has three types of locations. The white section contains empty locations that can be filled by the sending process (producer). The gray area holds bytes that have been sent but not yet acknowledged. TCP keeps these bytes in the buffer until it receives an acknowledgment. The colored areas are bytes to be sent by the sending TCP. However, as we will see later in this chapter, TCP may be able to send only part of this colored section. This could be due to the slowness of the receiving process or perhaps congestion in the network. Also note that after the bytes in the gray locations are acknowledged, the location is recycled and available for use by the sending process. This is why we show a circular buffer.

The operation of the buffer at the receiver site is simpler. The circular buffer is divided into two areas (shown as white and colored). The white area contains empty locations to be filled by bytes received from the network. The colored sections contain received bytes that can be consumed by the receiving process. When a byte is consumed by the receiving process, the location is recycled and added to the pool of empty locations.

Bytes and Segments

Although buffering handles the disparity between the speed of the producing and consuming processes, we need one more step before we can send data. The IP layer, as a service provider for TCP, needs to send data in packets, not as a stream of bytes. At the transport layer, TCP groups a number of bytes together into a packet called a **segment.** TCP adds a header to each segment (for control purposes) and delivers the segment to the IP layer for transmission. The segments are encapsulated in an IP datagram and transmitted. This entire operation is transparent to the receiving process. Later we will see that segments may be received out of order, lost, or corrupted and resent. All these are handled by TCP with the receiving process unaware of any activities. Figure 22.13 shows how segments are created from the bytes in the buffers.

Figure 22.13 *TCP segments*

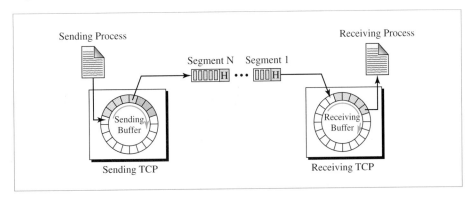

Note that the segments are not necessarily the same size. In the figure, for simplicity, we show one segment carrying 3 bytes and the other carrying 5 bytes. In reality segments carry hundreds, if not thousands, of bytes.

Full-Duplex Service

TCP offers full-duplex service, where data can flow in both directions at the same time. Each TCP then has a sending and receiving buffer, and segments are sent in both directions.

Connection-Oriented Service

TCP, unlike UDP, is a connection-oriented protocol. When a process at site A wants to send and receive data from another process at site B, the following occurs:

1. A's TCP informs B's TCP and gets approval from B's TCP.
2. A's TCP and B's TCP exchange data in both directions.
3. After both processes have no data left to send and the buffers are empty, the two TCPs destroy their buffers.

Note that this is a virtual connection, not a physical connection. The TCP segment is encapsulated in an IP datagram and can be sent out of order, or lost, or corrupted, and then resent. Each may use a different path to reach the destination. There is no physical connection. However, TCP creates a stream-oriented environment in which it accepts the responsibility of delivering the bytes in order to the other site. It's as if a bridge is created that spans multiple islands with traffic going from one island to another on one single connection.

Reliable Service

TCP is a reliable transport protocol. It uses an acknowledgment mechanism to check the safe and sound arrival of data. We will discuss this feature further in the section on error control.

Numbering Bytes

Although the TCP software keeps track of the segment being transmitted or received, there is no field for a segment number value. Instead, there are two fields called the **sequence number** and the **acknowledgment number.** These two fields refer to the byte number, not the segment number.

Byte Numbers

TCP numbers all data bytes that are transmitted in a connection. Numbering is independent in each direction. When TCP receives bytes of data from the process and stores them in the sending buffer, it numbers them. The numbering does not necessarily start from 0; it starts with a randomly generated number between 0 and $2^{32} - 1$. For example, if the random number happens to be 1057 and the total data to be sent are 6000 bytes, the bytes are numbered from 1057 to 7056. We will see that byte numbering is used for flow and error control.

> **The bytes of data being transferred in each connection are numbered by TCP. The numbering starts with a randomly generated number.**

Sequence Number

After the bytes have been numbered, TCP assigns a sequence number to each segment that is being sent. The sequence number for each segment is the number of the first byte carried in that segment.

Example 1

Imagine a TCP connection is transferring a file of 6000 bytes. The first byte is numbered 10010. What are the sequence numbers for each segment if data are sent in five segments with the first four segments carrying 1000 bytes and the last segment carrying 2000 bytes?

Solution

The following shows the sequence number for each segment:

Segment 1 $\longrightarrow$	sequence number: 10,010	(range: 10,010 to 11,009)
Segment 2 $\longrightarrow$	sequence number: 11,010	(range: 11,010 to 12,009)
Segment 3 $\longrightarrow$	sequence number: 12,010	(range: 12,010 to 13,009)
Segment 4 $\longrightarrow$	sequence number: 13,010	(range: 13,010 to 14,009)
Segment 5 $\longrightarrow$	sequence number: 14,010	(range: 14,010 to 16,009)

> **The value of the sequence number field in a segment defines the number of the first data byte contained in that segment.**

Acknowledgment Number

As we discussed before, communication in TCP is full-duplex; when a connection is established, both parties can send and receive data at the same time. Each party numbers the bytes, usually with a different starting byte number. The sequence number in each direction shows the number of the first byte carried by the segment. Each party also uses an acknowledgment number to confirm the bytes it has received. However, the acknowledgment number defines the number of the next byte that the party expects to receive. In addition, the acknowledgment number is cumulative, which means that the receiver takes the number of the last byte that it has received, safe and sound, adds 1 to it, and announces this sum as the acknowledgment number. The term *cumulative* here means that if a party uses 5643 as an acknowledgment number, it has received all bytes from the beginning up to 5642. Note that this does not mean that the party has received 5642 bytes because the first byte number does not normally start from 0.

> **The value of the acknowledgment field in a segment defines the number of the next byte a party expects to receive. The acknowledgment number is cumulative.**

Segment

The unit of data transfer between two devices using TCP is a **segment.** The format of a segment is shown in Figure 22.14.

Figure 22.14 *TCP segment format*

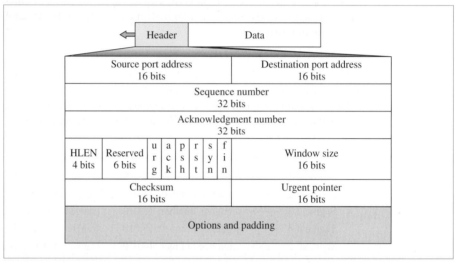

The segment consists of a 20- to 60-byte header, followed by data from the application program. The header is 20 bytes if there are no options and up to 60 bytes if it contains options. We will discuss some of the header fields in this section.

- **Source port address.** This is a 16-bit field that defines the port number of the application program in the host that is sending the segment.
- **Destination port address.** This is a 16-bit field that defines the port number of the application program in the host that is receiving the segment.
- **Sequence number.** This 32-bit field defines the number assigned to the first byte of data contained in this segment. As we said before, TCP is a stream transport protocol. To ensure connectivity, each byte to be transmitted is numbered. The sequence number tells the destination which byte in this sequence comprises the first byte in the segment.
- **Acknowledgment number.** This 32-bit field defines the byte number that the sender of the segment is expecting to receive from the other party. If the byte numbered x has been successfully received, $x + 1$ is the acknowledgment number.
- **Header length.** This 4-bit field indicates the number of 4-byte words in the TCP header. The length of the header can be between 20 and 60 bytes. Therefore, the value of this field can be between 5 ($5 \times 4 = 20$) and 15 ($15 \times 4 = 60$).
- **Reserved.** This is a 6-bit field reserved for future use.
- **Control.** This field defines 6 different control bits or flags, as shown in Figure 22.15. One or more of these bits can be set at a time. These bits enable flow control,

Figure 22.15 *Control field*

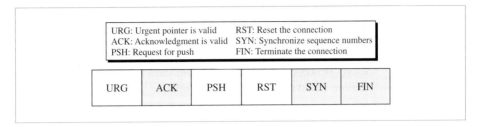

Table 22.3 *Description of flags in the control field*

Flag	Description
URG	The value of the urgent pointer field is valid.
ACK	The value of the acknowledgment field is valid.
PSH	Push the data.
RST	The connection must be reset.
SYN	Synchronize sequence numbers during connection.
FIN	Terminate the connection.

connection establishment and termination, and the mode of data transfer in TCP. A brief description of each bit is shown in Table 22.3.

■ **Window size.** This field defines the size of the window, in bytes, that the other party must maintain. Note that the length of this field is 16 bits, which means that the maximum size of the window is 65,535 bytes, unless the size of the window is augmented by some option fields.

■ **Checksum.** This 16-bit field contains the checksum. The calculation of the checksum for TCP follows the same procedure as the one described for UDP in the previous section.

■ **Urgent pointer.** This 16-bit field, which is valid only if the urgent flag is set, is used when the segment contains urgent data. The number is added to the sequence number to obtain the number of the last urgent byte in the data section of the segment. This is discussed later in this chapter.

■ **Options.** There can be up to 40 bytes of optional information in the TCP header. The discussion of these options is beyond the scope of this book. For more information see Forouzan's *TCP/IP Protocol Suite,* 2d ed., McGraw-Hill, 2003.

Connection

TCP is a connection-oriented protocol. It establishes a virtual path between the source and destination. All the segments belonging to a message are then sent over this virtual path. Using a single virtual pathway for the entire message facilitates the acknowledgment process as well as retransmission of damaged or lost frames. In TCP, connection-oriented transmission requires two procedures: **connection establishment** and **connection termination.**

Connection Establishment

TCP transmits data in full-duplex mode. When two TCPs in two machines are connected, they are able to send segments to each other simultaneously. This implies that each party must initialize communication and get approval from the other party before any data transfer. Four steps are needed to establish the connection, as discussed before. However, the second and third steps can be combined to create a three-step connection, called a **three-way handshake,** as shown in Figure 22.16.

Figure 22.16 *Three-step connection establishment*

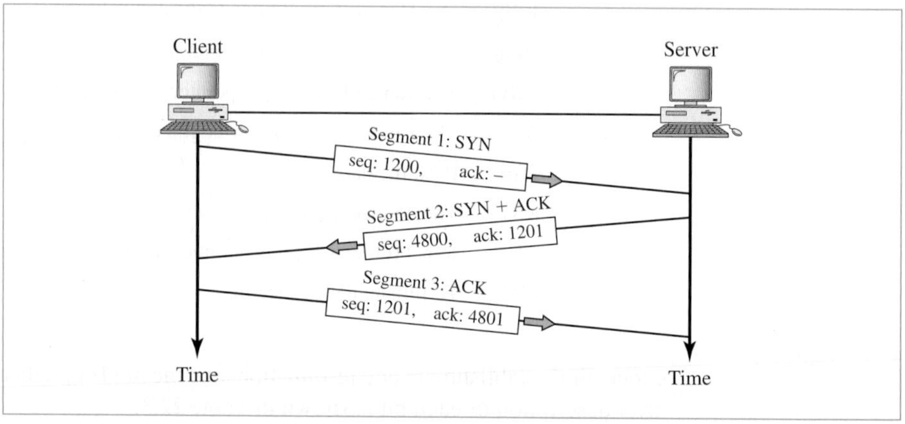

The steps of the process are as follows:

1. The client sends the first segment, a SYN segment. The segment includes the source and destination port numbers. The destination port number clearly defines the server to which the client wants to be connected. The segment also contains the client *initialization sequence number (ISN)* used for numbering the bytes of data sent from the client to the server.

2. The server sends the second segment, a SYN and an ACK segment. This segment has a dual purpose. First, it acknowledges the receipt of the first segment, using the ACK flag and acknowledgment number field. Note that the acknowledgment number is the client initialization sequence number plus 1 because no user data have been sent in segment 1. The server must also define the client window size. Second, the segment is used as the initialization segment for the server. It contains the initialization sequence number used to number the bytes sent from the server to the client.

3. The client sends the third segment. This is just an ACK segment. It acknowledges the receipt of the second segment, using the ACK flag and acknowledgment number field. Note that the acknowledgment number is the server initialization sequence number plus 1 because no user data have been sent in segment 2. The client must also define the server window size. Data can be sent with the third packet.

Connection Termination

Any of the two parties involved in exchanging data (client or server) can close the connection. When connection in one direction is terminated, the other party can continue sending data in the other direction. Therefore, four steps are needed to close the connections in both directions, as shown in Figure 22.17.

Figure 22.17 *Four-step connection termination*

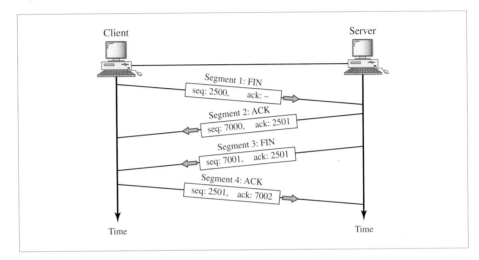

The four steps are as follows:

1. The client TCP sends the first segment, a FIN segment.
2. The server TCP sends the second segment, an ACK segment, to confirm the receipt of the FIN segment from the client. Note that the acknowledgment number is 1 plus the sequence number received in the FIN segment because no user data have been sent in segment 1.
3. The server TCP can continue sending data in the server-client direction. When it does not have any more data to send, it sends the third segment. This segment is a FIN segment.
4. The client TCP sends the fourth segment, an ACK segment, to confirm the receipt of the FIN segment from the TCP server. Note that the acknowledgment number is 1 plus the sequence number received in the FIN segment from the server.

Connection Resetting

TCP may request the resetting of a connection. *Resetting* here means that the current connection is destroyed. This happens in one of three cases:

1. The TCP on one side has requested a connection to a nonexistent port. The TCP on the other side may send a segment with its RST bit set to annul the request.
2. One TCP may want to abort the connection due to an abnormal situation. It can send an RST segment to close the connection.

3. The TCP on one side may discover that the TCP on the other side has been idle for a long time. It may send an RST segment to destroy the connection.

State Transition Diagram

To keep track of all the different events happening during connection establishment, connection termination, and data transfer, the TCP software is implemented as a finite state machine. A **finite state machine** is a machine that goes through a limited number of states. At any moment, the machine is in one of the states. It remains in that state until an event happens. The event can take the machine to a new state, or the event can make the machine perform some actions. In other words, the event is an input applied to a state. It can change the state and can also create an output. Table 22.4 shows the states for TCP.

Table 22.4   *States for TCP*

State	Description
CLOSED	There is no connection.
LISTEN	The server is waiting for calls from the client.
SYN-SENT	A connection request is sent; waiting for acknowledgment.
SYN-RCVD	A connection request is received.
ESTABLISHED	Connection is established.
FIN-WAIT-1	The application has requested the closing of the connection.
FIN-WAIT-2	The other side has accepted the closing of the connection.
TIME-WAIT	Waiting for retransmitted segments to die.
CLOSE-WAIT	The server is waiting for the application to close.
LAST-ACK	The server is waiting for the last acknowledgment.

To illustrate the concept we use a **state transition diagram.** The states are shown using ovals. The transition from one state to another is shown using the directed lines. Each line has two strings separated by a slash. The first string is the input, what TCP receives. The second is the output, what TCP sends. Figure 22.18 shows the state transition diagram for both client and server. The dotted lines of the figure represent the server, the solid lines represent the client. The diagram is more complex than what is shown in the figure.

Client Diagram

The client can be in one of the following states: CLOSED, SYN-SENT, ESTABLISHED, FIN-WAIT-1, FIN-WAIT-2, and TIME-WAIT.

- The client TCP starts in the CLOSED state.
- While in this state, the client TCP can receive an active open request from the client application program. It sends a SYN segment to the server TCP and goes to the SYN-SENT state.

Figure 22.18 *State transition diagram*

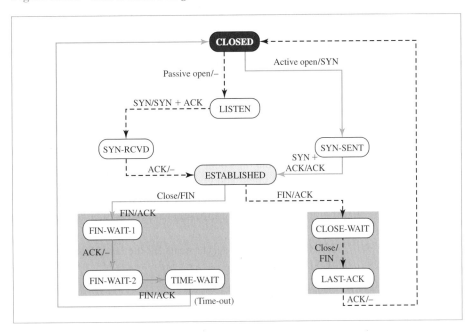

- While in this state, the client TCP can receive a SYN + ACK segment from the other TCP. It sends an ACK segment to the other TCP and goes to the ESTABLISHED state. This is the data transfer state. The client remains in this state as long as it is sending and receiving data.

- While in this state, the client TCP can receive a close request from the client application program. It sends a FIN segment to the other TCP and goes to the FIN-WAIT-1 state.

- While in this state, the client TCP waits to receive an ACK from the server TCP. When the ACK is received, it goes to the FIN-WAIT-2 state. It does not send anything. Now the connection is closed in one direction.

- The client remains in this state, waiting for the server to close the connection from the other end. If the client receives a FIN segment from the other end, it sends an ACK segment and goes to the TIME-WAIT state.

- When the client is in this state, it starts a timer and waits until this timer goes off. The value of this timer is set to double the lifetime estimate of a segment of maximum size. The client remains in the state before totally closing to let all duplicate packets, if any, arrive at their destination to be discarded. After the time-out, the client goes to the CLOSED state, where it began.

Server Diagram

Although the server can be in any one of the 11 states, in normal operation it is in one of the following states: CLOSED, LISTEN, SYN-RCVD, ESTABLISHED, CLOSE-WAIT, and LAST-ACK.

■   The server TCP starts in the CLOSED state.

■   While in this state, the server TCP can receive a passive open request from the server application program. It goes to the LISTEN state.

■   While in this state, the server TCP can receive a SYN segment from the client TCP. It sends a SYN + ACK segment to the client TCP and then goes to the SYN-RCVD state.

■   While in this state, the server TCP can receive an ACK segment from the client TCP. It goes to the ESTABLISHED state. This is the data transfer state. The server remains in this state as long as it is receiving and sending data.

■   While in this state, the server TCP can receive a FIN segment from the client, which means that the client wishes to close the connection. It can send an ACK segment to the client and goes to the CLOSE-WAIT state.

■   While in this state, the server waits until it receives a close request from the server program. It then sends a FIN segment to the client and goes to the LAST-ACK state.

■   While in this state, the server waits for the last ACK segment. It then goes to the CLOSED state.

Flow Control

Flow control defines the amount of data a source can send before receiving an acknowledgment from the destination. In an extreme case, a transport-layer protocol could send 1 byte of data and wait for an acknowledgment before sending the next byte. But this would be an extremely slow process. If the data are traveling a long distance, the source is idle while it waits for an acknowledgment.

At the other extreme, a transport-layer protocol can send all the data it has without worrying about acknowledgment. This speeds up the process, but it may overwhelm the receiver. Besides, if some part of the data is lost, duplicated, received out of order, or corrupted, the source will not know until all data have been checked by the destination.

TCP has a solution that stands somewhere in between. It defines a window that is imposed on the buffer of data delivered from the application program and is ready to be sent. TCP sends as many data as are defined by the sliding window protocol.

Sliding Window Protocol

To accomplish flow control, TCP uses a sliding window protocol. With this method, both hosts use a window for each connection. The window spans a portion of the buffer containing bytes that a host can send before worrying about an acknowledgment from the other host. The window is called a **sliding window** because it can slide over the buffer as data and acknowledgments are sent and received.

> A sliding window is used to make transmission more efficient as well as to control the flow of data so that the destination does not become overwhelmed with data. TCP's sliding windows are byte-oriented.

Figure 22.19 shows the sender buffer in Figure 22.12. However, instead of a circular buffer, we have shown a flat buffer for simplicity. Note that if we connect the two ends of the buffer, we get the circular buffer.

Figure 22.19 *Sender buffer*

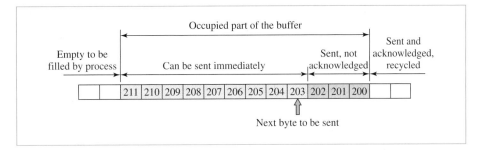

In Figure 22.19 the bytes before 200 have been sent and acknowledged. The sender can reuse these locations. Bytes 200 to 202 have been sent, but not acknowledged. The sender has to keep these bytes in the buffer in case they are lost or damaged. Bytes 203 to 211 are in the buffer (produced by the process) but have not yet been sent.

Let's examine the situation in which there is no sliding window protocol. In this case, the sender can go ahead and send all the bytes (up to 211) in its buffer, without regard to the condition of the receiver. The receiver's buffer, with its limited size, could completely fill up because the receiving process is not consuming data fast enough. The excess bytes discarded by the receiver will require retransmission. The sender must adjust itself to the number of locations available at the receiver site.

Receiver Window

Figure 22.20 shows the receiver buffer. Note that the next byte to be consumed by the process is byte 194. The receiver expects to receive byte 200 from the sender (which has been sent but not received). How many more bytes can the receiver store? If the total size of the receiving buffer is N and M locations are already occupied, then only $N - M$ more bytes can be received. This value is called the **receiver window.** For example, if $N = 13$ and $M = 6$, this means that the value of the receiver window is 7.

Figure 22.20 *Receiver window*

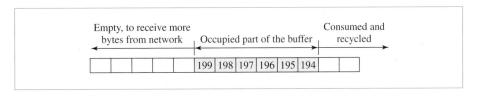

Sender Window

We have flow control if the sender creates a window—the **sender window**—with a size less than or equal to the size of the receiver window. This window includes the bytes sent and not acknowledged and those that can be sent. Figure 22.21 shows the sender buffer with the sender window.

Figure 22.21   *Sender buffer and sender window*

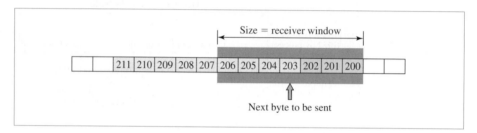

Note that the size of the sender window is equal to the size of the receiver window (7 in our example). However, this does not mean that the sender can send 7 more bytes; it can send only 4 more bytes because it has already sent 3 bytes. Note also that although bytes 207 to 211 are in the sending buffer, they also cannot be sent until more news arrives from the receiver.

Sliding the Sender Window

Let's see how messages from the receiver change the position of the sender window. In our example, suppose the sender sends 2 more bytes and an acknowledgment is received from the receiver (expecting byte 203) with no change in the size of the receiver window (still 7). The sender can now slide its window, and the locations occupied by bytes 200 to 202 can be recycled. Figure 22.22 shows the position of the sender buffer and the sender window before and after this event. In part b of the figure, the sender can now send bytes 205 to 209 (5 more bytes).

Figure 22.22   *Sliding the sender window*

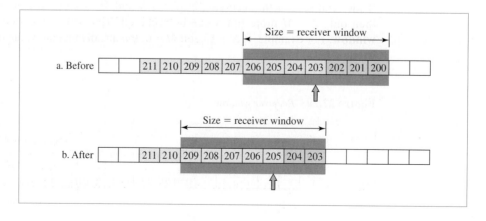

Expanding the Sender Window

If the receiving process consumes data faster than it receives, the size of the receiver window expands (the buffer has more free locations). This situation can be relayed to the sender, resulting in the increase (expansion) of the window size. In Figure 22.23, the receiver has acknowledged the receipt of 2 more bytes (expecting byte 205) and at the same time has increased the value of the receiver window to 10. In the meantime, the sending process has created 4 more bytes, and the sending TCP has sent 5 bytes.

Figure 22.23 *Expanding the sender window*

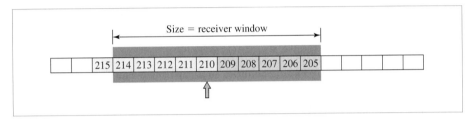

Shrinking the Sender Window

If the receiving process consumes data more slowly than it receives data, the size of the receiver window decreases (shrinks). In this case the receiver has to inform the sender to shrink its sender window size. In Figure 22.24, the receiver has received the 5 bytes (205 to 209); however, the receiving process has consumed only 1 byte, which means the number of free locations is reduced to 6 (10 − 5 + 1). It acknowledges bytes 205 to 209 (expecting 210), but also informs the sender to shrink its window size and not to send more than 6 more bytes. If the sender has already sent 2 more bytes when it receives the news and has received 3 more bytes from the sending process, we get the window and buffer as shown in Figure 22.24.

Figure 22.24 *Shrinking the sender window*

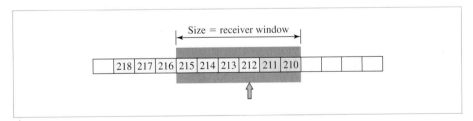

Closing the Sender Window

What happens if the receiver buffer is totally full? In this case, the receiver window value is zero. When this is relayed to the sender, the sender closes its window (left and right walls overlap). The sender cannot send any bytes until the receiver announces a nonzero receiver window value. We discuss this issue again when we talk about TCP timers.

> In TCP, the sender window size is totally controlled by the receiver window value (the number of empty locations in the receiver buffer). However, the actual window size can be smaller if there is congestion in the network.

> Some points about TCP's sliding windows:
>
> ■ The source does not have to send a full window's worth of data.
> ■ The size of the window can be increased or decreased by the destination.
> ■ The destination can send an acknowledgment at any time.

Silly Window Syndrome

A serious problem can arise in the sliding window operation when either the sending application program creates data slowly or the receiving application program consumes data slowly, or both. Either of these situations results in the sending of data in very small segments, which reduces the efficiency of the operation. For example, if TCP sends segments containing only 1 byte of data, it means that we are sending a 41-byte datagram (20 bytes of TCP header and 20 bytes of IP header) that transfers only 1 byte of user data. Here the overhead is 41/1, which indicates that we are using the capacity of the network very inefficiently. This problem is called the **silly window syndrome.** For each site, we first describe how the problem is created and then give a proposed solution.

Syndrome Created by the Sender

The sending TCP may create a silly window syndrome if it is serving an application program that creates data slowly, for example, 1 byte at a time. The application program writes 1 byte at a time into the buffer of the sending TCP. If the sending TCP does not have any specific instructions, it may create segments containing 1 byte of data. The result is a lot of 41-byte segments that are traveling through an internet.

The solution is to prevent the sending TCP from sending the data byte by byte. The sending TCP must be forced to wait as it collects data to send in a larger block. How long should the sending TCP wait? If it waits too long, it may delay the process. If it does not wait long enough, it may end up sending small segments. Nagle found an elegant solution.

Nagle's Algorithm   Nagle's algorithm is very simple, but it solves the problem. This algorithm is for the sending TCP:

1. The sending TCP sends the first piece of data it receives from the sending application program even if it is only 1 byte.

2. After sending the first segment, the sending TCP accumulates data in the output buffer and waits until either the receiving TCP sends an acknowledgment or enough data have accumulated to fill a maximum-size segment. At this time, the sending TCP can send the next segment.

3. Step 2 is repeated for the rest of the transmission. Segment 3 must be sent if an acknowledgment is received for segment 2 or enough data are accumulated to fill a maximum-size segment.

The elegance of Nagle's algorithm lies in its simplicity and in the fact that it takes into account the speed of the application program that creates the data and the speed of the network that transports the data. If the application program is faster than the network, the segments are larger (maximum-size segments). If the application program is slower than the network, the segments are smaller (less than the maximum segment size).

Syndrome Created by the Receiver

The receiving TCP may create a silly window syndrome if it is serving an application program that consumes data slowly, for example, 1 byte at a time. Suppose that the sending application program creates data in blocks of 1K, but the receiving application program consumes data 1 byte at a time. Also suppose that the input buffer of the receiving TCP is 4K. The sender sends the first 4 kbytes of data. The receiver stores them in its buffer. Now its buffer is full. It advertises a window size of zero, which means the sender should stop sending data. The receiving application reads the first byte of data from the input buffer of the receiving TCP. Now there is 1 byte of space in the incoming buffer. The receiving TCP announces a window size of 1 byte; the sending TCP, which is eagerly waiting to send data, takes this advertisement as good news and sends a segment carrying only 1 byte of data. The procedure will continue. One byte of data is consumed, and a segment carrying 1 byte of data is sent. Again we have an efficiency problem and a silly window syndrome.

Two solutions have been proposed to prevent the silly window syndrome created by an application program that consumes data more slowly than they arrive.

Clark's Solution   Clark's solution is to send an acknowledgment as soon as the data arrive, but to announce a window size of zero until either there is enough space to accommodate a segment of maximum size or until one-half of the buffer is empty.

Delayed Acknowledgment   The second solution is to delay sending the acknowledgment. This means that when a segment arrives, it is not acknowledged immediately. The receiver waits until there is a decent amount of space in its incoming buffer before acknowledging the arrived segments. The delayed acknowledgment prevents the sending TCP from sliding its window. After it has sent the data in the window, it stops. This kills the syndrome.

Delayed acknowledgment also has another advantage: It reduces traffic. The receiver does not have to acknowledge each segment. However, there also is a disadvantage in that the delayed acknowledgment may force the sender to retransmit the unacknowledged segments.

The protocol balances the advantages and disadvantages, and specifies that the acknowledgment should not be delayed by more than 500 ms.

Error Control

TCP is a reliable transport-layer protocol. This means that an application program that delivers a stream of data to TCP relies on TCP to deliver the entire stream to the application program on the other end in order, without error, and without any part lost or duplicated. Error control in TCP includes mechanisms for detecting corrupted segments, lost segments, out-of-order segments, and duplicated segments.

TCP uses three simple tools: checksum, acknowledgment, and time-out. Each segment includes the checksum field, which is used to check for a corrupted segment. If the segment is corrupted, it is discarded by the destination TCP. TCP uses the acknowledgment method to confirm the receipt of those segments that have reached the destination uncorrupted. No negative acknowledgment is used in TCP. If a segment is not acknowledged before the time-out, it is considered to be either corrupted or lost.

The source TCP starts one time-out counter for each segment sent. Each counter is checked periodically. When a counter matures, the corresponding segment is considered to be either corrupted or lost, and the segment will be retransmitted.

There is no negative acknowledgment in TCP.

Lost or Corrupted Segment   Figure 22.25 shows a lost segment. The situation is exactly the same as a corrupted segment. In other words, from the point of the source and destination, a lost segment and a corrupted segment are the same. A corrupted segment is discarded by the final destination; a lost segment is discarded by some intermediate node and never reaches the destination.

Figure 22.25 *Lost segment*

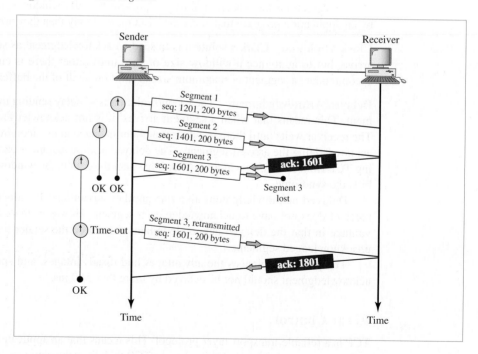

Duplicate Segment   A duplicate segment can be created, for example, by a source TCP when the acknowledgment does not arrive before the time-out. Handling the duplicate segment is a simple process for the destination TCP. The destination TCP expects a continuous stream of bytes. When a packet arrives that contains the same sequence number as another received segment, the destination TCP simply discards the segment.

Out-of-Order Segment   TCP uses the services of IP, an unreliable, connectionless network-layer protocol. The TCP segment is encapsulated in an IP datagram. Each datagram is an independent entity. The routers are free to send each datagram through any route they find suitable. One datagram may follow a route with a short delay; another may follow another route with a longer delay. If datagrams arrive out of order, the TCP segments that are encapsulated in the datagrams will be out of order as well. The handling of out-of-order segments by the destination TCP is very simple: It does not acknowledge an out-of-order segment until it receives all the segments that precede it. Of course, if the acknowledgment is delayed, the timer of the out-of-order segment may mature at the source TCP and the segment may be resent. The duplicates will then be discarded by the destination TCP.

Lost Acknowledgment   Figure 22.26 shows a lost acknowledgment sent by the destination. In the TCP acknowledgment mechanism, a lost acknowledgment may not even be noticed by the source TCP. TCP uses a cumulative acknowledgment system. Each acknowledgment is a confirmation that everything up to the byte specified by the acknowledgment number has been received. For example, if the destination sends an ACK segment with an acknowledgment number for byte 1801, it is confirming that bytes 1201 to 1800 have been received. If the destination has previously sent an acknowledgment for byte 1601, meaning it has received bytes 1201 to 1600, loss of the acknowledgment is irrelevant.

Figure 22.26   *Lost acknowledgment*

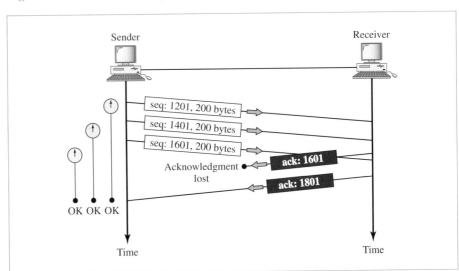

TCP Timers

To perform its operation smoothly, TCP uses the four **TCP timers** shown in Figure 22.27.

Figure 22.27 *TCP timers*

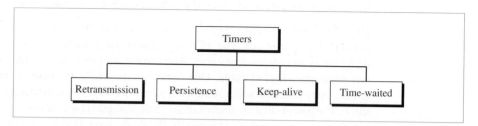

Retransmission Timer

To control a lost or discarded segment, TCP employs a **retransmission timer** that handles the retransmission time, the waiting time for an acknowledgment of a segment. When TCP sends a segment, it creates a retransmission timer for that particular segment. Two situations may occur:

1. If an acknowledgment is received for this particular segment before the timer goes off, the timer is destroyed.

2. If the timer goes off before the acknowledgment arrives, the segment is retransmitted and the timer is reset.

Calculation of Retransmission Time TCP is a transport-layer protocol. Each connection connects two TCPs that may be just one physical network apart or located on opposite sides of the globe. In other words, each connection creates a path with a length that may be totally different from another path created by another connection. This means that TCP cannot use the same retransmission time for all connections. Selecting a fixed retransmission time for all connections can have serious consequences. If the retransmission time does not allow enough time for a segment to reach the destination and an acknowledgment to reach the source, it can result in retransmission of segments that are still on the way. Conversely, if the retransmission time is longer than necessary for a short path, it may result in delay for the application program.

Even for one single connection, the retransmission time should not be fixed. A connection may be able to send segments and receive acknowledgments faster during nontraffic periods than during congested periods. TCP uses a dynamic retransmission time, a transmission time that is different for each connection and which may change during the same connection.

Retransmission time can be made dynamic by basing it on the **round-trip time (RTT).** Several formulas are used for this purpose. The most common is to set the retransmission time equal to twice the RTT:

$$\text{Retransmission time} = 2 \times \text{RTT}$$

Calculation of RTT The question now is, How do we calculate the RTT? The RTT, too, is calculated dynamically. There are two methods. In the first method, TCP uses the value from the TCP timestamp option. In the second method, TCP sends a segment, starts a timer, and waits for an acknowledgment. It measures the time between the sending of the segment and the receiving of the acknowledgment. Each segment has a round-trip time. The value of the RTT used in the calculation of the retransmission time of the next segment is the updated value of the RTT according to the following formula:

$$RTT = \alpha(\text{previous RTT}) + (1 - \alpha)(\text{current RTT})$$

The value of α is usually 90 percent. This means that the new RTT is 90 percent of the value of the previous RTT plus 10 percent of the value of the current RTT. For example, if the previous RTT is 250 μs and it takes a segment at this moment to be acknowledged in 70 μs, the values of the new RTT and the retransmission time are

$$RTT = 90\% \times 250 + 10\% \times 70 = 232 \text{ μs}$$

$$\text{Retransmission time} = 2 \times 232 = 464 \text{ μs}$$

Karn's Algorithm Suppose that a segment is not acknowledged during the retransmission period and it is therefore retransmitted. When the sending TCP receives an acknowledgment for this segment, it does not know if the acknowledgment is for the original segment or for the retransmitted one. This dilemma was solved by Karn. Karn's solution is very simple. Do not consider the RTT of a retransmitted segment in the calculation of the new RTT. Do not update the value of RTT until you send a segment and receive an acknowledgment without the need for retransmission.

Persistence Timer

To deal with the zero window-size advertisement, TCP needs another timer. Suppose the receiving TCP announces a window size of zero. The sending TCP then stops transmitting segments until the receiving TCP sends an acknowledgment announcing a nonzero window size. This acknowledgment can be lost. Remember that acknowledgments are not acknowledged in TCP. If this acknowledgment is lost, the receiving TCP thinks that it has done its job and waits for the sending TCP to send more segments. The sending TCP has not received an acknowledgment and waits for the other TCP to send an acknowledgment advertising the size of the window. Both TCPs can continue to wait for each other forever.

To correct this deadlock, TCP uses a **persistence timer** for each connection. When the sending TCP receives an acknowledgment with a window size of zero, it starts a persistence timer. When the persistence timer goes off, the sending TCP sends a special segment called a *probe*. This segment contains only 1 byte of data. It has a sequence number, but its sequence number is never acknowledged; it is even ignored in calculating the sequence number for the rest of the data. The probe alerts the receiving TCP that the acknowledgment was lost and should be resent.

The value of the persistence timer is set to the value of the retransmission time. However, if a response is not received from the receiver, another probe segment is sent and the value of the persistence timer is doubled and reset. The sender continues sending the probe segments and doubling and resetting the value of the persistence timer until the value reaches a threshold (usually 60 s). After that, the sender sends one probe segment every 60 s until the window is reopened.

Keep-Alive Timer

A **keep-alive timer** is used in some implementations to prevent a long idle connection between two TCPs. Suppose that a client opens a TCP connection to a server, transfers some data, and becomes silent. Perhaps the client has crashed. In this case, the connection remains open forever.

To remedy this situation, most implementations equip a server with a keep-alive timer. Each time the server hears from a client, it resets this timer. The time-out is usually 2 h. If the server does not hear from the client after 2 h, it sends a probe segment. If there is no response after 10 probes, each of which is 75 s apart, it assumes that the client is down and terminates the connection.

Time-Waited Timer

The **time-waited timer** is used during connection termination. When TCP closes a connection, it does not consider the connection really closed. The connection is held in limbo for a time-waited period. This allows duplicate FIN segments, if any, to arrive at the destination to be discarded. The value for this timer is usually 2 times the expected lifetime of a segment.

Congestion Control

We discuss TCP congestion control when we discuss congestion control in general.

Other Features

There are two other TCP features that we need to discuss: pushing data and handling urgent data.

Pushing Data

We saw that the sending TCP uses a buffer to store the stream of data coming from the sending application program. The sending TCP can choose the size of the segments. The receiving TCP also buffers the data when they arrive and delivers them to the application program when the application program is ready or when the receiving TCP feels that it is convenient. This type of flexibility increases the efficiency of TCP.

However, there are occasions in which the application program is not comfortable with this flexibility. For example, consider an application program that communicates interactively with another application program on the other end. The application program on one site wants to send a keystroke to the application at the other site and receive an immediate response. Delayed transmission and delayed delivery of data may not be acceptable to the application program.

TCP can handle such a situation. The application program on the sending site can request a *push* operation. This means that the sending TCP should not wait for the window to be filled. It must create a segment and send it immediately. The sending TCP can also set the push bit (PSH) to tell the receiving TCP that the segment includes data that must be delivered to the receiving application program as soon as possible and not to wait for more data to come.

Although the push operation can be requested by the application program, today most implementations ignore such requests. TCP can choose whether to use this operation.

Urgent Data

TCP is a stream-oriented protocol. This means that the data are presented from the application program to TCP as a stream of characters. Each byte of data has a position in the stream. However, there are occasions in which an application program needs to send *urgent* bytes. This means that the sending application program wants a piece of data to be read out of order by the receiving application program. Suppose that the sending application program is sending data to be processed by the receiving application program. When the result of processing comes back, the sending application program finds that everything is wrong. It wants to abort the process, but it has already sent a huge amount of data. If it issues an abort command (Control + C), these two characters will be stored at the end of the receiving TCP buffer. It will be delivered to the receiving application program after all the data have been processed.

The solution is to send a segment with the URG bit set. The sending application program tells the sending TCP that the piece of data is urgent. The sending TCP creates a segment and inserts the urgent data at the beginning of the segment. The rest of the segment can contain normal data from the buffer. The urgent pointer field in the header defines the end of the urgent data and the start of normal data.

When the receiving TCP receives a segment with the URG bit set, it extracts the urgent data from the segment, using the value of the urgent pointer, and delivers it, out of order, to the receiving application program.

22.4   KEY TERMS

client
client-server paradigm
connection establishment
connection termination
connectionless service
connection-oriented service
ephemeral port number
finite state machine
flow control
keep-alive timer
persistence timer
port number
process-to-process delivery
receiver window
retransmission timer
round-trip time (RTT)

segment
sender window
sequence number
server
silly window syndrome
sliding window
socket address
state transition diagram
TCP timer
three-way handshake
time-waited timer
Transmission Control Protocol (TCP)
user datagram
User Datagram Protocol (UDP)
well-known port numbers

22.5   SUMMARY

❏ UDP and TCP are transport-layer protocols that create a process-to-process communication.

❏ UDP is an unreliable and connectionless protocol that requires little overhead and offers fast delivery.

❏ In the client-server paradigm, an application program on the local host, called the client, needs services from an application program on the remote host, called a server.

❏ Each application program has a unique port number that distinguishes it from other programs running at the same time on the same machine.

❏ The client program is assigned a random port number called the ephemeral port number.

❏ The server program is assigned a universal port number called a well-known port number.

❏ The combination of the IP address and the port number, called the socket address, uniquely defines a process and a host.

❏ The UDP packet is called a user datagram.

❏ UDP has no flow control mechanism.

❏ Transmission Control Protocol (TCP) is a connection-oriented, reliable, stream transport-layer protocol in the Internet model.

❏ The unit of data transfer between two devices using TCP software is called a segment; it has 20 to 60 bytes of header, followed by data from the application program.

❏ TCP uses a sliding window mechanism for flow control.

❏ Error detection is handled in TCP by the checksum, acknowledgment, and time-out.

❏ Corrupted and lost segments are retransmitted, and duplicate segments are discarded.

❏ TCP uses four timers—retransmission, persistence, keep-alive, and time-waited—in its operation.

❏ Connection establishment requires three steps; connection termination normally requires four steps.

❏ TCP software is implemented as a finite state machine.

❏ The TCP window size is determined by the receiver.

22.6   PRACTICE SET

Review Questions

1. What is the difference between a process-to-process delivery and a host-to-host delivery?

2. How is a well-known port different from an ephemeral port?

3. What is a socket address?

4. When is a three-way handshake used?

5. Why would an application use UDP instead of TCP?

6. What is a UDP packet called? What is a TCP packet called?

7. What is the purpose of the sequence number in a TCP packet?

8. What is the purpose of flow control?

9. What is the silly window syndrome?

10. What is Nagle's algorithm?

11. What methods can prevent a silly window syndrome created at the receiver?

12. Name the timers used by TCP.

13. What is the purpose of the TCP push operation?

14. How can TCP handle urgent data?

Multiple-Choice Questions

15. UDP and TCP are both _____ layer protocols.
    a. Physical
    b. Data link
    c. Network
    d. Transport

16. Which of the following functions does UDP perform?
    a. Process-to-process communication
    b. Host-to-host communication
    c. End-to-end reliable data delivery
    d. All the above

17. UDP needs the _____ address to deliver the user datagram to the correct application program.
    a. Port
    b. Application
    c. Internet
    d. Physical

18. Which is a legal port address?
    a. 0
    b. 513
    c. 65,535
    d. All the above

19. The definition of reliable delivery includes _____.
    a. Error-free delivery
    b. Receipt of the complete message
    c. In-order delivery
    d. All the above

20. Which of the following does UDP guarantee?
    a. Sequence numbers on each user datagram
    b. Acknowledgments to the sender
    c. Flow control
    d. None of the above

21. The source port address on the UDP user datagram header defines _____.
    a. The sending computer
    b. The receiving computer
    c. The application program on the sending computer
    d. The application program on the receiving computer

22. Which of the following is *not* part of the UDP user datagram header?
    a. Length of header
    b. Source port address
    c. Checksum
    d. Destination port address

23. The _____ defines the client program.
    a. Ephemeral port number
    b. IP address
    c. Well-known port number
    d. Physical address

24. The _____ defines the server program.
    a. Ephemeral port number
    b. IP address
    c. Well-known port number
    d. Physical address

25. IP is responsible for _____ communication while TCP is responsible for _____ communication.
    a. Host-to-host; process-to-process
    b. Process-to-process; host-to-host
    c. Process-to-process; node-to-node
    d. Node-to-node; process-to-process

26. A host can be identified by _____ while a program running on the host can be identified by _____.
    a. An IP address; a port number
    b. A port number; an IP address
    c. An IP address; a host address
    d. An IP address; a well-known port

27. The _____ address uniquely identifies a running application program.
    a. IP address
    b. Host

c. NIC

d. Socket

28. The _____ field is used to order packets of a message.

    a. Urgent pointer

    b. Checksum

    c. Sequence number

    d. Acknowledgment number

29. The _____ field is used for error detection.

    a. Urgent pointer

    b. Checksum

    c. Sequence number

    d. Acknowledgment number

30. Multiply the header length field by _____ to find the total number of bytes in the TCP header.

    a. 2

    b. 4

    c. 6

    d. 8

31. Urgent data require the urgent pointer field as well as the URG bit in the _____ field.

    a. Control

    b. Offset

    c. Sequence number

    d. Reserved

32. In _____, data are sent or processed at a very inefficient rate, such as 1 byte at a time.

    a. Nagle's syndrome

    b. Silly window syndrome

    c. Sliding window syndrome

    d. Delayed acknowledgment

33. To prevent silly window syndrome created by a receiver that processes data at a very slow rate, _____ can be used.

    a. Clark's solution

    b. Nagle's algorithm

    c. Delayed acknowledgment

    d. (a) or (c)

34. To prevent silly window syndrome created by a sender that sends data at a very slow rate, _____ can be used.

    a. Clark's solution

    b. Nagle's algorithm

    c. Delayed acknowledgment

    d. (a) or (c)

35. An ACK number of 1000 always means that _____.
    a. 999 bytes has been successfully received
    b. 1000 bytes has been successfully received
    c. 1001 bytes has been successfully received
    d. None of the above

36. The _____ timer prevents a long idle connection between two TCPs.
    a. Retransmission
    b. Persistence
    c. Keep-alive
    d. Time-waited

37. The _____ timer is needed to handle the zero window-size advertisement.
    a. Retransmission
    b. Persistence
    c. Keep-alive
    d. Time-waited

38. Karn's algorithm is used in calculations by the _____ timer.
    a. Retransmission
    b. Persistence
    c. Keep-alive
    d. Time-waited

39. The _____ timer is used in the termination phase.
    a. Retransmission
    b. Persistence
    c. Keep-alive
    d. Time-waited

40. The _____ timer keeps track of the time between the sending of a segment and the receipt of an acknowledgment.
    a. Retransmission
    b. Persistence
    c. Keep-alive
    d. Time-waited

41. Connection establishment involves a _____ handshake.
    a. One-way
    b. Two-way
    c. Three-way
    d. None of the above

42. A special segment called a probe is sent by a sending TCP when the _____ timer goes off.
    a. Transmission
    b. Persistence

c. Keep-alive

d. Time-waited

Exercises

43. In cases where reliability is not of primary importance, UDP would make a good transport protocol. Give examples of specific cases.

44. Are both UDP and IP unreliable to the same degree? Why or why not?

45. Do port addresses need to be unique? Why or why not? Why are port addresses shorter than IP addresses?

46. What is the dictionary definition of the word *ephemeral?* How does it apply to the concept of the ephemeral port number?

47. What is the minimum size of a UDP datagram? What is the maximum size of a UDP datagram?

48. What is the minimum size of the process data that can be encapsulated in a UDP datagram? What is the maximum size of the process data that can be encapsulated in a UDP datagram?

49. A client uses UDP to send data to a server. The data are 16 bytes. Calculate the efficiency of this transmission at the UDP level (ratio of useful bytes to total bytes).

50. Redo Exercise 49 calculating the efficiency of transmission at the IP level. Assume no options for the IP header.

51. Redo Exercise 49 calculating the efficiency of transmission at the data link layer. Assume no options for the IP header, and use Ethernet at the data link layer.

52. What is the maximum size of the TCP header? What is the minimum size of the TCP header?

53. If the value of HLEN is 0111, how many bytes of option are included in the segment?

54. What can you say about the TCP segment in which the value of the control field is one of the following?

a. 000000

b. 000001

c. 010001

d. 000100

e. 000010

f. 010010

55. TCP is sending data at 1 megabyte per second (8 Mbytes/s). If the sequence number starts with 7000, how long does it take before the sequence number goes back to zero?

56. A TCP connection is using a window size of 10,000 bytes, and the previous acknowledgment number was 22,001. It receives a segment with acknowledgment number 24,001. Draw a diagram to show the situation of the window before and after.

57. Redo Exercise 56 if the receiver has changed the window size to 11,000.

58. Redo Exercise 56 if the receiver has changed the window size to 90,000.

59. A client uses TCP to send data to a server. The data are 16 bytes. Calculate the efficiency of this transmission at the TCP level (ratio of useful bytes to total bytes).

60. Redo Exercise 59, calculating the efficiency of transmission at the IP level. Assume no options for the IP header.

61. Redo Exercise 59, calculating the efficiency of transmission at the data link layer. Assume no options for the IP header, and use Ethernet at the data link layer.

CHAPTER 23

Congestion Control and Quality of Service

Congestion control and quality of service are two issues so closely bound together that improving one means improving the other and ignoring one usually means ignoring the other. Most techniques to prevent or eliminate congestion also improve the quality of service in a network.

We have postponed the discussion of these issues until now because these are issues related not to one layer, but to three: the data link layer, the network layer, and the transport layer. We waited until now so that we can discuss these issues once instead of repeating the subject three times. Throughout the chapter, we give examples of congestion control and quality of service at different layers.

23.1 DATA TRAFFIC

The main focus of congestion control and quality of service is data traffic. In congestion control we try to avoid traffic congestion. In quality of service, we try to create an appropriate environment for the traffic. So, before talking about congestion control and quality of service, we discuss the data traffic itself.

Traffic Descriptor

Traffic descriptors are qualitative values that represent a data flow. Figure 23.1 shows a traffic flow with some of these values.

Average Data Rate

The **average data rate** is the number of bits sent during a period of time, divided by the number of seconds in that period. We use the following equation:

$$\text{Average data rate} = \frac{\text{amount of data}}{\text{time}}$$

The average data rate is a very useful characteristic of traffic because it indicates the average bandwidth needed by the traffic.

Figure 23.1   *Traffic descriptors*

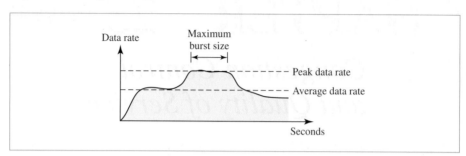

Peak Data Rate

The **peak data rate** defines the maximum data rate of the traffic. In Figure 23.1 it is the maximum *y* axis value. The peak data rate is a very important measurement because it indicates the peak bandwidth that the network needs for traffic to pass through the network without changing its data flow.

Maximum Burst Size

Although the peak data rate is a critical value for the network, it can usually be ignored if the duration of the peak value is very short. For example, if data are flowing steadily at the rate of 1 Mbps with a sudden peak data rate of 2 Mbps for just 1 ms, the network probably can handle the situation. However, if the peak data rate lasts 60 ms, there may be a problem for the network. The **maximum burst size** normally refers to the maximum length of time the traffic is generated at the peak rate.

Effective Bandwidth

The **effective bandwidth** is the bandwidth that the network needs to allocate for the flow of traffic. The effective bandwidth is a function of three values: average data rate, peak data rate, and maximum burst size. The calculation of this value is very complex.

Traffic Profiles

For our purposes, a data flow can have one of the following traffic profiles: constant bit rate, variable bit rate, or bursty. Note that there are people in this field who consider the last two as one category.

Constant Bit Rate

A **constant-bit-rate (CBR),** or a fixed-rate, traffic model has a data rate that does not change. In this type of flow, the average data rate and the peak data rate are the same. The maximum burst size is not applicable. This type of traffic is very easy for a network to handle since it is predictable. The network knows in advance how much bandwidth to allocate for this type of flow. Figure 23.2 shows constant-bit-rate traffic.

Variable Bit Rate

In the **variable-bit-rate (VBR)** category, the rate of the data flow changes in time, with the changes smooth instead of sudden and sharp. In this type of flow, the average

Figure 23.2 *Constant-bit-rate traffic*

data rate and the peak data rate are different. The maximum burst size is usually a small value. This type of traffic is more difficult to handle than constant-bit-rate traffic, but it normally does not need to be reshaped, as we will see later. Figure 23.3 shows variable-bit-rate traffic.

Figure 23.3 *Variable-bit-rate traffic*

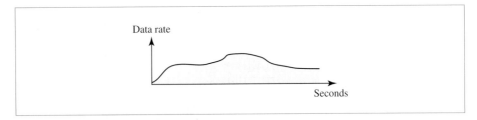

Bursty

In the **bursty data** category, the data rate changes suddenly in a very short period of time. It may jump from zero, for example, to 1 Mbps in a few microseconds and vice versa. It may also remain at this value for a while. The average bit rate and the peak bit rate are very different values in this type of flow. The maximum burst size is significant. This is the most difficult type of traffic for a network to handle because the profile is very unpredictable. To handle this type of traffic, the network normally needs to reshape it, using reshaping techniques, as we will see shortly. Bursty traffic is one of the main causes of congestion in a network. Figure 23.4 shows bursty traffic.

Figure 23.4 *Bursty traffic*

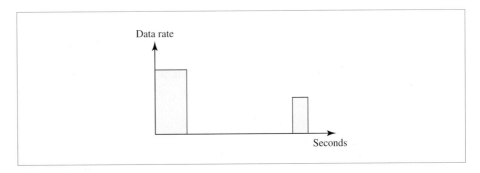

23.2   CONGESTION

An important issue in a packet-switched network is **congestion.** Congestion in a network may occur if the **load** on the network—the number of packets sent to the network—is greater than the *capacity* of the network—the number of packets a network can handle. **Congestion control** refers to the mechanisms and techniques to control the congestion and keep the load below the capacity.

We may ask why there is congestion on a network. Congestion happens in any system that involves waiting. For example, congestion happens on a freeway because any abnormality in the flow, such as an accident during rush hour, creates blockage.

Congestion in a network or internetwork occurs because routers and switches have queues—buffers that hold the packets before and after processing. A router, for example, has an input queue and an output queue for each interface. When a packet arrives at the incoming interface, it undergoes three steps before departing, as shown in Figure 23.5.

Figure 23.5   *Incoming packet*

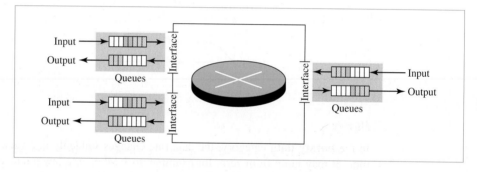

1. The packet is put at the end of the input queue while waiting to be checked.
2. The processing module of the router removes the packet from the input queue once it reaches the front of the queue and uses its routing table and the destination address to find the route.
3. The packet is put in the appropriate output queue and waits its turn to be sent.

We need to be aware of two issues. First, if the rate of packet arrival is higher than the packet processing rate, the input queues become longer and longer. Second, if the packet departure rate is less than the packet processing rate, the output queues become longer and longer.

Network Performance

Congestion control involves two factors that measure the performance of a network: **delay** and **throughput.**

Delay versus Load

Figure 23.6 shows the relationship between packet delay and network load.

Figure 23.6 *Packet delay and network load*

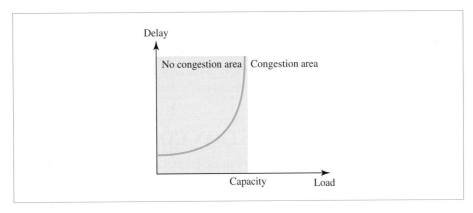

Note that when the load is much less than the capacity of the network, the delay is at a minimum. This minimum delay is composed of propagation delay and processing delay, both of which are negligible. However, when the load reaches the network capacity, the delay increases sharply because we now need to add the waiting time in the queues (for all routers in the path) to the total delay. Note that the delay becomes infinite when the load is greater than the capacity. If this is not obvious, consider the size of the queues when almost no packet reaches the destination, or reaches the destination with infinite delay; the queues become longer and longer. Delay has a negative effect on the load and consequently the congestion. When a packet is delayed, the source, not receiving the acknowledgment, retransmits the packet, which makes the delay, and the congestion, worse.

Throughput versus Load

We defined throughput in Chapter 3 as the number of bits passing through a point in a second. We can extend that definition from bits to packets and from a point to a network. We can define **throughput** in a network as the number of packets passing through the network in a unit of time. We can then plot the throughput versus the network load, as shown in Figure 23.7.

Figure 23.7 *Throughput versus network load*

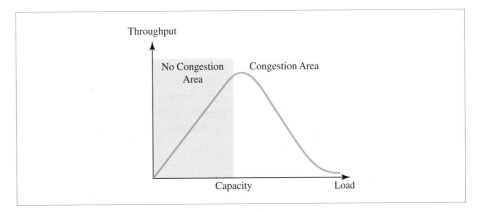

Notice that when the load is below the capacity of the network, the throughput increases proportionally with the node. We expect the throughput to remain constant after the load reaches the capacity, but instead the throughput declines sharply. The reason is the discarding of packets by the routers. When the load exceeds the capacity, the queues become full and the routers have to discard some packets. Discarding packets does not reduce the number of packets in the network because the sources retransmit the packets, using time-out mechanisms, when the packets do not reach the destinations.

23.3   CONGESTION CONTROL

Congestion control refers to techniques and mechanisms that can either prevent congestion, before it happens, or remove congestion, after it has happened. In general, we can divide congestion control mechanisms into two broad categories: open-loop congestion control (prevention) and closed-loop congestion control (removal).

Open-Loop Congestion Control

In **open-loop congestion control,** policies are applied to prevent congestion before it happens. In these mechanisms, congestion control is handled by either the source or the destination. We give a brief list of policies that can prevent congestion.

Retransmission Policy

A good retransmission policy can prevent congestion. The retransmission policy and the retransmission timers must be designed to optimize efficiency and at the same time prevent congestion.

Window Policy

The type of window at the sender may also affect congestion. The Selective Repeat window is better than the Go-Back-N window for congestion control.

Acknowledgment Policy

The acknowledgment policy imposed by the receiver may also affect congestion. If the receiver does not acknowledge every packet it receives, it may slow down the sender and help prevent congestion.

Discarding Policy

A good discarding policy by the routers may prevent congestion and at the same time may not harm the integrity of the transmission. For example, in audio transmission, if the policy is to discard less sensitive packets when congestion is likely to happen, the quality of sound is still preserved and congestion is prevented.

Admission Policy

An admission policy, which is a quality of service mechanism, can also prevent congestion in virtual circuit networks. Switches in a flow first check the resource requirement of a flow before admitting it to the network.

Closed-Loop Congestion Control

Closed-loop congestion control mechanisms try to alleviate congestion after it happens. Several mechanisms have been used by different protocols. We describe a few of them here.

Back Pressure

When a router is congested, it can inform the previous upstream router to reduce the rate of outgoing packets. The action can be recursive all the way to the router before the source. This mechanism is called *back pressure*.

Choke Point

A **choke point** is a packet sent by a router to the source to inform it of congestion. This type of control is similar to ICMP's source quench packet.

Implicit Signaling

The source can detect an implicit signal concerning congestion and slow down its sending rate. For example, the mere delay in receiving an acknowledgment can be a signal that the network is congested. We will see this type of signaling when we discuss TCP congestion control in Section 23.4.

Explicit Signaling

The routers that experience congestion can send an explicit signal, the setting of a bit in a packet, for example, to inform the sender or the receiver of congestion. Explicit signaling, as we will see in Frame Relay congestion control, can occur in either the forward or the backward direction.

Backward Signaling   The bit can be set in a packet moving in the direction opposite to the congestion. This bit can warn the source that there is congestion and that it needs to slow down to avoid the discarding of packets.

Forward Signaling   The bit can be set in a packet moving in the direction of the congestion. This bit can warn the destination that there is congestion. The receiver in this case can use policies, such as slowing down the acknowledgments, to alleviate the congestion.

23.4   TWO EXAMPLES

To better understand the concept of congestion control, let us give two examples: one in TCP and the other in Frame Relay.

Congestion Control in TCP

As we have said, an internet is a combination of networks and connecting devices (e.g., routers). A packet from a sender may pass through several routers before reaching its final destination. A router has a buffer that stores the incoming packets, processes them, and forwards them. If a router receives packets faster than it can process, congestion might occur and some packets could be dropped. When a packet does not reach the destination, no acknowledgment is sent for it. The sender has no choice but to retransmit the lost packet. This may create more congestion and more dropping of packets, which means more retransmission and more congestion. A point may then be reached in which the whole system collapses and no more data can be sent. TCP therefore needs to find some way to avoid this situation.

> **TCP assumes that the cause of a lost segment is due to congestion in the network.**

In Chapter 11, we talked about flow control and tried to discuss solutions when the receiver is overwhelmed with data. We said that the sender window size is determined by the available buffer space in the receiver. In other words, we assumed that it is only the receiver that can dictate to the sender the size of the sender's window. We totally ignored another entity here—the network. If the network cannot deliver the data as fast as they are created by the sender, it needs to tell the sender to slow down. In other words, in addition to the receiver, the network is a second entity that determines the size of the sender's window in TCP.

> **If the cause of the lost segment is congestion, retransmission of the segment does not remove the cause—it aggravates it.**

Congestion Window

In TCP, the sender's window size is determined not only by the receiver but also by congestion in the network.

The sender has two pieces of information: the receiver-advertised window size and the congestion window size. The actual size of the window is the minimum of these two.

> Actual window size = minimum (receiver window size, congestion window size)

Congestion Avoidance

To avoid congestion, the sender TCP has two strategies; one is called **slow start and additive increase,** and the second is called **multiplicative decrease.**

Slow Start   At the beginning of a connection, TCP sets the congestion window size to the maximum segment size. For each segment that is acknowledged, TCP increases the size of the congestion window by one maximum segment size until it reaches a threshold of one-half of the allowable window size. This is called *slow start,* which is totally misleading because the process is not slow at all. The size of the congestion window increases exponentially. The sender sends one segment, receives one acknowledgment, increases the size to two segments, sends two segments, receives acknowledgments for two segments, increases the size to four segments, sends four segments, receives acknowledgment for four segments, increases the size to eight segments, and so on. In other words, after receipt of the third acknowledgment, the size of the window has been increased to eight segments. The rate is exponential ($2^3 = 8$). Slow start is used with additive increase.

Additive Increase To avoid congestion before it happens, one must slow down this exponential growth. After the size reaches the threshold, the size is increased one segment for each acknowledgment even if an acknowledgment is for several segments. The additive-increase strategy continues as long as the acknowledgments arrive before their corresponding time-outs or the congestion window size reaches the receiver window value.

Multiplicative Decrease If congestion occurs, the congestion window size must be decreased. The only way the sender can guess that congestion has occurred is through a lost segment. If the sender does not receive an acknowledgment for a segment before its retransmission timer has matured, it assumes that there is congestion. Because networks today are to some extent noise-free, it is more probable that a segment is lost than that it is corrupted. The strategy says if a time-out occurs, the threshold must be set to one-half of the last congestion window size, and the congestion window size should start from 1 again. In other words, the sender returns to the slow start phase. Note that the threshold is reduced to one-half of the current congestion window size each time a time-out occurs. This means that the threshold is reduced exponentially (multiplicative decrease). Figure 23.8 shows the idea.

Figure 23.8 *Multiplicative decrease*

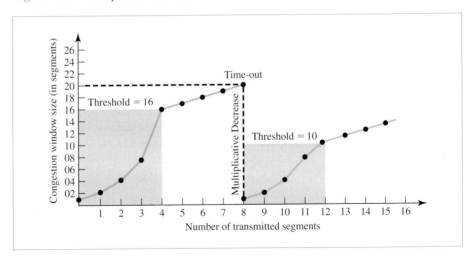

Congestion Control in Frame Relay

Congestion in a Frame Relay network decreases throughput and increases delay. A high throughput and low delay are the main goals of the Frame Relay protocol. Frame Relay does not have flow control. In addition, Frame Relay allows the user to transmit bursty data. This means that a Frame Relay network has the potential to be really congested with traffic, thus requiring congestion control.

Congestion Avoidance

For congestion avoidance, the Frame Relay protocol uses 2 bits in the frame to explicitly warn the source and the destination of the presence of congestion.

BECN   The **backward explicit congestion notification (BECN)** bit warns the sender of congestion in the network. One might ask how this is accomplished since the frames are traveling away from the sender. In fact, there are two methods: The switch can use response frames from the receiver (full-duplex mode), or else the switch can use a predefined connection (DLCI = 1023) to send special frames for this specific purpose. The sender can respond to this warning by simply reducing the data rate. Figure 23.9 shows the use of BECN.

Figure 23.9   *BECN*

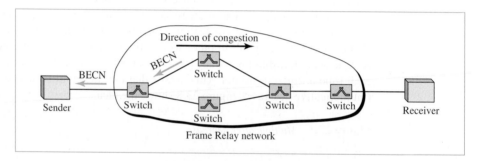

FECN   The **forward explicit congestion notification (FECN)** bit is used to warn the receiver of congestion in the network. It might appear that the receiver cannot do anything to relieve the congestion. However, the Frame Relay protocol assumes that the sender and receiver are communicating with each other and are using some type of flow control at a higher level. For example, if there is an acknowledgment mechanism at this higher level, the receiver can delay the acknowledgment, thus forcing the sender to slow down. Figure 23.10 shows the use of FECN.

Figure 23.10   *FECN*

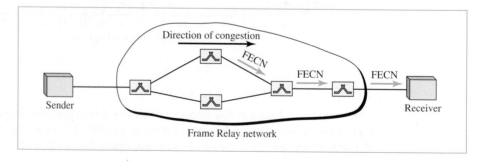

When two endpoints are communicating using a Frame Relay network, four situations may occur with regard to congestion. Figure 23.11 shows these four situations and the values of FECN and BECN.

Figure 23.11 *Four cases of congestion*

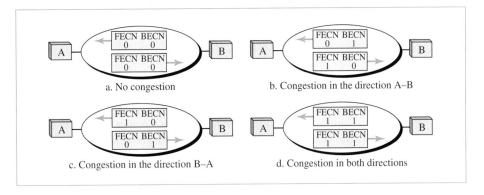

a. No congestion

b. Congestion in the direction A–B

c. Congestion in the direction B–A

d. Congestion in both directions

23.5 QUALITY OF SERVICE

Quality of service (QoS) is an internetworking issue that has been discussed more than defined. We can informally define quality of service as something a flow seeks to attain.

Flow Characteristics

Traditionally, four types of characteristics are attributed to a flow: reliability, delay, jitter, and bandwidth, as shown in Figure 23.12.

Figure 23.12 *Flow characteristics*

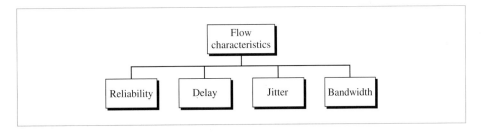

Reliability

Reliability is a characteristic that a flow needs. Lack of reliability means losing a packet or acknowledgment, which entails retransmission. However, the sensitivity of application programs to reliability is not the same. For example, it is more important that electronic mail, file transfer, and Internet access have reliable transmissions than telephony or audio conferencing.

Delay

Source-to-destination **delay** is another flow characteristic. Again applications can tolerate delay in different degrees. In this case, telephony, audio conferencing, video conferencing, and remote log-in need minimum delay, while delay in file transfer or email is less important.

Jitter

Jitter is the variation in delay for packets belonging to the same flow. Real-time audio and video cannot tolerate high jitter. For example, a real-time video broadcast is useless if there is a 2-ms delay for the first and second packets and a 60-ms delay for the third and fourth. On the other hand, it does not matter if packets carrying information in a file have different delays. The transport layer at the destination waits until all packets arrive before delivery to the application layer.

Bandwidth

Different applications need different bandwidths. In video conferencing we need to send millions of bits per second to refresh a color screen while the total number of bits in an email may not reach even a million.

Flow Classes

Based on the flow characteristics, we can classify flows into groups, with each group having similar levels of characteristics. This categorization is not formal or universal; some protocols such as ATM have defined classes, as we will see later.

23.6   TECHNIQUES TO IMPROVE QOS

In Section 23.5 we tried to define QoS in terms of its characteristics. In this section, we discuss some techniques that can be used to improve the quality of service. We briefly discuss four common methods: scheduling, traffic shaping, admission control, and resource reservation.

Scheduling

Packets from different flows arrive at a switch or router for processing. A good scheduling technique treats the different flows in a fair and appropriate manner. Several scheduling techniques are designed to improve the quality of service. We discuss three of them here: FIFO queuing, priority queuing, and weighted fair queuing.

FIFO Queuing

In **first-in, first-out (FIFO) queuing,** packets wait in a buffer (queue) until the node (router or switch) is ready to process them. If the average arrival rate is higher than the average processing rate, the queue will fill up and new packets will be discarded. A FIFO queue is familiar to those who have had to wait for a bus at a bus stop. Figure 23.13 shows a conceptual view of a FIFO queue.

Figure 23.13 *FIFO queue*

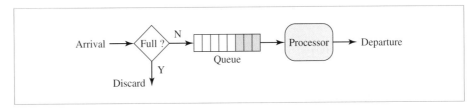

Priority Queuing

In **priority queuing,** packets are first assigned to a priority class. Each priority class has its own queue. The packets in the highest-priority queue are processed first. Packets in the lowest-priority queue are processed last. Note that the system does not stop serving a queue until it is empty. Figure 23.14 shows priority queuing with two priority levels (for simplicity).

Figure 23.14 *Priority queuing*

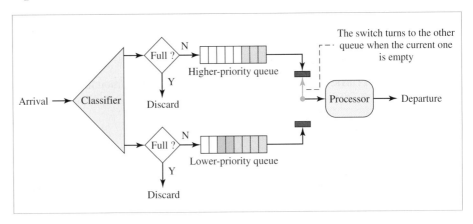

A priority queue can provide better QoS than the FIFO queue because higher-priority traffic, such as multimedia, can reach the destination with less delay. However, there is a potential drawback. If there is a continuous flow in a high-priority queue, the packets in the lower-priority queues will never have a chance to be processed. This is a condition called *starvation*.

Weighted Fair Queuing

A better scheduling method is **weighted fair queuing.** In this technique, the packets are still assigned to different classes and admitted to different queues. The queues, however, are weighted based on the priority of the queues; higher priority means a higher weight. The system processes packets in each queue in a round-robin fashion with the number of packets selected from each queue based on the corresponding weight. For example, if the weights are 3, 2, and 1, three packets are processed from the first queue, two from the second queue, and one from the third queue. If the system does not impose priority on the classes, all weights can be equal. In this way, we have fair queuing with priority. Figure 23.15 shows the technique with three classes.

Figure 23.15   *Weighted fair queuing*

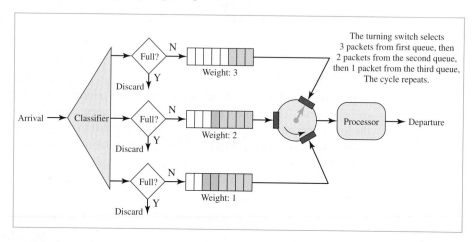

Traffic Shaping

Traffic shaping is a mechanism to control the amount and the rate of the traffic sent to the network. Two techniques can shape traffic: leaky bucket and token bucket.

Leaky Bucket

If a bucket has a small hole at the bottom, the water leaks from the bucket at a constant rate as long as there is water in the bucket. The rate at which the water leaks does not depend on the rate at which the water is input to the bucket unless the bucket is empty. The input rate can vary, but the output rate remains constant. Similarly, in networking, a technique called **leaky bucket** can smooth out bursty traffic. Bursty chunks are stored in the bucket and sent out at an average rate. Figure 23.16 shows a leaky bucket and its effects.

In the figure, we assume that the network has committed a bandwidth of 3 Mbps for a host. The use of the leaky bucket shapes the input traffic to make it conform to this commitment. In the figure the host sends a burst of data at a rate of 12 Mbps for 2 s, for a total of 24 megabits of data. The host is silent for 5 s and then sends data at a rate of 2 Mbps for 3 s, for a total of 6 megabits of data. In all, the host has sent 30 megabits of data in 10 s. The leaky bucket smooths the traffic by sending out data at a rate of 3 Mbps during the same 10 s. Without the leaky bucket, the beginning burst may have hurt the network by consuming more bandwidth than is set aside for this host. We can also see that the leaky bucket may prevent congestion. As an analogy, consider the freeway

Figure 23.16 *Leaky bucket*

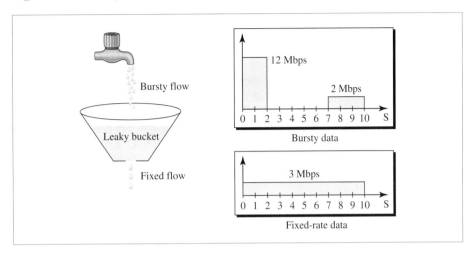

during rush hour (bursty traffic). If, instead, commuters could stagger their working hours, congestion on our freeways could be avoided.

A simple leaky bucket implementation is shown in Figure 23.17. A FIFO queue holds the packets. If the traffic consists of fixed-size packets (e.g., cells in ATM networks), the process removes a fixed number of packets from the queue at each tick of the clock. If the traffic consists of variable-length packets, the fixed output rate must be based on the number of bytes or bits.

Figure 23.17 *Leaky bucket implementation*

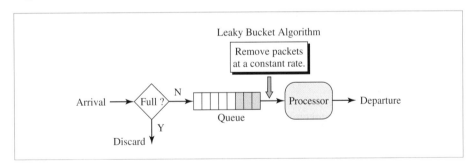

The following is an algorithm for variable-length packets:

1. Initialize a counter to *n* at the tick of the clock.
2. If *n* is greater than the size of the packet, send the packet and decrement the counter by the packet size. Repeat this step until *n* is smaller than the packet size.
3. Reset the counter and go to step 1.

A leaky bucket algorithm shapes bursty traffic into fixed-rate traffic by averaging the data rate. It may drop the packets if the bucket is full.

Token Bucket

The leaky bucket is very restrictive. It does not credit an idle host. For example, if a host is not sending for a while, its bucket becomes empty. Now if the host has bursty data, the leaky bucket allows only an average rate. The time when the host was idle is not taken into account. On the other hand, the **token bucket** algorithm allows idle hosts to accumulate credit for the future in the form of tokens. For each tick of the clock, the system sends *n* tokens to the bucket. The system removes one token for every cell (or byte) of data sent. For example, if *n* is 100 and the host is idle for 100 ticks, the bucket collects 10,000 tokens. Now the host can consume all these tokens in one tick with 10,000 cells, or the host takes 1000 ticks with 10 cells per tick. In other words, the host can send bursty data as long as the bucket is not empty. Figure 23.18 shows the idea.

Figure 23.18   *Token bucket*

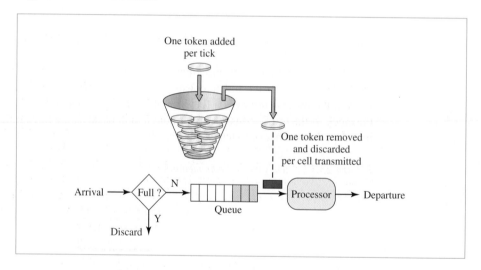

The token bucket can easily be implemented with a counter. The token is initialized to zero. Each time a token is added, the counter is incremented by 1. Each time a unit of data is sent, the counter is decremented by 1. When the counter is zero, the host cannot send data.

> **The token bucket allows bursty traffic at a regulated maximum rate.**

Combining Token Bucket and Leaky Bucket

The two techniques can be combined to credit an idle host and at the same time regulate the traffic. The leaky bucket is applied after the token bucket; the rate of the leaky bucket needs to be higher than the rate of tokens dropped in the bucket.

Resource Reservation

A flow of data needs resources such as a buffer, bandwidth, CPU time, and so on. The quality of service is improved if these resources are reserved beforehand. We discuss in this section one QoS model called Integrated Services, which depends heavily on resource reservation to improve the quality of service.

Admission Control

Admission control refers to the mechanism used by a router, or a switch, to accept or reject a flow based on predefined parameters called flow specifications. Before a router accepts a flow for processing, it checks the flow specifications to see if its capacity (in terms of bandwidth, buffer size, CPU speed, etc.) and its previous commitments to other flows can handle the new flow.

23.7 INTEGRATED SERVICES

Based on the discussion of Sections 23.5 and 23.6, two models have been designed to provide quality of service in the Internet: Integrated Services and Differentiated Services. Both models emphasize the use of quality of service at the network layer (IP), although the model can also be used in other layers such as the data link. We discuss Integrated Services in this section and Differentiated Service in Section 23.8.

As we learned in Chapter 20, IP was originally designed for *best-effort* delivery. This means that every user receives the same level of services. This type of delivery does not guarantee the minimum of a service, such as bandwidth, to applications such as real-time audio and video. If such an application accidentally gets extra bandwidth, it may be detrimental to other applications, resulting in congestion.

Integrated Services, sometimes called **IntServ,** is a *flow-based* QoS model, which means that a user needs to create a flow, a kind of virtual circuit, from the source to the destination and inform all routers of the resource requirement.

> **Integrated Services is a *flow-based* QoS model designed for IP.**

Signaling

The reader may remember that IP is a connectionless, datagram, packet-switching protocol. How can we implement a flow-based model over a connectionless protocol? The solution is a signaling protocol to run over IP that provides the signaling mechanism for making a reservation. This protocol is called **Resource Reservation Protocol (RSVP)** and will be discussed shortly.

Flow Specification

When a source makes a reservation, it needs to define a flow specification. A flow specification has two parts: Rspec (resource specification) and Tspec (traffic specification). Rspec defines the resource that the flow needs to reserve (buffer, bandwidth, etc.). Tspec defines the traffic characterization of the flow.

Admission

After a router receives the flow specification from an application, it decides to admit or deny the service. The decision is based on the previous commitments of the router and the current availability of the resource.

Service Classes

Two classes of services have been defined for Integrated Services: guaranteed service and controlled-load service.

Guaranteed Service Class

This type of service is designed for real-time traffic that needs a guaranteed minimum end-to-end delay. The end-to-end delay is the sum of the delays in the routers, the propagation delay in the media, and the setup mechanism. Only the first, the sum of the delays in the routers, can be guaranteed by the router. This type of service guarantees that the packets will arrive within a certain delivery time and are not discarded if flow traffic stays within the boundary of Tspec. We can say that guaranteed services are quantitative services, in which the amount of end-to-end delay and the data rate must be defined by the application.

Controlled-Load Service Class

This type of service is designed for applications that can accept some delays, but are sensitive to an overloaded network and to the danger of losing packets. Good examples of these types of applications are file transfer, email, and Internet access. The controlled-load service is a qualitative type of service in that the application requests the possibility of low-loss or no-loss packets.

RSVP

In the Integrated Service model, an application program needs resource reservation. As we learned in the discussion of the IntServ model, the resource reservation is for a *flow*. This means that if we want to use IntServ at the IP level, we need to create a flow, a kind of virtual circuit network, out of the IP, which was originally designed as a datagram packet-switched network. A virtual circuit network needs a signaling system to set up the virtual circuit before data traffic can start. The Resource Reservation Protocol (RSVP) is a signaling protocol to help IP create a flow and consequently make a resource reservation. Before discussing RSVP, we need to mention that it is an independent protocol separate from the Integrated Service model. It may be used in other models in the future.

Multicast Trees

RSVP is different from some other signaling systems we have seen before in that it is a signaling system designed for multicasting. However, RSVP can be also used for unicasting because unicasting is just a special case of multicasting with only one member in the multicast group. The reason for this design is to enable RSVP to provide resource reservations for all kinds of traffic including multimedia which often uses multicasting.

Receiver-Based Reservation

In RSVP, the receivers, not the sender, make the reservation. This strategy matches the other multicasting protocols. For example, in multicast routing protocols, the receivers, not the sender, make a decision to join or leave a multicast group.

RSVP Messages

RSVP has several types of messages. However, for our purposes, we discuss only two of them: **Path** and **Resv.**

Path Messages   Recall that the receivers in a flow make the reservation in RSVP. However, the receivers do not know the path traveled by packets before the reservation is made. The path is needed for the reservation. To solve the problem, RSVP uses *Path* messages. A Path message travels from the sender and reaches all receivers in the multicast path. On the way, a Path message stores the necessary information for the receivers. A Path message is sent in a multicast environment; a new message is created when the path diverges. Figure 23.19 shows path messages.

Figure 23.19   *Path messages*

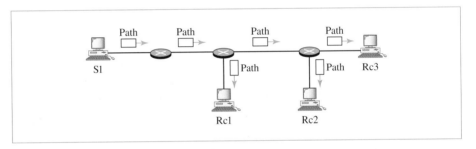

Resv Messages   After a receiver has received a Path message, it sends a *Resv* message. The Resv message travels toward the sender (upstream) and makes a resource reservation on the routers that support RSVP. If a router does not support RSVP on the path, it routes the packet based on the best-effort delivery methods we discussed before. Figure 23.20 shows the Resv messages.

Figure 23.20   *Resv messages*

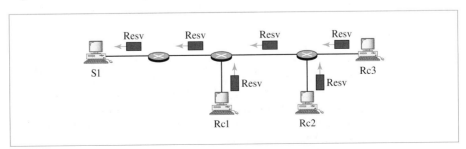

Reservation Merging

In RSVP, the resources are not reserved for each receiver in a flow; the reservation is merged. In Figure 23.21 Rc3 requests a 2-Mbps bandwidth while Rc2 requests a 1-Mbps bandwidth. Router R3, which needs to make a bandwidth reservation, merges the two requests. The reservation is made for 2 Mbps, the larger of the two, because a 2-Mbps input reservation can handle both requests. The same situation is true for R2. The reader may ask why Rc2 and Rc3, both belonging to one single flow, request different amounts of bandwidth. The answer is that, in a multimedia environment, different receivers may handle different grades of quality. For example, Rc2 may be able to receive video only at 1 Mbps (lower quality), while Rc3 may be able to receive video at 2 Mbps (higher quality).

Figure 23.21   *Reservation merging*

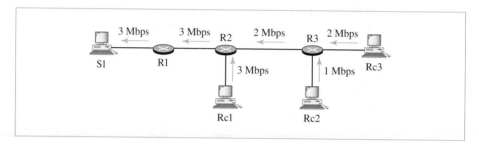

Reservation Styles

When there is more than one flow, the router needs to make a reservation to accommodate all of them. RSVP defines three types of reservation styles, as shown in Figure 23.22.

Figure 23.22   *Reservation styles*

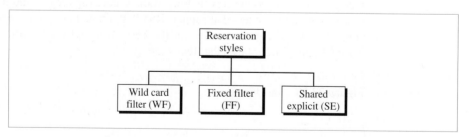

Wild Card Filter Style   In this style, the router creates a single reservation for all senders. The reservation is based on the largest request. This type of style is used when the flows from different senders do not occur at the same time.

Fixed Filter Style   In this style, the router creates a distinct reservation for each flow. This means that if there are *n* flows, *n* different reservations are made. This type of style is used when there is a high probability that flows from different senders occur at the same time.

Shared Explicit Style   In this style, the router creates a single reservation which can be shared by a set of flows.

Soft State

The reservation information (state) stored in every node for a flow needs to be refreshed periodically. This is referred to as a *soft state* as compared to the *hard state* used in other virtual circuit protocols such as ATM or Frame Relay, where the information about the flow is maintained until it is erased. The default interval for refreshing is currently 30 s.

Problems with Integrated Services

There are at least two problems with Integrated Services that may prevent its full implementation in the Internet: scalability and service-type limitation.

Scalability

The Integrated Services model requires that each router keep information for each flow. As the Internet is growing every day, this is a serious problem.

Service-Type Limitation

Integrated Services provides only two types of services, guaranteed and control-load. Those opposing this model argue that applications may need more than these two types of services.

23.8   DIFFERENTIATED SERVICES

Differentiated Services (DS or **Diffserv)** was introduced by the IETF (Internet Engineering Task Force) to handle the shortcomings of Integrated Services. Two fundamental changes were made:

1. The main processing was moved from the core of the network to the edge of the network. This solves the scalability problem. The routers do not have to store information about flows. The applications, or hosts, define the type of service they need each time they send a packet.
2. The per-flow service is changed to per-class service. The router routes the packet based on the class of service defined in the packet, not the flow. This solves the service-type limitation problem. We can define different types of classes based on the needs of applications.

> **Differentiated Services is a class-based QoS model designed for IP.**

DS Field

In Diffserv, each packet contains a field called the DS field. The value of this field is set at the boundary of the network by the host or the first router designated as the boundary router. IETF proposes to replace the existing TOS (type of service) field in IPv4 or the class field in IPv6 by the DS field, as shown in Figure 23.23.

Figure 23.23 *DS field*

The DS field contains two subfields: DSCP and CU. The DSCP (Differentiated Services Code Point) is a 6-bit subfield that defines the **per-hop behavior (PHB).** The 2-bit CU (currently unused) subfield is not currently used.

The Diffserv capable node (router) uses the DSCP 6 bits as an index to a table defining the packet-handling mechanism for the current packet being processed.

Per-Hop Behavior (PHB)

The Diffserv model defines per-hop behaviors for each node that receives a packet. So far three PHBs are defined: DE PHB, EF PHB, and AF PHB.

DE PHB   The DE PHB (default PHB) is the same as best-effort delivery, which is compatible with TOS.

EF PHB   The EF PHB (expedited forwarding PHB) provides the following services:
- Low loss
- Low latency
- Ensured bandwidth

This is the same as having a virtual connection between the source and destination.

AF PHB   The AF PHB (assured forwarding PHB) delivers the packet with a high assurance as long as the class traffic does not exceed the traffic profile of the node. The users of the network need to be aware that some packets may be discarded.

Traffic Conditioner

To implement Diffserv, the DS node uses traffic conditioners such as meters, markers, shapers, and droppers, as shown in Figure 23.24.

Meters   The meter checks to see if the incoming flow matches the negotiated traffic profile. The meter also sends this result to other components. The meter can use several tools such as a token bucket to check the profile.

Marker   A marker can re-mark a packet that is using best-effort delivery (DSCP: 000000) or down-mark a packet based on information received from the meter. Down-marking (lowering the class of the flow) occurs if the flow does not match the profile. A marker does not up-mark (promote the class) a packet.

Figure 23.24 *Traffic conditioner*

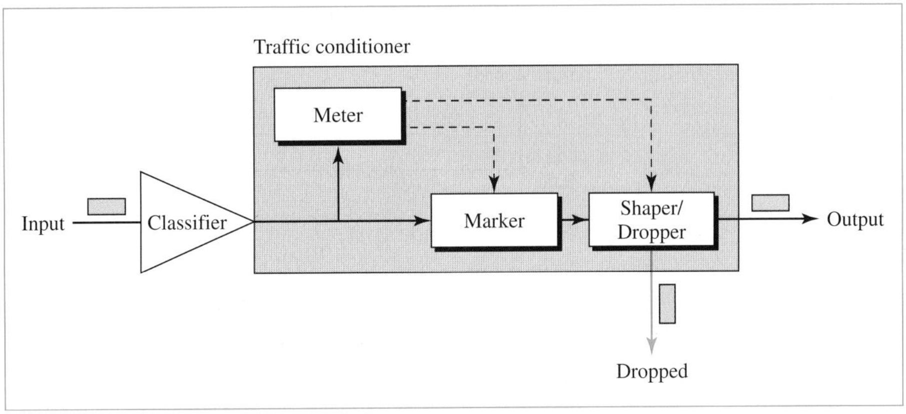

Shaper   A shaper uses the information received from the meter to reshape the traffic if it is not compliant with the negotiated profile.

Dropper   A dropper, which works like a shaper with no buffer, discards packets if the flow severely violates the negotiated profile.

23.9   QOS IN SWITCHED NETWORKS

We discussed the proposed models for QoS in the IP protocols. Let us now discuss QoS as used in two switched networks: Frame Relay and ATM. These two networks are virtual circuit networks that need a signaling protocol such as RSVP.

QoS in Frame Relay

Four different attributes to control traffic have been devised in Frame Relay: access rate, committed burst size B_c, committed information rate (CIR), and excess burst size B_e. These are set during the negotiation between the user and the network. For PVC connections, they are negotiated once; for SVC connections, they are negotiated for each connection during connection setup. Figure 23.25 shows the relationships between these four measurements.

Access Rate

For every connection, an **access rate** (in bits per second) is defined. The access rate actually depends on the bandwidth of the channel connecting the user to the network. The user can never exceed this rate. For example, if the user is connected to a Frame Relay network by a T-1 line, the access rate is 1.544 Mbps and can never be exceeded.

Committed Burst Size

For every connection, Frame Relay defines a **committed burst size B_c.** This is the maximum number of bits in a predefined period of time that the network is committed

Figure 23.25   *Relationship between traffic control attributes*

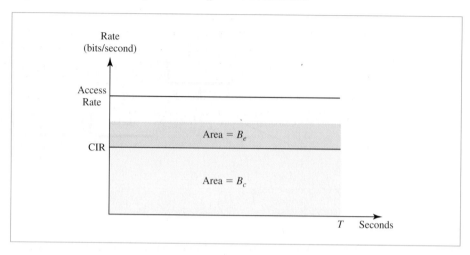

to transfer without discarding any frame or setting the DE bit. For example, if a B_c of 400 kbits for a period of 4 s is granted, the user can send up to 400 kbits during a 4-s interval without worrying about any frame loss. Note that this is not a rate defined for each second. It is a cumulative measurement. The user can send 300 kbits during the first second, no data during the second and the third seconds, and finally 100 kbits during the fourth second.

Committed Information Rate

The **committed information rate (CIR)** is similar in concept to committed burst size except that it defines an average rate in bits per second. If the user follows this rate continuously, the network is committed to deliver the frames. However, because it is an average measurement, a user may send data higher than the CIR at times or lower at other times. As long as the average for the predefined period is met, the frames will be delivered.

The cumulative number of bits sent during the predefined period cannot exceed B_c. Note that the CIR is not an independent measurement; it can be calculated by using the following formula:

$$\text{CIR} = \frac{B_c}{T} \text{ bps}$$

For example, if the B_c is 5 kbits in a period of 5 s, the CIR is 5000/5, or 1 Kbps.

Excess Burst Size

For every connection, Frame Relay defines an **excess burst size B_e**. This is the maximum number of bits in excess of B_c that a user can send during a predefined period of time. The network is committed to transfer these bits if there is no congestion. Note that there is less commitment here than in the case of B_c. The network is committing itself conditionally.

User Rate

Figure 23.26 shows how a user can send bursty data. If the user never exceeds B_c, the network is committed to transmit the frames without discarding any. If the user exceeds B_c by less than B_e (that is, the total number of bits is less than $B_c + B_e$), the network is committed to transfer all the frames if there is no congestion. If there is congestion, some frames will be discarded. The first switch that receives the frames from the user has a counter and sets the DE bit for the frames that exceed B_c. The rest of the switches will discard these frames if there is congestion. Note that a user who needs to send data faster may exceed the B_c level. As long as the level is not above $B_c + B_e$, there is a chance that the frames will reach the destination without being discarded. Remember, however, that the moment the user exceeds the $B_c + B_e$ level, all the frames sent after that are discarded by the first switch.

Figure 23.26 *User rate in relation to B_c and $B_c + B_e$*

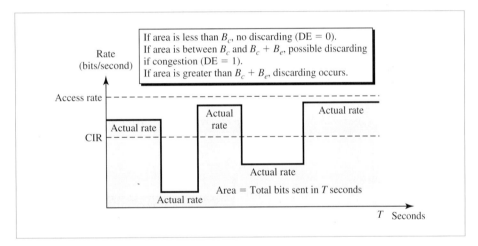

QoS in ATM

The QoS in ATM is based on the class, user-related attributes, and network-related attributes.

Classes

The ATM Forum defines four service classes: CBR, VBR, ABR, and UBR (see Fig. 23.27).

CBR   The **constant-bit-rate (CBR)** class is designed for customers who need real-time audio or video services. The service is similar to that provided by a dedicated line such as a T-line.

VBR   The **variable-bit-rate (VBR)** class is divided into two subclasses: real time (VBR-RT) and non-real-time (VBR-NRT). VBR-RT is designed for those users who need real-time services (such as voice and video transmission) and use compression techniques to create a variable bit rate. VBR-NRT is designed for those users who do

Figure 23.27 *Service classes*

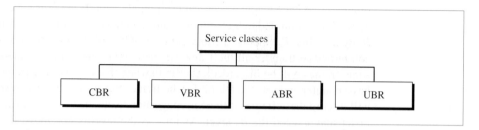

not need real-time services but use compression techniques to create a variable bit rate.

ABR The **available-bit-rate (ABR)** class delivers cells at a minimum rate. If more network capacity is available, this minimum rate can be exceeded. ABR is particularly suitable for applications that are bursty.

UBR The **unspecified-bit-rate (UBR)** class is a best-effort delivery service that does not guarantee anything.

Figure 23.28 shows the relationship of different classes to the total capacity of the network.

Figure 23.28 *Relationship of service classes to the total capacity of the network*

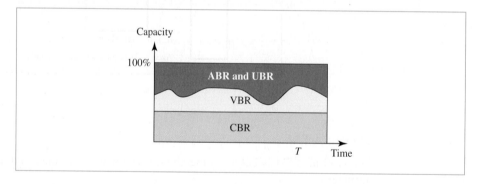

User-Related Attributes

ATM defines two sets of attributes. User-related attributes are those attributes that define how fast the user wants to send data. These are negotiated at the time of contract between a user and a network. The following are some user-related attributes:

SCR The sustained cell rate (SCR) is the average cell rate over a long time interval. The actual cell rate may be lower or higher than this value, but the average should be equal to or less than the SCR.

PCR The peak cell rate (PCR) defines the sender's maximum cell rate. The user's cell rate can sometimes reach this peak, as long as the SCR is maintained.

MCR   The minimum cell rate (MCR) defines the minimum cell rate acceptable to the sender. For example, if the MCR is 50,000, the network must guarantee that the sender can send at least 50,000 cells per second.

CVDT   The cell variation delay tolerance (CVDT) is a measure of the variation in cell transmission times. For example, if the CVDT is 5 ns, this means that the difference between the minimum and the maximum delays in delivering the cells should not exceed 5 ns.

Network-Related Attributes

The network-related attributes are those that define characteristics of the network. The following are some network-related attributes:

CLR   The cell loss ratio (CLR) defines the fraction of cells lost (or delivered so late that they are considered lost) during transmission. For example, if the sender sends 100 cells and one of them is lost, the CLR is

$$CLR = \frac{1}{100} = 10^{-2}$$

CTD   The cell transfer delay (CTD) is the average time needed for a cell to travel from source to destination. The maximum CTD and the minimum CTD are also considered attributes.

CDV   The cell delay variation (CDV) is the difference between the CTD maximum and the CTD minimum.

CER   The cell error ratio (CER) defines the fraction of the cells delivered in error.

23.10   KEY TERMS

access rate
additive increase
available bit rate (ABR)
average data rate
backward explicit congestion
   notification (BECN)
bursty data
choke point
closed-loop congestion control
committed burst size B_c
committed information rate (CIR)
congestion
congestion avoidance
congestion control
constant bit rate (CBR)
delay

Differentiated Services (DS or Diffserv)
effective bandwidth
excess burst size B_e
first-in, first-out (FIFO) queuing
forward explicit congestion notification
   (FECN)
Integrated Services (IntServ)
jitter
leaky bucket
load
maximum burst size
multiplicative decrease
open-loop congestion control
peak data rate
per-hop behavior (PHB)
priority queuing

quality of service (QoS)	token bucket
reliability	traffic shaping
Resource Reservation Protocol (RSVP)	unspecified bit rate (UBR)
slow start	variable bit rate (VBR)
throughput	weighted fair queuing

23.11 SUMMARY

❏ The average data rate, peak data rate, maximum burst size, and effective bandwidth are qualitative values that describe a data flow.

❏ A data flow can have a constant bit rate, a variable bit rate, or traffic that is bursty.

❏ Congestion control refers to the mechanisms and techniques to control congestion and keep the load below capacity.

❏ Delay and throughput measure the performance of a network.

❏ Open-loop congestion control prevents congestion; closed-loop congestion control removes congestion.

❏ TCP avoids congestion through the use of two strategies: the combination of slow start and additive increase, and multiplicative decrease.

❏ Frame relay avoids congestion through the use of two strategies: backward explicit congestion notification (BECN) and the forward explicit congestion notification (FECN).

❏ A flow can be characterized by its reliability, delay, jitter, and bandwidth.

❏ Scheduling, traffic shaping, resource reservation, and admission control are techniques to improve quality of service (QoS).

❏ FIFO queuing, priority queuing, and weighted fair queuing are scheduling techniques.

❏ Leaky bucket and token bucket are traffic shaping techniques.

❏ Integrated Services is a flow-based QoS model designed for IP.

❏ The Resource Reservation Protocol (RSVP) is a signaling protocol that helps IP create a flow and makes a resource reservation.

❏ Differential Services is a class-based QoS model designed for IP.

❏ Access rate, committed burst size, committed information rate, and excess burst size are attributes to control traffic in Frame Relay.

❏ Quality of service in ATM is based on service classes, user-related attributes, and network-related attributes.

23.12 PRACTICE SET

Review Questions

1. How are congestion control and quality of service related?

2. What is a traffic descriptor?

3. What is the relationship between the average data rate and the peak data rate?
4. What is the definition of bursty data?
5. What is the difference between open-loop congestion control and closed-loop congestion control?
6. Name the policies that can prevent congestion.
7. Name the mechanisms that can alleviate congestion.
8. What determines the sender window size in TCP?
9. How does Frame Relay control congestion?
10. What attributes can be used to describe a flow of data?
11. What are four general techniques to improve quality of service?
12. What is traffic shaping? Name two methods to shape traffic.
13. What is the major difference between Integrated Services and Differentiated Services?
14. How is Resource Reservation Protocol related to Integrated Services?
15. What are attributes used for traffic control in Frame Relay?
16. In regard to quality of service, how do user-related attributes differ from network-related attributes in ATM?

Multiple-Choice Questions

17. The maximum length of time that traffic is generated at the peak rate is called the
    _____.
    a. Average data rate
    b. Maximum burst size
    c. Effective bandwidth
    d. Constant bit rate
18. The _____ is the maximum data rate of the traffic.
    a. Average data rate
    b. Peak data rate
    c. Maximum burst size
    d. Effective bandwidth
19. The effective bandwidth is based on _____.
    a. Average data rate
    b. Peak data rate
    c. Maximum burst size
    d. All the above
20. _____ traffic features sudden data rate changes in very short periods of time.
    a. Constant-bit-rate
    b. Variable-bit-rate
    c. Bursty
    d. Peak-bit-rate

21. When the load is greater than the capacity, the delay _____.
    a. Decreases
    b. Increases linearly
    c. Goes to infinity
    d. Goes to zero

22. _____ is a closed-loop mechanism to alleviate congestion.
    a. A choke point
    b. Implicit signaling
    c. Explicit signaling
    d. All the above

23. For a system using TCP, the sender window size is determined by the _____ window size.
    a. Receiver
    b. Sender
    c. Congestion
    d. (a) and (c)

24. Slow start is used in conjunction with _____ as a TCP congestion control strategy.
    a. Additive increase
    b. Additive decrease
    c. Multiplicative increase
    d. Multiplicative decrease

25. The FECN informs the _____ of congestion while the BECN informs the _____ of congestion.
    a. Destination; interface
    b. Destination; sender
    c. Sender; destination
    d. Interface; sender

26. _____ is a flow characteristic in which the delay varies for packets belonging to the same flow.
    a. Choke point
    b. Throughput
    c. Additive increase
    d. Jitter

27. In _____ queuing the first packet into the queue is the first packet out of the queue.
    a. FIFO
    b. LIFO
    c. Priority
    d. Weighted fair

28. The _____ traffic shaping method gives a host credit for its idle time.
    a. Leaky bucket
    b. Token bucket

c. Traffic bucket

d. Bursty bucket

29. A flow-based QoS model designed for IP is called _____.

   a. Integrated Services

   b. Differentiated Services

   c. RSVP

   d. Multicast trees

30. A signaling protocol that helps IP create a flow is called _____.

   a. Integrated Services

   b. Differentiated Services

   c. RSVP

   d. Multicast trees

31. RSVP uses _____ messages.

   a. Path

   b. Resv

   c. Resource

   d. (a) and (b)

32. In an RSVP reservation style called _____ filter, the router creates a single reservation that can be shared by a set of flows.

   a. Wild card

   b. Fixed

   c. Shared explicit

   d. All the above

33. Differentiated Services was designed to handle the _____ problem associated with Integrated Services.

   a. Scalability

   b. Stability

   c. Reservation

   d. All the above

34. A _____ is a Differentiated Services traffic conditioner.

   a. Meter

   b. Marker

   c. Shaper

   d. All the above

35. When added to B_e, B_c should be less than the _____.

   a. CIR

   b. Access rate

   c. Committed burst size

   d. (a) and (b)

36. What is the relationship between the access rate and the CIR?
    a. CIR is always equal to the access rate.
    b. CIR is greater than the access rate.
    c. CIR is less than the access rate.
    d. CIR plus B_e is equal to the access rate.

37. A Frame Relay network is committed to transfer _____ bps without discarding any frames.
    a. B_c
    b. B_e
    c. CIR
    d. (a) and (b)

38. In Frame Relay the transmission rate can never exceed _____.
    a. B_c
    b. B_e
    c. CIR
    d. The access rate

39. The cell _____ is the difference between the CTD maximum and minimum.
    a. Loss ratio
    b. Transfer delay
    c. Delay variation
    d. Error ratio

40. The cell _____ is the ratio of lost cells to cells sent.
    a. Loss ratio
    b. Transfer delay
    c. Delay variation
    d. Error ratio

41. The _____ service class is particularly suitable for applications with bursty data.
    a. CBR
    b. VBR
    c. ABR
    d. UBR

42. The _____ service class is suitable for customers who need real-time video transmission without compression.
    a. CBR
    b. VBR
    c. ABR
    d. UBR

43. The _____ is greater than the SCR.
    a. PCR
    b. MCR

c. CVDT

d. All the above

44. _____ measures the variation in cell transmission time.

    a. SCR

    b. PCR

    c. MCR

    d. CVDT

45. If the SCR is 60,000, the PCR is 70,000, and the MCR is 55,000, what is the minimum number of cells that can be sent per second?

    a. 55,000

    b. 60,000

    c. 70,000

    d. 5000

46. The _____ is the fraction of the cells delivered in error.

    a. CLR

    b. CTD

    c. CDV

    d. CER

47. If the maximum CTD is 10 μs and the minimum CTD is 1 μs, the _____ is 9 μs.

    a. CLR

    b. CTD

    c. CDV

    d. CER

Exercises

48. The address field of a Frame Relay frame is 1011000100010110. Is there any congestion in the forward direction? Is there any congestion in the backward direction?

49. A frame goes from A to B. There is congestion in both directions. Is the FECN bit set? Is the BECN bit set?

50. In a leaky bucket, what should be the capacity of the bucket if the output rate is 5 gal/min, and there is an input burst of 100 gal/min for 12 s and there is no input for 48 s?

51. An output interface in a switch is designed using the leaky bucket algorithm to send 8000 bytes/s (tick). If the following frames are received in sequence, show the frames that are sent during each second.

    Frames 1, 2, 3, 4:   4000 bytes each

    Frames 5, 6, 7:   3200 bytes each

    Frames 8, 9:   400 bytes each

    Frames 10, 11, 12:   2000 bytes each

52. A user is connected to a Frame Relay network through a T-1 line. The granted CIR is 1 Mbps with a B_c of 5 million bits per 5 s and B_e of 1 million bits per 5 s. Answer the following questions.

    a. What is the access rate?

    b. Can the user send data at 1.6 Mbps?

    c. Can the user send data at 1 Mbps all the time? Is it guaranteed that frames are never discarded in this case?

    d. Can the user send data at 1.2 Mbps all the time? Is it guaranteed that frames are never discarded in this case? If the answer is no, is it guaranteed that frames are discarded only if there is congestion?

    e. Repeat the question in part (d) for a constant rate of 1.4 Mbps.

    f. What is the maximum data rate the user can use all the time without worrying about the frames being discarded?

    g. If the user wants to take a risk, what is the maximum data rate that can be used with no chance of discarding if there is no congestion?

53. In Exercise 52 the user sends data at 1.4 Mbps for 2 s and nothing for the next 3 s. Is there a danger of discarding if there is no congestion? Is there a danger of discarding if there is congestion?

54. If each cell takes 10 μs to reach the destination, what is the CTD?

55. A network has lost 5 cells out of 10,000 and 2 are in error. What is the CLR? What is the CER?

PART 6

Application Layer

This part of the book explores several application programs, available at the topmost layer, layer five, of the Internet model. The application layer allows people to use the Internet. We could say that the other four layers are created so that people can use these application programs.

Figure 1 shows the position of the application layer in the 5-layer Internet model. The application layer is the fifth layer in the model. Above it are the users and below it is the transport layer. This means the application layer receives services from the transport layer and provides services to users.

Figure 1   *Position of application layer*

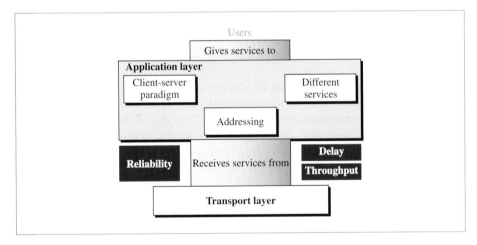

The application layer enables the user, whether human or software, to access the network. It provides user interfaces and support for services such as electronic mail, remote file access and transfer, and access to the World Wide Web.

Issues

We can say that there are three general issues related to this layer: the client-server paradigm, addressing, and types of services.

Client-Server Paradigm

The application layer programs are based on the concept of clients and servers. The purpose of a network, and in particular, the global Internet, is to provide a service to a user. A user at a local site wants to receive a service from a computer at a remote site. For example, a user wants to retrieve a file from a remote computer. Both computers must run programs. The local computer runs a program that requests a service from another program on the remote computer. We discuss the client-server paradigm in Chapter 24.

Addressing

A client and a server communicate with each other using addresses. When a client requests a service from a server, it must include the address of the server as the destination address, as well as its own address as the source address. The source address is required so that the server knows where to send the response. When the server responds to the request, it reverses the addresses; it uses its own address as the source and the address of the client as the destination.

However, the addressing mechanism in the application program is not like the ones in other layers; each application has its own address format. For example, an email address may look like *forouzan@fhda.edu,* while an address to access a web page may look like *http://www.fhda.edu.*

We can say that part of the address is related to the port address of the server and the directory structure where the server program is located. The main part, however, is an alias name for the address of the remote host. The application program uses an alias name instead of an IP address. Although this type of address is very convenient for human beings to remember and use, it is not suitable for the IP protocol when it opens a communication with the server. The alias address must be mapped to the IP address. An application program needs the service of another entity to map the alias address to the IP address. This entity is an application program, called DNS, in this layer. DNS is not directly used by the user; it is used by other application programs to perform the mapping. We discuss DNS in Chapter 25.

Types of Service

The application layer is designed to give different services to the user or user programs. The most common service, SMTP, allows a user to send a message to another user in the Internet. This service is electronic mail and has many similarities to the traditional postal mail. Another common service is file transfer. A user can transfer a file from its computer to the server or transfer a file from a server to its computer. This application program is called FTP. We discuss these two similar services in Chapter 26.

The invention of the World Wide Web heralds a new era for Internet users. WWW is a repository of information that the Internet user can access. To use the WWW requires a simple transfer protocol called HTTP. We discuss WWW and HTTP in Chapter 27.

Recently, multimedia in the form of audio and video data, has attracted the attention of Internet users. They can listen to music that is streamed from a server. They can listen to radio or TV broadcasts through the Internet. They can to talk to each other or create a teleconferencing environment. This type of service is new and growing. It has brought new concepts to the Internet. The quality of service that we discussed in the previous parts of the book plays a very important role when we use multimedia. We have devoted Chapter 28 to this issue.

Support

To be useful to the user, an application program must be supported by the services provided by the lower layer, the transport layer. The type of support needed is different for different applications. We can categorize this support into three categories: reliability, throughput, and delay.

Reliability

Some applications depend heavily on reliability. Among them are email and file transfer. We do not want to receive a corrupted email or a file that is missing some of its parts. These types of applications need either to include reliability as part of their protocol or use the services of a reliable transport-layer protocol such as TCP. Other application programs are not so sensitive to reliability. If a very small part of the music we download from the Internet is missing, it might not even be noticeable.

Throughput

Maximum throughput, the maximum amount of data that can be transferred in a unit of time is a criteria required by some applications. Multimedia applications need, in general, a high throughput to be effective. We see in Chapter 28 that transferring live video files involves transferring millions of bits in a short amount of time, even if the data are compressed. Throughput is intrinsically related to bandwidth. An application that requires a high throughput requires a high bandwidth.

Delay

Some applications are very sensitive to delay. An interactive real-time application program cannot tolerate delay. We do not want to use the Internet as a telephone service if there are long delays in the conversation. Some applications, on the other hand are not sensitive to delay. An email can wait for a few seconds or even hours before delivery.

Chapters

Part six of the book covers five chapters: Chapter 24 covers the concept of the client-server paradigm and the socket interface. Chapter 25 is devoted to DNS, a protocol that maps application-layer addresses to network-layer addresses. Chapter 26 explores two common protocols, SMTP and FTP, that allow users to transfer messages and files through the Internet. Chapter 27 discusses WWW and the protocol that accesses it, HTTP. Finally, Chapter 28 is an introduction to the use of multimedia in the Internet, an issue that is evolving rapidly.

CHAPTER 24

Client-Server Model: Socket Interface

Before discussing some application layer protocols in the next few chapters, we need to understand the nature of these application programs. We need to know that the Internet is based on a client-server model. To do a task, there must be a client and a server. In Section 24.1, we discuss this model. Although there are several ways to allow a client and a server to communicate, the most common one is the socket interface, which we discuss in Section 24.2. This book is not designed to teach client-server programming, but we introduce the idea, using flowcharts, one of the tools of programming. This gives the reader the basic concepts of client-server programming without getting bogged down by the details. For those who are interested in examples of client-server programming, see Appendix H.

24.1 CLIENT-SERVER MODEL

There are several ways that a computer can ask for the services of another computer. By far the most common is the **client-server model.**

Relationship

The purpose of a network, or an internetwork, is to provide services to users. A user at a local site wants to receive a service from a computer at a remote site. There is only one way for a computer to do the job; it must run a program. A computer runs a program to either request a service from another computer or provide a service to another computer. This means that two computers, connected by an internet, must each run a program, one to provide a service and the other to request a service.

It should be clear now that if we want to use the services available on an internet, **application programs,** running at two end computers and communicating with each other, are needed. In other words, in an internet, the application programs are entities that communicate with each other, not computers or users.

At first glance, enabling communication between two application programs, one running at the local site and the other running at the remote site seems simple. But many questions arise when we want to implement the approach. These are some of the questions that we may ask:

1. Should both the applications be able to request services and provide services, or should they just do one or the other? One solution is to have an application program, called the *client,* running on the local machine request a service from another application program, called the *server,* running on the remote machine.

Figure 24.1   *Client-server model*

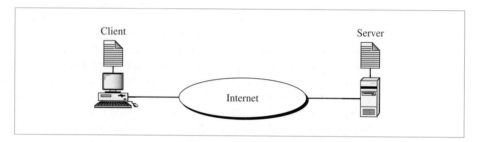

2. Should an application program provide services only to one specific application program installed somewhere in an internet, or should it provide services for any application program that requests this service? The most common solution is a server providing a service for any client, not a particular client (see Fig. 24.2).

Figure 24.2   *Client-server relationship*

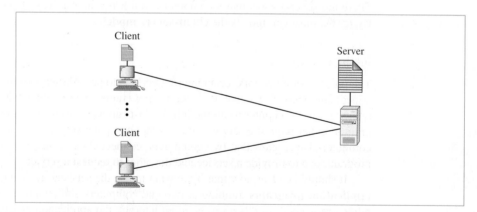

3. When should an application program be running—all the time or just when there is a need for the service? Generally, a client program, which requests a service, should run only when it is needed. The server program, which provides a service, should run all the time because it does not know when its services will be needed.

4. Should there be only one universal application program that can provide any type of service a user wants? Or should there be one application program for

each type of service? In the Internet, services needed frequently and by many users have specific client-server application programs. For example, we have separate client-server application programs that allow users to access files or send email. For services that are more customized, we should have one generic application program that allows users to access the services available on a remote computer.

Client   A **client** is a program running on the local machine requesting service from a server. A client program is started by the user (or another application program) and terminates when the service is complete. A client opens the communication channel using the IP address of the remote host and the well-known port address of the specific server program running on that machine. This is called an **active open.** After a channel of communication is opened, the client sends its request and receives a response. Although the request-response part may be repeated several times, the whole process is finite and eventually comes to an end. At that moment, the client closes the communication channel with an **active close.**

Server   A **server** is a program running on the remote machine and providing service to the clients. When it starts, it opens the door for incoming requests from clients, but it never initiates a service until it is requested to do so. This is called a *passive open.*

A server program is an infinite program. When it starts, it runs infinitely unless a problem arises. It waits for incoming requests from clients. When a request arrives, it responds to the request, either iteratively or concurrently, as we will see shortly.

Concurrency

Both clients and servers can run in concurrent mode.

Concurrency in Clients

Clients can be run on a machine either iteratively or concurrently. Running clients **iteratively** means running them one by one; one client must start, run, and terminate before the machine can start another client. Most computers today, however, allow **concurrent clients;** that is, two or more clients can run at the same time.

Concurrency in Servers

An **iterative server** can process only one request at a time; it receives a request, processes it, and sends the response to the requestor before it handles another request. A **concurrent server,** on the other hand, can process many requests at the same time and thus can share its time between many requests.

The servers use either UDP, a connectionless transport layer protocol, or TCP, a connection-oriented transport layer protocol. Server operation, therefore, depends on two factors: the transport layer protocol and the service method. Theoretically we can have four types of servers: connectionless iterative, connectionless concurrent, connection-oriented iterative, and connection-oriented concurrent.

Connectionless Iterative Server   The servers that use UDP are normally iterative, which, as we have said, means that the server processes one request at a time. The first and last are discussed here. The server uses one single port for this purpose, the well-known port. All the packets arriving at this port wait in line to be served, as is shown in Figure 24.3.

Figure 24.3 *Connectionless iterative server*

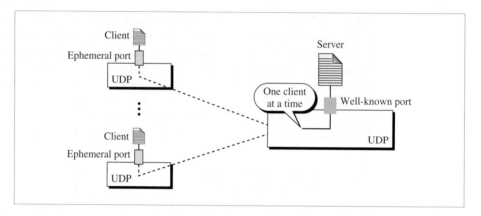

Connection-Oriented Concurrent Server The servers that use TCP are normally concurrent. This means that the server can serve many clients at the same time. Communication is connection-oriented, which means that a request is a stream of bytes that can arrive in several segments and the response can occupy several segments. A connection is established between the server and each client, and the connection remains open until the entire stream is processed and the connection is terminated.

This type of server cannot use only one well-known port because each connection requires a port and many connections may be open at the same time. Many ports are needed, but a server can use only one well-known port. The solution is to use one well-known port and many ephemeral ports. The server issues a passive open at the well-known port. A client can make its initial approach to this port to make the connection. After the connection is made, the server assigns a temporary port to this connection to free the well-known port. Data transfer can now take place between these two temporary ports, one at the client site and the other at the server site. The well-known port is now free for another client to make a connection. The idea is to push demultiplexing to TCP instead of the server. See Figure 24.4 for this configuration.

Processes

Understanding the concept of a process is necessary to comprehend the **client-server model.** In this section, we discuss this concept and its relationship to the client-server model, particularly concurrent processing.

Most operating systems, including UNIX, distinguish a program from a process. Whereas a program and a process are related to each other, they are not the same thing.

Figure 24.4   *Connection-oriented concurrent server*

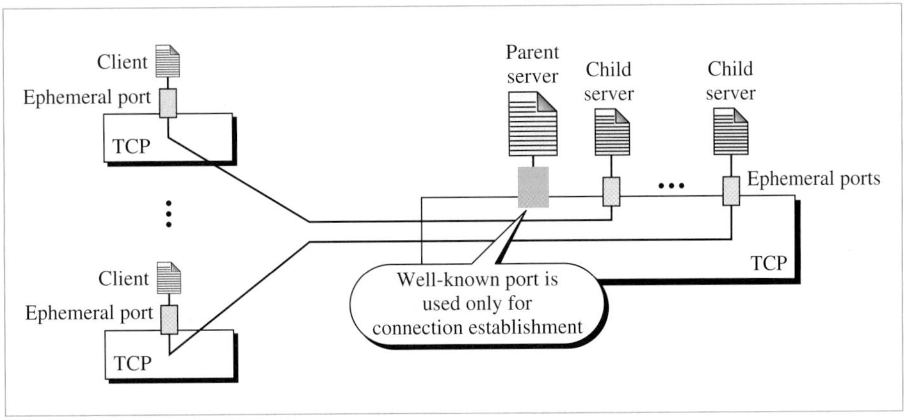

In UNIX, a program is code. The code defines all the variables and actions to be performed on those variables. A **process,** on the other hand, is an instance of a program. When the operating system executes a program, an instance of the program, a process, is created. The operating system can create several processes from one program, which means several instances of the same program are running at the same time (concurrently). Memory is allocated for each process separately.

24.2   SOCKET INTERFACE

The **Socket Interface** was originally based on UNIX and defines a set of system calls (procedures) that are an extension of system calls used in UNIX to access files. This section discusses the fundamentals of Socket Interface programming, though it, by no means, teaches Socket Interface programming; there are whole books devoted to this subject. Instead, we introduce the concept and idea and maybe provide motivation for those readers who want to learn more.

Sockets

The communication structure that we need in socket programming is a **socket.** A socket acts as an endpoint. Two processes need a socket at each end to communicate with each other.

A socket is defined in the operating system as a structure. Figure 24.5 shows a simplified version of a socket structure with five fields. These fields are listed below.

■ **Family.** This field defines the protocol group: IPv4, IPv6, UNIX domain protocols, and so on.

■ **Type.** This field defines the type of socket: stream socket, packet socket, or raw socket. These are discussed below.

■ **Protocol.** This field is usually set to zero for TCP and UDP.

Figure 24.5 *Socket structure*

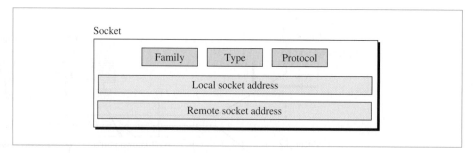

- **Local socket address.** This field defines the local socket address, a combination of the local IP address and the port address of the local application program.
- **Remote socket address.** This field defines the remote socket address, a combination of the remote IP address and the port address of the remote application program.

Socket Types

The socket interface defines three types of sockets: the stream socket, the packet socket, and the raw socket. All three types can be used in a TCP/IP environment (see Fig. 24.6).

Figure 24.6 *Socket types*

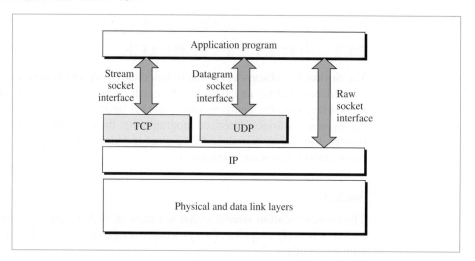

Stream Socket   A **stream socket** is designed to be used with a connection-oriented protocol such as TCP. TCP uses a pair of stream sockets to connect one application program to another across the Internet.

Datagram Socket   A **datagram socket** is designed to be used with a connectionless protocol such as UDP. UDP uses a pair of datagram sockets to send a message from one application program to another across the Internet.

Raw Socket Some protocols such as ICMP or OSPF that directly use the services of IP use neither stream sockets nor datagram sockets. **Raw sockets** are designed for these types of applications.

Connectionless Iterative Server

In this section, we discuss connectionless, iterative client-server communication using UDP and datagram sockets. As we discussed before, a server that uses UDP is usually connectionless iterative. This means that the server serves one request at a time. A server gets the request received in a packet from UDP, processes the request, and gives the response to UDP to send to the client. The server pays no attention to the other packets. These packets, which could all be from one client or from many clients, are stored in a queue, waiting for service. They are processed one by one in order of arrival.

The server uses one single port for this purpose, the well-known port. All the packets arriving at this port wait in line to be served. Figure 24.7 shows the flowchart of events in connectionless iterative communication.

Figure 24.7 *Socket interface for connectionless iterative server*

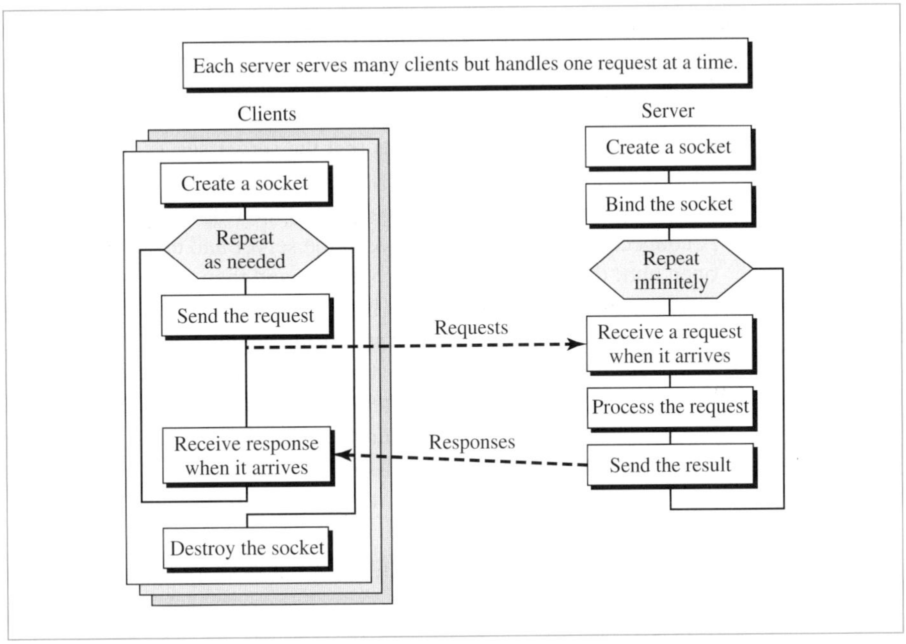

Server

The server performs the following functions:

1. **Create a socket.** The server asks the operating system to create a socket.
2. **Bind.** The server asks the operating system to enter information in the socket related to the server. This is called *binding the server socket*.

3. **Repeat.** The server repeats the following steps infinitely:
   a. **Receive a request.** The server asks the operating system to wait for a request destined for this socket and to receive it.
   b. **Process.** The request is processed by the server.
   c. **Send.** The response is sent to the client.

Client

The client performs the following functions:

1. **Create a socket.** The client asks the operating system to create a socket. There is no need for binding here. The operating system normally fills in the information in the socket.
2. **Repeat.** The client repeats the following steps as long as it has requests:
   a. **Send.** The client asks the operating system to send a request.
   b. **Receive.** The client asks the operating system to wait for the response and deliver it when it has arrived.
3. **Destroy.** When the client has no more requests, it asks the operating system to destroy the socket.

Connection-Oriented Concurrent Server

In this section, we discuss connection-oriented, concurrent client-server communication using TCP and stream sockets. As mentioned before, the servers that use TCP are normally concurrent. This means that the server serves many clients at the same time. Communication is connection-oriented, which means that a request is a stream of bytes that could arrive in several segments, and the response could occupy several segments. A connection is established between the server and each client; the connection remains open until the entire stream is processed, and then the connection is terminated.

The server must have one buffer for each connection. The segments from the clients are stored in the appropriate buffers and handled concurrently by the server.

To provide this service, most implementations use the concept of parent and child servers. A server running infinitely and accepting connections from clients is called a *parent server*. The parent server uses the well-known port. After the connection is made, the parent server creates a *child server* and an ephemeral port and lets the child server handle the client. It frees itself so that it can wait for another connection. In this section, we show how a server can serve several clients concurrently, using the services of TCP. Figure 24.8 shows the flowchart of events for a server and a client.

Server

The server performs the following functions:

1. **Create a socket.** The server asks the operating system to create a socket.
2. **Bind.** The server asks the operating system to enter information in the socket created in the previous step.
3. **Listen.** The server asks the operating system to be passive and listen to the client that needs to be connected to this server. Remember that TCP is a connection-oriented protocol. A connection needs to be made before data transfer.

Figure 24.8 *Socket interface for connection-oriented concurrent server*

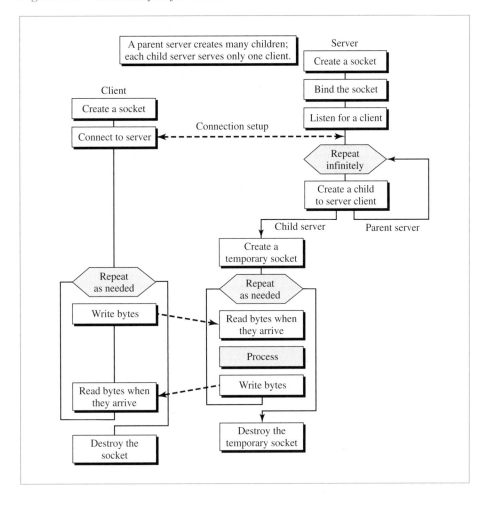

4. **Repeat.** The server repeats the following steps infinitely:
   a. **Create a child.** When a child requests a connection, the operating system creates a temporary child process and assigns the duty of serving the client to the child. The parent process is free to listen for new clients.
   b. **Create a new socket.** A new socket is created to be used by the child process.
   c. **Repeating.** The child repeats the following steps as long as it has requests from the client:

      Read. The child reads a stream of bytes from the connection. Remember that TCP is a byte-oriented protocol.

      Process. The child processes the stream of bytes.

      Write. The child writes the results as a stream of bytes to the connection.
   d. **Destroy socket.** After the client has been served, the child process asks the operating system to destroy the temporary socket.

Client

The client performs the following functions:

1. **Create a socket.** The client asks the operating system to create a socket.
2. **Connect.** The client asks the operating system to make a connection.
3. **Repeat.** The client repeats the following steps as long as it has data to send.
   a. **Write.** The client sends a stream of bytes to be sent to the server.
   b. **Read.** The client receives a stream of bytes from the server.
4. **Destroy.** After the client has finished, it asks the operating system to destroy the socket. The connection is also closed.

Client and Server Programs

Client-server programs are written in languages such as C, C++, Java, and Perl. This type of programming is very involved and requires an advanced knowledge of programming as well as knowledge of the particular language. These topics are beyond the scope of this book. However, we give some examples of client-server programs in Appendix H for those interested readers.

24.3   KEY TERMS

active close
active open
application program
application programming interface (API)
client
client-server model
concurrent client
concurrent server
connectionless iterative server
connection-oriented concurrent server

datagram socket
iterative client
iterative server
process
raw socket
server
socket
Socket Interface
stream socket

24.4   SUMMARY

❏ In the client-server model, the client runs a program to request a service and the server runs a program to provide the service. These two programs communicate with each other.

❏ One server program can provide services for many client programs.

❏ Clients can be run either iteratively (one at a time) or concurrently (many at a time).

❏ Servers can handle clients either iteratively (one at a time) or concurrently (many at a time).

❏ A connectionless iterative server uses UDP as its transport layer protocol and can serve one client at a time.

❑ A connection-oriented concurrent server uses TCP as its transport layer protocol and can serve many clients at the same time.

❑ When the operating system executes a program, an instance of the program, called a process, is created.

❑ If two application programs, one running on a local system and the other running on the remote system, need to communicate with each other, a network program is required.

❑ The socket interface is a set of declarations, definitions, and procedures for writing client-server programs.

❑ The communication structure needed for socket programming is called a socket.

❑ A stream socket is used with a connection-oriented protocol such as TCP.

❑ A datagram socket is used with a connectionless protocol such as UDP.

❑ A raw socket is used by protocols such as ICMP or OSPF that directly use the services of IP.

24.5   PRACTICE SET

Review Questions

1. Discuss the terms client and server and their relationship to each other in the client-server model.
2. What is the difference between an active open and a passive open?
3. How does a server that handles clients iteratively differ from a server that handles clients concurrently?
4. How is a program different from a process?
5. What is a socket interface?
6. What are the components of a socket address?
7. Name three types of socket interfaces.
8. Which socket interface is designed for use with TCP?
9. How can a connection-oriented concurrent server handle multiple clients?
10. What is a child server?

Multiple-Choice Questions

11. _____ can request a service.
    a. A socket interface
    b. A port
    c. A client
    d. A server

12. _____ can provide a service.
    a. An iterative server
    b. A concurrent server
    c. A client
    d. (a) and (b)

13. The client program is _____ because it terminates after it has been served.
   a. Active
   b. Passive
   c. Finite
   d. Infinite

14. The server program is _____ because it is always available, waiting for a client request.
   a. Active
   b. Passive
   c. Finite
   d. Infinite

15. A connection-oriented concurrent server uses _____ ports.
   a. Ephemeral
   b. Well-known
   c. Active
   d. (a) and (b)

16. A connectionless iterative server uses _____ ports.
   a. Ephemeral
   b. Well-known
   c. Active
   d. (a) and (b)

17. Machine A requests service X from machine B. Machine B requests service Y from machine A. What is the total number of application programs required?
   a. One
   b. Two
   c. Three
   d. Four

18. A client issues _____ when it needs service from a server.
   a. An active open
   b. A passive open
   c. An active request
   d. A finite open

19. A server program, once it issues _____, waits for clients to request its service.
   a. An active open
   b. A passive open
   c. An active request
   d. A finite open

20. _____ processes requests one at a time.

   a. An iterative client

   b. An iterative server

   c. A concurrent client

   d. A concurrent server

21. _____ processes many requests simultaneously.

   a. An iterative client

   b. An iterative server

   c. A concurrent client

   d. A concurrent server

22. In a connection-oriented concurrent server, the _____ is used for connection only.

   a. Infinite port

   b. Ephemeral port

   c. Well-known port

   d. (b) and (c)

23. A _____ is an instance of a _____.

   a. Process; program

   b. Program; process

   c. Process; service

   d. Structure; process

24. The _____ socket is used with a connection-oriented protocol.

   a. Stream

   b. Datagram

   c. Raw

   d. Remote

25. The _____ socket is used with a connectionless protocol.

   a. Stream

   b. Datagram

   c. Raw

   d. Remote

26. The _____ socket is used with a protocol that directly uses the services of IP.

   a. Stream

   b. Datagram

   c. Raw

   d. Remote

27. A _____ server serves multiple clients, handling one request at a time.

   a. Connection-oriented iterative

   b. Connection-oriented concurrent

   c. Connectionless iterative

   d. Connectionless concurrent

28. A _____ server serves multiple clients simultaneously.
    a. Connection-oriented iterative
    b. Connection-oriented concurrent
    c. Connectionless iterative
    d. Connectionless concurrent

Exercises

29. In Figure 24.7, explain why the loop on the server side is repeated infinitely, but the one on the client side is repeated a finite number of times.
30. In Figure 24.7, if more than one client accesses the same server, how does the transport layer on the client side know where to deliver an arriving response?
31. In Figure 24.7, if a client sends several requests and receives several responses, how can it match a response to a request?
32. In Figure 24.8, there are three loops. Explain why only of them is an infinite loop.
33. In Figure 24.7, the communication between a client and a server is based on the discrete requests and responses. On the other hand, the communication between a client and a server is based on stream of byes. Can you explain the reason?
34. In Chapter 22, we said that TCP is a connection-oriented protocol that uses a three-way handshaking for connection. Can you find the trace of this handshaking in Figure 24.8?
35. Why do we need the *listen* step in Figure 24.8, but not in Figure 24.7?
36. Iterative client-sever programs using UDP allow only one client at a time. Do you think a client can monopolize a server in the type of transaction? Explain your answer.
37. Do you think a child process can run infinitely? Explain your answer.
38. In Figure 24.7, why do we need a *bind* step in the server side, but not in the client side?
39. What do you think happens to a child server in Figure 24.8 after the child has finished serving a client?

CHAPTER 25

Domain Name System (DNS)

To identify an entity, the Internet uses the IP address, which uniquely identifies the connection of a host to the Internet. However, people prefer to use names instead of numeric addresses. Therefore, we need a system that can map a name to an address or an address to a name.

When the Internet was small, mapping was done using a **host file.** The host file had only two columns; one for the name and one for the address. Every host could store the host file on its disk and update it periodically from a master host file. When a program or a user wanted to map a name to an address, the host consulted the host file and found the mapping.

Today, however, it is impossible to have one single host file relate every address to a name, and vice versa. The host file would be too large to store in every host. In addition, it would be impossible to update all the host files in the world every time there is a change.

One solution would be to store the entire host file in a single computer and allow access to this centralized information to every computer that needs a mapping. But we know that this would create a huge amount of traffic on the Internet.

Another solution, the one used today, is to divide this huge amount of information into smaller parts and store each part on a different computer. In this method, the host that needs mapping can contact the closest computer holding the needed information. This method is used by the **Domain Name System (DNS).** In this chapter, we first discuss the concepts and ideas behind the DNS. We then describe the DNS protocol itself.

25.1 NAME SPACE

To be unambiguous, the names assigned to machines must be carefully selected from a **name space** with complete control over the binding between the names and IP addresses. In other words, the names must be unique because the addresses are unique. A name space that maps each address to a unique name can be organized in two ways: flat or hierarchical.

Flat Name Space

In a **flat name space,** a name is assigned to an address. A name in this space is a sequence of characters without structure. The names may or may not have a common section; if they do, it has no meaning. The main disadvantage of a flat name space is that it cannot be used in a large system such as the Internet because it must be centrally controlled to avoid ambiguity and duplication.

Hierarchical Name Space

In a **hierarchical name space,** each name is made of several parts. The first part can define the nature of the organization, the second part can define the name, the third part can define departments, and so on. In this case, the authority to assign and control the name spaces can be decentralized. A central authority can assign the part of the name that defines the nature of the organization and the name. The responsibility for the rest of the name can be given to the organization itself. Suffixes can be added to the name to define host or resources. The management of the organization need not worry that the prefix chosen for a host is taken by another organization because even if part of an address is the same, the whole address is different. For example, assume two colleges and a company call one of their computers *challenger.* The first college is given a name by the central authority such as *fhda.edu,* the second college is given the name *berkeley.edu,* and the company is given the name *smart.com.* When these organizations add the name *challenger* to the name they have already been given, the end result is three distinguishable names: *challenger.fhda.edu, challenger. berkeley.edu,* and *challenger.smart.com.* The names are unique without the need to be assigned by a central authority. The central authority controls only part of the name, not the whole name.

25.2   DOMAIN NAME SPACE

To have a hierarchical name space, a **domain name space** was designed. In this design, the names are defined in an inverted-tree structure with the root at the top. The tree can have only 128 levels: level 0 (root) to level 127. Whereas the root glues the whole tree together, each level of the tree defines a hierarchical level (see Fig. 25.1).

Label

Each node in the tree has a label, which is a string with a maximum of 63 characters. The root label is a null string (empty string). DNS requires that children of a node

Figure 25.1   *Domain name space*

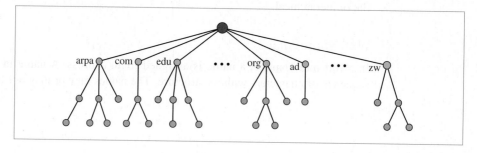

(nodes that branch from the same node) have different labels, which guarantees the uniqueness of the domain names.

Domain Name

Each node in the tree has a domain name. A full **domain name** is a sequence of labels separated by dots (.). The domain names are always read from the node up to the root. The last label is the label of the root (null). This means that a full domain name always ends in a null label, which means the last character is a dot because the null string is nothing. Figure 25.2 shows some domain names.

Figure 25.2 *Domain names and labels*

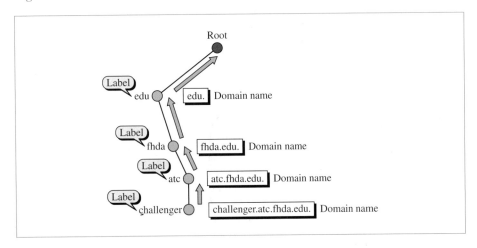

Fully Qualified Domain Name (FQDN)

If a label is terminated by a null string, it is called a **fully qualified domain name (FQDN).** An FQDN is a domain name that contains the full name of a host. It contains all labels, from the most specific to the most general, that uniquely define the name of the host. For example, the domain name

challenger.atc.fhda.edu.

is the FQDN of a computer named *challenger* and installed at the Advanced Technology Center (ATC) at De Anza College. A DNS server can only match an FQDN to an address. Note that the name must end with a null label, but because null here means nothing, the label ends with a dot (.).

Partially Qualified Domain Name (PQDN)

If a label is not terminated by a null string, it is called a **partially qualified domain name (PQDN).** A PQDN starts from a node, but it does not reach the root. It is used when the name to be resolved belongs to the same site as the client. Here the resolver can supply the missing part, called the **suffix,** to create an FQDN. For example, if a user at the fhda.edu. site wants to get the IP address of the challenger computer, he or she can define the partial name

`challenger`

The DNS client adds the suffix *atc.fhda.edu.* before passing the address to the DNS server.
   The DNS client normally holds a list of suffixes. The following can be some of the list of suffixes at De Anza College.

`atc.fhda.edu.`

`fhda.edu.`

`.`

Figure 25.3 shows some FQDNs and PQDNs.

Figure 25.3 *FQDN and PQDN*

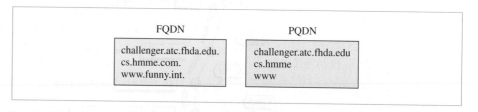

Domain

A **domain** is a subtree of the domain name space. The name of the domain is the domain name of the node at the top of the subtree. Figure 25.4 shows some domains.

Figure 25.4 *Domains*

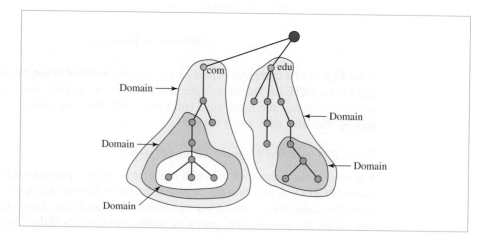

Note that a domain may itself be divided into domains, or **subdomains** as they are sometimes called.

25.3   DISTRIBUTION OF NAME SPACE

The information contained in the domain name space must be stored. However, it is very inefficient and also not reliable to have just one computer store such a huge amount of information. It is inefficient because responding to requests from all over the world places a heavy load on the system. It is not reliable because any failure makes the data inaccessible.

Hierarchy of Name Servers

The solution to these problems is to distribute the information among many computers called **DNS servers.** One way to do this is to divide the whole space into many domains based on the first level. In other words, we let the root stand alone and create as many domains (subtrees) as there are first-level nodes. Because a domain created this way could be very large, DNS allows domains to be divided further into smaller domains (subdomains). Each server can be responsible (authoritative) for either a large or a small domain. In other words, we have a hierarchy of servers in the same way that we have a hierarchy of names (see Fig. 25.5).

Figure 25.5   *Hierarchy of name servers*

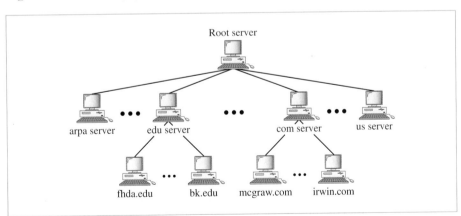

Zone

What a server is responsible for, or has authority over, is called a **zone.** If a server accepts responsibility for a domain and does not divide the domain into smaller domains, the *domain* and the *zone* refer to the same thing. The server makes a database called a *zone file* and keeps all the information for every node under that domain. However, if a server divides its domain into subdomains and delegates part of its authority to other servers, *domain* and *zone* refer to different things. The information about the nodes in the sub-domains is stored in the servers at the lower levels, with the original server keeping some sort of reference to these lower-level servers. Of course the original server does not free itself from responsibility totally: It still has a zone, but the detailed information is kept by the lower-level servers (see Fig. 25.6).

Figure 25.6   *Zones and domains*

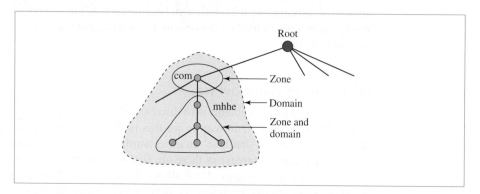

A server can also divide its domain and delegate responsibility but still keep part of the domain for itself. In this case, its zone is made of detailed information for the part of the domain that is not delegated and references to those parts that are delegated.

Root Server

A **root server** is a server whose zone consists of the whole tree. A root server usually does not store any information about domains but delegates its authority to other servers, keeping references to those servers. Currently there are more than 13 root servers, each covering the whole domain name space. The servers are distributed all around the world.

Primary and Secondary Servers

DNS defines two types of servers: primary and secondary. A **primary server** is a server that stores a file about the zone for which it is an authority. It is responsible for creating, maintaining, and updating the zone file. It stores the zone file on a local disk.

A **secondary server** is a server that transfers the complete information about a zone from another server (primary or secondary) and stores the file on its local disk. The secondary server neither creates nor updates the zone files. If updating is required, it must be done by the primary server, which sends the updated version to the secondary.

The primary and secondary servers are both authoritative for the zones they serve. The idea is not to put the secondary server at a lower level of authority, but to create redundancy for the data so that if one server fails, the others can continue serving clients. Note also that a server can be a primary server for a specific zone and a secondary server for another zone. Therefore, when we refer to a server as a primary or secondary server, we should be careful to which zone we refer.

> **A primary server loads all information from the disk file; the secondary server loads all information from the primary server.**

25.4 DNS IN THE INTERNET

DNS is a protocol that can be used in different platforms. In the Internet, the domain name space (tree) is divided into three different sections: generic domains, country domains, and inverse domain (see Fig. 25.7).

Figure 25.7 *DNS in the Internet*

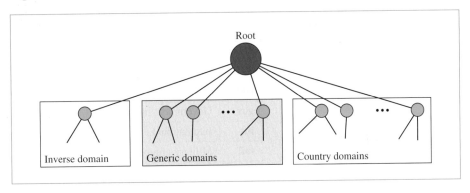

Generic Domains

The **generic domains** define registered hosts according to their generic behavior. Each node in the tree defines a domain, which is an index to the domain name space database (see Fig. 25.8).

Looking at the tree, we see that the first level in the generic domains section allows seven possible three-character labels. These labels describe the organization types as listed in Table 25.1.

Recently a few more first-level labels have been approved; these are shown in Table 25.2.

Figure 25.8   *Generic domains*

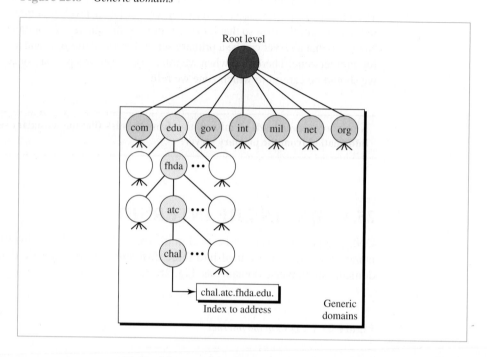

Table 25.1   *Generic domain labels*

Label	Description
com	Commercial organizations
edu	Educational institutions
gov	Government institutions
int	International organizations
mil	Military groups
net	Network support centers
org	Nonprofit organizations

Table 25.2   *New generic domain labels*

Label	Description
aero	Airlines and aerospace companies
biz	Businesses or firms (similar to com)
coop	Cooperative business organizations
info	Information service providers
museum	Museums and other nonprofit organizations
name	Personal names (individuals)
pro	Professional individual organizations

Country Domains

The **country domains** section follows the same format as the generic domains but uses two-character country abbreviations (e.g., *us* for United States) in place of the three-character organizational abbreviations at the first level. Second-level labels can be organizational, or they can be more specific, national designations. The United States, for example, uses state abbreviations as a subdivision of the country domain *us* (e.g., *ca.us.*).

Figure 25.9 shows the country domains section. The address *anza.cup.ca.us* can be translated to De Anza College in Cupertino in California in the United States.

Figure 25.9 *Country domains*

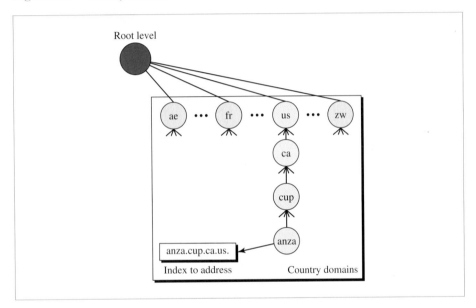

Inverse Domain

The **inverse domain** is used to map an address to a name. This may happen, for example, when a server has received a request from a client to do a task. Whereas the server has a file that contains a list of authorized clients, the server lists only the IP address of the client (extracted from the received IP packet). To determine if the client is on the authorized list, the server can send a query to the inverse DNS server and ask for a mapping of address to name.

This type of query is called an *inverse* or *pointer* (PTR) query. To handle a pointer query, the inverse domain is added to the domain name space with the first-level node called *arpa* (for historical reasons). The second level is also one single node named *in-addr* (for inverse address). The rest of the domain defines IP addresses.

The servers that handle the inverse domain are also hierarchical. This means the netid part of the address should be at a higher level than the subnetid part, and the subnetid part higher than the hostid part. In this way, a server serving the whole site is at a higher level than the servers serving each subnet. This configuration makes the domain look inverted when compared to a generic or country domain. To follow the convention of reading the domain labels from the bottom to the top, an IP address such as 132.34.45.121 (a class B address with netid 132.34) is read as 121.45.34.132.in-addr.arpa. See Figure 25.10 for an illustration of the inverse domain configuration.

Figure 25.10   *Inverse domain*

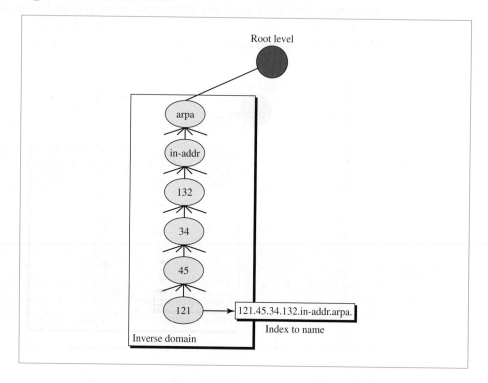

25.5   RESOLUTION

Mapping a name to an address or an address to a name is called **name-address resolution.**

Resolver

DNS is designed as a client-server application. A host that needs to map an address to a name or a name to an address calls a DNS client named a **resolver.** The resolver accesses the closest DNS server with a mapping request. If the server has the information, it satisfies the resolver; otherwise, it either refers the resolver to other servers or asks other servers to provide the information.

After the resolver receives the mapping, it interprets the response to see if it is a real resolution or an error and finally delivers the result to the process that requested it.

Mapping Names to Addresses

Most of the time, the resolver gives a domain name to the server and asks for the corresponding address. In this case, the server checks the generic domains or the country domains to find the mapping.

If the domain name is from the generic domains section, the resolver receives a domain name such as *chal.atc.fhda.edu.*. The query is sent by the resolver to the local DNS server for resolution. If the local server cannot resolve the query, it either refers the resolver to other servers or asks other servers directly.

If the domain name is from the country domains section, the resolver receives a domain name such as *ch.fhda.cu.ca.us.*. The procedure is the same.

Mapping Addresses to Names

A client can send an IP address to a server to be mapped to a domain name. As mentioned before, this is called a PTR query. To answer queries of this kind, DNS uses the inverse domain. However, in the request, the IP address is reversed, and two labels, *in-addr* and *arpa,* are appended to create a domain acceptable by the inverse domain section. For example, if the resolver receives the IP address 132.34.45.121, the resolver first inverts the address and then adds the two labels before sending. The domain name sent is *121.45.34.132.in-addr.arpa.,* which is received by the local DNS and resolved.

Recursive Resolution

The client (resolver) can ask for a recursive answer from a name server. This means that the resolver expects the server to supply the final answer. If the server is the authority for the domain name, it checks its database and responds. If the server is not the authority, it sends the request to another server (the parent usually) and waits for the response. If the parent is the authority, it responds; otherwise, it sends the query to yet another server. When the query is finally resolved, the response travels back until it finally reaches the requesting client. This is, **recursive resolution,** shown in Figure 25.11.

Figure 25.11   *Recursive resolution*

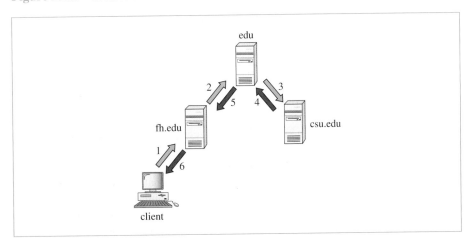

Iterative Resolution

If the client does not ask for a recursive answer, the mapping can be done iteratively. If the server is an authority for the name, it sends the answer. If it is not, it returns (to the client) the IP address of the server that it thinks can resolve the query. The client is responsible for repeating the query to this second server. If the newly addressed server can resolve the problem, it answers the query with the IP address; otherwise, it returns the IP address of a new server to the client. Now the client must repeat the query to the third server. This process is called **iterative resolution** because the client repeats the same query to multiple servers. In Figure 25.12 the client queries three servers before it gets an answer from the *csu.edu* server.

Figure 25.12   *Iterative resolution*

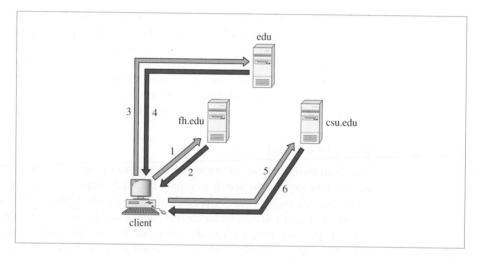

Caching

Each time a server receives a query for a name that is not in its domain, it needs to search its database for a server IP address. Reduction of this search time would increase efficiency. DNS handles this with a mechanism called **caching.** When a server asks for a mapping from another server and receives the response, it stores this information in its cache memory before sending it to the client. If the same or another client asks for the same mapping, it can check its cache memory and resolve the problem. However, to inform the client that the response is coming from the cache memory and not from an authoritative source, the server marks the response as *unauthoritative.*

Caching speeds up resolution, but it can also be problematic. If a server caches a mapping for a long time, it may send an outdated mapping to the client. To counter this, two techniques are used. First, the authoritative server always adds a piece of information to the mapping called *time-to-live (TTL).* It defines the time in seconds for which the receiving server can cache the information. After that time, the mapping is invalid and any query must be sent again to the authoritative server. Second, DNS requires that each server keep a TTL counter for each mapping it caches. The cache memory must be searched periodically, and those mappings with an expired TTL must be purged.

25.6 DNS MESSAGES

DNS has two types of messages: query and response. Both types have the same format. The **query message** consists of a header and the question records; the **response message** consists of a header, question records, answer records, authoritative records, and additional records (see Fig. 25.13).

Figure 25.13 *Query and response messages*

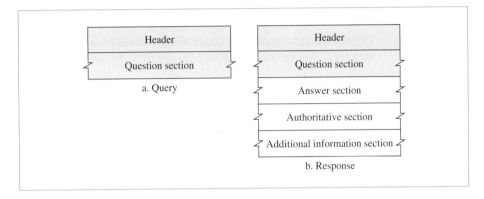

Header

Both query and response messages have the same header format with some fields set to zero for the query messages. The header is 12 bytes, and its format is shown in Figure 25.14.

Figure 25.14 *Header format*

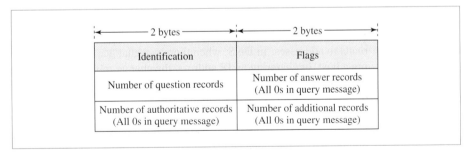

The *identification* is used by the client to match the response with the query. The client uses a different identification number each time it sends a query. The server duplicates this number in the corresponding response. *Flags* is a collection of subfields that define the type of the message, the type of answers requested, the type of desired resolution (recursive or iterative), and so on. *Number of question records* contains the number of queries in the question section of the message. *Number of answer records* contains the number of answer records in the answer section of the response message. Its value is zero in the query message. *Number of authoritative records* contains the number of authoritative records in the authoritative section of a response message. Its value is zero in the query message. Finally *Number of additional records* contains the number of additional records in the additional section of a response message. Its value is zero in the query message.

Question Section

This is a section consisting of one or more question records. It is present on both query and response messages.

Answer Section

This is a section consisting of one or more resource records. It is present only on response messages. This section includes the answer from the server to the client (resolver).

Authoritative Section

This is a section consisting of one or more resource records. It is present only on response messages. This section gives information (domain name) about one or more authoritative servers for the query.

Additional Information Section

This is a section consisting of one or more resource records. It is present only on response messages. This section provides additional information that may help the resolver. For example, a server may give the domain name of an authoritative server to the resolver in the authoritative section, and may include the IP address of the same authoritative server in the additional information section.

25.7   DDNS

When the DNS was designed, no one predicted that there would be so many changes made to addresses. In DNS, when there is a change, such as adding a new host, removing a host, or changing an IP address, the change must be made to the DNS master file. These types of changes involve a lot of manual updating. The size of today's Internet does not allow this kind of manual operation.

The DNS master file must be updated dynamically. The **Dynamic Domain Name System (DDNS)** therefore has been devised to respond to this need. In DDNS, when a binding between a name and an address is determined, the information is sent, usually by DHCP (see Chapter 19) to a primary DNS server. The primary server updates the zone. The secondary servers are notified either actively or passively. In active notification, the primary server sends a message to the secondary servers about the change in the zone, whereas in passive notification, the secondary servers periodically check for any changes. In either case, after being notified about the change, the secondary requests information about the entire zone (zone transfer).

To provide security and prevent unauthorized changes in the DNS records, DDNS can use an authentication mechanism.

25.8 ENCAPSULATION

DNS can use either UDP or TCP. In both cases the well-known port used by the server is port 53. UDP is used when the size of the response message is less than 512 bytes because most UDP packages have a 512-byte packet size limit. If the size of the response message is more than 512 bytes, a TCP connection must be used. In that case, one of two scenarios can occur:

■ If the resolver has prior knowledge that the size of the response message is more than 512 bytes, it must use the TCP connection. For example, if a secondary name server (acting as a client) needs a zone transfer from a primary server, it must use the TCP connection because the size of the information being transferred usually exceeds 512 bytes.

■ If the resolver does not know the size of the response message, it can use the UDP port. However, if the size of the response message is more than 512 bytes, the server truncates the message. The resolver now opens a TCP connection and repeats the request to get a full response from the server.

DNS can use the services of UDP or TCP, using the well-known port 53.

25.9 KEY TERMS

caching
country domain
DNS server
domain
domain name
domain name space
Domain Name System (DNS)
Dynamic Domain Name System (DDNS)
flat name space
fully qualified domain name (FQDN)
generic domain
hierarchical name space
host file
inverse domain

iterative resolution
name space
name-address resolution
partially qualified domain name (PQDN)
primary server
query message
recursive resolution
resolver
response message
root server
secondary server
suffix
zone

25.10 SUMMARY

❑ Domain Name System (DNS) is a client-server application that identifies each host on the Internet with a unique user-friendly name.

❑ DNS organizes the name space in a hierarchical structure to decentralize the responsibilities involved in naming.

❑ DNS can be pictured as an inverted hierarchical tree structure with one root node at the top and a maximum of 128 levels.

❑ Each node in the tree has a domain name.

❑ A domain is defined as any subtree of the domain name space.

❑ The name space information is distributed among DNS servers. Each server has jurisdiction over its zone.

❑ A root server's zone is the entire DNS tree.

❑ A primary server creates, maintains, and updates information about its zone.

❑ A secondary server gets its information from a primary server.

❑ The domain name space in the Internet is divided into three sections: generic domains, country domains, and inverse domain.

❑ There are seven traditional generic labels, each specifying an organization type. Recently some new labels have been added.

❑ Each country domain specifies a country.

❑ The inverse domain finds a domain name for a given IP address. This is called address-to-name resolution.

❑ Name servers, computers that run the DNS server program, are organized in a hierarchy.

❑ The DNS client, called a resolver, maps a name to an address or an address to a name.

❑ In recursive resolution, the client sends its request to a server that eventually returns a response.

❑ In iterative resolution, the client may send its request to multiple servers before getting an answer.

❑ A fully qualified domain name (FQDN) is a domain name consisting of labels beginning with the host and going back through each level to the root node.

❑ A partially qualified domain name (PQDN) is a domain name that does not include all the levels between the host and the root node.

❑ There are two types of DNS messages: queries and responses.

❑ There are two types of DNS records: question records and resource records.

❑ Dynamic DNS (DDNS) automatically updates the DNS master file.

❑ DNS uses the services of UDP for messages of less than 512 bytes; otherwise, TCP is used.

25.11 PRACTICE SET

Review Questions

1. What is an advantage of a hierarchical name space over a flat name space for a system the size of the Internet?

2. What is the difference between a primary server and a secondary server?

3. What are the three domains of the domain name space?

4. What is the purpose of the inverse domain?

5. How does recursive resolution differ from iterative resolution?
6. What is a FQDN?
7. What is a PQDN?
8. What is a zone?
9. How does caching increase the efficiency of name resolution?
10. What are the two main categories of DNS messages?
11. Why was there a need for DDNS?

Multiple-Choice Questions

12. In the domain name *chal.atc.fhda.edu,* _____ is the least specific label.
    a. *chal*
    b. *atc*
    c. *fhda*
    d. *edu*
13. In the domain name *chal.atc.fhda.edu,* _____ is the most specific label.
    a. *chal*
    b. *atc*
    c. *fhda*
    d. *edu*
14. Which of the following domain names would most likely use a country domain to resolve its IP address?
    a. chal.atac.fhda.edu
    b. gsfc.nasa.gov
    c. kenz.acct.sony.jp
    d. mac.eng.sony.com
15. A DNS response is classified as _____ if the information comes from a cache memory.
    a. Authoritative
    b. Unauthoritative
    c. Iterative
    d. Recursive
16. In _____ resolution the client is in direct contact with at most one server.
    a. A recursive
    b. An iterative
    c. A cache
    d. All the above
17. In _____ resolution the client could directly contact more than one server.
    a. A recursive
    b. An iterative
    c. A cache
    d. All the above

18. In address-to-name resolution the _____ domain is used.
    a. Inverse
    b. Reverse
    c. Generic
    d. Country

19. How is the lifetime of a name-to-address resolution in cache memory controlled?
    a. By the time-to-live field set by the server
    b. By the time-to-live counter set by the server
    c. By the time-to-live field set by the authoritative server
    d. (b) and (c)

20. In the string 219.46.123.107.in-addr.arpa, what is the network address of the host we are looking for?
    a. 219.46.123.0
    b. 107.123.0.0
    c. 107.123.46.0
    d. 107.0.0.0

21. A host with the domain name *pit.arc.nasa.gov.* is on the _____ level of the DNS hierarchical tree. (The root is level 1.)
    a. Third
    b. Fourth
    c. Fifth
    d. Not enough information given

22. A host with the domain name *trinity.blue.vers.inc* is on the _____ level of the DNS hierarchical tree. (The root is level 1.)
    a. Third
    b. Fourth
    c. Fifth
    d. Not enough information given

23. A DNS _____ server gets its data from another DNS server.
    a. Primary
    b. Secondary
    c. Root
    d. All the above

24. A DNS _____ server creates, maintains, and updates the zone file.
    a. Primary
    b. Secondary
    c. Root
    d. All the above

25. A DNS _____ server's zone is the entire DNS tree.
    a. Primary
    b. Secondary

  c. Root
  d. All the above
26. A resolver is the _____.
  a. DNS client
  b. DNS server
  c. Host machine
  d. Root server
27. To find the IP address of a host when the domain name is known, the _____ can be used.
  a. Inverse domain
  b. Generic domains
  c. Country domains
  d. (b) or (c)

Exercises

28. Determine which of the following is an FQDN and which is a PQDN.
  a. xxx
  b. xxx.yyy.
  c. xxx.yyy.net
  d. zzz.yyy.xxx.edu.
29. Determine which of the following is an FQDN and which one is a PQDN.
  a. mil.
  b. edu.
  c. xxx.yyy.net
  d. zzz.yyy.xxx.edu
30. Which domain is used by your system, generic or country?
31. Why do we need a DNS system, when we can directly use an IP address?
32. To find the IP address of a destination, we need the service of DNS. DNS needs the service of UDP or TCP. UDP or TCP needs the service of IP. IP needs an IP destination address. Is this a vicious circle here?
33. If a DNS domain name is *voyager.fhda.edu,* how many labels are involved here? How many levels of hierarchy?
34. Is a PQDN necessarily shorter than the corresponding FQDN?
35. A domain name is *hello.customer.info.* Is this a generic domain or a country domain?
36. Do you think a recursive resolution is normally faster than an interactive one? Explain.
37. Can a query message have one question section but the corresponding response message have several answer sections?

CHAPTER 26

Electronic Mail (SMTP) and File Transfer (FTP)

There are two popular applications for exchanging information. Electronic mail exchanges information between people; file transfer exchanges files between computers. In this chapter, we discuss these applications.

26.1 ELECTRONIC MAIL

One of the most popular network services is electronic mail (email). Electronic mail is used for sending a single message that includes text, voice, video, or graphics to one or more recipients. **Simple Mail Transfer Protocol (SMTP)** is the standard mechanism for electronic mail in the Internet.

Sending Mail

To send mail, the user creates mail that looks very similar to postal mail. It has an **envelope** and a **message** (see Fig. 26.1).

Figure 26.1 *Format of an email*

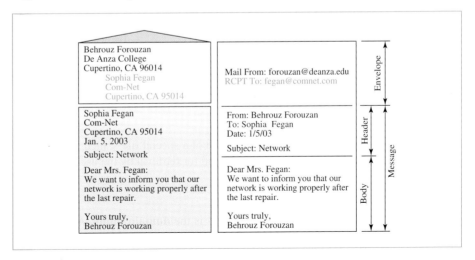

Envelope

The envelope usually contains the sender address, the receiver address, and other information.

Message

The message contains the *headers* and the *body*. The **headers** of the message define the sender, the receiver, the subject of the message, and other information. The body of the message contains the actual information to be read by the recipient.

Receiving Mail

The email system periodically checks the mailboxes. If a user has mail, it informs the user with a notice. If the user is ready to read the mail, a list is displayed in which each line contains a summary of the information about a particular message in the mailbox. The summary usually includes the sender mail address, the subject, and the time the mail was sent or received. The user can select any of the messages and display its contents on the screen.

Addresses

To deliver mail, a mail handling system must use an addressing system with unique addresses. The addressing system used by SMTP consists of two parts: a *local part* and a *domain name,* separated by an @ sign (see Fig. 26.2).

Figure 26.2 *Email address*

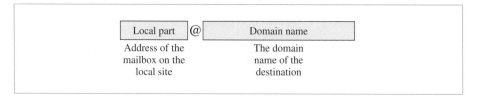

Local Part

The local part defines the name of a special file, called the user mailbox, where all the mail received for a user is stored for retrieval by the user agent.

Domain Name

The second part of the address is the **domain name.** An organization usually selects one or more hosts to receive and send email; they are sometimes called *mail exchangers.* The domain name assigned to each mail exchanger either comes from the DNS database or is a logical name (e.g., the name of the organization).

User Agent (UA)

The first component of an electronic mail system is the **user agent (UA).** A user agent sometimes is called a *mail reader,* but the terminology is confusing; we prefer to use the term *user agent* instead.

Services Provided by a User Agent

A user agent is a software package (program) that composes, reads, replies to, and forwards messages. It also handles mailboxes. Figure 26.3 shows the services of a typical user agent.

Figure 26.3   *User agent*

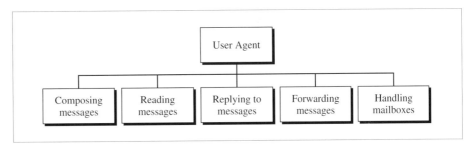

Composing Messages   A user agent is responsible for composing the email message to be sent out. Most user agents provide a template on the screen to be filled in by the user. Some even have a built-in editor that can do spell checking, grammer checking, and other tasks one expects from a sophisticated word processor. A user, of course, can use her or his favorite text editor or word processor to create the message and import it, or cut and paste, into the user agent.

Reading Messages   The second duty of the user agent is to read the incoming messages. When a user invokes a user agent, it first checks the mail in the incoming mailbox. Most user agents show a one-line summary of each received mail which contain the following fields.

1. A number field.
2. A flag field that shows if the mail is new, already read but not replied to, read and replied to, and so on.
3. The size of the message.
4. The sender.
5. The subject field if the subject line in the message is not empty.

Replying to Messages   After reading a message, a user can use the user agent to reply to a message. Normally, a user agent allows the user to reply to the original sender or to reply to all recipients of the message. The reply message normally contains the original message (for quick reference) and the new message.

Forwarding Messages   Replying is defined as sending a message to the sender or recipients of the copy. Forwarding means to send the message to a third party. A user agent allows the receiver to forward the message, with or without extra comments, to a third party.

Handling Mailboxes   A user agent normally creates two mailboxes: inbox and outbox. Each box is a file with special format that can be handled by the user agent. The inbox keeps all the received emails until they are deleted by the user. The outbox keeps all the sent emails until the user deletes them.

User Agent Types

There are two types of user agents: command-driven and GUI-based.

Command-Driven   Command-driven user agents belong to the early days of electronic mail. They are still present as the underlying user agents in servers. A command-driven user agent normally accepts a one-character command from the keyboard to perform its task. For example, a user can type the character r, at the command prompt, to reply to the sender of the message, or type the character R to reply to the sender and all recipients. Some examples of command-driven user agents are *mail, pine,* and *elm.*

Some examples of command-driven user agents are *mail, pine,* and *elm.*

GUI-Based   Modern user agents are GUI-based. They contain graphical user interface (GUI) components that allow the user to interact with the software by using both the keyboard and the mouse. They have graphical components such as icons, menu bars, and windows that make the services easy to access. Some examples of GUI-based user agents are Eudora, Microsoft's Outlook, and Netscape.

Some examples of GUI-based user agents are *Eudora, Outlook,* and *Netscape.*

Multipurpose Internet Mail Extensions (MIME)

SMTP is a simple mail transfer protocol. Its simplicity, however, comes with a price. SMTP can send messages only in 7-bit ASCII format. In other words, it has some limitations. For example, it cannot be used for languages that are not supported by 7-bit ASCII characters (such as French, German, Hebrew, Russian, Chinese, and Japanese). Also, it cannot be used to send binary files (files that store data as a stream of 0s and 1s without using any character code), video, or audio.

Multipurpose Internet Mail Extensions (MIME) is a supplementary protocol that allows non-ASCII data to be sent through SMTP. MIME is not a mail protocol and cannot replace SMTP; it is only an extension to SMTP.

MIME transforms non-ASCII data at the sender site to ASCII data and delivers them to the client SMTP to be sent through the Internet. The server SMTP at the receiving side receives the ASCII data and delivers them to MIME to be transformed to the original data.

We can think of MIME as a set of software functions that transform non-ASCII data to ASCII data and vice versa (see Fig. 26.4).

Figure 26.4 *MIME*

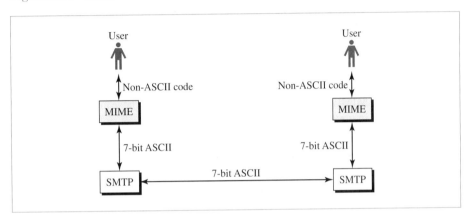

MIME defines five headers that can be added to the original SMTP header section to define the transformation parameters:

1. MIME-Version
2. Content-Type
3. Content-Transfer-Encoding
4. Content-Id
5. Content-Description

Figure 26.5 shows the original header and the extended header. We will describe each header in detail.

Figure 26.5 *MIME header*

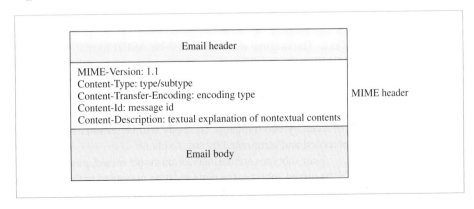

MIME-Version

This header defines the version of MIME used. The current version is 1.1.

MIME-Version: `1.1`

Content-Type

This header defines the type of data used in the body of the message. The content type and the content subtype are separated by a slash. Depending on the subtype, the header may contain other parameters.

Content-Type: `<type / subtype; parameters>`

MIME allows seven different types of data. These are listed in Table 26.1 and described in greater detail below.

Table 26.1 *Data types and subtypes in MIME*

Type	Subtype	Description
Text	Plain	Unformatted text
Multipart	Mixed	Body contains ordered parts of different data types
	Parallel	Same as above, but no order
	Digest	Similar to mixed, but the default is message/RFC822
	Alternative	Parts are different versions of the same message
Message	RFC822	Body is an encapsulated message
	Partial	Body is a fragment of a bigger message
	External-body	Body is a reference to another message
Image	JPEG	Image is in JPEG format
	GIF	Image is in GIF
Video	MPEG	Video is in MPEG format
Audio	Basic	Single-channel encoding of voice at 8 KHz
Application	PostScript	Adobe PostScript
	Octet-stream	General binary data (8-bit bytes)

- **Text.** The original message is in 7-bit ASCII format, and no transformation by MIME is needed. There is only one subtype currently used, *plain*.
- **Multipart.** The body contains multiple, independent parts. The multipart header needs to define the boundary between each part. The boundary is used as a parameter. It is a string token that is repeated before each part on a separate line by itself and preceded by two hyphens. The body will be terminated using the boundary token preceded and terminated by two hyphens.

  Four subtypes are defined for this type: *mixed, parallel, digest,* and *alternative*. In the mixed subtype, the parts must be presented to the recipient in the exact order as in the message. Each part has a different type and is defined at the boundary. The parallel subtype is similar to the mixed subtype, except that the order of the parts is unimportant. The digest subtype is also similar to the mixed subtype except that the default type/subtype is message/RFC822 as defined below. In the alternative subtype, the same message is repeated using different formats. The following is an example of a multipart message using a mixed subtype:

```
Content-Type: multipart/mixed; boundary=xxxx

    --xxxx
    Content-Type: text/plain;
    ...........................................
    --xxxx
    Content-Type: image/gif;
    ...........................................
    --xxxx--
```

■ **Message.** In the message type, the body is itself a whole mail message, a part of a mail message, or a pointer to a message. Three subtypes are currently used: *RFC822, partial,* or *external-body.* The subtype RFC822 is used if the body is encapsulating another message (including header and the body). The subtype partial is used if the original message has been fragmented into different mail messages and this mail message is one of the fragments. The fragments must be reassembled at the destination by MIME. Three parameters must be added: *id, number,* and the *total.* The id identifies the message and is present in all the fragments. The number defines the sequence order of the fragment. The total defines the number of fragments that comprise the original message. The following is an example of a message with three fragments:

```
Content-Type: message/partial;
id="forouzan@challenger.atc.fhda.edu";
number=1;
total=3;


.......................
.......................
```

The external-body subtype indicates that the body does not contain the actual message but is only a reference (pointer) to the original message. The parameters following the subtype define how to access the original message. The following is an example:

```
Content-Type: message/external-body;
name="report.txt";
site="fhda.edu";
access-type="ftp";


.......................
.......................
```

- **Image.** The original message is a stationary image, indicating that there is no animation. The two currently used subtypes are Joint Photographic Experts Group *(JPEG),* which uses image compression, and Graphics Interchange Format *(GIF).*
- **Video.** The original message is a time-varying image (animation). The only subtype is Motion Picture Experts Group *(MPEG).* If the animated image contains sounds, it must be sent separately using the audio content type.
- **Audio.** The original message is a sound. The only subtype is basic, which uses 8-KHz standard audio data.
- **Application.** The original message is a type of data not previously defined. There are only two subtypes used currently: *octet-stream* and *PostScript.* Octet-stream is used when the data must be interpreted as a sequence of 8-bit bytes (binary file). PostScript is used when the data are in Adobe PostScript format.

Content-Transfer-Encoding

This header defines the method to encode the messages into 0s and 1s for transport:

```
Content-Transfer-Encoding:   <type>
```

The five types of encoding are listed in Table 26.2.

Table 26.2   *Content-transfer encoding*

Type	Description
7bit	ASCII characters and short lines
8bit	Non-ASCII characters and short lines
Binary	Non-ASCII characters with unlimited-length lines
Base64	6-bit blocks of data are encoded into 8-bit ASCII characters
Quoted-printable	Non-ASCII characters are encoded as an equal sign followed by an ASCII code

- **7bit.** This is 7-bit ASCII encoding. Although no special transformation is needed, the length of the line should not exceed 1000 characters.
- **8bit.** This is 8-bit encoding. Non-ASCII characters can be sent, but the length of the line still should not exceed 1000 characters. MIME does not do any encoding here; the underlying SMTP must be able to transfer 8-bit non-ASCII characters. It is, therefore, not recommended. Base64 and quoted-printable types are preferable.
- **Binary.** This is 8-bit encoding. Non-ASCII characters can be sent, and the length of the line can exceed 1000 characters. MIME does not do any encoding here; the underlying SMTP must be able to transfer binary data. It is, therefore, not recommended. Base64 and quoted-printable types are preferable.
- **Base64.** This is a solution for sending data made of bytes when the highest bit is not necessarily zero. Base64 transforms this type of data to printable characters, which can then be sent as ASCII characters or any type of character set supported by the underlying mail transfer mechanism.

Base64 divides the binary data (made of streams of bits) into 24-bit blocks. Each block is then divided into four sections, each made of 6 bits (see Fig. 26.6).

Figure 26.6   *Base64*

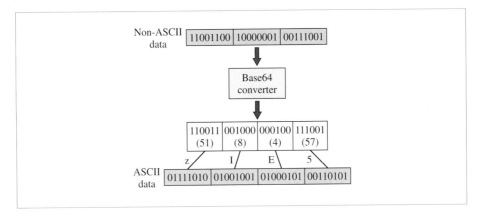

Each 6-bit section is interpreted as one character according to Table 26.3.

Table 26.3   *Base64 encoding table*

Value	Code	Value	Code	Value	Code	Value	Code	Value	Code	Value	Code
0	A	11	L	22	W	33	h	44	s	55	3
1	B	12	M	23	X	34	i	45	t	56	4
2	C	13	N	24	Y	35	j	46	u	57	5
3	D	14	O	25	Z	36	k	47	v	58	6
4	E	15	P	26	a	37	l	48	w	59	7
5	F	16	Q	27	b	38	m	49	x	60	8
6	G	17	R	28	c	39	n	50	y	61	9
7	H	18	S	29	d	40	o	51	z	62	+
8	I	19	T	30	e	41	p	52	0	63	/
9	J	20	U	31	f	42	q	53	1		
10	K	21	V	32	g	43	r	54	2		

■ **Quoted-printable.** Base64 is a redundant encoding scheme; that is, 24 bits becomes four characters and eventually is sent as 32 bits. We have an overhead of 33.3 percent. If the data consist mostly of ASCII characters with a small non-ASCII portion, we can use quoted-printable encoding. If a character is ASCII, it is sent as is. If a character is not ASCII, it is sent as three characters. The first character is the equals sign (=). The next two characters are the hexadecimal representation of the byte. Figure 26.7 shows an example.

Figure 26.7 *Quoted-printable*

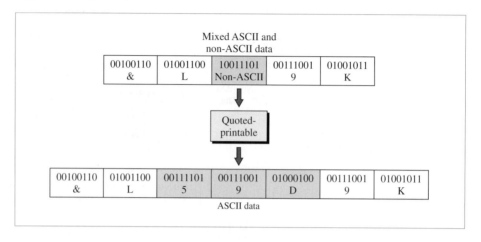

Content-Id

This header uniquely identifies the whole message in a multiple-message environment.

```
Content-Id: id=<content-id>
```

Content-Description

This header defines whether the body is image, audio, or video.

```
Content-Description:  <description>
```

Mail Transfer Agent (MTA)

The actual mail transfer is done through **mail transfer agents (MTAs).** To send mail, a system must have a client MTA; and to receive mail, a system must have a server MTA.

In the Internet, message transfer is done through a protocol (and software) named Simple Mail Transfer Protocol (SMTP). To send a message, we need a client SMTP and a server SMTP. In Figure 26.8 we show Alice sending an email to Bob with the SMTP clients and servers needed.

Note that mail transfer occurs between the two mail servers, one at Alice's site and the other at Bob's site. The mail servers can belong to the ISPs to which Alice and Bob are subscribers, or they can belong to the companies where Alice and Bob work.

Commands and Responses

SMTP uses commands and responses to transfer messages between an MTA client and an MTA server (see Fig. 26.9). Each command or reply is terminated by a two-character (carriage return and line feed) end-of-line token.

Figure 26.8 *MTA client and server*

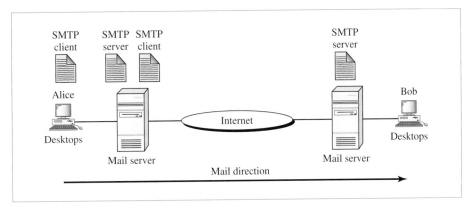

Figure 26.9 *Commands and responses*

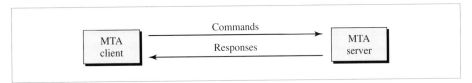

Commands   Commands are sent from the client to the server. A command consists of a keyword followed by zero or more arguments. SMTP defines 14 commands.

Responses   Responses are sent from the server to the client. A response is a three-digit code that may be followed by additional textual information.

Mail Transfer Phases

The process of transferring a mail message occurs in three phases: connection establishment, message transfer, and connection termination.

Connection Establishment   After a client has made a TCP connection to the well-known port 25, the SMTP server starts the connection phase.

Message Transfer   After connection has been established between the SMTP client and server, a single message between a sender and one or more recipients can be exchanged.

Connection Termination   After the message is transferred successfully, the client terminates the connection.

Mail Delivery

The delivery of email from the sender to the receiver consists of three stages (see Fig. 26.10).

Figure 26.10   *Email delivery*

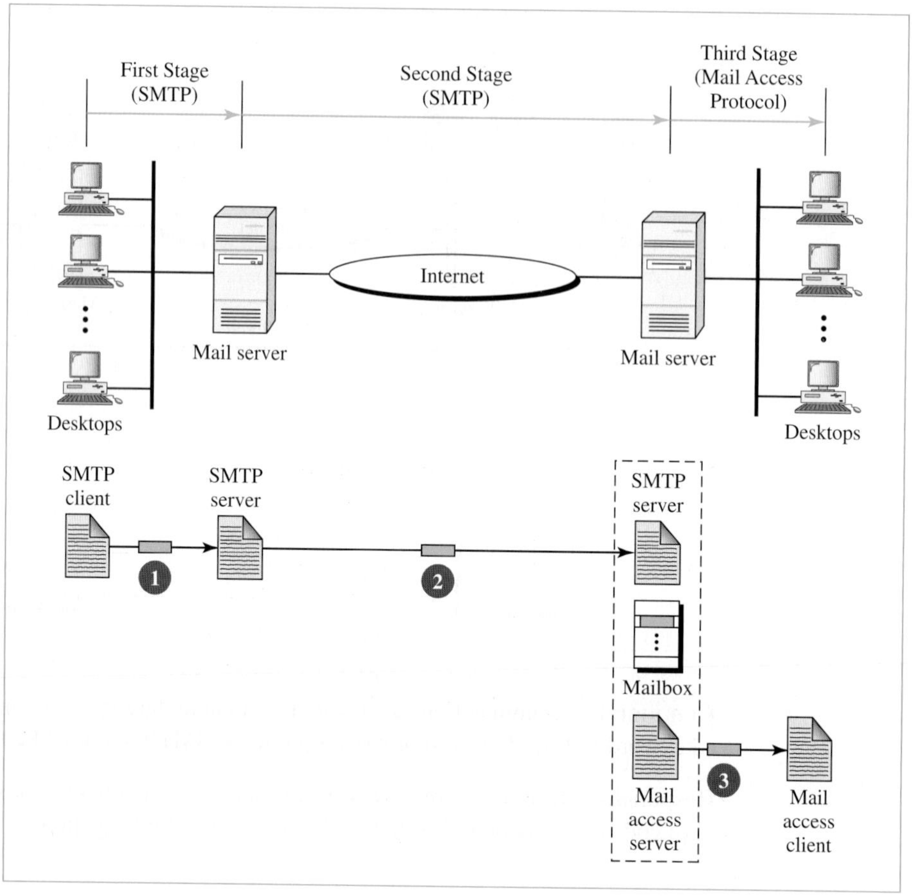

First Stage

In the first stage, the email goes from the user agent to the local server. The mail does not go directly to the remote server because the remote server may not be available at all times. Therefore, the mail is stored in the local server until it can be sent. The user agent uses SMTP client software, and the local server uses SMTP server software.

Second Stage

In the second stage, the email is relayed by the local server, which now acts as the SMTP client, to the remote server, which is the SMTP server in this stage. The email is delivered to the remote server, not to the remote user agent. The reason is that SMTP messages must be received by a server that is always running since mail can arrive at any time. However, people often turn off their computers at the end of the day, and those with laptops or mobile computers do not normally have them on all the time. So usually an organization (or an ISP) assigns a computer to be the email server and run the SMTP server program. The email is received by this mail server and stored in the mailbox of the user for later retrieval.

Third Stage

In the third stage, the remote user agent uses a mail access protocol such as POP3 or IMAP4 (both discussed in the next section) to access the mailbox and obtain the mail.

Mail Access Protocols

The first and the second stages of mail delivery use SMTP. However, SMTP is not involved in the third stage because SMTP is a *push* protocol; it pushes the message from the sender to the receiver even if the receiver does not want it. The operation of SMTP starts with the sender, not the receiver. On the other hand, the third stage needs a *pull* protocol; the operation must start with the recipient. The mail must stay in the mail server mailbox until the recipient retrieves it. The third stage uses a **mail access protocol.**

Currently two mail access protocols are available: Post Office Protocol, version 3 (POP3) and Internet Mail Access Protocol, version 4 (IMAP4).

POP3

Post Office Protocol, version 3 (POP3) is simple, but it is limited in functionality. The client POP3 software is installed on the recipient computer; the server POP3 software is installed on the mail server.

Mail access starts with the client when the user needs to download email from the mailbox on the mail server. The client (user agent) opens a connection with the server on TCP port 110. It then sends its user name and password to access the mailbox. The user can then list and retrieve the mail messages, one by one. Figure 26.11 shows an example of downloading using POP3.

Figure 26.11 *POP3*

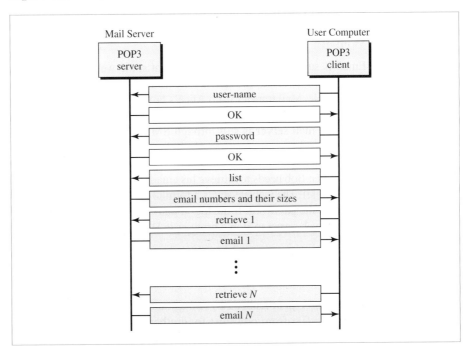

POP3 has two modes: the delete mode and the keep mode. In the delete mode, the mail is deleted from the mailbox after each retrieval. In the keep mode, the mail remains in the mailbox after retrieval. The delete mode is normally used when the user is working at his or her permanent computer and can save and organize the received mail after reading or replying. The keep mode is normally used when the user accesses mail away from the primary computer (e.g., a laptop). The mail is read but kept in the system for later retrieval and organizing.

IMAP4

POP3 assumes that each time a client accesses the server, the whole mailbox will be cleared out (transferred). This is not convenient when people access their mailboxes from different clients (at home, at work, on a trip, at a hotel, etc.).

POP3 is deficient in several ways. It does not allow the user to organize mail on the server; the user cannot have different folders on the server. (Of course, the user can create folders on her or his own computer.) In addition, POP3 does not allow the user to partially check the contents of the mail before downloading.

Another mail access protocol, **Internet Mail Access Protocol version 4 (IMAP4),** is similar to POP3, but has more features. IMAP4 is more powerful and more complex.

IMAP4 provides the following extra functions:

- A user can check the email header prior to downloading.
- A user can search the contents of the email for a specific string of characters prior to downloading.
- A user can partially download email. This is especially useful if bandwidth is limited and the email contains multimedia with high bandwidth requirements.
- A user can create, delete, or rename mailboxes on the mail server.
- A user can create a hierarchy of mailboxes in a folder for email storage.

Web-Based Mail

Email is such a common application that some websites today provide this service to anyone who accesses the site. Two common sites are Hotmail and Yahoo. The idea is very simple. Mail transfer from Alice's browser to her mail server is done through HTTP (see Chapter 27). The transfer of the message from the sending mail server to the receiving mail server is still through SMTP. Finally, the message from the receiving server (the web server) to Bob's browser is done through HTTP.

The last phase is very interesting. Instead of POP3 or IMAP4, HTTP is normally used. When Bob needs to retrieve his emails, he sends a message to the website (Hotmail, for example). The website sends a form to be filled in by Bob, which includes the log-in name and the password. If the log-in name and password match, the email is transferred from the web server to Bob's browser in HTML format.

26.2   FILE TRANSFER

File transfer protocol (FTP) is the standard mechanism provided by the Internet for copying a file from one host to another. Transferring files from one computer to another is one of the most common tasks expected from a networking or internetworking environment.

Although transferring files from one system to another seems simple and straightforward, some problems must be dealt with first. For example, two systems may use different file name conventions. Two systems may have different ways to represent text and data. Two systems may have different directory structures. All these problems have been solved by FTP in a very simple and elegant approach.

FTP differs from other client-server applications in that it establishes two connections between the client and the server. One connection is used for data transfer, the other for control information (commands and responses). Separation of commands and data transfer makes FTP more efficient. The control connection uses very simple rules of communication. We need to transfer only one line of command or a line of response at a time. The data connection, on the other hand, needs more complex rules due to the variety of data types transferred.

FTP uses two well-known TCP ports: Port 21 is used for the control connection, and port 20 is used for the data connection.

FTP uses the services of TCP. It needs two TCP connections. The well-known port 21 is used for the control connection, and the well-known port 20 is used for the data connection.

Figure 26.12 shows the basic model of FTP. The client has three components: user interface, client control process, and the client data transfer process. The server has two components: the server control process and the server data transfer process. The control connection is made between the control processes. The data connection is made between the data transfer processes.

Figure 26.12 *FTP*

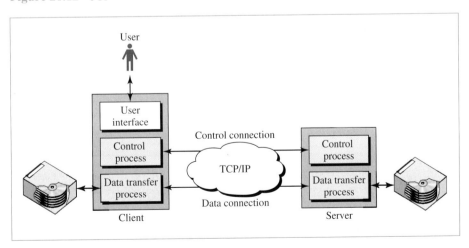

The control connection is maintained during the entire interactive FTP session. The data connection is opened and then closed for each file transferred. It opens each time commands that involve transferring files are used, and it closes when the file is transferred. In other words, when a user starts an FTP session, the control connection opens. While the control connection is open, the data connection can be opened and closed multiple times if several files are transferred.

Connections

The two FTP connections, control and data, use different strategies and different port numbers.

Control Connection

The **control connection** is created in the same way as other application programs described so far. The connection remains open during the entire process. The service type used by the IP is *minimize delay,* because this is an interactive connection between a user (human) and a server. The user types commands and expects to receive responses without significant delay.

Data Connection

The **data connection** uses the well-known port 20 at the server site. The data connection is opened when data are ready to transfer. It is closed when it is not needed. A data connection may be opened and closed several times during a session; the control connection is opened and closed once. The service type used by IP is *maximize throughput.*

Communication

The FTP client and server, which run on different computers, must communicate with each other. These two computers may use different operating systems, different character sets, different file structures, and different file formats. FTP must make this heterogeneity compatible.

FTP has two different approaches, one for the control connection and the other for the data connection. We will study each approach separately.

Communication over Control Connection

FTP uses the same approach as SMTP to communicate across the control connection. It uses the ASCII character set (see Fig. 26.13). Communication is achieved through

Figure 26.13   *Using the control connection*

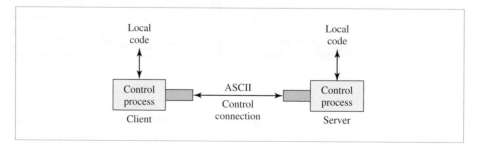

commands and responses. This simple method is adequate for the control connection because we send one command (response) at a time. Each command or response is only one short line, so we need not worry about file format or file structure. Each line is terminated with a two-character (carriage return and line feed) end-of-line token.

Communication over Data Connection

The purpose and implementation of the data connection are different from those of the control connection. We want to transfer files through the data connection. The client must define the type of file to be transferred, the structure of the data, and the transmission mode. Before sending the file through the data connection, we prepare for transmission through the control connection. The heterogeneity problem is solved by defining three attributes of communication: file type, data structure, and transmission mode (see Fig. 26.14).

Figure 26.14   *Using the data connection*

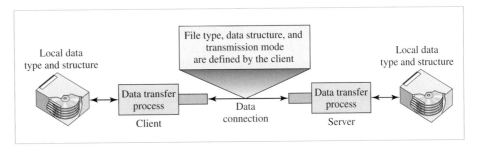

File Type   FTP can transfer one of the following file types across the data connection:

- **ASCII file.** This is the default format for transferring text files. Each character is encoded using ASCII. The sender transforms the file from its own representation to ASCII characters, and the receiver transforms the ASCII characters to its own representation.
- **EBCDIC file.** If one or both ends of the connection use EBCDIC encoding (used in IBM computers) the file can be transferred using EBCDIC encoding.
- **Image file.** This is the default format for transferring binary files. The file is sent as continuous streams of bits without any interpretation or encoding. This is mostly used to transfer binary files such as compiled programs or images encoded as 0s and 1s.

If the file is encoded in ASCII or EBCDIC, another attribute must be added to define the printability of the file.

1. **Nonprint.** This is the default format for transferring a text file. The file contains no vertical specifications for printing. This means that the file cannot be printed without further processing because there are no characters to be interpreted for vertical movement of the print head. This format is used for files that will be stored and processed later.

2. **TELNET.** In this format the file contains ASCII vertical characters such as CR (carriage return), LF (line feed), NL (new line), and VT (vertical tab). The file is printable after transfer.

Data Structure FTP can transfer a file across the data connection by using one of the following interpretations about the structure of the data:

- **File structure (default).** The file has no structure. It is a continuous stream of bytes.
- **Record structure.** The file is divided into records (or structs in C). This can be used only with text files.
- **Page structure.** The file is divided into pages, with each page having a page number and a page header. The pages can be stored or accessed randomly or sequentially.

Transmission Mode FTP can transfer a file across the data connection by using one of the following three transmission modes:

- **Stream mode.** This is the default mode. Data are delivered from FTP to TCP as a continuous stream of bytes. TCP is responsible for chopping data into segments of appropriate size. If the data are simply a stream of bytes (file structure), no end-of-file is needed. End-of-file in this case is the closing of the data connection by the sender. If the data are divided into records (record structure), each record will have a 1-byte end-of-record (EOR) character, and the end of the file will have a 1-byte end-of-file (EOF) character.
- **Block mode.** Data can be delivered from FTP to TCP in blocks. In this case, each block is preceded by a 3-byte header. The first byte is called the *block descriptor;* the next 2 bytes defines the size of the block in bytes.
- **Compressed mode.** If the file is big, the data can be compressed. The compression method normally used is run-length encoding. In this method, consecutive appearances of a data unit are replaced by one occurrence and the number of repetitions. In a text file, this is usually spaces (blanks). In a binary file, null characters are usually compressed.

File Transfer

File transfer occurs over the data connection under the control of the commands sent over the control connection. However, remember that file transfer in FTP means one of three things (see Fig. 26.15).

Figure 26.15 *File transfer*

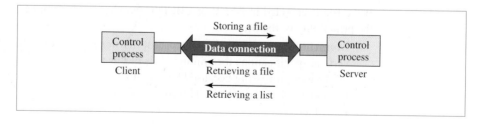

- A file is to be copied from the server to the client. This is called *retrieving a file*.
- A file is to be copied from the client to the server. This is called *storing a file*.
- A list of directory or file names is to be sent from the server to the client. Note that FTP treats a list of directory or file names as a file. It is sent over the data connection.

Example 1

Figure 26.16 shows an example of how a file is stored.

Figure 26.16   *Example 1*

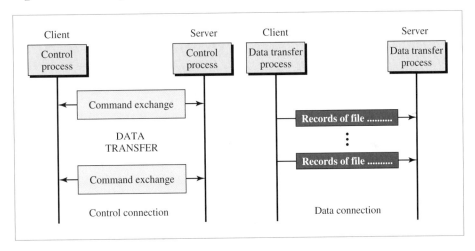

1. The control connection is created, and several control commands and responses are exchanged.
2. Data are transferred record by record.
3. A few commands and responses are exchanged to close the connection.

User Interface

Most operating systems provide a user interface to access the services of FTP. The interface prompts the user for the appropriate input. After the user types a line, the FTP interface reads the line and changes it to the corresponding FTP command. Table 26.4 shows the interface commands provided in UNIX FTP. Some of the commands can be abbreviated as long as there is no ambiguity.

Table 26.4   *List of FTP commands in UNIX*

Commands
!, $, account, append, ascii, bell, binary, bye, case, cd, cdup, close, cr, delete, debug, dir, discount, form, get, glob, hash, help, lcd, ls, macdef, mdelete, mdir, mget, mkdir, mls, mode, mput, nmap, ntrans, open, prompt, proxy, sendport, put, pwd, quit, quote, recv, remotehelp, rename, reset, rmdir, runique, send, status, struct, sunique, tenex, trace, type, user, verbose,?

Example 2

We show some of the user interface commands that accomplish the same task as in Example 1. The user input is shown in boldface. As shown below, some of the commands are provided automatically by the interface. The user receives a prompt and provides only the arguments.

```
$ ftp challenger.atc.fhda.edu
Connected to challenger.atc.fhda.edu
220 Server ready
Name: forouzan
Password: xxxxxxx
ftp > ls /usr/user/report
200 OK
150 Opening ASCII mode
. . . . . . . . . . .
. . . . . . . . . .
226 transfer complete
ftp > close
221 Goodbye
ftp > quit
```

Anonymous FTP

To use FTP, a user needs an account (user name) and a password on the remote server. Some sites have a set of files available for public access. To access these files, a user does not need to have an account or password. Instead, the user can use *anonymous* as the user name and *guest* as the password.

User access to the system is very limited. Some sites allow anonymous users only a subset of commands. For example, most sites allow the user to copy some files, but do not allow navigation through the directories.

Example 3

We show an example of using anonymous FTP. We connect to *internic.net,* where we assume there are some public data available.

```
$ ftp internic.net
Connected to internic.net
220 Server ready
Name: anonymous
331 Guest login OK, send "guest" as password
Password: guest
ftp > pwd
257 '/' is current directory
ftp > ls
200 OK
150 Opening ASCII mode
```

```
  bin
  ...
  ftp > close
  221 Goodbye
  ftp > quit
```

26.3   KEY TERMS

anonymous FTP
ASCII file
control connection
data connection
domain name
EBCDIC file
envelope
File Transfer Protocol (FTP)
header
image file

Internet Mail Access Protocol, version 4
   (IMAP4)
mail transfer agent (MTA)
message
Multipurpose Internet Mail Extensions
   (MIME)
Post Office Protocol, version 3 (POP3)
Simple Mail Transfer Protocol (SMTP)
user agent (UA)

26.4   SUMMARY

- ❑ The protocol that supports email on the Internet is called Simple Mail Transfer Protocol (SMTP).
- ❑ The UA prepares the message, creates the envelope, and puts the message in the envelope.
- ❑ The email address consists of two parts: a local address (user mailbox) and a domain name. The form is *localname@domainname*.
- ❑ The MTA transfers the email across the Internet.
- ❑ SMTP uses commands and responses to transfer messages between an MTA client and an MTA server.
- ❑ The steps in transferring a mail message are connection establishment, message transfer, and connection termination.
- ❑ Multipurpose Internet Mail Extension (MIME) is an extension of SMTP that allows the transfer of multimedia and other non-ASCII messages.
- ❑ Post Office Protocol, version 3 (POP3) and Internet Mail Access Protocol, version 4 (IMAP4) are protocols used by a mail server in conjunction with SMTP to receive and hold email for hosts.
- ❑ File transfer protocol (FTP) is a TCP/IP client-server application for copying files from one host to another.
- ❑ FTP requires two connections for data transfer: a control connection and a data connection.
- ❑ FTP employs ASCII for communication between dissimilar systems.

❏ Prior to the actual transfer of files, the file type, data structure, and transmission mode are defined by the client through the control connection.

❏ Responses are sent from the server to the client during connection establishment.

❏ There are three types of file transfer:

    a. A file is copied from the server to the client.

    b. A file is copied from the client to the server.

    c. A list of directories or file names is sent from the server to the client.

❏ Most operating systems provide a user-friendly interface between FTP and the user.

❏ Anonymous FTP provides a method for the general public to access files on remote sites.

26.5   PRACTICE SET

Review Questions

1. What is the name of the protocol used for electronic mail over the Internet?
2. What are the two main parts of an email?
3. Describe the addressing system used by SMTP.
4. What is a user agent?
5. What are the two types of user agents?
6. What is MIME?
7. What are the three mail transfer phases?
8. Name two mail access protocols.
9. What is the purpose of FTP?
10. Describe the functions of the two FTP connections.
11. What kinds of file types can FTP transfer?
12. What are the three FTP transmission modes?
13. How does storing a file differ from retrieving a file?
14. What is anonymous FTP?

Multiple-Choice Questions

15. The purpose of the UA is _____.

    a. Message preparation

    b. Envelope creation

    c. Transferral of messages across the Internet

    d. (a) and (b)

16. The purpose of the MTA is _____.

    a. Message preparation

    b. Envelope creation

    c. Transferral of messages across the Internet

    d. (a) and (b)

17. Which part of the mail created by the UA contains the sender and receiver names?
    a. Envelope
    b. Address
    c. Header
    d. Body
18. In the email address mackenzie@pit.arc.nasa.gov, what is the domain name?
    a. mackenzie
    b. pit.arc.nasa.gov
    c. mackenzie@pit.arc.nasa.gov
    d. (a) and (b)
19. The _____ field in the MIME header is the type of data and the body of the message.
    a. Content-type
    b. Content-transfer-encoding
    c. Content-Id
    d. Content-description
20. The _____ field in the MIME header uses text to describe the data in the body of the message.
    a. Content-type
    b. Content-transfer-encoding
    c. Content-Id
    d. Content-description
21. The _____ field in the MIME header describes the method used to encode the data.
    a. Content-type
    b. Content-transfer-encoding
    c. Content-Id
    d. Content-description
22. The _____ field in the MIME header has type and subtype subfields.
    a. Content-type
    b. Content-transfer-encoding
    c. Content-Id
    d. Content-description
23. A JPEG image is sent as email. What is the content-type?
    a. Multipart/mixed
    b. Multipart/image
    c. Image/JPEG
    d. Image/basic
24. An email contains a textual birthday greeting, a picture of a cake, and a song. The text must precede the image. What is the content-type?
    a. Multipart/mixed
    b. Multipart/parallel
    c. Multipart/digest
    d. Multipart/alternative

25. An email contains a textual birthday greeting, a picture of a cake, and a song. The order is not important. What is the content-type?
    a. Multipart/mixed
    b. Multipart/parallel
    c. Multipart/digest
    d. Multipart/alternative

26. A message is fragmented into three email messages. What is the content-type?
    a. Multipart/mixed
    b. Message/RFC822
    c. Message/partial
    d. Multipart/partial

27. A client machine usually needs _____ to send email.
    a. Only SMTP
    b. Only POP
    c. Both SMTP and POP
    d. None of the above

28. Which of the following is true?
    a. FTP allows systems with different directory structures to transfer files.
    b. FTP allows a system using ASCII and a system using EBCDIC to transfer files.
    c. FTP allows a PC and a SUN workstation to transfer files.
    d. All the above are true.

29. During an FTP session the control connection is opened _____.
    a. Exactly once
    b. Exactly twice
    c. As many times as necessary
    d. All the above

30. During an FTP session the data connection is opened _____.
    a. Exactly once
    b. Exactly twice
    c. As many times as necessary
    d. All the above

31. In FTP, what attributes must be defined by the client prior to transmission?
    a. Data type
    b. File structure
    c. Transmission mode
    d. All the above

32. In FTP, there are three types of _____: stream, block, and compressed.
    a. Files
    b. Data structures
    c. Transmission modes
    d. All the above

33. In FTP, ASCII, EBCDIC, and image define an attribute called _____.
    a. File type
    b. Data structure
    c. Transmission mode
    d. All the above
34. In FTP, when you _____, it is copied from the server to the client.
    a. Retrieve a file
    b. Store a file
    c. Retrieve a list
    d. (a) and (c)
35. In FTP, when you _____, it is copied from the client to the server.
    a. Retrieve a file
    b. Store a file
    c. Retrieve a list
    d. (a) and (c)
36. In anonymous FTP, the user can usually _____.
    a. Retrieve files
    b. Navigate through directories
    c. Store files
    d. Do all the above

Exercises

37. Convert the following bit stream into ASCII characters using the Base64 conversion method:
    11001110   11110000   11101111
38. Convert the following bit stream into ASCII characters using the quoted-printable conversion method:
    11001110   11110000   11101111
39. Why do you think there is a need for two connections in FTP, but only one for SMTP?
40. Why there is a need for an access protocol in SMTP, but not in FTP?
41. Why do we need conversion methods such as Base64 or quoted-printable in SMTP, but not in FTP?
42. What type of quality of service (QoS) is the most important in SMTP (minimum delay, maximum throughput, reliability)? Which one is less important?
43. Do you think SMTP is a suitable protocol for transferring stored audio and video?
44. Do you think SMTP is a suitable protocol for transferring live audio and video?
45. What do you think would happen if the control connection were accidentally severed during an FTP transfer?
46. Why should there be limitations on anonymous FTP? What could an unscrupulous user do?
47. Explain why FTP does not have a message format.

CHAPTER 27

HTTP and WWW

The World Wide Web (WWW) has changed the way we live. The public has become aware of the power of the Internet through WWW. In this chapter, we first discuss HTTP, a file transfer protocol specifically designed to facilitate access to the WWW. We then discuss the WWW itself.

27.1 HTTP

The **Hypertext Transfer Protocol (HTTP)** is used mainly to access data on the World Wide Web. The protocol transfers data in the form of plain text, hypertext, audio, video, and so on. It is called the Hypertext Transfer Protocol because it is used in an environment where there are rapid jumps from one document to another.

HTTP functions like a combination of FTP and SMTP. It is similar to FTP because it transfers files and uses the services of TCP. However, it is much simpler than FTP because it uses only one TCP connection (well-known port 80). There is no separate control connection; only data are transferred between the client and the server.

HTTP is like SMTP because the data transferred between the client and the server are similar to SMTP messages. In addition, the format of the messages is controlled by MIME-like headers. However, HTTP differs from SMTP in the way the messages are sent from the client to the server and from the server to the client. Unlike SMTP messages, the HTTP messages are not destined to be read by humans; they are read and interpreted by the HTTP server and HTTP client (browser). SMTP messages are stored and forwarded, but HTTP messages are delivered immediately.

The idea of HTTP is very simple. A client sends a request, which looks like mail, to the server. The server sends the response, which looks like a mail reply to the client. The request and response messages carry data in the form of a letter with a MIME-like format.

The commands from the client to the server are embedded in a letterlike request message. The contents of the requested file or other information are embedded in a letterlike response message.

HTTP uses the services of TCP on well-known port 80.

Transaction

Figure 27.1 illustrates the HTTP transaction between the client and server. Although HTTP uses the services of TCP, HTTP itself is a stateless protocol. The client initializes the transaction by sending a request message. The server replies by sending a response.

Figure 27.1   *HTTP transaction*

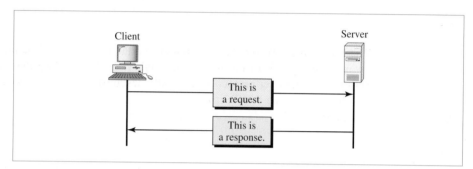

There are two general types of HTTP messages: request and response. Both message types follow almost the same format.

Request Messages

A request message consists of a request line, headers, and sometimes a body. See Figure 27.2.

Figure 27.2   *Request message*

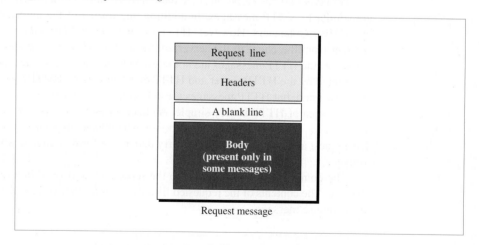

Request Line

The **request line** defines the request type, resource (URL), and HTTP version (see Fig. 27.3).

■ **Request type.** In version 1.1 of HTTP, several request types are defined. The request type categorizes the request messages into several methods, which we will discuss later.

Figure 27.3   *Request line*

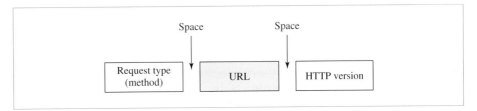

■ **Uniform Resource Locator (URL).** A client that wants to access a Web page needs an address. To facilitate the access of documents distributed throughout the world, HTTP uses the concept of uniform resource locators. The URL is a standard for specifying any kind of information on the Internet. The URL defines four things: method, host computer, port, and path (see Fig. 27.4).

Figure 27.4   *URL*

■ The *method* is the protocol used to retrieve the document. Several different protocols can retrieve a document; among them are FTP and HTTP. Note that this *method* is distinct from the request type *method*. The former is a protocol; the latter is a function.

■ The **host** is the computer where the information is located, although the name of the computer can be an alias. Web pages are usually stored in computers, and computers are given alias names that usually begin with the characters *www*. This is not mandatory, however, as the host can be any name given to the computer that hosts the Web page.

■ The URL can optionally contain the port number of the server. If the port is included, it is inserted between the host and the path, and it should be separated from the host by a colon.

■ **Path** is the path name of the file where the information is located. Note that the path can itself contain slashes that, in the UNIX operating system, separate the directories from the subdirectories and files.

■ **Version.** Although the most current version of HTTP is 1.1, HTTP versions 1.0 and 0.9 are still in use.

Methods

The request type field in a request message defines several kinds of messages referred to as *methods*. The request method is the actual command or request that a client issues to the server. We briefly discuss the purposes of some methods here.

GET   The GET method is used when the client wants to retrieve a document from the server. The address of the document is defined in the URL; this is the main method for retrieving a document. The server usually responds with the contents of the document in the body of the response message unless there is an error.

HEAD   The HEAD method is used when the client wants some information about a document but not the document itself. It is similar to GET, but the response from the server does not contain a body.

POST   The POST method is used by the client to provide some information to the server. For example, it can be used to send input to a server.

PUT   The PUT method is used by the client to provide a new or replacement document to be stored on the server. The document is included in the body of the request and stored in the location defined by the URL.

PATCH   PATCH is similar to PUT except that the request contains a list of differences that should be implemented in the existing file.

COPY   The COPY method copies a file to another location. The location of the source file is given in the request line (URL); the location of the destination is given in the entity header (discussed in the "Header" section).

MOVE   The MOVE method moves a file to another location. The location of the source file is given in the request line (URL); the location of the destination is given in the entity header.

DELETE   The DELETE method removes a document on the server.

LINK   The LINK method creates a link or links from a document to another location. The location of the file is given in the request line (URL); the location of the destination is given in the entity header.

UNLINK   The UNLINK method deletes links created by the LINK method.

OPTION   The OPTION method is used by the client to ask the server about available options.

Response Message

A response message consists of a status line, a header, and sometimes a body. See Figure 27.5.

Status Line

The **status line** defines the status of the response message. It consists of the HTTP version, a space, a status code, a space, and a status phrase. See Figure 27.6.

■ **HTTP version.** This field is the same as the corresponding field in the request line.

■ **Status code.** The status code field is similar to those in the FTP and the SMTP protocols. It consists of three digits.

■ **Status phrase.** This field explains the status code in text form.

Figure 27.5 *Response message*

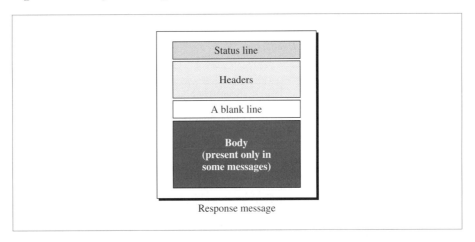

Response message

Figure 27.6 *Status line*

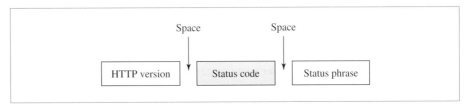

Headers

The headers exchange additional information between the client and the server. For example, the client can request that the document be sent in a special format, or the server can send extra information about the document.

The header can be one or more header lines. Each header line is made of a header name, a colon, a space, and a header value (see Fig. 27.7). We will show some header lines in the examples at the end of this section.

A header line belongs to one of four categories: general header, request header, response header, and entity header. A request message can contain only general, request, and entity headers. A response message, on the other hand, can contain only general,

Figure 27.7 *Header format*

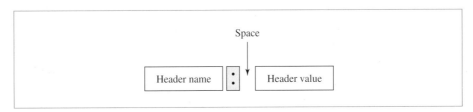

response, and entity headers. Figure 27.8 diagrams a request message and a response message.

Figure 27.8   *Headers*

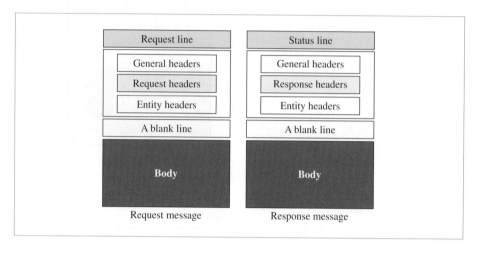

General Header

The **general header** gives general information about the message and can be present in both a request and a response.

Request Header

The **request header** can be present only in a request message. It specifies the client's configuration and the client's preferred document format.

Response Header

The **response header** can be present only in a response message. It specifies the server's configuration and special information about the request.

Entity Header

The **entity header** gives information about the body of the document. Although it is mostly present in response messages, some request messages, such as POST and PUT methods, that contain a body also use this type of header.

Some Examples

In this section we give two examples.

Example 1

This example retrieves a document. We use the GET method to retrieve an image with the path /usr/bin/image1. The request line shows the method (GET), the URL, and the HTTP version (1.1). The header has two lines that show that the client can accept images in GIF and JPEG format. The request does not have a body. The response message contains the status line and four lines of header. The header lines define the date, server, MIME version, and length of the document. The body of the document follows the header (see Fig. 27.9).

Figure 27.9 *Example 1*

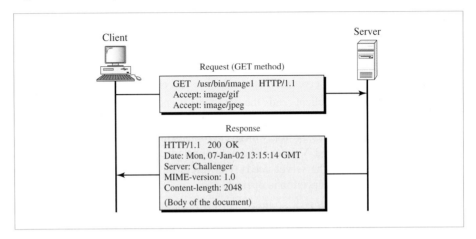

Example 2

This example retrieves information about a document. We use the HEAD method to retrieve information about an HTML document (see the next section). The request line shows the method (HEAD), URL, and HTTP version (1.1). The header is one line showing that the client can accept the document in any format (wild card). The request does not have a body. The response message contains the status line and five lines of header. The header lines define the date, server, MIME version, type of document, and length of the document (see Fig. 27.10). Note that the response message does not contain a body.

Figure 27.10 *Example 2*

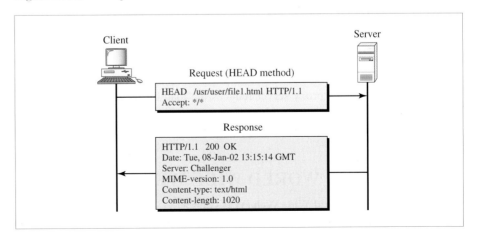

Some Other Features

In this section, we briefly discuss some other features of HTTP version 1.1.

Persistent versus Nonpersistent Connection

HTTP version 1.0 specified a nonpersistent connection, while a persistent connection is the default in version 1.1.

Nonpersistent Connection   In a **nonpersistent connection,** one TCP connection is made for each request/response. The following lists the steps in this strategy:

1. The client opens a TCP connection and sends a request.
2. The server sends the response and closes the connection.
3. The client reads the data until it encounters an end-of-file marker; the client then closes the connection.

In this strategy, for N different images in different files, the connection must be opened and closed N times. The nonpersistent strategy imposes high overhead on the server because the server needs N different buffers and requires a slow start procedure each time a connection is opened.

Persistent Connection   HTTP version 1.1 specifies a persistent connection by default. In a **persistent connection,** the server leaves the connection open for more requests after sending a response. The server can close the connection at the request of a client or if a timeout has been reached. The sender usually sends the length of the data with each response. However, there are some occasions when the sender does not know the length of the data. This is the case when a document is created dynamically or actively (see the next section). In these cases, the server informs the client that the length is not known and closes the connection after sending the data so the client knows that the end of the data has been reached.

> **HTTP version 1.1 specifies a persistent connection by default.**

Proxy Server

HTTP supports proxy servers. A **proxy server** is a computer that keeps copies of responses to recent requests. In the presence of a proxy server, the HTTP client sends a request to the proxy server. The proxy server checks its cache. If the response is not stored in the cache, the proxy server sends the request to the corresponding server. Incoming responses are sent to the proxy server and stored for future requests from other clients.

The proxy server reduces the load on the original server, decreases traffic, and improves latency. However, to use the proxy server, the client must be configured to access the proxy instead of the target server.

27.2   WORLD WIDE WEB

The **World Wide Web (WWW)** is a repository of information spread all over the world and linked together. The WWW has a unique combination of flexibility, portability, and user-friendly features that distinguish it from other services provided by the Internet.

The WWW project was initiated by CERN (European Laboratory for Particle Physics) to create a system to handle distributed resources necessary for scientific research.

The WWW today is a distributed client-server service, in which a client using a browser can access a service using a server. However, the service provided is distributed over many locations called *websites* (see Fig. 27.11).

Figure 27.11 *Distributed services*

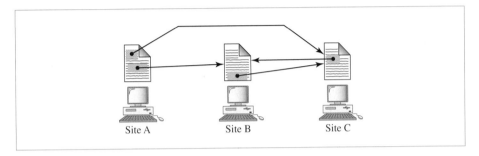

Site A   Site B   Site C

Hypertext and Hypermedia

The WWW uses the concept of hypertext and hypermedia. In a **hypertext** environment, information is stored in a set of documents that are linked using the concept of pointers. An item can be associated with another document by a pointer. The reader who is browsing through the document can move to other documents by choosing (clicking) the items that are linked to other documents. Figure 27.12 shows the concept of hypertext.

Figure 27.12 *Hypertext*

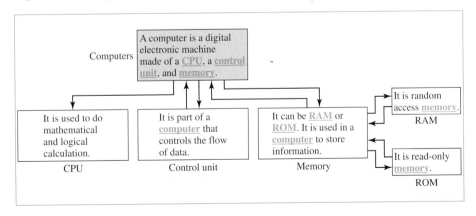

Whereas hypertext documents contain only text, **hypermedia** documents can contain pictures, graphics, and sound.

A unit of hypertext or hypermedia available on the Web is called a **page.** The main page for an organization or an individual is known as a **homepage.**

Information about one specific subject can be undistributed or distributed. In the first case, all the information may consist of one or more Web pages on the same server. In the second case, the information is made of multiple pages distributed on different servers.

Browser Architecture

A variety of vendors offer commercial browsers that interpret and display a Web document, and all use nearly the same architecture. Each **browser** usually consists of three parts: a controller, client programs, and interpreters. The controller receives input from the keyboard or the mouse and uses the client programs to access the document. After the document has been accessed, the controller uses one of the interpreters to display the document on the screen. The client programs can be one of the protocols described previously, such as HTTP, FTP, or SMTP. The interpreter can be HTML or Java, depending on the type of document (see Fig. 27.13).

Figure 27.13   *Browser architecture*

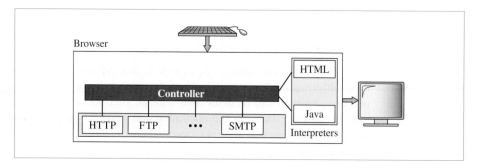

The documents in the WWW can be grouped into three broad categories: static, dynamic, and active (see Fig. 27.14).

Figure 27.14   *Categories of Web documents*

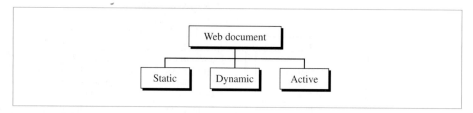

Static Documents

Static documents are fixed-content documents that are created and stored in a server. The client can get only a copy of the document. In other words, the contents of the file are determined when the file is created, not when it is used. Of course, the contents in the server can be changed, but the user cannot change it. When a client accesses the document, a copy of the document is sent. The user can then use a browsing program to display the document (see Fig. 27.15).

Figure 27.15   *Static document*

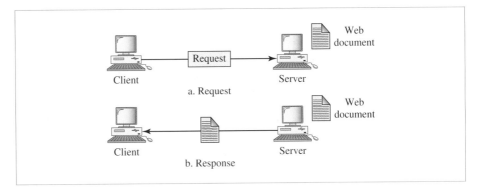

HTML

Hypertext Markup Language (HTML) is a language for creating Web pages. The term *markup language* comes from the book publishing industry. Before a book is typeset and printed, a copy editor reads the manuscript and puts a lot of marks on it. These marks tell the designer how to format the text. For example, if the copy editor wants part of a line to be printed in boldface, he or she draws a wavy line under that part. In the same way, data for a Web page are formatted for interpretation by a browser.

Let us clarify the idea with an example. To make part of a text displayed in boldface with HTML, we must include the beginning and ending boldface tags (marks) in the text, as shown in Figure 27.16.

Figure 27.16   *Boldface tags*

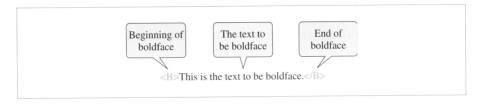

The two tags <B> and </B> are instructions for the browser. When the browser sees these two marks, it knows that the text must be made boldface (see Fig. 27.17).

A markup language such as HTML allows us to embed formatting instructions in the file itself. The instructions are stored with the text. In this way, any browser can read the instructions and format the text according to the workstation being used. One might ask why we do not use the formatting capabilities of word processors to create and save formatted text. The answer is that different word processors use different

Figure 27.17   *Effect of boldface tags*

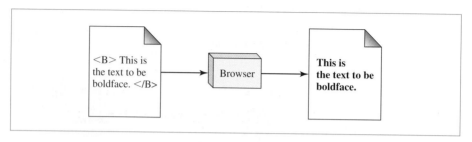

techniques or procedures for formatting text. For example, imagine that a user creates formatted text on a Macintosh computer and stores it in a Web page. Another user who is on an IBM computer is not able to receive the Web page because the two computers are using different formatting procedures.

HTML lets us use only ASCII characters for both the main text and formatting instructions. In this way, every computer can receive the whole document as an ASCII document. The main text is the data, and the formatting instructions can be used by the browser to format the data.

Structure of a Web Page

A Web page is made up of two parts: the head and body.

Head   The head is the first part of a Web page. The head contains the title of the page and other parameters that the browser will use.

Body   The actual contents of a page are in the body, which includes the text and the tags. Whereas the text is the actual information contained in a page, the tags define the appearance of the document.

Tags   The browser makes a decision about the structure of the text based on the **tags,** which are marks that are embedded into the text. A tag is enclosed in two signs (< and >) and usually comes in pairs. The beginning tag starts with the name of the tag, and the ending tag starts with a slash followed by the name of the tag.

A tag can have a list of attributes, each of which can be followed by an equals sign and a value associated with the attribute. Figure 27.18 shows the format of a tag.

Figure 27.18   *Beginning and ending tags*

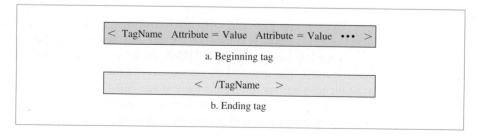

Table 27.1 lists some of the most common tags.

Table 27.1   *Common tags*

Beginning Tag	Ending Tag	Meaning
Skeletal Tags		
<HTML>	</HTML>	Defines an HTML document
<HEAD>	</HEAD>	Defines the head of the document
<BODY>	</BODY>	Defines the body of the document
Title and Header Tags		
<TITLE>	</TITLE>	Defines the title of the document
<Hn>	</Hn>	Defines different headers (n is an integer)
Text Formatting Tags		
<B>	</B>	Boldface
<I>	</I>	Italic
<U>	</U>	Underlined
_		Subscript
[	]	Superscript
Data Flow Tags		
<CENTER>	</CENTER>	Centered
 		Line break
List Tags		
<OL>	</OL>	Ordered list
<UL>	</UL>	Unordered list
<LI>	</LI>	An item in a list
Image Tags		
<IMG>		Defines an image
Hyperlink Tags		
<A>	</A>	Defines an address (hyperlink)
Executable Contents		
<APPLET>	</APPLET>	The document is an applet

Examples

In this section, we give some simple examples of HTML documents to show the implementation of the tags previously described.

Example 3

This example shows how tags are used to let the browser format the appearance of the text.

First HTML Program
<HTML>
<HEAD>
<TITLE> First Sample Document </TITLE>
</HEAD>
<BODY>
<CENTER>
<H1><B> ATTENTION </B></H1>
</CENTER>
You can get a copy of this document by:
<UL>
<LI> Writing to the publisher
<LI> Ordering online
<LI> Ordering through a bookstore
</UL>
</BODY>
</HTML>

Example 4

This example shows how tags are used to import an image and insert it into the text.

Second HTML Program
<HTML>
<HEAD>
<TITLE> Second Sample Document </TITLE>
</HEAD>
<BODY>
This is the picture of a book:
<IMG SRC="Pictures/book1.gif"   ALIGN=MIDDLE>
</BODY>
</HTML>

Example 5

This example shows how tags are used to make a hyperlink to another document.

Third HTML Program
<HTML>
<HEAD>
<TITLE> Third Sample Document </TITLE>
</HEAD>
<BODY>
This is a wonderful product that can save you money and time.
To get information about the producer, click on
<A HREF="http://www.phony.producer">
Producer </A>
</BODY>
</HTML>

Dynamic Documents

Dynamic documents do not exist in a predefined format. Instead, a **dynamic document** is created by a Web server whenever a browser requests the document. When a request arrives, the Web server runs an application program that creates the dynamic document. The server returns the output of the program as a response to the browser that requested the document. Because a fresh document is created for each request, the contents of a dynamic document can vary from one request to another. A very simple example of a dynamic document is getting the time and date from the server. Time and date are kinds of information that are dynamic in that they change from moment to moment. The client can request that the server run a program such as the *date* program in UNIX and send the result of the program to the client. Figure 27.19 illustrates the steps in sending and responding to a dynamic document.

Figure 27.19 *Dynamic document*

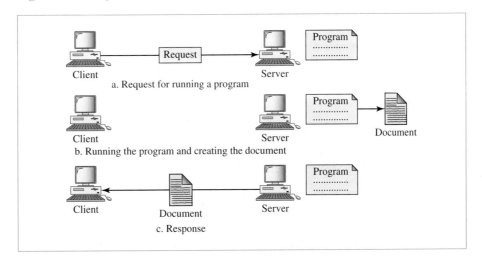

a. Request for running a program

b. Running the program and creating the document

c. Response

A server that handles dynamic documents follows these steps:

1. The server examines the URL to find if it defines a dynamic document.
2. If the URL defines a dynamic document, the server executes the program.
3. It sends the output of the program to the client (browser).

Common Gateway Interface (CGI)

Common Gateway Interface (CGI) is a technology that creates and handles dynamic documents. CGI is a set of standards that defines how a dynamic document should be written, how input data should be supplied to the program, and how the output result should be used.

CGI is not a new language; instead, it allows programmers to use any of several languages such as C, C++, Bourne Shell, Korn Shell, C Shell, or Perl. The only thing that CGI defines is a set of rules and terms that the programmer should follow.

The use of *common* in CGI indicates that the standard defines a set of rules that are common to any language or platform. The term *gateway* here means that a CGI program is a gateway that can be used to access other resources such as databases and graphic packages. The term *interface* here means that there is a set of predefined terms, variables, calls, and so on that can be used in any CGI program.

CGI Program

A CGI program in its simplest form is code written in one of the languages supporting CGI. Any programmer who can encode a sequence of thoughts in a program and knows the syntax of one of the above-mentioned languages can write a simple CGI program.

Examples

In this section, we have given some examples of CGI programming that show the concept and idea. Programs are written in different languages to show the reader that CGI is language-independent.

Example 6

Example 6 is a CGI program written in Bourne shell script. The program accesses the UNIX utility *(date)* that returns the date and the time. Note that the program output is in plain text.

First Example of CGI

```
#!/bin/sh
# The head of the program
echo Content_type: text/plain
echo
# The body of the program
now='date'
echo  $now
exit 0
```

Example 7

Example 7 is similar to Example 6 except that program output is in HTML.

Second Example of CGI
| ```
#!/bin/sh
# The head of the program
echo Content_type: text/html
echo
# The body of the program
echo <HTML>
echo <HEAD><TITLE> Date and Time </TITLE></HEAD>
echo <BODY>
now='date'
echo <CENTER><B> $now </B></CENTER>
echo </BODY>
echo </HTML>
exit 0
``` |

Example 8

Example 8 is similar to Example 7 except that the program is written in Perl.

Third Example of CGI
| ```
#!/bin/perl
# The head of the program
print  "Content_type: text/html\n";
print "\n";
# The body of the program
print "<HTML>\n";
print "<HEAD><TITLE> Date and Time </TITLE></HEAD>\n";
print "<BODY>\n";
$now = 'date';
print "<CENTER><B>  $now </B></CENTER>\n";
print "</BODY>\n";
print "</HTML>\n";
exit 0
``` |

Active Documents

For many applications, we need a program to be run at the client site. These are called **active documents.** For example, imagine we want to run a program that creates animated graphics on the screen or interacts with the user. The program definitely needs to be run at the client site where the animation or interaction takes place. When a browser requests an active document, the server sends a copy of the document in the form of byte code. The document is then run at the client (browser) site (see Fig. 27.20).

An active document in the server is stored in the form of binary code. However, it does not create overhead for the server in the same way that a dynamic document does. Although an active document is not run on the server, it is stored there as a binary

Figure 27.20   *Active document*

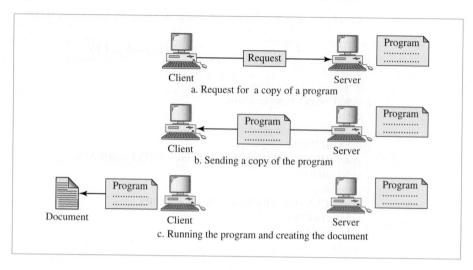

document that it is retrieved by a client. When a client receives the document, it can also store the document in its own storage area. In this way, the client can run the document again without making another request.

An active document is transported from the server to the client in binary form. This means that it can be compressed at the server site and decompressed at the client site, saving both bandwidth and transmission time.

Creation, Compilation, and Execution

The following steps show how an active document is created, compiled, and executed.

1. At the server site, a programmer writes a program, in source code, and stores it in a file.

2. At the server site, the program is compiled and binary code is created, which is stored in a file. The path name of this file is the one used by a URL to refer to the file. In this file, each program command (statement) is in binary form, and each identifier (variable, constants, function names, and so on) is referred to by a binary offset address.

3. A client (browser) requests a copy of the binary code, which is probably transported in compressed form from the server to the client (browser).

4. The client (browser) uses its own software to change the binary code into executable code. The software links all the library modules and makes it ready for execution.

5. The client (browser) runs the program and creates the result that can include animation or interaction with the user.

Java

Java is a combination of a high-level programming language, a run-time environment, and a class library that allows a programmer to write an active document (an applet) and a browser to run it. Java can also be a stand-alone program without using a browser.

Java is an object-oriented language which is, syntactically and semantically, very similar to C++. However, it does not have some of the complexities of C++ such as operator overloading or multiple inheritance. Java is also platform-independent and does not use pointer arithmetic. In Java, like any other object-oriented language, a programmer defines a set of objects and a set of operations (methods) to operate on those objects. It is a *typed* language which means that the programmer must declare the type of any piece of data before using it. Java is also a concurrent language, which means the programmer can use multiple threads to create concurrency.

Classes and Objects

Java, as an object-oriented language, uses the concept of classes and objects. An object is an instance of a class that uses methods (procedures or functions) to manipulate encapsulated data.

Inheritance

One of the main ideas in object-oriented programming is the concept of inheritance. Inheritance defines a hierarchy of objects, in which one object can inherit data and methods from other objects. In Java we can define a class as the base class that contains data and methods common to many classes. Inherited classes can inherit these data and methods and can also have their own data and methods.

Packages

Java has a rich library of classes, which allows the programmer to create and use different objects in an applet.

Skeleton of an Applet

An **applet** is an active document written in Java. It is actually the definition of a publicly inherited class, which inherits from the applet class defined in the java.applet library. The programmer can define private data and public and private methods in this definition (see Fig. 27.21).

Figure 27.21   *Skeleton of an applet*

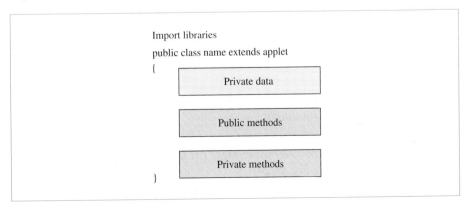

The client process (browser) creates an instance of this applet. The browser then uses the public methods defined in the applet to invoke private methods or to access data. Figure 27.22 shows this relationship.

Figure 27.22   *Instantiation of the object defined by an applet*

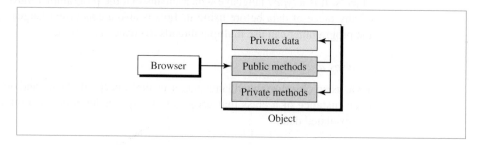

Creation, Compilation, and Running

The first step is to use an editor to create a Java source file. The name of the file is the same as the name of the publicly inherited class with the "java" extension. Next the Java compiler creates bytecode from this file, with the "class" extension. The next step creates an applet which can be run by a browser (see Fig. 27.23).

Figure 27.23   *Creation and compilation*

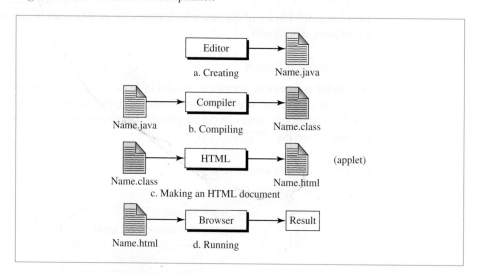

HTML Document

To use the applet, an HTML document is created and the name of the applet is inserted between the <APPLET> tags. The tag also defines the size of the window used for the applet (see Fig. 27.24).

Figure 27.24 *HTML document carrying an applet*

```
<HTML>

   <APPLET  CODE = "Name.class"
   WIDTH = mmm
   HEIGHT = nnn .... >
   </APPLET >

</HTML>
```

Examples

In this section, we give two very simple examples of Java programs. The purpose is not to teach Java but to show how Java can be used to create active documents.

Example 9

In this example, we first import two packages, java.awt and java.applet. They contain the declarations and definitions of classes and methods that we need. Our example uses only one publicly inherited class called *First*. We define only one public method, *paint*. The browser can access the instance of First through the public method paint. The paint method, however, calls another method called *drawString*, which is defined in java.awt.*. Three parameters are passed to drawString: a string that we want to display, the x coordinate, and the y coordinate. The coordinates are measured from the top left of the browser window in pixels.

```
                          First Example of Java
import java.applet.*;
import java.awt.*;

public class First extends Applet
{
    public void paint (Graphics  g)
      {
        g.drawString ("Hello World", 100, 100);
      }
}
```

Example 10

In this example, we modify the program in Example 9 to draw a line. Instead of method drawString, we use another method called *drawLine*. This method needs four parameters: the x and y coordinates at the beginning of the line and the x and y coordinates at the end of the line. We use 0, 0 for the beginning and 80, 90 for the end.

Second Example of Java

```
import java.applet.*;
import java.awt.*;

public class Second extends Applet
{
    public void paint (Graphics  g)
     {
       g.drawLine (0, 0, 80, 90);
     }
}
```

27.3   KEY TERMS

active document	nonpersistent connection
applet	page
browser	persistent connection
Common Gateway Interface (CGI)	proxy server
dynamic document	request header
entity header	response header
general header	static document
homepage	status code
hypermedia	status line
hypertext	tag
Hypertext Markup Language (HTML)	Uniform Resource Locator (URL)
Hypertext Transfer Protocol (HTTP)	Web
Java	World Wide Web (WWW)

27.4   SUMMARY

❑   The Hypertext Transfer Protocol (HTTP) is the main protocol used to access data on the World Wide Web (WWW).

❑   The World Wide Web is a repository of information spread all over the world and linked together.

❑   Hypertext and hypermedia are documents linked to one another through the concept of pointers.

❑   Browsers interpret and display a Web document.

❑   A browser consists of a controller, client programs, and interpreters.

❑   A Web document can be classified as static, dynamic, or active.

❑   A static document is one in which the contents are fixed and stored in a server. The client can make no changes in the server document.

❑   Hypertext Markup Language (HTML) is a language used to create static Web pages.

❑   Any browser can read formatting instructions (tags) embedded in an HTML document.

❑   A dynamic Web document is created by a server only at a browser request.

❏ The Common Gateway Interface (CGI) is a standard for creating and handling dynamic Web documents.

❏ A CGI program with its embedded CGI interface tags can be written in a language such as C, C++, shell script, or Perl.

❏ The server sends the output of the CGI program to the browser.

❏ The output of a CGI program can be text, graphics, binary data, status codes, instructions, or an address of a file.

❏ An active document is a copy of a program retrieved by the client and run at the client site.

❏ Java is a combination of a high-level programming language, a run-time environment, and a class library that allows a programmer to write an active document and a browser to run it.

❏ Java is used to create applets (small application programs).

❏ Java is an object-oriented typed language with a rich library of classes.

27.5   PRACTICE SET

Review Questions

1. How is HTTP related to WWW?
2. How is HTTP similar to SMTP?
3. How is HTTP similar to FTP?
4. What is a URL and what are its components?
5. What is a proxy server and how is it related to HTTP?
6. What is a homepage?
7. Name the common three components of a browser.
8. What are the three types of web documents?
9. What does HTML stand for and what is its function?
10. What is the difference between an active document and a dynamic document?
11. What does CGI stand for and what is its function?
12. Describe the relationship between Java and an active document.

Multiple-Choice Questions

13. HTTP has similarities to both _____ and _____.
    a. FTP; SNMP
    b. FTP; SMTP
    c. FTP; MTV
    d. FTP; URL
14. A request message always contains _____.
    a. A header and a body
    b. A request line and a header
    c. A status line, a header, and a body
    d. A status line and a header

15. Which of the following is present in both a request line and a status line?
    a. HTTP version number
    b. URL
    c. Status code
    d. Status phrase

16. What does the URL need to access a document?
    a. Path name
    b. Host computer
    c. Retrieval method
    d. All the above

17. Which of the following is a retrieval method?
    a. HTTP
    b. FTP
    c. TELNET
    d. All the above

18. A user wants to replace a document with a newer version; the request line contains the _____ method.
    a. GET
    b. POST
    c. COPY
    d. PUT

19. A user wants to copy a file to another location; the request line contains the _____ method.
    a. PUT
    b. PATCH
    c. COPY
    d. POST

20. A user needs to retrieve a document from the server; the request line contains the _____ method.
    a. GET
    b. HEAD
    c. POST
    d. PUT

21. A user needs to send the server some information. The request line method is _____.
    a. OPTION
    b. PATCH
    c. MOVE
    d. POST

22. A user needs to move a file to another location. The request line method is _____.
    a. MOVE
    b. PUT

    c. GET

    d. PATCH

23. A response message always contains _____.

    a. A header and a body

    b. A request line and a header

    c. A status line, a header, and a body

    d. A status line and a header

24. The _____ header supplies information about the body of a document.

    a. General

    b. Request

    c. Response

    d. Entity

25. The _____ header can specify the server configuration or provide information about a request.

    a. General

    b. Request

    c. Response

    d. Entity

26. The _____ header can specify the client configuration and the client's preferred document format.

    a. General

    b. Request

    c. Response

    d. Entity

27. Hypertext documents are linked through _____.

    a. DNS

    b. TELNET

    c. Pointers

    d. Homepages

28. Which of the following is not a client program in WWW?

    a. FTP

    b. TELNET

    c. HTTP

    d. HTML

29. Which of the following is an interpreter?

    a. HTTP

    b. HTML

    c. CGI

    d. FTP

30. What are the components of a browser?
    a. Retrieval method, host computer, path name
    b. Controller, client program, interpreter
    c. Hypertext, hypermedia, HTML
    d. All the above

31. Which type of Web document is run at the client site?
    a. Static
    b. Dynamic
    c. Active
    d. All the above

32. Which type of Web document is created at the server site only when requested by a client?
    a. Static
    b. Dynamic
    c. Active
    d. All the above

33. Which type of Web document is fixed-content and is created and stored at the server site?
    a. Static
    b. Dynamic
    c. Active
    d. All the above

34. The _____ of a Web page contains the title and parameters used by the browser.
    a. Tags
    b. Head
    c. Body
    d. Attributes

35. In <IMG SRC="Pictures/book1.gif " ALIGN=middle> ALIGN is _____.
    a. A tag
    b. The head
    c. The body
    d. An attribute

36. An ending tag is usually of the form _____.
    a. </tagname>
    b. <\tagname>
    c. <tagname>
    d. <tagname!>

37. Which category of HTML tags allows the listing of documents?
    a. Image
    b. List

    c. Hyperlink

    d. Executable contents

38. The _____ tags enclose binary code or byte code.

    a. Image

    b. List

    c. Hyperlink

    d. Executable contents

39. A program can use _____ to write a CGI program.

    a. Bourne shell script

    b. Perl

    c. C

    d. Any of the above

40. An unemployed actor has posted his resume on the Web. This is probably a(n) _____ document.

    a. Active

    b. Static

    c. Passive

    d. Dynamic

41. The server receives input from a browser through _____.

    a. An attribute

    b. A tag

    c. A form

    d. Any of the above

42. Output from a CGI program is _____.

    a. Text

    b. Graphics

    c. Binary data

    d. Any of the above

43. Which type of Web document is transported from the server to the client in binary form?

    a. Static

    b. Dynamic

    c. Active

    d. All the above

44. An applet is a small application program written in _____.

    a. C

    b. C++

    c. Shell script

    d. Java

45. _____ is used to enable the use of active documents.
    a. HTML
    b. CGI
    c. Java
    d. All the above
46. Java is _____.
    a. A programming language
    b. A run-time environment
    c. A class library
    d. All the above
47. An applet is _____ document application program.
    a. A static
    b. An active
    c. A passive
    d. A dynamic
48. Stock quotations are posted on the Web. This is probably a(n) _____ document.
    a. Active
    b. Static
    c. Passive
    d. Dynamic
49. Updates for a satellite's coordinates can be obtained on the WWW. This is probably a(n) _____ document.
    a. Active
    b. Static
    c. Passive
    d. Dynamic

Exercises

50. Compare HTTP and FTP. Which one is simpler? Explain your answer.
51. Compare the way SMTP and HTTP transfer images. Which one do you think is more efficient? Why?
52. What quality of service (QoS) is the most important in HTTP (minimum delay, maximum throughput, and reliability? Which one is less important? Explain your answer.
53. SMTP, FTP, and HTTP are protocols to transfer messages from one point to another. Compare and contrast their use.
54. Do you think HTTP can be used effectively for transferring stored audio and video? Explain your answer.
55. Do you think HTTP can be used effectively for transferring live audio and video? Explain your answer.

56. Do you think an HTTP client can monopolize an HTTP server?
57. Do you think HTTP uses iterative or concurrent client/server interaction?
58. Show the effect of the tags in the following line:

```
This is <BR> a line of <BR> HTML
```

59. Show the effect of the tags in the following line:

```
This is <BR><BR> another line of <BR><BR> HTML
```

60. Show the effect of the tags in the following lines:

```
<H1> DOCUMENT </H1>
<H2> This is an HTML document </H2>
<H1> It shows the effect of H-tags </H1>
```

61. Show the effect of the tags in the following lines:

```
<UL>
<LI> Last Name, First Name, Initial </LI>
<LI> Street Address, City </LI>
<LI> State, Zip Code </LI>
</UL>
```

62. Where will each figure be shown on the screen?

```
Look at the following picture:
then tell me what you feel:
<IMG SRC="Pictures/Funny1.gif" ALIGN=middle>
<IMG SRC="Pictures/Funny2.gif" ALIGN=bottom>
<B> What is your feeling? </B>
```

63. Show the effect of the following HTML segment.

```
The publisher of this book is <A HREF="www.mhhe">
McGraw-Hill Publisher </A>
```

CHAPTER 28

Multimedia

Recent advances in technology have changed our use of audio and video. In the past, we listened to an audio broadcast through a radio and watched a video program broadcast through a TV. We used the telephone network to interactively communicate with another party. But times have changed. People want to use the Internet, not only for text and image communications, but also for audio and video services. In this last chapter about the application layer, we concentrate on applications that use the Internet for audio and video services.

We can divide audio and video services into three broad categories: **streaming stored audio/video, streaming live audio/video,** and **interactive audio/video,** as shown in Figure 28.1. Streaming means a user can listen (or watch) the file after the downloading has started.

Figure 28.1   *Internet audio/video*

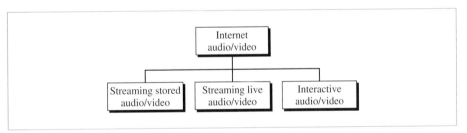

In the first category, streaming stored audio/video, the files are compressed and stored on a server. A client downloads the files through the Internet. This is sometimes referred to as **on-demand audio/video.** Examples of stored audio files are songs, symphonies, books on tape, and famous lectures. Examples of stored video files are movies, TV shows, and music video clips.

Streaming stored audio/video refers to on-demand requests for compressed audio/video files.

In the second category, streaming live audio/video, a user listens to broadcast audio and video through the Internet. A good example of this type of application is the

Internet radio. Some radio stations broadcast their programs only on the Internet; many broadcast them both on the Internet and on air. Internet TV is not popular yet, but many people believe that TV stations will broadcast their programs on the Internet in the future.

> **Streaming live audio/video refers to the broadcasting of radio and TV programs through the Internet.**

In the third category, interactive audio/video, people use the Internet to interactively communicate with one another. A good example of this application is Internet telephony and Internet teleconferencing.

> **Interactive audio/video refers to the use of the Internet for interactive audio/video applications.**

We will discuss these three applications in this chapter, but first we need to discuss some other issues related to audio/video: digitizing audio and video and compressing audio and video.

28.1   DIGITIZING AUDIO AND VIDEO

Before audio or video signals can be sent on the Internet, they need to be digitized. We discuss audio and video separately.

Digitizing Audio

When sound is fed into a microphone, an electronic analog signal is generated which represents the sound amplitude as a function of time. The signal is called an *analog audio signal*. We saw in Chapter 5 that an analog signal, such as audio, can be digitized to produce a digital signal. We learned that according to the Nyquist theorem, if the highest frequency of the signal is f, we need to sample the signal $2f$ times per second. There are other methods for digitizing an audio signal, but the principle is the same. We limit our discussion to what was discussed in Chapter 5.

Voice is sampled at 8000 samples per second with 8 bits per sample. This results in a digital signal of 64 Kbps. Music is sampled at 44,100 samples per second with 16 bits per sample. This results in a digital signal of 705.6 Kbps for monaural and 1.411 Mbps for stereo.

Digitizing Video

A video consists of a sequence of frames. If the frames are displayed on the screen fast enough, we get an impression of motion. The reason is that our eyes cannot distinguish the rapidly flashing frames as individual ones. There is no standard number of frames per second; in North America 25 frames per second is common. However, to avoid a condition known as flickering, a frame needs to be refreshed. The TV industry repaints each frame twice. This means 50 frames need to be sent, or if there is memory at the sender site, 25 frames with each frame repainted from the memory.

Each frame is divided into small grids, called picture elements or **pixels.** For black-and-white TV, each 8-bit pixel represents one of 256 different gray levels. For a color TV, each pixel is 24 bits, with 8 bits for each primary color (red, green, and blue).

We can calculate the number of bits in a second for a specific resolution. In the lowest resolution a color frame is made of 1024×768 pixels. This means that we need

$$2 \times 25 \times 1024 \times 768 \times 24 = 944 \text{ Mbps}$$

This data rate needs a very high-data-rate technology such as SONET. To send video using lower-rate technologies, we need to compress the video.

Compression **is needed to send video over the Internet.**

28.2   AUDIO AND VIDEO COMPRESSION

To send audio or video over the Internet requires **compression.** In this section, we discuss first audio compression and then video compression.

Audio Compression

Audio compression can be used for speech or music. For speech, we need to compress a 64-KHz digitized signal; for music, we need to compress a 1.411-MHz signal. Two categories of techniques are used for audio compression: predictive encoding and perceptual encoding.

Predictive Encoding

In **predictive encoding,** the differences between the samples are encoded instead of encoding all the sampled values. This type of compression is normally used for speech. Several standards have been defined such as GSM (13 Kbps), G.729 (8 Kbps), G.723.3 (6.4 or 5.3 Kbps). Detailed discussions of these techniques are beyond the scope of this book.

Perceptual Encoding: MP3

The most common compression technique that is used to create CD-quality audio is based on the **perceptual encoding** technique. As we mentioned before, this type of audio needs at least 1.411 Mbps; this cannot be sent over the Internet without compression. **MP3** (MPEG audio layer 3), a part of the MPEG standard (discussed in the video compression section), uses this technique.

Perceptual encoding uses the science of psychoacoustics, which is the study of how people perceive sound. The idea is based on some flaws in our auditory system: Some sounds can mask other sounds. Masking can happen in frequency and time. In

frequency masking, a loud sound in a frequency range can partially or totally mask a softer sound in another frequency range. For example, we cannot hear what our dance partner says in a room where a loud heavy metal band is performing. In **temporal masking,** a loud sound can numb our ears for a short time even after the sound has stopped.

MP3 uses these two phenomena, frequency and temporal masking, to compress audio signals. The technique analyzes and divides the spectrum into several groups. Zero bits are allocated to the frequency ranges that are totally masked. A small number of bits are allocated to the frequency ranges that are partially masked. A larger number of bits are allocated to the frequency ranges that are not masked.

MP3 produces three data rates: 96 Kbps, 128 Kbps, and 160 Kbps. The rate is based on the range of the frequencies in the original analog audio.

Video Compression

As we mentioned before, video is composed of multiple frames. Each frame is one image. We can compress video by first compressing images. Two standards are prevalent in the market. **Joint Photographic Experts Group (JPEG)** is used to compress images. **Moving Picture Experts Group (MPEG)** is used to compress video. We briefly discuss JPEG and then MPEG.

Image Compression: JPEG

As we discussed previously, if the picture is not in color (gray scale), each pixel can be represented by an 8-bit integer (256 levels). If the picture is in color, each pixel can be represented by 24 bits (3×8 bits), with each 8 bits representing red, blue, or green (RBG). To simplify the discussion, we concentrate on a gray scale picture.

In JPEG, a gray scale picture is divided into blocks of 8×8 pixels (see Fig. 28.2).

Figure 28.2 *JPEG gray scale*

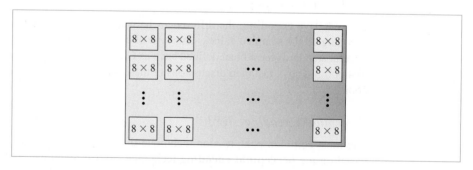

The purpose of dividing the picture into blocks is to decrease the number of calculations because, as you will see shortly, the number of mathematical operations for each picture is the square of the number of units.

The whole idea of JPEG is to change the picture into a linear (vector) set of numbers that reveals the redundancies. The redundancies (lack of changes) can then be removed by using one of the text compression methods. A simplified version of the process is shown in Figure 28.3.

Figure 28.3 *JPEG process*

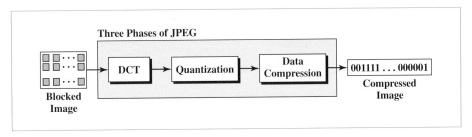

Discrete Cosine Transform (DCT) In this step, each block of 64 pixels goes through a transformation called the **discrete cosine transform (DCT).** The transformation changes the 64 values so that the relative relationships between pixels are kept but the redundancies are revealed. We do not give the formula here, but we do show the results of the transformation for three cases.

Case 1 In this case, we have a block of uniform gray, and the value of each pixel is 20. When we do the transformations, we get a nonzero value for the first element (upper left corner); the rest of the pixels have a value of 0. The value of $T(0,0)$ is the average (multiplied by a constant) of the other values and is called the *dc value* (direct current, borrowed from electrical engineering). The rest of the values, called *ac values,* in $T(m,n)$ represent changes in the pixel values. But because there are no changes, the rest of the values are 0s (see Fig. 28.4).

Figure 28.4 *Case 1: uniform gray scale*

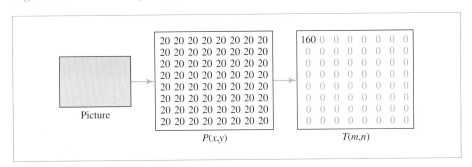

Case 2 In the second case, we have a block with two different uniform gray scale sections. There is a sharp change in the values of the pixels (from 20 to 50). When we do the transformations, we get a dc value as well as nonzero ac values. However, there are only a few nonzero values clustered around the dc value. Most of the values are 0 (see Fig. 28.5).

Figure 28.5 *Case 2: two sections*

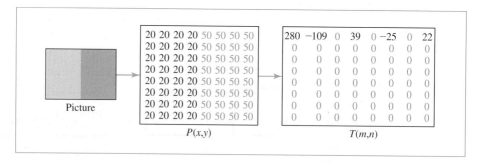

Case 3 In the third case, we have a block that changes gradually. That is, there is no sharp change between the values of neighboring pixels. When we do the transformations, we get a dc value, with many nonzero ac values also (Fig. 28.6).

Figure 28.6 *Case 3: gradient gray scale*

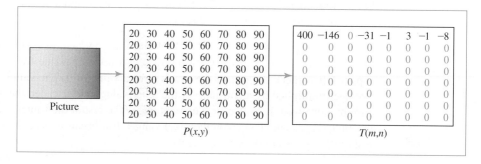

From Figures 28.4, 28.5, and 28.6, we can state the following:

- The transformation creates table T from table P.
- The dc value is the average value (multiplied by a constant) of the pixels.
- The ac values are the changes.
- Lack of changes in neighboring pixels creates 0s.

Quantization After the T table is created, the values are quantized to reduce the number of bits needed for encoding. Previously in **quantization,** we dropped the fraction from each value and kept the integer part. Here, we divide the number by a constant and then drop the fraction. This reduces the required number of bits even more. In most implementations, a quantizing table (8 by 8) defines how to quantize each value. The divisor depends on the position of the value in the T table. This is done to optimize the number of bits and the number of 0s for each particular application. Note that the only phase in the process that is not reversible is the quantizing phase. We lose some information here that is not recoverable. As a matter of fact, the only reason that JPEG is called *lossy compression* is because of this quantization phase.

Compression After quantization, the values are read from the table, and redundant 0s are removed. However, to cluster the 0s together, the table is read diagonally in a zigzag fashion rather than row by row or column by column. The reason is that if the picture does not have fine changes, the bottom right corner of the *T* table is all 0s. Figure 28.7 shows the process.

Figure 28.7 *Reading the table*

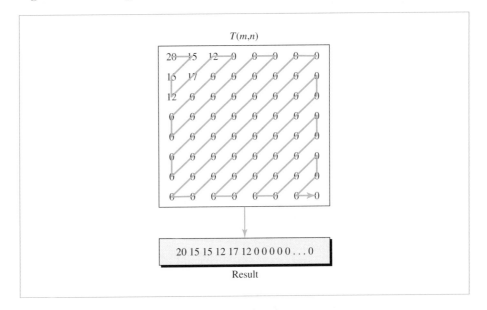

Video Compression: MPEG

The **Moving Picture Experts Group (MPEG)** method is used to compress video. In principle, a motion picture is a rapid flow of a set of frames, where each frame is an image. In other words, a frame is a spatial combination of pixels, and a video is a temporal combination of frames that are sent one after another. Compressing video, then, means spatially compressing each frame and temporally compressing a set of frames.

Spatial Compression The **spatial compression** of each frame is done with JPEG (or a modification of it). Each frame is a picture that can be independently compressed.

Temporal Compression In **temporal compression,** redundant frames are removed. When we watch television, we receive 50 frames per second. However, most of the consecutive frames are almost the same. For example, when someone is talking, most of the frame is the same as the previous one except for the segment of the frame around the lips, which changes from one frame to another.

To temporally compress data, the MPEG method first divides frames into three categories: I-frames, P-frames, and B-frames.

- **I-frames.** An **intracoded frame (I-frame)** is an independent frame that is not related to any other frame (not to the frame sent before or to the frame sent after). They are present at regular intervals (e.g., every ninth frame is an I-frame). An I-frame must appear periodically to handle some sudden change in the frame that the previous and following frames cannot show. Also, when a video is broadcast, a viewer may tune in his or her receiver at any time. If there is only one I-frame at the beginning of the broadcast, the viewer who tunes in late will not receive a complete picture. I-frames are independent of other frames and cannot be constructed from other frames.

- **P-frames.** A **predicted frame (P-frame)** is related to the preceding I-frame or P-frame. In other words, each P-frame contains only the changes from the preceding frame. The changes, however, cannot cover a big segment. For example, for a fast-moving object, the new changes may not be recorded in a P-frame. P-frames can be constructed only from previous I- or P-frames. P-frames carry much less information than other frame types and carry even fewer bits after compression.

- **B-frames.** A **bidirectional frame (B-frame)** is relative to the preceding and following I-frame or P-frame. In other words, each B-frame is relative to the past and the future. Note that a B-frame is never related to another B-frame.

Figure 28.8 shows a sample sequence of frames.

Figure 28.8   *MPEG frames*

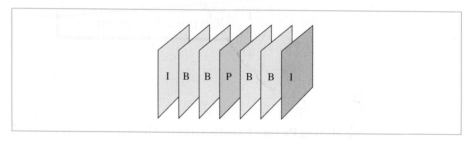

Figure 28.9 shows how I-, P-, and B-frames are constructed from a series of seven frames.

Figure 28.9   *MPEG frame construction*

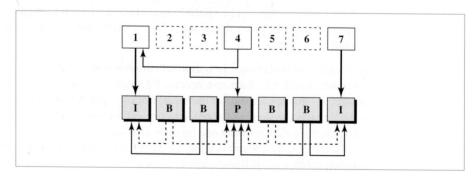

MPEG has gone through two versions. MPEG1 was designed for a CD-ROM with a data rate of 1.5 Mbps. MPEG2 was designed for high-quality DVD with a data rate of 3 to 6 Mbps.

28.3 STREAMING STORED AUDIO/VIDEO

Now that we have discussed digitizing and compressing audio/video, we turn our attention to specific applications. The first is streaming stored audio and video. Downloading these types of files from a Web server can be different from downloading other types of files. To understand the concept, let us use three approaches, each with a different complexity.

First Approach: Using a Web Server

A compressed audio/video file can be downloaded as a text file. The client (browser) can use the services of HTTP and send a GET message to download the file. The Web server can send the compressed file to the browser. The browser can then use a help application, normally called a **media player,** to play the file. Figure 28.10 shows this approach.

Figure 28.10   *Using a Web server*

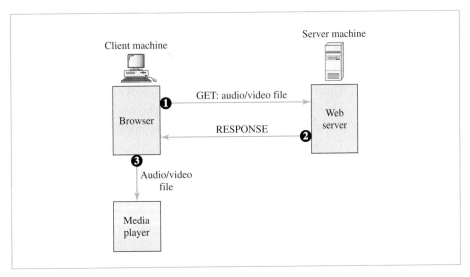

This approach is very simple and does not involve *streaming*. However, it has a drawback. An audio/video file is usually large even after the compression. An audio file may contain tens of megabits, and a video file may contain hundreds of megabits. In this approach, the file needs to download completely before it can be played. Using contemporary data rates, the user needs some seconds or tens of seconds before the file can be played.

Second Approach: Using a Web Server with Metafile

In another approach, the media player is directly connected to the Web server for downloading the audio/video file. The Web server stores two files: the actual audio/video file and a **metafile** that holds information about the audio/video file. Figure 28.11 shows the steps in this approach.

Figure 28.11   *Using a Web server with a metafile*

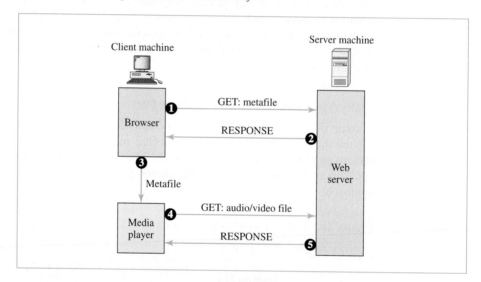

1. The HTTP client accesses the Web server using the GET message.
2. The information about the metafile comes in the response.
3. The metafile is passed to the media player.
4. The media player uses the URL in the metafile to access the audio/video file.
5. The Web server responds.

Third Approach: Using a Media Server

The problem with the second approach is that the browser and the media player both use the services of HTTP. HTTP is designed to run over TCP. This is appropriate for retrieving the metafile, but not for retrieving the audio/video file. The reason is that TCP retransmits a lost or damaged segment, which is counter to the philosophy of streaming. We need to dismiss TCP and its error control; we need to use UDP. However, HTTP, which accesses the Web server, and the Web server itself are designed for TCP; we need another server, a **media server.** Figure 28.12 shows the concept.

1. The HTTP client accesses the Web server using a GET message.
2. The information about the metafile comes in the response.
3. The metafile is passed to the media player.

Figure 28.12 *Using a media server*

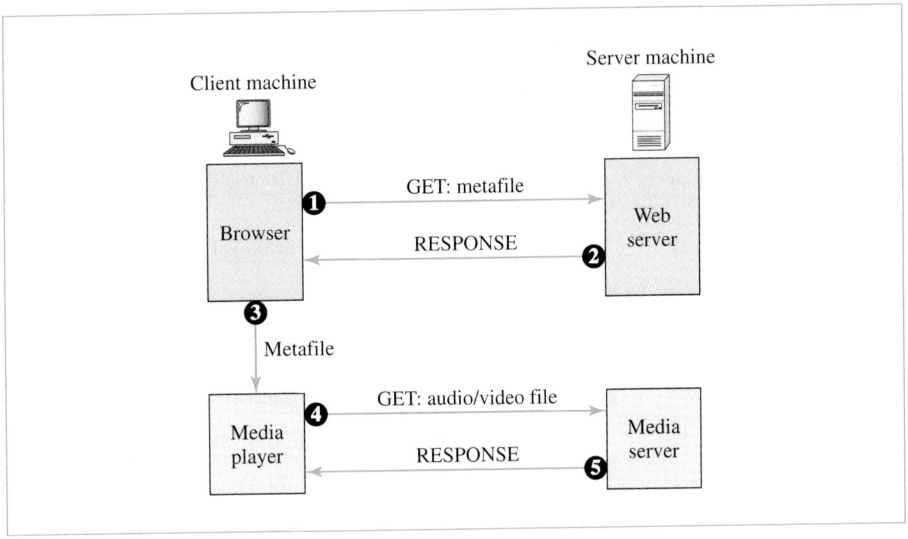

4. The media player uses the URL in the metafile to access the media server to download the file. Downloading can take place by any protocol that uses UDP.
5. The media server responds.

Fourth Approach: Using a Media Server and RTSP

The **Real-Time Streaming Protocol (RTSP)** is a control protocol designed to add some more functionalities to the streaming process. Using RTSP, we can control the playing of audio/video. RTSP is an out-of-band control protocol that is similar to the second connection in FTP. Figure 28.13 shows a media server and RTSP.

1. The HTTP client accesses the Web server using a GET message.
2. The information about the metafile comes in the response.
3. The metafile is passed to the media player.
4. The media player sends a SETUP message to create a connection with the media server.
5. The media server responds.
6. The media player sends a PLAY message to start playing (downloading).
7. The audio/video file is downloaded using another protocol that runs over UDP.
8. The connection is broken using the TEARDOWN message.
9. The media server responds.

The media player can send other types of messages. For example, a PAUSE message temporarily stops the downloading; downloading can be resumed with a PLAY message.

Figure 28.13   *Using a media server and RTSP*

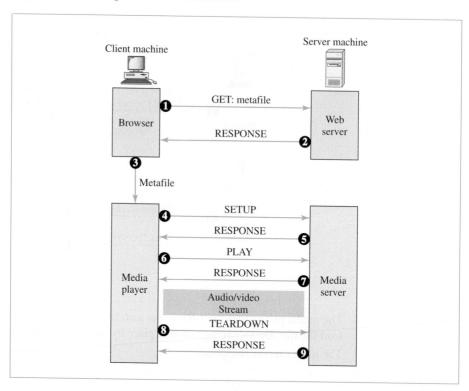

28.4   STREAMING LIVE AUDIO/VIDEO

Streaming live audio/video is similar to the broadcasting of audio and video by radio and TV stations. Instead of broadcasting to the air, the stations broadcast through the Internet. There are several similarities between streaming stored audio/video and streaming live audio/video. They are both sensitive to delay; neither can accept retransmission. However, there is a difference. In the first application, the communication is unicast and on-demand. In the second, the communication is multicast and live. Live streaming is better suited to the multicast services of IP and the use of protocols such as UDP and RTP (discussed later). However, presently, live streaming is still using TCP and multiple unicasting instead of multicasting. There is still much progress to be made in this area.

28.5   REAL-TIME INTERACTIVE AUDIO/VIDEO

In real-time interactive audio/video, people communicate with one another in real time. The Internet phone or voice over IP is an example of this type of application. Video conferencing is another example that allows people to communicate visually and orally.

Characteristics

Before discussing the protocols used in this class of applications, we discuss some characteristics of real-time audio/video communication.

Time Relationship

Real-time data on a packet-switched network require the preservation of the time relationship between packets of a session. For example, let us assume that a real-time video server creates live video images and sends them online. The video is digitized and packetized. There are only three packets, and each packet holds 10 s of video information. The first packet starts at 00:00:00, the second packet starts at 00:00:10, and the third packet starts at 00:00:20. Also imagine that it takes 1 s (an exaggeration for simplicity) for each packet to reach the destination (equal delay). The receiver can play back the first packet at 00:00:01, the second packet at 00:00:11, and the third packet at 00:00:21. Although there is a 1-s time difference between what the server sends and what the client sees on the computer screen, the action is happening in real time. The time relationship between the packets is preserved. The 1-s delay is not important. Figure 28.14 shows the idea.

Figure 28.14   *Time relationship*

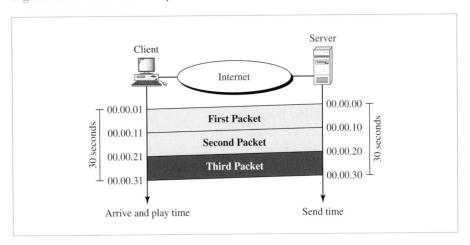

But what happens if the packets arrive with different delays? For example, the first packet arrives at 00:00:01 (1-s delay), the second arrives at 00:00:15 (5-s delay), and the third arrives at 00:00:27 (7-s delay). If the receiver starts playing the first packet at 00:00:01, it will finish at 00:00:11. However, the next packet has not yet arrived; it arrives 4 s later. There is a gap between the first and second packets and between the second and the third as the video is viewed at the remote site. This phenomenon is called **jitter.** Figure 28.15 shows the situation.

Jitter is introduced in real-time data by the delay between packets.

Figure 28.15   *Jitter*

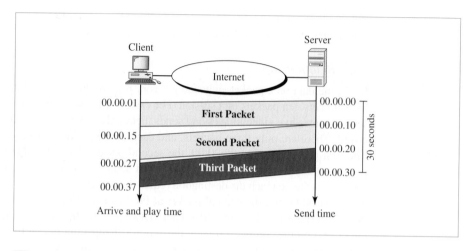

Timestamp

One solution to jitter is the use of a **timestamp.** If each packet has a timestamp that shows the time it was produced relative to the first (or previous) packet, then the receiver can add this time to the time at which it starts the playback. In other words, the receiver knows when each packet is to be played. Imagine the first packet in the previous example has a timestamp of 0, the second has a timestamp of 10, and the third a timestamp of 20. If the receiver starts playing back the first packet at 00:00:08, the second will be played at 00:00:18, and the third at 00:00:28. There are no gaps between the packets. Figure 28.16 shows the situation.

Figure 28.16   *Timestamp*

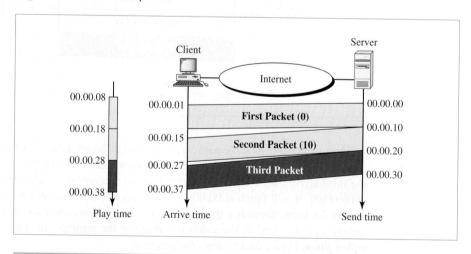

To prevent jitter, we can timestamp the packets and separate the arrival time from the playback time.

Playback Buffer

To be able to separate the arrival time from the playback time, we need a buffer to store the data until they are played back. The buffer is referred to as a **playback buffer.** When a session begins (the first bit of the first packet arrives), the receiver delays playing the data until a threshold is reached. In the previous example, the first bit of the first packet arrives at 00:00:01; the threshold is 7 s, and the playback time is 00:00:08. The threshold is measured in time units of data. The replay does not start until the time units of data are equal to the threshold value.

Data are stored in the buffer at a possibly variable rate, but they are extracted and played back at a fixed rate. Note that the amount of data in the buffer shrinks or expands, but as long as the delay is less than the time to play back the threshold amount of data, there is no jitter. Figure 28.17 shows the buffer at different times for our example.

Figure 28.17 *Playback buffer*

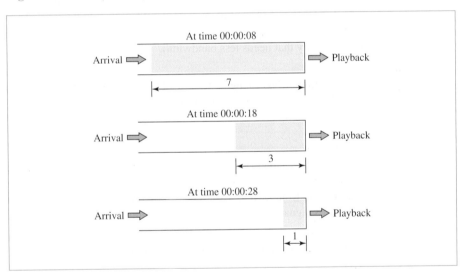

A playback buffer is required for real-time traffic.

Ordering

In addition to time relationship information and timestamps for real-time traffic, one more feature is needed. We need a *sequence number* for each packet. The timestamp alone cannot inform the receiver if a packet is lost. For example, suppose the timestamps are 0, 10, and 20. If the second packet is lost, the receiver receives just two packets with timestamps 0 and 20. The receiver assumes that the packet with timestamp 20 is the second packet, produced 20 s after the first. The receiver has no way of knowing that the second packet has actually been lost. A sequence number to order the packets is needed to handle this situation.

> **A sequence number on each packet is required for real-time traffic.**

Multicasting

Multimedia play a primary role in audio and video conferencing. The traffic can be heavy, and the data are distributed using **multicasting** methods. Conferencing requires two-way communication between receivers and senders.

> **Real-time traffic needs the support of multicasting.**

Translation

Sometimes real-time traffic needs **translation.** A translator is a computer that can change the format of a high-bandwidth video signal to a lower-quality narrow-bandwidth signal. This is needed, for example, for a source creating a high-quality video signal at 5 Mbps and sending to a recipient having a bandwidth of less than 1 Mbps. To receive the signal, a translator is needed to decode the signal and encode it again at a lower quality that needs less bandwidth.

> **Translation means changing the encoding of a payload to a lower quality to match the bandwidth of the receiving network.**

Mixing

If there is more than one source that can send data at the same time (as in a video or audio conference), the traffic is made of multiple streams. To reduce the traffic to one stream, data from different sources can be mixed into one stream. A **mixer** mathematically adds signals coming from different sources to create one single signal.

> **Mixing means combining several streams of traffic into one stream.**

Support from Transport Layer Protocol

The procedures mentioned in the previous sections can be implemented in the application layer. However, they are so common in real-time applications that implementation in the transport layer protocol is preferable. Let's see which of the existing transport layers is suitable for this type of traffic.

TCP is not suitable for interactive traffic. It has no provision for timestamping, and it does not support multicasting. However, it does provide ordering (sequence numbers). One feature of TCP that makes it particularly unsuitable for interactive traffic is its error control mechanism. In interactive traffic, we cannot allow the retransmission of a lost or corrupted packet. If a packet is lost or corrupted in interactive traffic, it must just be ignored. Retransmission upsets the whole idea of timestamping and playback. Today there is so much redundancy in audio and video signals (even with compression) that we can simply ignore a lost packet. The listener or viewer at the remote site may not even notice it.

> **TCP, with all its sophistication, is not suitable for interactive multimedia traffic because we cannot allow retransmission of packets.**

UDP is more suitable for interactive multimedia traffic. UDP supports multicasting and has no retransmission strategy. However, UDP has no provision for timestamping, sequencing, or mixing.

To use UDP and at the same time provide support for the missing features, we use UDP in conjunction with a new transport protocol, Real-Time Transport Protocol (RTP), for real-time traffic on the Internet.

> **UDP is more suitable than TCP for interactive traffic. However, we need the services of RTP, another transport layer protocol, to make up for the deficiencies of UDP.**

Real-Time Transport Protocol

Real-Time Transport Protocol (RTP) is the protocol designed to handle real-time traffic on the Internet. RTP does not have a delivery mechanism (multicasting, port numbers, and so on); it must be used with UDP. RTP stands between UDP and the application program. The main contributions of RTP are timestamping, sequencing, and mixing facilities. Figure 28.18 shows the position of RTP in the protocol suite.

Figure 28.18 *RTP*

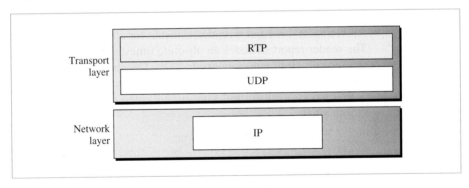

UDP Port

Although RTP is itself a transport layer protocol, the RTP packet is not encapsulated directly in an IP datagram. Instead, RTP is treated as an application program and is encapsulated in a UDP user datagram. However, unlike other application programs, no well-known port is assigned to RTP. The port can be selected on demand with only one restriction: The port number must be an even number. The next number (an odd number) is used by the companion of RTP, Real-Time Transport Control Protocol.

> **RTP uses a temporary even-numbered UDP port.**

Real-Time Transport Control Protocol (RTCP)

RTP allows only one type of message, one that carries data from the source to the destination. In many cases, there is a need for other messages in a session. These messages control the flow and quality of data and allow the recipient to send feedback to the source or sources. **Real-Time Transport Control Protocol (RTCP)** is a protocol designed for this purpose. RTCP has five types of messages as shown in Figure 28.19.

Figure 28.19 *RTCP message types*

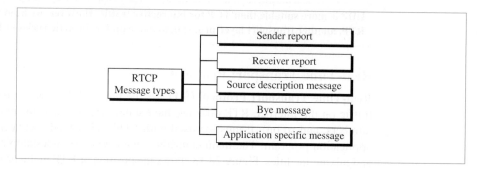

Sender Report

The sender report is sent periodically by the active senders in a conference to report transmission and reception statistics for all RTP packets sent during the interval. The sender report includes an absolute timestamp, which is the number of seconds elapsed since midnight January 1, 1970. The absolute timestamp allows the receiver to synchronize different RTP messages. It is particularly important when both audio and video are transmitted (audio and video transmissions use separate relative timestamps).

Receiver Report

The receiver report is for passive participants, those that do not send RTP packets. The report informs the sender and other receivers about the quality of service.

Source Description Message

The source periodically sends a source description message to give additional information about itself. This information can be the name, email address, telephone number, and address of the owner or controller of the source.

Bye Message

A source sends a bye message to shut down a stream. It allows the source to announce that it is leaving the conference. Although other sources can detect the absence of a source, this message is a direct announcement. It is also very useful to a mixer.

Application-Specific Message

The application-specific message is a packet for an application that wants to use new applications (not defined in the standard). It allows the definition of a new message type.

UDP Port

RTCP, like RTP, does not use a well-known UDP port. It uses a temporary port. The UDP port chosen must be the number immediately following the UDP port selected for RTP. It must be an odd-numbered port.

> **RTCP uses an odd-numbered UDP port number that follows the port number selected for RTP.**

28.6 VOICE OVER IP

Let us concentrate on one real-time interactive audio/video application: **voice over IP,** or Internet telephony. The idea is to use the Internet as a telephone network with some additional capabilities. Instead of communicating over a circuit-switched network, this application allows communication between two parties over the packet-switched Internet. Two protocols have been designed to handle this type of communication: SIP and H.323. We briefly discuss both.

SIP

The **Session Initiation Protocol (SIP)** was designed by IETF. It is an application layer protocol that establishes, manages, and terminates a multimedia session (call). It can be used to create two-party, multiparty, or multicast sessions. SIP is designed to be independent of the underlying transport layer; it can run on either UDP or TCP.

Messages

SIP is a text-based protocol like HTTP. SIP, like HTTP, uses messages. Six messages are defined as shown in Figure 28.20.

Figure 28.20 *SIP messages*

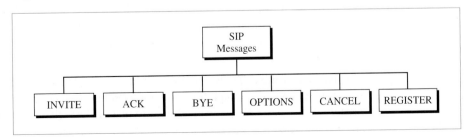

Each message has a header and a body. The header consists of several lines that describe the structure of the message, caller's capability, media type, and so on. We give a brief description of each message. Then we show their applications in the sample sessions.

The caller initializes a session with the INVITE message. After the callee answers the call, the caller sends an ACK message for confirmation. The BYE message terminates a session. The OPTIONS message queries a machine about its capabilities. The CANCEL message cancels an already started initialization process. The REGISTER message makes a connection when the callee is not available.

Addresses

In a regular telephone communication a telephone number identifies the sender, and another telephone number identifies the receiver. SIP is very flexible. In SIP, an email address, an IP address, a telephone number, and other types of addresses can be used to identify the sender and receiver. However, the address needs to be in SIP format (also called scheme). Figure 28.21 shows some common formats.

Figure 28.21   *SIP formats*

Simple Session

A simple session using SIP consists of three modules: establishing, communicating, and terminating. Figure 28.22 shows a simple session using SIP.

Establishing a Session   Establishing a session in SIP requires a three-way handshake. The caller sends an INVITE message, using UDP or TCP, to begin the communication. If the callee is willing to start the session, she sends a reply message. To confirm that a reply code has been received, the caller sends an ACK message.

Communicating   After the session has been established, the caller and the callee can communicate using two temporary ports.

Terminating the Session   The session can be terminated with a BYE message sent by either party.

Tracking the Callee

What happens if the callee is not sitting at her terminal? She may be away from her system or at another terminal. She may not even have a fixed IP address if DHCP is being used. SIP has a mechanism (similar to one in DNS) that finds the IP address of

Figure 28.22   *SIP simple session*

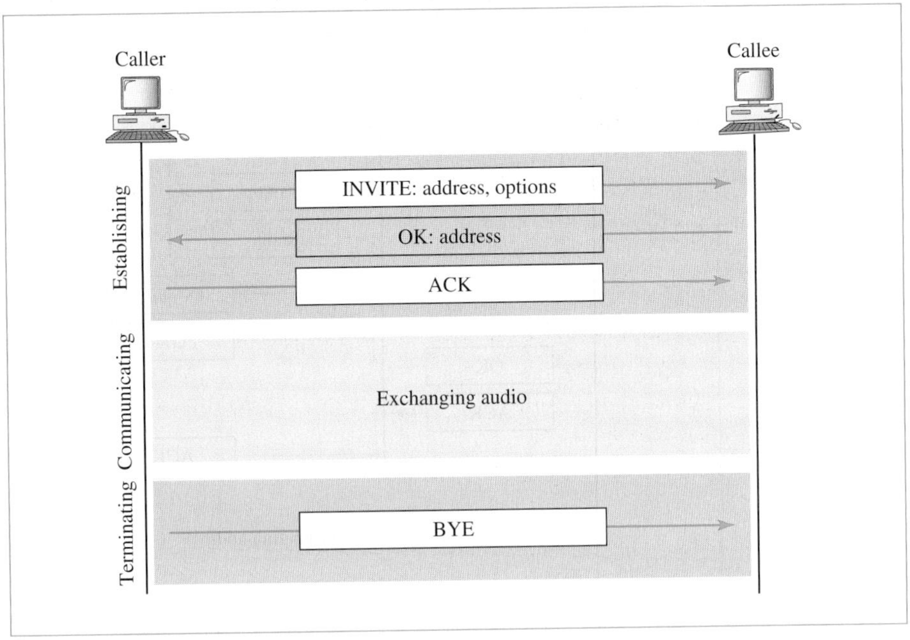

the terminal at which the callee is sitting. To perform this tracking, SIP uses the concept of registration. SIP defines some servers as registrars. At any moment a user is registered with at least one **registrar server;** this server knows the IP address of the callee.

When a caller needs to communicate with the callee, the caller can use the email address instead of the IP address in the INVITE message. The message goes to a proxy server. The proxy server sends a lookup message (not part of SIP) to some registrar server that has registered the callee. When the proxy server receives a reply message from the registrar server, the proxy server takes the caller's INVITE message and inserts the newly discovered IP address of the callee. This message is then sent to the callee. Figure 28.23 shows the process.

H.323

H.323 is a standard designed by ITU to allow telephones on the public telephone network to talk to computers (called *terminals* in H.323) connected to the Internet. Figure 28.24 shows the general architecture of H.323.

A **gateway** connects the Internet to the telephone network. In general, a gateway is a five-layer device that can translate a message from one protocol stack to another. The gateway here does exactly the same thing. It transforms a telephone network message to an Internet message. The **gatekeeper** server on the local area network plays the role of the registrar server, as we discussed in the SIP protocol.

Figure 28.23   *Tracking the callee*

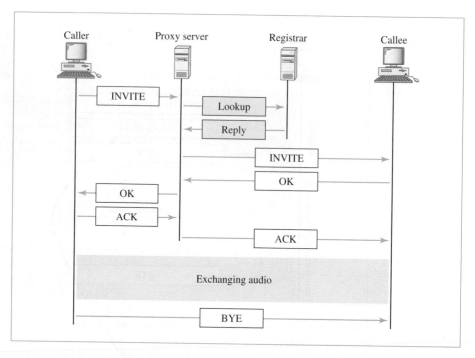

Figure 28.24   *H.323 architecture*

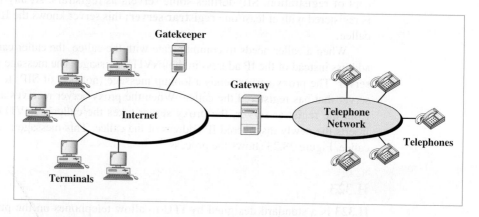

Protocols

H.323 uses a number of protocols to establish and maintain voice (or video) communication. Figure 28.25 shows these protocols.

H.323 uses G.71 or G.723.1 for compression. It uses a protocol named H.245 which allows the parties to negotiate the compression method. Protocol Q.931 is used for establishing and terminating connections. Another protocol called H.225, or RAS (Registration/Administration/Status), is used for registration with the gatekeeper.

Figure 28.25   *H.323 protocols*

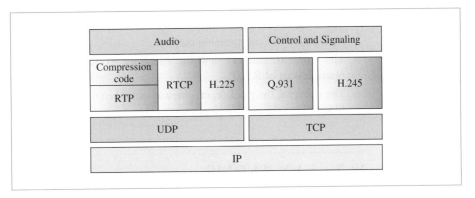

Operation

Let us show the operation of a telephone communication using H.323 with a simple example. Figure 28.26 shows the steps used by a terminal to communicate with a telephone.

1. The terminal sends a broadcast message to the gatekeeper. The gatekeeper responds with its IP address.

2. The terminal and gatekeeper communicate, using H.225 to negotiate bandwidth.

Figure 28.26   *H.323 example*

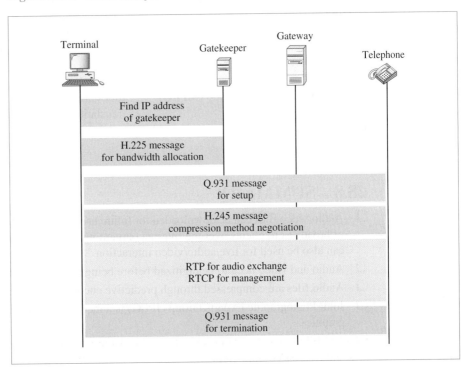

3. The terminal, the gatekeeper, gateway, and the telephone communicate using Q.931 to set up a connection.

4. The terminal, the gatekeeper, gateway, and the telephone communicate using H.245 to negotiate the compression method.

5. The terminal, gateway, and the telephone exchange audio using RTP under the management of RTCP.

6. The terminal, the gatekeeper, gateway, and the telephone communicate using Q.931 to terminate the communication.

28.7   KEY TERMS

bidirectional frame (B-frame)
compression
discrete cosine transform (DCT)
frequency masking
gatekeeper
gateway
H.323
interactive audio/video
intracoded frame (I-frame)
jitter
Joint Photographic Experts Group (JPEG)
media player
media server
metafile
mixer
Moving Picture Experts Group (MPEG)
MP3
on-demand audio/video

pixel
playback buffer
predicted frame (P-frame)
predictive encoding
Real-Time Streaming Protocol (RTSP)
real-time traffic
Real-Time Transport Control Protocol (RTCP)
Real-Time Transport Protocol (RTP)
registrar server
Session Initiation Protocol (SIP)
spatial compression
streaming live audio/video
streaming stored audio/video
temporal compression
temporal masking
timestamp
translation
voice over IP

28.8   SUMMARY

❏   Audio/video files can be downloaded for future use (streaming stored audio/video) or broadcast to clients over the Internet (streaming live audio/video). The Internet can also be used for live audio/video interaction.

❏   Audio and video need to be digitized before being sent over the Internet.

❏   Audio files are compressed through predictive encoding or perceptual encoding.

❏   Joint Photographic Experts Group (JPEG) is a method to compress pictures and graphics.

❏   The JPEG process involves blocking, the discrete cosine transform, quantization, and lossless compression.

❏ Moving Pictures Experts Group (MPEG) is a method to compress video.

❏ MPEG involves both spatial compression and temporal compression. The former is similar to JPEG, and the latter removes redundant frames.

❏ We can use a Web server, or a Web server with a metafile, or a media server, or a media server and RSTP to download a streaming audio/video file.

❏ Real-time data on a packet-switched network require the preservation of the time relationship between packets of a session.

❏ Gaps between consecutive packets at the receiver cause a phenomenon called jitter.

❏ Jitter can be controlled through the use of timestamps and a judicious choice of the playback time.

❏ A playback buffer holds data until they can be played back.

❏ A receiver delays playing back real-time data held in the playback buffer until a threshold level is reached.

❏ Sequence numbers on real-time data packets provide a form of error control.

❏ Real-time data are multicast to receivers.

❏ Real-time traffic sometimes requires a translator to change a high-bandwidth signal to a lower-quality narrow-bandwidth signal.

❏ A mixer combines signals from different sources into one signal.

❏ Real-time multimedia traffic requires both UDP and Real-Time Transport Protocol (RTP).

❏ RTP handles timestamping, sequencing, and mixing.

❏ Real-Time Transport Control Protocol (RTCP) provides flow control, quality of data control, and feedback to the sources.

❏ Voice over IP is a real-time interactive audio/video application.

❏ The Session Initiation Protocol (SIP) is an application layer protocol that establishes, manages, and terminates multimedia sessions.

❏ H.323 is an ITU standard that allows a telephone connected to a public telephone network to talk to a computer connected to the Internet.

28.9   PRACTICE SET

Review Questions

1. How does streaming live audio/video differ from streaming stored audio/video?
2. What is predictive encoding?
3. What is MP3?
4. How does frequency masking differ from temporal masking?
5. What is the function of a metafile in streaming stored audio/video?
6. What is the purpose of RTSP in streaming stored audio/video?
7. How does jitter affect real-time audio/video?
8. Discuss how SIP is used in the transmission of multimedia.
9. When would you use JPEG? When would you use MPEG?

10. How is MPEG related to JPEG?

11. In JPEG, what is the function of blocking?

12. Why is the DCT needed in JPEG?

13. How does quantization contribute to compression?

14. What is a frame in MPEG compression?

15. What is spatial compression compared to temporal compression?

16. Discuss the three types of frames used in MPEG.

Multiple-Choice Questions

17. For streaming stored audio/video, the _____ holds information about the audio/video file.
    a. Alpha file
    b. Beta file
    c. Metafile
    d. Jitter

18. _____ is a control protocol that adds functionalities to the streaming process.
    a. RTSP
    b. HTTP
    c. TCP/IP
    d. SIP

19. The audio/video stream is sent by the media server to the _____.
    a. Browser
    b. Web server
    c. Media player
    d. None of the above

20. A _____ shows when a packet was produced relative to the first or previous packet.
    a. Timestamp
    b. Playback buffer
    c. Sequence number
    d. Threshold

21. _____ are used to number the packets of a real-time transmission.
    a. Timestamps
    b. Playback buffers
    c. Sequence numbers
    d. Translators

22. In a real-time video conference, data from the server are _____ to the client sites.
    a. Unicast
    b. Multicast

c. Broadcast

d. None of the above

23. A _____ adds signals from different sources to create a single signal.

a. Timestamp

b. Sequence number

c. Mixer

d. Translator

24. A _____ changes the format of a high-bandwidth video signal to a lower-quality narrow-bandwidth signal.

a. Timestamp

b. Sequence number

c. Mixer

d. Translator

25. An RTP packet is encapsulated in a(n) _____.

a. UDP user datagram

b. TCP segment

c. IP datagram

d. RTCP packet

26. TCP is not suitable for real-time traffic because _____.

a. There is no provision for timestamping

b. There is no support for multicasting

c. Missing packets are retransmitted

d. All the above

27. JPEG encoding involves _____, a process that reveals the redundancies in a block.

a. Blocking

b. The DCT

c. Quantization

d. Vectorization

28. The last step in JPEG, _____, removes redundancies.

a. Blocking

b. Quantization

c. Compression

d. Vectorization

29. The RTCP _____ message shuts down a stream.

a. Application-specific

b. Bye

c. Source description

d. Farewell

30. The RTCP _____ report informs the sender and other receivers about the quality of service.
   a. Sender
   b. Receiver
   c. QoS
   d. Passive

31. Voice over IP is a(n) _____ audio/video application.
   a. Streaming stored
   b. Streaming live
   c. Interactive
   d. None of the above

32. _____ is an application layer protocol that establishes, maintains, and terminates a multimedia session.
   a. SIP
   b. RTCP
   c. DCT
   d. JPEG

33. _____ is a SIP message type.
   a. INVITE
   b. CANCEL
   c. OPTIONS
   d. All the above

34. A _____ is involved in an SIP mechanism to find the IP address of a callee.
   a. Proxy server
   b. Registrar server
   c. Media server
   d. (a) and (b)

35. A standard that allows a telephone (connected to a public telephone network) to talk to a computer connected to the Internet is _____.
   a. IEEE 802.3
   b. SIP
   c. H.323
   d. V.90bis

36. _____ is a protocol to set up and terminate a connection between a computer on the Internet and a telephone (connected to a public telephone network).
   a. H.323
   b. Q.931
   c. H.245
   d. H.225

Exercises

37. In Figure 28.17 what is the amount of data in the playback buffer at each of the following times?
    a. 00:00:17
    b. 00:00:20
    c. 00:00:25
    d. 00:00:30

38. Compare and contrast TCP with RTP. Are both doing the same thing?

39. Can we say UDP plus RTP is the same as TCP?

40. Why does RTP need the service of another protocol, RTCP, but TCP does not?

41. In Figure 28.12, can the Web server and media server run on different machines?

42. We discuss the use of SIP in this chapter only for audio. Is there any drawback to prevent using it for video?

43. Do you think H.323 is actually the same as SIP? What are the differences? Make a comparison between the two.

44. What are the problems for full implementation of voice over IP? Do you think we will stop using the telephone network very soon?

45. Can H.323 also be used for video?

PART 7

Security

We have devoted the last part of the book to network security, a subject that is becoming more important every day. This subject is so vast and involved that we can only give an overview in this text. The number of books dealing with Internet security is growing as are the number of hackers. We discuss just the fundamental concepts here.

Topics

We have chosen several topics related to Internet security for this part of the book. These are shown in Figure 1.

Figure 1 *Security topics*

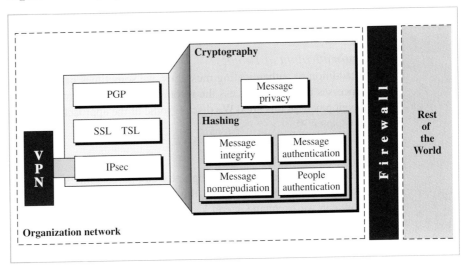

Cryptography

Cryptography is the heart of security. If we need to create privacy, we need to encrypt our message at the sender site and decrypt it at the receiver site. For thousands of years, people believed that cryptography required the use of a secret key between the two parties. Recently, a new method, public key cryptography has been devised that uses two keys: one public and one private. Using secret key cryptography is like using just one key that both locks and unlocks a door. Using public key cryptography is like using two separate keys; one can only lock, the other can only unlock. We have devoted Chapter 29 to the topic of cryptography.

Security Aspects

Today, security involves more than just privacy of the message. When Alice sends a message to Bob, both are concerned about privacy, but they also need to worry about other issues. Bob needs to be sure that the message from Alice really comes from Alice, and not somebody else; Bob needs to authenticate the message. Bob also needs to be sure that the message has not been changed during the transition; Bob needs to be sure of the integrity of the message. If Bob represents a bank and Alice represents a customer, Bob needs to be able to prove later that Alice has sent the message if she later denies it; this is nonrepudiation. We introduce these aspects of security in Chapter 30.

Hashing

A topic that is related to the cryptography is hashing. Hashing means creating a miniature version of a message that can be used instead of the message for some aspect of security. For example, the miniature can be checked for integrity. If the miniature has not been changed during the transmission, it means that the message has not been changed. We will discuss hashing in Chapter 30 when we discuss the digital signature.

Authentication of People

In addition to authenticating messages, we sometimes need to authenticate people or processes to let them access the resources of an organization. There has been a lot of development in this area. We discuss some of the approaches and provide some insight in Chapter 30.

Key Management

Although it appears that cryptography can solve some security problems, it creates others in a network as large as the Internet. One such problem is key management. How can we exchange secret keys between two parties who are thousands of miles away? How can we be sure that Alice's public key is actually her key? We introduce key management in Chapter 30.

Security and Internet Model

There was little provision for security in the original design of the Internet model. The OSI model, on the other hand, provided encryption/decryption services in the presentation layer, a layer that does not exist in the Internet model. The OSI model was never implemented.

Now the question is, "If we want to implement security in the Internet model, at which layer it should be added?" The experts have not come out with a solid solution, especially since a security breach can happen in all five layers. At the physical layer, an intruder can wiretap into the transmission media and read or alter a sequence of bits.

At the data link layer, frames can be captured and read or altered. This could be particularly common in a LAN where a transmission is broadcast and every station receives a copy of a frame. At the network layer, an IP datagram can be removed, altered, or inserted into the network. At the transport layer, a user datagram or a segment can be captured or altered. Finally, at the application layer, the whole message can be altered or read. Before applying or adding security to the Internet, several questions need to be asked.

1. In which layer is security more effective?
2. In which layer is security easier to provide?
3. If we have security at one level, do we need security at other levels?

Security at the Application Layer   The whole purpose of the Internet is to provide process-to-process communication, sending a message from one process to another. So some people believe that security must only be implemented at the application layer. If a message going from one process to another is secure, the two processes do not care about the security in other layers. There are those who see problems in this implementation:

a. The application programs in this level are very well established and independent from each other. If we want to implement security at this layer, we need to provide security for each application protocol such as DNS, SMTP, FTP, HTTP. This means that all of these application programs must be revised. Although this involves time and money, the idea is implemented in SMTP as we will see in Chapter 31.

b. Not all communication in the Internet is done at the application layer. Some services, such as RIP use the services of a transport layer, but are not an application layer service. An intruder can easily attack RIP and divert the updating message to confuse and mislead the routers.

c. Some other protocols use the services of IP directly without even using a transport layer protocol. For example, OSPF falls into this category.

Security at the Transport Layer   Many people argue that the transport layer is the best layer to implement security. We can include security measures in UDP or TCP. Every application uses either UDP or TCP. If these two are secure, the application program is secure. Opponents to this idea argue that UDP and TCP are well-established transport-layer protocols and changing them is not a trivial task. Although security has not been directly added to UDP or TCP, a security protocol called TLS has been designed that runs on the top of the transport layer.

Security at the Network Layer   Many believe that the optimum solution is to implement security at the network layer, to the IP. This argument has resulted in a new provision called IPsec that we studied in Chapter 21.

Security at the Data Link Layer   Although some argue that security can be easily implemented at the data link layer because the domain is just the link, others believe that node-to-node security does not guarantee end-to-end security. We do not discuss link security in this book.

Firewalls

Although we can keep a message confidential, preserve its integrity, authenticate its sender, and ensure nonrepudiation, these aspects of security do not prevent someone from deliberately sending a message to a system to cause damage. We need yet another tool. We need to filter the messages to allow only those that we want. The firewall is a technology that is used in this case. We discuss firewalls in Chapter 31.

Virtual Private Networks

In the past, an organization that needed internal privacy used a private network. However, if an organization has several branches in the world, connecting these private networks using private WANs can be very expensive. Instead, organizations can use the services of the Internet to connect their private networks together as though the Internet were a virtual private WAN. We discuss the virtual private network (VPN) technology in Chapter 31.

Chapters

We briefly discuss cryptography in Chapter 29. We discuss security aspects, people authentication, and key management in Chapter 30. We cover Internet security, firewalls, and VPNs in Chapter 31.

CHAPTER 29

Cryptography

We begin our discussion of network security with an introduction to cryptography and a discussion of the methods used in security management. The science of cryptography is very complex; there are entire books devoted to the subject. A cryptography expert needs to be knowledgeable in areas such as mathematics, electronics, and programming. In this chapter, we consider the concepts needed to understand the security issues discussed in Chapter 30 and network security discussed in Chapter 31.

We focus on symmetric-key cryptography, which is presently more common than public-key cryptography. Symmetric-key cryptography is less math-based than public-key cryptography, which has its origins in number theory.

Cryptography and its applications to the Internet are a relatively new field whose importance increases with every new attack on the Internet.

29.1 INTRODUCTION

The word **cryptography** in Greek means "secret writing." However, the term today refers to the science and art of transforming messages to make them secure and immune to attacks. Figure 29.1 shows the components involved in cryptography.

Figure 29.1 *Cryptography components*

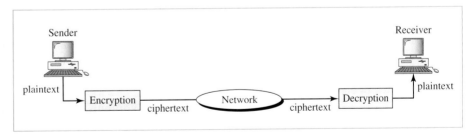

The original message, before being transformed, is called **plaintext.** After the message is transformed, it is called **ciphertext.** An **encryption** algorithm transforms the plaintext to ciphertext; a **decryption** algorithm transforms the ciphertext back to plaintext. The sender uses an encryption algorithm, and the receiver uses a decryption algorithm.

Throughout this chapter and Chapters 30 and 31, we discuss encryption and decryption algorithms. We refer to them as **ciphers.** The term *cipher* is also used to refer to different categories of algorithms in cryptography.

This is not to say that every sender-receiver pair needs its very own unique cipher for a secure communication. Instead, through the use of public ciphers with secret keys, one cipher can serve millions of communicating pairs. A **key** is a number (value) that the cipher, as an algorithm, operates on. To encrypt a message, we need an encryption algorithm, an encryption key, and the plaintext. These create the ciphertext. To decrypt a message, we need a decryption algorithm, a decryption key, and the ciphertext. These reveal the original plaintext. Figure 29.2 shows the idea.

Figure 29.2 *Encryption and decryption*

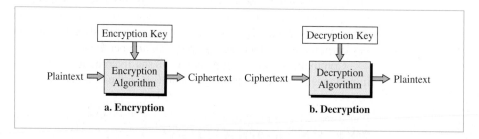

The encryption and decryption algorithms are public; anyone can access them. The keys are secret; they need to be protected.

> In cryptography, the encryption/decryption algorithms are public; the keys are secret.

It is customary to introduce three characters in cryptography; we use Alice, Bob, and Eve. Alice is the person who needs to send secure data. Bob is the recipient of the data. Eve is the person who somehow disturbs the communication between Alice and Bob by intercepting messages or sending her own disguised messages. These three names represent computers or processes that actually send or receive data, or intercept or change data.

We can divide all the cryptography algorithms in the world into two groups: symmetric-key (sometimes called secret-key) cryptography algorithms and public-key (sometimes called asymmetric) cryptography algorithms.

29.2   SYMMETRIC-KEY CRYPTOGRAPHY

In **symmetric-key cryptography,** the same key is used by both parties. The sender uses this key and an encryption algorithm to encrypt data; the receiver uses the same key and the corresponding decryption algorithm to decrypt the data (see Fig. 29.3).

Figure 29.3   *Symmetric-key cryptography*

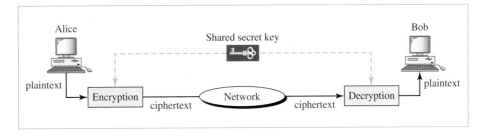

> **In symmetric-key cryptography, the same key is used by the sender (for encryption) and the receiver (for decryption). The key is shared.**

In symmetric-key cryptography, the algorithm used for decryption is the inverse of the algorithm used for encryption. This means that if the encryption algorithm uses a combination of addition and multiplication, the decryption algorithm uses a combination of division and subtraction.

Note that the symmetric-key cryptography algorithms are so named because the same key can be used in both directions.

> **In symmetric-key cryptography, the same key is used in both directions.**

Symmetric-key algorithms are efficient; it takes less time to encrypt a message using a symmetric-key algorithm than it takes to encrypt using a public-key algorithm. The reason is that the key is usually smaller. For this reason, symmetric-key algorithms are used to encrypt and decrypt long messages.

> **Symmetric-key cryptography is often used for long messages.**

A symmetric-key algorithm has two major disadvantages. Each pair of users must have a unique symmetric key. This means that if N people in the world want to use this method, there needs to be $N(N-1)/2$ symmetric keys. For example, for 1 million people to communicate, 500 billion symmetric keys are needed. The distribution of the keys between two parties can be difficult. We will see how we can solve this problem in Chapter 30.

Traditional Ciphers

In the earliest and simplest ciphers, a character was the unit of data to be encrypted. These traditional ciphers involved either substitution or transposition.

Substitution Cipher

A cipher using the **substitution** method substitutes one symbol with another. If the symbols in the plaintext are alphabetic characters, we replace one character with another. For example, we can replace character A with D and character T with Z. If the symbols are digits (0 to 9), we can replace 3 with 7 and 2 with 6. We will concentrate on alphabetic characters. Substitution can be categorized as either **monoalphabetic** or **polyalphabetic.**

Monoalphabetic Substitution In monoalphabetic substitution, a character in the plaintext is always changed to the same character in the ciphertext regardless of its position in the text. For example, if the algorithm says that character A in the plaintext must be changed to character D, every character A is changed to character D, regardless of its position in the text. The first recorded ciphertext was used by Julius Caesar and is still called the *Caesar cipher.* The cipher shifts each character down by three. Figure 29.4 shows idea of the Caesar cipher.

Figure 29.4 *Caesar cipher*

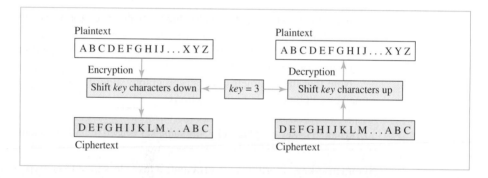

Before we go further, let us analyze the Caesar cipher which has an encryption algorithm, a decryption algorithm, and a symmetric key. As the figure shows, the encryption algorithm is "shift *key* characters down." The decryption algorithm is "shift *key* characters up." The key is 3. Note that the encryption and decryption algorithms are the inverses of each other; the key is the same in encryption and decryption.

We can think of monoalphabetic substitution in another way. We can assign numbers to the alphabet characters (A = 0, B = 1, C = 3, . . . , Z = 25). We can think of the encryption algorithm as simply "add the key to the plaintext number to get the ciphertext number." Decryption is the same, but we replace *add* with *subtract* and switch *plaintext* with *ciphertext*. Of course adding and subtracting are modulo 26, which means that 24 + 3 is 1, not 27; Y (24) is substituted with B (1).

In monoalphabetic substitution, the relationship between a character in the plaintext and a character in the ciphertext is always one-to-one. We can have many other encryption/decryption algorithms with other keys. We could change character A to J (shift of 9) and change character P to M (shift of −3). Figure 29.5 shows another example of monoalphabetic substitution. In this cipher, the two algorithms are still the inverse of each other. The key is the two rows as shown in the figure. Note that we still have a monoalphabetic substitution because the one-to-one relation is preserved.

Monoalphabetic substitution is very simple, but the code can be attacked easily. The reason is that the method cannot hide the natural frequencies of characters in the

Figure 29.5 *Example of monoalphabetic substitution*

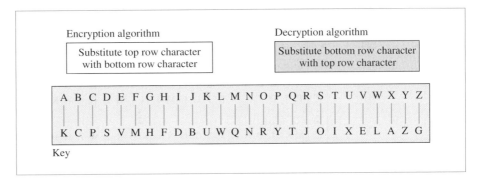

In monoalphabetic substitution, the relationship between a character in the plaintext to the character in the ciphertext is always one-to one.

language being used. For example, in English, the most frequently used characters are E, T, O, and A. An attacker can easily break the code by finding which character is used the most and replace that one with the letter E. It can then find the next most frequent and replace it with T, and so on.

Polyalphabetic Substitution   In *polyalphabetic substitution,* each occurrence of a character can have a different substitute. The relationship between a character in the plaintext to a character in the ciphertext is one-to-many. Character A can be changed to D in the beginning of the text, but it could be changed to N at the middle. There are many interesting polyalphabetic substitution ciphers. We discuss a very simple one. It is obvious that if the relationship between plaintext characters and ciphertext characters is one-to-many, the key must tell us which of the many possible characters can be chosen for encryption. Let us define our key as "take the position of the character in the text, divide the number by 10, and let the remainder be the shift value." With this scenario, the character at position 1 will be shifted one character, the character at position 2 will be shifted two characters, and the character in position 14 will be shifted four characters (14 mod 10 is 4).

An example of polyalphabetic substitution is the **Vigenere cipher.** In one version of this cipher, the character in the ciphertext is chosen from a two-dimensional table (26×26), in which each row is a permutation of 26 characters (A to Z). To change a character, the algorithm finds the character to be encrypted in the first row. It finds the position of the character in the text (mod 26) and uses it as the row number. The algorithm then replaces the character with the character found in the table. Figure 29.6 shows only some of the rows and columns. According to this table, A is encrypted as W if it is in position 0 and as M if it is in position 25.

A ciphertext created by polyalphabetic substitution is harder to attack successfully than a ciphertext created by monoalphabetic substitution. A simple observation of the frequencies does not help. As a matter of fact, a good polyalphabetic substitution may smooth out the frequencies; each character in the ciphertext may occur almost the same

Figure 29.6   *Vigenere cipher*

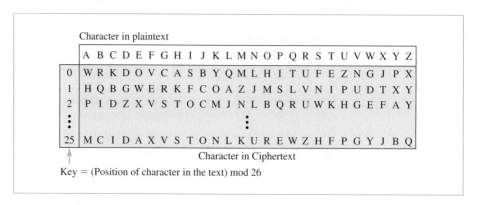

In polyalphabetic substitution, the relationship between a character in the plaintext and a character in the ciphertext is one-to-many.

number of times. However, attacking the code is not difficult; although the encryption changes the frequency of the characters, the character relationships are still preserved. A good trial-and-error attack can break the code. But we leave this as an exercise for students.

Transpositional Cipher

In a **transpositional cipher,** the characters retain their plaintext form but change their positions to create the ciphertext. The text is organized into a two-dimensional table, and the columns are interchanged according to a key. For example, we can organize the plaintext into an 8-column table and then reorganize the columns according to a key that indicates the interchange rule. Figure 29.7 shows an example

Figure 29.7   *Transpositional cipher*

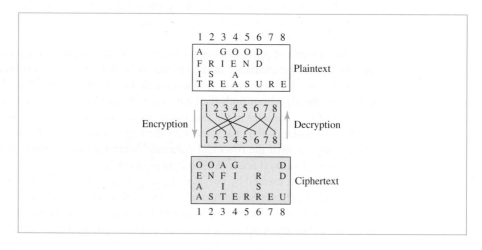

of transpositional cryptography. The key defines which columns should be swapped. As you have guessed, transpositional cryptography is not very secure either. The character frequencies are preserved, and the attacker can find the plaintext through trial and error. This method can be combined with other methods to provide more sophisticated ciphers.

Block Cipher

Traditional ciphers used a character or symbol as the unit of encryption/decryption. Modern ciphers, on the other hand, use a block of bits as the unit of encryption/decryption. Figure 29.8 shows the concept of the **block cipher;** the plaintext and ciphertext are blocks of bits.

Figure 29.8 *Block cipher*

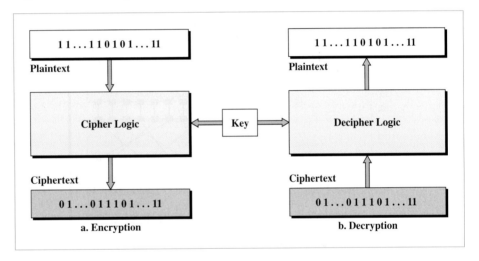

P-box

A **P-box** (P for permutation) performs a transposition at the bit level; it transposes bits as shown in Figure 29.9. It can be implemented in software or hardware, but hardware

Figure 29.9 *P-box*

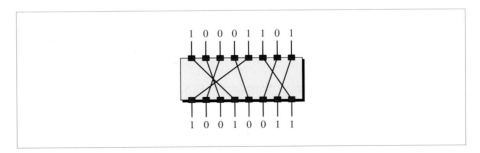

is faster. The key and the encryption/decryption algorithm are normally embedded in the hardware. Note that both the plaintext and ciphertext have the same number of 1s and 0s.

S-box

An **S-box** (S for substitution) performs a substitution at the bit level; it transposes permuted bits as shown in Figure 29.10. The S-box substitutes one decimal digit with another. The S-box normally has three components: an encoder, a decoder, and a P-box. The decoder changes an input of n bits to an output of 2^n bits. This output has one single 1 (the rest are 0s) located at a position determined by the input. The P-box permutes the output of decoder, and the encoder changes the output of the P-box back to a binary number in the same way as the decoder, but inversely.

Figure 29.10   *S-box*

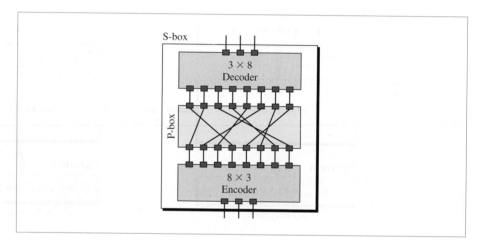

For example, if the number in the figure is 2 (010), the decoder changes it to 00000100. The position of the 1 bit is, counting from the right with the leftmost bit at position 0, at position 2. After the P-box transposition, in this configuration, we have 01000000. The 1 bit is at position 6. Therefore, the encoder encodes this as binary 110. The 2 has been changed to decimal digit 6.

Product Block

The P-boxes and S-boxes can be combined to get a more complex cipher block. This is called a **product block,** as shown in Figure 29.11.

Data Encryption Standard (DES)

One example of a complex block cipher is the **Data Encryption Standard (DES).** DES was designed by IBM and adopted by the U.S. government as the standard encryption method for nonmilitary and nonclassified use. The algorithm encrypts a 64-bit plaintext

Figure 29.11 *Product block*

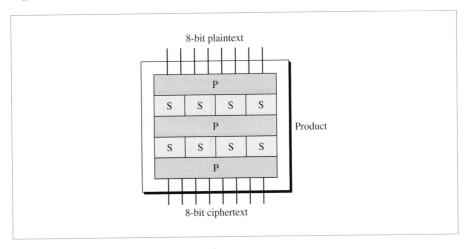

using a 56-bit key. The text is put through 19 different and complex procedures to create a 64-bit ciphertext, as shown in Figure 29.12. DES has two transposition blocks, one swapping block, and 16 complex blocks called iteration blocks. Figure 29.13 shows the general scheme.

Figure 29.12 *DES*

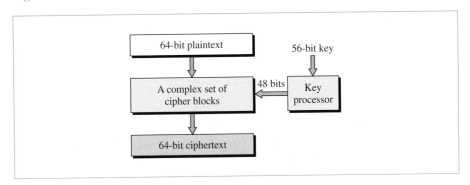

Although the 16 iteration blocks are conceptually the same, each uses a different key derived from the original key. Figure 29.14 shows the schematics of an iteration block.

In each block, the previous right 32 bits become the next left 32 bits (swapping). The next right 32 bits, however, come from first applying an operation (a function) on the previous right 32 bits and then XORing the result with the left 32 bits.

Note that the whole DES cipher block is a substitution block that changes a 64-bit plaintext to a 64-bit ciphertext. In other words, instead of substituting one character at a time, it substitutes 8 characters (bytes) at a time, using complex encryption and decryption algorithms.

Figure 29.13   *General scheme of DES*

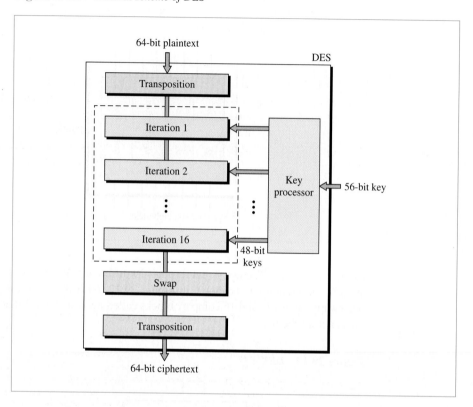

Figure 29.14   *Iteration block*

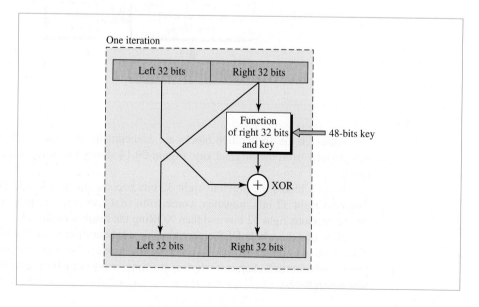

DES takes the data and chops them into 8-byte segments. However, the encryption and the key are the same for each segment. So if the data are four equal segments, the result is also four equal segments.

Triple DES

Critics of DES contend that the key is too short. To lengthen the key and at the same time keep the new block compatible with that of the original DES, **triple DES** was designed. This uses three DES blocks and two 56-bit keys, as shown in Figure 29.15. Note that the encrypting block uses an encryption-decryption-encryption combination of DESs, while the decryption block uses a decryption-encryption-decryption combination. It was designed this way to provide compatibility between triple DES and the original DES when K1 and K2 are the same.

Figure 29.15 *Triple DES*

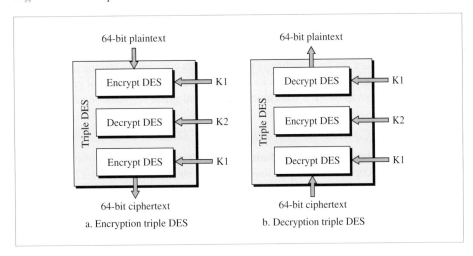

a. Encryption triple DES   b. Decryption triple DES

The DES cipher uses the same concept as the Caesar cipher, but the encryption/decryption algorithm is much more complex due to the sixteen 48-bit keys derived from a 56-bit key.

Operation Modes

DES and triple DES are actually long substitution ciphers that operate on eight-character segments (sometimes called long characters). Can we encrypt and decrypt longer messages (1000 characters, e.g.)? Several modes have been defined, and we briefly describe the four most common.

Electronic Code Block (ECB) Mode

In **electronic code block (ECB) mode,** we divide the long message into 64-bit blocks and encrypt each block separately, as shown in Figure 29.16. The encryption of each

Figure 29.16 *ECB mode*

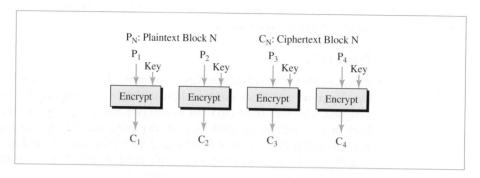

block is independent of the other blocks in ECB mode. Although the figure shows only four blocks, ECB is designed to handle many more.

The problem with the ECB mode is that the encryption of each 8-byte block is independent of the others; the encryption of each block does not depend on the other blocks in the processor. This means that Eve could exchange two blocks; Bob would not notice this change if both blocks were related to the same message. For example, if Eve knows that blocks 4, 8, 12, 16, . . . , are the student grade-point averages, she could swap block 8 with block 16 (her bad grade for someone else's top grade).

Cipher Block Chaining (CBC) Mode

In **cipher block chaining (CBC) mode,** the encryption (or decryption) of a block depends on all previous blocks, as shown in Figure 29.17.

Figure 29.17 *CBC mode*

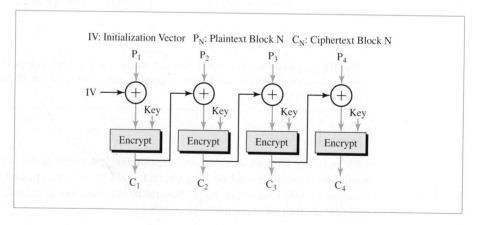

For example, to encrypt the second plaintext block (P_2), we first XOR it with the first ciphertext block (C_1) and then pass it through the encryption process. In this way, C_2 depends on C_1. If someone exchanges C_1 with C_3, for example, C_2 will not decrypt correctly; it will create garbage. The situation for the first block is different because there is no C_0. Instead, a 64-bit random number, called the *initialization vector* (IV), is used. The IV is sent with the data so that the receiver can use it in decryption.

Cipher Feedback Mode (CFM)

Cipher feedback mode (CFM) was created for those situations in which we need to send or receive data 1 byte at a time, but still want to use DES (or triple DES). One solution is to make a 1-byte C_N dependent on a 1-byte P_N and another byte, which depends on 8 previous bytes itself, as shown in Figure 29.18.

Figure 29.18 *CFM*

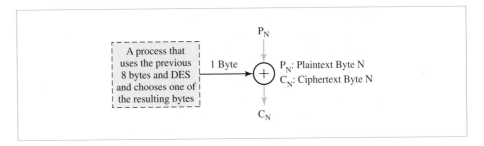

Cipher Stream Mode (CSM)

To encrypt/decrypt 1 bit at a time and at the same time be independent of the previous bits, we can use **cipher stream mode (CSM).** In this mode, data are XORed bit by bit with a long, one-time bit stream that is generated by an initialization vector in a looping process. The looping process, as Figure 29.19 shows, generates a 64-bit sequence that is XORed with plaintext to create ciphertext.

Figure 29.19 *CSM*

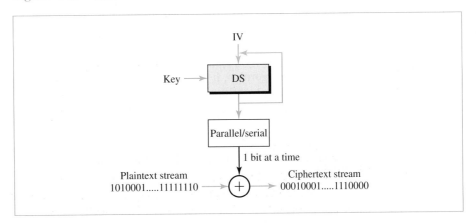

29.3   PUBLIC-KEY CRYPTOGRAPHY

In **public-key cryptography,** there are two keys: a **private key** and a **public key.** The private key is kept by the receiver. The public key is announced to the public.

Imagine Alice, as shown in Figure 29.20, wants to send a message to Bob. Alice uses the public key to encrypt the message. When the message is received by Bob, the private key is used to decrypt the message.

Figure 29.20   *Public-key cryptography*

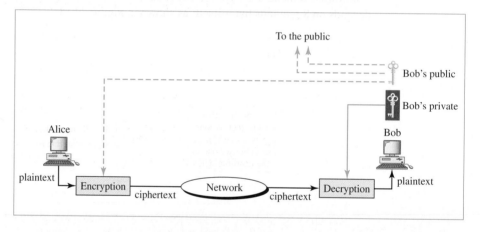

In public-key encryption/decryption, the public key that is used for encryption is different from the private key that is used for decryption. The public key is available to the public; the private key is available only to an individual.

Public-key encryption/decryption has two advantages. First, it removes the restriction of a shared symmetric key between two entities (e.g., persons) who need to communicate with each other. A shared symmetric key is shared by the two parties and cannot be used when one of them wants to communicate with a third party. In public-key encryption/ decryption, each entity creates a pair of keys; the private one is kept, and the public one is distributed. Each entity is independent, and the pair of keys created can be used to communicate with any other entity. The second advantage is that the number of keys needed is reduced tremendously. In this system, for 1 million users to communicate, only 2 million keys are needed, not 500 billion, as was the case in symmetric-key cryptography.

Public-key cryptography also has two disadvantages. The big disadvantage is the complexity of the algorithm. If we want the method to be effective, the algorithm needs large numbers. Calculating the ciphertext from plaintext using the long keys takes a lot of time. That is the main reason that public-key cryptography is not recommended for large amounts of text.

> **Public-key algorithms are more efficient for short messages.**

The second disadvantage of the public-key method is that the association between an entity and its public key must be verified. If Alice sends her public key via an email to Bob, then Bob must be sure that the public key really belongs to Alice and nobody else.

We will see that this certification is really important when we use public-key cryptography for authentication. However, this disadvantage can be overcome using a certification authority (CA) that we discuss in Chapter 30. Public-key encryption methods are relatively new. Several methods have been used during the last few decades, but the one most common today is based on the RSA algorithm.

RSA

The most common public-key algorithm is called the **RSA method** after its inventors (Rivest, Shamir, and Adleman). The private key here is a pair of numbers (N, d); the public key is also a pair of numbers (N, e). Note that N is common to the private and public keys.

The sender uses the following algorithm to encrypt the message:

$$C = P^e \bmod N$$

In this algorithm, P is the plaintext, which is represented as a number; C is the number that represents the ciphertext. The two numbers e and N are components of the public key. Plaintext P is raised to the power e and divided by N. The mod term indicates that the remainder is sent as the ciphertext.

The receiver uses the following algorithm to decrypt the message:

$$P = C^d \bmod N$$

In this algorithm, P and C are the same as before. The two numbers d and N are components of the private key. Figure 29.21 shows an example.

Figure 29.21 *RSA*

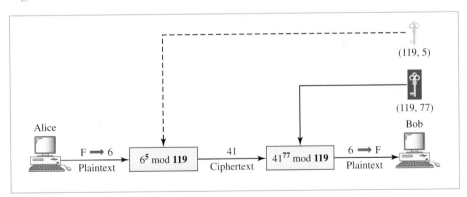

Imagine the private key is the pair (119, 77) and the public key is the pair (119, 5). The sender needs to send the character F. This character can be represented as number 6 (F is the sixth character in the alphabet). The encryption algorithm calculates $C = 6^5 \bmod 119 = 41$. This number is sent to the receiver as the ciphertext. The receiver uses the decryption algorithm to calculate $P = 41^{77} \bmod 119 = 6$ (the original number). The number 6 is then interpreted as F.

The reader may question the effectiveness of this algorithm. If an intruder knows the decryption algorithm and $N = 119$, the only thing missing is $d = 77$. Why couldn't the intruder use trial and error to find d? The answer is yes, in this trivial example an intruder could easily guess the value of d. But a major concept of the RSA algorithm is to use very large numbers for d and e. In practice, the numbers are so large (on the scale of tens of digits) that the trial-and-error approach of breaking the code takes a long time (years, if not months) even with the fastest computers available today.

Choosing Public and Private Keys

One question that comes to mind is, How do we choose the three numbers N, d, and e for encryption and decryption to work? The inventors of the RSA used number theory to prove that using the following procedure will guarantee that the algorithms will work. Although the proof is beyond the scope of this book, we outline the procedure:

1. Choose two large prime numbers p and q.
2. Compute $N = p \times q$.
3. Choose e (less than N) such that e and $(p-1)(q-1)$ are relatively prime (having no common factor other than 1).
4. Choose d such that $(e \times d) \bmod [(p-1)(q-1)]$ is equal to 1.

29.4   KEY TERMS

block cipher	P-box
cipher	plaintext
cipher block chaining (CBC) mode	polyalphabetic substitution
cipher feedback mode (CFM)	private key
cipher stream mode (CSM)	product block
ciphertext	public key
cryptography	public-key cryptography
Data Encryption Standard (DES)	Rivest, Shamir, Adleman (RSA) method
decryption	S-box
electronic code block (ECB) mode	symmetric-key cryptography
encryption	transpositional cipher
key	triple DES
monoalphabetic substitution	Vigenere cipher

29.5   SUMMARY

- Cryptography is the science and art of transforming messages to make them secure and immune to attack.
- Encryption renders a message (plaintext) unintelligible to unauthorized personnel.
- Decryption transforms an intentionally unintelligible message (ciphertext) into meaningful information.
- Cryptography algorithms are classified as either symmetric-key methods or public-key methods.

❑ In symmetric-key cryptography the same secret key is used by the sender and the receiver.

❑ Substitution ciphers are either monoalphabetic or polyalphabetic.

❑ The P-box, S-box, and product block are methods used by block ciphers.

❑ DES is a symmetric-key method adopted by the U.S. government, but it has been replaced by Triple DES or other methods.

❑ Operation modes to handle long messages include ECB mode, CBC mode, CFM, and CSM.

❑ In public-key cryptography, the public key is used by the sender to encrypt the message; the private key is used by the receiver to decrypt the message.

❑ One of the commonly used public-key cryptography methods is the RSA algorithm.

29.6 PRACTICE SET

Review Questions

1. What is the relationship between plaintext and ciphertext?
2. What are the two categories of cryptography methods? What is the main difference between the categories?
3. What is the concept behind substitutional cryptography?
4. Why is polyalphabetic substitution superior to monoalphabetic substitution?
5. What is the concept behind transpositional cryptography?
6. What is a block cipher?
7. What is the function of a P-box?
8. What is a product block?
9. How is triple DES different from the original DES?
10. Name four methods to encrypt and decrypt long messages.
11. What keys are needed for public-key cryptography?
12. What is a popular public-key encryption algorithm?

Multiple-Choice Questions

13. Before a message is encrypted, it is called _____.
    a. Plaintext
    b. Ciphertext
    c. Cryptotext
    d. Cryptonite
14. After a message is decrypted, it is called _____.
    a. Plaintext
    b. Ciphertext
    c. Cryptotext
    d. Cryptonite

15. A cipher is _____.
    a. An encryption algorithm
    b. A decryption algorithm
    c. A private key
    d. (a) or (b)

16. In the symmetric-key method of cryptography, which key is publicly known?
    a. Encryption key only
    b. Decryption key only
    c. Both
    d. None of the above

17. If 20 people need to communicate using symmetric-key cryptography, _____ symmetric keys are needed.
    a. 19
    b. 20
    c. 190
    d. 200

18. The _____ is an example of polyalphabetic substitution.
    a. P-box
    b. S-box
    c. Product block
    d. Vigenere cipher

19. The _____ is a block cipher.
    a. P-box
    b. S-box
    c. Product block
    d. All the above

20. We use a cryptography method in which the character Z always substitutes for the character G. This is probably _____.
    a. Monoalphabetic substitution
    b. Polyalphabetic substitution
    c. Transpositional
    d. None of the above

21. We use an cryptography method in which the plaintext AAAAAA becomes the ciphertext BCDEFG. This is probably _____.
    a. Monoalphabetic substitution
    b. Polyalphabetic substitution
    c. Transposition
    d. None of the above

22. One way to encrypt and decrypt long messages is through the use of the _____.
    a. ECB mode
    b. CBC mode

    c. CFM

    d. All the above

23. An initialization vector is needed in the _____.

    a. ECB mode

    b. CBC mode

    c. CVF

    d. CSM

24. In the _____ the encryption of each 8-byte block is independent of the others.

    a. ECB mode

    b. CBC mode

    c. CVF

    d. CSM

25. In the public-key method of cryptography, which key is publicly known?

    a. Encryption key only

    b. Decryption key only

    c. Both

    d. None of the above

26. In the public-key method of cryptography, only the receiver has possession of the _____.

    a. Private key

    b. Public key

    c. Both keys

    d. None of the above

27. The RSA algorithm uses a _____ cryptography method.

    a. Public-key

    b. Private-key

    c. Symmetric-key

    d. Denominational

Exercises

28. Encrypt the following message, using monoalphabetic substitution with key = 4.

          THIS IS A GOOD EXAMPLE

29. Decrypt the following message, using monoalphabetic substitution with key = 4.

          IRGVCTXMSR MW JYR

30. Decrypt the following message, using monoalphabetic substitution without knowing the key.

          KTIXEVZOUT OY ROQK KTIRUYOTM G YKIXKZ OT GT KTBKRUVK

31. Encrypt the following message, using polyalphabetic substitution. Use the position of each character as the key.

          One plus one is two, one plus two is three, one plus three is four.

32. Use the following encrypting algorithms to encrypt the message "GOOD DAY."
    a. Replace each character with its ASCII code.
    b. Add a 0 bit at the left to make each character 8 bits long.
    c. Swap the first 4 bits with the last 4 bits.
    d. Replace every 4 bits with its hexadecimal equivalent.
    What is the key in this method?

33. Use the following encrypting algorithm to encrypt the message "ABCADEFGH" (assume that the message is always made of uppercase letters).
    a. Treat each character as a decimal number, using ASCII code (between
    a. 65 and 90).
    b. Subtract 65 from each coded character.
    c. Change each number into a 5-bit pattern.

34. Using the RSA algorithm, encrypt and decrypt the message "BE" with key pairs (3, 15) and (5, 15).

35. Given the two prime numbers $p = 19$ and $q = 23$, try to find N, e, and d.

36. To understand the security of the RSA algorithm, find d if you know that $e = 17$ and $N = 187$.

37. In the RSA algorithm, we use $C = P^e \bmod N$ to encrypt a number. If e and N are large numbers (each hundreds of digits), the calculation is impossible and creates an overflow error even in a supercomputer. One solution (not the best one) using number theory involves several steps, where each step uses the result of the previous step:
    a. $C = 1$.
    b. Repeat e times:

    $$C = (C \times P) \bmod N$$

    In this way, a computer program can be written that calculates C using a loop. For example $6^5 \bmod 119$, which is 41, can be calculated as follows:

    $$(1 \times 6) \bmod 119 = 6$$
    $$(6 \times 6) \bmod 119 = 36$$
    $$(36 \times 6) \bmod 119 = 97$$
    $$(97 \times 6) \bmod 119 = 106$$
    $$(106 \times 6) \bmod 119 = 41$$

    Use this method to calculate $227^{16} \bmod 100$.

CHAPTER 30

Message Security,
User Authentication,
and Key Management

After studying cryptography in Chapter 29, we discuss some of its applications: message security, user authentication, and key management.

Message security involves confidentiality, integrity, authentication, and finally nonrepudiation.

User authentication means verifying the identity of the person or process that wants to communicate with a system. User authentication is also needed for key management.

Finally, we need key management: the distribution of symmetric keys and the certification of the public keys. Section 30.4 explains the methods used in key management.

30.1   MESSAGE SECURITY

Let us first discuss the security measures applied to each single message. We can say that security provides four services: privacy (confidentiality), message authentication, message integrity, and nonrepudiation (see Fig. 30.1).

Figure 30.1   *Message security*

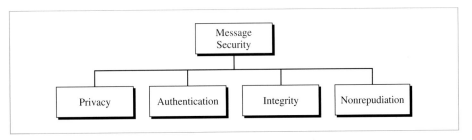

Privacy

Privacy means that the sender and the receiver expect confidentiality. The transmitted message must make sense to only the intended receiver. To all others, the message must be unintelligible.

The concept of how to achieve privacy has not changed for thousands of years: The message must be encrypted. That is, the message must be rendered unintelligible to unauthorized parties. A good privacy technique guarantees to some extent that a potential intruder (eavesdropper) cannot understand the contents of the message.

Privacy with Symmetric-Key Cryptography

Privacy can be achieved using symmetric-key encryption and decryption, as shown in Figure 30.2. As we discussed in Chapter 29, in symmetric-key cryptography the key is shared between Alice and Bob.

Figure 30.2   *Privacy using symmetric-key encryption*

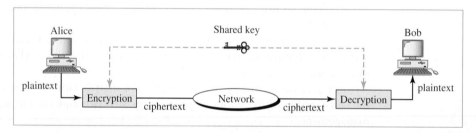

Using symmetric-key cryptography is very common for achieving privacy. Later in this chapter, we will see how to manage the distribution of symmetric keys.

Privacy with Public-Key Cryptography

We can also achieve privacy using public-key encryption. There are two keys: a private key and a public key. The private key is kept by the receiver. The public key is announced to the public. This is shown in Figure 30.3.

Figure 30.3   *Privacy using public-key encryption*

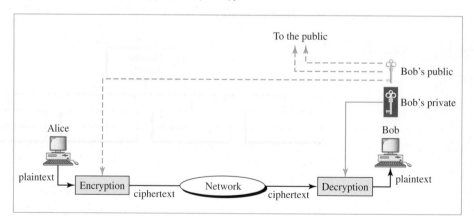

The main problem with public key encryption is its owner must be verified (certified). We will see how to solve this problem shortly.

Message Authentication

Message **authentication** means that the receiver needs to be sure of the sender's identity and that an imposter has not sent the message. We will see how digital signature can provide message authentication.

Integrity

Integrity means that the data must arrive at the receiver exactly as they were sent. There must be no changes during the transmission, either accidental or malicious. As more and more monetary exchanges occur over the Internet, integrity is crucial. For example, it would be disastrous if a request for transferring $100 changed to a request for $10,000 or $100,000. The integrity of the message must be preserved in a secure communication. We will see how digital signature can provide message integrity.

Nonrepudiation

Nonrepudiation means that a receiver must be able to prove that a received message came from a specific sender. The sender must not be able to deny sending a message that he or she, in fact, did send. The burden of proof falls on the receiver. For example, when a customer sends a message to transfer money from one account to another, the bank must have proof that the customer actually requested this transaction. We will see how digital signature can provide nonrepudiation.

30.2   DIGITAL SIGNATURE

We said that security provides four services in relation to a single message: privacy, authentication, integrity, and nonrepudiation. We have already discussed privacy. The other three can be achieved by using what is called **digital signature.**

The idea is similar to the signing of a document. When we send a document electronically, we can also sign it. We have two choices: We can sign the entire document, or we can sign a digest (condensed version) of the document.

Signing the Whole Document

Public-key encryption can be used to sign a document. However, the roles of the public and private keys are different here. The sender uses her private key to encrypt (sign) the message just as a person uses her signature (which is private in the sense that it is difficult to forge) to sign a paper document. The receiver, on the other hand, uses the public key of the sender to decrypt the message just as a person verifies from memory another person's signature.

In the digital signature, the private key is used for encryption and the public key for decryption. This is possible because the encryption and decryption algorithms used today, such as RSA, are mathematical formulas and their structures are similar. Figure 30.4 shows how this is done.

Figure 30.4   *Signing the whole document*

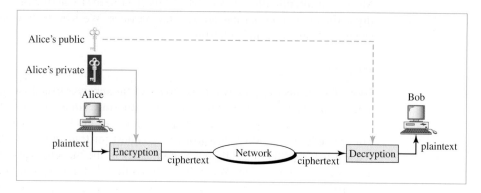

Digital signatures can provide integrity, authentication, and nonrepudiation.

Integrity   The integrity of a message is preserved because if Eve intercepted the message and partially or totally changed it, the decrypted message would be unreadable.

Authentication   We can use the following reasoning to show how a message can be authenticated. If Eve sends a message while pretending that it is coming from Alice, she must use her own private key for encryption. The message is then decrypted with the public key of Alice and will therefore be nonreadable. Encryption with Eve's private key and decryption with Alice's public key result in garbage.

Nonrepudiation   Digital signature also provides for nonrepudiation. Bob saves the message received from Alice. If Alice later denies sending the message, Bob can show that encrypting and decrypting the saved message with Alice's private and public key can create a duplicate of the saved message. Since only Alice knows her private key, she cannot deny sending the message.

> **Digital signature does not provide privacy. If there is a need for privacy, another layer of encryption/decryption must be applied.**

Signing the Digest

We said before that public-key encryption is efficient if the message is short. Using a public key to sign the entire message is very inefficient if the message is very long. The solution is to let the sender sign a digest of the document instead of the whole document. The sender creates a miniature version or **digest** of the document and signs it; the receiver then checks the signature on the miniature.

To create a digest of the message, we use a **hash function.** The hash function creates a fixed-size digest from a variable-length message, as shown in Figure 30.5.

Figure 30.5 *Signing the digest*

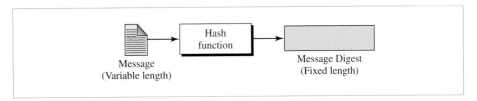

The two most common hash functions are called MD5 (Message Digest 5) and SHA-1 (Secure Hash Algorithm 1). The first one produces a 120-bit digest. The second produces a 160-bit digest.

Note that a hash function must have two properties to guarantee its success. First, hashing is one-way; the digest can only be created from the message, not vice versa. Second, hashing is a one-to-one function; there is little probability that two messages will create the same digest. We will see the reason for this condition shortly.

After the digest has been created, it is encrypted (signed) using the sender's private key. The encrypted digest is attached to the original message and sent to the receiver. Figure 30.6 shows the sender site.

Figure 30.6 *Sender site*

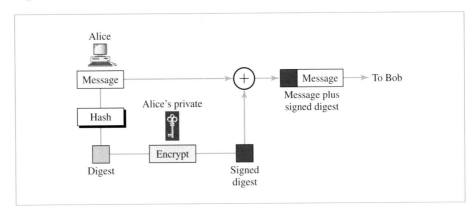

The receiver receives the original message and the encrypted digest. He separates the two. He applies the same hash function to the message to create a second digest. He also decrypts the received digest, using the public key of the sender. If the two digests are the same, all three security measures are preserved. Figure 30.7 shows the receiver site.

According to Section 30.1, we know that the digest is secure in terms of integrity, authentication, and nonrepudiation, but what about the message itself? The following reasoning shows that the message itself is also secured:

1. The digest has not been changed (integrity), and the digest is a representation of the message. So the message has not been changed (remember, it is improbable that two messages create the same digest). Integrity has been provided.

Figure 30.7 *Receiver site*

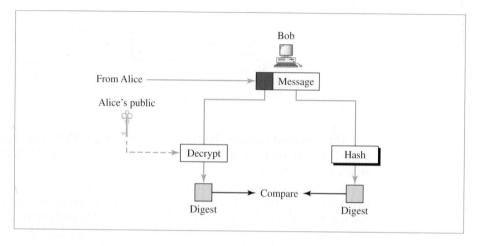

2. The digest comes from the true sender, so the message also comes from the true sender. If an intruder had initiated the message, the message would not have created the same digest (it is improbable that two messages create the same digest).

3. The sender cannot deny the message since she cannot deny the digest; the only message that can create that digest, with a very high probability, is the received message.

30.3   USER AUTHENTICATION

The main issue in security is key management, as we will see in Section 30.4. However, key management involves **user authentication.** We, therefore, briefly discuss these issues before talking about key management.

User Authentication with Symmetric-Key Cryptography

In this section, we discuss authentication as a procedure that verifies the identity of one entity for another. An *entity* can be a person, a process, a client, or a server; in our examples, entities are people. Specifically, Bob needs to verify the identity of Alice and vice versa. Note that entity authentication, as discussed here, is different from the message authentication that we discussed in the previous section. In message authentication, the identity of the sender is verified for each single message. In user authentication, the user identity is verified once for the entire duration of system access.

First Approach

In the first approach, Alice sends her identity and password in an encrypted message, using the symmetric key K_{AB}. Figure 30.8 shows the procedure. We have added the padlock with the corresponding key (shared key between Alice and Bob) to show that the message is encrypted with the key.

  Is this a safe approach? Yes, to some extent. Eve, the intruder, cannot decipher the password or the data because she does not know K_{AB}. However, Eve can cause damage

Figure 30.8 *Using a symmetric key only*

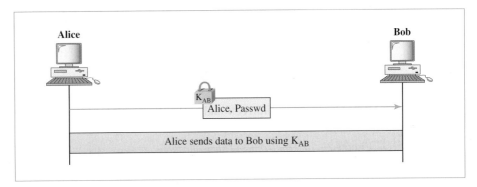

without accessing the contents of the message. If Eve has an interest in the data message sent from Alice to Bob, she can intercept both the authentication message and the data message, store them, and resend them later to Bob. Bob has no way to know that this is a replay of a previous message. There is nothing in this procedure to guarantee the freshness of the message. As an example, suppose Alice's message instructs Bob (as a bank manager) to pay Eve for some job she has done. Eve can resend the message, thereby illegally getting paid twice for the same job. This is called a **replay attack.**

Second Approach

To prevent a replay attack (or playback attack), we add something to the procedure to help Bob distinguish a fresh authentication request from a repeated one. This can be done by using a **nonce.** A nonce is a large random number that is used only once, a one-time number. In this second approach, Bob uses a nonce to challenge Alice, to make sure that Alice is authentic and that someone (Eve) is not impersonating Alice. Figure 30.9 shows the procedure.

Figure 30.9 *Using a nonce*

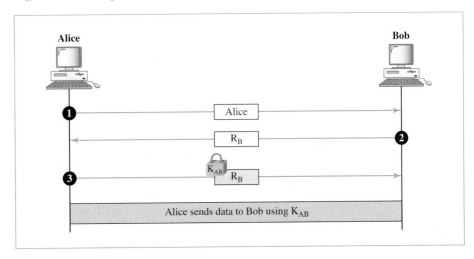

Authentication happens in three steps. First, Alice sends her identity, in plaintext, to Bob. Bob challenges Alice by sending a nonce, R_B, in plaintext. Alice responds to this message by sending back the nonce and encrypting it using the symmetric key. Eve cannot replay the message since R_B is valid only once.

Bidirectional Authentication

The second approach consists of a challenge and a response to authenticate Alice for Bob. Can we have **bidirectional authentication?** Figure 30.10 shows one method.

Figure 30.10   *Bidirectional authentication*

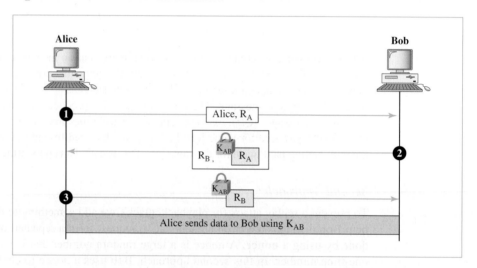

In the first step, Alice sends her identification and her nonce to challenge Bob. In the second step, Bob responds to Alice's challenge by sending his nonce to challenge her. In the third step, Alice responds to Bob's challenge. Is this authentication totally safe? It is on the condition that Alice and Bob use a different set of nonces for different sessions and do not allow multiple authentications to take place at the same time. Otherwise, this procedure can be the target of a **reflection attack;** we leave this as an exercise.

User Authentication with Public-Key Cryptography

We can use public-key cryptography to authenticate a user. In Figure 30.9, Alice can encrypt the message with her private key and let Bob use Alice's public key to decrypt the message and authenticate her. However, we have the man-in-the-middle (see next section) attack problem because Eve can announce her public key to Bob in place of Alice. Eve can then encrypt the message containing a nonce with her private key. Bob decrypts it with Eve's public key, which he believes is Alice's. Bob is fooled. Alice needs a better means to advertise her public key; Bob needs a better way to verify Alice's public key. We discuss public-key certification next.

30.4 KEY MANAGEMENT

We discussed how symmetric-key and public-key cryptography can be used in message security and user authentication. However, we never explained how symmetric keys are distributed and how public keys are certified. We explore these two important issues here.

Symmetric Key Distribution

There are three problems with symmetric keys.

1. First, if n people want to communicate with one another, there is a need for $n(n-1)/2$ symmetric keys. Consider that each of the n people may need to communicate with $n-1$ people. This means that we need $n(n-1)$ keys. However, symmetric keys are shared between two communicating people. Therefore, the actual number of keys needed is $n(n-1)/2$. This is usually referred to as the n^2 **problem.** If n is a small number, this is acceptable. For example, if 5 people need to communicate, only 10 keys are needed. The problem is aggravated if n is a large number. For example, if n is 1 million, almost half a trillion keys are needed.

2. Second, in a group of n people, each person must have and remember $n-1$ keys, one for every other person in the group. This means that if 1 million people want to communicate with one another, each must remember (or store) almost 1 million keys in his or her computer.

3. Third, how can two parties securely acquire the shared key? It cannot be done over the phone or the Internet; these are not secure.

Session Keys

Considering the above problems, a symmetric key between two parties is useful if it is dynamic: created for each session and destroyed when the session is over. It does not have to be remembered by the two parties.

> **A symmetric key between two parties is useful if it is used only once; it must be created for one session and destroyed when the session is over.**

Diffie-Hellman Method

One protocol, the **Diffie-Hellman (DH) protocol,** devised by Diffie and Hellman, provides a one-time session key for two parties. The two parties use the session key to exchange data without having to remember or store it for future use. The parties do not have to meet to agree on the key, it can be done through the Internet. Let us see how the protocol works when Alice and Bob need a symmetric key to communicate.

Prerequisite   Before establishing a symmetric key, the two parties need to choose two numbers N and G. The first number, N, is a large prime number with restriction that $(N-1)/2$ must also be a prime number; the second number G is also a prime number, but it has more restrictions. These two numbers need not be confidential. They can be sent through the Internet; they can be public. Any two numbers, selected properly, can serve the entire world. There is no secrecy about these two numbers; both Alice and Bob know these magic numbers.

Procedure   Figure 30.11 shows the procedure.

Figure 30.11   *Diffie-Hellman method*

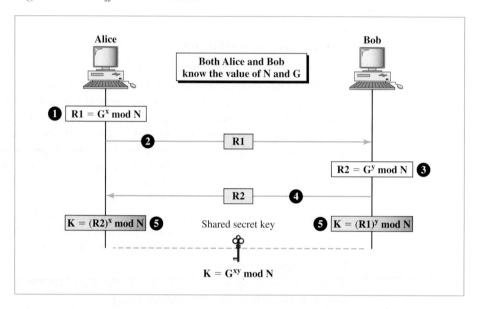

The steps are as follows:

Step 1   Alice chooses a large random number x and calculates $R1 = G^x$ mod N.

Step 2   Alice sends R1 to Bob. Note that Alice does not send the value of x; she only sends R1.

Step 3   Bob chooses another large number y and calculates $R2 = G^y$ mod N.

Step 4   Bob sends R2 to Alice. Again, note that Bob does not send the value of y; he only sends R2.

Step 5   Alice calculates $K = (R2)^x$ mod N. Bob also calculates $K = (R1)^y$ mod N. And K is the symmetric key for the session.

The reader may wonder why the value of K is the same since the calculations are different. The answer is an equality proved in number theory.

$$(G^x \bmod N)^y \bmod N = (G^y \bmod N)^x \bmod N = G^{xy} \bmod N$$

Bob has calculated $K = (R1)^y$ mod N = $(G^x$ mod N$)^y$ mod N = G^{xy} mod N. Alice has calculated $K = (R2)^x$ mod N = $(G^y$ mod N$)^x$ mod N = G^{xy} mod N. Both have reached the same value without Bob knowing the value of x or Alice knowing the value of y.

The symmetric (shared) key in the Diffie-Hellman protocol is $K = G^{xy}$ mod N.

Example 1

Let us give an example to make the procedure clear. Our example uses small numbers, but note that in a real situation, the numbers are very large. Assume $G = 7$ and $N = 23$. The steps are as follows:

1. Alice chooses $x = 3$ and calculates $R1 = 7^3 \bmod 23 = 21$.
2. Alice sends the number 21 to Bob.
3. Bob chooses $y = 6$ and calculates $R2 = 7^6 \bmod 23 = 4$.
4. Bob sends the number 4 to Alice.
5. Alice calculates the symmetric key $K = 4^3 \bmod 23 = 18$.
6. Bob calculates the symmetric key $K = 21^6 \bmod 23 = 18$.

The value of K is the same for both Alice and Bob; $G^{xy} \bmod N = 7^{18} \bmod 23 = 18$.

Man-in-the-Middle Attack The Diffie-Hellman protocol is a very sophisticated symmetric-key creation algorithm. If x and y are very large numbers, it is extremely difficult for Eve to find the key knowing only N and G. An intruder needs to determine x and y if R1 and R2 are intercepted. But finding x from R1 and y from R2 are two difficult tasks. Even a sophisticated computer would need perhaps a long time to find the key by trying different numbers. In addition, Alice and Bob change the key the next time they need to communicate.

However, the protocol does have a weakness. Eve does not have to find the values of x and y to attack the protocol. She can fool Alice and Bob by creating two keys: one between herself and Alice and another between herself and Bob. Figure 30.12 shows the situation.

Figure 30.12 *Man-in-the-middle attack*

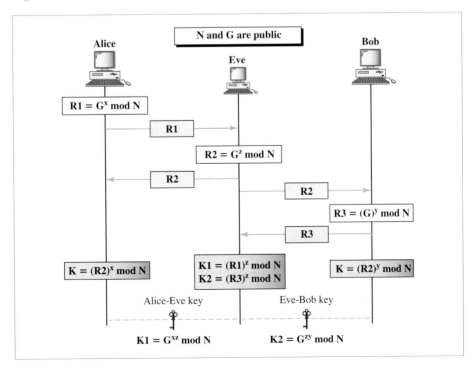

The following can happen:

1. Alice chooses x, calculates $R1 = G^x \bmod N$, and sends R1 to Bob.

2. Eve, the intruder, intercepts R1. She chooses z, calculates $R2 = G^z \bmod N$, and sends R2 to both Alice and Bob.

3. Bob chooses y, calculates $R3 = G^y \bmod N$, and sends R3 to Alice. R3 is intercepted by Eve and never reaches Alice.

4. Alice and Eve calculate $K1 = G^{xz} \bmod N$, which becomes a shared key between Alice and Eve. Alice, however, thinks that it is a key shared between Bob and herself.

5. Eve and Bob calculate $K2 = G^{zy} \bmod N$, which becomes a shared key between Eve and Bob. Bob, however, thinks that it is a key shared between Alice and himself.

In other words, two keys, instead of one, are created: one between Alice and Eve and one between Eve and Bob. When Alice sends data to Bob encrypted with K1 (shared by Alice and Eve), the data can be deciphered and read by Eve. Eve can send the message to Bob encrypted by K2 (shared key between Eve and Bob); or she can even change the message or send a totally new message. Bob is fooled into believing that the message has come from Alice. The same scenario can happen to Alice in the other direction.

This situation is called a **man-in-the-middle attack** because Eve comes in between and intercepts R1, sent by Alice to Bob, and R3, sent by Bob to Alice. It is also known as a bucket brigade attack because it resembles a short line of volunteers passing a bucket of water from person to person.

Key Distribution Center (KDC)

The flaw in the previous protocol is the sending of R1 and R2 as plaintext which can be intercepted by any intruder. Any private correspondence between two parties should be encrypted using a symmetric key. But this can create a vicious circle. Two parties need to have a symmetric key before they can establish a symmetric key between themselves. The solution is a trusted third party, a source that both Alice and Bob can trust. This is the idea behind a **key distribution center (KDC).**

Alice and Bob are both clients of the KDC. Alice has established one symmetric key between herself and the center in a secure way, such as going to the center personally. We call Alice's symmetric key K_A. Bob has done the same; we call his symmetric key K_B.

First Approach Using a KDC   Let us see how a KDC can create a session key K_{AB} between Alice and Bob. Figure 30.13 shows the steps.

Step 1   Alice sends a plaintext message to the KDC to obtain a symmetric session key between Bob and herself. The message contains her registered identity (the word *Alice* in the figure) and the identity of Bob (the word *Bob* in the figure). This message is not encrypted; it is public. KDC does not care.

Step 2   KDC receives the message and creates what is called a **ticket.** The ticket is encrypted using Bob's key (K_B). The ticket contains the Alice and Bob identities and the session key (K_{AB}). The ticket with a copy of the session key is sent to Alice. Note that Alice receives the message, decrypts it, and extracts the session key. She cannot decrypt Bob's ticket; the ticket is for Bob, not for Alice. Note also that we have a double encryption in this message; the ticket is encrypted, as well as the entire message.

Figure 30.13   *First approach using KDC*

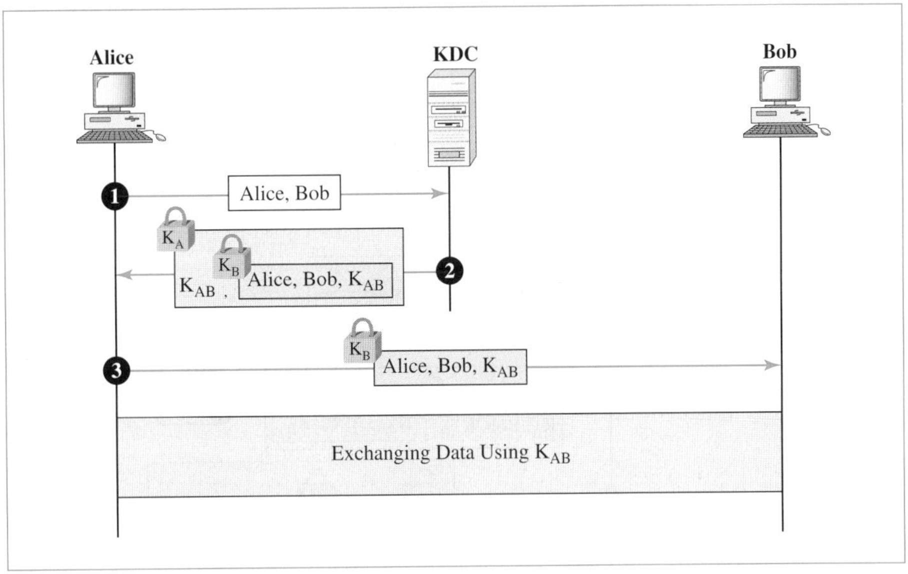

Step 3   Alice sends the ticket to Bob. Bob opens the ticket and knows that Alice needs to send messages to him using K_{AB} as the session key.

Sending data.   After the third step, Alice and Bob can exchange data using K_{AB} as a one-time session key.

Eve can use the replay attack we discussed previously. She can save the message in step 3 as well as the data messages and replay all.

Needham-Schroeder Protocol   Another approach is the elegant **Needham-Schroeder protocol,** a foundation for many other protocols. This protocol uses multiple challenge-response interactions between parties to achieve a flawless protocol. In the latest version of this protocol, Needham and Schroeder use four different nonces: R_A, R_B, R_1, and R_2. Figure 30.14 shows the seven steps of this protocol.

The following are brief descriptions of each step:

Step 1   Alice sends her identity to Bob, thereby declaring that she needs to talk to him.

Step 2   Bob uses nonce R_B and encrypts it with his symmetric key K_B. Nonce R_B is intended for the KDC, but it is sent to Alice. Alice sends R_B to the KDC to prove that the person who has talked to Bob is the same person (not an imposter) who will talk to the KDC.

Step 3   Alice sends a message to the KDC that includes her nonce, R_A, her identity, Bob's identity, and the encrypted nonce from Bob.

Step 4   The KDC sends an encrypted message to Alice that includes Alice's nonce, Bob's identity, the session key, and an encrypted ticket for Bob that includes his nonce. Now Alice has received the response to her nonce challenge and the session key.

Step 5   Alice sends Bob's ticket to him along with a new nonce, R_1, to challenge him.

Figure 30.14   *Needham-Schroeder protocol*

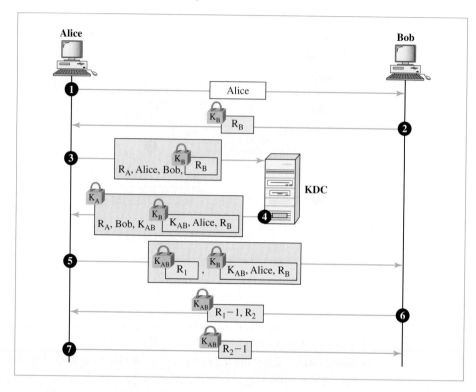

Step 6   Bob responds to Alice's challenge and sends his challenge to Alice (R2). Note that the response to Alice's challenge is the value $R_1 - 1$; this ensures that Bob has decrypted the encrypted R_1. In other words, the new encryption ensures that an imposter has not sent the exact encrypted message back.

Step 7   Alice responds to Bob's challenge. Again, note that the response carries $R_2 - 1$ instead of R_2.

Otway-Rees Protocol   A third approach is the **Otway-Rees protocol**, another elegant protocol, that has even fewer steps. Figure 30.15 shows this five-step protocol. The following briefly describes the steps.

Step 1   Alice sends a message to Bob that includes a common nonce R, the identities of Alice and Bob, and a ticket for KDC that includes Alice's nonce R_A (a challenge for KDC to use), a copy of the common nonce R, and the identities of Alice and Bob.

Step 2   Bob creates the same type of ticket, but with his own nonce R_B; both tickets are sent to KDC.

Step 3   KDC creates a message that contains R, the common nonce, a ticket for Alice and a ticket for Bob; the message is sent to Bob. The tickets contain the corresponding nonce, R_A or R_B, and the session key K_{AB}.

Step 4   Bob sends Alice her ticket.

Step 5   Alice sends a message encrypted with her session key K_{AB}.

Figure 30.15 *Otway-Rees protocol*

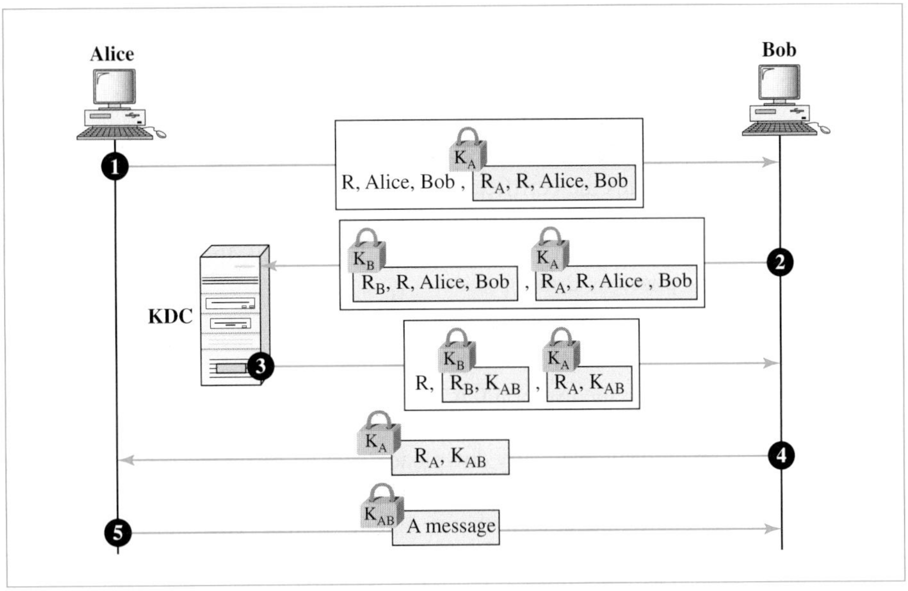

Public-Key Certification

In public-key cryptography, people do not need to know a symmetric shared key. If Alice wants to send a message to Bob, she only needs to know Bob's public key, which is open to the public and available to everyone. If Bob needs to send a message to Alice, he only needs to know Alice's public key, which is also known to everyone. In public-key cryptography, everyone shields a private key and advertises a public key.

> **In public-key cryptography, everyone has access to everyone's public key.**

The Problem

In public-key cryptography, everybody who expects to receive a message from someone else needs to somehow advertise his or her public key to the sender of the message. The problem is how to advertise the public key and make it safe from Eve's interference. If Bob sends his public key to Alice, Eve may intercept it and send her (Eve's) own public key to Alice. Alice, assuming that this is Bob's public key, encrypts a message for Bob with this key and sends it to Bob. Eve again intercepts and decrypts the message with her private key and knows what Alice has sent to Bob. Eve can even put her public key online and claim that this is Bob's public key.

Certification Authority

Bob wants two things: He wants people to know his public key, and he wants no one to accept a public key forged as Bob's. Bob can go to a **certification authority (CA),** a federal or state organization that binds a public key to an entity and issues a certificate. The CA has a well-known public key itself that cannot be forged. The CA checks Bob's identification (using a picture ID along with other proof). It then asks for Bob's public key and writes it on the certificate. To prevent the certificate itself from getting forged, the CA creates a message digest from the certificate and encrypts the message digest with its private key. Now Bob can upload the certificate as plaintext and the encrypted message digest. Anybody who wants Bob's public key downloads the certificate and the encrypted digest. A digest can then be created from the certificate; the encrypted digest is decrypted with the CA's public key. The two digests are then compared. If they are equal, the certificate is valid and no imposter has posed as Bob.

X.509

Although the use of a CA has solved the problem of public-key fraud, it has created a side effect. Each certificate may have a different format. If Alice wants to use a program to automatically download different certificates and digests belonging to different people, the program may not be able to do so. One certificate may have the public key in one format and another in another format. The public key may be in the first line in one certificate, and in the third line in another. Anything that needs to be used universally must have a universal format.

To remove this side effect, ITU has devised a protocol called **X.509,** which has been accepted by the Internet with some changes. Protocol X.509 is a way to describe the certificate in a structural way. It uses a well-known protocol called ASN.1 (Abstract Syntax Notation 1) that defines fields very familiar to C programmers.

We do not discuss ASN.1 here, but we list some of the fields and their meanings defined by X.509 in Table 30.1.

Table 30.1   *X.509 fields*

Field	Explanation
Version	Version number of X.509
Serial number	The unique identifier used by the CA
Signature	The certificate signature
Issuer	The name of the CA defined by X.509
Validity period	Start and end period that certificate is valid
Subject name	The entity whose public key is being certified
Public key	The subject public key and the algorithms that use it

Public-Key Infrastructure (PKI)

When we want to use public keys universally, we have a problem similar to one concerning DNS (Domain Name System) in Chapter 25. We found that we cannot have only one DNS server to answer the queries. We need many servers. In addition, we found that the best solution is to put the servers in a hierarchical relationship. If Alice needs to get Bob's IP address, Alice sends a message to her local server that may or may not have Bob's IP address. The local server can consult its parent server, up to the root, until the IP address is found.

Likewise, a solution to public-key queries is a hierarchical structure called a **public-key infrastructure (PKI).** Figure 30.16 shows an example of this hierarchy.

Figure 30.16 *PKI hierarchy*

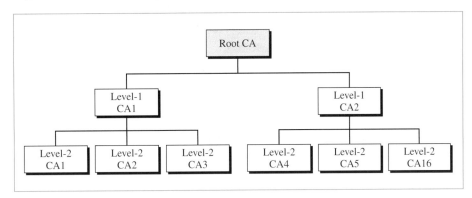

At the first level, we can have a root CA that can certify the performance of CAs in the second level; these level-1 CAs may operate in a large geographic area or logical area. The level-2 CAs may operate in smaller geographic areas.

In this hierarchy, everybody trusts the root. But people may or may not trust intermediate CAs. If Alice needs to get Bob's certificate, she may find a CA somewhere to issue the certificate. But Alice may not trust that CA. In a hierarchy Alice can ask the next-higher CA to certify the original CA. The inquiry may go all the way to the root.

PKI is a new issue in the Internet. It will undoubtedly broaden in scope and change in the next few years.

30.5 KERBEROS

Kerberos is an authentication protocol, and at the same time a KDC, that has become very popular. Several systems including Windows 2000 use Kerberos. Kerberos is named after the three-headed dog in Greek mythology that guards the gates of Hades. Originally designed at MIT, it has gone through several versions. We discuss only version 4, the most popular, and we briefly explain the difference between version 4 and version 5, the latest.

Servers

Three servers are involved in the Kerberos protocol: an **authentication server (AS),** a **ticket-granting server (TGS),** and a real (data) server that provides services to others. In our examples and figures, *Bob* is the real server and *Alice* is the user requesting service. Figure 30.17 shows the relationship between these three servers.

Figure 30.17   *Kerberos servers*

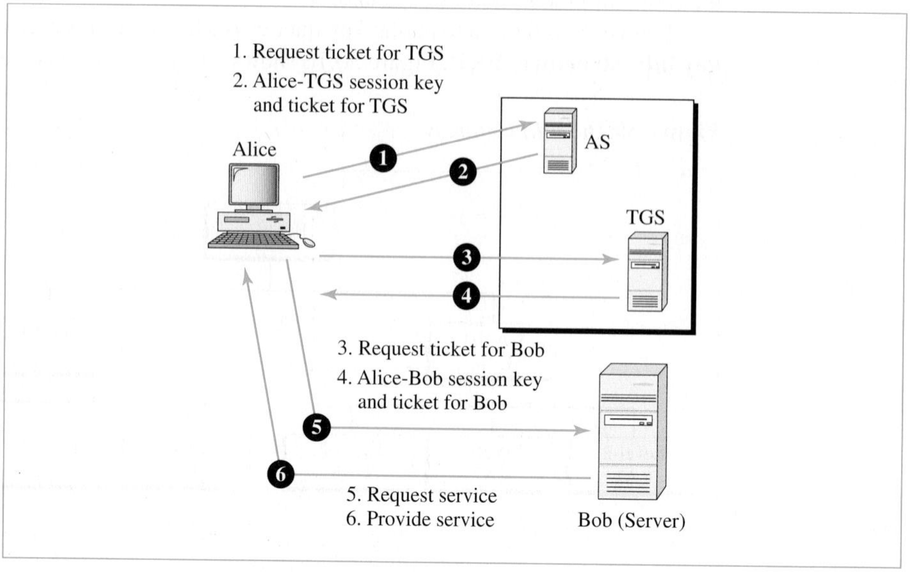

Authentication Server (AS)

The AS is the KDC in the Kerberos protocol. Each user registers with the AS and is granted a user identity and a password. The AS has a database with these identities and the corresponding passwords. The AS verifies the user, issues a session key to be used between Alice and the TGS, and sends a ticket for the TGS.

Ticket-Granting Server (TGS)

The TGS issues a ticket for the real server (Bob). It also provides the session key (K_{AB}) between Alice and Bob. Kerberos has separated the user verification from ticket issuing. In this way, although Alice verifies her ID just once with AS, she can contact TGS multiple times to obtain tickets for different real servers.

Real Server

The real server (Bob) provides services for the user (Alice). Kerberos is designed for a client-server program such as FTP, in which a user uses the client process to access the server process. Kerberos is not used for person-to-person authentication.

Operation

A client process (Alice) can receive a service from a process running on the real server (Bob) in six steps, as shown in Figure 30.18.

Step 1

Alice sends her request to AS in plaintext, using her registered identity.

Figure 30.18 *Kerberos example*

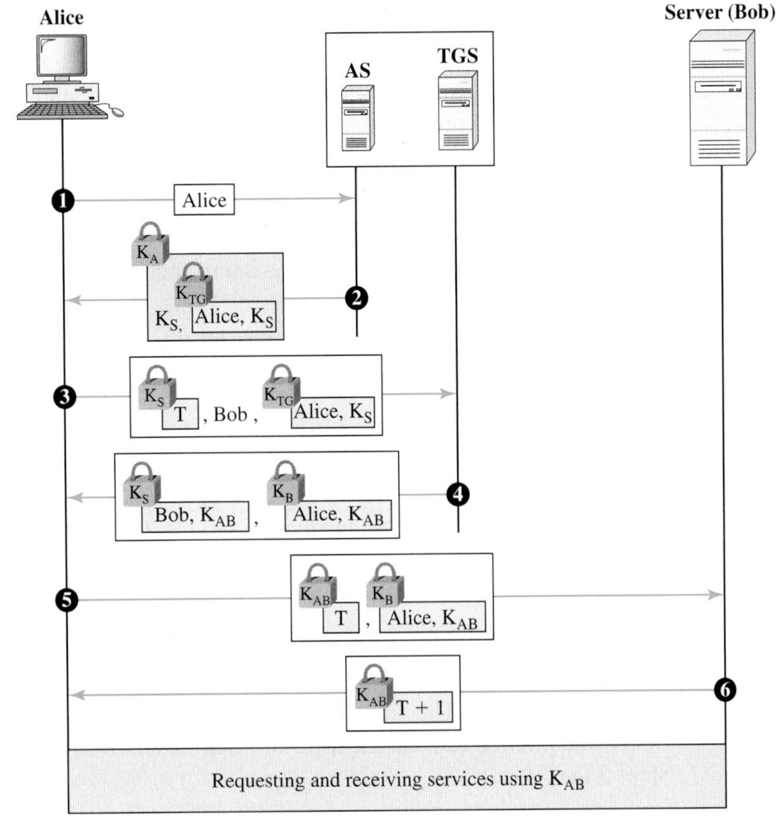

Step 2

The AS sends a message encrypted with Alice's symmetric key K_A. The message contains two items: a session key K_S that is used by Alice to contact TGS and a ticket for TGS that is encrypted with the TGS symmetric key K_{TG}. Alice does not know K_A, but when the message arrives, she types her password. The password and the appropriate algorithm together create K_A if the password is correct. The password is then immediately destroyed; it is not sent to the network, and it does not stay in the terminal. It is only used for a moment to create K_A. The process now uses K_A to decrypt the message sent; K_S and the ticket are extracted.

Step 3

Alice now sends three items to the TGS. The first is the ticket received from AS. The second is the name of the real server (Bob), and the third is a timestamp which is encrypted by K_S. The timestamp prevents a replay by Eve.

Step 4

Now, TGS sends two tickets, each containing the session key between Alice and Bob K_{AB}. The ticket for Alice is encrypted with K_S; the ticket for Bob is encrypted with Bob's key K_B. Note that Eve cannot extract K_{AB} because she does not know K_S or K_B. She cannot replay step 3 because she cannot replace the time-stamp with a new one (she does not know K_S). Even if she is very quick and sends the step 3 message before the time-stamp has expired, she still receives the same two tickets that she cannot decipher.

Step 5

Alice sends Bob's ticket with the time-stamp encrypted with K_{AB}.

Step 6

Bob confirms the receipt by adding 1 to the time-stamp. The message is encrypted with K_{AB} and sent to Alice.

Requesting and Receiving Services

After step 6, Alice can request and receive services from Bob using K_{AB} as the symmetric shared key.

Using Different Servers

Note that if Alice needs to receive services from different servers, she need repeat only the last four steps. The first two steps have verified Alice's identity and need not be repeated. Alice can ask the TGS to issue tickets for multiple servers by repeating steps 3 to 6.

Kerberos Version 5

The minor differences between version 4 and version 5 are briefly listed below:

1. Version 5 has a longer ticket lifetime.
2. Version 5 allows tickets to be renewed.
3. Version 5 can accept any symmetric-key algorithm.
4. Version 5 uses a different protocol for describing data types.
5. Version 5 has more overhead than version 4.

Realms

Kerberos allows the global distribution of ASs and TGSs, with each system called a realm. A user may get a ticket for a local server or a distant server. In the second case, for example, Alice may ask her local TGS to issue a ticket that is accepted by a distant TGS. The local TGS can issue this ticket if the distant TGS is registered with the local one. Then Alice can use the distant TGS to access the distant real server.

30.6 KEY TERMS

authentication server (AS)

bidirectional authentication

certification authority (CA)

Diffie-Hellman protocol

digest

digital signature

hash function

integrity

Kerberos

key distribution center (KDC)

man-in-the-middle attack

message authentication

n^2 problem

Needham-Schroeder protocol

nonce

nonrepudiation

Otway-Rees protocol

privacy

public-key infrastructure (PKI)

replay attack

ticket

ticket-granting server (TGS)

user authentication

X.509

30.7 SUMMARY

❏ The issues involved in single-message security are privacy, authentication, integrity, and nonrepudiation.

❏ Message privacy is achieved through encryption of the plaintext and decryption of the ciphertext.

❏ Message authentication, integrity, and nonrepudiation are achieved through a method called digital signature.

❏ We can use digital signature on the entire message or on a digest of the message. A hash function creates the digest from the original document.

❏ Encryption of a message using a shared symmetric key is vulnerable to a replay attack. The use of a nonce can prevent this type of attack.

❏ The use of symmetric keys for user authentication requires too many shared keys if the user population is large.

❏ The Diffie-Hellman method provides a one-time session key for two parties. However, it is vulnerable to a man-in-the-middle attack.

❏ A key distribution center (KDC) is a trusted third party that assigns a symmetric key to two parties.

❏ The Needham-Schroeder protocol for user authentication uses multiple challenge-response interactions between communicating parties. The Otway-Rees protocol for user authentication uses even fewer challenge-response interactions.

❏ A certification authority (CA) is a federal or state organization that binds a public key to an entity and issues a certificate.

❏ A public-key infrastructure (PKI) is a hierarchical system to answer queries about key certification.

❏ Kerberos is a popular authentication protocol that requires an authentication server and a ticket-granting server.

30.8   PRACTICE SET

Review Questions

1. Name two user authentication systems that are vulnerable to a replay attack.
2. What is a nonce?
3. What is bidirectional authentication?
4. What is the n^2 problem?
5. Discuss the variables needed in the Diffie-Hellman method of user authentication.
6. What is the man-in-the-middle attack? How can it be prevented?
7. Name two protocols that use a KDC for user authentication.
8. What is the purpose of the Kerberos authentication server? What is the purpose of the Kerberos ticket-granting server?
9. List three differences between Kerberos version 4 and Kerberos version 5.
10. What is the purpose of X.509?
11. What is a certification authority?

Multiple-Choice Questions

12. If user A wants to send an encrypted message to user B, the plaintext is encrypted with the public key of _____.
    a. User A
    b. User B
    c. The network
    d. (a) or (b)
13. When symmetric-key encryption is combined with private-key encryption, the _____ key is encrypted with the public key.
    a. Private
    b. Public
    c. Symmetric
    d. Skeleton
14. In the digital signature technique, the sender of the message uses _____ to create ciphertext.
    a. His or her own symmetric key
    b. His or her own private key
    c. His or her own public key
    d. The receiver's private key
15. In the digital signature technique, the receiver of the message uses _____ to create plaintext.
    a. Her or his own symmetric key
    b. Her or his own private key
    c. Her or his own public key
    d. The sender's public key

16. A _____ is a trusted third party that solves the problem of symmetric-key distribution.
    a. CA
    b. KDC
    c. TLS
    d. Firewall

17. A _____ certifies the binding between a public key and its owner.
    a. CA
    b. KDC
    c. TLS
    d. Firewall

18. In a _____ attack, a message captured by an intruder is illegally sent a second time.
    a. Return
    b. Man-in-the-middle
    c. Bucket brigade
    d. Replay

19. A _____ is a large number used only once that helps distinguish a fresh authentication request from a repeated one.
    a. Ticket
    b. Nonce
    c. Realm
    d. Public key

20. In an authentication using symmetric keys, if 10 people need to communicate, we need _____ keys.
    a. 10
    b. 20
    c. 45
    d. 90

21. In the _____ protocol, the symmetric key is $K = G^{xy} \bmod N$, where G and N are public numbers.
    a. Diffie-Hellman
    b. Needham-Schroeder
    c. Otway-Rees
    d. Kerberos

22. In a _____ attack, an intruder comes between two communicating parties, intercepting and replying to their messages.
    a. Return
    b. Man-in-the-middle
    c. Bucket-in-the-middle
    d. Replay

23. A _____ is a trusted third party that establishes a symmetric key between two parties who wish to communicate.
   a. KDC
   b. CA
   c. PKI
   d. TGS

24. In the _____ protocol, a nonce is decremented by 1 so that an intruder cannot send the exact same message a second time.
   a. Diffie-Hellman
   b. Needham-Schroeder
   c. Otway-Rees
   d. Kerberos

25. _____ is an authentication protocol that needs an authentication server and a ticket-granting server.
   a. Diffie-Hellman
   b. Needham-Schroeder
   c. Otway-Rees
   d. Kerberos

26. The _____ is the KDC in the Kerberos protocol.
   a. AS
   b. TGS
   c. Real server
   d. Data server

27. The _____ issues tickets for the real server.
   a. AS
   b. TGS
   c. Real server
   d. Data server

28. In _____-key cryptography, everyone has access to all the public keys.
   a. Private
   b. Symmetric
   c. Public
   d. Certified

29. A protocol called _____ describes the certificate issued by a CA in a structural way.
   a. X.509
   b. CA level 1
   c. KDC
   d. Kerberos

30. Windows 2000 uses an authentication protocol called _____.
   a. Diffie-Hellman
   b. Needham-Schroeder

    c. Otway-Rees

    d. Kerberos

Exercises

31. Add a layer of symmetric-key encryption/decryption to Figure 30.4 to provide privacy.

32. Add a layer of public-key encryption/decryption to Figure 30.4 to provide privacy.

33. Show that G^{xy} is the same as $(G^x)^y$ using $G = 11$, $x = 3$, and $y = 4$.

34. Prove that the result of $G^{xy} \bmod N$ is the same as the result of $(G^x \bmod N)^y \bmod N$, using $G = 7$, $x = 2$, $y = 3$, and $N = 11$.

35. The fact that the result of $G^{xy} \bmod N$ is the same as the result of $(G^x \bmod N)^y \bmod N$ can tremendously simplify the calculation of $G^{xy} \bmod N$. Use this fact to calculate $7^{18} \bmod 11$. *Hint:* Factor 18 and do three calculations.

36. What is the value of the symmetric key in the Diffie-Hellman protocol if $G = 7$, $N = 23$, $x = 3$, and $y = 5$?

37. What are the values of R_1 and R_2 in the Diffie-Hellman protocol if $G = 7$, $N = 23$, $x = 3$, and $y = 5$?

38. In the Diffie-Hellman protocol, what happens if x and y have the same value? That is, have Alice and Bob accidentally chosen the same number? Are the values of R1 and R2 the same? Is the value of the session key calculated by Alice and Bob the same? Use an example to prove your claims.

39. Which of the following numbers is a good candidate for N in the Diffie-Hellman protocol?   7, 11, 21, 33, 37, 15, or 47

40. In Figure 30.13 (First approach using KDC), what happens if the ticket for Bob is not encrypted in step 2 with K_B, but is encrypted by K_{AB} in step 3?

41. Why is there a need for four nonces in the Needham-Schroeder protocol?

42. In the Needham-Schroeder protocol, how is Alice is authenticated by the KDC? How is Bob authenticated by the KDC? How is the KDC authenticated for Alice? How is the KDC authenticated for Bob? How is Alice authenticated for Bob? How is Bob authenticated for Alice?

43. Can you explain why in the Needham-Schroeder protocol, Alice is the party that is in contact with the KDC; but in the Otway-Rees protocol, Bob is the party that is in contact with the KDC?

44. There are four nonces (R_A, R_B, R_1, and R_2) in the Needham-Schroeder protocol, but only three nonces (R_A, R_B, and R_1) in the Otway-Rees protocol. Can you explain why there is a need for one extra nonce, R_2, in the first protocol?

45. Why do we need only one timestamp in Kerberos instead of four nonces in Needham-Schroeder or three nonces in Otway-Rees?

46. In the bidirectional approach to authentication in Figure 30.10, if multiple-session authentication is allowed, Eve intercepts the R_B nonce from Bob (in the second session) and sends it as Alice's nonce for a second session. Bob, without checking that this nonce is the same as the one he sent, encrypts R_B and puts it in a message with his nonce. Eve uses the encrypted R_B and pretends that she is Alice, continuing with the first session and responding with the encrypted R_B. This is called a reflection attack. Show the steps in this scenario.

CHAPTER 31 ≡

Security Protocols in the Internet

All the security principles and concepts discussed in the previous two chapters can be used to provide all aspects of security for the Internet model. In particular, security measures can be applied to the network layer, transport layer, and application layer.

At the IP layer, implementation of security features is very complicated, especially since every device must be enabled. IP provides services not only for user applications, but also for other protocols such as OSPF, ICMP, and IGMP. This means that implementation of security at this level is not very effective unless all devices are equipped to use it. We discuss a protocol called IPSec that provides security at the IP level.

At the transport layer, security is even more complicated. We could modify the application or modify the transport layer for security. Instead, we discuss a protocol that "glues" a new layer to the transport layer to provide security on behalf of the transport layer.

At the application layer, each application is responsible for providing security. The implementation of security at this level is the simplest. It concerns two entities: the client and the server. We discuss a security method at the application layer called PGP.

A mechanism often used to ensure the integrity of an organization is a firewall. We give a brief discussion of firewalls in this chapter.

Finally, because this is the last chapter on security, we discuss an interesting technology—virtual private networks—that uses the public Internet but has the security level of a private network.

31.1   IP LEVEL SECURITY: IPSEC

IP Security (IPSec) is a collection of protocols designed by the IETF (Internet Engineering Task Force) to provide security for a packet at the IP level. IPSec does not define the use of any specific encryption or authentication method. Instead, it provides a framework and a mechanism; it leaves the selection of the encryption, authentication, and hashing methods to the user.

Security Association

IPSec requires a logical connection between two hosts using a *signaling protocol,* called **Security Association (SA).** In other words, IPSec needs the connectionless IP protocol changed to a connection-oriented protocol before security can be applied. An SA connection is a simplex (unidirectional) connection between a source and destination. If a duplex (bidirectional) connection is needed, two SA connections are required, one in each direction. An SA connection is uniquely defined by three elements:

1. A 32-bit security parameter index (SPI), which acts as a virtual circuit identifier in connection-oriented protocols such as Frame Relay or ATM.

2. The type of the protocol used for security. We will see shortly that IPSec defines two alternative protocols: AH and ESP.

3. The source IP address.

Two Modes

IPSec operates at two different modes: transport mode and tunnel mode. The mode defines where the IPSec header is added to the IP packet.

Transport Mode

In this mode, the IPSec header is added between the IP header and the rest of the packet, as shown in Figure 31.1.

Figure 31.1   *Transport mode*

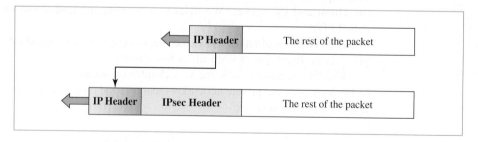

Tunnel Mode

In this mode, the IPSec header is placed in front of the original IP header. A new IP header is added in front. The IPSec header, the preserved IP header, and the rest of the packet are treated as the payload. Figure 31.2 shows the original and the new IP packet.

Two Security Protocols

IPSec defines two protocols: Authentication Header (AH) protocol and Encapsulating Security Payload (ESP) protocol. We discuss both of these protocols here.

Figure 31.2 *Tunnel mode*

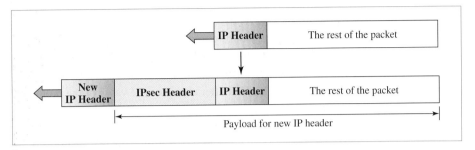

Authentication Header (AH) Protocol

The **Authentication Header (AH) protocol** is designed to authenticate the source host and to ensure the integrity of the payload carried by the IP packet. The protocol calculates a message digest, using a hashing function and a symmetric key, and inserts the digest in the authentication header. The AH is put in the appropriate location based on the mode (transport or tunnel). Figure 31.3 shows the fields and the position of the authentication header in the transport mode.

Figure 31.3 *AH*

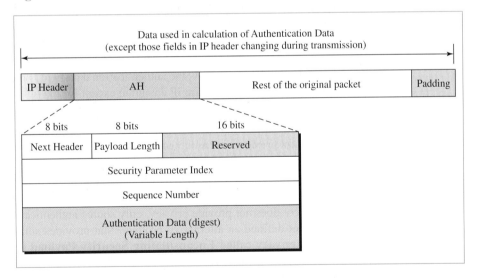

When an IP datagram carries an authentication header, the original value in the protocol field of the IP header is replaced by the value 51. A field inside the authentication header (next header field) defines the original value of the protocol field (the type of payload being carried by the IP datagram). Addition of an authentication header follows these steps:

1. An authentication header is added to the payload with the authentication data field set to zero.

2. Padding may be added to make the total length even for a particular hashing algorithm.

3. Hashing is based on the total packet. However, only those fields of the IP header that do not change during transmission are included in the calculation of the message digest (authentication data).

4. The authentication data are included in the authentication header.

5. The IP header is added after changing the value of the protocol field to 51.

A brief description of each field follows:

■ **Next header.** The 8-bit next-header field defines the type of payload carried by the IP datagram (TCP, UDP, ICMP, OSPF, and so on). It has the same function as the protocol field in the IP header before encapsulation. In other words, the process copies the value of the protocol field in the IP datagram to this field. The value of the protocol field in the IP datagram is changed to 51 to show that the packet carries an authentication header.

■ **Payload length.** The name of this 8-bit payload-length field is misleading. It does not define the length of the payload; it defines the length of the authentication header in 4-byte multiples, but it does not include the first 8 bytes.

■ **Security parameter index.** The 32-bit security parameter index (SPI) field plays the role of a virtual circuit identifier and is the same for all packets sent during a Security Association connection.

■ **Sequence number.** A 32-bit sequence number provides ordering information for a sequence of datagrams. The sequence numbers prevent playback. Note that the sequence number is not repeated even if a packet is retransmitted. A sequence number does not wrap around after it reaches 2^{32}; a new connection must be established.

■ **Authentication data.** Finally, the authentication data field is the result of applying a hash function to the entire IP datagram except for the fields that are changed during transit (e.g., time-to-live).

The AH protocol provides source authentication and data integrity, but not privacy.

Encapsulating Security Payload

The AH protocol does not provide privacy, only source authentication and data integrity. IPSec later defined an alternative protocol that provides source authentication, integrity, and privacy called **Encapsulating Security Payload (ESP).** ESP adds a header and trailer. Note that ESP's authentication data are added at the end of packet which makes its calculation easier. Figure 31.4 shows the location of the ESP header and trailer.

When an IP datagram carries an ESP header and trailer, the value of the protocol field in the IP header changes to 50. A field inside the ESP trailer (the next-header field) holds the original value of the protocol field (the type of payload being carried by the IP datagram, such as TCP or UDP). The ESP procedure follows these steps:

1. An ESP trailer is added to the payload.

2. The payload and the trailer are encrypted.

Figure 31.4 *ESP*

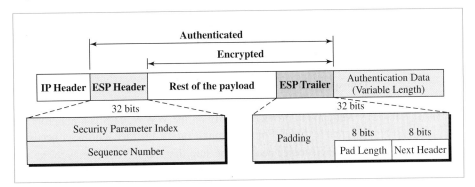

3. The ESP header is added.
4. The ESP header, payload, and ESP trailer are used to create the authentication data.
5. The authentication data are added at the end of the ESP trailer.
6. The IP header is added after changing the protocol value to 50.

The fields for the header and trailer are as follows:

- **Security parameter index.** The 32-bit security parameter index field is similar to that defined for the AH protocol.
- **Sequence number.** The 32-bit sequence number field is similar to that defined for the AH protocol.
- **Padding.** This variable-length field (0 to 255 bytes) of 0s serves as padding.
- **Pad length.** The 8-bit pad length field defines the number of padding bytes. The value is between 0 and 255; the maximum value is rare.
- **Next header.** The 8-bit next-header field is similar to that defined in the AH protocol. It serves the same purpose as the protocol field in the IP header before encapsulation.
- **Authentication data.** Finally, the authentication data field is the result of applying an authentication scheme to parts of the datagram. Note the difference between the authentication data in AH and ESP. In AH, part of the IP header is included in the calculation of the authentication data; in ESP, it is not.

ESP provides source authentication, data integrity, and privacy.

IPv4 and IPv6

IPSec supports both IPv4 and IPv6. In IPv6, however, AH and ESP are part of the extension header.

AH versus ESP

The ESP protocol was designed after the AH protocol was already in use. ESP does whatever AH does with additional functionality (privacy). The question is, Why do we need AH? The answer is that we don't. However, the implementation of AH is already included in some commercial products, which means that AH will remain part of the Internet until the products are phased out.

31.2 TRANSPORT LAYER SECURITY

Transport Layer Security (TLS) was designed to provide security at the transport layer. TLS was derived from a security protocol called Secure Sockets Layer (SSL), designed by Netscape to provide security on the WWW. TLS is a nonproprietary version of SSL designed by IETF. For transactions on the Internet, a browser needs the following:

1. The customer needs to be sure that the server belongs to the actual vendor, not an imposter. For example, a customer does not want to give an imposter her credit card number. In other words, the server must be authenticated.

2. The customer needs to be sure that the contents of the message are not modified during transition. A bill for $100 must not be changed to $1000. The integrity of the message must be preserved.

3. The customer needs to be sure that an imposter does not intercept sensitive information such as a credit card number. There is a need for privacy.

There are other optional security aspects that can be added to the above list. For example, the vendor may need to authenticate the customer. TLS can provide additional features to cover these aspects of security.

Position of TLS

TLS lies between the application layer and the transport layer (TCP), as shown in Figure 31.5.

Figure 31.5 *Position of TLS*

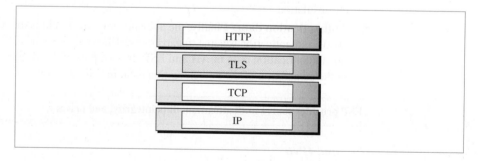

The application layer protocol, in this case HTTP, uses the services of TLS, and TLS uses the services of the transport layer.

Two Protocols

TLS is actually two protocols: the handshake protocol and the data exchange (sometimes called the record) protocol.

Handshake Protocol

The **handshake protocol** is responsible for negotiating security, authenticating the server to the browser, and (optionally) defining other communication parameters. The handshake protocol defines the exchange of a series of messages between the browser and server. We discuss a simplified version, as shown in Figure 31.6.

Figure 31.6 *Handshake protocol*

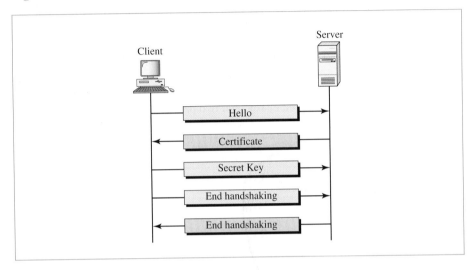

1. The browser sends a *hello* message that includes the TLS version and some preferences.
2. The server sends a *certificate* message that includes the public key of the server. The public key is certified by some certification authority, which means that the public key is encrypted by a CA private key. The browser has a list of CAs and their public keys. It uses the corresponding key to decrypt the certificate and finds the server public key. This also authenticates the server because the public key is certified by the CA.
3. The browser generates a secret key, encrypts it with the server public key, and sends it to the server.
4. The browser sends a message, encrypted by the secret key, to inform the server that handshaking is terminating from the browser side.
5. The server decrypts the secret key using its private key and decrypts the message using the secret key. It then sends a message, encrypted by the secret key, to inform the browser that handshaking is terminating from the server side.

Note that handshaking uses the public key for two purposes: to authenticate the server and to encrypt the secret key, which is used in the data exchange protocol.

Data Exchange Protocol

The **data exchange** (record) **protocol** uses the secret key to encrypt the data for secrecy and to encrypt the message digest for integrity. The details and specification of algorithms are agreed upon during the handshake phase.

31.3   APPLICATION LAYER SECURITY: PGP

The implementation of security at the application layer is more feasible and simpler, particularly when the Internet communication involves only two parties, as in the case of email and TELNET. The sender and the receiver can agree to use the same protocol and to use any type of security services they desire. In this section, we discuss one protocol used at the application layer to provide security: PGP.

Pretty Good Privacy (PGP) was invented by Phil Zimmermann to provide all four aspects of security (privacy, integrity, authentication, and nonrepudiation) in the sending of email.

PGP uses digital signature (a combination of hashing and public-key encryption) to provide integrity, authentication, and nonrepudiation. It uses a combination of secret-key and public-key encryption to provide privacy. Specifically, it uses one hash function, one secret key, and two private-public key pairs. See Figure 31.7.

Figure 31.7   *PGP at the sender site*

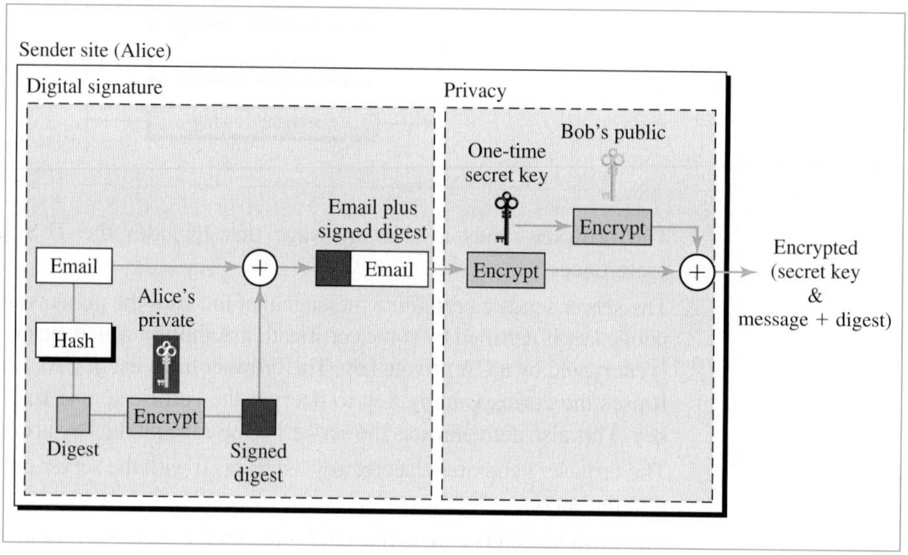

The figure shows how PGP creates secure email at the sender site. The email message is hashed to create a digest. The digest is encrypted (signed) using Alice's private key. The message and the digest are encrypted using the one-time secret key created by Alice. The secret key is encrypted using Bob's public key and is sent together with the encrypted combination of message and digest.

Figure 31.8 shows how PGP uses hashing and a combination of three keys to extract the original message at the receiver site. The combination of encrypted secret key and message plus digest is received. The encrypted secret key first is decrypted (using Bob's private key) to get the one-time secret key created by Alice. The secret key then is used to decrypt the combination of the message plus digest.

Figure 31.8 *PGP at the receiver site*

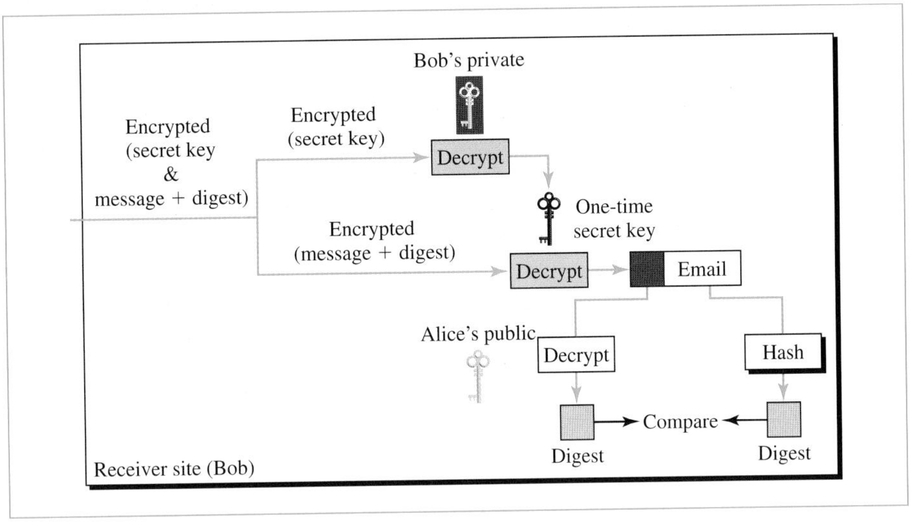

Bob's private
Encrypted
(secret key
&
message + digest)
Encrypted
(secret key)
Decrypt
One-time
secret key
Encrypted
(message + digest)
Decrypt
Email
Alice's public
Decrypt
Hash
Compare
Digest
Digest
Receiver site (Bob)

31.4 FIREWALLS

All previous security measures cannot prevent Eve from sending a harmful message to a system. To control access to a system we need firewalls. A **firewall** is a device (usually a router or a computer) installed between the internal network of an organization and the rest of the Internet. It is designed to forward some packets and filter (not forward) others. Figure 31.9 shows a firewall.

Figure 31.9 *Firewall*

Outgoing
Incoming
Global
Internet
Internal
network(s)
Firewall

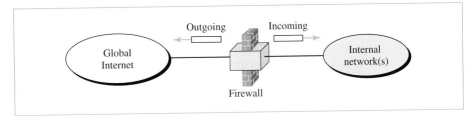

For example, a firewall may filter all incoming packets destined for a specific host or a specific server such as HTTP. A firewall can be used to deny access to a specific host or a specific service in the organization.

A firewall is usually classified as a packet-filter firewall or a proxy-based firewall.

Packet-Filter Firewall

A firewall can be used as a packet filter. It can forward or block packets based on the information in the network layer and transport layer headers: source and destination IP addresses, source and destination port addresses, and type of protocol (TCP or UDP).

A **packet-filter firewall** is a router that uses a filtering table to decide which packet must be discarded (not forwarded). Figure 31.10 shows an example of a filtering table for this kind of a firewall.

Figure 31.10   *Packet-filter firewall*

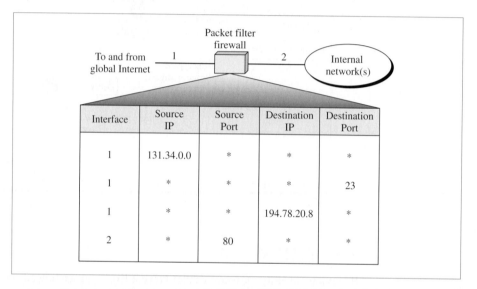

Interface	Source IP	Source Port	Destination IP	Destination Port
1	131.34.0.0	*	*	*
1	*	*	*	23
1	*	*	194.78.20.8	*
2	*	80	*	*

According to the figure, the following packets are filtered:

1. Incoming packets from network 131.34.0.0. are blocked (security precaution). Note that the * (asterisk) means "any."
2. Incoming packets destined for any internal TELNET server (port 23) are blocked.
3. Incoming packets destined for internal host 194.78.20.8. are blocked. The organization wants this host for internal use only.
4. Outgoing packets destined for an HTTP server (port 80) are blocked. The organization does not want employees to browse the Internet.

A packet-filter firewall filters at the network or transport layer.

Proxy Firewall

The packet-filter firewall is based on the information available in the network layer and transport layer headers (IP and TCP/UDP). However, sometimes we need to filter a message based on the information available in the message itself (at the application layer). As an example, assume that an organization wants to implement the following policies regarding its Web pages: Only those Internet users who have previously established business relations with the company can have access; access to other users must be blocked. In this case, a packet-filter firewall is not feasible because it cannot distinguish between different packets arriving at TCP port 80 (HTTP). Testing must be done at the application level (using URLs).

One solution is to install a proxy computer (sometimes called an application gateway), which stands between the customer (user client) computer and the corporation computer. When the user client process sends a message, the **proxy firewall** runs a server process to receive the request. The server opens the packet at the application level and finds out if the request is legitimate. If it is, the server acts as a client process and sends the message to the real server in the corporation. If it is not, the message is dropped and an error message is sent to the external user. In this way, the requests of the external users are filtered based on the contents at the application layer. Figure 31.11 shows a proxy firewall implementation.

Figure 31.11 *Proxy firewall*

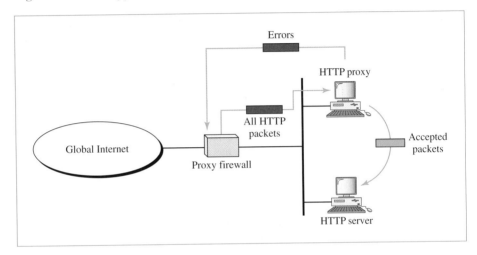

A proxy firewall filters at the application layer.

31.5 VIRTUAL PRIVATE NETWORK

Virtual private network (VPN) is a technology that is gaining popularity among large organizations that use the global Internet for both intra- and interorganization communication, but require privacy in their internal communication.

Private Networks

A private network is designed for use inside an organization. It allows access to shared resources and, at the same time, provides privacy. Before we discuss some aspects of these networks, let us define two commonly used related terms: *intranet* and *extranet*.

Intranet

An **intranet** is a private network (LAN) that uses the Internet model. However, access to the network is limited to the users inside the organization. The network uses application programs defined for the global Internet, such as HTTP, and may have Web servers, print servers, file servers, and so on.

Extranet

An **extranet** is the same as an intranet with one major difference: Some resources may be accessed by specific groups of users outside the organization under the control of the network administrator. For example, an organization may allow authorized customers access to product specifications, availability, and online ordering. A university or a college can allow distance learning students access to the computer lab after passwords have been checked.

Addressing

A private network that uses the Internet model must use IP addresses. Three choices are available:

1. The network can apply for a set of addresses from the Internet authorities and use them without being connected to the Internet. This strategy has an advantage. If in the future the organization decides to be connected to the Internet, it can do so with relative ease. However, there is also a disadvantage: The address space is wasted.

2. The network can use any set of addresses without registering with the Internet authorities. Because the network is isolated, the addresses do not have to be unique. However, this strategy has a serious drawback: Users might mistakenly confuse the addresses as part of the global Internet.

3. To overcome the problems associated with the first and second strategies, the Internet authorities have reserved three sets of addresses, shown in Table 31.1.

Table 31.1   *Addresses for private networks*

Prefix	Range	Total
10/8	10.0.0.0 to 10.255.255.255	2^{24}
172.16/12	172.16.0.0 to 172.31.255.255	2^{20}
192.168/16	192.168.0.0 to 192.168.255.255	2^{16}

Any organization can use an address out of this set without permission from the Internet authorities. Everybody knows that these reserved addresses are for private networks. They are unique inside the organization, but they are not unique globally. No router will forward a packet that has one of these addresses as the destination address.

Achieving Privacy

To achieve privacy, organizations can use one of three strategies: private networks, hybrid networks, and virtual private networks.

Private Networks

An organization that needs privacy when routing information inside the organization can use a **private network** as discussed previously. A small organization with one single site can use an isolated LAN. People inside the organization can send data to one another that totally remain inside the organization, secure from outsiders. A larger organization with several sites can create a private internet. The LANs at different sites can be connected to each other using routers and leased lines. In other words, an internet can be made out of private LANs and private WANs. Figure 31.12 shows such a situation for an organization with two sites. The LANs are connected to each other using routers and one leased line.

Figure 31.12 *Private network*

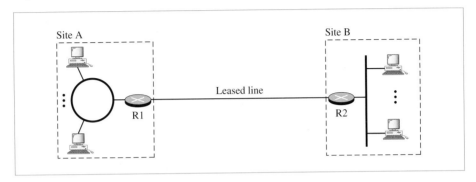

In this situation, the organization has created a private internet that is totally isolated from the global Internet. For end-to-end communication between stations at different sites, the organization can use the Internet model. However, there is no need for the organization to apply for IP addresses with the Internet authorities. It can use private IP addresses. The organization can use any IP class and assign network and host addresses internally. Because the internet is private, duplication of addresses by another organization in the global Internet is not a problem.

Hybrid Networks

Today, most organizations need to have privacy in intraorganization data exchange, but, at the same time, they need to be connected to the global Internet for data exchange with other organizations. One solution is the use of a **hybrid network.** A hybrid network allows an organization to have its own private internet and, at the same time, access to the global Internet. Intraorganization data are routed through the private internet; interorganization data are routed through the global Internet. Figure 31.13 shows an example of this situation.

An organization with two sites uses routers R1 and R2 to connect the two sites privately through a leased line; it uses routers R3 and R4 to connect the two sites to the rest of the world. The organization uses global IP addresses for both types of communication. However, packets destined for internal recipients are routed only through routers R1 and R2. Routers R3 and R4 route the packets destined for outsiders.

Virtual Private Networks

Both private and hybrid networks have a major drawback: cost. Private wide-area networks (WANs) are expensive. To connect several sites, an organization needs several leased lines, which means a high monthly fee. One solution is to use the global Internet for both private and public communications. A technology called virtual private network (VPN) allows organizations to use the global Internet for both purposes.

Figure 31.13   *Hybrid network*

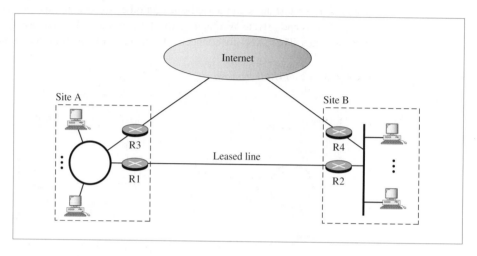

VPN creates a network that is private but virtual. It is private because it guarantees privacy inside the organization. It is virtual because it does not use real private WANs; the network is physically public but virtually private.

Figure 31.14 shows the idea of a virtual private network. Routers R1 and R2 use VPN technology to guarantee privacy for the organization.

Figure 31.14   *Virtual private network*

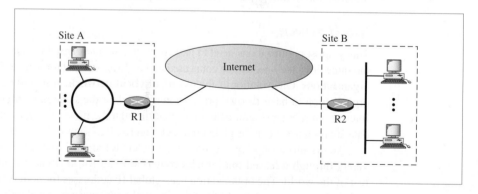

VPN Technology

VPN technology uses IPSec in the tunnel mode to provide authentication, integrity, and privacy.

Tunneling

To guarantee privacy and other security measures for an organization, VPN can use the IPSec in the tunnel mode. In this mode, each IP datagram destined for private use in the organization is encapsulated in another datagram. To use IPSec in the **tunneling** mode, the VPNs need to use two sets of addressing, as shown in Figure 31.15.

Figure 31.15 *Addressing in a VPN*

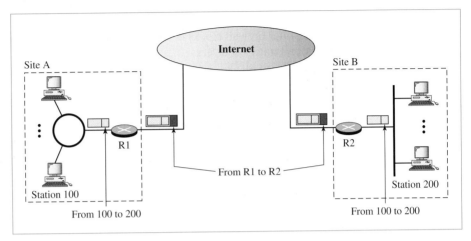

The public network (Internet) is responsible for carrying the packet from R1 to R2. Outsiders cannot decipher the contents of the packet or the source and destination addresses. Deciphering takes place at R2, which finds the destination address of the packet and delivers it.

31.6 KEY TERMS

Authentication Header (AH) protocol	packet-filter firewall
data exchange protocol	Pretty Good Privacy (PGP)
Encapsulating Security Payload (ESP)	private network
extranet	proxy firewall
firewall	Security Association (SA)
handshake protocol	Transport Layer Security (TLS)
hybrid network	tunneling
intranet	virtual private network (VPN)
IP Security (IPSec)	

31.7 SUMMARY

❏ Security methods can be applied in the application layer, transport layer, and IP layer.

❏ IP Security (IPSec) is a collection of protocols designed by the IETF to provide security for an Internet packet.

❏ The Authentication Header protocol provides integrity and message authentication.

❏ The Encapsulating Security Payload protocol provides integrity, message authentication, and privacy.

❏ Transport Layer Security (TLS) provides security at the transport layer through its handshake protocol and data exchange protocol.

❏ Pretty Good Privacy (PGP) provides security for the transmission of email.

❏ A firewall is a router installed between the internal network of an organization and the rest of the Internet.

❏ A packet-filter firewall blocks or forwards packets based on information in the network and transport layers.

❏ A proxy firewall blocks or forwards packets based on information in the application layer.

❏ A private network is used inside an organization.

❏ An intranet is a private network that uses the Internet model.

❏ An extranet is an intranet that allows authorized access from outside users.

❏ The Internet authorities have reserved addresses for private networks.

❏ A virtual private network (VPN) provides privacy for LANs that must communicate through the global Internet.

31.8 PRACTICE SET

Review Questions

1. What is IPSec?
2. Why does IPSec need Security Association?
3. What are the two protocols defined by IPSec?
4. What does AH add to the IP packet?
5. What does ESP add to the IP packet?
6. What are authentication data?
7. What is the security parameter index field?
8. Are both AH and ESP needed for IP security? Why or why not?
9. What are the two protocols defined by TLS?
10. What is the name of the protocol that provides security for email?
11. What is the purpose of a firewall?
12. What are the two types of firewalls?
13. What is a VPN and why is it needed?
14. How do LANs on a fully private internet communicate?
15. How do LANs on a hybrid internet communicate?

Multiple-Choice Questions

16. IPSec requires a logical connection between two hosts using a signaling protocol called _____.

    a. AH

    b. SA

c. PGP

d. TLS

17. The handshake protocol and data exchange protocol are part of _____.

a. CA

b. KDC

c. TLS

d. SSH

18. _____ is a collection of protocols that provide security at the IP layer level.

a. TLS

b. SSH

c. PGP

d. IPSec

19. _____ is an IP layer security protocol that only provides integrity and authentication.

a. AH

b. PGP

c. ESP

d. IPSec

20. _____ is an IP layer security protocol that provides privacy as well as integrity and authentication.

a. AH

b. PGP

c. ESP

d. IPSec

21. An IP datagram carries an authentication header if the _____ field of the IP header has a value of 51.

a. Next-header

b. Protocol

c. Security parameter index

d. Sequence number

22. A _____ can forward or block packets based on the information in the network layer and transport layer headers.

a. Proxy firewall

b. Packet-filter firewall

c. Message digest

d. Private key

23. The _____ field in the authentication header and the ESP header define the security method used in creating the authentication data.

a. Padding

b. Sequence number

c. Authentication data

d. SPI

24. _____ is a transport layer security protocol.
   a. TLS
   b. PGP
   c. IPSec
   d. AH

25. A method to provide for the secure transport of email is called _____.
   a. TLS
   b. SA
   c. PGP
   d. IPSec

26. A _____ can forward or block messages based on the information in the message itself.
   a. Proxy firewall
   b. Packet-filter firewall
   c. Message digest
   d. Private key

27. A _____ network is totally isolated from the global Internet.
   a. Private
   b. Hybrid
   c. Virtual private
   d. Any of the above

28. A _____ network can use a leased line for intraorganization communication and the Internet for interorganization communication.
   a. Private
   b. Hybrid
   c. Virtual private
   d. Any of the above

29. A VPN uses _____ to guarantee privacy.
   a. IPSec
   b. Tunneling
   c. Both (a) and (b)
   d. None of the above

30. In a VPN, _____ encrypted.
   a. The inner datagram is
   b. The outer datagram is
   c. Both inner and outer datagrams are
   d. Neither the inner nor the outer datagram is

31. Tunneling is a technique in which the IP datagram is first _____ and then _____.
   a. Encapsulated in another datagram; encrypted
   b. Encrypted; encapsulated in another datagram

c. Authenticated; encrypted

d. Encrypted; authenticated

32. An _____ is a private network with no external access that uses the TCP/IP suite.

a. Internet

b. internet

c. Intranet

d. Extranet

33. An _____ is a private network with limited external access that uses the TCP/IP suite.

a. Internet

b. internet

c. Intranet

d. Extranet

Exercises

34. Show the values of AH fields in Figure 31.3. Assume authentication data are only 128 bytes.

35. Show the values of ESP header and trailer fields in Figure 31.4.

36. Draw Figure 31.3 if AH is used in the tunnel mode.

37. Draw Figure 31.4 if ESP is used in the tunnel mode.

38. Draw a figure to show the position of AH in IPv6.

39. Draw a figure to show the position of ESP in IPv6.

40. Compare the handshaking protocol in Figure 31.6 with authentication protocols we discussed in Chapter 30. Can you find a protocol in Chapter 30 which is similar to the handshaking protocol?

41. The PGP protocol in Figure 31.7 uses three keys. Explain the purpose of each.

42. Does the PGP protocol need the services of a KDC? Explain your answer.

43. Does the PGP protocol need the services of a CA? Explain your answer.

44. Can a VPN use IPsec in transport mode? Explain your answer.

APPENDIX A

ASCII Code

The American Standard Code for Information Interchange (ASCII) is the most commonly used code for encoding printable and nonprintable (control) characters.

ASCII uses 7 bits to encode each character. It can therefore represent up to 128 characters. Table A.1 lists the ASCII characters and their codes in both binary and hexadecimal forms.

Table A.1   *ASCII table*

Decimal	Hexadecimal	Binary	Character	Description
0	00	0000000	NUL	Null
1	01	0000001	SOH	Start of header
2	02	0000010	STX	Start of text
3	03	0000011	ETX	End of text
4	04	0000100	EOT	End of transmission
5	05	0000101	ENQ	Enquiry
6	06	0000110	ACK	Acknowledgment
7	07	0000111	BEL	Bell
8	08	0001000	BS	Backspace
9	09	0001001	HT	Horizontal tab
10	0A	0001010	LF	Line feed
11	0B	0001011	VT	Vertical tab
12	0C	0001100	FF	Form feed
13	0D	0001101	CR	Carriage return
14	0E	0001110	SO	Shift out
15	0F	0001111	SI	Shift in
16	10	0010000	DLE	Data link escape
17	11	0010001	DC1	Device control 1
18	12	0010010	DC2	Device control 2
19	13	0010011	DC3	Device control 3

Table A.1   *ASCII table (Continued)*

Decimal	Hexadecimal	Binary	Character	Description
20	14	0010100	DC4	Device control 4
21	15	0010101	NAK	Negative acknowledgment
22	16	0010110	SYN	Synchronous idle
23	17	0010111	ETB	End of transmission block
24	18	0011000	CAN	Cancel
25	19	0011001	EM	End of medium
26	1A	0011010	SUB	Substitute
27	1B	0011011	ESC	Escape
28	1C	0011100	FS	File separator
29	1D	0011101	GS	Group separator
30	1E	0011110	RS	Record separator
31	1F	0011111	US	Unit separator
32	20	0100000	SP	Space
33	21	0100001	!	Exclamation mark
34	22	0100010	"	Double quote
35	23	0100011	#	Pound sign
36	24	0100100	$	Dollar sign
37	25	0100101	%	Percent sign
38	26	0100110	&	Ampersand
39	27	0100111	'	Apostrophe
40	28	0101000	(	Open parenthesis
41	29	0101001	)	Close parenthesis
42	2A	0101010	*	Asterisk
43	2B	0101011	+	Plus sign
44	2C	0101100	,	Comma
45	2D	0101101	-	Hyphen
46	2E	0101110	.	Period
47	2F	0101111	/	Slash
48	30	0110000	0	
49	31	0110001	1	
50	32	0110010	2	
51	33	0110011	3	
52	34	0110100	4	
53	35	0110101	5	
54	36	0110110	6	
55	37	0110111	7	

Table A.1   *ASCII table (Continued)*

Decimal	Hexadecimal	Binary	Character	Description
56	38	0111000	8	
57	39	0111001	9	
58	3A	0111010	:	Colon
59	3B	0111011	;	Semicolon
60	3C	0111100	<	Less than sign
61	3D	0111101	=	Equals sign
62	3E	0111110	>	Greater than sign
63	3F	0111111	?	Question mark
64	40	1000000	@	At sign
65	41	1000001	A	
66	42	1000010	B	
67	43	1000011	C	
68	44	1000100	D	
69	45	1000101	E	
70	46	1000110	F	
71	47	1000111	G	
72	48	1001000	H	
73	49	1001001	I	
74	4A	1001010	J	
75	4B	1001011	K	
76	4C	1001100	L	
77	4D	1001101	M	
78	4E	1001110	N	
79	4F	1001111	O	
80	50	1010000	P	
81	51	1010001	Q	
82	52	1010010	R	
83	53	1010011	S	
84	54	1010100	T	
85	55	1010101	U	
86	56	1010110	V	
87	57	1010111	W	
88	58	1011000	X	
89	59	1011001	Y	
90	5A	1011010	Z	
91	5B	1011011	[	Open bracket

Table A.1   *ASCII table (Continued)*

Decimal	Hexadecimal	Binary	Character	Description
92	5C	1011100	\	Backslash
93	5D	1011101	]	Close bracket
94	5E	1011110	^	Caret
95	5F	1011111	_	Underscore
96	60	1100000	`	Grave accent
97	61	1100001	a	
98	62	1100010	b	
99	63	1100011	c	
100	64	1100100	d	
101	65	1100101	e	
102	66	1100110	f	
103	67	1100111	g	
104	68	1101000	h	
105	69	1101001	i	
106	6A	1101010	j	
107	6B	1101011	k	
108	6C	1101100	l	
109	6D	1101101	m	
110	6E	1101110	n	
111	6F	1101111	o	
112	70	1110000	p	
113	71	1110001	q	
114	72	1110010	r	
115	73	1110011	s	
116	74	1110100	t	
117	75	1110101	u	
118	76	1110110	v	
119	77	1110111	w	
120	78	1111000	x	
121	79	1111001	y	
122	7A	1111010	z	
123	7B	1111011	{	Open brace
124	7C	1111100	|	Bar
125	7D	1111101	}	Close brace
126	7E	1111110	~	Tilde
127	7F	1111111	DEL	Delete

APPENDIX B

Numbering Systems and Transformation

Today's computers make use of four numbering systems: decimal, binary, octal, and hexadecimal. Each has advantages for different levels of digital processing. In Section B.1, we describe each of the four systems. In Section B.2, we show how a number in one system can be transformed to a number in another system.

B.1 NUMBERING SYSTEMS

All the numbering systems examined here are *positional*, meaning that the position of a symbol in relation to other symbols determines its value. Within a number, each symbol is called a digit (decimal digit, binary digit, octal digit, or hexadecimal digit). For example, the decimal number 798 has three decimal digits. Digits are arranged in order of ascending value, moving from the lowest value on the right to the highest on the left. For this reason, the leftmost digit is referred to as the most significant and the rightmost as the least significant digit (see Fig. B.1). For example, in the decimal number 1234, the most significant digit is the 1, and the least significant is the 4.

Figure B.1 *Digit positions and their significance*

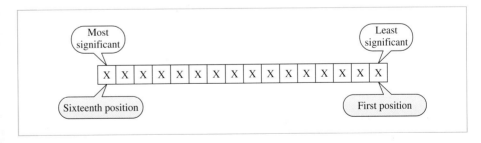

Decimal Numbers

The decimal system is the one most familiar to us in everyday life. All our terms for indicating countable quantities are based on it, and in fact when we speak of other

865

numbering systems, we tend to refer to their quantities by their decimal equivalents. Also called *base-10,* the name *decimal* is derived from the Latin stem *deci,* meaning 10. The decimal system uses 10 symbols to represent quantitative values: 0, 1, 2, 3, 4, 5, 6, 7, 8, and 9.

> **Decimal numbers use 10 symbols: 0, 1, 2, 3, 4, 5, 6, 7, 8, and 9.**

Weight and Value

In the decimal system, each weight equals 10 raised to the power of its position. The weight of the first position, therefore, is 10^0, which equals 1. So the value of a digit in the first position is equal to the value of the digit times 1. The weight of the second position is 10^1, which equals 10. The value of a digit in the second position, therefore, is equal to the value of the digit times 10. The weight of the third position is 10^2. The value of a digit in the third position is equal to the value of the digit times 100 (see Table B.1).

Table B.1   *Decimal weights*

Position	Fifth	Fourth	Third	Second	First
Weight	10^4 (10,000)	10^3 (1000)	10^2 (100)	10^1 (10)	10^0 (1)

The value of the number as a whole is the sum of each digit times its weight. Figure B.2 shows the weightings of the decimal number 4567.

Figure B.2   *Example of a decimal number*

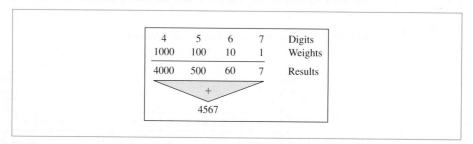

Binary Numbers

The binary number system provides the basis for all computer operations. Computers work by manipulating electric current on and off. The binary system uses two symbols, *0* and *1,* so it corresponds naturally to a two-state device, such as a switch, with 0 to represent the off state and 1 to represent the on state. Also called *base 2,* the word *binary* derives from the Latin stem *bi,* meaning 2.

> **Binary numbers use two symbols: 0 and 1.**

Weight and Value

The binary system is also a weighted system. Each digit has a weight based on its position in the number. Weight in the binary system is 2 raised to the power represented by a position, as shown in Table B.2. Note that the value of the weightings is shown in decimal terms next to the weight itself. The value of a specific digit is equal to its face value times the weight of its position.

Table B.2 *Binary weights*

Position	Fifth	Fourth	Third	Second	First
Weight	2^4 (16)	2^3 (8)	2^2 (4)	2^1 (2)	2^0 (1)

To calculate the value of a number, multiply each digit by the weight of its position, and then add the results. Figure B.3 demonstrates the weighting of the binary number 1101. As you can see, 1101 is the binary equivalent of decimal 13.

Figure B.3 *Example of a binary number*

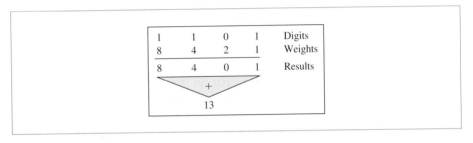

Octal Numbers

The octal number system is used by computer programmers to represent binary numbers in a compact form. Also called *base 8,* the term *octal* derives from the Greek stem *octa,* meaning 8. Eight is a power of 2 (2^3) and therefore can be used to model binary concepts. The octal system uses eight symbols to represent quantitative values: 0, 1, 2, 3, 4, 5, 6, and 7.

> **Octal numbers use eight symbols: 0, 1, 2, 3, 4, 5, 6, and 7.**

Weight and Value

The octal system is also a weighted system. Each digit has a weight based on its position in the number. Weight in octal is 8 raised to the power represented by a position, as shown in Table B.3. Once again, the value represented by each weighting is given in decimal terms next to the weight itself. The value of a specific digit is equal to its face value times the weight of its position. For example, a 4 in the third position has the equivalent decimal value 4×64, or 256.

Table B.3   *Octal weights*

Position	Fifth	Fourth	Third	Second	First
Weight	8^4 (4096)	8^3 (512)	8^2 (64)	8^1 (8)	8^0 (1)

To calculate the value of an octal number, multiply the value of each digit by the weight of its position, then add the results. Figure B.4 shows the weighting for the octal number 3471. As you can see, 3471 is the octal equivalent of decimal 1849.

Figure B.4   *Example of an octal number*

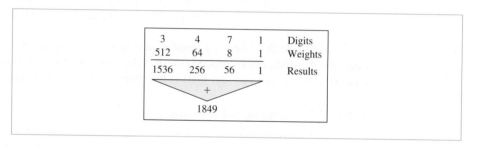

Hexadecimal Numbers

The term *hexadecimal* is derived from the Greek stem *hexadeca,* meaning 16 (*hex* means 6, and *deca* means 10). So the hexadecimal number system is *base 16.* Sixteen is also a power of 2 (2^4). Like octal, therefore, the hexadecimal system is used by programmers to represent binary numbers in a compact form. Hexadecimal uses 16 symbols to represent data: 0, 1, 2, 3, 4, 5, 6, 7, 8, 9, A, B, C, D, E, and F.

Hexadecimal numbers use 16 symbols: 0, 1, 2, 3, 4, 5, 6, 7, 8, 9, A, B, C, D, E, and F.

Weight and Value

Like the others, the hexadecimal system is a weighted system. Each digit has a weight based on its position in the number. The weight is used to calculate the value represented by the digit. Weight in hexadecimal is 16 raised to the power represented by a position, as shown in Table B.4. Once again, the value represented by each weighting is given in decimal terms next to the weight itself. The value of a specific digit is equal to its face value times the weight of its position. For example, a 4 in the third position has the equivalent decimal value 4×256, or 1024. To calculate the value of a hexadecimal number, multiply the value of each digit by the weight of its position, then add the results.

Table B.4   *Hexadecimal weights*

Position	Fifth	Fourth	Third	Second	First
Weight	16^4 (65,536)	16^3 (4096)	16^2 (256)	16^1 (16)	16^0 (1)

Figure B.5 shows the weighting for the hexadecimal number 3471. As you can see, 3471 is the hexadecimal equivalent of decimal 13,425.

Figure B.5 *Example of a hexadecimal number*

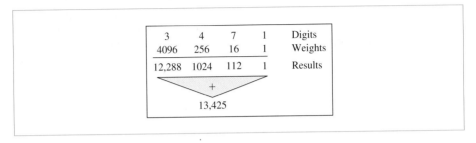

B.2 TRANSFORMATION

The different numbering systems provide different ways of thinking about a common subject: quantities of single units. A number from any given system can be transformed to its equivalent in any other system. For example, a binary number can be converted to a decimal number, and vice versa, without altering its value. Table B.5 shows how each system represents the decimal numbers 0 through 15. As you can see, decimal 13

Table B.5 *Comparison of four systems*

Decimal	Binary	Octal	Hexadecimal
0	0	0	0
1	1	1	1
2	10	2	2
3	11	3	3
4	100	4	4
5	101	5	5
6	110	6	6
7	111	7	7
8	1000	10	8
9	1001	11	9
10	1010	12	A
11	1011	13	B
12	1100	14	C
13	1101	15	D
14	1110	16	E
15	1111	17	F

is equivalent to binary 1101, which is equivalent to octal 15, which is equivalent to hexadecimal D.

From Other Systems to Decimal

As we saw in the discussions above, binary, octal, and hexadecimal numbers can be transformed easily to their decimal equivalents by using the weights of the digits. Figure B.6 shows the decimal value 78 represented in each of the other three systems.

Figure B.6 *Transformation from other systems to decimal*

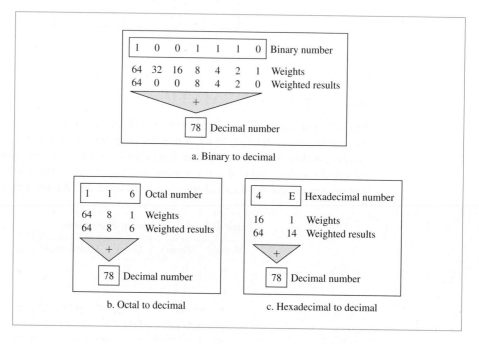

a. Binary to decimal

b. Octal to decimal

c. Hexadecimal to decimal

From Decimal to Other Systems

A simple division trick gives us a convenient way to convert a decimal number to its binary, octal, or hexadecimal equivalent (see Fig. B.7).

To convert a number from decimal to binary, divide the number by 2 and write down the resulting remainder (1 or 0). That remainder is the least significant binary digit. Now, divide the result of that division by 2, and write down the new remainder in the second position. Repeat this process until the quotient becomes zero.

In Figure B.7, we convert the decimal number 78 to its binary equivalent. To check the validity of this method, we convert 1001110 to decimal, using the weights of each position.

$$2^6 + 2^3 + 2^2 + 2^1 \longrightarrow 64 + 8 + 4 + 2 \longrightarrow 78$$

To convert a number from decimal to octal, the procedure is the same but the divisor is 8 instead of 2. To convert from decimal to hexadecimal, the divisor is 16.

Figure B.7 *Transformation from decimal to other systems*

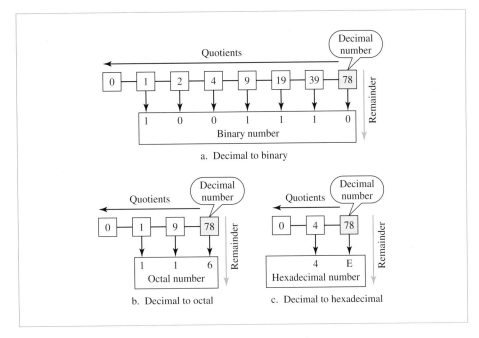

a. Decimal to binary

b. Decimal to octal

c. Decimal to hexadecimal

From Binary to Octal or Hexadecimal

To change a number from binary to octal, we first group the binary digits from right to left by 3s. Then we convert each tribit to its octal equivalent and write the result under the tribit. These equivalents, taken in order (not added), are the octal equivalent of the original number. In Figure B.8, we convert binary 1001110.

To change a number from binary to hexadecimal, we follow the same procedure but group the digits from right to left by 4s. This time we convert each quadbit to its

Figure B.8 *Transformation from binary to octal or hexadecimal*

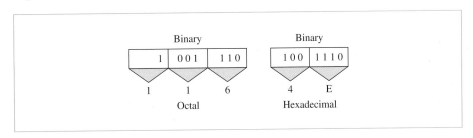

hexadecimal equivalent (use Table B.5). In Figure B.8, we convert binary 1001110 to hexadecimal.

From Octal or Hexadecimal to Binary

To convert from octal to binary, we reverse the procedure above. Starting with the least significant digit, we convert each octal digit into its equivalent three binary digits. In Figure B.9, we convert octal 116 to binary.

Figure B.9   *Transformation from octal or hexadecimal to binary*

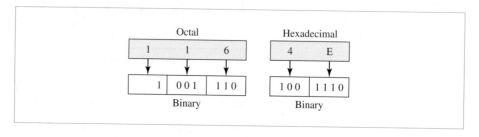

To convert a number from hexadecimal to binary, we convert each hexadecimal digit to its equivalent four binary digits, again starting with the least significant digit. In Figure B.9, we convert hexadecimal 4E to binary.

APPENDIX C

The OSI Model

The layered model that dominated data communication and networking literature before 1990 was the **Open Systems Interconnection (OSI) model.** Everyone believed that the OSI model would become the ultimate standard for data communication—but this did not happen. The Internet model became the dominant commercial architecture because it was used and tested extensively; the OSI model was never fully implemented.

In this appendix, we briefly discuss the OSI as a model and compare it to the Internet model.

C.1 THE MODEL

Established in 1947, the **International Organization for Standardization (ISO)** is a multinational body dedicated to worldwide agreement on international standards. An ISO standard that covers all aspects of network communications is the Open Systems Interconnection (OSI) model. It was first introduced in the late 1970s. An **open system** is a set of protocols that allows any two different systems to communicate regardless of their underlying architectures. The purpose of the OSI model is to show how to facilitate communication between different systems without requiring changes to the logic of the underlying hardware and software. The OSI model is not a protocol; it is a model for understanding and designing a network architecture that is flexible, robust, and interoperable. Figure C.1 shows the model.

C.2 LAYERS IN THE OSI MODEL

In this section we briefly describe the functions of each layer in the OSI model.

First Four Layers

The first four layers in the OSI model (physical, data link, network, and transport layers) and the corresponding layers in the Internet model are almost the same. We do not discuss these layers here.

7	Application
6	Presentation
5	Session
4	Transport
3	Network
2	Data link
1	Physical

ISO is the organization. OSI is the model.

Session Layer

The **session layer** is the network *dialog controller*. It establishes, maintains, and synchronizes the interaction between communicating systems.

Specific responsibilities of the session layer include the following:

- **Dialog control.** The session layer allows two systems to enter into a dialog. It allows the communication between two processes to take place in either half-duplex (one way at a time) or full-duplex (two ways at a time) mode. For example, the dialog between a terminal connected to a mainframe can be half-duplex.

- **Synchronization.** The session layer allows a process to add checkpoints (**synchronization points**) into a stream of data. For example, if a system is sending a file of 2000 pages, it is advisable to insert checkpoints after every 100 pages to ensure that each 100-page unit is received and acknowledged independently. In this case, if a crash happens during the transmission of page 523, the only pages that need to be resent after system recovery are pages 501 to 523. Pages previous to 501 need not be resent. Figure C.2 illustrates the relationship of the session layer to the transport and presentation layers.

Presentation Layer

The **presentation layer** is concerned with the syntax and semantics of the information exchanged between two systems. Figure C.3 shows the relationship between the presentation layer and the application and session layers.

Specific responsibilities of the presentation layer include the following:

- **Translation.** The processes (running programs) in two systems are usually exchanging information in the form of character strings, numbers, and so on. The information

Figure C.2 *Session layer*

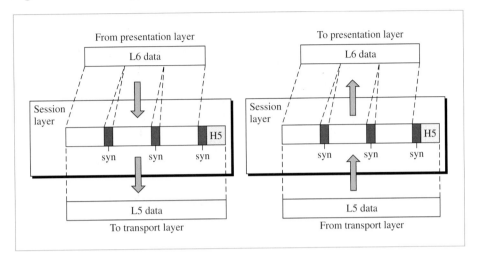

Figure C.3 *Presentation layer*

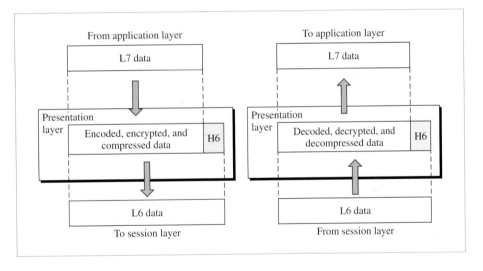

must be changed to bit streams before being transmitted. Because different computers use different encoding systems, the presentation layer is responsible for interoperability between these different encoding methods. The presentation layer at the sender changes the information from its sender-dependent format into a common format. The presentation layer at the receiving machine changes the common format into its receiver-dependent format.

■ **Encryption.** To carry sensitive information, a system must be able to ensure privacy. Encryption means that the sender transforms the original information to another form and sends the resulting message out over the network. Decryption reverses the original process to transform the message back to its original form.

■ **Compression.** Data compression reduces the number of bits contained in the information. Data compression becomes particularly important in the transmission of multimedia such as text, audio, and video.

Application Layer

The **application layer** enables the user, whether human or software, to access the network. It provides user interfaces and support for services such as electronic mail, remote file access and transfer, shared database management, and other types of distributed information services.

Figure C.4 shows the relationship of the application layer to the user and the presentation layer. Of the many application services available, the figure shows only three: X.400 (message-handling services), X.500 (directory services), and file transfer, access, and management (FTAM). The user in this example uses X.400 to send an email message.

Figure C.4   *Application layer*

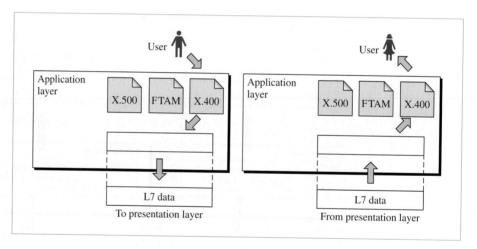

Specific services provided by the application layer include the following:

■ **Network virtual terminal.** A network virtual terminal is a software version of a physical terminal and allows a user to log on to a remote host. To do so, the application creates a software emulation of a terminal at the remote host. The user's computer talks to the software terminal, which, in turn, talks to the host, and vice versa. The remote host believes it is communicating with one of its own terminals and allows you to log on.

■ **File transfer, access, and management (FTAM).** This application allows a user to access files in a remote host (to make changes or read data), to retrieve files from a remote computer for use in the local computer, and to manage or control files in a remote computer locally.

■ **Mail services.** This application provides the basis for email forwarding and storage.

■ **Directory services.** This application provides distributed database sources and access for global information about various objects and services.

C.3 COMPARISON

The Internet model was developed prior to the OSI model. Therefore, the layers in the Internet model do not match exactly those in the OSI model. The Internet model is made of five layers; the OSI model has seven layers. The three topmost layers in the OSI model are represented in the Internet model by a single layer called the *application layer* (see Fig. C.5).

Figure C.5 *The Internet and OSI models*

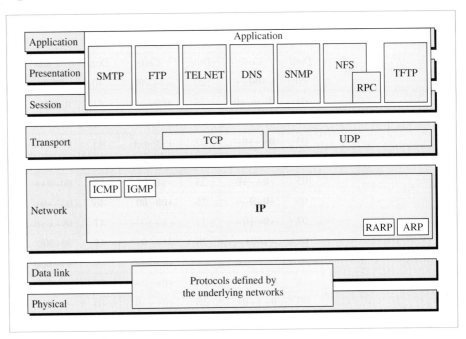

APPENDIX D

8B/6T Code

This appendix is a tabulation of 8B/6T code pairs. The 8-bit data are shown in hexadecimal format. The 6T code is shown as + (positive signal), – (negative signal), and 0 (lack of signal) notation. Because the table is very large, we have shown the first half of the code in Table D.1 and the second half in Table D.2.

Table D.1

Data	Code	Data	Code	Data	Code	Data	Code
00	–+00–+	20	–++–00	40	–00+0+	60	0++0–0
01	0–+–+0	21	+00+––	41	0–00++	61	+0+–00
02	0–+0–+	22	–+0–++	42	0–0+0+	62	+0+0–0
03	0–++0–	23	+–0–++	43	0–0++0	63	+0+00–
04	–+0+0–	24	+–0+00	44	–00++0	64	0++00–
05	+0––+0	25	–+0+00	45	00–0++	65	++0–00
06	+0–0–+	26	+00–00	46	00–+0+	66	++00–0
07	+0–+0–	27	–+++––	47	00–++0	67	++000–
08	–+00+–	28	0++–0–	48	00+000	68	0++–+–
09	0–++–0	29	+0+0––	49	++–000	69	+0++––
0A	0–+0+–	2A	+0+–0–	4A	+–+000	6A	+0+–+–
0B	0–+–0+	2B	+0+––0	4B	–++000	6B	+0+––+
0C	–+0–0+	2C	0++––0	4C	0+–000	6C	0++––+
0D	+0–+–0	2D	++00––	4D	+0–000	6D	++0+––
0E	+0–0+–	2E	++0–0–	4E	0–+000	6E	++0–+–
0F	+0––0+	2F	++0––0	4F	–0+000	6F	++0––+
10	0––+0+	30	+–00–+	50	+–––+0+	70	000++–
11	–0–0++	31	0+–––+0	51	–+–0++	71	000+–+

878

Table D.1 *(Continued)*

Data	Code	Data	Code	Data	Code	Data	Code
12	−0−+0+	32	0+−0−+	52	−+−+0+	72	000−++
13	−0−++0	33	0+−+0−	53	−+−++0	73	000+00
14	0−−++0	34	+−0+0−	54	+−−++0	74	000+0−
15	−−00++	35	−0+−+0	55	−−+0++	75	000+−0
16	−−0+0+	36	−0+0−+	56	−−++0+	76	000−0+
17	−−0++0	37	−0++0−	57	−−+++0	77	000−+0
18	−+0−+0	38	+−00+−	58	−−0+++	78	+++−−0
19	+−0−+0	39	0+−+−0	59	−0−+++	79	+++−0−
1A	−++−+0	3A	0+−0+−	5A	0−−+++	7A	+++0−−
1B	+00−+0	3B	0+−−0+	5B	0−−0++	7B	0++0−−
1C	+00+−0	3C	+−0−0+	5C	+−−0++	7C	−00−++
1D	−+++−0	3D	−0++−0	5D	−000++	7D	−00+00
1E	+−0+−0	3E	−0+0+−	5E	0+++−−	7E	+−−−++
1F	−+0+−0	3F	−0+−0+	5F	0++−00	7F	+−−+00

Table D.2

Data	Code	Data	Code	Data	Code	Data	Code
80	−00+−+	A0	−++0−0	C0	−+0+−+	E0	−++0−+
81	0−0−++	A1	+−+−00	C1	0−+−++	E1	+−+−+0
82	0−0+−+	A2	+−+0−0	C2	0−++−+	E2	+−+0−+
83	0−0++−	A3	+−+00−	C3	0−+++−	E3	+−++0−
84	−00++−	A4	−++00−	C4	−+0++−	E4	−+++0−
85	00−−++	A5	++−−00	C5	+0−−++	E5	++−−+0
86	00−+−+	A6	++−0−0	C6	+0−+−+	E6	++−0−+
87	00−++−	A7	++−00−	C7	+0−++−	E7	++−+0−
88	−000+0	A8	−++−+−	C8	−+00+0	E8	−++0+−
89	0−0+00	A9	+−++−−	C9	0−++00	E9	+−++−0
8A	0−00+0	AA	+−+−+−	CA	0−+0+0	EA	+−+0+−
8B	0−000+	AB	+−+−−+	CB	0−+00+	EB	+−+−0+
8C	−0000+	AC	−++−−+	CC	−+000+	EC	−++−0+
8D	00−+00	AD	++−+−−	CD	+0−+00	ED	++−+−0
8E	00−0+0	AE	++−−+−	CE	+0−0+0	EE	++−0+−

Table D.2   *(Continued)*

Data	Code	Data	Code	Data	Code	Data	Code
8F	00−00+	AF	++−−−+	CF	+0−00+	EF	++−−0+
90	+−−+−+	B0	+000−0	D0	+−0+−+	F0	+000−+
91	−+−−++	B1	0+0−00	D1	0+−−++	F1	0+0−+0
92	−+−+−+	B2	0+00−0	D2	0+−+−+	F2	0+00−+
93	−+−++−	B3	0+000−	D3	0+−++−	F3	0+0+0−
94	+−−++−	B4	+0000−	D4	+−0++−	F4	+00+0−
95	−−+−++	B5	00+−00	D5	−0+−++	F5	00+−+0
96	−−++−+	B6	00+0−0	D6	−0++−+	F6	00+0−+
97	−−+++−	B7	00+00−	D7	−0+++−	F7	00++0−
98	+−−0+0	B8	+00−+−	D8	+−00+0	F8	+000+−
99	−+−+00	B9	0+0+−−	D9	0+−+00	F9	0+0+−0
9A	−+−0+0	BA	0+0−+−	DA	0+−0+0	FA	0+00+−
9B	−+−00+	BB	0+0−−+	DB	0+−00+	FB	0+0−0+
9C	+−−00+	BC	+00−−+	DC	+−000+	FC	+00−0+
9D	−−++00	BD	00++−−	DD	−0++00	FD	00++−0
9E	−−+0+0	BE	00+−+−	DE	−0+0+0	FE	00+0+−
9F	−−+00+	BF	00+−−+	DF	−0+00+	FF	00+−0+

APPENDIX E

Checksum Calculation

This appendix shows how to calculate a checksum in both binary and hexadecimal notation.

E.1 BINARY NOTATION

To show a binary checksum calculation, we use Figure E.1.

Figure E.1 *Partial sum for binary notation*

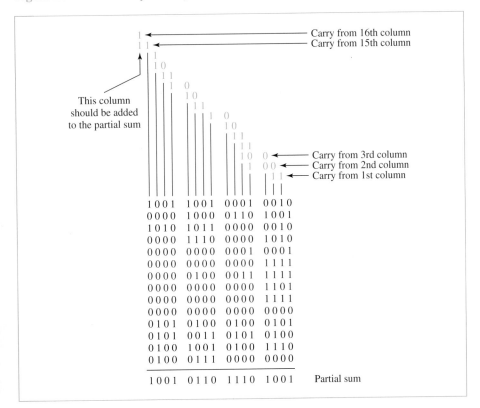

Partial Sum

First we calculate the partial sum as shown in Figure E.1. We add each column and carry to the next columns, if necessary. Note the following points:

- When we add the first (rightmost) column, we get 7. The number 7 in binary is 111. We keep the rightmost 1 and carry the rest to columns 2 and 3.
- When we add the second column, we include the carry from the first column. The result is 8, which is 1000 in binary. We keep the first bit (rightmost) and carry the rest (100) to columns 3, 4, and 5.
- We repeat the above procedure for each column.
- When we finish adding the last column, we have two 1s for which there is no column left for addition. We add these two 1s to the partial sum in the next step.

Sum

If there is no carry from the last column, the partial sum is the sum. However, if there are extra columns (in this example, there is one column with two rows), these are added to the partial sum to obtain the sum. Figure E.2 shows this calculation. Now we have the sum.

Figure E.2   *Sum and checksum for binary notation*

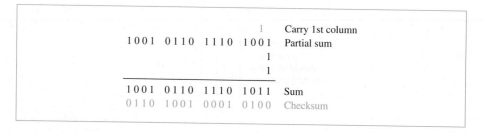

Checksum

After the sum is calculated, we complement each bit to get the checksum. Figure E.2 also shows the checksum.

E.2   HEXADECIMAL NOTATION

Now let us do the same calculation in hexadecimal.

Partial Sum

First we calculate the partial sum as shown in Figure E.3. We add each column and carry to the next columns, if necessary. Note the following points:

- We use 10, 11, 12, 13, 14, and 15 instead of A, B, C, D, E, and F when we do the actual addition.

Figure E.3 *Partial sum for hexadecimal notation*

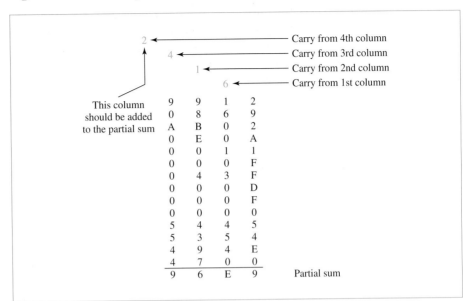

- When we add the first column, we get 105. This number in hexadecimal is 69_{16}. We keep the first digit (9) and carry the second digit (6) to column 2.
- We repeat the same procedure for each column.
- When we add the last column, we get 41. This number in hexadecimal is 29_{16}. We keep the first digit (9) and add the second digit to the partial sum in the next step.

Sum

If there are no carries from the last column, the partial sum is the sum. However, if there are extra columns (in this example, there is only one column), these are added to the partial sum to obtain the sum. Figure E.4 shows this calculation. Now we have the sum.

Figure E.4 *Sum and checksum for hexadecimal notation*

9	6	E	9	Partial sum
			2	Carry from last column
9	6	E	B	Sum
6	9	1	4	Checksum
0110	1001	0001	0100	Checksum (binary)

Checksum

After the sum is calculated, we complement each hexadecimal digit to get the checksum. Figure E.4 also shows the checksum. Note that when we calculate the complement, we subtract each digit from 15 to get the complement (ones complement in hexadecimal). The figure also shows how to represent the checksum in binary.

APPENDIX F

Structure of a Router

We discussed routing in Chapter 19 and routing algorithms in Chapter 21. In these two chapters, we represented a router as a black box that accepts incoming packets from one of the input ports (interfaces), uses a routing table to find the output port from which the packet departs, and sends the packet from this output port. In this appendix, we want to open the black box and look at the inside. However, our discussion won't be very detailed; entire books have been written about routers. We just give an overview to the reader.

F.1 COMPONENTS

We can say that a router has four components: **input ports, output ports,** the **routing processor,** and the **switching fabric,** as shown in Figure F.1.

Figure F.1 *Router components*

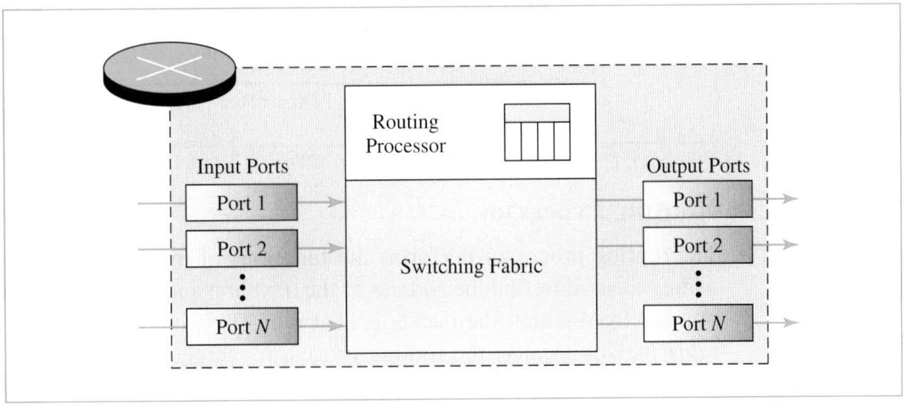

Input Ports

An input port performs the physical and data link functions of the router. The bits are constructed from the received signal. The packet is decapsulated from the frame. Errors are detected and corrected. The packet is ready to be routed by the network layer. In addition to a physical layer processor and a data link processor, the input port has buffers (queues) to hold the packet before being directed to the switching fabric. Figure F.2 shows a schematic diagram of an input port.

Figure F.2   *Input port*

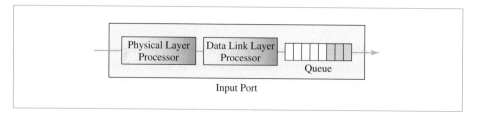

Output Ports

An output port performs the same functions as the input port, but in the reverse order. First the outgoing packets are queued, then the packet is encapsulated in a frame, and finally the physical layer functions are applied to the frame to create the signal to be sent on the line. Figure F.3 shows a schematic diagram of an output port.

Figure F.3   *Output port*

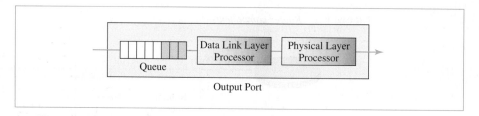

Routing Processor

The routing processor performs the functions of the network layer. The destination address is used to find the address of the next hop and, at the same time, the output port number from which the packet is sent out. This activity is sometimes referred to as *table lookup* because the routing processor searches the routing table. In the newer routers, this function of the routing processor is being moved to the input ports to facilitate and expedite the process.

Switching Fabrics

The most difficult task in a router is to move the packet from the input queue to the output queue. The speed with which this is done affects the size of the input/output queue and the overall delay in packet delivery. In the past, when a router was actually a dedicated computer, the memory of the computer or a bus was used as the switching fabric. The input port stored the packet in memory; the output port got the packet from the memory. Today, routers are specialized mechanisms that use a variety of switching fabrics. We briefly discuss some of these fabrics here.

Crossbar Switch

The simplest type of switching fabric is the crossbar switch discussed in Chapter 8 and repeated in Figure F.4.

Figure F.4 *Crossbar switch*

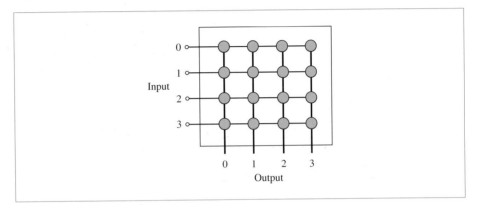

Banyan Switch

A more realistic approach is a switch called a **banyan switch** (named after the banyan tree). A banyan switch is a multistage switch with microswitches at each stage that route the cells based on the output port represented as a binary string. For *n* inputs and *n* outputs, we have $\log_2(n)$ stages with *n*/2 microswitches at each stage. The first stage routes the cell based on the high order bit of the binary string. The second stage routes the cells based on the second high order bit, and so on. Figure F.5 shows a banyan switch with eight inputs and eight outputs. The number of stages is $\log_2(8) = 3$.

Figure F.5 *A banyan switch*

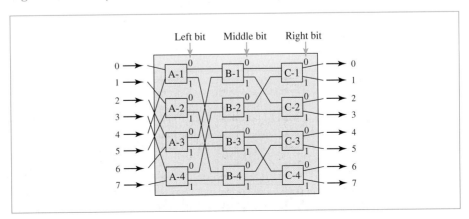

Figure F.6 shows the operation. In part a, a cell has arrived at input port 1 and must go to output port 6 (110 in binary). The first microswitch (A-2) routes the cell based on the first bit (1), the second microswitch (B-4) routes the cell based on the second bit (1), and the third microswitch (C-4) routes the cell based on the third bit (0). In part b, a cell has arrived at input port 5 and must go to output port 2 (010 in binary). The first microswitch (A-2) routes the cell based on the first bit (0), the second microswitch (B-2) routes the cell based on the second bit (1), and the third microswitch (C-2) routes the cell based on the third bit (0).

Figure F.6   *Examples of routing in a banyan switch*

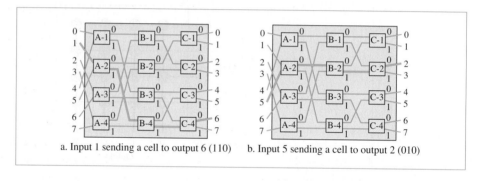

Banyan switch

a. Input 1 sending a cell to output 6 (110)   b. Input 5 sending a cell to output 2 (010)

Batcher-Banyan Switch

The problem with the banyan switch is the possibility of internal collision even when two cells are not heading for the same output port. We can solve this problem by sorting the arriving cells based on their destination port.

K. E. Batcher designed a switch that comes before the banyan switch and sorts the incoming cells according to their final destination. The combination is called the **Batcher-banyan switch.** The sorting switch uses hardware merging techniques, but we will not discuss the details here. Normally, another hardware module called a trap is added between the Batcher switch and the banyan switch (see Fig. F.7) The trap module prevents duplicate cells (cells with the same output destination) from passing to the banyan switch simultaneously. Only one cell for each destination is allowed at each tick; if there is more than one, they wait for the next tick.

Figure F.7   *Batcher-banyan switch*

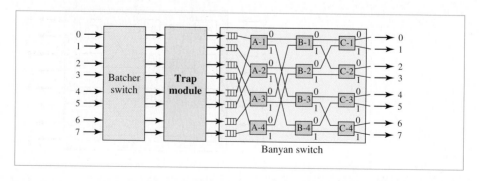

Banyan switch

APPENDIX G

ATM LANs

ATM is mainly a wide area network (WAN ATM); however, the technology can be adapted to local area networks (ATM LAN). In Chapter 18, we discussed ATM technology. In this appendix the technology is applied to LANs.

The high data rate of the technology (155 and 622 Mbps) has attracted the attention of designers who are looking for greater and greater speed in LANs. In addition, ATM technology has several advantages that make it an ideal LAN:

- ATM technology supports different types of connections between two end users. It supports permanent and temporary connections.

- ATM technology supports multimedia communication with a variety of bandwidths for different applications. It can guarantee a bandwidth of several megabits per second for real-time video. It can also provide support for text transfer during off-peak hours.

- An ATM LAN can be easily adapted for expansion in an organization.

G.1 ATM LAN ARCHITECTURE

Today, we have two ways to incorporate ATM technology in a LAN architecture: creating a **pure ATM LAN** or making a **legacy ATM LAN.** Figure G.1 shows the taxonomy.

Figure G.1 *ATM LANs*

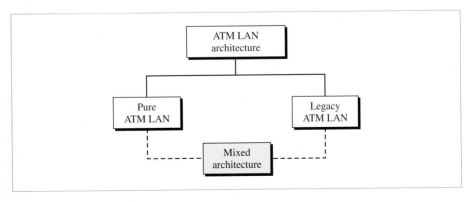

Pure ATM Architecture

In a pure ATM LAN, an **ATM switch** is used to connect the stations in a LAN, in exactly the same way stations are connected to an Ethernet switch. Figure G.2 shows the situation.

Figure G.2 *Pure ATM LAN*

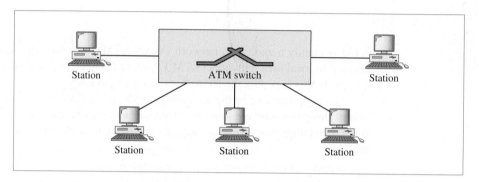

In this way, stations can exchange data at one of two standard rates of ATM technology (155 and 652 Mbps). However, the station uses a **virtual path identifier (VPI)** and a **virtual connection identifier (VCI),** instead of a source and destination address.

This approach has a major drawback. The system needs to be built from the ground up; existing LANs cannot be upgraded into pure ATM LANs.

Legacy LAN Architecture

A second approach is to use ATM technology as a backbone to connect traditional LANs. Figure G.3 shows this architecture.

Figure G.3 *Legacy ATM LAN*

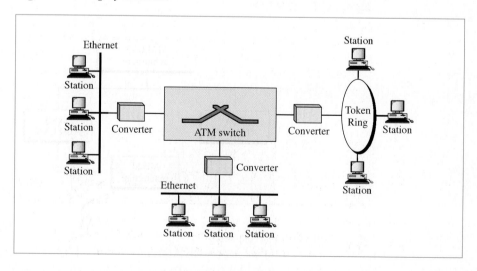

In this way, stations on the same LAN can exchange data at the rate and format of traditional LANs (Ethernet, Token Ring, etc.). But when two stations on two different LANs need to exchange data, they can go through a converting device that changes the frame format. The advantage here is that output from several LANs can be multiplexed together to create a high-data-rate input to the ATM switch. There are several issues that must be resolved first.

Mixed Architecture

Probably the best solution is to mix the two previous architectures. This means keeping the existing LANs and, at the same time, allowing new stations to be directly connected to an ATM switch. The **mixed architecture LAN** allows the gradual migration of legacy LANs onto ATM LANs by adding more and more directly connected stations to the switch. Figure G.4 shows this architecture.

Figure G.4 *Mixed architecture ATM LAN*

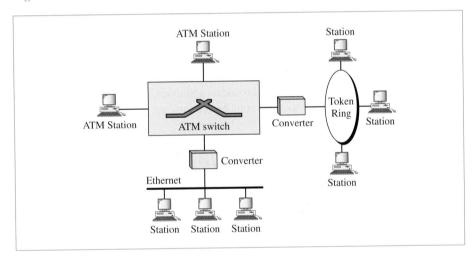

Again, the stations in one specific LAN can exchange data using the format and data rate of that particular LAN. The stations directly connected to the ATM switch can use an ATM frame to exchange data. However, the problem is, How can a station in a traditional LAN communicate with a station directly connected to the ATM switch or vice versa? We see how the problem is resolved now.

G.2   LAN EMULATION (LANE)

At the surface level, the use of ATM technology in LANs seems very natural. However, the similarity is only at the surface level; many issues need to be resolved, as summarized below:

■ **Connectionless versus connection-oriented.** Traditional LANs, such as Ethernet, are **connectionless protocols.** A station sends data packets to another station whenever the packets are ready. There is no **connection establishment** or **connection termination** phase. On the other hand, ATM is a **connection-oriented protocol;** a station that wishes to send cells to another station should first establish a connection and, after all the cells are sent, terminate the connection.

■ **Physical addresses versus virtual connection identifiers.** Closely related to the first issue is the difference in addressing. A connectionless protocol, such as Ethernet, defines the route of a packet through **source** and **destination addresses.** However, a connection-oriented protocol, such as ATM, defines the route of a cell through virtual connection identifiers (VPIs and VCIs).

■ **Multicasting and broadcasting delivery.** Traditional LANs, such as Ethernet, can both **multicast** and **broadcast** packets; a station can send packets to a group of stations or to all stations. There is no easy way to multicast or broadcast on an ATM network although point-to-multipoint connections are available.

■ **Interoperability.** In a mixed architecture, a station connected to a legacy LAN should be able to communicate with a station directly connected to an ATM switch.

An approach called **local area network emulation (LANE)** solves the above-mentioned problems and allows stations in a mixed architecture to communicate with one another. The approach uses emulation. Stations can use a connectionless service that emulates a connection-oriented service. Stations use the source and destination addresses for initial connection and then use VPI and VCI addressing. The approach allows stations to use unicast, multicast, and broadcast addresses. Finally, the approach converts frames using a legacy format to ATM cells before they are sent through the switch.

G.3 CLIENT-SERVER MODEL

LANE is designed as a **client-server model** to handle the four previously discussed problems. The protocol uses one type of client and three types of servers, as shown in Figure G.5.

Figure G.5 *Client and servers in a LANE*

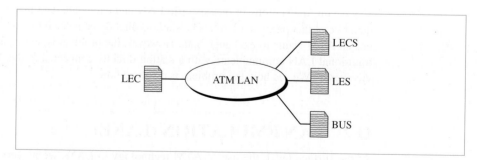

LAN Emulation Client (LEC)

All ATM stations have **LAN emulation client (LEC)** software installed on top of the three ATM protocols. The upper-layer protocols are unaware of the existence of the

ATM technology. These protocols send their requests to LEC for a LAN service such as connectionless delivery using MAC unicast, multicast, or broadcast addresses. The LEC, however, just interprets the request and passes the result on to the servers.

LAN Emulation Configuration Server (LECS)

The **LAN emulation configuration server (LECS)** is used for initial connection between the client and LANE. This server is always waiting to receive the initial contact. It has a well-known ATM address that is known to every client in the system.

LAN Emulation Server (LES)

LAN emulation server (LES) software is installed on the LES. When a station receives a frame to be sent to another station using a physical address, LEC sends a special frame to the LES. The server creates a virtual circuit between the source and the destination station. The source station can now use this virtual circuit (and the corresponding identifier) to send the frame or frames to the destination.

Broadcast/Unknown Server (BUS)

Multicasting and broadcasting require the use of another server called the **broadcast/unknown server (BUS).** If a station needs to send a frame to a group of stations or to every station, the frame first goes to the BUS; this server has permanent virtual connections to every station. The server creates copies of the received frame and sends a copy to a group of stations or to all stations, simulating a multicasting or broadcasting process. The server can also deliver a unicast frame by sending the frame to every station. In this case the destination address is unknown. This is sometimes more efficient than getting the connection identifier from the LES.

G.4   MIXED ARCHITECTURE WITH CLIENT-SERVER

Figure G.6 shows clients and servers in a mixed-architecture ATM LAN. In the figure, three types of servers are connected to the ATM switch (they can actually be part of the switch). Also we show two types of clients. Stations A and B, designed to send and receive LANE communication, are directly connected to the ATM switch. Stations C, D, E, F, G, and H in traditional legacy LANs are connected to the switch via a converter. These converters act as LEC clients and communicate on behalf of their connected stations.

Figure G.6 *A mixed-architecture ATM LAN using LANE*

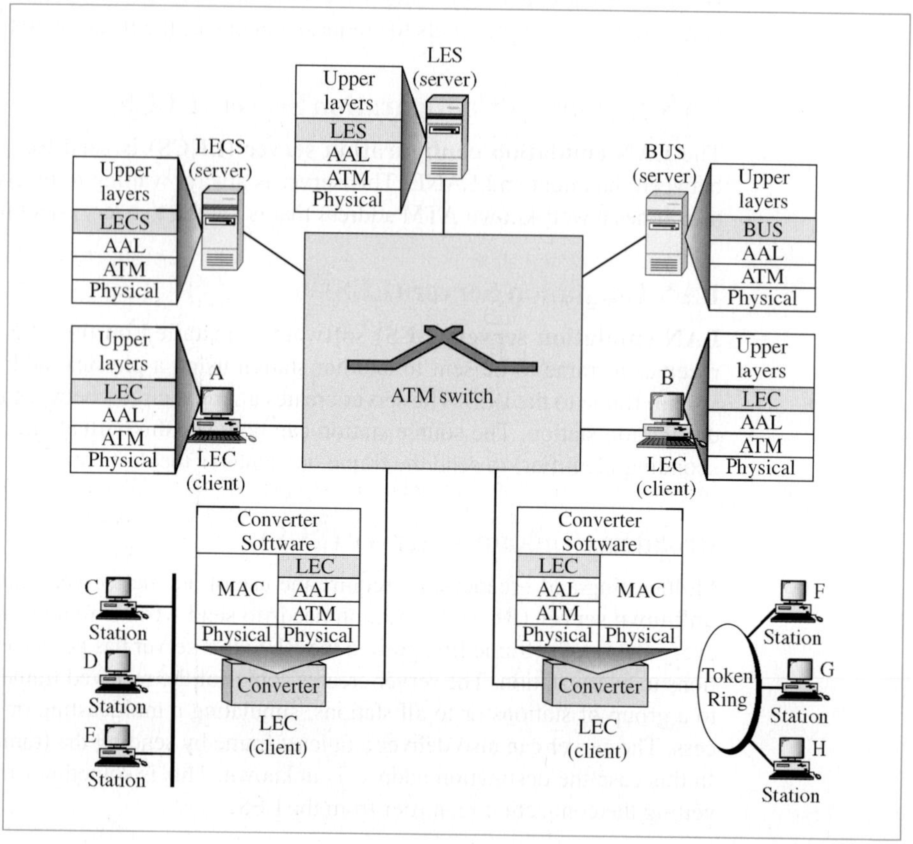

APPENDIX H

Client-Server Programs

In Chapter 24, we introduced socket programming. We gave the flowchart design of client and server programs for both UDP and TCP. In this appendix, we give an example of a client and server program for interested readers.

H.1 UDP CLIENT-SERVER PROGRAMS

This section contains one simple server program and one simple client program. The server is a generic server. We have included one PROCESS call that is used to define the server function. For the sake of simplicity, we have not included any error-checking or error-handling statements.

Server Program

The server program is shown in Program H.1.

Program H.1

UDP Server Program
#include <sys/types.h>
#include <sys/socket.h>
#include <netdb.h>
#include <netinet/in.h>
#include <stdio.h>
#include <string.h>
#define MAXBUF   256
void main (void)
{
char buf [MAXBUF] ;
int passiveSocket ;

Program H.1   *(Continued)*

socklen_t clientAddrLen ;
struct sockaddress   serverAddr ;
struct sockaddress   clientAddr ;
passiveSocket = socket (AF_INET, SOCK_DGRAM, 0) ;
memset (&serverAddr , 0 , sizeof (serverAddr)) ;
serverAddr.sin_family = AF_INET ;
serverAddr.sin_port = htons (a-well-known-port) ;
serverAddr.sin_addr.s_addr = htonl (INADDR_ANY) ;
bind (passiveSocket, &serverAddr, sizeof (serverAddr));
clientAddrLen = sizeof (serverAddr) ;
memset (buf , 0, MAXBUF) ;
for (; ;)
{
while (recvfrom (passiveSocket, buf, MAXBUF, 0,   &clientAddr, &clientAddrLen) > 0)
{
PROCESS (............) ;
sendto (passiveSocket, buf , MAXBUF , 0 ,   &clientAddr , clientAddrLen) ;
memset (buf , 0 , MAXBUF) ;
}
}
}

Client Program

The client program is shown in Program H.2.

Program H.2

UDP Client Program
#include <sys/types.h>
#include <sys/socket.h>
#include <netdb.h>
#include <netinet/in.h>
#include <stdio.h>
#include <string.h>
#define MAXBUF   256

Program H.2   *(Continued)*

```
void main (void)
{
  char buf [ MAXBUF] ;
  int activeSocket ;
  socklen_t remoteAddrLen ;
  struct sockaddress    remoteAddr ;
  struct sockaddress    localAddr ;
  struct hostent   *hptr ;
  activeSocket =  socket (AF_INET, SOCK_DGRAM, 0) ;
  memset (&remoteAddr , 0  , sizeof (remoteAddr) ) ;
  remoteAddr.sin_family = AF_INET ;
  remoteAddr.sin_port = htons (a-well-known-port)  ;
  hptr = gethostbyname (" a-domain-name") ;
  memcpy ((char*) &remoteAddr.sin_addr.s_addr,
       hptr ->h_addr_list[0], hptr ->h_length ) ;

  memset (buf , 0, MAXBUF) ;
  remoteAddrLen = sizeof (remoteAddr) ;
  while (gets (buf) )
  {
  sendto (activeSocket,  buf  , sizeof (buf) , 0 ,
       &remoteAddr ,  sizeof (remoteAddr) ) ;
  memset (buf, 0, sizeof (buf) ) ;
  recvfrom (activeSocket,  buf , MAXBUF, 0 ,
       &remoteAddr  ,  &remoteAddrLen ) ;
  printf ("%s\n", buf) ;
  memset (buf ,  0 , sizeof (buf) ) ;
  }
  close (activeSocket ) ;
}
```

H.2 TCP CLIENT-SERVER PROGRAMS

This section contains one simple server program and one simple client program. The server is a generic server. We have included one PROCESS call that is used to define the server function. For the sake of simplicity, we have not included any error-checking or error-handling statements.

Server Program

Program H.3 shows the server program.

Program H.3

TCP Server Program
#include <sys/types.h>
#include <sys/socket.h>
#include <netdb.h>
#include <netinet/in.h>
#include <stdio.h>
#include <string.h>
#define MAXBUF   256
void main (void)
{
char buf [MAXBUF] ;
int listenSocket ;
int acceptSocket ;
socklen_t clientAddrLen ;
struct sockaddress   serverAddr ;
struct sockaddress   clientAddr ;
listenSocket = socket (AF_INET, SOCK_STREAM, 0) ;
memset (&serverAddr , 0 , sizeof (serverAddr)) ;
serverAddr.sin_family = AF_INET ;
serverAddr.sin_port = htons (a-well-known-port) ;
serverAddr.sin_addr.s_addr = htonl(INADDR_ANY) ;
bind (listenSocket, &serverAddr, sizeof (serverAddr)) ;
listen (listenSocket , 1) ;
clientAddrLen = sizeof (clientAddr) ;
for (; ;)
{
acceptSocket = accept (listenSocket &clientAddr, &clientAddrLen) ;
pid = fork () ;
if (pid > 0)   /* parent */
{
close (acceptSocket) ;
continue ;
}

Program H.3 *(Continued)*

```
        else    /* child */
    {
      close (listenSocket) ;
      memset (buf , 0, MAXBUF) ;
      while (read (acceptSocket , buf, MAXBUF) > 0 )
      {
        PROCESS (............) ;
      memset (buf, 0, MAXBUF);
      write  (acceptSocket,  buf  , MAXBUF ) ;
      memset (buf , 0   , MAXBUF) ;
       } /* while */
      close (acceptSocket) ;
       } /* else */
     } /* for */
  }
```

Client Program

The client program is shown in Program H.4.

Program H.4

TCP Client Program
#include <sys/types.h>
#include <sys/socket.h>
#include <netdb.h>
#include <netinet/in.h>
#include <stdio.h>
#include <string.h>
#define MAXBUF   256
void main (void)
{
char buf [MAXBUF] ;
int activeSocket ;
struct sockaddress   remoteAddr ;
struct sockaddress   localAddr ;
struct hostent *hptr ;
activeSocket = socket (AF_INET, SOCK_STREAM, 0) ;

Program H.4   *(Continued)*

```
memset (&remoteAddr , 0  , sizeof (remoteAddr)) ;
remoteAddr.sin_family = AF_INET ;
remoteAddr.sin_port = htons (a-well-known-port)  ;
hptr = gethostbyname (" a-domain-name") ;
memcpy   ((char*) &remoteAddr.sin_addr.s_addr ,
    hptr ->h_addr_list[0], hptr ->h_length ) ;
connect (activeSocket, remoteAddr, sizeof struct sockaddress) ;
memset (buf , 0, MAXBUF) ;
while (gets (buf) )
{
    write  (activeSocket,  buf  , MAXBUF) ;
    memset (buf, 0, MAXBUF);
    read (activeSocket ,  buf , MAXBUF) ;
    printf ("%s\n", buf) ;
    memset (buf , 0 , MAXBUF) ;
}
close (activeSocket) ;
}
```

APPENDIX I

RFCs

There are approximately 2500 RFCs. In Table I.1 we list alphabetically, by protocol, those that are directly related to the material in this text. The main RFCs for each protocol are in boldface. For a complete listing, go to http://www.faqs.org/rfcs.

Table I.1 *RFCs for each protocol*

Protocol	RFC
ARP and RARP	**826, 903,** 925, 1027, 1293, 1329, 1433
BGP	1092, 1105, 1163, 1265, 1266, 1267, 1364, 1392, 1403, 1565, 1654, 1655, 1665, 1745, 1997, 2238, 2439
BOOTP and DHCP	**951,** 1048, 1084, 1395, 1497, 1531, 1532, 1533, 1534, 1541, 1542, 2131, 2132
DHCP	See BOOTP and DHCP
DNS	799, 811, 819, 830, 881, 882, 883, 897, 920, 921, **1034, 1035,** 1386, 1480, 1535, 1536, 1537, 1591, 1637, 1664, 1706, 1712, 1713, 1995, 2317
FTP	114, 133, 141, 163, 171, 172, 238, 242, 250, 256, 264, 269, 281, 291, 354, 385, 412, 414, 418, 430, 438, 448, 463, 468, 478, 486, 505, 506, 542, 553, 624, 630, 640, 691, 765, 913, **959,** 1635, 2460, 2577
HTML	1866
HTTP	**2068,** 2109
ICMP	777, **792,** 1016, 1018, 1256, 1788, 1885, 2521
IGMP	988, 1054, 1112, 2236
IP	760, 781, **791,** 815, 950, 919, 922, 1025, 1063, 1141, 1190, 1191, 1624, 2113
IPv6	1365, 1550, 1678, 1680, 1682, 1683, 1686, 1688, 1726, 1752, 1826, 1883, 1884, 2133, 2147, 2492, 2553, 2590, 2675
MIME	See SNMP, MIME, SMI
OSPF	1131, 1245, 1246, 1247, 1370, 1583, 1584, 1585, 1586, 1587, 2178, 2328, 2329, 2370
PIM	2362

Table I.1   *RFCs for each protocol (Continued)*

Protocol	RFC
PPP	1134, 1171, 1172, 1331, 1332, 1547, 1570, 1663
RARP	See ARP and RARP
RIP	1131, 1245, 1246, 1247, 1370, 1583, 1584, 1585, 1586, 1587, 1722, 1723, 2082, 2453
SMI	See SNMP, MIB, SMI
SMTP, MIME, POP	196, 221, 224, 278, 524, 539, 753, 772, 780, 806, **821,** 934, 974, 1047, 1081, 1082, 1225, 1460, 1496, 1426, 1427, 1652, 1653, 1711, 1725, 1734, 1740, 1741, 1767, 1869, **1870,** 2045, 2449, 2487, 2554, 2633, 2683
SNMP, MIB, SMI	1065, 1067, 1098, 1155, **1157, 1212, 1213,** 1229, 1231, 1243, 1284, 1351, 1352, 1354, 1389, 1398, 1414, 1441, 1442, 1443, 1444, 1445, 1446, 1447, 1448, 1449, 1450, 1451, 1452, 1461, 1472, 1474, 1537, 1623, 1643, 1650, 1657, 1665, 1666, 1696, 1697, 1724, 1742, 1743, 1748, 1749, 1905, 1906, 2001, 2037, 2320, 2593, 2581, 2582, 2579, 2677
TCP	675, 721, 761, **793,** 879, 896, 1078, 1106, 1110, 1144, 1145, 1146, 1263, 1323, 1337, 1379, 1644
TELNET	137, 340, 393, 426, 435, 452, 466, 495, 513, 529, 562, 595, 596, 599, 669, 679, 701, 702, 703, 728, 764, 782, 818, **854, 855,** 1184, 1205, 1411, 1412
TFTP	**1350,** 1782, 1783, 1784, 1785
UDP	768
WWW	1614, 1630, 1737, 1738

APPENDIX J

UDP and TCP Ports

Table J.1 lists the common well-known ports ordered by port number.

Table J.1 *Ports by port number*

Port Number	UDP/ TCP	Protocol
7	TCP	ECHO
13	UDP/TCP	DAYTIME
19	UDP/TCP	CHARACTER GENERATOR
20	TCP	FTP-DATA
21	TCP	FTP-CONTROL
23	TCP	TELNET
25	TCP	SMTP
37	UDP/TCP	TIME
67	UDP	BOOTP-SERVER
68	UDP	BOOTP-CLIENT
69	UDP	TFTP
70	TCP	GOPHER
79	TCP	FINGER
80	TCP	HTTP
109	TCP	POP-2
110	TCP	POP-3
111	UDP/TCP	RPC
161	UDP	SNMP
162	UDP	SNMP-TRAP
179	TCP	BGP
520	UDP	RIP

Table J.2 lists the ports ordered alphabetically by protocol.

Table J.2   *Port numbers by protocol*

Protocol	UDP/TCP	Port Number
BGP	TCP	179
BOOTP-SERVER	UDP	67
BOOTP-CLIENT	UDP	68
CHARACTER GENERATOR	UDP/TCP	19
DAYTIME	UDP/TCP	13
ECHO	TCP	7
FINGER	TCP	79
FTP-CONTROL	TCP	21
FTP-DATA	TCP	20
GOPHER	TCP	70
HTTP	TCP	80
POP-2	TCP	109
POP-3	TCP	110
RIP	UDP	520
RPC	UDP/TCP	111
SMTP	TCP	25
SNMP	UDP	161
SNMP-TRAP	UDP	162
TELNET	TCP	23
TFTP	UDP	69
TIME	UDP/TCP	37

APPENDIX K

Contact Addresses

The following is a list of contact addresses for various organizations mentioned in the text.

- **ATM Forum**
  Presidio of San Francisco
  P.O. Box 29920 (mail)
  572B Ruger Street (surface)
  San Francisco, CA 94129-0920
  Telephone: 415 561-6275
  Email: info@atmforum.com
  http://www.atmforum.com

- **Federal Communications Commission (FCC)**
  445 12th Street S.W.
  Washington, DC 20554
  Telephone: 1-888-225-5322
  Email: fccinfo@fcc.gov
  http://www.fcc.gov

- **Institute of Electrical and Electronics Engineers (IEEE)**
  Operations Center
  445 Hoes Lane
  Piscataway, NJ 08855-1331
  Telephone: 732 981-0060
  http://www.ieee.gov

- **International Organization for Standardization (ISO)**
  1, rue de Varembe
  Case postale 56
  CH-1211 Geneva 20
  Switzerland
  Telephone: 41 22 749 0111
  Email: central@iso.ch
  http://www.iso.org

International Telecommunication Union (ITU)
Place des Nations
CH-1211 Geneva 20
Switzerland
Telephone: 41 22 730 5852
Email: tsbmail@itu.int
http://www.itu.int/ITU-T

Internet Architecture Board (IAB)
Email: IAB@isi.edu
http://www.iab.org

Internet Corporation for Assigned Names and Numbers (ICANN)
4676 Admiralty Way, Suite 330
Marina del Rey, CA 90292-6601
Telephone: 310 823-9358
Email: icann@icann.org
http://www.icann.org

Internet Engineering Steering Group (IESG)
Email: iesg@ietf.org
http://www.ietf.org/iesg.html

Internet Engineering Task Force (IETF)
Email: ietf-infor@ietf.org
http://www.ietf.org

Internet Research Task Force (IRTF)
Email: irtf-chair@ietf.org
http://www.irtf.org

Internet Society (ISOC)
775 Weihle Avenue, Suite 102
Reston, VA 20190-5108
Telephone: 703 326-9880
Email: info@isoc.org
http://www.isoc.org

Acronyms

4D-PAM5	4-dimensional, 5-level pulse amplitude modulation	BECN	backward explicit congestion notification
AAL	application adaptation layer	B-frame	bidirectional frame
ABM	asynchronous balanced mode	BGP	Border Gateway Protocol
ABR	available bit rate	BnZS	bipolar n-zero substitution
ACK	acknowledgment	BOOTP	Bootstrap Protocol
ACL	asynchronous connectionless link	bps	bits per second
ADSL	asymmetric digital subscriber line	BSS	Basic Service Set
AH	Authentication Header	CA	Certification Authority
AM	amplitude modulation	CATV	community antenna TV
AMI	alternate mark inversion	CBC mode	cipherblock chaining mode
AMPS	Advanced Mobile Phone System	CBR	constant bit rate
ANSI	American National Standards Institute	CBT	Core-Based Tree
API	application programming interface	CCITT	Consultative Committee for International Telegraphy and Telephony
ARP	address resolution protocol		
ARPA	Advanced Research Projects Agency	CCK	complementary code keying
		CDMA	code division multiple access
ARPANET	Advanced Research Projects Agency Network	CFM	cipher feedback mode
		CGI	Common Gateway Interface
ARQ	automatic repeat request	CHAP	Challenge Handshake Authentication Protocol
AS	autonomous system or authentication server		
		CIDR	Classless Inter-Domain Routing
ASCII	American Standard Code for Information Interchange	CIR	committed information rate
		CLEC	competitive local exchange carrier
ASK	amplitude shift keying	CMTS	cable modem transmission system
ATM	asynchronous transfer mode		

CRC	cyclic redundancy check	EIA	Electronics Industries Association
CS	convergence sublayer	email	electronic mail
CSM	cipher stream mode	ESP	Encapsulating Security Payload
CSMA	carrier sense multiple access	ESS	Extended Service Set
CSMA/CA	carrier sense multiple access with collision avoidance	FCC	Federal Communications Commission
CSMA/CD	carrier sense multiple access with collision detection	FCS	frame check sequence
D-AMPS	digital AMPS	FDDI	fiber distributed data interface
DARPA	Defense Advanced Research Projects Agency	FDM	frequency division modulation
		FDMA	frequency division multiple access
dB	decibel	FECN	forward explicit error congestion notification
DC	direct current		
DCT	discrete cosine transform	FHSS	frequency hopping spread spectrum
DDNS	dynamic domain name system	FIFO	first-in, first-out
DDS	digital data service	FM	frequency modulation
DE	discard eligibility	FQDN	fully qualified domain name
DEMUX	demultiplexer	FRAD	Frame Relay assembler/dissembler
DES	data encryption standard	FSK	frequency shift keying
DHCP	Dynamic Host Configuration Protocol	FTP	File Transfer Protocol
		GMII	gigabit medium independent interface
Diffserv	Differentiated Services		
DIFS	distributed interframe space	GPS	Global Positioning System
DLCI	data link connection identifier	GSM	Global System for Mobile Communication
DMT	discrete multi-tone technique		
DNS	Domain Name System	HDLC	High-level Data Link Control
DOCSIS	Data Over Cable System Interface Specifications	HDSL	high bit rate digital subscriber line
		HFC network	hybrid-fiber-coaxial network
DS	Differentiated Services	HR-DSSS	High Rate Direct Sequence Spread Spectrum
DSL	digital subscriber line		
DSLAM	digital subscriber line access multiplexer	HTML	hypertext markup language
		HTTP	hypertext transfer protocol
DSSS	direct sequence spread spectrum	Hz	hertz
DSU	digital service unit	IAB	Internet Architecture Board
DVMRP	Distance Vector Multicast Routing Protocol	IANA	Internet Assigned Numbers Authority
		ICANN	Internet Corporation for Assigned Names and Numbers
DWDM	dense wave division multiplexing		
EBCDIC	extended binary coded decimal interchange code	ICMP	Internet Control Message Protocol
		ICMPv6	Internet Control Message Protocol, version 6
ECB	electronic code block		
EGP	Exterior Gateway Protocol	IEEE	Institute of Electrical and Electronics Engineers

IESG	Internet Engineering Steering Group	MBONE	multicast backbone
IETF	Internet Engineering Task Force	MDI	medium dependent interface
I-frame	intracoded frame	MEO	medium earth orbit
IGMP	Internet Group Management Protocol	MII	medium independent interface
IGP	Interior Gateway Protocol	MIME	Multipurpose Internet Mail Extension
ILEC	incumbent local exchange carrier		
IMAP4	Internet Mail Access Protocol, version 4	MLT-3 encoding	multiline transmission, 3-level encoding
INTERNIC	Internet Network Information Center	MOSPF	Multicast Open Shortest Path First
IntServ	Integrated Services	MPEG	motion picture experts group
IP	Internet Protocol	MSC	mobile switching center
IPCP	Internetwork Protocol Control Protocol	MTA	mail transfer agent
		MTSO	mobile telephone switching office
IPng	Internet Protocol, version 6	MTU	maximum transfer unit
IPSec	IP Security	NAK	negative acknowledgment
IPv4	Internet Protocol, version 4	NAT	network address translation
IPv6	Internet Protocol, version 6	NAV	network allocation vector
IR	infrared	NCP	Network Control Protocol
IRTF	Internet Research Task Force	NIC	network interface card
IS-95	Interim Standard 95	NNI	network-to-network interface
ISO	International Organization of Standardization	NRM	normal response mode
		NRZ	nonreturn to zero
ISOC	Internet Society	NRZ-I	nonreturn to zero-invert
ISP	Internet service provider	NRZ-L	nonreturn to zero-level
ITM-2000	Internet Mobile Communication for year 2000	NSP	national service provider
		NVT	network virtual terminal
ITU–T	International Telecommunications Union–Telecommunication Standardization Sector	OC	optical carrier
		OSI	open systems interconnection
		OSPF	open shortest path first
IXC	interexchange carrier	PAM	pulse amplitude modulation
JPEG	Joint Photographic Experts Group	PAP	Password Authentication Protocol
KDC	key distribution center	PCF	point coordination function
LAN	local area network	PCM	pulse code modulation
LANE	LAN emulation	PCS	Personal Communication System
LCP	Link Control Protocol	P-frame	predicted frame
LSA	link state advertisement	PGP	Pretty Good Privacy
LSP	link state packet	PHB	per hop behavior
MA	multiple access	PIM	Protocol Independent Multicast
MAC address	physical address	PIM-DM	Protocol Independent Multicast, Dense Mode
MAN	metropolitan area network		
MAU	medium attachment unit		

PIM-SM	Protocol Independent Multicast, Sparse Mode	SNR	signal to noise ratio
PING	Packet Internet Groper	SONET	Synchronous Optical Network
PKI	public key infrastructure	STP	shielded twisted pair
PLS	physical layer signaling sublayer	STS	synchronous transport signal
PM	phase modulation	SVC	switched virtual circuit
POP	point of presence	TCP	Transmission Control Protocol
POP3	Post Office Protocol, version 3	TCP/IP	Transmission Control Protocol/ Internetworking Protocol
PPP	Point-to-Point Protocol	TDD-TDMA	time-division duplexing TDMA
PQDN	partially qualified domain name	TDM	time-division multiplexing
PSK	phase shift keying	TDMA	time division multiple access
PVC	permanent virtual circuit	TELNET	Terminal Network
QAM	quadrature amplitude modulation	TFTP	trivial file transfer protocol
QoS	quality of service	TGS	ticket-granting server
RADSL	rate adaptive asymmetrical digital subscriber line	TLS	Transport Layer Security
		TOS	type of service
RARP	reverse address resolution protocol	TP	transmission path
RFC	Request for Comment	TSI	time-slot interchange
RIP	routing information protocol	TTL	time to live
ROM	read-only memory	UA	user agent
RPB	reverse path broadcasting	UBR	unspecified bit rate
RPF	reverse path forwarding	UDP	User Datagram Protocol
RPM	reverse path multicasting	UNI	user network interface
RSVP	Resource Reservation Protocol	URL	uniform resource locator
RTCP	Real-time Transport Control Protocol	UTP	unshielded twisted pair
		VBR	variable bit rate
RTP	Real-time Transport Protocol	VC	virtual circuit
RTSP	Real-time Streaming Protocol	VCI	virtual channel identifier or virtual connection identifier
RTT	round-trip time		
RZ	return to zero	VDSL	very high bit rate digital subscriber line
SA	source address or Security Association		
		VOFR	Voice Over Frame Relay
SAR	segmentation and reassembly	VPI	virtual path identifier
SDH	synchronous digital hierarchy	VPI/VCI	virtual path identifier/virtual channel identifier
SDSL	symmetric digital subscriber line		
SFD	start frame delimiter	VPN	virtual private network
SIFS	short interframe space	VT	virtual tributary
SIP	Session Initiation Protocol	WAN	wide area network
SMTP	simple mail transfer protocol	WATS	wide area telephone service
SNMP	simple network management protocol	WWW	World Wide Web

Glossary

1000Base-CX   A two-wire implementation of Gigabit Ethernet using shielded twisted pair cables.

1000Base-LX   A two-wire implementation of Gigabit Ethernet using optical fibers transmitting long-wave laser signals.

1000Base-SX   A two-wire implementation of Gigabit Ethernet using optical fibers transmitting short wave laser signals.

1000Base-T   A four-wire implementation of Gigabit Ethernet using twisted-pair cables.

100Base-FX   A two-wire implementation of Fast Ethernet using fiber-optic cable.

100Base-T4   A four-wire implementation of Fast Ethernet using twisted-pair cable.

10Base2   The IEEE 802.3 standard for Thin Ethernet.

10Base5   The IEEE 802.3 standard for Thick Ethernet.

10Base-FL   The IEEE 802.3 standard for fiber-optic Ethernet.

10Base-T   The IEEE 802.3 standard for twisted-pair Ethernet.

1-persistent strategy   A CSMA persistence strategy in which a station sends a frame immediately if the line is idle.

2B1Q encoding   A line encoding technique in which each pulse represents 2 bits.

4B/5B encoding   A block coding technique in which 4 bits are encoded into a 5-bit code.

4-dimensional, 5-level pulse amplitude modulation (4D-PAM5)   An encoding scheme used by 1000Base-T.

56K modem   A modem technology using two different data rates: one for uploading and one for downloading from the Internet.

800 service   A telephone service free to the caller.

8B/10B encoding   A block coding technique in which 8 bits are encoded into a 10-bit code.

8B/6T encoding   A block coding technique in which 8 bits are encoded into a 6-bit code.

900 service   A telephone service paid by the caller.

A

access control   The determination of link control through a data link protocol.

access rate   In Frame Relay, the data rate that can never be exceeded.

access point   A central base station in a BSS.

acknowledgment (ACK)   A response sent by the receiver to indicate the successful receipt and acceptance of data.

active close   In the client-server model, the closing of a communication by the client.

active document   In the World Wide Web, a document executed at the local site using Java.

active open   In the client-server model, the opening of a communication by the client.

add/drop multiplexer   A SONET device that multiplexes signals from different sources or demultiplexes a signal to multiple destinations.

additive increase   With slow start, a congestion avoidance strategy in which the window size is increased by just one segment instead of exponentially.

Address Resolution Protocol (ARP)   In TCP/IP, a protocol for obtaining the physical address of a node when the Internet address is known.

address space   The total number of addresses used by a protocol.

address-mask request and reply ICMP   Messages that find the network mask.

Advanced Mobile Phone System (AMPS)   A North American analog cellular phone system using FDMA.

Advanced Research Projects Agency (ARPA)   The government agency that funded ARPANET.

Advanced Research Projects Agency Network (ARPANET)   The packet-switching network that was funded by ARPA.

ALOHA   The original random multiple access method in which a station can send a frame any time it has one to send.

alternate mark inversion (AMI)   A digital-to-digital bipolar encoding method in which the amplitude representing 1 alternates between positive and negative voltages.

American National Standards Institute (ANSI)   A national standards organization that defines standards in the United States.

American Standard Code for Information Interchange (ASCII)   A character code developed by ANSI and used extensively for data communication.

amplitude   The strength of a signal, usually measured in volts, amperes, or watts.

amplitude modulation (AM)   An analog-to-analog conversion method in which the carrier signal's amplitude varies with the amplitude of the modulating signal.

amplitude shift keying (ASK)   A modulation method in which the amplitude of the carrier signal is varied to represent binary 0 or 1.

analog   A continuously varying entity.

analog data   Data that are continuous and smooth and not limited to a specific number of values.

analog hierarchy   A telephone company system in which multiplexed signals are combined into successively larger groups for more efficient transmission.

analog leased service   A service featuring a dedicated line between two users.

analog signal   A continuous waveform that changes smoothly over time.

analog switched service   A temporary analog connection between two users.

analog-to-analog modulation   The representation of analog information by an analog signal.

analog-to-digital conversion   The representation of analog information by a digital signal.

angle of incidence In optics, the angle formed by a light ray approaching the interface between two media and the line perpendicular to the interface.

anonymous FTP A protocol in which a remote user can access another machine without an account or password.

anycast address An address that defines a group of computers with addresses that have the same beginning.

aperiodic signal A signal that does not exhibit a pattern or repeating cycle.

applet A computer program for creating an active Web document. It is usually written in Java.

application adaptation layer (AAL) A layer in ATM protocol that breaks user data into 48-byte payloads.

application layer The fifth layer in the Internet model; provides access to network resources.

application programming interface (API) A set of declarations, definitions, and procedures followed by programmers to write client-server programs.

area A collection of networks, hosts, and routers all contained within an autonomous system.

area border router A router inside an area that summarizes the information about the area and sends it to other areas.

area identification A 32-bit field that defines the area within which the routing takes place.

asymmetric digital subscriber line (ADSL) A communication technology in which the downstream data rate is higher than the upstream rate.

asynchronous balanced mode (ABM) In HDLC, a communication mode in which all stations are equal.

asynchronous connectionless link (ACL) A link between a Bluetooth master and slave in which a corrupted payload is retransmitted.

Asynchronous Transfer Mode (ATM) A wide area protocol featuring high data rates and equal-sized packets (cells); ATM is suitable for transferring text, audio, and video data.

asynchronous transmission Transfer of data with start and stop bit(s) and a variable time interval between data units.

ATM LAN A LAN using ATM technology.

ATM layer A layer in ATM that provides routing, traffic management, switching, and multiplexing services.

ATM switch An ATM device providing both switching and multiplexing functions.

attachment unit interface (AUI) A 10Base5 cable that performs the physical interface functions between the station and the transceiver.

attenuation The loss of a signal's energy due to the resistance of the medium.

authenticating state In PPP, an optional state that verifies the identity of the receiver.

Authentication Header (AH) Protocol A protocol defined by IPSec at the network layer that provides integrity to a message through the creation of a digital signature by a hashing function.

authentication server (AS) The KDC in the Kerberos protocol.

authentication Verification of the sender of a message.

automatic repeat request (ARQ) An error-control method in which correction is made by retransmission of data.

automatic tunneling Tunneling in which the receiving host has an IPv6 compatible address; no reconfiguration is necessary.

autonegotiation   A Fast Ethernet feature that allows two devices to negotiate the mode or data rate.

autonomous system (AS)   A group of networks and routers under the authority of a single administration.

autonomous system boundary router   Routers responsible for dissipating information about other autonomous systems into the current system.

available bit rate (ABR)   The minimum data rate in ATM at which cells can be delivered.

B

back off   In multiple access, waiting before re-sending after a collision.

backbone router   A router inside the backbone.

backbone   A network that connects smaller networks in an organization.

backward explicit congestion notification (BECN)   A bit in the Frame Relay packet that notifies the sender of congestion.

bandwidth on demand   A digital service that allows subscribers higher speeds through the use of multiple lines.

bandwidth   The difference between the highest and the lowest frequencies of a composite signal. It also measures the information-carrying capacity of a line or a network.

bandwidth-delay product   A measure of the number of bits that can be sent while waiting for news from the receiver.

band-pass channel   A channel that can pass a range of frequencies.

base header   In IPv6, the main header of the datagram.

basic service set (BSS)   The building block of a wireless LAN as defined by the IEEE 802.11 standard.

baud rate   The number of signal elements transmitted per second. A signal element consists of one or more bits.

best-effort delivery   The unreliable transmission mechanism by IP that does not guarantee message delivery.

bidirectional authentication   An authentication method involving a challenge and a response from sender to receiver and vice versa.

bidirectional frame (B-frame)   An MPEG frame that is related to the preceding and following I-frame or P-frame.

bipolar encoding   A digital-to-digital encoding method in which 0 amplitude represents binary 0 and positive and negative amplitudes represent alternate 1s.

bipolar n-zero substitution (BnZS)   An encoding method to provide synchronization for long strings of 0s.

bit   binary digit; the smallest unit of information; 1 or 0.

bit interval   The time required to send one bit.

bit padding   In TDM, the addition of extra bits to a device's source stream to force speed relationships.

bit rate   The number of bits transmitted per second.

bit stuffing   In HDLC, the addition of an extra 0 to prevent the receiver from mistaking the data for a flag. In TDM, a technique that adds bits for synchronization purposes.

bits per second (bps)   A measurement of data speed; bits transmitted per second.

block cipher   An encryption/decryption algorithm that has a block of bits as its basic unit.

block coding   A coding method to ensure synchronization and detection of errors.

blocking   An event that occurs when a switching network is working at its full capacity and cannot accept more input.

blocking port   A port on a bridge that does not forward a frame.

Bluetooth   A wireless LAN technology designed to connect devices of different functions such as telephones and notebooks in a small area such as a room.

BNC connector   A common coaxial cable connector.

Bootstrap Protocol (BOOTP)   The protocol that provides configuration information from a table (file).

Border Gateway Protocol (BGP)   An interautonomous system routing protocol based on path vector routing.

bridge   A network device operating at the first two layers of the Internet model with filtering and forwarding capabilities.

broadcast address   An address that allows transmission of a message to all nodes of a network.

broadcasting   Transmission of a message to all nodes in a network.

browser   An application program that displays a WWW document. A browser usually uses other Internet services to access the document.

BSS-transition mobility   In a wireless LAN, a station that can move from one BSS to another but is confined inside one ESS.

burst error   Error in a data unit in which two or more bits have been altered.

bursty data   Data with varying instantaneous transmission rates.

bus topology   A network topology in which all computers are attached to a shared medium (often a single cable).

byte   A group of eight bits.

C

cable modem   A technology in which the TV cable provides Internet access.

cable modem transmission system (CMTS)   A device installed inside the distribution hub that receives data from the Internet and passes them to the combiner.

cable TV   A system using coaxial cable that brings multiple channels of video programs into homes.

caching   The storing of information in a small, fast memory used to hold data items that are being processed.

carrier sense multiple access (CSMA)   A contention access method in which each station listens to the line before transmitting data.

carrier sense multiple access with collision avoidance (CSMA/CA)   An access method in which collision is avoided.

carrier sense multiple access with collision detection (CSMA/CD)   An access method in which stations transmit whenever the transmission medium is available and retransmit when collision occurs.

carrier signal   A high frequency signal used for digital-to-analog or analog-to-analog modulation. One of the characteristics of the carrier signal (amplitude, frequency, or phase) is changed according to the modulating data.

cell   A small, fixed-size data unit; also, in cellular telephony, a geographical area served by a cell office.

cell network   A network using the cell as its basic data unit.

cellular telephony   A wireless communication technique in which an area is divided into cells. A cell is served by a transmitter.

Certification Authority (CA)   An agency such as a federal or state organization that binds a public key to an entity and issues a certificate.

Challenge Handshake Authentication Protocol (CHAP)   In PPP, a three-way hand-shaking protocol used for authentication.

channel   A communications pathway.

channelization   A multiple access method in which the available bandwidth of a link is shared in time.

checksum   A field used for error detection. It is formed by adding bit streams using one's complement arithmetic and then complementing the result.

chip   In CDMA, a number in a code that is assigned to a station.

choke point   A packet sent by a router to the source to inform it of congestion.

cipher   An encryption/decryption algorithm.

cipher block chaining (CBC) mode   A DES and triple DES operation mode in which the encryption (or decryption) of a block depends on all previous blocks.

cipher feedback mode (CFM)   A DES and triple DES operation mode in which data is sent and received 1 bit at a time, with each bit independent of the previous bits.

cipher stream mode (CSM)   A DES and triple DES operation mode in which data is sent and received 1 byte at a time.

ciphertext   The encrypted data.

circuit switching   A switching technology that establishes an electrical connection between stations using a dedicated path.

cladding   Glass or plastic surrounding the core of an optical fiber; the optical density of the cladding must be less than that of the core.

class A address   An IPv4 address with the first octet between 0 and 127.

class B address   An IPv4 address with the first octet between 128 and 191.

class C address   An IPv4 address with the first octet between 192 and 223.

class D address   An IPv4 multicast address.

class E address   An IPv4 address reserved for special purposes.

classful addressing   An IPv4 addressing mechanism in which the IP address space is divided into 5 classes: A, B, C, D, and E. Each class occupies some part of the whole address space.

classless addressing   An addressing mechanism in which the IP address space is not divided into classes.

Classless InterDomain Routing (CIDR)   A technique to reduce the number of routing table entries when supernetting is used.

client process   A running application program on a local site that requests service from a running application program on a remote site.

client-server model The model of interaction between two application programs in which a program at one end (client) requests a service from a program at the other end (server).

closed-loop congestion control A method to alleviate congestion after it happens.

coaxial cable A transmission medium consisting of a conducting core, insulating material, and a second conducting sheath.

code division multiple access (CDMA) A multiple access method in which one channel carries all transmissions simultaneously.

collision The event that occurs when two transmitters send at the same time on a channel designed for only one transmission at a time; data will be destroyed.

collision domain The length of the medium subject to collision.

committed burst size (B_c) The maximum number of bits in a specific time period that a Frame Relay network must transfer without discarding any frames.

committed information rate (CIR) The committed burst size divided by time.

common carrier A transmission facility available to the public and subject to public utility regulation.

Common Gateway Interface (CGI) A standard for communication between HTTP servers and executable programs. CGI is used in creating dynamic documents.

community antenna TV (CATV) A cable network service that broadcasts video signals to locations with poor or no reception.

competitive local exchange carrier (CLEC) A telephone company that cannot provide main telephone services; instead, other services such as mobile telephone service and toll calls inside a LATA are provided.

complementary code keying (CCK) An HR-DSSS encoding method that encodes four or eight bits into one symbol.

composite signal A signal composed of more than one sine wave.

concurrent client A client running the same time as another client of the same process.

concurrent server A server that can process many requests at the same time and share its time between many requests.

congestion avoidance In Frame Relay, a method using two bits that explicitly notify the source and destination of congestion.

congestion control A method to manage network and internetwork traffic to improve throughput.

congestion Excessive network or internetwork traffic causing a general degradation of service.

connecting device A tool that connects computers or networks.

connection control The technique used by the transport layer to deliver segments.

connection establishment The preliminary setup necessary for a logical connection prior to actual data transfer.

connection termination A message sent to end a connection.

connectionless iterative server A connectionless server that processes one request at a time.

connectionless service A service for data transfer without connection establishment or termination.

connection-oriented concurrent server A connection-oriented server that can serve many clients at the same time.

connection-oriented service   A service for data transfer involving establishment and termination of a connection.

constant bit rate (CBR)   The data rate of an ATM service class that is designed for customers requiring real-time audio or video services.

constellation   A graphical representation of the phase and amplitude of different bit combinations in digital-to-analog modulation.

Consultative Committee for International Telegraphy and Telephony (CCITT)   An international standards group now known as the ITU-T.

contention   An access method in which two or more devices try to transmit at the same time on the same channel.

control connection   The FTP connection used for control information (commands and responses).

controlled access   A multiple access method in which the stations consult one another to determine who has the right to send.

convergence sublayer (CS)   In ATM protocol, the upper AAL sublayer that adds a header or a trailer to the user data.

core   The glass or plastic center of an optical fiber.

Core-Based Tree (CBT)   In multicasting, a group-shared protocol that uses a center router as the root of the tree.

country domain   A subdomain in the Domain Name System that uses two characters as the last suffix.

CRC checker   The process that validates the CRC remainder.

CRC generator   The process that creates the CRC remainder.

critical angle   In refraction, the value of the angle of incidence that produces a 90-degree angle of refraction.

crossbar switch   A switch consisting of a lattice of horizontal and vertical paths. At the intersection of each horizontal and vertical path, there is a crosspoint that can connect the input to the output.

crosspoint   The junction of an input and an output on a crossbar switch.

crosstalk   The noise on a line caused by signals traveling along another line.

cryptography   The science and art of transforming messages to make them secure and immune to attacks.

CSNET   A network sponsored by the National Science Foundation originally intended for universities.

cycle   The repetitive unit of a periodic signal.

cyclic redundancy check (CRC)   A highly accurate error-detection method based on interpreting a pattern of bits as a polynomial.

D

data connection   The FTP connection used for data transfer.

data encryption standard (DES)   The U.S. government standard encryption method for nonmilitary and nonclassified use.

data exchange protocol   A protocol that uses the secret key to encrypt the data for secrecy and to encrypt the message digest for integrity.

data level   The number of different symbols used to represent a digital signal.

data link connection identifier (DLCI)   A number that identifies the virtual circuit in Frame Relay.

data link control   The responsibilities of the data link layer: flow control and error control.

data link layer   The second layer in the Internet model. It is responsible for node-to-node delivery.

Data Over Cable System Interface Specifications (DOCSIS)   A standard for data transmission over an HFC network.

data transparency   See *transparency.*

datagram approach (to packet switching)   A data transmission method in which each data unit is independent of others.

datagram   In packet switching, an independent data unit.

datagram socket   A structure designed to be used with a connectionless protocol such as UDP.

DC component   See *direct current.*

de facto standard   A protocol that has not been approved by an organized body but adopted as a standard through widespread use.

de jure standard   A protocol that has been legislated by an officially recognized body.

decibel (dB)   A measure of the relative strength of two signal points.

decryption   Recovery of the original message from the encrypted data.

default mask   The mask for a network that is not subnetted.

default routing   A routing method in which a router is assigned to receive all packets with no match in the routing table.

Defense Advanced Research Projects Agency (DARPA)   A government organization, which, under the name of ARPA funded ARPANET and the Internet.

delayed response strategy   A technique used by IGMP to prevent unnecessary traffic on a LAN.

demodulation   The process of separating the carrier signal from the information-bearing signal.

demodulator   A device that performs demodulation.

demultiplexer (DEMUX)   A device that separates a multiplexed signal into its original components.

dense wave-division multiplexing (DWDM)   A WDM method that can multiplex a very large number of channels by spacing channels closer together.

destination-unreachable message   An ICMP error-reporting message sent to a source when a router cannot route a datagram or a host cannot deliver a datagram.

dibit   A unit of data consisting of two bits.

differential Manchester encoding   A digital-to-digital polar encoding method that features a transition at the middle of the bit interval as well as an inversion at the beginning of each 1 bit.

Differentiated Services (DS or Diffserv)   A class-based QoS model designed for IP.

Diffie-Hellman protocol   A key management protocol that provides a one-time session key for 2 parties.

digest   A condensed version of a document.

digital AMPS (D-AMPS)   A second-generation cellular phone system that is a digital version of AMPS.

digital data   Data represented by discrete values or conditions.

digital data service (DDS)   A digital version of an analog leased line with a rate of 64 Kbps.

digital service unit (DSU)   A device that allows the connection of a user's device to a digital line.

digital signal (DS) service   A telephone company service featuring a hierarchy of digital signals.

digital signal   A discrete signal with a limited number of values.

digital signature   A method to authenticate the sender of a message.

digital subscriber line (DSL)   A technology using existing telecommunication networks to accomplish high-speed delivery of data, voice, video, and multimedia.

digital subscriber line access multiplexer (DSLAM)   A telephone company site device that functions like an ADSL modem.

digital-to-analog modulation   The representation of digital information by an analog signal.

digital-to-digital encoding   The representation of digital information by a digital signal.

Dijkstra's algorithm   In link state routing, an algorithm that finds the shortest path to other routers.

direct current (DC)   A zero-frequency signal with a constant amplitude.

direct sequence spread spectrum (DSSS)   A wireless transmission method in which each bit to be sent by the sender is replaced by a sequence of bits called a chip code.

discard eligibility (DE)   A bit that defines that a packet can be discarded if there is congestion in the network.

discrete cosine transform (DCT)   A JPEG phase in which a transformation changes the 64 values so that the relative relationships between pixels are kept but the redundancies are revealed.

discrete multitone technique (DMT)   A modulation method combining elements of QAM and FDM.

Distance Vector Multicast Routing Protocol (DVMRP)   A protocol based on distance vector routing that handles multicast routing in conjunction with IGMP.

distance vector routing   A routing method in which each router sends its neighbors a list of networks it can reach and the distance to that network.

distortion   Any change in a signal due to noise, attenuation, or other influences.

distributed interframe space (DIFS)   In wireless LANs, a period of time that a station waits before sending a control frame.

distributed processing   A strategy in which services provided for the network reside at multiple sites.

distribution hub   In an HFC network, a site that modulates and distributes signals.

DNS server   A computer that holds information about the name space.

domain   A subtree of the domain name space.

domain name   In the DNS, a sequence of labels separated by dots.

domain name space   A structure for organizing the name space in which the names are defined in an inverted-tree structure with the root at the top.

Domain Name System (DNS)   A TCP/IP application service that converts user-friendly names to IP addresses.

dotted-decimal notation   A notation devised to make the IP address easier to read; each byte is converted to its decimal equivalent and then set off from its neighbor by a decimal.

downlink   Transmission from a satellite to an earth station.

downloading   Retrieving a file or data from a remote site.

downstream data band   In an HFC network, the 550 to 750 MHz band for data from the Internet to the subscriber premises.

dual stack   Two protocols (IPv4 and IPv6) on a station.

duplex mode   See *full-duplex mode.*

dynamic document   A Web document created by running a CGI program at the server site.

Dynamic Domain Name System (DDNS)   A method to update the DNS master file dynamically.

Dynamic Host Configuration Protocol (DHCP)   An extension to BOOTP that dynamically assigns configuration information.

dynamic mapping   A technique in which a protocol is used for address resolution.

dynamic routing   Routing in which the routing table entries are updated automatically by the routing protocol.

E

E lines   The European equivalent of T lines.

echo-request and reply message   An ICMP query message that determines whether two systems (hosts or routers) can communicate with each other.

effective bandwidth   The bandwidth that the network needs to allocate for the flow of traffic; a function of three values: average data rate, peak data rate, and maximum burst size.

electromagnetic spectrum   The frequency range occupied by electromagnetic energy.

electronic code block (ECB) mode   A DES and triple DES operation method in which a long message is divided into 64-bit blocks before being encrypted separately.

electronic mail (email)   A method of sending messages electronically based on mailbox addresses rather than a direct host-to-host exchange.

Electronics Industries Association (EIA)   An organization that promotes electronics manufacturing concerns. It has developed interface standards such as EIA-232, EIA-449, and EIA-530.

email   See *electronic mail.*

Encapsulating Security Payload (ESP)   A protocol defined by IPSec that provides privacy as well as a combination of integrity and message authentication.

encapsulation   The technique in which a data unit from one protocol is placed within the data field portion of the data unit of another protocol.

encryption   Converting a message into an unintelligible form that is unreadable unless decrypted.

end office   A switching office that is the terminus for the local loops.

ephemeral port number   A port number used by the client.

error control   The detection and handling of errors in data transmission.

error correction by retransmission   The process of correcting bits by resending the data.

error-reporting message   An ICMP message sent to the source to report an error.

ESS-transition mobility   A station in a wireless LAN that can move from one ESS to another.

establishing state   In PPP, a state in which communication begins and options are negotiated.

Ethernet   A local area network using CSMA/CD access method. See *IEEE Project 802.3.*

even parity   An error-detection method in which an extra bit is added to the data unit so that the total number of 1s becomes even.

excess burst size (B_e) In Frame Relay, the maximum number of bits in excess of B_c that the user can send during a predefined period of time.

Extended Service Set (ESS)   A wireless LAN service composed of two or more BSSs with APs as defined by the IEEE 802.11 standard.

extension header   Extra headers in the IPv6 datagram that provide additional functionality.

exterior routing   Routing between autonomous systems.

external link LSA   A message that announces all the networks outside the AS.

extranet   A private network that uses the TCP/IP protocol suite that allows authorized access from outside users.

F

Fast Ethernet   See *100Base-T.*

Federal Communications Commission (FCC)   A government agency that regulates radio, television, and telecommunications.

fiber distributed data interface (FDDI)   A high-speed (100-Mbps) LAN, defined by ANSI, using fiber optics, dual ring topology, and the token-passing access method. Today an FDDI network is also used as a MAN.

fiber link Ethernet   Ethernet using fiber optic media.

fiber node   In an HFC network, the location of the optical fiber and coaxial fiber juncture.

fiber-optic cable   A high-bandwidth transmission medium that carries data signals in the form of pulses of light. It consists of a thin cylinder of glass or plastic, called the core, surrounded by a concentric layer of glass or plastic called the cladding.

File Transfer Protocol (FTP)   In TCP/IP, an application layer protocol that transfers files between two sites.

filtering   A process in which a bridge makes forwarding decisions.

finite state machine   A machine that goes through a limited number of states.

firewall   A device (usually a router) installed between the internal network of an organization and the rest of the Internet to provide security.

first-in, first-out (FIFO) queue   A queue in which the first item in is the first item out.

flag field   In an HDLC frame, an 8-bit synchronization sequence that identifies the beginning or end of a frame.

flat name space   A method to map a name to an address in which there is no hierarchical structure.

flooding   Saturation of a network with a message.

flow control   A technique to control the rate of flow of frames (packets or messages).

flow label   An IPv6 mechanism to enable the source to request special handling of a packet.

footprint   An area on Earth that is covered by a satellite at a specific time.

forward error correction   Correction of errors at the receiver.

forward explicit congestion notification (FECN)   A bit in the Frame Relay packet that notifies the destination of congestion.

forwarding port   A port on a bridge that forwards a received frame.

Fourier analysis   The mathematical technique used to obtain the frequency spectrum of an aperiodic signal if the time-domain representation is given.

fragmentation offset   A field in the IP header used in fragmentation to show the relative position of the fragment with respect to the whole datagram.

fragmentation   The division of a packet into smaller units to accommodate a protocol's MTU.

frame   A group of bits representing a block of data.

frame check sequence (FCS)   The HDLC error-detection field containing either a 2- or 4-byte CRC.

Frame Relay   A packet-switching specification defined for the first two layers of the Internet model. There is no network layer. Error checking is done on end-to-end basis instead of on each link.

Frame Relay assembler/disassembler (FRAD)   A device used in Frame Relay to handle frames coming from other protocols.

framing bit   A bit used for synchronization purposes in TDM.

frequency division multiple access (FDMA)   A multiple access method in which the bandwidth is divided into channels.

frequency hopping spread spectrum (FHSS)   A wireless transmission method in which the sender transmits at one carrier frequency for a short period of time, then hops to another carrier frequency for the same amount of time, hops again for the same amount of time, and so on. After N hops, the cycle is repeated.

frequency modulation (FM)   An analog-to-analog modulation method in which the carrier signal's frequency varies with the amplitude of the modulating signal.

frequency shift keying (FSK)   A digital-to-analog encoding method in which the frequency of the carrier signal is varied to represent binary 0 or 1.

frequency   The number of cycles per second of a periodic signal.

frequency-division multiplexing (FDM)   The combining of analog signals into a single signal.

frequency-domain plot   A graphical representation of a signal's frequency components.

full-duplex mode   A transmission mode in which communication can be two way simultaneously.

full-duplex switched Ethernet   Ethernet in which each station, in its own separate collision domain, can both send and receive.

fully qualified domain name (FQDN)   A domain name consisting of labels beginning with the host and going back through each level to the root node.

fundamental frequency   The frequency of the dominant sine wave of a composite signal.

G

gatekeeper   In the H.323 standard, a server on the LAN that plays the role of the registrar server.

gateway   A device used to connect two separate networks that use different communication protocols.

general header   A part of an HTTP request or response message that gives general information about the message.

generic domain   A subdomain in the domain name system that uses generic suffixes.

geographical routing   A routing technique in which the entire address space is divided into blocks based on physical landmasses.

geosynchronous Earth orbit   An orbit that allows a satellite to remain fixed above a certain spot on earth.

Gigabit Ethernet   Ethernet with a 1000 Mbps data rate.

gigabit medium independent interface (GMII)   In Gigabit Ethernet, a specification that defines how the reconciliation sublayer is to be connected to the transceiver.

global Internet   The Internet.

Global Positioning System (GPS)   An MEO public satellite system consisting of 24 satellites and used for land and sea navigation. GPS is not used for communications.

Global System for Mobile Communication (GSM)   A second-generation cellular phone system used in Europe.

Globalstar   An LEO satellite system with 48 satellites in six polar orbits with each orbit hosting eight satellites.

Go-Back-*N* ARQ   An error-control method in which the frame in error and all following frames must be retransmitted.

grafting   Resumption of multicast messages.

ground propagation   Propagation of radio waves through the lowest portion of the atmosphere (hugging the earth).

group   An analog signal created by 12 voice channels multiplexed together.

group membership   Belonging to a group.

group-shared tree   A multicast routing feature in which each group in the system shares the same tree.

guard band   A bandwidth separating two signals.

guided media   Transmission media with a physical boundary.

H

H.323   A standard designed by ITU to allow telephones on the public telephone network to talk to computers (called terminals in H.323) connected to the Internet.

half-duplex mode   A transmission mode in which communication can be two-way but not at the same time.

Hamming code   A method that adds redundant bits to a data unit to detect and correct bit errors.

handoff   Changing to a new channel as a mobile device moves from one cell to another.

handshake protocol   A protocol to establish or terminate a connection.

harmonics   Components of a digital signal, each having a different amplitude, frequency, and phase.

hash function   An algorithm that creates a fixed-size digest from a variable-length message.

head end   A cable TV office.

header   Control information added to the beginning of a data packet. Also, in an email, the part of the message that defines the sender, the receiver, the subject of the message, and other information.

header translation   Conversion of the IPv6 header to IPv4.

hertz (Hz)   Unit of measurement for frequency.

hexadecimal colon notation   In IPv6, an address notation consisting of 32 hexadecimal digits, with every four digits separated by a colon.

hierarchical name space   A name space made of several parts, with each succeeding part becoming more and more specific.

hierarchical routing   A routing technique in which the entire address space is divided into levels based on specific criteria.

high bit rate digital subscriber line (HDSL)   A service similar to the T1-line that can operate at lengths up to 3.6 km.

High Rate Direct Sequence Spread Spectrum (HR-DSSS)   A signal generation method similar to DSSS except for the encoding method (CCK).

High-level Data Link Control (HDLC)   A bit-oriented data link protocol defined by the ISO. It is used in X.25 protocol. A subset, called link access procedure (LAP), is used in other protocols. It is also a base for many data link protocols used in LANs.

homepage   A unit of hypertext or hypermedia available on the Web that is the main page for an organization or an individual.

hop count   The number of nodes along a route. It is a measurement of distance in routing algorithms.

hop limit   An IPv6 field that limits the number of routers that a packet can visit.

hop-to-hop delivery   Transmission of frames from one node to the next.

horn antenna   A scoop-shaped antenna used in terrestrial microwave communication.

host   A station or node on a network.

host file   A file, used when the Internet was small, that mapped host names to host addresses.

hostid   The part of an IP address that identifies a host.

host-specific routing   A routing method in which the full IP address of a host is given in the routing table.

hub   A central device in a star topology that provides a common connection among the nodes.

Huffman encoding   A statistical compression method using variable-length codes to encode a set of symbols.

hybrid network   A network with a private internet and access to the global Internet.

hybrid-fiber-coaxial (HFC) network   The second generation of cable networks; uses fiber optic and coaxial cable.

hypermedia   Information containing text, pictures, graphics, and sound that are linked to other documents through pointers.

hypertext   Information containing text that is linked to other documents through pointers.

HyperText Markup Language (HTML)   The computer language for specifying the contents and format of a web document. It allows additional text to include codes that define fonts, layouts, embedded graphics, and hypertext links.

HyperText Transfer Protocol (HTTP)   An application service for retrieving a web document.

I

idle state   In PPP, a state in which the link is inactive.

image file   In FTP, the default format for transferring binary files. The file is sent as continuous streams of bits without any interpretation or encoding.

incumbent local exchange carrier (ILEC)   A telephone company that provided services before 1996 and is the owner of the cabling system.

infrared wave   A wave with a frequency between 300 GHz and 400 THz; usually used for short-range communications.

inner product   A number produced by multiplying two sequences, element by element, and summing the products.

Institute of Electrical and Electronics Engineers (IEEE)   A group consisting of professional engineers which has specialized societies whose committees prepare standards in members' areas of specialty.

Integrated Services (IntServ)   A flow-based QoS model designed for IP.

integrity   A data quality of being noncorrupted.

interactive audio/video   Real-time communication with sound and images.

interautonomous system routing protocol   A protocol to handle transmissions between autonomous systems.

interexchange carrier (IXC)   A long-distance company that, prior to the Act of 1996, provided communication services between two customers in different LATAs.

interface   The boundary between two pieces of equipment. It also refers to mechanical, electrical, and functional characteristics of the connection.

Interim Standard 95 (IS-95)   One of the dominant second-generation cellular telephony standards in North America.

interior routing   Routing inside an autonomous system.

interleaving   Taking a specific amount of data from each device in a regular order.

International Organization of Standardization (ISO)   A worldwide organization that defines and develops standards on a variety of topics.

International Telecommunications Union–Telecommunication Standardization Sector (ITU–T)   A standards organization formerly known as the CCITT.

internet   A collection of networks connected by internetworking devices such as routers or gateways.

Internet   A global internet that uses the TCP/IP protocol suite.

Internet address   A 32-bit or 128-bit network-layer address used to uniquely define a host on an internet using the TCP/IP protocol.

Internet Architecture Board (IAB)   The technical adviser to the ISOC; oversees the continuing development of the TCP/IP protocol suite.

Internet Assigned Numbers Authority (IANA)   A group supported by the U.S. government that was responsible for the management of Internet domain names and addresses until October 1998.

Internet Control Message Protocol (ICMP)   A protocol in the TCP/IP protocol suite that handles error and control messages.

Internet Control Message Protocol, version 6 (ICMPv6)   A protocol in IPv6 that handles error and control messages.

Internet Corporation for Assigned Names and Numbers (ICANN) A private, nonprofit corporation managed by an international board that assumed IANA operations.

Internet draft A working Internet document (a work in progress) with no official status and a six-month lifetime.

Internet Engineering Steering Group (IESG) An organization that oversees the activity of IETF.

Internet Engineering Task Force (IETF) A group working on the design and development of the TCP/IP protocol suite and the Internet.

Internet Group Management Protocol (IGMP) A protocol in the TCP/IP protocol suite that handles multicasting.

Internet Mail Access Protocol, version 4 (IMAP4) A complex and powerful protocol to handle the transmission of electronic mail.

Internet Mobile Communication for year 2000 (ITM-2000) An ITU issued blueprint that defines criteria for third generation cellular telephony.

Internet model A 5-layer protocol stack that dominates data communications and networking today.

Internet Network Information Center (INTERNIC) An agency responsible for collecting and distributing information about TCP/IP protocols.

Internet Protocol (IP) The network-layer protocol in the TCP/IP protocol suite governing connectionless transmission across packet switching networks.

Internet Protocol, version 6 (IPv6) The sixth version of the Internetworking Protocol; it features major IP addressing changes.

Internet Research Task Force (IRTF) A forum of working groups focusing on long-term research topics related to the Internet.

Internet service provider (ISP) Usually, a company that provides Internet services.

Internet Society (ISOC) The nonprofit organization established to publicize the Internet.

Internet standard A thoroughly tested specification that is useful to and adhered to by those who work with the Internet. It is a formalized regulation that must be followed.

Internetwork Protocol Control Protocol (IPCP) In PPP, the set of protocols that establish and terminate a network layer connection for IP packets.

internetwork (internet) A network of networks.

internetworking Connecting several networks together using internetworking devices such as routers and gateways.

intracoded frame (I-frame) An independent frame that is not related to any other frame and appearing at regular intervals.

intranet A private network that uses the TCP/IP protocol suite.

inverse domain A subdomain in the DNS that finds the domain name given the IP address.

inverse multiplexing Taking data from one source and breaking it into portions that can be sent across lower-speed lines.

IP datagram The Internetworking Protocol data unit.

IP Security (IPSec) A collection of protocols designed by the IETF (Internet Engineering Task Force) to provide security for a packet carried on the Internet.

IrDA port A port that allows a wireless keyboard to communicate with a PC.

Iridium A 66-satellite network that provides communication from any Earth site to another.

iterative resolution   Resolution of the IP address in which the client may send its request to multiple servers before getting an answer.

iterative server   In the client-server model, a server that can serve only one client at a time.

J

Java   A programming language used to create active Web documents.

jitter   A phenomenon in real-time traffic caused by gaps between consecutive packets at the receiver.

Joint Photographic Experts Group (JPEG)   A standard for compressing continuous-tone picture.

jumbo group   An analog signal created by six multiplexed master groups.

K

Karn's Algorithm   An algorithm that does not include the retransmitted segments in calculation of round-trip time.

keepalive message   A message that establishes a relationship between the two routers.

keepalive timer   A timer that prevents a long idle connection between two TCPs.

Kerberos   An authentication protocol used by Windows 2000.

key   A number that a cipher operates on.

key distribution center (KDC)   In secret key encryption, a trusted third party that shares a key with each user.

L

layered architecture   A model based on ordered tiers.

leaky bucket algorithm   An algorithm to shape bursty traffic.

least-cost tree   An MOSPF feature in which the tree is based on a chosen metric instead of shortest path.

leave report   An IGMP message sent by a host when no process is interested in a specific group.

legacy ATM LAN   LAN in which ATM technology is used as a backbone to connect traditional LANs.

line-of-sight propagation   The transmission of very high frequency signals in straight lines directly from antenna to antenna.

Link Control Protocol (LCP)   A PPP protocol responsible for establishing, maintaining, configuring, and terminating links.

link state advertisement (LSA)   In OSPF, a method that disperses information.

link state database   In link state routing, a database common to all routers and made from LSP information.

link state packet (LSP)   In link state routing, a small packet containing routing information sent by a router to all other routers.

link state routing   A routing method in which each router shares its knowledge of changes in its neighborhood with all other routers.

link state update packet   A packet that provides information about a specific route or routes.

link The physical communication pathway that transfers data from one device to another.

load The number of packets sent to a network.

local access and transport area (LATA) An area covered by one or more telephone companies.

local access Using a terminal directly connected to the computer.

local address The part of an email address that defines the name of a special file, called the user mailbox, where all of the mail received for a user is stored for retrieval by the user agent.

local area network (LAN) A network connecting devices inside a single building or inside buildings close to each other.

local area network emulation (LANE) Software that enables an ATM switch to behave like a LAN switch.

local call service A telephone service handling local calls, usually charging a flat monthly fee.

local exchange carrier (LEC) A telephone company that handles services inside a LATA.

local Internet service provider The same as an Internet service provider.

local ISP The same as an Internet service provider.

local loop The link that connects a subscriber to the telephone central office.

local management information (LMI) A protocol used in Frame Relay to provide. management features.

logical address An address defined in the network layer.

logical link control (LLC) The upper sublayer of the data link layer as defined by IEEE Project 802.2.

Logical Link Control and Adaptation Protocol (L2CAP) A Bluetooth layer used for data exchange on an ACL link.

logical tunnel The encapsulation of a multicast packet inside a unicast packet to enable multicast routing by non-multicast routers.

low Earth orbit (LEO) A polar satellite orbit with an altitude between 500 and 2000 km. A satellite with this orbit has a rotation period of 90 to 120 minutes.

low-pass channel A channel that passes frequencies between 0 and f.

M

mail transfer agent (MTA) An SMTP component that transfers the mail across the Internet.

Manchester encoding A digital-to-digital polar encoding method in which a transition occurs at the middle of each bit interval for the purpose of synchronization.

man-in-the-middle attack A key management problem in which an intruder intercepts and sends messages between the intended sender and receiver.

mask For IPv4, a 32-bit binary number that gives the first address in the block (the network address) when ANDed with an address in the block.

master The one Bluetooth station in a piconet that controls all the others.

master group An analog signal created by 10 multiplexed supergroups.

maximum burst size The maximum length of time traffic is generated at the peak rate.

maximum transfer unit (MTU) The largest size data unit a specific network can handle.

media player A help application that plays an audio/video file; used by a browser.

media server   A server accessed by a media player to download an audio/video file.

medium access control (MAC) sublayer   The lower sublayer in the data link layer defined by the IEEE 802 project. It defines the access method and access control in different local area network protocols.

medium attachment unit (MAU)   See *transceiver.*

medium bandwidth   The difference between the highest and lowest frequencies a medium can support.

medium dependent interface (MDI)   In Fast Ethernet, implementation-specific hardware that connects the transceiver to the medium.

medium Earth orbit (MEO)   A satellite orbit positioned between the two Van Allen belts. A satellite at this orbit takes six hours to circle the earth.

medium independent interface (MII)   In Fast Ethernet hardware that connects an external transceiver to the reconciliation layer.

membership report   An IGMP message sent by a host or router interested in joining a specific group.

mesh topology   A network configuration in which each device has a dedicated point-to-point link to every other device.

message authentication   A security measure in which the sender of the message is verified for every message sent.

metric   A cost assigned for passing through a network.

metropolitan area network (MAN)   A network that can span a geographical area the size of a city.

microwave   Electromagnetic waves ranging from 2 GHz to 40 GHz.

minislot   In an HFC network, a time slot for timesharing of the upstream channels.

mixer   A device that combines real-time signals from different sources into one signal.

mobile host   A host that can move from one network to another.

mobile switching center (MSC)   In cellular telephony, a switching office that coordinates communication between all base stations and the telephone central office.

mobile telephone switching office (MTSO)   An office that controls and coordinates communication between all of the cell offices and the telephone control office.

modem   A device consisting of a modulator and a demodulator. It converts a digital signal into an analog signal (modulation) and vice versa (demodulation).

modulation   Modification of one or more characteristics of a carrier wave by an information-bearing signal.

modulator   A device that converts a digital signal to an analog signal suitable for transmission across a telephone line.

monoalphabetic substitution   An encryption method in which each occurrence of a character is replaced by another character in the set.

motion picture experts group (MPEG)   A method to compress videos.

MT-RJ   A fiber-optic cable connector.

multicast address   An address used for multicasting.

multicast backbone (MBONE)   A set of internet routers supporting multicasting through the use of tunneling.

Multicast Open Shortest Path First (MOSPF)   A multicast protocol that uses multicast link state routing to create a source-based least cost tree.

multicast router   A router with a list of loyal members related to each router interface that distributes the multicast packets.

multicasting   A transmission method that allows copies of a single packet to be sent to a selected group of receivers.

multiline transmission, 3-level (MLT-3) encoding   A line coding scheme featuring 3 levels of signals and transitions at the beginning of the 1 bit.

multimode graded-index fiber   An optical fiber with a core having a graded index of refraction.

multimode step-index fiber   An optical fiber with a core having a uniform index of refraction. The index of refraction changes suddenly at the core/cladding boundary.

multiple access (MA)   A line access method in which every station can access the line freely.

multiplexer (MUX)   A device used for multiplexing.

multiplexing   The process of combining signals from multiple sources for transmission across a single data link.

multiplicative decrease   A congestion avoidance technique in which the threshold is set to half of the last congestion window size, and the congestion window size starts from one again.

Multipurpose Internet Mail Extension (MIME)   A supplement to SMTP that allows non-ASCII data to be sent through SMTP.

multistage switch   An array of switches designed to reduce the number of crosspoints.

N

n^2 problem   A problem due to the large number of keys needed in symmetric key distribution.

Nagle's algorithm   An algorithm that attempts to prevent silly window syndrome at the sender's site; both the rate of data production and the network speed are taken into account.

name space   All the names assigned to machines on an internet.

name-address resolution   Mapping a name to an address or an address to a name.

national service provider (NSP)   A backbone network created and maintained by a specialized company.

Needham-Schroeder protocol   A key management protocol using multiple challenge-response interactions between 2 entities.

negative acknowledgment (NAK)   A message sent to indicate the rejection of received data.

netid   The part of an IP address that identifies the network.

network   A system consisting of connected nodes made to share data, hardware, and software.

network address   An address that identifies a network to the rest of the Internet; it is the first address in a block.

network address translation (NAT)   A technology that allows a private network to use a set of private addresses for internal communication and a set of global Internet addresses for external communication.

network allocation vector (NAV)   In CSMA/CA, the amount of time that must pass before a station can check the line for idleness.

Network Control Protocol (NCP)   In PPP, a set of control protocols that allows the encapsulation of data coming from network layer protocols.

network interface card (NIC)   An electronic device, internal or external to a station, that contains circuitry to enable the station to be connected to the network.

network layer   The third layer in the Internet model, responsible for the delivery of a packet to the final destination.

network link LSA   An LSA packet that announces the existence of all of the routers connected to the network.

Network Virtual Terminal (NVT)   A TCP/IP application protocol that allows remote login.

networking state   A PPP state in which packets of user data and packets for control are transmitted.

network-specific routing   Routing in which all hosts on a network share one entry in the routing table.

network-to-network interface (NNI)   In ATM, the interface between two networks.

next header   In IPv6, an 8-bit field defining the header that follows the base header in the datagram.

next-hop routing   A routing method in which only the address of the next hop is listed in the routing table instead of a complete list of the stops the packet must make.

node   An addressable communication device (e.g., a computer or router) on a network.

node-to-node delivery   Transfer of a data unit from one node to the next.

noise   Random electrical signals that can be picked by the transmission medium and result in degradation or distortion of the data.

nonce   A large random number that is used once to distinguish a fresh authentication request from a used one.

nonpersistent connection   A connection in which one TCP connection is made for each request/response.

nonpersistent strategy   A random multiple access method in which a station waits a random period of time after a collision is sensed.

nonrepudiation   A security aspect in which a receiver must be able to prove that a received message came from a specific sender.

nonreturn to zero (NRZ)   A digital-to-digital polar encoding method in which the signal level is always either positive or negative.

nonreturn to zero, invert (NRZ-I)   An NRZ encoding method in which the signal level is inverted each time a 1 is encountered.

nonreturn to zero, level (NRZ-L)   An NRZ encoding method in which the signal level is directly related to the bit value.

normal response mode (NRM)   In HDLC, a communication mode in which the secondary station must have permission from the primary station before transmission can proceed.

notification message   A BGP message sent by a router whenever an error condition is detected or a router wants to close the connection.

no-transition mobility   In wireless LANs, mobility confined inside a BSS or non-mobility.

Nyquist theorem   A theorem that states that the number of samples needed to adequately represent an analog signal is equal to twice the highest frequency of the original signal.

O

odd parity   An error-detection method in which an extra bit is added to the data unit such that the sum of all 1-bits becomes odd.

omnidirectional antenna   An antenna that sends out or receives signals in all directions.

on-demand audio/video   Another name for streaming stored audio/video.

one's complement   A representation of binary numbers in which the complement of a number is found by complementing all bits.

open message   A BGP message sent by a router to create a neighborhood relationship.

open shortest path first (OSPF)   An interior routing protocol based on link state routing.

open system   A model that allows two different systems to communicate regardless of their underlying architecture.

Open Systems Interconnection (OSI) model   A seven-layer model for data communication defined by ISO.

open-loop congestion control   Policies applied to prevent congestion.

optical carrier (OC)   The hierarchy of fiber-optic carriers defined in SONET. The hierarchy defines up to 10 different carriers (OC-1, OC-3, OC-12, . . . , OC-192), each with a different data rate.

optional attribute   A BGP path attribute that need not be recognized by every router.

orbit   The path a satellite travels around the earth.

Orthogonal Frequency Division Multiplexing (OFDM)   A multiplexing method similar to FDM, with all the subbands used by one source at a given time.

Otway-Rees protocol   A key management protocol with less steps than the Needham-Schroeder method.

overhead   Extra bits added to the data unit for control purposes.

P

packet switching   Data transmission using a packet-switched network.

packet   Synonym for data unit, mostly used in the network layer.

packet-filter firewall   A firewall that forwards or blocks packets based on the information in the network-layer and transport-layer headers.

packet-switched network   A network in which data are transmitted in independent units called packets.

page   A unit of hypertext or hypermedia available on the Web.

parabolic dish antenna   An antenna shaped like a parabola used for terrestrial microwave communication.

parallel transmission   Transmission in which bits in a group are sent simultaneously, each using a separate link.

parameter-problem message   An ICMP message that notifies a host that there is an ambiguous or missing value in any field of the datagram.

parity bit   A redundant bit added to a data unit (usually a character) for error checking.

parity check   An error-detection method using a parity bit.

partially qualified domain name (PQDN)   A domain name that does not include all the levels between the host and the root node.

passive open   The state of a server as it waits for incoming requests from a client.

Password Authentication Protocol (PAP)   A simple two-step authentication protocol used in PPP.

path layer   A SONET layer responsible for the movement of a signal from its optical source to its optical destination.

path overhead   Control information used by the SONET path layer.

path   The channel through which a signal travels.

path vector routing   A routing method on which BGP is based; in this method, the ASs through which a packet must pass are explicitly listed.

P-box   A hardware circuit used in encryption that connects input to output.

peak amplitude   The maximum signal value of a sine wave.

peak data rate   The maximum data rate of the traffic.

peer-to-peer process   A process on a sending and a receiving machine that communicate at a given layer.

per hop behavior (PHB)   In the Diffserv model, a 6-bit field that defines the packet-handling mechanism for the packet.

period   The amount of time required to complete one full cycle.

periodic signal   A signal that exhibits a repeating pattern.

permanent virtual circuit (PVC)   A virtual circuit transmission method in which the same virtual circuit is used between source and destination on a continual basis.

persistence timer   A technique to handle the zero window-size advertisement.

persistent connection   A connection in which the server leaves the connection open for more requests after sending a response.

persistent strategy   In CSMA, a strategy in which the station sends a frame after sensing the line.

Personal Communication System (PCS)   A generic term for a commercial cellular system that offers several kinds of communication services.

phase modulation (PM)   An analog-to-analog modulation method in which the carrier signal's phase varies with the amplitude of the modulating signal.

phase shift keying (PSK)   A digital-to-analog modulation method in which the phase of the carrier signal is varied to represent a specific bit pattern.

phase   The relative position of a signal in time.

PHY sublayer   The transceiver in Fast Ethernet.

physical address   The address of a device used at the data link layer (MAC address).

physical layer signaling (PLS) sublayer   An Ethernet sublayer that encodes and decodes data.

physical layer   The first layer of the Internet model, responsible for the mechanical and electrical specifications of the medium.

physical topology   The manner in which devices are connected in a network.

piconet   A Bluetooth network.

piggybacking   The inclusion of acknowledgment on a data frame.

pipelining   In Go-Back-*n* ARQ, sending several frames before news is received concerning previous frames.

pixel A picture element of an image.

plaintext In encryption/decryption, the original message.

playback buffer A buffer that stores the data until they are ready to be played.

point coordination function (PCF) In wireless LANs, an optional and complex access method implemented in an infrastructure network.

point of presence (POP) A switching office where carriers can interact with each other.

point-to-point access See *point-to-point connection.*

point-to-point connection A dedicated transmission link between two devices.

point-to-point link A dedicated transmission link between two devices.

Point-to-Point Protocol (PPP) A protocol for data transfer across a serial line.

polar encoding A digital-to-analog encoding method that uses two levels (positive and negative) of amplitude.

policy routing A path vector routing feature in which the routing tables are based on rules set by the network administrator rather than a metric.

poll In the primary/secondary access method, a procedure in which the primary station asks a secondary station if it has any data to transmit.

poll/final (P/F) bit A bit in the control field of HDLC; if the primary is sending, it can be a poll bit; if the secondary is sending, it can be a final bit.

poll/select An access method protocol using poll and select procedures. See *poll.* See *select.*

polyalphabetic substitution An encryption method in which each occurrence of a character can have a different substitute.

polynomial An algebraic term that can represent a CRC divisor.

port In a URL, the port number of the server.

port address In TCP/IP protocol an integer identifying a process.

port number An integer that defines a process running on a host.

Post Office Protocol, version 3 (POP3) A popular but simple SMTP mail access protocol.

p-persistent strategy A CSMA persistence strategy in which a station sends with probability p if it finds the line idle.

preamble The 7-byte field of an IEEE 802.3 frame consisting of alternating 1s and 0s that alert and synchronize the receiver.

predicted frame (P-frame) An MPEG frame which contains only the changes from the preceding frame.

predictive encoding In audio compression, encoding only the differences between the samples.

presentation layer The sixth layer of the OSI model responsible for translation, encryption, authentication, and data compression.

Pretty Good Privacy (PGP) A protocol that provides all four aspects of security in the sending of email.

primary server A server that stores a file about the zone for which it is an authority.

primary station In primary/secondary access method, a station that issues commands to the secondary stations.

priority queueing A queuing technique in which packets are assigned to a priority class, each with its own queue.

privacy   A security aspect in which the message makes sense only to the intended receiver.

private key   In conventional encryption, a key shared by only one pair of devices, a sender and a receiver. In public-key encryption, the private key is known only to the receiver.

private network   A network that is isolated from the Internet.

process   A running application program.

process-to-process delivery   Delivery of a packet from the sending process to the destination process.

product block   A combination of P-boxes and S-boxes to get a more complex cipher block.

Project 802   The project undertaken by the IEEE in an attempt to solve LAN incompatibility. See also *IEEE Project 802*.

propagation speed   The rate at which a signal or bit travels; measured by distance/second.

propagation time   The time required for a signal to travel from one point to another.

Protocol Independent Multicast (PIM)   A multicasting protocol family with two members, PIM-DM and PIM-SM; both protocols are unicast-protocol dependent.

Protocol Independent Multicast, Dense Mode (PIM-DM)   A source-based routing protocol that uses RPF and pruning/grafting strategies to handle multicasting.

Protocol Independent Multicast, Sparse Mode (PIM-SM)   A group-shared routing protocol that is similar to CBT and uses a rendezvous point as the source of the tree.

protocol   Rules for communication.

protocol suite   A stack or family of protocols defined for a complex communication system.

proxy firewall   A firewall that filters a message based on the information available in the message itself (at the application layer).

proxy server   A computer that keeps copies of responses to recent requests.

pruning   Stopping the sending of multicast messages from an interface.

public key   In public-key encryption, a key known to everyone.

public key infrastructure (PKI)   A hierarchical structure of CA servers.

public-key cryptography   A method of encryption based on a nonreversible encryption algorithm. The method uses two types of keys: The public key is known to the public; the private key (secret key) is known only to the receiver.

pulse amplitude modulation (PAM)   A technique in which an analog signal is sampled; the result is a series of pulses based on the sampled data.

pulse code modulation (PCM)   A technique that modifies PAM pulses to create a digital signal.

pulse rate   The number of symbols per second.

Q

quadbit   A unit of data consisting of four bits.

quadrature amplitude modulation (QAM)   A digital-to-analog modulation method in which the phase and amplitude of the carrier signal vary with the modulating signal.

quality of service (QoS)   A set of attributes related to the performance of the connection.

quantization   The assignment of a specific range of values to signal amplitudes.

query message An ICMP message that helps a host or a network manager get specific information from a router or another host. Or, an IGMP message that requests group information from a router or a host. Or, a DNS message that requests information.

queue A waiting list.

R

radio wave Electromagnetic energy in the 3-KHz to 300-GHz range.

random access A medium access category in which each station can access the medium without being controlled by any other station.

ranging In an HFC network, a process that determines the distance between the CM and the CMTS.

rate adaptive asymmetrical digital subscriber line (RADSL) A DSL-based technology that features different data rates depending on the type of communication.

raw socket A structure designed for protocols that directly use the services of IP and use neither stream sockets nor datagram sockets.

read-only memory (ROM) Permanent memory with contents that cannot be changed.

Real-Time Streaming Protocol (RTSP) An out-of-band control protocol designed to add more functionality to the streaming audio/video process.

Real-time Transport Control Protocol (RTCP) A companion protocol to RTP with messages that control the flow and quality of data and allow the recipient to send feedback to the source or sources.

Real-time Transport Protocol (RTP) A protocol for real-time traffic; used in conjunction with UDP.

receiver window In the TCP sliding window protocol, the window at the receiver site.

reconciliation sublayer A Fast Ethernet sublayer which passes data in 4-bit format to the MII.

recursive resolution Resolution of the IP address in which the client sends its request to a server that eventually returns a response.

redirection An ICMP message type that informs the sender of a preferred route.

redundancy The addition of bits to a message for error control.

reflection The phenomenon related to the bouncing back of light at the boundary of two media.

refraction The phenomenon related to the bending of light when it passes from one medium to another.

regenerator A device that regenerates the original signal from a corrupted signal. See also *repeater*.

regional cable head (RCH) In an HFC network, the main distribution site.

regional ISP A small ISP that is connected to one or more NSPs.

registrar server In SIP, a server that knows the IP address of the callee.

reliability A QoS flow characteristic; dependability of the transmission.

remote access Using a terminal that is not directly connected to a computer.

remote bridge A device that connects LANs and point-to-point networks; often used in a backbone network.

remote host   The computer that a user wishes to access while seated physically at another computer.

remote server   A program run at a site physically removed from the user.

rendezvous router   A router that is the core or center for each multicast group; it becomes the root of the tree.

rendezvous-point tree   A group-shared tree method in which there is one tree for each group.

repeater   A device that extends the distance a signal can travel by regenerating the signal.

replay attack   The resending of a message that has been intercepted by an intruder.

Request for Comment (RFC)   A formal Internet document concerning an Internet issue.

request header   A part of the HTTP request message that specifies the client's configuration and the client's preferred document format.

resolver   The DNS client that is used by a host that needs to map an address to a name or a name to an address.

Resource Reservation Protocol (RSVP)   A signaling protocol to help IP create a flow and make a resource reservation to improve QoS.

response header   A part of the HTTP response message that specifies the server's configuration and special information about the request.

response message   A DNS message type that returns information.

retransmission timer   A timer that controls the waiting time for an acknowledgment of a segment.

return to zero (RZ)   A digital-to-digital encoding technique in which the voltage of the signal is zero for the second half of the bit interval.

reuse factor   In cellular telephony, the number of cells with a different set of frequencies.

Reverse Address Resolution Protocol (RARP)   A TCP/IP protocol that allows a host to find its Internet address given its physical address.

reverse path broadcasting (RPB)   A technique in which the router forwards only the packets that have traveled the shortest path from the source to the router.

reverse path forwarding (RPF)   A technique in which the router forwards only the packets that have traveled the shortest path from the source to the router.

reverse path multicasting (RPM)   A technique that adds pruning and grafting to RPB to create a multicast shortest path tree that supports dynamic membership changes.

ring topology   A topology in which the devices are connected in a ring. Each device on the ring receives the data unit from the previous device, regenerates it, and forwards it to the next device.

Rivest, Shamir, Adleman (RSA) encryption   See *RSA encryption*.

RJ45   A coaxial cable connector.

roaming   In cellular telephony, the ability of a user to communicate outside of his own service provider's area.

root server   In DNS, a server whose zone consists of the whole tree. A root server usually does not store any information about domains but delegates its authority to other servers, keeping references to those servers.

rotary dialing   Accessing the switching station through a phone that sends a digital signal to the end office.

round-trip time (RTT)   The time required for a datagram to go from a source to a destination and then back again.

route   A path traveled by a packet.

router   An internetworking device operating at the first three OSI layers. A router is attached to two or more networks and forwards packets from one network to another.

router link LSA   An LSA packet that advertises all of the links of a router.

router-solicitation and advertisement message   An ICMP message sent to obtain and disperse router information.

Routing Information Protocol (RIP)   A routing protocol based on the distance vector routing algorithm.

routing table   A table containing information a router needs to route packets. The information may include the network address, the cost, the address of the next hop, and so on.

routing   The process performed by a router; finding the next hop for a datagram.

RSA encryption   A popular public-key encryption method developed by Rivest, Shamir, and Adleman.

S

sampling rate   The number of samples obtained per second in the sampling process.

sampling   The process of obtaining amplitudes of a signal at regular intervals.

satellite network   A combination of nodes that provides communication form one point on the earth to another.

S-box   An encryption device made of decoders, P-boxes, and encoders.

scatternet   A combination of piconets.

search algorithm   A rule for finding the next hop.

secondary server   In DNS, a server that transfers the complete information about a zone from another server (primary or secondary) and stores the file on its local disk.

secondary station   In poll/select access method, a station that sends a response in answer to a command from a primary station.

secret-key encryption   A security method in which the key for encryption is the same as the key for decryption; both sender and receiver have the same key.

Security Association (SA)   An IPSec signaling protocol that creates a logical connection between 2 hosts.

security   The protection of a network from unauthorized access, viruses, and catastrophe.

segment   The packet at the TCP layer. Also, the length of transmission medium shared by devices.

segmentation and reassembly (SAR)   The lower AAL sublayer in the ATM protocol in which a header and/or trailer may be added to produce a 48-byte element.

segmentation   The splitting of a message into multiple packets; usually performed at the transport layer.

select   In poll/select access method, a procedure in which the primary station asks a secondary station if it is ready to receive data.

selective-repeat ARQ   An error-control method in which only the frame in error is resent.

self-synchronization   Synchronization of long strings of 1s or 0s through the coding method.

semantics   The meaning of each section of bits.

sender window   In the TCP sliding window protocol, the window at the sender site.

sequence number   The number that denotes the location of a frame or packet in a message.

serial transmission   Transmission of data one bit at a time using only one single link.

server   A program that can provide services to other programs, called clients.

service-point address   See *port address*.

Session Initiation Protocol (SIP)   In voice over IP, an application protocol that establishes, manages, and terminates a multimedia session.

session layer   The fifth layer of the OSI model, responsible for the establishment, management, and termination of logical connections between two end users.

setup phase   In virtual circuit switching, a phase in which the source and destination use their global addresses to help switches make table entries for the connection.

S-frame   An HDLC frame used for supervisory functions such as acknowledgment, flow control, and error control; it contains no user data.

Shannon capacity   The theoretical highest data rate for a channel.

shielded twisted-pair (STP)   Twisted-pair cable enclosed in a foil or mesh shield that protects against electromagnetic interference.

short interframe space (SIFS)   In CSMA/CA, a period of time that the destination waits after receiving the RTS.

shortest path tree   A routing table formed by using the Dijkstra algorithm.

signal   Electromagnetic waves propagated along a transmission medium.

signal level   The number of values allowed in a particular signal.

signal-to-noise ratio (SNR)   The signal strength divided by the noise, both in decibels.

silly window syndrome   A situation in which a small window size is advertised by the receiver and a small segment sent by the sender.

simple bridge   A networking device that links two segments; requires manual maintenance and updating.

Simple Mail Transfer Protocol (SMTP)   The TCP/IP protocol defining electronic mail service on the Internet.

Simple Network Management Protocol (SNMP)   The TCP/IP protocol that specifies the process of management in the Internet.

simplex mode   A transmission mode in which communication is one way.

sine wave   An amplitude-versus-time representation of a rotating vector.

single-bit error   Error in a data unit in which only one single bit has been altered.

single-mode fiber   An optical fiber with an extremely small diameter that limits beams to a few angles, resulting in an almost horizontal beam.

sky propagation   Propagation of radio waves into the ionosphere and then back to earth.

slash notation   A shorthand method to indicate the number of 1s in the mask.

slave   In a piconet, a station under control of a master.

sliding window   A protocol that allows several data units to be in transition before receiving an acknowledgment.

sliding window ARQ   An error-control protocol using sliding window concept.

slow convergence A RIP shortcoming apparent when a change somewhere in the internet propagates very slowly through the rest of the internet.

slow start A congestion-control method in which the congestion window size increases exponentially at first.

socket address A structure holding an IP address and a port number.

socket An end point for a process; two sockets are needed for communication.

socket interface An API based on UNIX that defines a set of system calls (procedures) that are an extension of system calls used in UNIX to access files.

solicited response A RIP response sent only in answer to a request.

source address (SA) The address of the sender of the message.

source quench A method, used in ICMP for flow control, in which the source is advised to slow down or stop the sending of datagrams because of congestion.

source routing bridge A source or destination station that performs some of the duties of a transparent bridge as a method to prevent loops.

source routing Explicitly defining the route of a packet by the sender of the packet.

source-based tree A tree used for multicasting by multicasting protocols in which a single tree is made for each combination of source and group.

source quench message An ICMP message sent to slow down or stop the sending of datagrams.

source-to-destination delivery The transmission of a message from the original sender to the intended recipient.

space propagation A type of propagation that can penetrate the ionosphere.

space-division switching Switching in which the paths are separated from each other spatially.

spanning tree A tree with the source as the root and group members as leaves; a tree that connects all of the nodes.

spanning tree algorithm An algorithm that prevents looping when two LANs are connected by more than one bridge.

spatial compression Compressing an image by removing redundancies.

special-query message An IGMP query message sent by a router to ensure that no host or router is interested in continuing membership in a group.

specific host on this network A special address in which the netid is all 0s and the hostid is explicit.

spectrum The range of frequencies of a signal.

split horizon A method to improve RIP stability in which the router selectively chooses the interface from which updating information is sent.

spread spectrum A wireless transmission technique that requires a bandwidth several times the original bandwidth.

star backbone A backbone in which the logical topology is a star.

star topology A topology in which all stations are attached to a central device (hub).

start bit In asynchronous transmission, a bit to indicate the beginning of transmission.

start frame delimiter (SFD) A 1-byte field in the IEEE 802.3 frame that signals the beginning of the readable (nonpreamble) bit stream.

state transition diagram A diagram to illustrate the states of a finite state machine.

static document On the World Wide Web, a fixed-content document that is created and stored in a server.

static mapping A technique in which a list of logical and physical address correspondences is used for address resolution.

static routing A type of routing in which the routing table remains unchanged.

stationary host A host that remains attached to one network.

status line In the HTTP response message a line that consists of the HTTP version, a space, a status code, a space, a status phrase.

stop bit In asynchronous transmission, one or more bits to indicate the end of transmission.

stop-and-wait ARQ An error-control protocol using stop-and-wait flow control.

store-and-forward switch A switch that stores the frame in an input buffer until the whole packet has arrived.

straight tip connector A type of fiber-optic cable connector using a bayonet locking system.

stream socket A structure designed to be used with a connection-oriented protocol such as TCP.

streaming live audio/video Broadcast data from the Internet that a user can listen to or watch.

streaming stored audio/video Data downloaded as files from the Internet that a user can listen to or watch.

STS multiplexer/demultiplexer A SONET device that multiplexes and demultiplexes signals.

stub link A network that is connected to only one router.

subnet address The network address of a subnet.

subnet mask The mask for a subnet.

subnetwork A part of a network.

subscriber channel connector A fiber-optic cable connector using a push/pull locking mechanism.

substitution A bit-level encryption method in which n bits substitute for another n bits as defined by P-boxes, encoders, and decoders.

suffix For a network, the varying part (similar to the hostid) of the address. In DNS, a string used by an organization to define its host or resources.

summary link to AS boundary router LSA An LSA packet that lets a router inside an area know the route to an autonomous boundary router.

summary link to network LSA An LSA packet that finds the cost of reaching networks outside of the area.

supergroup A signal composed of five multiplexed groups.

supernet A network formed from two or more smaller networks.

supernet mask The mask for a supernet.

supervisory frame See *S-frame*.

switch A device connecting multiple communication lines together.

switched Ethernet An Ethernet in which a switch, replacing the hub, can direct a transmission to its destination.

switched virtual circuit (SVC) A virtual circuit transmission method in which a virtual circuit is created and in existence only for the duration of the exchange.

switched/56 A temporary 56-Kbps digital connection between two users.

switching office The place where telephone switches are located.

symmetric digital subscriber line (SDSL) A DSL-based technology similar to HDSL, but using only one single twisted-pair cable.

symmetric key The key used for both encryption and decryption.

symmetric-key cryptography A cipher in which the same key is used for encryption and decryption.

synchronization points Reference points introduced into the data by the session layer for the purpose of flow and error control.

synchronous connection oriented (SCO) link In a Bluetooth network, a physical link created between a master and a slave that reserves specific slots at regular intervals.

Synchronous Digital Hierarchy (SDH) The ITU-T equivalent of SONET.

Synchronous Optical Network (SONET) A standard developed by ANSI for fiber optic technology that can transmit high-speed data. It can be used to deliver text, audio, and video.

synchronous payload envelope (SPE) The part of the SONET frame containing user data and transmission overhead.

synchronous transmission A transmission method that requires a constant timing relationship between the sender and the receiver.

synchronous transport signal (STS) A signal in the SONET hierarchy.

syntax The structure or format of data, meaning the order in which they are presented.

T

tag A formatting instruction embedded in an HTML document.

TCP timer The timers used by TCP to handle retransmission, zero window-size advertisements, long idle connections, and connection termination.

TCP/IP protocol suite A group of hierarchical protocols used in an internet.

TDM bus A time-division switch in which the input and output lines are connected to a high-speed bus through microswitches.

teardown phase In virtual circuit switching, the phase in which the source and destination inform the switch to erase their entry.

telecommunications Exchange of information over distance using electronic equipment.

teleconferencing Audio and visual communication between remote users.

Teledesic A system of satellites that provides fiber-optic communication (broadband channels, low error rate, and low delay)

TELNET See *Terminal Network*.

temporal compression An MPEG compression method in which redundant frames are removed.

Terminal Network (TELNET) A general purpose client-server program that allows remote login.

terminating state A PPP state in which several packets are exchanged between the two ends for house cleaning and closing the link.

terminator An electronic device that prevents signal reflections at the end of a cable.

thick Ethernet See *10Base5*.

thin Ethernet See *10Base2*.

three-layer switch A switch at the network layer; a router.

three-way handshake   A sequence of events for connection establishment or termination consisting of the request, then the acknowledgment of the request, and then confirmation of the acknowledgment.

throughput   The number of bits that can pass through a point in one second.

ticket   An encrypted message containing a session key.

ticket-granting server (TGS)   A Kerberos server that issues tickets.

time division duplexing TDMA (TDD-TDMA)   In a Bluetooth network, a kind of half-duplex communication in which the slave and receiver send and receive data, but not at the same time (half-duplex).

time division multiple access (TDMA)   A multiple access method in which the bandwidth is just one time-shared channel.

time to live (TTL)   The lifetime of a packet.

time-division multiplexing (TDM)   The technique of combining signals coming from low-speed channels to share time on a high-speed path.

time-division switching   A circuit-switching technique in which time-division multiplexing is used to achieve switching.

time-domain plot   A graphical representation of a signal's amplitude versus time.

time-exceeded message   An ICMP message sent to inform a source that (1) its datagram has a time-to-live value of zero, or (2) the fragments of a message have not been received within a set time limit.

time-slot interchange (TSI)   A time-division switch consisting of RAM and a control unit.

timestamp   An IP header option used to record the time of datagram processing by a router. Also, a method to handle jitter in interactive real-time audio/video.

timestamp-request and reply message   An ICMP message sent to determine the round-trip time or to synchronize clocks.

time-waited timer   A TCP timer used in connection termination that allows late segments to arrive.

T-lines   A hierarchy of digital lines designed to carry speech and other signals in digital forms. The hierarchy defines T-1, T-2, T-3, and T-4 lines.

token   A small packet used in token-passing access method.

token bucket   An algorithm that allows idle hosts to accumulate credit for the future in the form of tokens.

token passing   An access method in which a token is circulated in the network. The station that captures the token can send data.

Token Ring   A LAN using a ring topology and token-passing access method.

toll call service   An inter-LATA or intra-LATA telephone service charged to the caller.

topology   The structure of a network including physical arrangement of devices.

touch-tone dialing   A telephone dialing method in which each key is represented by two small bursts of analog signals.

traffic   Messages on a network.

traffic control   A method for shaping and controlling traffic in a wide area network.

traffic shaping   A mechanism to control the amount and the rate of the traffic sent to the network to improve QoS.

trailer Control information appended to a data unit.

transceiver A device that both transmits and receives.

transceiver cable In Ethernet, the cable that connects the station to the transceiver. Also called the attachment unit interface.

transient link A network with several routers attached to it.

transition state The different phases through which a PPP connection goes.

translation Changing from one code or protocol to another.

Transmission Control Protocol (TCP) A transport protocol in the TCP/IP protocol suite.

Transmission Control Protocol/Internetworking Protocol (TCP/IP) A five-layer protocol suite that defines the exchange of transmissions across the Internet.

transmission medium The physical path linking two communication devices.

transmission path (TP) In ATM, the physical connection between two switches.

transmission rate The number of bits sent per second.

transparency The ability to send any bit pattern as data without it being mistaken for control bits.

transparent bridge Another name for a learning bridge.

transparent data Data that can contain control bit patterns without being interpreted as control.

Transport Layer Security (TLS) A security protocol at the transport level designed to provide security on the WWW.

transport layer The fourth layer in the Internet and OSI model; responsible for reliable end-to-end delivery and error recovery.

transpositional cipher A character-level encryption method in which the position of the character changes.

trellis-coded modulation A modulation technique that includes error correction.

triangulation A two-dimensional method of finding a location given the distances from 3 different points.

tribit A unit of data consisting of three bits.

triple DES An algorithm compatible with DES that uses three DES blocks and two 56-bit keys.

Trivial File Transfer Protocol (TFTP) An unreliable TCP/IP protocol for file transfer that does not require complex interaction between client and server.

trunk Transmission media that handle communications between offices.

tunneling In multicasting, a process in which the multicast packet is encapsulated in a unicast packet and then sent through the network. In VPN, the encapsulation of an encrypted IP datagram in a second outer datagram. For IPv6, a strategy used when two computers using IPv6 want to communicate with each other when the packet must pass through a region that uses IPv4.

twisted-pair cable A transmission medium consisting of two insulated conductors in a twisted configuration.

twisted-pair Ethernet An Ethernet using twisted-pair cable; 10Base-T.

two-dimensional parity check An error detection method in two dimensions.

two-layer switch A bridge with many ports and a design that allows better (faster) performance.

type of service (TOS) A criteria or value that specifies the handling of the datagram.

U

U-frame   An HDLC unnumbered frame carrying link management information.

unbalanced configuration   An HDLC configuration in which one device is primary and the others secondary.

unguided medium   A transmission medium with no physical boundaries.

unicast address   An address belonging to one destination.

unicast message   A message sent to just one destination.

unicast routing   The sending of a packet to just one destination.

unidirectional antenna   An antenna that sends or receives signals in one direction.

Uniform Resource Locator (URL)   A string of characters (address) that identifies a page on the World Wide Web.

unipolar encoding   A digital-to-digital encoding method in which one nonzero value represents either 1 or 0; the other bit is represented by a zero value.

unnumbered frame   See *U-frame.*

unshielded twisted-pair (UTP)   A cable with wires that are twisted together to reduce noise and crosstalk. See also *twisted-pair cable* and *shielded twisted-pair.*

unspecified bit rate (UBR)   The data rate of an ATM service class specifying only best-effort delivery.

update message   A BGP message used by a router to withdraw destinations that have been advertised previously or to announce a route to a new destination.

uplink   Transmission from an earth station to a satellite.

uploading   Sending a local file or data to a remote site.

upstream data band   In an HFC network, the 5 to 42 MHz band for data from the subscriber premises to the Internet.

user agent (UA)   An SMTP component that prepares the message, creates the envelope, and puts the message in the envelope.

user authentication   A security measure in which the sender identity is verified before the start of a communication.

User Datagram Protocol (UDP)   A connectionless TCP/IP transport layer protocol.

user datagram   The name of the packet in the UDP protocol.

user network interface (UNI)   The interface between a user and the ATM network.

user support layers   The session, presentation, and application layers.

user-to-network interface (UNI)   In ATM, the interface between an end point (user) and an ATM switch.

V

V series   ITU-T standards that define data transmission over telephone lines.

variable bit rate (VBR)   The data rate of an ATM service class for users needing a varying bit rate.

very high bit rate digital subscriber line (VDSL)   A DSL-based technology for short distances.

video band   In an HFC network, the band from 54 to 550 MHz for downstream video.

Vigenere cipher A polyalphabetic substitution scheme that uses the position of a character in the plaintext and the character's position in the alphabet.

virtual channel identifier (VCI) A field in an ATM cell header that defines a channel.

virtual circuit (VC) A logical circuit made between the sending and receiving computer. The connection is made after both computers do handshaking. After the connection, all packets follow the same route and arrive in sequence.

virtual circuit approach to packet switching A packet switching method in which all packets of a message or session follow the exact same route.

virtual circuit identifier (VCI) A field in an ATM cell header that defines a channel.

virtual circuit switching A switching technique used in switched WANs.

virtual connection identifier A VCI or VPI.

virtual link An OSPF connection between two routers that is created when the physical link is broken. The link between them uses a longer path that probably goes through several routers.

virtual local area network (VLAN) A technology that divides a physical LAN into virtual workgroups through software methods.

virtual path (VP) In ATM, a connection or set of connections between two switches.

virtual path identifier (VPI) A field in an ATM cell header that identifies a path.

virtual path identifier/virtual channel identifier (VPI/VCI) Two fields used together to route an ATM cell.

virtual private network (VPN) A technology that creates a network that is physically public, but virtually private.

virtual tributary (VT) A partial payload that can be inserted into a SONET frame and combined with other partial payloads to fill out the frame.

Voice Over Frame Relay (VOFR) A Frame Relay option that can handle voice data.

voice over IP A technology in which the Internet is used as a telephone network.

W

Walsh table In CDMA, a two-dimensional table used to generate orthogonal sequences.

wavelength The distance a simple signal can travel in one period.

wave-division multiplexing (WDM) The combining of modulated light signals into one signal.

web page A unit of hypertext or hypermedia available on the Web.

Web Synonym for World Wide Web (WWW).

weighted fair queueing A packet scheduling technique to improve QoS in which the packets are assigned to queues based on a given priority number.

well-known attribute Path information that every BGP router must recognize.

well-known port A port number that identifies a process on the server.

wide area network (WAN) A network that uses a technology that can span a large geographical distance.

wide area telephone service (WATS) A telephone service in which the charges are based on the number of calls made.

window size field The size of the sliding window used in flow control.

wireless communication   Data transmission using unguided media.

wireless LAN   A LAN which uses unguided media.

World Wide Web (WWW)   A multimedia Internet service that allows users to traverse the Internet by moving from one document to another via links that connect them together.

X

X.25   An ITU-T standard that defines the interface between a data terminal device and a packet-switching network.

X.509   An ITU-T standard for public key infrastructure (PKI).

Z

zone   In DNS, what a server is responsible for or has authority over.

Index

Numerics

1000Base-CX, 352
1000Base-LX, 352
1000Base-SX, 352
1000Base-T, 352, 353
1000Base-X, 351–353
100Base-FX, 347–348
100Base-T4, 347, 349–350
100Base-TX, 347–348
100Base-X, 346
10Base2, 340
10Base5, 339
10Base-FL, 341
10Base-T, 340
   full-duplex, 343
16-QAM, 125
1-persistent, 315
2B1Q, 94
   HDSL, 222
2-PSK, 122
3-slot frame, 377
4B/5B, 97, 349
4-dimensional, 5 level pulse
   amplitude modulation;
   see 4D-PAM5
4D-PAM5, 353
4-PSK, 123
4-QAM, 125
56K modem, 131
   ADSL, 219
800 service, 209
802.11, 370
8B/10B, 97, 353
8B/6T, 98
8B/6T code, 890
8-PSK, 123
8-QAM, 125
900 service, 209

A

AAL, 455
AAL1, 456
   CS, 456
AAL2, 457
   CS layer fields, 457
AAL3/4, 457
AAL5, 459
ABM, 281
AC value, 777
access control, 33
access method, 239, 334
access point; see AP
access rate, 655
   T-1, 655
ACK, 268, 873
   in poll, 319
   Stop-and-Wait ARQ, 269
ACK frame, 270
ACK message, 792
ACK segment, 610, 611
acknowledgment, 440, 620
   ALOHA, 313
   flow control, 240, 267
   Go-Back-N, 275
acknowledgment number, 598,
   606, 607
acknowledgment policy, 638
ACL, 377
active close, 673
active document, 747, 748
active open, 673
additive increase, 640, 641
address
   MAC, 240
   need for multiple, 514
   network, 484
   physical, 240

address format, 668
address mask messages, 528
Address Resolution Protocol;
   see ARP
address to name resolution, 695
addressing
   data link layer, 240
   Ethernet, 336
   transport layer, 591
   VPN, 867
admission control, 649
admission policy, 638
ADSL, 219, 223
   actual bit rate, 221
   adaptive, 220
   DMT, 221
   HDSL, 222
   local loop, 219
   VDSL, 223
ADSL modem, 221
Advanced Mobile Phone System;
   see AMPS
Advanced Research Projects Agency;
   see ARPA
AF PHB, 654
AH protocol, 855, 856, 857
AL field, 458
ALOHA, 312
alternate mark inversion; see AMI
AM, 133, 134, 135, 136
AM bandwidth, 134, 135
AM radio, 155
AM station, 134
American National Standards Institute;
   see ANSI
American Standard Code for Information
   Interchange; see ASCII
AMI, 93, 94, 222

amplifier, 388
  attenuation, 70
  cable TV, 223
amplitude, 115, 118
  ASK, 117
  FM, 136
  FSK, 120
  measurement, 51
  PM, 138
  PSK, 122
  QAM, 125
  sine wave, 54
amplitude modulation; *see* AM
amplitude shift keying; *see* ASK
AMPS, 412
analog bandwidth, 65
analog data, 49
analog hierarchy
  telephone system, 153
analog leased service, 153, 209
analog service, 208
analog signal, 49, 50, 115
  vs. digital, 66
analog switched service, 208
analog to analog conversion, 133
analog to digital conversion, 98
analog transmission
  T-line, 163
AND operation, 489
angle of incidence, 179
anonymous FTP, 724
ANSI, 5, 19, 20
antenna
  focus, 188
  horn, 188
  line of sight, 185
  parabolic dish, 188
  satellite, 421
anycast address, 531
AP, 361, 370
aperiodic signal, 50
applet, 749
application adaptation layer; *see* AAL
application layer, 39, 667, 888
  directory services, 889
  file manipulation, 39, 888
  Internet model, 889
  mail services, 39, 888
  NVT, 888
  PGP, 860
  remote login, 39
  responsibilities, 888
  security, 853
  services, 888
  transport layer, 589
  web access, 39

application program, 671
area, 549
area border router, 549
ARP, 514, 515
  broadcast query, 515
  encapsulation, 517
  four cases, 517
  hardware length field, 516
  hardware type field, 516
  host to host on different
      networks, 518
  host to host on single network, 518
  IP to physical address mapping, 515
  operation, 517
  operation field, 516
  packet components, 515
  packet format, 516
  protocol length field, 516
  protocol type field, 516
  query packet, 515
  response packet, 515
  response packet components, 515
  router to host on different
      networks, 518
  router to host on same
      network, 518
  sender hardware address field, 516
  sender protocol address field, 516
  steps involved, 517
  target hardware address field, 516
  target protocol address field, 516
  unicast response, 515
ARPA, 16
ARPANET, 16
ARQ, 268
  bandwidth-delay product, 280
AS, 843, 844
ASCII, 5, 873
  extended, 5
  table, 873
ASCII code, 243
ASK, 115, 117, 120
  bandwidth, 118
  bandwidth example, 119
  bandwidth formula, 118
  bit, baud rate example, 119
  carrier signal, 117
  concept, 118
  noise, 118
  with PSK, 125
  QAM, 126
ASN.1, 842
asymmetrical DSL; *see* ADSL
asynchronous balanced mode; *see* ABM
asynchronous connectionless link;
      see ACL

asynchronous TDM
  ATM, 448
asynchronous transmission, 103, 105, 106
Asynchronous Transmission Mode;
  see ATM
AT&T Bell System, 210
AT&T divestiture, 210
ATM, 446, 449, 451
  AAL1, 456
  AAL2, 457
  AAL3/4, 457
  AAL5, 459
  architecture, 449
  asynchronous TDM, 448
  ATM layer, 454
  available bit rate class, 658
  backward compatibility, 446
  cell, 452
  cell delay variation, 659
  cell error ratio, 659
  cell loss ratio, 659
  cell transfer delay, 659
  cell variation delay tolerance, 659
  connection establishment, 452
  connection release, 452
  connection types, 903
  connection-oriented, 906
  connections, 452
  constant-bit-rate class, 657
  design goals, 446
  example, 449
  header for NNI, 454
  hierarchical routing, 451
  Identifier, 450
  Information Super-Highway, 446
  layers, 453
  minimum cell rate, 659
  multimedia, 903
  multiplexing, 448
  network-related attributes, 659
  peak cell rate, 658
  physical layer, 454
  QoS, 657
  SONET, 453
  sustained cell rate, 658
  SVC, 452
  switching, 452
  switching fabric, 452
  unspecified bit rate class, 658
  user-related attributes, 658
  variable-bit-rate class, 657
  variable-bit-rate non-real time,
      657, 658
  variable-bit-rate real-time, 657
  virtual connection, 449
  WAN, 903

ATM Forum, 446
  address, 919
ATM LAN, 459, 903
  advantages, 903
  architecture, 903
  BUS, 907
  client/server, 907
  expansion, 903
  LANE, 906
  legacy, 904
  mixed architecture, 905
  pure, 904
ATM layer, 453
  cell loss priority, 455
  cell size, 454
  congestion control, 455
  function, 454
  Generic Flow Control (GFC), 455
  header error correction, 455
  header for UNI, 454
  header format, 454
  NNI level flow control, 455
  payload type, 455
  UNI level flow control, 455
  VCI field, 455
  VPI, 455
  VPI field, 455
ATM switch, 904
attachment unit interface; *see* AUI
attenuation, 69, 387
  amplifier, 70
  example, 70
  optical fiber, 184
audio signal, 774
  digitizing, 774
AUI, 337
  MII, 346
authenticating state, 297
  PPP, 304
authentication, 297, 300, 528, 827, 832
  AH protocol, 856
  bidirectional, 834
  digital signature, 829
  packet, 297
authentication data, 856
Authentication Header protocol;
    see AH protocol
authentication server; *see* AS
auto negotiation, 345
automatic repeat request; *see* ARQ
autonomous boundary router, 558
autonomous system, 544, 548
  area, 549
  backbone, 549
  path vector routing, 558
average data rate, 633

B
back off, 315
back pressure, 639
backbone, 549
  area id, 549
  bus, 12
  logical star, 398
  virtual link, 549
backbone network, 396
backbone router, 549
backoff, 316
  ALOHA, 313
backward explicit congestion
    notification; *see* BECN
band
  AMPS, 412
  Bluetooth, 375
  D-AMPS, 413
  DSSS, 364
  FHSS, 364
  GSM, 414
  HR-DSSS, 365
  IS-95, 416
  OFDM, 365
band-pass, 66
bands, 186
bandwidth, 59, 121, 124, 129, 135, 136,
    137, 441
  AM, 134
  AM radio, 134, 155
  ASK, 118
  audio signal, 134, 136
  bit rate, 64
  bridge, 341
  cellular telephone, 155
  for data transmission, 128
  Ethernet, 341
  example, 61
  FDM, 150
  flow characteristic, 644
  FM, 136
  FM station, 138
  FSK, 120, 121
  group, 154
  local loop, 205
  master group, 154
  optical fiber, 184
  PSK, 124
  QAM, 126
  real-time traffic, 788
  of signal, 118
  stereo audio signal, 138
  supergroup, 154
  of telephone line, 128
bandwidth on demand, 165
  bursty data, 441

bandwidth-delay product, 280
Banyan switch, 901
base 8, 879
base header, 531
base station (BS), 312, 409
base 16, 880
baseband layer, 375
basic service set; *see* BSS
BAsize, 458
Batcher, 902
Batcher-Banyan switch, 902
baud, 127
baud rate, 116, 121, 124
  ASK, 124
  and bit rate, 117
  dibit, 127
  example, 117, 128
  FSK, 127
  PSK, 124
Bc, 655
  bursty data, 657
Be, 656
  bursty data, 657
BECN, 444
  mechanism, 642
  sender, 642
Bell Operating Company;
    see BOC
Bellman-Ford algorithm, 546
best-effort delivery, 519
B-frame, 780
BGP, 544, 545, 557
  keepalive message, 560
  notification message, 560
  open message, 560
  path vector routing, 557
  port, 917
  types of messages, 560
  update message, 560
bidirectional authentication, 834
bidirectional edge, 552
bidirectional frame, 780
binary notation, 478
binary number, 878
binary system, 877
biphase encoding, 92
bipolar encoding, 88, 93
bipolar n-zero substitution;
    see BnZS
bit, 102, 103
  baud, 127
  baud rate comparison, 127
  phase relationship, 123
bit duration, 117
bit interval, 62
bit padding, 161

bit rate, 62, 86, 116
  bandwidth, 64
  and baud rate, 117
  dibit, 127
  example, 86, 117, 128
bit stuffing, 289
  exceptions, 289
  HDLC, 288, 289
  TDM, 161
bits per second, 62
block cipher, 813
block coding, 95
  4B/5B, 97
  8B/10B, 97
  8B/6T, 98
  division, 96
  error control, 96
  line coding, 96
  steps, 96
  substitution, 96
  synchronization, 96
block descriptor, 722
blocking, 201
blocking port, 394
Bluetooth, 361, 372
  applications, 372
  architecture, 373
  device, 374
  frame format, 377
  layers, 374
Bluetooth LAN, 373
BNC connector, 178
BnZS, 93
BOC, 210
body, 742
bootstrap process, 492
border gateway protocol;
  see BGP
bridge, 341, 390
  collision domain, 342
  connecting LANs, 391, 395
  dynamic, 391
  Ethernet, 341
  as a filter, 390
  function, 341, 390
  loop problem, 392
  multiple LAN issues, 395
  redundant, 392
  source routing, 395
  transparent, 391
  two-layer switch, 396
bridge protocol data unit
  (BPDU), 395
bridged Ethernet, 341
broadcast address
  Ethernet, 336

broadcast/unknown server; see BUS
broadcasting
  VLAN, 401
browser, 740, 741
  architecture, 740
  client program, 740
  components, 740
  controller, 740
  dynamic document, 745
  HTML, 741
  interpreter, 740
  markup language, 742
  streaming stored audio/video, 781
BSS, 361
BSS-transition mobility, 363
Btag, 458
bucket brigade attack, 838
buffer
  circular, 604
  flow control, 267
  receiver site, 605
  router, 900
  sender site, 605
  server, 678
  TCP, 604, 615
buffer allocation, 458
burst error, 243, 244
bursty data, 441
  Frame Relay, 441
  T-line, 441
  traffic control, 657
bursty flow, 635
bursty traffic
  leaky bucket, 647
  token bucket, 648
BUS, 907
bus, 10, 11, 12
bus topology, 197
BYE message, 792
byte, 478
byte number, 606
byte synchronization, 107

C

CA, 821, 841, 847
cable
  coaxial, 177
  twisted-pair, 174
cable modem; see CM
cable modem transmission system;
  see CMTS
cable TV, 223
  coaxial cable, 179
  head end, 223

caching, 696
Caesar Cipher, 810
CANCEL message, 792
capacities, 164
carrier
  AM, 134
  FM, 136
  inter-LATA, 206
  PM, 138
carrier frequency, 117
carrier sense multiple access;
  see CSMA
carrier sense multiple access with
  collision avoidance; see CSMA/CA
carrier sense multiple access with
  collision detection;
  see CSMA/CD
carrier signal, 117
CATV, 223
CBT, 574
  autonomous system, 574
  core router, 575
  encapsulation, 575
  leaving the group, 574
  multicast packet, 575
  rendezvous router, 574
CCITT, 19
CCK, 365
CDMA, 320, 321, 416, 417, 419
  demultiplexer, 323
  DSSS, 364
  encoding, 322
  multiplexer, 322
  sequence generation, 323
CDMA multiplexer, 416
CDMA2000, 420
cell, 240, 448, 452, 659
  ATM, 452
  definition, 448
  header, 452
  payload, 452
  size, 452
  structure, 452
cell network, 448
  concept, 448
  example, 448
  vs. frame network, 448
  multiplexing, 448
  real-time transmission, 448
  stream, 448
  VC, 450
cell relay, 446
cellular telephone, 155
cellular telephony, 409
  first generation, 411
  handoff, 411

MSC, 411
  placing a call, 410
  query signal, 411
  radius, 409
  receiving a call, 411
  second generation, 412
  third generation, 419
  tracking, 409
  transmission power, 409
  weak signal, 411
Cerf, Vint, 16
CGI, 746
Challenge, 300
Challenge Handshake Authentication
    Protocol; *see* CHAP
channel, 9, 150
channel identifier, 457
channelization, 320
CHAP, 300, 301
Cheapernet; *see* 10Base2
checker
  checksum, 254
  CRC, 251
checksum, 246, 253, 620, 895
  checker, 254
  complement, 253, 895, 898
  example, 255, 522
  field, 253
  generator, 253
  header coverage, 522
  hexadecimal, 896
  partial sum, 895, 896
  performance, 255
  procedure, 253
  receiver, 254
  receiver procedure, 254
  receiver rejection, 255
  sender procedure, 254
  sum, 895, 897
  UDP, 602
  undetectable error, 255
  value at receiver, 255
child server, 678
chip, 321
chip code, 364
choke point, 639
CIDR, 492, 501
  geographical routing, 502
  hierarchical routing, 502
  IPv6, 530
  routing table search algorithms, 502
  routing table size, 501
  table entries, 501
cipher, 808
  block, 813
  substitution, 809
  transposition, 812

Cipher Block Chaining (CBC), 818
Cipher Feedback Mode (CFM), 819
Cipher Stream Mode (CSM), 819
ciphertext, 807
  RSA, 821
CIR, 656
circuit switching, 197, 435
  example, 197
  inputs and outputs, 198
  link reduction, 197
circular buffer, 604
cladding, 180
Clark's solution, 619
class A, 481
class B, 482
class C, 483
class D, 484
class E, 484
classful addressing, 479, 491
  blocks, 481
  classes, 481
  routing table, 500
classless addressing, 479, 491
  beginning address, 491
  first address, 491
  mask, 491
  search algorithm, 502
  subnet, 492
  variable-length blocks, 491
Classless InterDomain Routing;
    see CIDR
Clear To Send (CTS), 366
CLEC, 206, 211
client, 594, 672, 673, 678
  active close, 673
  active open, 673
  concurrent, 673
  connect call, 680
  connection-oriented concurrent, 680
  definition, 673
  iterative, 673
  opening a socket, 678
  read call, 680
  repeated steps, 678, 680
  write call, 680
client program
  activity, 672
  port number, 594
  transport layer, 591
client-server model, 671
  addressing, 668
  application programs, 673
  concurrency, 673
  process concept, 674
client-server paradigm, 594
CLOSED state, 612, 613, 614

closed-loop congestion control, 638
CLOSE-WAIT state, 614
CM, 219, 226
CMTS, 226
coax; *see* coaxial cable
coaxial cable, 174, 177
  applications, 179
  cable TV, 179, 223
  conductor, 177
  connector, 178
  Ethernet, 179
  frequency range, 177
  HFC, 224
  performance, 178
  RG ratings, 178
  sheath, 177
  standards, 178
  structure, 177
  telephone network, 178
code, 5
code division multiple access;
    see CDMA
coding theory, 321
collision, 311
  backoff time, 315
  CSMA, 314
  MAC, 241
  wireless, 368
collision domain, 342
committed burst size; *see* Bc
committed information rate; *see* CIR
  calculation
common carrier, 205
  after 1996, 210
  before 1984, 210
  between 1984 and 1996, 210
  history, 210
Common Gateway Interface; *see* CGI
communication
  requirements, 267
community antenna TV, 223
competitive local exchange carriers;
    see CLEC
complement
  Walsh table, 324
complementary code keying;
    see CCK
composite signal, 56
  distortion, 71
  transmission medium, 59
compression
  FTP, 722
  MPEG, 779
  spatial, 779
concurrency, 673

conductor
  twisted-pair, 174
  unguided media, 184
confidentiality, 828
Configuration Packet, 299
congestion, 444, 636, 642
  additive increase, 641
  avoidance, 640
  concept, 639
  example, 636
  Frame Relay, 444
  leaky bucket, 646
  multiplicative decrease, 641
  prevention, 638
  queue, 636
  retransmission, 640
congestion control, 446, 624, 633, 636,
    638, 639
  closed-loop, 639
  Frame Relay, 642
  network role, 640
  open-loop, 638
  receiver role, 640
connecting device, 35, 387
connection, 9, 609
  persistent, 738
connection control, 37, 590
connection establishment, 598, 610
  procedure, 610
  SMTP, 715
connection resetting, 611
connection termination, 599, 611
  procedure, 599, 611
  SMTP, 715
connectionless iterative
    communication, 677
connectionless iterative server, 673
connectionless service, 597
connectionless transmission, 590
connectionless transport layer, 37
connection-oriented
  concept, 476
connection-oriented concurrent
    communication, 678
connection-oriented concurrent
    server, 674, 678
connection-oriented protocol, 906
connection-oriented service,
    598, 606
connection-oriented transmission, 590
connection-oriented transport layer, 37
connector, 176
  coaxial cable, 178
  optical fiber, 182
constant bit rate traffic, 634
constellation, 122, 123

Consultative Committee for International
    Telegraphy and Telephony;
    see CCITT
contact address, 919
control field
  HDLC, 283
  types, 284
control frame, 369
control variable, 268
controlled access, 317
controller, 11, 740
convergence sublayer; *see* CS
core, 180, 574
Core-Based Tree; *see* CBT
cosmic ray, 173
country domain, 693
CPI, 458, 459
CR, 873
CRC, 246, 249, 250, 459
  ATM, 455
  basis, 249
  checker, 251
  division, 250
  divisor, 250, 251
  divisor representation, 261
  generator, 250
  HDLC, 283
  modulo-2 division, 250
  overview, 249
  performance, 253
  polynomial, 251
  PPP, 296
  receiver, 250
  receiver function, 249
  redundancy bit, 249
  sender, 250
  sender function, 249
  standard polynomials, 251–253
CRC generator, 251, 261
CRC-32, 335
  Ethernet, 335
  wireless, 369
critical angle, 179
crossbar, 901
  multistage switch, 199
crossbar switch, 199, 901
crosspoint, 199, 201
crosstalk, 174
cryptography, 807
  public-key, 808
  symmetric-key, 807
CS, 456
CSMA, 312, 314
  collision, 314
  demultiplexer, 325
  inner product, 324
  multiplexer, 325

CSMA/CA, 316
  acknowledgment, 317
  wireless LAN, 317
CSMA/CD, 315, 334
  Ethernet, 316
  frame transmission, 334
  full-duplex switched Ethernet, 344
  minimum frame length, 335
  wireless, 366, 368
CU, 654
cycle, 50
  infinite, 53
  phase, 54
cyclical redundancy check; *see* CRC

D

DA, 335, 668
damaged frame, 268
D-AMPS, 413
data, 3, 49, 267
  transmission, 49
data communications, 3–4
data compression
  presentation layer, 888
data encryption standard;
    see DES
data exchange protocol, 858
data frame, 370
  in poll, 319
data level, 86
Data Link Connection Identifier;
    see DLCI
data link control, 267
data link layer, 32, 239
  access control, 33
  addressing, 33
  duties, 239
  error control, 33, 240, 267, 268
  flow control, 33, 240, 267
  framing, 33
  function, 32
  Internet model, 239
  local reponsibility, 239
  physical addressing, 33
  sublayers, 241
data link processor, 900
Data over Cable System Interface
    Specification; *see* DOCSIS
data traffic, 633
data transfer
  virtual circuit switching, 437
data transparency, 288
database
  DHCP, 492
datagram, 476, 520

datagram approach, 475, 476
datagram socket, 676
DC component, 89
DCF, 365
DCT, 777
  AC value, 777
  gradient case, 778
  sharp change case, 777
  uniform gray scale case, 777
DDNS, 698
DDS, 209, 210
  digital leased line, 210
de facto standard, 19
de jure standard, 19
DE PHB, 654
decibel, 70
decimal system, 877
  to binary, 882
  to hexadecimal, 883
  to octal, 883
  symbols, 878
  transformation from, 882
  transformation to, 882
  weight and value, 878
decryption, 807
default mask, 489
default router, 527
default routing, 499
DEL, 876
delay, 636
  load, 637
  real-time, 785
  in time-division switching, 203
delayed acknowledgment, 619
delayed response, 566
delivery
  host-to-host, 467
  process-to-process, 36
  source-to-destination, 34
demodulator, 151
  function, 129
demultiplexer, 149
  CDMA, 323
demultiplexing, 151, 597
  filters, 151
  transport layer, 597
DEMUX; *see* demultiplexer
dense WDM, 157
Department of Defense; *see* DOD
DES, 814
  triple, 817
designated bridge, 393
designated parent router, 571
designated port, 394
destination address; *see* DA
destination host
  reassembly, 524

destination unreachable, 526
DHCP, 492
  bound state, 494
  DDNS, 698
  dynamic configuration
    protocol, 492
  initializing state, 493
  leasing, 492
  rebinding state, 494
  renewing state, 494
  requesting state, 493
  selecting state, 493
  transition states, 493
DHCPACK, 493, 494
DHCPDISCOVER, 493
DHCPOFFER, 493
DHCPREQUEST, 493, 494
dialing, 207
dialog control, 40, 886
dibit, 123, 125
  baud rate, 127
differential Manchester, 90, 93
Diffie-Hellman method, 835
digest, 830
  hash function, 830
  PGP, 860
  receiver site, 831
  sender site, 831
digit, 877
  least significant, 877
  most significant, 877
  ordering of, 877
digital
  vs. analog, 49
digital AMPS; *see* D-AMPS
digital bandwidth, 65
digital data, 49, 115
Digital Data Service; *see* DDS
digital service, 209
digital service unit; *see* DSU
digital signal, 49, 50, 62
  vs. analog, 66
  bandwidth, 63
  characteristics, 50
  composite analog signal, 63
digital signal service; *see* DS
digital signature, 829
  authentication, 830
  hash function, 831
  integrity, 830
  non-repudiation, 830
  PGP, 860
  signing the digest, 830
  signing the whole document, 829
digital subscriber line; *see* DSL
digital subscriber line access multiplexer;
  see DSLAM

digital-to-analog modulation, 115
Dijkstra's algorithm, 556, 573
  BGP, 558
  least-cost tree, 573
Direct Sequence Spread Spectrum;
  see DSSS
directory services, 889
discarding policy, 638
Discrete Cosine Transform; *see* DCT
discrete multitone technique;
  see DMT
diskless workstation, 492
Distance Vector Multicast Routing
  Protocol; *see* DVMRP
distance vector routing, 546
  BGP, 558
  routing table, 546
  sharing at intervals, 546
  sharing information, 546
  sharing with neighbors, 546
distortion, 71
distributed coordination function; *see* DCF
Distributed Inter Frame Space
  (DIFS), 366
distributed processing, 8
distribution hub, 224
distribution system, 362
DLCI, 442
  Frame Relay, 444
DLE, 873
DMT, 220, 223
  division of bandwidth, 221
  FDM, 220
  QAM, 220
  VDSL, 223
DNS, 685
  caching, 696
  country domain, 693
  divisions, 691
  domain, 689
  encapsulation, 699
  generic domain, 691
  Internet, 691
  inverted-tree structure, 686
  labels, 686
  levels, 686
  message, 697
  primary server, 690
  resolver, 694
  reverse domain, 693
  root server, 690
  secondary server, 690
  server, 689
  TCP, 699
  UDP, 699
  updating, 698
  zone, 689

DNS message
 additional information section, 698
 additional records field, 698
 answer records field, 697
 answer section, 698
 authoritative records field, 698
 authoritative section, 698
 flags field, 697
 header, 697
 identification field, 697
 question records field, 697
DNS response, 698
do not fragment bit, 524
DOCSIS, 227
DOD, 16
domain, 688, 689
 country, 693
 generic, 691
 inverse, 693
domain name, 687
 full, 687
 SMTP, 706
Domain Name System; *see* DNS
dotted-decimal notation, 478
 finding the class, 480
downlink, 423
drop cable, 224
drop line, 11
dropper, 655
DS, 162, 653
 DS-0 service, 162
 DS-1 service, 162
 DS-2 service, 162
 DS-3 service, 162
 DS-4 service, 163
 field, 653
 hierarchy of digital signals, 162
DS-0, 162
DSCP, 654
DSL, 219
 limitation, 223
 PPP, 295
DSL modem, 219
DSLAM, 221
DSSS, 364, 416, 417
 HR-DSSS, 365
DSU, 210
dual stack, 533
dual tone, 207
duplex, 7
duplicate segment, 620
DVMRP, 570
dwell time, 363
dynamic, 543, 745
dynamic database, 492
dynamic document, 745

Dynamic Domain Name System;
 see DDNS
Dynamic Host Configuration Protocol;
 see DHCP
dynamic mapping, 514
dynamic port, 595
dynamic routing, 499
dynamic routing table, 500
dynamic table, 543

E

E line, 164
EBCDIC, 884
echo request and reply messages, 528
EF PHB, 654
effective bandwidth, 634
EHF, 186
EIA, 20
electromagnetic energy, 173
electromagnetic signals, 49
electromagnetic spectrum, 173, 185
Electronic Code Block (ECB), 817
Electronic Industries Association;
 see EIA
electronic mail; *see* email
electronic serial number (ESN), 416
email, 39, 705, 715
 first stage, 716
 PGP, 860
 second stage, 716
 third stage, 717
encapsulation
 ARP, 517
 DNS, 699
encapsulation security payload;
 see ESP
encoding
 1000Base-X, 353
 100Base-FX, 348
 100Base-TX, 348
 AMI, 93
 bipolar, 93
 differential Manchester, 93
 Manchester, 92
 NRZ, 90
 NRZ-I, 90
 NRZ-L, 90
 PCM, 99
 polar, 90
 RZ, 91
 unipolar, 89
encryption, 528, 807
 DES, 814
 monoalphabetic, 810
 presentation layer, 887

 symmetric-key, 808
 Vigenere Cipher, 811
end office, 204, 205
end switch, 206
ending tag, 458
enterprise network, 15
entity authentication, 832
envelope, 134
EOT, 873
ephemeral port number,
 594, 674
error, 38, 243, 591
error control, 33, 37, 267, 268,
 591, 619
 block coding, 95
 concept, 267
 data link layer, 240, 268
 duplicate segment, 620
 HDLC, 284
 lost acknowledgment, 621
 lost segment, 620
 out-of-order segment, 621
 retransmission, 268
 timers, 620
 transport layer, 37
error correcting code, 256
error correction, 243, 256
 bit states, 256
 burst error, 260
 forward, 256
 multiple-bit, 260
 redundancy bit, 256, 257
 redundancy bit formula, 257
 retransmit data, 256
 single-bit error, 256
error detection, 243, 245
 checksum, 253
 CRC, 249
 Ethernet, 335
 Frame Relay, 442
 HDLC, 283
 parity check, 246
error-reporting message
 ICMP, 526
ESC, 874
ESP, 856
ESS, 361
ESS-transition mobility, 363
established state, 613, 614
establishing state, 296
 PPP, 304
Etag, 458
ETB, 874
Ethernet
 acknowledgment, 334
 address transmission, 336

addressing, 336
AUI, 337
baseband implementations, 339
BNC, 178
bridged, 341
collision domain, 342
CRC, 335
CSMA/CD, 316, 334, 344
data field, 335
fields, 334
frame length, 335
full-duplex switched, 343
generations, 333
hexadecimal notation, 336
length/type field, 335
MAC control sublayer, 344
MAC frame, 334
MAU, 338
maximum frame length, 336
minimum data length, 336
multicast address, 336
physical address, 335
PLS sublayer, 337
preamble, 335
SA, 335
in sample network, 485
shared capacity, 341
switched, 342
thick, 339, 340, 341
thin, 340
traditional, 334
transceiver, 338
unicast address, 336
ETX, 873
even parity, 246
excess burst size; *see* Be
explicit signal, 639
extended address, 444
extended service set; *see* ESS
extension header, 532
exterior routing, 544, 545
extremely high frequency;
    see EHF

F

fall-back, 130
fall-forward, 130
Fast Ethernet, 334, 344
auto negotiation, 345
backward compatibility, 345
encoding, 345
implementation, 346
MAC sublayer, 345
MDI, 346
MII, 346

PHY sublayer, 346
reconciliation sublayer, 345
fault identification, 10
fault isolation, 13
FCC, 187, 419
address, 919
FCS, 283
FDM, 150
analogy, 150
applications, 155
carrier, 150
cellular telphone, 155
channels, 150
concept, 150
FDMA, 321
guard bands, 150
implementation, 155
OFDM, 365
process, 151
telephone system, 153
time-domain, 151
TV, 155
when to use, 150
FDMA, 320, 321, 412, 415, 419
FECN, 444
receiver, 642
Federal Communications Committee;
    see FCC
FF, 873
FHSS, 363
Bluetooth, 375
function, 363
fiber, 156, 228
fiber link Ethernet; *see* 10Base-FL
fiber-optic cable, 174
trunk, 205
FIFO queueing, 644
leaky bucket, 647
priority queueing, 645
file transfer, 718
file transfer protocol; *see* FTP
filter
ADSL, 221
local loop, 220
filtering, 390
FIN segment, 611
final, 284
finite state diagram
client, 612
server, 613
finite state machine
example, 612
FIN-WAIT-1, 613
FIN-WAIT-2, 613
firewall, 861
packet filter, 861
proxy, 862

fixed filter style, 652
flag field, 282
flickering, 775
flooding, 550, 561
flow characteristics, 643
flow class, 644
flow control, 33, 37, 267, 268,
    591, 614
buffer, 267
concept, 267
data link layer, 240, 267
Frame Relay, 641
HDLC, 284
in IP, 526
receiver, 267
sliding window, 614
transport layer, 37
flow label, 529
flow specification, 649
flowchart
ALOHA, 313
wireless LAN, 366
FM, 133, 136, 137
bandwidth, 136, 138
spectrum, 136
station, 136
FM bandwidth, 136, 137
FM radio, 136, 155
footprint, 421
LEO, 425
forum, 19, 20
forward error correction, 256
forward explicit congestion notification;
    see FECN
forward signal, 639
forwarding port, 394
Fourier analysis, 57
FQDN, 687
DNS server, 687
FRAD, 444
fragmentation, 469, 523, 532
definition, 523
do not fragment bit, 524
flags field, 524
fragmentation offset, 524
header fields, 524
ICMP error message, 524
identification field, 524
more fragment bit, 524
offset, 525
reassembly, 524
wireless, 368
frame, 33, 157, 283, 442, 444,
    641, 643
Bluetooth, 377
HDLC, 282

frame—*Cont.*
    MPEG, 779
    TDM, 157, 158
    video, 774
frame check sequence; *see* FCS
frame length, 335
frame network, 446
Frame Relay, 435, 441
    access rate, 655
    address field, 444
    architecture, 442
    Bc, 655
    Be, 656
    BECN, 444
    bursty data, 442
    CIR, 656
    command response, 305
    command response bit, 444
    congestion, 444
    congestion avoidance, 642
    congestion control, 295, 641
    congestion situation, 643
    cost, 442
    data link layer, 443
    data rate, 441
    discard eligibility bit, 444
    DLCI, 442
    extended address, 444
    FECN, 444
    flow control, 641
    FRAD, 444
    frame fields, 443
    frame format, 443
    frame size, 442
    HDLC, 443
    layers, 441, 443
    LMI, 445
    QoS, 655
    switch table, 442
    user rate, 657
    virtual circuit network, 442
    VOFR, 445
Frame Relay assembler/disassembler;
    see FRAD
frame tag, 403
framing bit, 160
frequency, 52, 53, 101, 115, 133
    AM, 134
    ASK, 117
    bandwidth, 59
    carrier signal, 117
    cellular telephony, 409
    FM, 136
    fundamental, 57
    high, 53
    infinite, 53

    inverse, 52
    low, 53
    PM, 138
    PSK, 122
    as rate of change, 53
    receiving device, 117
    sine wave, 54
    zero, 53
frequency band
    satellite communication, 422
frequency division multiple access;
    see FDMA
Frequency Hopping Spread Spectrum;
    see FHSS
frequency masking, 775
frequency modulation; *see* FM
frequency shift, 121
    FSK, 127
frequency shift keying; *see* FSK
frequency spectrum, 58
frequency-division multiplexing;
    see FDM
frequency-domain plot, 55
from DS, 370
FSK, 115, 118, 120, 121, 122, 124
    bandwidth, 120
    baud rate, 121
    frequency, 120
    limiting factor, 120
    noise, 120
FTAM, 888
FTP, 718, 733, 740
    anonymous FTP, 724
    ASCII file, 721
    attributes of communication, 721
    binary file, 721, 722
    binary file storage example, 723
    block mode, 722
    client components, 719
    client definitions, 720
    communication, 720
    compressed mode, 722
    connections, 719, 720
    control connection, 719, 720
    data connection, 719, 720
    data structure, 722
    EBCDIC file, 721
    file printability, 721
    file retrieval, 723
    file storage, 723
    file structure, 722
    file transfer, 722
    file type, 721
    HTTP, 731
    image file, 721
    minimize delay TOS, 720

    nonprint attribute, 721
    NVT, 720
    page structure, 722
    ports, 719, 917
    record structure, 722
    sending a directory or file name, 723
    server components, 719
    stream mode, 722
    TELNET, 722
    text file, 722
    transmission mode, 722
    UNIX interface, 723
    user interface, 723
full domain name, 687
full-duplex; *see* duplex
full-duplex service, 606
Fully Qualified Domain Name;
    see FQDN
fundamental frequency, 57

G

G.71, 794
G.723.1, 794
G.723.3, 775
G.729, 775
gamma ray, 173
gap
    asynchronous transmission, 105
gatekeeper, 793
gateway, 793
gateway link (GWL), 425
general query message, 565
generator
    checksum, 253
    CRC, 250
generic domain, 691
    first level, 691
    mapping, 695
GEO satellite, 422, 423
geosynchronous orbit, 423
geosynchronous satellite, 423
GET message, 781, 782, 783
gif, 712
Gigabit Ethernet, 334, 350
    half-duplex MAC, 350
    implementation, 351
    MAC sublayer, 350
    MDI, 351
    medium access, 350
    physical layer, 350
    reconciliation sublayer, 350
    sublayers, 350
    transceiver, 351
Gigabit Medium Independent Interface;
    see GMII

global address, 436, 471
Global Positioning System
    (GPS), 424
Global System for Mobile
    Communication; *see* GSM
Globalstar, 427
GMII, 351
Go-Back-N
    acknowledgment, 275
    bidirectional, 277
    control variable, 274
    lost ACK, 276
    lost frame, 276
    normal operation, 275
    receiver sliding window, 274
    receiver window size, 277
    sender sliding window, 273
    sender window size, 277
    sequence number, 273
Go-Back-N ARQ, 273
Go-Back-N window, 638
gopher, 733
    port, 917
government regulatory agencies, 19
GPS, 424
graded-index multimode
    optical fiber, 181
grafting, 572
ground propagation, 185
group, 153, 154
groupid, 563
group-shared tree, 567, 568
GSM, 414, 775
guard band, 150
    jumbo group, 154
    telephone system, 154
guest password, 724
guided media, 173, 174

H

H.225, 794
H.245, 794
H.323, 791, 793, 795
half-duplex, 6, 7
Hamming code, 257
handoff, 411
handshake protocol, 858
handshaking
    wireless, 368
hard handoff, 411
hard state, 653
harmonic, 57, 65
hash function, 830, 831
hashing
    AH protocol, 856

HDLC, 281, 286, 289
    aborted transmission, 289
    address field, 283
    bit stuffing, 288
    control field, 283
    data transparency, 288
    definition, 281
    error detection, 283
    flag field, 282
    flow chart for bit stuffing, 289
    flow management, 283
    frame format, 282
    Frame Relay, 443
    frame types, 282
    idle transmission, 289
    I-frame, 282
    information field, 283
    line configuration, 281
    NRM, 281
    PPP, 295
    station address, 283
    synchronization pattern, 282
    transmission mode, 281
HDSL, 222
head, 742
head end, 223
header, 31
    cell, 452
    transport layer, 590
header error, 527
header translation, 534
HEC, 457
hello packet, 560
hexadecimal colon notation, 529
hexadecimal system, 877, 880
HF, 186
HFC, 224–226
hidden terminal, 366
hierarchical name space, 686
hierarchy
    name server, 689
    subnet, 488
high bit rate digital subscriber line;
    see HDSL
High Rate DSSS; *see* HR-DSSS
High-level Data Link Control;
    see HDLC
homepage, 739
hop-count, 544
hop-to-hop, 33
horn antenna, 188
host
    ARP query, 515
    routing table, 527
host file, 685
hostid, 481, 486, 489

host-specific routing, 499
host-to-host delivery, 467, 472, 593
HR-DSSS, 365
HTML, 740, 741
HTTP, 731, 733, 740, 781, 782, 783
    client, 732
    data sending example, 738
    embedded commands, 731
    entity header, 736
    FTP similarity, 731
    general header, 736
    header, 735
    information retrieval example, 737
    message format, 731
    methods, 733
    MIME-like header, 731
    port, 917
    request header, 736
    response header, 736
    response message, 734
    server, 732
    SMTP similarity, 731
    status code field, 734
    status line, 734
    status phrase field, 734
    URL, 733
    version field, 733, 734
    WWW, 731
hub, 11, 389
hybrid network, 864, 865
hybrid-fiber-coaxial network; *see* HFC
hypermedia, 739
hypertext, 739
HyperText Markup Language;
    see HTML
Hypertext Transfer Protocol; *see* HTTP

I

IAB, 920
IANA, 595
ICANN, 920
ICMP, 525
    address mask messages, 528
    destination unreachable
        message, 526
    echo request and reply messages, 528
    encapsulation, 525
    error correction, 526
    error handled, 526
    error message, 526
    error reporting, 526
    message types, 526
    parameter problem message, 527
    purpose, 526
    query message, 527

ICMP—*Cont.*
  redirect message, 527
  router solicitation and
      advertisement, 528
  source quench message, 526
  time exceeded message, 527
  timestamp messages, 528
ICMP package
  output module, 535
ICMPv6, 532
idle state, 296
IEEE, 19
  address, 919
  Project 802, 241
IEEE 802.11, 361
IEEE 802.15, 373
IESG, 920
IETF, 791, 920
IFG, 317
I-frame, 780
IGMP, 561
  checksum field, 563
  delayed response, 566
  distributing router, 564
  function, 562
  group address field, 563
  host list, 564
  host membership, 564
  joining a group, 564
  leave report, 562
  leaving a group, 564
  loyal member, 563
  maximum response type field, 563
  membership report, 562
  monitoring group membership, 565
  query for membership
      continuation, 565
  query message, 562
  query router, 567
  router list, 564
  router membership, 564
  type field, 563
ILEC, 206, 211
  POP, 206
image, 5
IMAP4, 718
IMP, 16
implicit signal, 639
IMT-DS, 420
IMT-FT, 420
IMT-MC, 420
IMT-SC, 420
IMT-TC, 420
incumbent local exchange carrier;
    see ILEC
index of refraction, 180

information, 5, 49
information field
  HDLC, 283
information frame; *see* I-frame
Infrared Data Association (IrDA), 189
infrared light, 173
infrared waves, 186, 189
infrastructure network, 362
initialization sequence number;
    see ISN
inner product, 324
input port, 899
Institute of Electrical & Electronics
    Engineers; *see* IEEE
Integrated Services; *see* IntServ
integrity, 827
  AH protocol, 856
  digital signature, 829
inter frame gap, 317
Inter Frame Space (IFS), 366
interactive audio/video, 773
interconnectivity, 19
interexchange carriers; *see* IXC
interface
  Internet model, 30
interface message processor; *see* IMP
interference, 174
Interim Standard-95; *see* IS-95
interior routing, 544, 545
inter-LATA service, 206
interleaving
  cell network, 448
  frame building, 158
  synchronous TDM, 158
  TDM, 158
International Organization for
    Standardization; *see* ISO
International Standards Organization;
    see ISO
International Telecommunications
    Union; *see* ITU
International Telecommunications
    Union–Telecommunication
    Standards Sector; *see* ITU-T
Internet, 15, 16
  application programs, 671
  communication, 671
  concept, 514
  current, 16
  datagram approach, 476
  definition, 15, 543
  DNS, 691
  draft, 20
  example, 485
  history, 15
  info required by each computer, 492

link state routing graphical
    representation, 552
  logical address, 514
  packet, 514, 544
  packet delivery, 514
  packet-switched network, 474
  physical address, 514
  standard, 20
Internet address, 477
Internet Control Message Protocol;
    see ICMP
Internet Group Management Protocol;
    see IGMP
Internet Mail Access Protocol,
    version 4; *see* IMAP4
Internet Mobile Communication, 419
Internet model, 29, 889
  application layer, 39, 667, 889
  data link layer, 239
  header, 31
  layer communication, 29
  layer interface, 30
  layers, 889
  network layer, 34
  network support layers, 31
  organization, 31
  peer-to-peer process, 30
  physical layer, 30, 32
  trailer, 31
  transport layer, 36
  user support layers, 31
Internet phone, 784
Internet Protocol; *see* IP
Internet Protocol Control Protocol;
    see IPCP
Internet Protocol, Next Generation;
    see IPng
Internet Protocol, Version 6;
    see IPv6
Internet radio, 774
Internet Service Providers; *see* ISP
Internet standards, 20
Internet TV, 774
internetwork, 303, 471, 472;
    see also Internet
  purpose, 671
Internetworking Protocol; *see* IP
interoperability, 18
interpreter, 740
inter-satellite link (ISL), 425
intracoded frame, 780
intra-LATA service, 205
IntServ, 649
  DF, 653
  problems, 653
  RSVP, 650

inverse domain, 693
  mapping, 695
  server, 693
inverse multiplexing, 165
inverse query, 693
invite message, 792
ionosphere, 185
IP, 16, 513
  analogy, 519
  best-effort delivery, 519
  connectionless, 520
  datagram, 520
  deficiencies, 525
  lack of error handling, 525
  lack of management
      communication, 525
  multiplexing, 521
  paired with TCP, 519
  reliability, 519
  TCP/IP, 519
  unreliable, 519
IP address, 477, 594
  ARP, 515
  binary notation, 478
  classful addressing, 479
  dotted-decimal notation, 478
  finding the class, 479
  hierarchy, 486
  host, 595
  hostid, 481
  netid, 481
  notation, 478
  unique, 477
  universality, 477
IP datagram
  checksum field, 522
  destination address field, 522
  destination protocol, 521
  differentiated services field, 521
  fragmentation, 523
  header length calculation, 521
  header length field, 520
  hops allowed, 521
  identification field, 521
  option error, 527
  options, 525
  protocol field, 521
  reassembly, 524
  segment encapsulation, 605
  size, 521
  source address field, 522
  time-to-live field, 521
  total length field, 521
  version field, 520
IP layer security, 853; see also IPSec
IPCP, 303

IPng, 520
IPSec, 853
  modes, 854
  protocols, 854
  SA, 854
IPv4
  address space problems, 528
  audio and video problems, 528
  deficiencies, 528
  header translation, 534
  IPSec, 857
  security problems, 528
  transition to IPv6, 533
  tunneling, 533
IPv6
  address abbreviation, 529
  address notation, 529
  Address Space, 529
  CIDR, 530
  extension header, 532
  extension of the protocol, 529
  fragmentation, 532
  header format, 529
  header translation, 534
  IPSec, 857
  new features, 528
  new options, 529
  resource allocation, 529
  runs of zero, 530
  transition from IPv4, 533
  tunneling, 533
IPv6 address, 529
  abbreviation example, 530
  anycast, 531
  categories, 530
  consecutive zeros, 530
  multicast, 531
  shorthand notation, 530
  unicast, 531
IPv6 packet, 531
IrDA port, 189
Iridium, 426
IRTF, 920
IS-95, 416, 420
  data rate sets, 418
  reverse transmission, 417
ISN, 610
ISO, 5, 19, 40, 885
  address, 919
  purpose, 885
ISOC, 920
ISP, 491, 502
  local, 502
  national, 502
  PPP, 295
  regional, 502

iterative resolution, 696
ITM-2000, 419
ITU, 19
  address, 920
ITU-T, 19
  ATM, 446
IXC, 206, 210
  POP, 207

J
Java, 740, 748
  Applet, 749
  C++, 749
  class, 749
  concept, 748
  Inheritance, 749
  object, 749
  packages, 749
  typed language, 749
jitter, 644, 785
Joint Photographic Experts Group
    (JPEG); see JPEG
JPEG, 776, 796
  compression, 779
  DCT, 777
  quantization, 778
  redundancy, 776
  spatial compression, 779
jumbo group, 153, 154

K
Kahn, Bob, 16
Karn's algorithm, 623
KDC, 838
  AS, 844
  Kerberos, 843
  ticket, 838
keepalive message, 560
keepalive timer, 624
Kepler's law, 421
Kerberos, 843, 844
Kevlar, 182
key, 808, 809
Key Distribution Center; see KDC

L
L2CAP, 378
label
  country domain, 693
  generic domain, 691
LAN, 13, 333
  bridge, 395
  connectionless, 905

LAN—*Cont.*
  data rate, 14
  Internet, 333
  interoperability, 906
  layers, 334
  logical segments, 400
  media, 14
  multicasting, 906
  physical address, 906
  purpose, 13
  size, 13
  switched, 400
  virtual connection identifier, 906
  VLAN, 400
  wireless, 361
LAN emulation; *see* LANE
LANE, 905, 906
  ATM LAN, 906
  client/server model, 906
  connectionless protocol, 905
  LEC, 907
  LECS, 907
  LES, 907
LANE client; *see* LEC
LANE configuration server;
    see LECS
LANE server; *see* LES
LAST-ACK state, 614
LATA, 205, 210, 211
  communication, 206
  POP, 207
LCP, 297, 298
leaky bucket, 646
  token bucket, 648
least-cost tree, 573
leave report, 562, 564
LEC, 205, 210, 906
LECS, 907
legacy ATM LAN, 903
length field, 458
length indicator, 457, 459
LEO satellite, 422, 425
LES, 907
LF, 186, 873
LI, 459
light, 173, 174
line bandwidth, 129
line coding, 85
  aspects, 85
  block coding, 96
line-of-sight propagation, 185, 423
  microwave antenna, 185, 188
link, 9, 150, 299
  point-to-point, 551
  stub, 552
  transient, 551
  virtual, 552

Link Control Protocol; *see* LCP
Link State Advertisement; *see* LSA
link state database, 555
  Dijkstra algorithm, 556
link state routing, 550
  BGP, 558
  graphical representation, 552
  routing table, 556
LISTEN state, 614
LLC, 241, 334
LMI, 445
load, 636
Local Access Transport Area; *see* LATA
local area network; *see* LAN
local call service, 208
local central office, 205
local exchange carrier; *see* LEC
local Internet service provider;
    see local ISP
local ISP, 18
local loop, 204, 205
  ADSL, 219
  bandwidth, 220
  connections, 207
  filter, 220
  signal, 208
  switching office, 205
Local Management Information; *see* LMI
locator, 733
logical address, 514
logical link control; *see* LLC
logical star backbone, 398
long-distance company, 206
loop prevention, 559
lossy compression, 778
lost acknowledgment, 621
lost frame, 268
lost segment, 620
low-Earth orbit satellite, 425
low-pass, 66
LRC
  calculation, 248–249
LSA, 553
  external link, 555
  link state database, 555
  network link, 554
  router link, 554
  summary link to AS boundary
    router, 554
  summary link to network, 554

M

MA, 291, 311, 312
MAC, 241, 334
  specific protocols, 241

MAC address, 240, 594
MAC sublayer, 241, 334
  Fast Ethernet, 344
  function, 334
  Gigabit Ethernet, 350
  wireless LAN, 365
mail access protocol, 717
mail exchanger, 706
mailbox, 706
MAN, 14
  LANs, 14
  ownership, 14
  use of, 14
management frame, 369
Manchester encoding, 90,
  92, 337
man-in-the-middle attack,
  837, 838
mapping
  address to name, 695
  dynamic, 514
  host file, 685
  name to address, 695
  static, 514
marker, 654
markup language, 742
mask, 488
  classless addressing, 491
master group, 153, 154
master station, 373
MAU, 338
maximum burst size, 634
maximum transmission unit, 523
MBONE, 569
MD5, 831
MDI, 339, 346
  Gigabit Ethernet, 351
media
  guided, 174
  unguided, 184
media player, 781
medium, 3, 4
  band-limited, 63
  wide bandwidth, 63
medium access, 311
  Gigabit Ethernet, 350
  methods, 311
medium access control; *see* MAC
medium attachment unit;
    see MAU
medium dependent interface;
    see MDI
Medium Independent Interface;
    see MII
medium-earth orbit satellite, 424
membership report, 562, 564

MEO satellite, 422, 424
mesh, 10
mesh topology, 197
message, 4
message switching, 197
meta file, 782
metric, 544, 549
  OSPF, 549
  TOS, 544
  type of service, 549
metropolitan area network;
    see MAN
MF, 186
microswitch, 901
microwaves, 186, 188
  applications, 189
  band, 188
  frequencies, 188
  horn antenna, 188
  IrDA port, 190
  parabolic dish antenna, 188
  propagation, 188
  unidirectional, 188
  unidirectional antenna, 188
MID, 458
MII, 346
  AUI, 346
  Fast Ethernet, 346
  features, 346
  receive data, 346
MIME
  7bit encoding, 712
  8bit encoding, 712
  alternative multipart subtype, 710
  application data type, 712
  audio content type, 712
  audio data type, 712
  base64 encoding, 712
  basic audio subtype, 712
  binary encoding, 712
  concept, 708
  content subtype, 710
  content-description header, 714
  content-Id header, 714
  content-transfer-encoding
      header, 712
  content-type header, 710
  data boundary, 710
  digest multipart subtype, 710
  extended header, 709
  extension to SMTP, 708
  external-body message subtype, 711
  external-body subtype, 711
  gif, 712
  headers, 709
  id parameter, 711

image data type, 712
jpeg, 712
message data type, 711
message fragments, 711
message/rfc822, 711
mixed multipart subtype, 710
mpeg, 712
multipart data type, 710
number parameter, 711
NVT ASCII, 708
octet-stream application
    subtype, 712
parallel multipart subtype, 710
partial message subtype, 711
postscript application
    subtype, 712
quoted-printable encoding, 713
rfc822 message subtype, 711
text data type, 710
total parameter, 711
types of data, 710
version header, 710
video data type, 712
minimize delay, 720
minislot, 228
mixed architecture LAN, 905
mixer, 788
MLT-3, 94, 348
mobile station (MS), 409
mobile switching center; *see* MSC
modem, 128, 130, 131
  in communications link, 129
  data rate limitation, 131, 219
  function, 128
  standards, 130
  traditional, 131
  V.32, 130
  V.32bis, 130, 211, 232
  V.33, 211, 232
  V.34, 131
  V.92, 132
modulating signal, 117
modulation, 117
  AM, 134
  analog to analog, 133
  Bluetooth, 375
  digital to analog, 115
  DSSS, 364
  FHSS, 364
  FM, 136
  HR-DSSS, 365
  OFDM, 365
  PM, 138
  trellis coding, 130
modulator
  function, 128

monoalphabetic substitution, 810
more fragment bit, 524
MOSPF, 572
  least-cost tree, 572
  link state packet, 574
Motion Picture Experts Group;
    see MPEG
MP3, 775
  compression, 776
  data rates, 776
MPEG, 712, 776, 779
  B-frame, 780
  frame types, 779
  I-frame, 780
  P-frame, 780
  temporal compression, 779
  versions, 781
MPEG audio layer 3, 775
MSC, 409
  handoff, 411
  receiving a signal, 411
  transmission of signal, 411
MTA, 714
MT-RJ, 183
MTU, 523
  fragmentation, 532
  maximum length, 523
  minimum size, 532
multicast address, 336, 531
  IPv6, 531
multicast backbone; *see* MBONE
multicast communication, 481
Multicast Open Shortest Path First;
    see MOSPF
multicast router, 563
  groupid, 563
  purpose, 565
multicasting
  applications, 576
  DVMRP, 570
  group-shared tree, 568
  LAN, 906
  MOSPF, 572
  pruning, 572
  real-time, 788
  router interface, 561
  RPB, 571
  RSVP, 650
  source-based tree, 567
  tunneling, 568
  UDP, 602
multidrop, 9
multimode, 180
multiple access; *see* MA
multiple-bit error, 244
multiple-slave communication, 376

multiplexer, 149, 448
  CDMA, 322
multiplexing, 149, 597
  definition, 149
  many to one/one to many, 149
  transport layer, 597
multiplexing identification, 458
multiplicative decrease, 640, 641
multipoint, 8, 9, 11
Multipurpose Internet Mail Extensions;
    see MIME
multistage, 901
multistage switch, 199, 204
  Banyan, 901
  blocking, 201
  compared to crossbar, 199
  crosspoints needed, 201
  design considerations, 199
  first-stage, 200
  intermediate switch, 200
  multiple paths, 200
  space-time-time-space (STTS), 204
  third-stage, 200
  time-space-space-time (TSST), 204
  time-space-time (TST), 204
music
  sampling rate, 774
MUX; *see* multiplexer

N

n^2 problem, 835
Nagle's algorithm, 618
NAK, 278, 874
  in poll, 319
name server
  hierarchy, 689
name space, 685, 689
name-address resolution, 694
NAP, 17
NAT, 494
National Service Provider; *see* NSP
NAV, 368
NCP, 16, 302
Needham-Schroeder, 839
negative acknowledgment; *see* NAK
neighborhood concept
  path vector routing, 558
netid, 481, 486
  masking, 489
network, 8, 659
  categories, 13
  criteria, 8
  definition, 15
  hybrid, 865

performance, 8
  private, 864
  reliability, 8
network access point; *see* NAP
network address, 482, 484
Network Address Translation;
    see NAT
network capacity, 637
Network Control Protocol; *see* NCP
network layer, 34, 467, 471, 472
  address, 468
  at destination, 474
  duties, 468
  logical addressing, 34
  multiple addresses, 468
  packet, 34
  routing, 35, 469
  at source, 472
network layer reliability, 600
network interface card; *see* NIC
network performance, 636
network security, 8
network service, 476
network support layers, 31
network to network interfaces;
    see NNI
networking, 304
networking state, 297
  PPP, 304
network-specific routing, 498
next-hop routing, 497
nibble, 345
NIC, 336
  as device id, 515
  Ethernet, 336
NNI, 449, 451
node, 8
  in switching, 197
node-to-node delivery, 83, 593
noise, 71
  ASK, 118
  coaxial cable, 177
  crosstalk, 71
  digital service, 209
  effect on amplitude, 118
  impulse, 71
  PSK, 122
  QAM, 125, 126
  thermal, 71
noiseless channel, 67
noisy channel, 68
nonce, 833
  Needham-Schroeder, 839
non-persistent connection, 738
non-repudiation, 827
  digital signature, 829, 830

normal response mode; *see* NRM
notification message, 560
no-transition mobility, 363
NRM, 281
NRZ, 90, 353
  types, 90
NRZ-I, 90, 91
NRZ-L, 90, 91
NSP, 17
NUL, 873
null suffix, 688
number system, 877, 881
Nyquist
  bit rate, 67
  example, 102
  noiseless channel, 67
Nyquist theorem, 101, 774
  frequency, 101

O

octal system, 877, 879
octet, 478
odd parity, 247
OFDM, 365
omnidirectional antenna, 187
on-demand audio/video, 773
one's complement arithmetic, 253
one-slot frame, 377
one-time session key, 839
on-off-keying; *see* OOK
OOK, 118
open message, 560
open shortest path first; *see* OSPF
open system, 885
Open Systems Interconnection;
    see OSI
Open Systems Interconnection model;
    see OSI model
open-loop congestion control, 638
operation mode, 817
optical fiber, 179
  advantages, 184
  applications, 184
  ATM, 446
  attenuation, 184
  bandwidth, 184
  bandwidth capabilities, 228
  cable TV, 184
  cladding, 182
  composition, 182
  connectors, 182
  core, 182
  corrosive materials, 184
  cost, 184
  density, 181

disadvantages, 184
electromagnetic noise, 184
graded-index multimode, 180
HFC, 224
installation/maintenance, 184
Kevlar, 182
LAN, 184
light, 179
light weight, 184
multimode, 180
outer jacket, 182
performance, 183
propagation modes, 180
reflection, 180
single-mode, 180, 181
sizes, 182
standardization, 228
step-index multimode, 180
tapping, 184
unidirectional propagation, 184
WDM, 156
options, 299
function, 523
options message, 792
orbit, 420
Orthogonal Frequency Division
Multiplexing; *see* OFDM
orthogonal sequence, 323
OSI, 885
interoperability, 29
QAM, 126
OSI model, 31, 40, 885, 889
application layer, 888
data link layer, 32
Internet model, 889
layers, 40, 885
organization of the
layers, 31
physical layer, 30
presentation layer, 40, 886
session layer, 40, 886
upper layers, 807
OSPF, 545, 548
hello packet, 560
link state routing, 550
link types, 550
metric, 549
network as a link, 550
path vector routing, 558
point-to-point link, 551
stub link, 552
transient link, 551
virtual link, 552
Otway-Rees protocol, 828
out-of-order segment, 621
output port, 899

P

packet, 474, 476, 544
control information, 474
format, 474
length, 474
packet payload type, 457
packet switching, 197, 435
approaches, 475
datagram approach, 476
IP, 520
virtual circuit approach, 475
packet-filter firewall, 861
packetizing
data link layer, 240
transport layer, 590
packet-switching, 474
padding
AH protocol, 856
Ethernet, 336
page, 739
paging, 411, 417
PAM, 99
PAP, 300
parabolic dish antenna, 188
parallel transmission, 103, 104, 244
parameter problem message, 527
parent server, 678
parity bit, 246
in Hamming code, 258
parity check, 246
even number of errors, 248
odd number of errors, 248
simple, 246
two-dimensional, 248
parked state, 373
partial sum, 895
Partially Qualified Domain Name;
see PQDN
passive open, 673
password, 300, 301
Password Authentication Protocol;
see PAP
path attributes, 559
AS_PATH, 560
NEXT-HOP, 560
non-transitive, 560
origin, 559
transitive, 560
Path message, 651
Path MTU Discovery technique, 532
path vector routing, 557–559
P-Box, 813
PCM, 99, 101
binary encoding, 100
bit rate, 103

bits per sample, 102
line coding, 100
PAM, 99, 100
processes, 100
quantization, 100
PCS, 419
peak amplitude, 51
peak data rate, 634
peer-to-peer process, 30
per hop behavior; *see* PHB
perceptual encoding, 775
performance, 8, 253
checksum, 255
period, 50, 52, 421
inverse, 52
units, 52
periodic signal, 50, 51
permanent virtual circuit; *see* PVC
persistence strategy, 314
1-persistent, 315
non-persistent approach, 315
persistent approach, 315
persistence timer, 623
persistent connection, 738
personal area network (PAN), 373
Personal Communications System
(PCS), 419
P/F bit, 284
P-frame, 780
PGP, 860
phase, 54, 115, 133, 138
AM, 134
and bit value, 122
ASK, 117
definition, 54
FM, 136
FSK, 120
PM, 138
PSK, 122
QAM, 125
sine wave, 54
phase modulation; *see* PM
phase shift, 54
phase shift keying; *see* PSK
PHB, 654
PHY sublayer, 346
physical, 443
physical address, 33, 240, 514
ARP, 515
physical layer, 32, 45
ATM, 453
bit representation, 32
bit synchronization, 32
data rate, 32
Ethernet, 337
Fast Ethernet, 345

physical layer—*Cont.*
  Frame Relay, 443
  function, 32
  Gigabit Ethernet, 350
  Internet model, 30
  purpose, 32
  signals, 49
  tasks, 45
  transmission media, 173
physical layer processor, 900
piconet, 373
piggybacking, 272, 284, 287
pilot channel, 417
PIM, 576
PIM-DM, 576
PIM-SM, 576
pipelining, 281
pixel, 5, 775, 779
plaintext, 807
  RSA, 821
PLAY message, 783
playback attack, 833
playback buffer, 787
PLS sublayer, 337
  reconciliation sublayer, 345
PM, 133, 138
point of presence; *see* POP
pointer query, 693
point-to-point, 8, 10
  definition, 9
  mesh, 10
  sample network, 485
point-to-point access, 295
point-to-point connection, 197 ·
point-to-point link, 551
point-to-point protocol; *see* PPP
polar encoding, 88, 90, 115
  types, 90
polarity, 89
policy routing, 559
poll, 284, 318
polling, 284, 318
polyalphabetic substitution, 811
polynomial, 251, 252
  binary representation, 251
  CRC, 251, 261
  properties, 251
POP, 207
POP3, 717, 718
port
  ephemeral, 595
  registered, 595
  well-known, 595
port address, 37, 38
port number, 594
  ephemeral, 594

process, 595
  TCP, 603
  UDP, 601
  well-known, 595
Post Office Protocol, version 3;
  see POP3
POTS, 204
power, 173
  satellite, 422
p-persistent, 315
PPP, 295, 302
  address field, 296
  authenticating state, 297
  authentication, 300
  control field, 296
  data field, 296
  establishing state, 296
  FCS, 296
  flag field, 295
  frame, 295
  HDLC, 295
  idle state, 296
  ISP, 295
  link termination packet, 299
  loopback test, 299
  NCP, 302
  networking state, 297
  option negotiation, 299
  protocol field, 296
  stack, 297
  terminating state, 297
  transition states, 296
PQDN, 687
  suffix, 688
preamble, 335
predicted frame, 780
predictive encoding, 775
presentation layer, 40, 886
  compression, 888
  encryption, 887
  responsibilities, 886
  translation, 886
Pretty Good Privacy; *see* PGP
primary server, 690
primary station, 318
priority queueing, 645
privacy, 827, 828
  AH protocol, 856
private address
  NAT, 495
private key, 820, 828, 841
  PGP, 860
  RSA, 821
private network, 863, 864
probe, 623
process, 674

process-to-process communication
  UDP, 601
process-to-process delivery,
  36, 593
product block, 814
program
  process, 674
propagation delay
  CSMA, 314
  LEO, 425
propagation speed, 72
  wavelength, 74
propagation time, 72, 73
protocol, 4, 18, 30
protocol field
  AH protocol, 856
  CHAP, 301
  PAP packet, 300
Protocol Independent Multicast;
  see PIM
Protocol Independent Multicast, Dense
  Mode; *see* PIM-DM
Protocol Independent Multicast, Sparse
  Mode; *see* PIM-SM
proxy firewall, 862
proxy server, 738
pruning, 572
PSK, 115, 122, 123, 124, 129
  ASK, 122, 124, 125
  bandwidth, 124
  bandwidth example, 124, 125
  binary, 122
  bit rate, 124
  FSK, 122
  limitations, 125
  modem, 129
psychoacoustics, 775
public key, 820, 828, 835, 841
  RSA, 821
public key infrastructure (PKI), 843
public-key cryptography, 808,
  820, 841
  disadvantage, 820
  key verification, 820
  RSA algorithm, 821
pull protocol, 717
pulse amplitude modulation;
  see PAM
pulse code modulation; *see* PCM
pulse rate, 86
pure ATM LAN, 903
push operation, 624
push protocol, 717
PVC, 437, 452
  ATM, 452
  establishment, 452

Q

Q.931, 794
QAM, 116, 125, 126, 220
  ASK, 126
  bandwidth, 126
  selection error, 130
  trellis coding, 130
  variations, 125
QoS, 379, 643
  admission control, 649
  ATM, 657
  Bluetooth, 379
  DF, 653
  Frame Relay, 655
  how to improve, 644
  IntServ, 649
  leaky bucket, 646
  resource reservation, 649
  switched network, 655
  traffic shaping, 646
Q-PSK, 123
quadrature amplitude modulation;
  see QAM
quality of service, 446;
  see also QoS
quantization, 778
  PCM, 99
quantization noise
  modem, 131
query
  DNS, 697
query message, 527, 562
  ICMP, 526
  response time, 565
  special, 565
query router, 566, 567
queue, 636

R

radio government; *see* RG
radio layer, 375
radio wave, 173, 186
  AM radio, 187
  applications, 188
  band, 187
  frequencies, 186
  ionospheric propagation, 185
  omnidirectional, 187
  penetration, 187
RAM, 202
random access, 311
random access memory;
  see RAM
RARP, 514

raw socket, 677
RBOC, 210
RCH, 224
realm, 846
real-time
  playback buffer, 787
  threshold, 787
real-time audio, 528
real-time audio/video, 785
real-time data, 785
real-time interactive audio/video, 784
Real-Time Streaming Protocol
  (RTSP), 783
real-time traffic
  error control, 788
  mixer, 788
  multicasting, 788
  RTP, 789
  sequence number, 787
  TCP, 788
  timestamp, 786
  translation, 788
  translator, 788
  UDP, 789
real-time transmission, 4
Real-time Transport Control Protocol;
  see RTCP
Real-time Transport Protocol (RTP), 603;
  see also RTP
receive not ready; *see* RNR
receiver, 4
  flow control, 241, 267
  reservation, 651
receiver window
  TCP, 615
reconciliation sublayer, 345, 350
  PLS sublayer, 345
recursive resolution, 695
redirect message, 527
redundancy, 245, 776
  checksum, 253
  concept, 245
  CRC, 249
  send data twice, 245
  trellis coding, 130
redundancy bit, 257
redundancy check, 245, 246
reflection, 180
reflection attack, 834
refraction, 179
Regional Bell Operating System;
  see RBOC
regional cable head, 224
Regional Internet Service Providers or
  regional ISP; *see* regional ISP
regional ISP, 18

regional office, 204
register message, 792
registered port, 595
registrar server, 793
Registration/Administration/Status
  (RAS), 794
regulatory agencies, 20
REJ, 285
reject; *see* REJ
reliability, 8, 643
reliable service, 606
reliable transport layer service, 600
remote bridge, 398
rendezvous router, 574
repeater, 387
  amplifier, 388
  HDSL, 222
  hub, 389
  location, 389
  ring, 12
  segment, 388
replay attack, 833
  KDC, 839
Request for Comment; *see* RFC
Request to Send (RTS), 366
reservation, 318, 649
  refreshing, 653
reservation frame, 318
reserved address, 481
resolution, 775
  iterative, 696
  name to address, 694
  recursive, 695
resolver, 694
resource reservation, 649
Resource Reservation Protocol;
  see RSVP
response
  DNS, 697
Resv message, 651
retransmission, 640
retransmission policy, 638
retransmission time, 622
retransmission timer, 622
return to zero; *see* RZ
reuse factor, 410
  GSM, 416
  IS-95, 418
Reverse Address Resolution Protocol;
  see RARP
reverse path broadcasting; *see* RPB
reverse path forwarding; *see* RPF
reverse path multicasting; *see* RPM
RFC, 20, 915
  list, 915
  maturity levels, 20

RG, 178
  coaxial cable, 178
  ratings, 178
ring, 10, 12
  advantages, 13
  definition, 12
  disadvantages, 13
  dual, 13
  repeater, 12
RIP, 545, 546, 602
  encapsulation, 548
  path vector routing, 558
  port, 917
  updating algorithm, 546
RJ45, 176
RNR, 285
roaming, 411
root port, 393
root server, 690
rotary dialing, 208
round trip time; see RTT
router, 35, 543
  address, 528
  area border, 549
  autonomous system boundary, 548
  backbone, 549
  components, 899
  designated parent, 571
  fragmentation, 469, 523
  input port, 899
  multicast, 563
  output port, 900
  structure, 899
  subnet, 488
  switching fabric, 901
router solicitation and advertisement
      message, 528
routing
  default, 499
  distance vector, 546
  distance vector vs. link state, 550
  dynamic, 499
  host specific, 499
  interior and exterior, 544
  link state, 550
  network layer, 35
  network specific, 498
  next hop, 497
  static, 499
  subnet, 488
routing information protocol; see RIP
routing processor, 899, 900
routing protocol, 469, 543
routing table, 497, 543, 556
  dynamic, 500, 543
  entries, 546

intialization, 548
  link state routing, 550
  next hop field, 548
  shortest path tree, 556
  static, 500, 543
  updating of, 527, 548
routing techniques, 497
RPB, 571
RPC, 917
RPF, 570
RPM, 572
RR, 285
RSA encryption, 821, 822
Rspec, 649
RSVP, 649, 650
  IntServ, 650
  message, 651
  reservation merging, 652
  reservation style, 652
RTCP, 789
RTP, 789
RTT, 622
  as function of previous RTTs, 623
  calculation, 622
  Karn's algorithm, 623
run-length encoding, 722
RZ, 90, 91, 92

S

SA, 335, 668
sample and hold, 99
sampling, 98, 99
  PAM, 99
sampling rate, 101, 774
  Nyquist theorem, 101
  PAM, 101
  PCM, 101
SAR, 456
satellite, 420
  frequency band, 423
  geosynchronous, 423
  trunk, 205
satellite communication, 420
satellite network, 420
satellite orbit, 420
satellite period, 421
S-Box, 814
scalability, 653
scatternet, 373
scheduling, 644
  FIFO queue, 645
  priority queue, 645
  weighted fair queueing, 645
SCO, 377
SDSL, 222

SEAL, 459
secondary
  in polling, 319
secondary server, 690
secondary station, 318
secret key, 838
  PGP, 860
secret-key encryption
  key, 809
Secure Sockets Layer (SSL), 858
security, 8
  application layer, 853
  authentication, 829
  integrity, 829
  network layer, 853
  transport layer, 853
Security Association (SA), 854
security parameter index (SPI), 854;
      see also SPI
segment, 37, 342, 388, 605, 608
  format, 608
  header fields, 608
  size, 608
  TCP, 608
segment type, 458
segmentation
  L2CAP, 379
segmentation and reassembly; see SAR
select
  addressing, 318
  frame, 318
  polling, 318
selecting, 318
Selective Reject; see SREJ
Selective Repeat, 638
  bidirectional, 280
  operation, 278
  receiver window size, 278
  sender window size, 278
  window size, 279
Selective Repeat ARQ, 273
self-synchronization, 88
semantics, 18
sender, 4, 642
  flow control, 267
sender buffer
  TCP, 615
sender window, 616
  closing, 617
  expansion, 617
  shrinking, 617
  sliding, 616
  TCP, 616
sequence number, 273, 456, 458, 598,
      599, 606, 607, 787
sequence number protection, 456

serial transmission, 103, 104
  advantage, 104
  burst error, 244
  classes, 103
  conversion device, 104
  types, 104
server, 594, 672, 673
  accept call, 679
  bind call, 678
  buffer, 678
  clients, 672
  close accepting socket, 679
  closing the communicating
      socket, 679
  concurrent, 673
  connectionless iterative, 673, 677
  connection-oriented concurrent,
      674, 678
  definition, 673
  ephemeral port, 674
  iterative, 673
  listen call, 678
  opening a socket, 677
  passive open, 673
  primary, 690
  processing data, 679
  queue, 677
  read call, 679
  receive call, 678
  repeat call, 679
  repeated steps, 679
  root, 690
  secondary, 690
  TCP, 674, 678
  transport layer protocol, 673
  UDP, 673
  well-known port, 674
  write call, 679
server program, 595
  activity, 672
  port number, 595
server socket interface, 677
service class, 650, 657
  controlled-load, 650
  guaranteed, 650
service-type limitation, 653
Session Initiation Protocol; see SIP
session key, 835, 838
  Diffie-Hellman, 835
  TGS, 844
session layer, 40, 886
setup message, 783
setup request, 439
SFD, 335
S-frame, 282
SHA-1, 831

Shannon capacity, 68, 69
Shannon formula, 131
shaper, 655
shared explicit style, 653
shared-group tree
  CBT, 575
sheath, 177
SHF, 186
shielded twisted-pair, 175
shift keying, 117
Short Inter Frame Space (SIFS), 366
shortest path tree, 556
sign and magnitude, 100
signal
  amplitude, 51
  analog, 50
  analog and digital, 49
  aperiodic, 50
  composite analog, 50
  degradation, 12
  nonperiodic, 50
  periodic, 50
  types, 49, 66, 67, 69, 72, 74, 75
signal bandwidth, 128
signal fading, 366
signal level, 86
signal to noise ratio; see SNR
signal unit, 116
signals, 49
silly window syndrome, 618
  cause, 618
  Clark's solution, 619
  created by receiver, 619
  created by sender, 618
  delayed acknowledgment, 619
  Nagle's algorithm, 618, 619
simple and efficient adaptation layer;
      see SEAL
simple parity check, 246
  performance, 248
simplex, 6
sine wave, 51
  characteristics, 54, 115
  description, 51
  frequency, 52
  period, 52
single-bit error, 243, 244
single-mode, 181
  density, 181
  distortion, 182
  optical fiber, 181
single-slave communication, 375
single-stage switch
  blocking, 201
  crosspoints needed, 201
SIP, 791

sky propagation, 185
slash notation, 491
slave station, 373
sliding window, 273, 614
  buffer, 614
  silly window syndrome, 618
slow start, 640, 738
SMTP
  address system, 706
  client, 716
  client commands, 715
  commands, 714, 715
  connection establishment, 715
  connection termination, 715
  domain name, 706
  first stage, 716
  HTTP, 731
  limitations, 708
  local part of address, 706
  Mail Exchangers, 706
  mail transfer phases, 715
  message transfer, 715
  port, 917
  responses, 714, 715
  second stage, 716
  server, 716
  user mail box, 706
SNMP
  port, 917
SNR, 68
socket
  bind call, 677
  closing, 678
  datagram, 676
  definition, 675
  family field, 675
  Internet Socket Address
      Structure, 675
  local socket address field, 676
  protocol field, 675
  raw, 677
  receiving, 678
  remote socket address field, 676
  repeated steps, 678
  send call, 678
  sending, 678
  stream, 676
  type field, 675, 676
socket address, 596
  IP header, 597
  pair, 596
  port number, 597
socket interface
  client, 680
  connectionless iterative server, 677
  connection-oriented concurrent
      server, 678

soft handoff, 411
    IS-95, 418
soft state, 653
SOH, 873
SONET, 453
    ATM, 453
    video, 775
source quench message, 526
source quench packet, 639
source routing bridge, 395
source-based tree, 567
source-to-destination delivery, 34
SP, 874
space, 203
space-division switch, 199
space-division switching, 203
spanning tree algorithm, 392
spatial compression, 779
special query message, 565
spectrum, 58, 61, 62, 136
    AM, 134
    ASK, 118
    FM, 136
SPI, 856
splitter, 224
square wave, 58
SREJ, 285
ST, 458
standard, 18
    categories, 19
    creation committees, 19
    definition, 18
    Internet, 20
    need for, 18
    ratification, 20
standards organizations, 19
star, 10, 11
star topology, 197
start bit
    asynchronous transmission, 105
start frame delimiter; *see* SFD
state transition diagram, 612
static database, 492
static documents, 740
static mapping, 514
static routing, 499
static routing table, 500
static table, 543
step-index multimode, 180
stop bit
    asynchronous transmission, 105
Stop-and-Wait ARQ, 268, 270, 271
    ACK numbering, 268
    bidirectional, 272
    delayed acknowledgment, 271
    lost acknowledgment, 270

lost frame, 269
    normal transmission, 269
    piggybacking, 272
    sender, 268
    timer, 269
STP, 175
straight tip connector (ST), 182
stream delivery, 604
stream of bits, 45
stream socket, 676
streaming, 781
streaming live audio/video, 773, 784
streaming server, 782
streaming stored audio/video, 773
    streaming server, 782
    streaming server and RTSP, 783
    web server, 781
    web server and meta file, 782
streaming stored audio/visual, 781
stub link, 552
STX, 873
subnet, 487, 488
    classless addressing, 492
    hostid, 488
    prefix, 492
    router, 488
subnet mask, 489, 490
subnetting, 486
Subscriber Channel Connector
    (SC), 182
substitution, 96
    monoalphabetic, 810
substitution cipher, 809
suffix, 688
supergroup, 153, 154
supernet, 490
supernetting, 490
supervisory frame; *see* S-frame
SVC, 437, 452
    ATM, 452
switch, 35, 197, 343, 901
    Banyan, 901
    Batcher-Banyan, 902
    bridge, 343
    crossbar, 199, 901
    logical star backbone, 398
    table, 437
    telephone network, 205
    telephone system, 208
    time-space-time example, 204
    two-layer, 396
switched backbone, 398
switched Ethernet, 342
Switched Multi-Megabit Data Services
    (SMDS), 15
switched virtual circuit; *see* SVC

switched/56, 209
    bandwidth on demand, 210
    data rate, 209
    modem, 210
    subscriber, 209
    uses, 210
switching, 197
    circuit, 197
    folded switch, 198
    methods, 197
    multistage, 199
    need for, 197
    nodes, 197
    space- vs. time-division, 203
    space-division, 199
    TDM bus, 203
switching fabric, 899, 900
switching office, 204, 205
symmetric digital subscriber line;
        see SDSL
symmetric key, 832, 835, 838
    Diffie-Hellman, 837
symmetric key distribution, 835
    key, 809
symmetric-key cryptography, 807, 808
SYN segment, 610, 874
synchronization, 115
    asynchronous transmission, 105
    block coding, 95
    byte level, 105
    clock, 88
    differential Manchester, 93
    example, 88
    IS-95, 416
    Manchester, 92
    RZ, 91, 92
    unipolar encoding, 89
synchronization points, 886
synchronous transmission, 103, 106, 107
    advantage, 107
    grouping of bits, 106
    receiver function, 106
    synchronization, 107
SYN-RCVD state, 614
SYN-SENT state, 612
syntax, 18

T

T-1 line, 163
    access rate, 655
    capacity, 164
    data rate, 164, 655
    frame, 163
    overhead, 163
    synchronization bit, 163

table
    virtual circuit switch, 437
table lookup, 900
tag, 742
    attributes, 742
    common, 743
    format, 742
tandem office, 204
tandem switch, 206
    POP, 207
tap, 11, 224
TCP, 16, 519, 593, 600, 603
    acknowledgment number, 607
    buffer, 604, 624
    circular buffer, 605
    client program, 913
    client-server model, 673
    connection-oriented, 609
    connection-oriented service, 606
    DNS, 699
    duplicate segment, 620
    error control, 619
    flow control, 614
    full-duplex mode, 610
    and IP, 519
    out of order segment, 621
    persistence timer, 623
    port number, 603
    ports, 917
    push bit, 625
    push operation, 624
    pushing data, 624
    real-time traffic, 788
    reliable service, 606
    resetting, 611
    segment, 605, 608
    segmentation, 722
    sequence number, 607
    server program, 912
    SIP, 791
    sliding window, 614
    split, 16
    stream delivery, 604
    streaming live audio/video, 784
    stream-oriented protocol, 625
    timers, 621
    urgent data, 625
TCP header
TCP/IP
    application layer, 889
    datagram format, 520
    Version 5, 41
TDD, 375
TDD-TDMA, 375
TDM, 150, 157
    applications, 165

    bit padding, 161
    data rate, 157
    frame, 157
    framing bit, 160
    synchronization, 160
    TDMA, 321
    time slot, 157
TDM bus, 203
TDMA, 320, 321, 416, 419
    Bluetooth, 375
TEARDOWN message, 783
teardown phase, 440
telecommunication, 3
Telecommunications Act of 1996,
        205, 210
Teledesic, 427
telephone
    FDM, 151
telephone line, 128
    bandwidth, 128
    capacity, 68
telephone network, 204
    analog leased service, 209
    analog services, 208
    analog switched service, 208
    bandwidth, 208
    components, 204
    digital service, 209
    switch, 208
telephone system
    analog switched service, 153
    hierarchy, 154
    multiplexing, 153
telephone system categories, 153
TELNET, 733, 740
    port, 917
temporal compression, 779
temporal masking, 776
terminating state, 297, 304
TFTP
    port, 917
TGS, 843
    AS, 844
    Kerberos, 844
thick Ethernet; *see* 10Base5
Thicknet; *see* 10Base5
thin Ethernet; *see* 10Base2
three-way handshake, 610
throughput, 72, 636, 637, 638
ticket, 838
ticket-granting server; *see* TGS
Time Division Duplexing,
        see TDD
time division multiple access;
        see TDMA
time exceeded message, 527

time slot
    switching, 203
time-division multiplexing;
        see TDM
time-division switch, 199, 201
time-division switching
    pro and con, 203
    space-division, 203
time-domain plot, 54
time-out, 620
    dynamic retransmission, 622
timer
    Go-Back-N, 274
    keepalive, 624
    persistence, 623
    retransmission, 622
    time-waited, 624
timers, 621
time-slot interchange; *see* TSI
timestamp, 786
    sender report, 790
timestamp messages
    clock synchronization, 528
    round-trip time, 528
time-to-live
    caching, 696
time-wait state, 613
time-waited timer
    purpose, 624
timing, 18
T-line, 163
    analog transmission, 163
    bursty data, 441
    DS relationship, 163
    E-line, 164
    frame size, 163
    multiplexing, 163
    PCM, 100
TLS, 858
to DS, 370
token, 319
token bucket, 646, 648
    leaky bucket, 648
    meter, 654
token passing, 319
Token Ring
    in sample network, 485
toll call service, 209
toll free call, 206
topology, 9
touch-tone dialing, 208
TP, 449
traffic
    frame size, 447
traffic control
    Frame Relay, 655

traffic control—*Cont.*
   PVC, 655
   SVC, 655
traffic descriptor, 633
traffic profile, 634
traffic shaping, 646
trailer, 31, 33
transceiver, 338
   1000Base-T, 353
   1000Base-X, 352
   100Base-FX, 348
   100Base-T4, 349
   100Base-TX, 347
   Fast Ethernet, 346
   Gigabit Ethernet, 351
transient link, 551, 552
transition, 533
   IPv4 to IPv6, 533
   strategies, 533
transition state diagram, 296
transition strategy
   dual stack, 533
   header translation, 534
   tunneling, 533
translation, 788
   presentation layer, 886
translator, 788
transmission, 49, 449
   AMPS, 412
   D-AMPS, 413
   IS-95, 416
   serial, 103
Transmission Control Protocol; *see* TCP
transmission impairment, 69
transmission medium, 45, 49, 173;
    see also medium
   categories, 173
   composite signal, 58
   location, 173
   physical layer, 45
transmission mode, 103
transmission paths; *see* TP
transmission rate, 32
transport layer, 36
   addressing, 591
   application layer, 589
   connection control, 37, 590
   connection establishment, 591
   connection-oriented
     transmission, 590, 591
   demultiplexing, 597
   duties, 590
   error control, 37, 591
   flow control, 37, 591
   functions, 589
   header, 590

   as liaison, 589
   long message, 590
   multiplexing, 597
   ordering of datagrams, 476
   packetizing, 590
   port addressing, 37
   real-time traffic, 788
   reassembly, 37
   responsibilities, 36
   security, 853
   segmentation, 37
transport layer security; *see* TLS
transport mode, 854
transposition cipher, 812
tree
   least-cost, 573
trellis-coding, 130
triangulation, 424
tribit, 123, 125
triple DES, 817
trunk, 204, 205
TSI, 201, 203
Tspec, 649
tunnel mode, 854
tunneling, 533, 568
   VPN, 867
TV, 155
twisted pair, 174
   applications, 176
   categories, 175
   components, 174
   DSL, 176, 223
   HDSL, 222
   interference, 174
   LAN, 176
   local loop, 205
   performance, 176
   RJ45, 176
   telephone network, 176
twisted-pair Ethernet; *see* 10Base-T
twisting, 175
two-dimensional parity check, 248
   performance, 249
   undetectable error, 249

U

UA, 706, 707
UDP, 593, 598, 600, 601
   advantages, 601
   checksum, 602
   client program, 910
   client-server model, 673
   connectionless, 601
   DNS, 699
   internal control mechanism, 602

   multicasting and broadcasting, 602
   ports, 917
   real-time traffic, 789
   route-updating protocols, 602
   RTP, 789
   server program, 909
   for simple communication, 602
   SIP, 791
UDP port
   RTCP, 791
UDP programs, 909
U-frame, 282, 286
   codes, 285
   commands and responses, 286
   control field, 285
   function, 285
   HDLC, 285
   PPP, 296
   system management, 282
   types, 285
UHF, 186
ultraviolet light, 173
unguided media, 173, 184
UNI, 449
   VPI length, 451
unicast address, 336, 531
unicast communication, 481
unicasting
   router interface, 543
Unicode, 5
unidirectional antenna, 188
unipolar encoding, 88, 89, 97
UNIs, 451
unnumbered frame; *see* U-frame
unreliable transport layer service, 600
unshielded twisted pair; *see* twisted pair
update message, 560
uplink, 423
upper OSI layers, 807
upward multiplexing, 609
URG bit, 625
urgent byte, 625
urgent data, 625
URL
   alias, 733
   components, 733
   document retrieval, 733
   dynamic document, 746
   host, 733
   HTTP, 733
   locators, 733
   method, 733
   pathname, 733
   port number, 733
user datagram, 601
User Datagram Protocol; *see* UDP

user mobile link (UML), 425
user network interface; *see* UNIs
user support layers, 31
user-to-user ID, 459
UTP; *see* twisted pair
UU, 459
UUI, 457

V

V.32, 130
V.32bis, 130
V.34, 131
V.90, 131
V.92, 132
Van Allen belt, 422, 424
variable bit rate traffic, 634
variable-length packet
   leaky bucket, 647
VC, 449, 450
   cell network, 450
VCI, 436, 451
   length, 451
   VPC switch, 452
VDSL, 223
very high bit rate digital subscriber line;
   see VDSL
very low frequency; *see* VLF
VHF, 186
video, 6, 528, 774
   compression, 776
video conferencing, 784
Vigenere Cipher, 811
virtual circuit
   IntServ, 649
virtual circuit approach, 475
virtual circuit identifier; *see* VCI
virtual circuit switching, 435
   acknowledgment, 440
   data transfer phase, 437
   phases, 436
virtual circuits; *see* VC
virtual connection identifier
   (VCI), 904
virtual link, 549, 552
virtual local area network; *see* VLAN
virtual path; *see* VP
virtual path identifier (VPI), 904;
   see also VPI
virtual private network; *see* VPN
visible light, 173
VLAN
   802.1Q, 403
   advantages, 403

automatic configuration, 402
broadcast domain, 401
communication between
   switches, 403
concept, 399
configuration, 402
frame tagging, 403
grouping by IP address, 402
grouping by MAC address, 402
grouping by multiple
   characteristics, 402
grouping by port number, 402
logical LAN, 400
manual configuration, 402
membership characteristics, 401
multicast IP address, 402
semiautomatic configuration, 403
table maintenance, 403
TDM, 403
VLF, 186
VOFR, 445
voice
   sampling rate, 774
   transmission, 173
   VOFR, 445
Voice Over Frame Relay;
   see VOFR
voice over IP, 784, 791
VP, 449, 450
VPC switch
VPI, 451, 452
VPN, 863, 866
VRC, 248
   CRC, 249
   reliability, 247
VT, 873

W

Walsh table, 323
WAN, 15
WATS, 209
wave-division multiplexing;
   see WDM
wavelength, 73
   definition, 73
W-CDMA, 420
WDM, 150, 155
Web page, 741
web site, 739
weighted fair queueing, 645
well-known port, 595, 674, 677
   server, 674
   UDP and TCP, 917

well-known port number, 595
   list, 603
wide area network; *see* WAN
wide area telephone service;
   see WATS
wide-band CDMA, 420
wildcard filter style, 652
window size
   basis of, 640
window policy, 638
wireless, 361
   addressing mechanism, 370
   control frame, 369
   CSMA/CA, 366
   CSMA/CD, 366
   data frame, 370
   frame control field, 369
   frame types, 369
   MAC layer frame, 368
   MAC sublayer, 365
   management frame, 369
   NAV, 368
   physical layer, 363
wireless communication, 184
wireless Ethernet, 361
wireless LAN, 361
   CSMA/CA, 317
   station types, 363
wireless LAN station, 363
wireless transmission
   frame size, 368
World Wide Web; *see* WWW
WWW, 733, 738
   active document, 747
   concept, 739
   document types, 740
   dynamic document, 745
   homepage, 739
   hypertext and hypermedia, 739
   information distribution, 740
   pointers, 739
   static document, 740

X

X ray, 173
X.25, 441
X.509, 842
xDSL, 219

Z

zone, 689
zone file, 689